News
Reporting
and Writing

News Reporting and Writing

Ninth Edition

Melvin Mencher

Columbia University

Boston   Burr Ridge, IL   Dubuque, IA   Madison, WI   New York   San Francisco   St. Louis
Bangkok   Bogotá   Caracas   Kuala Lumpur   Lisbon   London   Madrid   Mexico City
Milan   Montreal   New Delhi   Santiago   Seoul   Singapore   Sydney   Taipei   Toronto

McGraw-Hill Higher Education

A Division of The McGraw-Hill Companies

NEWS REPORTING AND WRITING
Published by McGraw-Hill, a business unit of The McGraw-Hill Companies, Inc., 1221 Avenue of the Americas, New York, NY, 10020. Copyright © 2003 by Melvin Mencher. Previous editions © 2000, 1997, 1994, 1991, 1987, 1984, 1981 and 1977. All rights reserved. No part of this publication may be reproduced or distributed in any form or by any means, or stored in a database or retrieval system, without the prior written consent of the author, including, but not limited to, in any network or other electronic storage or transmission, or broadcast for distance learning.
Some ancillaries, including electronic and print components, may not be available to customers outside the United States.

This book is printed on acid-free paper.

1 2 3 4 5 6 7 8 9 0 FGR/FGR 0 9 8 7 6 5 4 3 2

ISBN 0-07-249194-9

Editorial director: *Phillip A. Butcher*
Editorial assistant: *Jennifer Van Hove*
Project manager: *Jill Moline*
Lead production supervisor: *Lori Koetters*
Producer, Media technology: *Jessica Bodie*
Supplement producer: *Nate Perry*
Photo research coordinator: *Judy Kausal*
Cover design: *Mary E. Kazak*
Typeface: *10/12 Times Roman*
Compositor: *Shepherd Incorporated*
Printer: *Quebecor World Fairfield Inc.*

Library of Congress Cataloging-in-Publication Data

Mencher, Melvin.
    News reporting and writing / Melvin Mencher.—9th ed.
      p. cm.
    Includes indexes.
    ISBN 0-07-249194-9 (alk. paper)
    1. Reporters and reporting. 2. Journalism—Authorship. I. Title.
PN4781 .M4 2003
070.4'3—dc21

2002019067

www.mhhe.com

Contents

PART FIVE

From Accidents to Education 403

PART SIX

Laws, Taste and Taboos, Codes and Ethics 579

Preface

This ninth edition of *News Reporting and Writing* marks its 25th year in journalism classrooms. In that time, much has changed. Computers have replaced typewriters. Broadcast journalism has become a powerful messenger of information. Online news services have found a niche. But the fundamentals remain, as does the purpose of *NRW:*

1. To teach the skills necessary for a variety of media work.
2. To provide the background knowledge essential to accurate and informed reporting and writing.
3. To suggest the values that direct and underline the practice of journalism.

Learning to report accurately and to write precisely and vigorously is no simple task. Digging through the clusters of events and the torrent of verbiage to find useful, relevant information and then capturing these nuggets in purposeful language require mastery of a demanding discipline.

To guide us, we will spend a lot of time with truth seekers—another way to describe journalists—as they go about their work. We will accompany a young reporter as he conducts his first interview, and we will watch an experienced reporter dig through records to expose a state's shameful treatment of its mentally ill. We will listen to a reporter's thinking as she works out the lead to her story about a city council meeting. We will peer over the shoulders of reporters using databases for key information, and we will look in on some online news operations.

We will sit in the press box with reporters covering high school football and major league baseball games. We will join a police reporter as she races to cover a triple murder.

We will watch a reporter labor over his story until "little beads of blood form on his forehead," as Red Smith described the agony of the journalist's search for the words that accurately portray the event. And we will share in the reporter's joy when the story is finished and is given a byline and placed on the front page or makes the evening network newscast.

In other words, we will be concerned with the processes of reporting and writing—how reporters gather information from sources and from their observations, how they verify the material, and how they put it together in stories.

The journalists we will be watching work for small newspapers in Iowa, South Dakota and Oregon, and they are on the staffs of metropolitan dailies in Chicago and Los Angeles. They serve online news services and online newspapers. One reporter writes for a network television station in New York; another covers local events for a television station in San Francisco. We will see how general assignment reporters and the men and women assigned to cover politics, sports, business, the police, city hall, education and other beats do their jobs.

The Basics

Whether covering a college basketball game, writing an obituary or reporting the president's State of the Union address, the journalist follows the same basic process. The sports reporter, the entertainment writer, the general assignment reporter in a town of 25,000 and the Associated Press's White House correspondent all share a way of thinking and a similar set of techniques that have guided journalists through the years, whatever the changes in technology.

In their reporting, journalists seek out the new, the significant, the material they decide will inform their readers, viewers and listeners. And they find a suitable form for this information in a story that satisfies the public's need to know.

Reporting and writing basics are explored in detail in this textbook. But without guiding principles about the function of journalism in a democracy, the basics don't go very far in developing the journalist. The journalists we will be following not only show a mastery of the basics. We will see that they share an ethic that directs and gives meaning to their work.

The Morality of Journalism

The literary critic Northrop Frye could have been describing journalistic morality: "The persistence of keeping the mind in a state of disciplined sanity, the courage of facing results that may deny or contradict everything that one had hoped to achieve—these are obviously moral qualities, if the phrase means anything at all."

Power of Knowing. "Knowledge will govern ignorance, and a people who mean to be their own governors must arm themselves with the power knowledge gives. A popular government without popular information or the means of acquiring it is but a prologue to a farce or a tragedy or perhaps both."
—*James Madison*

James O. Freedman, former president of Dartmouth, might have been speaking of the practice of journalism when he described his experience as a law clerk to Thurgood Marshall: "In that year, I learned from a great advocate that law must be practiced not only with craft and passion but also with a tenacious commitment to ideals."

Mary McGrory, the Washington columnist, described an aspect of how journalists approach their work in comments she made after interviewing 45 journalists who had applied for Nieman Fellowships at Harvard. She said she found these journalists to have a "great deal of commitment and compassion." Most had a trait in common, she said: "They knew a great deal about what they were doing. They did not think it enough."

The journalists I know—my former colleagues and students, from whom I have shamelessly taken time and borrowed ideas—would shrink at being described as moralists. Yet they consider their work to have a large moral component. Most of them worry about the abuse of power.

Although adversary journalism is often criticized and sometimes ignored, it is as old as the Republic. Today's journalists are descended from a press described by the historian Robert A. Ruthland as "obstreperous newspapers (that) signalled the rise of a new kind of journalism in America that would not truckle long to any officialdom."

The journalist knows that democracy is healthiest when the public is informed about the activities of captains of industry and chieftains in public office. Only with adequate information can people check those in power. Jack Fuller of the *Chicago Tribune* put this simply: "To me, the central purpose of journalism is to tell the truth so that people will have the information to be sovereign."

Ignorance and repression are the consequences of unchecked power and of a journalism that substitutes entertainment for information. Walt Whitman, journalist and poet, described the fragility of democracy and its source of strength this way: "There is no week nor day nor hour when tyranny may not enter upon this country, if the people lose their supreme confidence in themselves—and lose their roughness and spirit of defiance."

Confident, rough and defiant. An apt description of the journalist at work—but also characteristics that have aroused anger and animosity. In its role as watchdog for the public, the press has been relentlessly scrutinized and sometimes attacked for its revelations. Journalists understand that the path of the truth teller is not always smooth, that people are sometimes disturbed by what the journalist tells them.

This ninth edition is offered to students with a commitment to and a belief in the traditional role of the press as a means of enabling people to improve their lot and to govern themselves intelligently. *News Reporting and Writing* takes seriously the observation in the Book of Proverbs: "The instruments of both life and death are contained within the power of the tongue."

Public Service Journalism

The kind of journalism that animates this textbook can be described as public service journalism, a journalism that meets the needs of people by supplying them with the information essential to rational decision making. Public service journalism has a long and glorious history. It has attracted writers like Charles Dickens whose crusading newspaper *Household Words* carried stories that revealed his indignation at the indecencies visited on the young, the poor and the powerless—themes current today.

While many writers sat at their desks, Dickens visited orphanages, saw for himself the conditions under which homeless women lived. He saw the streets teeming with the uneducated young. He described what he saw.

Dickens said his ambition as an editor was that his newspaper "be admitted into many homes with confidence and affection," and it was. His biographer says the result of Dickens' revelations was a "huge and steadily growing audience ranging in both directions from the middle and upper middle classes."

Today's journalists are worthy inheritors of this tradition of public service journalism, and we will be looking at their work. We'll watch a reporter show how children born in a poor part of town receive an education inferior to the children born into a middle class neighborhood. We will listen to a reporter describe the ill-fated attempt of a group of people to escape tyranny.

Journalism intends to entertain us as well as to inform us, and we will also follow reporters as they show us the zany side of life. We'll drop in on a young woman as she tries to teach her students the tricks of the bartending trade, and we will eavesdrop on a truck-diner waitress as she trades quips and barbs with her burly customers.

Journalism's Tradition

Journalism has always had its down periods, and there has been no shortage of nostrums offered for a quick cure. Its survival, however, has rested on the bedrock of its tradition. Albert Camus, the French journalist and author, was sustained by that sense of his calling during the Nazi occupation of France when he wrote from the underground. Accepting the Nobel Prize for literature in 1957, Camus said, "Whatever our personal frailties may be, the nobility of our calling will always be rooted in two commitments difficult to observe: refusal to lie about what we know and resistance to oppression."

In much of what the journalist does, there is an awareness of the relevance of his or her work to human needs and purposes, for the reporter knows that news represents reality to most people. The reporter is interested in ideas but avoids the sin of making the concrete abstract.

Journalism "is something more than a craft, something other than an industry, something between an art and a ministry," says Wickham Steed, an editor of *The Times* of London. "Journalists proper are unofficial public servants whose purpose is to serve the community."

My model for this amalgam of artist, sentry, public servant and town crier is Ralph M. Blagden, who taught a generation of journalists their duty and introduced them to the power and splendor of their native language. Ralph's classrooms were the newsrooms of newspapers from New Hampshire to California, where he worked as reporter and editor.

Ralph was my competitor as a state capitol correspondent, and never was there such a mismatch. As a beginning reporter, I reported what people said and did and stopped there. Ralph generously took the youngster in tow and showed him that a good reporter never settles for the surface of the news, that the compelling commandment of the journalist is to dig out the truth. He refused to make reporting divisible: All good reporting is investigative reporting, he insisted.

Long before investigative reporting became the fashion, Ralph was digging out documents and records to disclose truths. His journalism was in the tradition of Joseph Pulitzer and that publisher's crusading editor, O. K. Bovard. Those of us who were fortunate to work with Ralph feel ourselves to be members of a journalistic family whose roots are embedded in a noble tradition.

Benjamin C. Bradlee of *The Washington Post* says of Blagden:

> Ralph taught me to be dissatisfied with answers and to be exhaustive in questions. He taught me to stand up against powers that be. He taught me to spot bullies and resist them. He taught me about patience and round-the-clock work. He taught me about ideas and freedom and rights—all of this with his own mixture of wit and sarcasm and articulate grace. He could also throw a stone farther than I could, which annoys me to this day.

Bradlee, who directed the *Post*'s coverage of the Watergate story that earned his newspaper a Pulitzer Prize for meritorious public service and led to the resignation of president, recalls his first story for Blagden when he was a young reporter.

"It had to do with the post-war housing mess, and he made me rewrite it 16 times. I've never done that to a reporter, but I suspect I should have. He had a great dollop of righteous indignation, which I learned to admire enormously."

"And of course he wrote with style and punch and clarity."

I recall the first story I covered with Ralph. He had heard that patients in a state hospital for the mentally ill were being mistreated. Some had mysteriously died. We interviewed doctors, nurses, attendants and former patients, and we walked through the wards and corridors of the institution. I learned that secondhand accounts are just a starting point, that direct observation and other techniques of verification are essential, and when we wrote the story I learned the power of the simple declarative sentence. I also learned that journalists can be useful members of society, for after the story appeared and both of us had moved on, the state built a modern hospital to replace that aging snake pit.

New to the Ninth

This Silver Anniversary edition is accompanied by a second CD. The first, "Brush Up: A Quick Guide to Writing and Math Skills," proved so popular that we decided to add "NRW Plus." In this new CD you will find entire stories, many of them accompanied by the comments of the reporters who wrote them.

For those who want more information about a subject in the textbook, supplementary material is provided in the CD. The executive editor of *USA Today* describes his newspaper's response to the Sept. 11 terror bombings and a reporter relates her search for a court document that reveals a sordid chapter in this country's troubled racial past.

"NRW Plus" has a self-teaching component as well. Notes, audio material and documents are provided for exercises, and these are followed by sample stories with which you can compare your work. Ethical dilemmas present some of the problems journalists face. Their resolutions are included in the CD.

"NRW Plus" allows you to follow a reporter doing computer-assisted reporting. Several guided CAR exercises are included.

The appendices that had been in the textbook are now included in "NRW Plus."

—Melvin Mencher

Additional Supplements for Students

Workbook for News Reporting and Writing: Used in conjunction with the textbook; contains writing exercises and reporting assignments, home assignments, skill drills and class discussion topics. A city map, directory and cross directory and a source list are provided for the exercises. (Mencher)
ISBN: 0-07-249195-7

Two CD-ROMs are packaged with the ninth edition textbook:

Brush-up: A Quick Guide to Basic Writing and Math Skills, an interactive, self-teaching CD designed for journalism students. (Mencher and Wendy P. Shilton)
ISBN: 0-07-249197-3

NRW Plus, contains full news and feature stories accompanied by the comments of reporters who handled them and self-teaching exercises, allowing students to check their work. (Mencher)
ISBN: 0-07-246022-3

Reporter's Checklist and Notebook, a handy guide to handling beats and covering a variety of stories. Checklists for 15 story types are included, as is "Useful Math for Reporters." Sold independently and can be packaged with the textbook. (Mencher)
ISBN: 0-69-729404-8

Package Options

News Reporting and Writing, 9/e + Two CD-ROMs.
ISBN: 0072564970

News Reporitng and Writing, 9/e + Two CD-ROMs + *Workbook.*
ISBN: 0074192809

News Reporting and Writing, 9/e + Two CD-ROMs + *Workbook* + *Reporter's Checklist and Notebook.*
ISBN: 0074182978

The *Instructor's Manual* is available to instructors on the Web at www.mhhe.com/mencher.

Acknowledgments

Many have contributed to *NRW*—my first city editor, George Baldwin, whose patience with a beginner lifted me from days of dark despair; former students whose journalism I have included here; academic colleagues whose suggestions have helped make *NRW* classroom-useful.

I learned from my student who stormed out of the classroom when I said I would not assign her to the story she said she wanted to cover because I was worried about her safety, and I am in debt to my bureau chief at the United Press who had worn down a pencil putting thick, black lines through my copy. "Just show us what the guy did," he told me. "Let the reader draw the conclusions."

The following list acknowledges some of those who shared in the preparation of the nine editions of *News Reporting and Writing.* Only I bear responsibility for the contents.

Marjorie Arnold
The Fresno (Calif.) *Bee*

Brian Barrett
Office of the New York County
District Attorney

Frank Barrows
Managing Editor, *The Charlotte*
(N.C.) *Observer*

Tom Bettag
"Nightline"

Joan Bieder
Columbia University

Mervin Block
Broadcast writing coach

Art Carey
Bucks County (Pa.) *Courier Times*
and *The Philadelphia Inquirer*

Marcia Chambers
The New York Times

Susan Clark
Associated Press

Kenneth Conboy
Coordinator of the New York City
Criminal Justice System

Claude Cookman
The Miami Herald

Jere Downs
The Philadelphia Inquirer

Robert A. Dubill
Executive Editor, *USA Today*

Jack Dvorak
Indiana University

Julie Ellis
Freelance writer

Fred Endres
Kent State University

Heidi Evans
Daily News, New York City

Ellen Fleysher
WCBS-TV, New York City

Thomas French
St. Petersburg Times

Joseph Galloway
UPI, *U.S. News and World Report*

Mary Ann Giordano
Daily News, New York City

Joel M. Gora
American Civil Liberties Union

Sara Grimes
University of Massachusetts,
Amherst

Susan Hands
The Charlotte Observer

Donna Hanover
WTVN-TV, Columbus, Ohio

Jena Heath
The News & Observer, Raleigh, N.C.,
Austin American–Statesman

Michael Hiltzik
Courier-Express, Buffalo, N.Y., and
Los Angeles Times

Anne Hull
St. Petersburg Times

Louis E. Ingelhart
Ball State University

Thomas H. Jones
Chicago Sun-Times

Melissa Jordan
Associated Press

Jack Kelley
USA Today

E.W. Kenworthy
The New York Times

Jeff Klinkenberg
St. Petersburg Times

Eric Lawlor
The Houston Chronicle

John Leach
The Arizona Republic

Elizabeth Leland
The Charlotte Observer

Lynn Ludlow
San Francisco Examiner

Jack Marsh
Argus Leader, Sioux Falls, S.D.

Paul S. Mason
ABC News

Tony Mauro
Gannett News Service

John McCormally
The Hawk Eye, Burlington, Iowa

Frank McCulloch
The Sacramento Bee

Bill Mertens
The Hawk Eye, Burlington, Iowa

John D. Mitchell
Syracuse University

Eric Newhouse
Great Falls Tribune

Merrill Perlman
The New York Times

Lew Powell
The Charlotte Observer

Ron Rapoport
*Los Angeles Times, Chicago Sun-
Times* and Los Angeles *Daily News*

Elizabeth Rhodes
The Charlotte (N.C.) *Observer* and
Seattle Times

Ronald Robinson
Augustana College, Sioux Falls, S.D.

Sam Roe
The Blade, Toledo, Ohio

Mort Saltzman
The Sacramento Bee

Sydney Schanberg
The New York Times

John Schultz
Columbia University

Wendy Shilton
University of Southern Maine,
University of Prince Edward Island

Allan M. Siegal
The New York Times

Rex Smith
Managing Editor *Times Union,*
Albany, N.Y.

Jeff C. South
Virginia Commonwealth University

Laura Sessions Stepp
The Washington Post

Herbert Strentz
Drake University

Diana K. Sugg
The Sacramento Bee

Lena H. Sun
The Washington Post

Mike Sweet
The Hawk Eye, Burlington, Iowa

Jeffrey A. Tannenbaum
The Wall Street Journal

Bob Thayer
The Providence Journal

Jim Toland
San Francisco Chronicle

Carolyn Tuft
Belleville (Ill.) *News-Democrat*

Mary Voboril
The Miami Herald

Howard Weinberg
Executive producer, "Bill Moyers'
Journal"

Elizabeth Weise
USA Today

Jan Wong
The Globe and Mail, Toronto

Emerald Yeh
KRON-TV, San Francisco

Phoebe Zerwick
Winston-Salem Journal

The affiliations of the contributors are given as of the time of their assistance.

A Personal Word

Some of you may be thinking of the future, the kind of journalism you will want to be doing and the best place to launch your careers. Fortunately for you, the field is wide open. Journalism is a gateway to a variety of opportunities.

You may choose the path to a newspaper, magazine or broadcast career. Or you may have a particular interest that leads you to one of the several thousand special publications, the so-called business newspapers, magazines and newsletters. Or you may choose to report and write online. One indication of the importance of online journalism is its recognition by the Pulitzer Prize Board, which accepts online material as a supplement to a newspaper's entry for the Public Service Gold Medal.

Starting Out

A reporter who had worked on several newspapers around the country advised a journalism student: "Find a small newspaper or station where you can keep learning, where you will be assigned to everything—schools, local politics, the courthouse, police, the city council and the Kiwanis Club."

This is sound advice. Why a small news operation? "If you're on a paper, say, of 20,000 circulation, during the run of the year you're probably going to cover every conceivable type of story—trials and floods and politics and crime and breaking news and nonbreaking news and features," says Gene Roberts. When he was managing editor of *The New York Times* and had his pick among the many job applicants, Roberts said he favored "the reporter who cut his professional teeth doing everything under the sun on a small newspaper."

Minutes before Howell Raines was to be introduced to the staff as the new executive editor of the *Times,* he stopped to make a telephone call. The call was to his first city editor, Clark Stallworth of the *Birmingham Post-Herald.* "It meant a lot to me to call Clark," Raines said later. "When I walked into his newsroom, I didn't know how to type, and when I left nine months later I had the basic tools of reporting from a really great editor and teacher." Raines said he has been lucky: "I've had the benefit of great mentors and role models through my career."

Listen to Maria T. Alvarez, whose first job was with *The News* in Southbridge, Mass., circulation around 6,500. Now with the *New York Post,* Alvarez says she tells the news clerks at the *Post* to get out of the city, to go to a small paper. "They aren't getting the basic training, they aren't well rounded." A small paper, she tells them, is "the best experience. It's what America is all about."

While at *The News,* she was given the time to investigate a charity that promised to help terminally ill children. She reported that donations actually went to expensive trips and furniture for the organizer of the charity.

Howard Gardner, professor of psychology at Harvard who is making a study of journalists, says the first job is important. "It's like an inoculation," he says. "If you don't have examples of good workers, it's difficult to know what good work is."

Not every small newspaper or station is worth your time. Some are understaffed and do little more than slap at the news. But there are many good ones, and it isn't difficult to find out which they are.

These are the newspapers and stations that win awards for their reporting. The Du Pont-Columbia and George Foster Peabody Awards honor broadcast journalists, the Pulitzer Prizes and the Associated Press Managing Editors awards are for newspaper journalists. Many honors exist for both print and broadcast journalists, such as the George Polk Awards and the Sigma Delta Chi Awards of the Society of Professional Journalists.

Reading through professional publications such as *Broadcasting* and *Editor & Publisher,* you will come across pieces about the good work being done by smaller staffs. Ever hear of the *News Chief* in Winter Haven, Fla., circulation 10,000? Probably not. This small central Florida daily newspaper was the subject of a long article in *Editor & Publisher.* The *News Chief* revealed that inadequate background checks were made of Florida teachers and, as a result, more than 35 convicted child molesters, rapists, drug sellers and other criminals were teaching children. After the stories appeared, a state law was adopted requiring more extensive background checks of applicants. Newspapers over the country followed the lead of the small Florida daily.

Prize Winners

Some newspapers regularly figure in lists of the country's best newspapers. At the head of the list, invariably, is *The New York Times,* the nation's newspaper of record. It has a large Washington and foreign staff, and its national correspondents span the continent. Right behind are *The Washington Post* and *Los Angeles Times,* both likely to do more investigative reporting than *The New York Times. The Wall Street Journal* is considered the best written newspaper of all. Much more than a daily chronicle of business, the *Journal* offers excellent Washington coverage and has an enterprising staff of digging reporters. *The Miami Herald* is considered to offer the best coverage of Latin America.

The Philadelphia Inquirer has stressed investigative journalism and has won many Pulitzer Prizes. *The Boston Globe, Newsday, Chicago Tribune, The Milwaukee Journal, The Courier-Journal* (Louisville, Ky.) and *St. Petersburg Times* are also among the nation's best.

Here are the call letters of some of the radio and television stations that have won prizes for outstanding reporting over the past few years:

WBAP, Arlington Tex. KVUE-TV, Austin, Tex. KMTW-TV, Auburn, Maine. WJZ-TV, Baltimore. WBRZ-TV, Baton Rouge, La. WGBH-TV, WCVB-TV, WBUR, Boston. KGAN-TV, Cedar Rapids, Iowa. WBBM-TV, WMAQ-TV, WTTW-TV, Chicago. WCPO-TV, WVXU-FM, Cincinnati. WFFA-TV, KRLD-AM, Dallas. KBDI, Denver. KTVS-TV, Detroit. WEHT, Evansville, Ind. KSEE-TV, Fresno, Calif. KHOU-TV, KPRC-TV, KTRH-AM, Houston. WTHR-TV, Indianapolis. WJXT-TV, Jacksonville, Fla. KAIT-TV, Jonesboro, Ark. KNX-AM, KNXT-TV, Los Angeles. WHAS, Louisville. WPLG-TV, Miami.

WCCO-TV, WTCN, Minneapolis. WSMV-TV, Nashville. WWL-AM, WWL-TV, New Orleans. WMTV-TV, Omaha. KWY, KWY-TV, WCAU-TV, Philadelphia. WRAL-TV, Raleigh. KXTV, Sacramento. KSBW-TV, Salinas, Calif. KSL-TV, KTUX-TV, Salt Lake City. KCST-TV, San Diego. KGO-AM, KGO-TV, KRON-TV, KPIX-TV, San Francisco. KCTS-TV, KING-TV, Seattle. KXLY-TV, Spokane. KMOX, KMOV, St. Louis. KGUN-TV, Tucson. KOTV, KTUL-TV, Tulsa. WDVM-TV. WRC-TV, WJLA, Washington, D.C. KWWL-TV, Waterloo, Iowa.

A number of online publications and services have been cited for excellent work, among them Channel 4000 (wcco.com) in Minneapolis, Salon magazine in San Francisco (salonmagazine.com) and NEWS.COM (news.com) also in San Francisco.

The Job Search

For tips on how to go about how to prepare a job resume, see Appendix G **The Journalism Job Hunt** in *NRW Plus*.

Part Opener Photos

Part One

A tornado strikes, and a reporter is there to gather information.

Photo by Charlie Riedel, *The Hays* (Kan.) *Daily News*

Part Two

Flood, then fire—a big story that calls for accuracy, clarity and complete coverage.

Photo by Bill Alkofer, *St. Paul Pioneer Press*

Part Three

A volcano erupts. Lava covers power lines. The story must be written.

Photo by Bruce Asato, *The Honolulu Advertiser*

Part Four

Shaken but safe, these firefighters emerge from a church fire that took the lives of three firemen.

Photo by Bill Miskiewicz, *Times/Record* (Fort Worth, Texas)

Part Five

There's a story in the losers as well as the winners.

Photo by Greg Latza, *Argus Leader* (Sioux Falls, S.D.)

Part Six

Should the reporter intrude on the grief-stricken?

Photo by Dave McDermand, *The Eagle* (Bryan, Texas).

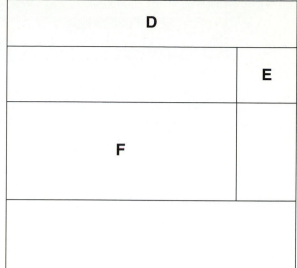

Cover Photos: Tragedy, Rescue, Restoration and Cooperation

The photographs on the front and back covers of the ninth edition of *News Reporting and Writing* illustrate and illuminate the scope and variety of journalism.

(A) Paul Buckowski of the *Times Union* in Albany, N.Y., took this photograph of a diver emerging with a batch of Eurasion watermilfoil for his newspaper's series on the water plant that is choking out native plant species and interfering with recreational use of the lakes in the Adirondacks.

(B) The 9/11 terror bombing of the World Trade Center left a vacuum in the New York skyline that was filled by two shafts of blue light to memorialize the 2,850 persons who died when the twin towers collapsed. Photo by Jasmina Nielsen.

(C) Chuck Liddy of *The News & Observer* of Raleigh, N.C., was on hand when a Marine Corps helicopter plucked this truck driver from swollen flood waters following a hurricane.

(D) Out for the exercise or the trophy, these marathon runners await the start of their long trek in the sun. Photo by Mike Roemer.

(E) After 10 months into the third year of a drought in West Texas, the skies opened up, and Ronald W. Erdrich took this feature photograph for the *Abilene Reporter-News*.

(F) Rescue workers dig frantically under logs used for the annual Texas A&M University bonfire. In seven seconds, the 40-foot stack of 5,000 logs collapsed, trapping more than a dozen underneath. Photo by Dave McDermand of *The Eagle* of Bryan, Texas.

PART ONE: The Reporter at Work

1 On the Job

Linda Cataffo

Picnic interrupted by late-breaking news story.

Preview

Watching reporters at work, we see that they are:

- Hard working
- Persistent
- Enterprising
- Curious
- Dependable
- Knowledgeable
- Compassionate
- Courageous
- Compassionate
- Fair

Reporters are tenacious in their search for facts that will give their readers and viewers information about events. They work quickly and efficiently against deadlines. They have a passion for accuracy and a determination to dig out all aspects of the story.

- 8:53 A.M.
AP NewsAlert
Plane crashes into World Trade Center, according to television reports
  - A killer tornado strikes a small South Dakota community, virtually wiping it out.
  - Freeport Parent–Teacher Association discusses raising teacher salaries $2,000 a year.
  - The State Board of Education decides to ask the Planned Parenthood Federation to help it develop a program to educate high school students about AIDS.
  - A candidate for the city council says he opposes a proposed city park and recreation bond issue.
  - Residents of Winston-Salem, N.C., are disturbed by a series of events: The mayor-elect joins the Council of Conservative Citizens in a

pledge to the Confederate battle flag; the board of aldermen splits along racial lines on police use of pepper spray; the Ku Klux Klan holds a rally downtown.

• A 2-year-old boy dies after his foster father throws him on the bathroom floor. Reporters for *The Denver Post* decide to check: Is this a unique incident or is it part of a systemic problem?

Journalists at Work

We hear about these events and much of what goes on around us from journalists. We see some of these events as they unfold on television, and some are described for us in the morning newspaper and on the 8 A.M. radio newscast. The journalist is the link between events and the public.

Journalists reported to us from the World Trade Center when terrorists struck, and they interviewed survivors of the killer tornado. They told us about the discussion at the Parent–Teacher Association meeting, and they described the possible consequences of the suggested AIDS-education program in city high schools.

News Consumers

Even when we have witnessed an event or seen it on TV, we want to know more about it if we think it's important. We want the details we may have missed, interpretations and explanations. The day after the World Trade Center bombings, *USA Today* sold a record 2.1 million copies of the newspaper.

Every sports fan in town wants to savor once more the victory of his team in the game he watched on TV. He reads every line of the sports writer's game story, and he learns that the reason the coach played a third-string quarterback was a hunch that the opposing team was vulnerable to the long pass.

The reporter who covered the Parent–Teacher Association meeting knows her readers will want to know what effect a teacher pay raise will have on the budget, whether property tax rates will have to be increased to pay for the raise. She checks with the city budget director, who tells her the city is on a thin financial edge and any extra expenditures may have to be met with tax increases.

The education reporter finds out that school authorities are caught between opposing pressures for the AIDS-education program. One group favors a "safe-sex education program." Another is lobbying for an "abstinence-based program." By explaining these opposing views, the reporter puts on the community agenda an important topic for discussion and resolution.

The Bombings

ABC news correspondent Don Dahler was looking out his window at home when the first airliner hit one of the World Trade Center towers. He watched a huge plume of smoke envelop the upper stories. He saw people jumping out of windows in a frantic attempt to escape the inferno.

Dahler grabbed his telephone and called ABC. "The whole building has collapsed," he reported. Then he ran downstairs to what became known as Ground Zero, the scene of twisted metal girders, smoke and fire and futile rescue attempts. He stayed there, on camera, for 18 straight hours.

Three weeks later, Dahler was sent to Pakistan to cover the unfolding war against the Taliban.

In Washington, several staffers of *USA Today* were on their way to work driving past the Pentagon when a third plane struck. Mike Waller said, "Time stood still as I watched the plane descend and then head for the building. There was a gigantic fireball and then sheer terror.

"I don't know how I am going to sleep after this," he thought. But he went on to the office to help put out the newspaper.

To see how the paper was put out under pressure, see *USA Today* in *NRW Plus*.

David Handschuh, a photographer for the *Daily News,* was nearby when the terrorists struck the World Trade Center. The force of the explosion threw him more than a hundred feet. He lost his glasses, his cellphone and his pager. But his digital camera was intact and despite broken bones and the loss of his eyeglasses, he stayed to record the continuing horror. As he scrambled through the ruins, he tripped, fell, lost his bearings.

Emergency crews pulled him from the rubble three times that day. "They saved my life," he said.

In the four hours following the terrorists' strike, the Associated Press moved on its wires 40 flashes, NewsAlerts and bulletins. See **Terror Bombings** in *NRW Plus* for a rundown of this coverage.

At Ground Zero

David Handschuh took this photograph the instant a hijacked airliner struck the second World Trade Center tower. Handschuh was caught in the falling debris and had to be rescued.

The Agreement

An implicit understanding exists between the reporter and the public.

1. **The reporter** will do his or her best to give the public a complete and accurate account of the event as soon as possible. After the AP learned of a school shooting in Jonesboro, Ark., the Little Rock bureau immediately put the information on its wire:

a0662 11:41 AM
BC—APNewsAlert, 0021 <
Shooting at Jonesboro, Ark., middle school; school office reports one dead, at least 13 hurt.

Then it informed news editors:

An AP reporter and photographer are heading to the scene of the school shootings in Jonesboro, Ark.

Within 15 minutes of moving its NewsAlert, the AP had this story on its wires:

JONESBORO, Ark. (AP)—Two youths wearing camouflage opened fire on middle school students Tuesday as they assembled outside during a fire alarm. At least one person was killed and other injured.

When reporters at the *Argus Leader* in Sioux Falls, S.D., heard about the storm moving toward southeastern South Dakota, they headed for the newsroom, though it was their day off.

2. **The public** presumes that the reporter's account is honestly and accurately reported and written. Although pollsters tell us that people are wary of the news they see and read, the reality is that people act on the information they obtain from their newspapers and broadcast stations:

The mother of three children in Little Rock schools who is disturbed by the Jonesboro shootings asks her state senator to press for stringent gun-control laws.

The last paragraph of the story on the Freeport Parent–Teacher Association meeting states that parents are invited to a dinner meeting Thursday at the local high school where teacher salaries will be discussed. A Freeport couple decides to attend.

A local parents' organization drafts a petition that opposes AIDS education in the high schools.

A mother of three small children, angered by the candidate's position on the park and recreation program, calls friends and tells them to vote against him.

Worried about a deepening racial gulf in Winston-Salem, citizens form interracial supper clubs. Carol Eickmeyer spends several hundred dollars to have 500 bumper stickers printed that read: **Hate? Not in MY town.**

Readers of *The Denver Post* articles about the foster care system demanded that the state legislature take action.

Continuous Coverage

Reporters stay with their assignments until they feel they have answered questions the public might have.

Freeport reporters continued their coverage of the proposed teacher-salary increase that the PTA approved. They watched the local school board discuss the issue, and one reporter wrote a story comparing local teacher salaries with those of teachers in other cities in the state. She found local teachers were among the lowest paid.

Local reporters also looked into the State Board of Education proposal for AIDS education in the high schools. How representative of local sentiment was the organization that was actively opposing the proposal? The city editor asked a reporter to find out.

Reporters for the *Argus Leader* spent a week in Spencer to tell the full story of the tragedy. Let's watch a couple of them go about their work. Then we will go out to Arkansas and look over the shoulder of Kelly P. Kissel, the news editor of the AP Little Rock bureau just as he sends newswoman Jenny Price to Jonesboro following state police reports of a shooting at the Westside Middle School.

First to Sioux Falls.

A Tornado Hits Spencer

The skies are darkening over southeastern South Dakota and they are growing more ominous by the minute. In the *Argus Leader* newsroom in Sioux Falls, the small Saturday night staff is alerted to the possibility of worsening weather. Assistant City Editor Rosemary McCoy calls reporter Rob Swenson at home to tell him he may have to go back to the newsroom to help with coverage. Swenson decides to return.

David Kranz, another reporter, has Saturday off but decides to go in when he hears of the gathering storm. "We have a limited staff on weekends," he says, "so I offered to help." He shows up at 9 P.M., just as a weather bureau warning of a tornado rushing toward Sioux Falls sends people into basements from 9 to 9:30 P.M., not the place to be with a 10:10 P.M. deadline for the first edition.

As the Sioux Falls alert is ended the newsroom hears that the tornado has hit the small town of Spencer, 50 miles west of Sioux Falls. The tornado struck the town with its full fury.

McCoy sends Swenson and a photographer to Spencer. "Our mission was to get there quickly and call back with observations in time for the Sunday edition," Swenson says. "The deadline was a major factor the moment we left the parking lot."

Blocked   But Swenson could not drive into town. "We were stopped at a roadblock by law officers," he says. They parked about a quarter of a mile outside town. "The town was dark except for a slow-moving parade of flashing lights from ambulances, fire trucks and other emergency vehicles, which stretched from where we stood to the center of town." Officers would not talk, so Swenson interviewed "terrified Spencer residents who had been out of town when the tornado struck. They were waiting at the roadblock to return to what was left of their homes."

When it was clear Swenson would not be able to contribute much more to the Sunday paper, he was sent to Salem, a nearby town to which Spencer residents had been evacuated, for interviews for the Monday paper.

In the Newsroom

Knowing that Swenson and photographer Ken Klotzbach were unable to get into Spencer, Kranz started to work the phones. He had good contacts, having been the editor of *The Daily Republic* in Mitchell, which serves the Spencer area. "I was fairly familiar with the town," Kranz says, "but I only knew a handful of people. I began calling them, suspecting the lines might be down, and got no answer. I then worked the phones in the area, thinking some rural Spencer people may have been in the town to check on things. No answer anywhere."

Enterprise   "At that point, I shifted my attention to law enforcement types. I called the wives of two law enforcement or emergency people that I knew would be there. First, I called the Minnehaha County Emergency Management director's wife. I asked for his cell phone number."

He continued to call and hit paydirt by finding the Davison County sheriff's cell phone number.

"The sheriff saved our day. He stood in the middle of the debris and described the situation to me. He pointed out areas familiar to me. He then handed the phone to the U.S. Marshal who gave us a vivid description of the way Spencer was and what he was now seeing.

"As deadline neared, the sheriff told us he knew there were fatalities. He saw one for sure, but expected there were others."

Governor's Comments   Kranz continued to call the sheriff and with 10 minutes before the deadline for the last Sunday edition, he asked the sheriff if the governor, Bill Janklow, were anywhere near.

"He told me he was standing five feet away. I asked him to hand the governor the phone and I asked the governor how many people were dead. He put the number at four. Without the source Kranz had, the local TV station could only confirm one death.

"The governor told me what he would have to do in the next few days and he gave me a plea for citizens not to visit Spencer the next day. He asked that they stay home and pray, that being there would only make the situation worse."

With the minute hand sweeping toward deadline, Kranz made one more call, this one to a woman in an area outside Spencer. Again, he was lucky. She had driven into Spencer to check on her mother. Her observations of the devastation in the town added a "real people" voice to the story, Kranz says.

Continued Coverage   Within minutes of putting the Sunday paper to bed, the staff began planning further coverage of the disaster. Jill Callison, the religion writer, was to cover church services. Six other reporters also would go to Spencer. In the Sioux Falls newsroom, several reporters would write obituaries and gather information on how people could help the town.

The full dimension of the disaster was reflected in the headline in Monday's newspaper:

'The town is gone'

Under this banner headline were two stories. One was about the tornado's effects. Written by Kranz and Swenson, it begins:

SPENCER—Shocked survivors wandered their ripped-apart community Sunday searching for tornado-scattered belongings and mourning six neighbors who died.

The whole community reeled from the devastation that Saturday's vicious storm left behind.

"It's just like a bomb hit us," Tom Simmons said. "Just like a bomb hit."

Most of the homes had been reduced to rubble.

"This whole town is gone," said Gov. Bill Janklow.

The other story began:

> Here are ways people may help victims
> of the Spencer tornado:

Red Cross

> Donations made to the American Red
> Cross may be earmarked to help with dis-
> aster relief for Spencer. . . .

The story went on to describe how people could donate food, collected at local markets, and send blankets and clothing to the victims.

Summing Up

Managing Editor Peter Ellis says, "We covered every angle of this story we could think of. We told about the heroes, the 8,000 volunteers who showed up to help, the governor who camped out there for a week, the prisoners who were happy to help, the minister who was spared while his wife died a few feet away from him.

Ken Klotzback, *Argus Leader*

The Morning After

"The main lesson from Spencer, I think, is that nothing beats good reporting, and lead reporter Dave Kranz is one of the best. He is always working his beat, including keeping up with former sources from years ago. It was because of this that we were able to get the sensational coverage, especially on the first day, that we did."

School Shooting

Next to the AP bureau in Little Rock. It is getting on to noon and Kelly Kissel, the bureau's news editor, is about to have his chicken lunch when he hears that the state police have been asked to set up a perimeter outside Westside Middle School. There has been a shooting at the school in Jonesboro. A person has been killed. This is a major story, and Kissell needs a reporter on the scene. He shoves his lunch aside, tells reporter Jenny Price to take off for Jonesboro.

He wants her to call him every half hour on the cell phone. During her first calls, Kissel, who knows northeastern Arkansas from having spent summers at his grandparents' farm there, gives Price shortcuts: Take a left a mile past the grain elevator, another left, then right just past the railroad tracks. But even with these instructions, it will take Price two hours to reach Jonesboro and Kissel must put something on the AP wire quickly.

Early Stories

Kissel calls state police, local reporters in Jonesboro, the school superintendent's office. It isn't until he has the superintendent's secretary on the line that he has something good enough for the wire. He writes these three paragraphs:

> BC—School Shooting, 0089
> URGENT
> Shooting at Arkansas school; more than a dozen injured
> JONESBORO, Ark. (AP)—Two men wearing camouflage opened fire on middle school students Tuesday as they assembled outside during a fire alarm. At least one person was killed.
> Connie Tolbert, secretary to the school district superintendent, said eight to 13 people, mostly students, were injured. Other reports put the number of injured at up to 16.
> Jonesboro is a city of 46,000 about 130 miles northeast of Little Rock.

This is a big story, and Kissel calls the AP general desk in New York to discuss coverage. He is given the green light to send another reporter, Peggy Harris, to the scene. Over the next week, seven AP staff members will be rotated in and out of Jonesboro.

As Price is making her way to Jonesboro, Kissel and other staffers gather more information to try to flesh out the story.

AP Photo by Mark Humphrey

False Alarm

Backpacks and cleaning supplies were dropped in the hallway of the Westside Middle School when students left as the fire alarm sounded. As the students and their teachers walked out, the two boys hidden in a wooded area opened fire.

Escalating Deaths   Bulletins, more NewsAlerts, new leads follow in rapid order through the day. At 12:07, a NewsAlert reports a second death. At 12:11, the second lead has 15 injured. In a few minutes, a third lead corrected the 15 to 13. Then, at 12:31, the AP reports two suspects, ages 11 and 13, have been taken into custody. Then a story with background about other school shootings and the figure of 13 injured is reduced to 12. At 13:03 (1:03 P.M.), a NewsAlert reports a third death. At 13:37, a NewsAlert about a fourth death.

Price has now reached the scene, and it is time to collect the bits and pieces for a definitive story. Price will write this, and it will be followed for the next six and a half hours by 10 Writethrus, each with new information. To read how this coverage unfolded, see **Jonesboro School Shooting** in *NRW Plus.*

An Announcement and a Fire

We are in the newsroom of a midwestern newspaper with a circulation of 25,000. The telephone on the city editor's desk rings and, after listening for a moment, the city editor calls out to a young reporter. "Bob, the publicity director of the Lions Club has a story."

The caller tells the reporter his club intends to donate some equipment to a city playground next Saturday at 10 A.M. at a ceremony the governor will attend.

The reporter calls the governor's press secretary to check the governor's itinerary in case he is making other local stops. In 15 minutes, he has written a short piece, putting the governor in the lead. He again checks the date, time and location of the ceremony against his notes.

A few minutes later, he is told to cover a fire with a photographer.

An hour later, Bob returns to the newsroom.

Human Interest   "It was a small fire, about $7,500 in damages, but there's some good human interest in it," Bob tells the city editor.

"Don't tell me you've got three columns on a three-paragraph fire, Bob," the city editor replies. "What's it about?"

Without looking at his notes, he answers. "The story isn't the fire but the background. I found out the family bought the house a few months ago. They had just remodeled it, and this week the wife went to work to help pay for it. She leaves their 10-year-old boy home with his 12-year-old brother for a few hours every day.

"Well, the 12-year-old wanted to make some money cutting grass. He knows they're short of money. He was filling the lawn mower with gasoline in the garage when the tank tipped over against the water heater. Woosh. Lucky he wasn't hurt."

The city editor thinks a moment.

"Got any good quotes from the older boy?" he asks.

"Yes."

"Well, it sounds as though it's worth more than a couple of paragraphs. But don't make it a chapter in the book, Bob."

At his desk, Bob pauses before writing. He can start his story like most accounts of fires he has read:

A fire of accidental origin caused $7,500 in damages to a dwelling at 1315 New Hampshire St. today.

No one was injured in the blaze that started in the garage when the 12-year-old son of the owners, Mr. and Mrs. Earl Ruman . . .

Direct Lead   He has put a direct news lead on the story, which he knows his newspaper prefers for stories of this sort. But he is unhappy with this start. This is not the way he described the fire to the editor, he recalls. Then he remembers advice he was given by a reporter: "Every story demands to be told a certain way. Don't impose a form or style on it. The way you write it has to flow from the nature of the event."

The nature of his story was the youngster's good intentions gone awry. So he starts again:

> Two months ago, Mr. and Mrs. Earl Ruman moved into a three bedroom house at 1315 New Hampshire St. It was their dream house.
> After years of skimping and saving . . .

At this rate, he will write the book his editor warned him against, he thinks. Although he wants a dramatic story—one that will build to a climax—he cannot take forever to develop the point. Readers will drift away.

Feature Lead   His editor has been telling his reporters to try for feature-type leads when the event makes it possible. Perhaps this is one of those events. The youngster is the heart of the story, Bob reasons, and the boy must go into the lead. He tries again:

> Teddy Ruman knew his father and mother had skimped and saved to put aside enough money to buy their dream house at 1315 New Hampshire St.
> This morning, he decided to help, too. But his well-intentioned efforts turned to tragedy.
> The 12-year-old . . .

That seems to be more like it. In 40 minutes, he has the story in good shape, he thinks.

The city editor reads through the copy.

"Yes, it's a sad story," he tells his cub reporter. "It's hardly a tragedy, but it would be sadder if they didn't have insurance to cover their loss."

Bob makes for the telephone on his desk. He remembers another bit of advice: "Don't leave unanswered any questions the reader may have. Don't leave any holes in your story."

Next, to another fire, this one far more serious, that is covered by a TV reporter.

TV Covers a Fire

It is Christmas Day in the newsroom of a television station. A teletype clicks off a story about a fire in a small town in New Jersey. The AP reports that while a family was asleep, a fire broke out and flames raced through their house. Four died. Only two boys escaped.

The news editor calls to a reporter, "Elaine, take this one on."

On the way to the fire, Elaine thinks of questions to ask and the locations in which to shoot the story.

"When I go out on an assignment I am conscious of the need for pictures," she said later. "I look for things that have an immediate impact, because I have a short time to tell the story—maybe two-and-a-half minutes.

"So I look for the strongest statement in a talk, the most emotionally appealing part of the running story. When I arrive at a story, I want to be the first one to interview the eyewitness, so that the person is still experiencing the event. The emotional facts have to tell the story."

On the scene, Elaine learns from the fire chief that the surviving youngsters had run to a neighbor's house during the fire. As crews from competing stations arrive, she and her crew approach the neighbor's house through the backyard to avoid being spotted.

"When I spoke to the woman next door, I asked her what happened when the boys burst into her home. She became tense and distraught as she described one boy's face, burned and blackened by the fire," Elaine recalled.

"On a breaking story, a broadcast journalist usually asks fewer questions than the print journalist. On this story all I needed to ask the neighbor was two or three questions and let her tell the story."

On the return drive, Elaine structures the script in her mind. She has pictures of the fire scenes and interviews of the neighbor and the fire chief. She works the script around these, the most dramatic shots.

A Child's Death

It was a drive-by shooting. The victim: 2-year-old Heather Brown. The family had been to church and stopped on the way home at McDonald's for ice cream. At home, Heather was fidgety and wouldn't go to sleep, so her father took her into the living room and began to rock her to sleep on the couch.

Suddenly, 60 high-caliber slugs tore into the house. One struck Heather in the head and she died in her father's arms.

For Diane Sugg of *The Sacramento Bee* the story was not so much the shooting death but the story of a lovable little girl. She found that story by driving out to the Valley Christian Church and waiting for its pastor, A.D. Olivan. He was close to Heather's parents and had spoken to them since the shooting.

Sugg had telephoned the minister but he didn't want to talk, so she drove to the church and waited. One hour. Two. After three hours, he arrived and Sugg persuaded him to talk to her about the child who used to run around the church singing to herself and hugging everyone she saw. There was something special about Heather, and everyone knew it.

"I would never have gotten Heather's story if I hadn't waited in a dark parking lot for three hours, hoping the family's pastor would come back to the church," Sugg says. "He did, and he could see I was sincere."

A Metro Daily

We are on West 33rd Street in New York City in the newsroom of the *Daily News* and the phone rings. An assistant city editor takes the call and turns to the city editor.

"This fellow says the governor's daughter is going to get a marriage license at 2:30. Maybe we ought to get a picture," he suggests.

The city editor is not enthusiastic.

"We had her announcement a few weeks ago," he says. But he decides they may as well take it. Nothing better may turn up for inside pages. (Nothing does, and the picture will run on page 3.)

A courthouse reporter calls about a suit he thinks will make a good story. A 21-year-old woman on welfare has won $925,000 from a car-rental company. The reporter is given the go-ahead and is told to slug the story "Suit." (The slug is important, for this is the story's identifying mark.) Usually, the desk will tell a reporter how long the piece should run, but the city editor knows that his courthouse man, an experienced reporter, will hold it to 450 to 500 words.

"Slay"

Early in the day, the city desk has made up a schedule of stories the local staff would work on. (See the next page.) One of these, a murder, had broken the day before in the *New York Post*. The *Post* story began:

> A 22-year-old American Airlines employee was slain by one of three holdup men in her Bronx apartment early today while her husband, bound hand and foot, lay helplessly in another room.

A *News* reporter in the Bronx is told to dig into the story, which is slugged "Slay." The reporter learns that the victim was a flight attendant, which gives the slaying what journalists describe as "class." The death of someone with a glamorous or out-of-the-ordinary job is assumed to perk up reader interest.

The *News* picks up a few other facts the *Post* did not have. The police report that the gunmen had asked for $25,000 and that the woman was slain with a shot from a pistol that was placed against her head. The rewriteman double-checks the names, and he learns that the victim's name was Gwendolyn Clarke, not Gwendolin Clark. Also, she was 27, not 22.

Mulligan's Theory The rewriteman, Arthur Mulligan, asks if there are any pictures of the victim. There is nothing available yet, he is told.

"I have a theory on this one," he says. A copy editor looks up. "Take it easy," she tells Mulligan. "Remember your theory on the Rainslayer?" (After three holdup victims were murdered during nighttime rainstorms several months before, Mulligan had theorized the killer was the "Roving Rainstorm Robber," who preyed on people when their heads were bent under umbrellas. Nope.)

Mulligan says, "My theory is that it was narcotics. Must be. Who has $25,000 sitting around the house? The guy has no job and drives a new Lincoln Continental. She'd just come in from a run, too."

It makes sense, the city editor agrees, and calls his Manhattan police headquarters man to check out the narcotics possibility.

CAREY—Names Joes Hynes and Morris Abrams as special nursing home prosecutor and Moreland Commissioner, respectively.

PROFILES—of Hynes and Abrams.

NURSE—Nearly half of the 175 nursing homes in city could face cutoff of federal funds, according to list made available to us.

BERGMAN—files libel suit against Times, Stein et al for $1 million.

SLAY—Robbers invade home, slay wife, bind hubby and escape with car.

SUIT—Good reader on young woman, blinded and severely hurt in car crash in France, living off welfare's $154 Month, wins $925,000.

JOBS—On deadline, city submits proposal for $46.7M in fed job funds.

UN—Ralph Bunche Institute report finds incompetence, cronyism and nepotism in the folks who work for our world body.

ABORT—Morgy OK's abortion for woman in her 28th week, 2 weeks late.

AUDIT—Levitt report says city isn't even close to coping with fraud in the welfare department, citing huge jump in fraudulent checks.

CIVIL—Service News column.

BRIEFS—Etc.

It is 3:40 P.M. and "Slay" has not yet taken shape. The reporters have not called in. At the news conference, the city editor had suggested that "Slay" might be page 1 material, and the managing editor gave the story the green light. (Murders are given good play in the *News*. The day before, a knifeslaying in New Jersey was displayed on page one of the *News*. *The New York Times*—the *News'* morning competition—played the story on page 39.)

It is now 4 P.M.—an hour before the copy should be off the city desk—and the activity in the newsroom picks up. Reporters are writing faster, copy is moving to the various desks in greater volume, and the tension increases. Copy should be in the hands of the news editor by 5 P.M., but on big stories the paper can hold until 6 P.M. for the first edition.

Drug Connection   At 4:30 P.M., the police reporter in Manhattan headquarters calls in with additional information on "Slay." He reports that the narcotics bureau is looking into the possibility that drugs were involved. Mulligan has enough information to go to work on the story.

Ten minutes later, the picture editor relays information from the police radio, which has been crackling with calls all day. "The police think they've spotted a suspect in that bank holdup where the cop was killed," he says. "They're stopping the subways around 42nd Street and Eighth Avenue."

This could be a good story—a chase for a cop killer through the New York subway system during the rush hour. But the desk takes the information calmly. Rather than send someone out, an editor calls the Manhattan police reporter—a busy man today—and asks him to pinpoint the search area. He had already started to do so.

At 4:58, Mulligan finished 500 words of "Slay." The city editor changes a couple of words, deletes others. It now reads:

> Bronx homicide police were puzzled yesterday by circumstances surrounding the murder of a 27-year-old American Airlines flight attendant who was shot in the head by one of three men who burst in on her and her husband shortly after midnight in the couple's apartment.

After describing the demands of the men and the details of the slaying, giving the address of the victim and explaining how the men got away, the story refers to "speculation by the police that the shooting involved narcotics. . . ."

At 5:01, the police radio carries the information that a man has been picked up in the subway for questioning. Later, he is released. No one is ruffled by the collapse of the story about the search for a cop killer in the darkened subway tunnels.

At 5:07, more of "Slay" is on the desk. At 5:15, the Manhattan police reporter calls Mulligan and says that the police think there may be a link between the murder of the flight attendant and the slaying of two men whose bodies were discovered in the Bronx. One of the victims was stuffed into a steamer trunk and the other was put into a wooden box. An insert is written for "Slay," and a short piece that had been written about the bodies and slugged "Trunk," is killed.

Folo Story   The next day, a general assignment reporter, Daniel O'Grady, is assigned to check out the narcotics angle. Police confirm Mulligan's theory about narcotics, and the lead in Sunday's newspaper reads:

> A gangland war for control of the lucrative narcotics trade in Harlem and the Bronx reportedly has left six dead in the last two months, including an American Airlines flight attendant who, police believe, may have smuggled drugs from the Caribbean for one faction of the mob.

Longer Stories

We have been looking at what reporters call breaking new stories or spot news stories. These are events and situations that have to be covered quickly, today, now. Let's next look at stories that take longer to develop, report and write, stories that are important but are not immediate.

First, to Jere Downs who moved to the transportation beat after covering breaking news for several years for *The Philadelphia Inquirer*. The switch was not easy, she says. She missed the excitement of breaking news and the quick reward of a byline in the next day's paper. Gradually, she found the reporting and writing a challenge that she enjoyed.

"I'm writing less—perhaps twice a week at most. But my stories have more impact," she says. Crucial to her coverage, she says, is her "habit of scooping up all paper from an agency whenever I have the chance: operating budgets, capital budgets, requests for proposals, studies, board meeting minutes." She organizes the material, after carefully reading it all, even the inch-thick 2002 operating budget of the local transit agency.

"This is going to be boring," she thought. But she kept reading and underlining budget items that seemed unusual. One jumped at her—$32 million for paying lawsuit claims. That turned into a story.

The Big Hole

Sources are essential for reporters, and Downs has lunch with one on Monday, visits the office of another Tuesday. Wednesday she was shooting the breeze with a highway construction engineer.

"In the course of our chat about the Route 202 construction project, he mentioned that construction was bogged down by a troublesome sinkhole that had so far swallowed $4 million in concrete," Downs said. Sinkhole repairs had been budgeted at far less, $30,400. But a warren of limestone caverns were discovered directly beneath the location of the $224 million interchange. Downs knew at once she had a story, and after her chat with the engineer she set out to gather information.

Her story begins this way:

The long-awaited solution to one of the state's worst highway traffic nightmares—King of Prussia's congestion of cloverleafs—will take longer and cost more money because of unexpected and huge sinkholes in the construction zone.

"There is no bottom to it," said Carmine Fiscina, the Federal Highway Administration engineer overseeing the Route 202 project. "We all knew there were sinkholes, but this is an unbelievable turn of events.

"This is a Pandora's box."

That was just the beginning. "PennDot is still pumping cement into the ground—$8.5 million to date," Downs says. The agency exhausted the region's supply of cement. "So it is building a cement plant on the construction site." More holes, more cement, more stories.

Downs is assigned to the transportation beat, as we have seen. There are education, court and police beats. There are politics, sports and local government beats. And then there are newer types of beats that seek to give readers information the traditional beats do not turn up—personal finance, health and fitness, families and children—this last the beat that Laura Sessions Stepp has carved out at *The Washington Post*.

Children and Families

"Readers devour issues presented up close and personal," Stepp says. One, she found, is adolescence, its perils and its promises. She wrote about the growing confidence of Josh, a 12-year-old she watched dig fence poles and stretch wire on his parents' farm in southwestern Kansas.

Josh told Stepp that if he "stretched the wire too tightly it might snap, and the herd of Hereford crossbreeds would wander onto the highway, perhaps into the path of an 18-wheeler."

Stepp told Josh's growing up story.

Sleep Problems   Stepp discovered that sleep deprivation is prevalent among many young people. "Beginning at age 15, kids need more sleep than younger children," she quotes a sleep researcher. They need nine hours of sleep but are getting only six, Stepp was told.

"This three-hour debt accumulates over a couple of days," her source told Stepp, "until their bodies take over and fall asleep regardless of what they're doing." When that happens, disaster can be moments away, and this is how Stepp begins her story about sleep deprivation among teen-agers:

There wasn't a day when Erik Utterman, a junior at Sidwell Friends School, didn't leave school a little tired. But on this particular March evening two years ago, he felt a little drowsier than usual. He had been up all night, finishing an English composition. He had skipped lunch, then spent two hours after school at baseball practice.

He was two miles from home as he steered the family van east down Westmoreland Street in Falls Church about 6 P.M. Edward Lee Rogers, an environmental lawyer who lived in nearby McLean, was driving west on the other side. . . .

Utterman dozed off and his van struck Rogers' Volvo on the driver's side, killing him almost instantly. Rogers' seat belt was of no avail.

Utterman, also belted, escaped without serious physical injury but with a vision he will carry always.

As he whispered to his mother when she arrived at the scene, "Mom, I know I killed him. I know what his head looked like."

Christmas Fund

When Cailin Brown took over the Christmas Fund stories for the *Times Union* in Albany, N.Y., the newspaper had been running brief pieces taken from material submitted by local social service agencies. Fictitious names were used for the people briefly profiled. The reporters handling the Fund drive never interviewed those whose stories they told.

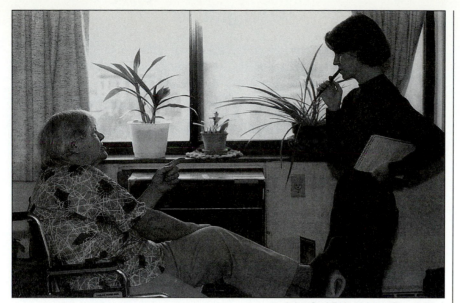

John Carl D'Annabile, *Time Union*

Downed, But Still Feisty

Stella Jabonaski makes her point emphatically to reporter Cailin Brown, who covers the Christmas fund drive for the *Times Union.* The drive is devoted to aiding the elderly needy in the Albany, N.Y., area. During the holiday season, Brown profiles 25 men and women for front-page stories of courage and perseverance despite debilitating physical conditions and too often forgetful families. Brown's stories have led to a steady increase in donations to the Christmas fund.

Brown decided to change everything. She believed that the "same tenets of journalism" that work for other stories should be applied to the fundraising drive.

"After countless meetings and some heated disagreements, the newspaper, social service workers and I came to terms on my plan," she says. She would interview the elderly the newspaper profiled and the paper would run their photographs. The pictures, Brown says, "made sense to me because newspaper readers are drawn to illustrated stories."

The stories, which appear on page 1 of the *Times Union,* are tales of courage and despair, devotion and loneliness. Brown, a general assignment reporter during the year, says that the people she interviews "are usually forgotten by their families, something unthinkable to our readers.

"I have covered my share of crime, both violent and white collar. I have written the story of a vibrant 3-year-old waiting for the death knell of leukemia. Yet never in 13 years as a reporter have I been so moved by the human condition as I have been listening to these people talk about getting old."

At "Nightline"

Let's drop in on Tom Bettag, the executive producer of "Nightline." It's 10 A.M. in Washington, D.C., and Bettag is making a conference call to the ABC News bureau chiefs around the world. The program won't air until 11:35 P.M., more than 13 hours later, but Bettag has been thinking about the news for that day from the moment he awoke.

In Moscow, Russia's president has been taken to the hospital with a serious heart condition. In Burma, Aung San Suu Kyi, the champion of the country's democratic movement, who had been under house arrest for six years, was suddenly released. Bettag asks his correspondents what these developments mean.

He takes a breather from the task of laying out the day's news agenda. "Our job is to illuminate the major issues of our time," he tells a visitor. He makes no apologies for the seriousness of the "Nightline" program. "People turn on 'Nightline' to find out if there's something they need to know, if there's something people are going to be talking about in the morning.

"They aren't interested in being entertained. 'Nightline' has its largest audience when there is real news." The program's high ratings attest to the public's appetite for serious news.

Quest for Freedom

The story had all the elements of a tragedy: A 6-year-old boy—Elian Gonzalez—was discovered clinging to an inner tube off Fort Lauderdale, Fla. Scooped up by fishermen, he was taken to a Florida hospital. The boy and his mother were in a group fleeing Cuba when their boat went down in heavy seas. The boy's mother drowned.

What would make so many Cubans want to risk the dangerous trip to the United States? How did Elian's mother and her friends arrange to find the boat? *USA Today* sent foreign correspondent Jack Kelley to Cardenas, Cuba, to find out.

In Cuba, Kelley gained the trust of the boy's family and their friends. After two weeks of what Kelley calls "delicate prodding," they introduced him to four men who had helped to organize some of the illegal boat trips from Cardenas to Florida.

It took another two weeks of clandestine conversations and promises of confidentiality before two of the four took him into their confidence. They introduced him to some Cubans who were planning to leave.

Kelley then spent three weeks interviewing members of the planned voyage, including a 29-year-old, Yacqueline, in whose small kitchen the interviews took place.

Because Yacqueline feared government retribution if she were caught, she asked Kelley and her fellow passengers to enter her house from the rear after dark. "She even worked out a signal—all lights on in the house—if it was unsafe to enter because the neighbors might be watching," Kelley said.

Once inside, Yacqueline would whisper behind closed curtains or speak in the dark. She would also play salsa music to drown out her voice. If she heard a car approach, she hid Kelley in a closet.

After more than 100 hours of interviews with Yacqueline and her friends, Kelley had established his credibility. They persuaded the smugglers to let him watch the group depart. It was 5:16 in the morning when Kelley, hidden in nearby mangroves, watched the boat slip into the water with the two guides and their passengers.

Here is how Kelley's story begins.

CARDENAS, Cuba—Guided by the dim light of a crescent moon, nine people, one pregnant and one carrying a young child, crept from a grove of mangrove trees bordering a deserted beach and walked quickly toward shore.

They carried only their allotted supplies: four boiled eggs, five apples and six bottles of water. It would be enough, they had been told, to last five days at sea.

As they left the cover of trees, they grew more afraid. Some began walking backward toward the shore to see whether anyone was watching. Two started running to the water's edge. One woman, shaking with fright, tripped over her feet and broke her bottles on the rocky shore. . . .

Kelley had planned to fly to Florida a few days after the departure to meet the group on its arrival in the United States.

The Storm   A few hours after their departure, high seas and gusty winds whipped the water. Three-foot-high waves crested, then grew higher.

Twelve miles out at sea, the passengers in Yacqueline's boat were fighting for their lives. "Raul kept yelling, 'Hold on! Hold on!'" Silvia, 31, recalled, "We knew we were in trouble. We knew the end was near."

Six-foot-high waves were washing over the boat and tossing it "like a toy," she said. Some of the passengers cupped their hands to try to bail the water. But it was useless; more kept pouring in.

"We just held onto the sides and to each other," one of the passengers, Roberto, 26, said. "The boat was rocking. We were tipping."

Suddenly, one wave propelled the back of the boat into the air, catapulting Ulices out of Yacqueline's arms and into the

water. Yacqueline screamed. She rose to jump in after him. Ignacio, another passenger, pushed her back down. He reached overboard, grabbed the child's arm and yanked him into the boat.

"Tie him to the tube! Tie him to the tube!" Raul yelled from behind them. He then pointed to another passenger, the widow Guadeloupe. She had covered her face with her hands. She was crying.

They couldn't hear what Raul was saying. The winds sounded like a tornado and the waves crashed down like thunder, drowning out his words, Silvia said. It was the last anyone saw of them.

Kelley continues his detailed description of the battering of the craft. A wave hits, knocking Ignacio, Yacqueline and Ulices into the water. Ignacio struggles to keep the child's head above water.

Yacqueline, who didn't know how to swim, flailed her arms as if trying to climb out of the water. She opened her mouth to scream but swallowed seawater instead. She never saw Ulices in the water behind her.

Then, "they all disappeared," Silvia said.

For the complete story as it appeared in *USA Today* see **Quest for Freedom** in *NRW Plus*.

Television Documentaries

The TV documentary is another form of the long story. Born in robust form during the early days of television, the documentary is considered TV's most ambitious and most worthwhile public service. It's also expensive, and it became a near casualty when the networks began to cut costs. Still, good work is being broadcast every so often.

Sports Mania

The U.S. is sports obsessed, and the media respond to the obsession with large sports staffs and acres of newsprint and hours of TV and radio time. The name of the game is winning, Howard Weinberg, a TV producer and director, learned, and this led him to develop a documentary for Bill Moyers about the price paid for the drive to win on the field.

His documentary begins:

America is a society obsessed with winning.
Many American universities have made a business of winning.

And then:

BILL MOYERS, Host: (voice-over) The name of the game is winning, to be number one, to sell the university's image and gain the money to do it all again, especially by getting on television. It's mass entertainment and America's colleges are providing more of it than ever before. The top 100 big-time sports universities, the ones you see on TV, now take in total revenues of more than a billion dollars a year.

Investigative Stories

We expect the media to do more than keep us informed of the day's news. While that's important enough, we also want the media to keep track of those in power, to tell us how well and how honestly they are performing. This is the watchdog function of the journalist.

With the Disabled   A few weeks after Cammy Wilson took a reporting job with the *Minneapolis Tribune,* her city editor gave her a feature assignment: Spend a day with a woman in a wheelchair to see how disabled people get around in the city. Wilson accompanied the woman as she went about her chores, shopped and had lunch. At the end of the day, the woman remarked to Wilson, "Isn't it awful how much we have to pay to be taken to the doctor?" "How much?" Wilson asked. "Forty to fifty dollars," she replied.

Wilson sensed a story of greater impact than the feature she was assigned to write. Wilson asked the woman if she had a receipt for a trip to the doctor. The woman did.

Overbilling   By the time she finished her reporting, Wilson had a major scandal laid out: The transportation of the disabled was a multimillion-dollar operation in which people were being billed $40 to $120 for a round-trip to a medical facility. Companies were billing at an individual rate even when they took groups from a nursing home or a senior citizen center to a clinic.

Her stories interested the Health, Education and Welfare Department in Washington D.C., and, because Medicaid money was involved, HEW investigated. The Minnesota legislature held hearings and enacted several laws to regulate the transportation firms.

Exploitation   A couple of weeks later, Wilson was house hunting. In one house, she noticed that every item was for sale. From worn-out washcloths to underwear, everything had a price tag. "Has the owner died?" she asked the realtor. "No," he said, "the owner is in a nursing home." "Why is he selling?" "He's not selling. The conservator is," the realtor replied.

Once again, Wilson had a story. She learned that the owner, Ludvig Hagen, 86, suffered a fall and was taken to a nursing home to recover. While there, the church that he had named in his will marked the house and all of Hagen's possessions for sale. Wilson began her story this way:

> "4415 17th Ave. S."
> "4415 17th Ave. S."
> The old man in his wheelchair repeated
> the address, tears beginning to well.
> "I don't have to sell my house. It's
> paid for."
> But his house is for sale. It and all his
> possessions are part of an estate valued at
> $140,000. . . .

As a result of the story, the county attorney launched an investigation.

Wilson then looked at probate, the handling of wills and estates by the courts. She learned that the county probate court had appointed a management firm to handle the estates of various people and that the firm had sold their homes for well under the market price to the same buyer, who within six months resold the houses for 50 to 100 percent more than the purchase price.

A Tip and an Exposé

"The message on my answering machine was straightforward: 'I have a story that may be of interest to you.'

An Ethic. "Making a living is nothing; the great difficulty is making a point, making a difference—with words."
—Elizabeth Hardwick

"Although reporters often get calls like this, many of which lead nowhere, I was intrigued, given the source, someone I had interviewed from time to time during the three years I covered the health, hospital and AIDS beat for the New York *Daily News* . . . someone who had never called me before . . . someone who sounded troubled."

Heidi Evans returned the call. The caller told her that the city health department had quietly stopped giving Pap smear tests to thousands of low-income women who depended on its clinics for free gynecological care.

"Since many of the clients of these clinics fit the profile of women most at risk of developing cervical cancer—sexually active women who have had several partners and little access to medical care—I knew I had the start of an important story," she said.

She dug into the records, interviewed people and found an even bigger story—the health department had endangered the lives of many women.

Here is how Evans began her story:

> More than 2,000 Pap smears languished in a city health department laboratory for as long as a year, leaving hundreds of women at high risk of developing cervical cancer without knowing it.

These stories take time to report and write, and editors usually have more pressing work for their reporters. They are sometimes reluctant to give a reporter the time to develop a hunch or a tip.

Gang Rape

Loretta Tofani went face-to-face with her editors at *The Washington Post* about a discovery she had made while covering the Prince George's County Courts. During a sentencing, a lawyer told the judge, "Your honor, my client was gang raped in the county jail." The assertion shook Tofani. "I asked the judge how often he heard about the rapes. 'Oh, it happens all the time,' he said."

Tofani decided to check. She continued to cover her beat, but on her days off and when she finished work, she went to see jail guards at their homes, and she interviewed rape victims. After six weeks, she went to her editor. About a dozen men a week were being raped, most of them held in jail because they lacked bail money.

"They were gang raped because the jail failed to enforce its rules and permitted prisoners to block the view of guards with black trash bags," she told her editor. "Jail policies actually promoted the gang rapes because the jail failed to separate the weak from the strong, to separate those charged with drunk driving, shoplifting and trespassing, who became rape victims, from convicted murderers and armed robbers, the typical rapists."

Her editor replied: "Let's put it on the back burner." She went over his head to another editor. He turned her down. "Spend your time on daily stories," he told her. Her third try was successful, and the metropolitan editor ordered her immediate editor to give Tofani time to do the story.

The stories about gang rapes in the county jail won a Pulitzer Prize.

Number Crunching

Reporters are using the vast resources of the Internet to gather information for stories. Much of that information is numerical.

Cities, states and the federal government put their records into databases, which makes the information fingertip accessible. Mike Trautmann of the *Argus Leader* cross matched the computerized list of private lawyers doing state work with another computerized list of contributors to gubernatorial and legislative races.

In Austin, Stuart Eskenazi and Jeff South analyzed Texas public safety records and found more than 118,000 motorists were driving without insurance, and that a fourth of all accidents involved uninsured drivers.

A frequent use of city databases is the determination of how much city-worker overtime is costing. Trautmann found $1 million was paid out by Sioux Falls, and in Austin South and Mike Todd discovered dozens received more than $15,000 a year each in overtime payments.

Polluters *The Plain Dealer* in Cleveland checked records of the Nuclear Regulatory Commission to find that sewage plants were routinely accepting radioactive waste from hospitals, universities and other sources. In California, the McClatchy Newspapers analyzed pesticide reports to learn that a health threat existed in the populated area of the Central Valley.

A reporter for *The Times-Picayune* in New Orleans who was working on the decline of the world's fisheries navigated among the Internet e-mail discussion groups. He read the messages scientists were sending each other and gathered useful material. Then he identified himself and asked for help with his reporting project. "It was amazing," he said. "Not only were they eager to help, but they bent over backwards to get things to us."

Contributors "The power of the database is that you can make connections that were difficult before," says Stephen Miller of *The New York Times*. One of the most frequently used databases during political campaigns is the one maintained by the Federal Election Commission, www.tray.com/fecinfo. The commission lists the names of donors, their occupations and employers, zip codes, how much money they donated and to whom. Reporters use the information to see what influence money seeks to buy from officials.

"It's tough to find a story that doesn't have numbers in it," says Miller, and "the spreadsheet is the key to digging into these stories."

Foster Care

It took reporters for *The Denver Post* seven months to answer the question we posed at the beginning of this chapter: Was the death of a 2-year-old an isolated instance of anger, or did it reveal a deeper pattern?

The reporters had a hunch that the foster child system was at fault, that some, perhaps many, of the foster parents were unfit for the task, that some had criminal records. To verify their hunch, they crunched 1.8 million computer records, created computer tables to track inspection reports and looked over a database of Colorado criminals and matched it with a database of foster parents.

They found matches: A foster father had spent more than half his adult life in prison, a foster mother had pleaded guilty to solicitation for prostitution, a woman who operated a daycare center had been charged with selling drugs out of the center. The state legislature took action.

It's a short hop from Denver to Las Vegas, Nev., where Brendan Riley of the Associated Press has been working on a story about crime in the fastest-growing city in the U.S. Riley is especially interested in the effectiveness of the Las Vegas Metro Police Department in solving crimes.

At the Bottom

By digging into the FBI's database, www.fbi.gov, Riley has discovered that the Las Vegas police force solves only a fifth of the violent crimes committed in the city. This is the worst record in the country.

Riley runs the data by the police and asks for comments. The response he gets sends him scurrying back to his figures. The police say their data shows Las Vegas has problems solving crimes, but it definitely isn't the lowest-ranking city in the country in this category. Miami, San Francisco and several others are worse, they tell him. In fact, a department spokesman says, Las Vegas is seventh or eighth worst.

Riley checks his data and compares it with the material the Las Vegas police have made available to him.

He spots the reason for the difference. "Either accidentally or deliberately, Metro failed to count one of the lesser crime categories," Riley says. "That has the effect of skewing the numbers so Las Vegas doesn't look so bad." Riley stands by his numbers. But he will need comments from the police about the reasons for the low ranking.

He will also need comments from an outside authority, someone at the University of Nevada who is an expert on criminal justice. And he wants human interest. After all, a numbers story is not the most interesting reading.

Human Interest   The logical person to try to reach is a crime victim, someone involved in an unsolved crime. Riley locates Joyce McKay in Fresno, Calif. Her son and his girlfriend were shot to death in Las Vegas. Riley puts this human interest as high in the story as he can. He quotes McKay: "There's no closure. It's an ugly thing and an ugly feeling to be left with."

Expert's Comment   For an interpretation of the figures from outside the police department, Riley turns to Grant Stitt, chairman of the Criminal Justice Department at the University of Nevada, Reno, who is quoted as saying, "To a certain extent, it shows what the police are up against. You can have a very effective police force, but also have a community full of criminals. The police may be as effective as possible, but that's all they can do."

Riley quotes the police as saying the force has 1.54 officers per 1,000 Las Vegas residents, well below the national average. Add tourists to the population figure, and the ratio is even lower. Also, Riley quotes Stitt as saying, the voters refused to approve a bond issue that would have expanded the jail. "We live in a democratic society," Stitt says, "and the police are an agency of government. We pay for government, and we get what we pay for." With this quotation, Riley ends his story.

Online Journalism

Corpus Christi, Texas, is home to many Navy families, and when the USS Inchon, an aircraft carrier, and four sister ships were making their way to home port, the *Corpus Christi Caller-Times* provided readers with stories on the newspaper's Web site. The stories were filed by the newspaper's on-board reporter, Stephanie Jordan.

"My kids rush to the computer every night to see where Daddy is," a Navy wife told the newspaper. "I would like to thank the *Caller-Times* for this wonderful Web page."

When Hurricame Bret threatened the Gulf Coast, the newspaper put its staff to work filing frequent stories on the site, www.caller.com. One story quoted Omar Garza, "I wasn't scared. The wind was only 120 mph." Stories like this increased the viewership fourfold and included weather buffs from around the country.

Web Versions

Some newspapers provide an online version of the newspaper, rewriting newspaper stories. At a few newspapers, the online staff may initiate coverage.

"We try to avoid looking like the newspaper on the Web," says Andrea Panciera, the online editor at www.projo.com, the Web site of *The Providence Journal.* Her staff produces three set reports a day and covers breaking stories as well.

The site carries stories that the newspaper's reporters write—but most are rewritten to suit the site's style, "radio/TV style," Panciera says.

At the *Times-Record News* in Wichita Falls, Texas, Carroll Wilson advises writers for www.trnonline.com: Write short. Keep as close to one computer screen as possible. People scan and surf the Web, Wilson says. "This is different from reading a newspaper. When you go to the Web for information you go for quick bites, quick hits."

Let's take a step back and see what marks the reporters we have been reading about.

The Characteristics of the Reporter

Different as these journalists may appear at first glance, they share certain characteristics, and there are many similarities in the way they handle their assignments.

One characteristic we notice is the reporter's attitude. He or she is curious. The reporter wants to know what is happening—firsthand. This curiosity is not born of nosiness. Journalists learn early that seeing and hearing for themselves is better than secondhand accounts. The firsthand account rings with authenticity.

Persistent

The journalist knows how important persistence is in getting to the truth. "Let me tell you the secret that has led me to my goal," said Louis Pasteur, the French chemist whose studies of bacteria led to the pasteurization process. "My only strength lies in tenacity."

Persistence allowed Lisa Newman to tell the story of how a Chicago police officer was transferred as punishment for giving the daughter of the police superintendent a traffic ticket. Newman heard about the incident from an officer, but when she talked to the officer who issued the ticket he refused to confirm her tip.

Newman, a reporter for *The Daily Calumet and Pointer,* gradually lessened the police officer's resistance, and he finally gave her the details. She also learned that the ticket was dismissed in traffic court.

With the information, Newman wrote several stories that led to an investigation.

Asking Questions   Persistence also means asking question after question until the issue is clarified, the situation made understandable for the reader or viewer. The columnist Dave Barry says, "I was a pretty good writer and I thought that was all that mattered. But journalism isn't about writing. You learned that what it's really about is asking hard questions, being persistent."

Dangerous Drug   David Willman of *The Los Angeles Times* Washington bureau learned that a drug to treat diabetes had been removed from the market in Great Britain but was still being sold in the United States. A year's investigation led to his two-part series on the deaths the drug Rezulin had caused. But the Federal Drug Administration took no action. For the next 14 months he wrote about the mounting death toll and the growing concern of physicians in 25 follow-up stories. The FDA finally removed the drug from the market. An editor described Willman as "the most tenacious guy I ever met as far as grabbing something and never letting it go." Willman won a Pulitzer Prize in 2001 for investigative reporting for his stories.

Confronting Editors   Sometimes, a reporter has to move beyond persistence. "You must be a little pushy, a little bit abrasive, a little bit obnoxious," says Bill Kovach, former executive editor of the Atlanta *Journal and Constitution* and Curator of the Nieman Foundation at Harvard. He is talking about the behavior that may be necessary "to get important subjects into the newspaper. You have to be up-front, confronting editors face-to-face."

Night Owl. The juror was the lone holdout in a major trial, but finally gave in and allowed the Oakland Raiders to move to Los Angeles. All the reporters in both cities wanted to interview the juror, but he wasn't talking. Andy Furillo, then with the *Herald Examiner,* followed the juror home and camped on the curb in front of the juror's house. He stayed the night, and next morning the juror, obviously impressed by Furillo's persistence, invited him in and gave him the interview.

GOYA/KOD

When *The Washington Post* was digging up exclusives in its Watergate coverage, the national editor of *The Los Angeles Times* was disturbed by the failure of the *Times'* Washington bureau to match the coverage. The *Times'* reporters were trying to cover the scandal by telephone, the editor learned.

"Tell them to get off their asses and knock on doors," the editor shouted to the Washington news editor. The advice went out with increasing frequency and ferocity, until the Washington editor decided to post a sign in the office:

GOYA/KOD
Get Off Your Asses
and
Knock On Doors

Fair

In journalism's younger days there was a newsroom saying, "Never check out a good story." Today's journalist always looks for the rejoinder, the defense, the reply, the other side of the story. A survey of working journalists found near unanimous agreement on two reporting necessities—getting the facts right and getting both sides of the story. Later in this chapter we will watch a reporter as he tries to steer a middle course in a conflict over school reading material.

Knowledgeable

Stanley Walker, one of the great city editors, was once asked, "What makes a good reporter?"

"The answer is easy," he replied, with a show of a smile around his eyes. "He knows everything. He is aware not only of what goes on in the world today, but his brain is a repository of the accumulated wisdom of the ages." Walker, who helped make *The New York Herald Tribune* into a writer's newspaper, continued: "He hates lies and meanness and sham, but keeps his temper. He is loyal to his paper and to what he looks upon as his profession; whether it is a profession, or merely a craft, he resents attempts to debase it."

The wider the reporter's knowledge base, the quicker the reporter can bring the story into focus. As soon as the reporter heard the speaker say that the country's politics had gone wrong with Franklin Roosevelt's New Deal, he knew his story was about a conservative take on politics. Reporters always try to get a jump on their stories, given the short time they have to do their reporting and writing. The more they know, the faster they can find the theme of the event.

Enterprising

News conferences, interviews and ball games present few problems. But for every easily accessible situation there is a tougher assignment, a less accessible source. The lore of journalism includes tales of enterprising reporters such as the one about the Chicago reporter who was blocked from a crime scene. He noticed doctors being waved into the building. He sprinted down the street to a pawn shop, pointed to a small suitcase, handed over a few dollars and raced back. Holding the case in his most professional manner, the reporter was allowed to pass.

Finding the Casualties   When Chinese troops shot down hundreds of students demonstrating in Tiananmen Square for democratic reforms, reporters were prevented from entering the area. Officials denied that any of the young men and women were killed. Jan Wong realized she could learn about casualties by going to local hospitals. She found the front doors were barred to outsiders.

"But no one guards the back door," and she went in. "Dozens of corpses, mostly unrefrigerated, decompose on the fifth day after Chinese troops slaughtered unarmed demonstrators near Tiananmen Square," she wrote for her newspaper, *The Globe and Mail* of Toronto.

A week later, the authorities decided Wong was finding out too much. As she was walking down a street, a car with no license plate cut her off, secret servicemen grabbed her and tried to shove her in the car. She kicked and screamed, attracting passersby who protested. The police released her.

Naming the Coach   In the days of intense competition between the United Press International and the Associated Press, reporters knew that a beat would result in a major play in newspapers and on stations. Sources did not want to show preference, so they would hold news conferences which allowed all the media an even shot. The trick was to break down the wall of silence before the scheduled conference, and the UPI did just that when a new football coach was to be announced at Rice University.

The Houston UPI bureau called around the country to the coaches who had been mentioned as candidates. No luck. The only one left was the assistant coach at Rice, and a call went out to his home. The maid answered. No, the coach wasn't in. Nor his wife.

"Is she going to go to the news conference this afternoon?" the UPI reporter asked.

"Yes, sir. She wouldn't miss that for the world," the maid answered.

In seconds, the bureau put out a story about the assistant coach's new job.

You might say that was risky. But would the assistant coach's wife be going to a news conference to hear someone else named coach?

Sending a Bulletin   Sometimes, getting the news out is a problem. During the Truman–Dewey presidential campaign when the candidates toured the country by train, there were long stretches without a stop, which meant the reporters could not get out to phone in their stories.

Merriman Smith, the United Press White House reporter, was aboard the Dewey train during a stop in St. Louis when the candidate was pelted with eggs, a far better story than the routine political talks Dewey had been giving.

But the train quickly pulled out of the station and there was no scheduled stop for four hours. The reporters complained, to no avail. (Remember, this was long ago, 1948, and there were no cellular phones then.) They would miss all the afternoon newspapers.

Smith didn't join in the complaining. He sat down and with paper and pencil began to jot down bulletins, which he rolled up and wrapped in $5 bills with a "Note to finder." The note instructed the finder to call the United Press collect and read the bulletin.

Every time the train passed a station, Smith would toss out one of his packets. Then he would return to the rest of the reporters and join in on the grousing.

Smith's packets did the trick. The United Press had a four-hour beat.

Courageous

For Ian Stewart of the Associated Press, the question was simple: Rely on people to tell him what was happening, or see for himself? Should he and an AP cameraman and an AP television cameraman venture to Freetown in Sierra Leone, which was being threatened by rebel gunmen? For 10 months, the rebels had rampaged across the countryside, earning a fearsome reputation by hacking off the hands and feet of villagers in a campaign of intimidation.

"The choice was simple," Stewart said. "We had to go to give the people of Sierra Leone a voice and to tell their story."

They went and they met with disaster. Myles Tierney, the TV cameraman, was killed, and Stewart suffered a bullet to his brain that left an arm and hand useless.

Given the disastrous outcome, was his choice wise? "I could not in clear conscience ignore the plight of an innocent people," Stewart said. Not go? "That is not why I entered journalism, nor is that what I was trained to do."

Courage of another sort motivated Ellen Whitford of *The Norfolk Virginian-Pilot* to go into an abortion clinic and allow herself to be examined and prepared for an abortion. Whitford wanted to prove what she had learned secondhand, that abortions were being performed on women who were not pregnant.

At the Square One of the standard stories from China is the visit to Tiananmen Square on the anniversary of the massacre. Although protests are banned by the authorities, some Chinese manage to register their desire for democracy. This is dangerous for the protesters and for journalists. It proved a disaster for Todd Carrel, an ABC news correspondent who was interviewing a lone protester as he unfurled a banner of complaint.

"Undercover Chinese policemen attacked me," Carrel says. "And that beating changed my life." The Chinese police beat him so severely that Carrel is disabled. The protester, Carrel learned, had his life changed as well. He was confined to a mental institution.

Martyred. In 1837, Elijah Lovejoy, an anti-slavery editor, was slain by a mob in Alton, Ill., as he tried to defend his press. Lovejoy is considered the first martyr to freedom of the press in the United States.

Murdered

Daniel Pearl, the South Asia bureau chief for *The Wall Street Journal,* wanted to find out what motivated the hatred of Islamic militants for the United States. He arranged to meet several of them in a restaurant in Karachi, Pakistan. Shortly after he arrived, the militants kidnapped Pearl and took him to a hiding place where they put him in chains and photographed him with a gun to his head. His captors accused him of being a CIA and an Israeli agent.

Four weeks later, a videocassette was delivered to Pakistani authorities. They said it showed Pearl had been "brutally slaughtered," his throat cut. Pearl was the tenth journalist to die covering the conflict in Afghanistan and Pakistan.

Reporters and photographers have died covering wars and disasters. Mark Kellogg, a correspondent for the *Bismarck* (Dakota Territory) *Tribune,* fell while riding with Custer and the 7th Cavalry at Little Big Horn in 1876. Ernie Pyle, the legendary war correspondent, was shot by a sniper in the closing days of World War II. Several journalists were shot and killed covering the war in Afghanistan.

Every journalist is familiar with harassment. A reporter needs a dash of courage and confidence to refuse the official version and to ask questions that seem to challenge an official's probity. Reporters question authority, and those in command dislike being questioned.

Also, the reporter needs courage to face facts that contradict his or her beliefs.

Compassionate

The stereotype of the reporter as a hard-boiled, toughened observer of the passing scene lies buried with the 1930s movies that created the image. Journalists do care. But they find too often that the public isn't interested in stories about, for example, the one of five children living in poverty, the more than 40 million without health insurance.

James Fallows, national correspondent for *The Atlantic Monthly,* describes as "the highest achievement" of journalism making "people care about and understand events or subjects they had not previously been interested in." Here are some examples of journalists trying to make their readers care:

- *The Orange County Register:* "We did not want yet another trend story that no one would pay attention to," deputy editor Robin Doussard said. The reporter–photographer team, Laura Saari and Daniel Anderson, let the children speak, and they spoke of living in roach-infested motels, scouring garbage cans for abandoned toys, moving so often they could not stay in school.

Journalists: Some Vintage Versions

Reporters are "a cross between a bootlegger and a whore . . . a lot of lousy, daffy buttinskis, swelling around with holes in their pants, borrowing nickels from office boys. And for what? So a million hired girls and motormen's wives'll know what's going on."

—*Ben Hecht and Charles MacArthur, "Front Page"*

". . . reporters tend to be dilettantes who know a little bit about a lot of things and not very much about any one thing. And the nature of the game, the dailiness of it, never gives them very much opportunity to learn very much about any one thing."

—*Victor Navsky, editor of* The Nation

". . . I see a pale-skinned man in his early forties . . . at two in the morning. He's divorced, his wife has taken his children to another town and when he goes home in the morning there's nothing in the ice box."

—*Thomas Powers, former United Press International reporter*

• *The Atlanta Journal and Constitution:* Children were also this paper's focus. These were 844 children who had died of neglect and abuse over a five-year period. Most were poor children. To attract readers, the paper made a graphic of 844 pairs of children's shoes to represent each of the dead children. The series examined 10 families living in poverty in affluent Gwinnett County.

• *The St. Paul Pioneer Press:* Its focus was on the working poor, a single father whose $920 a month barely held the family together, a woman who worked 11 hours a day at a fast-food restaurant.

Let's follow a reporter who exhibits some of these characteristics as he tries to background a press release that challenged his values and assumptions.

A Press Release That Needs Backgrounding

In the newsroom of a daily newspaper in Maryland, the editor calls the education reporter over to his desk. "Dick, here's something pretty important. Overnight took these notes from a fellow who said he is the publicity chairman of an organization called the Black Parents Association. See if the outfit amounts to anything and, if it does, let's have some comments. Write it down the middle. It's a touchy issue."

The notes read as follows:

The association has just sent a complaint to the state board of education. We are disturbed by the use of certain books our children are being given in the city's schools and school libraries.

Some of this reading gives the children—black or white—a stereotyped view of minority people. At a time when we are in danger of becoming two societies, every effort must be made to understand each other. Some of the books our children are being asked to read do not accomplish this. They portray black people as ignorant, lacking in culture, childlike, sexually loose, etc.

We are asking that certain books be removed from the library and the classroom—<u>Huck Finn, Manchild in the Promised Land</u> and <u>Down These Mean Streets.</u> We intend to add to the list.

"The picture of Jim in the Twain book is that of the stereotyped black man of slave days," says James Alberts, association president. "Impressionable children are led to think of black people as senseless, head-scratching, comic figures. We object to that portrayal of Nigger Jim."

Alberts said that in 1957 the Finn book was banned from elementary and junior high schools in New York City by the city board at the request of the NAACP. Later, he said, black students at Brandeis University picketed a school near the university that used the book. In recent years, some cities have removed the book from reading lists. In Waukegan, Ill., it was removed on the ground that it was offensive to blacks. Dr. John H. Wallace, an educator on the Chicago School Board, calls it "the most grotesque example of racist trash ever written."

"If it is to be read, it should be read at home under the direction of their parents," Alberts said.

The group met in Freedom Hall of the Mt. Zion Baptist Church tonight.

Background Check

Dick checks his newspaper's digital story archive to see if there are any stories about the association. He finds a 1990 story that says that the association was formed in 1955, one year after the U.S. Supreme Court ruling on school desegregation, and has been active in local school affairs.

He telephones the president of the association to ask if any particular incident provoked the action. The president tells him a parent brought up the issue at a meeting last month. Dick asks for the name of the parent, but the president has forgotten it.

For reaction from the schools, he looks up the telephone numbers of the city school superintendent, some high school principals and the head of the board of education. He calls for their comments. If he has time, he thinks he will try to go over to a high school. It would be appropriate to interview black students, he decides. But that may have to wait for a folo (follow-up story).

He rereads the release. Many readers will know *Huckleberry Finn,* but what about the other books? He will have to find out something about them.

Balance   He remembers that, when he took a course in American literature, one of his textbooks described *Huckleberry Finn* as the greatest of all American novels. Maybe he will work that in to give the story some balance. He read the book for the course and remembers Jim as a man of dignity. But his reactions certainly are not those a black high school student might have, he concedes. Yes, he will have to talk to students and to their parents as well. He also will have to guard against putting his opinions into the story.

Dick looks under *Twain* in the encyclopedia and, to his surprise, he finds that the book is properly titled, *The Adventures of Huckleberry Finn.* He had better check the other titles.

Censored Writers

Dick admits to himself he does not like what the association is doing. It is too close to censorship, he thinks. After all, Mark Twain is a great writer. And people are always objecting that some authors are dangerous reading for the young—Hemingway, Salinger, Vonnegut, Steinbeck. But Mark Twain?

Can a great writer be prejudiced? There's a running debate about Shakespeare's *The Merchant of Venice* and Dickens' *Oliver Twist.* He recalls reading a wire story about some parents asking that *The Merchant of Venice* be restricted to high school seniors on the ground that younger students are vulnerable to the anti-Semitic stereotypes in the play.

He also recalls reading that, when Twain was a young reporter in San Francisco, he wrote an account of an attack by a gang of young whites on a Chinese man. Several policemen stood by and watched, Twain had written.

Censored Books. "Cumulative findings since 1982 show that the most frequently attacked books are American classics. The top three targets since we began our monitoring have been John Steinbeck's *Of Mice and Men,* J.D. Salinger's *The Catcher in the Rye* and Mark Twain's *The Adventures of Huckleberry Finn.*"
—*People for the American Way, a constitutional liberties group*

Twain's story, a straightforward account of the incident, never ran in the newspaper. Even so, it's possible Twain could have been a racist by today's definition.

Dick has a vague recollection of reading a story about Twain helping a black student at Yale. Better look into that, too. He will need time to check out all these recollections, he decides. He will not trust his memory.

Also, he will need to look into the whole issue of book censorship, which, he knows, has been in the news for some time. He knows that battles are being waged across the country over appropriate material for the school curriculum. He will have to use the Internet to obtain a lot of background material for his story, and he will have to interview parents, school officials and teachers—and why not students?

To follow Dick as he gathers information for his story, see **Huckleberry Finn** in *NRW Plus*. Then see **Internet Basics** in *NRW Plus* to see how to use this valuable tool.

Summing Up

Journalists live in a world of confusion and complexity. Nevertheless, they manage through enterprise, wit, energy and intelligence to move close to the truth of the event and to shape their understanding into language and a form that can be understood by all. The task ahead of us in this book is to help you develop the journalist's craft and to find a personal credo to work by. A reporter who worked her way from small newspapers in New Mexico, Pennsylvania and New Jersey to the AP and then to *The New York Times* says her motto is "Keep cool but care." This philosophy seems to describe the reporters we will be following in the rest of this book.

Journalists make mistakes. It is important to learn from mistakes and not to be discouraged. Although mistakes can be embarrassing and humiliating, they are unavoidable. Look at the Corrections box on page two of any issue of *The New York Times,* which is staffed by some of the best journalists in the business. Day after day, two to five admissions of error are published—wrong names, wrong addresses, wrong figures. Don't live in fear of making a mistake; that will cut down your range. Do the best you can. That's all anyone can ask of you.

Further Reading

At the end of each chapter, suggested supplementary reading is listed. The listed books have been recommended by journalists and by authorities in the fields discussed in the chapter.

This list includes, for example, the autobiography of a major figure in American journalism, Lincoln Steffens. It also includes Vincent Sheean's recollections of his life as a foreign correspondent, a book that persuaded many young men and women that journalism is for them. Also listed is a biography of Edward R. Murrow, the eminent broadcast journalist, and a study of the country's most influential newspaper, *The New York Times*. One book describes the women journalists who broke through barriers at the *Times*. Finally, no journalism bibliography would be complete without the book that describes how two young reporters, Bob Woodward and Carl Bernstein, toppled a president.

Alabiso, Vincent, Kelly Smith Tunney and Chuck Zoeller, eds. *Flash! The Associated Press Covers the World.* New York: Abrams, 1998.

Bogart, Leo. *Commercial Culture: The Media System and the Public Interest.* New York: Oxford University Press, 1995.

Frankel, Max. *The Times of My Life and My Life with The Times.* New York: Random House, 1999.

Kendrick, Alexander. *Prime Time: The Life of Edward Murrow.* Boston: Little, Brown, 1969.

Kroeger, Brooke. *Nellie Bly: Daredevil, Reporter, Feminist.* New York: Times Books, 1994.

Robertson, Nan. *The Girls in the Balcony: Women, Men, and The New York Times.* New York: Random House, 1992.

Sheean, Vincent. *Personal History.* Boston: Houghton Mifflin, 1969.

Steffens, Lincoln. *The Autobiography of Lincoln Steffens.* New York: Harcourt Brace, 1931.

Talese, Gay. *The Kingdom and the Power.* New York: World Publishing, 1969.

Waldron, Ann. *Hodding Carter: The Reconstruction of a Racist.* Chapel Hill, N.C.: Algonquin Books of Chapel Hill, 1993.

Woodward, Bob, and Carl Bernstein. *All the President's Men.* New York: Simon & Schuster, 1974.

PART TWO: The Basics

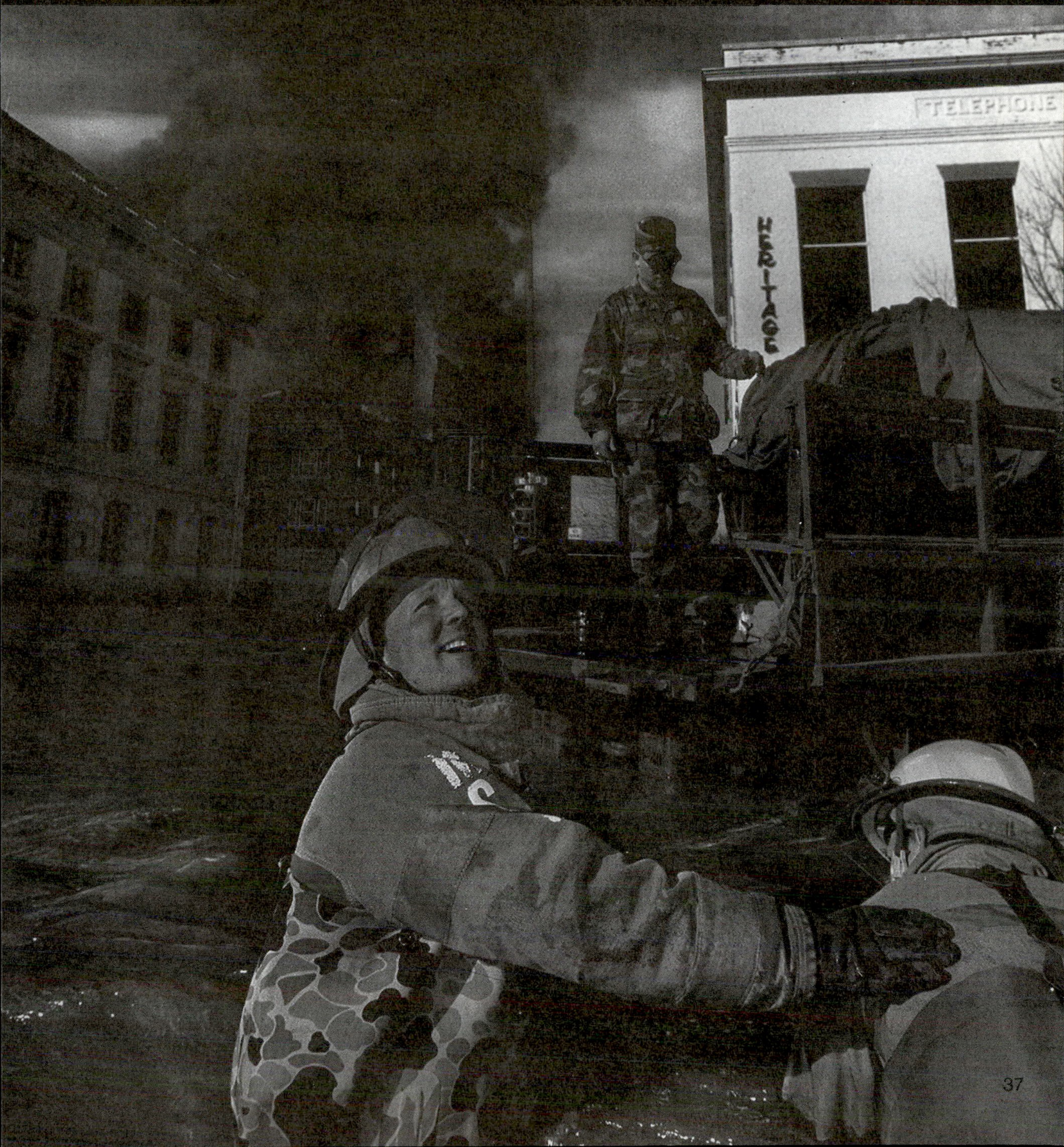

Wayne Miller

Spell the name, please. What's the address? The exact charge. . . .

Preview

News stories must be:

- **Accurate.** All information is verified before it is used.
- **Properly attributed.** The reporter identifies his or her sources of information.
- **Complete.** The story answers all the questions of the reader or viewer. It contains the specifics that illustrate, prove, and document the main point of the story.
- **Balanced and fair.** All sides in a controversy are presented.
- **Objective.** The news writer does not inject his or her feelings or opinions.
- **Brief and focused.** The news story gets to the point quickly and keeps to the point.
- **Well-written.** Stories are clear, direct, interesting.

Direct observation is the surest way to obtain accurate information. With secondhand and thirdhand accounts, the reporter tries to verify the material by seeking out documents and records. When only human sources are available for verification, reporters check the source's reliability.

If we were to generalize from the work of the reporters we have been watching, we might conclude that the reporter:

1. Attempts to report accurately the truth or reality of the event through:
    A. Direct observation.
    B. The use of (a) authoritative, knowledgeable and reliable human sources and (b) relevant and reliable physical sources.
2. Tries to write an interesting, timely and clearly written story. Quotations, anecdotes, examples and human interest enliven the story.

If journalism needs rules, these would be the starting points.

Underlying and directing the application of these rules or guidelines is the reporter's imperative: The story must be accurate. Whether news story or feature, conveyer of fact or entertainment, accuracy is essential.

Accuracy

The highest praise A. J. Liebling, a master reporter for newspapers and *The New Yorker* magazine, could pay a colleague was, "He is a careful reporter," by which Liebling meant that the reporter took great care to be accurate. Although the reporter often works under severe space and time limitations, he or she makes every effort to check the accuracy of information through verification and documentation.

Joseph Pulitzer, a towering figure in U.S. journalism, had a cardinal rule for his staff: "Accuracy, accuracy, accuracy." There may be arguments in newsrooms about writing style, about the best way to interview a reluctant source, but there is no debate about errors. A journalist may be tolerated if his or her writing does not sparkle, but reporters won't last the week if they are error-prone.

Check and Check Again

Mistakes occur when the reporter fails to check an assumption or a source's assertion.

When she was the public editor at *The Oregonian,* Michele McLellan recalls, "The newspaper featured a local high-school band member in a photo on the local news cover. The picture was tailor-made to brighten the family scrapbook. And it might have been the only time Julia Carr would see herself in her local newspaper.

"But we misspelled her name in the caption. I cringed that we had failed a young person in such a basic way. The bandleader provided the wrong spelling, but our photographer accepted responsibility. I was proud we didn't just shrug, blame the source and move on."

When the news editor of *The New York Times* spotted a line in a story that described the Canadian city of Sudbury as a "suburb of Toronto," he checked an atlas. Sudbury, he found, is 250 miles north of Toronto. The reporter blamed the source, an FBI agent, but the editor found that to be no excuse. "It should have been second nature to check," he said.

And These   The headline writer put the famous mountain peak El Capitan in Yellowstone National Park.

In one story, *The New York Times* writer wrote of "the University of Wisconsin at Ann Arbor" and Los Alamos in "the desert sands of New Mexico."

A caption in a *Times* story about a documentary film refers to the "Ida P. Wells housing project in Chicago."

In another *Times* story, a westward train makes several stops "before arriving in Santa Fe." The writer also describes Santa Fe as being "in New Mexico's desert."

Costly Difference. The recipe in *Gourmet* magazine called for a dash of wintergreen *oil.* While the magazine was on the press, someone discovered that wintergreen *extract* was called for. Wintergreen *oil* is poisonous. Oops. The magazine printed the proper ingredients on a sticker and put it on the 750,000 copies of the magazine.

Unanimous. A poll of 550 journalists on journalistic values ranked highest (1) getting the facts right and (2) getting both sides on record.

The caption in a midwestern newspaper refers to 22 women in the Washington State Senate. The picture shows 23 women.

Newsweek recommends parents let their 5-month-olds feed themselves raw carrot sticks and zweiback.

No, El Capitan isn't where the headline put it, but west in Yosemite National Park. And we all know where the University of Wisconsin is located. It's Ida B. Wells. No trains stop in Santa Fe, which is hardly in the desert being some 7,000 feet high, as is Los Alamos. As for *Newsweek*'s recommendation for feeding children, the magazine had to call back several hundred thousand copies of the issue. Its recommendation of carrots and zweiback could cause 5-month-olds to choke.

Corrections

When mistakes are made, corrections follow so that the record is accurate.

Correction

In last week's edition of the Michigan Chronicle, the story "Fauntroy stirs breakfast crowd," Congressman Walter Fauntroy's grandmother was misidentified. The matriarch was known to Fauntroy family members as "Big Ma," not "Big Mouth" as reported.

Language, Too

Accuracy also applies to the use of language. Words are chosen carefully to match the situation, event or individual. The writer who settles for the imprecise rather than the exact word or words lives dangerously, teetering on the brink of being misunderstood or misleading readers and listeners.

Precision   We don't say she was "unusually tall." We write she was "an inch over six feet tall." No matter how concise our broadcast news item is, we don't write that "the ship damaged the pier." We write, "the tanker (freighter, battleship, ferry) caused $500,000 in damage to the pier."

Hold It   Speed, the essential ingredient of much journalism, is accuracy's enemy. Checking—whether it involves calling another source or consulting the dictionary for the proper shade of a word's meaning—takes time. That extra 2 minutes, even 30 seconds, may mean the story won't make the 6 o'clock broadcast or the first edition. But check we must, even on the biggest stories that are the most competitive.

At 3:22 a.m., a note appeared on the AP news wire: Frank Sinatra was dead. A big story, all right, for Sinatra was probably the best-known singer of the last half of the 20th century. On the AP's general desk in New York, overnight editor Dave Zelio immediately checked the report. He called the Los Angeles bureau for confirmation, and in less than two minutes this moved over the wire:

```
A0487 (03:23:43 EDT)
abx
bBC—APNewsAlert
+Frank+   +Sinatra dies of heart attack, publicist says.
```

In 90 seconds, a bulletin ran, and at 3:38 a.m., a 1,200-word story was moving to newspapers and broadcast stations.

Firsthand Observation

The reporter knows that a story based on direct observation is superior in accuracy and reader interest to one based on secondhand information.

As Bertrand Russell, the British philosopher, advised his students:

> Make the observation yourself. Aristotle could have avoided the mistake of thinking that women have fewer teeth than men by the simple device of asking Mrs. Aristotle to keep her mouth open while he counted. Thinking you know, when in fact you don't, is a fatal mistake to which we are all prone.

During the Vietnam War, a wire service reporter wrote a graphic account of a battle from a government press release, a secondhand account. Homer Bigart, one of the great war correspondents, was appalled to find the young reporter's story on page 1 of *The New York Times*. Bigart had been to the front and knew the release made exaggerated claims.

Bigart took the reporter to the scene. "See," he told the reporter, "it isn't there."

Peter Arnett, another much-respected war reporter, says his motto is "to write only what I saw myself."

Despite the air of certainty in the tone of news stories, a close reading reveals that many are not based on the reporter's direct observation. The reporter rarely sees the burglar breaking in, the policy being drafted, the automobile hitting the telephone pole. The reporter obtains information about these events from authoritative sources such as documents and records (police files for the burglary and the accident) and from reliable individuals (policy makers and participants and witnesses).

News Filters

When the reporter bases his or her story on direct observation, the story is a firsthand account. But when the reporter is not on the scene and information is obtained from those who were present, the reporter's story is a secondhand account. It has been filtered through the source.

Some stories are based on accounts that have been filtered twice before reaching the reporter. For example, an official agency holds a meeting at which the participants are sworn to secrecy. The reporter learns that one of

Two Types. "In Vietnam, it was said that there were two kinds of observers, those who heard about the war from others and those with muddy boots. I preferred the latter."
—*Malcolm W. Browne,*
Muddy Boots
and Red Socks

those attending the meeting described it to a member of his staff, who happens to be a good source of news for the reporter. The reporter manages to obtain the staff member's account of the executive's account of what occurred.

Here are examples of stories based on direct observation and on secondary sources:

SHREWSBURY—About 250 anti-abortion demonstrators were arrested yesterday and charged with trespassing and violating a court order after they blocked the doors to the Planned Parenthood clinic for several hours.

The protesters, who prayed and sang as they were dragged and carried to police vans and a rented bus, were part of a new national group, called Operation Rescue, which has targeted abortion clinics. The group takes its name from a Bible passage in the Book of Proverbs: "Rescue those who are being drawn away to death."

WASHINGTON, Oct. 7—Striking at night from aircraft carriers and distant bases, the United States and Britain launched a barrage of cruise missles and long-range bombers against Afghanistan today. Their aim was the destruction of the terrorist training camps of Osama bin Laden and the Taliban government that has protected it.

The president ordered the strike. "These carefully targeted actions are designed to disrupt the use of Afghanistan as a terrorist base of operations and to attack the military capability of the Taliban regime," President Bush said in a televised statement from the White House at 1 p.m., half an hour after the attack began.

FBI agents have established that the Watergate bugging incident stemmed from a massive campaign of political spying and sabotage conducted on behalf of President Nixon's re-election and directed by officials of the White House and the Committee for the re-election of the President.

The activities, according to information in FBI and Department of Justice files, were aimed at all the major Democratic presidential contenders and—since 1971—represented a basic strategy of the Nixon re-election effort.

During their Watergate investigation federal agents established that hundreds of thousands of dollars in Nixon campaign contributions had been set aide to pay for an extensive undercover campaign aimed at discrediting individual and Democratic presidential candidates and disrupting their campaigns. . . .

—*The Washington Post*

Covering a Riot

Reporters want to be on the scene, to let the reader see the event through their eyes, hear the sounds of conflict through their ears. When Miami's black section erupted in violence following the police shooting of an unarmed motorcyclist, Will Lester of the Associated Press went to police headquarters to obtain police reaction.

He spotted a city commissioner leaving the headquarters. She told him she was on her way to Overtown, which had been torched by rioters. "Mind if a reporter comes along?" Lester asked. No, the commissioner replied, and with police permission they left the closed-off area. They rode in an unmarked car, through barricades, past police officers on every corner. When they sped down

How the News Is Filtered

The story is based on direct observation of the event by the reporter.

Secondhand Account.
The story is based on the account passed on by a participant or witness.

Thirdhand Account.
The story is based on information supplied by a source who was informed by a participant.

one darkened street, Lester said, "policemen at the end of the street ducked behind closed car doors and leveled pistols at our heads." They heard gunfire as they sped on. Flames leaped from shops. Snipers' bullets whizzed by.

The commissioner talked to a group of young people. "The police are too quick to use their guns," one told her. "The Cubans take our jobs." Lester jotted it down. He noted that, as the rioters spoke, they grew angrier. A rock flew into the street near them. Police officers leveled their rifles. The crowd grew ugly, and police fired tear gas to back people away from the street.

"One of the young men standing by the street gave me a look of desperation," Lester said. "You put it in the paper. Tell them how we feel," the man told Lester. Lester said he understood, but the young man countered, "You can't understand."

But Lester wrote his story, describing what he had seen and heard, hoping that his readers would understand.

Clinton and the Intern   The most dazzling display of secondhand and thirdhand journalism occurred during the grand jury investigation of possible perjury by President Clinton in his relationship with the White House intern Monica Lewinsky. It was, said a University of Virginia professor, a "feeding frenzy" with unsourced, poorly-sourced, judgmental and opinionated pieces passing for reporting. Because grand juries operate in secrecy, there was no first-hand reporting. But reporters, anxious not to be out-reported by the competition, grabbed at anything and everything that floated by.

"The picture that emerges," said the Committee of Concerned Journalists, "is of a news culture that is increasingly involved with disseminating information rather than gathering it."

We now turn to attribution, the sourcing of stories. Proper attribution increases the credibility of the news story.

Attribution

The farther the reporter is from direct observation, the more concerned he or she is about the accuracy of the report. Accurate and comprehensive direct observation is difficult enough. After the information has been filtered once or twice, only the most foolhardy journalist would stake his or her reputation on the accuracy of the report. To make clear to the reader that secondhand and third-hand accounts are not based on the reporter's direct observation of the event, the reporter attributes the information about the event to a source.

Here are the first two paragraphs from a story in *The Detroit News:*

> For six minutes, a Detroit police operator listened on the telephone as 24 bullets were fired into the bodies of an East Side couple.
>
> But, according to the police, the civilian mistook the shots for "someone hammering or building something" and dispatched the call as a routine burglary.

Bill Carter, *The Norman Transcript*

Attribute?

Not necessary. No reporter from *The Norman Transcript* was on hand when this tractor plowed into this house at lunchtime, but the evidence speaks for itself.

The lead may give the reader the impression the reporter was at the phone operator's elbow. But the second paragraph attributes the information to the police.

Attribution refers to two concepts:

1. **Statements** are attributed to the person making them.
2. **Information** about the events not witnessed by the reporter is attributed to the source of the information.

Here is a story that contains both types of attribution:

Mike Roemer

Attribute?

Of course. We attribute statements to those making them.

(**1**) Mayor Stanley Kretchmer said yesterday the city probably could balance its budget this year and next without laying off any workers.

(**1**) The decision, he said, "depends on a number of factors—the passage of a new tax package, the cooperation of municipal labor unions, general prosperity that keeps revenues high."

(**2**) At a meeting last week, the mayor told department heads they should consider the possibility of layoffs of about 10 percent of their work force, according to city officials who attended the meeting.

(**2**) Police and fire department personnel would be exempt from the cuts, sources reported.

Generally, we attribute what we do not observe or know to be factual. Although the reporter may take the information from a police record, the document does not necessarily attest to the truth of the information, only that some source—the police, a victim, the suspect, a witness—said that such-and-such occurred. The reporter attributes the information to this source.

Some news organizations such as the AP demand rigid adherence to the following policy: Always attribute what you do not see unless it is common knowledge.

Let us examine three stories to see how this policy is carried out. Under each story is the speculation of an experienced reporter about the reasons attribution was or was not used. (Her direct quotes follow each story.)

YMCA

(**1**) NEW YORK AP—Dr. Jesse L. Steinfeld, former Surgeon General of the U.S. Public Health Service, has been appointed chairman of the National YMCA Health and Physical Education Advisory Council.

(**2**) Steinfeld is professor of medicine at the University of California at Irvine, Calif., and chief of medical services for the Veterans Hospital in Long Beach, Calif.

(**3**) The advisory council will play an important role in the setting of future directions of the Y's nationwide programs, national board chairman Stanley Enlund said today in announcing Steinfeld's appointment to the nonsalaried post.

(**1**) There is no need for attribution of the appointment because the action is obviously on the record.

(**2**) Steinfeld's background is taken from records and needs no attribution.

(**3**) The role of the council is an opinion offered by the chairman of the board and must be attributed to him.

Hotel Fire

(1) BRANFORD, Conn. AP—The Waverly Hotel, popular earlier in the century, was destroyed by a two-alarm fire today.

(2) The roof collapsed into the heart of the building. At daylight the burned-out hotel was still smouldering.

(3) Myrtle Braxton, 73, who lived alone in the massive three-story building, was reported in fair condition at Yale-New Haven Hospital suffering from smoke inhalation.

(4) Officials said the fire was reported by Mrs. Braxton at 3:41 a.m. They said it apparently started in the kitchen area where Mrs. Braxton was living after having closed off most of the rest of the building. She was living there without central heating or electricity, officials said.

(5) A neighbor said that a large number of antiques on the third floor were destroyed. Also lost was a huge ship's wheel from a sailing ship, a centerpiece in the dining room.

(6) The bank that holds the mortgage said the land and hotel were worth $40,000 to $50,000.

(1)(2) The condition of the hotel is a physical fact about which the reporter has no doubt.

(3) The attribution is implied as coming from the hospital.

(4) "Officials," presumably fire department officials, are cited as the authority because only they could have known this. In the second sentence, the cause is attributed. (Always attribute the cause of a fire.)

(5)(6) Attribution gives the information credibility.

CBC

(1) The Citizen's Budget Commission, a private taxpayer's organization, said today that the proposed city budget of $185 million is more than the city can afford.

(2) The budget was submitted two weeks ago.

(3) Mayor Sam Parnass described it as an austerity budget.

(4) The Commission said it concluded after studying the budget that "significant cuts can be made."

(5) The $185 million spending plan is up 12 percent from the current year.

(6) When he submitted the budget, Mayor Parnass said anticipated revenues would cover the increase. The Commission is supported by the city's business community.

(1) A charge, allegation or opinion is always attributed, usually at the beginning of the lead. Here, the Commission is immediately identified as the source of the allegation.

(2) Background need not be attributed because it is part of the record.

(3) Attribute the mayor's opinion to him.

(4) Attribution to the source of the material.

(5) Background needing no attribution.

(6) Attribute the mayor's statement. (The last sentence is the reporter's attempt to give the reader the why of the Commission's opposition—it's a taxpayer's group that likes austerity budgets because it means lower taxes. Nice touch.)

"Remember," the editor cautioned, "attribution does not guarantee the accuracy or truth of the material. All it does is place responsibility for the material with a source.

"If it turns out the information is inaccurate, the publication or station isn't responsible for the misinformation. The source is.

"If you don't identify the source, the reader or listener is going to assume that we stand behind the statements because we know they are true."

Types of Attribution

Generally, reporters presume that those who speak to them can be named as the source of the information. Occasionally, a source will request he or she not be named. The reporter then has to determine whether the source can be referred to in a general way, as a "city hall official" or a "state legislator" or a "bank executive," for example.

The source may say the information is for *background* only or *off the record.* These terms have specific meanings to reporters but may not have the same meanings to sources. The reporter must clarify with the source whether the material can be used without direct attribution or not used at all but is being provided solely for the reporter's information, or somewhere in between.

Some reporters refuse to accept material if there is a condition that it may not be used in any form. They may bargain with the source, asking if they can go to another source to obtain confirmation. Or they may ask if the material can be used without using the source's name.

Caution: Many editors refuse to accept copy that contains charges or accusations with no named source. They will not accept attribution to "an official in city hall," "a company spokesperson."

Background and off-the-record information pose problems for conscientious reporters because they know that backgrounders can be used to float *trial balloons.* These stories are designed by the source to test public reaction without subjecting the source to responsibility for the material. Reporters, eager to obtain news of importance and sometimes motivated by the desire for exclusives, may become the conduits for misleading or self-serving information.

When a reporter attributes assertions to a source, the reader can assess the accuracy and truth of the information on the basis of the general reliability of the source and his or her stake in the information.

The lesson for reporters is clear: Avoid commitments not to use names of sources.

Anonymous Sources

The reporter's job is to put sources on record, by name. Readers and listeners trust such a report. "When we write 'sources say,' they're convinced we're making it up," writes David Shaw, media critic of the *Los Angeles Times.*

Four Types

On the Record: All statements are directly quotable and attributable, by name and title, to the person who is making the statement.

On Background: All statements are directly quotable, but they cannot be attributed by name or specific title to the person commenting. The type of attribution to be used should be spelled out in advance: "A White House official," "an Administration spokesman."

On Deep Background: Anything that is said in the interview is usable but not in direct quotation and not for attribution. The reporter writes it on his or her own.

Off the Record: Information is for the reporter's knowledge only and is not to be printed or made public in any way. The information also is not to be taken to another source in hopes of getting confirmation.

Some publications and stations insist that all material be attributed to a named source, but others will use nonattributed information when the reporter is sure the material is reliable. In these cases, the editor usually wants to know the name of the source.

Special care must be exercised when an anonymous source makes a charge of wrongdoing. *The New York Times* tells its staff:

> We do not want to let unidentified sources (like "law enforcement officials") use us to circulate charges against identifiable people when they provide no named complainants or other verifiable evidence.

Here is the policy of the Associated Press:

> We do not routinely accede to requests for anonymity. We want information on the record. When a news source insists that he or she not be identified by name, we say so. If we accept the condition of anonymity, we keep our word. But within the rule set by the newsmaker, we do everything possible to tell readers the source's connections, motivations and viewpoints.

Warning

Attributing secondhand and thirdhand accounts to their sources does not absolve reporters of responsibility for libelous statements in their stories. A reporter for a Florida newspaper reported that a county employee smoked marijuana, and the worker brought suit. "The reporter's own testimony indicated she had relied on second- and thirdhand accounts when writing the story," *Editor & Publisher* reported. A jury awarded the employee $70,000. (See Chapter 25 for further discussion of libel.)

See for Yourself Journalists sometimes go astray when they rely on human sources and neglect to ask for proof of assertions the sources make. Records, documents, reports are more reliable than a source's version of them. But a physical source must be examined by the reporter.

A cornerstone of a journalist's allegation about Hillary Clinton's honesty in the Whitewater scenario was that she had vastly overstated the value of the Clintons' real estate holdings in a loan application.

The allegation was given widespread attention. Then a reporter who checked the document found that at the bottom of the front page was the notation: "Both sides of this document must be complete." On reading the other side, the reporter found that Mrs. Clinton had accurately stated the value.

The journalist who had attacked Mrs. Clinton defended his story by stating that his source had not provided the back of the page.

Verification

Attributing material to a source does not prove its truth. All a reporter does when attributing information is to place responsibility for it with the source named in the story. Attribution says only this: It is true that the source said this.

The reporter who cares about truth is reluctant to settle for this half step but often is prevented from moving on by deadline pressures and the difficulty of verifying material. If a reporter tried to check every bit of information, most stories would never be written. There are, of course, certain routine verifications a reporter must make:

- Names, addresses and telephone numbers are checked in the newspaper's library, the telephone directory and the city directory.
- Background information is taken from clips in the library.
- Dubious information is checked against records, with other sources.

Check the Farm   Harlyn Riekena was worried, he told *New York Times* reporter David Cay Johnston. He had heard all this talk about how the federal estate tax would hurt farmers like him. His 950 acres planted in soybean and corn in central Iowa was valuable, worth about $2.5 million. Riekena "fretted that estate taxes would take a big chunk of his three grown daughters' inheritance," Johnston wrote.

President George W. Bush had made the point repeatedly: "To keep farms in the family, we are going to get rid of the death tax," the president said. (Opponents of the estate tax had taken to calling it the death tax, a more ominous title.) Bush had rounded up enough votes in the House to reduce the tax and then abolish it. But how true was the administration's dire prediction of the death of the family farm unless the tax was repealed?

Johnston went to farm country to check, and he did find fear of loss. The administration's warnings had found roots. But was the prediction true? Johnston asked Neil Harl, an Iowa State University economist whose tax advice "has made him a household name among Midwest farmers," Johnston wrote.

Harl told Johnston: "It's a myth." Harl said "he had searched far and wide but had never found a case in which a farm was lost because of estate taxes."

Johnston checked with the American Farm Bureau Federation, a supporter of the repeal. But, Johnston wrote, "It could not cite a single example of a farm lost because of estate taxes."

Check the Documents   Too often, the assertions of officials and authorities are considered nonverifiable, and they are allowed to stand without checking. That, says Marie Cocco, a columnist for *Newsday,* in unfair to the reader and doesn't help the reporter's reputation. When she read a press release during the 2000 presidential campaign that said the Clinton administration had allowed government spending to explode, she paused.

"I knew from years of covering federal budget and tax policy that the essence of this claim was wrong," she says. "By the time of the 2000 presidential election, the federal government was running large surpluses, which means the government was taking in more money than it was spending."

She went to the public budget tables and looked at the numbers. She found, and she wrote, that despite the rhetoric about a spending spree, "Government has been shrinking. Don't take it from me. Take it from the nonpartisan

---

Historic Bet: Pastrami vs. Crab

When the Giants and the 49ers met in a National Football League playoff, Mayor Edward Koch of New York wagered a New York deli feast—pastrami, corned beef, dill pickles with cornrye bread—against Mayor Dianne Feinstein's cracked crab and California wine. The Giants and Koch lost. *The New York Times* reported the food was shipped by the Second Avenue Deli. *The Washington Post* said the Carnegie Deli supplied the sandwiches.

Big deal. Who cares what delicatessen shipped the corned beef and pastrami? Whoa, hold the mayo. The delis care. And we care, as journalists. It's trifles such as this that make the reader shake his or her head knowingly—journalists just can't get the simplest things right.

Congressional Budget Office." The Office, she reported, found that "government spending as a share of the economy dropped again last year, to 18.2 percent. You have to go back a generation—to 1966—to find a year when government ate up such a small piece of national output."

Nonverifiable Information

The reporter can verify this statement: "The mayor submitted a $1.5 million budget to the city council today." All the reporter needs to do is examine the minutes of the meeting or the budget. But he or she cannot verify the truth of this statement: "The budget is too large (or too small)." A city councilman might have indeed stated that he would oppose the budget because it was too large, whereas the head of the Municipal League might have declared her organization's distress at the "paltry budget that endangers health and welfare projects." We can determine that the statements were made, but we cannot determine the truth of opinions and judgments. All we can do is to quote the source accurately, seek countering opinions and let the reader or viewer decide.

The Techniques of Verification

Verification is not the use of another opinion to counter the view of one source with that of another on controversial issues. Journalists should offer several views on controversial matters, and they should seek out the victims of charges. But that is balance, not verification.

When President Clinton sent U.S. planes to bomb sites in Iraq, Sen. Trent Lott, the Republican leader in the Senate, said it was done in an attempt to divert attention from Clinton's impeachment. He was quoted as saying that in 1991 when President George Bush asked for authorization to use force against Iraq, "I don't believe there was a single Democrat that voted for that."

Then the reporter inserted in his story: "In fact, 86 Democrats in the House and 10 in the Senate, including Al Gore, voted for the authorization."

The reporter, David E. Rosenbaum, checked the files rather than allow an accusation to appear in print without verification.

Not all assertions can be verified, of course, and when this happens and the source has not offered proof, the news writer says so. Here is how one reporter handled such a situation:

> She said that test scores have improved
> "substantially," although she offered no
> documentation.

During wartime, journalists depend on official sources because so much happens out of range of the reporter. Sometimes, however, a reporter will try to verify material from an official source. The result can be illuminating.

In Vietnam When the United States announced its planes had accidentally bombed the Cambodian village of Neak Luong, the U.S. Embassy told correspondents that the damage was minimal. Sydney H. Schanberg, a *New York*

Times correspondent, decided to see for himself and sought air transportation to the village. The Embassy intervened to keep him from flying there, but Schanberg managed to find a boat.

Schanberg stayed in Neak Luong long enough to interview villagers and to see for himself whether the damage was minimal. It wasn't.

To see more about Schanberg's coverage, see **In Neak Luong** in *NRW Plus*.

Verification adds a degree of truth to a news story, an ingredient too often missing in the rush to be first with claims, assertions, opinions. In the climate of competition among the various forms of media, the rule seems to be assertion first, verification second—if we can get around to it. Readers and viewers are entitled to verifying information and to all relevant information. Stories are not complete when essential information is lacking. Let's begin with a couple of examples.

Complete

Here is a brief story that ran in the business section of a major newspaper:

The United States' highest-paid chief executive officer resigned his post as Computer Associates International Inc., the world's largest independent software company, reshuffled its senior ranks and announced plans to spin off key divisions in an attempt to bolster its lackluster stock.

Company founder Charles Wang handed the CEO's reins to chief operating officer Sanjay Kumar, but will stay on as chairman and play an active role in the company with the responsibility of developing news initiatives.

Complete? Does the story leaves unanswered any questions the reader might have? If you noticed that the story does not follow up the generality "highest paid chief executive officer" with the amount Wang is paid, go to the head of the class.

There isn't a reader of this piece who isn't wondering how high in the stratosphere of executive salaries Wang's ascends. The reader leaves the piece dissatisfied.

Complete stories are written by reporters who anticipate and answer the questions their readers, viewers and listeners will ask.

Example No. 2 The radio reporter began her 60-second piece about summer rentals in an exclusive area this way:

Once, renters fought for space at the Hamptons. Now, there are dozens of listings and few takers. The prices have gone way down. Still, there are long lists of available rentals.

After this beginning, what do you expect to hear? You want to know just how high those rentals were and what they have descended to now. But our reporter forgot to follow her generality with a specific. Her piece was not complete because she never gave us a single specific price.

Some More Examples   How would you follow these lines taken from some stories:

1. The temperature reached an all-time high yesterday at noon.
2. While in college, she set records in 100 and 200 meter races.
3. He said that today's rap stars will join yesterday's "in the dustbin of forgotten groups."

You would expect:

1. The temperature hit 102 degrees, breaking the record of 98 degrees set on April 10, 1999.
2. Her times of 11.2 in the 100 meter dash and 22.03 in the 200 meter race remain standing at the college to this day.
3. "Who remembers 'Four Hot Dogs' today? Or 'The Malignants'?"

The complete story is also fair and balanced.

Fairness

When Walter Anderson, the editor in chief of *Parade,* was a young reporter he interviewed a woman whom he described as the "unmarried mother of five." After the story appeared, the woman's son called to ask Anderson, "Why did you write that? Why is that anyone's business?"

On reflection two decades later, Anderson said, "The article I wrote was accurate, but I don't think it was fair. I had gotten the facts right, but I was not right."

The Essentials

• No story is fair if it omits facts of major importance or significance. So fairness includes completeness.
• No story is fair if it includes essentially irrelevant information at the expense of significant facts. So fairness includes relevance.
• No story is fair if it consciously or unconsciously misleads or deceives the reader. So fairness includes honesty—leveling with the reader.
• No story is fair if reporters hide their biases or emotions behind such subtly pejorative words as "refused," "despite," "admit." So fairness requires straightforwardness ahead of flashiness.
• No story is fair if innocent people are hurt.

Balance

During political campaigns, editors try to balance—in some cases down to the second of air time or the inch of copy—candidate A and candidate B.

Balance is important. But some journalists contend that balance does not mean they must station themselves precisely at the midpoint of an issue. If candidate A makes an important speech today, the speech may be worth page 1 play. If, on the same day, opponent B repeats what he said yesterday or utters nonsense, the newspaper or station is under no obligation to balance something with nothing. A journalism of absolute balance can add up to zero. Balance is a moral commitment and cannot be measured by the stopwatch or the ruler.

The same common sense is applied to matters that require fair play. Should candidate A make a serious accusation against opponent B, the reporter seeks out B for a reply. The targets of charges and accusations are always given their say, and the reply is placed as closely to the allegation as possible.

When *The Atlanta Journal-Constitution* revealed that a state legislator was helping his son sell computers to the state, the newspaper carried the senator's reply as well as the charge.

Here is the AP's policy on balance:

> We make every reasonable effort to get comment from someone who has a stake in a story we're reporting—especially if the person is the target of an attack or allegations. . . . If someone declines comment, we say so. If we can't get comment from someone whose side of a story should be told, we spell out in our copy the steps we took to try to get that comment. . . . Whenever possible we also check our files to see what, if anything, the person has said in the past relating to the allegations. Including past comment may provide needed balance and context.

Objectivity

Lack of balance and the absence of fairness are often inadvertent. Because writing is as much an act of the unconscious as it is the conscious use of controlled and disciplined intelligence, the feelings of reporters can crop up now and then.

In describing an official the reporter dislikes, a reporter might write, "C. Harrison Gold, an ambitious young politician, said today. . . ."

Or, writing about an official the reporter admires, that reporter might write, "Gerald Silver, the dynamic young state controller, said today. . . ."

It is acceptable for a young man or woman to be "ambitious," but when the word is used to describe a politician, it has a negative connotation. On the other hand, the "dynamic" politician conjures up an image of a young man or woman hard at work serving the public. Maybe the reporter is accurate in these perceptions. Maybe not. The reporter's job is to let the reader draw conclusions by describing what the politician says and does.

In other words, it is the reporter's method that takes precedence, and the method is to be objective. If the reporter feels that Gold is overly ambitious to the point of sacrificing the nonpartisanship of his office, then it is the reporter's job to prove it through meticulous reporting. The reporter must verify his or her suspicions, feelings or hunches.

Edward Reed

Self-Discipline

Whatever the reporter feels about a candidate for office, the account of his campaign is written objectively. The reporter quotes the candidate on his positions, on issues, asks him questions and describes his appearances at street rallies. The reporter allows the reader to make judgments.

No one is free of opinions. Actually, they can be right on target, these sudden insights. The task for the journalist is to do the reporting that verifies them.

Unfair and unbalanced journalism might be described as a failure in objectivity. When journalists talk about objectivity, they mean that the news story is free of the reporter's opinion or feelings, that it contains facts and that the account is from an impartial and independent observer. Stories are objective when they can be checked against some kind of record—the text of a speech, the minutes of a meeting, a police report, a purchase voucher, a payroll, unemployment data, or vital statistics. Stories are objective when material in them is borne out by evidence.

If readers want to weep or laugh, write angry letters to their senators or send money to the Red Cross for tornado victims, that is their business. The reporter is content to lay out the facts. Objective journalism is the reporting of the visible, what people say and do.

Objectivity's Limitations

In the 1950s, social and political problems that had been proliferating since the end of World War II began to cause cleavages in society, and reporters found their methodology—the prevailing concept of objective reporting—inadequate in finding causes and fixing responsibility.

Journalists were concerned about the attention they had given Joseph McCarthy, the Wisconsin senator whose charges of Communist conspiracies had been given front-page play over the country. Their tortured self-analysis led them to assume collective responsibility for the senator's rise to power. They realized it was not enough to report what McCarthy had said—which was objective reporting. McCarthy had indeed made the charges, but many of the charges were later found to be false.

Frustrated Journalists   Elmer Davis, a radio journalist, pointed to the limitations of objective journalism during the McCarthy period. He described the frustrations of reporters who knew officials were lying but were unable to say so in their stories.

Davis said that the principle of objectivity holds that a newspaper or station will run "everything that is said on both sides of a controversial issue and let the reader make up his mind. A noble theory; but suppose that the men who talk on one side (or on both) are known to be lying to serve their own personal interest, or suppose they don't know what they are talking about. To call attention to these facts, except on the editorial page, would not, according to most newspaper practice, be objective."

Davis wondered whether readers have enough background on many subjects and he asked, "Can they distinguish fact from fiction, ignorance from knowledge, interest from impartiality?"

The newspaper is unworthy of the reader's trust, Davis continued in his book *But We Were Born Free,* "if it tells him only what somebody says is the truth, which is known to be false." The reporter has no choice, he wrote, but to put into "the one-dimensional story the other dimensions that will make it approximate the truth." The reporter's obligation is to the person who goes to the news "expecting it to give him so far as humanly possible not only the truth and nothing but the truth, but the whole truth." Then, in a paragraph that influenced many journalists, Davis wrote:

> The good newspaper, the good news broadcaster, must walk a tightrope between two great gulfs—on one side the false objectivity that takes everything at face value and lets the public be imposed on by the charlatan with the most brazen front; on the other, the "interpretive" reporting which fails to draw the line between objective and subjective, between a reasonably well-established fact and what the reporter or editor wishes were the fact. To say that is easy; to do it is hard. No wonder that too many fall back on the incontrovertible objective fact that the Honorable John P. Hoozis said, colon quote—and never mind whether he was lying or not.

Adjustments

Another broadcast journalist, Edward R. Murrow, who had moved from radio to television, pioneered in-depth reporting. He sought to make television journalism more than a bulletin board with news for the middle class. In his work in the 1950s, Murrow demonstrated passion to get at underlying truths along with curiosity and journalistic discipline.

Davis, Murrow and a few other journalists gave a broader scope to objective reporting. Journalists—with their unique nonpartisan perspective and their commitment to democratic values, accurate observation and truth—began to see how they could provide insights for the public and for policy-makers. To do so more effectively, they knew they had to change some of their traditional practices. Underlying their conviction that change was needed was their assumption that journalists are publicly useful men and women.

Providing Context   Some of these journalists found support and justification for their attempt to widen journalism's scope in a report that had been issued in 1947 by a group of academicians, *A Free and Responsible Press. A General Report on Mass Communications: Newspapers, Radio, Motion Pictures, Magazines, and Books*. The report told journalists that they are most useful when they give "a truthful, comprehensive, and intelligent account of the day's events in a context which gives them meaning. . . . It is no longer enough to report *fact* truthfully. It is now necessary to report the *truth about the fact*."

Journalists began to find ways to go beyond reporting assertions and claims. They sought to give an added dimension to their stenographic function by checking statements and by looking for causes and consequences of actions. This kind of journalism, demonstrated in Schanberg's reporting from Vietnam, takes the public closer to the truth.

Such reporting is now commonplace. It is expected of all reporters that they will report the *truth about the fact*. In Elizabeth Rosenthal's report from China about Chinese officials wooing the International Olympic Committee for the 2008 games, she quotes a Chinese Foreign Ministry spokesman, "Most Chinese believe that the human rights situation in China is the best ever."

That satisfied the stenographic function. Then she placed the statement in context, "But that was not true for all Chinese this week," she wrote. She described the detention of members of a human rights group and the imprisonment of a woman for signing a petition urging the Olympic Committee to call on China to release jailed human rights advocates. Rosenthal also reported the stepped-up surveillance of demonstrators at Tiananmen Square where human-rights advocates try to speak out.

Brevity

In our generalization about the reporter's job at the outset of this chapter, we pointed out that the news story is succinct. The tersely told story is admired by editors and by busy readers and listeners. Here is a two-paragraph story that says a great deal although it contains only four sentences:

JOHANNESBURG, South Africa, Nov. 8—The bodies of 60 victims of an accidental dynamite explosion a mile and a half down a gold mine 100 miles southwest of Johannesburg were brought to the surface today.

Of the dead, 58 were Basuto tribesmen from Lesotho, chosen for the dangerous job of shaft-sinking, or blasting a way down to the gold-bearing reef. The two others were white supervisors. The black Africans will be buried in a communal grave tomorrow.

—*The New York Times*

Creative work is based on the art of omission. When Beethoven was struggling with the music to his opera "Fidelio," he realized that the leisurely pace of the music did not meet the demands of the theater, and for years he pared down his work. David Hamilton, the music critic, describes Beethoven's effort as a "ruthless piece of self criticism . . . Beethoven expunged balancing phrases, trimmed decorative expansions, excised anything that did not move forward, eventually achieving the terse urgency that now marks the opera's crucial scenes."

In eliminating large sections of his music, Beethoven rejected three overtures he had written. One, "Leonore No. 3," became one of the most popular pieces in the orchestral repertory. Despite its obvious beauty and power, Beethoven found it unsuited to his opera.

Joseph G. Herzberg, an editor on several New York City newspapers, said, "Newspapering is knowing what to leave out and condensing the rest." But stories can be so brief they omit essential information. As we saw earlier in this chapter, the balance between too-brief and just-enough can be struck when the reporter asks himself or herself: "Have I answered the reader or listener's questions?"

Selectivity

The way out of the dilemma of being brief but not writing telegrams is through Herzberg's advice, which can be summed up in one word—selectivity. Brevity is a function of selectivity—knowing what to leave out.

Selectivity also involves the use of language that makes the point succinctly. Edna Buchanan, the police reporter for *The Miami Herald,* began her account of a record-breaking week of violence in Dade County this way:

> Dade's murder rate hit new heights this
> week as a wave of violence left 14 people
> dead and five critically hurt within five days.

A couple of paragraphs compared these figures with murder figures of previous years, and then Buchanan summarized most of the deaths:

In the latest wave of violence, a teenager's throat was cut and her body dumped into a canal. A former airline stewardess was garroted and left with a pair of scissors stuck between her shoulder blades. Four innocent bystanders were shot in a barroom gun battle. An 80-year-old man surprised a burglar who battered him fatally with a hammer. An angry young woman who "felt used" beat her date to death with the dumbbells he used to keep fit. And an apparent robbery victim was shot dead as he ran away from the robbers.

Strain   A natural tension exists between the editor and the reporter. The editor, confronted with ever-decreasing space and time, wants shorter stories. The reporter, excited by the event and driven by a compulsion to tell the full story, wants more time and more space. Online journalists are even more pressed to compress their work.

Some editors contend that if Genesis can describe the earth's creation in a thousand words, then no reporter needs any more for any event of human dimension. But some events are so complex that only an extended account will do. Important stories often require scene setting and background that consume time and space. The guide for the length of stories is: Make it brief but clear and complete.

Clarity

The executives of 40 daily newspapers in Iowa and journalism instructors at the state's three journalism schools were asked to rank characteristics considered most important for beginning reporters. Both groups put the ability to write clearly and interestingly first.

Clear prose follows comprehension. That is, the reporter must be able to understand the event before he or she can explain it clearly and succinctly. You cannot clarify what you do not understand.

Clarity is enhanced by simplicity of expression, which generally means short sentences, everyday language, coherence and logical story structure. We shall be looking at these in detail in Chapter 7.

Human Interest

To make certain the story is read, the journalist recounts events in ways that substitute for the drama of the personal encounter. One of the ways the journalist does this is to tell the story in human terms. Reporters personalize and dramatize the news by seeking out the people involved in the event. Human interest is an essential ingredient of news.

A change in city zoning regulations is dramatized by pointing out that now low-income families can move into an area that had been effectively sealed off to them by the previous two-acre zoning rule. A factory shutdown is personalized by talking to workers who must line up at the unemployment office instead of at a workbench.

Polluting   In a story about chemicals polluting the Hudson River and ruining the fishing industry, Barry Newman of *The Wall Street Journal* begins:

Grassy Point, N.Y.—In the gray-shingled shack at water's edge, four fishermen sit playing cards around an old kitchen table, ignoring the ebb tide laden with the spring run of shad. The wall is hung with foul-weather gear; rubber boots are piled in the corner. On the refrigerator door somebody has taped up a newspaper clipping about the awful chemical in the fish of the Hudson River.

"I do my fishing from the window here," an old man says, looking off to the quiet hills on the east bank, three miles across the river from this small valley town.

"No nets for me this year," another man says. "No pay," says the third. And the fourth: "A lot of trouble, this."

Localizing   In Washington, the talk was of budget cutting. Members of Congress used the podium as a pulpit to expound on the morality of frugality.

Back home in Minneapolis, the *Star Tribune* decided to see just what role federal spending played in Anoka County. "This was an attempt to bring down to a personal level the debate in Washington over extremely intricate financial and policy issues," said Mike Kaszuba, suburban affairs reporter. He teamed with the newspaper's Washington bureau chief Sharon Schmickle to do the reporting and writing.

The reporters found that billions of dollars had flowed into the county since the New Deal built the Anoka high school stadium. Federal money "built the bridge that carries traffic over the Rum River into downtown. Now it pays Mary Wellman, hired last year as Anoka's only female police officer."

The series gave faces and names to people helped by federal funds—students eating school lunches, students attending the local technical college, people using the Anoka ambulance, people who need help with their heating bills, salaries for teachers who help special education students.

Responsibility

Ted Williams was one of baseball's greatest players. The Boston Red Sox outfielder won six batting titles over a span of 17 years and was one of the few to win the Triple Crown twice, leading the league in 1942 and in 1947 in batting, runs batted in and home runs. To many baseball fans, he was heroic. To some sports writers, he was, as Roger Kahn put it, "a pill."

It was possible for readers to know the real Williams because, Kahn says, when nine writers covered Red Sox games "it was impossible to conceal" the truth about Williams. "If one writer courted The Thumper by refusing to report a tantrum as news, another inevitably seized the tantrum as news. Regardless of each reporter's skill, an essential, imperfect system of checks and balances worked. If you cared enough about Williams, and I did, you could find a portrait that was honest by consensus."

But many of the Boston newspapers that covered Williams are gone, as are others in many cities. There are fewer than 30 cities with competing daily newspapers. This means that the responsibility for truth telling falls on fewer shoulders. It falls, in most U.S. cities, in fact, on a single reporter, for most local news beats are covered by only one journalist.

Responsibility is not a visible part of a news story. It is an attitude that the reporter carries to the job. It encompasses all the components we have discussed in this chapter.

Responsibility is the reporter's commitment to the story, to journalism and to the public. Responsibility demands of the reporter that the story be accurate, complete, fair and balanced, that it be so clear anyone can understand it.

Nothing in the law requires a reporter to be responsible. In fact, journalists sometimes flinch at the word. The reason for their discomfort is that some people and some groups use the word as a club with which to beat journalists when the newspaper or station presents material they dislike.

Journalists testily reply that they can be as irresponsible as they like. That's understandable, and it is true. But beneath the surface, reporters and editors understand that journalism is a moral enterprise, that theirs is a calling practiced with honesty and diligence within the limits of verifiable truth and scant time.

Summing Up

Editors tell their new news writers that journalism begins with the ABCs—accuracy, brevity and clarity. Of course, there is more required of the journalist, but these are good for starters.

Misspelled Name

Accuracy of fact and language.

Brevity in making the point succinctly.

Clarity so there is no doubt about what happened.

These can be seen as moral requirements as well as necessities of the practice of the craft. Journalists take on the responsibility of telling people about the world around them so that they can act on what they read, see and hear. But action depends on clear, understandable and accurate information. Without such information, action may be misdirected or, just as bad, never taken.

Polls tell us that much of the public is suspicious of journalists. This is dangerous for democracy, which functions only when an informed public is involved in the give-and-take of communal life.

Returning journalism to its status as trusted and reliable informer may begin simply with spelling names correctly, getting the address right, quoting the source accurately, and sticking around to see for yourself. Public distrust can begin with such simple mistakes as leaving the event before it's over as a *Boston Globe* music reviewer did. He praised the Allman Brothers Band's "show-climaxing" song "Revival." Trouble is, "Revival" was not the last piece the band played. The *Globe*'s critic had relied on the planned song list and left early to beat the traffic.

Writing

Finally, a word about writing. A news story may be accurate, properly attributed, balanced and fair, objective and brief. The reporter may be compassionate and understanding, may have carried out his or her tasks with responsibility. The story may have something interesting and exciting to say. But unless it is written with some skill, the reader or listener will not bother.

Good writing—direct and clear, simple and straightforward—is an important component of the story. Good writing avoids clichés and redundancies. It does not strain for effect. It does not call attention to itself but to the story it tells.

Further Reading

Benjamin, Burton. *Fair Play: CBS, General Westmoreland, and How a Television Documentary Went Wrong.* New York: Harper & Row, 1988.

Bensman, Joseph, and Robert Lilienfield. *Craft and Consciousness.* New York: Wiley, 1973.

Chancellor, John, and Walter R. Mears. *The News Business.* New York: Harper & Row, 1983.

Commission on Freedom of the Press. *A Free and Responsible Press.* Chicago: University of Chicago Press, 1947.

Edwards, Julia. *Women of the World: The Great Foreign Correspondents.* Boston: Houghton Mifflin, 1988.

Liebling, A. J. *The Press.* New York: Ballantine Books, 1964.

Mills, Kay. *A Place in the News: From the Women's Pages to the Front Page.* New York: Dodd, Mead, 1988.

Schiller, Dan. *Objectivity and the News: The Public and the Rise of Commercial Journalism.* Philadelphia: University of Pennsylvania Press, 1981.

Siebert, Fred S., et al. *Four Theories of the Press.* Urbana: University of Illinois Press, 1956.

PART THREE: Writing the Story

3 What Is News?

U.S. Navy Photo

Impact . . . timeliness . . . conflict.

Preview

Journalists look to a set of news values to help them determine the newsworthiness of events. These values are:

- Timeliness.
- Impact, consequence or importance.
- Prominence of the people involved.
- Proximity to readers and listeners.
- Conflict.
- The unusual nature of the event.
- Currency—the sudden interest people have in an ongoing situation.
- Necessity—a situation the journalist feels compelled to reveal.

At least three-fourths of all stories fall into the categories of impact or importance and the unusual.

We have discussed several essentials of journalism—accuracy, attribution, verification, completeness, balance and fairness, objectivity, brevity, clarity, human interest and responsibility. These elements are the reporter's guides to reporting and writing the story. But in what kinds of events is the public interested? And once on the scene of such an event, what aspects of it are newsworthy?

Some Answers Past and Present

We know that several subjects draw people to the media—news of the weather, crime, money, health, sports, entertainment and local activities. Parents want to find out how to dress their children for school and themselves for the trip to the shopping mall. The result: The morning newspaper and broadcasts stress weather news.

We know that women over the age of 50 are avid followers of news about health. The result: Daytime TV, radio and cable have plenty of news about illness and new cures. Men under 40 make up, almost exclusively, the followers of sports. Radio, TV and the print media are heavy on sports in the morning before men leave for work and in the evening when they are at home.

We have known for a long time what interests people and what we think they should know about the events that affect them.

Realizing that Roman citizens needed to know about official decisions that affected them, Julius Caesar posted reports of government activities in the *Acta Diurna*. In China, the T'ang dynasty (618–906 A.D.) published a gazette—handwritten or printed by woodblock—to inform court officials of its activities. The more immediate predecessor of the newspaper was the handwritten newsletter, containing political and economic information, that circulated among merchants in early 16th-century Europe.

Wars, Dragons and Business

The first printed newsbook, published in 1513 and titled *The trewe encounter,* described the Battle of Flodden Field in which James IV of Scotland was killed during his invasion of England. The Anglo-Scottish wars that followed provided printers with material for more newsbooks. The elements of our modern-day journalism were included in these accounts—names of officers in the wars and their deeds. Adventure, travel and crime were featured, along with accounts of disasters.

As one printer-pamphleteer put it, people are interested in "and most earnestly moved with strange novelties and marvelous things." These early day journalists favored stories of monsters and dragons, not unlike our own day's tales of the Abominable Snowman and the Loch Ness monster.

During the 17th century, news sheets spread to the business centers of Europe, reporting news of commerce. In this country, as historian Bernard Weisberger has pointed out, the newspaper "served as a handmaiden of commerce by emphasizing news of trade and business."

To this day, much of our news is about the actions of government and business, and our journalism continues to stress the drama of war and other calamities.

Day and Bennett

The newspaper editors of the 19th century understood the need to appeal to a large audience to stay in business, and their acumen led to definitions of news that hold to this day. The papers in the large cities were printing news for the newly literate working class. One of the first penny papers—inexpensive enough for working people—contained the ingredients of popular journalism. In 1833, the first issue of Benjamin H. Day's *New York Sun* included a summary of police court cases and stories about fires, burglaries and a suicide. Other stories contained humor and human interest.

Several years later, James Gordon Bennett—described by historians as the originator of the art, science and industry of news gathering—used the recently developed telegraph to give the readers of his *Herald* commercial and political news to go along with his reports of the everyday life of New York City, its sins and scandals. His formula of news for "the merchant and man of learning, as well as the mechanic and man of labor" guides many editors today.

Definition. "Journalism is in fact history on the run. It is history written in time to be acted upon; thereby not only recording events but at times influencing them. Journalism is also the recording of history while the facts are not all in."
—*Thomas Griffith,* Time *magazine*

The Library of Congress

Joseph Pulitzer

Pulitzer

Day and Bennett followed the tastes and appetites of their readers, but they also directed and taught their readers by publishing stories they deemed important. This blend of entertainment, information and public service was stressed by Joseph Pulitzer, who owned newspapers in St. Louis and New York. He, too, gave his readers what he thought they wanted—sensational news and features. But Pulitzer was not content with entertainment. He also used his news staff for his campaigns to curb business monopolies and to seek heavy taxes on income and inheritance. In 1883, Pulitzer charged the staff of his New York *World* with this command:

> Always fight for progress and reform, never tolerate injustice or corruption, always fight demagogues of all parties, never belong to any party, always oppose privileged classes and public plunderers, never lack sympathy with the poor, always remain devoted to the public welfare, never be satisfied with merely printing news, always be drastically independent, never be afraid to attack wrong, whether by predatory plutocracy or predatory poverty.

Hearst

Pulitzer and William Randolph Hearst were locked in a circulation war for New York readers when Cuba rebelled against its Spanish rulers. Spain was severe in repressing the insurrection and the New York newspapers seized on the story of helpless Cubans trying to free themselves from oppression.

Hearst's *Journal* was particularly imaginative. After the United States declared war in 1898 and the troops were slow in making it to Cuba, Hearst urged them on with an inventive news story that had 5,000 troops on their way.

"Over the next week," writes Arthur Lubow in *The Reporter Who Would Be King,* "the *Journal* reported an exciting sequence of landings, bombardments and fleet battles, all admirably detailed, all entirely fictitious. The *Journal* was selling so well thanks to its apocryphal scoops that its rivals began to play the same game, often rewriting the accounts of the creative *Journal* writers."

Today's Editors

Modern mass media editors overseeing newsrooms humming with the latest electronic wonders apply many 19th-century concepts of news. They would define their news menu as a blend of information, entertainment and public service. They would also agree with the definition of news offered by Charles A. Dana, who ran the *New York Sun* from 1869 to 1897. Dana said news is "anything that interests a large part of the community and has never been brought to its attention before."

One of Dana's editors, John B. Bogart, contributed the classic definition, "When a dog bites a man, that is not news, because it happens so often. But if a man bites a dog, it's news."

Another enduring definition of news was offered by Stanley Walker, a Texan gone East to succeed as city editor of *The New York Herald Tribune* in the early 1930s. He said news was based on the three W's, "women, wampum, and wrongdoing." By this he meant that news was concerned with sex, money and crime—the topics people desired to know about. Actually, Walker's formula is as old as the contents of Caesar's *Acta Diurna* 2,000 years ago, which, along with information about public affairs, offered news of sports, crime and sensational events. And in England, while newspapers were carrying material directed at the commercial class, handbills and pamphlets were carrying sensational crime news.

By the mid–1970s, the United States had been through three crises: a war in Vietnam that wound down with guilt and defeat for many Americans; the Watergate scandals; and the failure of some political, social and economic experiments of the 1950s and 1960s that had been hailed as solutions to international conflict, racial tension and poverty.

It was not surprising, then, to see a shift in the criteria used to determine the news. Av Westin, the executive producer of the American Broadcasting Company's "Evening News" program, said Americans wanted their news to answer the following questions: Is the world safe? Are my home and family safe? If they are safe, then what has happened in the last 24 hours to make them better off? Is my pocketbook safe?

People not only wanted more pocketbook stories but escape stories as well. Reflecting the interests of their readers, editors asked for more entertainment in the form of copy about lifestyles, leisure subjects and personalities.

In the 1990s, editors devised the "reader-friendly" story. Readers, they argued, want to learn how to diet, how to raise their children, where to invest their money. The news agenda was being shaped to conform to the interests of middle-class readers and viewers. Also, editors became aware that a major segment of the female population consists of working women. Coverage followed this awareness.

Three Views

"A news sense is really a sense of what is important, what is vital, what has color and life—what people are interested in. That's journalism."
—*Burton Rascoe,*
Chicago Tribune, *1920s*

"Marketing should be the king of all editors. They should forget what university professors stuffed into their heads, find out what readers really want and give it to them."
—*Stuart Garner,*
Thomson Newspapers, *1980s*

"News is truth that matters."
—*Gerry Goldstein,* The
Providence Journal, *1990s*

News in the New Century The 21st century opened with proof of Walker's wampum and Westin's pocketbook theories of news. Stories abounded of the high-flying economy and its new dot-com millionaires. In short order, the news focus shifted to an economy in retreat, jobs lost, dot-coms collapsing, the Dow Jones declining.

At any given time, news in the mass media follows two general guidelines:

• News is information about a break from the normal flow of events, an interruption in the expected, a deviation from the norm.
• News is information people need to make sound decisions about their lives.

How does a reporter or editor determine what events are so unusual and what information is so necessary that the public should be informed of them? Journalists have established some guides, called news values, for answering these questions.

News Values

The following eight factors determine the newsworthiness of events, personalities and ideas:

1. Timeliness

Events that are immediate, recent. The daily newspaper, the online news services and the hourly newscast seek to keep readers and listeners abreast of events. Thus, broadcast news is written in the present tense, and most leads on newspaper stories contain the word today. No matter how significant the event, how important the people involved, news value diminishes with time. André Gide, the French novelist, defined journalism as "everything that will be less interesting tomorrow than today."

The media are commercial enterprises that sell space and time on the basis of their ability to reach people quickly with a perishable commodity. The marketplace rewards a fast news carrier. Although newspapers place less emphasis on speed than do the electronic media, a newspaper that offers its readers too much rehashed news will not survive. Radio, which was being prepared for its funeral when television captured a large segment of the listening audience, staged a comeback with the all-news station.

Online journalism provides Internet surfers with a running report on everything from hourly stock market prices to traffic flows and the scores of various games. When *The Dallas Morning News* was told that Timothy McVeigh, the Oklahoma City bomber, confessed his guilt to his lawyer, the newspaper put the story on its online version rather than hold it for the print version.

Recognizing the importance of timeliness, the Associated Press and other news providers pump out a steady stream of urgents, bulletins and Writethrus on breaking stories. As we saw in Chapter 1, the AP met the public's need for the latest information with a steady stream of material on the World Trade Center bombings. Sometimes, speed leads to misinformation. For a glimpse at the trouble the media encountered in calling the 2000 presidential election, see **Calling Bush or Gore** in *NRW Plus.*

Timely Information Essential   There is another side to our need to know quickly. Timeliness is important in a democracy. People need to know about the activities of their officials as soon as possible so they can assess the directions in which their leaders are moving. Told where they are being led, citizens can react before actions become irreversible. In extreme cases, the public can rid itself of an inefficient or corrupt official. Officials also want quick distribution of information so that they can have feedback from the public. This interaction is one of the reasons the Constitution protects the press. Without the give-and-take of ideas, democracy could not work.

Timeliness is also the consequence of advertising necessities. Because most businesses are based on the quick turnover of goods, advertisements must appear soon after goods are shipped to stores. The news that attracts readers to the advertisements must be constantly renewed.

2. Impact

Events that are likely to affect many people. Journalists talk about events that are significant, important. They talk about giving high priority in their coverage to situations that people need to know about to be well informed. The more people that are affected by the event, the bigger the story. An increase in the postal rates will be given major attention because so many are affected. An increase in a town's property tax will receive considerable play in that town and nowhere else, but a change in the federal income tax rate will receive national attention.

Journalists may take the initiative in digging up situations that have considerable impact. David Willman, a reporter in the Washington bureau of the *Los Angeles Times,* suspected that the federal Food and Drug Administration had lost its effectiveness as the guardian of public health. He spent two years examining the FDA's work and discovered it had approved seven prescription drugs that were believed to have caused the deaths of more than 1,000 people. Despite warnings from its own specialists about the drugs—among them a painkiller, a diet pill and a heartburn medicine—approval had been granted.

Some events take time for their significance to be realized. When Gen. George C. Marshall, the secretary of state, gave a commencement address at Harvard in 1947 and proposed what became known as the Marshall Plan for the reconstruction of war-torn Europe, it received scant media attention. Two reporters who saw its impact were discouraged by their editors from filing full stories. The AP reported that Marshall, "among others, spoke."

Marshall's 1,200-word address took less than 12 minutes to deliver at the commencement exercise. "Though few sensed it at the time," says John T. Bethell, senior editor of *Harvard Magazine,* "it would go down as the most important commencement address ever given at Harvard."

The lesson: Only the well-informed are able to make decisions about newsworthiness.

3. Prominence

Events involving well-known people or institutions. When the president trips disembarking from an airplane, it is front-page news; when a city councilmember missteps, it is not worth a line of print. A local banker's embezzlement is more newsworthy than a clerk's thievery, even when the clerk has stolen more. When Michael Jackson sprains a thumb while working on a Walt Disney movie, it is network news. Names make news, goes the old adage, even when the event is of little consequence.

Two events that probably received the most massive media coverage of the 1990s were the result of prominence—the pursuit, arrest and trials of O.J. Simpson and the sexual affair of President Clinton with a young White House intern. Never mind that the economies of several large countries were crumbling, that the Middle East and Northern Ireland saw carnage amidst peace efforts, that nuclear proliferation arose and that ethnic warfare killed hundreds of thousands and made refugees of many more. Names made news, big and bigger news.

Prominence applies to organizations as well, and even to some physical objects. The repair of a major bridge in Akron is given coverage in that city and not elsewhere. But when the Golden Gate Bridge shuts down that action merits national coverage.

In 1884, the American poet and journalist Eugene Field was moved by the journalism of personalities to write:

Now the Ahkoond of Swat is a vague sort of man

Who lives in a country far over the sea;

Pray tell me, good reader, if tell me you can,

What's the Ahkoond of Swat to you folks or me?

Despite Field's gentle poke, journalists continue to cater to what they perceive as the public's appetite for newsworthy names.

4. Proximity

Events that are geographically or emotionally close to people interest them. In Chapter 1, we read about the tornado that ripped apart the small town of Spencer, S.D. The *Argus Leader,* the state's major newspaper, sent reporters and photographer's 50 miles west to the town. In 1½-inch type on page 1, the newspaper quoted the governor:

'The town is gone'

If 42 people die in an airplane crash in the Andes and one of the passengers is a resident of Little Rock, the news story in Little Rock will emphasize the death of the local person. This is known as *localizing* the news. When two tour buses collided in Wales, injuring 75 peoples, *USA Today* began its account this way:

> Teen-agers from Lancaster, Pa., Houston and St. Louis were among 75 people hurt when two tour buses returning from Ireland collided in Wales.

For six days, the *Argus Leader* kept its staffers in Spencer covering the aftermath of the tornado. Elsewhere, the media turned to other news. But when 11 Texas A&M students and a former student died under a 40-foot stack of logs they were building for the annual bonfire, the news was carried for days everywhere in the country. In this event, several news values were in play, perhaps the most compelling was the emotional tie.

Emotional Closeness   People are interested in events and individuals that seem close to them. In the Texas A&M tragedy, the students who were the victims reminded friends and parents of students away at college. What sort of activities are my children, my friends involved in that could have such terrible consequences?, people asked themselves.

The tie may be religious, ethnic, racial. Newspapers and stations with large Catholic or Jewish populations give considerable space and time to news from the Vatican or the Middle East. After the space shuttle Challenger exploded and sent seven crew members to their deaths, the *Amsterdam News,* a weekly in New York with a predominantly black readership, headlined on page 1 the death of the black astronaut who was abroad.

A report by Human Rights Watch and the Sentencing Project showed that throughout the country 3.9 million parolees, ex-prisoners and prisoners cannot vote. In 14 states, most of them in the South, 2 million will never be able to vote because they were convicted of a felony. Of the 2 million, 1.4 million are black men. One in three black men in Alabama and Florida cannot vote. *The Miami Herald* ran a front page story; *USA Today* and *The Wall Street Journal* did not cover the story. NBC did not use the story; CBS ran a brief segment; ABC devoted three minutes to it. The African-American-run American Urban Radio Network gave the report 30 minutes.

Dave McDermand, *The Bryan-College Station Eagle*

Bonfire Tragedy

Twelve deaths and several injuries followed the collapse of logs being prepared for the annual Aggie Bonfire on the Texas A&M campus.

5. Conflict

Strife, antagonism, warfare have provided the basis of stories since early peoples drew pictures on their cave walls of their confrontations with the beasts that surrounded them. People and their tribes and their countries have been at war with each other, and with themselves, since history has been kept, and the tales that resulted have been the basis of saga, drama, story and news.

Mike Roemer

Political Conflict

The opponents on the issue of abortion do battle with placards, parades and politics. This long-running conflict has erupted in violence.

To journalists today, conflict has a more nuanced meaning. "The most effective stories I've read," says Peter St. Onge, a staff writer for *The Charlotte Observer,* "involved ordinary people confronting the challenges of daily life."

Although critics of the press condemn what they consider to be an overemphasis on conflict, the advance of civilization can be seen as an adventure in conflict and turmoil. Indeed, one way to define, and to defend, journalism is that it provides a forum for discussion of the conflicts that divide people and groups, and that this peaceful debate makes conflict resolution possible.

6. The Unusual

Events that deviate sharply from the expected, that depart considerably from the experiences of everyday life make news. We know that. But here we are talking about the truly different, the bizarre, strange and wondrous.

When a dog bites a man, it isn't news. But when a police dog, a tried and true member of the K-9 Corps, sinks his teeth into the arm of his police handler, that's unusual, and it's news. We've all seen big watermelons in the supermarket, but the 40-pound monster makes page 1 of the B section of *The Freeport News* when the farmer offers it to the First Baptist Church for its annual picnic.

Domestic Violence   Domestic spats are not news, unless they are so violent murder is committed. But when Lorena Bobbitt tired of her husband's mental and physical attacks and cut off his penis. . . . Yes, that was news for several weeks.

In fact, media fascination with the Bobbitt family surgery led Peter Kann, publisher of *The Wall Street Journal,* to condemn "media fascination with the bizarre, the perverse and pathological—Lorena Bobbitt journalism."

But it was over in a few weeks, and today few people can identify Lorena Bobbitt or recall the reason for her 15 seconds of media attention. The bizarre has the lifespan of a firefly's momentary flash.

To some, though, the attention was important and worthwhile, for the incident made people think about domestic violence and its victims, and in its wake some governors pardoned women imprisoned for killing husbands who had for years tormented and beaten them. Cause and effect? Possibly.

A Symbol   The young man who stood alone before a column of tanks on their way to bloody Tiananmen Square struck everyone who saw the photograph and read the accompanying story as so amazing, so wondrous that the act quickly became a symbol. To some, it was a symbol of defiance of tyranny. To others, it was, as the writer and critic Ian Buruma wrote, a symbol "of the futility of empty-handed opposition to brute force."

This tragic figure came to represent the end to the student demonstration in the Square for freedom and democracy. But, some say, the bizarre episode may well symbolize "the beginning of the end of the Communist Party rule in China," as Buruma put it.

AP Photo by Jeff Widener

A Lone Man's Plea

As the tanks headed down Cangan Boulevard in their show of strength in Beijing, a young man darted in front of the column. The tanks stopped. The man looked up and called out to the soldiers to stop the killing. The tanks tried to weave around him, easing him aside. He cried out again, pleading for no more violence. Bystanders finally pulled him away, fearing he would be crushed under the treads.

7. Currency

Occasionally, a situation long simmering will suddenly emerge as the subject of discussion and attention. Historians might describe the situation as an idea whose time has come. When it does, the media catch up.

In the early 1960s, President Kennedy called attention to the plight of the poor. Then President Johnson declared a "war on poverty." Newspapers responded by covering health and welfare agencies and by going into poor areas of their cities in search of news. Television produced documentaries on the blighted lives of the poor. More than 30 years later, poverty, although as pervasive, receives less attention.

The plight of women and members of minority groups in achieving recognition for their talents was long ignored. Victims of the glass ceiling and discrimination in the executive suites, they finally broke through to the media and became the subject of coverage. Progress followed.

Generally, journalists have not been in the vanguard of these discoveries but have been propelled into making news of them by others. Sometimes, journalists will decide that a situation needs attention and will make it newsworthy. We saw a few pages back how a *Los Angeles Times* reporter revealed that a federal agency had approved the sale of prescription drugs that were killing people. He stayed with the story for two years before the agency pulled the drugs from the market.

The work of David Willman falls in an eighth category, a category that stems from the reporter's feelings that he or she must act.

8. Necessity

The seven previous categories of newsworthiness involve people, events and situations that call out for coverage—meetings, speeches, accidents, deaths, games and the like. This final category is of the journalist's making. That is, *the journalist has discovered something he or she feels it is necessary to disclose.* The situation or event, the person or idea may or may not come under any of the previous seven categories of newsworthiness, or may meet one or more of these values. The essential element is that the journalist considers the situation to be something everyone should know about, and usually it is a situation that needs to be revealed or remedied. Here are some examples:

WMAQ, Chicago—The TV station revealed that U.S. Customs officers at O'Hare International Airport were using racial and gender profiling to target black women for invasive strip searches of passengers. The story led to a class-action suit and an investigation by the Customs Service of the practice at all international airports.

San Antonio Express-News—Reporter John Tedesco wondered about the safety record of amusement rides at two large local theme parks. An accident at one had killed a woman. He found: Rides are not subject to state inspection; although state law requires parks to report accidents, many serious injuries were not reported.

WTVF, Nashville—Reporters found wholesale theft of food and clothing at a Feed the Children Warehouse.

The Detroit News—Melvin Claxton and Charles Hurt disclosed the inadequate financial support for the city's fire department resulted in loss of lives and unnecessary property damage.

Chicago Tribune—Reporters Ken Armstrong and Maurice Possley pored through the records of 11,000 homicide cases from around the country, a two-year investigation. They found prosecutors hid and manufactured evidence. They documented 381 wrongful homicide convictions. Later, Armstrong and Steve Mills looked through the records of the 285 Illinois prison inmates on Death Row and discovered so many irregularities that the governor declared a moratorium on executions.

Reportorial Enterprise These stories were reporter-initiated. Reporters felt it necessary to look deeply into a situation. In many cases, reporters dug into situations that one reporter described as affecting "the least of them," the men, women and children that journalism usually overlooks. Noreen Turyn, an anchor at WSET in Lynchburg, Va., heard about a state law that allowed the forced sterilization of women considered unfit to have children. She felt it necessary to call to public attention this intrusion on the rights of women, and her stories overcame legislative lack of interest to bring about a change in the law.

Katherine Boo of *The Washington Post* describes this reporting as traveling through "the shadowlands of the disadvantaged and disenfranchised." In two separate series, Boo disclosed the horrible conditions in which the city's retarded lived—and died. She documented beatings, robberies, rapes and the use of the retarded for slave labor in so-called training programs.

Abortions for All   When Heidi Evans of the *Daily News* was told by a caller that every woman who went to a cash-only abortion clinic was informed that she was pregnant, Evans raced over to the clinic the next day with a urine sample of her own.

"The owner, who did the tests himself, told me I was pregnant and tugged at my arm to have the procedure right then," Evans said.

"The following day, I sent another reporter with a sample from one of our male colleagues. The urine also tested positive." After two more weeks of reporting, in which she showed how poor, mostly immigrant women were herded by the clinic owner to a back room where a fly-by-night doctor operated, the state shut down the clinic.

Evans had been called by the clinic owner's receptionist with the tip because Evans had a reputation as a reporter who could do something, could correct injustice. She had just completed a series after finding that the city had 2,000 unread Pap tests sitting in a box. Thousands more had just been sent out for analysis after sitting in an office for as long as a year unread.

"The women had been told by clinic doctors to assume their Pap tests were normal if they didn't hear back in six weeks," Evans said. "Ninety three learned later that they had precancerous conditions and 11 had cervical cancer."

The result: The city's testing program was overhauled and women now are given their test results in a week. Four of the officials responsible were fired or demoted. Evans was awarded the prestigious George Polk Award for local reporting for her Pap smear series.

Evans is not reluctant to say that her journalism is an activist, advocacy journalism. She makes news out of the undercurrents and the hidden activities of those in power.

Hog Heaven   Despite journalism's tardiness and the complexity of the beat, major stories have been developed about the threat to the environment by accident and design. *The News & Observer* examined an unlikely source of environmental degradation—hog lagoons.

Raising hogs is big business, and the bigger the hog farm the better the business because the slaughterhouse can be next door, eliminating the expense of hauling the hogs to the meat cutters. But the big hog farms—some have a million animals—do the following, the newspaper revealed:

Contaminate Ground Water

Through the emission of ammonia gas into the atmosphere that is returned with rain, streams are being choked with algae.

Waste from the hogs—which produce as much as four times as much waste per hog as do humans—is piling up in open fields.

The series on the hog farms contamination won a Pulitzer Prize.

Help Offered

When the *Daily News* prodded the city to act, it set up a Hot Line for women whose Pap tests had been ignored.

Chris Seward, *The News & Observer*

Hazard

When Hurricane Floyd hit North Carolina, thousands of hogs were drowned. Officials estimated 28,000 hogs were killed. The decaying carcasses became a health hazard and had to be incinerated.

The Society of Environmental Journalists has a Web page with links to authoritative sources: www.sej.org, and one of the links is to the National Library for the Environment: www.cnie.org/nel/index.shmtl.

Questionable Deaths   In North Carolina, disability advocates had complained about the state's mental health system. The governor didn't listen. Parents complained about the lack of services for their children. Legislators weren't interested. Debbie Cenziper of *The Charlotte Observer* listened and became interested. The result: More than 30 stories beginning with a five-part series that revealed that 34 people with mental disabilities—many of them young—died under questionable circumstances while in the care of the state's mental health facilities. "They died from suicide, murder, scalding, falls," Cenziper says. "They suffocated, starved, choked, drowned." Most of the deaths were never investigated because the state had not been told of them.

The stories led to increased mental health funding, money for hiring 27 inspectors for mental health facilities and two laws to correct the dangerous flaws Cenziper had described.

See **Broken Trust** in *NRW Plus.*

Does It Work?   In all these stories that reporters initiated the common element is that something was not functioning properly, that something was wrong with the system. David Burnham, a former *New York Times* reporter, says the increased bureaucratization of public life calls for a new approach to news. The media need to spend more time asking: How are the bureaucracies that affect our lives working? Are they deviating from our expectation that they are there to serve us?

Is the police department engaged in crime prevention; is the power company delivering sufficient energy at a reasonable price; are the high schools graduating college-entry seniors? To the *Times Union* in Albany, N.Y., the question was whether the method of handling state prison rule-breakers is humane.

Inside the Box   Prisons in the state have 5,700 special housing units used for disciplining prisoners. Known to prisoners and their guards as The Box, these special cells house prisoners for 23 hours a day. To prison officials, The Box reduces violence by isolating dangerous inmates. To human rights advocates, The Box erases human dignity, impairs mental health and reduces its inmates to less-than-human status.

Despite official opposition, Paul Grondahl was able to visit several prisons. He also was able to obtain letters from prisoners. Prisoners who talked to Grondahl faced punishment. But as one prisoner said, "I've got nothing to lose. They can't do anything to us that's worse than this."

Dying Lakes   The *Times Union* also felt it necessary to track the progress, if any, being made to cope with the effects of acid rain in the nearby Adirondacks Park, the largest wilderness area east of the Rockies. What it found did not make for optimism.

Changing Times . . . Changing Beats

A century ago, 50 percent of the workforce in the United States made a living from agriculture. Farm news was big news. Today, with 2.5 percent so employed, farm news is important outside agricultural areas only when the cost of food goes up. At the beginning of the 20th century, fewer than 115,000 students attended college and journalists paid little attention to them. Today, more than 50 times as many are enrolled and higher education is a major beat.

Reporter Dina Cappiello found that 500 of the 6-million-acre park's 2,800 lakes are dead. Unless something is done, she wrote, within 40 years a thousand more lakes will be lost to acid rain, lakes empty of plant and animal life.

See **Dying Lakes** in *NRW Plus*.

News Is Relative

These eight news values do not exist in a vacuum. Their application depends on those who are deciding what is news, where the event and the news medium are located, the tradition of the newspaper or station, its audience and a host of other factors.

Personal Factors

When the economy took a downturn in 2001, companies cut back their workforces, stocks tumbled, retirement investments shrank. It was natural, then, for journalists to report the effects of the shift from an expanding economy to a no-growth economy.

The Times Union in Albany, N.Y., ran its story under this headline:

Simple Tastes Keep Family on an Even Financial Keel

The reporter selected a middle-aged dentist, his wife and their three grown children. They manage to water ski "behind their boat on Great Sacandaga Lake and have just finished renovating their kitchen. They have hopes of putting new siding on their garage next year."

How badly were they affected by the receding economy? "They hold a diversified portfolio managed by a financial adviser and made up mostly of blue-chip stocks," the reporter wrote.

The story was too much for a *Times Union* reader, who wrote the newspaper that the couple "do not have a simple life style with a boat, a remodeled kitchen, money to pay for their daughter's Ph.D. and law education and blue-chip stocks. This article is an insult to those people who are struggling to put food on their tables."

The newspaper's managing editor, Rex Smith, agreed with the letter writer. The reporter, the wife of a doctor, had imposed her tastes, her upper middle-class lifestyle on the situation, Smith said.

Economic Pressures

The media are a business, a profit-seeking enterprise. Most stations and newspapers are no different from General Motors, Microsoft and Home Depot. Their operations are designed to maximize profits.

Advertising is the engine that drives the media. This can be seen quickly enough when the newspaper has 48 pages because the department stores are advertising white sales. The result is a large news hole, with plenty of space for stories. On days when the advertising is slim, the newspaper may run to 32 pages and stories are cut to the bone, or not run at all.

More broadly, when times are good and advertisers clamor for space and time, staffs are large, coverage deep. When there is a hitch in the economy, foreign bureaus are closed, staffs are cut. Some events simply are not covered.

Increasingly, media outlets are owned by large companies whose stock is traded on the stock market. The result: "The pressure to maximize stockholder return has become ever more intense," says Larry Jinks, for more than 40 years an executive with Knight-Ridder. "That affects how news is gathered and presented."

A Wall Street analyst put the matter bluntly: "Some reporters don't understand that they work for a company that sells advertising. They're in the advertising business, not in the journalism business. They don't get it. Without the bottom line, they don't have jobs. They're in a business and the business is to sell ads and make money. The people that own the company are the shareholders, not the reporters."

Advertisers Muscle the Media Hardly a month goes by without the report of some advertiser or commercial group deciding to hold back on advertising because of news coverage. When a newspaper exposed shoddy sales techniques by used car dealers, the local dealers declared an advertising moratorium.

Conflicting Goals: Sales vs. Truth

Advertising is the principal source of revenues that supports our media system. That dependence creates an incongruity between the public's preferences and the criteria employed by the people in charge. As consumers of communication, we judge it by its value and meaning for us; advertisers judge it by its efficiency in disseminating what they call "exposure opportunities."

Media content has been driven primarily by the need to maximize audiences for sale rather than by the desire to communicate the truth about our world or express deep thoughts and feelings. To this end, broadcasting and film have vied with each other in pursuit of violence and vulgarity. The largest of our mass media, the daily press, traditionally the forum for contention and irreverence, has undergone a steady attrition of competition and a general retreat to the safety of the middle ground. Left to its own devices, the public persistently drifts toward amusement rather than enlightenment, avoiding confrontation with the pressing, perhaps overwhelming, problems that confront the nation and the world.

—Leo Bogart

In New York, a series of articles in the *Daily News* reported that "more than half the city's supermarkets fail inspections because of vermin, filth and rotting food." The reaction of the markets was swift. All but one pulled their advertising. The *News,* battling declining revenue and serious circulation losses, apologized in a four-page advertorial carried out by the business department of the newspaper. The material, *The New York Times* reported, was "effusively complimetary."

Asked if the section righted matters, the manager of one of the market chains replied, "I'll go back if they fire the reporter and the editor." That, said the *News*'s executive editor, was not going to happen.

In California, the California Health Services Department sent TV stations a series of ads in its $12 million campaign to curtail smoking. One ad drew the ire of the R. J. Reynolds Tobacco Company. The commercial attacked the industry's contention that nicotine is not addictive and that secondhand cigarette smoke is not dangerous.

Reynolds sent a warning letter to nine stations, saying the commercial was "false and defamatory" and that libel may be involved.

Seven stations ignored the Reynolds warning, but KABC of Los Angeles and KBHK of San Francisco pulled the 30-second commercial.

No Capitulation   After a Connecticut newspaper printed a front-page story about a kidnapping at a shopping center, the merchants at the center told the publisher that the newspaper's survival depended on the economic health of local business and that such stories would drive shoppers elsewhere. The newspaper replied that crime was always covered by the newspaper and that no individual or group could be given special treatment.

Cause and Effect. The news article quoted producers as saying that the new Brad Pitt movie was "loathsome," "absolutely indefensible," "deplorable on every level." The movie review in the same newspaper, *The Hollywood Reporter,* said the movie "is exactly the kind of product that lawmakers should target for being socially irresponsible. . . . The production company, 20th Century Fox, stopped all its movie advertising in an obvious attempt, *The New York Times* reported, "to damage the trade paper financially."

U.S. Cities with Competing Daily Newspapers

■ Two separate newspapers

● Newspapers under joint operating agreements

- ● Birmingham (Ala.) News
- ● Birmingham Post-Herald

- ● Tucson Arizona Daily Star
- ● Tucson Citizen
- ● Tucson Territorial

- ■ San Francisco Chronicle
- ■ San Francisco Examiner

- ● Denver Post
- ● Denver Rocky Mountain News

- ■ Washington Post
- ■ Washington Times

- ■ Honolulu Advertiser
- ■ Honolulu Star-Bulletin

- ■ Chicago Defender
- ■ Chicago Daily Herald
- ■ Chicago Southtown Economist
- ■ Chicago Sun-Times
- ■ Chicago Tribune

- ● Salt Lake City Deseret News
- ● Salt Lake City Tribune

- ● Fort Wayne (Ind.) News-Sentinel
- ● Fort Wayne Journal-Gazette

- ■ Boston Globe
- ■ Boston Herald

- ● Detroit Free Press
- ● Detroit News

- ■ Columbia (Mo.) Missourian
- ■ Columbia Daily Tribune

- ● Lincoln (Neb.) Journal
- ● Lincoln Star

- ● Las Vegas (Nev.) Sun
- ● Las Vegas Review-Journal

- ■ Trenton (N.J.) Times
- ■ Trenton Trentonian

- ● Albuquerque (N.M.) Journal
- ● Albuquerque Tribune

- ■ New York Daily News
- ■ New York Post
- ■ New York Times
- ■ Staten Island (N.Y.) Advance

- ● Cincinnati Enquirer
- ● Cincinnati Post

- ■ Wilkes-Barre (Pa.) Times Leader
- ■ Wilkes-Barre Citizens' Voice

- ■ York (Pa.) Dispatch
- ■ York Daily Record

- ■ Kingsport (Tenn.) News
- ■ Kingsport Times-News

- ● Seattle Post-Intelligencer
- ● Seattle Times

- ● Charleston (W. Va.) Gazette
- ● Charleston Daily Mail

- ● Green Bay (Wis.) Press-Gazette
- ● Green Bay News-Chronicle

- ● Madison (Wis.) Capital Times
- ● Madison Wisconsin State Journal

Dying Competition

The number of cities with competing newspapers has steadily declined, and the number of chain-owned newspapers has spiraled over the past three decades, the result of declining advertising income and a decrease in the circulation of afternoon newspapers. Twenty-eight states have no competing newspapers.

At *The Washington Post,* reporter Leonard Downie had been looking into an arrangement between corrupt real estate speculators and local savings and loan institutions to gouge inner-city residents. The bankers got wind of Downie's checking and told the managing editor that if the *Post* ran the series, they would pull their advertising.

Downie, who later became the *Post*'s executive editor, recalls Benjamin C. Bradlee, his editor, telling him about the visit and the threat. Bradlee looked at Downie and said simply, "Just get it right."

The reporting continued, the series ran and the banks pulled their advertising, costing the newspaper $750,000 in lost advertising revenue.

The Pressure of Competition

"If my competition has it, I want it." This is the unwritten rule of journalism in the era of stepped-up competition. It led newspapers and stations to carry the Drudge report that a major Clinton adviser had a record of wife beating. The report was false. The rule led *The Wall Street Journal*'s Interactive Edition to report that President Clinton and Monica Lewinsky had been seen disposing of evidence of their liaison, and *The Dallas Morning News* Web site to report that a federal employee would testify to having seen Clinton and Lewinsky in a "compromising situation." Both reports were found to be false, but not after the story was carried on the front pages of major newspapers and on many newscasts.

The Influence of Owners

In addition to putting their imprint on their products by deciding how much money to take out of the enterprise, owners can exert a powerful tonal influence. Some are cautious, unwilling to dig into news that might stir controversy. Their papers and stations cover the surface of the news, what we describe in Chapter 10 as Layer 1 news, the stenographic report of what people say and do. Some go further, imposing a particular political point of view and slant on the news. And some combine avarice and political slant.

Cave In   When the Chinese government was upset by the British Broadcasting Corporation's news coverage of developments in China, it made its displeasure known to Rupert Murdoch, the owner of a massive global media conglomorate that includes large holdings in China. Murdoch's Hong Kong broadcast operation had been airing the BBC newscasts that irritated Chinese Communist Party leaders.

Murdoch acted quickly. He eliminated BBC news. He said that using the BBC, considered the provider of the finest broadcast journalism in the world, would jeopardize his business in China.

Murdoch again made the news with a move motivated by his business interests in China. HarperCollins, a book publisher owned by Murdoch, planned to publish a book by Chris Patten, the last British governor of Hong Kong. Patten was an outspoken critic of China's authoritarianism and miserable human rights record. When Murdoch learned of the publication plans he ordered Harper-Collins to drop the book.

A British newspaper published a "private and confidential" memo circulated in the publishing house that set out a strategy to disguise the reason for abandoning the book. The memo, according to the newspaper, "expressed great anxiety over how a 'hostile press' might report the move."

Murdoch's son, James, head of the business in Asia, criticized Western news organizations for their coverage of China. He said their reporting of the arrest, torture and death of members of the Falun Gang religious group in China was wrong-headed, that China rightly considered the group dangerous. Human

Murdoch's Empire

"Murdoch uses his diverse holdings, which include newspapers, magazines, sports teams, a movie studio and a book publisher, to promote his own financial interests at the expense of real newsgathering, legal and regulatory rules and journalistic ethics. He wields his media as instruments of influence with politicians who can aid him, and savages his competitors in his news columns. If ever someone demonstrated the dangers of mass power being concentrated in few hands, it would be Murdoch."

—*Russ Baker, "Murdoch's Mean Machine," Columbia Journalism Review*

rights groups saw the comments as further evidence of the Murdoch media empire's effort to ingratiate the company with Chinese leaders because of the company's extensive business plans in China.

Owners' Politics Murdoch is politically conservative, and his politics impose a deep imprint on his media properties. When Sen. James Jeffords of Vermont changed his party membership from Republican to Independent, thus giving control of the U.S. Senate to the Democrats, the front page of Murdoch's *New York Post* put a photo of Jeffords on page 1 that was doctored to show him in Revolutionary-era clothes next to the headline:

BENEDICT

JEFFORDS

Turncoat

senator

imperils

Dubya's

agenda

In Pittsburgh, the *Tribune-Review* offers its readers a perspective on the news that is influenced by its owner, billionaire Richard Mellon Scaife. An article in *Brill's Content* reported that Scaife's "political and personal interests directly affect the newspaper's content, sometimes damaging its journalism. For instance, because Scaife doesn't like Senator Arlen Specter, a Pennsylvania Republican, mentions of Specter are sometimes stricken from reporters' drafts. Scaife funds many right-wing groups, which in turn are often quoted in the newspaper without any hint of the connection."

During the Bush–Gore presidential race, all photos of Al Gore were pulled from the election-day issue, and on Scaife's orders the AP election story was rewritten to minimize mention of Gore.

Courage In contrast, there is Katherine Graham, publisher of *The Washington Post.* In the darkest days of the newspaper's coverage of Watergate, when President Nixon threatened economic reprisals to *Post* properties, Graham stood steadfast. In a tribute to Graham on her death, Hendrik Hertzberg wrote in *The New Yorker:*

> The courage she summoned in the face
> of serious, and at that time frightening,
> abuses of power put democracy in her debt
> in a way that few other American publish-
> ers, perhaps none, have ever equalled.

Chains

The media are spiraling toward a concentration of ownership in fewer and fewer large corporations. Fifty years ago, families owned almost all the daily newspapers. Today, four of five newspapers are owned by groups, known as chains. The Chicago Tribune, Gannett and Knight-Ridder alone own a fourth of all daily newspapers. "The family-owned newspaper is an endangered species," says H. Brandt Ayers, whose family has owned *The Anniston Star* in Alabama for parts of three centuries.

The *Star's* ownership is happy if it can make 10 percent profit, Ayers says. Chain owners want twice as much to placate dividend-hungry stockholders.

Most media commentators find the concentration worrisome. "The pressure on them is to produce dollars," says Ben Bagdikian. Profits come before good journalism, he says.

Group ownership has its defenders. Their large resources enable local editors to take on the community power structure without fear of economic retaliation, the defenders say.

The reality is mixed. Some group-owned media do provide minimal coverage. Some continue to dig and provide their readers and viewers with illuminating journalism. The difference often lies with the staffs, their leadership and the tradition of the newspaper or station.

The Charleston (W.Va.) *Gazette* has long spoken for protection of its environment. This Scripps Howard paper has encouraged reporter Ken Ward, Jr., to take a strong point of view to his work. "The area is economically depressed and controlled by a few large companies that rape and pillage and don't leave much for the people," he says. "If there is any place in the United States that needs good investigative reporting that comes at things with a good set of values, it's here."

Tradition

Some publications and broadcast stations have a history of public service journalism that guides them in their selection of what is worthy of their reporters' time and the owners' funds. Some are content to cover the surface, rarely allowing reporters the time to dig into a situation.

The Charlotte Observer challenged the tobacco industry. More recently it took on the home builders. Reporters Ames Alexander and Rick Rothacker accompanied building inspectors on their rounds, watched houses being built, pored through public records and interviewed more than 400 homeowners, builders, inspectors and others. The paper's database editor, Ted Mellnick, helped them examine "4 million computer records on all building inspections conducted in Mecklenburg County since the 1970s," says Alexander.

The project took eight months. The reporters concluded that "North Carolina's laws favor builders over buyers."

See **Home Buyer Beware** in *NRW Plus*.

The Audience

When the TV actress Ellen DeGeneres announced that she is a lesbian, the *San Francisco Chronicle* put the story on page 1 alongside a four-column photo of a crowd in town watching the show on a big screen. *The New York Times* national edition put the story on page 17A. The reason for the difference in play: San Francisco has a large percentage of gay men and women in its population.

Threat. "It is daily becoming more obvious that the biggest threat to a free press and the circulation of ideas is the steady absorption of newspapers, television and radio stations, networks and other vehicles of information into corporations that know how to turn knowledge into profit—but are not equally committed to inquiry or debate or to the First Amendment."
—*Reuven Frank, former head of NBC News*

Corporate Journalism. ". . . one can argue that considering there are nearly 1,500 daily papers in the United States, and considering that most of these are handsomely profitable, the percentage of excellence is abysmally low. Today's typical daily is mediocre, with a strong overlay of provincialism. And industry trends are only making matters worse."
—*Leaving Readers Behind: The Age of Corporate Journalism by Thomas Kunkel and Gene Roberts*

Five Packs a Day

Although *The Charlotte Observer* circulates among farmers who grow two-thirds of the tobacco used to make cigarettes, the newspaper published a 20-page special report "Our Tobacco Dilemma" that called attention to the health hazards of smoking. On the front page of the section was this photograph of James McManus, 62, who has, the newspaper reported, "smoking-caused emphysema" and requires an "oxygen tank to survive." The tobacco industry spends more than $1 billion a year on advertising.

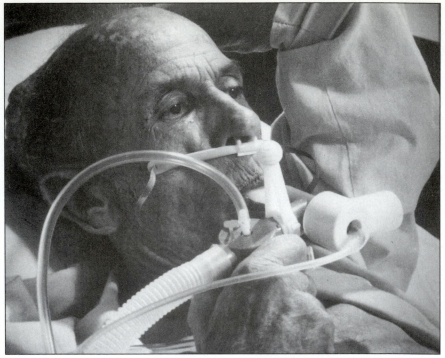

Mark Sluder, *The Charlotte Observer*

Everything media writers do is aimed at an audience, and the nature of that audience may well be the most important influence in media performance.

Look at the magazines for teen-age girls. Long preoccupied with articles about pop music, personal appearance and dating, they have shifted focus to more serious subjects. "We have to give girls tools that they have not needed in past generations," says Atoosa Rubenstein, the editor in chief of *CosmoGirl*. "The intricacies of being a teen-ager have definitely changed." To appeal to this new kind of audience—readers that these magazine editors consider miniaturized versions of adults—the magazines are running articles on racism, depression, adoption. Jane Rinzler Buckingham, the president of a market research firm that studies the buying habits of teen-agers, says that teen-agers are more troubled than ever before. "They don't know if they are supposed to grow up to be corporate working women and conquer the world, or be stay-at-home moms, or Miss America or Hillary Clinton. The typical teen-age girl isn't quite sure whether to worry about her pimple or whether to go out and win a Pulitzer," Buckingham says.

Demographics The surge in the country's Hispanic population caught the media by surprise. The 2000 census showed that in 20 years the Hispanic population had increased 115 percent, whereas the black population increased 32 percent. Long concentrated in California and southwestern farm areas, Spanish-speaking workers have fanned out across the country, and they brought their families with them. The influx challenged blacks as the nation's largest minority group.

The *Evansville* (Ind.) *Courier & Press* learned that more than 10,000 Hispanics live in its 20-county region and assigned a reporter–photographer team to cover the new arrivals. In a six-part series, "Hola, Amigos," the newspaper reported the efforts of the immigrants to adjust to the American way of life

"What we tried to do," said Rich Davis, the reporter assigned to the story, "was to put faces on the word 'immigration' and convey the human experience behind changes we were all observing in our region."

"The highlight for me came one October evening when, amid pealing church bells, Narda Marmolejo walked down the aisle of a cathedral. It was her 15th birthday party, or quinceañera, and she looked like Cinderella at her ball, an event that amazed her Anglo friends. Narda's parents toil at factory jobs to give their children opportunities they didn't have."

We know that demographics influence story selection. Av Westin, a veteran broadcaster, took the truism to a study he made. He interviewed more than 100 TV news executives, producers and correspondents and their crews. His conclusion is that TV journalists "are not thinking about journalism: Demographics and minute-by-minute Nielsen analyses have influenced story selection. And that, in turn, has prompted my project's most sobering discovery: Every week—every day—stories about African-Americans, Hispanics and Asians are kept off the air."

"Race," he concluded, "is a criterion for story selection."

The Reporter

Given all of the pressures under which the media operate, it remains true today what has been operative through the years: For the most part the reporter, the man or woman on the beat, makes the news. The court reporter who looks through a dozen court filings chooses the one or two that she will write about. The police reporter, whose daily rounds begin with the examination of the dozen arrests made overnight, decides which two or three he will report. The feature writers with a dozen ideas swirling through their heads have time for a couple.

Yes, the guidelines do help, the news values that we have discussed—timeliness, prominence, impact and the others. But there is wide latitude within these categories. For example: Just who is prominent? To Karen Garloch, a medical writer for *The Charlotte Observer,* a local building contractor named Vernon Nantz may not have been prominent, but his situation qualified him for her attention. Nantz was dying of cancer and had decided to forgo chemotherapy. He wanted to die at home, close to his family.

"The idea for this story was born out of my interest, as a medical writer, in the end of life care," Garloch says. "I had written many stories about living wills and advance directives, the forms people sign to declare their expectations about extraordinary medical care. I had also written about the growth of the hospice movement and discussions among ethicists and doctors when to stop treatment that appears to be futile."

"With millions of Americans facing these choices, I wanted to tell the story of the end of life through a real person who made the choice to reject extraordinary medical care and die with dignity at home."

Garloch's series about Vernon Nantz began this way:

> When Vernon Nantz was diagnosed with a recurrence of cancer, his doctor told him: "We can treat it, but we're not gonna beat it." Vernon had just months. He decided to use Hospice at Charlotte, stay at home with his wife and be around his family and friends.
>
> More and more we want a choice about how and where we die.
>
> This is the story of one man's choice.

Garloch was with Nantz when he decided not to get out of bed to dress for the visit of the hospice nurse. She was there when the family gathered around his bed, sure he was dying, and she was there when he rallied and ate an entire fried fish dinner with french fries and hush puppies. And she arrived at the Nantz home shortly after he died at 2 A.M.

Reader response was overwhelming, said Garloch's editor, Frank Barrows.

Like many of the reporters we have seen at work, Garloch could be said to have made the news with this story of Vernon Nantz. She and the others could be described as activist journalists.

For Garloch's story, see **Vernon's Goobye** in *NRW Plus*.

Activist Journalists   To some journalists, news consists of overt events—an automobile accident, a city council meeting, a court document, the State of the Union Address. Their journalism is denotative, pointing to what has happened. Necessary as this reporting is, some journalists consider it a passive type of journalism because the journalist essentially is responding to events. They would complement denotative journalism with a more active, seeking-out journalism.

Activist journalists seek to place on the public agenda matters that they believe require consideration, civic discussion that could lead to some kind of action. The action could be simply an awareness of another way to end one's days, as the Garloch feature demonstrated. Or it could lead to remedial action, as Willman's stories about deadly prescription drugs accomplished. The sociologist Herbert Blumer says that issues come to public attention, not because of the "intrinsic gravity of the social problem," but because they have been given status by some respected group that has called attention to the problem. These groups can legitimatize an issue as a matter of concern requiring action, Blumer says.

Among those that can legitimatize situations Blumer lists educational organizations, religious leaders, legislators, civic groups and the press. Once legitimatized, the issue can be acted upon quickly, Blumer says.

Summing Up

Impersonal and objective as journalists would like to make the determinants of news, much of journalism is based on selection, and choice is a highly personal affair. It derives from the journalist's professional background, his or her education and the intangible influences of family, friends and colleagues.

The professional decisions—what people need to know—are framed by other considerations as well: The need to entertain to keep readers and viewers who are constantly being seduced by entertainment media; the pressures of the business of journalism such as budgeting restrictions, meeting the competition, considering the needs of advertisers.

Even more elusive in our search for absolutes in the area of news determinants are the decisions that have their origin in the arena where ambition and conscience battle.

Vague as these influences may be, the reporter must cope with them. Fortunately, the reporter's handiwork is tangible. Once the heat of reporting and writing has cooled, the reporter can examine the story. Then, alone or with a trusted friend or colleague, the reporter can try to pinpoint the reasons for decisions. This self-questioning—directed by some of the principles we have discussed in this chapter and those we'll tackle in Chapter 27 on the morality of journalism—is part of the journalist's continuing education.

Further Reading

Bagdikian, Ben H. *The Media Monopoly.* Boston: Beacon Press, 1987.

Clurman, Richard. *To the End of Time: The Seduction and Conquest of a Media Empire.* New York: Simon & Schuster, 1992.

Gans, Herbert J. *Deciding What's News.* New York: Pantheon Books, 1979.

Kunkel, Thomas and Gene Roberts. *Leaving Readers Behind: The Age of Corporate Journalism.* Little Rock: The University of Arkansas Press, 2001.

Roshco, Bernard. *Newsmaking.* Chicago: University of Chicago Press, 1975.

Schudson, Michael. *Discovering the News.* New York: Basic Books, 1978.

Sloan, Bill. *"I Watched a Wild Hot Eat My Baby"—A Colorful History of Tabloids and Their Cultural Impact.* Amherst, N.Y.: Prometheus Books, 2001.

Westin, Av. *Newswatch: How TV Decides the News.* New York: Simon & Schuster, 1983.

The Tools of the Trade

The telephone . . . a basic reporting tool.

Preview

Journalists rely on a variety of tools to do their work. These include the computer, tape recorder, telephone and many information sources such as census data, polls, official documents and reports, most of which are available online.

The journalist:

• Understands how to use basic references.
• Knows public-record laws.
• Uses the computer to gather and to analyze information for stories.
• Is able to conduct and interpret a public opinion poll.

Journalists use several kinds of instruments for their reporting—pencils, pads, cell phones, tape recorders and computers. They use reference materials and such analytic tools as mathematics and polling techniques. Then there is the special language the journalist uses to communicate with co-workers.

Learning the language is essential, as the apprentice electrician finds out the first day on the job when he is told to get a bucket of volts, or the chemistry student who is immortalized in the couplet:

Johnny was a chemist; Johnny is no more.

What Johnny thought was H_2O was H_2SO_4.

Newsroom ignorance may not prove fatal, but it can lead to inclusion in journalism's hall of horrors. Take the case of the afternoon newspaper in Walsenburg, Colo., that wanted to carry the name of the winner of the Indianapolis 500 car race in its late edition. The newspaper's AP wire shut off at 3 p.m., too early for the result. So the editor asked the Indianapolis AP bureau to let him know the winner by telegram.

The Indianapolis bureau acknowledged the newspaper's request with this message: "Will overhead winner of Indianapolis 500." The AP was telling Walsenburg it would telegram the winner's name. In wire service lingo, the word *overhead* was used for *telegram.*

But the sports department didn't know that, and a reporter who was handed the message wrote this story:

Indianapolis, Ind., May 30—(AP)—Will Overhead won the Indianapolis Memorial Day race today. At the two hundred fifty mile post Babe Stapp was leading the string of racing cars, but gave way to Overhead on the last half of the 500 mile grind.

Bannered Blunder

A glossary of journalism terms is provided in the back of the book. When in doubt about any term, consult it. You may want to pencil in additions.

The Tangible Tools

Unlike the reporter's vocabulary, the tangible tools are supplied by the employer:

The **computer** is used to type and to edit stories, to call up background information and to do computer-assisted reporting from databases.

A **pad** with a hard back like a stenographer's notebook is best for note taking. The stiff backing makes jottings clear, and the spiral binding keeps notes in order.

The **tape recorder** is a necessity for the radio reporter, optional for the print reporter. The tape recorder is useful in covering speeches. It is an aid for stories requiring precise quotes. The broadcast journalist may not tape the voice of the source without asking permission.

A **laptop computer** is useful for out-of-office assignments.

The **telephone** is a basic tool of the trade but it cannot substitute for the face-to-face interview. (See Chapter 25 for legal restrictions.)

The **cellular phone** and the computer, powered by battery, allow reporters to send in their stories from any location. The system can be carried in a briefcase.

The **microcomputer** makes charts, graphs and diagrams. With the microcomputer it is possible for even the smallest newspapers and stations to expand their use of visual material produced in the newsroom.

New Media Journalist

With the expansion of multimedia ownership has come the multimedia journalist, also known as the new media journalist. This reporter will be asked to gather material that can be used for print, online and broadcast news media. This means carrying an array of equipment into the field. John Pavlik, director of Columbia University's Center for New Media, lists 13 instruments and utensils the new media journalist should or will carry into the field as follows:

1. Megapixel still and digital video camera for high resolution photos and digital movies.
2. Laptop computer.

Mobile Workstation

The reporter–photographer–videographer of the future sets out to cover a story for his multimedia employers. He is carrying a dozen of the tools he requires as a new media journalist.

Steven Feiner

3. Handheld computer, such as the Palm, "not only a personal organizer with calendar and address book but also increasingly a fully functional computer."

4. Digital audio recorder for recording interviews.

5. Digital cell phone, not only for making and receiving phone calls "but increasingly Internet enabled."

6. Mobile e-mail device such as the Blackberry to stay in touch in the field from anywhere in the United States.

7. Mobile GPS receiver for location finding; can be stamped directly on photos and video as a digital watermark to protect copyright and to authenticate time and date.

8. Wireless Internet access device. Useful for real-time communications from the field (e-mail), Web searching, locating sources, getting directions, maps.

9. Portable digital storage device with massive—multiple gigabyte—capacity.

10. A variety of software packages installed on laptop—video editor, image/photo/graphics editor, audio editor, word processing, spreadsheet, e-mail/Web browser with various plug-ins, and so forth.

11. Instant Messenger software and Voice over IP (VoIP) for real-time, no-cost communications (text, voice, graphics, images) over the Internet between any two locations on earth.

12. Electronic fax service and online hard drive, enabling the reporter to create a virtual newsroom.

13. Satellite telephone, small enough to fit in a briefcase and carried on an airplane as hand luggage; the instrument, also known as the video phone, is increasingly used for breaking stories too difficult to reach with satellite uplink facilities.

Newsroom Resources

Newspapers and stations subscribe to a variety of news services. The major supplier of news is the Associated Press. Syndicates formed by large newspapers such as the Los Angeles Times–Washington Post News Service, the Chicago Tribune Press Service, the New York Times News Service and others are increasingly used.

Local reporters use the wire services for special coverage. A newspaper will ask the AP to follow a local team in a national tournament and the service will write a story aimed at that paper's readers. The wire service also will make special checks. A member newspaper could ask the AP to check a senator's vote on a farm bill, for example.

Basic References

Every reporter has a few reference works handy—the newspaper or station stylebook, a dictionary and the telephone directory. The stylebook assures consistency in spelling, capitalization, punctuation and abbreviation. Is it 18 Fifth Ave. or 18 Fifth Avenue? The stylebook tells us. Do newspapers use postal abbreviations for states? The stylebook tells us to use Calif., not CA. A **Stylebook,** included in this textbook for your use, begins on p. S-1.

Reporters use the dictionary to verify spellings and to make certain that the words they want have the shades of meaning they intend.

The cross-indexed or reverse directory, a listing of telephone numbers by address, is invaluable on a late-breaking story when the reporter cannot go to the event but needs details from the scene.

New Tool. A new type of video telephone enabled CNN reporter Lisa Rose Weaver to score a scoop. She had the only images of the crew of a downed American spy plane as it left Chinese detention. The video telephone enabled Weaver to avoid the required use of Chinese transmission facilities, to evade the censors and to report live without government permission.

Searching the Past

For her feature on changes in fashions, this reporter turns to the *Reader's Guide* for magazine articles about men's and women's clothing in the 1960s. She could also have used a CD-ROM of the *Guide*.

ALPHABETICAL DIRECTORY WHITE PAGES

(h) HOUSEHOLDER   (r) RESIDENT OR ROOMER

correct full name —————————— Landon Edw G & Charlotte D; servmn B F Goodrich
h1215 Oak Dr

occupation and employer —————— Landon Fred M & Mary E; supvr Reliance Elec h60
Norman Av

complete street address
including apartment number ———— Landon Kenneth A & Carol L; clk First Natl Bk
h1400 E Main St Apt 14

Landon Kenneth A Jr studt r1400 E Main St Apt 14

Landon Virginia E r1641 W 4th St

student 18 years of age or older ——— Lane See Also Layne

cross reference of surnames ———— Lane Allen M & Joan M (Allen's Bakery) h1234
Grand Blvd

Lane Avenue Restaurant (Ernest G Long) 216
Lane Av

out-of-town resident employed
in area ——————————— Lane James M & Betty B; brkmn Penn Central
r Rt 1 Jefferson O

Lane Marvin L USA r1234 Grand Blvd

armed force member and
branch of service ——————— Lane Robt B & Margt E; retd h1402 N High St

Lane Walter M r1234 Grand Blvd

Layne See Also Lane

Layne Agnes E Mrs v-pres Layne Co h2325
Eureka Rd

wife's name and initial —————— Layne Albert M & Minnie B; slsmn Hoover Co h19
Bellows Av

corporation showing officers and
nature of business ——————— Layne Co Inc Thos E Layne Pres Mrs Agnes E
Layne V-Pres Edw T Layne Sec-Treas bldg
contrs 100 N High St

Layne Edw T & Diane E; sec-treas Layne Co h140
Oakwood Dr

Layne Ralph P & Gladys M; formn Layne Co h1687
Maple Dr

Layne Thos E & Agnes E; pres Layne Co h2325
Eureka Rd

suburban designation ————— Leach See Also Leech

retiree ——————————— Leach Wm E USMC r1209 Ravenscroft Rd (EF)

Lee Alf M & Celia J; retd h2106 Oakwood Dr

business partnership showing
partners in parenthesis ————— Lee Bros (Louis J And Harry M Lee) plmbs 151
Abbott St

Lee Harry M & Karen L (Lee Bros) h2023 Stone Rd

Lee Louis J & Martha B (Lee Bros) h1616 Fulton

husband and wife employed ———— Lee Martha B Mrs ofc sec Lee Bros h1616 Fulton

Lee Minnie M Mrs h87 Eastview Dr

"r" resident or roomer —————— Lee Muriel E r810 LaForge St

Lee Sterling T & Nadine S; mtcemn Eastview Apts
h202 Wilson St Apt 1

"h" householders ——————— Lee Thos W & Effie M (Tom's Men's Wear) r Rt 23

owner of business showing name
of business in parenthesis ————— **LEE'S PHARMACY (Lee A Shaw) Prescriptions
Carefully Compounded, Complete Line Of
Toiletries And Cosmetics, Fountain Service,**

bold type denotes paid listing ——— **Greeting Cards, 1705 N High St (21505) Tel**

Leech See Also Leach

business firm showing name of
owner in parenthesis —————— Leech Doris E tchr North High Sch
h1323 W McLean St

Leech Joseph B & Lucy V; slsmn Metropolitan Dept
Store h824 Wilson St

unmarried and unemployed
resident ——————————— Leech Joseph B Jr studt r824 Wilson St

Leech Marcia M clk Community Hosp r1323 W
McLean St

more than one adult in household —— Lewis Anne M Mrs clk County Hwy Dept h914
Wilson Av

Lewis Ernest W studt r914 Wilson Av

Lewis Harold G & Anne M; mgr Cooper Paint Store
h914 Wilson Av

Lewis Robt B lab County Hwy Dept r1410 Union
Hwy Rt 2

church showing name of pastor ——— Lewistown Methodist Church Rev John R Allen
Pastor 515 Maple Valley Rd

Every reporter should know how to use these references, most of which are available online as well as in print form:

- **A world almanac.**
- *The Reader's Guide to Periodical Literature.*
- *The New York Times Index.*
- *Bartlett's Familiar Quotations.* Who penned, "How do I love thee? Let me count the ways"? Had a Chicago journalist consulted Bartlett's, the newspaper might have been spared embarrassment. The quotation was used under a large page-1 picture of a couple sitting on a statue of Shakespeare in a Chicago park—with attribution to William Shakespeare. (If you do not know the author, look it up.)
- *National Five-Digit Zip Code and Post Office Directory.* Use this for locating cities in states and for finding the ZIP code.
- **City directory.** Several firms produce directories with information about people living in the community. A typical entry will include correct full name; occupation and employer; complete street address including apartment number; spouse's name and initial; whether the person owns or rents, is retired, is employed, is a student. In the street directory, a reporter can find the name of the resident and his or her telephone number from a given address. Some directories are based on telephone numbers; given a number, the reporter can find the name of the telephone subscriber. The directory companies also make up classified business directories that list, at no charge, all businesses.
- *Who's Who in America.* This resource contains biographical information about 72,000 living North Americans and is an essential source for information about leaders in social, economic, cultural and political affairs. Biographical information is supplied by the person listed. Other biographical directories published by the same firm, Marquis Who's Who Inc., include regional directories and directories on biographees' professions. For biographies of long-dead people, the *Dictionary of American Biography* is useful. For people who have died within the last several years, consult back volumes of *Who's Who, Who Was Who* or *Current Biography.*

Using the Computer

"Five years ago, I thought database reporting was a skill only specialists needed," says Debbie Cenziper of *The Charlotte Observer.* She learned better, she says. For her stories about the abuses in the North Carolina mental health system—which we described in Chapter 3—she went to a database that recorded 600,000 deaths. She went there, she says, every day during her work on the series. "I've learned that without these skills I cannot complete my work."

The computer has put information of incredible variety at the fingertips of journalists, and it has helped them process information—crunch the data—with speed and accuracy. Let's take a deeper look at these two indispensable tasks the computer performs for the reporter: first—locating information; second—processing the information.

Using the Internet

A survey of 500 journalists throughout the country showed that 98 percent check their e-mail daily. They use the Internet to correspond, to find story ideas, develop new sources and check for news releases that could lead to stories.

The average reporter spends three hours a day reading or sending e-mail, the *Middleberg/Ross Survey of Media in the Wired World* reports.

"I can find out if a person has been sued, or divorced, or whether he or she has a criminal record. I can locate within five minutes any person in the United States who uses a credit card or has a bank account, and I can probably locate his or her family members and address history in less than thirty minutes. . . ."

—*J. Robert Port, Associated Press*

Locating Information

If you know what you want and where to find it, it takes seconds to locate the Web site or other Internet source with the necessary information. If you have a subject in mind but are unsure of where to nail it down, a search engine will put you on track.

Websites   Let's say you want to do a story on the changes in population in your city or state. You want the overall figures, and you want the demographic changes. You know that the Census Bureau keeps these figures. (**Appendix E, "Sources Online,"** in the CD *NRW Plus* lists the bureau's address, www.census.gov.)

When the local school board reported that a proposed high school site may have had a factory making toxic products on it 50 years ago, you can check with the Environmental Protection Agency, (www.epa.gov).

Used with care, Web sites provide quick and useful information, ranging from the general to the specific.

Several organizations provide journalists with background material and access to experts. FACSNET, (www.facsnet.org), makes available background papers and documents on public policy issues and has links, organized around beats, to sources for interviews.

ProfNet (www.profnet.com) provides sources for interviews. ProfNet is a collaborative of 4,000 public information officers linked by the Internet who can provide quick and convenient access to experts. Half the members of ProfNet are colleges and universities. The remainder consist of think tanks, laboratories, government agencies, nonprofit organizations and public relations agencies. ProfNet also can be reached by e-mail, info@profnet.com.

Donations   Want to know who donated to a candidate for Congress and how much, consult the Federal Election Commission Reports, www.tray.com.

Much journalistic Web work involves obtaining material kept by various governmental agencies—city building permits, names of school bus drivers, planning and zoning actions, county tax receipts, election results by precinct and voting district, census data, drunk driving convictions, prison populations, violent and property crimes on campus. The list is longer than imaginable. If there is a document kept by a governmental department, chances are that it is available through the Internet.

When you have a subject in mind but are not sure of where to find information that could be stored on a Web site, you use a search engine.

Search Engines   Search engines like Google (www.google.com), AltaVista (www.altavista.com) and HotBot (www.hotbot.com) locate information by searching Web pages. Google, one of the largest of the engines, searches 1.4 billion Web pages.

To make a quick and efficient search, you should be certain of the information you need so that you can provide a *search term* or *keyword* to initiate the search. If you want to write a story about the growth of enrollment in two- and four-year colleges, you might use the search term "college enrollment."

Search terms are refined by using a relationship term: *and, or, not.* Let's say you want only the enrollment changes in four-year schools. You could enter "college enrollment not two year colleges."

Let's say you want to find out what is the most popular major among college students. You use one of the search engines, Google, and you write: "Most popular college major." Google asks whether you mean "Most popular college majors." That will do, so you type that term in. The reply comes quickly in the synopsis of an article. Business is the leading undergraduate major, you find. If you want to see the entire article from which the summary was made, Google provides a Web site you can consult.

Limits. These search engines search the free part of the Internet. Many newspapers and magazines offer free access for a limited period, then place the material in a paid archive service. Commercial information services such as Lexis-Nexis and Dow Jones News Retrieval allow for more comprehensive searches.

Listservs   The computer lets reporters toss out a question to reporters on a similar beat. Investigative reporters regularly turn to the IRE (Investigative Reporters and Editors) listserv for help.

The Library of Congress

Newsday

The Old . . . and the New Newsrooms

Before the computer revolution, paper, pencils, glue pots and spikes were the tools of the trade for copy editors. Under the harsh light of bright bulbs overhead, the editors slashed at the copy. In today's newsroom, stories are edited on the screen, and no one jams his or her hand on the copy spike. And women are slowly taking over.

Julie Poppen, higher education reporter for the *Rocky Mountain News* in Denver, sent an e-mail to the listserv of the Education Writers Association asking about school districts that require students to attend summer school if their scores are low on standardized tests. She received responses from reporters in Greenville, S.C., Richmond and Chicago.

Enterprise   A reporter wanted to know the identity of a candidate for a Des Moines school job who was rebuffed by the school board. The reporter and a photographer managed to catch the applicant for a moment, just long enough for a picture to be taken. The reporter posted the photo on the education writers listserv and asked if anyone could identify him. One did, and the reporter had his story.

The Grateful Dead   When Elizabeth Weise covered a story about the reopening of a remodeled auditorium in San Francisco, she wrote that the Grateful Dead had played the night the hall opened 35 years before. Weise had the bad luck to have an editor in AP's New York headquarters who was a Deadhead. She messaged Weise that the Grateful Dead didn't exist then. Check your facts, she told Weise.

Weise knew that there is a Grateful Dead Usenet news group, and she posted a query on it. She was right, they told her, but at that time the group was using the name The Warlocks.

Crunching the Numbers

The computer is an organizing tool. It can take the information fed into it and performs these functions:

- **Alphabetizing:** Similar jobs, similar names can be placed in a series.
- **Rank ordering:** Instructed to put any list in some kind of order, the computer will rank low to high, best to worst, biggest to smallest, etc.
- **Correlating or matching:** The computer will compare two different lists.

Let's see how these functions have been used by reporters for stories.

Double Pay   Reporters at the *Dayton* (Ohio) *Daily News* fed the names of all county workers into their computer, which alphabetized the lists from the different departments and agencies into a master list. The master list showed that several workers held two jobs and were receiving two paychecks. The reporters also learned the names of those receiving unusually large amounts of overtime pay.

Smoke and Drink   Bob Sanders had heard that alcohol and cigarette distributors target minority neighborhoods. To check, he obtained billboard locations from the city planning commission and the minority population concentrations from tract material of the Census Bureau and correlated them. Here is how his story for *The Post-Standard* in Syracuse, N.Y., begins:

Jeff Scruggs has a blue ribbon on his front door on Seymour Street proclaiming his opposition to drugs.

But when he opens that door each day he is confronted by a different message: a long smoldering cigarette gracing a 12-by-25-foot billboard, providing a backdrop on a corner neighbors say is a hot spot for drug dealers. . . .

All up and down Salina Street and Erie Boulevard, outside the mom-and-pop stores on South Avenue and on the near west side, more than half the city's 247 street-level billboards give residents two major messages: smoke and drink.

Behind the Tests In the Hartford bureau of the AP, reporters compiled economic factors for Connecticut's 169 cities and towns. Then it obtained tests scores in reading, writing and math. The bureau staff correlated the scores with the economic factors and found a strong relationship. The best predictor of the scores, they found, was the cost of the homes in which the children live.

Playgrounds, Murders and Ballplayers Reporters like stories that show how their city, their county, their state or their team stands in comparison with others. A TV reporter in Kansas used a computerized list of how much cities spent per capita on their playgrounds. His city was way down on the list.

The FBI's annual report *Crime in the United States* was culled by a Florida newspaper reporter to see where his state ranked for murders last year. Five of the ten states with the highest murder rates were in the South, he found, but Florida was not.

A sports reporter wondered why the baseball team was consistently out of the playoffs. Was management tightfisted in this era of multi-million-dollar salaries? How did the Reds compare with other team salaries? The ranking confirmed the reporter's suspicions of a miserly management.

> **Spreadsheets.** Reporters use spreadsheets to sort, summarize, combine and do calculations with data. For a demonstration of spreadsheet use, see **CAR Spreadsheet Demo** in *NRW Plus*.

Drivers–Violators *The Providence Journal* took a list of the names of bus drivers and matched it with a list of traffic violations. It found some drivers had been ticketed as many as 20 times. Some drivers were convicted felons, it found in matching the driver list with a criminal conviction list.

Court Racism The *Los Angeles Times* analyzed criminal court sentences and found that first-offender blacks were much more likely to be jailed than first-offender whites for the same crimes.

Deadly Nursing For a description of how a *Chicago Tribune* reporter used databases to expose the fatal consequences of shortages of nurses see **Deadly Nursing** in *NRW Plus*.

Database Types

There are three types of databases:

    1. **Full text:** Articles from newspapers and magazines, documents, reports, files.
    2. **Bibliographic:** References to full text; summaries of full text.
    3. **Numeric:** Data such as crime statistics, census figures, economic material.

Patrick Lee, a business reporter for the *Los Angeles Times,* says he prefers "statistics, official reports, full documents" to the press releases that flood his desk. "The advantage of the Internet," he says, "is that you can go directly to the primary sources without an intermediary."

Public Records

Reporters know what records are available to them on their beats. Among the many records usually accessible to the public are:

- Assessment and tax records, deeds, property transfers.
- Records dealing with licenses—restaurant, dog, liquor, tavern and the many other business and professional licenses.
- City engineer's records—streets, alleys, property lines, highways.
- City building permits, variances, unpaid taxes, liens, violations.
- Automobile ownership.
- Election returns.
- Articles of incorporation. Most states require officers to file their names and holdings in the corporation. Partnerships.
- Bills and vouchers for all governmental purchases. Copies of the checks (warrants) paid out for goods and services.
- Minutes of city council, county commission meetings. All appropriations, budgets.
- Most records in the judicial area—indictments, trials, sentences, court transcripts.
- Wills, receiverships, bankruptcies.
- Most police records on a current basis.

All the states have "sunshine laws" that require records to be available for public examination.

Freedom of Information Act

Access to one of the vast areas of information—federal records—was limited until Congress enacted the Freedom of Information Act in 1966. The act, and important amendments in 1975, unlocked millions of pages of federal docu-

No Secrets. The journalist's insistence on freedom to seek out information has a distinguished heritage. In 1644, John Milton's *Areopagitica, "A Speech for the Liberty of Unlicensed Printing,"* contended that truth might be learned if all ideas were let loose for discussion.

Joseph Pulitzer put the matter in journalistic terms:

"There is not a crime, there is not a dodge, there is not a trick, there is not a swindle which does not live by secrecy. Get these things out in the open, describe them, attack them, ridicule them in the press, and sooner or later public opinion will sweep them away."

ments. The FOIA states that the public has the right to inspect any document that the executive branch possesses, with nine exceptions. These exceptions prevent reporters, or anyone else, from examining income tax returns, secret documents vital to national defense or foreign policy, intra-agency letters and other sensitive material.

The 1975 amendments give the federal courts the power to review classified documents to make sure that they are properly classified, and they put a limit on the time an agency can take to reply to a request.

The *Mercury-News* in San Jose, Calif., used a Freedom of Information request to the FBI to obtain material that revealed that President Reagan had been an FBI informer in the late 1940s. The documents obtained by the newspaper identified Reagan as "T-10" and said that he and his first wife had "provided the FBI with names of actors they believed were members of a clique with a pro-Communist line." The *Mercury-News* also learned from FBI files on the author John Steinbeck that the FBI had tracked Steinbeck for years because of his involvement with labor causes. Steinbeck wrote *The Grapes of Wrath,* which won a Pulitzer Prize for literature in 1940.

See **Appendix C, "How to Use the FOIA—Freedom of Information Act,"** in *NRW Plus.*

Cautions and Warnings

Neil Reisner, a training director for the National Institute for Computer-Assisted Reporting, says the Internet is "just another tool for journalists. Use the same methods you use to verify any other source."

Revisionists   In *The New Republic,* Brian Hecht says of the Internet, "It is impossible to know where information comes from, who has paid for it, whether it is reliable and whether you will ever be able to find it again. A student looking for information on the Internet about, say, World War II cannot know whether a given 'page' has been posted by a legitimate historian or by a Holocaust revisionist." (Revisionists assert there was no Holocaust in which Nazi Germany murdered millions of Jews, gypsies, the mentally ill, homosexuals and political opponents.)

Polluters   Bill Kovach, former curator of the Nieman Foundation at Harvard, worries about the "careless, even ignorant misuse of technology." He says that too many reporters "routinely rummage around in the electronic databases for information which, as often as not, is a public-relations handout, self-serving market tip or other self-seeking, self-serving trash.

"As a result, plagiarism and facile rewriting masquerade as real reporting and further pollute the electronic databases with more useless, inaccurate information." Kovach worries that because databases may not be recharged "with new and important information based on active and aggressive reporting of what is truly new" that the database will grow "more toxic and dangerous to the health of democracy."

Too Distant. "Technology is the knack of so arranging the world that we don't have to experience it."
—*Max Frisch, Swiss playwright*

Useful Data

Journalists have always used numbers to enlighten us. Economic data can warn us that inflation may be getting out of hand. Alcohol-related traffic deaths may indicate that we had better lower the blood alcohol level at which a person can be arrested for drunk driving. An increase in childhood diseases may be a sign that immigrant children are not getting immunization shots.

Much of the data that the journalist had to dig out of printed reports, documents and files are now stored in easily accessible databases. Let's start with one of the more useful sets of data.

Census Data

The reporter who wants to track social change in his or her community will find census data essential. Working mothers, children in nursery school, shifts in family patterns and demographic changes—data on all this are available. Reporters have used census data to find pockets of the elderly and of ethnic groups. Changes in the racial makeup of neighborhoods can be charted with census data.

For Civic Profiles   For a story about the housing stock in the community, the reporter can find the number of houses that lack toilets, private baths and hot water. The number of people living in housing units (density) also can be determined. By analyzing who lives in a representative's district, it is possible to indicate how he or she is most likely to vote or to determine the pressures exerted on the legislator regarding public housing, Social Security and other social issues. The data also can be used to document depth reporting—the need for additional day-care centers, low cost housing or senior citizen facilities.

Printed census reports are available at public and university libraries and at many local, state and federal agencies. The best place to obtain local census material is the State Data Center, where experts can help with interpretations and make comparisons with previous censuses. Detailed information is available from the centers on computer tapes and floppy disks as well as on CD-ROM (compact disc-read-only memory) and through the Bureau's Web site, www.census.gov.

The Bureau takes more than 250 sample surveys a year to monitor trends in employment, population growth, fertility, living arrangements and marriage. It makes surveys of a number of activities every five years, including housing, agriculture, business, construction, government, manufacturing, mineral industry and transportation.

Disease and Death Data

Some of the best-kept official records are those for disease and death. Doctors, clinics and hospitals are required to keep scrupulous records. These are sent to city and county health offices, which relay them to state and federal agencies.

Because this information has been kept for many years, it can provide the journalist with an insight into changing community health standards. Infant mortality rates are sometimes described as the measure of the civilization of a society.

The United States' infant mortality rate is 23rd among industrialized nations, and the rates in some of its cities are even higher than those in some developing countries.

The figures are highest in urban areas and poor rural areas, and they are unusually high among minority, teen-age, and unwed mothers. Geographic comparisons also can be made because most local health agencies break the city into health districts. Districts with low-income residents can be compared with those with middle-income residents, and comparisons can be made between districts with white and nonwhite populations.

Some of the stories developed from infant mortality are stark:

	Black	White
Infant mortality rate	13.8	5.9

Correlations can be made between the infant death rate and such factors as low birth weight, marital status of mother, prenatal care, family income.

Data on death and disease are available from the state health department, which usually has the figures in an available database, and from the Centers for Disease Control and Prevention, (www.cdc.gov) and the National Center for Health Statistics, (www.cdc.gov/nchswww/products/htm).

You can see that a lot of the material reporters gather is in the form of numbers, quantitative data. This takes us to another useful tool, but one that makes some journalism students shudder.

Mathematics for the Reporter

The wire service dispatch reads:

The average American who lives to the age of 70 consumes in that lifetime the equivalent of 150 cattle, 24,000 chickens, 225 lambs, 26 sheep, 310 hogs, 26 acres of grain and 50 acres of fruits and vegetables.

A Nevada newspaper reader who saw the story was puzzled. That seemed like a lot of meat to consume in a lifetime, he thought. He consulted his butcher who estimated the dressed weights of the various animals listed in the story. They came up with a total of 222,695 pounds of meat. The reader wrote the wire service that he had done some figuring. He multiplied 70 years by 365 days to find the total number of days in the average person's lifetime. The figure was 25,500 days. He divided the total meat consumption of 222,695 pounds by 25,500 days. "That figures out to a whopping 8.7 pounds of meat a day," he wrote.

The wire service retired the reference work from which the item was gleaned.

The reporter who handled the story would have avoided embarrassing the wire service had he observed Rule No. 1 for numbers: Always check them.

Big Harvest   If the reporter who handled the Postal Service food drive story for his Florida paper had checked the numbers he was given, he would have avoided looking as silly as the wire service reporter. He wrote that letter

carriers had collected 11 million tons of food last year in three Florida counties. A reader checked: 11 million tons equals 22 billion pounds. Divide that by the U.S. population of 261 million.

The reader calculated that the letter carriers would have had to have collected 84 pounds of food from each man, woman and child in the United States. Hardly likely.

It turns out that it wasn't tons but pounds—11 million pounds. That's still a lot, but it's 1/2,000th of the newspaper's figure.

Tangled Numbers   A CBS newscast during the bombing of the Taliban in Afghanistan reported on a poll asking men and women whether the United States should send its troops into battle. "Women were more in favor than men," the newscaster read. "Three of ten women approved, whereas only two of three men approved sending in U.S. troops."

Hold everything. A CBS spokesman clarified the mess his mathematically-challenged newswriter had created. "The number three seemed larger than two, so the writer got his numbers and sexes jumbled." There's more to it than that. Even if the newswriter had written that two of three men approved and only three of ten women approved, the listener would be left trying to compare thirds and tenths. Obviously, the newswriter could not do the simple mathematics that would have enabled him to write:

> Men were more in favor than women. Almost 70 percent of the men approved sending in U.S. land troops, but only 30 percent of the women polled approved.

Or he could have used fractions:

> Two-thirds of the men approved, but less than a third of the women supported sending in U.S. land troops.

Basic Calculations

To avoid embarrassing errors like these, reporters need to be able to handle three fairly simple calculations—how to figure a percentage, an average and a rate.

Percentages   This is probably the most useful calculation in the journalist's toolbox. It is used to compare this year's traffic deaths with last year's; the increase, or decrease, in felonies; population increases or declines. The list is endless. Here's a percentage calculation a Florida radio reporter made when he saw the 2000 census figures.

> The South made the biggest percentage population gain in the last decade. Its 13.3 percent increase edged out the gain in the Far West of 12.5 percent.

To find the percentage increase, the reporter took the 2000 census figure for the South and compared it with the 1990 figure:

2000	96.9 million
1990	85.5 million

He subtracted the old from the new, getting 11.4 million, and he divided that by the 1990 figure:

$$\frac{11.4 \text{ million}}{85.5 \text{ million}} = 13.3 \text{ percent}$$

Averages We're all familiar with averages. There's your grade point average (GPA) and the baseball player's batting average. There's the weather reporter's average temperature for last month. You know all about these, right? Just take all the numbers and divide by the number of incidents. What's that? Yes, it's not as simple as it sounds, and as we shall see, it's even more complicated than that.

But let's get down to basics.

Take the first baseman who is in a batting slump. The sportswriter says that in his last 45 appearances at the plate he has had only nine hits. The sports fan wants to know: What's that mean in terms of his batting average? And so the reporter calculates: Hits divided by plate appearances—

$$\frac{9}{45} = \frac{1}{5} \quad \text{or .2} \quad \text{or .200}$$

We drop the decimal point. Our star first baseman is batting a dismal 200. He'd better improve or his $4 million salary will go down the drain next year when he renegotiates his contract.

Average temperature for January? Take all the daily measurements for the 31 days, add them up and divide by the number of days to get the daily average.

$$\frac{807}{31} = 26.03$$

So you can write that average temperature last month was a cold 26 degrees. You can compare that with January of last year and make any other comparisons.

Averages can be more complicated than those we have just calculated, as we shall soon demonstrate. But first, let's look at the third of the basic calculations the reporter must be able to do.

Rates Reporters deal with rates all the time—murder rates, death rates, divorce rates, infant mortality rates. Rates tell us more than raw numbers because they take factors like population into consideration.

The University of California at Los Angeles has more property crime on campus than any other four-year school, 1,439 in a recent year, according to FBI statistics. Duke University is way down the list with 931 property crimes that year.

But the total numbers are misleading. It's actually riskier to have property in a Duke dormitory than it is at UCLA. The rates tell us why. UCLA is a huge school, with a student enrollment of about 36,000. Duke is small,

11,600 students. Let's take the number of property crimes per student, which is what a rate consists of—so many incidents per some other factor:

UCLA:

$$\frac{1439}{36000} = .03997$$

Duke:

$$\frac{931}{11600} = .08026$$

To make these decimals more easily understandable, let's figure the number of property crimes per hundred students. We'll multiply the decimals by 100 and we get:

UCLA = 3.997, which is about 4
Duke = 8.026, which is about 8

So a Duke student is twice as likely to have his Walkman stolen than a UCLA student. The rate of 8 is twice the rate of 4.

More Rates   We can make the same sort of analysis when we consider other crime statistics. Take murder. If you go over the figures, you will see that the cities and states with the highest totals are not those with the highest rates.

The same can be said for a number that many people consider a measurement of how well a society takes care of its citizens—infant mortality. The states with the largest number of infant mortalities are not among the states with the highest rates.

Remember: Rates are a better indicator than raw numbers.

Refining the Data

Unfortunately, just when we think we're getting somewhere, we encounter an obstacle. In this case, our infant mortality numbers and our murder numbers are actually masking something essential to understanding life in the United States. Just as we saw in the case of the computer, machinery without a mind behind it is useless. Here, we have to think about a basic fact of life in the United States, race.

If we break both murder victims and infant mortality deaths into racial categories we find data that tell us more than our overall rates tell us. When we do this, we find that the black murder victimization rate is 6 to 10 times greater than the white rate, depending on which age groups are compared. In some states black infant mortality rates are as much as three times as great as those for white infants.

Next, the problem of averages. Darrell Huff, the author of books about mathematics says, "When you are told something is an 'average' you still don't know very much about it unless you can find out what kind of average it is: mean, median, or mode."

Means, Modes and Medians

How would you describe the average salary at J.C. Walnut and Co., an upholstery shop whose employees are on strike? Walnut says it is $31,140, and he has put a sign in his window saying so and telling his customers that the employees are ungrateful.

Here is how the annual salaries for the company break down:

- $72,500 (1) Mr. Walnut
- 59,600 (1) Son Theodore
- 30,500 (4) Master craftsmen
- 25,200 (6) Upholsterers
- 20,600 (3) Laborers

If we add up the salaries, being careful to multiply by the number of workers in each category, we reach a total payroll of $467,100. To find the average Walnut reached, we divide by 15, the total number of people on the payroll. The average is $31,140. So Walnut is right, right? Wrong.

First let's consider the word *average,* which covers three kinds of figures:

Mean: This is the average Walnut used. To derive it, we add up all the figures in our set and divide by the total number of individual components.

Mode: The component occurring most often in a listing of components.

Median: The midpoint in a grouping.

The mean distorts when there are unusually high or low components, as there are here with Walnut and son Theodore's salaries making the average tilt toward the high end.

The mode here is $25,200, which is the most frequently occurring salary.

The median, which is used most often in computing averages, requires you list all the salaries to find the midpoint:

```
                        72,500
                        59,600
                        30,500
                        30,500
                        30,500
                        30,500
                       ┌25,200
                        25,200      ←──── Median
            Mode        25,200
                        25,200
                        25,200
                       └25,200
                        20,600
                        20,600
                        20,600
```

Look at this list of 15 numbers. The midpoint is the eighth on the list because there are seven salaries above it and seven below it. The eighth salary on the list is $25,200, which is the same as the mode.

Our figure of $25,200 is considerably less than Walnut's average of $31,140. And if we use some common sense, we realize that only the employees are on strike, so what is Walnut doing putting his and his son's salaries in the computation?

Take out the top two on the list and we get 13 salaries. The mode and the median are still $25,200. The mean is $25,769.

Let's take this a step further before we leave the delightful realm of mathematics. Let's look behind the median. There's more here than meets the eye.

Analyzing Averages

The federal government announces that the median household income last year was $46,737. Not bad. But wait a minute. Common sense, based on our reading and experience, tells us that income is widely disproportionate in this country among whites, blacks and Hispanics and between men and women. We want a breakdown of the median. Look at what we find:

Household Income

White	$49,023
Black	29,404
Hispanic	29,608

These figures tell us something about the nature of our society: The median family income of blacks and Hispanics is 60 percent that of whites.

As for working women, here are the median incomes:

Income of Women

White	$27,687
Black	23,697
Hispanic	20,483

Dissecting data gives us specifics, and, as we know, journalism is the art of the specific. The same agency that gave us median income figures reports that 32.3 million people were living in poverty last year, poverty being designated as a household income that is less than $17,030 for a family of four. With each additional family member, the poverty threshold increases by about $2,500.

We ask for particulars. Who are these 32.3 million people? The largest number, 24.5 million, are white and make up two-thirds of the total poor. But if we make a further check to see what percentage of the total number of whites live in poverty, we derive a much smaller percentage, 9.8 percent. Let's make a similar calculation for other groups:

Black:	23.6 percent
Hispanic:	22.8 percent

Personalizing Numbers

Numbers do tell us a great deal about the way we live. But for journalists numbers are the starting point. Behind the percentages, rates and averages are human beings, and it is their story that the journalist is obliged to tell. When Phoebe Zerwick of the *Winston-Salem Journal* learned that the infant mortality rate in North Carolina was among the highest in the nation, and that the death rate of black infants in the *Journal*'s home county hovered around 20, more than twice the state's average, she gave the figures a human dimension. One of her stories calling attention to the toll begins this way:

Yvette Johnson took her punishment for smoking crack day after day as she watched her 3-pound son struggle to live.

"Even today, after being clean for four years, I still remember those months," Johnson said.

"Seeing this baby suffer, seeing those needles and tubes and seizures, I really felt it was my fault," she said. "The only way I could say I was sorry was to go there every day and stay clean.

"Basically my son died about 10 times in the hospital. That was the worst punishment that I could actually say a person could have given me. Jail wouldn't have done no good. A whipping would have done no good.

"For the first three-and-a-half months I didn't do nothing. I just sat there and looked at my baby and cried."

Personalizing the Smoker

"An estimated 50 million Americans smoked 600 billion cigarettes last year," the story about a local anti-smoking proposal said. The city editor calls you, the reporter handling the story, to the desk.

"Let's put this and a lot of the other figures into some understandable terms," he tells you. "In this case, why not follow the sentence with one that says, 'This means the average smoker lit up so many cigarettes a day.'"

Back at your desk, you make a few simple calculations: 600 billion cigarettes smoked a year ÷ 50 million smokers = 12,000 cigarettes per smoker a year.

You want average daily use, so you make the next calculation: 12,000 cigarettes a year ÷ 365 days = 32.87 cigarettes per smoker a day.

You round that off to 33—a pack and a half a day. A reader can see the smoker crumpling up a pack and smoking halfway through a second pack for his or her daily dose. This is more graphic than the millions and billions, which depersonalize the story.

For more about the use of mathematics, see **More Math** in *NRW Plus*.

Public Opinion Polling

Abortion. Prayer in school. Gun control. Tax increases. Voting for the president, the mayor. How do we stand on these issues; how will we vote? In the past, the answers were hardly convincing. Reporters would chat with politicians, those supposedly perceptive insiders with delicate olfactory organs attuned to the mildest breezes. The result might be interesting reading, but it had no predictive value whatsoever.

Now, the science of surveying gives the journalist a surer hand to reach into areas of coverage that before had been handled with impressions and conjecture.

Polls are used for a variety of stories. The well-designed poll can tell with a fair degree of accuracy not only what people think of a president's performance, but also whether a proposed school bond issue is popular in a middle-class section of the community or what types of day care are favored by working mothers. Polls have been used to determine whether Catholics approve of abortion, how people feel about the death penalty, what blacks think of affirmative action. *The New York Times* even ran a survey that established that 87 percent of 3- to 10-year-olds believe in Santa Claus.

Recognizing the value of polls and surveys, many newspapers and television stations have hired pollsters and polling organizations. The reporter is still essential, for the poll can supply only the information. The reporter must make the poll into news. To do this, he or she must understand how polls work and their possibilities and limits.

Use with Care The poll is a systematic way of finding out what people are thinking at a given time by questioning a sample population. It can provide a fairly accurate stop-action photo of a situation. This does not mean that all polling data should be taken at face value. There are some inherent problems in polling, and there are pollsters whose purpose is to promote their clients. Reporters who understand polls know what to accept, what to discard. Reporters who are overwhelmed by data, who believe there is some mystery about figures, will be victimized, just as they will be misled by any public relations gimmick.

Polls are "able to establish with great accuracy the extent to which an opinion is held, and they can successfully predict behavior over the short run," writes Sheldon S. Wolin of the Department of Politics at Princeton University. "Once the period is extended," he cautions, "the reliability of the findings diminishes rapidly."

Political Polls

There are hundreds of polling organizations and firms. The majority are local groups that conduct marketing surveys. The big firms—Gallup, Harris, and Roper—handle commercial clients, too, but are best known for their political polls and surveys. It is this political polling that so often finds its way into newspapers and news broadcasts. During a political campaign, as much as one-third to one-half of the news is about the public's reaction to a candidate or an issue.

Unfortunately, the emphasis on predicting winners, on who's ahead, rather than on interpreting the data leads to the waste of huge amounts of fascinating material about how people are voting and why, whether some groups—blacks, Jews, Catholics, farmers—have switched their allegiances.

Stealth Candidates. When the former grand wizard of the Ku Klux Klan, David Duke, ran for governor of Louisiana, polls consistently underestimated his actual vote. Why? Voters are unwilling to admit their true feelings when race is an issue, says pollster Paul Maslin. To correct for this, pollsters divide the undecided white vote 4:1 for the white candidate in a race of a white versus a black candidate. Some interviewers will ask general questions to gauge whether interviewers have racist sentiments.

Although reputable pollsters pretest their questions, ambiguities do creep in. Reporters always should examine the questions behind the polling data to make sure that they are clear and, for polls conducted for private clients, to ascertain whether they are loaded.

Winners and Losers

Journalists must be careful about their tendency to heed the demands of readers and listeners for definitive opinions and for winners and losers. A poll can only state what people **say** they are thinking or how voters **say** they will vote at the time they are polled, and sometimes even then the contests are too close to call.

Journalists should remember this: People change their minds; polls cannot guarantee that behavior will be consistent with intentions.

Reputable pollsters know just how far they can take their data. But they are often under pressure to pick winners in election contests. When preelection polls indicate a 60–40 percent breakdown, a pollster feels at ease in choosing the winner. But when an editor, reflecting the desire of readers and listeners, asks for a choice in a 44–42 race with 14 percent undecided, then trouble lies ahead.

Although editors and broadcast producers tend to be most interested in the top of the poll—who's ahead—most of the significant material in the poll usually is found in why the candidate is ahead or behind and how the candidate is faring with certain groups. This can make interesting and significant news. There may be a good story in the candidate who does well with a certain religious group and poorly with another because of his or her stand on abortion or prayer in schools.

For a more detailed explanation of polling, see **More about Polls** in *NRW Plus*.

Summing Up

Journalists have an array of research and reporting tools that if used with intelligence and care lead to accurate and thorough stories. The tools enable reporters to call up the newspaper or station's library, access a range of basic reference material, reach out to other reporters with queries and obtain a vast amount of online material.

Reporting. "There is no substitute for what you see and hear. This is as true in the age of the Internet as before it, perhaps more so, because the temptations to shortcuts and the means to take them have multiplied beyond measure."
—*Roger Cohen, foreign correspondent,* The New York Times

Further Reading

Aueletta, Ken. *The Highwaymen: Warriors of the Information Superhighway.* New York: Random House, 1997.

Barzun, Jacques, and Henry F. Graff. *The Modern Researcher.* New York: Harcourt Brace Jovanovich, 1985.

Croteau, Maureen, and Wayne Worcester. *The Essential Researcher.* New York: HarperCollins, 1993. (A one-volume sourcebook for journalists written by University of Connecticut journalism faculty members.)

Huff, Darrell, and Irving E. Gers. *How to Lie with Statistics.* New York: Norton, 1954.

Meyer, Philip. *Precision Journalism,* 2nd ed. Bloomington: Indiana University Press, 1979.

Paul, Nora. *Computer Assisted Research: A Guide to Tapping Online Information,* 2nd ed. St. Petersburg, Fla.: The Poynter Institute for Media Studies, 1994.

Pavlik, John. *Journalism and the New Media.* New York: Columbia University Press, 2001.

Williams, Frederick. *Reasoning with Statistics.* New York: Holt, Rinehart and Winston, 1968.

5 The Lead

Mike Roemer

**Picketing city council—
a direct lead.**

Preview

The lead gives the reader the sense of the story to follow. There are two basic types of leads:

• **Direct:** This lead tells the reader or listener the most important aspect of the story at once. It is usually used on breaking news events.

• **Delayed:** This lead entices the reader or listener into the story by hinting at its contents. It often is used with feature stories.

The lead sentence usually contains one idea and follows the subject-verb-object sentence structure for clarity. It should not exceed 35 words.

The effective story lead meets two requirements. It captures the essence of the event, and it cajoles the reader or listener into staying awhile.

> We slept last night in the enemy's camp.
> —By a correspondent for the *Memphis Daily Appeal,* after the first day of the Civil War Battle of Shiloh

> Millionaire Harold F. McCormick today bought a poor man's youth.
> —Carl Victor Little, UP, following McCormick's male gland transplant operation in the early 1920s. UP's New York Office quickly killed the lead and sent out a sub (substitute lead)

> The million-to-one shot came in. Hell froze over. A month of Sundays hit the calendar. Don Larsen today pitched a no-hit, no-run, no-man-reach-first game in a World Series.
> —Shirley Povich, *The Washington Post & Times Herald,* on the perfect game the Yankee pitcher hurled against the Brooklyn Dodgers in 1956

"I feel as if I had been pawed by dirty hands," said Martha Graham.
    —Walter Terry, dance critic of *The New York Herald Tribune,* after two members of Congress denounced Graham's dancing as "erotic"

What price Glory? Two eyes, two legs, an arm—$12 a month.
    —St. Clair McKelway, *Washington Herald,* in a story about a disabled World War I veteran living in poverty

Snow, followed by small boys on sleds.
    —H. Allen Smith, *New York World-Telegram,* in the weather forecast

Rule Breakers, but Memorable

These leads defy almost every canon decreed by those who prescribe standards of journalistic writing. The first lead violates the rule demanding the reporter's anonymity. The UP lead is in questionable taste. Povich's lead has four sentences and three clichés. Terry's lead is a quote lead and McKelway's asks a question—both violations of the standards. Smith's weather forecast is a little joke.

Yet, the leads are memorable.

They work because they meet the two requirements of lead writing: They symbolize in graphic fashion the heart of the event, and they entice the reader to read on. Here are two leads from New York City newspapers that appeared the morning after the mayor announced his new budget. Which is better?

Mayor Lindsay listed facilities for public safety yesterday as his top spending priority for next year, shifting from his pledge of a year ago to make clean streets his first objective in capital expenditures.
    —*The New York Times*

Mayor Lindsay dropped his broom and picked up the nightstick yesterday, setting law enforcement facilities as the top priority in the city's construction plans for the coming fiscal year.
    —*Daily News*

Great Beginnings

The business of luring the reader into a story is hardly confined to journalistic writing. Andrew E. Svenson, the prolific author of many of the Nancy Drew, Bobbsey Twins and Hardy Boys juvenile books, said that the trick in writing is to set up danger, mystery and excitement on page 1 to convince the child to turn the page. He said he had rewritten page 1 as many as 20 times.

Plato knew the importance of the first words of a written work. "The beginning is the most important part of the work," he wrote in *The Republic.*

The great Russian writer Leo Tolstoy said the idea behind good writing is jumping "straight into the action."

The Old Testament begins with simple words in a short sentence: "In the beginning God created the heavens and the earth."

Everyone remembers great beginnings:

> It was the best of times, it was the worst of times, it was the age of wisdom, it was the age of foolishness, it was the epoch of belief, it was the epoch of incredulity, it was the season of Light, it was the season of Darkness, it was the spring of hope, it was the winter of despair.

As most high school students know, that is how Charles Dickens began *A Tale of Two Cities*. Another book, written 92 years later, is also familiar to high school readers, possibly because of the beginning that trapped them into reading further:

> If you really want to hear about it, the first thing you'll probably want to know is where I was born, and what my lousy childhood was like, and how my parents were occupied, and all that David Copperfield kind of crap, but I don't feel like going into it, if you want to know the truth.

The writer—J. D. Salinger. The book—*Catcher in the Rye*.

Another famous beginning from literature:

> It is a truth universally acknowledged, that a single man in possession of a good fortune, must be in want of a wife.

That's the way Jane Austen began *Pride and Prejudice*.

Finding the Lead

New Yorker writer John McPhee says, "The first part—the lead, the beginning—is the hardest part of all to write. I've often heard writers say that if you have written your lead you have 90 percent of the story." Locating the lead, he says, is a struggle.

"You have tens of thousands of words to choose from, after all—and only one can start the story, then one after that, and so forth. . . . What will you choose?" McPhee asks.

But before the words can be selected, the facts must be sorted out. How does the reporter select the one or two facts for a lead from the abundance of material he or she has gathered? What's the focus of the story?

The fact sifting begins well before the reporter sits down to write. Experienced reporters agree with journalists John W. Chancellor and Walter R. Mears who say:

> We have found that a way to write good leads is to think of them in advance—to frame the lead while the story is unfolding.

The Importance of the Lead

Why this stress on finding and writing the lead? Some beginning reporters believe that if they simply start writing, the lead will come to them. Possibly. But given the time constraints under which journalists write, that's unlikely. It may work for the veteran reporter given a week or two to come up with a series on the city's economy. We'll soon see how they operate. But for day-to-day writing, the reporter think leads early and often.

Also, as McPhee points out, once crafted, the lead helps to organize the story. "The story flows from the lead," is an old newsroom saying. The reporter Henry Fairlie describes the importance of the lead this way: "Every journalist who has ever struggled with [a lead] knows why it can take so much effort. It is as important to him as to the reader. Writing it concentrates the mind wonderfully, forcing him to decide what in the story is important, what he wants to emphasize, and can eventually give the shape to the rest of the story as he writes it."

Thomas Boswell, columnist for *The Washington Post,* says, "The most important thing in the story is finding the central idea. It's one thing to be given a topic, but you have to find the idea or the concept within that topic. Once you find that idea or thread, all the other anecdotes, illustrations and quotes are pearls that hang on this thread. The thread may seem very humble, the pearls may seem very flashy, but it's still the thread that makes the necklace."

Finding the Thread

A thief broke into an auto parts store and stole a batch of batteries. Here's how a reporter for *The Charlotte Observer* wrote the story along with an analysis provided by her editor:

Thieves Get 36 Batteries

Thieves who entered a Charlotte auto parts store stole 36 Delco batteries, police were told yesterday.

Crowell Erskine, 49, manager of the Piedmont Auto Exchange at 410 Atando Ave., told officers the store was broken into between 5 p.m. Tuesday and 8 a.m. Wednesday by thieves knocking a hole in the rear wall of the one-story brick building.

Erskine said the batteries were valued at $539.18.

—*The Charlotte Observer*

Analysis

1. The lead focuses on the basic idea, the theft of a batch of batteries. The reporter knows the reader opens the newspaper each day with the question, "*What* happened today?"

2. The reporter answers what he or she thinks will be the logical questions a reader might ask, "*Where* did the break-in occur? *When* did it happen? *How* was it done?" The answers to those questions explain and amplify the lead.

3. Background is provided. The reporter knows the reader will want to be told the value of the goods stolen.

Other Scenarios Let's say that the thief had somehow managed to bring off the job in broad daylight. Then *when* the theft occurred and *how* it was managed would be the main elements in the lead, the thread along which the story would be written.

Had the thief scaled a 15-foot wall to gain entry, *how* the theft was managed would be placed in the lead.

If the thief left a note in the store apologizing for his act and saying he needed the money to pay medical bills for his sick wife, *why* the theft occurred—according to the thief—would be put into the lead.

The most important element always forms the basic idea for the lead. To find that basic element, the reporter anticipates the questions the reader will ask and then answers them. These questions have been summarized as *who, what, when, where, why,* and *how*—the Five W's and an H.

Burying the Lead

The most common mistake young reporters make is burying the lead. That is, the main idea is swimming somewhere in the body of the story instead of being placed in the lead. Here are a couple of examples taken from student news stories:

> The Student Council met last night to discuss and adopt next year's budget.

> The university has changed its stand on admissions policies and will put them into effect in two years.

The reader has to wade through a few paragraphs before getting to the point: that the budget for next year includes $4,500 to bring "diverse speakers" to the campus; that the university adopted a "need-blind admission policy" that should make for a more diverse student body. These belong in the lead.

Let's watch a student write a story about the local United Way Campaign, which was in the middle of a fund drive. The student thought that the midpoint of the drive might be a good time to check progress. Here is the story he turned in:

> The local United Way Campaign today issued its second weekly report in its current campaign to raise $750,000 for next year's activities.
>
> Tony Davis, the campaign chairman, said that donations in the first two weeks had exceeded last year's fund raising at a similar time.
>
> "We've collected $350,000, and that's about $25,000 ahead of last year," Davis said. "Thanks to the work of our downtown volunteers, the local merchants have been canvassed more thoroughly than ever before, and their gifts have been very generous."
>
> The month-long drive seeks funds for 28 local organizations, including the Big Brothers, Senior Citizens House and a new program to aid crippled children.

The Problem   The story is clear but it has a glaring fault: The basic idea or theme was placed in the second paragraph. Occasionally, a reporter will intentionally delay the lead, usually for dramatic effect. This was no such instance. The most significant fact the student reporter gleaned from his reporting was that the campaign was running ahead of last year's receipts. And because this is a straightforward or spot news story, the progress report should have been placed in the lead. Given this advice by his instructor, the student rewrote the story:

> The United Way Campaign to raise $750,000 is running ahead of last year's drive at the midway point.

Tony Davis, the campaign chairman, said today that in the first two weeks of the month-long fund drive, $350,000 had been collected. That is $25,000 ahead of last year's collections at this time.

"Thanks to the work of our downtown volunteers, the local merchants have been . . ."

The same set of facts was given to a reporting and writing class. Here are some of the leads that emerged:

Tony Davis, the chairman of the United Way Campaign, reported today that the fund drive is running ahead of schedule.

The United Way Campaign has collected $350,000, which is $25,000 ahead of last year's drive at this time.

Local merchants were credited today with helping to push the United Way Campaign closer and faster toward its goal of $750,000.

In each of these leads, the basic idea is the same: Collections are ahead of those of last year. This is the most important element and it must be the basis of the lead.

Pregnant Teen-Agers

Let's accompany Sarah as she works on a story about a talk she has just covered. A Harvard sociologist spoke about teen-age pregnancy to a campus audience. He said that the bill for social services, special schools, lost work hours and hospital care for the infants, who are often born prematurely, adds up to several billion dollars a year.

"Last year," he said, "about 375,000 unmarried teen-agers gave birth, and almost as many teen-agers had abortions. The dollar costs have been enormous, to say nothing of the social costs."

Sarah is writing for the campus newspaper. She has a couple of hours before deadline. If she were working for a radio or TV station, she would not have the luxury of time to think about her lead and story. As Chancellor and Mears state in their book *The News Business:*

When you've got to run to a telephone to start dictating, or when you've got to go on camera and start talking, the one thing you really need is to have a lead in your head. It doesn't have to be fancy, but if you frame it properly, the rest of the story will flow from it in a natural and graceful way.

Sarah knows that if she can identify the heart of the talk, her story will just about organize itself because the next several paragraphs after the lead will consist of quotes that buttress and amplify the lead material she has selected. Easier said than done, she muses.

Well, what's her lead? She had better start writing, and she does:

A Harvard sociologist studying teen-age pregnancy gave a speech last night to more than 200 students and faculty members in Hall Auditorium.

Sarah isn't happy with her lead. She talks to herself:

Trouble. That's called backing into the lead. All this kind of lead tells the reader is that the speaker spoke to an audience, which is hardly interesting or important enough t) merit anyone's attention. He did say something interesting—in fact, he made several interesting points.

Sarah had been surprised by the large number of teen-agers who gave birth and the number of abortions among these young women. Lead material?

Not really, she reasons, because the speaker devoted most of his talk to the cost of teen-age pregnancy. This information was clearly the most important. She could work the figures into the second and third paragraphs to explain the reasons for the high cost. Sarah writes:

A Harvard sociologist said last night that teen-age pregnancy is costing the country billions of dollars a year.

Gerald Cantor told 200 students and faculty members in Hall Auditorium that the annual costs associated with the pregnancies of almost 750,000 unmarried women under the age of 20 "are vastly greater than we had thought."

He attributed the costs to social services. . . .

Sarah pauses to read what she has written. She is satisfied that she has found the most important part of the talk for her lead, that she has identified the speaker properly and placed the talk. . . . Wait. She isn't happy with the word *said* in her lead. Not very exciting.

Should I make it *warned*? Or is that too strong? He really didn't warn. I'll leave it as is.

Sarah has answered the first three of our five questions for lead writing:

1. **What:** The high cost.
2. **Who:** Harvard sociologist.
3. **Direct or delayed:** Direct.

We take leave of Sarah as she ponders the fourth and fifth questions. If you wish, lend her a hand.

A Race for Congress

Here is a lead a reporter wrote about a congressional race. He thought he had answered the first two questions writers ask themselves when writing a lead:

Replies of Rep. Ronald A. Sarasin and William R. Ratchford, candidates in the Fifth Congressional race, to a Connecticut League of Women Voters questionnaire were released today.

He did include *what* had happened and *who* was involved. But he did not make his answer to the first question sufficiently specific. What did they say in their replies? The reporter reached this answer down in the story, but his editor pointed out that voters want to know the opinions and positions of their candidates quickly in stories about politics. Such events do not lend themselves to delayed leads.

A better lead for the political story might have been:

Ronald A. Sarasin and William R. Ratchford, candidates for Congress in the Fifth District, agree that financing Social Security is the major domestic issue facing the nation.

The next paragraph might have included the background information that the reporter had mistakenly put into his lead:

Their positions on Social Security and on other issues were released today by the Connecticut League of Women Voters. The League had sent its questionnaires to all major candidates for office.

The subsequent paragraphs would expand the Social Security theme and introduce additional material from the replies of the candidates.

Help for the Airlines

After terrorists struck at New York and Washington, people stayed away from airline travel, and the industry went into a tailspin. Thousands of jobs were cut by the airline companies, but income dwindled and they asked for help from the government. The lead on a network newscast told the story simply and directly:

Major airline executives are asking Congress for help. They say they need 24 billion dollars in emergency aid.

Types of Leads

If you look back at the leads we have been discussing—pregnant teenagers, a race for Congress and the airline aid request—you will see that they took the reader and the listener directly to the main idea or theme of the story. They are appropriately called direct leads. Although young journalists are offered long lists of lead types, there are really only two types, the *direct* and the *delayed* lead. The *who* and the *what* leads, the *anecdotal, contrast* and *shotgun* leads, the *question, quote* and *gag* leads—they all fall into these two categories.

Let's look more closely at the direct lead, and then we will examine the delayed lead.

Direct Lead

The direct lead is the workhorse of journalism. It is used on most stories. As we have seen, the direct lead focuses on the theme of the event in the first paragraph. The surest way to test a reporter's competence, editors say, is to see whether his or her leads on spot news events move directly to the point. Here are some direct leads:

The temperature reached 102 degrees at noon yesterday and set a record high for the city.

On a day of unspeakable horror for New York and the nation, terrorists crashed plans into the World Trade Center and the Pentagon yesterday in the deadliest assault on the United States in its history.

NASHVILLE—The Tennessee Titans very nearly pulled off Music City Miracle II before falling to Baltimore 16-10 Monday.

WASHINGTON—The House of Representatives voted today to impeach President Clinton.

A local couple was awarded $150,000 in damages yesterday in Butte County Court for injuries they suffered in a traffic accident last March.

SPENCER—Shocked survivors wandered their ripped-apart community Sunday, searching for tornado-scattered belongings and mourning six neighbors who died.

Another in a series of snowstorms is expected to hit the Sierra today.

SAN FRANCISCO—The California Supreme Court ruled today that newspapers and television stations can be held liable for news-gathering techniques that intrude on privacy.

WASHINGTON—The U.S. Senate this afternoon acquitted President Clinton of the two impeachment charges brought against him by the House of Representatives. The vote on both charges fell far short of the two-thirds required for conviction.

For more leads on the terror bombing story see **Terror Bombings** in *NRW Plus*.

Lead Essentials

Direct leads usually contain:

- Specific information about what happened or what was said.
- When the event occurred.
- The location of the event.
- The source of the information.

Lively Leads   Direct leads need not be dry and dull. Here's a direct lead by Aljean Harmetz of *The New York Times* for a business story, which we usually think of as a dry subject with prose to match:

> Two veteran motion picture industry executives were chosen today by the board of Walt Disney Productions to head the troubled company a mouse built.

When a fire struck a high-rise apartment building in Queens, New York, the AP put this lead on its story:

> A late-morning fire in the upper floors of an 18-story apartment building in the Lefrak city project in Elmhurst, Queens, killed three people Thursday, the Fire Department said.

Now look at how the *Daily News* began its story about the same fire:

> Strong winds combined lethally with a fire in a Queens high-rise building yesterday, creating a "blowtorch" that roared through an apartment building and into a hallway, killing three people and injuring 22.

The image of a blowtorch searing its way through the building is powerful. A battalion fire chief used that word in an interview and the reporter had the good sense to put it in the lead. Good reporting makes for good writing.

Here is how a *New York Times* reporter used an image in a direct lead:

UNION, S.C.—A jury today decided that Susan Smith should not be put to death for the drowning of her two young sons and instead should spend the rest of her life in prison, to remember.

It took the jury two and one-half hours to reject the prosecution's request for the death penalty and settle on the life sentence. The jury's unanimous decision saved Mrs. Smith, 23, from death row, but left her alone in a tiny cell with the ghosts of her dead children for at least the next 30 years, her lawyer said.

Those two words added to the first paragraph give Rick Bragg's story an added dimension to the picture of a woman who drowned her two boys because her lover did not want to continue a relationship with a woman with two children.

The next paragraph continues with the news and also fills in the picture he drew for us in his lead.

Online Leads The direct lead is the mainstay of stories on the Web sites of newspapers and online news services. Studies have shown that online readers want their news in capsule form. They want to know what happened and to whom as soon as possible.

Online editors tell their writers to try to answer the Five W's and an H— who, what, when, where, why and how—in the leads of their stories.

Kickers

All these leads are direct leads for breaking or hard news stories. But there are times when writers back into the lead on a breaking news story—intentionally. Edna Buchanan began a story for *The Miami Herald* this way:

> Bad things happen to the husbands of the Widow Elkin.
> Someone murdered husband No. 4, Cecil Elkin, apparently smashing his head with a frying pan as he watched "Family Feud" on TV.
> Husband No. 3, Samuel Smilich, drowned in a weedy South Dade canal.
> Husband No. 2, Lawrence Myers, cannot be found. . . .

Anyone out there who isn't hanging on every word? Notice the detail Buchanan supplies: It was not just any pan but a frying pan with which No. 4 was dispatched. And he wasn't just watching television but "Family Feud." The canal where No. 3 was found was "weedy."

Buchanan goes on to write about Widow Elkin and then concludes the piece:

> It is the murder of her fourth husband that got Margaret Elkin in trouble. She is accused of trying to hire a beekeeper to kill him. The trial is set for Sept. 9.

The prosaic way to have started this story would have put the date set for the trial in the lead. But Buchanan's reporting turned up a remarkable series of events, and she gave us a modern morality tale with a climax.

Journalists call these lead-type endings *kickers,* probably in recognition of the jolt the climax gives the reader.

The story that delays presenting the main element uses the delayed lead.

Delayed Lead

The delayed lead is often used on features and news features, the kinds of stories that are not about developing or fast-breaking events. The delayed lead usually sets a scene or evokes a mood with an incident, anecdote or example.

Here is a mood-setting lead on a feature by AP Newsfeatures writer Sid Moody:

> Jack Loizeaux is a dentist of urban decay, a Mozart of dynamite, a guru of gravity. Like Joshua, he blows and the walls come tumbling down.

What does Loizeaux do? Our interest is aroused. The delayed lead purposely does not provide essential information to the reader or listener. This suspense is part of the attraction of the delayed lead. (Loizeaux runs a demolition company, revealed to us a few paragraphs later.)

Evicted   Here is a scene-setting delayed lead by Jon Glass from *The Virginia-Pilot* in Norfolk, Va.:

> VIRGINIA BEACH—It's 6 on Monday evening and the "happy hour" meeting is just starting at the Side Door.

We wonder just what is going to happen at this meeting, and Glass proceeds to tell us in the fourth and subsequent paragraphs:

Alcohol is what brought them, but the drink of choice is brewing in two industrial-sized coffee makers and served strong and black in Styrofoam cups. About 50 people, fewer than usual for this after-work meeting, sit in a circle on folding metal chairs to share their stories and words of hope.

For more than 20 years, this room at the Open Door Chapel Church has been a gathering place for people trying to overcome drinking problems.

Soon, it will be "last call" at the place members of Alcoholics Anonymous call the Side Door.

The church, in the 3100 block of Virginia Beach Blvd., wants to use the room to expand its K-12 school program, said the chapel's new pastor, the Rev. Bill Clevenger. He also said there were concerns about foul language and loitering around the meeting room, which is next to classes attended by children.

The church's board of elders and Clevenger sent a letter to AA leaders last week giving them until June 1 to find another place to meet. . . .

A Killer's Trial   Leonora Bohen LaPeter was assigned to cover the death penalty trial of the killer of a family of four for the *Savannah Morning News:*

The second I walked into the courtroom I started to think about how I was going to write it. I was thinking, "Where's my lead? How am I going to use that? Who am I going to talk to during the breaks?"

Notice LaPeter's priority—the lead is first in her thinking. She knows that once she has it, her story will take shape.

I was looking for the moment that's different, for something that starts my story. I was looking for details, for things people were doing that might be a detail in the story. Obviously, my lead changed several times throughout the day.

Here is one of LaPeter's leads, based on a detail she observed among the people in the courtroom.

MONROE—Connie Smith bowed her head and kept it there.

Sitting in the front row of a Monroe courtroom Tuesday—surrounded by family and friends—she couldn't bear to look at the television screen.

It showed the inside of her sister, Kim Daniels', home in Santa Claus the morning of Dec. 4, 1997, about seven hours after Kim, 33, her husband, Danny, 47, and their two children, Jessica, 16, and Bryant, 8, died from shotgun blasts as they slept in their beds.

In an interview for the Poynter Institute's *Best Newspaper Writing* series, LaPeter says that when the woman bowed her head she thought, "There it is. There's my scene."

"Children of Fire" Delayed leads are often used on narratives. Here is how Thomas French of the *St. Petersburg Times* began the first of four articles about the children of Southeast Asian refugee families and their adjustment to life in the United States:

Quietly, she weaves among the other children. She stands at the edge of the playground and waits her turn at the swings. She runs with the other girls, all of them holding hands and laughing, their black hair blowing in the wind, their bodies forming a line that ripples and curves. When it is time to go inside and rest, she lies on her towel and stares out the classroom window, gazing at the ocean of blue sky where her mother will soon be going to live.

Mari Truong is in her first year at preschool. Her teachers keep close tabs on her and her situation at home. They worry in the way of all mothers, and they watch in the way of all teachers, and they make sure she knows she is not alone. In the middle of class, one of them pulls her onto her lap and brushes her hand across the child's cheek.

"You have to stay little," the teacher tells her. "Or else I'll miss you, and I'll cry."

Mari smiles, returns the hug, then slips away. She is only 4 and still shines with the radiance of the very young. Yet there is something elusive about her, something fierce that refuses to be pinned down, captured, categorized. Already she looks at the world with the eyes of someone who will never surrender.

They are astonishing, Mari's eyes. Impossibly big and round, sharp and piercing, so dark brown they almost blossom into black. Despite her age, they seem to be charged with decades of emotion and experience. What have her eyes seen that Mari does not yet have words to explain? Do they carry memories, passed along in stories, of what her parents witnessed on the other side of the globe? Do they open at night, in her bed, and replay scenes from the refugee camp in Thailand where she was born? Does she see visions of her mother, like she used to be, before the doctors and the hospital and the wasting away?

For more about Mari and her friends, see **The Girl Whose Mother Lives in the Sky** in *NRW Plus*.

Stinger Here's a lead by Jonathan D. Salant that draws the reader in with a list of star coming attractions, then comes crashing to political ground zero:

> WASHINGTON (AP)—Hear country music stars Lyle Lovett and Tanya Tucker. Meet athletes Troy Aikman and Nolan Ryan. Get your picture taken with a 2,500-pound Brahma bull. Dine on your share of 7,000 pounds of beef brisket and 1,200 pounds of peach cobbler.
>
> This preinaugural bash is being brought to you by Boeing, Visa and dozens of other companies with issues before the federal government.

News Magazines The delayed lead is a favorite approach of the news magazines for events that readers are already familiar with through newspaper and broadcast coverage. Here is how *U.S. News & World Report* began its long piece on the week's big story:

> He had a temper so combustible that he once ejected Lana Turner and Ava Gardner from his Palm Springs house, screaming "Out, out, out!" and then hurling Gardner's cosmetics, clothes and records into the driveway. His buddies included mobsters and thugs, and he divided the world, Sicilian style, into friends—recipients of lavish gifts—and enemies. Face to face, the blue eyes could drill through you, and he could be unpredictable, foul-mouthed and crude, taking swings at anyone who got in his way.

Compare this beginning with the AP's direct lead on the same event:

> LOS ANGELES (AP)—Frank Sinatra, the dashing teen idol who matured into the premier romantic balladeer of American popular music and the "Chairman of the Board" to his millions of fans, died Thursday night of a heart attack. He was 82.

On Track Just any incident or anecdote will not do for the delayed lead. The lead must be consistent with the news point, the theme of the story. It must *lead* the reader straight to the heart of the event. Notice how John Rebchook of the *El Paso Herald-Post* takes this delayed lead to the news point in the fourth paragraph, the current status of the drive to collect unpaid traffic fines. Rebchook illustrates his point about unpaid traffic warrants by using in his lead a specific driver who has avoided paying:

> In less than three miles, Joseph L. Jody III ran six stop signs, changed lanes improperly four times, ran one red light, and drove 60 mph in a 30 mph zone—all without a driver's license. Two days

Example

later, he again drove without a driver's license. This time he ran a stop sign and drove 80 mph in a 45 mph zone. For his 16 moving violations Jody was fined $1,795.

He never paid. Police say that Jody has moved to Houston. Of the estimated 30,000 to 40,000 outstanding traffic warrants in police files, Jody owes the largest single amount.

Still, Jody's fines account for a small part of at least $500,000 owed to the city in unpaid traffic warrants.

In February, Mayor Jonathan Rogers began a crackdown on scofflaws in order to retrieve some $838,000 in unpaid warrants. As of mid-March, some $368,465 had been paid.

News point (Theme)

Leads on News Features

As the movement of news and information speeded up with all-day, all-news radio and TV stations and the Internet, print publications with a much slower access to readers turned to writing techniques to attract readers who already had some idea of the event. One of the techniques is the news feature. The writer "featurizes" the breaking news event by putting a delayed lead on the story. We've already seen how news magazines do this. Newspapers do, too.

Custody   By the time *The New York Times* was on newsstands and doorsteps, everyone knew the end to a legal battle over custody of 2½-year-old Jessica. The Supreme Court had dashed the hopes of Jessica's adoptive parents to keep her. This meant the child would have to be turned over to her biological mother, who had given her up for adoption shortly after Jessica was born.

Don Terry put this lead on his news feature:

> BLAIRSTOWN, Iowa, Aug. 2—When she is grown up, maybe Jessica DeBoer will understand why the adults in her young but complicated life have caused so much hurt in the name of love.
>
> But starting today, the 2½-year-old has more immediate lessons to learn, namely how to live without the only people she has ever known as Mommy and Daddy, Roberta and Jan DeBoer of Ann Arbor, Mich.

Slaying   The Associated Press, which takes a conservative approach to newswriting, put this beginning on a murder story:

DECATUR, Ga., Jan. 26 (AP)—Aster Haile, an Ethiopian immigrant, was delighted when her cousin arranged a marriage for her—so excited that she bought clothes for her first date with the man and showed them off.

But the day after the date, Ms. Haile called a friend and said that the man was too old and that she could not marry him. A day later, she was found dead along an Atlanta highway, shot in her head.

In the third paragraph is the arrest, which in times past would have been the lead to this story.

The police have charged the man who set up the date, Arega Abraha, with murder. Mr. Abraha was arrested on Friday at the Cincinnati-Northern Kentucky International Airport on a Federal charge of unlawful flight to avoid prosecution.

Impeachment   When the House of Representatives voted to impeach President Clinton, the *St. Louis Post-Dispatch* put this lead on the momentous story:

New York Democrat Charles Rangel rose Saturday to utter one of the rare sentences on which both sides of the House of Representatives could agree: "Mr. Speaker, the whole world is watching."

President Clinton's name was not mentioned until the fifth paragraph, and the actual vote was near the bottom of the 34-inch story. The editor, Cole C. Campbell, explained the choice of a delayed lead: "We knew people would know the outcome of the vote when they picked up the paper, so we wanted to do a story that conveyed the historicity of the moment."

Dr. Ruth's Blooper In her story for *USA Today,* Barbara S. Rothschild describes a sex therapist's boo-boo with this delayed lead:

There may finally be a question that embarrasses Dr. Ruth Westheimer. It's about the accuracy of her book.

Teens who read the new sex book coauthored by the USA's best-known sex therapist could get more than they asked for.

A baby, perhaps.

First Love: A Young People's Guide to Sexual Information, by Dr. Ruth and education professor Nathan Kravetz, has a major error on page 195.

In a chapter on contraception, the $3.50 book says it's "safe" to have sex the week before and the week of ovulation.

It should read "unsafe"—since those are the times a woman is *most* likely to become pregnant. . . .

Direct or Delayed?

As should be clear by now, there are no absolute rules about when the direct or the delayed lead should be used. True enough, on large-scale events the direct lead is usually called for, and on features the delayed lead works best. But the lines tend to blur between these extremes.

Usually, publications, stations and the online servers establish a style their reporters follow. When a study of bank lending practices found that whites are more likely than blacks to receive mortgage money, Michael Quint of *The New York Times* began his story with a direct lead:

> WASHINGTON, Oct. 21—The most comprehensive report on mortgage lending nationwide ever issued by the Government shows that even within the same income group whites are nearly twice as likely as blacks to get loans.

For its page 1 story the same day, *The Wall Street Journal* writer John R. Wilke preferred a delayed lead that focused on the effect of the discriminatory practices on an individual. Here is how his story began:

> BOSTON—When Sterling Saunders needed a home-repair loan, he turned to two of New England's largest banks, Shawmut Bank and Bank of Boston. He had a steady job, equity in the house and little debt, but they turned him down.
>
> In desperation, he arranged a $35,000, two-year loan from a small Massachusetts mortgage lender, Resource Equity Inc., at a stratospheric 34.09% interest rate. When Resource wouldn't refinance Mr. Saunder's loan he fell even deeper into debt through

Adrift

The storm was expected, but it seemed to catch everyone by surprise. Direct or delayed lead on the story? Here's how the *Daily News* began its story:

Didn't anyone see this coming? And were emergency officials caught napping?

These questions surged to the top in the wake of the raging storm that caught most New Yorkers by surprise and produced startling scenes of motorists nearly drifting into the East River.

City officials were warned and should have passed their alert on to the public, the National Weather Service said last night.

Jim Hughes, *Daily News*

refinancings with other high-rate lenders. Now the 42-year-old city employee, his wife and three daughters face eviction from their home of 16 years by a third lender.

"This might never have happened if we'd been able to find a bank loan in the first place," Mr. Saunders says. The banks decline to address specifics of his case, but judging by recent studies of lending patterns, one reason he couldn't get bank loans may have had to do with his address: He lives in a low-income, mostly black Boston neighborhood with few bank branches. A big survey by the Federal Reserve and analyses by others show these areas get a disproportionately small share of mortgage money from banks. . . .

Theme

The *Journal* also ran a direct-lead story reviewing the study inside the newspaper.

The Dangers

The narrative style has influenced papers across the country, but the style sometimes has spread by contagion rather than by healthy example. The delayed lead requires a talented hand. Moreover, it cannot be used at the reporter's whim.

In an attempt to sell their editors on their stories, ambitious reporters use delayed leads on routine news stories, and some reporters play with delayed leads when they are unable to write direct news leads. By taking the narrative or chronological approach or by focusing on an individual or an incident, they hope that the reader will somehow figure out just what the news point is.

Editors are aware of these tactics and the abusers of the delayed lead find themselves confined to taking scores from the local bridge and bowling leagues and explaining to the wrestling promoters why the sports editor doesn't consider wrestling results worthy of space.

The Combo Lead

Some reporters have mastered a technique that combines the direct and delayed leads. The story begins with a few general sentences. Then the reporter hits the reader with a karate chop at the end of the first paragraph. Edna Buchanan, the Pulitzer Prize-winning police reporter for *The Miami Herald,* is master of this kind of lead. Here are two typical Buchanan leads:

The man she loved slapped her face. Furious, she says she told him never, ever to do that again. "What are you going to do, kill me?" he asked, and handed her a gun. "Here, kill me," he challenged. She did.

On New Year's Eve, Charles Curzio stayed later than planned at his small TV repair shop to make sure customers would have their sets in time to watch the King Orange Jamboree Parade. His kindness cost his life.

Direct, with a Difference Buchanan covered a story about an ex-convict, Gary Robinson, who pushed his way past a line at a fried-chicken outlet. He was persuaded to take his place in line, but when he reached the counter there was no fried chicken, only nuggets, whereupon he slugged the woman at the counter. In the ensuing fracas, a security guard shot Robinson. Buchanan's lead was:

Gary Robinson died hungry.

Buchanan says her idea of a successful lead is one that could cause a reader who is breakfasting with his wife to "spit out his coffee, clutch his chest, and say, 'My god, Martha. Did you read this?' "

For her lead on a story about a drug smuggler who died when some of the cocaine-filled condoms that he had swallowed began to leak in his stomach, Buchanan wrote:

His last meal was worth $30,000 and it killed him.

A Difficult Choice

Let us listen to Margaret as she mulls over the notes she has taken at a city council meeting:

There were 13 items on the agenda. Well, which were the important ones? I'll circle them in my notes—
• General traffic program to route heavy trucks to Stanley Street and keep Main for lighter traffic.

- **56 stop signs to be bought.**
- **Paving program for Kentucky Street that will later fit into the bypass.**
- **OK'd contract to White Painting Co. to paint City Hall, $28,000.**
- **Hired consulting firm for traffic study.**

Clearly, I need a direct lead here. Four of them seem to deal with traffic. Should I summarize them or should I pick out the truck route or the traffic study? They seem equally important, so maybe I'll summarize the four. I'll drop the stop signs way down and then go into the painting contract.

She writes:

The City Council today took three significant actions to cope with the city's downtown traffic congestion.
The Council:
1. Approved the employment of Rande Associates, a consulting firm from Burbank, Calif., to make a study of traffic patterns.
2. Called for bids on paving 12 blocks of Kentucky Street, which is planned as part of a downtown bypass.
3. Endorsed the city traffic department's proposal to route heavy vehicles to Stanley Street away from Main Street.

At this point, some doubts assail Margaret. She remembers that the truck traffic issue has been argued for several months. Downtown merchants complained to the mayor about the truck traffic, and Stanley Street home owners petitioned the Council to keep the trucks away. Her newspaper and the local radio station have editorialized about it. In her haste to structure a complicated story, her news judgment went awry, she thinks. She writes:

The City Council today decided to route truck traffic to Stanley Street and away from downtown Freeport.

The city hall reporter is pleased with the lead she has written. But then more doubts. Maybe the overall pattern is more important than the single item about Stanley Street. After all, she thinks, the Council's three major actions will affect more people than those involved in the Stanley Street situation. Margaret decides that she needs some advice and she shows the city editor both leads.

"That's a tough one," he tells her. "Sometimes you flip a coin. Why don't you use your first lead and move up the third item, the one on Stanley Street, and put it first in the list?"

If we look closely at the two leads Margaret prepared, we notice that the single-element lead about the routing of truck traffic to Stanley Street denotes a specific action the council took. The summary lead about the council taking three "significant" actions to "cope with" traffic congestion is the reporter's conclusion or interpretation. Editors allow experienced reporters to interpret the news.

Good Reporting Equals Good Leads

Many weak leads are the result of inadequate reporting. Consider this lead:

Barbara Elizabeth Foster, 19, St. Mary's University
sophomore, will be queen of the city's Rose Festival.

Immediately, the city editor knows he is in for a tedious trek through the copy. The reporter failed to single out an interesting characteristic of the new queen to add to her age and year in school. Glancing through the copy, the editor notices that her mother was named Maid of Cotton 25 years ago. At the end of the story, there is a fleeting mention that her father enjoys gardening.

The editor runs his fingers through thinning hair. Masking his exasperation, he circles two sections and suggests to the reporter that there just might be a lead in the mother-daughter relationship and that a logical question to have asked the new queen was whether her father grew roses. Without good reporting no story can shine, much less be complete.

Color

Next, to the fourth and fifth of our five guides to writing leads. The fourth question the reporter has to answer is, "Is there a colorful word or dramatic phrase that I want to work into the lead?"

When Florida conducted the first execution in the United States in a dozen years, many reporters were assigned to the event. The nation had engaged in a debate about the morality of the death penalty. How best to put the Florida execution into words? Here is the lead Wayne King wrote for *The New York Times:*

STARKE, Fla., May 25—The state of
Florida trussed Arthur Spenkelink immo-
bile in the electric chair this morning,
dropped a black leather mask over his face
and electrocuted him.

The choice of the verb "trussed" is inspired. Not only does it mean to secure tightly; its second definition is "to arrange for cooking by binding close the wings or legs of a fowl."

S-V-O

The basic construction of the lead should be subject-verb-object, S-V-O. That is, the lead should begin with the subject, should be closely followed by an active verb and should conclude with the object of the verb.

The S-V-O structure has an internal imperative: It directs the reporter to write simple sentences, sentences with one main clause. This kind of construction keeps leads short, another major requirement for a readable beginning.

Here are two direct leads:

> In the past decade, David Blake has overpaid the city $7,635 in property fees on his small pharmacy in East Harlem.
>
> —*Newsday*

S = David Blake; V = has overpaid; O = the city.

> SAN FRANCISCO—A federal judge has ordered the City of San Francisco to hire 60 women police patrol officers within the next 32 weeks.
>
> —UPI

S = judge; V = has ordered; O = San Francisco.

The S-V-O construction is a staple of journalistic writing. Even in complex leads, the structure is used as in this Pulitzer Prize AP story:

> It was a story no one wanted to hear:
> Early in the Korean War, villagers said, American soldiers machine-gunned hundreds of helpless civilians under a railroad bridge in the South Korean countryside.

S = no one; V = wanted; O = hear story.
S = soldiers; V = machine-gunned; O = civilians.

Most Used   Three-fourths or more of the sentences reporters write follow the S-V-O pattern. It parallels the usual pattern of discourse and conforms to the command, "Write as you talk." Also, the S-V-O construction is functional. It is consistent with the thinking pattern of the reporter as he or she structures the lead. It is the most direct way of answering the first two questions the reporter asks when trying to find the lead: What happened? Who was involved?

Variety Is Possible

Although the S-V-O guideline may seem rigid, it does permit a variety of leads. When Supreme Court Justice Thurgood Marshall died, the leads showed the reporters' assessment of his significance:

> WASHINGTON—Thurgood Marshall, one of the most influential Americans of the 20th century and the first black to be elevated to the U.S. Supreme Court, died Sunday at the Bethesda Naval Medical Center in suburban Washington. He was 84.
>
> —Glen Elsasser and Nicholas M. Horrock, *Chicago Tribune*

> WASHINGTON—Thurgood Marshall, who championed the causes of the downtrodden, the imprisoned and the defenseless in almost a quarter-century on the Supreme Court, died yesterday at the Bethesda Naval Medical Center near here. He was 84.
>
> —*The Boston Globe*

Retired Supreme Court Justice Thurgood Marshall, the first black to serve on the nation's highest court and a key figure in the civil rights movement, died yesterday of heart failure at 84.

—Newsday

WASHINGTON—Retired Justice Thurgood Marshall, the first black to sit on the U.S. Supreme Court and a towering figure in the civil rights movement, died Sunday of heart failure. He was 84.

—The Associated Press

All the leads, however different, hewed to the basic S = (Marshall); V = (died); O = (yesterday, Sunday) structure.

Lead Length

When a reporter writes a lead, he or she navigates between divergent currents. One pull is toward writing a longer-than-average sentence, as the lead must offer significant information. The other is toward a short sentence because short sentences are more easily understood than long ones. The long sentence may be difficult to grasp; the short sentence may be uninformative or misleading.

Lead sentences should adhere to a 35-word limit whenever possible, for visibility as well as readability. Long leads occupy so much of the narrow newspaper or online column that they appear forbidding. For broadcasting, all sentences tend to be short for quick comprehension.

The AP tells its reporters, "When a lead moves beyond 20–25 words it's time to start trimming." Some of the extra baggage that can be jettisoned:

- Unnecessary attribution.
- Compound sentences joined by *but* and *and*.
- Exact dates and times unless essential.

Momentous Events   When an event is compellingly important, all rules and guidelines are tossed aside and the writer is allowed to jam the facts into the first paragraph. Here's the lead in *The New York Times* after the Sept. 11, 2001, terror bombings in New York and Washington:

Hijackers rammed jetliners into each of New York's World Trade Center towers yesterday, toppling both in a hellish storm of ash, glass, smoke and leaping victims, while a third jetliner crashed into the Pentagon in Virginia. There was no official count, but President Bush said thousands had perished, and in the immediate aftermath the calamity was already being ranked the worst and most audacious terror attack in American history.

Look at this lead in *The Washington Post* that runs 39 words long:

Five men, one of whom said he is a former employee of the Central Intelligence Agency, were arrested at 2:30 a.m. yesterday in what authorities described as an elaborate plot to bug the office of the Democratic National Committee.

Not much artistry here, just the facts. But what facts. This was the opening salvo in the *Post*'s exposure of the Watergate scandal that led to the resignation of Richard Nixon from the presidency.

Leads for Folos

When the Supreme Court ruled that principals can censor high school newspapers, *The Christian Science Monitor,* the *Kennebec* (Maine) *Journal, The Augusta* (Ga.) *Chronicle* and scores of other newspapers around the country assigned staff reporters to find out what effect the ruling would have on local high schools.

These local stories are known as *folos.* The *folo* can run alongside the major story, or it can be published a day or so after the major piece has run.

The lead to a *folo* includes some information from the major piece:

> Local high school principals say they
> will continue to allow student journalists a
> free hand, despite a Supreme Court deci-
> sion that gives them the power to censor
> school publications.

Updated or freshened stories fall into the category of the *folo* story. Usually, it is possible to find someone to comment on a new development or to track down people affected by a new program or policy.

Readability

A reporter handed in this lead:

> The city planning office today recommended adding a section
> to the zoning code regulations on classification for residential
> use of property.

The editor puzzled over it and then instructed the reporter to say specifically what the proposed section would do. The reporter tried again:

> The city planning office today recommended that property
> zoned for two-acre, one-family dwellings be rezoned to allow the
> construction of cooperative apartment houses for middle- and
> low-income families.

The city editor looked this over and seemed pleased. "Let's take it a step further," he said. "What's the point of the recommendation?" He answered his own question. "To change the code so ordinary people, not only the rich, can move into that wooded area north of town near the Greenwich Estates section. Let's try to get people into the lead." The reporter returned in 10 minutes with these two paragraphs:

> Low- and middle-income families may be able to buy
> apartments in suburban areas north of the city.

Roundups. A *roundup* is a story that joins two or more events with a common theme. Roundups usually take multiple-element direct leads. They are often used for stories on traffic accidents, weather, crime. When the events are in different cities and are wrapped up in one story, the story is known as an "undated roundup." Here's an example.

Torrential rains in Missouri and Kansas left five persons dead, hundreds homeless and crop losses of more than $1 million.

This is the intention of a proposal made today by the city planning office. The recommendation to the city council would rezone property in the area from the present restrictions that permit only single-family dwellings on two-acre lots.

In this process of writing and rewriting, the reporter went from a jargon-loaded, impenetrable lead to one that stated succinctly and clearly what the proposed regulation was intended to bring about. Accuracy was not sacrificed for simplicity and readability.

Readability Components

Readability stems from the ideas that make up the sentence, the order in which they are written and the words and phrases chosen to give the ideas expression:

Ideas: When possible, the lead should contain one idea. "The sentence is a single cry," says Sir Herbert Read, the British critic and author, in his *English Prose Style*. Too many ideas in a sentence make for heavy going. Also, the idea selected should be easy to grasp; complexities should be simplified.

Sentence order: The subject-verb-object construction is the most easily understood.

Word choice: Because the lead moves on its subject and verb, the choice of nouns and verbs is essential for readability. Whenever possible, the subject should be a concrete noun that the reader can hear, see, taste, feel or smell. It should stand for a name or a thing. The verb should be a colorful action verb that accelerates the reader to the object or makes the reader pause and think. It is not so much the presence or absence of the verb that matters, but the choice between a transitive and an intransitive verb.

Don't Write Writing

Immersed in words, the reporter is tempted to write writing, to make meaning secondary to language. This is fine when a poet plays with words, but it is dangerous for a journalist, whose first allegiance is to straightforward expression. Word play can lead to tasteless flippancies such as this lead:

> JACKSONVILLE, Fla.—Like justice,
> the new judge of the Duval County Court
> is blind.

Some reporters seem to think that using a direct quotation in the lead or injecting *you* into the lead makes for classy writing. They're wrong. Editors consider this weak writing. When you are tempted, consider this lead and imagine the editor's explosion when it popped out on his screen:

> You don't have to go to a doctor to find out whether you are pregnant. Test kits can be bought over the counter.

Good journalism is the accurate communication of an event to a reader, viewer or listener. As Wendell Johnson, a professor of psychology and speech pathology at the University of Iowa, put it, "Communication is writing about something for someone . . . making highly reliable maps of the terrain of experience." Johnson would caution his students, "You cannot write writing."

The reporter who makes the facts conform to clever writing will achieve notoriety of a sort, if he or she is clever enough. Such fame is fleeting, though. Editors and the public eventually flush out the reporter whose competence is all scintillation.

This is not a red light to good writing. In fact, the fashioning of well-crafted stories is an essential part of the journalist's work.

Summing Up

Good leads are based on the writer's clear understanding of the theme of the story. All else follows. This is why finding the theme is No.1 in our list of guidelines for writing readable leads:

1. Find the essential element(s) of the story.
2. Decide whether a direct or a delayed lead better suits the event.
3. If one element is outstanding, use a single-element lead. If more than one is, use a multiple-element lead.
4. Use the S-V-O construction.
5. Use concrete nouns and colorful action verbs.
6. Keep the lead short, under 30 or 35 words.
7. Make the lead readable, but do not sacrifice truthful and accurate reporting for readability.

Further Reading

Howarth, W. L. *The John McPhee Reader*. New York: Vintage Books, 1977.

Murray, Donald. *Writing for Your Readers*. Chester, Conn.: The Globe Pequot Press, 1983.

Roberts, Gene, and David R. Jones. *Assignment America*. New York: Quadrangle/Times Books, 1974. (An anthology of good writing by correspondents for *The New York Times*.)

6 Story Structure

Mike Roemer

**Picketing the legislators—
single-element story.**

Preview

Planning precedes writing. Reporters see the news story as an organized whole. Each sentence, every paragraph is purposely placed. Even while reporting, reporters try to visualize the shape and content of their stories, especially the beginning, the lead. The lead gives the story its structure.

Most news stories have a linear structure:

• The beginning includes a summary of the most important material. It tells the reader what to expect.
• The remainder of the story—the body—amplifies, buttresses, gives examples and explains the beginning. It also contains background and secondary material. The ending can sum up the story.

First the idea. Then the words.

As the young reporter struggled with his story, he recalled this advice that his city editor gave him the day before. Having written the obituary of a banker in 45 minutes, he was proud of his speed. But the editor said that the story was disorganized, without a focus. "Think the story through before you write," he told the reporter. The reporter read his story carefully, keeping in mind his editor's comment. Yes, he was writing without a firm idea of what he wanted to say and how it would fit together.

Suddenly, he was struck by what he had just told himself: "What do I want to say? Where do I put it?" That was the key to putting his notes into some kind of structured shape.

• What do I want to say?
• Where does it go?

This reporter's discovery is made all the time by young journalists. Usually, it is followed by another revelation: The news story form or structure is simple and most stories fit into the following structure:

• The lead.
• The material that explains and amplifies the lead.
• The necessary background.
• The secondary or less important material.

The Main Idea

The city editor's advice about thinking before writing has been offered to generations of students. As an essay in the *Fifth Reader,* a grade school textbook of the 1880s, puts it, "In learning to write, our first rule is: '*Know what you want to say.*' " (The italics are those of the author of the essay, Edward Everett Hale, the Boston clergyman who wrote the short novel *The Man Without a Country.*) Hale had a second rule: "*Say it.* That is, do not begin by saying something else which you think will lead up to what you want to say."

Every writer who has written about the writer's craft—whether journalist, poet or novelist—has understood these first principles of writing. George Orwell, the British journalist and novelist, was concerned that the English language was being endangered by unclear thinking. In an essay, "Politics and the English Language," he wrote that the first question scrupulous writers ask themselves before writing is, "What am I trying to say?" The next step is to find the appropriate form or structure for what you want to say.

The Structure

In *The Elements of Style,* the "little book" that generations of college students have used, authors William Strunk Jr. and E. B. White begin their section on writing this way: "Choose a suitable design and hold to it." They continue: "A basic structural design underlies every kind of writing. . . . The first principle of composition, therefore, is to foresee or determine the shape of what is to come, and pursue that shape."

Henry James, the American novelist, said that without form "there is absolutely no substance." Form, he wrote, "*takes,* holds, and preserves, substance—

Wandering in Wonderland

The inability to fix on the point causes writers to go on and on and on. They believe that as long as they keep going, they will hit on something newsworthy. They are like Lewis Carrol's Alice in her conversation with the Cheshire Cat:

"Would you tell me, please, which way I ought to go from here?"
"That depends a good deal on where you want to get to," said the Cat.
"I don't much care where—" said Alice.
"Then it doesn't matter which way you go," said the Cat.
"—so long as I get *somewhere,*" Alice added as an explanation.
"Oh, you're sure to do that," said the Cat, "if you only walk long enough."

No editor will permit a writer to wander aimlessly through a story on the way to *somewhere.*

saves it from the welter of helpless verbiage that we swim in as in a sea of tasteless tepid pudding, and that makes one ashamed of an art capable of such degradations."

Sometimes plans change. A writer may develop new ideas in the act of writing and the original plan has to be discarded. But even then a new plan is substituted.

Nevertheless, many reporters start to write without a plan in mind. As a result, their stories exhibit one of the most common faults of journalistic writing—disorganization or lack of focus. Henry Fairlie, a British journalist, calls this deficiency "shapelessness." He attributes it to "an intellectual inability, on the part both of the reporter and copy editor, to master the story." This mastery, Fairlie says, must be put to use "before writing."

Once the writer decides on the key element or elements of the story, its shape is determined.

Eight Steps to the Organized Story

1. Identify the focus or main idea of the story from notes.
2. Write a brief summary of the main idea.
3. Using the summary, separate in notes the material relating to the main idea from secondary matter.
4. Organize the secondary matter in order of importance.
5. Begin to write, making sure that the separate parts are linked with transitions.
6. Read the completed copy for accuracy, brevity, clarity.
7. Read the completed copy for grammar, style, word usage.
8. Rewrite if necessary—and it usually is.

The Single-Element Story

A story that consists of one important action or is based on one major fact or idea is a single-element story. Also known as the single-incident story, it is probably the story form most often used. The story requires:

- Lead.
- Explanatory and amplifying material.
- Background (if necessary).
- Secondary material (if any).

The single-element spot news story may contain several themes or ideas, but in this type of story the reporter decides that only one is important. A story of this kind may have the following structure:

- Lead: Idea A.
- Explanatory material. Elaboration of Idea A.
- Secondary material. Subthemes of B, C, D, E.
- Background.
- Further elaboration of Idea A.

**Single-Element
Story Structure**

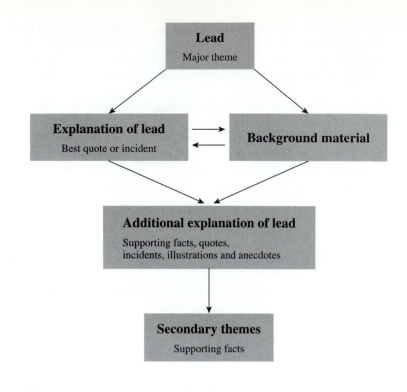

Short pieces written this way usually can be cut after the lead or two paragraphs, and longer pieces can be cut after a few paragraphs.

Here are the beginnings of two single-element stories:

> Road flooding from Hurricane Floyd has caused a logistical nightmare for Eastern North Carolina stores and businesses that can't deliver products or get replacements for food staples and other items.
>
> —*The News & Observer*

> The number of students of color enrolling and graduating from the nation's colleges and universities continues to increase modestly, but the rate of increase is beginning to slow, reports the American Council on Education.
>
> —*USA Today*

Two-Element Story

Here are 11 paragraphs from an election story in the *Daily News*. The story is based on two major themes: (A) rejection of the bond issue and (B) Republican control of the legislature. The reporter uses the effect of the voting on Gov. Hughes to attract readers to the story of the balloting:

Gov. Hughes Loses Bonds & Legislature

by Joseph McNamara

(1) New Jersey Gov. Richard J. Hughes took a shellacking all around in yesterday's statewide election. The voters rejected the $750 million bond issue proposal on which he had hung much of his political prestige, and the Republicans gained control of both houses of the Legislature.

(2) Hughes, who had warned during the campaign that if the bond issue were defeated he would ask the Legislature in January for a state income tax and sales tax to meet the state's financial needs, announced early today that he "may have to do some rethinking" about the size of the need. And he made it clear that the "rethinking" would increase his estimate of the amount required.

(3) "I accept the verdict rendered by the people," he said in a written statement.

Behind from the Start

(4) The bond issue proposal, which was broken into two questions—one on institutions and the other on roads—trailed from the time the polls closed at 8 p.m. With the count in from 4,238 of the state's 4,533 districts, the tally early today was:

(5) Institutions: No, 868,586; Yes, 736,967.

(6) Highways: No, 866,204; Yes, 681,059.

(7) As a measure of Hughes' defeat, in the Democrats' Hudson County stronghold—where the Governor had hoped for a plurality of 150,000—he got only a 100,501 to 64,752 vote in favor of the institutional bonds and 93,654 to 66,099 in favor of the highway bonds.

(8) Four other referendums had no great opposition, and passed easily. They were on voter residency requirements, a tax break on farm land and a change in exemptions from the ratables to the finished tax for both veterans and the elderly.

(9) The Republicans have controlled the State Senate for the last half century, and smashing victories yesterday in crucial Essex, Burlington and Camden Counties increased their majority—which had shrunk to a hairsbreadth 11–10—to two-thirds.

(10) Democrats swamped in the avalanche included Gov. Hughes' brother-in-law Sen. Edward J. Hulse of Burlington County. He was unseated by Republican Edwin B. Forsythe who ran up a convincing 6,000-vote majority.

(11) In populous Essex County, Republican C. Robert Sarcone defeated Democrat Elmer M. Matthews—who conceded shortly after 11 p.m. without waiting for the final count. And in Camden County, Republican Frederick J. Scholz unseated incumbent Joseph W. Cowgill. . . .

Analysis (1)

(1) The lead contains a colloquial phrase in the first sentence to emphasize the effect of the voting. The second sentence summarizes the two themes, A and B.

(2–7) These six paragraphs refer to theme A. In 2, the reporter gives a possible consequence of the loss of the bond issue.

In any election, vote tallies are essential, and the reporter supplies them in 5 and 6, which set up a good example in 7 of the extent of the governor's shellacking.

(8) Secondary information about other items on the ballot.

(9–11) Elaboration of theme B. Examples of specific races are given.

Three-Element Story

The following is an example of a story that begins with a three-element lead. The reporter would have singled out one element had she thought that one was the most important of the three. She decided the three were of equal importance.

Study Links 3 Factors to Heart Ills

By Jane E. Brody

(1) A new study conducted among 110,000 adult members of the Health Insurance Plan of Greater New York has once again demonstrated that smoking, an overweight condition and physical inactivity are associated with a greatly increased risk of death and disability from heart disease.

Analysis (2)

(1) The lead has a three-part theme: A study concludes that smoking, A, overweight, B, and physical inactivity, C, increase risk of heart disease.

(2) Brody tells the reader the source of the material and where it came from and then gives more information about theme A.

(3) More detail on A.

(4) Here she jumps to C, physical inactivity. It might have been better to have followed the A, B, C order.

(5) More on physical inactivity.

(6) Brody moves on to theme B, overweight.

(7) More on B; its relationship to A and C.

(8) Brody considered this secondary information.

A less cluttered lead might have put the attribution in the second paragraph and started, "Smoking, an overweight condition and physical inactivity. . . ."

(2) The study, published yesterday in the June issue of The American Journal of Public Health, reported that men and women who smoke cigarettes face twice the risk of suffering a first heart attack as do non-smokers.

(3) The annual incidence of first heart attacks among pipe and cigar smokers was also found to be higher than among non-smokers, but not as high as among cigarette smokers.

(4) Men who are "least active," both on and off the job, are twice as likely as "moderately active" men to suffer a first heart attack and four times as likely to suffer a fatal heart attack.

(5) Men who were classified as "most active" showed no advantage in terms of heart attack rate over men considered "moderately active." The authors reported that other differences between active and inactive men, such as the amount they smoked, could not account for their different heart attack rates.

(6) The heavier men in the study had a 50 percent greater risk of suffering a first heart attack than the lighter-weight men. An increased risk was also found among women who had gained a lot of weight since age 25.

(7) None of the differences in risk associated with weight could be explained on the basis of variations in smoking and exercise habits, the authors stated.

(8) The incidence of heart attacks was also found to be higher among white men than among non-whites and among Jewish men than among white Protestants and Catholics. But the heart attack rate among Jewish women was not markedly different from that among non-Jewish women.

—*The New York Times*

Some reporters might have found a lead in the information Brody places in the last paragraph. Although most events have obvious leads, a number do not. News judgment is essential on multiple-element stories, and judgments differ. Brody was on target. The last paragraph is secondary.

Brody's story also illustrates another basic guideline for structuring a story: Put related material together.

Story Units

In organizing their stories, news writers move from one theme to another in the order of the importance of the subjects or themes. The lead is elaborated first, and then the next-most-important theme is stated and then elaborated and explained. The rule of thumb is this: Put everything about the same subject in the same place.

When his editor explained the rule "like things together" to the journalist Dwight Macdonald, his first reaction was, "Obviously." His second, he said, was, "But why didn't it ever occur to me?" His third was, "It was one of those profound banalities 'everybody knows'—after they've been told. It was the climax of my journalistic education."

The Inverted Pyramid

The story structure explained in this chapter—important elements at the beginning, less important at the end—has for decades been taught to students as the "inverted pyramid" form. The term can be misleading. An inverted pyramid is an unbalanced monolith, a huge top teetering on a pinpoint base. It is a monstrous image for journalists, for the top of a story should be deft and pointed. Discard the picture of this precariously balanced chunk and remember that all it means is that the most important material is usually placed at the beginning of the story and the less important material is placed at the end.

The news story takes its shape from the requirements and limitations of the craft as measured by the clock—a silent but overwhelming presence—and the available space and time for copy. Given these realities, most stories must be written in such a way that they can be handled quickly and efficiently. If the 10 inches of available space suddenly shrinks to 8 and the 40 seconds of air time to 20, no problem. The story structure makes it possible to cut the bottom two paragraphs without losing key information.

If the only justification for the standard news story form were its utility to the people writing and editing the news, it would not have stood up over the years, even for as modern a media outlet as online journalism. The form has persisted because it meets the needs of media users. People usually want to know what happened as soon as the story begins to unfold. If it is interesting, they will pay attention. Otherwise, they turn elsewhere. People are too busy to tarry without reward.

Sometimes the pleasure may come from suspense, a holding of the breath until the climax is revealed deep in the story. When the reporter senses that this kind of structure is appropriate for the event, a delayed lead will be used.

Memorable Parts   Research tells us that structure can help increase the veiwer's and reader's understanding of the story and his or her involvement in it. For those who stay with the story from beginning to end, the start and the conclusion seem to be the best-remembered portions of the piece. Now that page layout can be more precisely designed, the reporter can put a kicker or summary at the end of a story without worrying that it might be squeezed out.

The Wall Street Journal Story Formula

Here is a story structure the *Journal* uses:

Anecdote: Begin with an example or illustration of the theme.

Explicit statement of theme: The lead. It should be no lower than the sixth paragraph. Sometimes this paragraph is called the *nut graph*.

Statement of the significance of the theme: Answers the reader's question, "Why should I be reading this?"

Details: Proof, elaboration of the theme.

Answers to reader's questions: Why is this happening? What is being done about it?

News forms may be said to be utilitarian or pragmatic, in the tradition of the hustle and bustle of American life. But there is also an aesthetic component in the standard news form that its detractors sometimes fail to detect. If the expression "form follows function" implies beauty in the finished work, then the news story is a work of art, minor as it may be. The news story meets the demands of art: It reveals a harmony of design.

Storytelling Form

Editors are concerned about the failure of the newspaper to attract new readers. They believe that the standard fare and form are unappetizing, that a generation reared on MTV, 15-second TV commercials, rock music and docudramas seeks more excitement than most newspapers have been offering. As a consequence, there is increasing use of the storytelling or narrative form. The reader is invited into the story with an interesting, amusing or exciting incident. The story then builds to a climax.

Scene Setting Here is how Jere Downs of *The Philadelphia Inquirer* began a story:

Driving to Easter services yesterday about 1:45 p.m., James Freeman saw a man standing on the South Street bridge.

"I knew he wanted to jump," said Freeman. "I made a U-turn right on the bridge and stopped traffic."

Freeman left his wife, his granddaughter and four foster children—all dressed in their Easter finery—watching from their minivan. Then, Freeman walked toward the lone figure staring down into the Schuykill 60 feet below.

The reader is hooked. Will Freeman talk the would-be suicide into backing off? Downs lets Freeman show us what happened:

"I've been where you want to go," Freeman said he told the man. "Whatever it is, it's not worth it."

Freeman said the man, in his mid-40s, looked at him with a pinched face lined with tears.

Then the man looked back across the river toward the University of Pennsylvania campus.

"I gotta do it," Freeman recalled saying. "Nobody loves me. I'm a Vietnam vet. My being here is like a burden on everybody."

Downs has used a column of type to this point, and she goes on to describe how others stopped their cars to help. A minister approached the distraught man and said to him, "You're looking down when you should be looking up to God."

The Climax Finally, in the 24th paragraph, the man climbs down from the concrete abutment.

(Postscript: A few days later, Downs received a handwritten note in the mail. "I enclose a check which I made out to you. Would you possibly be able to funnel this money in some way to allow Mr. X to receive some quality psychotherapy. I must remain anonymous. My reasons for doing this are (1) I was once where Mr. X was. (2) I have come back and am a successful businessman. Thank you for writing a terrific article." The check was for $1,000.)

Structure Necessary

At first glance, this storytelling form seems to release the writer from the task of structuring carefully. Not so. As we will see in the next chapter, the storyteller is just as scrupulous in the choice of material for the beginning of the piece as is the user of the traditional form. Both forms require the writer to identify the major theme and to make clear at the outset that the story will be concerned with that theme. The incident or example selected to begin the storytelling article must fit neatly into the theme of the piece.

That theme may come in the first paragraph, the third paragraph or the last. The ending is as carefully crafted as is the beginning. In all cases, the writer must first identify the theme and then decide where it will be placed in the piece.

Look at a story a reporter wrote about the search for a new city hall. She began with a general observation and then moved into the significant action:

> Modern buildings of glass and steel mark the downtown section.
> But the city's business is conducted in an old brick building that many residents liken to a warehouse.
> Last night, city officials went shopping for a new city hall. They looked at a modern 10-story office building. . . .

The third paragraph contains the news element, the lead idea. The first two paragraphs take the reader to the theme in an interesting way.

But suppose the reporter is covering a fire in city hall that led to two deaths. This story must begin with the news of the deaths. That news cannot be delayed. The structure of a story takes its shape from the nature of the event.

Story Necessities

Take any event and play the reporter's game. What are the necessary facts for an automobile accident story, a fire story, an obituary? Let us say an automobile hits a child. What must the story include? It will have to contain the child's name, age and address; the driver's name, age, address and occupation; the circumstances and location of the accident; the extent of the child's injuries; the action, if any, taken against the motorist. Any other necessities?

Given an assignment, the reporter has in mind a list of necessities for the story. The necessities guide the reporter's observations and direct the questions he or she will ask of sources. But there can be a problem.

Seeing the Differences Unless the reporter can spot the significant differences between stories of a similar type, one accident story will be like another, one obituary like a dozen others. The reporter on the "automobile hits child" story tries to discover the unusual or unique aspects of the event that should be given priority: Was the youngster playing? If so, was he or she running after a ball, playing hide-and-seek? Was the child looking for a dog, cat, younger brother? Was the child crossing the street to go to school? How seriously was the child injured? Will the youngster be able to walk normally?

Once the reporter has (a) thought about the necessities of stories he or she is assigned and (b) sought out the facts that differentiate this story from others like it, the story is on its way to being organized. The final step is to construct a lead around the important or unique element. There is no simple formula for determining what should go into the lead. The criteria for news we developed in Chapter 2 are helpful.

Basically, news judgment is an exercise in logical thinking. When a fire destroys a hotel worth $30 million and takes 14 lives, the reporter focuses the lead on the lives lost, not the destruction of the hotel, no matter how costly. The reporter reasons that life cannot be equated with money. If no one was killed or hurt in the fire, then the significance may well be that it was a costly structure, not a three-story hotel for transients that had seen better times. If there were no injuries and the hotel had some historical interest, the lead might be that a landmark in town was destroyed by fire. Finally, if no one was hurt and the hotel was a small, old building like many others in town, the fire would rate only two or three paragraphs and a single sentence, maybe two, on the 11 p.m. newscast.

Covering a Strike Threat

Let's watch a reporter assigned to the education beat. Told to check a report that public school teachers might not report for work next fall, she thinks of several essential questions:

- Is the report true?
- How many teachers are involved?
- What are the reasons for the strike?
- When will the decision be made about whether to strike?
- What are the responses of authorities to the threat?
- What plans are being made for the students should there be a strike?

The answers to these questions and other observations made during her reporting are the building blocks for the story. The reporter knows what her lead will be from the minute she receives the assignment—the possibility of a teacher strike and schools not opening. She has a simple formula for finding the basic theme: What do I know today that I did not know yesterday and that everyone would like to know?

These are the first few paragraphs of the story she writes:

Teachers in all 15 public schools in the city today threatened to strike next September unless they are given an 8 percent wage increase in next year's contract.

Spokesmen for the local unit of the American Federation of Teachers, which represents 780 Freeport school teachers, said the strike threat will be presented to the City Board of Education at Thursday's negotiating session.

"Without a contract that contains pay levels reflecting the increased cost of living, we will not report for work in September," said Herbert Wechsler, the president of the local unit. "No contract, no work."

When the Thursday session led to no resolution of the issue, the reporter's story about this development began this way:

The possibility of a strike of public school teachers next September loomed larger today when six hours of contract talks failed to settle the wage issue.

The teachers' union seeks an 8 percent pay increase over the current pay levels for next year's contract. The school board has offered 4 percent.

More than 15,000 school children would be affected by a strike.

The nonstop discussion between the union and the city school board failed to produce a settlement, said Herbert Wechsler, the president of the local unit of the American Federation of Teachers. The union, which represents the city's 780 public school teachers, issued its strike threat Tuesday and presented it formally at today's session.

Joseph Foremen, the state superintendent of education, who is attending the contract talks at the invitation of both sides, said:

"The two groups are widely separated. We need a cooling-off period. Unless one side or the other makes some kind of concession, we may have no teachers in the schools Sept. 9. And a concession is the last thing on their minds now."

The General, Then the Specific

The best advice she received from an editor, a reporter remarked, was "Follow every generality with a specific."

Every story has a logical structure, the editor told her, of general to specific. For example, when a council member says that next year's budget will set a record high, the reporter asks how high that will be, what the amount will be:

Riggio said next year's budget will set "a record high." He estimated it would amount to $725 million.

Here's another example:

Miles said, "Vince Lombardi was wrong when he said that winning is everything." It's more important, Miles said, to develop an athlete's sense of fair play and his or her love of sport.

Dirty Dining

Not only is this technique used internally in a story, but the general-then-specific form is used to organize the news story or feature. The *Daily News* spent five months investigating New York City's restaurant inspections. It found that restaurants that frequently failed were not closed, that several of the elite eating places where the rich and royalty dine had some of the worst records for filth. More than a fourth of the 18,812 restaurants were not inspected though the law required it.

Here is how the series began:

Hundreds of city restaurants—from Manhattan's swankest establishments to corner delicatessens—are rife with violations that are hazardous to your health.

They crawl with rats, roaches and other vermin.

They serve food that has been sitting for hours at temperatures that breed dangerous bacteria.

They store food perilously close to toxic chemicals or raw sewage back-ups.

Their kitchen workers don't wash their hands or wear gloves—and feel free to touch the food they serve.

Order room service at the luxurious Waldorf-Astoria. Your coffee could have had a funny odor because fish juice dripped from a tray into an open carton of milk.

Have dinner at Chin Chin, an up-scale E. 49th St. restaurant recommended by the noted Zagat's restaurant guide; its pantry has been found crawling with roaches.

Stop for lunch at the Times Square Deli, on 43rd St. at Broadway; the woman who just worked the cash register was spotted slicing cold cuts—and never put on gloves.

Dash into Kaplan's at the Delmonico on E. 59th St.; the chicken, tuna and shrimp salads have a history of being dangerously warm.

These are not isolated or unusual cases.

A five-month Daily News investigation has found alarming, pervasive failures in New York's system for insuring that the city's 18,812 restaurants maintain clean and healthful conditions.

The Health Department does not meet federal guidelines for inspections and inspects restaurants far less frequently than authorities do in most other cities.

The specifics—names, dates, incidents—fill out the general overview and provide the convincing detail. Another story in the series, "The Daily News Dining Hall of Shame," began this way:

These are the worst restaurants in the city—33 places the Daily News identified as having the most horrendous inspection histories and a diner's menu of violations.

Next, the newspaper checked off the 33 places, one by one, detailing their violations.

Specific-to-General

The reverse story structure is also used when the specific highlights the generality. This structure is often used for news features.

Antoinette Trotter couldn't figure out what was wrong with her boy. Shawn seemed so clumsy, the way he dropped dishes and sent cups clattering to the floor. He was restless, always squirming at the dinner table, unable to sit still.

This is the way Stephanie Armour began her story about workers who bring toxins from the job into their homes, putting family members in danger. Here is how the *USA Today* story continued:

Concerned, the mother brought the 6-year-old to doctors, who ran tests and told her that Shawn's blood contained nearly four times the acceptable level of lead for children, according to a lawsuit filed by the family.

Antoinette was surprised, but she was even more stunned when investigators told her why.

The boy, they told her, was being poisoned by her husband's job.

Shawn's father, Lashla, repaired and rebuilt batteries, work that brought him into contact with lead dust. . . .

After seven paragraphs of the specifics of the Trotter family's problem, Armour presents her generality:

> In a health risk that is often overlooked and undocumented, people of all ages are being exposed to workplace hazards so potent that they can change cell structures, slow mental development and unleash life-threatening tumors. But these are people who have never set foot in the workplaces that are poisoning them. All have been exposed to toxins that their family members unknowingly brought home from the job.

DAD: Dialogue, Action, Description

To the news writer, form and content are one. Each reinforces the other. We've already noted that no matter how well-reported a story is, if it zigs here and zags there, the reader or viewer will not bother to try to make sense out of the chaos. Also, if the story lacks dialogue, action or description, the bored reader will move on.

Dialogue, action, description: DAD. Let's look at a story that contains these essential elements, a religion story. This story by Jena Heath that appeared in *The Charlotte Observer* stirred a tempest.

Letters showered down on the newspaper for a month, and Heath received calls of support and outrage from Virginia and the District of Columbia as well as from North Carolina after the piece was put on the Knight-Ridder wire and run on the front page of the religion section of *The Washington Post.*

Women Priests

Heath, who now is the White House correspondent for the *Austin American-Statesman,* initiated the story. She thought it was time to write something about the role of Catholic women in their church. Her editor suggested she talk to women who want to be priests. Newsroom colleagues came up with names of sources.

Heath worked on the story for two weeks. The story ran at the top of page 1 of the Sunday newspaper. Look at how Heath blends description, action and dialogue in these opening paragraphs:

Sister Carol Symons

It was seven winters ago, but Sister Carol Symons hasn't forgotten.

She was ministering to the sick in Boone. The day the call came, the town's only priest was away. Sister Carol raced the seven minutes from her home to the hospital, where she found anguish. A Mexican migrant worker had given birth to a stillborn girl.

As she entered the dimly lit recovery room, the nun murmured to the woman's husband, tears glistening on his face. She walked across the room and took the woman's hand. Looking up from her stretcher, the woman choked out the words in Spanish.

Quiero confesar mis pecados, she pleaded. I want to confess my sins.

Sister Carol couldn't help. In the Roman Catholic Church, only priests can offer the peace of absolution.

"For me, the heart of the story is that there I was, a person in ministry and I couldn't help her," Sister Carol said.

Change is coming for Catholic women, not fast enough for some, too fast for others. One door, though, remains firmly shut: the door to the priesthood.

The image of a female priest at the altar is an emotional one for Catholics. Traditionalists say Jesus chose 12 men as his disciples, that Jesus himself was a man and that the church's long history of an all-male clergy means the priesthood was never intended for women.

Many Catholic women, meanwhile, have seen female priests in the Episcopalian Church since 1976, when it began ordaining women. They've seen female rabbis since 1972 and a host of female ministers, including Southern Baptists, since 1964.

Yet Catholic women who feel called to the priesthood say they must live with the pain of knowing they cannot serve God as their hearts dictate.

Good story structure depends on the blending of these three basic elements of the news story.

Alcoholism

Eric Newhouse's yearlong series in the *Great Falls* (Mont.) *Tribune,* "Alcohol, Cradle to Grave," begins with a scene at the Great Falls Rescue Mission, "which has been called the final pit stop before the graveyard for those unable to handle their addictions," Newhouse writes.

Breakfast is at 6 a.m. Today it's grits and eggs, and clients are expected to clean up the cafeteria and sweep out the dayroom before they head out. . . .

Tom Jerome, a former ranch hand from Miles City, is sitting on a bench in the Rescue Mission, already drunk and waiting for coffee at 9 a.m. Considering the Mission's rules, how did he spend the night there?

"I didn't," he says. "I usually spend the nights out."

But the gray-tiled dayroom can be a dry place, so Jerome periodically slips out into the alley where he has a cache of beer waiting for him.

When the reporter is conscious—as Newhouse was—of the need to organize the story around dialogue, action and description, the story tends to write itself. Newhouse's series won a Pulitzer Prize.

For more stories from Newhouse's series and his explanation of how the series came about and how he did his reporting, see **Alcohol: Cradle to Grave** in *NRW Plus*.

An Editor's Lament

When dialogue, action and description flow, the reader or listener is swept along, compelled to stay with the narrator. Increasingly, print publications are asking their reporters to write narratives, to engage in storytelling. Michael Kelly, editor of *The Atlantic* magazine, says that what he and his readers want and what writers submit are very different. He says that "most people who write for newspapers or magazines cannot write a narrative. And the reason is that they cannot or have not learned to write that which is at the core of narrative, which is physical description and dialogue."

In reading manuscripts submitted to *The Atlantic,* Kelly has found that even good writers show a "stunning lack of physical description.

"A writer will go to some interesting, fascinating and dangerous place, and file a piece that will contain a great deal of terrific reporting on all sorts of levels—interviews, analysis and so on—and the story will simply be bereft of physical description, of the colorful, vivid scene painting that readers continue to love. It's a myth that readers have turned away from this and that in the age of the picture and now the age of Internet, that readers don't want it."

Physical Description   Let's walk into Langan's, an Irish bar in New York City, with John Cassidy, who is doing a profile for *The New Yorker* of journalist Steve Dunleavy, at 62 a veteran of decades of opinion-laced journalism. Cassidy describes Dunleavy's face: "creased like an old pair of leather shoes." Cassidy approaches Dunleavy:

> He was smartly dressed, in a gray three-piece suit, white monogrammed skirt with French cuffs, gold cufflinks, red silk tie, and shiny black shoes. His pallor was that of a rotting cod. His silver pompadour, which makes him resemble an aging. Elvis, shot from his crown in glorious defiance of taste and gravity.

Summing Up

A lot of work goes into writing a news story. As a reporter with more than 30 years of experience on California newspapers put it to a beginner, "Those of us who survive work on our stories from the minute we get the assignment." The

Description "I am a great believer in description. I try to make the reader feel that he can see and taste and smell and touch and hear whatever the incident is. I've just listed the five senses."
—Everett Allen, The Standard Times

work the reporter was talking about takes the form of projecting at each level of reporting and writing the story as it will appear in its final form.

Reporters try to visualize and structure their stories at these stages:

- Immediately on receiving the assignment.
- While gathering material at the event.
- Before writing.
- During writing.

Further Reading

Snyder, Louis L., and Richard B. Morris. *A Treasury of Great Reporting.* New York: Simon & Schuster, 1949.

Wilson, Ellen. *The Purple Decades: A Reader.* New York: Farrar, Straus and Giroux, 1982.

7 The Writer's Art

Bob Thayer, *The Providence Journal.*

Sentences so sharp they cast a shadow.

Preview

The well-written story:

• Makes its point clearly.
• Engages the reader or listener with human-interest material, quotations, incidents and examples.
• Guides the reader or listener with a pace and a style appropriate to the event or personality being described.
• Leaves the reader or listener satisfied that the story is complete and is truthful.

Journalists write to be read and to be heard. They know that unless their stories are clear, interesting and well written their readers, viewers and listeners will move on to something else. To attract, keep and satisfy this fickle public, journalists have developed ways of telling stories—techniques and tactics—that make their stories compelling.

Journalists know that good writing helps people visualize the event, the personality being profiled, that good writing moves people to the scene. George Orwell, whose writing influenced and inspired many journalists, said, "Good prose is like a window pane."

The window pane, unlike the stained glass window, does not call attention to itself. Good writing calls attention to the people in the story, the event, the information.

Writers Write . . . and Read, Too

The men and women who write for a living—whether journalists, poets, novelists or essayists—work at learning and mastering their trade. They have an "idea of craft," as the writer-teacher Frank Kermode puts it, a drive toward "doing things right, making them accurate and shapely, like a pot or a chair."

> **Love Affair.** "Reading usually precedes writing. And the impulse to write is almost always fired by reading. Reading, the love of reading, is what makes you dream of becoming a writer."
> —*Susan Sontag*

Every writer is familiar with the agony of chasing elusive words. The writer knows that words can be brought to life only by strenuous and continued effort. The aim is perfection of expression, the absolute fit of words to the event. Walt Whitman, journalist and poet, described the writer's goal this way:

> A perfect writer would make words sing, dance, kiss, do the male and female act, bear children, weep, bleed, rage, stab, steal, fire cannon, steer ships, sack cities. . . .

Poet or police reporter, the writer is engaged in a struggle to find words and phrases to match his or her observations. When Ernest Hemingway covered the police court for the *Kansas City Star,* he would take his notes home and work over them hour after hour to simplify the testimony of witnesses until he had captured in a few words the essence of the evidence. He would use the language he had heard in court. This practice, as much as the influence of Ezra Pound and Gertrude Stein, may have been responsible for Hemingway's objective prose, what the critic Maxwell Geismar called "his famous flat style: the literal, factual description of the 'way things are.' "

This style, more brother than cousin to journalism, is evident in the ending to *A Farewell to Arms.* Frederic has just pushed the nurses out of the room where Catherine has died so that he can be alone with her:

> But after I had got them out and shut the door and turned off the light it wasn't any good. It was like saying good-bye to a statue. After a while I went out and left the hospital and walked back to the hotel in the rain.

Journalists read widely to master style and technique, to learn the tricks of the writer's trade. Stephen King, the prolific writer of best-selling horror stories, says, "Writing is a matter of exercise . . . if you write for an hour and a half a day for ten years you're gonna turn into a good writer." In his book *On Writing, A Memoir of the Craft,* King lists first in his suggestions for aspiring writers, "Read a lot of books."

Doing It Right—in a Hurry

Novelist or journalist, said Hal Boyle, for years one of the AP's top reporters, the writer has the same task: "The recognition of truth and the clear statement of it are the first duties of an able and honest writer."

Unlike the novelist, the journalist cannot spend hours in the search for the right word, a couple of days to devise a beguiling beginning. The journalist is asked to write—and to write well—now, quickly, before the clock's hands sweep to the inexorable deadline. No other writer is asked to perform with such speed. Yet journalists manage to do the job, creating stories that are, in Kermode's words, "accurate and shapely."

Preliminaries

It is impossible to write for the public unless you understand what you are writing about. Comprehension precedes clarity. You cannot "be wholly clear about something you don't understand," says John Kenneth Galbraith, the Harvard economist whose books and articles about what is called "the dismal science" of economics are models of clarity.

Once you understand the situation, you have to know just what you want to say. The focus or theme of the story must be clearly in mind. "You cannot start to write until you know what you want to say," the editor told his new reporter.

With a firm grip on writing mechanics and the theme clearly in mind, the story will spin out of the computer. Well, almost.

"I don't know anybody who writes well who writes easily," says Joan Beck, a columnist for the *Chicago Tribune*. After journalism school, she went to work at the *Tribune* and was, she says, "surprised to see people whose bylines I had admired for a long time sitting there, head in hand, trying to write. It was a great revelation to me that writing did not come easily to anybody I know."

A reminder: Don't write writing. Don't make the purpose of your writing clever prose. Your job is to communicate information. "I never heard a reader praise the quality of writing," says Henry McNulty, for many years the ombudsman for *The Hartford Courant*. "They are only interested in the facts in a story and their accuracy." Write well, the best you can to attract and retain readers, listeners and viewers. But never at the expense of a truthful telling of the story.

And last: Writers who try to write well are always asking themselves whether the words they are using make their stories clear, succinct, direct. When they are dissatisfied with the answer, they revise and rewrite. As Hemingway told an interviewer who asked him what the problem was that caused him to rewrite the last paragraph of *A Farewell to Arms* 39 times: "Getting the words right."

Show, Don't Tell

In our effort to find some guides to help us write well, we might start with Leo Tolstoy who, in describing the strength of his masterwork *War and Peace,* said, "I don't tell; I don't explain. I show; I let my characters talk for me."

Journalists rediscover Tolstoy's maxim in newsrooms everywhere. Rick Bragg, a reporter for *The New York Times,* recalls that as a new reporter in Birmingham a senior editor would take him aside and tell him his "one basic rule of good writing: Show me, don't tell me. Let me see what you see. Paint me a picture. Then I'll follow you anywhere, even past the jump." Bragg says the technique can be used for hard news stories as well as for features.

Oklahoma City   Here is the beginning of Bragg's story from the scene of the Oklahoma City bombing. The story, he says, "was written in less than two hours because it had to be. As I sat there in front of my laptop I had no time to craft pretty sentences. I just had to reach into my mind for the sadness I had seen . . . and it wrote itself."

OKLAHOMA CITY—Before the dust and the rage had a chance to settle, a chilly rain started to fall on the blasted-out wreck of what had once been an office building, and on the shoulders of the small army of police, firefighters and medical technicians that surrounded it.

They were not used to this, if anyone is. On any other day, they would have answered calls to kitchen fires, domestic disputes, or even a cat up a tree. Oklahoma City is still, in some ways, a small town, said the people who live here.

This morning, as the blast trembled the morning coffee in cups miles away, the world came crashing hard onto Oklahoma City.

"I just took part in a surgery where a little boy had part of his brain hanging out of his head," said Terry Jones, a medical technician, as he searched in his pocket for a cigarette. Behind him, firefighters picked carefully through the skeleton of the building, still searching for the living and the dead.

"You tell me," he said. "how can anyone have so little respect for human life."

Terror Bombings   At another catastrophe, *Daily News* reporter Dave Goldiner captures the scene of Sept. 11, 2001:

Tears streaming down his face, Fire Lt. Vincent Boura stumbled yesterday out of The Pit—and wondered if anything would ever be the same.

Along with thousands of other soot-covered firefighters, Boura spent hour after exhausting hour climbing in and out of a huge hole rescuers carved into the World Trade Center rubble.

They rappelled down 30-foot ropes as bright sunshine glinted off their helmets amid smoke.

They stumbled through the debris-choked blackness that once housed stores on the concourse. They searched—mostly in vain—for any signs of life.

"I'm going to go home and kiss my daughter," said Boura, who lurched down the street, soot covering him from head to toe. "She's just starting to say 'Daddy.' Unfortunately, a lot of kids are not going to be able to say 'Daddy' anymore."

Enduring Lesson   Louis Lyons, a Boston newspaperman and later curator of the Nieman Foundation for journalists at Harvard, never forgot the lesson his night editor taught him. "When I was a cub reporter I had a story to do on the quarterly report of the old Boston Elevated system, whose history then as now was a nearly unbroken record of deficits," Lyons recalled. "This time they were in the black. I knew just enough to know how extraordinary that was.

"I wrote: 'The Boston Elevated had a remarkable record for January—it showed a profit. . . .'

"The old night editor brought my copy back to my typewriter. He knew I was green. In a kindly way, quite uncharacteristic of him, he spelled out the trouble.

"He pointed out that the word remarkable 'is not a reporting word. That is an editorial word.' " Then he advised Lyons to write the story so that the reader would say, "That's remarkable."

One way journalists show their readers is through reporting the effects on people of the situation about which they are writing. The Department of Health and Human Services reported that 1.1 million minors run away or are thrown out of their homes every year. Most runaways are physically or sexually abused by a parent. About a third have an alcoholic parent, and many are from foster homes.

Troubled Teens   To give the report life and meaning, Sonia L. Nazario of *The Wall Street Journal* found some troubled teen-agers in California. Her account begins:

HOLLYWOOD—Five teen-agers crouch over a candle in a dark, fetid cavern under a busy roadway. Around them, the dirt floor seems to move as rats look for food. As the teen-agers pass around a half-gallon bottle of Riesling, they talk about their latest sexual scores. This is the place the teens call, simply, the Hole. "This is my home," reads a graffito scrawled on a concrete wall.

Here at the Hole, an ever-changing group of about 30 teen-agers, who have run away from home or been thrown out, have banded together to form a grotesquely modern kind of family. Predominantly white, middle-class and from troubled backgrounds, the "Trolls," as they call themselves, come to the Hole to find empathy and love. They have adopted a street father, a charismatic ex-con named John Soaring Eagle, or "Pops" to his flock. In return for his affection and discipline, the Trolls support Pops—and themselves—by panhandling, prostitution and mugging.

Teen Priorities   In a three-sentence paragraph, Sam Blackwell of the Eureka, Calif., *Times-Standard* shows us a lot about teen-age romance:

They had met cruising the loop between Fourth and Fifth Streets in Eureka. She fell in love with Wes' pickup truck, then fell in love with Wes. Wes gave her an engagement ring the day she graduated from high school.

DAD   Notice how Bragg and Goldiner blend description, action and dialogue to show us what happened at these tragic scenes.

Showing can be accomplished in small ways as well, even within the confines of a single sentence. Consider the science reporter who wanted to describe the size of a very small worm. She wrote, "Although they strongly caution against inferring too much about human life spans from worms no bigger than a comma at the end of this clause, they say that evolution. . . ."

If one of the writer's most impelling directives is to make the reader see, then the science writer did just that. Telling not only makes for dull reading, it makes readers passive. Showing engages readers by making them visualize, draw conclusions, experience insights.

Let Them Talk, Act

"Isn't anybody in this town can beat me. I'm invincible." This is Bella Stumbo of *The Los Angeles Times* quoting a politician. She doesn't have to tell us the man has a gigantic ego.

> **32,000 Times Better.** Henry James, the writer, advised young writers that "an ounce of example is worth a ton of generalities."

Good writers let the words and the actions of their subjects do the work. John Ciardi says, "Make it happen; don't talk about its happening."

When the reporter makes it happen, the reader moves into the story. The writer disappears as intermediary between the event and the reader.

Covering the funeral of a child killed by a sniper, a reporter wrote, "The grief-stricken parents wept during the service." Another reporter wrote, "The parents wept quietly. Mrs. Franklin leaned against her husband for support." The first reporter **tells** us the parents are "grief-stricken." The other reporter **shows** us the woman's grief.

To show the effects of the disappearance of dairy farms in the northeast, the reporter wrote of the farmers who stick around after selling their farms and can be seen "in the general store buying their morning beer."

Details show us more than generalities do. A story about a former Minnesota beauty queen pleading guilty to shoplifting described her loot as "several items." When the story reached an AP editor, she found out what had been stolen and put the items in the story—a swimsuit, silk scarves and hairpieces.

Good Quotes Up High

The reporter is alert to the salient remark, the incisive comment, the words of a source that sum up the event or that will help the reader visualize the person who is speaking. Also, a person's words help achieve conviction, the feeling that the reporter is telling the truth. After all, if these are the words of a participant, the reader reasons, the story must be true. The higher in the story the quote appears, the better, although good quote leads are rare.

Notice the use of the poignant remark of the child in the second paragraph of this story:

> Mary Johnson, 9, lay alongside the bodies of her slain family for nearly two days. She believed she, too, would die of the bullet wounds inflicted by her mother.
>
> But Mary lived, and told ambulance attendants on her way to the hospital yesterday: "Don't blame mother for the shootings."

Quote Them. "Realistic dialogue involves the reader more completely than any other single device. It also defines character more quickly and effectively than any other single device. (Dickens has a way of fixing character in your mind so that you have the feeling he has described every inch of his appearance—only you go back and discover that he actually took care of his physical description in two or three sentences; the rest he has accomplished with dialogue.)"
—*Tom Wolfe*

Taking the Gospel to College Students

The careful reporter listens closely to the message of this young evangelist as she proclaims the gospel at the University of Arkansas. The writer quotes her, describes her intention, watches students' reactions. The reporter also interviews the students to whom she is preaching and talks to the evangelist about her successes and failures.

In an interview with an opponent of the U.S. government's policies in El Salvador, a reporter used this quote high in her story:

> "Why are we on the side of those who
> are killing the nuns?" he asked.

Reporters have an ear for the telling quote. In a story about the record number of murders in Miami-Dade, Edna Buchanan of *The Miami Herald* quoted a homicide detective as saying, "In Dade County, there are no surprises left."

The astronomer James Jeans provided a startling image of the universe: "Put three grains of sand inside a vast cathedral and the cathedral will be more closely packed with sand than space is with stars."

Ten Guides to Good Writing

1. Make sure you understand the event.
2. When you have found the focus for your story—when you know what you want to say—start writing.
3. Show, don't tell.
4. Put good quotes and human interest high in the story.
5. Put relevant illustrations or anecdotes up high in the story.
6. Use concrete nouns and colorful action verbs.
7. Avoid adjectival exuberance and resist propping up verbs with adverbs.
8. Avoid judgments and inferences. Let the facts talk.
9. Don't raise questions you cannot answer in your copy.
10. Write simply, succinctly, honestly and quickly.

The actress Farrah Fawcett was quoted in a story, "The reason that the all-American boy prefers beauty to brains is that he can see better than he can think."

Unprintable Unfortunately, some of the best quotes never make it into print or to broadcasts. But they live on in journalism lore. There's the story about Frank Sinatra and the 1952 Democratic national convention, where, after Sinatra sang the national anthem, the audience erupted. Sam Rayburn, Speaker of the House of Representatives and the convention chairman, walked across the platform toward Sinatra.

Rayburn, a towering figure in politics and in demeanor, reached out to shake Sinatra's hand. As Rayburn put his left arm around Sinatra's shoulder, Sinatra snarled:

"Get your hands off me, you creep."

Adored by his fans, Sinatra was known to journalists as much for his nasty temper as for his generosity to friends. But the nastiness rarely emerged in stories about Sinatra until late in his career.

Human Interest Up High

As with good quotations, we try to place as close to the lead as possible the human-interest example, incident or anecdote that spotlights the theme of the story:

> The steady increase in tuition is driving some students away from the colleges of their choice and keeping them in schools close to home.
>
> Ralph Cramer, a high school senior, was admitted to an Ivy League college, but the $25,000 plus tuition was out of his family's reach. . . .

Life. William Maxwell, one of the great editors and a writer, said: "After 40 years, what I came to care about most was not style, but the breath of life."

As you see, the example amplifies and humanizes the story theme. When delayed leads are used, the human interest incident begins the story. With direct leads—which often stress the formal aspect of the event—the human-impact illustration or example should be close to the lead.

We are all a little like Alice (of *Alice's Adventures in Wonderland*). " 'What is the use of a book,' thought Alice, 'without pictures or conversations?' " The reporter lets the anecdotes serve as pictures, and the quotations as conversations.

Mark Twain's Principles

Mark Twain had volunteered to read the essays submitted for a writing contest by the young women at the Buffalo Female Academy. He was delighted by what he read, and in his report to the Academy he pointed out the virtues of the two prize essays. He described them as "the least artificial, least labored, clearest, shapeliest and best carried out."

The first-prize essay "relates a very simple little incident in unpretentious language," he said. It has "the very rare merit of *stopping when it is finished."* (Twain's emphasis.) "It shows a freedom from adjective and superlatives, which is attractive, not to say seductive—and let us remark, in passing, that one can seldom run his pen through an adjective without improving his manuscript.

"We can say further that there is a singular aptness of language noticeable in it—denoting a shrewd facility of selecting just the right word for the service needed, as a general thing. It is a high gift. It is the talent which gives accuracy, grace and vividness in descriptive writing."

Four Principles   Good writing has four characteristics. It is:

• **Accurate:** The language fits the situation. This is what Twain means by "accuracy of wording," "using just the right word."
• **Clear:** Through proper use of form and content, the story is free of vagueness and ambiguity.
• **Convincing:** The story is believable. It sounds true.
• **Appropriate:** The style is natural and unstrained. In Twain's words, "unpretentiousness, simplicity of language . . . naturalness . . . selecting just the right word for the service needed."

The four principles are not islands unto themselves. Causeways connect them. If we write that a congressman "refuted" charges that his proposal will cause unemployment, when he actually "denied" the charges, the language we use is inaccurate and the story is not clear. When we quote people as they use the language—not in the homogenized dialogue that passes for the spoken word in too many news stories—the language is appropriate and our stories are more likely to convince readers they are true.

Before we go on, a reminder and a qualifier.

The reminder: A great deal of work is done before the reporter writes. Good journalistic writing is the result of good reporting and clear thinking. Clever writing cannot conceal a paucity of facts, stale observations or insensitive reactions to people. But bad writing can nullify superior reporting.

The qualifier: In the rest of this chapter—and in other chapters, too—rules, formulas and injunctions are presented. They are offered as guidelines, as ways to get going. They should not be considered inviolate laws. But it is best for the beginner to accept them for the time being, until his or her competence is proved. After this apprenticeship has been served, the experienced journalist can heed Anton Chekhov's comments about writing in his play *The Seagull.* "I'm coming more and more to believe that it isn't old or new forms that matter. What matters is that one should write without thinking about forms at all. Whatever one has to say should come straight from the heart."

Accuracy of Language

The city editor of a medium-size Iowa daily stared at the lead in disbelief. A reporter who had covered a city commission meeting the night before had written that the commission adopted a controversial resolution "with one descending vote." The proper word is *dissenting,* the city editor informed his errant reporter.

Without accuracy of language, the journalist cannot make the story match the event. The obvious way to check words for accuracy is to use the dictionary. But reporters who misuse language often do so without knowing their words are misfits. They could be saved from embarrassment by widening their reading.

Ernest Hemingway's writing was simple, but it was not simplistic. He shaved language to the bone, but at no sacrifice to meaning. This required hard work. Reaching for a baseball metaphor, Hemingway said of the writer that "he has to go the full nine even if it kills him."

Use Words with Referents

A reporter's vocabulary comes from a feel for words, for the way people use language, which sometimes differs from dictionary usage. "The true meaning of a term is to be found by observing what a man does with it, not by what he says about it," says the scientist P.W. Bridgeman.

Also, journalists use words that correspond to specific objects. When the journalist writes about the state treasurer's annual report, she is describing a specific person who has issued a document that can be examined. But when the reporter takes it upon herself to describe the report as *sketchy* or *optimistic,* she is moving into an area in which there are no physical referents. She may use such words in an interpretative story, but only if she anchors them to specific facts and figures.

Words such as *progress, freedom, patriotism, big business, militant, radical* cause trouble because they float off in space without being anchored to anything specific, concrete or identifiable. Reporters do quote sources who use these words and phrases, but they make sure to ask sources to explain just how they are using these vague terms.

Unwary reporters can become accomplices in brainwashing by using vague language. When an oil company distributed a press release announcing the construction of an "oil farm" outside a Massachusetts town and the reporter

Talk of the Town

A young reporter assigned to the police beat used his enterprise to develop a story about youth gangs for the *Omaha World-Herald.* The editor told Charles Robins that his story had more impact on the community than any other in months. The editor outlined the reasons:

1. It began with a "vivid, graphic description of specific, real-life events, things that happened to real people." He said too many enterprise stories use pseudonyms, "losing at least 50 percent of their effectiveness when they do.

2. "The story had a hard-news peg. A man had just been mugged.

3. "It had confirmation from named sources.

4. "You used direct quotations, but you were selective in what you used. You weren't just a stenographer tapping out everything your sources said in long, repetitive quotations.

5. "You used specific, colorful description. You noted the color of their (the gang members') 'uniforms,' including the color-coded shoelaces, the $300 jogging suits and the cellular telephones.

6. "The story was told economically in 24 inches. There were other angles you probably could have gone after, but doing so might have delayed publication and made the story more difficult to digest."

Ever since the day the story was printed, the editor said, it has been Topic No. 1 "in every age and demographic group in Omaha."

---

dutifully wrote in her lead that the "oil farm will occupy a tract southeast of the city," the reporter was not only using language inaccurately, she was helping the oil firm obscure reality. The so-called "farm" was to be used for oil storage tanks, which have a grimy image. A farm, with visions of white barns and green pastures, is what the oil company wanted readers to imagine so that potential opposition would be diverted. *Farm* as used by the oil company and the reporter is a euphemism.

Euphemisms

When Congress was discussing *taxes,* it sought to soften the impact of that dread word by substituting the words *revenue enhancement.* In Northern California, where marijuana is a major agricultural product, the polite term for its cultivation is *cash-intensive horticulture.* A company does not demote an employee; it hands him or her a *negative advancement.* When the *Challenger* shuttle exploded, the bodies were placed not in coffins but in *crew transfer containers.*

When a pleasant word or phrase is used in place of one that may be grim, the substitute is called a *euphemism.*

Veiling Reality. The State Department said that it would no longer use the word *killing* in its reports on human rights. In its place, the department said, will be "unlawful or arbitrary deprivation of life."

For its program to train dolphins to kill enemy swimmers, the Navy said the purpose was "swimmer nullification."

Some journalists may consider themselves compassionate for letting euphemisms slip by. After all, what is the harm in permitting people who work with convicts to describe prisoners as the *consumers of criminal justice services?* What, for that matter, is wrong with *senior citizens* for older people or *sight deprived* for the blind? Surely, these euphemisms hurt no one.

Actually, they do damage us because they turn us away from reality. If the journalist's task can be reduced to a single idea, it is to point to reality. Words should describe the real, not blunt, blur or distort it.

Years ago, a Chicago police reporter who was covering a rape was reminded by his desk of the newspaper's prohibition of what the publisher considered earthy language. *Rape,* he was told, was taboo. In his second paragraph, he wrote, "The woman ran down the street screaming, 'Help, I've been criminally assaulted! Help, I've been criminally assaulted!' "

Said

These misuses of language are dangerous shoals on which many reporters have run aground. If we could mark the reefs that threaten writers, the most dangerous would be where reporters have gone under while fishing for synonyms for the verb *to say.*

The newswriter wrote that a candidate "disclosed" that his opponent had received donations from foreign businesses, a violation of the law. The word *disclosed,* his editor told the reporter, "suggests that we believe the assertion to be true. Make it *said,* a neutral word."

Michael Gartner, editor of *The Daily Tribune* in Ames, Iowa, tells of his experiences with his editor as a young reporter. Bill Kreger, a news editor at *The Wall Street Journal,* would spot a "he laughed," "he sputtered," "he grimaced" in the attribution. He would call Gartner, or the other miscreant, to his desk.

"Laugh me this sentence," he would say. "Sputter me this sentence." Or: "Grimace me this sentence."

Then he would make the copy read, "he said."

In Stephen King's five suggestions to aspiring writers, he says, "Use *said* and *says* for attributing in dialogue."

Let it be said at once, loud and clear, the word *said* cannot be overused for attribution. If tempted to replace it with *affirmed, alleged, asserted, contended, declared, pointed out, shouted, stated* or *whispered,* see the dictionary first. Better still, recall Ring Lardner's line: "Shut up he explained."

Facts First, Words Second

One of the impediments to accuracy stems from the reporter's unceasing desire for language that will perk up the reader. The desire is healthy, but it can lead to the selection of words—as well as facts—that are more colorful and exciting than the event merits. Reporters sometimes are so stimulated by the urge to be creative that their language and their stories diverge from the reality that inspired them. As writers, they believe that an occasional liberty with facts and language should be granted them.

Use the Senses. "Generally speaking, if he can't see it, hear it, feel it and smell it, he can't write it."
—*William Burroughs*

When a researcher pointed out that a feature about a Vietnam War veteran included some erroneous information—claims about medals won—the reporter was unmoved, not interested in making a correction. "I'm not an investigative reporter," he said. "I'm a features reporter."

To some writers, words are ends in themselves. But the objective is to communicate information accurately, not to display technical brilliance with the zoom lens or tape splicer, not to play with words. Technique has its place; its proper role is to aid in accurate communication. As Pauline Kael, the movie critic, put it, "Technique is hardly worth talking about unless it's used for something worth doing."

Spelling

A few words about the bane of the copy editor, the misspelled word. A word incorrectly spelled is a gross inaccuracy. It is like a flaw in a crystal bowl. No matter how handsome the bowl, the eye and mind drift from the sweeping curves to the mistake. A spelling error screams for attention, almost as loudly as an obscenity in print.

Maybe not. These days we see *alright* for all right, *its* for it's, *cemetary* for cemetery. Even *The New York Times,* surely one of the most scrupulously edited newspapers, has its share of misspellings. A story about nuns who support the ordination of women stated, "They want nuns to have a visible role at the *alter.*"

Spell-Check Limited   Some reporters put their trust in computer programs that check spelling. But such programs will not flag correctly spelled words that are misused, such as *alter* for *altar.* The program was of no use to the student journalists who wrote these headlines for the Columbia University daily student newspaper:

Baker Field Sight of Football Triumph

Soccer Hopes for Tourney Birth after 2–1 Win

Intelligent reporters—good spellers or bad spellers—use the dictionary. Many editors associate intelligence with spelling ability because they consider the persistent poor speller to be stupid for not consulting the dictionary—whatever his or her native intelligence.

The saying has it that doctors bury their mistakes and architects cover them with ivy. Journalists have no such luck. Their blunders are forever committed to public view:

> Letters must be signed and should include address and phone number. The Monitor reserves the right to edit letters for spelling, grammer and punctuation, as well as possibly libelous material.
>
> *The Monitor*

R. L. Chambers

Oops

The city parks department needs to invest in a dictionary, and learn how to use it.

Internet Spelling. Patricia T. O'Conner, author of a grammar book *Woe Is I*, trolled Internet newsgroups to check on spelling and grammar. She landed a boatload. "Leaving aside the misuse of *its*, the misspelling of *grammar* seemed to be the most common mistake of all," she says.

Question is, how to tell roommates your gay

—Forum (Fargo, N.D.)

Blind girl servives first round of bee

—Gazette (Indiana, Pa.)

Five Fatal Flaws

After reading through dozens of freshman compositions, Loretta M. Shpunt, an English teacher at Trinity College in Washington, D.C., said she seriously considered buying a red ink pad and a set of rubber stamps that read:

Not a Sentence
"It's" Equals "It Is"
"Its" Is Possessive
Dangling Participle
"I" Before "E" Except After "C"

Clarity

Required. "The newspaper writer's first obligation is to be clear."
—*Saul Pett, AP*

The words and phrases the journalist selects must be put into a setting, into sentences and paragraphs that make sense to readers. "If you're going to be a newspaper writer you've got to put the hay down where the mules can reach it," said Ralph McGill of the *Atlanta Constitution.* Although his reporting ranged over subjects as complex as race relations and foreign affairs, McGill's writing was clear to all the paper's readers. A reader of the King James version of the Bible, he learned early the strength, vigor and clarity of the precise word in the simple declarative sentence.

"A word fitly spoken is like apples of gold in pictures of silver," McGill said of the journalist's craft, quoting from Proverbs in the Old Testament. We know several ways to make these pictures—these sentences and paragraphs—clear to our readers.

Grammar

First, there are the essentials of grammar and punctuation. In our grandparents' day, students stood at the blackboard and diagrammed sentences. They broke sentences down into nouns, verbs, pronouns, adjectives, adverbs, prepositions, conjunctions and interjections. From there, they went into phrases—verbal, prepositional, participial, gerund and infinitive. Then they examined clauses—main and subordinate. This is how they learned sentence construction. In most schools today, the only grammar students learn is taught in foreign language classes. For a journalist, this is inadequate training.

One way the beginning journalist can cope with this inadequacy is to invest in a handbook of grammar. It will not only solve grammatical problems quickly, but also help expand the student's writing range.

Punctuation

Punctuation is the writer's substitute for the storyteller's pauses, stops and changes in voice level. The proper use of punctuation is essential to clarity. Misuse can change emphasis or meaning:

"Let's eat, Grandma."

"Let's eat Grandma."

We know that readers pause at the ends of sentences and paragraphs. These short intervals in the flow of the story help readers absorb what they have read. Broadcast copy needs even shorter sentences, because the listener cannot reread unclear material.

Sentence Length

Spurred by an anxiety to cram facts into sentences, some inexperienced reporters write blockbuster sentences that send the reader down line after line in increasing confusion. When you have a sentence running three lines or more, think of the self-editing of Isaac Babel, a Russian writer whose short stories are highly polished gems:

I go over each sentence, time and again. I start by cutting all the words it can do without. You have to keep your eye on the job because words are very sly. The rubbishy ones go into hiding and you have to dig them out—repetitions, synonyms, things that simply don't mean anything.

Before I take out the rubbish, I break up the text into shorter sentences. The more full stops the better. I'd like to have that passed as a law. Not more than one idea and one image to a sentence.

A paragraph is a wonderful thing. It lets you quietly change the rhythm, and it can be like a flash of lightning that shows the landscape from a different perspective. There are writers, even good ones, who scatter paragraphs and punctuation marks all over the place.

The maxim that each sentence should, if possible, carry only one idea has been assumed to be an injunction limited to journalism. Not so, as we see from Babel's comment. Good journalistic writing is based upon the principles of good writing. Journalism is a part of the world of letters.

Punctuation Pains. It is said of the novelist Gustave Flaubert that he spent an entire morning laboring over where to place a comma, then took the afternoon to fret about whether to remove it.

James Thurber, the great *New Yorker* writer, said of his editor Harold Ross, "He used to fuss for an hour over a comma. He'd call me in for lengthy discussions about the Thurber colon."

Guide   The press associations have concluded after a number of studies that one of the keys to readable stories is the short sentence. Here is a readability table:

Average Sentence Length	Readability
8 words or less	Very easy to read
11 words	Easy to read
14 words	Fairly easy to read
17 words	Standard
21 words	Fairly difficult to read
25 words	Difficult to read
29 words or more	Very difficult to read

One sentence after another under 17 words would make readers and listeners feel as though they were being peppered with bird shot. The key to good writing is variety, rhythm, balance. Short and long sentences are balanced. Also, a long sentence that is well-written can be as understandable as an eight-word sentence, if it is broken, usually by punctuation, into short clauses and phrases.

Transitions

Quickie. Groucho Marx uttered the most succinct transition ever made: "Hello, I must be going."

Some reporters have trouble writing short sentences because they cannot handle transitions, the links between sentences and paragraphs. Because these reporters have no mastery of the device that enables a writer to move smoothly from sentence to sentence, their tendency is to think in large clots of words. The journalist with control of transitions thinks in smaller sentence clusters.

There are four major types of transitions:

1. **Pronouns:** Use pronouns to refer to nouns in previous sentences and paragraphs:

> *Dr. Braun* began teaching history in 1977. *He* took *his* Ph.D. that year. *His* dissertation subject was the French Impressionists.

2. **Key words and ideas:** Repeat words and ideas in preceding sentences and paragraphs:

> He has been accused of being an *academic purist. Those words* make him shudder.
> "*Academic purist* is made to sound like an epithet," he said.

3. **Transitional expressions:** Use connecting words that link sentences. A large array of expressions function as connectors. Here are most of the major categories of conjunctions and some of the words in each category that can be used as transitions:

> **Additives:** again, also, and, finally, furthermore, in addition, next, thus, so, moreover, as well.

> **Contrasts:** but, however, nevertheless, instead, on the other hand, otherwise, yet, nonetheless, farther.

> **Comparisons:** likewise, similarly.

A Pulitzer Prize Story: Workings of the Brain

Here is the beginning of the first story in a series by Jon Franklin that won a Pulitzer Prize for explanatory journalism for *The Evening Sun*. The word count in these 12 sentences runs 16, 24, 34, 9, 13, 18, 14, 21, 19, 5, 13, 21. The average sentence length is 17 words, standard reading fare. Notice the way Franklin varies the length of his sentences to set up a rhythm—long, short. The longest sentence in the sample—the third, 34 words—is followed by a short sentence—9 words.

Since the days of Sigmund Freud the practice of psychiatry has been more art than science. Surrounded by an aura of witchcraft, proceeding on impression and hunch, often ineffective, it was the bumbling and sometimes humorous stepchild of modern science.

But for a decade and more, research psychiatrists have been working quietly in laboratories, dissecting the brains of mice and men and teasing out the chemical formulas that unlock the secrets of the mind.

Now, in the 1980s, their work is paying off.

They are rapidly identifying the interlocking molecules that produce human thought and emotion. They have devised new scanners that trace the flickering web of personality as it dances through the brain. Armed with those scanners, they are mapping out the terrain of the human psyche.

As a result, psychiatry today stands on the threshold of becoming an exact science, as precise and quantifiable as molecular genetics. Ahead lies an era of psychic engineering, and the development of specialized drugs and therapies to heal sick minds.

But that's only the beginning: The potential of brain chemistry extends far beyond the confines of classic psychiatry.

Many molecular psychiatrists, for instance, believe they may soon have the ability to untangle the ancient enigma of violence and criminality.

Place: adjacent to, beyond, here, near, opposite.

Time: afterward, in the meantime, later, meanwhile, soon.

He tried twice to obtain permission to see the paintings in the private museum. *Finally,* he gave up.

Dr. Braun's *next* project centered on the music of Berlioz. *But* his luck remained bad. An attempt to locate a missing manuscript proved a *similar* failure.

In the meantime, he continued his study of Spanish so that he would be able to do research in Spain.

4. **Parallel structure.** Sentences and paragraphs are linked by repeating the sentence pattern:

No one dared speak in his classes. *No one* ventured to address him in any but the most formal manner. *No one,* for that matter, had the courage to ask questions in class. His lectures were nonstop monologues.

Transitions link major story elements as well as the smaller units, the sentences. Transitions are the mortar that holds the story together so that the story is a single unit.

Logical Order

A news story should move smoothly. When natural sequence is disrupted, the story loses clarity. Here are two paragraphs from a story in an Oklahoma daily newspaper:

> "There is nothing new in the allegations," Bartlett said. "We've heard them all before."
>
> "When we first heard them we thought there was nothing to it, but then we had a second look," Tillman said.

Although the first paragraph is closed by quotation marks, which means that the speaker (Bartlett) is finished, most readers jump ahead to the next quote and presume that Bartlett is still talking. They are jolted when they find that Tillman is speaking. The solution is simple: When you introduce a new speaker, begin the sentence or paragraph with his or her name. Also, jumps in time and place must be handled carefully to avoid confusion:

NEW YORK (April 13)—A criminal court judge who last month ruled that a waiter had seduced but not raped a college student sent the man to jail for a year **yesterday** on a charge of escaping from the police after his arrest.

On March 19, Justice Albert S. Hess acquitted Phillip Blau of raping a 20-year-old Pembroke College student. The judge said a man could use guile, scheme, and be deceitful, but so long as he did not use violence, rape did not occur.

At that time, women's groups protested the decision.

"Despite the protests of outraged feminists who demand your head, or other and possibly more appropriate parts of your anatomy," the judge told Blau **yesterday,** "I shall punish you only for crimes of which you have been found guilty."

The changes in time are clearly indicated at the start of the second and third paragraphs. From "yesterday" in the lead, the reader is taken to "March 19" in the second paragraph and is kept there in the third paragraph by the transition "At that time" beginning the paragraph. When the quote begins the fourth paragraph, the reader is still back in March with the women. Midway through the paragraph the reader suddenly realizes the judge is speaking and that he spoke yesterday. The jolts in time and place could have been avoided with a transition at the beginning of the fourth paragraph:

> In sentencing Blau **yesterday,** Justice Hess commented on the protests. He said: . . .

This may seem to be nitpicking. It is not. The journalist knows that every sentence, every word, even every punctuation mark must be carefully selected. Readers read from word to word, and are maneuvered, teased, pushed, sped and slowed through the story by the way it is written. Major disturbances of logic and order in the story confuse readers, just as a quick jump cut on television can destroy the continuity of the story for the viewer.

Chronological Order   Logical order is based upon the organizing concept that the reporter selects. The most frequently used organizing principle is chronology, a narrative device that is particularly useful on longer pieces.

The chronological approach has two forms. The writer can use the storytelling approach by beginning sometime before the climax:

Two college sophomores began the day yesterday in a hurry.

Judy Abrams had studied late the night before and had slept late. She gulped her breakfast of coffee and jumped into her car, five minutes before her 9 A.M. class.

Franklin Starrett did not have time for breakfast before he, too, sped off in his car for the campus. He had an appointment with his English instructor at 9 A.M.

Within minutes of their departures, the cars they were driving collided on Stanford Avenue south of the campus. . . .

Or the writer can put a direct news lead on the story and then, a few paragraphs down in the story, begin the chronological account:

Two Mallory College students were critically injured when the cars they were driving collided head-on yesterday morning on Stanford Avenue south of the campus.

Community Hospital officials said the students suffered multiple fractures and internal injuries. They called on students to volunteer blood for transfusions.

The students began the day in a hurry. . . .

Movement

Stories must move, and the nature of the event determines the pace at which the story progresses. A story about a tornado or hurricane striking a community will move at the speed of the wind, but the piece about the burial service for the victims will follow the deliberate cadence of the prayers of the minister as he speaks of those called too soon to their maker.

Fast or slow, the story has to move along. It cannot stop to explore secondary roads. Stan Grossfeld, associate editor of *The Boston Globe,* profiled the filmmaker Spike Lee as he taught a class at Harvard. In one of the class sessions, Lee describes how he edited the opening scene of *Jungle Fever:*

In the opening scene, which was shot but later cut, Lee descends in front of the Brooklyn Bridge on a crane and announces, "All you people who think I'm anti-Semitic can kiss my black ass two times."

Lee said the scene was extraneous: "When you write a script, you think everything's gonna be great, but once the film is shot and put together, sometimes a lot of the stuff is redundant. We had a whole subplot between me and my wife, eight scenes that had to go, 'cause it wasn't moving the plot forward. It didn't matter that I was in the scene, the [expletive] had to go."

AP Photo by Jerome Delay

Mourners

Schoolchildren weep outside St. Martin Bascilica in Liege, Belgium, for two slain classmates who were kidnapped by a child rapist. The story of the funeral had longer-than-average sentences, muted verbs.

Conviction

Some people find the news they read, hear and see as unconvincing as some of the advertising that accompanies it.

"What's the real story?" reporters are asked, as though they were prevented from revealing the truth by powerful advertisers or friends of the publisher or station manager. These pressures rarely influence reporters. More often, the pressures of time and the inaccessibility of documents and sources impede truth telling, and just as often, reporting and writing failures get in the way of the real story. Here are the components of a story that is accurate, complete and credible:

Reporting:

1. Relevant factual material from personal observation and physical sources. Details, specifics.

2. Authoritative and knowledgeable human sources for additional information.

3. Significant and complete background information.

Writing:

1. Simple language.
2. Illustrations, examples and quotes that document the lead.
3. Human interest.
4. Appropriate style.

Let's examine these story necessities.

Reporting

The journalist uses details just as any writer does—to build a picture that shows us what is going on and that convinces us of the truth of the account. The journalist's eye catches the tears of the child whose puppy takes third place instead of first at the dog show. Such specific observations convince the reader that the reporter's account can be trusted.

Details, Specifics   In his series about the shooting of a policeman, Robert L. Kaiser of the *Chicago Tribune* put his readers on the scene with these details:

As they prepared for their shift, one of the officers put his "9 mm SIG-Sauer P22—black and silver with a 13-shot magazine" in his holster. They rode in a "Ford Crown Victoria." The radio "crackled with news of a shooting near 43rd and State Streets" and the driver "mashed the accelerator with his size 9 boot and headed north." A gang member in a housing project notorious for drug dealing fired his gun, "a .357 can travel up to 1,350 feet per second—faster than the speed of sound. This one seared at least 60 feet in less than a heartbeat. With a muffled thump it tore into Ceriale. The bullet had a copper jacket and a core of lead. It opened a half inch hole in the lower left abdomen just below the protective vest, flattening as it burrowed down below the pubic bone toward the hip."

The journalist is conscious of the backdrop, the scene. It may be that the news conference took place in the mayor's office, the rescue made in a calm sea at dusk. Then the particulars: The mayor spoke from his desk, with seven microphones from radio and television stations in front of him and a dozen journalists in attendance; the Coast Guard boat was manned by six seamen and an officer.

Authoritative Sources

Here are the first four paragraphs of a speech story:

This country must return to law and order if America's free institutions are to survive, Lexington businessmen were told Monday night.

And, it is the responsibility of businessmen on the local level to educate Americans, particularly the youth, in the importance of these free institutions and what they mean.

Speaking at a general membership meeting of the Greater Lexington Area Chamber of Commerce, Dr. Kenneth McFarland, author, educator and businessman, said that the current situation must be turned around.

"We can no more co-exist with this than we can co-exist with a cancer," he said. "We've got to take the handcuffs off the police and put them back on the criminal where they belong."

These are serious statements, and we wonder who is making them. We are given the source's background in the third paragraph. But the identifying material raises more questions than it answers: Author of what? Educator where? What kind of business? Does he own or manage the business?

Because the story is so vague about the qualifications of the source, readers will be reluctant to accept his analysis. He may be qualified, but the story does not give his qualifications.

Readers and listeners find some news unconvincing because the sources that journalists use are officials or so-called experts who have not experienced the situations they are describing. A local story about unemployment that quotes only officials and data is inadequate. Unemployment is more than figures released by an official sitting at a desk. It is men and women standing idle on street corners or waiting anxiously in front offices day after day for job interviews.

Complete Background

In an AP story about the Army's pleasure over an unusually heavy crop of volunteers, the "story cited every factor except the main one: The economy was down, unemployment up, and enlistments always rise under those circumstances," said Jack Cappon, AP's general news editor. The reporter had failed to gather sufficient information.

An event that is not placed in context lacks meaning. Context can provide the how and why of the event. As Cappon put it, "In news writing, nothing is more basic than making sure that any event, speech, situation or statistic is reported in sufficient context to fix the meaning accurately."

> **Details, Details.** When reporting a murder, Edna Buchanan says she wants to know "what movie they saw before they got gunned down."
>
> "What were they wearing? What did they have in their pockets? What was cooking on the stove? What song was playing on the jukebox?"
>
> "I always ask what the dog's name is, what the cat's name is."

One of the biggest best sellers in this country's history was a political treatise, *Common Sense,* by Thomas Paine. Within three months of its publication in 1776, 120,000 copies were sold in the Colonies, whose population was about 2.5 million. Today, a book selling as well would reach 10 million readers in this country. Paine used the language of the people. He began his pamphlet, "In the following pages I offer nothing more than the simple facts, plain arguments, and common sense."

Look at the power of this section of a speech given by Sojourner Truth, an abolitionist and an advocate of equality for women. This is from her talk on women's rights, given in 1867:

> I am above 80 years old; it is about time for me to be going. I have been 40 years a slave and 40 years free, and would be here 40 years more to have equal rights for all. I suppose I am kept here because something remains for me to do; I suppose I am yet to help to break the chain. I have done a great deal of work; as much as a man, but did not get so much pay. I used to work in the field and bind grain, keeping up with the cradler; but men doing no more, got twice as much pay. . . . We do as much, we eat as much, we want as much. I suppose I am about the only colored woman that goes about to speak for the rights of the colored women. I want to keep the thing stirring, now that the ice is cracked. . . . I am glad to see that men are getting their rights, but I want women to get theirs, and while the water is stirring I will step into the pool.

Quotations

Wallace Stevens, the insurance company executive who wrote poetry that influenced a generation of poets, commented with some incredulity on events that were swirling around him: "In the presence of extraordinary actuality, consciousness takes the place of imagination." Fact has supplanted fiction.

Why, then, is so much journalism dull and unconvincing? Possibly because writers do not use in their stories what they see and hear. They paraphrase good quotes. They explain instead of letting the example show the reader.

Here are two paragraphs from a book by Studs Terkel, *Working: People Talk About What They Do All Day and What They Think of While They Do It.* Terkel, a radio reporter based in Chicago, interviewed a 14-year-old newsboy, Terry Pickens:

> I don't see where being a newsboy and learning that people are pretty mean or that people don't have enough money to buy things with is gonna make you a better person or anything. If anything, it's gonna make a worse person out of you, 'cause you're not gonna like people that don't pay you. And you're not gonna like people who act like they're doing you a big favor paying you. Yeah, it sort of molds your character, but I don't think for the better. If anybody told me being a newsboy builds character, I'd know he was a liar.

Tribute. "His writing always sparkled. He liked concrete nouns and active verbs, and each paragraph was solid as a brick."

—*Pete Hamill, an obituary of Lars-Erik Nelson of the* Daily News *and* Newsday

Plain Talk.

"If any man were to ask me what I would suppose to be a perfect style of language, I would answer, that in which a man speaking to five hundred people, of all common and various capacities, idiots or lunatics excepted, should be understood by them all, and in the same sense which the speaker intended to be understood."

—*Daniel Defoe*

"If language is not correct, then what is said is not what is meant; if what is said is not what is meant, then what ought to be done remains undone."

—*Confucius*

I don't see where people get all this bull about the kid who's gonna be president and being a newsboy made a president out of him. It taught him how to handle his money and this bull. You know what it did? It taught him how to hate the people on his route. And the printers. And dogs. . . .

No paraphrase or summary would have the impact of Terry Pickens' own words. For that matter, few psychologists with their understanding of the problems of adolescence can express so succinctly and convincingly—and with such emotion—the realities of growing up. Journalists can.

When the Virginia State Bar Association voted to admit its first black member despite a determined effort by some senior members to block the move, a news story quoted a Richmond lawyer as praising the applicant as a "commendable person with a high standing as a lawyer." Then the story quoted him as adding, "But he is a Negro and therefore I am opposed to accepting him as a member of this association. . . . I have a good many Negro friends, but I don't invite any of them to my home or club to socialize with me."

In three sentences, the reporter crystallized an aspect of racism by letting one of the participants speak.

Distant Judges Sara Grimes covered juvenile court in Philadelphia. The judges were generations away from the reality of street life. Here are sections of a story Grimes wrote to show the distance between the court and the young offenders. A judge is speaking to two boys in court:

"You should stand still and be respectful when approached by a police officer. Then the officers will respect you. . . .

"I imagine they roughed you up a little bit, huh? I'd have given you a couple of good ones, too, before I took you in.

"In the old days, we used to have Irish policemen and we'd get it over the legs and then we'd get it again at home when the police took us to our fathers.

"We didn't call it police brutality then, and I'm concerned about the disrespect shown here for the policemen. . . .

"The next time you see a policeman, think positively. You can even say, 'Officer, what can I do for you?' The police are paid to protect us. When I see them I feel safe.

"You work, you pay taxes, the police are there to protect you."

Slaughter's Witness Let sources talk and you often will find a vivid image, a colorful phrase, a passionate vehemence, a deep sadness. After a riot at the New Mexico State Penitentiary during which 33 prisoners were beaten, burned and hacked to death by fellow inmates, a reporter asked what it had been like inside as prisoners wielded blowtorches, hammers and hacksaws. An inmate replied:

Man, what can I tell you? It was like the devil had his own butcher shop and you could get any cut you wanted.

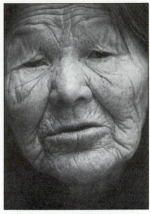

Mark Henle,
The Phoenix Gazette

'Magical Door'

"With envy, I listen to my grandchildren and greatgrandchildren speak the beautiful language. Speaking English is like a magical door to anywhere for them."
—Irene Begody, 77, Navajo Reservation

Words. "Don't go for ordinary words. Pick something else. Look at each word and use another word, especially when it comes to verbs. That's something we all should do, but reporters don't have the confidence to try a new word. Some words don't work and are forced and clichéd. But take a risk."

—*Anne Hull,* The Washington Post

In her story in *The Washington Post* about depression among youngsters, Laura Sessions Stepp balances the statements of authorities with the comments of adolescents like Darrell.

"Right over there," she quotes Darrell as he points across the street, "some boy got shot. I was at the skate rink across the street when it happened. You never know when it's going to be pointing your way. You shouldn't have to worry about getting shot when you're a kid."

Caution: Important as quotations are, it is improper to put into direct quotation what has been heard second- or thirdhand. This device, used by "imaginative" reporters influenced by the New Journalism, is unethical. Reconstructed quotes are best left to the novelists.

Human Interest

When a television reporter returned with a feature about a local store that was selling books, posters, pictures and other material based on television's "Star Trek," his editor praised his enterprise. But the tape concentrated on the material sold. There was little about the customers, the "Star Trek" fans.

"We missed," the editor said. "We should have followed a customer around and used him as the center of the story."

Frederick C. Othman, a veteran reporter for UPI, advised young reporters to put as many personal references as possible into each sentence, "he, she, King George, uncle, boy, girl or any such word describing a human being. The more such words, the more interesting the story."

Sometimes reporters fail to personalize events that easily lend themselves to human interest. When a puppy fell into the shaft of an abandoned well in Carlsbad, N.M., the rescue operation became a front-page story in many newspapers. One press service story that used the name of the puppy, Wimpy, was widely preferred to the competition's story that lacked the pup's name.

Dull   **Interesting**

Poison Center   Compare these versions of another story:

All doctors hope their patients never have occasion to use the Poison Control Center recently established in the emergency room of the Community General Hospital. However, it should be reassuring to citizens, particularly parents, to know the center exists for use in an emergency.

A frantic mother called her physician and cried that her two-year-old had been at the oven cleaner. The child's lips were smudged with the liquid.

The label said poison. What should she do?

Her call set in motion a series of checks and other calls. In a short time her physician knew precisely what chemicals were in the cleaner, which were poisonous, and what should be done.

The child was treated and beyond a few small burns on the lips and tongue the toddler is doing well.

This was the first case for the Freeport Poison Information Center in the Community General Hospital.

Springfield is one of only eight cities in the state which have official "recognized" centers to handle poisoning cases. The other seven cities are . . .

The journalist who wrote the second piece did a better job of writing because his reporting was superior. Also, he contributed a greater public service because the picture he painted of a mother and child is etched in the minds of parents. The second story is also more appropriate to the event—it *shows* what the Center does.

The style of the second piece is consistent with the event. The average sentence length of the first five sentences, which describe the poisoning incident, is around 11 words. The next three average 21 words because the reporter was seeking to give an air of calm after the frenzy of the incident. This brings us to the fourth and last of our guidelines for good journalistic writing.

Appropriate Style

The story began this way:

It was in midtown Manhattan, one of those new high-rises where the lobby rug is so thick you trip over it, and the walls are so thin you can hear the plumbing rushing. The office was on the 21st floor, at the end of a long corridor. I knocked on a door. The man who opened it looked like a private investigator. That was O.K. by me. I was there to write about private investigators.

"Joe Mullen," the man said. He stuck out a paw and I pumped it. He looked to be in his early 40s, medium height, silver hair. His eyes went with the hair, only darker. . . .

No, this isn't the beginning of one of Dashiell Hammett's hard-boiled detective novels. It's the way Carey Winfrey began his story about a real private investigator for *The New York Times.*

Every event has its own tone, texture and pace that writers try to reflect in their stories. The way a story is written is known as its *style.* An understanding of style might start with Cicero, the Roman statesman and orator: "Whatever his

In the Sty, on the Griddle

In his exposé of the living conditions in tenement housing owned by New York's Trinity Church, the muckraker Charles E. Russell wrote that no Iowa farmer "would house hogs the way 100,000 people are housed in New York City." The church, the city's biggest slum landlord, was forced to clean up its housing.

In his story about those who had invested in the stock of Minnie Pearl's Fried Chicken—which was to compete with Kentucky Fried Chicken—Floyd Norris wrote that they "were left holding shares worth less than a crispy gizzard."

theme he will speak it as becomes it; neither meagerly where it is copious, nor meanly where it is ample, not in this way where it demands that; but keeping his speech level with the actual subject and adequate to it."

In the following story of a murder, the short sentences reflect the starkness of the event:

Fight for Hat Cited as Motive in Boy's Slaying

Sixteen-year-old Kenneth Richardson was killed Thursday over a floppy brown hat, police said.

"It was just a plain old hat," Metro Homicide Detective Hugo Gomez said.

Richardson was wearing it. Someone tried to take it. Richardson refused.

Others entered the fray. The youth ran. They chased him.

"It was a running and shooting type thing. They were shooting directly at him," Gomez said.

Richardson still had the hat when taken to International Hospital, where he died in surgery. Dade's 554th homicide this year.

He was shot in the parking lot of the Miami Gardens Shopping Plaza at 12:15 A.M., soon after the nearby Gardens Shopping Skating Center closed for the night, police said.

No arrests have been made.

"They were all Carol City kids," Gomez said. "There was talk of several guns."

About 25 youths were in the area at the time, police say. "But there was nothing but the dust settling when we got there," Gomez said.

—*The Miami Herald*

Making Words Fit the Event

Because journalists are obliged to tell their stories briefly, they must choose words that count, words that quickly and efficiently paint pictures. The story is most effective when the journalist selects words in which the denotative and connotative meanings, the explicit and implicit meanings, mesh.

When New York City was close to bankruptcy, the city appealed for federal aid. President Ford brusquely said no, that the city's profligacy and incompetence had caused its fiscal misery and that it had to put its house in order itself. Pondering the story on the president's refusal, William Brink, the managing editor of the *Daily News,* cast about for the five or six words he could fit into the *News'* page 1 headline for the story. He tried:

FORD REFUSES AID TO CITY

The headline was dull, and the top line was half a unit too long. He tried again:

FORD SAYS NO TO CITY AID

This fit, but it was as dull as the first. Brink recalls that in the back of his mind was the idea that "Ford hadn't just declined to help us. He had, in effect, consigned us to the scrap heap." He then wrote two words on a piece of copy paper. After a few moments, he put three other words above them.

The headline in the margin here was instantly famous. Television news stations displayed it that night, and *Time* and *Newsweek* ran it in their summaries of the city's plight. It not only presented the information succinctly (denotative), it also suggested the president's disdain for New York (connotative) in language New Yorkers understand. The headline was appropriate to the subject.

Vocabulary Helps   The key to stylistic excellence is a wide vocabulary and a sensitivity to language that guides word choice. For instance, when the treasurer of a large utility is convicted of stealing $25,000 in company funds, a reporter can write:

- The *employee* was xxx.
- The *official* was xxx.
- The *executive* was xxx.

Each noun has a different connotation. *Employee* would be appropriate for a lower-ranking worker. Although he is an *official* of the company, the word usually is used in connection with public officials. *Executive* seems most appropriate.

Let us look at some verbs:

- He *pilfered* $25,000 xxx.
- He *took* $25,000 xxx.
- He *appropriated* $25,000 for his own use.
- He *embezzled* $25,000 xxx.
- He *stole* $25,000 xxx.

Pilfered seems to trivialize the event. *Took* is prosaic: We *take* a rest, *take* cream in our coffee. *Appropriated* suggests an official action: Congress *appropriates* funds. *Embezzled* and *stole* are strong words and probably the best to use.

Good writing is anchored in control, but sometimes the words take off on their own:

Thoughts flew like spaghetti in his brain.
"Marvin," she hissed.
The muscles on his arms rose slowly, like a loaf of bread taking shape.

The Stylist

The stylist is prized in every newsroom, just as an individual style is valued in every field. Yet reporters often are unimaginative in their selection of facts, and their writing is uninspired. A vapid writing style begets stereotyped observations and vice versa. Compare these two stories about Memorial Day. Which one is more appropriate to the event?

Historic Headline

The *Daily News* headline is recognized as the height of the art. Contrast it with this headline from a competing morning newspaper:
    Ford, Castigating City,
        Asserts He'd Veto
        Fund Guarantee
    This headline was in *The New York Times.*

Colorful. Columnists are allowed more leeway than newswriters, but sometimes they are checked, even when their reputations are based on straight talk. Molly Ivins, whose column is written from Texas, wrote of a local politician that "if his IQ slips any lower, we'll have to water him twice a day." But when she wrote of "a fella . . . havin' a beergut that belongs in the Smithsonian," her editors made it read, "a man with a protuberant abdomen."

Topeka Reminded of Debts to Dead

An Army general officer and a Navy lieutenant commander reminded Topekans of their debt and responsibility to America's war dead in two Memorial Day services Tuesday morning.

Brig. Gen. John A. Berry, commanding general of Fort Riley, spoke to representatives of 18 veterans organizations at ceremonies at Mount Hope Cemetery.

Earlier, Lt. Cmdr. John G. Tilghman, U.S. Navy Reserve, talked briefly at services on the Topeka Avenue Bridge.

"It is good for us to gather this morning to think of—and thank—those men and women who gave their lives in wars past that you and I may have the full benefits and privileges and responsibilities of our American heritage," said Cmdr. Tilghman.

"Many men in our wars did not always understand all the causes behind the war in which they fought, but they were sure they wanted those of us at home to continue to enjoy the birthright and heritage which is ours, and gave their lives that we might do so.

"You and I must realize our responsibilities in making sure our children and those to come in future generations will be sure of the same promise.

"Today, thousands are fleeing from those who would take away their birthright and their heritage. You and I may someday join their flight unless we get off the fence and take a stand for that which is right—morally right and right patriotically."

Tilghman told his audience protection of its heritage may not always be in combat dress and on a battlefield.

—*The State Journal*

Fresno Rites Honor Fallen War Heroes

Walk with me early this Memorial Day through the Liberty Cemetery before the ceremonies begin and a thousand feet scatter the dust over these quiet gravestones.

Here are the dead of many of our nation's wars.

A Flag flutters beside each grave and flowers grace them all. No one is forgotten.

Some died in uniform. Others, like Sergeant William J. Dallas of the 2nd Tennessee Infantry in the Spanish-American War, went to war and returned to live a long life—80 years long.

Many stones stand upright, their marble veined with the passage of time. What stories lie behind some of these stones? The passerby cannot tell. The inscriptions simply say:

Michael O'Connor, US Navy, Spanish-American War.

Or, in the Civil War section: Isaac N. Ulsh, Company B, 13th Kansas infantry.

Other markers tell more:

Jack T. Martin, Jr., 1922–1942, USS Langley, Lost At Sea.

James S. Waggoner, CEM, USN, USS Kete, 1917–1945, Lost At Sea.

Sergeant Keith A. Matthew, 877th Bomber Squadron, USAAF, 1918–1945, Lost At Sea.

Two Petersons

Side by side are these two:

T. Sergeant Maurice Peterson, 9th Air Corps, 330th Bomber Group, 1917–1944, Ploesti, Roumania.

Sergeant Sterling Peterson, Airborne Infantry, Company B, 1919–1944, Normandy, France . . . .

The sun rises higher and friends and relatives of the dead come bearing flowers.

Families come and decorate graves with snapdragons, roses, stocks, hydrangea, marigolds and others. While the adults place the flowers, the children roll in the grass and shout to one another.

Then the ceremonies begin.

Objectivity = Credibility. Primo Levi, an Italian chemist, was sent to a concentration camp by the Nazis. On his return to Italy, he decided to write of his experiences. Asked why his books seem so dispassionate, lacking any anger or desire for revenge, he replied:

I have deliberately assumed the calm and sober language of the witness, not the lamenting tones of the victim or the irate voice of someone who seeks revenge. I thought that my account would be more credible and useful the more it appeared objective, the less it sounded overly emotional; only in this way does a witness in matters of justice perform his task, that of preparing the ground for the judge. The judges are my readers.

Veterans organizations march to the cemetery, and the Colors are massed at the War Veterans Memorial Shaft.

"Let us pray that we may always honor those who have given the last full measure of devotion to their country," Dean Emeritus James M. Malloch says.

"Let us pray that the United States may ever be the land of the free and the home of the brave and the advocate of peace in the councils of nations."

—*The Fresno Bee*

The first story is like dozens of Memorial Day stories. The oratory, although perhaps passionately uttered, has little emotional impact because it ignores those the event commemorates—the victims of war. The second story teeters on the edge of sentimentality in the lead, but soon settles into understated narrative that seeks to match the solemn nature of the event.

The Aftermath   In his Oklahoma City hotel room, Rick Bragg watched the Denver jury convict Timothy J. McVeigh. "This was a man who had wrecked a city, wrecked lives. My story had to carry that import," he says. "It would have failed otherwise. But I also did not want to overwrite it, to lend drama to a story already so dramatic. It would have been like putting a scary mask on a face already so horribly disfigured.

"So I though the best thing to do was borrow a snippet, a snapshot, from every tale of great sadness I had heard since covering the story. Let that be the picture the reader saw."

Here is how his story begins:

After the explosion, people learned to write left-handed, to tie just one shoe. They learned to endure the pieces of metal and glass embedded in their flesh, to smile with faces that made them want to cry, to cry with glass eyes. They learned, in homes where children had played, to stand the quiet. They learned to sleep with pills, to sleep alone. Today, with the conviction of Timothy J. McVeigh in a Denver Federal court, with cheers and sobs of relief at the lot where a building once stood in downtown Oklahoma City, the survivors and the families. . . .

Changing Styles

Journalistic writing is an evolving, changing form of writing. It has been at times lush and imaginative, then spare and direct. Writers now are searching for ways to tell stories that will grab and hold the attention of people increasingly distracted by the clamor of everyday life and the enticements of an entertainment culture.

Tom Wolfe   Over the past 40 years, journalistic style embraced the New Journalism of Tom Wolfe and other rule-breakers. In a review of an anthology of Wolfe's journalism, *The Purple Decades: A Reader,* Ellen Wilson describes Wolfe's inspiration for this new way of writing:

In the early Sixties, Tom Wolfe went to the New York Coliseum to cover a Hot Rod and Custom Car show, and came back with the New Journalism. As he tells it in the introduction to "The Kandy-Kolored Tangerine-Flake Streamline

Baby," he felt frustrated by his inability to recreate the atmosphere of the show, with its "nutty-looking, crazy baroque custom cars, sitting in little nests of pink angora angels hair," in standard journalese. He needed a style flexible and uninhibited enough to capture everything a straight news story would miss: the carnival atmosphere and the thoughts and emotions of the participants.

He came up with a style incorporating slang and contemporary speech patterns, stream of consciousness and abrupt switches in perspective. The first step was painstaking research and close attention to detail. After that, he was free to select from the novelist's whole bag of tricks.

Storytelling   The New Journalism has been succeeded by narrative writing, storytelling that takes some of its components from the techniques of fiction writers, as Wolfe recommended. These tools include emphasis on individuals through whom the action is advanced, dialogue, scene-setting, suspense. It takes to the outer limit the injunction "show me, don't tell me."

Sometimes, the drive to storytelling can be rewarded with enthralled readers. Sometimes, the writer is carried away by the technique. One of the most common problems of the beginner who attempts storytelling is the collapse of the lead halfway through the piece.

An interesting anecdote, a fascinating character may begin the piece and then when the meat of the piece is under way, the writer suddenly realizes the anecdote and the characters are irrelevant.

"This is why frequently the narrative approach is abandoned once the going gets heavy and why stories with anecdotal beginnings are so full of disposable people, characters thrown away as soon as their work of getting readers into the story is finished," says William F. Woo, former editor of the *St. Louis Post-Dispatch* and now teaching at Stanford University.

The storytelling form, some critics argue, tends to overstate the dramatic and the colorful, sometimes at the expense of nuance and ambiguity, the irritating details that complicate the story line. Others, such as Jack Lule in his book *Daily News, Eternal Stories: The Mythological Role of Journalism,* counter that the news media are in trouble because they have strayed from storytelling. The result, says Lule, is that "news has become less valuable, less central."

Clearly, some events are best told using the standard news form of direct lead and then the body of the story that buttresses the lead. Some events lend themselves to the storytelling form.

When the police finally solved a triple murder in Florida and put the killer on trial, Tom French of the *St. Petersburg Times* knew that he had the makings of a narrative.

French spent three years on and off to gather information about the disappearance and death of a woman and her two daughters while they were on vacation in Florida. His work led to a seven-part series and the Pulitzer Prize. For excerpts from French's narratives, see **Angels & Demons** in *NRW Plus.*

Writing for the Medium

A lot of what we have discussed so far concerns the requirements of writing for print. There are other media, of course, and these have special needs the newswriter must master.

Radio newswriting is more condensed than writing for print. The reader can always go back and reread something she was unclear about. The radio listener has to grasp meaning on his first and only hearing. The radio news writer will not have much detail, few nuances.

The television news writer often writes to pictures, which are left to speak for themselves. The TV news writer has a more complicated script than the radio news writer because the TV writer is usually jumping back and forth—the interviewer, the burned-out family being interviewed, the house in flames, back to the studio.

We will go into greater detail about broadcast newswriting in Chapter 9.

Online Writing

Writing for the Internet also answers to the special needs of the medium, in this case a screen, usually with material on one or both sides of the news text. Most of those who work in online journalism agree with Mark Fitzgerald of *Editor & Publisher* who says, "The computer screen is notoriously inhospitable to long stories. Even a story that amounts to just 10 inches on the newspaper page seems endless on a computer screen."

Studies of online news readers indicate that they are attracted by headlines and brief summaries and will read a short piece. "Web readers tend to be impatient and tend to skim," says John Leach, online editor for *The Arizona Republic*. "The average amount of time spent reading a page on our Web sites is about a minute."

The story form preferred by Web writers is our old friend the inverted pyramid style in which the key elements of the event are placed at the beginning of the story. "Our readers want to get straight to the heart of the story," says Leach. "An 18-year-old reader describes what he wants from an online news site as 'the straight dump,' which an older reader might describe as 'just the facts ma'am.' "

MSNBC.com uses a story form it calls the Model T. The top of the T is a summary lead that gives the reader the point of the story at once. The vertical part of the T, the body of the story, can be told in any fashion the writer finds appropriate—straight news story, feature or narrative.

Ruth Gersh, editor of multimedia services at the AP, says the screen "seems to beg for a simpler writing style."

Convergence   Some media companies are experimenting with a one-style-fits-all form of writing. The same story is supposed to be used online, in print and on radio and TV. Generally, the converged style tends toward broadcast writing. In print form, these stories seem thin and some early enthusiasts have backed off from the one-style format.

But there have been some successful newsroom convergences in shared news gathering, and some stations have used newspaper reporters to discuss the news on their regularly scheduled broadcasts. The general manager of Channel 17-KIVA in El Paso, Kevin Lovell, said, "Newspapers are much better at doing in-depth reporting. But by bringing our different resources together we can enhance our news coverage."

The *El Paso Times* installed a television system in the newsroom that allows it to transmit news to the local stations.

Reading for Writers

"You can't write well if you don't read," says veteran reporter Joe Galloway, who put in stints as a foreign correspondent. "Don't show me your resumé," he says of job applicants. "Show me your library card." Wide reading—novels, essays, the work of journalists—helps writers learn to write, a task that is never-ending. The writing coach Don Murray says, "Professional writers never learn to write; they continue to learn writing all their professional lives. The good writer is forever a student of writing."

One journalist whose work would repay study is Ernie Pyle, a Scripps Howard newsman who wrote features for the news organization, then requested to be sent to cover World War II for the United Press.

Scripps Howard Foundation

Ernie Pyle

Reporter's Reporter

Pyle was loved by the soldiers he accompanied to battle. One of Pyle's memorable dispatches was of the death of Captain Waskow during the Italian campaign of 1944. It has become a journalistic classic. Here is part of Pyle's story:

Then a soldier came and stood beside the officer, and bent over, and he too spoke to his dead captain, not in a whisper but awfully tenderly, and he said:

"I sure am sorry, sir."

Then the first man squatted down, and he reached down, took the dead hand, and sat there for a full five minutes, holding the dead hand in his own and looking intently into the dead face, and he never uttered a sound all the time he sat there.

And finally he put the hand down, and then reached up and gently straightened the points of the captain's shirt collar, and then he sort of rearranged the tattered edges of his uniform around the wound. And then he got up and walked away down the road in the moonlight, all alone.

The Army Signal Corps operator who sent Pyle's dispatch over shortwave radio to United Press headquarters in New York told Pyle's biographer, "I had to struggle through that piece to make my voice override my tears." (*Ernie Pyle's War: America's Eyewitness to World War II*, James Tobin.)

For the full story, see **Captain Waskow** in *NRW Plus*.

With the Troops   Murray Kempton, the reporter and columnist admired by many journalists for his dogged reporting and distinct writing style, paid homage to Pyle who, Kempton wrote, "stands above the rest because he most fully incarnated what a reporter ought to be. Pyle went again and again wherever the worst extremes waited, the unconscripted man bound by conscience to the comradeship of the conscripted and enduring by free will what they were compelled to endure by necessity."

Pyle understood the use of understatement. Reread the four paragraphs about Captain Waskow's death. The emotion comes from you, the reader. When he went ashore with the troops on D-Day, Pyle wrote of what he saw strewn on Omaha Beach as men were mowed down—socks, sewing kits, family pictures. The details gave a personal cast to the body counts.

Jack Foisie, also a World War II combat correspondent, said of Pyle that he "seldom injected himself into his writings. He never mentioned his own close calls with death, although he had a number of them."

With the Navy   When the war in Europe ended, Pyle went to the Pacific to cover the sea war against Japan. There, Pyle felt uncomfortable about what he saw as the Navy caste system.

Soon after he was aboard a ship he found that his dispatches were being censored. The names of the sailors he had written about were deleted and only the names of high-ranking officers were left untouched. He also balked at the system that relegated black sailors to the food services. Pyle was able to change the first by threatening to abandon Navy coverage for the Marine and Army GIs, and the Navy gave in and stopped censoring his stories.

But he could not change the discrimination against black servicemen. That took three more years and the action of President Truman in 1948.

The Pyle Style   Malcolm W. Browne, who served as a war correspondent in Indochina, Pakistan and the Persian Gulf, says that Pyle was "a master of language, the equal of any first-rank novelist. He constantly struggled for the precise phrase and the telling verb; whereas a less careful correspondent might write that a shell 'howled' or 'screamed' overhead, Pyle wrote that it 'rustled.' "

The writer John Hersey said of Pyle that he was "the great artist" of the "human aspects of warfare—of bravery, loss, wounds, humor, self-sacrifice, pain and yes, death—and, by the way, he always added the name and home address of the person he was talking about."

The End   The death of good men haunted Pyle, and when he was shot by a sniper on Ie Shima in 1945, the soldiers who had risked their lives to bring back his body found in his pocket a column he had written for the end of the fighting in Europe. Here is some of it:

> Those who are gone would not wish themselves to be a millstone of gloom around our necks.
> But there are many of the living who have had burned into their brains forever the unnatural sight of cold dead men scattered over the hillsides and in the ditches along the high rows of hedge throughout the world.

Dead men by mass production—in one country after another—month after month and year after year. Dead men in winter and dead men in summer.

Dead men in such familiar promiscuity that they become monotonous.

Dead men in such monstrous infinity that you come almost to hate them.

For the entire column Pyle wrote, see **Cold Dead Men** in *NRW Plus.*

Pyle is buried beside GIs in the Punchbowl Cemetery in Hawaii.

Write . . . and Rewrite

Someone said nothing good was ever written as a first draft. Journalists often do not have the leisure of a second look at their copy. Too often, the job requires writing on the run, doing a story with facts gathered close to the deadline. Nothing can be done about that. But when there is time, the rewrite is almost always a good idea and usually necessary.

With practice, writing comes easier and is accomplished with less anguish and more speed. But every writer knows that his or her work can be improved with rewriting, and even the veteran journalists rewrite when they have time. The discipline of editing your own words is handy. When Jan Wong was writing a book about her experiences in China, *Red China Blues,* she was worried about putting together her many experiences.

"As a reporter, I sometimes got bogged down structuring a thousand-word article. Would I be able to put together 150 times that much—and still make the words flow?" she wondered.

Not to worry. She wrote . . . and rewrote. "I rewrote some chapters many times," she says. "But I enjoyed that. Rewriting was a skill I had honed as a journalist."

Using Printouts

Reporters who write long will often make printouts to work with. They find it easier to shuffle the pages to reorganize the structure and to make major changes in the copy.

The Round File. "The wastepaper basket is the writer's best friend."
—*William Kerrigan*

Mencken on Writing

H.L. Mencken was a master of invective. A columnist for *The Baltimore Sun,* he was never so masterfully abusive as when skewering writing he considered contemptible. Here is perhaps the most famous writer-bashing on record. Mencken is commenting on the writing of President Warren G. Harding:

> I rise to pay my small tribute to Dr. Harding. Setting aside a college professor or two and a half a dozen dipsomaniacal newspaper reporters, he takes the first place in my Valhalla of literati. That is to say, he writes the worst English that I have ever encountered. It reminds me of a string of wet sponges; it reminds me of tattered washing on the line; it reminds me of stale bean-soup, of college yells, of dogs barking idiotically through endless nights. It is so bad that a sort of grandeur creeps into it. It drags itself out of the dark abysm (I was about to write abscess!) of pish, and crawls insanely up to the topmost pinnacle of posh.

Let's see if we can wrap up this long chapter with a few conclusions about the art of writing.

Word Choice

Here is some practical advice from John Ciardi, poet, essayist and writer on writing:

> Count the adjectives and verbs; good writing (active writing) will almost invariably have more verbs. . . . A diction in which every noun is propped up by an adjective may be almost flatly said to be a bad one.

Mark Twain advised, "Whenever you see an adjective, kill it." And that vast source of material, Anonymous, is quoted on writing as saying, "The adjective is the enemy of the noun."

As for verbs, the action verb is our object. Mervin Block, the television writing coach, received a script with this lead: "The Dow was down more than 62 points." Block commented: "The verb *was* doesn't convey any action. The writer needs a vigorous verb like *fell.* Or *sank.* Or *slid.* Or *skidded.* Or *dropped.* Or *plunged.* Or *tumbled.* But *was* doesn't move."

Sentences

Red Smith's teacher at Notre Dame, John Michael Cooney, wanted sentences from his students that were "so definite they would cast a shadow." He was an enemy of vague writing and began class by intoning, "Let us pray for sense."

Sense for whom? Harold Ross, the founder and longtime editor of *The New Yorker* wanted his magazine never to contain "a sentence that would puzzle an intelligent 14-year-old."

The sentences should be put to good use, and that means using them for quotations, anecdotes and illustrations. Donald Murray, the writer and writing coach, comments on the use of examples, illustrations and anecdotes:

> You tell them the anecdote and they say, "Boy, this is a bad situation." That's the art in it—not to tell the reader how to think, how to feel, but to give the reader the old Mark Twain thing, "Don't say the old lady screamed. Drag her on stage and make her scream."

Advice

Perhaps the next to last word should be given to the copy editor. Here's Joel Rawson's lament about the copy he sometimes read when he was a copy editor at the *Providence Journal Bulletin:*

> The thing that I resent most is sloppiness. I resent getting a story with misspellings in leads and errors of fact, and I resent getting a story that I know somebody didn't sit down and reread. Even on deadline I expect somebody to go back and reread that

story and fix up what is obviously wrong with it. You're taking up a lot of people's time and you're also ruining your credibility and mine if work like that goes through the copy desk or other editors on this newspaper. And if somebody else doesn't catch (the mistakes) and they go into print, it hurts us all.

The final bit of advice comes from an assistant city editor on the now-defunct *Kansas City Times* via William F. Woo, then a young reporter on the staff. Woo was struggling to write an obituary for page 1. His effort was visible to Ray Lyle, the assistant city editor.

"Bill," he told Woo, "just write what happened."

Summing Up

Those of us who write for a living strive to blend information-giving with a bit of artistry if we can. So it's natural here to turn to a writer who wrote well and thought a lot about the writing craft.

Robert Louis Stevenson was the author of highly readable novels—*Treasure Island, Kidnapped* and *The Strange Case of Dr. Jeykll and Mr. Hyde*—as well as essays, poetry and travel accounts. Here's what he had to say about writing:

- **Accuracy:** ". . . there is only one way to be clever and that is to be exact. To be vivid is a secondary quality which must presuppose the first; for vividly to convey a wrong impression is only to make failure conspicuous. . . ."
- **Brevity:** ". . . the artist has one main and necessary resource which he must, in every case and upon any theory, employ. He must, that is, suppress much and omit more. He must omit what is tedious or irrelevant. . . ." But he must retain the material essential to the "main design."
- **Language:** The words with which the writer works should be from "the dialect of life."
- **Structure:** ". . . every word, phrase, sentence and paragraph must move in a logical procession." No word or phrase is selected unless it is "what is wanted to forward and illustrate" the work.

Further Reading

Clark, Roy Peter. *The American Conversation and the Language of Journalism.* St. Petersburg: The Poynter Institute for Media Studies, 1994.

Ghiglione, Loren, ed. *Improving Newswriting: The Best of the American Society of Newspaper Editors.* Washington, D.C.: ASNE Foundation, 1982.

Ivins, Molly. *Molly Ivins Can't Say That, Can She?* New York: Random House, 1991.

Kluger, Richard. *The Paper: The Life and Death of The New York Herald Tribune.* New York: Random House, 1987.

Lule, Jack. *Daily News, Eternal Stories: The Mythological Role of Journalism.* New York: The Guilford Press, 2001.

Nichols, David, ed. *Ernie's War: The Best of Ernie Pyle's World War II Dispatches.* New York: Random House, 1986.

Nichols, David, ed. *Ernie's America: The Best of Ernie Pyle's 1930s Travel Dispatches.* New York: Random House, 1989.

Ross, Lillian. *Reporting.* New York: Dodd Mead & Co., 1981.

Scanlan, Christopher, ed. *Best Newspaper Writing.* Chicago: Bonus Books; St. Petersburg: Poynter Institute for Media Studies.

Terkel, Studs. *Working: People Talk About What They Do All Day and What They Think While They Do It.* New York: Pantheon, 1972.

Terkel, Studs. *The Good War: An Oral History of World War Two.* New York: Pantheon, 1984.

Tobin, James. *Ernie Pyle's War: America's Eyewitness to World War II.* New York: Free Press, 1997.

8 Features, Long Stories and Series

Anita Henderson, *Beloit* (Wis.) *Daily News*

Features make us laugh and cry.

Preview

Features are written to entertain and to inform. The writer lets the actions and comments of the personalities carry the story. Features usually begin with a delayed lead—an incident or anecdote that illuminates the point of the feature. The body contains additional incidents, many quotes and the news peg. The ending may summarize the piece or provide a climax.

Long stories are written to provide readers with information about a complicated idea or situation. The reporter outlines the theme before reporting so that material relevant to it can be gathered. In writing, a tone or style appropriate to the main idea is adopted, and ample quotes and incidents are used to keep the story moving.

Series are written when the subject is too complex for the long story format. Each article has a major theme; sidebars may be used to develop subthemes.

Some editors say there are three types of news stories:

Spot news story: Contains material of such significance that it must be reported immediately to the public.

News feature: Uses information that supplements the spot news, usually by providing the human element behind the breaking news event or by giving background through interpretation and explanation.

Feature: Aims to entertain and/or inform with writing that emphasizes storytelling.

The Feature

The feature has had a reputation much like Canadian mining stock, slightly suspect. Although it has worthy antecedents in the satire and parody of poets and essayists who used the pen to attack individuals in public and private life, the feature was approached gingerly by editors. Many editors subscribed to the philosophy of Richard Draper, who wrote in his Boston *News-Letter* in the 18th century that he would use features only when "there happens to be a scarcity of news."

At First Distasteful

Conservative editors of the 19th century reacted with distaste to the features published by the penny press from the 1830s to the Civil War. Directed to the working class, which had been enlarged by the country's industrial revolution, these inexpensive newspapers ran stories about domestic tragedy and illicit sex, stories that editors such as Horace Greeley found unworthy of journalism. When he established the *Tribune* in New York in 1841, Greeley announced that his newspaper would avoid the "immoral and degrading Police Reports, Advertisements and other matters which have been allowed to disgrace the columns of our leading Penny Papers." But Greeley was soon running the kind of material he had condemned.

The feature story was a weapon in the great circulation wars between Pulitzer and Hearst in New York at the turn of the 20th century. Crime stories, sports, society news, science news—all of it embroidered with sensational details often as much invented as factual—were used to attract readers. This type of feature became synonymous with Yellow Journalism.

The Hearst newspapers were perhaps the most successful of the sensational and flamboyant papers of their day. W.A. Swanberg, in his biography *Citizen Hearst,* describes them:

> They were printed entertainment and excitement—the equivalent in newsprint of bombs exploding, bands blaring, firecrackers popping, victims screaming, flags waving, cannons roaring, houris dancing and smoke rising from the singed flesh of executed criminals.

A reporter for a Hearst newspaper described a typical Hearst paper as "a screaming woman running down the street with her throat cut." The Chief, as Hearst was known to his employees, had the man fired.

In the days of Front Page Journalism, the feature writer's job was to wring tears from the bartender, smiles from the policeman and gasps of wonderment from the tenement dwellers. The tales of the city, as spun out by the feature writers of the day, were long on drama, short on fact.

Tale of the Cat   During the circulation war between the Hearst and Pulitzer papers, a reporter for Pulitzer's *New York World* who covered shipping described what happened when reporters tried to make features of straight news:

One of those wrecked ships had a cat, and the crew went back to save it. I made the cat a feature of my story, while the other reporters failed to mention the cat and were called down by their city editors for being beaten. The next time there was a shipwreck, there was no cat but the other ship news reporters did not wish to take chances and put the cat in. I wrote the report, leaving out the cat, and then I was severely chided for being beaten. Now when there is a shipwreck, all of us always put in a cat.

The Decline   As the United States grew into a world power and its citizens had to confront the consequences of World War I and then a pervasive depression, some of the press graduated to more serious pursuits. The feature came to be seen as too frivolous for the responsible newspaper. Newspapers that held on to the old formulas declined in popularity. The Hearst chain dwindled from 22 newspapers to 8.

In 1947, when Joseph G. Herzberg, city editor of *The New York Herald Tribune,* put together a series of essays by *Tribune* staffers for the book *Late City Edition,* not one of the 29 chapters was devoted to the feature story.

Now Thriving

Today, the feature thrives. First, editors discovered that serious journalism does not have to be abstract. They rediscovered the fact known to Greek playwrights 2,300 years ago—events have a human dimension. Indeed, it is the human aspect of the event that makes it worth communicating. In his play *The Frogs,* Aristophanes has the playwright Euripedes say, "I made the drama democratic. I staged the life of every day, the way we live." This is an excellent description of our approach to the feature today.

The contemporary journalist tries to present the full dimension of how we live now, from how we are governed, make a living, raise a family and spend our money to the ways we entertain ourselves and make our way through the trials and triumphs life holds for us. The feature has proved a useful writing tool to tell many of these stories. So useful, in fact, that in 1979, after many years of ignoring the feature, the Pulitzer Prize board established a category for a distinguished example of feature writing, "giving prime consideration to high literary quality and originality."

The Somber   The Prize has gone to Lisa Pollak of *The Baltimore Sun* for her "compelling portrait of a baseball umpire who endured the death of a son while knowing that another son suffers from the same deadly genetic disease." The Prize has honored features about inner-city youngsters' determination to succeed and personal accounts by journalists, one a reminiscence by Howell Raines of *The New York Times* about Raines' childhood friendship with his family's black housekeeper. The first Prize in the new category went to Jon Franklin for a story about brain surgery, which we will be looking at in a few pages.

The Cheerful   But an unvarying diet of the somber does not tell the full story of how we live now. Also, any mass medium given over to a steady diet of the serious will be rejected by the audience. So the media offer a variety, and one of the items is the entertaining feature.

The news story might be a piece from Washington, D.C., about a sudden rise in the cost of living. The feature writer will use that as a takeoff for a feature about how the candy bar he used to buy for a nickel now costs 10 times as much. Where, he wonders, do kids these days get the money for a Babe Ruth or a Mars bar? He lurks around candy counters to find out.

The Difference. "The news writer tells you the bridge fell in and how many cars fell off. The feature writer tells you what it was like to have been there: 'When Joe Smith began to walk across the bridge, it began to tremble, and he grabbed the railing'— that sort of detail."

—*Jules Loh,*
AP feature writer

A Feature: A Man Beset

By making every word count, a reporter for *The Fresno Bee* captured the mood of a man with a problem:

> Ben Karp is a patient man. Like most of us he can shrug off life's little onslaughts in hopes of a better day.
>
> But Karp has been shrugging and dodging and hoping for six months now, and his patience finally snapped. He called the *Bee* and asked for a reporter to see him at his general merchandise business at 1837 Mariposa Street.
>
> "Very important," he said. On the scene, Karp whipped off his hat, pointed a slightly trembling finger at a brownish spot the size of a half dollar on it and then wordlessly pointed skyward.
>
> There, cooing happily and roosting comfortably in corners and on window sills, were pigeons. Dozens of pigeons.
>
> "I've called the mayor, the public works commissioner, the health department," Karp said. "They promised me to do something. Nothing is done. It's ruining my business. People don't like to walk in here past that line there.
>
> "I'd like to get a shotgun and scare them off. But you can't shoot a gun in the city. The health department says it can't do anything because it can't prove pigeons carry disease. The humane society says I can't trap or poison them. The mayor's office says he was going to have a meeting on it. Nothing happened.
>
> "This is bad for the city. I tell you. Thousands of people go in and out of the bus depot and they see this and I hear them say to each other, 'Fresno can't be such a clean city. Look at this.'
>
> "I don't blame people for not wanting to come into the store. What can I do about it?"
>
> And Karp looked up at his feathered friends and shrugged.

What he learns astounds him. Some youngsters are rolling in dough. Even poor kids are sporting $125 athletic shoes, he notices. One story begets another. But first, for the candy bars. It won't be nominated for a Pulitzer Prize, but that's all right. It's a fun story to write. And, he hopes, for people to read.

Caution: Some young reporters say they prefer to write features rather than hard news because the feature is easier to handle. This is the blather of the uninformed. The momentum of the news event carries most spot news stories. True, it is not easy to learn to organize a tight news story, and the skill to devise succinct leads that quickly take the reader to the news point is not easily mastered. But the feature writer must carry these burdens and more.

The feature is an exception to some of the writing rules, and this imposes on the writer the task of pioneering in each piece, beginning anew to find a form, a story tone, the appropriate words and the telling scenes for this particular story. Readers demand more of feature writers than of straight news writers and so do editors.

Sleepers The feature writer also sees the absurd and hears the preposterous. In his piece about the Southern Furniture Market in High Point, N.C., where the new styles in furniture are previewed each year, Lew Powell of *The*

Charlotte Observer tells us about Dr. Samuel Dunkell, "psychotherapist and author of the best-selling 'Sleep Positions.' " Just to make sure we know this event is hardly the stuff of which significant news is made, Powell sets the mood in the first paragraph:

> Today in Washington reporters are awaiting Koreagate revelations. In Memphis, the latest on Elvis. In Minneapolis, the Billy Graham audit. In High Point we're crowded into a mattress showroom waiting for the inside poop on sleep positions.

From the serious to the silly. Powell does this in a few sentences. The words "inside poop" tell the reader that what follows is going to be fun:

Enrico Caruso slept with 18 pillows. Neil Sedaka rubs his feet over each other. The late Hannah Arendt, author of "The Origins of Totalitarianism" and not someone you'd expect to be spilling this kind of stuff, favored the "water wings" position.

And have we got a photo opportunity for you! As Dunkell discusses the "royal" position, the "flamingo," the "mummy," the "sphinx" and the "swastika," model Norma demonstrates. Her yellow sleep-shirt keeps riding up, ensuring undivided attention. When she's joined by a male model for the "hug" and "spoon" position, a sock-footed TV cameraman clambers onto an adjacent Maxipedic for a better angle.

"Republicans sleep face down, Democrats on their backs," Dunkell says. Scribble, scribble. "Surprisingly few people fall out of bed—perhaps 20 percent in their lifetime." Scribble, scribble. . . .

The feature writer sees universals as well as aberrations. What is there about that pianist, this drummer with dreams that strike chords common to all of us? The feature writer knows that great writers inspire us to see ourselves in Tolstoy's Natasha, Fitzgerald's Nick Carraway and Melville's Captain Vere. The feature writer must be open to human experience. It was said of Rembrandt that he rejected nothing human. Neither does the feature writer.

Guidelines

- Show people doing things.
- Let them talk.
- Underwrite. Let the action and the dialogue carry the piece.
- Keep the piece moving.

Making the individuals carry the action requires a discerning eye to see the telling action and a discriminating ear to catch the illuminating quote.

Frontier Nurse Showing people doing things and letting them speak requires that the reporter be on the scene. Jim Warren of the *Lexington Herald-*

Leader accompanied Glenna Allen of the Frontier Nursing Service as she made her rounds in the eastern Kentucky mountains. His story begins this way:

HYDEN—The road that snakes up from Coon Creek is hard-packed dirt in some places and bottomless mud in others, all of it pitted with cavernous potholes.

Slide one way and you hit a mountain wall; slide the other and you go off a cliff into space.

Driving is tricky, especially when a mountainous coal truck—in this case a Tennessee Orange Mack with a full load of bituminous coal—looms around a blind curve.

Glenna Allen handled the situation with skill that comes from long practice, steering her battered tan Toyota almost to the drop-off at the right edge of the road. . . .

Tom Woods II, *The Lexington Herald-Leader*

Backwoods Care

Warren lets Allen talk:

"My mother hates it that I'm doing this," Miss Allen said with a laugh. "She thinks I'm going to get myself killed by a rattlesnake or run over some cliff, and she keeps asking when I'm coming home. . . ."

Conforming Kids Lena H. Sun, *The Washington Post* Beijing bureau chief, took her readers into a kindergarten to show how Chinese children are made into conforming, obedient citizens:

BEIJING—It is a playtime at the Tongren Kindergarten. As 3-year-olds run relay races in the schoolyard, the teacher suddenly calls out to one girl.

"You didn't run on the dotted line," the teacher says disapprovingly. The girl, pigtails bobbing, immediately retraces her steps on faded red spots painted on the concrete. The teacher smiles and nods. No one else makes the same mistake.

"Show people doing things," our first guideline, is the thrust of Sun's lead.

We said that the feature writer tries to tell us how we live now, our successes and failures, our dreams and our defeats. Sometimes, the feature writer looks back, too.

Elizabeth Leland did that in her feature for *The Charlotte Observer* that put a shaft of light on a dismal chapter in U.S. history.

An American Tragedy

Here is how she began her story of a family tragedy that illuminates a part of our past:

Gene Cheek was 12 when a judge took him from his mother.

It was a Monday morning, Nov. 18, 1963, and Gene remembers being excited because he didn't have to go to school.

He put on his best clothes—a white shirt and his Sunday coat, a size too small—and rode with his mother on a city bus to the courthouse in downtown Winston-Salem. They were going to get the $413

Before the Separation

Gene Cheek holds his half brother Randy. Next to him are his mother Sally and her boyfriend Cornelius Tucker. Seventeen months after this family portrait was made, a judge gave Gene's mother a choice: Give up Randy or give up Gene. For years, Gene wanted the story told, and when Elizabeth Leland did so, Gene Cheek said, "It's a cleansing to tell this story."

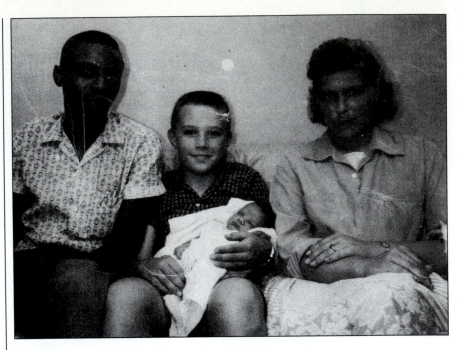

in child support his father owed them. They'd go shopping afterward.

His mother sat up front in the courtroom to the right of the judge. His father and an uncle sat to the left. Gene remembers goofing off by himself on a bench a few rows back, not paying attention to what anyone was saying, when he heard his mother crying. He walked up front.

The gray-haired judge in the black robe was telling her something, and as Gene listened he realized it was not about money. It was about her boyfriend.

The judge said it wasn't good for Gene to live with her because she was seeing a Negro man and had a Negro baby.

Gene's mother pleaded. I'm a good mother, she said, her voice breaking, tears wetting her cheeks.

The judge gave her a choice: Give up the baby or give up the boy.

When Gene Cheek told her about the separation, Leland was skeptical. She said she found it "incredible" that a judge would issue such an order. Even when relatives verified the story, she was uneasy.

Leland knew that only documentation—a court file—would be persuasive to readers. Without it, it was just a tale told by upset people.

For Leland's complete story and how she managed to find the documentation she needed, see **An American Tragedy** in *NRW Plus*.

Planning

Frank Barrows, Leland's managing editor at *The Charlotte Observer,* says careful planning of the feature is essential. "Simply because a feature is not written to be cut from the bottom—as a news story might be—does not mean that the material can be randomly set down on paper.

"For a feature to be something other than puffery, you must do the type of serious preparation and thinking that lead to organization. For instance, you might not want to put all the straight biographic data in one place."

Barrows knows that such material is usually tedious. Beginners tend to bunch up background. More experienced hands break up background such as biographical material and place bits and pieces into the moving narrative. For example, he says, when a reporter comes to a place in the story where she is showing how the subject's hometown influenced his life, that is the place to put something about his birthplace and a few other routine details. In other words, the necessary background is spotted or blended into the on-going story.

Another fault of beginners is the leisurely pace they set at the outset of the piece, as though they are feeling their way toward the theme of the story.

"Too often in features the writer does not tell his reader soon enough what he is writing about," Barrows says.

Truck Stop   Look at how Eric Lawlor of the *Houston Chronicle* slides the reader right into his piece about a truck stop outside town. He sets a scene in the first paragraph, pulls us into the restaurant in the second and in the third we meet Tina and then listen in on the chatter:

The truck stop on the North Freeway is ringed with rigs. Trucks glide past one another with the grandeur of sailing ships: 16-wheel galleons bearing—not spices from the Indies or gold from the New World—but auto parts and refrigerators.

Truckers weave as they enter the restaurant; like sailors on shore leave, they are still finding their legs.

Tina Hernandez, an 18-year-old waitress here, serves an order of ham and eggs.

"Where are my grits?" asks the recipient.

"You don't get grits unless you ask for them," she tells him. "If you want grits, you gotta say, 'I want grits.' "

If this sounds unnecessarily acerbic, it's not, in fact: Tina and her customers are actually fond of one another. An affection that masquerades as good-natured abuse.

"Give me a bowl of split-pea soup," says a man whose face looks curiously flat.

Perhaps someone sat on it. "Is there any meat in there?"

"There's meat in there all right," says Tina. "The problem is finding it."

"How are you and Billy (not his real name) doin'?" he wants to know.

"We don't talk anymore," says the waitress. "He got scared. Just checked out."

"Oh, I don't believe that. I'll bet you are goin' out and just don't want anyone to know about it."

"I'm tellin' ya: that man is scared of women."

"Maybe, he just doesn't like YOU," offers Myrtle, another waitress.

At a nearby table, a driver is telling a colleague about a recent fling.

"I had to leave her finally because she was so cold-blooded. You could get pneumonia sitting next to a woman like that."

Techniques

Feature writers call on all sorts of approaches to their writing. When the occasion calls for it, a writer may compose an all-quotation story, letting the characters carry the action with their words. Sometimes, the writer will inject himself or herself in the story, though most editors are not pleased when they are handed a first-person narrative. Here's the beginning of a first-person feature that works:

I don't drive a Mercedes. I don't smoke Cuban cigars, or drink Dom Perignon (unless you're buying). I'm more likely to dine at Burger King than a four-, three-, or two-star restaurant. But I do have one thing higher rollers would envy. I own a racehorse.

No, I don't own the horse by myself. I have a few partners; there are an even dozen of us, actually. We're not the types you'd expect to be in this game. We're a locksmith, an investment banker, a journalist, the director of a rape crisis center, a retired businessman, two therapists, a prosecutor, three lawyers in private practice, and a law student. Four of us are women.

David Hechler's experience as a horse owner lasted a year. Gypsy Flame proved to be nice to look at but slow afoot.

Cinematic Approach   One way to look at feature writing style is through the lens of a movie camera. If we did that, we would first focus through the telescopic lens on a small part of the scene and magnify it, then use the wide angle lens to show the big picture. Here is how Ellen Graham handled an assignment for *The Wall Street Journal* to see how the Girl Scout cookie crumbles. Let's zoom in on her work:

Eleven-year-old Kathleen Totz is a small but important cog in a sales effort unique in the annals of American enterprise. This year, the slim, bespectacled Girl Scout was the top cookie seller in Wallingford, Conn.'s Troop 265, toting up $498 in receipts for 266 boxes.

Then Graham takes a step back for the big picture:

By dribs and drabs, the door-to-door earnings of volunteers like Kathleen add up: The annual cookie sale—the Girl Scouts' main funding source—generates an estimated $400 million in revenue.

And still another step back to deliver in the fourth paragraph the point Graham is leading up to:

But many in this volunteer cadre—the Scouts, troop leaders and parents who provide the free labor—are starting to question the annual cookie drive, saying the troops simply don't see enough of the profits. Tax-free cookie proceeds mainly support the Girl Scouts' sprawling bureaucracy, critics say, while the girls themselves are left with the crumbs.

Using All the Techniques

In his feature about a school for bartenders, Lawlor gets down to business at once, taking the reader into the classroom in the lead:

> K. C. Stevens is explaining the difference between a godfather and a godmother.
>
> "To make a godfather," she tells her class at the Professional Bartenders School, "use amaretto and scotch. A godmother, on the other hand, combines amaretto and vodka."

Steve Campbell, *Houston Chronicle*

Learning the Trade

K. C. Stevens displays the proper blend of savvy and cordiality as she instructs budding bartenders. Then her students take over.

Then Lawlor steps back for a few paragraphs to let the reader survey the scene, telling us something about the teacher and her students:

K. C., a onetime barmaid, has been teaching people to mix drinks for four years now.

"I didn't want to find myself at the age of 40 wearing orthopedic shoes behind some crummy bar," she says. "Being a bartender is a young person's game."

Her class nods agreement. If that isn't to exaggerate this barely perceptible movement of heads. This is a pretty lethargic group. They slump at the school's mock bar as if drink had ravaged them. They wouldn't look out of place in Pompeii.

It's hard to imagine these people doing anything as animated as tending bar. Indeed it's hard to imagine them doing anything as animated as standing up.

K. C., a good soul, is inclined to agree.

"A lot of them are spaced off somewhere," she says. "I was telling a couple of them just this morning, 'Look, you're gonna have to put more time into studying.' But once they get the picture, things usually work out. Many people come in here expecting to party. They don't realize there's a lot of work involved."

From the first sentence, the reader is hooked on this story, a story that occupies a full column of type. Every line was read. Why? First, the subject is interesting. Even if you can't tell a Hot Toddy from a hot buttered bun—and care less—you wonder about these people who are able to throw together scores of different concoctions from their amazing array of bottles.

Second, Lawlor knows what he is doing. The most interesting subject in clumsy hands will be dulled. Let's analyze Lawlor's craft:

- The story moves quickly.
- The quotations are vivid.
- The characters interact. They talk, do things.

Tone and Style

In any discussion with feature writers, the words *tone* and *style* usually come up. A feature writer uses one tone—one kind of voice—for a piece about a classical guitarist, another for a guitarist with a rock group. Tone is established by selection of facts, quotes, illustrations, by word choice, length of sentences, even by the length of paragraphs. The rock musician may be quoted in short, one- or two-sentence paragraphs to match the rock beat, whereas the classical musician's quotes may run on longer to give the reader the sense of the sonority of classical music.

The Monster

The new field of neuroscience interested Jon Franklin, chief science writer for *The Evening Sun* in Baltimore. Franklin had been talking to Dr. Thomas Ducker, chief of neurosurgery at the University of Maryland Hospital, about brain surgery, and Ducker had agreed to call him the next time he planned an especially difficult surgical procedure. When Ducker called, Franklin set out to follow the story of Edna Kelly, who was afflicted with what she called her "monster," a tangled knot of abnormal blood vessels in the back of her brain. She was born with the malformation, but in recent years the vessels had ballooned inside her skull and were crowding out the healthy brain tissue.

Kelly agreed to be interviewed, and she allowed Franklin to use her name. She also permitted Franklin to watch the surgery. Ducker agreed to cooperate.

Preparation   Here is how the first story in Franklin's two-part series begins:

In the cold hours of a winter morning, Dr. Thomas Barbee Ducker, University Hospital's senior brain surgeon, rises before dawn. His wife serves him waffles but no coffee. Coffee makes his hands shake.

Downtown, on the 12th floor of the hospital, Edna Kelly's husband tells her goodbye.

For 57 years Mrs. Kelly shared her skull with the monster. No more. Today she is frightened but determined.

It is 6:30 a.m.

"I'm not afraid to die," she said as this day approached. "I've lost part of my eyesight. I've gone through all the hemorrhages. A couple of years ago I lost my sense of smell, my taste, I started having seizures. I smell a strange odor and then I start strangling. It started affecting my legs, and I'm partially paralyzed.

"Three years ago a doctor told me all I had to look forward to was blindness, paralysis and a remote chance of death. . . .

Operation   Franklin's intentions are made clear at the outset. This is to be a detailed account of the confrontation between a skilled surgeon and disease. Franklin takes the reader into the operating room:

Now, at 7:15 a.m. in Operating Room 11, a technician checks the brain surgery microscope and the circulating nurse lays out bandages and instruments. Mrs. Kelly lies still on a stainless steel table.

A small sensor has been threaded through her veins and now hangs in the antechamber of her heart. Dr. Jane Matjasko, the anesthesiologist, connects the sensor to a 7-foot-high bank of electronic instruments. Wave forms begin to move rhythmically across a cathode ray tube.

With each heartbeat a loudspeaker produces an audible popping sound. The steady pop, pop, pop, pop isn't loud, but it dominates the operating room.

Dr. Ducker enters the operating room and pauses before the X-ray films that hang on a lighted panel. He carried those brain images to Europe, Canada and Florida in search of advice, and he knows them by heart. Still he studies them again, eyes focused on the two fragile aneurisms that swell above major arteries. Either may burst on contact.

The one directly behind Mrs. Kelly's eyes is the most dangerous, but also the easiest to reach. That's first.

Ducker has managed to find and clip off one of the two deadly aneurisms. The next article begins with Ducker peering into the neurosurgery microscope in search of the second. The going is slow, dangerous.

Problems   Five hours into the operation there is trouble and Ducker worries that his patient's heart has been slowed too many times. He decides not to continue. If she recovers, he says, he will try again.

If she survives. If. If.

"I'm not afraid to die," Mrs. Kelly had said. "I'm scared to death . . . but . . . I can't bear the pain. I wouldn't want to live like this much longer."

Her brain was too scarred. The operation, tolerable in a younger person, was too much. Already, where the monster's tentacles hang before the brainstem, the tissue swells, pinching off the source of oxygen.

Mrs. Kelly is dying.

The clock in the lounge, near where Dr. Ducker sits, says 1:40.

"It's hard even to tell what to do. We've been thinking about it for six weeks. But, you know, there are certain things . . . that's just as far as you can go. I just don't know. . . ."

He lays the sandwich, the banana and the fig newtons on the table before him neatly, the way the scrub nurse laid out instruments.

"It was triple jeopardy," he says, finally, staring at his peanut butter sandwich the same way he stared at the X-rays. "It was triple jeopardy."

It is 1:43, and it's over.

Dr. Ducker bites, grimly, into the sandwich.

The monster won.

Franklin holds the reader in suspense until the jolting final sentences. The three sentences are short, quick—consistent with the abrupt end of Mrs. Kelly's life.

You might want to go back to our four rules for writing the feature and note in the margins of the sections from Franklin's pieces where he follows these guidelines.

The News Feature

The news feature usually has its origins in some news event. When Carl Hiassen of *The Miami Herald* dug into the court case involving a doctor and his millionaire wife, he came up with a tale of greed preying on loneliness. His story begins:

To Dr. Edward Gordon, love meant never having to say he was out of money.

Six years ago, the solicitous Miami Beach physician married a patient who was worth more than $8 million. Her name was Elizabeth Buffum, and she was a lonely alcoholic.

With Gordon, she stayed lonely and she often stayed drunk. She just barely stayed wealthy.

Today, as lawyers doggedly try to retrieve her scattered fortune from all over the globe, the former Mrs. Gordon lies in a Fort Lauderdale nursing home, permanently brain-damaged. Relatives say her life was destroyed by four ruinous years as the doctor's wife. They say it wasn't a marriage, it was a matrimonial Brink's job.

"Unbelievable," says one son, Peter Beaumont. "It's sort of a classic: elderly lady with lots of bucks heads down to Retirement City and gets fleeced by local doctor."

It began as a September love affair. He was 62, silver-haired and single, with a new medical practice in Florida. She was 60, a bit overweight and twice divorced, given to irascibility and depression. . . .

The lead is inviting. Nobody, every writer knows, ever tires of reading about love, money and violence. The second and third paragraphs are like the coming attractions at a movie, or the come-on advertising of television. The fourth paragraph drives home the theme: A woman ruined by her marriage. And in the fifth paragraph, a quote is used to sum up the theme. The sixth paragraph introduces us to the chronological narrative the writer will spin.

Feature Ideas

The advertisement read:

HEARTBROKEN Anyone who purchased (at my Garage Sale last week) a small white canister with blue flowers, please call me. It contains remains of a dearly departed family member.

There's a story in that canister. How did it find its way into the garage? Who bought it? Was it returned? And if so, where will the dearly departed be placed now?

Just look around. Notice that group sitting in the cafeteria, those high school students? They are griping. About what? Listen in: His mother doesn't like his girlfriend: "She thinks I'm too young to be going steady. She thinks I should spend my time on school work. But me and my girl were meant for each other."

A young woman says to no one in particular, "I don't fit in, not even here. I don't think I look good enough. I don't like the way my body is. Everyone else is popular. Not me."

Another teen-ager says he just had some news that has relieved him after a couple of weeks of stress: "I thought that my girlfriend was pregnant. Lost a lot of sleep, and weight. I just found out she isn't.

Ideas are everywhere. A letter writer to Ann Landers says that college students consume an average of 34 gallons of alcoholic beverages a year and quotes the chancellor of the University of Wisconsin as saying that the biggest problem on campus today is alcoholism. A reporter wonders:

What's happening on the local campus?

James J. Malloy, *The Providence Journal*

Saying Goodbye to a Good Buddy

The story by W. Zachary Malinowski of *The Providence Journal* about the burial of a teen-ager killed in a drive-by shooting begins this way:

Tears streamed down Wayne Tucker's face as he led the funeral procession down the center aisle at St. Teresa's Church yesterday. Behind Tucker stood eight teen-age pall-bearers in black sweatshirts and loose-fitting jeans, bearing the silver casket holding their friend, Tommy DeGrafft, who died in a barrage of gunfire last weekend. In Tucker's hands was a basketball covered with the scrawled signatures of DeGrafft's former teammates. One said simply, "To Tommy from All of Us."

Humor: Approach with Caution

Asked for advice about writing humor, most writers reply, "Don't try."

That's a two-pronged answer. Humor may be the most difficult kind of writing there is. There are probably 50 excellent Washington correspondents, a score of top-notch foreign correspondents. Every newspaper has a master reporter. But there are fewer than half a dozen good humorists writing for newspapers.

The other prong of the response is that if you have the urge to write a funny piece, or you are ordered to do so, don't try too hard. The strain will show.

Mark Twain, the country's greatest humorist, said, "There are several kinds of stories, but only one difficult kind—the humorous."

In his essay, "How to Tell a Story," he wrote, "The humorous story depends for its effect upon the manner of the telling. . . . The humorous story is told gravely; the teller does his best to conceal the fact that he even dimly suspects that there is anything funny about it."

Avoiding the Pitfalls

The following suggestions are from a dozen feature writers:

• "Good stories come from good material. Good material comes from good reporting—and that is just as true if not more so with feature writing as with news writing," says Sheryl James of the *St. Petersburg Times.* As Tom Wolfe puts it, "Style can't carry a story if you haven't done the reporting."

• Single-source stories are not as good as multisource stories. No one cares to read about the author who talks about his life unless his personal account is supplemented by interviews with fellow writers, critics, his family, friends, even some readers.

• Do not have such a love affair with quotes that you fail to paraphrase routine material. Worse: Do not use quotes chronologically from the interview as a prop for failing to organize the piece.

• Know what you are going to say and the tone in which it is to be said before starting. Otherwise, the story will never get off the ground.

• Develop an enthusiasm for the piece. Features can be marred by an objectivity that keeps the reader at a distance. "The idea of a feature is to involve the reader," a reporter said. "This is often taken to mean good craftsmanship through colorful writing. That's not enough. The writer needs to take a point of view, not simply to say, 'Look at this guy who was put into an institution for the retarded at the age of six, and when he was 18 some worker in the place saw that the kid wasn't retarded at all but had a learning disability.'

Steve Ueckert,
Houston Chronicle

Duck Talk

"You've got to tell those ducks what they want to hear," says Jimmy Goddard, a master duck caller Eric Lawlor interviewed for his piece about that fine art.

Lawlor let Goddard speak:

"Talk to them the way you'd talk to your lady. Say 'I love you honey, please come on back. . . .' You have to mean everything you say.

"Nothing alive spots a fraud faster than a duck. . . . You must be able to tell a duck's mood. I watch the bird. If he's happy, I'm happy. I tell him, 'If you'll just come on down here, the two of us can have a fine old time.' That's if he's happy. If he's lonesome, then you have to be lonesome. Ask him if he'd like to cry on your shoulder."

"The writer of this kind of piece has to be indignant at the tragedy. How can you be objective about this kind of inhumanity? A reader should be moved to indignation—not by the reporter's sounding off. We don't want that. But this kind of piece has to have the kind of facts and a story tone that gives a strong sense of human waste and bureaucratic inefficiency."

- Make sure the story has a good plot and is unusual enough to hold our interest. This means the central idea should have possibilities for drama, conflict, excitement, emotion.
- Don't tell us when you can show us people doing things.
- Avoid first-person stories. They are usually less interesting than you think.

Brights

The *bright* is to the feature what the short story is to the novel—a distillation, a tightly written gem that brightens the reader's day. The bright can be one paragraph or several. The following article is about as long as a bright should run:

POOLE, England—(AP)—"It was God who took out my tonsils," the little boy told his mother after his operation at Poole General Hospital.

"When I was taken into the big white room, there were two lady angels dressed in white. Then two men angels came in. Then God came in."

"How did you know it was God?" the mother asked.

"Well, one of the men angels looked down my throat and said, 'God, look at that child's tonsils.'

"Then God took a look and said, 'I'll take them out at once.' "

The conversation was reported by the hospital's staff newsletter.

The last paragraph is an anti-climax. It belongs in the running story, probably at the end of the second paragraph. Then the reader would be left with that wonderfully innocent quotation from the child.

The Long Story

Despite the pressure on news writers to compress, to boil down the already distilled, long stories and broadcast documentaries are being written all the time, even online. Some events and situations are so complicated, only a lengthy treatment suffices. Or the situation may be so interesting that length is an asset. Readers and viewers and listeners will stay with it all the way through, fascinated by every twist and turn.

Body Damage

The financial news was well known to those who follow business: The Body Shop franchises were in trouble, and the home office was undergoing a shakeup. Competition from similar merchandisers like Bath & Body Works had turned profits into losses.

To put a human face on the dollars-and-cents, profit-and-loss business story, Jeffrey A. Tannenbaum of *The Wall Street Journal* went to Mississippi to report the story of a couple who operate a Body Shop franchise and were not doing well. The full-page story, blending the experiences of Jim and Laura White with the company's woes, begins:

DOTTIE HITT, a trim 25-year-old real-estate agent, pops into the Body Shop outlet in Ridgeland, Miss. In less than a minute, she scoops up a pair of $5.95 nylon "scrubbing" gloves used for rubbing off flaky skin.

So far, so good for Body Shop franchisees Jim and Laura White, who run the store.

But hooked to Ms. Hitt's arm is a brown shopping bag from the Body Shop's archrival, Bath & Body Works. Minutes earlier, in the same shopping mall, Ms. Hitt had bought three bars of soap and four other products from the larger, cheerier Bath & Body Works store. She spent about $33 there—and would have bought the gloves at Bath & Body Works, too, if the store had them in stock.

Bath & Body "is the chain people talk about," Ms. Hitt says.

Phrases like that crush Mr. White, the franchisee. "It turns my stomach to come in here every day," he says. "I have to take an anti-depressant"—Zoloft, a drug he says he didn't need until a year ago.

Body Shop's performance has indeed been depressing in the U.S., where its competitors are winning big. In the fiscal year ended Feb. 28, sales declined about 5% at Body Shop outlets open a year or more, on top of declines of 6% and 3% for the previous two years. More than 20 U.S. franchisees—some with multiple units—have quit the chain during the past two years, often citing financial and emotional distress.

The delayed lead to Tannenbaum's story provides the reader with a dramatic example of the downward spiral of Body Shop. The business slide—really the theme of his piece—comes in the fourth paragraph. Tannenbaum has followed the two requirements of this type of feature story:

1. The anecdotal lead must be consistent with the theme of the story.
2. The theme must be no lower than the sixth paragraph.

Time and Labor

The long story travels on the legs of the reporter. "The first point about the long story," says Tannenbaum, "is that it usually requires a log of work. For a profile of Rockefeller University, I conducted at least 20 interviews in person, and the typical interview lasted 90 minutes. I also did several more interviews by phone and read a great deal of background material."

Balance The long story, he says, "is an interplay between the specific and the general." By "general" he means the key points or themes that the reporter has selected as the basis of the piece. A story about a breaking news event may have one or two points. The long story may have half a dozen. "Specific" refers to the details that illustrate and amplify the general points.

"For every generalization in the story," Tannenbaum continues, "there should be specific illustrations to buttress it. This means the reporter has to identify the themes and then must dig out the proof for them. The more specific and colorful the details that are used as proof or buttressing material, the more effectively the generalization or theme will be brought home to the reader."

Early Planning Like all experienced journalists, Tannenbaum tries to sketch out his major ideas or key points as early as possible. This may come before any reporting is done, or soon after the reporting begins. A theme can come from a tip, an editor's assignment, the reporter's hunch. Or it may simply be the logical step following a series of developments on a beat.

"For each key point, I want two things: Good quotes stating the point and colorful illustrations, anecdotes, examples," he says. "I know exactly what I am looking for from each interview subject."

In the reporting, additional points often will develop, and these, too, must be buttressed with specific quotes, illustrations, data and anecdotes.

Organizing the Story

No reader, viewer or listener will stay with a long story or a documentary unless the reporting develops interesting material and the writing is a cut above that acceptable for shorter pieces. The long article also must be well-organized to carry the reader or viewer through the long journey.

John McPhee, whom many consider one of the best reporters writing, had a formula when he wrote long pieces for *Time* magazine. "Each had to have a beginning, a middle and an end, some kind of structure so that it would go somewhere and sit down when it got there," McPhee says.

Saul Pett, for many years one of the AP's stellar writers, was called on often to write long pieces. He had a procedure he followed:

> There is my basic material. But it's all kind of in bunches. So then I sit down, and this is just dull donkey work, and I hate it, but I find it necessary, and I kind of outline my material. I don't outline my story because I don't know that yet. I'm outlining the material. I try to put it in piles.

He describes how he went about organizing a story about tempestuous New York Mayor Ed Koch:

> Here's stuff about Koch's wit. Here's stuff about his independence. Here's stuff about how he can be tough with minorities. Here's stuff about his background. All that exists in my notebooks scattered throughout. So the advantage of the outline is that I've got it on paper in logical segments. . . .
>
> I'm getting more familiar with the material so that when I'm ready to write I don't have to go fishing around in notebooks or in stacks of clips. By then I almost don't have to consult my notebooks.

McPhee's Procedure   McPhee admits that he goes "nuts trying to put it all in focus." But his procedure gets him through the thicket of notes. First, he identifies the major themes of his piece, puts them on index cards and tacks the cards on a bulletin board. Then the cards are arranged in the order the themes will appear in the final version.

"Strange as it may seem to the beginner anxious to set words to paper, structuring the story challenges a reporter's creative talents as much as the writing. What's most absorbing is putting these stories together," says McPhee. "I know where I'm going from the start of the piece. It's my nature to want to know. Because I'm interested in structure, I must sound mechanistic," he told an interviewer. "But it's just the opposite. I want to get the structural problems out of the way first so I can get to what matters more. After they're solved, the only thing left for me to do is tell the story as well as possible."

Anne Hull's Method   Like McPhee, Hull keeps index cards. On them she puts her key observations. She refers to them often in writing. "At some point you have to figure out what shape the story is going to take. I am not an organized thinker, an organized writer." For long series: "I break the story into scenes, but scenes have to fit together, and there have to be peaks, and there have to be waves. I make an outline after I create a time line."

Four Steps

1. Identify all themes. Summarize in a sentence or two.
2. Place each summarized theme on a separate index card. Put the cards in the order that the themes will follow in the story.

The Magazine-Story Formula

The most common problem that Art Carey, associate editor of *The Philadelphia Inquirer Magazine,* finds with long stories is poor organization. "So many writers, it seems, sit down with no plan, no idea of how to arrange the mass of information they've assembled in an understandable and engaging way."

He says that over the years the magazine has developed "a reliable magazine-story formula." This is it:

• A scene-setter lead that introduces the story's protagonist in a colorful situation that seems to epitomize his or her character or the quest, adventure or trend in which the protagonist is involved.

• A "nut" section or "hoohah" that explicitly states the premise of the story, outlines the major points and sells the story by tempting readers with some of the most engaging quotes, tidbits of information and previews of coming attractions.

This section should also tell readers why the story is so important, or new or different. There should be enough fanfare about the story's significance to convince readers that it's well worth the investment of the next 20 minutes of their lives.

• A background section that explains how the main character got to be the way he or she is or how a certain situation or controversy evolved.

• Several sections dealing in detail, and in an orderly progression, with the meat of the story and the themes heralded earlier.

• A concluding "kicker" section that packs some dramatic wallop, wraps everything up in a neat bow, tells the reader what it all means and perhaps leaves the reader with something profound to ponder.

---

3. Cut up notes by theme and place them next to theme cards. Reread and again arrange cards and notes in the order in which they will be written.

4. Look through the cards for the major theme that will serve as the lead or the integrating idea for the article. Write it on another card.

As the notes are lined up (Step 3), a reporter may discover a lack of adequate documentation or illustrative material to buttress some of the themes. More reporting will be necessary.

Reporters check their notes at this stage for the high-quality quotes and illustrations that can be placed high up in the various sections of the story. One might be used to begin the article if the piece lends itself to a delayed lead. Some reporters use a colored pencil or pen to mark these high-quality quotes, anecdotes and incidents to call them out for use.

Caution: Resist the temptation to use a dramatic quote or telling incident simply because it is attention getting. The material must illustrate the theme it accompanies. If the fit is loose, put the example with a more appropriate theme or toss it out—however much work went into digging it up, however exciting the material.

Remember: Keep clearly in mind or in view the major theme for the piece (Step 4). Toss out any material that is irrelevant to this integrating idea.

Changing Directions

Once the story is organized, do not assume that the structure cannot be changed. If the piece does not seem to be flowing properly, shift some of the elements around.

Some of the other problems that come up are:

• A theme has too much material to organize: Divide it into subthemes that can be handled more easily. Consider dropping, or at least drastically subordinating, some themes.

• A theme is too minor to be worth the space being given it: Blend it into another theme or discard it.

• The transition from one theme to another is awkward: To go from one theme to another smoothly, reorder the themes so that the linkage is more natural.

• A long block of background material does not move; it impedes the flow of the article: Break up this background, history, explanatory material and blend sections into the narrative.

Rewriting–Rereading   Most long pieces require rewriting, sometimes a top-to-bottom rewrite. The first version usually reflects the writer's need to get the story straight, to make sure the good quotes are there, the salient facts included.

Debbie Cenziper of *The Charlotte Observer* reads her stories three times, each time for a different purpose:

1. Her first reading is for "rhythm, for the flow of the story, for good writing."

2. "This is a gut check. How will my sources feel when they read this story? Is the criticism fair? Did I give all sides a chance to respond?"

3. "The third read is for basic fact-checking. I read each line on paper, check out the facts."

A Television Documentary

Let us watch the producer of a television documentary as he tries to focus on a theme for his subject—the decline of many of the country's older cities.

The deterioration of the inner city has had the attention of planners, politicians and journalists since the 1950s. If the city is the heart and brain of civilization, then the troubles afflicting the city cores of Denver, Detroit, Cleveland, Philadelphia, Boston, Baltimore, St. Louis, Los Angeles, New York and dozens of others threaten a way of life—cultural, commercial, educational, religious. For in the heart of the cities are the opera houses and philharmonic halls, the factories and the offices, the schools, and the temples and the cathedrals. The city gives a center to modern life.

To make journalism out of the tribulations of the large city is no easy task. The decline is the result of complex social, political and economic forces. Reporters with a national audience cannot write about all the cities in trouble. They must make one or two illustrate the plight of the many. They must draw common elements from the tangled problems of many cities and then find a city that symbolizes most of these elements.

The Racial Factor

Howard Weinberg, a producer of "Bill Moyers' Journal," cast about for some central themes and a city to symbolize them. Weinberg first defined the scope and limits of his piece. He then settled on a point of view. His idea was to show the forces, especially racism, at work in causing neighborhood deterioration.

"I went to Chicago," Weinberg says. "My associate and I spent a week there, interviewing real estate agents, mortgage bankers, open housing leaders, community leaders, journalists, government officials and others on the south, west, north sides of Chicago."

When he returned to New York he had no idea how he would tell such a complicated story in half an hour. Tentatively, he decided to use the neighborhood of Austin where black and white community groups had organized to preserve and improve their neighborhood. Also, one organizer, Gale Cincotta, lived in Austin, and Weinberg wanted to have a person as a focus for the program.

"In discussions with Bill Moyers, I was forced to rethink and refine my outline," he says. In looking back at his original outline, Weinberg found he had written, "It is beginning to be understood in communities of the inner cities that deterioration is not an accident, it is the inevitable result of a lack of faith. Expect deterioration—and you'll get it."

Redlining

This idea of a self-fulfilling prophecy kept coming back to Weinberg, and he continued to do more reporting. Gradually, a theme and a strong point of view emerged. "It became clearer that 'redlining' was the story I wanted to tell, not the FHA abuses, not the efforts to relocate blacks in the suburbs or to 'stabilize' a threatened neighborhood."

Redlining takes its name from the red circles that banks and other lending agencies reportedly draw on maps around certain neighborhoods. The banks decide that people in these neighborhoods will not be given mortgage money because the banks consider the neighborhoods to be deteriorating. The practice makes it difficult for residents to improve their homes or for buyers to move into the neighborhood. Further deterioration results.

Weinberg was struck by the material he turned up in his reporting. "A savings and loan association was licensed to serve a neighborhood—and clearly, it was not doing that when it openly admitted that it received 80 percent of its deposits from its neighborhood and reinvested 20 percent in its neighborhood," Weinberg says.

Weinberg visualized the booming suburbs—which the savings of inner-city residents were helping to build—and the deteriorating inner city. This would make for dramatic pictures.

He decided to shift the main focus from Austin to Rogers Park, which was beginning to go the way of Austin. Here is how the script of "This Neighborhood Is Obsolete" begins:

BILL MOYERS: The skyline of Chicago thrusts a handsome profile above the shores of Lake Michigan, suggesting the serene self-assurance of a city and its architecture, its wealth and its power and its tolerance for new ideas in urban living. But opulent skylines point up and away from the reality in their shadows. And in Chicago, as in every large American city, the grand vista is misleading.

Out beyond the soaring, secular temples of commerce, before you reach the shopping centers of suburbia, the future of Chicago is being decided every day in less spectacular surroundings: in neighborhoods where drugstores and delicatessens, taverns, laundromats, barbershops, and small churches on treelined corners express a lifestyle in danger of extinction.

For the way the economic game is played these days, these neighborhoods hardly have a chance. There's a profit in moving people out and hang the human cost.

In the next half hour, we'll look at two Chicago neighborhoods where the neighbors are fighting back.

I'm Bill Moyers.

This neighborhood is obsolete.

The people who live here don't think so, but some of the banks and savings and loan associations do. They stopped lending money because they believe the community's deteriorating and the risk is too great. But without money to improve people's homes or to give them a chance to buy another, the decay speeds up and the fear becomes a self-fulfilling prophecy.

In this and similar neighborhoods in Chicago, people accuse the savings and loan associations and the banks of redlining. Redlining means an entire geographic area can be declared unsuitable for conventional loans and mortgages. A redline is, in effect, drawn like a noose around a neighborhood until for want of good housing the working and middle classes are driven to the suburbs and the neighborhood is left to the very poor.

A side effect of redlining is something called disinvestment. You probably haven't heard of that term before. I hadn't until I came here. Disinvestment is a process of collecting deposits in one neighborhood and investing them somewhere else. The lending agents say it's necessary to spread the risk, but it leaves a neighborhood like this short of capital and hope. Gasping for its very life.

The people who could afford to, move on. And that's what the savings and loan associations would like to do. After they've helped to build up the suburbs and make them affluent and attractive, they want to move there, too, or at least to open a suburban branch. Only then does an old neighborhood like this discover where its money has gone, but by then it's too late.

The Results   Like much good journalism, the documentary had results. The month after the Moyers documentary, the Illinois Savings and Loan Commissioner issued a regulation against redlining that prohibits savings and loan associations from refusing to lend money in a neighborhood because of its age or changing character. Then Congress passed legislation to end redlining by banks.

Notice that Weinberg had to reduce his ideas to the dimension of his program. Like the writer of a 300-word story or a 30-second news item, he had to focus on a single theme and toss out all extraneous material. The journalist never escapes the chore of boiling down material, of eliminating anything not related to the theme.

The Test   That basic theme can always be expressed in a simple sentence or two. David Belasco, the American theatrical producer, once remarked, "If you can't write your idea on the back of my calling card, you don't have a clear idea."

Steve Lovelady, a veteran editor, uses the Belasco method. "After all those interviews," he says, "after weeks or months of document-digging, trail-sniffing, blind alleys, discoveries, dry holes, and amazing finds, synthesizing all that material is a daunting task." If after applying the Belasco test, Lovelady finds the reporter hasn't a clue about what all that work adds up to, he advises the reporter to take a walk, think, then go back to the material.

"I have yet to run across the story too complex or too nuanced or too important to be summed up in twenty-five words or less," Lovelady says. Once that is done, he says, "the heart of the story—the incisively stated, powerful paragraph—has been essentially written." This summary then is the blueprint for the long story or the series.

The Series

Some subjects are too broad, too deep, too complex for even the long story. Faced with such a problem, the reporter finds that the series of articles is the way out. When Sam Roe of *The Blade* decided to examine the decline in Great Lakes shipping, he knew that he could not handle the topic in a single article. Only a series would do the job.

Roe's task was to show how the collapse of the steel industry struck lake shipping with devastating effect. Most of the ships served U.S. steel firms, carrying iron ore to the giant plants. Toledo's port on Lake Erie handled 43.8 million tons of cargo in 1966. Two decades later, it handled 17.9 tons.

Tom O'Reilly, *The Blade*

A Port's Relentless Decline

As the steel industry collapsed, Great Lakes shipping went into decline. For the main story in his series on the slump in shipping, Sam Roe of *The Blade* went aboard a freighter and accompanied the crew on its voyage.

"To capture and hold a reader's attention throughout a series is no easy task," Roe says. "That's why it is important to have stories with action, particularly in the first installment." Roe's first part in his four-part series begins with a delayed lead:

ABOARD THE AMERICAN REPUB-LIC—"Damn! She's swinging too wide."

Capt. Robert Tretter cuts the throttle, curses the current, and prays that the *American Republic,* a freighter longer than two football fields, can negotiate one final hairpin bend on the Cuyahoga River. A strong current is denying her a lefthand turn and is pushing her toward a concrete embankment.

"You got 12 feet over here," says wheelsman John Norton. "She'd better not get closer."

The men on the bridge are as tense as sailors aboard a battleship in combat. For the past two hours, the *Republic,* carrying 21,000 tons of iron ore from Lorain, has inched her way down the narrow river toward Cleveland's inner docks.

Just what does this have to do with his theme, the decline of Great Lakes shipping? In a deft maneuver, the journalistic equivalent of Capt. Tretter's handling of his freighter, Roe sets his story in the right direction:

Now, just when it appears the *Republic*'s port side will ram the embankment, the current lets her go. . . .

This time, the *American Republic* prevailed.

But ahead of her lies a far more formidable obstacle, one that her crew and all others in the shipping industry fear they can't beat: the relentless decline of Great Lakes shipping.

Numbers tell the story. This year there were only . . .

"This lead is more captivating, I thought, than diving into the statistics," Roe says.

Roe says he finds it useful to "walk the reader through" main stories. "For example, the main Great Lakes story was reported and written from the vantage point of a single ship on a single voyage.

"A cook in the mess talking about tough times allowed me to cite unemployment figures. Two decks below, in the cargo holds, an engineer pointing out new equipment allowed me to discuss technological changes in the industry. And so on. The story never really had to move off the ship."

Outlining

Roe says an outline ensures a successful series. As soon as he has in mind a clear picture of what he wants to say, the outline is written. Too soon and the reporter cannot single out what is significant. Too late and the reporter will have wasted time gathering information irrelevant to the theme.

The outline has a practical use. "A solid, detailed outline helps a reporter sell a series to editors," Roe says. Editors are reluctant to give the OK to a reporter who has in hand only an idea and some scattered notes. Series require a large amount of space, and editors won't provide it unless they have some assurance of the probability of a successful series.

Roe suggests writing nut grafs, the paragraphs that contain the basic idea, for each story in the series. "Keep in mind when writing them: Why is this story significant? What am I trying to say?"

Roe's series, "Struggling to Stay Afloat," won first place in an AP contest for enterprise reporting.

For more examples of Roe's enterprise journalism, see **Tecumseh Street** in *NRW Plus*.

The Crab Pickers

Anne Hull told her editor at the *St. Petersburg Times* that she thought the story would take a week or two. The story was to be a description of how Mexican women are recruited to work in North Carolina picking the meat out of hardshell blue crabs caught off the coast. The recruitment was done under a federal program that permitted U.S. businesses to bring in foreign workers for jobs that U.S. workers will not do.

But as Hull dug into the story, her ideas shifted and she realized that there was a bigger, better story in the young women from a small town in central Mexico and their experiences.

She ended up becoming involved in a six-month journey that took her to Mexico, then with the women to the Outer Banks of North Carolina, and then home again. The reporting for a series often is intense and long, but Hull's was truly extended.

Hull was with the young women when the call summoning them north came. Here is how she begins her series:

It was early afternoon when the girl stepped into the shade of Señor Herrera's small store. She unfolded her mother's shopping list and set it on the wooden counter. A hot wind blew outside.

Señor Herrera was cutting down a rope of chorizo for her when the telephone rang. "Ay," he said, wiping his knife.

Señor Herrera owned the only telephone in Palomas. When news came, he would step outside and shout the bulletin through cupped hands, knowing it would be passed from house to house. The priest is delayed. The medicine for the sick horse is coming.

But this time, he leaned on the counter and spoke to the young girl.

Ve dile a las señoras que ya es hora.

Go tell the ladies it is time.

The girl ran into the daylight, past the mesquite fences and the burro braying in the dusty street. She stopped at a blue iron gate, where a woman was pinning laundry to a clothesline.

The girl called out. *Señora, señora, teléfono.*

Juana Cedillo stood in her patio, blown with the powdery shale of the desert highlands. She'd been expecting the message. Now it had arrived. There would be no more waiting with the empty suitcase under the bed.

She went inside and gave her daughter the news.

Ya es hora de irnos.

The hour has come for us to go.

For more about the women leaving Palomas and Hull's comments about writing long pieces see **Una Vida Mejor—A Better Life** in *NRW Plus*.

Investigative Series

Some series are so complex that their writers have trouble putting the material in focus, an essential step before a lead can be written.

When Donald Barlett and James Steele investigated a new federal tax law that exempted many rich individuals and a number of large corporations, they found they had seven themes, one for each piece in the series. They then started to write. But as they moved along they had trouble distilling some of the pieces into leads.

Rather than stop their writing, they continued with the series. They would write the leads later.

Their editor, Steve Lovelady, was looking over the third of the articles, soon to appear in *The Philadelphia Inquirer*.

"What does this mean to the average reader?" he asked himself. And he answered—"That you'll never get a break"—unlike the well-connected taxpayers the reporters had uncovered.

Reaching into the Past for a Feature

Features based on historical material in libraries and letters make for good reading, especially if there are interesting photographs to accompany the article. This photograph of a homestead in Wyoming reveals a lot about the roles of men and women on the frontier. The head of the household is seated comfortably at the center, and around him the women are shown with the tools of their work. One poses with her spinning wheel, and grandma is shown knitting. To the man's left a young woman poses with the butter churn, and to her left a mother fans a child in her lap.

Lovelady showed Barlett what he had scribbled on an envelope, and Barlett said, "Forget part three, this is now part one."

Barlett and Steele worked it over, polished it. Here is the lead for the series they came up with:

Imagine, if you will, that you are a tall, bald father of three living in a Northeast Philadelphia row house and selling aluminum siding door-to-door for a living. Imagine that you go to your congressman and ask him to insert a provision in the federal tax code that exempts tall, bald fathers of three from paying taxes on income from door-to-door sales. Imagine further that your congressman cooperates, writes that exemption and inserts it into pending legislation. And that Congress then actually passes it into law. Lots of luck.

Long. Very long. The reader is directly addressed twice in the first few words. But it works. The series had an enormous readership, and the newspaper was swamped with requests for copies. The series led to changes in the law.

Summing Up

The feature, long story and series join the direct or hard news story as the staples of journalistic writing. Despite criticism of the longer forms, if they are interesting, clear, well-organized and written with vigor they are read. The *Inquirer*'s lengthy tax series was read. Avidly. The *Oregonian* in Portland picked it up from the Knight-Ridder News Service. John Harvey, the *Oregonian*'s news editor, said:

> Your series touched off the greatest response of any series I have ever run in the *Oregonian*. Our readers were outraged. Were a certain senator on the ballot this year I doubt he could be reelected. Congratulations on a first-class job of reporting.

The book from the series became a big seller.

Further Reading

Buchwald, Art. *You Can Fool All of the People All the Time.* New York: Putnam, 1985.

Halberstam, David. *The Powers That Be.* New York: Knopf, 1979.

Mitchell, Joseph. *McSorley's Wonderful Saloon.* New York: Grosset & Dunlap, 1943.

Moffitt, Donald, ed. *The American Character: Views of America from* The Wall Street Journal. New York: George Brogiller, 1983.

Nasaw, David. *The Chief: The Life of William Randolph Hearst.* New York: Houghton Mifflin Co., 2000.

Swanberg, W. A. *Pulitzer.* New York: Scribner, 1967.

Note: Ben Hecht's book of the rough-and-tumble Chicago journalism period, *Gaily, Gaily,* is no longer in print, but copies can be found in libraries. It was published by Doubleday in 1963. Also hard to locate is *The Front Page,* a play about the same period written by Hecht and Charles MacArthur.

9 Broadcast Newswriting

Frank Woodruff, *Press & Sun-Bulletin*

**Teen-age runaway—subject
for a documentary.**

Preview

Broadcast stories are written to be easily understood. Radio and television writers:

- Use everyday language.
- Write short sentences.
- Limit every sentence to one idea.
- Use the present tense whenever appropriate.
- Usually confine their stories to one major theme.

In addition to writing local stories, broadcast writers rewrite into broadcast form the stories they obtain from news wires. The material is compressed, sentences are shortened and tenses are changed.

Television journalists must cope with a technology that emphasizes the image. What is written and how it is written often depends on the available video.

Broadcast news is written to be read aloud by newscasters and to be heard or seen by listeners or viewers. Stories are written according to rules different from those for print journalism.

Watch the evening news, stopwatch in hand. Most of the *tell* stories on television—brief items read by an anchor without tape—run two to five sentences for 10 to 30 seconds. Few broadcast stories run more than 90 seconds. If all the news on a half-hour newscast were to be printed, it would not fill two-thirds of a page of a standard-size newspaper.

Broadcast news serves a purpose different from that of the newspaper. Its intent is to provide the public with basic information quickly and succinctly. The broadcast writer's job is to get the story idea across without detail. To communicate events in such short bursts to an audience that cannot read or hear the material again, the broadcast journalist follows a special set of guidelines.

Like the jockey or the weight watcher who thinks twice about every slice of bread, the broadcast journalist examines every word and idea. Too many words and the story may squeeze out another item. Too many ideas and the listener or viewer may be confused.

Broadcast newswriters set their writing rhythm to a few guidelines: Keep it tight. Write simple sentences. One idea to a sentence. When attribution is necessary, begin the sentence with it.

An Early Guide

When the United Press hired reporters they were handed a green booklet about the size of a small greeting card. It was titled *United Press Radio News Style Book* and was written by Phil Newsom, the UP Radio News Manager.

Though more than 50 years old, and written before the days of television, Newsom's advice holds up today. Here are some of Newsom's guidelines:

> To write effectively for radio you must unlearn the prose writer's rules about sentence structure. Disregard such forms as dependent clauses and balanced sentences. You can even forget the first grammatical rule you ever learned—that a sentence must have a subject and a verb.
>
> Some of radio's most effective sentences are not complete sentences at all. They are descriptive phrases. They save a lot of words and go over very smoothly on the air.
>
> Ordinarily, short sentences are the best for radio. But the real test is whether they can be read aloud, whether the announcer finally can arrive at the end without gasping for breath.
>
> Don't try to tell too much in your opening sentence. The radio listener requires a little time to get adjusted after each story. We call it "warming up the listener."
>
> Never lead into a story with a question. The similarity between such leads and commercials is apt to be confusing.
>
> There has always been a rule in radio news reporting against hanging phrases, since they break up the flow of thought. For example, a newspaper lead might say:
>
> "Fourteen persons were killed today in an explosion at King's Powder Mill, state police announced."
>
> The radio news report would say:
>
> "State Police announce that 14 persons have been killed in an explosion at the King's Powder Mill."

These days we would not have the state police "announce" the 14 deaths. If it's an established fact, we would not even have to attribute the deaths.

Newsome suggests that broadcast writers study their notes for the "most interest-compelling angle" and use it for the lead. He goes on to advise writers to emphasize the aspects of the event that affect people personally. Stories written with people in mind hold their attention, he says.

Rewriting the Wires

Most of radio's nonlocal news is rewritten from the news wires. The wire stories are condensed and simplified. On television, most of the brief items—the *tell* stories—are also taken from the wires and rewritten. Let's see how this is done.

News Wire

SAN FRANCISCO (AP)—Leaders of the University of California on Thursday voted to drop race-based admissions following a tumultuous meeting in which Jesse Jackson and other demonstrators drove the panel from its meeting room.

The 14–10 decision by the UC Board of Regents was a major victory for those working to roll back affirmative action programs around the nation, including Republican Gov. Pete Wilson, who has made that fight the key plank of his presidential campaign.

"It means the beginning of the end of racial preferences," said Wilson, who grabbed the national spotlight from his vantage point as president of the regents. "We believe that students at the University of California should achieve distinction without the use of the kind of preferences that have been in place."

Jackson said after the vote, "California casts either a long shadow or a long sunbeam. This is a long shadow. July 20 will live a long time in California history."

(Ten more paragraphs follow.)

Radio Wire

[San Francisco]—The University of California Board of Regents voted tonight to end race-based preferences in school admissions.

The vote came soon after demonstrators interrupted the regents' meeting, singing "We Shall Overcome." The regents were forced to another room to vote on the admissions policy.

Earlier tonight, the regents voted to eliminate the school's affirmative action-based policies on the hiring of faculty and contractors.

Nixon Library   Let's watch Mervin Block rewrite a wire story for a 20-second tell story for network television news. Here is the wire copy Block had before him:

News Wire

Yorba Linda, Calif [AP]—Construction of the long-delayed Richard M. Nixon presidential library and museum will require the demolition of the home of a 93-year-old widow who doesn't want to move, officials say.

"I love my house. I don't want them to take it from me," said Edith Eichler, who knew Nixon as a boy here and supported him for president.

"Why should I have to move into a more crowded, dinky retirement place away from my family and friends? Do you think Richard Nixon would want his mother to move?"

Yorba Linda, Nixon's birthplace 30 miles southeast of Los Angeles, was chosen for the $25 million library last month after a nine-year search. Years of delays by San Clemente city officials forced Nixon to give up building the library in that coastal community, where he kept the western White House during his presidency.

At a news conference Monday night, city officials said they would appraise Eichler's one-story, wood-frame cottage within a month and make her an offer.

Eichler, a former schoolteacher who has lived in the house for 65 years, will be the only person displaced by the museum.

Eichler said she knew the Nixon family well.

"Richard was a nice enough little boy, always running around like any other kid. Who would believe he would become a president?

"And who would ever imagine they'd want to build this big library for him right in my own back yard?" she asked.

Here is Block's story:

Broadcast Version

They're putting up a library for former President Nixon near Los Angeles, but they say they first have to tear down the home of a 93-year-old widow. She says she loves her home and does not want to move. Officials of the city of Yorba Linda say they'll appraise her wood-frame cottage and make her an offer. The woman says she knew Nixon as a boy and supported him for president.

Here is how Block, now a broadcast writing coach, thought the story through:

I tell news writers, "Avoid premature pronouns." Yet I started my script with "they." Why? Although I refrain from starting a story with a pronoun, I know that in conversation we often start tidbits with "they." F'rinstance: "They say onions and garlic are good for you—but not for your companions."

I certainly don't want to start with a yawner: "Officials in Yorba Linda, California. . . ." In the first sentence, I want to mention *Nixon, library* and *L.A.*, but I don't see how I can sensibly start with any of them. So I turn to our old friend "they." I make it clear that it's "they" who say the home must be torn down.

I don't use the widow's name because it doesn't mean anything outside Yorba Linda. I defer mentioning the name of the town, because it's not widely known. I save words wherever I can: I don't call it a *presidential* library; what other kind would they put up for a former president? And I'm just as stingy with facts: I don't mention San Clemente, the western White House, the widow's background and other details in the wire copy.

"Newsbreak"

"Newsbreak" runs on the CBS television network several times a day. In less than a minute, several major stories are read. One day, Block compressed seven wire stories into 50 seconds. Here are three items from the script and his explanation of how he wrote them:

Script	Explanation
A former employee of the Westchester Stauffer's Inn, near New York City,	Rather than start a story with a place name, "In White Plains, New York," I always try to fix the place up high but unobtrusively. In

was arrested today and charged with setting the fire that killed 26 corporate executives last December.

The government's index of leading economic indicators last month rose slightly, one-point-four percent. The increase reversed three straight months of declines.

A British truck driver admitted today he was the "Yorkshire Ripper," pleading guilty to manslaughter in the deaths of 13 women. By not pleading guilty to murder, Peter Sutcliffe could be sent to a hospital for the criminally insane— and not prison.

the fourth line, I wrote "outside," then realized that "near" is closer and shorter. I didn't use his name because he was an unknown and his name wouldn't mean anything to anyone outside White Plains, which is largely unknown itself except as the site of a Revolutionary battle.

To save words, I didn't say the U.S. Department of Commerce issued the statistics. It's sufficient to say "the government." I originally wrote, "rose slightly last month." Then I caught myself, remembering Strunk's rule to "place the emphatic words of a sentence at the end."

This is a simple, straightforward, no-frills account of a dramatic development in a sensational story. But there's no need here for any supercharged language to "sell" the story. (As the architect Ludwig Mies van der Rohe used to say, "Less is more.") My second sentence gives the "why" for his plea. I underlined "murder" because I thought it was a word the anchor should stress. (Some anchors welcome this. In any case, in the pressure-cooker atmosphere of a network newsroom, the stress is usually on the writer.)

Voice-Over Videotape

Television writing is complicated by the need to write to visuals. Block was told to write a lead-in and 20 seconds of voice-over videotape for the "CBS Evening News" from this wire service story:

CRESTVIEW, Fla. [AP]—Tank cars carrying acetone exploded and burned when a train loaded with hazardous chemicals derailed here today. Thousands were evacuated as the wind spread thick yellow sulfur fumes over rural northwest Florida.

Only one injury was reported. A fisherman trekking through the woods near the wreck inhaled some of the fumes and was hospitalized for observation.

Oskaloosa County Civil Defense director Tom Nichols estimated that 5,000 people had fled homes or campsites in the 30-square-mile evacuation area, which included several villages and about half of Blackwater River State Forest.

"It's a rural area and houses are scattered all through it," said Ray Belcher, a supervisor for the Florida Highway Patrol. "It's about half woods, half farms."

Civil Defense officials put the approximately 9,000 residents of nearby Crestview on alert for possible evacuation as approaching thunderstorms threatened a wind-shift that would push the fumes in that direction. . . .

Block was writing "blind" in the tape. That is, he did not have access to the videotape his copy would refer to. Here is Block's thinking:

> First, I see the dateline, Crestview, Fla., and I know that in writing for broadcast I have to put the dateline up near the top as unintrusively as possible. It has to be done deftly.
>
> When I started writing for broadcast, I was told by an editor that it's inadvisable to begin a story by saying, "In Crestview, Florida. . . ." The editor told me that was a lazy man's way of starting a story. In London today . . . in Paris today. . . . He didn't say never. But in 90 or 95 percent of the cases, it's best not to begin that way.
>
> We see in the first line of the AP story that one of the trains is carrying acetone. My reaction is that most people don't know what acetone is. That probably is a reflection of my ignorance. If we were to use it on the air, it could sound like acid-own. In any case, there's no need to identify the chemical, or any of the chemicals, perhaps. The most important element is the explosion and the evacuation.
>
> In the second paragraph of the story, it says that only one injury was reported. I didn't mention the injury. It seems slight. The third paragraph gives the name of the county. In writing news for broadcast, you have to eliminate details and focus on the big picture.
>
> In my script, beginning with the second paragraph, I had to write 20 seconds of voice-over. As so often happens, I had no chance to see the videotape in advance, so I had to write in a general way without getting specific. I made an assumption at this point, and although it's dangerous to assume, I have seen so many derailments on TV films or tape that I figured the opening shot would be of derailed cars. So I presumed my paragraph covering the tape of the accident would be appropriate.
>
> I was looking for facts in the AP story that would be essential in my script. As you can see, my script consists of about a five-second lead-in and 20 seconds of voice-over for the tape. Within the tight space, I can use only the most important facts because a script cannot consist of a string of dense facts.

Rewrite. Looking over his handiwork later, Block regretted burying a good verb in a noun. He should have made it: "A tank car exploded in the Florida Panhandle today and caused the evacuation of about five thousand people from their homes."

Here is the script as Block wrote it:

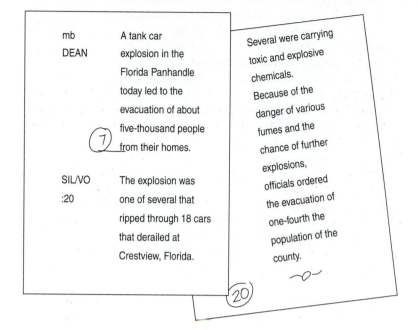

```
mb              A tank car
DEAN            explosion in the
                Florida Panhandle
                today led to the
                evacuation of about
           ⑦    five-thousand people
                from their homes.

SIL/VO          The explosion was
:20             one of several that
                ripped through 18 cars
                that derailed at
                Crestview, Florida.

                Several were carrying
                toxic and explosive
                chemicals.
                Because of the
                danger of various
                fumes and the
                chance of further
                explosions,
                officials ordered
                the evacuation of
                one-fourth the
                population of the
                county.
                          ⑳
```

Sentence Structure and Language

From our window into the thinking of a broadcast newswriter, we can generalize about writing for the ear.

Write short, simple sentences. Use everyday language. Make most sentences conform to the S-V-O structure (subject-verb-object). Keep one idea to a sentence. Here are some other guidelines and examples:

- **Begin sentences with a source, with the attribution, if needed:**
  WRONG: The city needs new traffic lights, the mayor said.
  RIGHT: The mayor says the city needs new traffic lights.
- **Avoid starting a story with a participial phrase or a dependent clause:**
  WRONG: Hoping to keep the lid on spiraling prices, the president called today for wage-price guidelines for labor and industry. (Participial phrase.)
  RIGHT: The president is calling for wage-price guidelines to keep prices down.
  WRONG: When the bill was passed, he was absent. (Dependent clause.)
  RIGHT: He was absent when the bill was passed.
- **Use ordinary, one-syllable words whenever possible:**
  WRONG: The unprecedented increase in profits led the Congress to urge the plan's discontinuance.
  RIGHT: The record profits led Congress to urge an end to the plan.

Who Is She? A feature about a mail carrier who found a puppy inside a mail box ends:

She took the terrier-mix puppy to the humane society.
She's being treated for dehydration and parasites but is expected to be just fine.

- **Use vigorous verbs.** Avoid adjectives and adverbs:
  WEAK: He made the task easy for his listeners.
  BETTER: He simplified the task for his listeners.
  WEAK: She walked slowly through the field.
  BETTER: She trudged through the field.
- **Use the active, not the passive, voice:**
  WEAK: He was shown the document by the lawyer.
  BETTER: The lawyer showed him the document.
- **Use familiar words in familiar combinations.**
- **Write simply, directly.** Omit useless words.
- **Write in language that can be read easily.** The writer should test his or her writing by reading it aloud. Not only will the reading catch sounds that do not work, it will reveal whether a newscaster can read one idea in a single pulse. The newscaster must be able to breathe, and each breath closes out an idea.

Simple, direct writing can be elegant. This is the language of Mark Twain, Charles Dickens, and Edward R. Murrow. Here is a lead by Charles Kuralt, a correspondent for CBS television who was doing a piece about exploitation of the environment:

Men look at hillsides and see board feet of lumber. Men look at valleys and see homesites.

- **Use a phrase to indicate someone is being quoted:** as he said, as he put it, and these are his words. For routine quotes, paraphrase.
  WEAK: He said, "I am not a crook."
  BETTER: He said, and these are his words, "I am not a crook."
- **Place titles before names.** Spell out all numbers through 11. (Why 11? Because it resembles two 1's.) Do not use initials for agencies and organizations unless they are widely known, such as FBI and CIA. Use contractions for informality. Keep sentences to fewer than 20 words.

Tenses

The anchoring tense for broadcast copy is usually the present or the present perfect tense:

The state highway department **says** it will spend six million dollars this year improving farm-to-market roads.
The state highway department **has announced** it will spend six million dollars this year improving farm-to-market roads.

When the present tense is used in the lead, the story often continues in that tense. When the present perfect tense is used in the lead, the story shifts to the past tense to indicate when the event occurred:

A federal judge **has issued** a temporary order stopping efforts to put a reservist on active army duty because he refused to shave off his beard.

Yesterday, the judge **gave** the army ten days to answer a suit filed by the American Civil Liberties Union for the reservist.

Following the past tense, the story can shift back to the present perfect or even to the present tense if the writer believes the situation is still true or in effect. The AP radio story continues:

The ACLU **filed** the suit on behalf of a high school teacher, John Jones of Bristol, Rhode Island.

The suit **asks** the court to declare unconstitutional a regulation forbidding beards and **claims** the teacher was marked absent from several drills that the suit **says** he attended.

Attribution

Broadcast copy places attribution at the beginning of sentences. This makes for clarity.

News Wire

ALBUQUERQUE [AP]—The death of a man whose body was found set in 500 pounds of concrete in a 55-gallon drum may be connected to a counterfeiting case, a federal agent says.

"I believe there is a connection. We won't be 100 percent certain until we know if the guy is who we think he is," said David Saleeba, special agent in charge of the U.S. Secret Service office in Albuquerque. . . .

Broadcast Wire

(Albuquerque)—A federal agent says the death of a man whose body was found set in 500 pounds of concrete in a 55-gallon drum may be connected to a counterfeiting case. Albuquerque police and federal agents say they believe the body recovered is that of 21-year-old Derek Suchy.

More on Writing

Block conducts broadcast newswriting workshops around the country, scrutinizes news scripts and, in his columns for the *Communicator,* the monthly magazine of the Radio–Television News Directors, examines bloopers, blunders and questionable writing. "Too many of us think we're not only the messengers but also part of the message," he writes. For example:

Carrollton police tell us one person was injured during a car chase overnight.

Sometimes, the broadcast writer will introduce the station into copy, or the media, as this Nebraska news writer did:

It was a full-fledged media event that brought every TV station in the state to northwest Nebraska today.

"The media are not the story," says Block. "The *story* is the story."

In one of his columns, Block culled these sentences from clips. Look at the words in italics:

- The attorney for defendant Henry Watson *dropped a bombshell* in his closing argument.
- City officials and union leaders have been *burning the midnight oil.*
- The workers were *visibly shaken* but not hurt.
- Lopez was sitting with friends on a courtyard bench at the Marlboro Houses in Coney Island when *shots rang out* Sunday.

Yes, you are right. They are clichés, the "language of newspeople churning out copy in a race against the clock," Block says. And he goes on to quote George Orwell's warning to writers: "Never use a metaphor, simile or other figure of speech you are used to seeing in print."

The Lead

Some events are too complex to plunge into immediately. Or there may be a confusing array of personalities or numbers. The listener then has to be set up for the theme of the piece.

Newspaper Lead

As Gov. Alfred Caster neared the end of his seven-day working vacation aboard a riverboat today, his aides said that he was unconcerned about some editorial criticism that he had become an absentee governor whose administration was adrift.

Broadcast Lead

Some newspaper editorials have criticized Governor Caster as an absentee governor. But officials aboard a riverboat with the governor say that the criticisms don't bother him. The governor is nearing the end of his seven-day working vacation on the boat.

Broadcast Reporting

Let's look at how broadcast reporters work. First, we go to an all-news radio station.

Each evening, the news director makes up an assignment sheet for reporters for the next day. The editor goes through the futures file, notes continuing stories and consults the wire services' schedules of stories. About 6 A.M., reporters begin to check with the editor for their assignments.

In the field, the reporters, who carry tape recorders, may each cover three or four stories—a feature, a running story from city hall, a talk by a congressman and a traffic accident that tied up a major artery. For each, the reporter phones the editor, who decides whether the reporter should go on live or be recorded.

If the reporter is to go on live, the editor places the reporter on a newscast. If recorded, the reporter talks to an aide, who makes sure the material is being recorded properly by an engineer. The recording, called a *cart* (for *cartridge*), is labeled by slug and time and given to the editor.

Radio reporters cannot rely on pictures, so they supply much of the descriptive material for their stories. Sound bites from their interviews are essential to give the listener a sense of immediacy and participation. The radio reporter develops a keen ear for the high-quality quote, the quotation that sums up the situation. The rest is ruthlessly discarded.

One of the most important tasks of the broadcast journalist is to ask relevant questions. Good interviews are made by the right questions.

As tape can be edited, the reporter can ask a question again if the answer is too long or complicated.

Television journalism involves a more complicated technology than print or radio. The TV reporter is always conscious of the need for a picture, for action of some sort. If the reporter is to be on air, the prevailing wisdom has it, she or he should be speaking over action.

Newsreaders. "Most local television stations hire readers, not journalists or newspeople. Local anchors are hired for their personalities or their looks, good hair, for instance. . . . They should be called newsreaders, as they are in Europe."
—*Walter Cronkite*

Reporting and Writing to Tape

The feature or timeless piece may include an interview, voice-over silent tape, or tape with sound of an event and the reporter's summarizing the event. The story may take days of planning and hours of shooting, editing and writing, and then when it is finally broadcast it may run for only a minute and a half.

For a story on a new reading program in the city schools, an interview with the superintendent of schools may set out the intent of the curriculum change. Additional interviews will allow viewers to hear the specific plans of teachers. School children will be interviewed. Locations might include classrooms, teachers discussing the program, the superintendent in his office.

The producer will want a variety of shots—medium, close-up and cutaway—to build a picture story to accompany the reporter's narration and interviews.

Stories for newspapers usually follow a straight-line form—most important material at the beginning, least important at the end. But for longer broadcast pieces, the form is a circle because the ending usually has a reminder of the theme.

The reporter's task is to marry natural sound, visuals and interviews. Sometimes the reporter muffs the opportunity. In a piece about a cloistered order of nuns who vow perpetual silence, the reporter wrote a narration with no pauses. He wrote about silence but never stopped talking. In effect, the viewer could not hear the silence. The event would have been captured had he stopped talking in some places, a few seconds at a time, to allow viewers to hear the clatter of knives and forks at a silent dinner, the footsteps of nuns in darkened hallways. The tone of the story should match the event.

Blunt Writing

The news all week had been grim. The World Trade Center ruins were still smoldering, and there was little hope of any one of the thousands missing being found alive. The intro for the weekend edition of ABC's *World News Tonight* reflected the state of affairs.

```
the president prepares the country
for a war, he says, unlike any we
have fought. a sixth grueling day of
digging and searching in the world
trade center rubble, and at the
pentagon. the victims of  tuesday's
terrorist attacks are remembered in
services near and far.
```

For more of the script prepared for the program, see **Terror Folo,** in *NRW Plus.*

Top Tips of the Trade

1. Start strong. Well begun is half done.
2. Read—and understand—your source copy.
3. Underline or circle key facts.
4. Think. Don't write yet. Think.
5. Write the way you talk.
6. Apply the rules for broadcast newswriting.
7. Have the courage to write simply.
8. Refrain from wordy warm-ups.
9. Put attribution before assertion.
10. Go with S-V-O: subject-verb-object.
11. Limit a sentence to one idea.
12. Use short words and short sentences.
13. Use familiar words in familiar combinations.
14. Humanize your copy. And localize it.
15. Activate your copy: use active voice—and action verbs.
16. Avoid a first sentence whose main verb is any form of *to be: is, are, was, were, will be.*
17. Avoid *may, could, seems.*
18. Put your sentences in a positive form.
19. Use present tense verbs where appropriate.
20. Don't start with a quotation or a question.
21. Use connectives—*and, also, but, so, because*—to link sentences.
22. Put the word or words you want to stress at the end of your sentence.
23. Use contractions—with caution.
24. Pep up your copy with words like *new, now, but, says.*
25. Watch out for *I, we, our, here, up, down.*
26. Omit needless words.
27. Hit only the highlights.
28. Don't parrot source copy.
29. Place the time element, if you need one, *after* the verb.
30. When in doubt, leave it out.
31. Don't raise questions you don't answer.
32. Read your copy aloud. If it sounds like writing, rewrite it. The art of writing lies in rewriting what you've already rewritten.

Adapted from Block, Mervin, *Writing Broadcast News—Shorter, Sharper, Stronger,* 2nd ed. (Chicago: Bonus Books, 1998)

Packaging Short News Features

Let's watch a television news student, Cathy, as she puts together a news feature. The story is about a program designed to prevent children from committing crimes when they grow up. Cathy has an interview with the psychologist who developed the program. She also has videotaped the children in the program as they talk to the psychologist and play. Cathy has interviewed the children for their reactions to the program.

After her reporting, Cathy has 40 minutes of tape. On her way back to the station Cathy starts blocking out her story:

I'll tell the editor to start with pictures of the children in a circle for 20 seconds while in my script I'll give some facts about the project.

Then a 20-to-30-second sound bite from the psychologist explaining the "substitute family" technique. As he talks about the substitute parents, the editor will show pictures of the children and parents greeting one another affectionately.

Then I'll write a short transition into the interviews. I think that to get into this section I'll pose the question, "But does the program work?" and have three or four short interviews with the answers.

She'll close with a quote from the psychologist and then her own wrap-up from the scene to answer questions she thinks have been left unanswered. She estimates the feature will run from 2:30 to 2:45, just what the producer wants.

Interviewing

Much of what Cathy did was the result of planning. For her interviews, she devised questions that sought to get to the heart of the story quickly. Interviews have to be kept short, to the point. This requires gentle but firm direction by the reporter. Here are some interviewing guidelines:

1. Don't ask questions that can be answered yes or no.
2. Don't ask long, involved questions.
3. Don't suggest answers to interviewees.
4. Build on the subject's answers—don't ask questions just because you prepared them. Listen to his or her answers and ask questions about what he or she says.
5. Ask only one question at a time. Don't ask multiple questions.
6. Develop a sense of timing. Cut in if the subject starts to be repetitive or long-winded. Don't cut the subject off just when he or she is about to say something important.

7. Make the subject comfortable before shooting the interview.

a. Describe the general area your questions will cover, but don't tell the subject exactly what the questions will be. The first, spontaneous response to a question is often the truest.

b. Explain the setting—which mike the subject should speak into and so on. Tell him or her to look at *you* or other questioners—not the camera—unless he or she is going to show the audience how to do something that requires direct communication between speaker and audience.

c. Before the interview chat easily to dispel any nervousness. Show an interest in the subject's area so he or she will gain confidence.

d. Don't act like you know it all. *Prepare* so you *do* know enough and so that your subjects believe you understand what they say.

e. Know what you are looking for. Most short news items must be carefully focused because of time limits.

8. Try to stick to one topic.

9. Adjust the tone of the questions to the interviewee's experience. A politician may need to be pushed and asked direct questions.

Long Pieces

Most broadcast stories are short. The better stations give their staffs the time to do longer pieces and series. Public broadcasting stations have a commitment to long-form television, as do several commercial stations such as WCCO-TV (Minneapolis), WBRZ-TV (Baton Rouge) and WSMV-TV (Nashville).

WSMV-TV has won many awards for its in-depth pieces. One of its prizewinning series was "A Matter of Taste." It was a penetrating examination of whether Tennessee was losing its natural beauty to development.

"Visual Chaos"

"When we started brainstorming about the series, the first location that came to mind was Pigeon Forge," says Don Heider, the writer for the WSMV-TV series. "This community had seen a remarkable amount of development in a short time, primarily due to its strategic location as an entry way to the Smoky Mountains. It was obvious this was a place where there had been unchecked development."

Heider needed someone to express those concerns, and he thought an artist would see the situation from a visual perspective. He also needed someone who would speak in support of the path the town took to its newfound prosperity. The Pigeon Forge Chamber of Commerce supplied some names. He also found an architect who was with a group pushing for stronger sign laws in the state.

"Key to the success of the piece," says Heider, "was a lot of set-up time on the front end, interviewing a number of people over the phone until I knew I had the right people to tell the story, and also ensuring that we had strong visuals.

Disappearing Viewers. About half of TV viewers look at local news, a steep decline from a decade ago. A survey of viewers found why: the same stories are covered over and over; there's not enough reporting on the real issues people need to know about; stations should show more respect for viewers' intelligence. The local news diet of accidents, fires and crime—cheap and easy to produce—doesn't mean much to most viewers' lives. Too much style; not enough substance.

"Also essential was good communication between myself and the photojournalist." They discussed ideas before Heider made his first calls, and the discussion continued throughout the planning and shooting. "We were still talking about what the story should say and look like when we edited it."

Here is the beginning of Heider's script:

SLUG ANCHOR WRITER WSMV-TX NEWS STATUS TIME
TACKY #1   HEIDER MON JUL 25 09:02 READY 4:54

NAT SOUND

SOUNDBITE 4/10:43 LEE ROBERSON/ARTIST [I SUPPOSE MOST PEOPLE WHO LIVE HERE KIND OF TAKE IT FOR GRANTED BUT I NEVER REALLY HAVE. I'M HERE BY CHOICE. I LIVE ADJACENT TO THE SMOKY MOUNTAINS NATIONAL PARK AND THAT'S BECAUSE I WANTED TO, IT'S **JUST NOT** SOMETHING THAT HAPPENED.]

NESTLED AWAY IN A SMALL COVE NEXT TO THE SMOKIES LIVES LEE ROBERSON.

SOUNDBITE 4/11:53 LEE [THESE MOUNTAINS ARE LIVEABLE AND THEY'RE HOSPITABLE AND THEY'RE COMFORTABLE, THEY KIND OF WELCOME YOU.]

LEE IS AN ARTIST. HE DRAWS HIS INSPIRATION FROM THIS LAND WHERE HE WAS RAISED.

SOUNDBITE 4/12:24 LEE [MY GRANDPARENTS LIVED IN CADE'S COVE.]

WHERE LEE LIVES, IT'S PEACEFUL . . . QUIET . . . RESTFUL. BUT JUST A FEW MILES AWAY, THINGS ARE DIFFERENT.

NAT SOUND—PIGEON FORGE

SOUNDBITE 2/13:34 LEON DOWNEY/PIGEON FORGE [IT IS A BOOM TOWN, SURE, AND IT HAS BEEN A BOOM TOWN FOR THE PAST SEVERAL YEARS.]

IT'S TENNESSEE'S NEWEST MECCA FOR TOURISM. PIGEON FORGE.

NAT SOUND

PIGEON FORGE IS A PUTT-PUTT PARADISE. A GO-CART KINGDOM. A UTOPIA FOR ANYONE UNDER THE AGE OF 15.

SOUNDBITE 2/17:27 DOWNEY [WHEN A FAMILY COMES IN HERE WITH A CARLOAD OF CHILDREN, WITH ONE OR TWO CHILDREN OR WHATEVER, THEIR HEADS ARE ON A SWIVEL AS SOON AS THEY GET HERE. THEY JUST CAN'T BELIEVE ALL THE FUN THINGS THERE ARE TO DO IN PIGEON FORGE. IT'S SORTA LIKE MYRTLE BEACH IN THE MOUNTAINS.]

THIS IS A COMMUNITY DESIGNED AROUND THE NEEDS AND WANTS OF CHILDREN. CHILDREN WHO CAN TALK THEIR PARENTS INTO SPENDING MONEY.

PIGEON FORGE WAS A GROWING TOURIST TOWN UNTIL 1986. THAT WAS THE YEAR DOLLY PARTON CAME BACK TO EAST TENNESSEE. SHE CONVERTED AN OLD AMUSEMENT PARK INTO DOLLYWOOD. THE PARK AND THE TOWN TOOK OFF.

NAT SOUND

IN JUST A YEAR DOLLYWOOD DOUBLED ITS ATTENDANCE. IN 1987, THE YEAR AFTER DOLLYWOOD OPENED, COMMERCIAL CONSTRUCTION IN PIGEON FORGE QUADRUPLED.

PIGEON FORGE ISN'T JUST A TOURIST TOWN NOW. IT'S A PHENOMENON. DEVELOPMENT HAS BEEN GOOD FOR BUSINESS. BUT DEVELOPMENT ALSO THREATENS SOMETHING HERE.

SOUNDBITE 4/17:04 ROBERSON [WHILE THERE'S NOTHING WRONG WITH PROVIDING ACCOMMODATIONS AND ENTERTAINMENT AND THE VARIOUS THINGS PEOPLE ARE LOOKING FOR I GUESS WHAT WE'RE A LITTLE CONCERNED ABOUT IS THAT WE MIGHT LOSE SIGHT OF WHY THEY COME HERE. NOW IF WE ALLOW WHY THEY CAME HERE AND COME HERE TO BE DESTROYED, WE ALL LOSE.]

PIGEON FORGE GOT ITS START AS THE GATEWAY TO THE SMOKIES. A STOPOVER POINT AS YOU ENTERED ONE OF THE SOUTH'S MOST SPECTACULAR NATURAL WONDERS.

BUT NOW AS YOU DRIVE THROUGH PIGEON FORGE YOU CAN BARELY SEE THE SMOKIES. THE VIEW IS BLOCKED BY SIGN AFTER SIGN.

SOUNDBITE BURR/5:14 EUGENE BURR/ARCHITECT-PLANNER [IT'S ESSENTIALLY A VISUAL CHAOS.]

EUGENE BURR IS A KNOXVILLE ARCHITECT AND PLANNER WHO HAS ALSO NOTICED SOME OF PIGEON FORGE'S GROWTH PROBLEMS.

SOUNDBITE BURR/2:56 BURR [YOU DON'T HAVE A SENSE OF CITY WHEN YOU ENTER PIGEON FORGE, THERE'S THIS WALL OF GARISH ADVERTISING WHERE EACH BUSINESS IS TRYING TO COMPETE WITH THE NEXT.]

BURR BELIEVES IF THE CITY DOESN'T TAKE STEPS TO IMPROVE ITSELF, ITS GROWTH MAY NOT LAST LONG.

Pregnant 14-Year-Old

Carolyn Mungo, a reporter for KPNX in Phoenix, noticed a crumpled piece of paper on her husband's dresser. It was a note from one of his eighth grade students:

Dear Mr. Niezgoda, I just got back from the hospital after being treated for an overdose. I also found I am 2 months pregnet. Well gotta go. Angie.

Mungo knew that Arizona has one of the highest rates of births to teens in the nation. "It was convinced this was a story viewers would connect with," she says.

"I knew that I could connect with this 14-year-old and eventually be able to carry the process through."

The process was a seven-month story on local news that followed Angie through her pregnancy to her child's birth. It was done, Mungo says, by working around her regular daily assignments. She and her photographer managed to follow Angie at school, after school, and in one sequence they watched as she tried to persuade the father of her child to stay off drugs.

"During this narrative piece, I told Angie's story but I also told the story of what happens to so many young girls who find themselves in a situation like hers," Mungo says.

Angie decided to raise the child, though she had no idea of how to support herself and the baby. "I don't know where the diapers are going to come from," she said on camera. "I had to use a washrag this morning."

Shifting Emphasis

More stations and the networks are blending the day's headlines with features and theme stories.

Juvenile Crime

"The CBS Evening News" began one of its in-depth pieces this way:

RATHER: In the streets of America, those domestic priorities include what to do about the plague of violent crime by the young against the young. Dallas today became the latest city to turn to one increasingly popular and controversial solution. Scott Pelley has a report.

SCOTT PELLEY: Each night the body count grows—American teen-agers victims of gangs, drugs and violence. It is a deadly trend that is prompting a growing number of cities to impose curfews on youth.

AL LIPSCOMB (Dallas city councilman): The figures are astoundin' on young people—the killin', the maimin'.

PELLEY: Dallas City Councilman Al Lipscomb is sponsoring a curfew measure.

LIPSCOMB: Since we cannot have any type of a curfew on parents, who cannot control their youth, we have to do the next best thing.

PELLEY: The proposal says kids under 17 must be home by 11, unless they work. Parents could be fined. Businesses that let kids in after the curfew face fines up to $2,000.

SARAH SLOBEN (dance-club manager): It's—it's solving a problem with a chain saw that needs to be dealt with with a scalpel.

PELLEY: Sarah Sloben manages a dance club for teenagers.

SLOBEN: It's an infringement of the rights of teen-agers. It's an unnecessary burden on business owners, and it's gonna tie up the police. The police are not baby-sitters. They're policemen.

Sexual Harassment

KTRH NewsRadio in Houston had cultivated sources in the Houston Police Department over the years of covering its activities. One of its sources told a KTRH reporter that women officers and other workers who complained of harassment suffered retaliation.

Stephen Dean investigated and verified the tip. Some women officers were transferred to desk jobs or to distant posts. Nothing was done to the officer against whom the complaint was filed.

Here's the lead-in to the first story:

Charges of retaliation and unfair treatment are raised by cops who claim they are victims of sexual harassment on the job. NewsRadio's Stephen Dean has the results of an exclusive KTRH investigation.

Dean then picks up the story:

Women who wear Houston police badges find themselves quickly transferred to desk jobs or cross-town assignments when they file sexual harassment complaints.

Some say they're treated harshly by supervisors and co-workers as the complaints are being processed.

Internal Affairs Sergeant Patsy Chapman filed a complaint against an office supervisor, saying he made repeated advances and stuck his tongue in her ear. When she turned him away, overtime requests she turned in for his approval suddenly disappeared. She was out $800 of pay.

So her last resort was a written complaint, and she says it caused her life to get even worse.

She was quickly transferred to another part of the city, while the supervisor was able to stay put in his job.

Attorney Cathy Butler is handling two cases of harassment in the department.

NewsRadio finds at least four cases within the past year where the victims claim they were forced to transfer after filing complaints.

And one female officer says she'd rather be touched all the time than go through the hassles in her new job.

Butler says if the department handled crime the way they handle sexual harassment, they wouldn't be catching many criminals.

Disappearing Songbirds

As cities expand into the countryside and as industry replaces forest and grassland, the environment changes. Pavement replaces grass, duplexes and factories rise where pine and birch once grew. KOTV in Tulsa wondered whether in this changing environment the songbird would be silenced.

Pervasive Prejudice

Public radio station KNAU-FM in Flagstaff, Ariz., used "real people and real voices," the judges said in awarding the station a prize for its documentary about persistent "tension and discrimination" in the cities bordering the Navajo and Hopi reservations. Producer Sandy Tolan (shown here) included a first-person narrative on what it's like to grow up Navajo in Flagstaff alongside the dominant white culture. His goal, he said, was to stimulate discussion of the issue.

KANU-FM photo

It embarked on a documentary, an "ecocampaign," the station called it, to alert viewers to the plight of grassland songbirds. One of the imperiled birds is the state bird, the scissortailed flycatcher. The reporting and filming took more than three months of arduous work.

"For those who've never noticed, once a songbird alights on a perch, it generally doesn't stay very long," says Scott Thompson, the reporter for the documentary. "We would spend hours in nearly inaccessible prairie draws and sloughs and desolate mesa plateaus, waiting for a chance encounter with a songbird or raptor."

The photographers shot vast amounts of videotape to be able to capture a few seconds of usable footage.

Result The public responded. KOTV distributed more than 12,000 viewer guides, and proceeds from the sale of videotapes went to a research center.

"Songs of the Prairie" is unusual for television, judges for Sigma Delta Chi's annual awards stated, although the subject "is just as important as it was when Rachel Carson published *Silent Spring*. The writing, photography were excellent, practically lyrical. The videography deserves special recognition."

The documentary won the Public Service Award.

A Dozen Deadly Don'ts

Thou shalt not:

1. Scare listeners.
2. Give orders.
3. Start a story with
   - "as expected."
   - "in a surprise move."
   - "a new development today."
   - "our top story tonight is."
   - *there is* or *it is.*
   - a participial phrase.
   - a personal pronoun.
   - a question.
   - a quotation.
   - an unknown or unfamiliar name.
   - someone's "making news" or "making history."
   - *another, more* or *once again.*
4. Characterize news as "good" or "bad."
5. Use any form of *to be* as the main verb in your lead.
6. Bury the verb in a noun.
7. Use *yesterday* or *continues* in your first sentence.
8. Use *no, not* and negatives in your first sentence.
9. Use newspaper style, language or rituals.
10. Cram too much information into a story.
11. Lose or mislead a listener.
12. Make a factual error.

Adapted from Block, Mervin, *Writing Broadcast News—Shorter, Sharper, Stronger,* 2nd ed. (Chicago: Bonus Books, 1998)

Copy Preparation

Copy is written to give the newscaster as much help as possible. The rules for copy preparation differ from station to station. Some require the slug in the upper left-hand corner and the time it takes to tell the story above it.

Copy for television is written on the right half of the page. The left half is kept open for technical instructions. Some stations also ask that radio copy be written this way, but most radio copy is written across the page.

A line of 45 to 50 characters will take four seconds to read. By keeping lines to the same length, it is easy to estimate the time it will take to read the story without the use of a stopwatch.

End each page with a full sentence. Better still: End on a paragraph. Do not leave the newscaster hanging in the middle of a sentence or an idea as he or she turns the page. Keep paragraphs short.

Each page should be slugged. For pieces running more than one page, each page should be numbered, and the writer's name or initials should appear on all pages.

Place the word *more,* circled, at the bottom of stories of more than one page, and use a clear, large-end mark—30, #, END—when finished.

Copy should be written in cap and lowercase. For television, visual directions should be written in all caps.

Telling the Whole Story

Little of what goes through the broadcast station's editing rooms reaches the public. Interviews are ruthlessly cut as editors search for the brief sound bite. Background material, if any, is compressed. Sometimes, the meaningful shades of gray that make the story complete don't make the broadcast, especially when they complicate the theme or story line.

Critics have accused broadcast journalists of allowing office holders and candidates to pass on to the public what one disparagingly described as "sound bites that were simply advertising."

A Conveyor Belt

People in public life have long considered broadcast news a more direct route to the citizen and a more congenial medium than print. Franklin D. Roosevelt was famous for his radio fireside chats in which he soothed a country mired in a deep depression. Dwight D. Eisenhower began the televised presidential news conference to reach the public directly, without the interpretations and possible criticism of the print press. Eisenhower used television, historian Stephen Ambrose wrote, to "set the national agenda" and also to "obfuscate an issue when he was not sure how he would deal with it."

Mario Cuomo of New York, when governor, told newspaper reporters, "Don't flatter yourselves into thinking you're the best way to reach the public.

"When I go to you, I don't reach the public directly; you do. When I go electronically, I reach the public. If I want to reach the public, I shouldn't be talking to you. I should be talking to a radio microphone."

Ethical Imperatives

Broadcast journalists are aware of attempts to use them as the conveyors of messages, and they are as careful of being exploited as are print journalists. Although broadcast journalists operate within tighter deadlines and are called on to be more concise than print journalists, they try to give fair, well-rounded and accurate accounts of events.

The TV camera has enormous power, and its users are conscious of this. When they were slow to arrive in Somalia, a CBS medical reporter said, hundreds of thousands of starving people died.

The Power of TV. In 1958, Edward Murrow said, "This instrument can teach, it can illuminate, yes, and it can even inspire. But, it can only do so to the extent that humans are determined to use it to those ends. Otherwise it is merely wires and lights in a box. There is a great and perhaps decisive battle to be fought against ignorance, intolerance and indifference. This weapon of television can be useful."

Today, the United States is the only Western nation without a network newscast in the prime-time evening hours.

A TV Newsman's Critique

The power of television to inform and influence the public worried Charles Kuralt, a veteran network reporter and writer. He thought too many stations follow the advice of news consultants who "would cut the Iliad or King Lear to 90 seconds." He was disturbed by the inadequate news training of the "earnest young man or woman" who opens the six o'clock news: "'Good evening, here is the news.' This is said very urgently and with the appearance of sincerity—most often by an attractive person who would not know a news story if it jumped up and mussed his or her coiffure."

In a talk at the University of Nevada-Reno, he told journalism students and their instructors:

> The real rewards—both in the giving and the receiving—are in the patient, hard work of the careful writer who seizes a fact or an event out of the air as it flashes past and hammers it like a blacksmith on his anvil, and tempers it, and dissatisfied, discards it and rekindles the fire in the forge, and comes back to it until at length it becomes a useful and pretty thing—and a bit of truth. Television news is papier-mâché. Real writing is wrought iron.

Local News: Mostly Crime

Studies of local news on TV stations show that they are the number one source of news for the public. But the studies also show that most of the news focuses on crime and little on social issues, education, race relations.

A study of local TV news by eight journalism schools found almost a third of news time went to crime and criminal justice stories, and a sixth to government and politics. Education averaged a miniscule one-fiftieth of news time. A study of 100 local TV newscasts by the Rocky Mountain Media Watch found crime took up 30 percent of newscast time.

Patricia Dean, head of broadcast journalism at Northwestern University, said, "What was surprising to me was what wasn't being reported at all, education and race relations especially." She said these were "very big issues" in the eight markets studied: Austin, Chicago, Indianapolis, New York, Syracuse, Eugene, Miami and Los Angeles.

An Exception In Austin, KVUE-TV instituted "community standards" guidelines for deciding whether to broadcast a story about a local crime. Under the direction of Carole Kent Kneeland, vice president for news, the station decided it would use a crime story if news executives could answer yes to questions such as: Is there an immediate threat to public safety? Is there a significant community impact? Do viewers need to take some kind of action?

The Reason. Marty Haag, senior news vice president for the A.H. Belo stations, says that "covering crime is the easiest, fastest, cheapest, most efficient kind of new coverage for TV stations. News directors and station owners love crime because it has a one-to-one ratio between making the assignment and getting a story on-air."

Austin was recorded in the study as devoting 5.7 percent of airtime to crime, whereas Indianapolis devoted 36.7 percent of airtime to the subject. KVUE has held the top ratings position for news in the Austin area for several years.

Kneeland influenced many stations. At KGUN9, the result was a "Viewers' Bill of Rights". For this ethical code, see **Appendix D** in *NRW Plus.*

Comments: Pluses and a Few Minuses

See Appendix D for the Code of Ethics of the Radio-Television News Directors Association.

Entertainment. "If people who listen to the news, and watch the news, become so conditioned by the frivolous treatment of news that they come to regard news primarily as entertainment, how can they really care about the news? Or really *think* about the news, think about what they see and hear in terms of meaning in their community, in their country, in their world?"
—*Edward Bliss, Jr.*

Values. "Most of the decisions made in television news are not about news; they're about money."
—*Andy Rooney, CBS*

Dan Rather, anchor, "CBS Evening News": The feel-good alleged news correspondents, the good-news pretenders are a dime a dozen and on every station. They're everywhere now. . . . One of the reasons, Dear Listener, is that not enough of you care, nor of us, those of us still in the craft, in the profession of what is supposed to be the public service of broadcast news.

Joan Barrett, KVUE-TV, Austin, Tex.: One of the first questions we ask at our morning meeting is, "What are people talking about today?" And then it's, "What do people need to know? What should they know? What do they want to know?" You know, producers play a key role in our shop. Yet we don't get many students who say "I want to be a producer." But they're the ones shaping the decisions in the newscasts for the most part.

Andrew Lack, president, NBC News: We are spawning a generation of reporters and news directors who no longer place any value on the written word, the turn of phrase, the uncut, long, hard question. All we care about are the almighty pictures, the video, the story count—and that it moves like a bat out of hell. We barely listen to what is said any more.

Tom Bettag, executive producer, "Nightline": I like to think of Nightline as a broadcast that attempts to illuminate the major issues of our time. They turn on Nightline to find out if there's something they need to know, if there's something people are going to be talking about in the morning. They aren't interested in being entertained. Nightline has its largest audiences when there is real news.

Kirk Winkler, KTVK-TV, Phoenix, Ariz.: The most important problem (among journalism students) is a simple lack of curiosity. One in ten students now graduating has enough of it to make it as a successful reporter. Also: They do not know how to report on deadline and some don't know what a city directory is and don't read a daily newspaper.

Walter Cronkite, "CBS Evening News" anchor and managing editor for 19 years: Some anchorpersons are inadequately educated and poorly trained. Their only qualifications seem to be pretty clothes and stylish hairdos—and this applies to both sexes. Too many are interested in becoming stars rather than journalists. They aren't interested in news except as it resembles show business. However, a talented generation of young people is coming out of journalism schools with the hearts and guts—and educational background—to be called journalists.

Summing Up

Preparation: Examine notes and all material for the broadcast to determine the key material. Highlight it. Know the time allotted for the segment you are writing. Decide on the lead.

Writing: Begin with the best. Make it short, to the point, interesting. Use S-V-O construction, present tense, familiar words and phrases.

Last-minute check: Read what you have written. If you sound too formal, stumble on a word or run out of breath, then rewrite.

Further Reading

Arlen, Michael J. *The Camera Age: Essays on Television.* New York: Farrar, Straus & Giroux, 1981.

Auletta, Ken. *Three Blind Mice: How the TV Networks Lost Their Way.* New York: Random House, 1991.

Bliss, Edward, Jr. *Now the News: The Story of Broadcasting.* New York: Columbia University Press, 1991.

Block, Mervin. *Writing Broadcast News—Shorter, Sharper, Stronger,* 2nd ed. Chicago: Bonus Books, 1998.

Block, Mervin. *Rewriting Network News: WorldWatching Tips from 345 TV and Radio Scripts.* Chicago: Bonus Books, 1990.

Block, Mervin. *Broadcast Newswriting: The RTNDA Reference Guide.* Chicago: Bonus Books, 1994.

Cloud, Stanley, and Lynne Olson. *The Murrow Boys: Pioneers on the Front Lines of Broadcast Journalism.* Boston: Houghton Mifflin, 1996.

Cronkite, Walter. *A Reporter's Life.* New York: Knopf, 1996.

Ellerbee, Linda. *And So It Goes: Adventures in Television.* New York: Putnam, 1986.

Hewitt, Don. *Minute by Minute.* New York: Random House, 1985. Hewitt is the executive producer of "60 Minutes."

Kimball, Penn. *Downsizing the News: Network Cutbacks in the Nation's Capital.* Washington: Woodrow Wilson Center Press; Baltimore: Johns Hopkins University Press, 1994.

Persico, Joseph E. *Edward R. Murrow: An American Original.* New York: McGraw-Hill, 1988.

Schonfeld, Reese. *Me and Ted Against the World: The Unauthorized Story of the Founding of CNN.* New York: HarperCollins, 2001. A quick-paced account of how entrepreneur Turner, who had no real interest in news, and Schonfeld, a veteran TV newsman, made what in its early days was called Chicken Noodly News into a major cable news service.

Schorr, Daniel. *Staying Tuned: A Life in Journalism.* New York: Pocket Books, 2001. From CBS, where he worked with Morrow, to CNN and PBS, Schorr has covered power in all its shades and voices.

Smith, Howard K. *Events Leading Up to My Death: The Life of a Twentieth Century Reporter.* New York: St. Martin's Press, 1996.

Smith, Sally Bedell. *In All His Glory: The Life of William S. Paley, the Legendary Tycoon and His Brilliant Circle.* New York: Simon & Schuster, 1990.

Sperber, Ann M. *Murrow: His Life and Times.* New York: Freundlich Books, 1986.

PART FOUR: Reporting Principles

Curt Hudson

Fatalities? Cause? Rescues?

Preview

The reporter's job is to gather information that helps people understand events that affect them. This digging takes the reporter through the three layers of reporting:

1. **Surface facts:** source-originated material—press releases, handouts, speeches.
2. **Reportorial enterprise:** verification, investigative reporting, coverage of spontaneous events, background.
3. **Interpretation and analysis:** significance, causes, consequences.

The reporter always tries to observe events. The reporter is alert to the media event, an action staged to attract media attention.

Verification, background checking, direct observation and enterprise reporting amplify and sometimes correct source-originated material.

Reporters are allowed to interpret events when appropriate.

The reporter is like the prospector digging and drilling the way to pay dirt. Neither is happy with the surface material, although sometimes impenetrable barriers or lack of time interfere with the search, and it is necessary to stop digging and to make do with what has been turned up. When possible, the reporter keeps digging until he or she gets to the bottom of things, until the journalistic equivalent of the mother lode—the truth of the event—is unearthed.

The reporter, like the prospector, has a feel for the terrain. This sensitivity—the reporter's street smarts or nose for news—helps unearth information for stories. Equally helpful is the reporter's general knowledge.

Let's watch a reporter for a Florida newspaper do some digging.

Finding the Lottery Winner

The word from Tallahassee was that the single winning ticket in the $5 million Florida lottery had been sold in Port St. Lucie. Sarah Jay, a reporter for *The Port St. Lucie News,* had heard rumors about the winner—that someone in a meat market knew the winner's name; that the winner could be found by talking to someone in the Roma Bakery. Jay tried the market. No luck. She fared better at the bakery, where a woman told Jay that her niece was the winner.

She gave Jay the woman's name—Pat Lino—but no phone number or address. Jay checked the telephone company—the number was unlisted. But she did find some Linos in the directory and called, thinking she might reach a relative.

"One guy was totally unrelated," Jay says. "Another was the winner's brother-in-law, and although he wouldn't give me her phone number he did mention that she lives in St. Lucie West, a new housing development."

Knowing that property tax records that list addresses are available, Jay checked the files for Pat Lino. She found the address and drove to the location, only to find no one there.

"It was all locked up. It looked as though I'd hit a dead end, but just to be sure I talked to a neighbor. He didn't know them, he said. Nor did another. But then I tried one more neighbor, and she knew Pat Lino. She had Pat Lino's daughter's phone number."

The neighbor called and Pat Lino was there. But she said she didn't want to be interviewed. "I told the neighbor that I only wanted to speak with her for a minute, that I'd been looking for her all day," Jay said. Lino gave in.

"In this small bedroom community, the naming of a $5 million lottery winner was the talk of the town. And we had it first."

The Reporting Process

As reporters go about their work of digging up information, they are guided by an understanding of the nature of reporting: Reporting is the process of gathering relevant material through a variety of means (direct observation, interviews, examination of reports and documents, use of databases and Internet resources) and subjecting the material to verification and analysis. When assembled, the material gives the reader, listener or viewer a good idea of what happened.

Reporting. "It's the hardest job in the world that doesn't involve heavy lifting."
—*Pete Hamill*

The Layers

Sometimes, the reporting process involves using source-originated material. The state's senior senator is planning to give a talk tomorrow at a fundraising dinner for the state Republican Party. The story that gives the time, place and purpose of the senator's talk is a Layer I story. That is, it simply relays information from a source.

If the reporter handling this story were to dig a bit deeper and ask the senator's press secretary whether the senator will support a particular gubernatorial candidate in the party primary, we can say that the reporter is now operating at a deeper layer, Layer II. We have seen how Sarah Jay worked Layer II by not waiting for the state to announce the winner of the lottery.

As we move on in our examination of journalistic work we will meet reporters who are allowed to interpret their findings, to find causes and consequences of the events they examine. They work in Layer III.

The News Story and Its Layers of Truth

Layer I—Handouts, press conferences, speeches, statements.

Layer II—Reportorial enterprise, verifying material, background, reporter's observations, spontaneous events.

Layer III—Significance, impact, causes, consequences, analysis, interpretation.

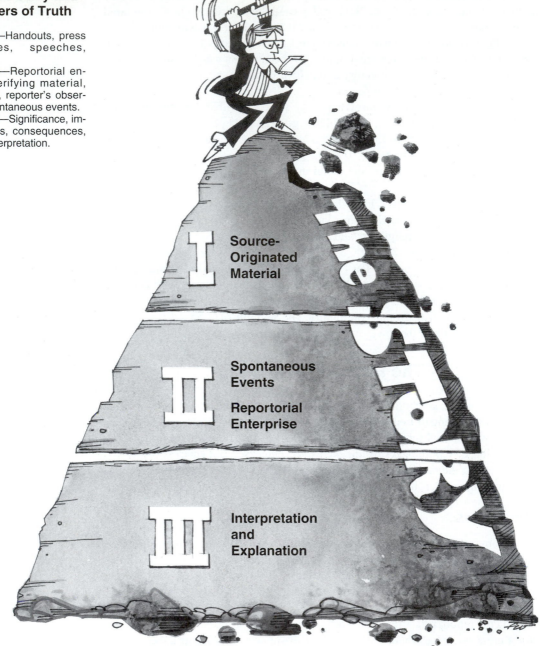

I — Source-Originated Material

II — Spontaneous Events / Reportorial Enterprise

III — Interpretation and Explanation

The Story

Digging for the Story

Most journalists say that their most important task is to look beneath the surface for the underlying reality. Lincoln Steffens, the great journalist of the muckraking period, said the reporter's task is "the letting in of light and air." Reporters base their work on the same conviction that guided Steffens. Their job is to seek out relevant truths for people who cannot witness or comprehend the events that affect them.

Layer I Reporting

Layer I reporting is the careful and accurate transcription of source-originated material—the record, the speech, the news conference. Its strengths and its limitations are those of objective journalism.

Layer I is the source for the facts used in most news stories. Information is mined from material that originates with and is controlled by the source. Fact gathering at this level of journalism may involve going to the mayor's office to pick up a transcript of the speech he is to deliver this evening or it may involve calling the mortuary holding the body of the child who drowned last night. The stories based on these facts rely almost wholly on information a source has supplied.

Fact gathering at Layer I is the journalistic equivalent of surface mining. The reporter sinks no shafts into the event but is content to use top-layer material, some of which is presented by public relations and information specialists. Much of the reporter's task is confined to sorting out and rearranging the delivered facts, verifying addresses and dates and checking the spelling of names. Most stories appearing in newspapers and on radio and television are based on source-originated material.

Essential Information   Despite criticism of it, Layer I reporting serves an essential function. At its most basic level, it gives the community information about the happenings in the community. The local newspaper will publish photos of dogs awaiting adoption at the County Animal Shelter and tell parents that the school lunch on Monday will be hot dogs, junior salad bar, veggie dippers and fruit salad. Tuesday, meatball sandwich, salad, buttery corn and raisins. . . .

The newspaper also will provide an hour-by-hour police incident report:

> 1:03 a.m.: A loud party was reported on Lincoln Street. On request, the responsibles agreed to quiet down.
> 2:24 a.m.: William Young of 42 Broadway was arrested for driving under the influence of alcohol. He was booked in the county jail. . . .

In Layer I, journalists report city council meetings, legislative hearings, United Way fund raising, street closings, traffic accidents, basketball games, appointments of the new university president and human rights commissioner, the verdicts at trials—an enormous range of activities. These stories tell people what's happening and to whom. Such coverage is essential, especially in the area of public affairs. The public must have access to the statements and activities of its officials, and these officials must have access to the people so they know what's on the mind of the public. This give and take makes responsive, consensual government possible.

Manipulation and Acceptance

News organizations, as well as sources, have thrived under the arrangement implicit in Layer I journalism. Material for news can be obtained quickly and inexpensively by relying on source-originated information.

In totalitarian countries journalists are restricted in coverage, as they are during wars and armed conflicts. The pictures journalists drew of these countries were often exactly the opposite of the grim reality. John K. Fairbank, an esteemed scholar of Chinese history and a major source for journalists, at one time wrote that the Chinese peasants had found Mao's revolution "a magnificent achievement." He admitted later, "Our reporting was very superficial. Steven Mosher, a historian, says in his book *China Misperceived: American Illusions and Chinese Reality* that while journalists were sending back glowing reports of the progress in reducing crime and massive improvement in health, millions were dying of starvation.

Despite considerable coverage of the Soviet Union, its swift collapse came as a shock to newspaper readers and television viewers. They were surprised by the revelations of the ruinous state of the economy and the pervasive hatred of the Communist Party among the people. There was no indication of this in many reporters' accounts of Soviet life. The manipulators of the media had been able to hide the true state of affairs in these repressive societies.

Pseudo-Events

As the mass media, particularly television, became the dominant dispensers of experience in American life, sources sought to manipulate reality to accommodate the media, especially television's need for pictures. The information sources realized that press releases and announcements unaccompanied by visual material of events would not merit more than 20 seconds on most newscasts, if that. As a result, sources learned to stage events for the press that resembled spontaneous events (Layer II) but were, in fact, as much under the control of the source as the press release and the prepared speech. These staged events are known as *media-events* or *pseudo-events.*

Following a presidential State of the Union speech, Russell Baker of *The New York Times* asked one of the president's advisers if the speech "was not mostly a media event, a nonhappening staged because reporters would pretend it was a happening."

"It's *all* media event," the adviser replied. "If the media weren't so ready to be used, it would be a very small splash."

Daniel J. Boorstin, the social historian, originated the term *pseudo-event* to describe these synthetic occurrences. He says that a "larger and larger proportion of our experience, of what we read and see and hear, has come to consist of pseudo-events." In the process, he says, "Vivid image came to overshadow pale reality." His book about image making opens with this short dialogue:

ADMIRING FRIEND: "My, that's a beautiful baby you have there!"
MOTHER: "Oh, that's nothing—you should see his photograph."

Boorstin says the pseudo-event has these characteristics: "It is not spontaneous, but comes about because someone has planned, planted or incited it. . . . It is planted primarily (but not always exclusively) for the immediate purpose of being reported or reproduced. Therefore, its occurrence is arranged for the convenience of the reporting or reproducing media. . . . Its relation to the underlying relativity of the situation is ambiguous. . . ."

Media Manipulation

The orchestration of events for public consumption is a frequent occurrence in government and politics. Needing public attention and approval, politicians often resort to media manipulation, and they often get away with their contrivances.

Perhaps one of the most dramatic pictures of the civil rights movement in the South in the early 1960s showed a determined Gov. George C. Wallace blocking the entrance to a University of Alabama building, refusing to allow two black students to enroll. For Wallace, a symbol to southerners of resistance to federally imposed desegregation, this was a powerful image. He refused to give way when confronted by federalized National Guard troops with a court order.

Grudgingly, however, in the face of firepower, he stood aside.

The reality was far different: In secret meetings, the Justice Department and Wallace had worked out a scenario that would make President John Kennedy and Wallace look good. Wallace would be allowed to take a stand against desegregating the university but would permit the black students to enroll under the Guard's protection.

Wallace thus was able to make political capital in the South, and Kennedy appeared decisive to people who wanted the country to move faster toward desegregating its educational system.

Another well-plotted scenario developed during the 1972 Republican presidential convention. But this pseudo-event was exposed by enterprising reporters who discovered a script that called for "spontaneous" cheering.

Limo Liberal During the U.S. Senate race between Hillary Clinton and her Republican opponent Rick Lazio, each tried to woo the large New York City vote, usually Democratic. On his first campaign stop, Lazio took the subway and remarked that Clinton was hardly a true New Yorker as she was being taken around the city in "a chauffeured limousine."

Spinsters. People, wrote Walter Lippmann in his 1922 book *Public Opinion,* do not react rationally to information but respond to the "pictures inside their heads." This marked "the birthing moment of spin," says Stuart Ewen, Hunter College historian and author of *PR! A Social History of Spin.*

"We live in a world where everyone is always battling for the public mind and public approval," Ewen says. "I think the public believes there is no truth, only spin—in part because much of the educated middle class spins for a living."

As he boarded a subway car, Lazio said to the reporters as cameras whirred and clicked, "This is the way New Yorkers travel." Yes, he said, he knew subways all right.

The reporters weren't buying. "How much is a MetroCard?" one reporter asked. (The card is a plastic inserted in the turnstile.) "I think it's about $3," Lazio answered.

The New York Times reporter covering this pseudo-event wrote:

> Well, not exactly. Yes, a round trip subway fare is $3. But the cheapest MetroCard you can buy is a one-day, $4 fun pass that tourists use. Most regular subway riders buy cards ranging in price from $15 to $120.

Trial Balloons

One of the ways government officials manage the media is through the floating of trial balloons. The technique involves letting reporters in on inside information, usually about an appointee or a new program. The material is to be used without attribution. The information is published or used on television, and public reaction is gauged. If the public rejects the idea floated, no one can be blamed as there is no source named. If there is acceptance, then the nominee may be named, the program adopted.

Early in his administration, President Clinton floated several nominees before the public. One, a candidate for attorney general, pulled out when negative response developed. The administration also leaked the possibility of freezing cost-of-living increases for Social Security recipients. When the reaction was negative, the administration sent up another balloon—increasing the taxes on Social Security benefits. That met with less opposition but was still considered politically risky.

Dangers of Layer I

When reporting is confined to Layer I, the distinction between journalism and public relations is hard to discern. The consequences for society can be serious, as Joseph Bensman and Robert Lilienfield, sociologists, explain:

> When "public relations" is conducted simultaneously for a vast number of institutions and organizations, the public life of a society becomes so congested with manufactured appearances that it is difficult to recognize any underlying realities.
>
> As a result, individuals begin to distrust all public facades and retreat into apathy, cynicism, disaffiliation, distrust of media and public institutions. . . . The journalist unwittingly often exposes the workings of the public relations man or information specialist, if he operates within a genuine journalistic attitude.

Conduit. "Increasingly, information is generated by those who wish to promote something or someone—a product, a cause, a political candidate or officeholder—without arguing their case on its merits or explicitly advertising it as self-interested material either. Much of the press, in its eagerness to inform the public, has become a conduit for the equivalent of junk mail."
—*Christopher Lasch*

Tom Wicker of *The New York Times* said that the press—because of its concentration on Layer I—has been weak at picking up new developments before they have become institutionalized and their sponsors have learned to stage media events to attract attention.

Worthwhile Information

Some staged events do produce news—the civil rights demonstrations in the 1960s, picketing by the local teachers union. Certainly, dozens of source-originated events are newsworthy—the text of the mayor's speech, the details the mortuary supplies about the child's death, the announcement that the university football program has been placed on probation for booster activities that included payment to athletes.

Handling the Handout

"Don't be a handout reporter," Harry Romanoff, a night city editor on the *Chicago American,* would tell young reporters. One of Romanoff's charges was Mervin Block, who recalls an encounter with Romanoff:

I remember his giving me a fistful of press releases trumpeting movie monarch Louis B. Mayer's expected arrival at the Dearborn Street Railroad Station. An hour later, Romy asked me what time Mayer's train would be pulling in. I told him, and when he challenged my answer, I cited the handouts: one from the Santa Fe, one from Mayer's studio (MGM), and one from his destination, the Ambassador East Hotel. All agreed on the time. But that wasn't good enough for Romy.

"Call the stationmaster and *find out.*"

More Costly   When handouts from food chains in Chicago announced price cuts on thousands of items, the Chicago newspapers bannered the stories on their front pages. One such headline:

Inflation Breakthrough—Food Prices to Drop Here

Despite the rash of stories about how the shopper "may save 15% in price battle," as one paper said in a headline over one of its stories, consumers were actually paying more on a unit, or per-ounce, basis.

The Chicago commissioner of consumer affairs demonstrated that the city's consumers were being misled by the store announcements and consequently by the newspaper stories that took the handouts at face value. Many of the items that were reduced in price were also reduced in weight. Peanut clusters went from 72 cents a packet to 69 cents, an apparent saving of 3 cents. But the packet went from 6 ounces to 5 1/4 ounces. With a little arithmetic, a reporter could have figured out that this was actually an increase of 6 cents a packet. Some items were publicized because they stayed at the same price "despite inflation," according to the handouts and the stories. True enough. A 70-cent can of beef stew was still 70 cents. But the new can contained half an ounce less than the old can.

The moral of this little tale of the peanut clusters and beef stew is: Even when operating in Layer I, check and check again.

The Internet as Source

Journalists mine the Internet for background information, as a tip source for stories and as a communication channel with other reporters and with sources. The Internet extends the reach of the journalist enormously. A reporter with *The Knoxville News-Sentinel* says he refers to the World Wide Web "as much as to the city directory, telephone book and the newspaper morgue."

But there is a difference between the material obtained via the Internet and that from standard references. The references are checked and verified. When the journalist turns to the Web, often as not he or she is operating in Layer I with unverified, source-originated material—and sometimes the source may be spurious.

You can see what happened to a reporter who thought she had discovered on the Internet an idea for a fabulous feature. See **The Backyard Archaeologist** in *NRW Plus,* Chapter 10.

Layer II Reporting

When reporters initiate information-gathering and when they add to Layer I material, they are digging in Layer II. We could say that the ordinary beat reporting that journalists engage in has much of Layer II involved. When sports reporters cover a game, they are working in Layer II, for example.

Whenever the situation moves beyond the control of those trying to manage it, the reporter is working in Layer II.

The transition from Layer I to Layer II can be seen at a news conference. The reading of a statement provides the source-originated material (I). The give-and-take of the question and answer period is spontaneous (II). When the source declines to answer questions, the reporter should understand that he or she is back in Layer I, dealing with material controlled by the source.

The reporter who seeks verification from a second source that the governor will appear at the Lions Club ceremony is moving into Layer II. So is the reporter who, after she is told by the police that the hotel was burglarized at 5:46 A.M., looks up the time of sunrise that day. Her enterprise enables her to write, "The holdup man left the hotel in early morning darkness."

The reporter who writes that the state purchasing agent has awarded to a local dealer a contract for a fleet of automobiles is engaged in Layer I journalism. The investigative reporter who digs into the records to learn that the contract was awarded without bids is working at the second level.

Checking a City Proposal

When an official of a city undergoing a recession recommends a city-financed plan that he says will increase employment, the reporter will ask him for precise details, questions that belong mostly in Layer I reporting. Then the reporter will check the data the official has supplied. He will look into the program the official said has been working in another city in the South. This checking moves the reporter into Layer II. Finally, the reporter will seek comments from other city officials about the feasibility of the proposal and its prospects for adoption.

Untold numbers of stories have been written about proposals that went nowhere because they were badly drafted or were introduced or recommended by people with no influence. Local newspapers usually play up a legislator's proposals or intentions, but give no attention to the fact that he is a freshman with no influence, a member of the minority party, or that the committee chairwoman has vowed never to let such legislation move through her committee.

Standard Practice   If we look back at the reporters at work in Chapter 1, we can see how often journalists move from Layer I to II:

- Much of the work Dick did on his story about the Black Parents Association after receiving the handout from the group was on his initiative.
- The investigative stories by Cammy Wilson and Heidi Evans were carried out entirely in Layer II.

Mark Avery

Seeking Out Dissidents

Jan Wong of *The Globe and Mail* of Toronto maintained contacts with those working for a democratic China in the face of suppression and prison. To avoid wiretaps and inquisitive police, she would meet in public places.

These reporters moved beyond merely relaying information originated and controlled by a source. Each checked the information, supplied missing facts, explained complicated details. None of these efforts is the activity of a reporter content with Layer I information. When they have time, reporters usually move from I to II.

Let's look at some other examples of Layer II reporting.

The Cost of the Gender Gap

After California passed a law prohibiting gender price discrimination, reporters for KRON-TV in San Francisco checked to see whether it was being complied with. The law had come about after a survey by a legislative office showed that women paid on average $1.79 more to launder an identical shirt than men, that they paid $5 more for a similar haircut and that clothing alterations were considerably more costly for women than for men.

KRON-TV reporters found "women were still being taken to the cleaners." Emerald Yeh and Christine McMurry found that of 30 hair salons in San Francisco, a third quoted higher prices for women than for men. When a woman took in a size 4 men's style shirt to be cleaned, she was charged $2.50. When a man took in the same shirt, he was charged $1.

Car Leasing The TV team did a similar investigation on the hidden costs of car leasing. They found a couple that had signed a lease for a Toyota Corolla that would end up costing them more than twice a cash purchase would have cost them. They investigated "the seductive pitch of leasing—more car for less money" and they found high costs for those who lease. They found lease agreements do not have to state the price of the car on which monthly payments are based. Hidden charges such as extra mileage could cost thousands extra, they reported.

Women for Sale

When Lena H. Sun, *The Washington Post*'s correspondent in China, heard of the practice of selling women to men seeking wives, she looked for a victim so she wouldn't have to rely on secondhand accounts. On the outskirts of Beijing, she found Ma Linmei who was, Sun wrote, "a virtual prisoner. The main road is more than an hour away by foot, down a steep, rocky path. She has no money, and she can barely speak the local dialect. No one will help her escape."

Her husband had been unable to find a bride locally and traveled thousands of miles to Yunan Province in southwestern China to buy a wife.

Sun interviewed Ma, who told her, "I miss my home. I miss my mother. I'm always sick. If I had money I would run away."

But in a way, Ma was luckier than many women, Sun found. Thousands of others "are abducted by traders in human flesh, who trick them with promises of good jobs and a better life far from home. The traffickers often rape and beat the women before selling them into virtual bondage, often with the full knowledge and cooperation of local Communist Party officials. . . ."

Lena H. Sun,
The Washington Post

Sold for $363

Although Ma Linmei is far from home and is married to a man she does not like, she is luckier than most bought wives. Many are brutalized, kept in virtual captivity.

Some of the victims, she reported, are as young as 14. Some are locked up, others shackled to keep them from running away. "Some have had their leg tendons cut to prevent them from escaping," Sun reported.

Searching the Files

In the darkest days of Southern resistance to desegregation, the state of Mississippi set up a Sovereignty Commission to spy on people who officials thought were engaged in anti-segregation activities. In 1989, Jerry Mitchell, a reporter for *The Clarion-Ledger,* heard that the files contained incriminating material. But he was told they were to remain sealed until 2027.

"I gradually developed several sources who shared what was in the sealed files," Mitchell says. "Those files showed that the State of Mississippi had secretly assisted the defense of Ku Klux Klan member Byron De La Beckwith, who was tried but never convicted in the 1963 assassination of NAACP leader Medgar Evers.

"I printed that story. Prosecutors reopened the case. Beckwith was convicted in 1994."

Mitchell continued his digging and located a man who had pleaded guilty to taking part in the firebombing of the home of another NAACP leader but had never been sent to prison. Mitchell's work led to the conviction of a Klan Imperial Wizard who had masterminded the murder.

Prizewinners

Mitchell's stories were recognized by a Sigma Delta Chi prize for Public Service Reporting. Let's take a quick survey of some prize-winning journalism. We'll see that the reporters who won them worked in Layer II journalism:

- More than 100,000 women in Third World countries have been sterilized, often against their will, usually without their knowledge. *(The Wall Street Journal.)*
- The military provides inadequate medical care to military families. (WRAL-TV, Raleigh.)
- Racial discrimination was common in strip searches at O'Hare International Airport. (WMAQ-TV.)
- Weak truck-safety laws, spotty enforcement and a friendly political climate are the causes of the state's No. 1 ranking for safety violations. *(Winston-Salem* (N.C.) *Journal.)*
- Medical mistakes kill thousands every year in U.S. hospitals. *(The Philadelphia Inquirer.)*
- Faulty construction and bogus hiring of minority and female subcontractors existed in stadium construction. (WCPO-TV.)
- Brutality in Maryland boot camps injured juveniles convicted of crimes. *(The Baltimore Sun.)*
- U.S. troops in Korea murdered innocent civilians. (AP.)
- The Grammys, music industry's richest awards program, helped far fewer unemployed, infirm and disabled musicians than it claimed. *(Los Angeles Times.)*

Computer-Assisted Reporting Projects

Journalists who use the computer to analyze material work in Layer II. When he was database editor of the *Austin American-Statesman* Jeff South teamed up with reporters to write informative stories. Here's how one begins:

Some of the highest-paid employees of Austin city government aren't doctors, lawyers and department heads. They're electricians, water workers and mechanics who add thousands of dollars to their salaries through overtime.

Dozens of city employees regularly earn more than $15,000 a year in overtime. Ninety have received more than $50,000 in overtime pay over the past four and a half years, and two-thirds of those employees work for one department: the electric utility.

By examining city payroll records, South and Mike Todd found the city had paid out more than $8 million in overtime in a year. A union official said the amount raises questions about proper staffing, equity in salaries and safety.

Dams, Drivers, Teachers In computer analyses of database and other material, South found 402 dams in Texas "could collapse" with heavy rains, that despite the law a sixth of Texas drivers do not have auto insurance, and a fourth of Texas public schools had no black or Hispanic teachers.

South, now teaching journalism at Virginia Commonwealth University, said computer-assisted reporting widens the reporter's scope.

"When a bureaucrat announces the bottom line—appraisals went up 5 percent—the CAR-savvy reporter knows the real story is in the details, South says." The announcement is Layer I journalism. The details take the reporter into Layer II. South asks:

"What was the biggest appraisal increase? Where did appraisals go down? Who owns those homes? Can we map changes by neighborhoods?

"Hey, let's run the appraisal database against the list of City Council members and appraisal office employees."

Notice the way Layer II journalism encompasses the watchdog function of the press.

Peter Eisler of *USA Today* dug into old records—100,000 pages of declassified documents—for his series on government contracts that put workers at risk and led to the pollution of many areas in the country. The material was placed in an Excel spreadsheet. For Eisler's detailed explanation of how he handled the reporting, and excerpts from his stories, see **Poisoned Workers & Poisoned Places** in *NRW Plus,* Chapter 10.

Usually, such journalistic revelations lead to remedial action. But sometimes, the anger at Layer II journalism by those in power can be overwhelming to a journalist. Raymond Bonner of *The New York Times* paid a high price for his reporting of the El Mozote massacre in El Salvador.

Questioning Authority

In January 1982, Bonner found the charred skulls and other remains of dozens of men, women and children in a village in El Salvador. His story began, "From interviews with people who live in this small mountain village and surrounding hamlets, it is clear that a massacre of major proportions occurred here last month." Bonner described bones scattered through the El Mozote area. Hundreds were killed, he reported, quoting those who said they had witnessed government troops killing with abandon.

Bonner quoted Rufina Amaya, a survivor. She said she had hidden in trees when the soldiers arrived at El Mozote. They killed her blind husband and her four children, ages 9, 5 and 3 years and 8 months.

The story appeared at a time U.S. foreign policy supported the military regime in El Salvador. Worried by the leftist Sandinista government in nearby Nicaragua, the Reagan administration wanted to contain guerilla movements in Central America. El Mozote was the key to a guerilla stronghold.

The Reagan foreign policy was under attack as supporting the El Salvadoran military regime's abuse of human rights, and Bonner's story in the prestigious *Times* threatened to undermine the policy still more.

Denials and Accusations

The government said no massacre had occurred. *The Wall Street Journal*'s editorial page, which was a strong supporter of the Reagan foreign policy, described Bonner as "overly credulous," and "a reporter out on a limb," that he had been taken in by a rebel "propaganda exercise." In a 36–inch editorial titled "The Media's War," the *Journal* editorialized:

> Much of the American media, it would seem, was dominated by a style of reporting that grew out of Vietnam—in which Communist sources were given greater credence than either the U.S. Government or the government it was supporting.

The ambassador to El Salvador described Bonner as an "advocate journalist," meaning Bonner had a desire to see events to fit a social or political agenda.

The *Times* buckled under the pressure. It ordered Bonner home and put him on the business desk.

Vindication

In time, Bonner was proved right. A team of forensic archaeologists dug into the ruins of El Mozote in 1992 and uncovered dozens of skeletons, most of children. They found shell casings and other indications of a massacre.

After reading Mark Danner's book *The Massacre at El Mozote: A Parable of the Cold War*, *New York Times* columnist Tony Lewis wrote, "After the Danner report, no rational person can doubt that Salvadoran forces carried out a massacre. They killed hundreds of people in El Mozote and other hamlets nearby: men, women, children, infants. They killed with a savagery that is hard even to read about." Lewis wrote that the incident proved "again how essential it is to be skeptical of convenient government denials."

At *The Washington Post,* its reporter Alma Guillermoprieto had written a report similar to Bonner's. *Post* editor Ben Bradlee did not back down in the face of pressure. Bradlee supported his reporter.

Vince Heptig, Courtesy of Alicia Patterson Foundation

A People's Suffering

For six years, the Guatemalan army waged a brutal war against Indian villagers it said were helping leftist guerrillas. The villagers said the thousands of killings were indiscriminate, and years after the deaths forensic specialists exhumed many bodies. Writer-photographer Vince Heptig accompanied forensic anthropologist Luis Minguel Alonso as he dug up remains. In *The APF Reporter,* Heptig tells the story simply and directly. Here are some excerpts:

Layer by layer, Luis brushed away the rich soil to reveal what the onlooking people already knew—the boy had been shot in the head. As he continued, Luis revealed the rope that tied the young boy's hands behind his back had also reached around his neck.

Luis deducted that the boy had been killed by "tiro de gracia," or a shot to the head at close range. The other twelve bodies the anthropologists unearthed suffered similar fates.

This mass grave contained 13 skeletons, bringing the total number of bodies exhumed in this tiny village to 26.

A Boy's Death: Hands Tied, Shot in Head

In an article in *Harper's* 10 years after the Bonner story and his recall, Michael Massing asked, "Did the *Times* bow to pressure from the government? When does official criticism of a reporter amount to a threat? What happens to a reporter when his or her interpretation of events contradicts that of the powers that be?"

After Bonner's exile, a new editor at the *Times* restored Bonner as a foreign correspondent.

Killings in Guatemala

This was not the first time that the *Times* acceded to government pressure in placing foreign correspondents. In 1954, the publisher of the newspaper agreed with the CIA to keep Sydney Gruson out of Guatemala. The CIA suggested that Gruson was "politically suspect." At the same time the CIA was clearing Guatemala of an inquisitive reporter, it was planning a coup to overthrow the elected president.

The coup was successful and the country began a slide into rule by a government "in the grip of homicidal fiends," as one reporter put it. The coup led to a lengthy guerrilla war with government troops engaging in the same kind of village cleansing that took place in El Salvador. More than 200,000 civilians died, 90 percent of them slain by government troops.

Investigative Reporting

Those who dig deepest in Layer II are called investigative reporters. Their work falls into two categories—checking on illegal activities and looking into systemic abuses. The city purchasing agent who awards contracts without offering them for bids violates the law. The police department that regularly stops black motorists is engaging in a systemic abuse.

Victimizing the Poor

An investigation that exposed a systemic abuse began when Judy Johnson of *The Anniston Star* heard that some people in an Alabama community were having trouble getting credit from banks and finance companies. She decided to investigate. She spent months examining records of mortgages and land transfers. "I compiled them into lists year by year, looking for patterns, building a history," she said.

She talked to people turned down by banks. Through the years of borrowing from a local businessman, one woman had accumulated $50,000 in loans. Among her loans was one for a four-year-old car she and her husband had bought from the businessman's used car lot. The model she bought cost her slightly less than a new car would have cost her.

Johnson showed how the poor, who cannot obtain credit from large lending institutions, are victimized by private lenders. Her series won national recognition.

A Tax Giveaway

As soon as the massive Tax Reform Act was passed by Congress and signed by the president, Donald L. Barlett and James B. Steele of *The Philadelphia Inquirer* began to examine it. They discovered hundreds of tax breaks for corporations and specific individuals. But the language was so intricate that identities were hidden.

Here is a typical provision:

> The amendments made by Section 201 shall not apply to a 562-foot passenger cruise ship, which was purchased in 1900 for the purpose of returning the vessel to United States service, the approximate cost of refurbishment of which is approximately $47,000,000.

The two investigative reporters set out to find who was profiting, why they were being helped and what the cost would be to taxpayers. They searched through financial disclosure statements by members of Congress, looked at documents of the Securities and Exchange Commission, used databases to examine thousands of newspapers, magazines, newsletters and government reports.

The digging took 15 months, and Barlett and Steele found that Congress had made the largest giveaway in the history of the federal income tax. (The beneficiaries of the provision involving the 562-foot passenger cruise ship, incidentally, were a group of wealthy investors in the *S.S. Monterey* who were given an $8 million tax break.)

They named the people and the companies that had been allowed to escape taxes by a law that stenographic journalists working in Layer I had hailed as a "tax reform." The rich were being helped by the new law at the expense of the average taxpayer.

In the face of massive public reaction—the lengthy series was reprinted around the country—Congress shelved its so-called reform legislation and passed a new tax bill without a single tax break for an individual or company. Barlett and Steele won the Pulitzer Prize for national reporting for their seven-part series.

Illegalities

Shortly after his graduation from journalism school, James Dwyer of *The Dispatch* in Hudson County, N.J., was checking the bids of merchants hoping to sell supplies to a vocational school. His instructor had told Dwyer that bids sometimes are manipulated and that looking them over can be rewarding.

Strange Bids Dwyer noticed that some seemed to be typed on the same typewriter. He also noticed that the prices for ladders, dust cloths, shovels and other items were high. Even when the supplies were purchased in quantity, prices were higher than they would have been for goods sold as individual items in hardware stores. For example, the school paid $564 for ladders that local stores sold for $189. He visited the school and found enough dust cloths to keep the school's furniture glowing for a couple of centuries.

Dwyer tried to locate the firms that made the unsuccessful bids. He could not find them. He theorized that the agent through whom the goods were sold had invented bidders, and using these fake firms to enter high bids on faked stationery, the agent made his firm the low bidder. Dwyer's investigation confirmed his theory and a grand jury took over after his stories appeared.

CAR Project   A reporter had been told by an out-of-office politician that some city workers were political appointees who never showed up for work. An idea: Examine parking tickets in resort areas issued to vehicles with New York license plates. He compared the names on the tickets with names on the city payroll. Lo and behold, he found tickets for city employees on days they were supposed to be working.

Finding Sources

As you may already have gathered, there are two basic types of sources, physical and human. Physical sources range from databases of political campaign donations to the minutes of city council sessions. They include census data and crime statistics. We will be looking at sources in greater detail in Chapter 13, but we'll pause a moment here to look at how a veteran reporter handles human sources.

Jeffrey A. Tannenbaum of *The Wall Street Journal* puts the names of the most helpful sources in his files. "Someday, they may come in handy," he says. But what about finding sources for a subject entirely new to the reporter?

"First, look for institutional sources," Tannenbaum says. "If you're writing about pizzas, there's a national association of pizza chefs." For his story about the growing power of the states' attorney generals, he asked the New York attorney general if there was an association of all 50 officers. He was given a telephone number.

In gathering information from news sources, he says, "One source leads to another. Perhaps only the seventh one in the chain has what you need."

When do you know you have gathered all you need? "Only after the information the sources have provided is getting redundant, and the sources are failing to supply new sources."

Layer III Reporting

Reporters face a public increasingly interested in knowing all the dimensions of the events and personalities that affect their lives. The result has been a journalism that has expanded beyond accounts of what happened. Now, reporters with proven competence are encouraged to tell readers, viewers and listeners how and why it happened, to describe the causes and consequences of the event and to analyze and interpret it.

Layer III reporting tells people how things work, why they work that way, or why they don't work. And if they don't, reporters explore alternatives.

Bad Swap   When *The Seattle Times* learned that the U.S. Forest Service had traded away a verdant area along the Green River for a logged-over, debris filled stubble, reporters dug into the program that permitted such disadvantageous exchanges. Then reporters went beyond their investigation to suggest ways to fix the program.

The *Times* suggested seven reforms, from selling unwanted government land to the highest bidder to allowing the public to have a voice in determining what land should be exchanged or sold and in negotiating the sale or exchange.

Quick Passage   In the early days of the presidency of George W. Bush, Congress enacted a law making it harder for people to erase their debts by filing for bankruptcy. Philip Shenon of *The New York Times* pointed out that President Clinton had vetoed a similar bill in his last weeks in office but that the current version had quick and easy sailing. Shenon showed why:

> The bill's quick resurrection after Mr. Bush's inauguration was seen as evidence of the generous campaign contributions made to each party by the credit industry. It also reflected the growing power of lobbyists in a government in which the White House and Congress are run by business-friendly Republicans.

Easy Credit   The AP story from Chicago began:

> William Rodriguez trudged home through rain and snow and wee-hour darkness.
>
> He was only 23, in good health and known as a happy-go-lucky fellow.
>
> Yet he would be dead before sunrise.

Rodriguez had purchased rat poison on his way home from work, and as he walked he ate the poison. Why? The AP assigned two reporters to find out. Their digging turned up the answer—easy credit. Rodriguez owed $700 to merchants for furniture, clothing, a television set. He couldn't meet the payments, and the creditors were threatening to tell his employer.

The story galvanized the city's enforcement agencies. Rodriguez had been sold low-grade merchandise and had been given credit at usurious rates. The legislature reacted by lowering interest rates. The law is known as the "Rodriguez Law."

Voter-Conscious   When the New Jersey state legislature passed a bill banning state Medicaid payments for abortions, it ignored nine federal district court decisions in eight states that ruled similar bills were unconstitutional. The reason for the legislators' action was described in this Layer III sentence from *The New York Times:* "Approval of the measure reflects the influence of the Catholic Church, which opposes abortion, in New Jersey: About 55 percent of the state's registered voters are Catholic."

The battle over the need for interpretative reporting has long been over, although some newspaper and broadcast station editors are adamant about its dangers and rarely permit it. Dangers there are, but the risks are only slightly greater than those inherent in other areas of journalism. The benefits to the reader outweigh these risks.

Putting I, II and III to Work

Let us watch a reporter mine these three layers for his story.

City Planner Arthur calls the local stations and newspaper to read to reporters a statement about a new zoning proposal. The release contains facts 1, 2 and 3. At the newspaper, reporter Bernard looks over the handout, tells his city editor that 1 and 2 are of no news value but that 3—elimination of two-acre zoning north of town—is important and worth exploring in an interview with Arthur. The editor agrees and assigns Bernard to the story.

Before leaving for the interview, Bernard checks the newspaper library for a story about a court decision he recalls that may be related to the proposed regulation. He telephones another city official and a real estate developer to obtain additional information. With this background and Arthur's statement, Bernard begins to develop ideas for questions. He jots down a few, 4, 5 and 6.

During the interview, City Planner Arthur repeats 1, 2 and 3. Reporter Bernard asks for more information about 3, the elimination of the minimum two-acre requirement for home building. Bernard also brings up his own subjects by asking questions 4, 5 and 6. New themes develop during the interview: 7, 8 and 9.

Back in the newsroom, Bernard looks over his notes. He sees that his hunch about 3 was correct. It was important. Arthur's answer to question 5 is newsworthy, he decides, and fact 7—the possibility of low-and medium-cost housing in the area—which developed during the interview, may be the lead, especially because the broadcast stations probably will not have it. Bernard needs comments on the impact of 7 from developers. A couple of calls and the

possible consequences, 10, emerge. The developers confirm their interest in building inexpensive housing. Looking over his notes, he spots background from the library, 11, that is now relevant and also will go into the story.

The story will contain facts 3, 5, 7, 10 and 11. Bernard decides he will fashion 7 and 10 into a lead, and he worries about how to blend 11 into the story at a fairly early stage without impeding the flow of Arthur's explanation. Background is important, but sometimes it is difficult to work smoothly into the story. He writes this lead:

> A proposed change to eliminate the two-acre zoning requirement for home building north of town could open the area to people who can afford only low- and medium-cost housing.

Bernard's story will consist of the following:

Facts	Layer
3	I
5, 7, 11	II
10	III

Bernard has used almost all the techniques reporters have at their command to gather facts for stories. He was given information by a source. Then he used the newspaper library—a physical source—for background. He then interviewed his original source—a human source—and made independent checks by calling up additional sources.

Here is a guide to how the reporting process begins:

- Know what to look for.
- Gather the information.
- Record it accurately.
- Weigh the information.

All this precedes writing.

Summing Up

Here is some down-to-earth advice about reporting from working reporters:

- Stay ready for any breaking news story by keeping up-to-date on developments in the community.
- There is a story behind almost any event. Remember, it was a third-rate break-in in a Washington building that began the Watergate revelations and ended in the resignation of a president.
- Always check all names in the telephone book, the city directory and the library to make absolutely sure they are spelled correctly.
- Follow the buck. Find out where money comes from, where it is going, how it gets there and who's handling it. Whether it is taxes, campaign contributions, or donations, keep your eye on the dollar.

- Be counterphobic. Do what you don't want to do or are afraid to do. Otherwise you'll never be able to dig into a story.
- Question all assumptions. The people who believed the emperor was clothed are legion and forgotten. We remember the child who pointed out his nudity.
- Question authority. Titles and degrees do not confer infallibility.

Further Reading

Behrens, John C. *The Typewriter Guerrillas.* Chicago: Nelson-Hall, 1977.

Boorstin, Daniel J. *The Image: A Guide to Pseudo-Events in America.* New York: Atheneum, 1961.

Crouse, Timothy. *The Boys on the Bus.* New York: Random House, 1973.

Hersey, John. *The Algiers Motel Incident.* New York: Knopf, 1968.

Hess, Stephen. *The Washington Reporter.* Washington, D.C.: Brookings Institution, 1981.

Kovach, Bill, and Tom Rosenstiel. *The Elements of Journalism.* New York: Crown Publishers, 2001.

McGinniss, Joe. *The Selling of the President 1968.* New York: Pocket Books, 1973.

Weir, David, and Dan Noyes. *Raising Hell: How the Center for Investigative Reporting Gets the Story.* Reading, Mass.: Addison-Wesley, 1983.

11 Making Sound Observations

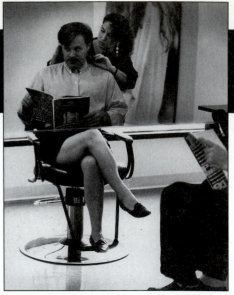

Bob Thayer, *The Providence Journal*

Seeing isn't always believing.

Preview

To gather the reliable and relevant information essential to a story, the reporter must:

• Know what readers and listeners are interested in, what affects them and what they need to know.
• Find a theme for the story early in the reporting.
• Look for the different, the unusual, the unique aspect of the event that illustrates it and that sets it apart from other events like it.

Reporters face restraints on their fact gathering. Time is always limited; it is not always easy to find vantage points from which to see the event; sources will not cooperate.

For some stories, journalists use unobtrusive observation (the identity of the reporter is unknown to those being observed) and participant observation (the reporter becomes part of the event being reported).

The Congo was torn by civil war. Because the war had serious international implications, the United Nations dispatched a peacekeeping force and sent Secretary-General Dag Hammarskjold to the African republic to try to arrange a cease-fire.

At dusk, reporters at the Ndola airport in Northern Rhodesia awaiting Hammarskjold's arrival saw a plane land and a fair-haired man emerge. The reporters, who had been held behind police lines a hundred yards away, ran to file bulletins on the secretary-general's arrival. Anticipating Hammarskjold's next move, the press associations soon had stories describing Hammarskjold's conferring with President Moise Tshombe about a cease-fire. Many of these stories ran in early editions of the next day's newspapers.

But the man the reporters saw disembark was not Hammarskjold. He was a British foreign affairs official on a fact-gathering tour. At the time the reporters were filing their stories, Hammarskjold was aboard another plane that later crashed in a forest 10 miles north of Ndola, killing the secretary-general and the others on board.

The UPI reporter told his boss later, "I saw a man I thought looked like Hammarskjold. Other reporters claimed they were sure it was. After comparing notes, we all agreed to file stories."

The incident reveals some of the problems reporters face in covering spot news stories. To make sound observations, the reporter has to see and hear the event clearly, but this is not always possible. In this case, rather than wait to be certain of their man's identity, the reporters did what reporters do when their observations are uncertain and they are under pressure—they made an inference.

Because the man had light hair and his build approximated that of the secretary-general, the reporters jumped to the conclusion that he was Hammarskjold. They had violated the reporter's maxim, "Beware of inferences. Do not jump from the known to the unknown."

To guard against individual error, they checked with each other and formed a consensus. The difficulty in covering events often causes journalists to consult each other for reassurance, which leads to what is known as *herd* or *pack journalism.* Reporters tend to chat about the lead, the credibility of the source, the reliability of the documentation they have been offered. They seek agreement in resolving the uncertainties.

Accurate observations are the basis of news stories and features. Learning how to report accurately—more difficult than it seems—begins with an understanding of the methods that are used in the search for relevant information for the task of truth telling.

The Art of Observation

In his short story, "The Murders in the Rue Morgue," Edgar Allan Poe has his character C. Auguste Dupin expound on the art of observation as Dupin goes about solving the grisly murders of Madame L'Espanaye and her daughter, which have stumped the Parisian police. He dismisses the way the police work:

> There is no method in their proceedings, beyond the method of the moment. . . . The results obtained by them are not unfrequently surprising, but, for the most part are brought about by simple diligence and activity. When these qualities are unavailing, their schemes fail.

Although hard work is essential to good reporting, activity is not enough. A method is essential. Dupin says that the detective makes "a host of observations and inferences. So, perhaps, do his companions; and the difference in the extent of the information obtained lies not so much in the validity of the inference as in the quality of the observation. The necessary knowledge is of *what* to observe."

In other words, the vacuum-cleaner collector of information wastes time. Dupin says the proper method is to follow "deviations from the plane of the ordinary." This is how "reason feels its way, if at all, in its search for the truth. In investigations such as we are now pursuing, it should not be so much asked 'what has occurred,' as 'what has occurred that has never occurred before.'"

Mistakes "Accurate observation of complex situations is extremely difficult, and observers usually make many errors of which they are not conscious."
—*W.I.B. Beveridge*

France's Fiction = New York's Fact

Dupin may be Poe's invention, but his method of observation is as useful in New York City as in Paris. Robert T. Gallagher, a private detective who spent 18 years on the New York City police force, disarmed more than 1,200 gun-toting thugs before they could draw their weapons. He had, everyone on the force agreed, an uncanny ability to spot people carrying guns on the street. How did he do it?

"If you're not looking for the clues you don't notice them," Gallagher said. "But if you're looking for them, they're so obvious they begin to jump out at you."

The easy one, "the classic bulge," Gallagher dismisses. He knew that most street criminals stick their guns in their waistbands. As a consequence, when they walk the leg on the gun side takes a shorter stride and the arm a shorter swing.

Another clue: the "security feel." Those carrying guns unconsciously reach to touch the weapon. They also adjust it after getting out of a car, going up or down stairs and stepping off a curb.

He notices the way jackets hang in the front. Buttoned, one side clings more tightly to a thigh than the other.

Like Dupin, Gallagher looks for the different, the unusual, what Dupin calls the "deviations from the plane of the ordinary." Dupin talks of seeing the "matter as a whole," and Gallagher's procedure is to examine the clothing, the gait, the mannerisms of his suspect. Out of this picture may emerge the clue for Gallagher, the deviation for Dupin and the lead for the journalist.

The Reporter's Task   For the reporter, every assignment is a mystery to be unraveled. With a method of observation, the reporter can find the significant information that becomes the core of the story. What makes this basketball game decided in the last 30 seconds different from the dozens of others that are also won with a last-second basket? How does this school board meeting differ from the last one, and the one before that? What is the outstanding evidence in the prosecution's case, who among the many is the defense's key witness, the judge's most significant quote in his sentencing comments?

The journalist cannot leave it up to the reader, viewer or listener to decide. By knowing how to make the important, the pertinent, the relevant observation the reporter provides the public with insight.

'Make Me See'

When reporters see clearly and see as a whole, they are on their way to communicating not only truthfully, but graphically. Gene Roberts, former managing editor of *The New York Times,* learned this on his first job as the farm columnist for the 9,000-circulation *Goldsboro News-Argus* in Wayne County, N.C. Roberts' editor was Henry Belk, who was blind.

Roberts recalls that when he showed up for work in the morning, Belk would call him over and inform the young reporter that his writing was insufficiently descriptive.

"Make me see," he would order.

On Trial for Murder

"At times, he came across as harmless, anonymous, utterly forgettable; your eyes would sweep over him and barely register his presence. A minute later, he would shift in his chair or turn his head a certain way, and all at once he seemed intimidating, even menacing. It was there in his size and obvious physical strength, in the enormous forearms that rested on the table before him, in the way he stepped so jauntily in and out of the courtroom under the bailiff's escort. For someone so big, he was surprisingly light on his feet."
—Thomas French, *St. Petersburg Times*

Roberts says, "It took me years to appreciate it, but there is no better admonition to the writer than 'Make me see.' There is no truer blueprint for successful writing than making your readers see. It is the essence of great writing."

Murderer In his series that traced the search for and the trial of the killer of a woman and her two daughters aboard a boat in Tampa Bay, Thomas French of the *St. Petersburg Times* lets us see the accused through the eyes of jurors:

The jurors could not stomach Oba Chandler.

Some of them, sick of the smile he had worn through so much of the trial, wanted to slap him. Others were terrified of him.

Especially the women.

Linda Jones, an office administrator seated in the back row of the jury box, could hardly make eye contact with Chandler. If he looked her way, she averted her gaze. Evelyn Calloway, a school bus driver who sat in the front row, next to the witness stand, had looked into Chandler's eyes as he testified and had seen such coldness in him, she did not think he was human. Calloway began to worry that he might actually lunge for her from the witness box.

Rose Welton, a grandmother at the other end of the front row, was also struck by the chill in Chandler's stare. When he looked into her eyes, Welton thought she could feel his spirit, crawling inside her body.

A single word went through her, over and over:

Devil, devil, devil.

French's exhaustive reporting and vivid writing—the seven-part series was three years in the making—earned him a Pulitzer Prize.

Relevant Observations

The reporter on assignment is confronted by a flood of facts. A meeting can last two hours, cover seven different topics and include four decisions. A speaker may deliver an address containing 4,500 words. To handle these stories, the reporter may have at most a column for each story, about 750 words, or 90 seconds on a newscast, much less for an online report.

There are three guides to the selection of relevant facts:

1. **Know the community:** Develop a feeling and understanding of what readers need and want to know.

2. **Find the theme:** Carefully identify the theme of the story as soon in the reporting as possible. This way facts that support, buttress and amplify the theme can be gathered, the rest ignored as irrelevant.

3. **Look for the dramatic:** Seek out the unique, the different, the unusual, the break from the normal and routine.

Know the Community

The way to know the people in a community is to talk to them, to watch them at work and play, to study their past and to listen to their aspirations for themselves and their families. Talk to people in the Home Depot, chat with the service station attendant at Exxon, ask the first-grade teacher what her most pressing problems are. Go to a Little League game, read the clips about past news events, talk to old-timers and newcomers, to doctors and to the men and women who clean offices in the early-morning hours.

A Texas Tale   Reporters who move from one area to another often have trouble adjusting to their new readers and listeners. The story is told about the veteran reporter for a Chicago newspaper who decided to forsake the big city for a more relaxed life in Texas. He accepted a job as the city editor of a west Texas daily newspaper. One day a fire broke out in town and the reporter's blood stirred in the city editor. He decided to go out on the story himself.

On his return, he batted out a story, Chicago style—dramatic and well-written. The managing editor was pleased with his city editor's handiwork except for one hole in the story.

"How much water did they use to put out the fire?" he asked. In parched west Texas, that fact was as important to readers as the number of fire units answering the call would have been to Chicago readers.

Find the Theme

Our second guideline is based on the form of the news story, which places certain demands on the reporter that he or she must satisfy in fact gathering. We know that the story consists of the statement of a central theme or idea (the lead) and the elaboration of that theme or idea (the body). The reporter must find the theme quickly so he or she can ask the relevant questions and make the appropriate observations to flesh out the story.

The sociologist Irving Kristol observed, "A person doesn't know what he has seen unless the person knows what he is looking for." In his book, *The Art of Scientific Investigation,* the British scientist W.I.B. Beveridge writes that developing ideas or hypotheses helps a person "see the significance of an object or event that otherwise would mean nothing."

Let's watch two reporters at work.

On the Street   When the Salvation Army dispatched 4,000 of its soldiers to New York City to do battle against "sin and evil," a reporter for *The New York Times* accompanied some of the troops through the streets. Impressed by the work of the Army men and women, the reporter decided early in her reporting to emphasize their dedication and singled out this detail in her account to illustrate her theme:

"The Army believes in total abstinence," a young soldier was saying to a disheveled-looking man, whose breath reeked of alcohol. "You are the temple of the Lord and if you destroy yourself, you're destroying Him."

"Am I?" the older man asked, as they stood in front of the entranceway of the Commodore. "No, I'm not."

"Sure you are," the soldier replied, resting his hand on the man's shoulder. The man reached out his hand, too, and began to cry. So did the Salvation Army soldier.

At a Party   In another part of town, the veteran *New Yorker* reporter Lillian Ross is at a party for a Broadway opening. She notices many cast members of "The Sopranos" and a bunch of pre-teen-agers and their parents. Ross decides to stay close to "eleven-year-old Bianca Bethuna, a pretty girl with long dark hair" and Bianca's mother. Ross describes Bianca as wearing "a stiff, full-skirted, long white organdie dress, white stockings, white patent-leather slippers, a diamond necklace, a gold bracelet, a gold Mickey Mouse wristwatch, and a sparkling silver tiara, which she won in a 'Sunhurst Beauty Pageant' a few years ago."

Clearly, Bianca is being groomed for something, and this gives Ross her theme, and this theme guides Ross's observations and her questions. Ross learns that Bianca is driven from her home in New Jersey every day after school for dance lessons, and on weekends as well, "has a piano lesson once a week. She gets weekly private lessons with a voice teacher and an acting coach." Her mother tells Ross, "All this started when I took Bianca at eighteen months to Mommy and Me classes. As they say, you do what you got to do."

Mourner

For the reporter who seeks out the unusual, the sting of defeat may make as good a theme as the joy of victory.

The unusual is not always at center court. It may be on the sidelines where the losers bury their heads in grief. It could be found in the half-hidden gesture of capitulation when the candidate betrays a bold front. It could be buried in the small print in a document, the last sentence in a press release that begins with optimism and self-congratulation but ends with the admission of an unprofitable business year.

Looking deeply, listening intently, the reporter discovers truths that fascinate readers and viewers.

Gregg Lovett

It is almost midnight at the party and Bianca is at last being photographed with the play's leading actress. Ross writes, "Someone asked Bianca's mother if she was ready to take the limo and go home with Bianca. 'No way,' Bianca's mother said. 'We've got to work the room' " This is the concluding line in Ross's piece. It is not difficult to see what Ross has been getting at, what her theme is. Ross hasn't **told** us; she has **shown** us through her observations and the quotations she uses.

Caution   If the reporter discovers facts that contradict the theme, it is discarded and a new theme is adopted. In this way, the reporter is like the scientist whose conclusion can be no stronger than his or her evidence.

Of course, some events will have secondary themes. The same rule about gathering only material that buttresses the main theme applies to the secondary ideas as well.

Devising Themes   Experienced reporters almost always have a theme or tentative idea as soon as they receive an assignment or at the outset of a story they originate. If a reporter is sent to cover a fire in a college dormitory, the reporter immediately thinks of deaths and injuries and the cause as the theme or possible lead. If the assignment is about the rescue of a drowning man, the lead could be the courage or ingenuity of the rescuer. Six youths die in an automobile accident; the reporter cannot help but immediately think of alcohol and drugs or speeding.

As soon as the Bethesda Naval Center announced that Supreme Court Justice Thurgood Marshall had died, reporters knew the theme of their story and the direction it would take. The fact that a Supreme Court Justice had died was not the theme but that the first black to join the Court and a leading figure in the civil rights movement had died. And that is just how the AP story began:

> WASHINGTON—Retired Justice Thurgood Marshall, the first black to sit on the U.S. Supreme Court and a towering figure in the civil rights movement, died Sunday of heart failure. He was 84.

Reporters knew what to write because of their knowledge of Marshall and his career.

These themes or ideas tell the reporter "what to observe," to use Poe's language. They guide the reporter in asking questions, in doing background checks. In short, they allow the reporter to structure the reporting.

The theme or idea originates in the reporter's experience, knowledge of the subject, understanding of the essentials or necessities for this kind of story and in a vague area we can only describe as the reporter's feel for the subject.

Intuition   Some reporters call these ideas or insights hunches. (We will discuss hunches and reportorial intuition in Chapter 17.) Ideas also can originate in a reporter's prejudices or biases.

"Look, I have advance prejudices," says Seymour Hersh. "Any reporter who says he doesn't is kidding. But that doesn't mean I would deliberately report something wrong or not tell the truth about something. I would not change a story to make it fit what I think.

The reporter's theme or idea throws a broad shaft of light on the subject, allowing the reporter to see his or her way through the dense undergrowth of material. Reporters know that they also need to make a pencil-light penetration of the material to come up with the specific news pegs or news angles for their stories. To do this they fall back on their knowledge and experience to help them distinguish the new from the old, the unusual from the usual, the unexpected from the routine.

These "deviations from the plane of the ordinary," as Poe put it, provide the newsworthy element for the story.

The reporter can spot these deviations, these interruptions in the expected, by knowing a lot about the situation that is being reported. The extraordinary shouts out for attention to the reporter who is open to the significant, the novel.

Look for the Different

Learning to distinguish the unique from the routine is difficult enough, let alone for the sports reporter covering her 33rd basketball game, the education reporter covering his fifth school board meeting. Events seem to settle

Bob Thayer
The Providence Journal

Turning Point?

Did the steal open up a big inning? Or did the second baseman's grab of a poor throw keep the runner at second and prevent a rally? This play could be the lead for the game story.

Different Reason

Thousands cross the Rio Grande in search of work, but this pregnant woman wants her child born in the United States.

into a familiar pattern. Spotting differences is difficult. We grow up seeing likenesses, similarities. How many can distinguish the Jonathan from the Delicious, the Jersey from the Guernsey? To most of us, all apples are alike, and cows are just cows.

But journalists see differently. They learn early on to look at the world through the eyes of the innocent child while applying the discerning eye of the wise elder who can distinguish between the significant and the unimportant, the dramatic and the routine.

Red Smith, a sportswriter who covered so many baseball games he lost count, explained the basis of the journalist's artistry: "Every ball game is different from every other ball game—if the reporter has the knowledge and wit to discern the difference."

When Gustave Flaubert, the French novelist, was teaching Guy de Maupassant to write, he told the young man to pick out one of the cab drivers in front of a railway station in Paris and to describe him in a way that would differentiate him from all the other drivers. To do so, Maupassant had to find the significant details that would single out that one man. The moustache? No, four others have one. That slouch? No, they all seem to be collapsing. Ah, one has a red beret. The others are wearing black hats. Also, he is the only one without a cigarette dangling from his mouth.

Little differences make for big stories.

The Obvious   Sometimes the different is so obvious, so dramatic it needs no searching eye or finely attuned ear. The task, then, is to walk the fine line between writing that is overly flashy and writing that understates the drama. The event, situation should speak for itself.

When Jack Kelley, a foreign correspondent for *USA Today,* was talking to an Israeli official a suicide bomber made his move nearby. Thirty yards from Kelley he blew himself up and killed 15 men and women and injured 90.

The pizza restaurant had been packed with young people and the carnage was horrendous. *USA Today*'s front page editor did not hesitate to describe the scene graphically in this headline:

Explosion, then Arms and Legs Rain Down

For Kelley's equally graphic account, see **Terror Bombing** in *NRW Plus.* It is accompanied by his comments about how he handled the story.

Individuality

Experienced reporters usually agree on the themes of the stories they cover. Beyond that, each reporter puts his or her individual stamp on the story. Some of that individuality comes from writing style. Much is based on the particular observations the reporter makes. What is relevant to one reporter may be irrelevant to another.

When Homer Bigart, the winner of two Pulitzer Prizes and one of the country's great reporters, was sent to cover the military trial of Lt. William Calley, who had been accused of murdering civilians in the My Lai massacre during the Vietnam War, Bigart observed how Calley was brought into court. He linked this observation to his observations at another army officer's trial he had covered, and he wrote:

> Although he had just been found guilty of twenty-two murders, Calley was treated far more gently than was Army doctor Captain Howard B. Levy four years ago after receiving a sentence for refusing to give medical training to Green Berets on the grounds that the training would be used unlawfully in Vietnam.
>
> Unlike Levy, Calley was not handcuffed and left the court unfettered. An officer explained: "His conduct has been exemplary throughout and he'll continue to be treated as an officer."

Bigart's editors at *The New York Times* apparently considered his references to the Levy trial to be irrelevant, for the section read simply:

> Lieutenant Calley was not handcuffed
> when driven to the stockade.

Whose judgment was better, Bigart's or his editors'? Bigart's reference to the Levy trial provides the reader with some idea of the intense feeling of the military against the peace movement—of which Levy was a symbol—and its consideration for the accused murderer of civilians, a career army man.

Looking, Listening

A journalist may be sharp of sight, acute of hearing and blessed with wide experience and the best of news sense. But unless that journalist is in a position to see and hear what is happening, all these qualities are meaningless. Good observation begins with good vantage points. This usually means being close to the action.

At a news conference, Gov. Kirk Fordice of Mississippi told reporters, "The United States of America is a Christian nation. . . . The less we emphasize the Christian religion the further we fall into the abyss of poor character and chaos in the United States of America."

Gov. Carroll A. Campbell Jr. of South Carolina differed, he wanted reporters to know. "The value base of this country comes from the Judeo-Christian heritage that we have and that is something we need to realize." Richard L. Berke, who covered the conference for *The New York Times,* watched Campbell as he returned to his seat on the dais next to Fordice.

"I just wanted to add the 'Judeo' part," Campbell told Fordice. Berke then writes, "Mr. Fordice responded tartly, 'If I wanted to do that I would have done it.' "

The exchange, brief as it was, provided a shaft of light for the reader, an insight into the positions and the feelings of the conservative and center factions of the Republican Party.

Berke had positioned himself so that he could overhear the conversation of the governors.

Listening In

Rodger Mallison of the *Fort Worth Star-Telegram* took photos and conducted interviews for a series on local crime. Here's what he wrote about the arrest of the young driver he photographed taking a sobriety test:

"In two hours I'll be out," the man says.

"I don't think so, dude. I'm not taking you to the drunk tank. I'm taking you to jail for DWI," Johnson says.

"You can't do that. I'm a very intelligent man."

"I can see that. It takes a lot of intelligence to get behind the wheel drunk. You could've killed somebody."

"That's right, and I'll kill you," the man says. "Stupid ----. You'll get killed; we've already got your name. Come to Stop Six. You'll be six feet under. Your --- is going. I hate a black man that takes another black man down. . . . I'll kill you. I will slit your whole throat."

It is a long nine-minute ride to the jail.

"I had to bite my tongue a few times," Johnson says at the jail. "You definitely have to have a thick skin. You can't take it personally."

Checking It

So, not only get up close, but when what you think you've heard sounds strange, check it out. Look into that seemingly wild statement, rumor or situation. Don't write it off. The reward could be a footnote in journalism history, or a Pulitzer Prize.

Editors attending a luncheon at a convention of the American Society of Newspaper Editors were astonished when they saw Fidel Castro, the guest of honor, reach across the table and swap plates with the president of the Society.

Had an editor acted on that astonishment at the 1961 banquet and done what reporters are supposed to do—ask why—that editor might have been informed that Castro feared assassination. And that editor might have had a major story. For in 1975, the Central Intelligence Agency admitted that during the administrations of presidents Eisenhower, Kennedy and Johnson the United States government had indeed tried to murder Castro.

Down the Drain   No one could believe the rumors: The Internal Revenue Service was botching a huge number of returns. Some weren't being examined, some were tossed away. Arthur Howe of *The Philadelphia Inquirer* decided to check the rumors and he learned that the IRS had mishandled one of three returns for the previous year. In Atlanta, a worker flushed returns down a toilet. In Memphis, complicated returns were destroyed.

The IRS denied it all. But Howe persisted, and he corroborated everything. He was awarded the Pulitzer Prize for National Reporting.

Unbelievable   Deborah E. Lipstadt maintains in her book *The American Press and the Covering of the Holocaust* that many newspapers refused to publish reports of the Nazi Final Solution because the reports of death squads and gas chambers were "beyond belief." If the newspapers and radio stations had been less skeptical of the reports of refugees, she writes, they might have had an accurate description of Hitler's rise to power and his policies.

The Holocaust and the Castro incident point to an unseen dimension of reporting. Although the reporter is guided by logic, he or she must be open to the most implausible facts and observations. Time after time reporters find aberrant facts and extraordinary observations and put them aside as too unusual for further examination. No report should be dismissed—no matter how outlandish it seems—without at least a quick check.

Caution: Notice the word *check*. The journalist's term for this is verification. By verification journalists mean direct observation and when that is not possible they mean statistical data, documents, reports, some kind of physical evidence. An anecdote or an isolated incident is not verification. These serve to buttress the observation and the evidence, give it a human dimension.

When physical evidence is impossible to obtain and direct observation is blocked, then human sources are acceptable if there is confirmation from several such sources.

Limitations of the Story

Although we may agree that the reporter's task is to continue the search for relevant facts until the theme is adequately supported, we also must admit that the search can never be completed, that there are facts beyond the reporter's reach. Just as a map can never be the complete guide to a territory, so a news story is rarely the definitive statement of reality.

Here are some of the obstacles reporters face:

- The deadline.
- The source the reporter cannot locate.
- The missing record, document or newspaper clipping.
- The incident the reporter cannot see or hear properly.
- The facts the source will not divulge.
- The material the copy editor cuts out of the story.
- The reporter's own limitations.
- The book or magazine the reporter fails to read. Yesterday's newspaper left unread beyond page 1.
- The phone call not returned.
- The question not asked.
- The appointment missed.

For those who like ideas expressed in formulas, we can represent the concept of the limitations of the story with the Reporter's Equation:

$$\textbf{Truth = Story + X}$$

Actually, the capital letter X represents a series of small x's—those that we have listed as the obstacles reporters face.

From our quick trip into the realm of math, let's take a turn down the hall to talk to a semanticist about truth and certainty.

Certainty's Boundaries

As the semanticist Wendell Johnson put it, "There is always at least a small gap between the greatest probability and absolute certainty." But we can be certain, Johnson does say, about some statements.

"It is certain that $2 = 2$," Johnson says, "because we say so. We agree to treat it as certain." But there is no certainty that two lawyers equal two lawyers. "No two things are the same, and no one thing stays the same," he says.

This concept is helpful to the journalist, for it guarantees—if it is followed—the reporter will take a fresh eye to people and events, that the first impression is helpful but not decisive.

"In the realm of direct experience," Johnson says, "whether we look backward in memory or forward in anticipation, nothing is absolutely certain. Each new situation, problem, or person is to be approached, therefore, not with rigidly fixed habits and preconceived ideas, but with a sense of apparent probabilities."

We will be discussing how journalists formulate "apparent probabilities" in Chapter 17 when we examine hunches, feelings and thinking patterns. But it should be said here that reporters covering their 5th football game, 10th basketball game, 15th city council meeting or 20th speech need to keep Johnson's advice in mind: (1) no two things are the same and (2) approach a reporting situation with an open mind but with some idea of the story.

Red Smith, whom many consider the best of all the sportswriters, went to every game. "He was horrified that someone might actually cover a game by watching TV or listening to radio," Gene Roberts said. Smith "needed the material, the sense of being there," Roberts said. It was his "being there" that gave Smith material that made his story of **this** game different from the story about yesterday's game.

Smith also approached each game with some idea of "probabilities," which he derived from the names of the starting pitchers, the possible continuation of streaks, animosities left over from the last time the teams played and a dozen other factors.

The Tyranny of Time

The clock is the journalist's major obstacle. Unlike the historian or the sociologist, who face few daily or weekly deadlines in their work, the journalist submits to the requirements of publication and airtime while still seeking to present a complete and accurate account.

Complex events require the time to find relationships that link seemingly disparate events. The reporter may find that the newspaper or station will not provide time. Discouraged, the reporter sometimes settles for a rudimentary form of truth, the recital of what sources declare (Layer I journalism), which is truth of a sort.

Style as a Barrier

The journalistic style also may obstruct truth. The journalist is instructed to tell a story in simple, dramatic, personalized prose. Some important events are complicated. The reporter who seeks to make these events—usually ideas, trends, concepts—come alive may distort them by using exciting details that are colorful but misleading. For years, the newsmagazines emphasized this kind of detail. Their correspondents named the wines the diplomat drank, counted the cigarettes he smoked during a tense hearing. The significance of the event often was lost in the human-interest trivia.

The Reporter as Intruder

The act of reporting can itself be an impediment to accurate observations. Walter Lippmann characterized the journalist as a "fly on the wall," a detached observer whose presence does not affect the event being observed. But if reporting requires close-at-hand observation, scrupulous note taking, photographs, or tape, how unobtrusive can the reporter be? The fly descends and buzzes around the event.

We know what happens when a television crew arrives at an event. Drones become animated. Reserved people begin to gesticulate. Reality is altered.

At a political rally in Central America, a reporter noted the calm, almost serene atmosphere. Even when a speaker released a dove from the center of the plaza, the crowd was hushed. Then the television and still photographers arrived, and the event suddenly took another shape. Fists were shaken. A Cuban flag was unfurled for the photographers, and revolutionary slogans were shouted into the recording equipment. When the photographers departed, the rally returned to its placid state. In the next day's newspaper, accompanying the reporter's story of a quiet protest against United States policy, was a shot of what seemed to be a fist-shaking mob.

Even the reporter's pencil and paper can distort the event. Every reporter experiences the trying moment when, after chatting with a source to put him or her at ease, it is time to reach for a pencil and notepad. In an instant, the mood changes. The simple tools of the reporter's trade have spooked the source.

Unobtrusive Observation

This type of reaction can be avoided by nonreactive or unobtrusive observation, methods that have the merit of allowing the reporter to be a fly on the wall. Let us follow a reporter as he uses this reporting technique.

Among the dozens of reporters gathered in central California to attend a Republican state conference was a reporter who was unknown to the delegates. He was able to mix freely, smiling and shaking hands with delegates. He knew he was being mistaken for a young delegate, and when one of the central committee secretaries told him there was an important meeting, he went along with her. They walked into the meeting together, and he sat near her, apparently doodling absent-mindedly on a pad in front of him.

All day long he moved in and out of caucuses, meetings and powwows. He heard Orange County delegates denounce the president, a Republican, as a liberal, a spendthrift, an enemy of the party's conservative principles. He listened as deals were made to try to attract labor and minority votes.

The week before when another political group held a convention, the reporter had plumped down in a soft chair in the lobby of the hotel and listened. He had heard delegates talk about bringing back the gold standard, the threat of communism from minorities, the radicalism of the labor movement and the dangers of sex education in the public schools.

Ethics Debated

Some journalists condemn this kind of reporting. They point out that journalists have exposed intrusions into privacy by credit investigators and some governmental agencies. Journalists cannot, they say, set themselves apart from the rules they would apply to others.

A reporting techinique that avoids the dilemma about concealing the reporter's identity is described by Helen Benedict of Columbia as "watch-and-wait" journalism. Sources know a reporter is present, but the reporter eases into the background, rarely asking a question. Lillian Ross, whose piece about an aggressive mother and her 11-year-old daughter we examined a few pages back, practices this kind of journalism. It is as close to the fly-on-the-wall reporting as journalism can reach.

Journalistic ethics are discussed further in Chapter 27.

Going Along for the Morning Collection

For her story about sanitation men, Phoebe Zerwick of the *Winston-Salem Journal* rides along on the orange garbage truck as the men make their morning rounds. She absorbs the sights and the sounds—and the smells, too. "A mist lingers on an unusually cool August morning. A few dogs bark, lunging at fences. Once in a while someone starts a car engine and backs out of a driveway. . . . The smell, sometimes sweet, sometimes sour, is still faint at 8 a.m. before the heat of the day cooks up stronger odors." She observes the workers: "The men keep up a furious pace, with Casey, 28, taking long strides in knee-high rubber boots and McLaurin, 34, running."

Participant Observation

Another research method—participant observation—links social science and journalism strategies. An Oregon reporter who managed to fold his six-foot frame into a third grader's seat at school was a participant observer. The reporter who worked as a telephone operator and then wrote a series of articles based on her observations was basing her stories on personal experience. At the simplest level, a reporter can spend a day with a meter reader, a public health nurse.

In participant observation, the reporter discards his or her role as the uninvolved, detached observer and joins the activity of the person or group he or she is covering. The reporter who became a third-grader for a story participated in the children's school work, ate lunch with them and played ball at recess. The school children took him for a friend, a bit older and awkward about some things, but a companion nevertheless. They talked to him as an equal. His relationship with the students enabled him to gather material that the usual interview and observation techniques would not have revealed.

News vs. Reality

William Foote Whyte, in his classic study of an Italian-American slum, *Street Corner Society* (Chicago: The University of Chicago Press, 1943), talks about the difference between the traditional perception of what is news and the reality of the way people live, which participant observation allows the reporter to view:

> If the politician is indicted for accepting graft, that is news. If he goes about doing the usual personal favors for his constituents, that is not news. The newspaper concentrates on the crisis—the spectacular event. In a crisis the "big shot" becomes public property. He is removed from the society in which he functions and he is judged by standards different from his own group. This may be the most effective way to prosecute the lawbreaker. It is not a good way to understand him. For that purpose, the individual must be put back into his social setting and observed in his daily activities. In order to understand the spectacular event, it is necessary to see it in relation to the everyday pattern of life. . . .

Whyte learned how to be accepted by the street corner people. "If you ask direct questions, people will just clam up on you," he writes. "If people accept you, you can just hang around, and you'll learn the answers in the long run without even having to ask the questions."

When Whyte used some obscenities to try to gain acceptance, one of his new friends advised him, "Bill, you're not supposed to talk like that. That doesn't sound like you." Whyte had to be careful about influencing the group he was observing. "I tried to be helpful in the way a friend is expected to be helpful." The results of his observations allowed the reader to have a moving picture of the street corner society, not the still photograph that the brief glimpse allows.

New Directions

The influence of social scientists like Whyte, Margaret Mead and others who studied people in their settings influenced journalists. Traditionally, journalism focused on centers of authority with their formalities—ceremonies, meetings, announcements. This was insufficient, journalists came to realize. They understood that they were not describing the reality of human experience and they became anxious to develop techniques that enabled them to expand their reporting. Sara Grimes, a reporter in Philadelphia, said after she had been covering the juvenile court for a year, "I wonder why so many reporters insist on quoting people in positions of power rather than observing people who are affected by power."

Listening to Youngsters   She listened closely to the young defendants in court, and she sought to understand the effect of the system on youngsters by talking to them. One day she learned that an 11-year-old boy—who was brought into court in handcuffs—had been held in a detention center for nine months although he had not committed a crime. He was a runaway. Grimes asked to talk to the youngster, who had been sent to foster homes after his parents were judged neglectful. He had not liked the foster homes and had run away. Here is part of the story she wrote:

"Jones, Jones," the guard's voice could be heard as he walked up and down the cell-block. Amid a few undistinguishable low grumblings behind the rows of bars came a small, high voice. "Yes, that's me."

Johnny was brought out to an anteroom. No longer crying, he sat with downcast eyes in dungarees and a gray sweatshirt. Quietly and slowly he answered questions.

He wished he had somebody to bring him soap because the institutional soap gives him a rash. He would like to leave YSC (Youth Study Center) and would go "any place they send me."

How does it feel to be handcuffed? In a barely audible voice, he answered: "It makes me feel like a criminal."

The Epidemic   Barbara Ferry of *The New Mexican* in Santa Fe found worry and fear in the usually placid northern New Mexico villages and towns. Drugs. Everywhere. In the village of Chimayo, she wrote, there are more than 30 dealers. "Villagers don't seem to be getting noticeably richer," she wrote. "They are dying." Her series included portraits of some of the victims, most of them young men and women. Some of these are in *NRW Plus* **The Damage Done.**

With an Addict   Loretta Tofani of *The Philadelphia Inquirer* watched as the young woman dropped her maternity pants past her swollen stomach. The woman, eight months pregnant, picked up a syringe and injected heroin into her right calf.

"He won't stop moving, this baby," the woman told Tofani. "When he moves a lot it means he's sick. He needs a fix."

Tofani stayed with the 30-year-old addict for months, watched her wheedle money from relatives for her drugs, stayed in her kitchen when she entertained a visitor for the $20 she needed for a fix.

And she stayed through the birth of the baby and watched the woman fight to retain custody of her daughter, who was born addicted to heroin, methadone and a pill the woman was popping before the birth.

Going behind the Doors

These reporters who contend that journalism has not dug deeply enough into the lives of people would agree with Chekhov's observation in his short story "Gooseberries":

We see the people who go to market, eat by day, sleep by night, who babble nonsense, marry, grow old, good-naturedly drag their dead to the cemetery, but we do not see or hear those who suffer, and what is terrible in life goes on somewhere behind the scenes. Everything is peaceful and quiet and only mute statistics protest: so many people gone out of their minds, so many gallons of vodka drunk, so many children dead from malnutrition. And such a state of things is evidently necessary; obviously the happy man is at ease only because the unhappy ones bear their burdens in silence, and if there were not this silence, happiness would be impossible. It is a general hypnosis. Behind the door of every contented, happy man there ought to be someone standing with a little hammer and continually reminding him with a knock that there are unhappy people, that however happy he may be, life will sooner or later show him its claws, and trouble will come to him—illness, poverty, losses, and then no one will see or hear him, just as now he neither sees nor hears others. But there is no man with a hammer. The happy man lives at his ease, faintly fluttered by small daily cares, like an aspen in the wind—and all is well.

Some reporters see themselves as the man behind the door. Their hammer is pad and pencil, camera and tape recorder. Let's look closely at a journalist who devoted considerable time to such reporting.

A Ghetto Family

In Depth Dash, now a member of the journalism faculty at the University of Illinois, calls the technique he used to write about the troubled family "immersion journalism."

Leon Dash, a reporter for *The Washington Post,* spent several years with a woman and her family in a relationship so close that he was able to gather the most intimate details of their lives. Although sympathetic to the family, Dash was unsparing in his presentation of a family wracked by poverty, drugs, prostitution, crime and illiteracy.

The book Dash wrote later is dedicated to "unfettered inquiry."

The head of the family, Rosa Lee, in her 50s on welfare and food stamps, supports herself through shoplifting and drug dealing. She has eight children by five different men. Dash shows her strengths as well as her weaknesses—her love for her children, aspiration to a decent life, resourcefulness. But he is no soft touch for the tales his sources tell him. Ducky, Rosa Lee's youngest son, informs Dash that he has had a religious conversion and will hereafter serve Christ.

Dash tells Ducky, "You cook powdered cocaine into crack for New York City dealers . . . and you have been addicted to crack for some time now."

Drugs emerge as the major destructive force in the life of the family Dash portrays. Two sons manage to escape from the dysfunctional home life, and Dash says three factors were involved: They attended school longer than their brothers and sisters; an adult became concerned about them (one a school teacher, the other a social worker), and each was able to obtain a full-time job.

The Live In

Dash's extended participant observation can also be described as a Live In, a reporting technique introduced 35 years ago at the Graduate School of Journalism at Columbia University. Based on the work of Margaret Mead, Oscar Lewis and Robert Coles, the Live In sends students into homes and workplaces. To move closer to their sources, students have tutored addicts in drug rehabilitation centers and children in schools. They have slept on the floors of mission houses in the Bowery, in sleeping bags at a residence of the Catholic Workers and on cots in shelters for the homeless.

Students have walked the beat with police officers, gone on home visits with social workers and accompanied ambulance drivers on their calls. These experiences were not one-shot affairs. Students met the policeman's family, talked to the welfare mother's children and went into wards to talk to patients.

The Students

Charles Young, a white, middle-class student from Wisconsin, did his Live In at a junior high school in West Harlem in New York City. Let's join Young while he waits for the assistant principal in his office. The room is filled with students. Young describes the scene at the beginning of his Live In:

Gus Marinos, known simply as "Marinos" to everybody, a Greek immigrant in his twenties with dazed but kindly eyes beneath his Coke-bottle glasses, returns to his office on the fourth floor. The room erupts with a deafening chorus of his name.

"MAH-*REE*-NOS! HER FINGERNAILS BE POISON!" a girl screams, holding up her scratched right hand.

"So die," says Marinos, examining some smudged papers on his desk.

"WHY 'ON'T CHEW DIE!"

"You wanna go home?"

"YEAH, BUT CHEW CAN'T TELL ME HER NAILS AIN'T POISON!"

"So go home."

"HER NAILS GOT DIRT AN' SHIT IN 'M!" The girl leaves with a pass home.

"MAH-*REE*-NOS!" another girl demands, "GIMME A PENCIL!" He hands her a pencil from his desk. "I 'ON'T WANT NO PENCIL LIKE THAT! I WANNA BLACK PENCIL!"

"This *is* a black pencil."

"I MEAN A YELLOW PENCIL THAT WRITES BLACK!"

"We don't sell those here."

"I 'ON'T WANT TO BUY NO PENCIL! I WANT CHEW TO GIMME IT!" She grabs the pencil from his hand and in the process drops a textbook. "NOW SEE YOU MADE ME DONE DIRTY MY BOOK!"

"I made you done what?"

"DIRTY MY BOOK!" She leaves for class.

These girls read an average of two years below the national norm for their grade level (slightly ahead of the boys), but the ghetto has already taught them how to get what they want from life: yell until somebody gives it to you. The lesson is apt, because when they are graduated in three years or so, they won't be equipped to do anything anyway.

That these girls (all sent to the office for disciplinary reasons) want something is obvious. What they want is less obvious and increasingly important as the market for unskilled labor dries up.

The first step in finding out what they want is learning a new vocabulary, some of which would be useful to define here. To "come out your mouth" is to communicate. "On time" is an adjective or adverb of approbation meaning you have done something according to socially accepted procedure. "On cap" is synonymous with "in your head," referring to intelligence. . . .

The Disciplinarian

Young interviewed the assistant principal in charge of discipline, who, he writes, "carries a cane in one hand and a leather whip in the other when she wades into a group of warring Dominican and Puerto Rican youths."

His description continues:

She resembles an army tank—solid, low-to-the-ground, unstoppable, paradoxically maternal.

She is in fact known as the mother of the school. Teachers speak with awe of the dedication that brings her to the otherwise deserted building on weekends and vacations. Students speak with equal awe of her omniscience. Because they trust her, she knows exactly who is pushing what drugs and who is fighting with whom.

Standing at the main entrance to the building at 3 o'clock one Friday afternoon in anticipation of a gang fight, Williams catalogues a gathering of a dozen or so Puerto Rican school alumni.

"That one is on parole now. . . . That one is pushing. Look at his station wagon. . . . That one has a sawed-off .38 in his pocket. We'd tell the police about it, but it will pass fifty hands by the time they can react. . . ."

On Thursday, one of their little brothers dropped a piece of chalk from the fourth floor that hit a Dominican on the head. In the ensuing melee, another Puerto Rican was badly cut on the arm with a broken bottle. The Puerto Ricans seek vengeance.

Having no stake in the matter, the blacks are blasé and leave the area immediately. They've seen it all before and even the prospect of serious violence is a bore. The Hispanics gather in groups along the sidewalk and buzz with rumors, with more energy than they have shown all day in class.

Williams crosses the street and puts her arm around one of her former students who has an Afro bigger than the rest of his body. She makes small talk for a couple of minutes, then kisses him on his pockmarked cheek as the gang scatters off down the street. A group of Dominicans, observing the enemy from a block away, disappears to its lair on 133rd Street.

The aborted fight is typical of junior highs anywhere in that the participants seem willing to do battle over nothing. What is frightening is that the involved alumni range in age from 16 to the mid-twenties. They never grew up, just became better armed. They are the fruit of the American system of education.

"Even five years ago they at least expressed an interest in college," says Williams back in the dormitory-room-sized office which she shares with three other school officials and usually seven or eight students who have been thrown out of class. . . .

The Basketball Player

Young befriended a bright young black student in the school. After Young graduated and went to work for *Rolling Stone,* he decided to look up the youngster for a story for the magazine about his dream of becoming a basketball star. He found the youth in high school, playing basketball, struggling with his classes and still filled with hope. Young's piece, "Above 125th Street: Curtis Haynes' New York," begins:

"I'm growin' plants all the time," says Curtis Haynes, pouring half a glass of water over a geranium. The floor and window ledge of his bedroom are covered with leafy pots. "Plants are everything. They give us oxygen and food. They also a home for insects." He brushes an aphid off a leaf. "Insects gonna inherit the earth."

He continues the tour of his room—recently painted electric blue by his mother—by pulling a picture off a shelf full of basketball trophies. Judging by his fleeting eyes and reticent tone of voice, he doesn't know what to make of me—a pale, white, 26-year-old, bearded magazine editor with thick glasses from a myopic childhood of too much TV watching and book reading in Madison, Wisconsin. Nor do I know what to make of him—a handsome, ebony-skinned, 16-year-old, short-haired high-school student with sharp vision from a childhood spent on the basketball courts of Harlem. "This is my brother, Footie," he says, holding a blurred photograph of a teenager bearing a strong resemblance to Curtis. "Remember, remember, remember . . ." is inscribed around the margins. "We named him that because he had such big feet," he says. Curtis' Pro Ked basketball shoes equal my own 11 1/2 Adidas—and I am 6' 2" while he is just 5' 10". "He died in a fight two years ago. Puerto Rican friend got in an argument at a party and the other dude pulled a gun. My brother jumped between them. I never go to parties no more."

The Crab Pickers

In Chapter 8 we read about the departure of a group of young women from a village in Mexico to North Carolina where they were to work in a crab plant. The elderly black women who had worked at the task of picking out the slivers of crab from the hard shells had gradually retired and a new source of workers was found in Mexico.

Two days after the phone call came, Hull was aboard a bus with the women for the four-day trip to the Outer Banks. She stayed with the women on and off for the length of their stay and returned home with them. Her four months of reporting was a Live In.

For more of Hull's work, see **Una Vida Mejor—A Better Life—(II)** in *NRW Plus*.

Anne Hull on Reporting   She wrote of a police officer that the officer wears "size 4, steel-toe boots."

"I asked her because I noticed she had small feet. And I said, 'Are those steel-toe boots?' A lot of it is just conversation. It's not conscious reporting. They think it's chit chat, but it's my job. I'm writing down everything."

How does she gather so much intimate and specific material?

"I don't think you can ever study someone too much, or be around them too much. It's hanging out with people. It's observing, which is just as important as the words that come out of their mouth."

On her interviewing style:

"It's very casual. Lots of eye contact. I tend to give my two cents and say, 'Oh yeah. I know what you mean. That happened to me once.' That makes people comfortable. But you can't do too much of it. It's not just what they say. It's how they look and how they say something."

Problems of Involvement

Participant observation can cause problems. In addition to the possibility that the reporter's presence may affect the event, the participant observer can become too deeply involved with his or her sources, risking the possibility that feelings may override responsibility to the facts.

Participant observation also has been criticized as exploitation of the source. After all, the journalist is using the lives of people as the basis of a story, which could lead to the reporter's acclaim, help him or her win a pay raise and possibly a promotion. But the alcoholic, the addict, the welfare mother and the police officer are not reimbursed for their contributions. Nor is much done about the problems that overwhelm some of these people.

Prying Indefensible The journalist James Agee agonized over prying into the lives of Southern sharecroppers. He and the photographer Walker Evans were assigned to do an article on cotton tenantry, the system by which farmers worked the fields of landowners in return for a share of the crop less what was advanced to them for seed, living quarters and tools. The sharecroppers were poorer than dirt poor, for not even the earth they tilled was theirs. The magazine article was not published, but in 1940 the work became a book, *Let Us Now Praise Famous Men.* Agee knew the justifications for his intimate observations, but they did not console him. Early in the book, he describes his reservations:

> It seems to me curious, not to say obscene and thoroughly terrifying, that it could occur to an association of human beings drawn together through need and chance and for profit into a company, an organ of journalism, to pry intimately into the lives of an undefended and appallingly damaged group of human beings, an ignorant and helpless rural family, for the purpose of parading the nakedness, disadvantage and humiliation of these lives before another group of human beings, in the name of science, of "honest journalism" (whatever that paradox may mean), of humanity, of social fearlessness, for money, and for a reputation for crusading and for unbias which, when skillfully enough qualified, is exchangeable at any bank for money (and in politics, for votes, for job patronage, abelincolnism, etc.). . . .

In Defense of Prying

In rebuttal to these criticisms, reporters who use the technique say that public awareness is increased by stories about the lives of people. They say this awareness can lead to reform by involving the public emotionally in the situations described by the reporter.

Steven Almond, a reporter for the *Miami New Times,* spent weeks at the James E. Scott housing project to reveal "what life is really like for the women and children living in Miami's inner city." Almond said he was bothered by one aspect of his work:

> By far, the most difficult aspect of the work was realizing that I was merely another male figure who would eventually abandon the kids that I had befriended. And facing that, in some deep sense, I was exploiting the kids by using their lives as journalistic fodder. It was betrayal.

Hopefully, The Canyon managed to convey a little bit about what it is like, day to day, for women and children who live in inner-city housing projects. That's not a story often told.

A Corrective for Detachment

Participant observation can help correct a detachment that can lead to callousness. A student who said he considered drug addicts weak and worthless conducted a Live In with a young female addict. The woman's daughter was being put up for adoption because the mother had been judged unfit to raise her. The woman's agony at the prospect of losing her daughter—which the student felt intensely—led him to do a series of revealing articles about the city's adoption laws.

The experience of participant observation allows the reporter to step outside routines and familiar environments to achieve new insights and to avoid another trap—the tendency to stereotype. Working under pressure, reporters fall back on stereotyping people, which permits them to simplify complicated events and to communicate complexities in easily understood terms. Forgetting that life is endless variety and change, some reporters look at the world through a kaleidoscope that is never turned. As a consequence, their observations reflect only a narrow, static vision. In Chapter 17, we will examine these stereotypes and the ways of thinking that determine how reporters look at events.

Everyday Reporting

Whether the reporter is involved in participant observation or covering a city council hearing, the principles and the methods of reporting are the same.

The reporter has a sense of what is newsworthy from his or her familiarity with the community and the beat. On assignment, the reporter tries to come up with a story idea quickly. Then the reporter documents the idea.

But the reporter is not so transfixed by the broad theme that he or she ignores details. When Christopher Ringwald of the *Watertown Daily Times* covered the disappearance of a young mother, he noted in his story, "The only item missing with Miss McDonald was a quart bottle of Bacardi rum." She had taken nothing else with her when she left.

Six weeks later, a partially decomposed body was found in a remote area. The identity was uncertain, and the police were not talking. But Ringwald did learn one fact that made his story have some certainty about the identification of the woman:

> To the side of the corpse, which was found in a reclining position as if the woman had fallen asleep there, according to Chief King, was a quart bottle of Bacardi rum.

Ringwald said that when he interviewed the family he asked what the woman took with her. On learning it was rum, "it seemed unnecessarily nosey to ask what brand. But I did."

Not only do reporters ask questions that they think will elicit useful replies, they note relevant and specific physical characteristics: Are there fewer spectators than anticipated? Were the bookcases empty? Is the block on which the murder took place a quiet residential street? Was the highway slick with rain when the accident occurred? Was it dark or dusk when the game ended?

They note whether the bird in the cage of the apartment in which the crime took place was a parakeet, canary or parrot. And they listen if it is a parrot. A reporter for a California newspaper put up high in his story the cries of the parrot at the scene of a murder-suicide: "Where's mommy? Where's daddy?"

Summing Up

The key to first-rate observation is the quality of the theme the reporter has in mind. The reporter's theory or idea—call it the possible lead to the story—"suggests and coordinates observations," says the scientist and teacher-writer Stephen Jay Gould of Harvard. "Theory can prod, suggest, integrate and direct in fruitful ways."

But it "can also stifle, mislead and restrict," Gould adds. He calls the business of devising themes as a prelude to making observations the "double-edged sword . . . as both liberator and incarcerator. . . ." It is liberating when the theme is borne out by information gathered by detached observation. It is incarcerating when the reporter's observations are made with eyes and ears determined to see and hear on the basis of hope and belief that the theme or lead is on target.

In the next chapter, we will look at how reporters build the background on which they structure sound observations for their stories.

Further Reading

Agee, James. *Let Us Now Praise Famous Men*. Boston: Houghton Mifflin, 1960.

Beveridge, W.I.B. *The Art of Scientific Investigation*. New York: Vintage Books, 1962.

Dash, Leon. *Rosa Lee: A Mother and Her Family in Urban America*. New York: Basic Books, 1996.

Lipstadt, Deborah E. *The American Press and the Covering of the Holocaust, 1933–1945*. New York: Free Press, 1985.

Sanders, Marlene, and Marcia Rock. *Waiting for Prime Time: The Women of Television News*. Urbana: University of Illinois Press, 1988.

12 Building and Using Background

Dorothea Lange, The Library of Congress

Classic photo. What is the subject?

Preview

Journalists are always at work building two kinds of background knowledge:

• **General:** The overall knowledge that the reporter takes to the job. This storehouse is based on wide reading and general experience.

• **Specific:** The specialized information that helps the reporter handle his or her beat. It includes, for example, knowing about one judge's preference for jail sentences and another's for probation, or the mayor's determination to reassess property values to increase revenues.

A command of background allows the reporter to see connections among facts and incidents; this grouping of material leads to stories that are more revealing than is the bare recital of the news event.

The journalist is expected to know it all. An error, a missing fact or a misinterpretation cannot be explained away.

Demanding as this may seem, it is the lot of the professional to be unfailingly certain in performance. The doctor is expected to identify the ailment that plagues the patient. The attorney is an authority on the law. The teacher is a wise, unfaltering guide who takes students through the complexities of phonics, irregular French verbs and William Blake.

But we know professionals are fallible. Doctors misdiagnose, and sometimes their operations fail. Lawyers lose cases they should win. Teachers are human, too, like the grade school teacher who assigned her class the task of writing sentences containing words from a list she supplied. One youngster, who consulted his collection of baseball cards for inspiration, chose the word *cap,* and he wrote, "Catfish Hunter wears a cap." The teacher returned the boy's paper with the sentence corrected: "**A** catfish hunter wears a cap."

Should the teacher have known Catfish Hunter was a baseball player? Well, perhaps we do make excuses for teachers, as well as for doctors and lawyers. But we do not excuse the journalist who errs through ignorance.

Should the journalist really be expected to know everything? "Yes," said the reporter Murray Kempton. "When you're covering anything, and you're writing about it at length, you use everything you know. And in order to use everything you have to be interested in an extraordinary range of things."

Should you have known that the photograph that opens this chapter—the most reproduced photo of all time—is titled "Migrant Mother" and portrays the anxiety about the future of a pea picker left destitute in California during the Great Depression of the 1930s? At age 32, she is the mother of seven children.

For more photographs with which you can test your background knowledge, see **Important Parts of the Past** in *NRW Plus.*

Twain's and Mencken's Complaints

In Mark Twain's *Sketches,* he describes his experiences as a newspaperman in "How I Edited an Agricultural Paper." Twain is telling a friend that little intelligence is needed to be a journalist:

> I tell you I have been in the editorial business going on fourteen years, and it is the first time I ever heard of a man's having to know anything in order to edit a newspaper. You turnip! Who write the dramatic critiques for the second-rate papers? Why, a parcel of promoted shoemakers and apprentice apothecaries, who know just as much about good acting as I do about good farming and no more. Who review the books? People who never wrote one. Who do up the heavy leaders on finance? Parties who have had the largest opportunities for knowing nothing about it. Who criticise the Indian campaigns? Gentlemen who do not know a war whoop from a wigwam, and who never have had to run a foot race with a tomahawk, or pluck arrows out of the several members of their families to build the evening camp-fire with. Who write the temperance appeals, and clamor about the flowing bowl? Folks who will never draw another sober breath till they do it in the grave.

H.L. Mencken, a journalist whose prose skewered presidents, poets and bartenders with equal vigor, used some of his most choice execrations to denounce his fellow journalists. In an editorial in the *American Mercury,* October 1924, he wrote of journalists:

> The majority of them, in almost every American city, are ignoramuses, and not a few of them are also bounders. All the knowledge that they pack into their brains is, in every reasonable cultural sense, useless; it is the sort of knowledge that belongs, not to a professional man, but to a police captain, a railway mail-clerk or a board boy in a brokerage house. It is a mass of trivialities and puerilities; to recite it would be to make even a barber or a bartender beg for mercy. What is missing from it is everything worth knowing—everything that enters into the common knowledge of educated men. There are managing editors in the United States, and scores of them, who have never heard of Kant or Johannes Müller and never read the Constitution of the United States; there are city editors who do not know what a symphony is, or a streptococcus, or the Statute of Frauds; there are reporters by the thousand who could not pass the entrance examination for Harvard or Tuskegee, or even Yale. It is this vast ignorance that makes American journalism so pathetically feeble and vulgar, and so generally disreputable no less. A man with so little intellectual enterprise that,

dealing with news daily, he goes through life without taking in any news that is worth knowing—such a man, you may be sure, is as lacking in true self-respect as he is in curiosity. Honor does not go with stupidity. If it belongs to professional men, it belongs to them because they constitute a true aristocracy—because they have definitely separated themselves from the great masses of men. The journalists, in seeking to acquire it, put the cart before the horse.

GBS: Two Views

The practice of journalism arouses considerable passion among outsiders, sometimes leading them to excesses of inconsistency. George Bernard Shaw, the eminent playwright and critic, was of two minds regarding journalism. In a note to a journalist, he wrote:

> Dear Sir,
> Your profession has, as usual, destroyed your brain.

But he also wrote:

> Journalism can claim to be the highest form of literature. For all the highest literature is journalism, including Plato and Aristophanes trying to knock some sense into the Athens of their days and Shakespeare peopling that same Athens with Elizabethans. Nothing that is not journalism will live as long as literature or be of any use while it does live. So let others cultivate what they may call literature. Journalism for me.

Improvements?

These comments were made years ago. Journalists are now college trained, often in schools of journalism (a hopeful sign, Mencken said in the same editorial we have quoted from). And yet: What are we to make of the current generation, one of whose representatives wrote in a college newspaper about a presentation of *The Merchant of Venus,* instead of *The Merchant of Venice?*

And what can we say to the journalism student who wrote of the sculptor Michel Angelo? Or to the reporter who wrote when crimes in town doubled that they went up 200 percent?

Should the journalist be expected to know the plays of Shakespeare, the country's history, the world of art and how to derive a percentage, calculate a ratio and find the median in a group of figures? Would it terrify would-be journalists to suggest that the answer has to be yes?

This storehouse of knowledge is the reporter's background. As Kempton, Twain and Mencken suggest, it should be kept full and constantly replenished. Reporters need to have at their fingertips a wide assortment of information: They should know dates, names, policies made, policies defeated, what leads the best-seller list and what agency compiles the list of the 10 most-wanted criminals. All of this has to be put into some kind of schematic, some kind of pattern, or reporters will eventually see themselves in the sad comment of T.S. Eliot, "We had the experience but missed the meaning."

Background Defined

The term *background* has three definitions:

- A reporter's store of information. This knowledge may be amassed over a long period or picked up quickly in order to handle a specific assignment. Without background knowledge, a reporter's fact gathering can be nondirected.
- Material placed in the story that explains the event, puts it into perspective. Without background, a story may be one-dimensional.
- Material a source does not want attributed to him or her. It may or may not be used, depending on the source's instructions.

Here, we are dealing with the first two meanings.

The Contents of the Storehouse

Journalists have a deep and wide-ranging fund of general information that they have developed through extensive reading, a variety of experience and their continuing education. Much of this stored information is about how things work, processes and procedures: the workings of the political system; the structure of local government; the arrest process; how governments pay for schools, streets and police and fire protection. The list is long.

Such knowledge is important because it is the bedrock on which news stories are built. The American philosopher John Dewey said, "We cannot lay hold of the new, we cannot even keep it before our minds, much less understand it, save by the use of ideas and knowledge we already possess." Irving Kristol, a writer on social and political affairs, says, "When one is dealing with complicated and continuous events, it is impossible to report 'what happened' unless one is previously equipped with a context of meaning and significance."

Specific knowledge is also required. When a candidate for the school board refers to "Brown versus Board of Education," the reporter knows the school desegregation court ruling she is referring to. When a luncheon speaker says that "the country took the wrong turn under the New Deal," the reporter knows the speaker is talking from a conservative perspective. And when a reporter does a profile of a country singer, he knows what the singer means when he says he is drifting from the "Nashville sound."

Zoning Favoritism   The knowledge of how things work can turn a routine assignment into a significant story. When a reporter for a Long Island newspaper was sent to cover a fire in a plastics factory, she noticed that the plant was located in a residential zone. On her return to the office, she told her editor, "I've got the information on the fire, but I want to check out why that factory was built there in a residential zone. Was it zoned industrial when the factory was built, or did the company get a variance?" The reporter knew that variances—exceptions to general zoning patterns—are sometimes awarded to

What They Don't Know

The National Assessment of Educational Progress tested 8,000 17-year-olds of different races, both sexes and in all regions of the United States.

Some of the findings:

- 20 percent or fewer could identify Joyce, Dostoyevsky, Ellison, Conrad or Ibsen.
- 36 percent knew Chaucer is the author of *The Canterbury Tales.*
- 37 percent could equate Job with patience during suffering.
- Fewer than 25 percent knew that Lincoln was president between 1860 and 1880.
- 32 percent could place the Civil War between 1850 and 1900.
- 57 percent could place World War II between 1900 and 1950.
- 30 percent could identify the Magna Charta.

friends or political donors. Although the reporter was not a city hall reporter or a specialist in real estate, she knew about zoning through her overall understanding of city government. Her curiosity and knowledge led to a significant story.

Election Caution   In the suspenseful election night coverage of the 2000 presidential race, the three networks, CNN, the AP and the Fox News Channel declared Al Gore the winner in an 11-minute span, 7:49 to 8 P.M. EST, based on exit polls conducted by the Voter News Service to which the media subscribed.

Within two hours, the networks and others pulled back their prediction of a Gore victory. As the evening wore on, the outlets swung over to a Bush prediction. The AP, however, declined to declare a winner. It did not, said AP Executive Editor John Wolman, because AP staffers who knew the state of Florida and its voting patterns saw that uncounted votes in heavily Democratic counties could swing the election the other way.

As it turned out Bush did win, but in a count much closer than the networks and others had indicated in their predictions.

The Clone   When Gina Kolata, science reporter for *The New York Times,* was thumbing through her copy of *Nature,* a magazine for scientists, she came across an article titled "Viable Offspring Derived from Fetal and Adult Mammalians." She leaped up.

"It didn't say the word clone and there was no clue in the article that there was anything interesting," she said. "People missed this story because they had to be able to understand the title and the abstract," which, she says, "was in the most abstruse scientific language in the whole world."

Vacuums. ". . . while they may be trained to write and while they may be trained to articulate what is written, the fact remains that many who call themselves journalists and are employed in local stations have no notion whatsoever about history, geography, political science, economics and other things about which an informed individual should have some grasp."
—*Frank Magid, CEO, Frank N. Magid Associates, TV consultants to 140 local stations*

Lost. "The unprepared mind cannot see the outstretched hand of opportunity."
—*Alexander Fleming, discoverer of penicillin*

Joe Munson, *The Kentucky Post*

Cutting the Turn Too Closely: Crack-Up at the 500

But she immediately called her editor and said, "Do you know what? I think they have actually done something amazing. I think they've cloned an adult."

Kolata's understanding of the abstruse technical article led to an exclusive page 1 story.

Covering the 500   When Joe Munson, a photographer for *The Kentucky Post* in Covington, Ky., was covering the Indianapolis 500, the daring tactics of a driver caught his eye. Munson knew that there is an imaginary line that race car drivers must follow around bends in order to keep their cars under control.

"I noticed driver Danny Ongais straying six inches from that imaginary line and I suspected he was destined for a crash," Munson recalled.

"So I kept my camera focused on him."

Munson was ready when Ongais lost control and his car cracked into the wall. Munson was able to gun off 20 shots of the fiery crash that seriously injured Ongais. One of them took first place in the sports category of a National Press Photographers Association regional competition.

A Reminder   During the 2000 presidential race, the Bush team had Sen. Strom Thurmond, R-S.C., attack Al Gore for trying to be "Trumanlike." Sen. Thurmond said, "Mr. Gore, I knew Harry Truman, I ran against Harry Truman, and you are no Harry Truman." The line merited a few sentences in the political stories of that day. But Michael Powell of *The Washington Post* put the aged senator's remark in context. He told readers that Thurmond had run against Truman on the Dixiecrat ticket and had accused Truman of "stabbing the South in the back" by integrating the armed forces. Powell quoted Thurmond's attacks on blacks and wrote that he was widely acknowledged as a "white supremacist and segregation's champion" during the period Thurmond claimed to "know" Truman.

Set Point   Christopher Keating, chief of *The Courant*'s Hartford capital bureau, noticed an item on the state bond commission's agenda that struck a bell. The item called for raising $800,000 in bonds for construction and renovation of tennis courts and other park facilities. The "tennis courts" was the bell ringer. Keating knew that during the gubernatorial campaign John G. Rowland had criticized the incumbent governor for winning approval of more than 100 projects in the final meeting of the bond commission.

"We're not going to be bonding tennis courts in my administration" Rowland said, and a month later he was governor.

"Now, six months later," Keating wrote, "the Rowland-led bond commission is scheduled to vote today on a similar item: $800,000 for construction and renovation of tennis courts and other improvements at three parks—in Rowland's hometown of Waterbury."

The story hit home. Rowland withdrew the $800,000 request that day.

Knowing the Records   Marcia Chambers, who covered the Criminal Courts Building for *The New York Times,* scored many exclusives because she had mastered the procedures of the criminal justice system. Chambers used files, records and background that led to an exclusive she wrote on the arrest of a mass-murder suspect. Here is her description of how she went about digging up the information for her story:

On the day Calvin Jackson was arrested, I covered the arraignment where the prosecutor announced that Jackson had been charged with the murder of one woman and had "implicated himself" in several others. At the time, we wanted to find out more about Jackson's prior criminal record, but given the hour—5:30 p.m.—we couldn't get the information. In a sidebar story that appeared the next day, Joe Treaster, the police reporter, said Jackson's previous arrest had occurred 10 months before. But the disposition of the case, the story said, was unknown.

From my experience, I knew that nearly all cases are disposed of through plea bargaining, the process whereby a defendant agrees to plead guilty in exchange for a lesser charge. Several weeks before I had obtained from the Office of Court Administration data that showed that last year only 545 out of 31,098 felony arrests went to trial, including drug cases. The rest were plea bargained.

On Monday, at 10 a.m., I went to the court clerk's office. My premise was that Jackson's last arrest, like the thousands of others that pass through the criminal court system, had probably involved plea bargaining, a reduction of charges and a minimal sentence.

From the docket book, I obtained the docket number of the mass-murder case, and since case records are public information, I asked the clerk for the case. I took it to the side of the room, and quickly copied the file that contained information about his previous arrests. (In addition to carrying change and a phone credit card for phone calls, reporters should carry at least two dollars in change at all times for the copying machine as well as a backup pen or pencil.)

Jackson's previous arrests (listed on what is called a rap sheet) were described by penal code designations, which sent Chambers to the newspaper's library to check the numbers in one reference and then to another reference to see what the maximum penalty was for the felonies for which he was convicted.

She found Jackson had been convicted of two felonies for which the punishment was up to 15 years in prison. By then it was 5:15 and Chambers started to write for the 7 P.M. deadline.

Blunders

Reporters with ample background knowledge do not embarrass themselves or their editors by blundering in print or on the air. Witness these bloopers, the result of a lack of background:

- In one of her columns, Harriet Van Horne referred to Canada as having a "tough and happily homogeneous population. . . ." (The columnist ignored the large Indian and Inuit populations and the almost six million French-speaking Canadians. Not only is the country not homogeneous, the French- and English-speaking Canadians are hardly happily ensconced together. Many of the French-speaking people contend that they are second-class citizens, which has led to the separatist movement in the province of Quebec.)
- When the basketball coach at Boston College accepted the head coaching job at Stanford, a CBS sports announcer said that the coach had "followed Horace Mann's advice to go west." (The advice is attributed to Horace Greeley, founder and editor of *The Tribune:* "Go west young man." Horace Mann was an educator.)
- In a feature on food served during the Jewish holidays, a reporter for the *Press-Enterprise* in Riverside, Calif., described Yom Kippur as "marked by rich, indeed lavish meals." (Yom Kippur, known as the Day of Atonement, is the most solemn of all Jewish holy days and is observed by fasting.)
- A *New York Times* story of mourning for victims of a terrorist bombing in Jerusalem said the mourners' clothing was "rented." (In funerals, clothing is *rent*—torn—not rented.)
- During a televised National Basketball Association game, a player let the man he was covering drive past him for a basket. The player looked disgusted with himself, and from the broadcast booth the sportscasters could see his lips moving. "What do you think he's saying, Bill?" one asked his colleague, Bill Russell, one of the great defensive stars in basketball and the first black coach in the NBA.

Botched. In the journal for journalism faculty, *Journalism & Mass Commun-ication Educator,* an author referred to the American philosopher "Thomas Dewey." Wrong Dewey. Thomas Dewey was the Republican candidate for president in 1944 and 1948, losing once to Franklin D. Roosevelt and then to Harry S Truman. John Dewey is the philosopher, considered one of the most influential theorists in education as well as philosophy.

The Past Illuminates the Present

To those who despair over today's racism and environmental damage, a knowledge of the past provides perspective. For years after gold was discovered in California, mining companies used hydraulic water cannons to wash down mountains for the gold ore they contained. Silt clogged once pristine rivers, causing floods downstream and irreparable damage was done to the terrain. After considerable public pressure, the practice was outlawed.

Now only a fringe movement of the far right, the Ku Klux Klan once elected governors and paraded its cause down the main avenues of cities and state capitals. Klanswomen even paraded down Pennsylvania Avenue in Washington, D.C.

Plumas County Museum

National Archives in Washington, D.C.

Russell replied, "I know how Walt feels. I can hear him muttering a four-syllable word." Russell's colleague laughingly corrected him, "You mean four-letter word, Bill." Slowly, deliberately, Russell said, "No, I mean four-syllable word."

There was a long pause, a smothered gasp and then a commercial. (Russell's long playing career had given him a vast store of knowledge about the game, from strategy to the obscenities players use.)

Anticipatory Journalism

A solid grasp of the past and the present is essential to a growing area of reporting—*anticipatory journalism.* It consists of spotting trends, identifying movements in their earliest stages, locating individuals with an important message.

Journalism has not been good at this kind of reporting. It ignored the feminist movement, was late to sense the civil rights surge, was hesitant about the lifestyle changes of teen-agers.

But anticipatory journalism need not confine itself to spotting trends and movements to be useful. It can be as simple as making journalism out of the realization that the city's revenues are inadequate to meet new expenses and that payrolls and services will have to be cut or taxes increased. With this knowledge, the reporter can interview the mayor, city council members and community leaders about what solutions they recommend.

This is public service journalism, for its practice gives people time to discuss and decide issues rather than having to react quickly when last-minute problems arise.

An essential to the practice of anticipatory journalism along with a grasp of background is a good string of sources, a subject we shall next look into after a final doleful note.

Don't Guess   Speculative reporting is not anticipatory journalism. The reporter who speculates about events or predicts outcomes is guessing. The reporter who anticipates uses evidence and makes no leaps to judgment or opinion.

When Vicente Fox challenged the candidate of the Institutional Revolutionary Party, which had governed Mexico for 71 years, his candidacy was written off by a speculative article in *The Christian Science Monitor.* The basis for the write-off?

". . . the so-called 'family' issue is taking on decisive importance," the reporter wrote. Fox is divorced and his four children are adopted, the newspaper reported, and it quoted several women voters as saying that Francisco Labistida, the candidate of the IRP, was their favorite because he stood for "strong families."

The result: Fox defeated Labistida.

Summing Up

The best journalists know a lot. They know the past as well as the present. They are exceptions to the charge leveled by *The New York Times* columnist Bob Herbert who describes the United States as "a nation of nitwits." As evidence, he cites a Gallup Poll that found:

- Sixty percent of Americans are unable to name the president who ordered the atomic bomb dropped on Japan. (Truman)
- One of four didn't know Japan was the target of the bomb.
- A fifth didn't know that such an attack had occurred.

"We are surrounded by a deep and abiding stupidity," he writes.

To ply their trade well journalists know that they must be informed. Otherwise, they are a menace to their readers, listeners and viewers.

Further Reading

Lewis, Anthony. *Gideon's Trumpet.* New York: Random House, 1964.
Steel, Ronald. *Walter Lippmann and the American Century.* Boston: Atlantic Monthly Press, 1980.

13 Finding, Cultivating and Using Sources

Chris Hardy, *San Francisco Examiner*

Sources come in all sizes.

Preview

The reporter relies on three types of sources:

• **Human sources,** which consist of authorities and people involved in news events. They can be less reliable than physical sources because some may have interests to protect or are untrained observers. When using human sources, reporters find the person most qualified to speak—an authority on the subject, an eyewitness, an official, a participant.

• **Physical sources,** which consist of records, documents, reference works, newspaper clippings.

• **Online sources,** which include a vast array of human and physical sources, from academicians to government data.

Journalists have a saying that a reporter can be no better than his or her sources. These sources include officials, spokesmen and -women, participants in events, documents, records, tape recordings, magazines, online search engines, libraries, films and books. The quality of the reporter's story depends on the quality of the sources.

Reporters spend a lot of time looking for and cultivating people who can become sources and contacts. A county courthouse reporter in California puts in a couple of hours a day passing time with his sources. He also chats with guards, secretaries, elevator operators, all of whom he describes as contacts, people who can provide tips for stories. An elevator operator tipped him off about a well-known businessman who had been summoned by a grand jury and was taken to the jury room by a back elevator.

Jere Downs, who covers transportation for *The Philadelphia Inquirer,* heard that the local transit agency, SEPTA, was considering a fare hike. "I called sources at the agency and requested that we have a cup of coffee and talk about the new prices," she says. "That was how I learned that the agency was raising prices against the advice of $1 million in consultant studies that advised dropping fares was the best course of action."

Making Nice at the Courthouse

Jeff Klinkenberg of the *St. Petersburg Times* shows us Milt Sosin, the Associated Press courthouse reporter in Miami, at work:

He pokes his head into offices and makes small talk with secretaries. He chats with a lawyer in an elevator. He shares respectful words with a newspaper reporter outside a courtroom. With a charming smile, he even opens a hallway door for a sweaty man in a three-piece suit.

For Sosin, who is probably the best reporter you *never* heard of, charm is part of his giant bag of journalist's tricks. His job is getting information. Being chummy, though it may come unnatu-

rally, could pay off one day: He may need these courthouse people to provide news that might lead to an Associated Press exclusive.

"It's no big deal," Sosin says later, sounding almost embarrassed. "They're just sources. You treat them right. You stop by and ask them if anything is going on, that's all. If they give you something you can use, you protect them. You never betray their confidences."

Sosin's way with sources pays off. One of his biggest scoops was the indictment of Gen. Manuel Noriega of Panama for drug crimes. All the major newspapers were working on the story.

Klinkenberg writes:

> "I was sure he had been indicted," Sosin says now. "But the U.S. attorney was keeping it secret. He wanted to announce it at a press conference. I made a few phone calls. All my sources said Noriega's name was on the indictment. I told AP to go with the story."

Massive Tire Recall

It was a "call from a source who does research for trial lawyers," says Sara Nathan, that led her to a major story. The source told her that Firestone tires on Ford Explorers were being recalled in six foreign countries but not in the United States. Nathan checked with several safety organizations, and they confirmed the tip and told her that they had urged a tire recall in the United States.

After first denying that their tires were defective, Firestone recalled 6.5 million tires in the face of stories like this one by Nathan and fellow *USA Today* reporter James R. Healey that began a series of articles:

Millions of people in the USA are riding on tires that are the focus of a federal safety probe, and that have been recalled and replaced in six other countries, according to government files.

The National Highway Traffic Safety Administration (NHTSA) also said Tuesday that it has reports of 21 deaths—up from just four it knew of earlier this week—and 193 crashes involving Firestone ATX, ATX II and Wilderness tires. Reports of the incidents say the treads inexplicably peeled off the tire casings, causing skids.

For more from the original series in *USA Today,* see **Tire Recall** in *NRW Plus.*

Reliability of Sources

The distinction between human and physical sources, and their relative reliability, was nicely put by Sir Kenneth Clark, the British writer and critic: "If I had to say who was telling the truth about society, a speech by the Minister of Housing or the actual buildings put up in his time, I would believe the buildings."

The difference is often on the reporter's mind, for even though much of his or her work depends on interviews, the reporter seeks physical evidence whenever possible. This kind of material includes newspaper clippings, books, records and documents as well as the reporter's direct observation.

Because of the possibility of hoaxes, rumor passed as fact and old information, reporters are careful about using online material. It is verified before use. Reliable online sources are listed in **Appendix F** in *NRW Plus.*

Human Sources

A person with information the reporter needs for a story or for background is called a *source*. Sources include the woman who saw an airplane fall short of the landing strip and Deep Throat, the informant who cooperated with *Washington Post* reporters Woodward and Bernstein on their Watergate investigation. The stockbroker friend of a reporter who explains complicated financial matters is a source, although his name may never appear in a story.

Arthur L. Gavshon, diplomatic reporter for the AP, says:

> To me anyone on the inside of any given news situation is a potential source. But they only turn into real sources when they come up with a bit, or a lot, of relevant information.

Gavshon says he finds sources anywhere and everywhere. He develops his sources "just as you would get to know a friend and nurture a relationship in everyday life (always assuming you can live a normal life as a journalist)—through the exercise of patience, understanding and a reasonable capacity to converse about shared interests."

Authoritative Sources   Sometimes an assignment is so complex or so unfamiliar that a reporter hardly knows where to begin. The clips on the subject prove to be too sketchy, and the references presume some knowledge of the subject. The reporter needs a crash course in the topic, but the assignment is due and there is no time for in-depth research.

On her second day as the marine news reporter for *The Gazette* in Montreal, Jan Wong was given an assignment and told to handle it quickly because her editor had another story for her to cover.

Wong did what reporters do in such circumstances. She turned to people who know, authoritative sources:

"I must have called 20 people," she says. "I called everyone I could find in the marine directory. People were very helpful."

Sources need not be mayors or directors of companies. The city hall reporter knows that the town clerk who has served a succession of mayors has a comprehensive knowledge of the community and the inner workings of town government. The courthouse reporter befriends law clerks, court stenographers and security guards. Business reporters cultivate switchboard operators, secretaries, mailroom help.

Tactics   Reporters have gone out of their way to do favors for their sources. At one newspaper in California, the reporters who handle obituaries send birthday candy and flowers to the mortuary employees who call to report the deaths of important people. A death called in near deadline means the newspaper or station telephoned first will have that much more time to write the obituary. A difference of two minutes can be the difference between making or missing the last edition or the 6 P.M. newscast.

Some reporters cultivate sources by reversing the news-gathering process. One Midwestern newsman says that instead of always asking sources for news, he puts his sources on the receiving end. "I see to it personally that they hear any gossip or important news. When I want news, I get it," he says.

The source needed for information on a single story need not be cultivated with the care reporters lavish on sources essential to a beat. But courtesy and consideration are always important. In speaking to a source for the first—and perhaps the only—time, the reporter identifies himself or herself immediately and moves to the questions quickly. A different pace is necessary for the source essential to a beat. Gavshon cautions:

> Don't ever rush things. Don't make the ghastly mistake of thinking only in terms of tomorrow's headline. . . . One-night stands rarely satisfy anybody.

Be Careful

Sources may not be what they seem. When a federal agency called for a moratorium on silicon-gel breast implants, a woman made herself available to reporters, saying she was a breast cancer patient and had implants. She said she was satisfied with them. Three local television stations and *The Boston Globe* used her comments.

Terry Schraeder of WCVB-TV in Boston checked out the woman and found she was a paid spokeswoman for Dow Corning, manufacturer of the implant material, which had provided her with training in handling the media and a list of reporters to contact.

Pseudo-Sources

Then there are the sources who are hardly qualified to speak on a subject but appear authoritative. When some members of Congress wanted to find out the plight of farmers hard hit by rising costs and falling income, they called Sissy Spacek and Jane Fonda to testify. The women had played the wives of farmers in films.

Who's Being Quoted?

Journalists have been criticized for calling upon a narrow band of sources for information for stories—business executives, bankers, government officials, college presidents, political leaders—usually white, middle-class men. This narrow demographic bandwidth skews stories, the critics say.

For stories about the economy, experts at the think tanks are called upon—the Cato Institute for the conservative point of view, the Urban Institute for the liberal and the Brookings Institution for the centrist positions. But the economy is about people—whether they keep their jobs, how inflation affects them. And the people make up a wide range of individuals.

To make up a representative sample of the community, as the polling people would say, it's important to have a mix of ages, races, ethnic groups and, of course, men and women. And if the story is about the economy sagging or soaring, we will want to hear how it affects families.

Susanne M. Schafer is the AP's chief military correspondent. Her beat includes the Pentagon, where official sources are notorious for "handling" reporters. To do her job properly, she says, she has "to get out there and interview the soldier in the trench, the lady in the cockpit. It's very hard to do, but that's the only way you're going to get beyond what I call death by briefing."

Tips

A disgruntled office worker tells a reporter that her boss has been using the city's money to take vacations, buy expensive furniture and go to a gambling resort. The reporter checks and the result is a story in *The New York Times* citing official documents obtained by the Freedom of Information Act. The official is quickly dismissed.

A member of the university's social science department tells a reporter on the university beat that he read a study that found that the favorite newspaper reading of those 21 to 25 years of age are the comics, television and movie listings and the classified ads. Maybe there's a story there, he suggests to the reporter. There is.

A city hall employee tells the beat reporter that anticipated property tax revenues have failed to materialize and the city may be caught short at year's end. A service station owner tells the radio reporter who stops by for gas that he has heard the street will be widened and many merchants on the three blocks to be widened plan to protest at the next meeting of the city planning and zoning commission. A woman working in a drugstore tells a customer—a TV reporter—that

Bias. ". . . there is no such thing as an independent source, and the first thing a reporter should ask himself when he is talking to anyone whom he thinks may be a source is, 'Why is this source talking to me? What is in it for him?' First, I have to find out what is in it for him before I find out what is in it for me. . . . I would never assume that any source is telling me the whole truth, because I don't think the source knows the whole truth. . . ."

—*Murrey Marder*

her daughter is excited about "the new reading program." The reporter checks the information and breaks a story about the city schools switching from the whole language approach to teaching reading with the old-fashioned phonics method.

Keeping the Source

The source is the reporter's life blood. Without access to information through the source, the reporter cannot function. The reporter is just as necessary to most sources, for without the journalist the source has no access to the public. Sources in the public sector need reaction to their ideas and policies.

Out of this mutual need a source-reporter relationship develops: The source will provide the reporter with information and will brief him or her on developments. In return, the reporter will write a fair account of the material.

As events become more complex, the reporter's dependence on sources increases. When a reporter learns of a probable future event, such as the presentation of the municipal budget to the city council, he or she may ask a source for background so that the difficult story can be written authoritatively. The courthouse reporter who learns through the grapevine that the grand jury is about to return an indictment against the city clerk will ask the district attorney for a briefing, promising not to break the story before the indictment is returned. Sources usually are happy to comply because they prefer an accurate story to a rush job.

Bob Greene, a former *Newsday* reporter now teaching journalism, says that it's necessary to build a "personal bond" with sources to keep them. "Show an interest in them, their work, their activities, their family. Get the names of children, husbands, wives, and use them. Every now and then, say, 'Let's have dinner, breakfast.' "

Protecting Sources

Occasionally, a reporter is asked to protect a source's identity. An investigative reporter learns from a police officer that a convict serving a life term for murder was convicted on perjured police testimony. In return for the tip about the frame-up, the reporter must promise not to name the source.

The reporter can make this promise because shield laws in most states protect confidential sources. All states have some kind of protection, but in some states, a reporter who tries to protect a confidential source may face contempt charges and jail. State press associations usually distribute pamphlets about reporters' rights.

Sometimes reporters have to overcome their reluctance to embarrass a friendly source with a tough story. Walter Lippmann said there must be a "certain distance between the reporter and the source, not a wall or a fence, but an air space." Once a friend becomes an official, he said, "you can't call him by his first name anymore."

Protecting Michael   Early in Michael Jordan's career with the Chicago Bulls basketball team, he asked reporters not to reveal that he had a child since he wasn't married. They went along, says Robert Blau, associate managing editor for projects and investigations at the *Chicago Tribune*. "They liked him. They

Paying Sources. "We pay for information," says Steve Coz, editor of *The National Enquirer.* "We pay them to be sources." Among the recipients of handsome checks from the weekly supermarket tabloid are chauffeurs, maids, bartenders, caterers, the modestly paid people who work for the famous. Payment for information, known as checkbook journalism, is frowned upon by the mainline media, though sometimes, tempted by the possibility of exclusive information, a newspaper or network will write a check.

wanted to be liked by him. And they needed him," Blau says. "There's a healthy debate to be had over whether the out-of-wedlock child born to a basketball player, even a superstar, is newsworthy. It certainly has nothing to do with performance on the court. But given Jordan's carefully choreographed image, the information might have been useful in assessing the man," Blau says.

"Protecting sources and currying their favor so they will remain sources, whether in a sweaty locker room or a swank boardroom, too easily crosses the line from common sense to conspiracy, cheating the public and betraying the truth," he says.

The Expert

Who knows the most about any given subject? The expert, of course. As obvious as this is, reporters sometimes use sources because of who they are, what they are, not because of what they know.

People tend to believe those in authority. The more impressive the title, the higher the social position, the more prestigious the alma mater, the more faith people have in the expert or authority. This trust in authority is known as the "hierarchy of credibility"—the higher on the scale the authority is, the more believable the source is thought to be. When the journalist surrenders to this tendency, he or she allows those in power to define events and situations.

Reporters must be careful to use sources only within their areas of expert knowledge. Asked questions within the narrow range of their expertise, sources are useful. A banker can talk about banking, a general about the strategy and

James Woodcock,
The Billings Gazette

She Knows Best

For a story on crowded classrooms, the best sources are the teachers and the students, not the president of the board of education.

tactics of war. But it is dangerous to rely on a banker for comments on the nation's economy or on a general as an authority on international affairs. They may be less useful than the lesser-known labor department area representative or the assistant professor of international affairs at a local college.

A reporter's best sources are those who have demonstrated their knowledge and competence as accurate observers, interpreters and forecasters of events. Reporters should drop sources who are proved wrong in their observations and assessments, whether they served in the president's cabinet, ran a multimillion-dollar import business or graduated *summa cum laude* from Harvard.

Reliability Tests

For sources on the beat, those the reporter is in touch with on a regular basis, reliability is usually determined by consistency. That is, the source is considered reliable if in the past the information he or she supplied proved accurate.

For transient sources, those interviewed for a particular story, the test is more complicated:

• Was the person an observer of the incident, or did he or she hear about it from someone else?
• Is the person a competent observer? An airline employee would be a better source for information about an airplane crash than would a student or a salesperson.
• Can the source supply precise details that have the ring of truth and seem consistent with the facts?
• Are several sources offering the same information? Generally, when several people provide the same version of an event, chances are good that the accounts are reliable.

Increasingly, as journalism covers complex events, experts are called upon as sources. These can be academicians, scientists, financial analysts and so on. As we have seen, not all are independent, down-the-middle in their expertise. The university scientist who issues skeptical reports about what he calls the "so-called greenhouse effect" may have his research funded by coal and oil interests. This funding does not necessarily mean the information is slanted, but a reporter would be wise to find someone without industry funding for research in this area.

Chris Bowman of *The Sacramento Bee* suggests these checks on the scientific expert:

Where does the funding come from for his or her research?
Is this original research, or material from some outside source?
Does the expert distinguish between his or her scientific observations and personal beliefs?

Checking the Prospectors   Kevin Krajick's magazine story about diamond prospectors led him to think about making a book out of the prospectors—a strange and secretive group—and the forbidding far north country in Canada where they searched.

"When I started on the book, I discovered that my reporting work had just begun," Krajick says. "In digging deeper into the details, I found all sorts of subsidiary characters who also had tales to tell—some in conflict with those of the main characters. Sometimes people who were in the same spot at the same time had differing versions.

"This led me to examine more deeply who had a stake in the story coming out a certain way—and who could be considered an impartial witness.

"Sometimes it even came down to a rough sort of vote. If four people saw the same event and three told the same story, it seemed likely the fourth guy was either misremembering or fudging it.

"Sometimes I would go back to the fourth person and run the other version of the story past him. Human memory is a funny thing. Even the smartest people forget things, remember things that never happened, are open to suggestions afterwards. They make their own myths, about themselves and others. Eyewitnesses are not always reliable.

"The best a writer can do is to get reasonable agreement among the parties, or else give the conflicting versions, point out no one agrees and move on fast . . . unless you *really* know what happened and can prove it."

Krajick's book is *Barren Lands: An Epic Search for Diamonds in the North American Arctic,* Henry Holt and Company, 2001.

Internet Reliability

Those who use the Internet—and most journalists do—are cautious. They know that Web pages can remain for years without being updated and that little is available about events before 1995 because that was when material began to be placed on the Web.

Liars, hoaxsters, promoters and leakers thrive on the Internet. "You can't be sure of any of it," said Henry Stokes, managing editor of *The Commercial Appeal.*

Flash: Navy Downs TWA Airliner The claim was sensational: A former newsman and presidential adviser, Pierre Salinger, announced he had proof that the U.S. Navy had accidentally shot down a TWA plane with 230 passengers while it was conducting missile tests off Long Island. "The mainline reporters hit the phones," says Elizabeth Weise, a *USA Today* reporter.

"Then there were the online reporters. They rushed not to the phones but to their keyboards, where they unleashed a torrent of e-mail, laughing maniacally all the while. Their fingers flew as they gasped out, 'Oh my god, they think it's real.' " The report, unsourced, unreliable, had been "filling up electronic mailboxes on the Net" for two months, Weise says.

"The Net is a place of intrigue, rumor and fabrication," she continues. "Salinger's problem was using an unsourced tip. The report Salinger thought he was breaking came to my e-mail box with several pages worth of headers, or return addresses. We traced it through numerous companies, several universities and even a government agency or two, but there was no true return address, just a list of people who had been passing it along."

Internet Checks "Check and confirm before using Internet material," Weise says. To confirm, Weise will talk to someone she knows to be reliable or make a telephone call to the source to verify the information. "Unless the person is already known to you, as a general rule never quote an individual without speaking to him or her on the telephone to confirm his or her identity."

Jan Alexander and Marsha Ann Tate, librarians at Widener University, have five tests for Web page reliability:

Authority—Who put the page together? Can you reach the people who put it together? Can you tell who wrote the information on the page and what their qualifications are?

Accuracy—Is there a source for information that you can check with to verify the information?

Currency—Is the page updated? Can you tell when the information was written, when posted?

Coverage—Is the material thorough? Are issues neglected?

Objectivity—Is advertising clearly separated from information? If there is bias, is it made clear?

These tests are useful for information whatever its source. Let's apply them to an organization that sought to have its slant on events relayed to the public, the Population Research Institute.

Authoritative? The Population Research Institute seems a straightforward organization. But a check of Internal Revenue Service files discloses that the Institute is a public relations arm of Human Life International, a partisan anti-abortion organization. It is headed by Paul Marx, whose book *Confessions of a Prolife Missionary* contains this sentence: "Note the large number of abortionists (consult the Yellow Pages) and pro-abortion medical professors who are Jewish."

The foreign advisor to Human Life International is Dr. Siegfried Ernst, about whom a German court stated: "The things he says are so racially discriminating that any impartial observer can see parallels to the ideology of the Third Reich." Clearly, the Institute fails the authority test.

Why, then, the media's use of Institute material? Possibly because journalists confuse the Population Research *Institute* with the authoritative and independent Population Research *Bureau*.

On issues like abortion, gun control, affirmative action, school prayer and others that have divided the country, it is important that journalists not pass on to the public propaganda in the guise of information from an independent source.

"The motives of those who press their views upon journalists must be routinely examined and, where appropriate, revealed to the reader," says Dr. Judith Lewis Herman of the Harvard Medical School. She warns against relying on anecdote and speculation in reporting on controversial issues. Anecdotes and personal experiences do not constitute proof, she says.

Online Evaluation   Here is a reliability scale devised by Steve Miller of *The New York Times:*

1. **Government data**—Material from federal, state and local sources. The figures, not the comments about them, are almost always reliable.
2. **Studies by universities and colleges**—These materials, usually in the form of articles in scholarly journals, are peer-reviewed before publication.
3. **Special-interest groups**—Although these have agendas they pursue, some have reputations as reliable sources.
4. **Home pages**—The least reliable and most questionable.

In all cases, specific attribution is essential.

Physical Sources

The range of physical information is enormous. The availability of physical sources is limited only by the reporter's knowledge of their existence.

Databases provide quick access to dozens of excellent sources, from census material to local arrest records. Donald Barlett and James Steele turned to *The Philadelphia Inquirer* databases for material for their prize-winning series about the federal Tax Reform Act. "Once you would come up with a name of somebody, you could go right to one of these databases and see what was known about him very quickly," Steele said. The database made it possible to pack large amounts of convincing detail into their stories, such as the description of the widow who inherited $4 million more from her late husband's estate under the giveaway terms of the act.

Scoop. The Virginia State Police posted for the first time on the Internet a list of all state residents convicted of violent sexual offenses. Names and addresses were included, and a weekly newspaper breathlessly reported that Culpeper County had 225 sexual offenders, more than those in its "four adjacent counties." In his haste, the reporter failed to notice that all 225 had the same post office box number—the address of the nearby state prison.

Specialized Publications. If you are doing a piece on the fast food industry, says a reporter, look at the *Nation's Restaurant News.* Want to know whether Americans drink more soda pop than water, consult *Beverage Industry.* These publications are part of the massive trade press, and they are a valuable source of specialized information.

Not All Sources Are Equal

Not all physical sources are of equal reliability. Tables of vital statistics are more reliable than the city official's summary introducing the tables. The world almanac is more reliable than a newspaper clipping of the same event, for the almanac is usually the work of professional researchers, and the news story may have been written in a hurry before all the facts were in.

Paper Trail

Much can be learned by tracking a person through the many documents he or she leaves behind. Such searches are described as "following the paper trail." The trail is strewn with material: a birth certificate, hospital records, school records, real estate transfers, marriage and death certificates.

The material can be found in newspaper clippings, court records, reference works and government agency files. Two examples of what can be learned:

Home: What it cost; what was paid and what was borrowed for the down payment; who holds the mortgage and how much it amounts to; liens on the property; the amount of property taxes paid and any delinquencies.

Automobile: Registration number; title information; name and model of vehicle; year of manufacture; license plate number. Automobile records also include data on the owner—name, age, height, weight, offenses.

Databases

Reporters mine the vast array of databases available:

Drunk Drivers When the Paddock papers in the Chicago area wanted to know what happened to people arrested for drunk driving, reporters fed into the computer 1,500 drunk driving arrests and their dispositions. The finding: More than two-thirds of those arrested avoided conviction. Only 1 in 15 was jailed or fined heavily. The *Atlanta Constitution* used local bank records to show a pattern of racial discrimination in housing loans, and it won a Pulitzer Prize for its stories.

Led to Slaughter Martha Mendoza of the AP used the computer to track the handling of a multimillion dollar federal program designed to protect thousands of wild horses on public lands. Under the direction of the Bureau of Land Management, the program allows individuals to adopt up to four horses each and care for them. After a year, the adopters are given legal title to the animals. At that point, Mendoza found, many of the owners, some of them BLM employees, were selling the horses to slaughterhouses—at a profit of $700 a horse. After her revelation, the BLM admitted that about 90 percent of the horses in the program were sold for slaughter.

Overtime   For his examination of overtime payments to city employees, Mike Trautmann obtained the city payroll. For one of his stories in a series for the *Argus Leader,* Trautmann put the mayor's salary into the computer to find out if anyone in the city's employ was earning more. The story he wrote began:

> When does an assistant make more than the boss? When he works for the city of Sioux Falls.
>
> Last year, the city paid three employees more than Mayor Gary Hanson's $77,250—including his chief of staff, Dean Nielsen.
>
> Three other employees earned nearly as much.

School Inspections   For his two-part series on the lack of adequate fire inspections of South Dakota schools, Trautmann developed a database for the more than 800 school buildings. His first story began:

More than half of South Dakota's schools have not had fire inspections in the past two years, as state law requires, making it uncertain whether some of those schools are fire safe.

Officials with the state fire marshal's office acknowledge that inspections have seriously lagged for many public and private schools. They say they will institute wholesale administrative changes to catch up.

"It's an embarrassment," said Mike Mehlhaff, director of the Division of Commercial Inspection and Regulation, the office responsible for overseeing school inspections.

Approximately 430 of the state's 850 public and private school buildings have not been inspected within the two-year legal requirement. Some haven't been inspected for as long as 10 to 15 years, according to inspection reports filed in the state fire marshal's office.

More than two dozen schools have no record of ever being inspected.

Computer Viruses   Weise began to think about the prevalence of virus warnings online, "and especially how they seem to increase around April Fools Day." Most of the warnings, she knew, are fakes. "But I realized that many readers probably didn't."

Here is how she went about gathering material for her story:

> First I called CERT, the Computer Emergency Response Center at Carnegie Mellon University in Pittsburgh, Penn. Then I did a search on the Web for Fraud pages, found several, one of which proved to be run by Rob Rosenberger, who runs the Computer Virus Myths site and proved to be an excellent interview.

Here is how her story began:

With *April Fools'* Day on Wednesday, computer security experts have but one plea: Don't believe everything you read in e-mail.

The Internet is awash in warnings about viruses that don't exist and scams that don't work, created by the malicious and passed on by the innocent, who think they're helping the Internet by spreading the word. With the day of tricks here, experts expect the river to turn into a flood.

"It's amazing what people will believe because they got it over the Internet," says Rob Rosenberger, who runs the Computer Virus Myths site *(kumite.com/myths)*. "Be sure to add fresh batteries to your clue meter come *April Fools'*."

Here is how Weise ended the piece:

> Finally, there's a simple test you can use to detect almost every deceptive message, says Bill Orvis, a security specialist with the Department of Energy's Computer Incident Response Advisory. "You can tell a **hoax** because it always ends with 'Tell all your friends.' "

For a listing of sources on the Internet, see **Appendix E, Sources Online** in *NRW Plus*.

How Reporters Use Sources

Let us accompany some reporters as they work with various kinds of sources for their stories. The first story is the type that puts reporters on their mettle, the late-breaking event that must be handled quickly and accurately.

A Fatality

The story takes us to a New Jersey newsroom where a reporter is making late police checks, which consist of calling area police departments not personally covered by the police reporter. Here, the reporter must rely on human sources. There is little opportunity to examine police records.

The reporter is told that a car plowed into a motorcycle at a stoplight and the two young people on the motorcycle were killed. The driver was arrested three miles down the highway and charged with drunken driving. The reporter knows this is a good story, but little time remains before the last edition closes. The rule in the newsroom, she remembers her editor telling her, is simple: "In baseball, if you get your glove on the ball and don't handle it cleanly, it's an error, no matter how hard it's hit to you. If you get a story before deadline and don't have it written for the next edition, you're not a reporter."

She has seen baseball games in which fielders managed to touch a ball but were not given errors when they failed to throw the batter out. But she had not called that to her editor's attention. She knows better.

Basic Information She quickly learns the names of the victims and the driver as well as the location and circumstances of the accident. Knowing that the investigating officers are still writing their report, she asks if they are available at the station. They will have details she needs, especially about the chase for the driver. She then calls the mortuary to obtain background about the victims. Mortuaries usually have the exact spelling of a victim's name, and his or her age, address and occupation.

She glances at the clock to see whether she has time to call the parents of the victims for more precise information. Also, relatives often are around after an emergency to help out, and they might be able to tell her something about the deceased. But she decides that first she will see whether the victims' names are in the newspaper library.

During her interviews with the investigating officers, one of them mentions that this was the third motorcycle accident in the last month. She notes that on her pad for a quick check in the library, too.

The check of the library discloses this was actually the fourth motorcycle accident in the county, one of the others having been fatal to a young man. She also finds a story about the young woman who was killed. She was the daughter of a prominent local family, and the story indicates she used a middle name, which was not in the reporter's notes.

The reporter then decides to locate the parents of the man who died in the accident. She realizes that she had decided not to make those calls because of her distaste for intruding on the family's tragedy. At some newspapers, reporters do not have to make such calls, she recalls a colleague telling her, but that is not the case at this one. The younger sister of the man answers the telephone and is able to supply some details about him.

The reporter used physical and human sources. One key to the story is her knowledge that the investigating police officers might be at the police station writing up the report of the accident. She knows that the best sources are those close to the scene. Although they had not seen the accident, they had arrived quickly and had conducted the investigation. The names of the officers will add authenticity to the story.

She begins to write, some 20 minutes before the last edition closes. She knows she has time because she had been organizing her notes as she was reporting.

The Spy Who Wasn't

Stories usually blend human and physical sources. When Art Jester of the *Lexington Herald-Leader* heard a speaker describe his hair-raising exploits during World War II, he became suspicious. The tales were just too dramatic, Jester felt, and he decided to dig.

The speaker claimed that Winston Churchill sent him to parachute behind German lines. A check of his birth certificate showed that he would have been 16 at the time. He claimed he was in a spy exchange at the Berlin Wall in 1957. The Wall was built in 1961.

He asserted he was an ordained Anglican priest, and in his talks he often wore clerical garb. An Anglican bishop Jester reached said, "We believe him to be a fraud." He claimed to be a model for a character in two of John Le Carré's novels. Jester reached the novelist, who told him, "I'm getting fairly irritated by the man. I've never heard of him, and there's no question of him being the basis of characters in my work. He is either mad or a fraud."

Jester wrote that the speaker gave 70 to 75 talks a year and his fee was $2,500 a speech.

A Shooting

Although reporters sometimes use the telephone when they should be on the street talking to people or at meetings observing the give-and-take of open debate, there are times when direct observation is impossible. We have just seen a reporter handle a fatal accident by telephone. When the deadline is imminent and the source or the event is more than a short walk or trip away, the only recourse is the telephone.

Using the telephone can be an art. Properly used, it is a boon to reporting. Let us watch a television news reporter cover a shooting 50 miles north of her station, WKTV in Utica, N.Y.

Early one fall evening, Donna Hanover is told by a cameraman that he has picked up an interesting police report: Two people had been shot in separate incidents as they drove past an Indian encampment near the town of Big Moose. Hanover knows immediately this is a big story. Some Mohawk Indians had moved onto state-owned land in the Adirondack Mountains six months before and had refused to leave.

Hanover's major problem is her impending deadline and the distance to Big Moose. Her newscast is at 11 P.M., which gives her no time for the trip up, reporting and the return trip. She has to use the telephone.

By 10:15 P.M., her calls to the state police have turned up little information—a few details on the shooting and the names and ages of the injured. Apparently both were wounded by shots fired at the cars in which they were riding. Hanover then calls a medical center near Big Moose to check the condition of the victims, a 22-year-old man and a 9-year-old girl. She also hopes to learn something more about the incident. She is told that the young man was taken to a hospital in Utica and that the girl is on her way.

Hospital Check   She asks for the names of the relatives of those who were injured, and a hospital attendant gives her the name of the injured man's father. She then calls "information for the home telephone number, hoping that some member of the family would have stayed at home in Big Moose," Hanover says.

She is lucky. The father is not there, but the victim's brother answers her call, and he had been riding in the car with his older brother at the time of the shooting.

This piece of good fortune enables Hanover to use an eyewitness, a better source than someone with a secondhand account. He tells Hanover that they had been fired at twice by the Indians. The first time the shots missed. But on the return trip, the car had come under heavy fire and his brother was hit in the shoulder.

The girl was in a car that passed by the Indian encampment a few hours after the boys were fired at. One bullet entered the trunk, went through the rear seat and struck the girl in the back.

As a result of her calls, Hanover is able to make the 11 o'clock news with a report of the incident. She does not have all the information she needs, but she does have the interview, information from the state police, the condition of the 22-year-old and the name of the 9-year-old girl who was also injured.

To the Scene   The next day, with plenty of time, Hanover and two photographers drive to Big Moose to do an on-the-scene report. She interviews the injured man's brother again, this time in front of a camera, photographs the damaged automobile and interviews local residents and the state police.

"The interview with the brother was important," Hanover says later, "because he was a primary source. The police report wasn't, and our job is to give our viewers the best and most accurate information about what has happened." The interview also added an essential ingredient for television news—visual identification.

"I always try to make the viewers feel close to the scene, to make them feel they were there as it happened," says Hanover.

One patrolman was photographed indicating bullet holes in the car. The Mohawk Indians were not available for interviews. Later, they told her they had been shot at and were returning the fire.

Her script begins:

New York state police are manning roadblocks near Eagle Bay and are escorting cars on Big Moose Road where two people in passing cars were shot Monday. Nine-year-old April Madigan of Geneva, New York, is in critical condition at St. Luke's Memorial Hospital Center. . . .

An Enterpriser

We turn from these spot news stories to a story that begins with a chat between friends.

Jeffrey A. Tannenbaum, a reporter with *The Wall Street Journal,* is in the newsroom when a call comes in from a former college classmate, Ralph Sanders.

Sanders, who is blind, tells Tannenbaum he is active in an organization called the National Federation of the Blind and that the group is planning a demonstration. Sanders says that the blind are tired of being denied rights granted to sighted people.

Sanders suggests the demonstration will make a good story. Sensing a broader story than the coverage of an event that is being staged for the media, Tannenbaum arranges to have lunch with Sanders.

"I was fascinated with the possibility of writing a story about the blind comparable to early stories on the civil rights movement," Tannenbaum says later. "In the course of a long interview, Sanders provided the theme for the story. I used it in the sixth paragraph of the finished story.

THE WALL STR

VOL. CLXXXVI NO. 7   ★ ★   EASTERN EDITION   THURSDAY, JU

New Crusaders

Angry Blind Militants, Seeking 'Equal Rights,' Try Tougher Tactics

---

Sightless Stage Walkouts, Sue Landlords, Bosses, Reject 'Excessive' Pity

---

The Fight With Sky Glider

By JEFFREY A. TANNENBAUM
Staff Reporter of THE WALL STREET JOURNAL

Keith and Elizabeth Howard were all set to board an Allegheny Airlines flight from Washington, D.C., to Philadelphia. The airplane wasn't fully booked. Yet an airline official suddenly insisted they must take separate flights.

The reason: The Howards are both blind.

The couple say they were told the pilot didn't want more than one blind passenger on the flight because he assumed that blind people might cause a safety problem or require extra service. While his wife went on ahead, the 43-year-old Mr. Howard waited for the next flight.

Far from being helpless nuisances, the Howards both successfully manage their own lunch counters in Washington. They angrily protested to Allegheny, which confirms their story. Allegheny apologized, and says that Ransome Airlines, which operated the flight under contract, has changed its policies to prevent a repeat of the incident. But the Howards figure their problems are far from over. They say the airline incident was typical of the "common discrimination—a normal thing" that society practices almost routinely against the blind.

But nowadays, blind people like the Howards are moving with increasing fervor to protest such discrimination. They are voicing complaints, turning to the courts and even staging strikes and demonstrations. As a result, employers, landlords and businesses generally are finding they must either change their policies or face protests and lawsuits.

"A Dash of Leprosy"

"Society will give charity to the blind, but it won't allow us to be first-class citizens," charges Ralph W. Sanders, president of the Arkansas unit of the National Federation of the Blind. "Like the blacks, we've come to the point where we're not going to stand for it anymore," he adds.

Ironically, this militancy occurs at a time when conditions for the blind are improving significantly, particularly in the realm of jobs. Several states in recent ~~~~~~ approve ~~~ broa~

What's News—

* * *

Business and Finance

OIL'S EXPORT PRICE was cut by Ecuador in what may be the first major crack in the oil cartel's pricing structure. Ecuador's cut was through a reduction in the income-tax rate charged oil companies.

(Story on Page 3)

* * *

A tax on most crude oil and refined petroleum products of up to three cents a barrel was proposed, as expected, by President Ford to help pay for damages caused by oil spills.

(Story on Page 3)

* * *

A Honduran commission urged steps to nationalize the concessions and property of units of United Brands and Castle & Cooke to increase that country's participation in the banana-export business.

(Story on Page 2)

* * *

Developing nations' efforts to negotiate new international agreements fixing commodities prices will be resisted by the U.S., a top Treasury official said.

(Story on Page 2)

* * *

General Motors is being countersued by a former dealer for $33 million in connection with a tangled series of criminal and civil cases involving alleged warranty fraud. Separately, GM said its supplemental benefit fund for laid-off employees could soon resume payouts for a brief period.

(Stories on Page 4)

* * *

Ford Motor confirmed that it quietly paid for repairing about 69,000 rust-damaged 1969-73 models even though normal warranties had expired.

(Story on Page 4)

* * *

Great Atlantic & Pacific Tea reported a $6.5 million loss, less than predicted, for its May 24 first quarter; a year earlier it earned $10.3 million.

(Story on Page 4)

* * *

International Paper's second quarter earnings slid 37% to $47.2

World-Wide

A MIDEAST AGREEMENT isn't "anywhere near," Kissinger said.

The Secretary of State, beginning a European trip during which he will meet with Israeli Prime Minister Rabin, said reports that an Egyptian-Israeli accord had been all but wrapped up are "totally wrong." Hearst Newspapers quoted Egyptian President Sadat as indicating that basic terms of a new interim Sinai agreement had been worked out. But Prime Minister Rabin said some key issues remain to be settled.

Sources suggested that an agreement would involve an electronic surveillance system, operated by the U.S., to warn of any attack through the Gidi and Mitla mountain passes in the Sinai.

Rabin conferred with West German Chancellor Schmidt in Bonn, who urged the Israeli premier to take advantage of the current chance for a settlement with Egypt. Kissinger arrived in Paris and will meet with Soviet Foreign Minister Gromyko in Geneva before seeing Rabin Saturday in Bonn.

The Palestine Liberation Organization said in Beirut that it had failed to win the release of an American Army colonel kidnapped last week. It said the colonel was being held by two radical Palestinian groups that don't belong to the PLO. The deadline the abductors set for the U.S. to meet their ransom demands passed.

* * *

A TURKISH-ARMS COMPROMISE was offered to the House by Ford.

After meeting with 140 House members, the President proposed legislation partially lifting the ban on military aid that was imposed after Turkey used U.S. weapons in invading Cyprus. Under the plan, undelivered arms already paid for by Turkey would be shipped and more weapons could be bought for cash, but Turkey wouldn't be eligible for grants. Ford would report to Congress every two months on arms sales and on the chances for a Cyprus settlement.

The three leading House opponents of arms for Turkey weren't invited to the meeting with Ford. One of them, Rep. John Brademas (D., Ind.), denounced the proposal as a fraud.

Speaker Carl Albert predicted the House would approve Ford's plan. The Senate last month voted 41-40 to end the arms embargo. Turkey has demanded that negotiations on the status of U.S. bases begin next Thursday if the embargo hasn't been lifted by then. It wasn't known whether Turkey would accept Ford's compromise.

* * *

PORTUGAL'S ARMED FORCES will form local units bypassing political ~~~~~

An Enterpriser: A Reporter-Initiated Story

"What I needed to do after the interview was to document the central thesis. I needed to find examples of ways in which blind people are discriminated against. And I needed to find cases of discrimination in which blind people were militant."

At lunch, Sanders provides some sources and examples of militancy. Tannenbaum finds other examples by calling organizations of the blind. He learns about discrimination by checking with social agencies and human rights commissions. He is able to find more than a dozen examples of discrimination.

Examples "As a rule of thumb," Tannenbaum says, "I like to have half-a-dozen highly readable, colorful, to-the-point examples in a story. Each one should illustrate a different aspect of the general problem, buttressing the main theme but not duplicating one another."

He checks with people who might have another point of view on what the blind charge is discrimination. Tannenbaum says, "More than fairness is involved here. A good reporter knows that the best stories are multidimensional. Conflict and controversy do make a better story, but they also accurately reflect reality."

Tannenbaum now has sources with specific complaints and incidents. He has a feeling an incident at a Washington, D.C., airport described by Keith and Elizabeth Howard should be well up in his story, perhaps the lead.

He interviews the head of Sanders' organization and a blind professor of American history at Seton Hall College in New Jersey, who provides an excellent quote that gives an overview. He consults some references for data about the blind. He has now interviewed 40 people and is ready to write.

Tannenbaum finds the writing goes quickly. "A well-reported story—one reported logically with a central theme in mind—tends to write itself," he recalls an editor telling him. He begins with the Howards in a delayed lead and presents the theme in his words in the fifth paragraph and then in Sanders' words in the sixth paragraph. The next two paragraphs are background.

Tannenbaum's first version had the blind professor's quote lower in the story, but he remembered the guideline that good quotes should be put up high in a story and so he raised the quote as high as he could.

Do Jane and Johnny Read?

The reporter, Mullins, is told by his city editor to find out whether people "are reading as much as they used to." It's a vague assignment, but Mullins thinks he knows what his editor has in mind. The editor has talked often about "cretinization by television," and recently he walked through the newsroom brandishing a photo from a college newspaper of roommates talking to each other on their computers. The photo shows them three feet apart.

"It says here that college students spend three to four hours a day surfing the Internet," he exploded. "No wonder they don't know anything. They have no time to read."

Ken Elkins,
The Anniston (Ala.) *Star*

Pitts?

The reading scores in local schools have been declining in recent years, and the newspaper has played up those stories. So Mullins decides to pass on the Net surfers and look at the young readers.

First, he wants to compare local reading scores with those of other school systems in the state and with national reading scores, which will take him to databases. He makes a note to do that. Maybe this is not just a local situation.

"If you find anyone is still reading, tell us what's being read," is the editor's parting comment as Mullins leaves the newsroom.

So his first stop will be a nearby library and another near a grade school.

He will also want to talk to some teachers. A reporter on the newspaper whose wife is a fourth-grade teacher told him that she is convinced her students cannot spell because they rarely read outside class and are unfamiliar with words. "Nobody can spell," Mullins told her, having put in time on the copy desk.

Library Users   In one library, he notices some youngsters chatting at a table near the window. Unobtrusively, he moves over to listen.

"What did you find out about the clipper ships?" one of the boys asks another. A few minutes later, a girl asks the boy next to her if he knows when the first transcontinental railroad was completed. Apparently they are doing research for an assignment on transportation. Mullins asks one of the boys, and he is told the work is for an honors history class in one of the local high schools. That is worth noting, Mullins decides.

As he passes three other students, he glances at the books they are reading—Jack Kerouac's *On the Road,* Hermann Hesse's *Demian,* and a book that appears to be about race car driving, judging by its title. That, too, goes into Mullins' notes. Suddenly, it strikes him that this is just what he needs to be doing, to rely on his observations and to support them with interviews of library users.

Mullins strolls around the library. As he passes one shelf, he observes that most of the books, which bear numbers ranging from 200 to 300 on their spines, are hardly used but that a few are well-worn. The well-read books are on eastern religions. He jots down their titles, and he makes a note to look into that by talking to the librarian. She might have some of the titles of the books that have been borrowed frequently.

Older Readers   The physical evidence seems to show that youngsters on school assignments are major library users, as are older people with time on their hands. The older readers congregate around the newspaper rack, and much of their borrowing and reading is of the historical romances, adventure novels and mysteries. Considerable activity by all age groups focuses on the how-to books that offer instruction on investments, gardening, home repair and sex. He learns videotapes are a big item with library users.

Mullins' story is a blend of human and physical sources, the one supplementing the other. His observation of the library users injects human interest into the story. He *shows* his readers students and adults using books, newspapers and magazines, and he names these publications, remembering the guideline that journalism is the art of the specific.

Summing Up

Good reporters rely on human and physical sources. A study by Kathleen A. Hansen of the University of Minnesota journalism faculty found that Pulitzer Prize winners used a greater variety of physical sources in their stories than did nonwinners. The winners used more documents, reports, books and other printed matter and fewer interviews than did the nonwinners.

Yet many reporters rely on the interview for almost all their reporting. Stephen Hess found in his study of Washington reporters that journalists used no documents in almost three-fourths of their stories. When reporters are given more time to do stories, he says, "they simply do more interviews."

The reporters we have been studying know the value of physical and human sources, and they know their limitations. We also can make these generalizations about reporters:

- They make direct observations whenever possible.
- When it is necessary to use secondhand accounts, they find the best human sources available, backed by physical evidence.
- They understand that the official version is not necessarily the true account, so they seek verification.
- They know the limitations of human and physical sources.

Interviews are, of course, essential to reporting. We will next examine how to conduct them and we will consider their place in the reporter's arsenal of methods for digging out useful and relevant material.

Further Reading

Abel, Elie. *Leaking: Who Does It? Who Benefits? At What Cost?* Winchester, Mass.: Unwin Hyman, 1987. (This is a 20th Century Fund study that examines leaks and their consequences to government and to journalism.)

Downie, Leonard J.V. *The New Muckrakers.* Washington, D.C.: New Republic, 1976.

Kovach, Bill, and Tom Rosenstiel. *Warp Speed.* New York: The Century Foundation Press, 1999.

Sigal, Leon V. *Reporters and Officials.* Lexington, Mass.: Heath, 1973.

Will Waldron, *Times Union*

Celebrity interviews are avidly read.

Preview

Reporters conduct two kinds of interviews:

• **News interview:** The purpose is to gather information to explain an idea, event or situation in the news.

• **Profile:** The focus is on an individual. A news peg often is used to justify the profile.

For effective interviews, reporters prepare carefully, and they ask questions that induce the source to talk freely. Questions are directed at obtaining information on a theme that the reporter has in mind before beginning the interview. If a more important theme emerges, the reporter develops it.

The reporter notes what is said, how it is said and what is not said. Sources are encouraged by the reporter's gestures and facial expressions to keep talking.

In the stadium locker room, the half-dressed hurdler was stuffing his warm-up suit and track shoes into a battered black bag. Seated on a bench nearby, a young man removed a pencil and a notepad from a jacket pocket.

"I'm from the paper in town," the young man said. "You looked sharp out there. Mind if I ask you some questions?"

The athlete nodded and continued his packing.

"First time you've been to this part of the West or this city?" the reporter asked. Another nod. This was not going to be easy, the reporter worried. The editor had told him to make sure he brought back a good story for tomorrow's paper, the day the National Association of Intercollegiate Athletics would begin its outdoor track meet at the local college. The tall, lithe young man standing in front of the bench was a world record holder in the hurdles, the editor had said, and worth a story for the sports section.

The reporter tried again. "What do you think of our town?" The athlete seemed to see the reporter for the first time.

"I don't know anything about this town," he replied. "I'm here to run. I go to the East coast, the West coast, here. They give me a ticket at school and I get on a bus or a plane and go. My business is to run." He fell silent.

Rebuffed, the reporter struggled to start the athlete talking again. In the 20-minute interview, the hurdler never really opened up.

Back in the newsroom, the reporter told the editor about his difficulties. They seemed to begin with his first question about whether the athlete had been to the town before, he said. His boss was not sympathetic.

"First, you should have checked the clips and called the college for information about your man," the editor said. "That way you could have learned something about him, his record or his school. You might have used it to break the ice. Or you could have asked him about the condition of the track, something he knows about."

Then the editor softened. He knew that interviewing is not easy for young reporters, that it can be perfected only through practice.

"I think you have a good quote there about the business of running," he told the reporter. "Did you get anything else about the places he's been? That could make an interesting focus for the piece."

Yes, the reporter said, he had managed to draw the hurdler out about where he had been in the last few months. With the editor's guidance, the reporter managed to turn out an acceptable story.

Types of Interviews

The major story on page 1 of a September issue of *The Hawk Eye* in Burlington, Iowa, was about a three-alarm fire that destroyed a two-story building that housed an automobile sales agency and a body repair shop. The reporter interviewed several people for information to supplement his observations. Here are the people he interviewed and a summary of their comments:

- **The owner:** 15 cars destroyed; exact loss as yet unknown.
- **A fire department lieutenant:** The building could not have been saved when firefighters arrived. They concentrated on saving the adjoining buildings.
- **An eyewitness:** "I didn't know what it was. It just went all at once. I seen it a-burning and I was scared to death."
- **The fire chief:** The state fire marshal will investigate the cause of the fire.

News Interview

Although the reporter was not present when firefighters battled the fire during the early morning hours, the interviews with the lieutenant and the eyewitness give his story an on-the-scene flavor. Because these interviews help explain the news event, we describe them as *news interviews*.

Another local front-page story also relies on a news interview. A head-on automobile crash on Iowa Route 2 near Farmington took the life of a Van Buren County woman and caused injuries to four others. The story is based on an interview with the Iowa Highway Patrol.

Personality Interview

The other type of interview story is the *profile* or *personality interview* in which the focus is a person rather than an event or situation.

Phoebe Zerwick of the *Winston-Salem Journal* frequently writes profiles for a feature called "Tarheel Sketch." In one, she profiled a federal district judge with a reputation as a hero to the disadvantaged.

"Over the past 20 years," Zerwick writes, "advocates for black children sent to inferior schools, poor people awaiting public assistance, disabled people who have been kicked off the Social Security rolls, and mentally disturbed children locked away in state hospitals have climbed the stairs to that courtroom. And over the years, McMillan has provided them with relief."

Before we examine the two types of interviews in detail, let's look at the principles that guide journalists when they interview sources.

Four Principles

From our examination of the interview of the hurdler, the coverage of the fire at the Iowa auto dealer's agency and Phoebe Zerwick's profile of a federal judge, we can settle on a few basics for the interviewer. Our sportswriter went off on the wrong foot when he failed to obtain background about the athlete he was to interview. Lacking this information, he was unable to draw out his subject, much less to establish a relationship with him.

Zerwick's profile is successful because she was well prepared before she interviewed the judge, having examined his decisions in key cases and talked to people who had appeared in the judge's courtroom.

The reporter who covered the local fire asked the people involved with the incident questions whose answers developed the information essential to the story.

Here are the four basic guides to good interviewing:

1. Prepare carefully, familiarizing yourself with as much background as possible.

2. Establish a relationship with the source conducive to obtaining information.

3. Ask questions that are relevant to the story and that induce the source to talk.

4. Listen and watch attentively.

Preparation

There's a saying in newsrooms that good interviews follow the two "P's"—persistence and preparation. Persistence is necessary to persuade people to be interviewed, and it is essential in following a line of questioning that the subject may find objectionable.

Tarheel Sketch

James McMillan

Big Mac's understanding of the Constitution
made him into a champion of the oppressed

By Phoebe Zerwick
JOURNAL REPORTER

CHARLOTTE — Something about the way the attorney was arguing his case didn't sit too well with Judge James B. McMillan.

The case before McMillan, a federal judge in the Western District, concerned a judge who had been opening court with prayer.

The judge, H. William Constangy, said that prayer helped him set a dignified tone for the day's proceedings and also expressed his reverence for the Lord.

But five public defenders in Charlotte were offended by the prayer. They thought that it came too close to government endorsement of religion and violated the First Amendment to the Constitution. Several weeks ago they brought their complaint to McMillan.

As McMillan said afterward, the case was riveting. The evidence was succinct, and the attorneys were well organized. But still, as Constangy's attorney delivered his closing argument, McMillan kept interrupting, fixing on a seemingly minor detail, the possessive pronoun his.

"I'm interested in the theory that it's his courtroom," McMillan asked, at least four or five times, each time raising more extreme examples. Does the judge have a right to pray even though he offends some and bores others? What if he wanted to turn toward Mecca and kneel upon a prayer rug? Does he have the right to do that?

Looking up from the bench, McMillan said, "It's not my courtroom. It's a place where I work."

McMillan's place of work is the federal courthouse in Charlotte, which faces Trade Street, a broad, tree-lined avenue that runs into the city's downtown. He works in a courtroom on the second floor.

Over the past 20 years, advocates for black children sent to inferior schools, poor people awaiting public assistance, disabled people who have been kicked off the Social Security

---

RESUMÉ

FULL NAME:
James B. McMillan.

AGE: 73.

PUBLIC POSITION:
U.S. District Court judge in the Western District.

BIRTHPLACE:
McDonald, Robeson County

EDUCATION:
B.A., University of North Carolina at Chapel Hill; Law degree, Harvard University.

FAMILY:
Married to Holly Neaves McMillan; one son, one daughter.

---

rolls, and mentally disturbed children locked away in state hospitals have climbed the stairs to that courtroom. And over the years, McMillan has provided them with relief.

In 1970, he ordered the Charlotte-Mecklenburg Board of Education to bus black children into schools in white neighborhoods and white children into schools in black neighborhoods. The case was the first busing case to be upheld by the U.S. Supreme Court and led to the desegregation of schools across the state and nation.

That was the first major case McMillan heard, and no case since then has triggered the kind of controversy that raged around him during those years. But since then, he has become a kind of hero among advocates for the poor by ruling in favor of the disadvantaged in numerous lesser-known cases.

Theodore O. Fillette, the deputy director of Legal Services of Southern Piedmont, said, "I can say without a doubt he has had the greatest impact on improving the rights of low-income people than anyone else in the state. I would include people without power, racial minorities, prisoners, and physically and mentally handicapped people."

In 1975, McMillan ordered the N.C. Department of Human Resources to process applications for welfare and Medicaid, the federal insurance program for the poor, within the required 45 days.

Some applicants were waiting as long as six months. During that time, some were evicted because they couldn't pay their rent. Others went hungry or cold.

The state is still under court order,

See McMILLAN, Page A20

Preparation may consist of a few minutes spent glancing through a story in last week's newscast before dashing out to interview a congresswoman on a flying visit to look at the local Veterans Hospital where cutbacks have affected care. It may be a prolonged examination of clippings and material that databases have turned up for a profile of the new university president.

Clyde Haberman, a *New York Times* columnist, says "exhaustive research is the basic building block of a successful interview."

Research   A.J. Liebling, a master reporter who moved from the newspaper newsroom to *The New Yorker* magazine, is quoted in *The Most of A.J. Liebling,* edited by William Cole: "The preparation is the same whether you are going to interview a diplomat, a jockey, or an ichthyologist. From the man's past you learn what questions are likely to stimulate a response."

Research begins with the library's clippings about the subject. If the interviewee is well-known, *Who's Who in America* and other biographical dictionaries can be consulted. Most reference works are on CD-ROM and are accessible online. People who know the interviewee can be asked for information.

These resources provide material for three purposes: (1) They give the reporter leads to tentative themes and to specific questions. (2) They provide the reporter with a feel for the subject. (3) They provide useful background.

Earning Trust

When Sheryl James of the *St. Petersburg Times* was interviewing sources for her prize-winning series on abandoned infants, she realized that many of those she was interviewing were unaccustomed to talking to a reporter. "I was dealing with good but somewhat unsophisticated people," she says, "who would have been easy to manipulate. It was a challenge to be sure they understood what I was doing and to keep promises made during the reporting process that I could have broken with impunity."

James focused on a woman who was charged with leaving her baby in a box near a dumpster. She had to develop a relationship with the woman. "I simply tried to be straightforward about what I was doing," James said, "and get her to trust me, to know that I would keep my word to her.

"Aside from that, when I finally did interview her, I felt as I do with many people I interview—I try to establish a relaxed rapport, to be human myself so that they know I'm not a media monster."

Opening Up   This was the fifth session reporter Claudia Dreifus was spending with Dan Rather and they both knew that a mile-high barrier separated them. "This isn't working," she said finally. Rather agreed and he invited her to accompany him in his pickup from Sam Houston State University in Huntsville, from which he graduated, south to Wharton, where he was born, and then over to Austin for dinner. The trip seemed to relax them both, and Dreifus was able to see Rather in a less formal setting.

Back home, Rather relaxed and opened up, complaining about his ill-fated pairing with Connie Chung on "The CBS Evening News" and worrying about the cost-cutting that has affected news coverage.

"At CBS News, we're down to the bone, past the bone, and we've been there a long time," he told Dreifus.

With experienced subjects, interviews usually go smoothly as both stand to gain from the interview: The subject will have his or her ideas and comments before the public, and the reporter will have a story.

Give and Take   The early stage of the interview is a feeling-out period. The interviewee balances his or her gains and losses from divulging information the reporter seeks, and the reporter tries to show the source the rewards the source will receive through disclosure of the information—publicity, respect and the feeling that goes with doing a good turn.

When the source concludes that the risks outweigh the possible gains and decides to provide little or no information or is misleading, the reporter has several alternatives. At one extreme, the reporter can try to cajole the source into a complete account through flattery—or by appearing surprised. At the other extreme, the reporter can demand information. If the source is a public official, such demands are legitimate because officials are responsible to the public. The reporter can tell the source that the story—and there will be some kind of story—will point out that the official refused to answer questions. Usually, the source will fall into line.

The Questions

Careful preparation leads the interviewer to a few themes for the interview, and these, in turn, suggest questions to be asked. But before the specific questions are put to the interviewee, a few housekeeping details usually are attended to, vital data questions. For some interviews, these may involve age, education, jobs held, family information. For well-known people, the questions may be about their latest activities.

Questions of this sort are nonthreatening and help make for a relaxed interview atmosphere. Also, they are sometimes necessary because of conflicting material in the files, such as discrepancies in age or education.

People want to know these details. Harold Ross, the brilliant and eccentric former newspaperman who founded and edited *The New Yorker,* slashed exasperatedly at the pages of profiles and interviews that lacked vital data. "Who he?" Ross would scrawl across such manuscripts.

Even the obvious questions about background can result in fascinating and revealing answers. For a personality profile, the interviewer asked Whoopi Goldberg why she adopted Goldberg as her stage name. She replied:

"It was my mother's idea. It's a name from the family past. There are lots of names hangin' on our family tree, Jewish, Catholic, Asian. . . . Black folks, white folks. I'm just the all-American mutt."

Simple question. Fascinating answer.

Direct Questions   Most questions flow from what the reporter perceives to be the theme of the assignment. A fatal accident: Automatically, the reporter knows that he or she must find out who died and how and where the death occurred. The same process is used in the more complicated interview.

A reporter is told to interview an actor who had been out of work for two years and is now in a hit musical. The reporter decides that the theme of the story will be the changes the actor has made in his life. He asks the actor if he has moved from his tenement walk-up, has made any large personal purchases and how his family feels about his being away most nights. These three questions induce the actor to talk at length.

Another reporter is to interview a well-known entertainer. The reporter decides to ask about the singer's experiences that led him to write songs that call attention to war, poverty, sexism and racism. "Bread," says the singer in answer to the first question the reporter asks. "Money," he explains. There is a good market in such songs. The reporter then quickly shifts themes and asks questions about the economics of popular music and the singer's personal beliefs.

Open- and Closed-Ended Questions   When the sportswriter asked the hurdler, "What do you think of our town?" he was using what is known as an *open-ended question,* which could have been answered in general terms. The sports editor's suggestion that the reporter ask the athlete about the condition of the track would have elicited a specific response—fast, slow, or slick—as it was a *closed-ended question.*

The open-ended question does not require a specific answer. The closed-ended question calls for a brief, pointed reply. Applied properly, both have their merits. Two months before the budget is submitted, a city hall reporter may ask the city manager what she thinks of the city's general financial situation—an open-ended question. The reply may cover the failure of anticipated revenues to meet expectations, unusually high increases in construction costs, higher interest rates and other factors that have caused trouble for the city. Then the reporter may ask a closed-ended question, "Will we need a tax increase?"

As we have seen, reporters often begin their interviews with open-ended questions, which allow the source to relax. Then the closed-ended questions are asked, which may seem threatening if asked at the outset of the interview.

Television and radio interviews usually end with a closed-ended question because the interviewer wants to sum up the situation with a brief reply.

The reporter who asks only open-ended questions should be aware of their possible implications. To some sources, the open-ended question is the mark of an inadequately prepared reporter who is fishing for a story.

Tough Questions   Sometimes a young reporter finds that posing the right question is difficult because the question might embarrass or offend the interviewee. There is no recourse but to ask.

Oriana Fallaci, an Italian journalist famous for her interviews, says that her success may be the result of asking the world leaders she interviews questions that other reporters do not ask.

"Some reporters are courageous only when they write, when they are alone with their typewriters, not when they face the person in power. They never put a question like this, 'Sir, since you are a dictator, we all know you are corrupt. In what measure are you corrupt?' "

Remarkably, heads of state, kings and guerrilla leaders open up to Fallaci. One reason for this is her presumption that the public is entitled to answers and her unwillingness to be treated with indifference. When the heavyweight champion boxer Muhammad Ali belched in answer to one of her questions, she threw the microphone of her tape recorder in his face.

Another reason for her effectiveness is "her talent for intimacy," as one journalist put it. "She easily establishes an atmosphere of confidence and closeness and creates the impression that she would tell you anything. Consequently, you feel safe, or almost safe, to do the same with her," writes Diana Loercher in *The Christian Science Monitor.*

Kissinger the Cowboy   In her interview with Henry Kissinger, the U.S. secretary of state at the time, Fallaci had him admit that his position of power made him feel like the "lone cowboy who leads the wagon train alone on his horse." His image of himself as the Lone Ranger caused an embarrassed Kissinger to say later that granting Fallaci the interview was the "stupidest" act in his life.

A political reporter who accompanied Sen. Don Nickles on a tour of Oklahoma towns noticed an apparent inconsistency in Nickles' public statements. Nickles often described himself as a conservative who was tough on federal spending. Yet in Eufaula, Nickles announced "good news" from Washington, a commitment of federal funds for a new housing project.

The Right Moment

When an interview begins, says Carol McCabe of *The Providence Journal,* people are wary, stiff. Gradually "they lean back, they are open. Then you can begin to move," she says. "The time to ask your most sensitive question is when the 'mirroring' starts. Mirroring is when they are doing the same thing you are doing. You begin the test: You push back in your chair and watch to see if they push back in theirs. You cross your right leg over the left one and see if they do it. You put one arm on the other arm, and see if they do it. That means they like you, you are together and that's the time to ask your tough questions."

The reporter then asked if the Republican senator's approach was consistent—condemning government spending in one place and welcoming it in another. Nickles' answer: He would vote against federal housing funds but as long as they were available, "I will try to see that Oklahoma gets its fair share."

The quote ends the story, and the reader is left to decide whether the senator is an opportunist.

Intrusive Questions   Still, there are questions that few reporters like to ask. Most of these concern the private lives of sources—the mental retardation of a couple's son, the fatal illness of a baseball player. Some questions are necessary, some not. The guidelines for relevance and good taste are constantly shifting, and reporters may find they are increasingly being told to ask questions that they consider intrusive. This is the age of intimacy.

Reporters who dislike asking these questions, preferring to spare sources anguish, are sometimes surprised by the frank replies. A reporter for *Newsday* was assigned to follow up on an automobile accident in which a drunken youth without a driver's license ran a borrowed car into a tree. One of the passengers, a 15-year-old girl, was killed. In doing his follow-up story, the reporter discovered that most of the parents were willing to talk because, as one parent said, the lessons learned from the accident might save lives.

Junk Questions   Wendell Rawls Jr., a veteran newsman, describes his interviewing technique:

> Don't tell people what you know. Ask questions. Then back off. Use diversion. I love to do that—talk with people about things you're not there to talk to them about. You ask a question that may be very meaningful. Then you move away from it. I do it sometimes even if the person doesn't get particularly fidgety, because I don't want him to think that I think what he has told me is necessarily important to me. I'll move to another question and say, "What is that on the wall? That's an interesting sort of. . . ." Whatever. Anything that will divert him, and he will start talking about that. And then maybe ask two or three questions about junk, and then come back and ask another very pointed question.

Questioning Candidates   Candidates for public office face questions from reporters who defend their probing on the basis of the public's right to know before they vote. Know what? About the candidate's stand on issues relevant to the office, of course. About their health, their income, the books they read, the movies they like, their sex lives, their religion? Yes and no, says the historian Arthur Schlesinger Jr.

In the 1884 presidential campaign, Schlesinger says, Grover Cleveland was accused by opponents of fathering an illegitimate child. Reporters did not pursue the matter.

"It was not until 1987 that a reporter, who has since repented, asked a presidential aspirant whether he had ever committed adultery," Schlesinger says. As for religion, only in 1928 and in 1960—when Catholics Al Smith and John

---

Sandpaper Sam. Some viewers find the questions of Sam Donaldson of ABC abrasive. He defends his tough, boring-in style:

There's a perception that I'm always asking some rude or confrontational question. That's absolutely wrong. I'm not trying to make the president say something foolish or trip him up. But I think it's proper to ask him a question that confronts him with the critics of his policy.

Kennedy ran for president—were candidates asked to define their positions on church and state. "But in general, the religious test had appeared to be safely drummed out of politics," Schlesinger says.

"Where to draw the line? The electorate is surely entitled to information that bears on a president's public responsibilities," he says. "That includes candidates' views on all aspects of public policy. It includes the release of health and income records. . . . Religion is a private matter. Voters are entitled to know where candidates stand on abortion, a public issue. Questions about husbands and wives should be off limits. So, too, should questions about whether candidates have slept with persons not their spouses, though any candidate who could command the adultery vote might very well sweep the country."

Listening, Watching

"Great reporters are great listeners," says Carl Bernstein of the Woodward-Bernstein reporting team that exposed the Watergate cover-up that led to President Nixon's resignation.

The good listener hears relevant quotes, revealing slips of the tongue, the dialect and diction of the source that sets him or her apart.

In an interview with Luis Manuel Delgado whom Diana Griego Erwin encounters at a motor vehicle office in Santa Ana, Calif., she finds Delgado unable to tell the English-speaking clerks what he needs. Does that bother him? Erwin asks. Here is an excerpt of their conversation from *The Orange County Register:*

"I should know how to speak English," he said with a quiet simplicity. "This is the United States."

"My kids are very good," he said. "They get good marks in school. They speak English. No accent. One wants to be a doctor. When they first came here I told them to study English and learn it well. Don't let them treat you like a donkey like they treat your papa."

I asked him if it didn't hurt, being treated "como un burro," as he said.

"No, I am not a donkey and my children know it. They know I do all this for them.

"They are proud of me. Nothing anyone else says or does can make me sad when they have pride in me.

"And they will never be donkeys."

Sometimes, a single quote can capture the person or illuminate the situation the interview is about. In an interview with a former governor of Arkansas, Sid McMath, a single quotation told a great deal. First, the background.

School Desegregation   In 1957, Gov. Orval Faubus defied a federal court order to desegregate Little Rock's Central High School. Although President Eisenhower responded by ordering the 101st Airborne to enforce the court order, Faubus had legitimatized resistance and there was violence when the few black students tried to enter the high school.

Faubus had been a small-time politico when McMath plucked him out of Madison County.

Listener. Lynn Hirschberg, whose profiles of Hollywood's stars appear in many magazines, skewers her subjects as often as she applauds them. Yet they rarely turn down her request for an interview, and they always open up to her. Why? "It comes down to how interested you are in what they have to say. It's just a matter of how much you want to listen."

Years after the Little Rock spectacle, McMath was asked about Faubus and he replied: "The sorriest thing I ever did as governor was to build a paved road into Madison County so Orval Faubus could come down it."

School Cruelty   Listen to Wendy Williams, a bright 13-year-old, talk to a reporter. She lives in a trailer park in Dixon, Ill. Her teacher recommended her for an advanced math class, but she said no. "I get picked on for my clothes and for living in a trailer park," she said. "I don't want to get picked on for being a nerd."

Louisiana Politics   Earl K. Long, a member of the powerful Long political dynasty, was getting on and a reporter interviewed him for a profile. Long told his interviewer, "When I die—if I die—I want to be buried in Louisiana so I can stay active in politics."

The Interviewer's Ground Rules

Both parties in an interview have certain assumptions and expectations. Generally, the reporter expects the interviewee to tell the truth and to stand behind what he or she has told the interviewer. The interviewee presumes the reporter will write the story fairly and accurately. Both agree, without saying so, that the questions and answers mean what they appear to mean—that is, that there are no hidden meanings.

Having said this, we must admit to the exceptions. Sources may conceal, evade, distort and lie when they believe it is to their advantage. The reporter must be alert to the signs of a departure from truth.

The rules that govern the reporter's behavior in the interview can be detailed with some certainty. Reporters, too, conceal, mislead and, at times, lie. Few reporters justify these practices. Most agree the reporter should:

1. Identify himself or herself at the outset of the interview.
2. State the purpose of the interview.
3. Make clear to those unaccustomed to being interviewed that the material will be used.
4. Tell the source how much time the interview will take.
5. Keep the interview as short as possible.
6. Ask specific questions that the source is competent to answer.
7. Give the source ample time to reply.
8. Ask the source to clarify complex or vague answers.
9. Read back answers if requested or when in doubt about the phrasing of crucial material.
10. Insist on answers if the public has a right to know them.
11. Avoid lecturing the source, arguing or debating.
12. Abide by requests for nonattribution, background only or off-the-record should the source make this a condition of the interview or of a statement.

Reporters who habitually violate these rules risk losing their sources. Few sources will talk to an incompetent or an exploitative reporter. When the source realizes that he or she is being used to enhance the reporter's career or to further the reporter's personal ideas or philosophy, the source will close up.

Sources also risk trouble when they exploit the press. Reporters understand that their sources will float occasional trial balloons and give incomplete, even misleading, information. But constant and flagrant misuse of the press leads to retaliation by journalists.

The News Interview

It's a rare news story that doesn't contain information obtained by interviewing someone. The interview may be as brief as asking the police dispatcher for the names of the officers who investigated a traffic accident, or as lengthy as seeking background from the dean of the English department about the reasons for the new requirement that all students must pass an "English proficiency test" to graduate.

Depth Interviews   During his coverage of a man accused of extortion and tax evasion, Douglas Watson of *The Washington Post* heard the testimony of a witness who, Watson was told, was being held in a special facility. Known as "safe houses," these installations are run by the United States Marshal's Service.

"In the interviews, I learned about other interesting and unreported aspects of the organization besides 'safe houses.'" Watson said. "One of the Service's activities is giving new identities to people who had been government witnesses. This enables them to start new lives in another part of the country."

Here is how Watson's story begins:

"Restricted Area—U.S. Govt. Training Center," says the sign on the barbed wire-topped fence surrounding a barracks at Ft. Holabird on the edge of Baltimore.

The sign doesn't say it, but the barracks is one of several "safe houses" that the U.S. Marshal's Service operates for the special care and feeding of very important prisoner-witnesses such as Watergate conspirator E. Howard Hunt, political saboteur Donald Segretti and stock manipulator Joel Kline.

Three to five "safe houses" have been in existence around the country for about a year, usually holding about 50, mostly white collar, "principals," as they like to call themselves. They are federal prisoners who usually were involved in organized crime and who are considered too valuable as government witnesses or too endangered by threats to be incarcerated in the usual prison. . . .

Watson does not need to attribute the material he has obtained in his interviews. Later in his story, he will quote some of his sources about particular activities of the Service.

Back Then   For a retrospective piece about the 1980 University of Georgia championship football team, *U.S. News & World Report* interviewed the starting offense and the punter in the team's Sugar Bowl victory over Notre Dame. The magazine found: 9 of the 12 did not graduate; none of the 6 black starters received degrees.

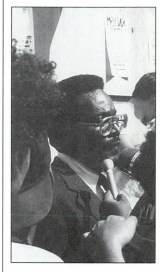

On the Scene

A radio reporter interviews a speaker following his address at a campus rally to protest alleged unfair hiring practices.

In a series of miniprofiles, the magazine reported on the players' careers in school and later. Herschel Walker, the star of the team, left the team after three years. "I had to worry about what was best for Herschel—and leaving school was best for Herschel," he is quoted as saying. He was signed for a reported $5.5 million by a professional team.

Not so fortunate was Walker's gridiron blocker, Jimmy Womack. Like Walker, he did not graduate. But he had no professional career and regrets his role in Walker's shadow. "If I had gone to Florida State, I could have been in the NFL somewhere," he said. For the players, there were, the magazine reports, "compensations . . . in the form of wadded-up $100 bills, passed along in 'padded handshakes' from alumni and boosters." Off the field, he remembered, there were "these girls that liked football players, not one at a time either."

Suicide Bomber   *USA Today* reporter Jack Kelley managed to pierce the secretive world of Palestinian Hamas suicide bombers for his page 1 story that begins:

> ZARQA, Jordan—The Hotaris are preparing for a party to celebrate the killing of 21 Israelis this month by their son, a suicide bomber.
>
> Neighbors hang pictures on their trees of Saeed Hotari holding seven sticks of dynamite. They spraypainted graffiti reading "21 and counting" on their stone walls. And they arrange flowers in the shapes of a heart and a bomb to display on their front doors.

Then Kelley goes directly to a high-quality quotation:

> "I am very happy and proud of what my son did and, frankly, am a bit jealous," says Hassan Hotari, 54, father of the young man who carried out the attack June 1 outside a disco in Tel Aviv. It was Israel's worst suicide bombing in nearly four years. "I wish I had done (the bombing). My son has fulfilled the Prophet's (Mohammed's) wishes. He has become a hero! Tell me, what more could a father ask?"

Kelley visits Hamas-run schools and talks to 11-year-old Ahmed whose "small frame and boyish smile are deceiving," Kelley writes. "They mask a determination to kill at any cost." He quotes Ahmed:

> "I will make my body a bomb that will blast the flesh of Zionists, the sons of pigs and monkeys. I will tear their bodies into little pieces and cause them more pain than they will ever know."

Kelley's piece is made convincing by his extensive interviews. He ends his piece with this chilling and prophetic quotation:

> "My prayer is that Saeed's brothers, friends and fellow Palestinians will sacrifice their lives, too," Saeed's father says. "There is no better way to show God you love him."

For the complete story and Kelley's comments about handling the story, see **The Secret World of Suicide Bombers** in *NRW Plus*.

The Profile

The profile is a minidrama, blending dialogue, action and description. Through the words and actions of the subject, along with those of his or her friends and associates, and with the reporter's insertion of background and explanatory matter, a life is illuminated.

Momentum is the key requirement for the profile. One of the obstacles to movement is the necessary background of the person profiled. Inserted in clots, the background brakes the story, stills its movement. The writer's task is to blend background into the moving narrative.

> On most days, his commute from Burlingame to his downtown law office in San Francisco took about half an hour. But on that Tuesday, he left at 8 a.m. as usual, turned on the radio and did not. . . .

The writer is describing how her subject heard a news story that influenced a career change. She is telling us that he pulled off the highway, parked his car in a Wendy's lot and began to think about becoming a teacher. Along the way, we learn that he lives in an affluent suburb and is a lawyer.

Reporting Is the Key

Reporting makes the profile. Joseph Mitchell, whose profiles for *The New Yorker* are considered the standard for the form, is described by Brendan Gill in *Here at The New Yorker,* a history of the magazine, as having had the ability to ask "just the right questions." The questions would open up his sources, and Mitchell would closely attend their recollections and reflections. He encouraged sources to a loquacity no one suspected they possessed. Mitchell knew that everyone has a good story and that good reporting will flush it out.

In the dedication of one of his books, Calvin Trillin, a *New Yorker* writer, wrote, "To the *New Yorker* reporter who set the standard, Joseph Mitchell." Note Trillin's description of Mitchell as a "reporter." Trillin, like all good writers, knows that reporting is at the heart of the journalist's work.

Quotes, Quotes

Track Talk. In her book *Seabiscuit,* Laura Hillenbrand describes a famous match race between Seabiscuit and War Admiral. Seabiscuit's regular rider, Red Pollard, was unable to ride because of an injury and George Woolf was substituted. Pollard advised Woolf to let Seabiscuit run eye-to-eye with War Admiral, that the Admiral was not game.

When Seabiscuit left War Admiral behind, Woolf said he saw "something pitiful" in the Admiral's eyes. "He looked all broken up. Horses, mister, can have crushed hearts just like humans."

Straight Talk. In a profile of Jeffrey M. Duban, a lawyer who represents professors denied tenure, students in disciplinary proceedings and those involved in sexual harassment claims, Piper Fogg of *The Chronicle of Higher Education,* quotes Duban:

I was a professor. I know the system. They're sons of bitches. These people are relentless. University administrators are unsparing. They will not say "uncle" unless you have them against the wall with your knee on their crotch.

Look back, and chances are that you will recall that your interest perked up when you came across quotation marks. As the novelist Elmore Leonard says, "When people talk, readers listen." In interviews, the writer listens for the telling remark that illuminates the person or the situation. Leonard says he lets his characters do the work of advancing his story by talking. He gets out of the way.

"Readers want to hear them, not me."

Love Song   Listen to the singer Lorrie Morgan talk about her problems: After her husband, the singer Keith Whitley, died of alcohol poisoning, Morgan was only offered slow, mournful ballads by her songwriters, she said in an interview with *The Tennessean* of Nashville.

"I mean, it was all kinds of dying songs," she said. But then she fell in love with Clint Black's bus driver, and she decided to change her tunes.

"I said, 'I'm not going to do that. I'm not basing my career on a tragedy.' I live the tragedy every day without it being in my music." Her life, she said, has turned around, thanks to her new love. "He's a wonderful, wonderful guy. This guy is very special, and I'm into him real bad." However, not too long afterward Lorrie's love life took a detour—her affections switched to a politician.

Memorable Quotation   What could be more revealing than the quotation TV newsman Daniel Schorr elicited from Sen. Roman Hruska, the ranking Republican on the Senate Judicial Committee when Richard Nixon sent Harrold Carswell's nomination for a seat on the Supreme Court to the committee. Carswell was widely regarded as a mediocrity. Hruska went to Carswell's defense: "There are a lot of mediocre judges and people and lawyers. They are entitled to a little representation, aren't they?"

Colorful Quotes

"A $400 suit on him would look like socks on a rooster."
—Gov. Earl Long of Louisiana

"Nixon is the kind of politician who would cut down a redwood tree and then mount the stump to make a speech for conservation."
—Adlai Stevenson

"Bill Clinton's foreign policy experience stems mainly from having breakfast at the International House of Pancakes."
—Pat Buchanan

A Tryout   Barry Singer of *The New York Times* lets Anne Wiggins Brown talk. Brown was the original Bess in George Gershwin's famous folk opera *Porgy and Bess* in 1935. The first African-American vocalist admitted to the prestigious Juilliard School of Music, she was a graduate student when at the age of 21 she heard that Gershwin was writing an opera "about Negroes in South Carolina." She applied and was called for an audition at which she sang Brahms, Schubert and Massenet for Gershwin, who then asked her, "Would you sing a Negro spiritual?" She flared at the request. She explains:

I was very much on the defensive at that age. I resented the fact that most white people thought that black people should or only could sing spirituals. "I am very sorry," I said, "but I haven't any of *that* music with me." And then I broke out, "Why is it that you people always expect black singers to sing spirituals?"

He just looked at me. He didn't say anything or do anything at all; he didn't appear angry or disturbed. But I saw that he understood my reaction. And as soon as I saw that, my whole attitude just melted away and I wanted more than anything else to sing a spiritual for this man. I said, "I can sing one spiritual without an accompaniment, if that's O.K." He told me it was. And I sang "City Called Heaven." It's a very plaintive, very melancholy spiritual. And I knew when I finished that I'd never sung it better in my life, because I was so emotionally involved at that moment.

He was very quiet for some time. Finally he spoke: "Wherever you go, you must sing that spiritual without accompaniment. It's the most beautiful spiritual I've ever heard." And we hugged one another.

Brown continues her reflections on her career, and then she thinks of what might have been:

"If I had been born 20 years later, I might have sung at the Metropolitan Opera," she mused.

"I might have marched for civil rights. I would have been here for that. I would certainly not have lived in Norway and my life would have been very different."

"Of course," she conceded, her eyes bright, "I would not have met Mr. Gershwin and that would have been a shame."

A Guide for the Profile

Let the reader:

- See the person—physical characteristics.
- Hear the person—lots of quotations.
- Watch the person—lots of action.
- Know the person—education, job, age, family, income, likes-dislikes, hobbies, successes-failures.

Interview Others   When appropriate, the reporter interviews friends, associates, relatives of the main subject. The profile of a popular psychology professor would be incomplete without comments from her students. After all, it's their reactions to her lectures and her personal interest in them that makes her popular.

When a young *New York Times* reporter turned in a piece about a nun who was an alcoholic and who counsels other similarly afflicted nuns, the story did not move past Charlotte Evans, an editor.

"As it stands," Evans told the reporter, "all you have is a moderately interesting interview with Sister Doody. You sat in a chair, and she sat in a chair and you had a chat. That's not very good, considering the story material."

"Did you talk to any nuns in treatment or just out of it?"

"Where is the anguish, the embarrassment, the guilt?"

"It doesn't sound as if you had done any real reporting, digging, pushing. Where are the people, the quotes, the color?"

For her profile of Les Brown, a black preacher and radio personality, Itabari Njeri of *The Miami Herald* talked to other ministers, a community activist and the directors of the local chapters of the Urban League and the National Association for the Advancement of Colored People, as well as to Brown. Assessments of Brown diverged widely: "I will not allow anyone to manipulate or prostitute the black community, and that is what Les Brown is doing to the nth degree," an Urban League official said. The activist had a different view: "He is different . . . he's got guts. He is a challenge to the traditional black leaders here."

The Veep   For its profile of Vice President Dick Cheney, *talk* magazine didn't bother to speak to Cheney but assembled quotations from more than a dozen people, ranging from his wife and school-days chums to political opponents:

Lynn Cheney—"There were two A&W Root Beer stands, and one was at one end of town and one was at the other. The really cool thing to do, if you wanted to win anyone's affection, was to drive endlessly back and forth between them. Dick never understood the appeal of this. It took me a long time to understand that Dick was indeed a cool person."

Joseph Meyer (a boyhood and college friend)—"When he and I roomed together (at the University of Wyoming) he would cook up one of those big blue pots of chili on Sunday night, and we'd just eat out of it, and every time we wanted to eat during the week we'd heat it up and scoop some out and eat it again."

Tony Coelho—"Cheney was friendly. Then he turned around and voted against you. But that is sort of the old-style politics. During the day you kicked the shit out of each other and at night you went out and drank together."

Bad Advice

Several articles have appeared in journalism publications that advocate paraphrasing as an efficient way to tell a story. Efficient? Maybe. But hardly effective. For reader interest, there is no substitute for letting people speak.

Research shows that direct quotations are helpful in establishing the reporter's credibility. S. Shyan Sundar of Pennsylvania State University found "the credibility and quality of stories with quotations to be significantly higher than identical stories without quotations."

The Miner   Listen to Linda Raisovich-Parsons, one of the first women to go into the coal mines, talk to Bharati Sadasivam:

> I went into the mines when I was 18 years old and had just finished high school. There was not a whole lot of career opportunities for a girl back then in West Virginia. My father was a coal miner. He had multiple sclerosis and I didn't want to burden him with the expense of a college education. . . .
>
> Initially, he didn't like the idea because he didn't want his daughter working in that kind of environment. But when he saw that I was not just testing the waters and was determined to make a go of it, he taught me the ropes and looked out for his baby daughter. . . .
>
> There was a lot of heavy lifting and carrying to do and that was what I found the most difficult. Most of the men took the position that well, if you're here, you've got to pull your weight and I was determined that no one was going to prove that I wasn't able to do the job.

Sadasivam's magazine article consists entirely of direct quotes. She allows Raisovich-Parsons to tell her story. After several years in the mines, the United Mine Workers union offered her a job as a mine inspector. She would have been the first female inspector. At first, it was not easy.

> There were some safety committees that simply couldn't accept a woman and would bypass me and go to my male co-workers. And I often got the same reactions from the coal companies. But there were others that were more accepting of me. I found the older miners more helpful and respectful than the younger ones. Sexual harassment was a problem initially but we've grown with these men and I think we're just one of the crew now.
>
> I found women on the whole more safety-conscious than men. They took all precautions, made sure that all the equipment was working properly. You find a very low accident rate among women.
>
> I'm comfortable here, but there are times when I've felt like a token woman. But the few women that are there are very outspoken, the type of people who get out and get involved because they've had to be fighters and scrappers to get the job. I have a button from a women miners' conference that says, "Just Another Mouthy Union Woman."

Sadasivam wrote the story just this way, a first-person account.

The Miniprofile

When Mark Patinkin and Christopher Scanlan were assigned to profile the black community in Rhode Island for *The Providence Journal-Bulletin,* they focused on individuals—the people who symbolize the facts and figures they were gathering.

For a story about the high rate of unemployment among blacks, they talked to a black man who was looking for work:

Voices: Stephen Gordon on Unemployment

"I felt like everything I was trying to build was worthless," said Stephen Gordon. "I was back at the bottom. Quite a few times, I'd just break down and cry. I couldn't even get a job on a garbage truck. I felt less than a man."

Stephen Gordon sits in the darkness of his kitchen in a Newport housing project, speaking of being black and jobless.

Back from Vietnam in 1971, he had gone through three years of the hardest of times. He had no high school diploma. He had no job. He had two children. His family survived on welfare.

Then came a federal job program that reached out and gave him hope, gave him training as a welder. He was a tradesman. For nine months, he strove to build the good life.

He was fired. He appealed the firing to the State Human Rights Commission, which found the company guilty of racial discrimination. That was two years ago, but the case remains on appeal. Meanwhile, Gordon went on unemployment, then welfare. He remembers the feeling.

"My inspiration was destroyed again," he said. "It was the same old rut."

Recently, he climbed out of the rut by finding a job as a cook in a Newport inn. For other black adults in the state, joblessness remains chronic.

Unemployment among Rhode Island blacks is higher than for any other group. There were 8,880 blacks in the labor force. . . .

There is hope in the black community, however, and with the careful use of quotes and the selection of incidents, Patinkin and Scanlan showed black success:

Voices: Ed Blue on Moving Up

"I wanted the good life," said Ed Blue. "I wasn't going to settle. I figured, I'm a citizen, I'm a taxpayer. I have as much a right as anybody else. Just give me a chance."

Twenty-eight years ago, Ed Blue came to Rhode Island with a suitcase and $300, another poor black immigrant from a small town in the South. Today he is the state's chief bank examiner and lives with his family in the state's wealthiest suburb, Barrington. Barbara, his wife, is running for Town Council.

For most blacks, Rhode Island has not been a place of opportunity. It wasn't for Ed Blue either. It was a place of slammed doors.

They slammed as soon as he got out of college. One large retailer put an "X" on his application for a clerk's job. He demanded to know why. The interviewer admitted it was to mark black applicants. Next he went to a bank. The bank told him he'd never be anything more than a guard.

Ed Blue saw other blacks told the same thing and saw them accept it. Don't bother, they told him, you won't make it, they won't let you make it. Blue would not accept that. "I was new here," he recalled, "I figured hell, I'll give it a shot. I'm going to break that down."

He put his shoulder against the door and he pushed hard. And when it finally gave, and a higher door slammed, he broke that one, too. He did it, he said, by proving he was so qualified they had no choice but to hire him. Ed Blue made it because he believed in Ed Blue.

"This is one of the things I've instilled in my children," he said. "Don't say you can't. I don't want to hear 'You can't.' "

For their report on crime in the Providence ghetto, the reporters interviewed a prostitute:

Voices: Debbie Spell on Hustling

"Being a hooker is all I know," said Debbie Spell. "It's how my mother supported me. That's all I seen when I was a kid, broads jumping into cars. Put me in a factory and I just couldn't hack it."

In poor neighborhoods, where unemployment and welfare rates are high, many blacks turn to hustling to survive. Debbie Spell turned to prostitution. Although she is 20, she looks 15. She is already the mother of three children. She normally works on Pine Street in Providence, where most of her customers are white.

"If it wasn't for them, then I wouldn't have food for my kids," she said, "or Pampers for my baby." Nor would she have her color television and living-room furniture.

"I'm not proud of it," she added, "but it's the way I make a living. Why should I work in a factory for $100 a week when I can make that much on a Thursday night?"

Although blacks make up only 3.4 percent of the population in Rhode Island, they make up 24 percent of the population at the Adult Correctional Institutions and 7.5 percent of admissions to state drug abuse programs.

In Providence, blacks account for about 10 percent of the population, but a much higher percentage ends up in the city's arrest books. Last year, of the 243 juveniles Providence police arrested for major crimes, 37 percent, or 90, were black. As blacks get older, their arrest percentage grows. . . .

Andy Dickerman, *The Providence Journal-Bulletin*

Follow-Up to a Tragedy

After he had written a profile of Debbie, a young woman who spoke freely of her life as a street walker, Christopher Scanlan learned that she had hanged herself in jail two days after her arrest.

To find out something about Debbie's life, Scanlan returned to the streets Debbie frequented. He interviewed the women who engaged in the same trade as Debbie. They spoke freely but did not want their faces to appear in the newspaper.

Getting Close "Tim Madigan can talk to anybody," says Madigan's editor at the *Fort Worth Star-Telegram.* "A convicted child molester trying to live a normal life in the suburbs. An aging war veteran. A major league baseball manager who almost destroyed his marriage in his obsession with the game."

Madigan interviewed 10 people for the newspaper's "Angels Among Us." Among them was a school crossing guard who embraces the children she escorts across the street each morning, a Methodist minister battling homelessness, gangs and hunger in his parish as cancer saps his strength. Here is one of Madigan's miniprofiles:

Jeanette Martin: Inspired Teacher

Dominique entered Jeanette Martin's Forth Worth classroom still in diapers, a profoundly handicapped 3-year-old boy barely able to walk, speak or eat solid foods. When he left three years later, Dominique graduated to a regular kindergarten class.

"You'll have to excuse me," says Martin, the ex-banking executive, who for the last seven years has taught disabled children in Forth Worth public schools "I get kind of emotional when I talk about this. I'm doing something now I would do for free."

That sense of making a difference was absent in her 20-year banking career, she says now. So when her Arlington bank closed in 1989, Martin, then a senior vice president, began to volunteer at the Jo Kelly School for disabled students in Forth Worth.

"You're a natural," Jo Kelly Principal Leslie James told her then.

With that encouragement, and support from her husband, Don, she set off on a career path that would pay her roughly half of what she earned as a banker. In purely financial terms, that is.

"If I have influenced their lives even half as much as they've influenced mine, then I'll consider myself a success," Martin says now. "I see these kids every day who have to struggle for things you and I take for granted or the things that are so easy for us.

"But they are so willing to do that and they try so hard. To me that's an inspiration more than any football player or politician. They inspire me. Every day they inspire me to do the best that I can."

Summing Up

Good interviews make for good stories. They provide insights into people and events. Here is some advice from practitioners of the trade.

Helen Benedict, author of a book on writing profiles, says: "People who are interviewed a lot get tired of the same old questions. You want to stand out as an interviewer and get a good story, and that depends on preparation and intelligence."

Benedict writes out her questions and takes her list with her to the interview. During the interview, she gently guides her subject after establishing his or her trust. "Don't interrupt too much, and don't challenge too early so the person is put on the defensive. Don't talk too much."

She likes to interview in her subjects' homes so she can observe their clothes, objects on walls and desks—their taste. She watches their mannerisms, how they move, sit, drink their coffee, answer the phone, speak to others.

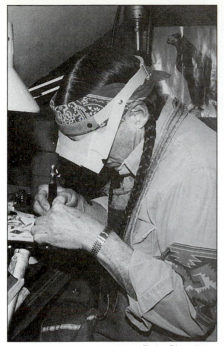

R. L. Chambers

Bharati Sadasivam

Working People

The diverse ways people make a living are worth chronicling: The Indian jewelry craftsman, the coal mine inspector, the railroad worker, the sign painter. Each has a fascinating story to tell.

Joseph Noble, *The Stuart* (Fla.) *News*

Mike Roemer

To get at the person behind the personality, good interviewers talk to the friends, associates, relatives of the subject. Samuel Johnson, the brilliant 18th-century English writer, advised writers that "more knowledge may be gained of a man's real character by a short conversation with one of his servants than from a formal and studied narrative, begun with his pedigree and ended with his funeral."

Some Guides

Fred L. Zimmerman, a *Wall Street Journal* reporter and editor, suggests the following:

1. Almost never plunge in with tough questions at the beginning. Instead, break the ice, explain who you are, what you are doing, why you went to him or her. A touch of flattery usually helps.

2. Often the opening question should be an open-ended inquiry that sets the source off on his or her favorite subject. Get the person talking, set up a conversational atmosphere. This will provide you with important clues about his or her attitude toward you, the subject and the idea of being interviewed.

3. Watch and listen closely. How is he or she reacting? Does he seem open or secretive? Maybe interrupt him in the middle of an anecdote to ask a minor question about something he is leaving out, just to test his reflexes. Use the information you are obtaining in this early stage to ascertain whether your preinterview hunches about him were right. Use it also to determine what style you should adopt to match his mood. If he insists upon being formal, you may have to become more businesslike yourself. If he is relaxed and expansive, you should be too, but beware of the possibility the interview can then degenerate into a formless conversation over which you have no control.

4. Start through your questions to lead him along a trail you have picked. One question should logically follow another. Lead up to a tough question with two or three preliminaries. Sometimes it helps to create the impression that the tough question has just occurred to you because of something he is saying.

5. Listen for hints that suggests questions you had not thought of. Stay alert for the possibility that the theme you picked in advance is the wrong one, or is only a subsidiary one. Remain flexible. Through an accidental remark of his you may uncover a story that is better than the one you came for. If so, go after it right there.

6. Keep reminding yourself that when you leave, you are going to do a story. As she talks, ask yourself: What is my lead going to be? Do I understand enough to state a theme clearly and buttress it with quotes and documentation? Do I have enough information to write a coherent account of the anecdote she just told me?

7. Do not forget to ask the key question—the one your editors sent you to ask, or the one that will elicit supporting material for your theme.

8. Do not be reluctant to ask an embarrassing question. After going through all the preliminaries you can think of, the time finally arrives to ask the tough question. Just ask it.

9. Do not be afraid to ask naive questions. The subject understands that you do not know everything. Even if you have done your homework there are bound to be items you are unfamiliar with. The source usually will be glad to fill in the gaps.

10. Get in the habit of asking treading-water questions, such as "What do you mean?" or "Why's that?" This is an easy way to keep the person talking.

11. Sometimes it helps to change the conversational pace, by backing off a sensitive line of inquiry, putting your notebook away, and suddenly displaying a deep interest in an irrelevancy. But be sure to return to those sensitive questions later. A sudden pause is sometimes useful. When the subject finishes a statement just stare at her maybe with a slightly ambiguous smile, for a few seconds. She often will become uneasy and blurt out something crucial.

12. Do not give up on a question because the subject says "no comment." That is only the beginning of the fight. Act as if you misunderstood her and restate the question a little differently. If she still clams up, act as if she misunderstood you and rephrase the question again. On the third try, feign disbelief at her refusal to talk. Suggest an embarrassing conclusion from her refusal and ask if it is valid. Later, ask for "guidance" in tracking down the story elsewhere, or suggest nonattribution, or get tough—whatever you think might work.

13. Occasionally your best quote or fact comes after the subject thinks the interview is over. As you are putting away your notebook and are saying goodbye the subject often relaxes and makes a crucial but offhand remark. So stay alert until you are out the door. (Sid Moody of the AP says that interviewing gems can come after the notebook is snapped shut. "I've found almost as a rule of thumb that you get more than you've gotten in the interview.")

These are starting points only, not absolute rules. They, and the material in the next chapter, will get you going. After a while, you will develop your own interviewing style. Zimmerman says, "Pick the techniques you think you can use and then practice them. Eventually, they'll become so natural you won't have to think about them."

Further Reading

Benedict, Helen. *Portraits in Print: The Art of Writing Profiles.* New York: Columbia University Press, 1990.

Capote, Truman. *In Cold Blood.* New York: New American Library, 1971.

Fallaci, Oriana. *Interview with History.* Boston: Houghton Mifflin, 1976.

Garrett, Annette. *Interviewing: Its Principles and Methods.* New York: Family Association of America, 1982.

Kadushin, Alfred. *The Social Work Interview.* New York: Columbia University Press, 1983.

Mitchell, Joseph. *Up in the Old Hotel.* New York: Vintage Books, 1993.

Note: The books by Garrett and Kadushin, which are used in schools of social work, are excellent guides for journalists.

Speaking for attribution.

Preview

Sources respond to interviewers they consider trustworthy and competent. They pick up clues about the reporter from the questions he or she asks and from the reporter's appearance and behavior.

A successful interview depends on:

• Questions that elicit information relating to the major theme of the story.
• Role-playing by the reporter that puts the interviewee at ease.
• Careful listening and accurate observation. The reporter listens for what is said, how it is said and what is not said. Also, the reporter observes the physical surroundings and any revealing interaction between the subject of the interview and others.

When A. J. Liebling interviewed the jockey Eddie Arcaro, the first question he asked was, "How many holes longer do you keep your left stirrup than your right?"

"That started him talking easily, and after an hour, during which I had put in about twelve words, he said, 'I can see you've been around riders a lot.'

"I had," Liebling said later, "but only during the week before I was to meet him." In his preparations, Liebling had learned that most jockeys on counterclockwise U.S. tracks help balance their weight and hug the rail by riding with the left stirrup longer than the right. A rail-hugging journey is the shortest distance from start to finish.

Starting Off Right

Careful preparations such as Liebling's enable reporters to establish an open, friendly relationship with sources, who are pleased that reporters took time to learn something about them.

Usually, it is not necessary to spend much time on the preliminaries with sources the reporter knows. But people who are infrequently interviewed—the atomic physicist in town for a lecture at the university, the engineer sent out by the company to survey the area north of town for industrial development—must be put at ease.

Intrusion. "Reporting never becomes any easier simply because you have done it many times. The initial problem is always to approach total strangers, move in on their lives in some fashion, ask questions you have no natural right to expect answers to, ask to see things you weren't meant to see, and so on. Many journalists find it so ungentlemanly, so embarrassing, so terrifying even, that they are never able to master this essential first move. . . ."
—*Tom Wolfe*

Reporters use all sorts of techniques to start interviews. One reporter usually glances around the source's home or room upon arriving. He tries to find something about which he can compliment the source. Before one interview, he noticed an ivy growing up one wall of the source's office.

"How do you keep the leaves against the wall?" he asked. "Magnets and small clasps," she replied, and she talked about her plants for several minutes.

Who's in Control?

Some sources take over the interview situation, and if they supply the needed information, the reporter should be willing to assume the passive role. Most sources, unaccustomed to being interviewed, need guidance with explanations, helpful questions, encouraging gestures and facial movements.

The source who dominates the interview and intentionally or inadvertently avoids the issue in which the reporter is interested is a challenge. The reporter must wrest control, subtly if possible. Control need not be overt. Indeed, a reporter bent on demonstrating that he or she is in charge will fail to achieve the balance of listening, watching and guidance that is necessary for the successful interview.

A subject may allow the reporter to direct the interview on the strength of the reporter's reputation or on the basis of his or her experience with the reporter. Some first-time sources consider reporters to be authority figures and become submissive. Generally, a source's cooperation and willingness to be guided depend on the source's reaction to the reporter's demeanor and first questions. Some of the questions that the interviewee may ask himself or herself at the outset of the interview are:

- Why is the reporter talking to me?
- What is her purpose? Is she here to hurt, embarrass or help me?
- What sort of story does she intend to write?
- Is she competent, or will she misunderstand and misquote me?
- Is she mature, trustworthy?

Chairmanship. In an interview Carol McCabe was doing for *The Providence Journal,* she said it became obvious that her subject was determined to control the conversation. To deflect his efforts, she sat in the subject's chair and conducted the interview from it.

• Is she bright enough to grasp some of the complexities, or should I simplify everything?

• Will I have to begin at the beginning, or does she seem to have done her homework?

Appearance and Behavior

One afternoon a journalism student cornered his instructor.

"Professor X (and here he named the journalism school's senior professor) told me I had better get my hair cut," the student said. "He said I would offend people I'm sent to interview."

The student's hair was long. "Have it cut and stop worrying," the instructor replied. "Most of the people you will be interviewing will be very proper people."

The student nodded dejectedly. "But it will ruin my love life," he said.

The instructor and the student thought over the problem, the student in deep despair.

"Why not have it trimmed, and see what happens?" the instructor suggested.

The student took an inch or so off his locks and had no further trouble with Professor X. Nor, presumably, did his love life suffer, for there were no further anguished visits from the young man, who, after graduation, became a long-haired and successful rock music critic for *The Village Voice*.

Fads A few years later, when the hirsute look had become common on assembly lines and in offices and faculty clubs, the issue became women in pants, then tattoos and body piercing. And so it goes: Youth expresses its independence through dress and grooming. And traditionalists take offense and condemn the new ways, until sometimes they join in and the fad becomes a trend and later a tradition. Until then, reporters in the vanguard risk offending sources, many of whom are traditionalists in politics, social activities, business and education.

A carefree, casual attitude and dress can tell a subject that you, the reporter, do not take him or her seriously. Hair and dress, tone of voice, posture, gestures and facial expressions convey messages to a source. Anthropologists say that what people do is more important than what they say, and the first impressions the reporter conveys with his or her dress, appearance, posture and hand and facial movements may be more important than anything the reporter says.

A reporter can choose his or her garb, practice speaking in a steady, modulated voice and learn to control gestures. But age, race, sex and physical characteristics are beyond the reporter's control, and some sources are affected by these.

Where there is identification with the reporter, the source is much more likely to speak freely than he or she is with an interviewer of another sex, race, religion or age. People feel comfortable with those who are like them.

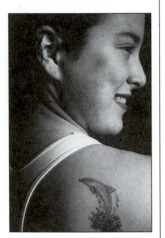

Mike Roemer

Cover Up, Remove

The tattoo can be discreetly covered by a sleeve, but the pierced tongue may prove so fascinating to the interviewee that it becomes the subject of discussion rather than the topic the reporter came to ask about.

Most small- and moderate-size newspapers and stations are staffed by young reporters, and it may well be that the prejudice among sources against youth is the most pervasive. Youth must prove itself. And until a source is sure that a young reporter can be trusted, the source may be tentative about cooperating.

Role-Playing

Sent to interview a pioneer developer of the polygraph, a reporter sensed that the man was easygoing and relaxed. In an attempt to be humorous, the reporter's opening remark was, "You're described as the country's leading polygraph expert. That's a lie detector, right?"

The interviewee suddenly stiffened. "If that's all you know, I'm going to call your city editor and have him send someone else over," he said. The reporter apologized, adopted a matter-of-fact approach, and the interview was conducted satisfactorily for both of them.

The reporter was intelligent and had carefully prepared for the interview, but had decided to appear naive to open up the source. He was role-playing, and although this interview just narrowly averted disaster, role-playing is generally successful if the reporter acts out a role appropriate to the subject and situation. Experienced sources expect a neutral, businesslike attitude from their interviewers. Sources who are unaccustomed to being interviewed respond best to the

Rich Turner, *The Stockton Record*

Interviewing Klansmen

Peter Francis of *The Stockton* (Calif.) *Record* questions two leaders of the Ku Klux Klan about their plans to organize additional California chapters. The KKK national leader (on left) and the head of the California Klan said their program, which included racial segregation, was attracting new members "every day." Although the men were wary of the reporter's intentions, Francis was able to draw them out about their plans for enlarging their base in California.

stereotypical journalist they see on television or in the movies, the knowledge-able expert. Some talk more freely to the opposite type, the reporter who confesses he or she needs help from the source.

Obviously, the best role for the journalist is the one he or she finds most comfortable, which for most journalists is the impersonal, unemotional and un-involved professional. Sometimes, the reporter finds that he or she must become involved or the story will slip away. When one reporter was assigned to cover the rush week activities at a local college, she was struck by the depression of the young women who were rejected by sororities. She felt she was unable to break through the reserve of the young women until she remarked to one of them, "I know how you feel. I went through the same thing in school."

From Friend to Authority Figure

Reporters can adopt the role of friend, confidant and companion when sources appear to need encouragement before they will talk. When a source indicates he will cooperate only if he is sure that he will benefit from the story, the reporter is reassuring, promising that her story will be fair and balanced and that this kind of story can only be helpful.

Some stories require pressing sources to the point of discomfort or implying a threat should they fail to respond. Journalism often becomes the business of making people say what they would prefer to keep to themselves. Much of this is properly the public's business, and the reporter who shifts roles from friend to authority figure or threatening power figure may justify his or her role as being in the public interest.

Compassionate Listener

The compassion and understanding that Diana Sugg of *The Sacramento Bee* took to the police beat resulted, she says, in "incredible stories about ordinary people."

She wrote about Connie Cornelius, a 44-year-old mother of four who was a girl scout troop leader, PTA member and volunteer school worker. One night, returning from a high school alcohol-free party for seniors, Cornelius drove her car into an intersection at the same instant a speeding car driven by a drunken driver careened through. Cornelius died instantly. Sugg interviewed family members and friends for her story of a tragic loss.

The suicide of a homeless man, Joseph King Jr., recorded in a brief note in the police reports, interested Sugg. "The detective who had worked the case knew me, and he told me how sad it was because before the suicide King and his homeless friend had been talking about trying to get jobs." Sugg tracked down King's friend. "He told me how shy and skinny King was, and that he always needed protection. 'I wasn't finished teaching him yet about how to live on the streets, about how to deal with the cold,' his friend said."

Sugg began her story of the death of an anonymous street man this way:

Joseph King Jr. was a tall guy, but he wasn't a fighter, and on the streets where he lived, his best friend had to watch out for him.

Even in the Sacramento parks where they sometimes slept, King was in the middle, with a friend on either side of him as protection through the night.

But the 49-year-old man was weary, friends said. Tired of moving from homeless shelter to homeless shelter. Tired of missing his former wife.

About 7 p.m. Thursday, after discussing with his best friend ways to get a job, the homeless man dove 20 feet over a ledge behind the Sacramento Memorial Auditorium.

With his buddy crying at his side in the dark loading area, King died.

"He was my best friend. That was the only friend I ever had that was something to me," said Michael Lockhart, 31, who had been living on the streets with King for the past four years.

Attention to the Victims Sugg says good police reporting should focus on the victims, make them "the human beings that they are." To accomplish this she devotes time to extensive interviews with friends, relatives, investigating officers. "If we can give readers some sense of the loss, if we can give them some insight and context into what is going on out there they might not become so callous. They might better understand why there are so many shootings and stabbings. And they won't be able to dismiss these victims as anonymous faces."

Sugg spent two hours interviewing the family of a youngster who had died. When Randy Ray Harlan was four weeks old, his father—strung out on drugs and alcohol—had beaten Randy mercilessly. Since that beating, the child had been blind and brain damaged. Randy's grandmother provided constant, loving care. Now, Randy could fight no longer. Five years after he was beaten so badly, he died.

As Sugg drove back to the newsroom, she passed the funeral home. She knew she had little time to write. But she was unsure of just how to handle the story. Maybe stopping here would help. She eased her car to the curb.

She recalled her interview with Randy's grandmother:

"He was beautiful before all this happened," the grandmother told Sugg, "perfect in every way." When Randy's sister asked, "Where's Randy? Where's Randy?" Sugg noted the grandmother's reply: "I told you, he's in heaven." Then the grandmother turned to Sugg and said, "He was very special to Carrie. She would hold onto him and hug him and kiss him, but she knew he couldn't do it back. All we could do was tell her he was sick."

Again, the grandmother recalled Randy:

"That little boy was a real fighter. I can imagine what he would have been like if this had never happened. He would have gone places.

"But it happened."

Viewing Randy Sugg got out of her car and walked over to the funeral home. She went in:

Pushing the doorbell and peering through the lace curtains, I realized that the viewing hours had started only minutes before. A man in a suit silently motioned me past the blank guest book. I turned the corner and found myself alone, staring at the baby blue coffin. It was small. I could have reached out and carried it away.

But I stood back, several feet from the open casket, noticing the music that hummed lightly in the background. The song sounded like it was coming from a music box in a nursery two or three rooms away. Pushing my fingers deep into my palms to avoid getting upset, I didn't want to get any closer.

Already I could see Randy's skin was tinged the grayish color I had faced too often. I was angry at myself for intruding into this peaceful place, for thinking that Randy was somehow going to tell me what I should feel, what I should write. Several minutes went by before I walked up slowly to his coffin.

Dressed in dark blue pants and a matching blue tie, his arms were wrapped around his teddy bear. Long, brown lashes hung heavy over his eyes. Looking down at him, I felt I owed him an explanation. Randy Harlan deserved to know why his father got strung out one afternoon on Jack Daniels and methamphetamine and began throwing him—a four-week-old infant—against the nursery walls. But I was lost. I didn't know what to say.

For a second, I thought I could almost see his chest move. I wanted to believe that maybe Randy was only sleeping in that white satin, and I stayed by his side for several minutes, watching him. I fought back an urge to reach out and pick him up, to hold him and rock him, make him forget about the pain he had endured in only five years of life.

This little boy is finally resting, I thought.

Here is how her story began:

A little boy rests at last.

Randy died shortly after dawn Sunday, at age 5. His foster mother was rocking him when the blind boy opened his eyes wide.

"He looked straight up at her, as if to say, 'I gotta go. I can't hang on any longer,' " said his grandmother, Velda Wills.

Randy let out a sigh, his thick, long lashes closing over his blue eyes. His short life was over—a life of pain and seizures, of barely hearing and never seeing. He couldn't hold his head up; he couldn't move his arms or legs.

Wednesday, Randy lay in a small, blue coffin, looking as though he had just fallen asleep in his church clothes. His arms were wrapped around his small teddy bear.

"Most of these people don't understand, but they don't have a 5-year-old baby to bury because of drugs," Wills said.

And here is the ending:

"That little boy was a real fighter," his grandmother said. "I can imagine what he would have been like if this had never happened. He would have gone places.

"But it happened."

Wednesday night, in his coffin, Randy was dressed in blue pants and a matching bow tie.

Long, brown lashes hung over his eyes, and just for a second his chest seemed to move—as if he were only sleeping.

Randy's funeral will be held at 11 A.M. Friday at the New Testament Baptist Church in North Highlands. The family has asked that any donations be made to child-abuse and drug-abuse prevention programs.

Nonjudgmental

The spacious brick home is indistinguishable from those that surround it in the middle-class neighborhood of South Arlington. . . . But something is different about this place and the couple who live here. The man of the house, Dean Jones, a high-paid supervisor in the aerospace industry, is rarely seen. It is Mary Jones who comes to the front door, always Mary Jones lest the visitor be a child selling candy. Her husband does not engage in neighborly fraternization, and is especially careful to stay clear of the boys across the street or the teen-age girl living on the corner.

This is how Tim Madigan begins "The Man Next Door," his interview with a convicted child molester. Madigan, you may remember, is the *Forth Worth Star-Telegram* reporter who wrote a series of miniprofiles, one of which you read in Chapter 14. His editor said Madigan "can talk to anybody." And those Madigan talks to speak openly to him:

" 'The fact is,' concedes Jones, a heavyset man with brown hair and eyeglasses. 'I have a deviant attraction to young females.'

"With great reluctance, Jones says he has come to terms with the truth. 'Pedophile' applies to him."

Jones tells Madigan about his attempts to control his deviant tendencies. "He has thrown out his collection of pornographic movies. . . . He does not visit a shopping mall unaccompanied by his wife."

Mrs. Jones is also open with Madigan, telling him that she has learned to stand between her husband and any children that may be nearby in a line at a restaurant.

"If my daughter comes and spends the night and I wake up and Dean's not in my bed and I find him coming from the front of the house, I should call his probation officer," she tells Madigan.

Jones goes along with all this, he says. "I've had the therapy. I've seen it work. As long as I'm not around kids, I haven't molested any kids.

"I can't control what trips my triggers. Just like you can't control what trips your triggers. What I can do is control what I do with it next."

Alcoholics   Eric Newhouse took the same nonjudgmental approach to his series about alcohol abuse when he dealt with the alcoholics in his area. He was neutral in interviewing Tara Fatz, manager of the Lobby Bar, who tells him that people are lined up at the door when she opens for business at 8 A.M. And he was nonjudgmental when he talked to Tom Jerome, drunk at 9 A.M. from the stash he keeps in an alley.

For Newhouse's comments about how he gathered material for his Pulitzer Prize–winning series in the *Great Falls Tribune* and excerpts from some of his stories, see **Alcohol: Cradle to Grave** in *NRW Plus*.

Limits to Role-Playing

The line limiting how far a reporter can go before role-playing becomes unethical is difficult to draw. There is a line between a reporter posing as a coroner to speak with the widow of a murder victim and a reporter feigning ignorance in an interview, a common tactic. Yet, in both cases the reporter is lying. What is the difference?

One well-known Washington reporter said she did not mind letting a senator pat her on the fanny if it meant he would be more inclined to give her a story—an attitude many of her female colleagues find abhorrent. But is that much different from some role-playing that is considered acceptable?

Balancing Act. "An interview is frequently the course you chart between what you came in knowing and what you're finding out as it's happening."
—*Terry Gross, National Public Radio's "Fresh Air"*

There are other questions. How well, after all, can a reporter assess a source so that role-playing is useful? We saw how one reporter failed. Even psychiatrists admit to no special ability to make lightning diagnoses.

The answers to these questions reside in the personal ethic of the reporter, which we will deal with in Chapter 27. Here, we can say that lying and deception are unacceptable but that the reporter is no different from the physician or the lawyer who is not obligated to tell patient or client all he or she knows in the professional relationship.

Invasive Questions

Thousands died when terrorists struck the Pentagon in Washington, D.C., and the World Trade Center towers in New York City. One of the tasks reporters faced was to interview survivors.

"It was one of the most emotionally gruelling assignments I've had in years," one *USA Today* reporter said. "To have to talk to people who lost loved ones was shattering," says Haya El Nasser.

Some of those whom reporters reached were angry. "Many people wanted nothing to do with me," says Traci Watson, another member of the *USA Today* reporting team assigned to write obituaries. "One person even sent an e-mail saying that everything possible should be done to stop us from writing about a particular victim. My correspondent, who'd been a good friend of the victim, seemed to think it would be demeaning to have the victim reduced to 'a blurb in a national newspaper.' "

But some friends and family did want to talk and "seemed to draw some comfort from doing so," Watson says.

Mel Antonen says, "I started every conversation with, 'I don't want to be invasive or insensitive, but we are gathering stories about the victims, and if you'd like to answer some questions we'd appreciate it. If not, we certainly understand.' "

One reporter looked back on the assignment, which lasted several days, and remembered: "The most heart-wrenching experience was hearing victims' voices on answering machines. I'm known as a pretty tough cookie around here. But I'll admit it: I cried many evenings."

Sensitive Questions

For his series "Unmarried . . . With Children," Sam Roe had to touch on touchy subjects. He wanted to know about the birth control practices of the single mothers, "not the most comfortable topic to be discussing with a male reporter," he says.

"Instead of blurting out, 'So, were you using birth control? What kind? What happened?' I said: 'Some women say they were using birth control and got pregnant anyway; others thought they were safe; still others say they just didn't think about it. What was the situation in your case?' "

Roe has found that "being polite, friendly, compassionate, honest helps. There is no substitute for being likeable."

The goal of the interview, Roe says, "is to get your subjects talking and to build up their confidence in you." He says that in his work with youngsters for his stories about Tecumseh Street (See Chapter 8), his first questions were "easy ones." He would phrase his first question as though he were seeking the advice of the youngster: "Before we start, I was hoping you could clear something up for me. I have been talking to a lot of guys in your neighborhood about the gang situation and some say that gangs are a thing of the past, while others say they are just less visible. What do you think?"

Roe said he used this tactic on a 17-year-old awaiting trial for shooting a man in the back of the head. "By the end of the interview he was acknowledging that he only had himself to blame for his problems—a rare admission for a kid."

Roe subscribes to the "share-the-pain" interviewing strategy. When the reporter talks about a similar painful event in his or her life, the reporter is seen to be human and compassionate. "The interview can then work toward being a conversation between two people."

Besides, he says, "If you ask people to spill their guts, you can spill some of your own."

He always leaves his name and phone number, so that "if they want to talk further they can call at any time. This lets them know they are important to you."

Despite the sensitivity of some questions, Roe asks them. "It never ceases to amaze me what strangers will tell you if you just ask."

Tough Questions

Reporters who work on investigative stories use a reporting technique that requires a straight face and a knowing tone of voice. Bruce Selcraig, a special contributor to *Sports Illustrated,* calls this the "assumed-truth question."

"You're trying to confirm whether the FBI has begun an investigation at Steroid University," he says. "You may get nowhere if you simply ask an agent, 'Can you confirm this or that?' Instead, try: 'What's the bureau's jurisdiction in this case?' 'Which agent will be supervising the investigation of the university?' "

Selcraig suggests reporters watch how their subjects handle questions:

Notice stress indicators like frequent crossing and uncrossing of legs, constant handling of desk items (paper clips, pencils), picking at one's clothing, and obvious signs like sweating or stuttering. He may not be lying yet, but you may be getting uncomfortably close to the right question. Try asking: "Have I made you nervous?" or "You seem bothered by something today."

With difficult stories and closed-mouthed sources, Bob Greene would take an approach he calls "building a circle." He would conduct many interviews for his investigative stories. The first one, he says, is general, "far off the goal. Then you move closer and closer until the person you are checking becomes tense. He or she is then primed for the final interview." Along the way, Greene says, a subject hears that you have been calling on people to check him. "He suggests that you might want to come over and talk to him."

"Interviewing is intimidation. Do they or you have the edge? But be cooperative. Say things like, 'We want to be right. Maybe we're wrong, but we've drawn this conclusion. You can see how a reasonable person can come to this conclusion, can't you?'

"Then they will admit about 80 percent of what you're alleging. They'll gradually back down. You can say, 'Please, give us something that proves we are wrong.' "

Greene follows these rules:

- Never debate or argue.
- Never make statements.
- Ask brief questions that are based on evidence.
- Be cooperative.

The Careful Observer

You are entering the office of the chairman of the English department. You had telephoned to ask if you could interview him about the department's plans to cope with the increasing numbers of high school graduates who arrive on campus poorly trained in reading and writing. He had told you to drop in about 3 P.M.

As you enter, you notice two paintings of sea scenes on a wall and two novels, a dictionary and a world almanac on his desk. Books in a floor-to-ceiling bookcase line one wall. These impressions do not particularly interest you because this will be a news interview focused on the situation, not the individual.

The chairman is worried, he says, about the growing numbers of students unable to understand college-level material. The chairman pauses often in his answers and occasionally goes to a shelf to take down a book that he reads to amplify a point.

"A friend of mine calls this the cretinization of American youth, and I used to laugh at him," he says. He reads from a copy of *McGuffey's Readers.*

"This grade-school material is now at the high school level," he says. "I wonder if anyone cares." He then reads from a Wordsworth poem that he says used to be memorized in grade school. No more, he says.

Musings "I wonder just what they are teaching students in high school," he says, "Not much, I fear, and that continues in college." He stops speaking to toy with a battered cigarette lighter. You wonder whether to ask about it.

"A member of our department told me the other day that he received a note from a publisher that his book proposal made too many demands on students. Said the vocabulary was beyond college students. And the publisher gave a couple of examples—'incomprehensible' and 'pernicious.' I am afraid we are living in a period of lowered expectations, and students pick up on that. They know that they don't have to do much to get by."

He goes back to his cigarette lighter. "Am I asking too much of students? Am I damaging their self-esteem by suggesting that their reliance on the spell checker is foolish, that they should read more than the comics and the movie ads?"

The Human Element   Suddenly, you decide that the interview should include more than the plans of the department to offer more courses in remedial writing and grammar. The story will include the chairman's musings, worries and personality as well as his plans. That will help personalize it, make it more readable.

Quickly, you reexamine the office to make note of the artists of the paintings, the titles of the books on the desk, and you ask about the cigarette lighter. (You learn the chairman uses it to relieve tension; he is trying to stop smoking.)

As the chairman talks, you note his mannerisms, his slow speech, his frequent stares out the window. A student enters the office and asks for permission to drop a course, and you watch him persuade the freshman to give the course another week.

Noticing the family pictures on the chairman's desk, you ask for their identities. Smiling, the chairman complies and then says, "You must be a believer in Whitehead's remark that genius consists of the minute inspection of subjects that are taken for granted just because they are under our noses."

You make a note of that, too, more for yourself than for the story.

Back in the newsroom, the editor agrees that the story is worth two columns, and he sends a photographer to take a picture of the chairman—toying with his cigarette lighter.

Details, Details

The reporter was acting in the best reportorial manner by noting specific details of the setting and the interviewee's mannerisms as well as watching for any interaction with third parties. In looking for details, the reporter was seeking the material that gives verisimilitude to an interview.

It was not enough to say that the chairman toyed with a cigarette lighter. The reporter wrote of the "lighter that he fingered to remind him of his no-smoking pledge." The reporter did not write that the chairman had read from an elementary school reader used in U.S. grade schools generations ago. He gave the book's title. The reporter did not merely quote the chairman when he spoke about the low scores of entering freshmen on the English placement test. The reporter noted the dejected slope of the chairman's shoulders, and he checked with the college admissions office to obtain the scores.

Too much for you, these warnings to be alert to every little detail? Then ponder the bewilderment of the *Baltimore Sun* reporter who turned in a story about a murder and was asked, "Which hand held the gun?"

The question is asked in newsrooms when a reporter writes a story that lacks convincing detail.

Listening and Hearing

There is an adage that says most people hear but few listen. Words assail us on all sides: Newspapers every day, magazines in the mail, books to be read, e-mail to read, the omnipresent radio and television sets, and the questions, advice and endless chatter of friends, neighbors, relatives and teachers. It is a wonder that anyone hears anyone amidst the clatter. But reporters must hear, must listen carefully. Their livelihood depends on it.

So many people are talking and so few listening with attention and courtesy that the reporter who trains himself or herself to hear will find people eager to talk to someone who cares about what they are saying.

To become a good listener:

- Cut down your ego. You are conducting an interview to hear what others say, not to spout your opinions.
- Open your mind to new or different ideas, even those you dislike.
- Grant the interviewee time to develop his or her thoughts.
- Rarely interrupt.
- Concentrate on what the person is saying and make secondary the person's personality, demeanor or appearance.
- Limit questions to the theme or to relevant ideas that turn up in the interview.
- Don't ask long questions.

Swallowed   Good listeners will have in their notes the quotations that give the reader or listener an immediate sense of the person being interviewed—what are known as high-quality quotes. Oscar Lewis, the anthropologist who wrote about Spanish-speaking peoples, began his article, "In New York You Get Swallowed by a Horse," about Hector, a Puerto Rican, this way:

We had been talking of this and that when I asked him, "Have you ever been in New York, Hector?"

"Yes, yes, I've been to New York."

"And what did you think of life there?"

"New York! I want no part of it! Man, do you know what it's like? You get up in a rush, have breakfast in a rush, go to work in a rush, go home in a rush, even shit in a rush. That's life in New York! Not for me! Never again! Not unless I was crazy.

"Look I'll explain. The way things are in New York, you'll get nothing there. But nothing! It's different in Puerto Rico. Here, if you're hungry, you come to me and say, 'Man I'm broke, I've had nothing to eat,' and I'd say, 'Ay, Benedito! Poor thing!' And I'd give you some food. No matter what, you wouldn't have to go to bed hungry. Here in Puerto Rico you can make out. But in New York, if you don't have a nickel, or twenty cents, you're worthless, and that's for sure. You don't count. You get swallowed by a horse!"

A Champion   Ira Berkow, a sportswriter for *The New York Times,* lets Rulon Gardner talk. Gardner had defeated Aleksander Karelin in the Olympic superheavyweight wrestling division for the gold medal. Gardner describes himself in the interview as a standard-bearer for wrestling and "maybe some kind of inspiration, a way of giving some people a little hope." Berkow continues quoting Gardner, "a school teacher who grew up on a farm in the metropolis of Afton, Wyo. (pop 1,394)":

"I had a learning disability," Gardner said. "People were always telling me that I wasn't good enough: 'You're not going to make it in junior college, then four-year college.' Then, 'You're not going to get a degree.' People were always putting restrictions on me, or trying to. I don't think they were being mean. They were just being honest, as they saw it.

"But I never listened to those people. I might have. Coming from a small town, the rest of the world looked very big. It was a big event if we were able to get to Salt Lake City once a year. But I was very competitive. I just kept giving myself opportunities in difficult situations."

With these few quotations, we are shown a good man, a man large in spirit and generosity as well in girth.

Alert Listening

The interviewer sits there, pad on her knee, pencil poised. She makes a note of what he is saying, pauses, asks a question, listens. She writes again, stops to let him go on and she thinks:

Is he really answering my question? No. But he has something here that's interesting. Maybe this line he's opening up is better than the one I came in with. I don't think he's avoiding the question. Maybe he is. Is this really important? No. How do I get him back on track? I'll let him talk, then prod him a bit.

All the time she is thinking she is also taking notes. She knows that she will have more than she needs for the story, but she doesn't want her subject to be discouraged from talking by stopping her note taking.

Note Taking

As the subject goes on, the reporter is writing about the books in his office, the dozens of plants scattered on shelves and the window sill, most of them orchids. She will have to ask about that. Suddenly he returns to the sensitive area she is interested in, just why the likable young assistant professor was turned down for tenure. She doesn't want to let him know that he has inadvertently wandered into important terrain, so she stops her note taking and appears to focus on a nearby plant. Then she doodles on the newspaper folded in her lap. Her seemingly absentminded doodles are key words from the department head's remarks that she will use to reconstruct his comments about the animosity the assistant professor stirred up in the department by attacking the university speech code.

To Tape or Not to Tape?

The tape recorder can provide large chunks of quotes, and the quotes will have the flavor of the person's speech. The tape recorder also protects against charges of misquotation. However, some sources freeze in front of a recorder or become so careful the interview is stilted.

Cautions. Studies of memory and the use of handwritten notes have found that those who rely on their memories may omit some material, but copious note takers sometimes irritate sources or influence their responses.

The author Truman Capote said that note taking makes people say "what they think you expect them to say." Annette Garrett, author of a book on interviewing, said that note taking can interfere with the interviewer's participation in the interview. Experienced reporters rely on notes to jog their memories, but few take verbatim notes.

One technique, suggested by a magazine interviewer for subjects who do not mind being taped, is to put the machine out of sight so that the subject is not conscious of the merciless machine with its ability to record every word.

"I tape, therefore I am," says Studs Terkel, whose radio programs and books utilize the tape recorder. For his books, Terkel, an excellent interviewer, transcribes his taped material, then edits it carefully. "It's like prospecting," he says. "The transcripts are the ore. I've got to get to the gold dust. It's got to be the person's truth, highlighted. It's not just putting down what people say."

Lillian Ross of *The New Yorker* has no use for the tape recorder and says flatly, "Do not use a tape recorder. The machine, surprisingly, distorts the truth. The tape recorder is a fast and easy and lazy way of getting a lot of talk down. . . . A lot of talk does not in itself make an interview. . . . A writer must use his own ears to listen, must use his own eyes to look."

Another *New Yorker* writer, John McPhee, often described as the country's foremost journalist, says, "All writing is a process of selection, and a tape is unselective. When you are writing without a recorder you make your selection right then. The tape is intrusive. When do you turn it off and on?"

Retroactive Requests

Sometimes a person being interviewed will suddenly stop and realize that he has said something he does not want to see in print or hear on television or the radio.

"Please don't use that," he will say. "It's off-the-record."

Should the reporter honor that request? It depends: If the source is a good contact and the material is not crucial to the story, the reporter probably will go along, particularly if the source is not a public figure or official. However, if the source has said something important, or the information is of concern to the public, then the reporter will usually reply that because the source knew he was talking to a reporter, he cannot suddenly go off-the-record retroactively.

When Jessica Mitford was interviewing Bennett Cerf, one of the owners of the Famous Writers School, he chatted freely with the amiable but sharp-penned writer. In the middle of his discourse, Cerf realized he sounded contemptuous of the people who took the school's correspondence course.

Here is how Mitford describes what happened, in her *Atlantic Monthly* article "Let Us Now Appraise Famous Writers":

While Mr. Cerf is by no means uncritical of some aspects of mail-order selling, he philosophically accepts them as inevitable in the cold-blooded world of big business—so different, one gathers, from his own cultured world of letters. "I think mail-order selling has several built-in deficiencies," he said. "The crux of it is a very hard sales pitch, an appeal to the gullible. Of course, once somebody has signed a contract with the Famous Writers School he can't get out of it, but that's true with every business in the country." Noticing that I was writing this down, he said in alarm, "For God's sake, don't quote me on that 'gullible' business—you'll have all the mail-order houses in the country down on my neck!" "Then would you like to paraphrase it?" I asked, suddenly getting very firm. "Well—you could say in general I don't like the hard sell, yet it's the basis of all American business." "Sorry, I don't call that a paraphrase, I shall have to use both of them," I said in a positively governessy tone of voice. "Anyway, why do you lend your name to this hard-sell proposition?" Bennett Cerf (with his melting grin): "Frankly, if you must know, I'm an awful ham—I love to see my name in the papers!"

When the source states beforehand that something is off-the-record and the reporter agrees to hear it on that condition, the material may not be used. Never? Well, hardly ever. Witness how Clifford D. May handles his source in this article, "Whatever Happened to Sam Spade?" in the *Atlantic Monthly.* A private detective, Jeremiah P. McAward, has been describing his difficulties in shadowing people:

"It's harder than you'd think," McAward continues. "Don't print this, but I once lost a pregnant Indian who was wearing a red blanket and had a feather in her hair, in Macy's." I reply that he cannot tell me something like that and expect that I won't use it. "Really?" he asks. I nod. "All right, then." There is a pause and then he adds. "But she just evaporated. A two-hundred-pound Indian."

Confidences

Reporters develop a sense of when to quote someone and when to consider the material off-the-record. The objective of the reporter is to gather important information for the public, not to embarrass or intimidate individuals. A reporter suggests this guideline:

A public official who talks to a reporter about public matters is presumed to be on-the-record. A person who has little contact with the press—even though he or she may be a public employee—should be presumed to be speaking off-the-record during a chat. Where there is uncertainty by the source or by the reporter, set the situation straight.

Reporters always keep in mind the fact that they rely on their sources, and a minor story that is based on quotes that the source presumes are off-the-record may shut off that source for good. However, no reporter will allow an official or a public figure to presume what he or she says is off-the-record unless that is clear at the outset of the interview.

Using and Abusing Quotes

Many reporters cleanse the language of free-speaking sources before putting their quotes into stories. They also correct grammatical errors and ignore absurd and meaningless statements that are not central to the story.

When the Canadian track star Donovan Bailey defeated the American Michael Johnson, Bailey was quoted in *The New York Times,* "He's afraid to lose. We should run this race again so I can kick his rear one more time." A reader e-mailed the newspaper to say that he had heard Bailey on Canadian TV and that Bailey had actually said, ". . . so I can kick his ass one more time." In a note to the staff, an editor wrote, "We shouldn't have changed it to 'rear.' We don't change quotes. (Since we also wouldn't want to use the word 'ass,' the proper course would have been a paraphrase.)"

On the other hand, several newspapers quoted Rep. Patricia Schroeder's response when she was asked how her congressional colleagues treat women. She replied, "A lot of men still don't know that harass isn't two words."

Use It? Fix It? or Cut It?

When an exact quote is ungrammatical and may cause the source embarrassment, do we rephrase it? Another question: Can we eliminate three or four sentences between the two that are relevant? The answers: Yes, and Yes.

"You ain't did nothing wrong," the mother was quoted in the first edition as telling her son. In the next edition, it was paraphrased: Telling her son he had done nothing wrong. . . .

When the exact quotation captures the character of the speaker, most writers let it stand. Speaking of the blues, the musician John Lee Hooker said, "Since I was a kid it's been a healing force for me. Since I was 12 years old. The blues done followed me. And I'll never get out alive."

Carol McCabe of *The Providence Journal-Bulletin* says, "I feel very strongly that it is condescending to make everyone sound as if they're speaking Standard English when they're not."

As for cutting in between sentences, it's done all the time so long as it does not change meaning.

Legal Angle

Alice Neff, a media lawyer, has these suggestions about quotations in the light of court decisions:

- If you use a tape recorder, listen to it to verify quotes.
- Corrections of grammar, syntax, stuttering and filling in explanatory words are all acceptable changes to quotations.
- It is acceptable to edit out irrelevancies and wandering.
- It is acceptable to substitute words, without changing the meaning.
- If you do make changes, consider the whole. Have you conveyed accurately what you think the person meant to say?

The Tabloid Approach

Compare these approaches to quotations with that of the weekly supermarket tabloids. Listen to Jack Alexander of the *Weekly World News* describe his interviewing technique:

> I always tell them I'm doing a series of articles, that I'm a religious editor or a travel editor. That puts them at ease. I say I'm with *The News* in Palm Beach and I try not to say more than that. I want to put questions in (the source's) mouth, so he just says "yes" or "no." Then we will quote him as saying that. (I ask the source,) "Could this happen?" He says, "Oh yeah." Then as far as we're concerned, it did happen.

Holy Writ or Amendable?

"We regard quotations as absolutely sacrosanct. If there is any reason at all to be tempted to change them, then you take the quotation marks off and paraphrase it."

—The New York Times

"Quotations should be exact. The words should not be rearranged for more felicitous phrasing."

—The Washington Post

"We can trim quotes to fit stories. The biggest problem . . . is how you use quotes and how you edit quotes in the story. . . ."

—Newsweek

The magazine engages in "what is commonly known as cleaning up the quotes."

—The New Republic

"(W)riters and reporters by necessity alter what people say, at the very least to eliminate grammatical and syntactical infelicities. If every alteration constituted the falsity required to prove actual malice, the practice of journalism, which the First Amendment standard is designed to protect, would require a radical change, one inconsistent with our precedents and First Amendment principles."

—Justice Anthony Kennedy, U.S. Supreme Court

Sal Ivone, managing editor of the *News,* describes his paper's news policy: "If someone calls me up and says her toaster is talking to her, I don't refer her to professional help. I say, 'Put the toaster on the phone.' "

Wendy Henry, editor of the *Globe,* explains the philosophy of these newspapers: "The great thing about working here is the simplemindedness that sales are everything, and a great honesty about what sort of paper we are and who we are aiming at."

Literal Quotes

To some sources, reporters apply the whip of exact quotations. They know the validity of the statement by Arnold Gingrich, former editor in chief of *Esquire* magazine, "The cruelest thing you can do to anybody is to quote him literally."

One of the delights for the reporters covering Chicago Mayor Richard Daley was quoting him exactly as he spoke. Angry at being attacked, Daley was quoted as saying, "They have vilified me; they have crucified me—yes, they have even criticized me." And, on another occasion when he sought to inspire the citizens of his city, he said, "We will reach greater and greater platitudes of achievement."

Daley had an uneasy relationship with reporters, who frequently pointed to corruption in his administration. Once, while lecturing reporters, he said that "the policeman isn't there to create disorder; the policeman is there to preserve disorder." Reporters delighted in quoting Daley's introduction of the poet Carl Sandburg as Chicago's "poet lariat."

Chicago journalists are equal-opportunity quoters—everyone is fair game. When a candidate for mayor attacked aides of an opponent for visiting a "house of prosecution," he was quoted as he spoke. And when another candidate remarked that he would be a "drum major for education" and would "get out in front and beat the banner," he, too, was quoted as he misspoke.

Generous Journalists

Lest you conclude from all this that reporters are always intent on humiliating their sources and that you are much too compassionate to join this cutthroat company, here's evidence to the contrary:

When a politician took the microphone at a meeting to defend a fellow political candidate and said, "He is not the orgy some people think he is," reporters did substitute *ogre* for *orgy*. When Sen. Dennis DeConcini of Arizona endorsed a balanced budget amendment to the Constitution at a news conference by announcing, "It's going to be a great day because we're going to finally wrestle to the ground this gigantic orgasm that is just out of control, that absolutely can't put itself together."—well, what would you have done?

Bushisms   When president, George Bush was known to mangle a noun now and then, but his verbal versatility was topped by his son's, candidate and then President George W. Bush:

The great thing about America is everybody should vote.

They misunderestimated me.

They want the federal government controlling Social Security like it's some kind of federal program.

Families is where our nation takes hope, where wings take dream.

Our priorities is our faith.

The important question is, How many hands have I shaked?

Rarely is the question asked: Is our children learning?

Mercifully, reporters overlook the mangled syntax and the misused nouns and verbs and paraphrase Bush so that his meaning is presented.

Instructive   No such generosity was shown by a *New Yorker* writer who attended a press conference for entrants in the Miss Universe contest. Miss U.S.A. is introduced and is telling reporters that the Miss Universe contest has helped her express her feelings and widen her knowledge:

"For instance, Miss India has a red spot on her forehead. And do you know what? She says it's an Indian custom. . . .

"One of the experiences I've had was just this morning," Miss U.S.A. says. "I'm rooming with Miss South Africa, and I just saw their money. You see people, but you never realize their money was different."

The reporters try to think of another question. Finally, one of them says, "What do you think of the feminist movement?"

"Oh, I think femininity is the best thing on this earth," she says.

"What about masculinity?"

"That's just as wonderful."

Anonymous and Confidential

Sources do not always want to be identified, for a variety of reasons. The low-level official whose boss demands all material from the office go out under his name requests anonymity for the information she provides. The whistle-blower does not want to endanger his job by being identified.

As the press digs deeper to get to the truths of events, anonymous and confidential sources increase. People with information demand they not be named. The most notable example of an unknown source is Deep Throat, the source for a considerable amount of information about Richard Nixon during his presidency. The reporters who handled the Watergate revelations, Carl Bernstein and Bob Woodward, never disclosed the identity of this key source—if indeed it was one person.

Plus and Minus   The anonymous source is not accountable for the information he or she provides, which in the case of the whistle-blower is helpful to the journalist seeking to uncover an unsavory situation. But without being accountable, the source can be less than fully forthcoming, can even mislead or lie.

"No newspaper worth its name could fulfill its mission without using confidential sources," says Harry M. Rosenfeld, former editor of the *Times-Union* in Albany, N.Y. "Without them, much of the very best in journalism would not be possible. At the same time, nothing so much brings our blood to boil. We decry their use and we despair of their ubiquity."

"I don't think we ever named a source," Carl Bernstein says of his and Bob Woodward's coverage of Watergate. "Because it would have been impossible to pursue the story without the use of anonymous sources."

Joel Kramer, executive editor of the Minneapolis *Star Tribune,* says, "Anonymous sources are like fireworks. Used properly, they can produce a spectacular display. But they can also explode in one's pocket."

On the other hand, *USA Today* will not use such sources: "Unidentified sources are not acceptable at *USA Today,*" a policy memo states. Michael Gartner, editor of the *Ames Daily Tribune* in Iowa and former president of NBC News in New York, likes the *USA Today* policy. He worries that "the anonymous source is taking over journalism. It's a lousy trend that is eroding the credibility of newspapers and adding to the unresponsibility of newspapers."

Some Guides

• Use of anonymous and confidential sources should be avoided if at all possible.

• Sources should be told exactly what is being promised them in terms of anonymity or confidentiality.

• Anonymous sources must not be used to criticize a person's character or credibility. The exception is rare, and then only with the permission of the editor.

• A source should be told that although his or her name will not appear, the reporter is obligated to give the source's name to the editor.

Clear at the Outset. ". . . the identification of a source now is one of the opening parts of the negotiation in a journalistic conversation. . . . the first thing you say is we have to agree on how you are to be described. That's a negotiating point."
—*David Shribman, Washington bureau chief,* Boston Globe

Monicagate. During the grand jury investigation of the Clinton-Lewinsky relationship, the use of anonymous sources escalated to epic proportions with the White House and the prosecutor's office feeding an insatiable media supposedly inside information. It was, said one media critic, a "feeding frenzy."

A Television Interview

Let us watch a television reporter as he puts into practice some of the principles and techniques we have been discussing in this and the preceding chapter on interviewing.

It is 6:30 A.M. and we are in an automobile with J.J. Gonzalez, a reporter for WCBS-TV, in New York City. Gonzalez and the crew are driving to J.F. Kennedy International Airport. Louis Treitler, the electrician, is at the wheel. Gonzalez is next to him. William Sinnott, the soundman, and Joe Landi, the cameraman, are in the back seat.

Gonzalez unfolds the note from the assignment editor and reads it again: "Go to Overseas National Headquarters at 175th St. off Farmers Blvd. (Right near the airport.) We will be able to get interviews with the passengers. Afterwards, we were told, we would be able to get on the runway to film the boarding which has been delayed until 8:30 or 9. Crew should arrive 7:30 A.M."

The passengers the assignment refers to are airline personnel who had been on a DC-10 the previous week en route to the Middle East. Their plane had run into a flock of seagulls on the runway, an engine ingested several of the birds, and before the plane could take off, one engine stopped turning over and dropped to the ground. The pilot managed to stop the plane and quickly ordered everyone out. Within seconds, the 10 crew members and 139 passengers were spilling out of the exits and down the escape chutes. The plane caught fire and in

Burning Jetliner

Clouds of black smoke rise from the burning fuselage of a jetliner when its takeoff was aborted. Ten crew members and 139 passengers scrambled to safety before the airplane erupted in flames. A television reporter used tape of the burning wreckage in his follow-up piece the next day when the passengers were interviewed as they resumed their trip to Saudi Arabia.

United Press International

five minutes was a charred hulk. No one was injured. But if those aboard had been the usual run of passengers, Gonzalez says, there might have been a catastrophe. The metropolitan editor had instructed Gonzalez to find out how the airline personnel felt about taking off a second time.

The Planning

It is a 45-minute drive to the airport, and Gonzalez and the crew have plenty of time to chat about the assignment. They will be going to three locations—first, to the airlines building where the passengers will be assembling, then to the airplane the passengers will board and finally to a runway to watch the plane take off. Film of the plane heading off into the rising sun will make a good closing shot, they agree. But they are not sure that they will be allowed on a runway, and they discuss going to the airport control tower. Sinnott doubts that the tower will be available either, and they talk about using the public observation platform.

Gonzalez knows there is tape at the station that was shot of the burning plane the previous week. He will want to insert some of that dramatic tape into what he anticipates will be unexciting tape from today's assignment.

"This is really a bunch of talking heads," Gonzalez says. He means that the tape shot today will show individuals talking for the camera.

Gonzalez will need a number of transitions, or bridges, to move the viewer from one place to the next smoothly. Gonzalez begins to think of possible bridges—long shots of the airport, the passengers milling about.

Gonzalez makes mental notes of the questions he will ask. If he is lucky, he will be able to interview the pilot of the plane that burned. He knows the pilot will not be on this morning's flight, but if he should happen to be around the airline office, an interview with him could liven up the story. It also would be useful as a transition to the tape of the burning plane and might even carry through as a voice-over (VO) of the firefighters battling the flames.

On the Scene

Fortunately for Gonzalez, the pilot is there, and after chatting with him to obtain some background about the first flight, Gonzalez asks him, "What went through your mind at this time?"

The pilot answers, "Basically, I thought we should be doing it some other way."

His reply makes everyone in the office laugh and it seems to break the tension.

"It's the understatement of the week," mutters a young woman who was aboard the first flight. But when Gonzalez and the crew look toward her she has put on a sparkling smile. In answer to Gonzalez's question about the mood of her fellow passengers, she says that as professional airline people they are not too nervous.

Gonzalez is excited about his interview with the pilot. "This is the only real news here," he says. "No one else has had an interview with the pilot."

In his interviews, Gonzalez did not ask many questions. He knew that viewers are more interested in the interviewee than the interviewer. To keep from intruding when a source began to slow down in the interview, he would encourage the source with a smile or a head shake.

"I also use facial questions a lot," he remarked later. "When someone tells me something that is unclear or hard to believe, I will look incredulous or give the person a blank stare. This encourages them to go on and talk.

"Sometimes, the best question you can ask is one word, a simple 'Why?' "

On the drive to the airport, Gonzalez had estimated the story to be worth "a pound and a quarter," a minute and 15 seconds. But it is Saturday, usually a dull news day, and there may not be many other local stories to compete with this story, so Gonzalez interviews several of the waiting passengers.

"How do you feel about taking the flight now? Uneasy?" he asks a young woman.

"No, I feel good," she answers as the cameraman shoots her reply. "I just want to get going."

Putting It Togeher

Back in the newsroom, Gonzalez engages in another set of preparations. Before he writes his script, he jots down what he has on tape and the voices that will accompany it. In one column, he lists the order in which he thinks the tape will be put together and in another column, he indicates the lead-in for the anchorman, his own voice and those of the interviewees.

Later, Gonzalez learns his hunch about the length of the story was correct. There are few breaking news stories, and CRASH, as he slugged it, is given more than two pounds on the 7 o'clock news.

Summing Up

A pleasant appearance, a neutral first question, a willingness to listen usually put an interviewee at ease. Jules Loh of the AP says the first question he asks is, " 'When were you born?' He replies, '1945.' I say, 'What date?' He says, 'October 1.' Now you pull the notebook out.

"You're getting a matter of fact. Then a couple more questions like that. This impresses the subject that you are interested in accuracy. The first thing they've heard about reporters is that they get everything wrong."

Sometimes you deliberately avoid taking notes, says Dan Wakefield, journalist, novelist and screenwriter. "If people were saying something I thought really embarrassing I would try not to be writing because I didn't want them to see my hand moving and clam up," he says. "I would wait until they said something kind of innocuous and that's when I would write down the awful thing they said."

Studs Terkel, the master radio interviewer and author of books based on interviews, puts people at ease by saying, " 'Oh yeah, that happened to me.' If I bring some of my own stuff in, maybe that person will feel more akin."

Sometimes, the results can be a disaster for the source . . . and troubling for the reporter. Here's the experience of Emily Yoffe, senior editor of the *Texas Monthly:*

Once I did a story about congressional press secretaries. And one of the press secretaries I interviewed lost his job over the story. I felt absolutely awful; it was never my intention to have anyone lose his job and, in fact, he lost his job because he was being too honest about what it was he did and because it made his boss look like the publicity hound he was.

It was a case where I was sitting there interviewing him, thinking, "I can't believe you are telling me this stuff." And he was very young and I was very young. If I were doing such a piece now and it was someone very young, I don't know if I'd warn him—through the tone of my questions—about what he was saying.

But then again, what he did was describe his job and I just wrote down what he told me. It was his boss who fired him—simply for telling the truth—not me.

Further Reading

Cole, William, ed. *The Most of A. J. Liebling*. New York: Simon & Schuster, 1963.

Mitford, Jessica. *Poison Penmanship*. New York: Vintage Books, 1980.

Webb, Eugene J., et al. *Unobtrusive Measures: Nonreactive Research in the Social Sciences*. Chicago: Rand McNally, 1966.

Speeches, Meetings and News Conferences

Bob Thayer, *The Providence Journal*

Watch the gestures, the mannerisms.

Preview

• **Speech** stories include the name and identification of the speaker, the theme of the talk, the setting and ample quotations. When a prepared text is used for the story, it is checked against the actual delivery.

• **Meeting** stories usually begin with the major action taken. They include the purpose of the meeting, background to the major action and quotations from those who spoke, including comments by the public.

• **News conference** stories begin with the major point made unless a better lead turns up in the question-and-answer period.

Speeches

"Ours is not to wonder why but to cover the speech or die," the reporter muttered as he put on his overcoat and stepped into the cold for a three-block walk to a downtown hotel where a testimonial dinner for the mayor was to be held. "I'll bet it's creamed chicken again," he said to himself.

The reporter's exasperation was caused as much by the fare he thought the speaker would offer as by the menu.

Speeches, hardly the most exciting stories a reporter covers, are a major part of the journalist's day-to-day work. Realizing that not every speech can be covered, speakers and organizations often deliver a prepared text to the newspaper and broadcast station ahead of time so that the story can be written in the office. (The reporter inserts the phrase, "In a speech prepared for delivery tonight . . ." or something similar.)

Speeches by prominent people are usually covered, whatever the subject. Nothing could have been more mundane than the testimonial dinner set for Betty Ford, wife of President Ford, at the New York Hilton one warm June evening. She was to be honored at the dinner launching a $6 million fund drive for an American Bicentennial Park in Israel. Her remarks were expected to be routine. Indeed, as the evening wore on, reporters became restless. A few of them left, asking those who remained to cover for them should anything unusual turn up.

Naturally, the unusual did occur, and it was front-page news in newspapers and a major item on evening newscasts. As Mrs. Ford was being introduced, the president of the Jewish National Fund of America, who had just finished speaking, slumped in his chair at the head table. In the confusion, Mrs. Ford went to the microphone and spoke to the stunned guests: "Can we bow our heads for a moment and say a prayer for Rabbi Sage," she said. The New York *Daily News* began its story this way:

> First lady Betty Ford led a stunned benefit dinner audience in prayer at the New York Hilton last night for a Zionist leader who collapsed at the affair honoring Mrs. Ford, and died of an apparent heart attack at a hospital a short time later.

Checklist: The Speech Story

The speech story includes:

- What was said: speaker's main point.
- Who spoke: name and identification.
- The setting or circumstances of the speech.
- Any unusual occurrence.

Any of these can provide the lead and theme of the story, although most speech stories emphasize what was said. Itabari Njeri of *The Greenville* (S.C.) *News* began her story with a delayed lead and moved to the speaker's main point in the second paragraph:

The three greatest lies, according to Dr. Eula Bingham, assistant secretary of labor: "The check is in the mail; Darling, I haven't looked at another woman in 27 years; and, I'm from the government and I'm here to help you."

The punchline got the desired laugh. But Dr. Bingham, who also directs the Labor Department's Occupational Safety and Health Administration, said she really is trying to help business and labor by eliminating or streamlining unnecessary government health and safety regulations.

Addressing the annual spring meeting of the South Carolina Occupational Safety Council, the former college professor and zoologist said: "We are attempting to revamp regulations that are burdensome and not meaningful. Our mandate is to protect the health, life and limb of working men and women. We are not interested in harassing or catching anybody."

Locate the Theme   The most important task the reporter faces is finding the theme. A tip-off to the theme may be the title of the speech. Often, speakers will use forensic devices to drive home their major points—pounding the podium, raising the voice, suddenly slowing down the delivery. Sometimes, the main point is in the summary at the end.

When the reporter is unsure of the theme, it makes sense to interview the speaker after the talk. When combining material from a speech and an interview, the journalist should tell the reader or listener where the information came from. Otherwise, those who attended the speech or heard it on radio or television will find the story puzzling.

Occasionally, a reporter will find a lead in what the speaker considers a secondary theme. Then, the reporter should lead with what he or she considers the more important element but summarize high in the story what the speaker considers the major theme.

For example, the president of a large investment firm is speaking to a local civic club about the role of the small investor. The morning papers have a story from New York about a sudden selling wave on the stock exchange late yesterday that sent prices tumbling. The speaker sticks to his subject that noon but in a digression predicts that the bottom of the market has not been reached. Obviously, the lead is his prediction of a continued decline. The reporter will probably want to ask the speaker after his talk for his comments on the market decline to give still more information to readers about his newsworthy prediction.

A speech consists of spoken words. So must the story. Unless there is an incident during the talk that would make the circumstances and the setting the most newsworthy item, the story will emphasize what was said with ample quotations at the top of the story. But writers resist the quote lead unless there is a highly unusual statement.

Tough to Handle

Now and then a reporter sits through an incoherent speech in which illogic and vagueness prevail. What should he or she do—confuse the reader with an accurate account? The reader will only blame the reporter.

The reporter should seek out the speaker and attempt to clarify the confused points and ask others who know about the situation the speaker tried to discuss. If these tactics fail, the only recourse is to write a brief story.

John R. Hunt, who turned from prospecting in the wilds of northwestern Quebec to newspapering, has been covering the North country of Ontario for the *North Bay Nugget* for more than 40 years, "As a small-town newspaperman, I have covered hundreds of speeches," Hunt says. "It is an interesting fact that a dull and boring speech can often become an interesting story. But I don't know of anything more difficult to write about than a funny speech." The best tactic is to use plenty of quotations and hope the humor carries through.

Off-the-Record

Reporters have the right to be present at an official, public meeting and can use anything they see and hear there. But they have no legal right to attend a meeting or talk by a private group, and they have to leave if asked. But the reporter can report what he or she learns from those who were there. A talk heard by dozens of people cannot be kept confidential, and the reporter usually points this out to those making the request for confidentiality. He or she also points out that because those attending the session will talk to the reporter about the speech, the speaker may find the material somewhat garbled in the telling and should welcome an accurate report. This argument usually wins the reporter's battle.

Remember, the reporter is not bound by requests for off-the-record status of any item if the request is made after the information has been disclosed.

Meetings

Meetings provide newspapers and broadcast stations with enormous amounts of news. Public bodies—school boards, city councils, legislatures, planning and zoning commissions—conduct much of their business at open meetings. Then there are the meetings of private groups—baseball club owners, the directors of corporations, protesting citizens.

On her first day as writing coach at the *Winston-Salem Journal,* Phoebe Zerwick encountered a reporter who confessed to her, "I think meetings are dull." Zerwick decided to find out the reason for this resistance and then to compile a tip sheet for "turning dull meeting stories into gems."

The Basics

At the outset of her investigation, Zerwick says she "found that reporters aren't doing some of the things that need to be done." She listed them:

Check the clips.

Obtain the agenda ahead of time.

Write out questions for interviews.

At the meeting, look for the offbeat and unusual.

Think about the people affected by a decision or policy.

In examining past stories on subjects the meeting will consider, reporters accumulate background that can put the issues in perspective. Also, the clips may lead to additional sources and to people affected by an item on the meeting agenda.

A *Journal* reporter confessed to Zerwick that he missed a good story by ignoring an item on the agenda of the zoning board of adjustment. People in Boone complained about a sign advertising a flea market. The sign was in the shape of a lion, and people in Boone were angered by the size of the lion's penis.

"Not bad for a zoning story," Zerwick comments.

Checklist: Meetings

The essentials of meeting stories are:

- Major business transacted: votes, decisions, adoption of policies.
- Purpose, time and location of meeting.
- Items on agenda.
- Discussion and debate. Length of session.
- Quotes from witnesses and experts.
- Comments and statements from onlookers, authorities and those affected by decision, vote or policy.
- Background.
- Unusual departures from agenda.
- Agenda for next session.

Delayed Lead Not all meeting stories will contain every one of these items. Notice the items stressed in the first five paragraphs of this meeting story from *The Brattleboro Reformer* of Brattleboro, Vt. The reporter used a delayed lead to emphasize the unusually large number of people who turned out. The first paragraph sets the scene for the major business transacted by the town school board, which is described in the second paragraph:

Public Protests Budget Cuts In Elementary Programs

By Gretchen Becker

Nearly 300 people came to an emotional Brattleboro Town School Board meeting at Green Street School Tuesday night to protest proposed cuts in the elementary school art, music, and physical education programs.

Purpose
Day
Location

Caught between the strong public opinion at the meeting not to make these cuts and a strong Town Meeting mandate to cut 5 percent from their budget, the school directors reluctantly approved almost $35,000 in budget reductions.

Major business transacted

Approved were elimination of the elementary art instructor's position, the second physical education position, a part-time vocal instructor's position, the fifth and sixth grade basketball program, and rental of space at Centre Church.

The board took no action on the administration's proposals to eliminate the instrumental music position and the part-time principal's position at Canal Street School. Approval of these cuts would have brought the total cuts to $46,000.

Salary Controversy

At Town Meeting March 22, the representatives voted to cut 5 percent, or $74,200, from the elementary budget. Those urging the cuts requested that teachers' salaries be frozen. However, WSESU Superintendent James Cusick has noted several times that the proposed budget included only $25,000 for increases in salaries. . . .

Background

Direct Lead   Most often, the lead will focus on the major action taken at the meeting, as in this lead:

City Councilwoman Elizabeth T. Boskin persuaded council members to approve additional funds for the city police department last night.	**Major action take**
The council had been cutting requested funds for the 2002–2003 budget because of anticipated declines in tax revenues.	**Purpose of meeting**
But Boskin said violent crimes had increased 18 percent last year.	**Amplification of major theme that includes direct quote on theme**
"The only way to handle this is with more police officers," she said.	
The department had asked for a 15 percent increase in funds over the current year's allocation for hiring an additional dozen officers.	**Background**
The council has been making cuts in the requests of city departments and agencies ranging from 10 to 20 percent.	
Boskin's plea was persuasive, and the council voted unanimously to approve the request for an additional $287,000, an increase of 14 percent.	**Amplification of theme**
Then the council returned to wielding the hatchet. . . .	**Transition to other actions**

Seating Plan. Wayne Worcester of the University of Connecticut recommends making a seating plan for covering meetings when you are unfamiliar with the participants. "Key the people to numbers, and as you take quotes and notes assign your numbers to them. When you write, refer to your seating plan."

On Deadline   Sometimes a meeting continues past the reporter's deadline, and the reporter has to make do with what he or she has. It is possible, however, to catch the sense or drift of a meeting, as Robert T. Garrett did in this story in *The* (Louisville) *Courier-Journal:*

LEXINGTON, Ky.—The Fayette county school board appeared likely last night to reject the teaching of "scientific creationism" alongside the theory of evolution in local science classes.	**Probable major action**
The five-member board, which had been deadlocked 2–2 on the issue, heard opposing views from residents for several hours last night before a packed house at school headquarters.	**Setting**
The board had taken no vote as of 11:15 p.m.	
But the fifth and previously undecided member of the school board, Harold	**Buttressing of lead with quotes and paraphrases**

Steele, hinted that he would vote against the proposed "two-model" science curriculum.

Steele said he had concern that "very definite parameters will endure" that ensure the separation of church and state.

As the school board prepares to face the question of tuition tax credits in coming weeks, it must remember that public education "is not permitted to teach sectarian courses," Steele said.

Before last night's debate, school board Chairman Barth Pemberton and board member Carol Jarboe were on record opposing introduction of creationism in the schools.

Probable position of others on major action

Board members Mary Ann Burdette and David Chittenden had said they support the teaching of creationist views. Mrs. Burdette moved that the creationist proposal be adopted, and Chittenden seconded it.

Scientific creationism is a theory closely aligned to the biblical account of creation.

Background

It holds that man and the Earth were created by an outside force, such as God, in a short span of time less than 10,000 years ago and have changed little since. . . .

The school board did vote 3–2 to reject creationism in classrooms.

News Conferences

The Day Book, a listing of daily events used by New York City newspapers and broadcast stations as an aid in making local assignments, carried this item one Wednesday evening:

Manhattan District Attorney Robert Morgenthau holds news conference to produce evidence that confirms existence of ancient civilization in Israel between 2000–1500 B.C., 155 Leonard Street 10:30 A.M.

To local editors, it sounded like a good yarn. Moreover, many New Yorkers feel a kinship with Israel. So, when the district attorney began his conference, half a dozen reporters and two television crews were on hand. But the story took an interesting turn.

AP photo by Mike Wintroath

Press Briefing

County Prosecutor Brent Davis informs the media that he will charge the two boys involved in the Jonesboro, Ark., school shooting with capital murder in Juvenile Court.

The reporters were told that a Manhattan school teacher visiting Israel had taken a clay tablet out of the country that was found to be an antiquity. Under Israeli law, no historical objects may leave the country, and the teacher was therefore in possession of stolen property, a criminal offense.

The DA's Compassion

The district attorney had decided not to prosecute. He had worked out an arrangement between the teacher and the Israeli government. Although all of this could have been announced in a press release, a news conference was called so that the district attorney could play midwife in the delivery of an important historical tablet to an Israeli representative. The district attorney, an elected official, would appear to the public as a man of compassion and wisdom. The media would benefit as well, for the story would interest readers and viewers.

The incident illustrates the mutuality of interests that the news conference serves. It permits an individual, group or organization to reach many reporters at one time with an announcement that will receive more attention than a press release because of the photo possibilities and the staging, and it is an efficient and economical way for the media to obtain newsworthy material.

Usually, the news conference has a prescribed form. A prepared statement is read or distributed to the reporters beforehand. Then reporters ask questions.

At the district attorney's news conference, reporters wanted to know the size of the tablet, when it was discovered, how it was recovered and other details. The news stories that appeared differed substantially from the press release.

District Attorney Robert Morgenthau's press release on the recovery of an antiquity by his office. Compare this with the story a reporter wrote that was based on the release and additional information provided at the news conference.

District Attorney—New York County

For Release: November 20
Contact: Gerda Handler
732-7300
Ext. 603/4

Robert M. Morgenthau, District Attorney, New York County, announced today the recovery of a priceless antiquity from ancient biblical times. The object is a sherd—a fragment of a clay tablet—bearing a cuneiform inscription of unique archaeological significance.

Mr. Morgenthau today returned this antiquity, dating from between 1500 and 2000 B.C., to Amos Ganor, Acting Consul General of the State of Israel.

The sherd was originally found at the site of the archaeological excavation of the ancient city of Hazor, located about ten miles north of the Sea of Galilee in Israel.

It was removed from Israel in violation of that country's Antiquities Ordinance, which requires the finder of any antiquity to notify the Government of the discovery and afford it an opportunity to acquire the object. A complaint was filed with the District Attorney by the Government of Israel through Dr. Avraham Biran, former Director of the Department of Antiquities in Israel. An investigation was undertaken by the District Attorney which resulted in the recovery of the sherd.

The sherd records a case of litigation, conducted in the presence of the king, concerning real estate in Hazor. It is of great historical value because it confirms that the excavation, begun in 1955 near the Sea of Galilee, is the ancient city of Hazor. According to Professor Yigal Yadin, who headed a four year archaeological expedition at Hazor, the sherd is a major link in the identification of the excavation as the ancient city of Hazor, that was mentioned in the Egyptian Execration Texts of the 19th Century B.C., the Annals of the Pharaohs Thut-mose III, Amen hotep II and Seti I and in several chapters of the Bible.

Here is how Marcia Chambers began her account that appeared in *The New York Times*. Note that some material in the lead is not contained in the handout and was obtained through questioning. Also, the story places the district attorney in the third paragraph, whereas the press release begins with the district attorney's name:

A fragment of a clay tablet 3,500 to 4,000 years old that confirms the existence of the biblical city of Hazor in Israel was returned yesterday to the Israeli Government after a teacher who smuggled it out of Israel agreed to surrender it to avoid prosecution.

The odyssey of the 2-by-2-inch fragment, with a cuneiform inscription, began last year when the young teacher was on his honeymoon. The teacher, an amateur archaeologist, found the tablet at the site of an archaeological excavation some 10 miles north of the Sea of Galilee.

It ended yesterday, at a news conference, when Robert M. Morgenthau, the Manhattan District Attorney, turned over the priceless piece to Amos Ganor, Israel's acting consul general here. . . .

Checklist: News Conferences

The essentials of news conference stories are:

- Major point of speaker.
- Name and identification of speaker.
- Purpose, time, location and length of conference.
- Background of major point.
- Major point in statement; major points in question-and-answer period.
- Consequences of announcement.

Panel Discussions

In symposia and panel discussions, the presence of several speakers can pose a problem. But experienced reporters usually make their way through the tide of talk by emphasizing a thematic approach. They will find a basic theme—often an area of agreement—and write a summary based on that theme:

> Four members of the local bar agreed last night that probation is no longer a useful means of coping with criminal offenders.
>
> Although the speakers disagreed on most matters at the symposium on "How to Handle Crime," they did agree. . . .

Disagreement Even when there is disagreement, this can be the theme of the story. Here are two leads based on disagreements:

Space exploration can be man's salvation, a physicist said today, but an astronomer worried that man might overreach himself and pollute the universe as well as his own planet.

The disagreement was voiced at a symposium last night, on "Space Travel," sponsored by the Science Club and held in the Civic Auditorium. More than 250 people turned out, obviously drawn by the promise of hearing one of the speakers discuss Unidentified Flying Objects.

But if they came expecting to hear a defense of UFO's they were disappointed, for Dr. Marcel Pannel said flatly, "They do not exist."

The above lead works because only two speakers are involved. The following summary lead was used because several speakers were involved:

There was no accord at the College Auditorium last night as four faculty members discussed "Discord in the Middle East."

The political scientists and historians disagreed on the causes of unrest in that troubled area, and they disagreed on solutions.

All they agreed upon was that the situation is thorny.

"We really don't know whether peace will break out tomorrow, or continued conflict is in the offing," said Professor Walter. . . .

Bob Thayer,
The Providence Journal

'No Way'

Opposition can be made the theme of a panel discussion story as well as agreement. Opposition, in fact, is usually intense, whereas agreement is routine, tepid, neutral.

After the theme is developed for a few paragraphs, each speaker is given his or her say. Obviously, the more newsworthy statements come first.

Singled Out   When one speaker says something clearly more interesting and significant than what the others are discussing, the newsworthy statement is the lead rather than a general theme. Here is how such a story runs:

A California research team may have found a potent opponent of the virus that causes the common cold sore.

The information was disclosed today at a discussion of bioscientists and physicians at the School of Public Health on the campus.

Dr. Douglas Deag, a naval biochemist, said that the enemy of the herpes simplex virus (types 1 and 2) may well be the popular seafood delicacy, seaweed. The red variety—known as Rhodophyta—contains a species that has an active agent that prevents the herpes virus from multiplying.

Herpes is responsible for keratitis—a severe eye infection—and a genital disease as well as the cold sore. But the research is in the early stages, Dr. Deag said.

He was one of five speakers who discussed "Frontiers of Medicine," which was concerned primarily with careers in the medical sciences. . . .

Summing Up

Here's a guide to establishing a procedure for covering speeches, news conferences and panel discussions:

1. Find the **subject.** The title is an indicator.
2. Determine the **purpose.** Generally, the speaker will be trying to report, explain or persuade, perhaps all three.
3. Locate the **main idea.** Here we get to the specific point that will constitute your lead.
4. Gather the **evidence** used to prove the point. This provides the body of the story.

Remember: These stories are based on spoken words. Your story must include plenty of quotations. The story always matches the nature of the event.

Also, show up early. That's the best way to talk to participants, to get a sense of what will follow.

17 Hunches, Feelings and Stereotypes

John Walker, *The Fresno Bee*

**Compassion can lead
to revealing stories.**

Preview

Reporters rely on their hunches and feelings as well as rational, disciplined thinking:

• Hunches and intuition spring from the interaction of new information with the reporter's accumulated knowledge. Hunches lead reporters to seek relationships among apparently unrelated facts, events and ideas. The patterns the reporter discovers help readers move closer to the truth of events.
• Feelings and emotions can motivate the reporter to seek out systemic abuses and illegalities.

But hunches and feelings can distort reporting, as can a reporter's stereotypes.

Reporters go about their work in a rational, almost scientific manner. They cover events with detachment, break down their observations and weigh them against their general knowledge and the background of the event and then draw conclusions on the basis of their observations, not in accordance with their hopes and beliefs. Then they reconstruct these observations in coherent, logical stories.

Analysis and synthesis, the application of reason to experience—these are the processes that underlie the journalist's work.

Yet, this summary is misleading. It ignores hunches and intuition and emotional reactions that include feelings such as prejudice, hatred, friendship and love.

Hunches and Intuition

Every reporter has had the experience on assignment of sensing the meaning of an event, of suddenly seeing through the thicket of details to the underlying concept that shapes the event. Some reporters seem to possess an extrasensory perception that enables them to detect the real story, the actuality that lies beneath surface details. "I can smell something a mile away. It's just a fact of life," says Seymour Hersh, whose stories of the My Lai massacre by U.S. troops in Vietnam was the first of his many investigative stories.

Hunches, guesswork and intuition come into play as soon as the reporter is given an assignment. Before leaving the newsroom, before gathering information, the reporter has feelings and insights about the story, and these shape the reporter's coverage of the event.

There is nothing wrong with this. These intuitive concepts are sound starting points for reporting. "Feelings are not only reasonable but are also as discriminating and as consistent as thinking," said the psychiatrist Carl Jung. Even scientists admit the nonrational to their universe. Albert Einstein wrote approvingly of "intuition, supported by being sympathetically in touch with experience."

The Cuban Missile Crisis Murrey Marder of *The Washington Post* glanced at the check-in book at the State Department one Saturday evening. Strange, he thought, two people from the CIA (Central Intelligence Agency) had just checked in. On a Saturday night? Marder had a hunch: A crisis was at hand. But where?

He noticed the only lights on that late were in the Latin American Bureau and the Bureau of International Organization Affairs. As he raced around the building, Marder came upon Harlan Cleveland, who was attached to the International Bureau.

Katherine Graham, publisher of the *Post*, recalls what happened:

> Marder had to think quickly of a question that might elicit a useful answer, which an open-ended one like, "What's going on?" clearly would not. So he asked, "How bad does it look to you, Harlan?" to which Cleveland replied, "Well, pretty bad."
>
> Marder felt he was on to something big. But what? He knew the United States was at sword's point with Cuba, then on intimate terms with the Soviet Union. Marder had his question. It was about "this Cuban thing," whether the administration was confronting Cuba. Cleveland responded, "I think we are."
>
> With a little more checking, Marder had an exclusive story—the onset of what was to become the Cuban Missile Crisis.

The Kennedy Assassination In the turmoil minutes after President Kennedy was struck down in Dallas, reporters heard rumors they had little time to check. They had to make quick decisions. Tom Wicker of *The New York Times* said he had to set these reports against what he knew about the people supplying the information, what he knew about human behavior, what two isolated facts added up to—above all on what he felt in his "bones."

In looking back on his on-the-scene coverage, Wicker said, "I see that it was a hard story to put together, but at the time you really didn't have much time to think about what you were doing. You just had to do what you could do.

"In a crisis, if a reporter can't trust his instinct for truth, he can't trust anything."

The Agnew Payoffs   Jerry Landauer, a superb investigative reporter for *The Wall Street Journal,* had a gut feeling when he first saw Spiro Agnew, then being nominated for vice president:

> There was something too tanned, too manicured, too tailored for the guy to have been living on a governor's salary, with no other known source of income. So I started going down to Towson, seat of Baltimore County, the bedroom community where Agnew got his political start; talked to lawyers who frequently appeared to be on the losing side of zoning cases, to engineers who didn't seem to be getting a fair share of state business. After a couple of visits some started talking.

Landauer found out Agnew was receiving payoffs.

Hunches Develop from Experience

We have watched four reporters develop big stories from feelings, hunches, intuition. But if we look closely at their reporting another pattern emerges. Marder and Landauer noticed a break in the normal, the expected, the routine. Wicker had experience with the people he was interviewing, and Hersh had learned that official versions cover up untidy and embarrassing truths.

In other words, experience and prior knowledge provided them with the mind set or memory to put the new material in perspective. They built the new on a foundation of the old, what they already had experienced, what they knew.

What seem to be intuition, hunches and luck is the crystallization of what is already known, a leap from the reporter's storehouse of knowledge to a higher plane of insight. A new situation, fact, observation or statement suddenly fuses with material from the storehouse.

In a review of R. A. Ochse's *Before the Gates of Excellence: The Determinants of Creative Genius,* Mary L. Tenopyr, testing director of AT&T, wrote of intuitive breakthroughs: "Nothing that was not already in the creator's mind comes forth, but what is produced is old information put to a new use or configured differently than it was before."

Reporters store thousands of facts about people, events, policies and the many incidents of their daily experience. This vast storehouse is organized subconsciously. When a new piece of information strikes the reporter as important, it triggers the subconscious into releasing related material.

Hunches and instinct usually work for the good reporters, rarely for the lazy or the talentless.

Gretzky's Genius   Ability plus practice and experience equals excellence in all fields. During the 1982 hockey season, a talented young center for the Edmonton Oilers set records no one thought possible. Wayne Gretzky had fans comparing his feats with those in other sports. His goals, 82, and his assists, 120, for the season were the equivalent of a .425 batting average in baseball, 55 points a game over a basketball season, 3,000 yards gained in a season of professional football.

Pure instinct, said those who watched him. Not so, says Gretzky.

"Nine out of ten people think my talent is instinct," he said. "It isn't. It's all practice. I got it all from my dad."

When Gretzky was a 3-year-old in Brantford, Ontario, his father iced down the backyard and had the youngster practicing. At the age of 10 he was skating five hours a day.

Reporters make use of this same combination of talent, hard work and experience. Reporters who rarely develop good stories attribute the success of their colleagues to luck. It doesn't work that way. "Luck is what happens when preparation meets opportunity," says Raymond Berry, a former coach of the New England Patriots.

Awed by a technological society in which computers and data processing machinery seem to minimize human ability, reporters should retain their faith in their own reasoning. "The largest computer now in existence lacks the richness and flexibility in the brain of a single honeybee," writes Peter Sterling, a brain researcher at the University of Pennsylvania Medical School.

Einstein's Model for Thinking

This diagram is a way of looking at the kind of thinking we have been describing.

Albert Einstein drew this diagram for a friend who asked the famous physicist to explain the roles of experience, intuition and logic in making discoveries or in formulating a theory. Einstein did not limit his ideas about thinking to science. The "whole of science is nothing more than a refinement of everyday thinking," he said.

Einstein's diagram shows a cyclical process. The process begins and ends at **E,** of which Einstein says, "The **E** (experiences) are given to us." E represents the range of sense experiences and observations that Einstein referred to as a "labyrinth of sense impressions," a "chaotic diversity."

Intuitive Leap   Out of this plane of experiences a curved line rises toward **A** at the top of the model. This leap is the intuitive reach of the thinker, the reporter's hunch, the scientist's sudden breakthrough.

"**A** are the axioms from which we draw consequences," Einstein said. "Psychologically, the **A** are based upon the **E.** There is, however, no logical path from the **E** to the **A,** but only an intuitive (psychological) connection, which is always subject to revocation."

In his first paper on relativity, Einstein referred sketchily to some experiments and then wrote that they "lead to the conjecture," which he called the Theory of Relativity. "There is no logical path to these elementary laws; only intuition, supported by being sympathetically in touch with experience."

In the diagram, lines lead downward from **A** to **S´, S˝, S˝´.** These are deductions from the central idea, and they can be tested in the plane of experience.

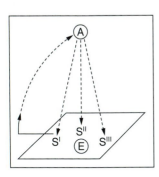

Everyday Thinking

Scientist or shopkeeper, mechanic or journalist . . . we all think this way, making the leap to some conclusion from our experiences. Einstein said the leap follows no logic, "only intuition." The more diverse the experience, the more insightful the theory or hunch for a story.

This model and Einstein's concepts are useful to the journalist, for they illustrate in simple fashion the reportorial process. Reporters develop ideas, **A,** based on their experiences, observations and readings symbolized by **E.** From **A,** reporters draw consequences, **S′, S″, S‴**—which we can call tentative leads or story ideas. These leads or themes are the basis of reporting, which is the validating or disproving of the leads in the plane of experience, **E.**

This discussion of Einstein's theory about thinking may seem theoretical to you. The fact is that reporters apply it often. Look at how Marder developed his exclusive story about the sudden worsening in U.S.-Cuban relations.

He made the leap to **A** from his experiences, **E,** as a State Department reporter: the unusual Saturday night meeting; the fact that it was taking place in the Latin American Bureau; his knowledge that relations between the two countries were strained.

Once he concluded that the meetings might involve Cuba, he devised a story lead, **S′,** that the situation had become serious. He tested this idea or story theme by asking an official questions based on his theory. The replies confirmed Marder's hunch.

Feelings

Reporters welcome their hunches and intuitive guesses, but they are less cordial toward their feelings—that uncontrollable emotion that can hold us captive without warning, lift us to ecstasy at a glance or a touch and plunge us to bleakest despair with a word or a gesture.

This wilderness of feeling frightens most people, and it terrifies those who depend on their rationality, as reporters do. But reporters are human and must function within the limitations of the rationality of human behavior.

Feelings, in fact, can be an asset. "How can you write if you can't cry?" asked Ring Lardner. The poet Robert Frost commented, "No tears in the writer, no tears in the reader." Feelings help us develop value systems and keep them nourished. Moral indignation can direct a reporter to crowning achievements. The muckrakers, whose journalism was the supreme journalistic achievement in the last century, were propelled by a monumental moral indignation. Anyone who reads their work can sense the intensity of feeling behind it.

Exploited Women   One muckraker wrote of a girl of 17 who had been working in department stores for three and a half years. Uneducated, from a poor family, the girl worked at a New York City department store "at a wage of $2.62 1/2 a week; that is to say, she was paid $5.25 twice a month. Her working day was nine and a half hours long through most of the year. But during two weeks before Christmas it was lengthened from twelve to thirteen and a half hours, without any extra payment in any form. . . ."

Rheta Childe Doar described maids' quarters that consisted of a den partitioned off from the coal bin; a maid's bed that consisted of an ironing board placed over a bathtub. Maids were rarely let out of the houses in which they worked.

The Library of Congress

Ida Tarbell

One of the band of muckrakers who exposed the monopolistic practices of big business, Tarbell revealed the ruthless drive to power of John D. Rockefeller and his Standard Oil Company. She and Lincoln Steffens ran *American* magazine from 1906 to 1915 and attacked municipal and federal corruption and the robber barons of industry.

The Library of Congress

Boys in the Coal Pits

Mary Alden Hopkins described unsafe factories in which women worked . . . and died. In Newark, N.J., 25 young women died when a fire broke out in a factory. Some leaped out of their top-floor workplace. Some stayed and died. "They lost their lives because they worked in a building that was not decently safe for human beings to work in," wrote Hopkins. She said there were at least 100 more unsafe factories in Newark, some without fire escapes.

Child Labor   The exploitation of child labor was another theme of the muckrakers. Edwin Markham wrote in *Cosmopolitan* of Helen Sisscak, who worked in the silk mills in Pennsylvania, "a girl of eleven who had for a year worked nights in the mill, beginning at half-past six in the evening and staying till half-past six in the morning. Haggard, hungry, and faint after the night's work shifting and cleaning the bobbins, this child had an hour's walk in the chill of the morning over the lonesome fields to her home." Her pay: three cents an hour.

Then there was Annie Dinke, a silk-twister, 13, who worked on her feet 13 hours, and Theresa McDermott, 11, whose wage was $2 a week.

John Spargo wrote in *Bitter Cry of the Children* of the 12- and 13-year-olds who worked for 50 and 60 cents a day in West Virginia coal mines:

> Crouched over the chutes, the boys sit hour after hour, picking out the pieces of slate and other refuse from the coal as it rushes past the washers. From the cramped position they have to assume most of them become more or less deformed and bent-backed like old men. . . . The coal is hard and accidents to the hands, such as cut, broken, or crushed fingers, are common among the boys. Sometimes there is a worse accident; a terrified shriek is heard, and a boy is mangled and torn in the machinery or disappears in the chute to be picked out later, smothered and dead.

This strong emotional reaction to the abuses of power of public officials and the titans of commerce and industry propels investigative reporters to their discoveries. The Teapot Dome scandal was exposed by a reporter for the *St. Louis Post-Dispatch* who spent years gathering evidence to prove that powerful oil interests had bribed the secretary of the interior in the Harding administration. The reporter, Paul Y. Anderson, was driven throughout his journalistic career by the need to expose wrongdoers.

Today's Crusaders

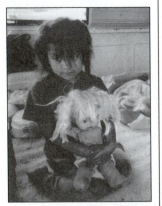

John Walker,
The Fresno Bee

**Baby sitter—
a child herself.**

These feelings—compassion, indignation at injustice, the need to right wrongs—constitute a powerful, continuing force in journalism. Look at the photograph that opens this chapter and the one on the left. The photos are from a series in *The Fresno Bee* titled "Children: The Forgotten Farmworkers." The photograph that opens the chapter shows Melissa Hernandez collecting onions in the field for her parents who cut off the tops. Melissa is 4 years old. On this page, Aida Cruz Sanchez, hardly more than a child herself, is left at the migrant labor camp to care for her 10-month-old brother while her parents work in the fields.

Alex Pulaski, who wrote the articles, describes the children he has watched working in the fields as "part of a work force intentionally ignored by federal lawmakers, who have carved out exemptions for agriculture. They allow children to labor in the fields at a younger age, in more hazardous jobs and for longer hours than their counterparts at fast-food outlets, retail stores and nearly every other business."

The newspaper estimates that 100,000 children "labor illegally in U.S. fields, forgotten because their sweat keeps down the price of the raisins, chilies and pickles we buy at the grocery store." These children work "in the cucumber fields of Ohio, the chili fields of New Mexico and the onion fields of Oregon and Idaho." Melissa was photographed in an onion field near Ontario, Ore.

Auditing Feelings

Despite the usefulness of strong feelings, the reporter is wise to check his or her emotions every so often, for they can distort observations and impede the processes of analysis and synthesis that are the foundation of reporting and writing.

A city hall reporter who finds the personal lifestyle and ideas of a council-woman abhorrent may discover he is looking only for negative facts about her. A political reporter whose personal allegiance is to the Democratic Party may find she is overly critical of the Republican Party and its leaders. The idea of welfare payments to the able-bodied poor—or subsidies to farmers—might so violate a reporter's beliefs that his coverage is distorted.

Here are some questions a reporter might ask himself or herself every so often:

- Have I so committed to myself to a person, an organization or an idea or belief that I ignore negative information about the person or group?
- Does my need for ego gratification—which runs high among journalists—lead me to see an event a certain way? (The blandishments of governors and presidents can lead to a journalism of cronyism and self-censorship. Clever sources know how to play to a reporter's need for praise.)
- Does my need for immediate and frequent reward—a byline, a front-page story, the lead on the evening news—make me write a story before all necessary facts are gathered? (The journalist often must write before every fact is in. Journalism is legitimately described as history in a hurry or, more poetically, "Journalism is history shot on the wing," as E. B. White put it.
- Is my competitive drive so great that I will ignore, underplay or try to knock down another reporter's legitimate story on my beat?

Cautions   Reporters cannot be neutral about life. Nor should they be. Enthusiasms, feelings, generalizations can be useful, as we have seen. But reactions that swing to an extreme should be examined carefully for their causes. Reporters must watch for uncritical enthusiasm and unreasonable hostility.

Some reactions may be based on what the semanticists call "short-circuited responses," ideas that burst forth without thought. A reporter may be positive about doctors or judges and negative about salespeople or stockbrokers without distinguishing among the individuals in these groups. This kind of thinking is known as *stereotyping,* a dangerous way to think, particularly for a reporter.

Stereotypes, Biases, Fears

Racism. In 1902, President Theodore Roosevelt invited Booker T. Washington to the White House and people were scandalized that a black man was being entertained by the president. Not until 1930 was another black person invited to the White House.

We like to think that we are reasonable, modern folk. Unlike our distant ancestors who resolved issues through violence, we turn to reasoned argument, to evidence, physical proof. Yet, what are we to make of the fact that while viewing the same television programs, reading the same newspaper accounts of the O. J. Simpson civil trial, 74 percent of white Americans agreed with the verdict that held Simpson liable for murdering his wife and her friend, whereas only 23 percent of black Americans agreed with the verdict?

The fact is that we carry with us attitudes, assumptions, biases, fears, desires, inclinations and stereotypes from an early age. We see the world the way our parents, friends, schools and racial and religious communities have defined it for us. We are also creatures of the culture that surrounds us—our jobs, the reading we do, the television programs we watch and our government and economic system.

All these influence the way we think and how we see and hear. And the way we think, see and hear affects the accuracy of our journalism. In a famous experiment, journalism students were shown to have made more errors when they wrote stories about a report that was contrary to their biases and predispositions than they did when the report supported their feelings.

The journalist sees much of the world through lenses tinted by others. The maker of images and stereotypes, the journalist is also their victim.

Victim of Images

Since Plato's time, philosophers have speculated about how and what people see. In the "Simile of the Cave" in *The Republic,* Plato describes a cave in which people are shackled so that they can only look straight ahead at one of the walls in the cave. They cannot see themselves or each other. Outside, a fire burns, and between the fire and the cave dwellers there runs a road in front of which a curtain has been placed. Along the road are men carrying figures of men and animals made of wood, stone and other materials. The shadows that these figures cast upon the wall are all the cave dwellers can see.

"And so in every way they would believe that the shadows of the objects we mentioned were the whole truth," Socrates says of what the prisoners can see.

The parable is striking, almost eerie in its perception of image making. It takes little imagination to replace the cave with the movie theater or to visualize the shadows on the wall as the images on a television or computer screen.

Stereotypes: Necessary . . . and Blinding

In the empirical world of human beings there are some two and a half billion grains of sand corresponding to our category "the human race." We cannot possibly deal with so many separate entities in our thought, nor can we individualize even among the hundreds whom we encounter in our daily round. We must group them, form clusters. We welcome, therefore, the names that help us perform the clustering.

The most important property of a noun is that it brings many grains of sand into a single pail, disregarding the fact that the same grains might have fitted just as appropriately into another pail. To state the matter technically, a noun *abstracts* from a concrete reality some one feature and assembles different concrete realities only with respect to this one feature. The very act of classifying forces us to overlook all other features, many of which might offer a sounder basis than the rubric we select.

—Gordon Allport, *The Language of Prejudice*

I knew a man who had lost the use of both eyes. He was called a "blind man." He could also be called an expert typist, a conscientious worker, a good student, a careful listener, a man who wanted a job. But he couldn't get a job in the department store order room where employees sat and typed orders which came over the telephone. The personnel man was impatient to get the interview over. "But you're a blind man," he kept saying, and one could almost feel his silent assumption that somehow the incapacity in one aspect made the man incapable in every other. So blinded by the label was the interviewer that he could not be persuaded to look beyond it.

—Irving Lee

Shadow Reality. A woman customer of a dating service that uses videotapes tells this story: She was reading the biographies of men in the service's reading room when she saw a young man who obviously was the man she was reading about. He seemed eminently suited for a young woman also in the room, and the woman whispered to the young man that he ought to introduce himself to the young woman. He did, and he spoke to the young woman for some time. When he suggested a date, she replied, "Oh no. Not until I see your videotape."

Plato goes still further with his insight into how images pass for reality. He examines what happens when the prisoners are "released from their bonds and cured of their delusions." Told that what they have seen was nonsense, they would not believe those who free them. They would regard "nothing else as true but the shadows," Socrates tells us. The realities would be too dazzling, too confusing.

The Seduction of Stereotypes

Now let us jump ahead some 2,250 years to the speculations of Walter Lippmann, whose classic description of how people see is contained in his book *Public Opinion.* Here is that description:

> For the most part we do not first see, and then define, we define first and then see. In the great blooming, buzzing confusion of the outer world we pick out what our culture has already defined for us, and we tend to perceive that which we have picked out in the form stereotyped for us by our culture.

Lippmann says that the "attempt to see all things freshly and in detail rather than as types and generalities is exhausting. . . ." Stereotypes allow us to fit individuals into categories defined for us, categories that are comfortable because they save time in a busy life and defend our position in society, Lippmann says. They also "preserve us from all the bewildering effects of trying to see the world steadily and see it whole," he writes.

Historical Notes

In 1873, the Supreme Court ruled that a woman was not constitutionally entitled to practice law. The opinion of Justice Joseph B. Bradley stated, "The natural and proper timidity and delicacy which belongs to the female sex evidently unfits it for many of the occupations of civil life. The paramount destiny and mission of women are to fulfill the noble and benign office of wife and mother. This is the law of the Creator."

Despite the prejudice against hiring women as reporters and editors, the media had to bend because of the manpower shortage during World War II. One of those hired by the United Press was Priscilla Buckley, who recalls that when she was promoted to the sports desk, "I was never to mention it to anyone. My copy, even the nightly feature story, was unsigned. If anyone called for a clarification I was instructed to have a copy boy take the call."

But the reporter must try to see it whole. When a student movie reviewer at Barnard College saw a film made by Luis Buñuel, she wrote, in amazement, "How Buñuel at age 70 can still direct such marvelous, memorable, intelligent and worthwhile films is beyond me." Her comment illustrates one of the stereotypes common to youth, the belief that with age comes decrepitude. Stereotypes are held by every age group, by religious groups, nationalities and the sexes.

Racial, Religious Stereotyping

The most persistent stereotyping in the United States has been directed at Jews, African Americans, Native Americans and Spanish-speaking people. Newspapers and broadcast stations have lent themselves to this stereotyping.

In the 1900s when mass migration brought many Jews to the United States, anti-Semitism spread rapidly, and newspapers were no deterrent. It was not unusual to see a criminal suspect described as a Jew or Jewish. "Jew banker" and "Jew peddler" were common descriptions, as was "Jew store." Bargaining was known as "Jewing down."

This persistent stereotyping had tangible consequences. In 1942, during World War II, a public opinion poll asked which groups menace the country most. Jews were third, just behind Germans and Japanese. Hotels and restricted neighborhoods carried signs, "No Jews or dogs allowed."

The media no longer set Jews apart in derogatory fashion, but other minorities contend they are stereotyped. Jesse Jackson accused the media of projecting black people in "five deadly ways every day. It projects us as less intelligent than we are, as less hard-working than we are, as less patriotic than we are, as less universal than we are, as more violent than we are. . . ."

Native Americans

"If Indians want to get the media's attention, they should focus on issues much more important than whether a team has an Indian for a mascot or over a beer named Crazy Horse." The advice stunned the audience of Native Americans. It was offered by the host of a major television network news show at a conference on the American Indian and the media.

The advice, well meaning though it may have been, revealed the insensitivity of whites to the feelings and frustrations of minority groups, in this case Native Americans.

"It has to do with self-esteem," said Tim Giago, then publisher of *Indian Country Today,* a national weekly published in Rapid City, S.D. "It has to do with children growing up believing they are better than mascots." Crazy Horse, Giago said, is a spiritual leader of the Lakota.

"What would happen if this company named a beer Martin Luther King Jr. malt liquor?" Giago asked. He went on, "Sure, there are more important issues facing us, but if we can't be treated as human beings in the small things, we will never be heard when it comes to the big things." Giago concluded his newspaper column with this warning:

"Like the blacks who were forced to sit in the back of the bus, we will no longer serve as mascots for the sports fanatics of this nation. We refuse to move to the back of the bus anymore."

Success   Some protests have paid off. Colgate University, whose nickname was the Red Raiders, dropped "Red," which is considered offensive to Native Americans. In Minneapolis, the *Star Tribune* does not use nicknames for American Indians in its sports reporting, replacing Braves, Chiefs, Tribe, Skins and others with the city or another suitable identifier.

Sexism

One of the most persistent stereotypings has been that of women. They have been seen as emotional and dependent, whereas men are stoic and self-sufficient. They have been accused of being intellectually inferior.

Jeanette Rankin, the first woman elected to Congress, voted against the United States entering World War I, which led *The New York Times* to comment that her vote was the "final proof of feminine incapacity for straight reasoning."

That same year, 1917, the *Times* was upset when suffragettes picketed the White House for the right to vote. The *Times* described the women's picketing as "monstrous." The women were arrested and jailed for six months without trial.

How to Tell a Businessman from a Businesswoman

An acute observer of the office scene compiled this telling commentary:

A businessman is aggressive; a businesswoman is pushy.

He is careful about details; she's picky.

He loses his temper because he's so involved in his job; she's bitchy.

He's depressed (or hungover), so everyone tiptoes past his office; she's moody, so it must be her time of the month.

He follows through; she doesn't know when to quit.

He's firm; she's stubborn.

He makes wise judgments; she reveals her prejudices.

He is a man of the world; she's been around.

He isn't afraid to say what he thinks; she's opinionated.

He exercises authority; she's bossy.

He's discreet; she's secretive.

He's a stern taskmaster; she's difficult to work for.

Those days are past, but sexism persists in some ways, one of them in media writing that identifies women through their relationships with men. Our language itself often reflects male-centered thinking. The column on the left contains what is considered to be sexist language. The column on the right contains nonsexist forms:

Sexist	Preferred
policeman	police officer
fireman	firefighter
postman	letter carrier
newsman	reporter

There are also inconsistencies in referring to men and women:

Sexist	Nonsexist
man and wife	husband and wife
men and ladies	men and women
Jack Parsons and Ms. (Miss, Mrs.) Burgess	Jack Parsons and Joan Burgess
Parsons and Joan	Jack and Joan (or) Parsons and Burgess

Gay and Lesbian Stereotyping

Some of the most pervasive stereotyping has been directed at the gay and lesbian community. The Gay and Lesbian Alliance Against Defamation (GLAAD) made the media a "major target of gay activists because of the often derogatory images of gays and lesbians in mainstream media content," says Jack Banks of the University of Hartford. "These activists charge that such portrayals have nurtured homophobic attitudes in society at large and fostered self-loathing by gays and lesbians."

GLAAD and other organizations conferred with TV producers and moviemakers, conducted letter-writing campaigns, sit-ins and boycotts. This activism has been fairly successful, and yet the stereotyping persists in some areas. People for the American Way reported that the media's tolerance for gay themes has aroused a counterattack from some groups.

GLAAD reported "a proliferation of Web sites devoted to hate and anti-gay rhetoric."

Substitutes for Observation

A news story grows out of the interaction between reporters and events. If reporters see the event in prefixed forms, they will prejudge the event, making it conform to the stereotyped pictures they carry. Robert L. Heilbroner describes an experiment performed with college students that shows how powerful these pictures can be. The students were shown "30 photographs of pretty but unidentified girls, and asked to rate each in terms of 'general liking, intelligence, beauty' and so on," Heilbroner says.

© Mark Geller

"Two months later," he continues, "the same group were shown the same photographs, this time with fictitious Irish, Italian, Jewish and 'American' names attached to the pictures. Right away the ratings changed. Faces which were now seen as representing a national and religious group went down in looks and still farther down in likability, while the 'American' girls suddenly looked decidedly prettier and nicer."

Stereotypes are, as the semanticist S. I. Hayakawa points out, "substitutes for observation."

Journalists who settle for stereotyped responses to events might heed the warning of F. Scott Fitzgerald: "Begin with an individual and before you know it you have created a type; begin with a type and you have created—nothing."

Patterns and Relationships

John Dewey said that "the striving to make stability of meaning prevail over the instability of events is the main task of intelligent human effort." These meanings are the patterns that establish relationships among facts and events. The great journalist of the muckraking period, Lincoln Steffens, said that his thinking about reporting was transformed by a prosecuting attorney during his investigation into municipal corruption in St. Louis.

"He was sweeping all his cases of bribery together to form a truth out of his facts," Steffens wrote later. "He was generalizing . . . he was thinking about them all together and seeing what they meant all together." Steffens said that this thinking led the prosecutor to conclude that the corruption was systemic.

Ten lives in 10 hours. Such was the appalling toll yesterday of two head-on crashes that chalked up the grimmest period in Bay Area traffic history.

Not one person in the four cars involved survived. An entire family of five was snuffed out. That family, and a sixth individual, were innocent victims.

Speed was the killer. And liquor a confederate.

Three died in an explosive, flaming smashup on the Bay Bridge at 11:40 p.m. yesterday. The killer car was going 90 miles an hour.

Just 10 hours earlier, at 1:40 p.m., seven met death in a jarring smackup. . . .

Or, as the poet Robert Frost put it, thinking "is just putting this and that together."

Causal Relationships

The causal relationship is one of the most common patterns we form. The first state-by-state comparison of how public schoolchildren do on national tests showed that only one in seven eighth graders is proficient in mathematics. Why? Authorities said the data showed:

The states whose students had the best performances are also states with the lowest proportion of families headed by single parents.

Students with the worst performances came from southeastern states where poverty is high and from states with large, disadvantaged urban areas.

The top 10 states in student performance were also the 10 lowest-ranked states in the percentage of students who reported watching more than six hours of television a night.

Here we have to be careful. Just because a situation occurs before or in tandem with an event does not qualify the situation as the cause of the event. Scientists worry about ozone depletion in the atmosphere, but they don't think beer consumption is the cause although it has been shown that the decline in the ozone parallels the increase in beer drinking.

Make the Connection When a reporter has the necessary information, he or she should be willing to state the possibility of a causal relationship. When Gov. Mike Huckabee overruled a ban on smoking in restaurants voted by the Arkansas health board, reporters included in their stories that "Huckabee, a non-smoker, has received tobacco industry campaign contributions." Reporters for the *Minneapolis Star Tribune* found that the milk producers lobby had channeled hundreds of thousands of dollars into the Republican Party treasury through dummy committees. Following these contributions, the reporters wrote, the White House decided to increase milk support prices.

There was no absolute proof that the contributions had caused the policy decisions. But the reporters decided that the suggestion of a causal relationship was legitimate.

In the obituaries of Joe Pyne, a television and radio talk show host, and Hal March, a master of ceremonies on television quiz shows, *The New York Times* reported the men died of lung cancer. Then the stories noted that Pyne had been a "heavy smoker" and that "Mr. March had smoked two packs of cigarettes a day for many years." There was no proof their cigarette smoking had caused their cancer, but the data collected by the surgeon general's office had indicated a high probability of such a relationship, and the newspaper was willing to suggest the cause-and-effect relationship for its readers.

Making causal relationships in print or on the air represents a certain risk to the reporter, but experienced reporters know when to take risks. In fact, risk taking may be one of the marks of a successful journalist. The British mathematician

G. B. Hardy remarked that high intelligence is not important to the success of most people. No one, he said, can make the most of his or her talents without constant application and without taking frequent risks.

Polar Alternatives

Another potentially dangerous line of thinking common among harried reporters is the polar alternative. For instance, the reporter may think. "Either the Black Parents Association is right or it is wrong in its stand on school books." This either-or thinking can save the reporter time and energy, but it can lead to superficial journalism.

The reporter who looks only for the black and white of situations will be limiting observations to the most obvious elements of the event. The world is hardly bilateral and the reporter should resist what is called *bilateral consciousness* by being aware of the infinite colors and shades between black and white.

Linking Facts

Navigating a multitude of facets, faces and facts is half the task. The reporter's most difficult job is to put them into some meaningful pattern, to synthesize them in a story. But that is what journalism is about—linking facts to make stories.

As we have seen, these leaps to significant relationships are launched from solid ground. They are based on experience and the logical thinking of the kind described by the philosopher Isaiah Berlin: "To comprehend and contrast and classify and arrange, to see in patterns of lesser or greater complexity is not a peculiar kind of thinking, it is thinking itself."

This ability to arrange and rearrange, to categorize and recategorize, to pattern and to organize is recognized as basic to thinking. Israel Rosenfeld wrote, "We do not simply store images or bits but become more richly endowed with the *capacity to categorize* in connected ways. . . . Human intelligence is not just knowing more, but reworking, recategorizing, and thus generalizing information in new and surprising ways."

The technique of patterning is described by T. S. Eliot, the poet, this way: "The poet's mind is a receptacle for seizing and storing up numberless feelings, phrases, images, which remain there until all the particles which can unite to form a new compound are present together." In describing the emotion in a poem, he says it "is a concentration and a new thing resulting from the concentration, of a very great number of experiences which to the practical and active person would not seem to be experiences at all; it is a concentration which does not happen consciously or of deliberation."

There is not much difference in the ways poets and journalists think, indeed in the ways all creative people think. The ability to pattern observations and feelings is the mark of the thinking person, whether we look at a reporter covering a story or a composer at her piano.

The good reporter has what the philosopher Alfred North Whitehead describes as an "eye for the whole chessboard, for the bearing of one set of ideas on another." In his book *The Powers That Be,* David Halberstam describes "the great reporter's gifts" as "limitless energy, a fine mind, total recall and an ability to synthesize material."

Finding the Links

Reporters are always looking for facts that relate to each other. The obituary writer wants to know the cause of death, especially if the death is sudden, unexpected.

A reporter covering such a death was given the explanation—accidental gunshot wound. But the reporter wonders. The death seems staged. Could it have been a suicide? That's playing games, he says to himself. Still, the death looks like that of a character in a novel. Thinking of this sort led the reporter to write that Ernest Hemingway had killed himself, contrary to the explanation put out by the authorities, who had agreed to cover up the truth to save the family from embarrassment.

A Story Possibility   A reporter assigned to write a year-end summary of traffic fatalities begins with the data the police department has supplied. As she scans the figures of deaths and injuries on city streets, she notices that pedestrian deaths and injuries are up 16 percent, whereas the overall increase over the previous year is 8 percent. She decides to concentrate on pedestrian accidents.

Further examination indicates that most of those killed and injured were 14 years old and under. The reporter recalls that some months ago a parents' organization petitioned the city council to provide more play streets for the warm-weather months in areas where there is a heavy concentration of low-income families and few open spaces. She wonders whether the number of children who were killed and hurt in traffic accidents was high in the summer. She also checks the location of the accidents. A pattern is beginning to take shape. Now she must determine whether the facts support her ideas.

As she moves through the data, she notices the traffic department lists the times at which deaths and injuries occurred. She is surprised at the number of children who were killed or hurt in the evening. Well, she reasons, perhaps that is logical. Where else can kids play on hot summer evenings, especially youngsters from homes without air conditioning? She looks at her newspaper's clip file to check her recollections of the city council meeting. All this takes less than an hour. Next, she makes several telephone calls to gather additional information.

A reporter's approach to the story is as important as the fact gathering. She could have settled for Layer I reporting. Had she done so, her story might have begun this way:

> Pedestrian deaths and injuries in the city last year were
> 16 percent higher than the previous year, a year-end summary
> of traffic accidents disclosed today.

Dangerous Streets   Instead, after her first hour of thinking and checking the clips and another 45 minutes of calls, she is ready to write a story that she begins this way:

> For 10 of the city's children the streets they played on last summer became a death trap.

She then gives the total figures for all deaths and injuries to children under 14 and the total traffic deaths for the city. Then she works into her story the petition the parents had presented to the city council. Her finding that the evening hours were particularly dangerous for youngsters had not been discovered by the parents, who had asked for daytime restrictions on traffic.

Before writing, the reporter had called the head of the parents' group and told her about the evening accident rate. The reporter was told that the group probably will renew its petitioning, this time with the request that in the summer some streets be permanently blocked off to traffic. This new material—the concept of 24-hour play streets— went into the story also.

The reporter not only turned out a meaningful story by linking certain facts but performed a public service for her community as well.

Summing Up

Journalists use their intuition and feelings to provide new insights into events and situations. Hunches and emotions are valuable but must be checked to see whether they are legitimate.

Particularly sensitive are the sentiments we carry with us from childhood—some positive, some negative. Some of these stereotypes stigmatize people.

Further Reading

Hayakawa, S. I. *Language in Thought and Action.* New York: Harcourt Brace Jovanovich, 1978.

Lippmann, Walter. *Public Opinion.* New York: Free Press, 1965.

Ochse, R. A. *Before the Gates of Excellence: The Determinants of Creative Genius.* New York: Cambridge University Press, 1990.

Part Five: Introduction

The preceding chapters have described the processes that underlie reporting and writing. Now we are ready to move to specific areas of coverage, beats. To help the new reporter handle these, we can devise a checklist of the necessary elements for any type of story.

For example: An obituary requires the name and identification of the deceased; the cause, time, place and location of death; the survivors; funeral and burial plans and some background about the deceased. We can make similar lists of necessities for other story types.

Using the Checklist

When a reporter goes out on an assignment, the aim should be to gather information on the checklist, the essentials of the story. The checklist is a starter, a takeoff point for imagination and enterprise. No rote learning of what to look for and how to structure a particular kind of story can substitute for creative journalism, just as no memorization of writing techniques can transmute slaglike prose into soaring sentences.

The elements on the checklist are not in the order they should appear in the story. Any one of the elements could be made into a lead, depending upon the circumstances. Reporters must use their judgment to determine what constitutes the news angle or theme of the event. Also, not all of the elements will appear in every story, but most will.

Students should not regard the checklist as a cook approaches a recipe for flapjacks—a cup of pancake mix, one large egg, a cup of milk, a tablespoon of liquid shortening; stir until fairly smooth and then pour on a preheated, lightly greased griddle. That may make for a satisfying short stack, but this is a textbook, not a cookbook. Creative cooks always depart from recipes anyway. The reporter's task is to put his or her personal stamp on copy. The checklist is designed to help point the reporter in the right direction.

Types of Beats

There are two kinds of beats—topical and geographical. Some of the topical beats are education, politics, business—beats that take reporters over a wide physical area in pursuit of stories. Some of the geographical beats are the courthouse, city hall, police—beats that require the reporter to report from a specific location.

Specific beats come and go. When many Americans made their living on the farm, agriculture was a major beat. It remains so in only a few areas. With the invention of the computer and the soaring progress in technology, beats were developed to cover these developments. With the awareness of the importance of race and ethnicity, these became centers of coverage, complete with workshops for reporters covering these beats.

Deskbound. "The biggest problem I have in the newsroom is getting the reporters off their asses and into the communities they are supposed to be covering."
—*Malcolm A. Borg, publisher*
The Record, Hackensack, N.J.

The beats listed in the next seven chapters cover areas of reporting to which beginning reporters are most likely to be assigned.

Covering a Beat

The reporter starting on a beat tries to meet everyone—clerks, secretaries, typists, assistants as well as those in charge of the offices and agencies on the beat. A sound idea is to give sources a business card or a note with your name, address and phone number.

"Shoot the breeze," says an experienced beat reporter. "That's the way to develop sources and how you find good stories. People usually are happy to chat with a reporter."

"You need to establish a relationship of trust with sources. But you make no promises you cannot fulfill or that interfere with your responsibilities as a reporter."

When he was the editor of *The Charlotte* (N.C.) *Observer,* Rich Oppel, distributed to his staff eight tips for managing a beat. Here, in summarized form, are his suggestions:

1. **Get started fast** and get out of the office. Don't waste time. Not many stories are found in newsrooms.
2. **Set daily goals.**
3. **Build sources.** There is no substitute for regular, perhaps daily, contact.
4. **Do favors.** Where appropriate, do a favor for a source. The council member's daughter needs a copy of a month-old edition for a class project. Why not?
5. **Ask the sweeping questions;** ask the dumb questions. What's taking most of your time these days? What's the biggest problem you face in your job?
6. **Listen carefully, watch carefully.**
7. **Look at the record.** In managing a beat, go for original source material.
8. **Set up calls.** Make phone checks. Phone calls are a supplement, not a substitute, for direct contact.

Know the Beat

We can add a No. 9 to this list: **Know the beat.** A survey of editors found that they rated their reporters' knowledge of their beats mediocre at best. They said their staffers were poorly prepared to cover education, police and the courts, budgets, business and local government.

The following chapters will help you master the fundamentals of these beats.

18 Accidents and Disasters

Ted S. Warren, *Austin American-Statesman*

Tornado's aftermath—a son, a mother, a home lost.

Preview

Local stories about accidents and disasters must include:

- Names and addresses of dead and injured.
- Extent and cost of property damage.
- Time, location and cause of accident.
- Comments from eyewitnesses and authorities.

Because many of these stories tend to read alike, an attempt is made to find an aspect of the event that sets it apart from others like it. Eyewitness accounts can provide a unique perspective of the event.

For natural disasters, rescue and relief operations are highlighted along with casualties and property damage.

Motor Vehicle Accidents

Motor vehicles kill, injure and maim an enormous number of people each year. News of collisions, of trucks and cars careening into trees and smashing into each other on fog-bound freeways is given good play in newspapers and on local radio and television news programs. Only the routine "fender benders," as reporters describe minor accidents, are ignored or summarized. Rare is the reporter who has never written a *fatal,* a story about an accident in which at least one person died. Newsrooms frequently check so that they have the latest accident reports right up to deadline.

One accident story tends to read like another. But the enterprising reporter finds an aspect of the event that sets his or her story apart. In this story from *The News-Gazette* in Champaign-Urbana, Ill., the location of the fatality was newsworthy:

DANVILLE—A 55-year-old Martinsville, Ind., man was killed Wednesday night as he was walking across the highway in the 2500 block of Georgetown Road.

Harold Owens was killed when he was struck by a car and a pickup truck while walking across Illinois 1 in the Hegler area south of Danville at 9:40 p.m.

That dark stretch of the road has been the scene of numerous fatal pedestrian accidents, according to Vermilion County Coroner Lyle Irvin.

Mr. Owens was with a logging crew that is working in the county. He was staying at a motel in the area and was walking across the road to a tavern, Irvin said.

The "dark stretch of road" has an ominous sound to it. We all know dangerous places like that. The story would have been more effective had those words in the third paragraph been worked into the lead.

Quotes Useful

We look for good quotes that set this particular accident apart from other accident stories:

CADIZ, Ky., Dec. 16 (AP)—Seven teen-age boys who had squeezed into a compact car were killed in a head-on collision on Wednesday, plunging this small town into mourning.

None of the boys was wearing a seatbelt when their car crossed the center line and collided with a four-wheel-drive vehicle outside this town of 1,600 in southwest Kentucky.

"No community this size can take seven at one time," David Goodcase, administrator of Trigg County Hospital, said as the hospital filled with friends and relatives. Boys and girls sat in clusters and wept.

Sometimes the remarks of the coroner or an official can provide material for the lead, as in this story from the *Herald-Dispatch* in Huntington, W. Va.:

ELK CREEK, W. Va.—Two brothers died early yesterday when their car went off W. Va. 65 and struck a tree, a county official said.

The deaths were the second and third traffic fatalities in Mingo County in two days, said interim County Coroner Larry Wood.

He identified the victims as Jimmy Nichols, 16, of Varney, and Clyde R. Nichols, 18, of Columbus.

He said their car left the highway about 12:15 a.m., wrapped around a tree and "practically disintegrated."

Although wreckage was scattered over a wide area, evidence at the scene indicated that Jimmy Nichols was driving, the coroner said.

"From the appearance of the car and where it left the road, excessive speed probably caused the accident," said Deputy Bill Webb of the Mingo County Sheriff's Department.

There were no witnesses to the crash, he said. . . .

That partial quote in the fourth paragraph is too good to be buried. Try your hand at including it in the lead.

Here's a quote from someone who witnessed the path of a car after it hit an abutment on a bridge overpass:

"I looked up and saw him flipping
through the air and coming at me head-
first," said John Pender of Havertown.

It, too, was too far down in the story, as was the fact that the car traveled 250 feet in the air before striking cars when it landed. For the full story, see **Spectacular Crash** in *NRW Plus.*

Ricardo Ferro,
St. Petersburg Times

Daring Rescue

Eyewitness accounts of accidents can provide detail and drama. Here, motorists extricate a driver as a vehicle burns dangerously close.

Caution: Pedestrians

Walking is the most dangerous way to get from one place to another, 20 times more dangerous than traveling by car and a thousand times more dangerous than air travel. But few reporters pay attention to the dangers to foot travelers, more than 5,000 of whom are killed annually.

The most dangerous places to take a walk, according to the Surface Transportation Policy Project, are:

1. Orlando, Fla.
2. Tampa–St. Petersburg, Fla.
3. Miami–Fort Lauderdale, Fla.
4. Providence–Pawtucket, R.I.; Fall River, Mass.
5. Phoenix
6. Houston–Galveston–Brazoria, Tex.
7. Atlanta
8. Los Angeles–Anaheim–Riverside
9. Buffalo–Niagra Falls, N.Y.
10. Charlotte–Gastonia, N.C.; Rock Hill, S.C.

In this the age of the car, most streets are built for vehicles, not pedestrians, says the author of the study, Barbara McCann. "Some subdivisions don't even have sidewalks, let alone crosswalks," she says. Although 12 percent of all motor vehicle fatalities are pedestrians, only 1 percent of federal highway safety funds go to pedestrian safety.

Checklist: Motor Vehicle Accidents

___ Victims: names, identification of dead and injured.

___ Type of vehicles involved.

___ Location.

___ Time.

___ Cause (from official source).

___ Names and identification of other drivers and passengers.

___ Cause of death, injuries.

___ Where dead taken.

___ Where injured taken and how.

___ Extent of injuries.

___ Heroism, rescues.

___ Latest condition of critically injured.

___ Funeral arrangements if available.

___ Damage to vehicles.

___ Arrests or citations by police.

___ Unusual weather or highway conditions.

___ Accounts by eyewitnesses and investigating officers.

___ Speed, origin and destination of vehicles.

Sources

State highway patrol; local, suburban police; sheriff's office; hospital; ambulance service; mortuary; coroner.

Cautions

Art Carey of *The Philadelphia Inquirer* says that one of the first warnings he received about covering accidents was to be careful of inadvertently attributing blame when writing about the cause. Unless one of the drivers has been cited or arrested, it is best to avoid a detailed description of the cause. The reporter must be especially careful about saying which vehicle struck the other because such statements may imply responsibility. Also, be wary of eyewitness accounts, and verify addresses and the spelling of names in police reports.

Airplane Accidents

Airplane accidents make headlines. A motor vehicle collision in which two are killed will not receive the attention given the crash of an airplane with the same number of fatalities. Airline crashes are big news. Local newspapers and stations will scan the casualty list carried on the wires for the names of local residents.

Checklist: Airplane Accidents

___ Number of dead and injured.

___ Time, location and official cause of crash.

___ Origin and destination of plane.

___ Airline and flight number.

___ Type of plane: manufacturer, number of engines.

___ Victims: names and identification (including hometown).

___ Survivors by name.

___ Condition of injured.

___Where dead and injured taken.

___ Cause of death: impact, fire, exposure.

___ Altitude at time of trouble.

Careful. Resist the temptation to write that airplanes collided in midair, a word that has no meaning. Just write that they collided, says the AP. If they collide on the ground, say so in the lead.

Resist pressure to give the cause. The National Transportation Safety Board usually takes a year or more to find the reason. The Aviation/Space Writers Association advises, "Don't jump to conclusions. Avoid oversimplifications. Attribute statements and conclusions."

___ Weather and flying conditions.

___ Last words of crew from black box.

___ Police, fire, rescue units at scene.

___ Unusual incidents; heroism.

___ Eyewitness accounts of survivors.

___ Eyewitness accounts of people on ground.

___ Comments by air controllers, officials, airline company.

___ Cost of aircraft.

___ Prominent people aboard.

___ Fire and other destruction as result of crash.

___ Direction aircraft heading before crash.

___ Flight recorder recovered?

___ If aircraft was missing, who found wreckage and how.

___ Funeral arrangements, if available.

___ Survivors of deceased, if available.

___ Official inquiry.

___ Previous crashes in area.

___ Previous crashes of same type of plane or same airline.

Sources

Airline; police, fire, and other rescue units; Federal Aviation Administration (which in many large cities has a special telephone number for accident information); air traffic controllers; airport officials; National Transportation Safety Board; hospital; mortuary; coroner; morgue.

Cautions

Eyewitnesses on the ground are notoriously inaccurate about aircraft crashes. Early reports of casualties tend to be exaggerated. Passenger flight lists can be erroneous; verify if possible.

Storms, Floods, Disasters

Floods, earthquakes, hurricanes, storms and drought—nature's excesses are the media's regular fare. Everyone is interested in the weather, and when it turns really bad it becomes front-page news and leads the evening newscast. Hurricane Floyd weakened when it struck eastern North Carolina, but it killed five, knocked out power to a million homes and caused massive flooding. It was news on page 1 of *The News & Observer* of Raleigh for two weeks, and stations sent out waves of teams to cover the damage.

The line separating accidents and storms from disasters is difficult to draw. If the difference is the number of lives lost, the amount of property damaged or destroyed, then who would set down the numbers that separate them? To the Texas A&M community, the death of several students and a former student when a pile of logs collapsed was a disaster.

So was the loss of three volunteer firemen in the fire in a church in the small town of Lake Worth, Texas. When the Precious Faith Temple in Lake Worth, Texas, caught fire, several companies of volunteer firefighters answered the alarm. As the blaze spread, the roof collapsed, trapping three of the men inside. They were pronounced dead at the scene. To the small community, this was a disaster. The weekly *Times/Record* ran a banner headline across its front page: **Firefighters perish,** and below the headline a photo of the fire ran across the width of the page.

Some define a disaster as massive, widespread destruction of the kind usually associated with the vagaries of nature—floods, earthquakes, hurricanes, storms and drought. It might be a famine in Ethiopia, an earthquake in Mexico, a volcanic eruption in Colombia that takes 22,000 lives in one hellish night. Generally, journalists use the word *disaster* to cover large loss of life.

When a major disaster strikes, the entire newsroom is sent to the scene, as occurred when the terror bombers struck the World Trade Center in New York.

Handling a Disaster

Dave Saltonstall was the rewriteman at the *Daily News* who wrote the major story following the bombings. He describes the day in the newsroom:

> I learned about noon that I'd be writing the "main bar," a story that was in fact an enormous group effort. *The News* had over 120 reporters and photographers on the street that day, some of whom were nearly killed by the collapsing towers. My job was to sort through the dozens of feeds that came in and weave them into something that was hopefully accurate, concise and clear-headed. In that, the story was not unlike any other major disaster take-out. But of course this wasn't like any other story.
>
> I think we all knew that Sept. 11th was one of those rare moments when the national psyche is transformed instantaneously and forever. And in a way, I think the weight of the day almost made the writing easier—the events were so powerful, so cataclysmic, that little flourish was needed.
>
> What was required was a clear recounting of an extraordinarily confusing and frightening day. We tried to do that, without losing sight of the deep emotional scars that the attacks would surely leave. Capturing the sheer scope of the damage and loss became the biggest rhetorical challenge, and at first the lead called it "the deadliest assault on the U.S. since the Japanese bombed Pearl Harbor." But by nightfall, it was slowly becoming clear that the loss of life would be much greater than Pearl Harbor or any other American conflict. That is well established now but seemed like much more of a reach in those first uncertain hours, when the death toll was still largely a guessing game.
>
> So we changed the lead at the last minute to "the deadliest assault on the U.S. in its history," which I think aptly and correctly conveyed the gravity of the day. The first edition left my desk at about 9 p.m., but we were able to update most stories until about 1 a.m.

'Deadliest Assault'

Here is how Saltonstall began his story on the World Trade Center bombings:

On a day of unspeakable horror for New York and the nation, terrorists crashed planes into the World Trade Center and the Pentagon yesterday in the deadliest assault on the U.S. in its history.

"Thousands of lives were suddenly ended by evil, despicable acts of terror," President Bush said in an address to the nation last night.

The attacks involved four synchronized plane hijackings, two from Boston, one from Newark and one from Dulles International outside Washington. Each was bound for the West Coast, loaded with fuel for the cross-country flight, and they crashed within 90 minutes of one another.

The challenge then became delivering the newspaper, which was a serious issue at the time since all bridges and tunnels into the city were closed and *The News* has been printed in New Jersey for years. But my understanding is that calls were made to Gov. Pataki's office and, given the obvious public service that all print media provided that day, our trucks were brought into the city under police escort. They hit the stands a little late but, like every other daily, were gone from most neighborhoods by 10 a.m. or so.

Rescues   Storm and disaster coverage includes stories of the work of rescuers:

Hurricane Floyd's drenching rain turned parts of Interstates 95 and 40 into treacherous passages Thursday, leading to at least two deaths and a pair of dramatic rescues in Nash and Pender counties.

The two victims couldn't be identified. But there were plenty of witnesses to rescues by Marine Corps helicopters in Nash and a mix of Highway Patrol troopers and volunteers in Pender, both daring acts that kept the death toll from climbing.

—*The News & Observer*

Failure

As floodwaters make footing difficult, these rescue workers try desperately to save an elderly driver trapped in his minivan underwater. The effort failed and the driver died.

Christobal Perez, *The News & Observer*

OKLAHOMA CITY (AP)—Choking through dusty smoke and the overpowering stench of the decaying dead buried around them, they push on. At times forced to inch along on their backs through foot-high crawl spaces, they push on.

Haunted by creaks, groans and cracks, they eye small chunks of rubble that shower them sporadically and stay alert for the scream of "Get out!," the signal that the collapse of tons of debris may be imminent.

At Ground Zero

The firefighters refused to leave.

Sweaty and soot-covered, they were beaten down with exhaustion, pain and anger.

At ground zero, amid the twisted and ash-coated rubble that had rained down on Battery Park City, they sat stunned, resting their aching bodies against buildings like the homeless.

"If any of you have already completed your 24-hour shift, please go home and report back here at 0900 hours," a deputy chief barked through a bullhorn.

Two dozen shell-shocked firefighters stood up, as if to leave—only to sit down again once the supervisor left.

"Some guys have been here since 9 a.m., and they won't go home," explained one Bronx firefighter.

"Our brothers, our friends, our relatives are buried there. I'm not going anywhere," he said.

"My uncle is a firefighter assigned to a house near here, and we haven't heard from him."

The dozens of smashed-up and ash-covered emergency vehicles nearby graphically illustrated the disaster facing their buried comrades.

—*New York Post*

Folo Stories   The coverage also includes what is known as a folo, a follow-up story that assesses damages, physical and emotional. The folo may also tell stories of courage and endurance. Peter St. Onge wrote folos for *The Charlotte Observer* when the storm receded, leaving in its wake the homeless and the penniless and some with stories of their rescue. For two stories St. Onge wrote about Hurricane Floyd's aftermath, see **The Storm That Shocked N.C.** in *NRW Plus*. St. Onge also describes how he reported and wrote these stories.

Checklist: Storms, Floods and Disasters

As in the accident story, the human toll is more important than the loss of property.

___ Dead.

___ Injured.

___ Total affected or in danger.

___ Cause of death.

___ Estimated death and injury toll.

___ Eyewitness accounts.

Lloyd B. Cunningham,
Argus Leader

Tornado Cleanup

___ Property loss:

    ___ Homes.

    ___ Land.

    ___ Public utilities.

    ___ Permanent damage.

___ Rescue and relief operations:

    ___ Evacuations.

    ___ Heroism.

    ___ Unusual equipment used or unique rescue techniques.

    ___ Number of official personnel and volunteers.

___ Warnings: health department, public utility commission, police and highway department statements.

___ Looting.

___ Number of spectators.

___ Insurance.

___ Suits.

___ Arrests.

___ Investigations.

___ Cleanup activities.

Sources

In storm and disaster coverage, statements may be issued by presidents and prime ministers, local police and priests. The destruction may be so vast no single source is adequate for coverage. Usually, the first place the reporter turns is to the experts—meteorologists for the weather picture, the Federal Aviation Administration for plane crashes, the Red Cross for disaster assistance.

Experts sometimes speak in technical language and the reporter should know some of these terms. In a flood situation, for example:

Flood stage—The height of the river above which damage begins to occur, usually because the river overflows its banks.

Crest—The highest level that a river reaches.

Human Interest

When a cold wave swept through the East over Christmas, it left seven dead in New Jersey. For his story of the disaster, Jim Dwyer chose five of the dead and began his story with vignettes: One man had in his pocket a 16-year-old newspaper clipping about his son's death; another was found dead in the front seat of a truck in which he had sought shelter.

A homeless man had dozed off under the Atlantic City boardwalk. "The temperature was basically warm when John went to sleep," said a friend, "but then it dropped rather drastically. In that drastic drop was when he died."

Caution: Eyewitness accounts should be treated with care, especially if they are of events that unfold rapidly and particularly if the witness to the event is emotionally involved.

R. Edward Geiselman of the psychology department at the University of California at Los Angeles and Ronald P. Fisher of the psychology department at Florida International University make recommendations useful to reporters:

1. Ask the eyewitness to reconstruct the incident "in general." Ask the witness to describe the scene. This will stimulate recall.

2. Tell the witness not to hold back just because he or she thinks the detail isn't important. Report everything.

3. Tell the eyewitness to recall the event in different order. "Now that you have told it from the beginning, start with the most impressive incident, or start at the end."

4. Have the witness change perspectives. "Think about the event from the view of others who were there."

Writing the Disaster Story

With stories of the dimension of a disaster, the reporter is tempted to pull out every writing device he or she knows. Resist. If resisting is difficult, pause and reflect on the story—part fact, part fiction—told of the reporter from a Philadelphia newspaper sent to cover a mine disaster in Donora, Pa., where hundreds of miners were entombed dead or facing imminent death from mine gas. The mine was surrounded by weeping relatives, and when it was opened 200 bodies were taken out.

The reporter looked at this scene of death and grief and wired his newspaper the lead: "God sits tonight on a little hill overlooking the scene of disaster. . . ."

As these words came over the telegraph machine in the newsroom in Philadelphia, an editor shouted out, "Stop," and he handed the telegraph editor a message to send back to the reporter in Donora: "Never mind disaster—interview God."

Dave McDermand,
The Bryan-College Station Eagle

Mourning fellow students

Preview

Obituaries are among the most frequently read stories in the newspaper. The obituary sums up the activities and outstanding qualities of the individual and includes:

• Name, age, occupation and address of deceased.
   • Time, place and cause of death.
   • Survivors.
   • Funeral and burial plans.

The obituary usually centers on the person's most noteworthy accomplishment or activity. Useful information is obtained from the news library and from reference material and the friends and relatives of the deceased. The obituary is enlivened with anecdotes about the person.

Here are two views of the obituary:

1. "The obituary is a routine story that no reporter enjoys writing."
2. "On the obituary page may be found the summing up of the glories, the achievements, the mediocrities, and the failures of a life which the rest of the paper chronicled day by day."

The first description is taken from a journalism textbook, the second from a veteran journalist's article about writing obituaries. Both summaries are accurate. Most obituaries are indeed routine, written by writers who rigorously follow a formula so that only names, addresses, ages and the other vital statistics differentiate one obituary from another. However, the writers who use their reportorial and writing skills on obituaries develop interesting stories and devoted subscribers. Obituaries are among the best-read staples in the newspaper.

No reporter should approach any story with the intention of writing routinely. Of course, some stories are difficult to make interesting, but the obituary hardly falls into this category, for the reporter has a wide panorama from which to select material—a person's entire life. No life lacks drama, if the reporter has the intelligence and the time and the desire to look for it.

Guideline William Buchanan of *The Boston Globe* was guided in writing obituaries by the thought "that what I wrote would probably be the last words ever printed about the person. That's why I always worked hard to include something in that person's life of which he or she would have been most proud."

I recall one woman who worked for years in the office of a candy factory. The part of her life she loved most was playing the violin at special Masses at St. Peter's and St. Paul's Churches in Dorchester. Or, for another example, there was a man who started as a busboy in a restaurant and later became the owner; after he became the owner, no job was too menial for him to handle. That clearly showed his character.

Even when the life is brief, the obituary can be interesting or moving. Here is an obituary of a 12-year-old boy written by a young reporter, James Eggensperger, for the *Sanders County Ledger* in Thompson Falls, Mont.

Goodbye, Ron

Ronald Laws, a rising star in Thompson Falls athletic competition, died Friday night doing one of the things he liked best, playing baseball. He was 12 years old.

Ron, as his friends and teachers and coaches called him, was batting in a Little League baseball game when he was hit in the chest by a pitched ball.

Then, according to one witness, he started running. After about 20 feet, he turned to the call of his coach, fell to the ground and never rose.

Spectators at the game rushed Ron to the Clark Fork Valley Hospital at Plains where the game was being played, but efforts there to start his heart failed.

His funeral was Monday in Thompson Falls. The Rev. Bruce Kline performed the service with special feeling because he had known Ron through Sunday school and liked him greatly. The Rev. Kline also performed graveside services at the Whitepine cemetery.

In fact, everyone who knew Ronnie liked him, teachers, classmates and teammates. He was a good sportsman and student and took pleasure in anything he undertook.

He left behind his parents, Mr. and Mrs. Larry Laws, and two brothers, Larry Lee and Timothy, and a sister, Lori.

Fittingly, the Thompson Falls and Plains All Star baseball teams are planning a two-game fund-raising baseball marathon for the 8th and 9th of July. Proceeds from the games will go to a memorial fund in Ron's name, a fund which will be used to support sports activities in both towns.

Other memorials for the fund may be sent to his parents.

Eggensperger recalls the day he took the call about the accident:

I remember feeling sick that such a thing should happen to such a good kid. But even more, that he had not had a chance to bloom into his potential and to enjoy all the things in life there are to enjoy. I put myself in his shoes and thought of all the memories, good and bad times, people and places I would have missed if I had not lived past 12, and the impact was overwhelming.

And in the back of my head was something I had been taught, which ran something like this: "An obit may be the only time a guy gets into the paper, and it's his last chance."

So I talked to some people and wrote what I felt.

Obituaries Can Enlighten Us

The obituary can tell us something about our past along with details of the life of the deceased. In the obituary of S. I. Hayakawa, a noted scholar on language usage who also served as a U.S. senator from California, it was reported that in 1937, while teaching at the University of Wisconsin, he married one of his students. "At the time, marriages between whites and Asians were not recognized in some states, including California, and the couple lived for nearly two decades in Chicago," the obituary reported.

Emma Bugbee was a pioneer woman reporter in New York. When she died, her obituary stressed the unique niche she had filled in the days when women were a rarity on newspaper reporting staffs.

Bugbee worked for *The New York Herald Tribune* for 56 years. For many of those years, she was one of only two women reporters at the newspaper. They were not allowed to sit in the city room, the obituary recalled, "but had to work down the hall."

In the obituary of Louis Loss, a professor of law at Harvard, the writer noted that after Loss's graduation from Yale Law School "he was attracted to Washington by the excitement of the New Deal, and because he knew he could not go to the big Wall Street law firms because he was Jewish." And then the writer, no doubt with a smile on his face, writes: "He would eventually become the William Nelson Cromwell Professor of Law at Harvard, a chair financed by one of those firms, Sullivan & Cromwell, in the name of one of its founders."

Online Obits. Several Web sites specialize in making obituaries available through arrangements with newspapers, and a number of newspapers have put into databases the obituaries they have printed.

Causes Informative   The causes of death inform us of some of our personal and social problems:

- The obituary of Eddie Kendricks, the former lead singer of the Temptations, who died of lung cancer at the age of 52, stated, "He said the disease was caused by 30 years of smoking."
- The deadly combination of cold weather and alcohol—a too-frequent cause of death among Native Americans—was Jerry Reynolds' theme for this obituary in the newspaper *Indian Country Today:*

MARTIN S.D.—The icy claw of winter claimed another young life in Indian Country last week.

Twenty-year-old Sidney Brown Bear of Allen was found dead in the back seat of a car in Martin the morning of March 5. Companions said he had been drinking at a bar in nearby Swett, S.D., the night before and fell down twice before leaving.

A preliminary autopsy report placed his blood alcohol content at almost four times the legal limit. . . .

The preliminary report indicated that exposure appeared to be the cause of death. . . .

Checklist: Obituaries

The following items are required in all obituaries:

___ Name, age, occupation and address of deceased.

___ Time, place and cause of death.

___ Birthdate, birthplace.

___ Survivors (only immediate family).

___ Memberships, military service.

___ Funeral and burial arrangements.

Many obituaries also will include:

___ Outstanding or interesting activities and achievements.

___ Memberships in fraternal, religious or civic organizations.

___ Anecdotes and recollections of friends and relatives.

Sources

First news of deaths can come from different sources. Many newspapers rely on the death notices mortuaries send newspapers to be placed in the classified advertising section. The news department is given a copy. Some mortuaries will call in the death of a prominent person, and on some newspapers and stations reporters regularly make the rounds of mortuaries by telephone.

The police and the coroner's office will have news of deaths caused by accidents. Reporters scan wire service stories for the names of local people who may have been involved in disasters or accidents out of town.

Background material for the obituary is gathered from many sources. The starting point is the newspaper or station library. Friends and relatives can provide information, some of it human interest material that makes an obituary interesting, and they can clarify questionable or vague information. Here are the various sources:

- Mortuary.
- Relatives, friends.
- Newspaper clippings.
- References such as *Who's Who*.
- Police, coroner and other officials.
- Hospital.
- Attending physician.

Digging Pays Off

By checking the files and by talking to different people—his boss, her college classmates, a co-worker, the teacher's students, the merchant's customers—the writer can turn up the nuggets that make an obituary glitter. In the obituary of Saul Pett, the AP's gifted feature writer, *Los Angeles Times* writer Mathis Chazanov wrote that Pett wrote scores of profiles, including one of the writer Dorothy Parker that began with Parker asking Pett for assistance:

> "Are you married, my dear?"
> "Yes, I am."
> "Then you won't mind zipping me up."

The following incident was recalled by Robert D. McFadden in his obituary of *New York Times* reporter Peter Kihss:

> On the night of Nov. 9, 1965, moments after a huge power failure plunged the Northeast into darkness, an assistant metropolitan editor of *The New York Times*—candle in hand—groped his way through the newspaper's darkened newsroom.
>
> "Peter," he called. "Peter."
>
> In the face of crisis, it seemed only right for the editor to call on Peter Kihss, his best reporter, to do the story.

In an obituary of James B. Reston of *The New York Times,* a colleague, Tom Wicker, said of Reston, "He had far and away the best sense of where to look for a story and whom to question. Scotty was lucky, too, and nobody who isn't lucky will ever be a good reporter."

Much is available about well-known people. In the AP's obituary of Frank Sinatra, material was included that had appeared in a magazine 18 years before the singer's death. Sinatra, Pete Hamill had written, "was the original working class hero. Mick Jagger's fans bought records with their allowances; Sinatra's people bought them out of wages."

In checking the files for an obituary of A. Leon Higginbotham Jr., one of the country's most prominent black judges, the writer came across a talk Higginbotham had given to the graduating seniors at Wesleyan University in 1966. He ended the obituary with Higginbotham's words:

> "I will make two requests of you. They are that you always attempt to see those human beings who become invisible to most people, and that you always try to hear the pleas of those persons who, despite their pain and suffering, have become voiceless and forgotten."

Writing the Obit

Richard G. West, whose comments on the obituary are quoted as No. 2 at the start of this chapter, says of the obituary, "Preparing an obituary is a delicate and exacting task, demanding the utmost diligence, insight and imagination. His obituary should be, as far as human judgment and ability may create it in the limits of a newspaper's space, a man's monument."

Monuments take time to carve, and the newspapers that attempt to carry obituaries for most of those who die within their circulation area cannot possibly devote much time or space to each. Still, some should be thoroughly reported and carefully written.

Beginning reporters often are broken in by a stint of obituary writing, because it tests the journalist's accuracy in reporting names and dates and his or her ability to work under pressure—people are always dying on deadline.

Some reporters consider obituary writing a dull assignment of little importance. "What nonsense. What an opportunity," says Joseph L. Galloway, senior writer for *U.S. News & World Report,* who wrote his share of obituaries when he broke into newspaper work on a small Texas daily:

> The obits are probably read by more people with greater attention to detail than any other section of a newspaper. Nowhere else is error or omission more likely to be noticed.
>
> A good reporter gives each obit careful and accurate handling. He or she searches in the stack for the one or two that can be brought to life.
>
> Veteran of World War II, the funeral home sheet says. Did he make the D-Day landing on the beaches of Normandy? Taught junior high school English for 43 years? Find some former pupils who can still quote entire pages of Longfellow because somehow she made it live and sing for them.

Two Types   The circumstances of the death determine how the obituary is written. When the death is sudden, unexpected—as in a traffic accident, a disaster, an airplane crash—the lead highlights the circumstances of the death. When the death is anticipated, as it is for the elderly and those who are seriously ill, the obituary concentrates on the individual's background and accomplishments.

FDR Dies at Age 63

Here are some examples of the two types:

Unexpected

MISSION VIEJO, Calif. (AP)—Florence Griffith-Joyner, the glamorous Olympic speed sensation who won three gold medals at the 1988 Games, was found dead Monday at 38 after a history of heart trouble.

FloJo, as she was known, apparently died at home during the night. Her husband and coach, Al Joyner, called 911 to report she was not breathing. An autopsy was scheduled.

Track champion Greg Foster said he was told by Griffith-Joyner's sister-in-law, Olympic track-and-field medalist Jackie Joyner-Kersee, that Griffith-Joyner apparently died of a heart problem. She had also suffered a seizure in 1996. . . .

CHICAGO (AP)—Chris Farley, the blubbery "Saturday Night Live" comic whose specialty was sweaty, tightly wound characters who erupted in vein-popping frenzies, was found dead Thursday in his apartment. He was 33.

The cause of death was not immediately known.

Farley died young like his comic idol, John Belushi. Both had a hearty appetite for food, drink and drugs.

Police said Farley's brother John called 911 after finding his brother in his 60th floor apartment in the 100-story John Hancock Building on a stretch of Michigan Avenue known as the Magnificent Mile. There was no sign of foul play.

The Cook County Medical Examiner's Office said Farley's body, clad in pajama bottoms, was found on the floor. . . .

Anticipated

LOS ANGELES (AP)—Frank Sinatra, the dashing teen idol who matured into the premier romantic balladeer of American popular music and the "Chairman of the Board" to his millions of fans, died Thursday night of a heart attack. He was 82.

> Walter Lippmann, the retired columnist and author and the elder statesman of American journalism, died today in New York City at the age of 85.

Find the Theme

As with any story, the obituary should emphasize a major theme. The writer usually finds the theme in the person's occupation or main accomplishment. When Richard Harwood, a journalist for *The Washington Post,* died, his newspaper based its obituary on Harwood's work:

> He was an exhaustive reporter, with a keen eye for distinctive detail. He understood and was able to communicate the

structure of things—not just the politics of government programs but the underlying substance, how they worked, whom they did and didn't help, their histories.

Accomplishments   When Charles M. Schulz died, every obituary began with the fact that he had created the comic strip "Peanuts" that starred Charlie Brown and Snoopy, and that 355 million people around the world read it.

When Tom Landry died, the obituaries emphasized that as coach of the Dallas Cowboys for 29 years he had led the team to five Super Bowls.

Frank Wills died at 52 in Augusta, S.C., of what friends said was a brain tumor. Frank Wills? He was the night watchman, as all his obituaries noted, who discovered the 1972 Watergate burglary that ultimately led to the resignation of President Richard Nixon.

Nat Fein took thousands of pictures in his work as a newspaper photographer. His obituary singled out one in the lead: a rear-view photograph of a dying Babe Ruth as he received applause in Yankee Stadium, known to baseball fans as the House That Ruth Built.

Just a Singer   Unlike Sinatra's obituaries, which emphasized his trigger-temper, notorious Mafia friendships and many tangled romances along with his fabulous voice, the obituaries of Perry Como were quiet, restrained—much like the man himself and his voice. Como's marriage lasted six decades, they noted. One obituary reported, "Mrs. Como always did the cooking and Mr. Como frequently dried the dishes."

It was his career—sales of 100 million records, a Grammy and several Emmys—that the obituary writers emphasized, not his personal life. The obituary in *The New York Times* ended this way:

> "I don't have a lot to tell the average interviewer," Perry Como once told a reporter. "I've done nothing that I can call exciting. I was a barber. Since then I've been a singer. That's it."

Yet this unexciting life merited five columns in the *Times* at its end.

Courthouse Man   In Chapter 13 we met Milt Sosin, Miami federal courthouse reporter for the AP. When Sosin died, *The New York Times* gave his obituary by Rick Bragg 20 inches plus a four-inch photo. The obituary consists of one anecdote after another:

Mr. Sosin, who often referred to editors as "amateurs," reacted with his usual contempt when an editor at The News once ordered the staff to write shorter, punchier paragraphs.

He sat down at his old typewriter, banged out his answer and stuck it on the bulletin board.

"Quit," it said. . . .

He regularly beat his competitors, scooping them even when he was old. In a time before cellular phones, when reporters raced to the courthouse pay phones to call in news of a verdict, Mr. Sosin carried a pad of yellow "out of order" stickers, which he would slap onto a phone before going into the courtroom.

One day a young reporter, Martin Merzer, now with The Miami Herald, sat beside Mr. Sosin in the courtroom.

"Hey, kid," Mr. Sosin asked him, "have you filed yet?"

Mr. Merzer told him the phone was out of order.

Mr. Sosin reached into his pocket and showed him the pad of stickers.

"He had this wonderful, evil smile on his face," Mr. Merzer remembered.

A Crusader   When William H. Jones, managing editor of the *Chicago Tribune,* died at the age of 43 of leukemia, his professional accomplishments as an investigative reporter and an eminent editor were emphasized. The obituary noted his "tireless work, creative thinking and total integrity."

The obituary writer found in the newspaper files a story about a talk Jones gave to a graduating class at the Medill School of Journalism at Northwestern University. The reporter quoted from that talk in order to show Jones' philosophy of journalism. Jones had spoken about journalism as a career:

> It's a commitment to use your skills to improve your community, to speak loudly for the victims of injustice and to speak out against those who perpetuate it. Some of the best reporting begins with a single, voiceless citizen who seeks help from a newspaper that is willing to listen, and to dig out the facts.

The obituary quoted an investigator with the city's Better Government Association who worked with Jones on a series of stories that exposed widespread corruption in Chicago's private ambulance companies, which won Jones a Pulitzer Prize when he was 31. The investigator said, "Bill hated to see people abused, especially the helpless."

A Humorist   Henry Morgan was a radio and television performer years before the days of talk shows. Admired for his quick wit—he usually worked without a script—he was derisive about the media and his sponsors. It was natural, then, for his obituary to dwell on some of Morgan's caustic comments and their consequences.

Richard Severo's obituary in *The New York Times* recalled that one of Morgan's sponsors was the candy bar Oh! Henry. The sponsors thought that the similarity of names would incline Morgan to sheathe his rapier wit. Hardly.

"Yes, Oh! Henry is a meal in itself," the obituary quoted a Morgan monologue, "but you eat three meals of Oh! Henrys and your teeth will fall out."

"On another broadcast," the obituary continued, "Mr. Morgan said that if children were fed enough of such candy bars they would 'get sick and die.' The makers of Oh! Henry withdrew."

When he was working for WCAU in Philadelphia as an announcer, Morgan broadcast a list of missing persons, and he included in the list the names of station executives. "It was days before they discovered it," Morgan recalled. WCAU let him go.

Then a serious note that recalled the Communist scare of the 1950s when self-appointed Communist hunters snared entertainers as well as politicians and foreign service personnel in their nets:

> His mordant humor did not sit well with certain people, and some of them concluded that he must be either a Communist or friendly to Communists. Mr. Morgan was amazed to find himself named in the book "Red Channels," which was issued in the 1950s and listed television entertainers thought to be either Communists or friendly to Communists.

He was blacklisted and "despite a proven ability to attract audiences, had a hard time finding work."

Serious stuff. But the obituary ended on a humorous note: Morgan said little about his origin, contending that he was of "mixed parentage"—one parent was a man, the other a woman.

Terrorism's Victims Soon after the World Trade Center was struck, killing 3,000 people, the local newspapers began to print thumbnail obituaries of the dead. Most of the victims were young, and the reporters used as their theme death's sudden interruption in the lives of the victims and their families:

Joseph Ianelli's personal and professional lives were taking off. The 28-year-old Hoboken resident and his fiancee, Monica Palatucci-Lebowitz, had decided they would marry next September. Three months ago, Ianelli went to work for. . . .

Just before school started this year, Victoria Alvarez-Brito and her husband, Mario, took their children on a weeklong vacation to Cancún, Mexico. It was part of a yearly ritual: pick a part of the world and explore it.

During the Cancún vacation, the Britos took pictures and made a video. On Tuesday, Sept. 10 Mr. Brito took the pictures to be developed. On Sept. 11, Mrs. Alvarez-Brito left home early to her job in the World Trade Center. . . .

Use Human Interest

Too many obituaries read like the label on a bottle. The major ingredients are listed, but the reader has no idea of the actual flavor. Details, human details, help the obituary writer move readers close to the person being written about. Few lives lack interest, even drama, if the reporter digs deeply enough to find it.

In an obituary of Helen Childs Boyden, who taught science and mathematics at Deerfield Academy, the reporter used several incidents from her life. When Mrs. Boyden had applied for work, the obituary reported, the principal

The Boy Is a Man.
Some alert students at Syracuse University point out that the writer of the Boyden obituary has a "boy" doing the recalling in the second paragraph when obviously it is a man recalling something Boyden told him when he was a boy.

was "not at all enthusiastic about the young applicant. But the school was too poor to insist on someone more experienced. He hired her on a temporary basis." She taught there for 63 years. The obituary continues:

> . . . In a highly personal style she cajoled thousands of students through the intricacies of mathematics and chemistry.
>
> Even in a large class she taught the individual, not the group. Her tongue was quick but never cutting. One boy, later a college president, recalls her telling him:
>
> "Victor! When will you stop trying to remember and start trying to think?"

Use Quotations and Incidents

Baseball Player   Willie Stargell, his obituary noted, "was an inspiration in a clubhouse where he forged unity across racial and ethnic lines." Playing for the Pittsburgh Pirates, he was known as Pops, the team as the Family, the obituary stated. But when he broke in with Pirates farm teams in Roswell, N.M., and San Angelo, Texas, racism was rampant.

In the obituary, the writer recalled the day Stargell was going into a ballpark in Plainview, Texas:

> Two men wearing trench coats approached him. One of them pulled out a revolver, uttered a racial epithet and said that if he played that day, "I'm gonna blow your brains out."
>
> Stargell remembered: "I was real scared. But by the time the rest of the team got there, I decided that if I was gonna die, I was gonna die doing exactly what I wanted to do. I had to play ball."

Teacher, Principal   In the obituary of Abraham H. Lass, author and educator, Robert D. McFadden, master of many story styles at *The New York Times,* takes us back to Lass's childhood. Lass was "the son of Russian Jewish immigrants who settled in America early in the century. . . ." Young Lass "spoke only Yiddish when he entered elementary school in 1913. But he learned English in the streets and in schools where the teachers, he recalled, were women in pince-nez and high lace collars." Then he quotes Lass:

Quotes That Weren't Quoted

At the funeral of Louis B. Mayer, a tyrannical Hollywood studio head, Red Skelton observed the huge crowd and remarked, "It only goes to show that when you give the public what it wants, it will turn out."

In Paris for the funeral of French President Georges Pompidou in 1974, Richard Nixon said, "This is a great day for France."

> "They didn't seem to like us or love us. . . . But they taught us—firmly, thoroughly, relentlessly. They did not ask, nor did they seem to care, who we were, where we came from, what we wanted or what language we spoke. They knew what they were in school for: to civilize us, Americanize us, give us a common tongue and a common set of traditions."

Stargell's and Lass's quotations give us a sense of the men and also an insight into the eras in which they lived.

Who Is Chosen

Most small newspapers run at least a short item on every death in town. In large cities, where 50 or more people die daily, newspapers will run an obituary on a handful. Alden Whitman, for years the chief obituary writer for *The New York Times,* said for a person to rate an obituary in a metropolitan newspaper, a person has to be "either unassailably famous or utterly infamous."

Mostly Men   The majority of those selected are men. A study of 1,803 obituaries in *The New York Times* over a three-year period showed that 84 percent were of men. Traditionally, women have been housewives, teachers, clerks, typists and secretaries, not the activities that lead to careers in business, politics and law. The *Times* study also examined the obituaries of those who died at 45 and younger, those less affected by gender roles. The same ratio—five to one male—held up.

The perceptive reporter knows there is more to a person's life than his or her occupation. There is as much drama—perhaps more—in the life of a women who reared three children or struggled to educate herself as there is in a man whose obituary is justified by his having run a local business for 35 years.

Here is the beginning of an obituary in a Maine newspaper:

> Mrs. Verena C. Hornberger, 92, died Tuesday at a Waldoboro nursing home. She was the widow of Hiester Hornberger.
>
> She was born at Bremen, daughter of Franklin and Emma (Hilton) Chaney. . . .

No Reporting   Not only is the obituary routinely written, it finds Mrs. Hornberger's prominence to be in her relationship to her husband, which might be newsworthy if he is shown to be prominent. He is not. But the obituary does contain some clues that, if followed up, might have made a fascinating story:

> . . . She graduated in 1910 from Colby College where she was a member of Chi Omega sorority.
>
> She was a teacher, first working in local schools. She also taught in Essex, Conn., and Verona, N.J., following graduate work in Germany at the University of Jena and Columbia's Teachers College.

Was she the last surviving member of the class of 1910? Does the college have any information about her? Do some of her students recall her? It was unusual for women in those days to finish high school, much less to graduate from

Paid   Obits. Many newspapers publish paid-for obituaries that friends or relatives submit. These allow a record for those of the deceased who do not make the news columns of the obit page.

The Rockford, Ill., *Register Star* runs free a "six-to nine-line obituary that lists the basic information," says Linda Grist Cunningham, executive editor. "Families who desire longer, more detailed obituaries pay for them."

Fame = Inches. A study of obituaries in *The New York Times* from 1993 through 1998 found the longest (510 inches) was of Richard M. Nixon. Next in space allotted was Frank Sinatra, and third was the obituary of Jacqueline Kennedy Onassis. (*Fame at Last: Who Was Who According to The New York Times Obituaries* by John C. Ball and Jill Jones.)

college, and graduate work abroad was rare. Can someone cast light on this? Obviously, the writer simply took the mortuary form and rewrote the data. No one was interviewed. Contrast this obituary with the work of Nicolaas Van Rijn of *The Toronto Star:*

Ann Shilton didn't become the first woman principal of an academic secondary school by being a pussycat.

The principal of Jarvis Collegiate Institute from 1975 to 1983, Miss Shilton "was a very strong single woman, with strong opinions and the will to make them known," her brother Paul said yesterday.

Miss Shilton, 69, died Thursday of abdominal cancer in Princess Margaret Hospital. . . .

Ordinary Folk   Deborah Howell, managing editor of the *St. Paul Pioneer Press,* says that "too many big-city dailies report just the deaths of important people—captains of industry and political leaders. That's a mistake. These newspapers ignore the woman who always feeds the ducks in the late afternoon at the city lake, the tireless youth worker at the neighborhood park, the druggist dispensing sage advice along with medicine for 50 years."

Howell recalled the obituary of a woman who died of cancer and who had asked for a party after her funeral. She was memorialized this way in the *Pioneer Press:*

The ladies sat in a circle of lawn chairs
in the neatly clipped backyard, between
the pea patch on the right and the tomatoes
and cucumbers on the left, sipping their
gentle scotches and bourbons and beers,
while the mosquitoes buzzed around their
ears, and the evening slowly faded without
pain into the night.

Of Tom Flaherty, Howell said, "To most folks, Tom might have seemed quite ordinary. He worked his whole life as a laborer on the Great Northern Railroad, as did many of the Irish immigrants in St. Paul. At first, I worried how I was going to make an obit on Tom interesting. Then I decided that his life represented so much that is so Irish, so Catholic, so railroad, so St. Paul. When any Irish railroadman died, Tom was at the wake. At the St. Patrick's Day parade, Tom led the Flaherty section.

"I explained the kind of obit I wanted to one of our better writers. His obit began:

Tom Flaherty was an Irishman's Irishman, a John Henry of a man who for
50 years matched his mighty muscle against
the hardest work the railroad had to offer.

"The trick is to make the dead person come alive again in an obituary, to remind family and friends and co-workers why someone was important," Howell said.

"Too often reporters come away with just the basic facts about birth, education, marriage, vocation and perhaps a few war medals. Obituaries can be examples of the paper's best writing, meaning reporters must search for the kind of detail—the unusual facts—that makes any news story interesting to read."

Accuracy Essential

When possible, all information from relatives and friends of the deceased should be checked. Assumptions should not go into print without checking. In the obituary of a physicist who worked in the development of the atomic bomb, the reporter wrote that he carried out his work "in the research center in the sands of Los Alamos." Los Alamos is high in the mountains of northern New Mexico.

In describing the physicist's background as a student, the reporter wrote that on the way to an eastern university "he stopped at the University of Wisconsin at Ann Arbor. . . ."

For a glimpse at some well-written sections of obituaries, see **Writing with a Flair** in *NRW Plus,* Chapter 19.

Frequently Asked Questions

Here are answers to some questions about writing obituaries.

Q. Does it make sense to prepare obituaries in advance?

A. Yes, even before a prominent person is ill. The AP keeps some 700 "biographical sketches" on hand, frequently brought up-to-date. A newspaper, depending on its size, may have a score or a handful. When a well-known person dies, the background, or *B Matter,* is ready so that all the reporter need write is a lead and the funeral arrangements.

Late Reports

Q. If we are days late with our obituary, do we try to bury the old time element?

A. This is an old wire service practice:

NAJA, Mexico, Jan. 1 (AP)—Chan K'in Viejo, the spiritual leader of the Lacadone Indians in southeastern Mexico, has died. A son said he was 104.

The son, Kayum Garcia, said his father died at his home on Dec. 23 and was buried the following day. . . .

This practice deserves interment. Be straightforward with the reader and state the date of death in the lead.

Verification

Q. Do I verify reports of deaths?

A. Always. Do so by telephoning relatives, the funeral home or mortuary, the police or hospital.

KING D. ROME

AGE: 1½ • HIGHLAND PARK

King Demarest Rome died yesterday. He was 1½ years old.

He was born in New Brunswick and lived with his family in Highland Park.

Surviving are his mother, Debra; four brothers, Billy, Thorndyke, Kate, and Alex Demarest, and a sister, Sarah Meredith.

Cremation will be private.

A few days later, the following appeared in the New Jersey newspaper:

Correction

Due to a reporter's error, The Home News & Tribune mistakenly published an obituary for a family pet in Sunday's editions. The obituary was published under the name King D. Rome. The error occurred because the newspaper's procedure of verifying all obituaries was not followed.

Embarrassing Material

Q. Should I omit material from a person's life that might offend some readers or embarrass survivors or friends?

A. Follow the policy of the newspaper or station. Generally, newspapers have become more frank since the 1930s when a new reporter for *The New York Herald Tribune* would be told by City Editor Stanley Walker that there were two rules for writing obits: "First, make sure he's dead. Second, if he's a rich drunk, call him a clubman and philanthropist."

We follow Walker's first rule by verifying reports of deaths. The second rule may be applied to a local businessman everyone in town knows was a heavy and habitual drinker in the last years of his life and lost most of his business because of his drinking.

In its obituary of D. Tennant Bryan, founder of the communications giant Media General Inc., *The New York Times* made a point of Bryan's opposition to the desegregation of public schools despite a Supreme Court ruling. In the second paragraph of the *Times* obituary that

Edward Wyatt wrote, Bryan was described as "a leading voice against school desegregation in Virginia in the mid-1950's," and later in the story Wyatt said Bryan's newspapers "were leading supporters of the campaign of 'massive resistance' to racial integration in public schools. . . ."

Jerry Garcia's obituaries all stated that he died in a California residential drug treatment center, and *The New York Times* said in the third paragraph of its page 1 obituary, "In the 1960s, he was known as Captain Trips, referring to his frequent use of LSD, and he struggled through the years with a heroin addiction."

Incidents well known to the public cannot be disregarded. On the other hand, when a man or woman had led a useful life after making a mistake years past, no harm to truth is done by passing over the incident. The obituary of the former city treasurer who was sentenced to the penitentiary for graft 30 years before his death will be handled differently by different newspapers. Some will include his crime; others will not, on the ground that he paid for his mistakes and thereafter led a blameless life.

Please Omit Flowers

Q. When people request no flowers, what do I write?

    A. Ask the caller if the family prefers that donations be made to an organization, scholarship or charity and name it: The family requests that remembrances be sent to the Douglas County Heart Association. Do not write that the family requests no flowers be sent.

Interviewing Survivors

Q. Do I press grieving survivors to speak to me even though they may not want to?

    A. Editors usually want background about the deceased that only people close to the person can provide. An obituary celebrates the person's life, and an interview with relatives can help capture that life. Few subjects have ample material in the clip file.

        Still, reporters must be sensitive to grief. If the source is unwilling to talk, do not press. But give reasons for needing the information, and try to conduct a personal interview if there is no deadline problem.

Reporters at *USA Today* faced the task of calling dozens of survivors and friends of men and women killed in the terror bombings at the Pentagon in Washington and at the World Trade Center in New York. "Talking to victims'

R. L. Chambers

Memorials

Posters were put up in New York City's Times Square subway station of those missing in the World Trade Center terror bombings. Soon they became memorials when the few survivors were accounted for.

families is the worst part of our jobs," says Andrea Stone. "I've done it many times, most memorably in the Gulf War, when I chased around western Pennsylvania for families of SCUD victims. That was bad enough. But this time was different.

"I got one 18-year-old whose father, an Army officer, died at the Pentagon. I felt like a sleaze talking to him. But he gave me some nice details about how his father sang barbershop music and loved his speedboat."

Mike Dodd said writing about sudden deaths is difficult "because of the circumstances and the families' uncertainty, the lack of closure." In the terror bombings, he said he found most people helpful, though occasionally a close relative would hand the phone to someone nearby. Dodd said that on this assignment the usual deadline pressures did not exist. Still, he said, "I left here both days feeling drained. These are good people, and they're hurting, and they hadn't begun the healing process."

Those Donna Leinwand called were "almost desperate to let us know about the people lost in the disasters. They want to let the world know none of these people were ordinary and that the terrorists stole some very special people. The families were devastated, of course. But most were receptive to our calls."

Cause of Death

Q. Do I always use the cause of death?

A. The cause is given, unless policy is otherwise. For years, cancer—the country's second leading cause of death—was replaced in many obituaries by the euphemisms "long illness" or "lingering illness." For some reason, many people regarded cancer as a disease too horrible to name. Under the educational program of the American Cancer Society, newspapers were encouraged to mention the disease. The cause of death should be reported whenever possible so that the public becomes aware of the major causes of death.

When lung cancer is the cause of death, reporters ask whether the deceased was a heavy smoker. For a time, newspapers ignored the deceased's smoking habit. But in recent years—after considerable criticism of this reluctance to list this possible cause of death—smoking is included, if not played up, as in this AP story:

COSTA MESA, Calif. (AP)—Wayne McLaren, who portrayed the rugged "Marlboro Man" in cigarette ads but became an anti-smoking crusader after developing lung cancer, has died. He was 51.

McLaren, who smoked for about 25 years and was diagnosed with the disease about two years ago, died Wednesday.

"He fought a hard battle," his mother, Louise McLaren, said. "Some of his last words were: 'Take care of the children. Tobacco will kill you, and I am living proof of it.' "

On the other hand, when Sammy Davis Jr. died, the cover story in *People* did not mention that he died of cancer presumably caused by his two-pack-a-day cigarette habit.

Suicide

Q. How do I handle suicides?

A. Follow the newspaper's policy. Most are frank; some avoid the word. *The Morning Record and Journal* in Meriden, Conn., describes the cause of death in the final paragraph of the obituary, which allows the family to cut off the paragraph before preserving the story or sending it to others. Be careful to attribute suicide to an authority, the medical examiner or the coroner. Without such attribution, do not state suicide was the cause of death. Avoid details about the method of death.

First Person

Q. If I knew the deceased well, can I write a first-person obituary?

A. Rarely. Obituaries are almost always in the straight news form. Now and then, a reporter may be permitted a personal reminiscence, but this is usually done in a column.

For an example, see **A Small Town, Hit Hard by Recent Tragedies** in *NRW Plus*. A reporter, Christopher Keating, recalls childhood friends who died in the terror bombings.

Localizing Obituaries

Q. Should I try to localize obituaries?

A. Yes, if the person is a resident of your community and died elsewhere or was a former well-known resident. For example:

> John A. Nylic, 68, a retired maintenance worker at General Electric Co., died Friday night after suffering an apparent heart attack while visiting in Lebanon Springs, N.Y.
>
> Mr. Nylic, who lived at 78 W. Housatonic St. . . .
>
> —*The Berkshire Eagle* (Pittsfield, Mass.)

Humorous Obituaries

Q. Must the obituary always be solemn?

A. Most are and should be. Now and then the subject lends himself or herself to lighter treatment. When the screenwriter Al Boasberg died, the lead to his obituary shocked some readers. Others found it appropriate. Boasberg had written many of the gags that were used in the Marx Brothers' movies. Some of his most famous sequences involved death, such as the one of Groucho Marx posing as a doctor taking a patient's pulse and intoning: "Either this man is dead or my watch has stopped." For the lead on Boasberg's obituary, Douglas Gilbert wrote:

The joke's on Al Boasberg. He's dead.

But humor can backfire, even when unintended. When Jorge Mas Canosa, a leader in Miami of the anti-Castro Cuban-American National Foundation, died, the weekly *Tropic* magazine of *The Miami Herald* had a cover photo of his funeral procession. The headline over the photo read "No Mas." (In Spanish, *no mas* means *no more* or *enough.*) The edition was withheld and the following week the headline read "Farewell."

The Specialist

A few newspapers assign specialists to write obituaries. Alden Whitman, for years the master obituary writer for *The New York Times,* was allowed to comment on the personal habits and the accomplishments of his subjects. When he wrote the obituary of Mies van der Rohe, the prophet of an austere modern architectural style, Whitman noted that the architect chose to live on the third floor of an old-fashioned apartment house on Chicago's north side.

In his obituary of André Malraux, the French writer, Whitman wrote that he was "a chain smoker of cheap cigarettes." In his lengthy obituary of the American socialist, Norman Thomas, Whitman said Thomas' socialism "was to Marxism what Musak is to Mozart."

Further Reading

Mitford, Jessica. *The American Way of Death.* New York: Fawcett Crest, 1978.
Whitman, Alden. *The Obituary Book.* New York: Stein and Day, 1971.
Whitman, Alden. *Come to Judgment.* New York: Viking Press, 1980.

Richard Green, *The Californian*

Fleeing robbery suspect.

Preview

Police reporters cover a vast array of news. Their beat calls upon them to handle:

• **Breaking stories:** Accidents, crimes, arrests, fires.

• **Features:** Profiles of police personnel, criminals; stories about police investigations.

• **Interpretative articles:** Law enforcement policies, changes in personnel and procedures.

• **Investigative reporting:** Examination of false arrests, corruption, lax enforcement.

Police news is given prominent play in most newspapers because of its dramatic nature and the fact that so many people are affected. Millions of Americans are victims of crimes each year.

Few beats produce as much news as the police beat, and few reporters are called upon to do as much as quickly as the police reporter. Each day, a dozen or more potential stories develop on the beat. The police reporter covers:

• **Crime:** reports of crime, investigation, arrest, booking, arraignment.

• **Accidents:** traffic, airplane, drowning, rescue.

• **Fires:** reports and on-the-scene coverage.

• **Departmental activity:** coverage of police department personnel, policies, efficiency and accountability.

• **Departmental integrity:** standards, policies and procedures for dealing with internal and external allegations, assumptions and attitudes about corruption that is systemic or sporadic.

• **Other law enforcement agencies:** sheriff's office, state highway patrol, suburban police departments, federal marshals.

The Beat with Everything. "The police beat is about people and what makes them tick, what turns them into homicidal maniacs, what brings out the best in them, what drives them berserk. It has it all: greed, sex, violence, comedy and tragedy. You learn more about people than you would on any other newspaper job."

—*Edna Buchanan,*
The Miami Herald
police reporter

The Range and Cost of Crime

Crime affects everyone, and news of crime interests most of us. One of four households is hit by crime every year, mostly by burglary and theft. One in 35 households is struck by a violent crime—murder, rape, robbery, assault. A rape is committed every 6 minutes, a murder every 34 minutes. We all know someone who has been the victim of some kind of crime.

The number of crime victims approaches 26 million. Of these, a fourth are the victims of violent crimes. The U.S. Department of Justice reports that almost 7 million people were the victims of murder, rape, robbery or assault last year.

Prison officials report that the prison population grew from 300,000 in the mid-1970s to more than 2 million 25 years later. More than 3.5 million are on probation or parole.

The crowded jails and prisons are the result of several converging forces—the public demand for longer sentences, the elimination of parole in some states, the belief that taking criminals off the streets will lower violent crime rates and the imprisonment of increasing numbers of men and women convicted of crimes involving drugs. In 25 years, the number of inmates in prisons for drug offenses went from 1 in 16 inmates to 1 in 5.

The incarceration rate in the United States is 445 per 100,000 population. The rates for other countries—South Africa, 311; England, 97; France, 81; Japan, 45. The prison population in the past decade grew by 168 percent despite a gradual decline in the number of violent crimes.

Fewer Crimes

No one is sure why the crime rate is dropping. One theory is that tougher law enforcement and longer prison sentences are keeping criminals off the streets. Another is that there are fewer men in their 20s, the high-crime age group.

Decline. For a graphic representation of the decreasing number and rate of crimes see **Crime Index Offenses** in *NRW Plus*.

Disorder Theory   Another suggested cause is the increase in what is known as "community-oriented policing." The standard police strategy is "incident-oriented policing," whereby police respond to a call about a crime. This practice permits a crime-permissive environment, some police authorities contend. By moving quickly when windows in a housing project are broken, when loitering youths insult passersby, when graffiti mars stop signs, when playgrounds are vandalized—when the police react to these low-level activities that disrupt public order, more serious crimes decline. Crime, the community sees, is not tolerated. The police presence frightens away the drug dealers. The gangs stop loitering.

When the police began making disorder arrests, as they did in New York, they found the people they arrested were carrying guns and many were wanted on felony warrants.

The "Disorder Theory," as the low tolerance for minor crimes is known, is common police practice now.

Table 20.1 Crime Rate

	Metropolitan Areas	Other Cities	Rural	National Average
Murder	5.9	3.8	3.8	5.5
Forcible rape	33.2	35.2	22.2	32.0
Robbery	173.0	59.9	15.9	144.9
Aggravated assault	349.2	302.5	167.8	323.6
Burglary	754.9	759.2	512.3	728.4
Larceny-theft	2631.9	3125.1	999.7	2475.3
Motor vehicle theft	479.9	199.2	122.3	414.2

Rates per 100,000 residents. From *Crime in the United States.*

Crime Rates by Areas

Traditionally, crimes have been highest in big cities and in the southern states. The growth of suburbs, however, has changed this pattern in some crime categories (see Table 20.1). Good roads, throughways and the bypasses allow for quick getaways for thieves who prey on the suburban areas.

Contrary to accepted wisdom, the large cities in the northeast are not the centers of violent and property crime. The southern states lead in both categories. For a breakdown of these crime rates see **Regional Crime Rates** in *NRW Plus.*

Costs   More than $150 billion is spent each year on the police, and on courts, prisons and jails and the parole and probation systems by cities, states and the federal government.

The cost of confining an inmate can run to $60,000 a year in large cities. And when the public demands, as it has, less probation, more confinement and longer sentences, the costs skyrocket. Handling criminals costs more than $300 a person in taxes.

Interest in Crime News

You might think that over the years of intense crime coverage the public's appetite would reach the saturation point. Not so. Crime news remains high on the media agenda.

Perhaps it is the increasingly bizarre nature of crimes:

• The perfect neighbor who stabbed his next-door neighbor 13 times after she resisted his sexual advances.

• The Mormon church leader who had an entire family executed to protect his standing in the church.

• The teen-ager who persuaded his college classmates to kill his stepfather.

• The lawyer who had his buddies on the police force shoot his wife and dump her and her car into a Chicago canal.

• The widow who rid herself of a series of husbands by feeding them arsenic.

Senseless Murders

Perhaps it is our sympathy for the victims. Daily, we read about and watch coverage in evening newscasts of the deaths of innocent people caught in drive-by shootings, children shot as they cowered in their apartments during drug wars. We read of seemingly senseless stabbings and shootings during holdups:

When the two men demanded his leather jacket and her shearling coat, the couple did not resist.

Alexander Ortiz, 22, took off his jacket. Arlyn Gonzales, 23, terrified, fumbled over a buckle at the collar of her coat. One of the men roughly tugged at her coat.

"Don't do it," Ortiz said. "Don't hurt her. She's pregnant."

In response, one of the men shot Ortiz, once in the throat and once in the left chest.

"C'mon, c'mon, Get her jacket," Ms. Gonzales said the gunman told his associate.

Though fatally wounded, Ortiz spoke to his girlfriend. "I don't want to die. I'm afraid. Take care of the baby for me. Take care of my baby, please." He died two hours later at Jamaica Hospital.

School Fears

Perhaps it is the fear parents live with when they send their children to school. The Bureau of Justice reports 9 percent of students aged 12 to 19 were crime victims in or near their schools over a six-month period; 15 percent said their schools had gangs; 16 percent said a student had attacked or threatened a

Rodolfo Gonzales,
San Antonio Light

Juvenile Crime

Law enforcement agencies devote considerable resources to juvenile crime. Gang membership totals about 650,000; 60 percent of the gang members are concentrated in California, Illinois and Texas.

teacher; 30 percent said marijuana was easy to obtain at school; 9 percent said crack and 11 percent said cocaine were easy to obtain in school; 31 percent said alcohol was easy to obtain.

Among black students in the central cities, 24 percent said they were afraid of being attacked while going to and from school. Three percent of students in central cities reported taking some kind of weapon to school to protect themselves.

The Police

To cope with crime there are almost 600,000 state and local police officers, and efforts are constantly being made to add to police power.

One response to the threat of crime has been the growth of private police, who number about 1.5 million. They guard office buildings, apartment complexes, shopping malls, gated communities and even the streets of some residential communities. Most universities use their own police to monitor campuses.

Those who can afford private protection do so. The commercial and residential areas that cannot afford to do so rely on police forces usually spread thin.

Police Department Organization

The police department is organized around the three police functions—(1) enforcement of laws, (2) prevention of crime and (3) finding and arresting criminals.

The department is headed by a chief or commissioner who is responsible to the mayor, director of public safety or city manager. The chief or commissioner is appointed and although he or she makes departmental policy, broad policy decisions affecting law enforcement come from a superior and are often made in a political context. The chief's second in command may be an assistant chief or inspector. Commissioners have deputy commissioners under them.

The rest of the organizational chart depends upon the size of the city. In large cities, deputy inspectors are put in charge of various divisions or bureaus—homicide, detective, robbery, juvenile, rape, arson, traffic. The larger the city, the more bureaus. As the patterns of criminal activity change, organizational changes are made. These changes make good stories.

The next in command in large cities are captains, who are assigned to run precincts and are assisted by lieutenants. Sergeants are placed in charge of shifts or squads at the precinct house. The private in the organization is the police officer.

The beat reporter's day-to-day contacts are for the most part with sergeants and lieutenants. Reporters, trained to be suspicious of authority, are sometimes irritated by the paramilitary structure, secretiveness and implicit authoritarianism of the police department.

Schooled. "The only education I ever had that amounted to anything was when I was a police reporter on the Lower East Side of New York. One could learn there more about life as it really was than in any formal school."

—Charles E. Russell, reporter and editor in the muckraking period

Diana K. Sugg, a police reporter for *The Sacramento Bee,* circulation 250,000, is blunt: "In most cities around the country, big or small, the cops don't like reporters." Often the reporter and the police work at cross purposes. "We want the information they can't or won't release." Let's accompany Sugg as she works her beat.

Making Her Rounds

Diana K. Sugg

It's 9 a.m. and Sugg is in the police station with her portable police scanner, pager, map and notepad. Some days she takes the sheriff's office first and then the police station.

She flips through the watch summaries of the significant events of the previous day and night. With her scanner buzzing in the background, she carefully reads every page, every notation. "I'm looking for anything strange, anything particularly cruel.

"Once a woman managed to catch a rapist by running into her bathroom with a portable telephone and calling 911. Another time a man tied up three children and then raped their mother in front of them. Or you may find material for a short feature story—like the man named the 'inept robber' by the police because he made four robbery attempts at markets—and made off with only one beer."

She also reads the arrest reports, sometimes as many as 200 a day. For the detailed reports and the watch summaries, her eyes go automatically to the name, age and, she says, "particularly the occupation. A 45-year-old unemployed man arrested for theft isn't much of a story. But a 45-year-old teacher? Why would he need to steal? When you contact him, will he tell you the arrest was a mistake?"

She looks at the section marked "Comments" at the bottom of the arrest sheets for unusual circumstances the officers may note. "Once a man threw a rock through a window and waited for the police to come because he wanted to be arrested—he was homeless and he had AIDS. He figured the jail officers would at least take care of him."

Consulting the Penal Code   Sugg occasionally consults a small handbook, the penal code, as crimes sometimes are listed only by the code number. "That's done to keep reporters from noticing certain arrests," she says.

She makes a point of looking in on the sergeant in charge that day. "Even if things are slow and I don't have anything to ask the sergeant, I always make a point to talk with him, sometimes sharing the hard parts of my job so he could understand why some stories were shorter, or why we weren't interested in covering some.

"During all this checking, the scanner is babbling and my pager is ringing as I am talking with a secretary. It can get nerve-wracking, because I am afraid I might miss something." Her ear is tuned to the code numbers for kidnappings, shootings, homicides, and she knows the police codes, too, those they use when they report they are going to eat, taking a bathroom break or going off duty.

To the Newsroom   Her morning checks completed, Sugg drives to the newsroom with a couple of items to run by her editor to see whether they are worth pursuing. She has to return a phone call to someone who read one of her stories and had something to add to it.

It's noon and she takes a break, her second Mounds bar, a diet Coke, maybe a giant chocolate chip cookie. The *Bee* is a morning paper, and Sugg has the afternoon to continue to gather information, to look deeper into some items, to call people on continuing stories.

Then she's off in the paper's Ford Bronco with her pager, scanner, portable radio, map and notebook. On the way to the scene, she's listening to officers talk to their supervisors. She moves fast. One day while working the night police shift—the newspaper covers the beat 'round the clock—she heard on her scanner a report of a shooting. She was off. On the way to the crime scene she heard officers report that one shooting was fatal, and then a second . . . and then a third. "Within half an hour I was dictating the story of a triple shooting over the portable radio," Sugg says. She made the deadline.

On the Scene   "Neighbors are incredible sources," Sugg says. "Especially if you find the one busybody who watches the street like a hawk and knows everything about the neighbors. People like this know where someone works, the hours he or she keeps, the age of his children, when he was divorced. All this information has to be checked out, but it's a starting point."

Many crimes do not have eyewitnesses, but Sugg looks for the neighbor who heard a shot, a scream. "Once I interviewed a 7-year-old boy who watched a shooting through his apartment window."

She always tries to interview the victims. "Often, when they discover your sincerity they open up and give you unbelievable details." She makes sure to absorb the scene—the ambulance door slamming shut, the smell of the burned house, the cold fog over the scene of the triple shooting.

Smaller-City Coverage

The Sacramento area, like many fast-growing regions, has more than its share of crime, and so crime receives considerable coverage. But even in smaller cities, crime is thoroughly covered. Although these newspapers and stations may not have a regular reporter covering the environment or business, education or county government, all assign a staffer to cover the police on a daily basis.

The items may include "juveniles throwing snowballs in front of the City Center, hindering pedestrians" and "moose on the highway" (*The Times Argus* in Barre-Montpelier, Vt.) and the kidnapping of a scarecrow

Table 20.2 The Most Dangerous Cities in the United States

Violent Crime Rate		Property Crime Rate	
Pine Bluff, Ark.	1,443.6	Miami	6,855.8
Lubbock, Tex.	1,093.6	Pine Bluff, Ark.	6,682.9
Baltimore	1,064.1	Tucson, Ariz.	6,213.1
Tallahassee, Fla.	1,049.1	Alexandria, La.	6,209.8
Miami	1,027.4	Albuquerque, N.M.	6,093.1
Memphis	1,006.1	Amarillo, Tex.	6,076.5
Gainesville, Fla.	998.0	Gainesville, Fla.	6,024.0
Nashville	973.3	Monroe, La.	5,990.4
Albuquerque, N.M.	945.7	Tacoma, Wash.	5,973.6
Los Angeles	944.4	Oklahoma City	5,829.5

Rates per 100,000 residents. From *Crime in the United States*.

"value $15" (*The Quincy Herald-Whig* in western Illinois). In larger cities they will include the following items from a daily listing in the *Argus Leader* in Sioux Falls, S.D.:

Police Log

VANDALISM: Vandals spray-painted a pentagon, a pitchfork and assorted other graffiti on the Knights of Columbus hall at 315 N. Summit Ave. on Monday, police said. The graffiti, which was found on the back wall of the hall, caused $50 damage.

VANDALISM: Vandals uprooted a fence post and threw display items such as wooden geese into the Laurel Oaks Pool at 3401 E. 49th St. on Saturday or Sunday, police said. The damage amounted to $100.

VANDALISM: A 57-year-old Sioux Falls man told police someone broke the windshield on his 1970 Ford Galaxy with rocks while it was parked at 1021 W. Bailey Ave. on Saturday, police said. Jerome K. Salwei, 521 S. Ebenezer Ave., said the damage amounted to $250, police said.

VANDALISM: Someone broke the left headlight, removed the hood ornament and scratched and dented the driver's side of a 1984 Cadillac El Dorado, causing $725 damage, on Friday or Saturday, police said. The car's owner, Alvin R. Clausen, 69, 816 W. 15th St., said he wasn't sure where the vandalism occurred.

AGGRAVATED ASSAULT: A 15-year-old boy and his 14-year-old friend told police three boys pulled what resembled a black automatic handgun on them as they rode their bikes on Westview Road from their homes to a convenience store and back Friday, police said. The "handgun" turned out to be a squirt gun.

AGGRAVATED ASSAULT: A 16-year-old Sioux Falls girl told police that her ex-boyfriend slapped and punched her on the back of her head and then struck her with a green garden hose May 31, police said. The girl said the assault occurred at her ex-boyfriend's residence in the 3300 block of South Holly Avenue and was not the first time he had struck her, police said. No arrest was made.

New on the Beat

Editors like to assign their younger reporters to the police beat in the belief there is no faster way to test a reporter's ability and to teach him or her about the city. The new police reporter immediately becomes acquainted with the organization of the police department and sets about making contacts with key officers.

With the Police: Drugs, Teens, Death

Randy Piland, *The Macon* (Ga.) *Telegraph*

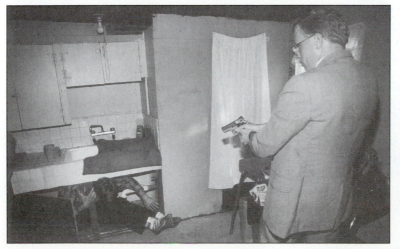

Other photos: Rodger Mallison, *Fort Worth Star-Telegram*

Survival depends on establishing a routine and developing good sources. Otherwise the police beat can become an impenetrable maze, and the reporter may be given only the information that the department deigns to hand out.

The new police reporter quickly learns the difference between a minor crime, which can be a violation or misdemeanor, and a major crime, a felony. Stealing a scarecrow may violate a city regulation, but stealing $10,000 from the local A&P is a felony as defined in state law. Misdemeanors are punishable by less than a year in jail and/or a fine, whereas felonies send the convicted perpetrator to the state prison, or a federal prison, for more than a year.

Types of Felonies

There are seven types of felonies, which fall into two general categories, not including the so-called possessory felonies involving weapons and drugs.

- **Violent crime:** murder, rape, robbery, aggravated assault.
- **Property crime:** burglary, larceny-theft, motor-vehicle theft.

The FBI keeps crime data in these categories, as do local police. Ten percent of all felonies are violent and 90 percent are crimes against property.

Sources Are Essential

Police reporters depend on inside sources. Without them—given the guarded nature of the police—the reporter has a hard time covering the beat. This is why big-city media keep at least one reporter on the police beat for years. It takes time to cultivate the police.

Edna Buchanan of *The Miami Herald* is a veteran of the beat. "I talk to cops a lot," she says. "Talking to cops is the only way to get a lot of the stories I do. Of course, a lot of policemen don't recognize a good story, so you just have to keep talking to them so it'll come up in conversation."

Many police departments have gone to computerized reports which, Buchanan says, require that the officers only fill in blanks. The old reports, handwritten by arresting officers, had color and the officers' comments. What this means, Buchanan says, is that reporters have to go to "hands-on, person-to-person human contacts." She recalls learning about a robbery where "a guy got robbed and knocked down. No big deal." But she learned from a contact that the victim had artificial legs and was pushed off his legs "for something like a dollar and forty cents."

Crime Coverage Changes

"If it bleeds, it leads" is an old newsroom guide to handling crime stories. But in recent years the media's hot pursuit of tabloid crime has resulted in re-assessments of crime coverage. Instead of concentrating on headline-type crimes, the suggestions center on examining crime prevention policies and the effectiveness of the criminal justice system.

Background. Profiles of those arrested show that most had a history of crime—65 percent had served time or had been sentenced to probation. Two-thirds were regular drug users. At the time of arrest, half tested positive for drug use. Almost half said they had been in substance abuse programs.

David Simon, crime reporter for *The Baltimore Sun,* wants crime reporting to cover substantive issues—the effectiveness of drug legislation, the crime bills introduced in Congress and state legislatures, the effect of crime in the minority community.

One Station's Response

At KVUE-TV in Austin, Tex., the station decided to respond to complaints of viewers about crime coverage. Viewers told management they were tired of "seeing violent crimes that didn't affect them." Michelle Kemkes, a news producer at the station, said viewers called such coverage "sensation crime reporting." They asked for "responsible and balanced reporting," she said.

Guidelines   The station responded by setting up the following guidelines. "If we can't answer yes to one of these questions, we don't report the story," she said:

1. Is there an immediate threat to the public?
2. Is there a threat to children?
3. Does someone need to take action?
4. Does the crime have a significant impact on the community?
5. Is there a crime prevention element?

Kemkes said that the approach differed from what she was taught in journalism school about covering crime. "We didn't learn to put our stories in perspective, but that's what everyone in the newsroom is learning now."

Application   She describes a crime story the station covered:

A husband shoots his wife, child and then himself at the University of Texas. We send a crew, and they call back with all the facts. We go through the guidelines and none of them seem to fit. The suspect is dead, so there's no threat to children or the public. Viewers don't need to take any kind of action, and it's definitely not about crime prevention. We try "significant community impact." None of the neighbors knew the family because they had just moved into their apartment. So, on the 5:30 p.m. news we didn't report the story. Other stations led with the story, which made me think twice about what I'd done.

Then our crew dug deeper. That night the apartment complex held a community meeting to talk about what happened and if they could have stopped it. Obviously this crime did have an impact on the neighbors, and that was the story we went with at 10.

Another story that generated heated discussion in the newsroom—the man who opened fire on a schoolyard of kindergartners in Scotland, killing 17 and then killing himself. How could I not run this heartbreaking story? Once again we applied the guidelines. I found out that this was a huge crime for Great Britain: only one percent of their crimes are committed with guns, compared with the U.S., in which about 32 percent of crimes involve guns. This was the bigger story.

The Arrest Process

Jails, Prisons. Jails are locally administered and hold persons who are awaiting trial or sentence or are serving sentences of a year or less. Prisons, state and federal, hold inmates with sentences of more than a year.

The police reporter knows arrest procedures, and because on some smaller newspapers and on many radio and television stations the same reporter who covers an arrest might stay with the case through the trial, a knowledge of the criminal court process is necessary, too. Here, we will discuss the arrest process. In the next chapter, criminal court procedures are outlined.

A person may be arrested on sight or upon issuance of a warrant. Let us follow a case in which a merchant spots in his store a man he believes robbed him the previous week.

The store owner calls a police officer who arrests the man. The suspect is searched on the scene and taken to the station house. The suspect is then searched again in front of the booking desk. His property is recorded and placed in a "property" envelope. The suspect's name and other identification and the alleged crime are recorded in a book known to old-time reporters as a *blotter*. (The blotter supposedly takes its name from the work of turn-of-the-century police sergeants who spilled considerable ink in their laborious efforts to transcribe information and then had to sop up the splotches with a blotter.)

Miranda Warning The police are required to tell a suspect at the time of arrest that he has the right to remain silent and to refuse to answer questions. (This is called the Miranda warning.) He also has the right to consult an attorney at any time and is told that if he cannot afford a lawyer one will be provided. Unless the suspect waives these rights, his statements cannot be used against him at his trial.

The signed waiver permits the police immediately to interrogate the suspect about his actions, background and whereabouts in connection with the crime. If it is a homicide case, the practice is to call in an assistant prosecutor to ensure the admissibility of any admission or confession.

The officer then prepares an arrest report, which is written in the presence of the suspect who also supplies "pedigree information"—age, height, weight, date and place of birth and other details.

The Complaint The suspect may then be photographed and fingerprinted and he'll be permitted to make a telephone call. A record is made of the number and person called and the suspect is returned to a detention cell to await arraignment. The arresting officer goes to the complaint room to confer with the victim and an assistant district attorney so that a complaint can be drawn up. The police officer may ask the complainant to identify the suspect again in a lineup.

The assistant district attorney has to decide whether the case is strong enough, the witness reliable, the offense worth prosecuting before a complaint is drawn. The prosecutor must also decide whether to reduce a felony charge to a

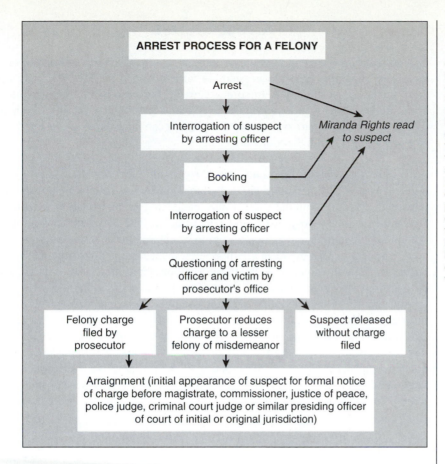

ARREST PROCESS FOR A FELONY

Arrest

Interrogation of suspect by arresting officer

Miranda Rights read to suspect

Booking

Interrogation of suspect by arresting officer

Questioning of arresting officer and victim by prosecutor's office

Felony charge filed by prosecutor

Prosecutor reduces charge to a lesser felony of misdemeanor

Suspect released without charge filed

Arraignment (initial appearance of suspect for formal notice of charge before magistrate, commissioner, justice of peace, police judge, criminal court judge or similar presiding officer of court of initial or original jurisdiction)

The Arrest Process

The police reporter covers all aspects of the arrest process, from the report of the arrest through the arraignment of the suspect. Most arrests receive bare mention, but the high-profile crimes are covered fully. Reporters rely for information on the police, the district attorney and the suspect's lawyer. The reporter is aware that the original charge often is reduced by the prosecutor because either the original charge cannot be sustained or the prosecutor believes the suspect is more likely to plead guilty to a lessened charge than he or she would to the original charge.

lesser felony or to a misdemeanor. She may reduce the charge if she feels the reduction would lead to a guilty plea and thus avoid the expense of a trial for the prosecution.

The police officer may have to file additional reports. If he fired his weapon, he must file an "unusual incident report," as it is described in some jurisdictions, and if he shot someone, he files an "inspector's report."

The fingerprints are checked in a central state agency to determine whether the suspect has a record, and the suspect's file is sent to the courts, which require the information before arraignment. The presiding judge decides whether bail should be set and the amount. A suspect with no record who is arrested for a minor crime may be released on his own recognizance—that is, without putting up bail.

Most large cities have overcrowded detention facilities and a backlog of untried cases. To cope, they may release suspects on low bail or none at all. Later, plea bargaining may be arranged in which the defendant agrees to plead guilty to a lesser charge so that the case can be disposed of at arraignment (see Chapter 21).

Arrest Stories

Most crimes are committed by young men, and a growing number involve teen-agers. Juveniles who are arrested are turned over to the juvenile court and their names are not released. In some states, in response to the rise in violent crime by youngsters, serious offenses by youths, particularly murder, are handled by the regular court system and their names can be used, as an upstate New York newspaper did in the following crime.

Murder The battered body of a 77-year-old man was discovered in his home at 11 P.M. by a neighbor who called the police. The neighbor said she saw two youths running from the scene. Police conducted an investigation and within five hours arrested a 16-year-old and a 14-year-old. The two were charged with second-degree murder and at their arraignment entered pleas of not guilty.

The reporter for the local afternoon newspaper learns all this on his 7 A.M. check. He calls the coroner to obtain information about the cause of death, and he questions the police about the murder weapon and the motivation. He also asks where the youths are being held and the time they were arrested. With the information on hand, he calls his desk to report what he has and the city editor tells him to give the story 200 words. The dead man was not prominent.

The editor asks about the neighbor: Did she identify the youngsters, and if not, how did the police learn their identities? The reporter says the police will not comment about the neighbor. Nor will the neighbor talk. The story will have to be a straight murder-and-arrest piece. Here is how the reporter wrote it:

Two Saratoga youths were arrested early today and charged with the murder of 77-year-old Anthony Hay, a local fuel oil and coal dealer, whose battered body was found last night in his home.

Police identified the youths as Arthur Traynor, 16, of 61 Joshua Ave., and John Martinez, 14, of 15 Doten Ave. Police said a neighbor saw two youths fleeing from Hay's residence at 342 Nelson Ave. The arrests were made within five hours of the slaying.

The youths entered pleas of not guilty at their arraignment this morning on charges of second-degree murder and were being held in the county jail pending a preliminary hearing.

Hay's body was found at 11 p.m. in the business office of his home. He was "badly beaten about the head and face and had a fractured skull," Coroner Clark Donaldson reported. Police said they recovered the death weapon, a three-foot wooden club. They declined to give any motive for the slaying.

Caution: Be careful about identifying the arrested. A libel suit resulted when a newspaper identified a crime suspect who had stolen a wallet from which police took the name. "Use special care in reporting the arrest of a public figure," advises the AP. "It is not uncommon for crime suspects to give police false names, and frequently those they provide are from sports figures, politicians, etc." Press authorities for authentication of the identification.

Be especially careful about identifying anyone as a suspect before the person has been formally charged. This had been common practice until a suspect in a bombing at the 1996 summer Olympics in Atlanta filed suit against the media that used his name in their accounts. *The Atlanta Journal-Constitution*

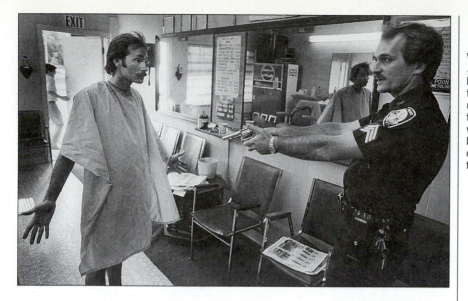

reported the man had become a suspect and NBC and CNN picked up the story. Three months later, he was cleared. Rather than have to fight a libel suit, the networks settled out of court for large sums, but the newspaper claimed it accurately quoted authorities. The newspaper would not settle out-of-court and won its case when a court ruled that the suspect was a public figure and that the newspaper had not been malicious in naming him, a key element in bringing a successful libel suit against a public figure.

In Dallas, a woman who named two football players on the Dallas Cowboys team as having raped her was later charged with perjury. But the police department had released the names of the players to the media and they were the subject of massive coverage. The police later announced a policy of not identifying suspects until they are arrested or charged.

Crime Classification

Crimes are classified as violations, misdemeanors or felonies. The classifications are made by the states and differ slightly from state to state. Generally, the length of the sentence and the fine determine the classification. Violations are low-level crimes, punishable by small fines or short jail terms—loitering, committing a public nuisance. Misdemeanors are more serious and can lead to a jail sentence of less than a year—petty larceny, minor burglaries, traffic offenses.

Felonies are serious crimes punishable by a sentence of more than a year in a state prison. These crimes are the subject of most police reporting. They include murder, rape, robbery, arson, assault with a deadly weapon, burglary and motor vehicle theft.

Hate Crimes

In 1990, in response to growing concern over bias crimes, Congress passed a law requiring the U.S. attorney general to collect data "about crimes that manifest evidence of prejudice based on race, religion, sexual orientation or ethnicity."

A recent year showed 8,152 incidents, with California leading the nation, reporting 1,942 incidents. Most incidents involved anti-black actions and anti-Jewish actions.

For a breakdown of these offenses, see **Hate Crimes** in *NRW Plus.*

Murder

In some areas, murder is rare—Vermont may have two homicides a year. When one is reported, coverage is intense. In metropolitan areas, where one to three murders are reported each day, only the prominence of the victim or the suspect merit full-scale coverage. Prominence clearly was the news value that motivated the minute coverage of the death of O. J. Simpson's ex-wife—not hers, of course, but his. Look at how the AP wrote the first lead on the discovery of the bodies:

> LOS ANGELES, (AP)—Hall of Fame football player O. J. Simpson's ex-wife and a man were found dead early Monday outside the woman's condominium, and Simpson was being interviewed by police.

This began what some critics described as a "media circus" or a "media feeding frenzy." Journalists countered by pointing to the near-insatiable public appetite for the story.

Story leads about the progress of the investigation and then the arrest of Simpson are in **O. J. Simpson** in *NRW Plus.*

Table 20.3 Murder and Non-negligent Manslaughter Rates

Metropolitan Areas		States	
New Orleans	20.4	Louisiana	12.5
Pine Bluff, Ark.	16.5	Mississippi	9.0
Shreveport, La.	15.8	Maryland	8.1
Memphis	14.6	New Mexico	7.4
Savannah, Ga.	13.9	Alabama	7.4
Baltimore	12.2	Illinois	7.2
Montgomery, Ala.	12.2	Tennessee	7.2
Birmingham, Ala.	11.8	North Carolina	7.0
Columbus, Ga.	11.5	Michigan	6.7
Greenville, N.C.	11.3	Nevada	6.5

Rates per 100,000 residents. From *Crime in the United States.*

Checklist: Homicide

Crime

___ Victim, identification.

___ Time, date, place of death.

___ Weapon used.

___ Official cause of death or authoritative comment.

___ Who discovered body.

___ Clues; any identification of slayer.

___ Police comments; motivation for crime.

___ Comments from neighbors, friends.

___ Any police record for victim; any connection with criminal activity.

___ Consequences to victim's family, others.

Arrest

___ Name, identification of person arrested.

___ Victim's name; time, date, place of crime.

___ Exact charge.

___ Circumstances of arrest.

___ Motive.

___ Result of tip, investigation.

___ Officers involved in investigation, arrest.

___ Booking.

___ Arraignment; bail, if any.

___ Suspect's police record (in states where it is not illegal to publish such information).

Homicide

Jose Flores, a foreman on a California strawberry farm, was furious when Mauricio Cruz picked some green berries. They argued. Flores went home and returned with a gun. Witnesses say he then shot Cruz in the back and while the worker was lying on the ground, he shot Cruz in the head. Flores fled and the sheriff's department in Santa Cruz County issued this poster.

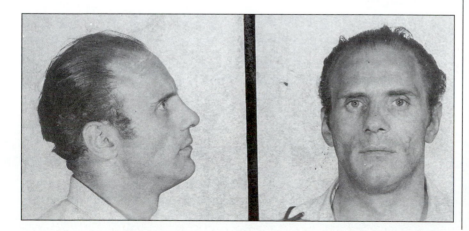

Mug Shot

After a suspect is arrested, booked and interrogated, he or she is photographed. The pictures, called *mug shots,* go into the suspect's file, which also contains his or her criminal record, known as a *rap sheet.* This is a photo of Joseph (Crazy Joe) Gallo, whose rap sheet showed an extensive record. Gallo was gunned down by rival mob hit men as he celebrated his 43rd birthday in Umberto's Clam House a block away from New York City police headquarters.

Burglary, Robbery

Burglary (B) is a crime against property, usually involving a home, office, or store break-in. Robbery (R) is a crime against a person, involving the removal of the person's goods or money with force or threat of force and is categorized as a violent crime.

Checklist: Burglary, Robbery

Crime

___ Victim, identification.

___ Goods or money taken; value of goods.

___ Date, time, location of crime.

___ (R) Weapon used.

___ (B) How entry made.

___ (R) Injuries and how caused.

___ Clues.

___ Unusual circumstances (overlooked valuables, frequency of crime in area or to victim, etc.).

___ Statements from victim, witness.

Arrest

___ Name, identification of person arrested.

___ Details of crime.

___ Circumstances of arrest.

Additional Elements   Some newspapers and stations have added these essentials to their stories about violent crime:

___ Where was the weapon obtained?

___ Were alcohol or drugs involved?

___ Did the victim and the perpetrator know each other?

Note: Half or more of those arrested are not formally charged with the crime for which they were arrested. The names of those arrested but not charged can be used without worrying about legal action. The question is one of fairness.

Crime Coverage and Race

High crime rates in the inner cities have led to considerable coverage of the perpetrators and the victims, who are mostly members of minority groups. And this, in turn, has been the cause of criticism of the media.

One area of controversy has been racial profiling, the police practice of using race as a significant factor in stop-and-search activities. For an analysis of this practice see **Racial Profiling** in *NRW Plus*.

For a case study of how a reporter went about exposing racism practiced by a police department see **Targeting Blacks** in *NRW Plus*.

Database Reporting

Police departments keep good records, and most are available to reporters online. It is not difficult, for example, to take the list that the state provides of all school bus drivers and correlate that list with the names of those arrested in a given period. Reporters regularly do this to check whether child molesters, drunk drivers or felons are driving children to and from school.

Drunk Drivers   You know drunk drivers are involved in traffic accidents. But how many of them are responsible for highway fatalities in your state? Easy. Ask the U.S. Department of Transportation, www.dot.gov, for the percentage of fatalities in the state in accidents involving alcohol. The DOT's National Highway Traffic Safety Administration keeps the data.

You'll find Texas, Louisiana, Alaska, North Dakota, Nevada, New Mexico and Washington are high in the rankings, usually with more than half the fatal accidents involving drivers with a blood alcohol content of .10 or higher.

And that takes you to another story. If many fatal traffic accidents involve drunk drivers, perhaps the state should clamp down on those drivers. Many states have lowered the acceptable blood alcohol content to .08 and have increased the penalties. What is your state doing? You can find out by using another website, www.hwysafety.org, the Insurance Institute for Highway Safety.

Police Efficiency

How well the local police force does its work can be checked by using a few figures: What percentage of reported crimes led to arrests? Another comparison: What percentage of arrests led to complaints filed by the district attorney? Prosecutors will not take a case unless the police provide them with sufficient evidence and solid witness support.

Can a force be too forceful? Using databases with police figures, *The Washington Post* found that District of Columbia police killed more people per capita than any other police force. Its series on quick-trigger cops won a Pulitzer Prize for public service.

Another check of departmental efficiency can be made by examining the response to calls made to the police. A study of 2,000 calls to the St. Louis Police Department found that 25 percent of the calls were ignored. Of the 75 percent to which the police responded, arrests were made 50 percent of the time. Ten percent of those arrested went to trial, and 4 percent of those arrested were convicted.

Arrests. The states with the highest rates of arrests for rape were Delaware, Michigan, Alaska, Missouri and Mississippi.

The states with the highest arrest rates for offenses against the family and children were Ohio, New Jersey, New Mexico, Hawaii and Mississippi.

Data Available

Along with their monitoring of individual crimes, police reporters keep track of crime patterns. Are certain types of crimes increasing, others decreasing? How does the city's crime rate compare with cities of the same size? Is there a relationship between drug and alcohol use and crime?

Data of this sort is available from several sources, much of it broken down by cities and states. The National Criminal Justice Reference Service e-mail, askncjrs@ncjrs.org, fields questions of all kinds. Its files contain extensive information on criminal justice.

The FBI publishes an annual report, Crime in the United States, Uniform Crime Reports, which is also available online at www.fbi.gov/ucr.CIUS/02CRIME/02CRIME2.PDF. (Insert the year for which you want the data.) The material includes total number of crimes and crime rates by state and city.

The Bureau of Justice Statistics makes available free copies of its reports that cover a wide range: national crime surveys, domestic violence, parole and probation, ages of rape victims, sentencing patterns, juvenile crime.

To be placed on the Bureau's mailing list, call toll-free 1-800-732-3277 or write: Justice Statistics Clearinghouse, P.O. Box 179, Dept. BJS-236, Annapolis Junction, MD 20701-0179. The website is www.ojp.usdoj.gov/bjs/.

Single copies are free. Public-use tapes of Bureau data sets are available from the Criminal Justice Archive and Information Network, P.O. Box 1248, Ann Arbor, MI 48106, telephone (313) 763-5010.

The Bureau also makes crime and justice data and a wide range of its publications available on CD-ROM, which can be purchased for $15 a CD. Order through the Maryland address.

The Victims

Crime falls heaviest on the poor, the young and members of minority groups. Half the victims of violent crimes are aged 12 to 24 although they represent only a fourth of the population. Blacks and Hispanics across all age groups are more at risk from violence than whites of comparable age: 1 in 30 blacks, 1 in 35 Hispanics, 1 in 58 whites.

Murder rates for blacks are 8 times higher than that for whites—1 in every 894 blacks, 1 in every 7,334 whites. The lifetime chance of being a murder victim is 1 in 131 for white males, 1 in 21 for black males. Blacks and Hispanics have robbery rates twice those for whites.

Reporters have studied victimization rates in their communities. In St. Louis, they found 1 in 13 black males will be murdered by age 45. In Philadelphia, the *Daily News* examined 433 murders committed in one year and found 340 of the victims were black. The city's black population amounted to 39 percent of the total population but 78.5 percent of the murder victims were black. Half the victims were 16 to 31, and 84 of the 89 victims under 20 years of age were black.

The *News* found the murder rate in a white working-class neighborhood was 2, but in the predominantly poor, black north Philadelphia area it was 66. In the heart of the black area known as the Badlands the rate was more than 100 per 100,000 residents.

Two-thirds of murder victims are killed by firearms, most by handguns.

Violence against Women

About 2.5 million women are the victims of violent crime each year. The most frequent crime committed against them is assault, often domestic assault. Studies by the Bureau of Justice found that the women "most vulnerable as the victims of violence are black, Hispanic, in younger age groups, never married, with lower family income and lower education levels and in central cities."

More than two-thirds of the women victims knew their attackers. Almost one-third of the attackers were husbands, boyfriends, or relatives; a third were acquaintances. Women victimized by strangers were six times more likely to report their attack to police as were those women attacked by relatives or friends. These women said they feared reprisals from their attackers.

Although the violent crime victimization rate for males has declined, the rate for females has not.

"In general," states the Bureau, "violent crime against women was primarily intra-racial. Eight of 10 violent crimes against white women were perpetrated by white offenders. Similarly, nine of 10 violent victimizations sustained by black women were committed by black offenders."

Rape

More than 350,000 rapes and sexual assaults are reported a year. Only about half the women report their victimizations to the police. The Bureau of Justice found about half of all rapes were perpetrated by someone known to the victim and that in one-fifth of the cases the offender was armed.

Table 20.4 Forcible Rape Rate

Metropolitan Areas		States	
Rapid City, S. D.	104.7	Alaska	79.3
Waco, Tex.	84.2	New Mexico	50.7
Pine Bluff, Ark.	81.5	Michigan	50.6
Anchorage	74.7	Washington	46.4
Kalamazoo–Battle Creek, Mich.	74.4	Florida	44.2
Bryan, College Station, Tex.	71.6	Nevada	43.0
Benton Harbor, Mich.	71.5	New Hampshire	42.2
Gainesville, Fla.	68.6	Oklahoma	41.2
Redding, Calif.	68.4	South Dakota	40.4
Beaumont, Tex.	66.7	Rhode Island	39.3

Rates per 100,000 residents. From *Crime in the United States*.

"Of female rape victims who took some self-protective action such as fighting back and yelling and screaming, most reported that it helped the situation rather than made it worse," the Bureau reported.

The Bureau estimates that one in six rape victims is under the age of 12. Of the 14 states that reported the age of the victim, Florida reported a total of 7,280 rapes, 14 percent of them of girls under age 11; Michigan, 4,731 rapes, 28 percent under age 11; Pennsylvania, 2,996 rapes, 14 percent under age 13; North Carolina, 2,397 rapes, 20 percent under age 16; South Carolina, 2,193 rapes, 16 percent under age 13. (States reported differently on age data.)

Of the states reporting, one in three rape victims was under age 13 in Delaware, Michigan and North Dakota; under 16 in Nebraska, Pennsylvania and Wisconsin; under 17 in Alabama; under 18 in Idaho and Washington, D.C.

See *NRW Plus* "**Cracking An Unsolved Rape Case Makes History**" for an article on how DNA was used in California.

Domestic Violence

The home, figures tell us, is more dangerous for women than the streets. Domestic violence is the single greatest cause of injury to American women. The American Medical Association considers family violence a public health menace and estimates it affects one-fourth of all families in the United States. The AMA reports domestic violence is responsible for a third of all murders of women.

Yet, coverage of the subject is minimal, lost in the reporting of murders, gang wars and drug busts. Also, the actual dimension of the crime is not reflected in the police reports. Close to half of all incidents of domestic violence

Child Abuse. The Justice Department reported child abuse and neglect reports tripled over the past decade, rising from one million to three million. The department said studies link the victims of child abuse and neglect to future delinquency and adult criminality.

Idaho, Alaska and Washington have the highest rates of physical and sexual child abuse.

Behind Closed Doors

Domestic abuse is the silent plague of American households. Half the occurrences are not reported to police, and journalists rarely cover the crime. Yet it affects about a quarter of households and is the single greatest cause of injury to women.

Donna Ferrato, *Domestic Abuse Awareness Project*

against women are not reported to police. Of married women not reporting their husbands, 41 percent were subsequently assaulted by them within six months. Of those who did report their husbands, 15 percent were reassaulted.

A Reporter's Perspective

Edna Buchanan, the prizewinning police reporter for *The Miami Herald,* says:

Sometimes, we are all the victim has got.

Sometimes you feel like Wonder Woman, or Superman, going to the rescue. Reporters can find missing kids, lost grandmothers, and misplaced corpses. We fish out people who fall through the cracks. Publicity rescues people tangled in the hopeless mazes of government and bureaucracy. We recover stolen cars and priceless family heirlooms. A story in the newspaper can secure donations of blood, money, and public support—and occasionally that rarest gift of all: justice.

Cynicism   Police reporters say cynicism comes with the job. Things are seldom what they seem. A heartbroken father tells police a hitchhiker he picked up forced him out of his car at gunpoint and drove off with his 2-year-old daughter in the back seat. A distraught mother reports her 4-year-old daughter and 2-year-old son disappeared in a department store on Christmas Eve. Newspapers and television carry the woman's prayer for the safe return of her children.

Two days after the hitchhiker story is played up by newspapers and television, the child's body is found in a garbage bin. The father is charged with second-degree murder; authorities say he left the child in the car on a hot day and she was asphyxiated.

Two days after a mother's tearful prayer on TV, this lead appears on a story in a New York newspaper:

Two small Queens children whose mother had reported losing them in a crowded Flushing department store on Christmas Eve were found dead in a rubblestrewn lot in East Harlem last night, and the mother and a man with whom she lives were charged with the murders.

Hardened   Reporters say it is difficult not to become calloused by the endless array of tragedy and senseless, vicious crimes. Elinor J. Brecher of *The Courier-Journal* in Louisville, Ky., moved to features after five years on the police beat. She decided to move after she covered the murder of an elderly shopkeeper. The behavior of onlookers bothered her.

"If the senseless death of an innocent human being means no more to people than the fantasy television deaths they gorge on daily, I wanted no further part of it."

Meaningless. ". . . the media have done an increasingly poor job of developing a balance between what is interesting and what is important. This is the difference between a crime story and crime coverage, between a story about yet another anecdotal crime and one that identifies the anecdote as either representative of a trend or representative of absolutely nothing."
—*David J. Krajicek* (*"Scooped! Media Miss Real Story on Crime While Chasing Sex, Sleaze, and Celebrities," Columbia University Press, 1998.*)

Buchanan has covered 5,000 murders, and many affect her: A young father had spent six months at the bedside of his 2-year-old, who had gone into a coma after strangling herself in a recliner chair. He finally could endure no more and shot the child to death as he rocked her in his arms. The man was sent to prison with a mandatory 25-year sentence. Buchanan remains on the beat.

Cautions

Garish details of rapes, homicides, suicides and assaults are considered unnecessary. Details essential to an investigation are not used, although there is no legal prohibition against using information obtained legally. Usually, police will not give reporters confessions, statements, admissions, or alibis by suspects; names of suspects or witnesses; details of sex crimes against women. (Publication of a confession or statement can jeopardize a defendant's rights.)

Double Checks All names, addresses, occupations should be double-checked against the city directory, telephone book and any other available source.

Beware of sudden cleanup drives for vice, gambling. Usually, they are designed for public consumption.

When the police arrest a suspect, reporters ask for his or her arrest record or rap sheet. In many cities and states, the record may be denied or only a portion of it released. Sometimes the refusal is the result of state law. There has been a growing sensitivity among officials concerning the need to guarantee the accused a fair trial. Revelations about past crimes might compromise the defendant's rights.

Using Prior Convictions Conviction data—information about a guilty plea, a conviction, or a plea of *nolo contendere*—usually can be used. Half the states make it illegal to use nonconviction data.

State laws that seal arrest records take precedence over sunshine laws. Where there are no explicit prohibitions against the use of such records, it is permissible to use them, whatever the disposition of the arrests. Reporters can use nonconviction information that they find in public documents that are traditionally open to the press: court records of judicial proceedings, police blotters, published court opinions, wanted announcements, traffic records.

Causes. Studies show that 75 percent of violent juvenile offenders have suffered abuse by a family member and more than 60 percent of juveniles in custody have parents who abused alcohol or drugs. Says John J. DiIulio, Jr., of Princeton, "Very bad boys come disproportionately from very bad homes in very bad neighborhoods."

Juvenile Records Juvenile records usually are sealed, and family court rules almost always prohibit press coverage. But there are few state laws that make it illegal to identify a juvenile as a suspect or that prohibit stories about a juvenile's conviction. Generally, the press has gone along with the contention that such publicity could make rehabilitation of the young offender more difficult.

When a 9-year-old boy turned himself in to the FBI as a bank robbery suspect, newspapers and television stations gave the story huge play. The youngster, who took $118 from a teller, held what looked like a pistol.

The newspapers and stations were unhappy about using the story but said they had no recourse. It was "pointless" not to publish a picture of the youngster, said the metropolitan editor of *The New York Times,* that was already "on television all over town."

Remember: An arrest is just that. It does not mean that the person has been charged with a crime. Charges are brought by the district attorney and indictments are made by a grand jury. When a person is arrested, the reporter can write that Jones was "arrested in connection with the robbery of a drugstore at 165 Massachusetts Ave." Or: "Jones was arrested in an investigation of the embezzlement of $45,000 from the First National Bank of Freeport."

The U.S. Department of Justice has found that half the arrests are disposed of prior to indictment.

Covering Campus Crime

A federal law requires colleges to release statistics on crimes on campus by October 1 each year. The figures are available to the public.

Data collected over the past several years show a continued increase in arrests for sex offenses, burglaries, robberies, motor vehicle thefts and hate crimes. Drug arrests increased significantly, violations of liquor laws increased slightly. A recent compilation showed that Michigan State University and the University of Michigan had the most arrests for violations of liquor laws. The University of California at Berkeley and the University of Maine had the most drug arrests.

Michigan State police say that most of the liquor arrests occur during the football season and involve visitors. About a third of the arrests occur on a game day, and two-thirds of those arrested are visitors.

Data Available

The U.S. Department of Education maintains a Web site that includes reported criminal offenses for more than 6,300 public and private colleges and universities. The institutions provide criminal offenses that have been reported to campus security authorities and to local police agencies. The Department of Education Web site is www.ope.ed.gov/security for campus crime data.

Table 20.5 Violent Crimes and Rape on Campus

Violent Crimes		Forcible Rape	
University of Maryland	32	University of Wisconsin at Madison	19
Arizona State Univ.	29	Univ. Calif. at Los Angeles	8
Univ. Calif. at Los Angeles	29	Colorado State University	8
Univ. Calif. at Riverside	29	Indiana University	7
Univ. Mass. at Amherst	29	Arizona State Univ.	6
Ohio State University	27	Boston University	6
Univ. Calif. at Irvine	27	James Madison University	6
Florida A&M Univ.	26	University of Maryland	6
Michigan State Univ.	26	Northern Arizona University	6
S.W. Louisiana Univ.	26	Eight schools	5

Number of offenses reported to police and campus authorities. From *Crime in the United States.*

Open Records

In 1998, as part of the Higher Education Act, all schools, public and private, that receive federal funds were asked to:

1. Maintain daily logs of criminal incidents reported to their police or security offices. The nature, date, time, location and disposition of each complaint must be added to the log within two business days of the initial report, and any further information learned after the initial report also must be disclosed within two days of its availability. The logs must be open for 60 days and available to the public. Thereafter, the logs must be opened within two business days of a request.

2. Make annual reports on the following crimes: murder and non-negligent manslaughter, sex offenses (forcible and nonforcible), robbery, aggravated assault, burglary, arson, and motor vehicle theft. Statistics are also required for those arrested or referred to campus courts for violations of the laws regarding liquor use and possession, drug and weapon possession.

The report must also indicate whether any incident or any crime involving bodily injury was the result of a hate crime. The hate crime must be categorized as the result of prejudice based on race, religion, gender, sexual orientation, ethnicity or disability.

The new regulations stress the responsibility of all campus officials, not only those directly involved with security, for reporting incidents and crimes they handle: deans, director of athletics, faculty advisers to student groups, coaches.

Crime statistics for each campus that reports are available online at http://ope.ed.gov/security.

A college that deliberately misrepresents any crime data is subject to a fine.

Table 20.6 Car Thefts and Property Crimes on Campus

Car Thefts		Property Crimes	
Georgia Inst. Technology	80	University of Michigan	1,605
Univ. Calif. at Northridge	71	Univ. Calif. at Los Angeles	1,426
Univ. South Florida	64	Ohio State University	1,333
University of Florida	62	Georgia Inst. Technology	1,255
Arizona State University	59	University of Arizona	1,181
Univ. Calif. at San Diego	57	Duke University	1,037
Calif. State Poly., Pomona	57	Arizona State University	942
Univ. New Mexico	55	Univ. Calif. at Berkeley	930
San Diego State Univ.	55	University of Florida	908
Univ. Calif. at Los Angeles	54	Michigan State University	897

Number of offenses reported to police and campus authorities. From *Crime in the United States.*

Source

The Student Press Law Center has booklets on campus crime for guidance of student journalists and offers advice to students needing information. It can be reached at Student Press Law Center, 1101 Wilson Blvd., Suite 1910, Arlington, VA 22209; www.splc.org.

Fire Coverage

The police reporter monitors the police radio for reports of fires. If a fire is serious or involves a well-known building or downtown area, the reporter will go to the scene. Importance can be determined by the number of units dispatched, usually expressed in terms of the number of alarms.

When a fire broke out in a downtown tire store at noon, it was too late for the staff of *The Anniston* (Ala.) *Star* to cover it for that day's newspaper. The presses had already started to roll. Because of the intensive radio coverage of the fire, the reporter assigned to the story knew that her piece for the next day's newspaper would have to feature some aspect other than the basic facts. Pam Newell Sohn found a feature angle and put a delayed lead on her story.

On the jump page, Sohn wrapped up the details of the fire under this lead:

> Virgil Coker Tire Service officials said today they are considering whether to re-build a downtown Anniston warehouse blitzed by a spectacular fire Thursday.

Ask for Information   At fires, as with any emergency situation, reporters seem to be in the way, and some hesitate to grab a police officer or firefighter to ask for details. Ask. Wayne Dawkins recalls covering a fire for his New Jersey newspaper:

> Firefighters were coming out of the building gasping for oxygen, and there I was, trying to ask questions about what it was like inside. I expected to hear, "Get the hell away from me. I don't want to talk to you." But they made an effort, once they caught their breath.

Here are the beginnings of two fire stories that appeared in *The Tennessean* of Nashville:

A resident of an East Nashville rooming house suffered massive burns early today before fellow residents braved flames and yanked him to safety through a second-floor window.

The house at 256 Strouse Ave. was gutted by the blaze, which Metro fire officials have labeled "suspicious."

A 3-month-old Nashville girl asleep on a sofa-bed perished last night as her house went up in flames and relatives clawed in vain at an outside wall to rescue her.

The victim is the daughter of Janice Holt, who shares her 1925 16th Ave. N. home with several relatives, police said.

Firefighters arrived at the one-story dwelling off Clay Street shortly after the 6:45 p.m. call, and found the house consumed by flames, said Metro District Fire Chief Jordan Beasley.

Entire block endangered by disabled

butane truck too near flaming building

Heroes

By PAM NEWELL SOHN
Star Staff Writer

They talked like it was all in a day's work.

. . . like anyone would work on a disabled, half-filled butane truck a few feet from a building burning out of control.

. . . like the expectation the truck might explode and level the entire block was of no more consequence than answering a ringing phone.

Their apparent attitude: It had to be done. And the handful of men did it.

WHILE POLICE were evacuating about 100 spectators from the scene of a savage fire Thursday at Virgil Coker Tire Service on Noble Street, and while firemen were trying to tame the flames, four men ignored warnings and made fast, makeshift repairs on the tank truck. Then they half-drove, half-dragged it out of immediate danger.

The four men were Anniston Police Sgt. Mike Fincher, wrecker driver Kenneth Garrett and brothers Lamar Crosson and Buford Crosson, both employees of Virgil Coker Tire Service.

The Southern Butane Co. truck, carrying about 400 gallons of highly flammable gas, was parked for repairs near the rear of the building when a fire broke out there at about 11:20 a.m.

The front-end of the truck was near a telephone pole and could not be moved forward. Two rear wheels and the drive axle had been removed from the truck. The empty wheel space was on the side of the burning building. Coker employees said work on the truck had reached a standstill waiting for the delivery of a new wheel hub.

WHEN IT BECAME apparent that the fire could not be extinguished quickly, some firemen and the four men began contemplating how to move the disabled truck.

Lamar Crosson said he heard mention of pulling the truck away from the blaze just as it stood. "But the (gas) valve was right there on the bottom and it could have broke and burned," said Crosson.

Crosson said that at about that time, the new hub was delivered and he and his brother began to reassemble the wheel hub and mount the tire, working between the truck and the burning building. They were assisted by fireman Jimmy Crossley, fincher and Garrett.

The men said they had to work "on and off" because of the intense smoke from the fire. And at times, according to Garrett, flames were as close as 10 feet away. When the smoke wasn't blinding and choking them, they were being doused with water from a fire pumper truck spraying cooling water on the butane tank, they said.

FINALLY, the men were able to secure one

(See Truck, Page 12A)

Checklist: Fires

___ Deaths, injuries.

___ Location.

___ Cause.

___ When, where started.

___ How spread.

___ When brought under control.

___ Property loss: how much of structure damaged.

___ Estimated cost of damage.

___ Type of structure.

___ Measures taken to protect public safety.

___ If rescue involved, how carried out.

___ Who discovered fire.

___ Number of fire companies, firefighters assigned. (How much water used.)

___ Exact cause of deaths, injuries.

___ Where dead, injured taken.

___ Quotes from those burned out; effect on their lives.

___ Comments of neighbors, eyewitnesses.

___ Insurance coverage.

___ Arson suspected?

___ Any arrests.

___ Unusual aspects.

Sources

- Fire chief, marshal, inspector.
- Police department.
- Hospital.
- Morgue, mortuary.
- Welfare agencies, rescue groups (Red Cross).
- City building, fire inspection reports.

If a fire is serious enough to merit a follow-up story, possible themes are the progress of the investigation into the cause of the fire and the conditions of the injured. Another may be the cost of replacing the destroyed structure.

Cautions

A newspaper sent a young reporter to cover a fire in the business section. The fire had started in a hardware store, and the reporter asked one of the fire-fighters about the cause. "Looks like he had naphtha in the place," he replied, and the reporter wrote that. After the newspaper appeared, the store owner called the editor to complain that he never kept naphtha in the store. Statements about causes should be carefully handled. Only the chief, a marshal, or the fire inspector should be quoted about the cause.

Further Reading

Benedict, Helen. *Virgin or Vamp, How the Press Covers Sex Crimes.* New York: Oxford University Press, 1992.

Buchanan, Edna. *Never Let Them See You Cry: More from Miami, America's Heart Beat.* New York: Random House, 1992.

Capote, Truman. *In Cold Blood.* New York: Signet, 1967.

Coté, William, and Roger Simpson. *Covering Violence—A Guide to Ethical Reporting about Victims & Trauma.* New York: Columbia University Press, 2000.

Krajicek, David J. *Scooped! Media Miss Real Story on Crime While Chasing Sex, Sleaze, and Celebrities.* New York: Columbia University Press, 1998.

Reiss, Albert. *The Police and the Public.* New Haven, Conn.: Yale University Press, 1971.

Reuss-Ianni, Elizabeth. *Street Cops and Management Cops.* New Brunswick, N.J.: Transaction Publishers, 1993.

21 The Courts

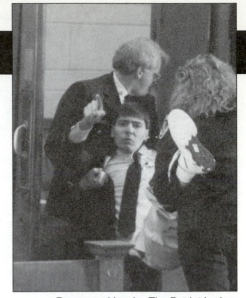

Rosemary Lincoln, *The Patriot Ledger*

Courtroom drama—forcible removal of defendant.

Preview

Coverage of state and federal courts involves:

• **Civil law**—actions initiated by an individual, usually a person suing another individual or an organization for damages. Many actions are settled out of court.

• **Criminal law**—actions initiated by the government for violation of criminal statutes. The process begins with the arraignment of the accused and concludes with dismissal or a not-guilty verdict or sentencing after a conviction.

Stories about aspects of the legal system interest readers:

- Plea bargaining.
- Sentencing patterns.
- Pretrial detention, probation, judges' efficiency.
- Politics and the courts.

For every one of the 2 million men and women behind the bars of jails and prisons, five others are being processed in the criminal justice system. At the same time, increasing numbers of lawsuits flood the civil courts. People are turning to civil courts to claim damages for impaired health from toxic waste dumps, for what survivors claimed were cigarette-induced deaths and for injuries from automobile accidents.

The courts over the land have become overwhelmed. They are at the confluence of a swollen tide of lawmaking, arrests and litigation. Watching over all this, pencil poised, is the reporter.

The only way the reporter maintains stability in this swelling tide of words—most of which are dense and arcane—is through knowledge of the judicial system, good sources and the ability to pick out the significant and interesting cases.

The Basics

There are two judicial systems, state and federal. State systems differ in detail but are similar in essentials. There are two kinds of law, criminal and civil. In criminal law, the government is the accuser. In civil law, an individual

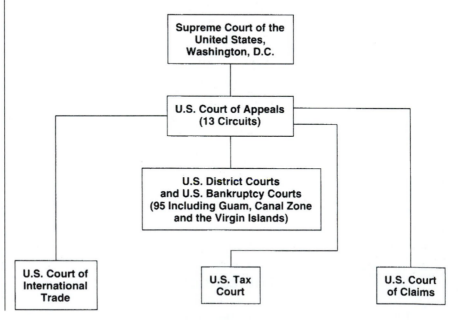

or group usually initiates the action; the government also can bring an action in the civil courts. Because crime stories make dramatic reading, the criminal courts receive the most media attention. Reporters cover the civil courts for damage suits, restraining orders and court decisions on such issues as taxes, business operations and labor conflicts.

These criminal and civil proceedings take place in state courts with a variety of titles—district, circuit, superior, supreme. The lower-level courts of original jurisdiction at the city and county levels—criminal, police, county, magistrate and the justice of the peace courts—handle misdemeanors, traffic violations and arraignments. The federal court system includes the federal district courts, the circuit courts of appeals and the Supreme Court.

The county courthouse or court reporter covers state and local courts and the office of the district attorney. The federal courthouse reporter covers the U.S. attorney, the federal magistrate and the federal courts. The magistrate arraigns those arrested and sets bail.

There are special state and local courts, such as the domestic relations or family court, sometimes called juvenile or children's court; small claims; surrogate's court (where wills are probated) and landlord-tenant court.

The court reporter's attention is directed to the civil and criminal proceedings in the state courts of superior jurisdiction—district, superior, circuit or supreme courts—and in the federal system.

Before we go into our examination of court coverage, a note of caution: Reporting the courts has been the subject of considerable legal action. Some areas are off-limits—grand jury deliberations, certain activities of jurors—and

The Federal Court System

The federal judicial system has three tiers:

District courts: Trial courts located throughout the nation.

Circuit courts: Intermediate regional appeals courts that review appeals from the district courts.

Supreme Court: Takes appeals on a discretionary basis from circuit courts.

The federal courts have power only over those matters the Constitution establishes: "controversies to which the United States shall be a party; controversies between two or more states; between a State and a citizen of another State; between citizens of different states. . . ."

some have been hemmed in by judicial decree. Chapter 25 surveys the continuing push-and-pull between journalists, who seek freedom to cover all aspects of the judicial system, and the courts, which have sought to limit coverage on the ground that it can compromise the defendant's right to a fair trial. Many states have press-bar guidelines.

Civil Law

Civil law consists of two major divisions: actions at law and equity proceedings.

Actions at Law

These suits are brought—mostly in state courts—for recovery of property, damages for personal injury and breach of contract. The reporter who thumbs through the daily flow of suits filed in the county courthouse singles out those that have unusual, timely or important elements. They are on the lookout for well-known people who may bring suit or against whom a suit is filed.

The Unusual Here is a brief story about a freak accident in a baseball game. The circumstances made the suit worth writing about:

OREGON CITY—A 13-year-old who broke both arms during a Little League baseball game has filed a $500,000 suit in Clackamas County Circuit Court through his guardian. It charges the Lake Oswego School District and Nordin-Schmitz, Inc., a private corporation, with negligence.

According to the suit, plaintiff Martin K. McCurdy was injured when he fell into a ditch on the boundary between the school district and Nordin-Schmitz property as he was chasing a ball during a Little League game May 16.

Explanation Essential Some cases involve complexities that the reporter has to explain so the reader or listener can make sense of the courtroom processes. Here is an example of how a radio reporter handled a court case that would have mystified listeners without an explanation:

The wife of a Dallas minister was found near death from what appeared to be an attempt to strangle her. Her husband was suspected, but police said they had no evidence to charge him. The woman is in a coma.

The woman's mother sued her son-in-law in civil court and has won a $16 million judgment, the money to be used for the lifetime care of the minister's wife.

Whoa, the listener says. How can a man be ordered to pay for a crime the police say they cannot charge him with? The reporter answered the question with this sentence:

> Unlike the criminal system, which requires proof beyond a reasonable doubt to convict a defendant, a civil suit requires only a preponderance of credible evidence.

The Key Differences   In a criminal trial, the issue is the guilt *beyond a reasonable doubt* of the accused. In a civil trial, in which damages, contracts and the like are involved, the issue is the *likelihood of the defendant's liability.*

In a criminal trial, the verdict must be unanimous. In a civil trial, 9 of the 12 jurors constitutes a verdict.

This difference between a criminal and a civil trial was a factor in one of the most heavily covered civil trials of the decade—the damage suit against O. J. Simpson that followed his acquittal of murder in a criminal trial.

O. J.'s Civil Trial   In Simpson's criminal trial for the murder of his ex-wife and her friend, a jury returned a unanimous verdict of not guilty. The families of the two victims then filed a civil action, asking for monetary damages for their loss.

The fact that the former football star had been acquitted in a criminal trial did not count for much with the civil jury. It found Simpson "liable" for the deaths and awarded a total of $35.5 million in damages to one of the families.

Although there is a constitutional prohibition against double jeopardy, private civil suits have not been considered a violation of the prohibition.

Prominence   The name Mike Tyson is well-known to more than just boxing fans. His escapades outside the ring were as well-known as those inside the ropes. So when a 26-year-old New York woman brought a $4.5 million punitive damage suit against Mike Tyson, it was news.

The woman claimed that Tyson, a former heavyweight boxing champion, had grabbed her breasts and buttocks in a disco after she rejected his advances. The jury was not impressed and refused her punitive damage claim but did award her $100 in compensatory damages.

Caution: Lawyers often file damage suits seeking large sums. A $1 million lawsuit is commonplace. Most damage suits are settled for far less or tossed out of court. Relatively few go to trial. The reporter examines the suit to see whether it has newsworthy elements in addition to the amount sought.

Equity Proceedings

The courts can compel individuals, organizations and government bodies to take an action or to refrain from an action. When such an order is requested,

---

Criminal and Civil Actions

Jay-Z, the Grammy Award–winning rapper, was placed on probation for three years after pleading guilty yesterday in State Supreme Court to stabbing a record producer in a Times Square nightclub two years ago.

Jay-Z, 31 years old, whose real name is Shawn Carter, admitted stabbing Lance Rivera, 35, at the Kit Kat Club. Rivera dropped a civil suit against Jay-Z after they made an out-of-court settlement for an undisclosed amount.

the complainant is said to seek equitable relief. Reporters come across these legal actions in the form of injunctions and restraining orders. Here is a story about a restraining order from the radio news wire of the UPI:

> PROVIDENCE, R.I.—A federal judge has issued a temporary order stopping efforts to put a reservist on active army duty because he refused to shave off his beard.
>
> District Judge Edward Day in Providence, R.I., yesterday gave the army 10 days to answer a suit filed Friday by the American Civil Liberties Union. . . .

Temporary injunctions, also known as preliminary injunctions, are issued to freeze the status quo until a court hearing can be scheduled. Thus, it makes no sense to write that the petitioner has "won" an injunction in such a preliminary proceeding (which is also called an "*ex parte* proceeding") because a permanent injunction cannot be issued until an adversary hearing is held in which both sides are heard. The respondent is ordered to show cause at the hearing—usually set for a week or two later—for why the temporary injunction should not be made final or permanent.

In this equity proceeding, a party asked the court to compel another party to take an action:

> The developers of a proposed shopping center and office complex at the intersection of Route 13 and West Trenton Avenue have asked Bucks County Court to order Falls Township to issue a building permit.
> —*Bucks County Courier Times*

Most stories that emanate from the courts are written in a straightforward news style. The lead usually describes the winner and the loser. If money is won, the lead will state the amount and the reason it was awarded.

But when the occasion warrants it, the reporter tells a story. This is the story of a wrong righted and a son recognized.

Music Man   Rick Bragg of *The New York Times* did some extra reporting and used the narrative writing style to give an added dimension to a ruling by the Mississippi Supreme Court. Here is how his piece begins:

JACKSON, MISSISSIPPI—The legend was that if you touched Robert Johnson you could feel the talent running through him, like heat, put there by the devil on a dark Delta crossroad in exchange for his soul. It is why Claud Johnson's grandparents would not let him out of the house that day in 1937 when Robert Johnson, his father, strolled into the yard.

Robert Johnson, the famous, almost mythical blues man, had come to Lincoln County, Miss., to see Virgie Jane Smith, a young woman he had been intimate with, and a son he had never seen.

"They told my daddy they didn't want no part of him. They said he was working for the devil, and they wouldn't even let me go out and touch him. I stood in the door, and he stood on the ground, and that is as close as I ever got to him. Finally, he said, 'Well, I might as well go on.' He wandered off and I never saw him again."

Mr. Johnson has always wondered what would have happened if he had run across that porch to him, so that everyone would know he was Robert Johnson's son. Now, the Mississippi Supreme Court ruled that he is the son and legal heir of. . . .

Bragg says, "I don't know if I would have read that story if it had begun: 'Today, the Mississippi Supreme Court ruled. . . .' Sometimes, the narrative makes the difference between a story that is read and one that is merely glanced at."

Pretrial and Trial

A complaint lists the cause of action, the parties to the action, and the relief sought. The defendant has several alternatives. He or she may file a motion seeking to delay, alter or halt the action. He or she can ask for a change of venue or a bill of particulars or can file other motions. When the defendant is ready to contest the action, or if motions to stop the action have not been granted, the defendant files an answer.

The case may then move to trial. Although there are more civil trials than criminal trials, few civil trials are covered. Reporters rely on records, lawyers and court personnel for information. Civil court stories are written on filing of the action and at the completion of the trial or at settlement.

Checklist: Civil Actions

___ Identification of person or organization filing action.

___ Background of plaintiff or petitioner.

___ Defendant; respondent.

___ Type of damage alleged.

___ Remedy sought.

___ Date of filing; court of jurisdiction.

___ Special motivation behind action, if any.

___ History of the conflict, disagreement.

___ Similar cases decided by courts.

___ Could suit lead to landmark decision? Is it a precedent?

___ Possibility of an out-of-court settlement.

___ Significance of action; effect on others.

___ Lawyers for both sides; types of firms they are associated with.

___ Date and presiding judge for trial, hearing.

___ Judge's reputation with similar cases.

Should the reporter cover the trial, key points for reporting are selection of the jury; relevant evidence; identification and expertise of witnesses; demeanor of witnesses on the stand; judge's rulings; pertinent material from opening and closing statements of attorneys; the damages, if any are assessed; whether the losing party intends to appeal.

Checklist: Verdict Stories

Here are the essentials of verdict stories for civil actions:

___ Verdict; damages, if awarded (same, less, greater than those sought).

___ Parties involved.

___ Judge's statement, if any; deviations by judge from jury's findings.

___ Summary of allegations by plaintiff.

___ Key testimony and attorneys' points.

___ Length of jury deliberations.

___ Comment by jurors on deliberations, verdict.

___ Any appeals or motions.

Sources

Private attorneys representing plaintiff and defendant; judges and their law clerks and clerks of the court; court stenographers; county courthouse clerk or assistant who is in charge of filing such actions. The clerk is usually the best source for tips on important cases.

Court Documents Privileged   Documents filed in the clerk's office usually are privileged as soon as the clerk stamps the material received. The reporter is free to use privileged material without fear of libel because it has been given official status. Statements in court also are privileged.

Cautions

Negotiations between the sides often will continue even after a trial begins, and the reporter should be aware of the possibility of a sudden settlement. In many damage suits, the plaintiff threatens to go to court to support his or her demand for a certain sum or other remedy. In turn, the defendant appears to be unconcerned about the possibility of a court battle. In reality, neither side welcomes the inconvenience, cost and unpredictability of a trial. The judge, too, wants a settlement. The civil courts are overwhelmed.

Attorneys for the losing side usually indicate an appeal will be filed. Do not overplay these assertions, but when an appeal is filed it can be a good story.

In civil cases, the defendant may ask the judge to dismiss the plaintiff's complaint or cause of action. Make sure to use the word *dismiss*, not *acquit*, which is a criminal term and refers to a verdict, after a full trial, by either a judge or a jury. In either a civil or criminal case, after the matter is finally decided, the judge usually orders a *judgment* to be entered in favor of the party prevailing in the action.

Criminal Law

Whether it is night court where the sweepings of the city streets are gathered for misdemeanor charges, or a high-paneled district courtroom where a woman is on trial for the murder-for-hire of her wealthy husband, the criminal courts offer endless opportunities for coverage.

The assumption that underlies the criminal justice system is that an injury to the individual affects the general public. Crimes are therefore prosecuted in the name of the state as the representative of the people.

The public prosecutor, an elected official, is usually known as the district attorney, state's attorney, county attorney or people's attorney. In the federal system, the prosecutor, a presidential appointee, is called the United States attorney.

Criminal Court Process

The criminal court system goes into operation shortly after the arrest and consists of pretrial and trial periods.

The pretrial period can be divided into four phases: arraignment, preliminary hearing, grand jury action and jury selection. Usually, these are accomplished in line with the constitutional provision: "In all criminal prosecutions, the accused shall enjoy the right to a speedy and public trial. . . ."

Arraignment

At arraignment, the defendant is told of the charges and of his or her right to an attorney and can enter a plea to the charge. If the defendant cannot afford a lawyer, the court assigns one. Arraignments are held in courts of original or least jurisdiction. These courts are empowered to try only misdemeanors and violations, such as gambling, prostitution, loitering and minor traffic offenses. In a felony case, the court will determine bail. The prosecutor is present at arraignment, and he or she may decide to dismiss or lower the charge. If a felony charge is lowered to a misdemeanor, the case can be disposed of then and there.

The arraignment court, often called the criminal or city police court, acts like a fine-necked funnel, allowing only those felonies to pass through that the district attorney considers serious. Others are reduced to violations and misdemeanors and handled forthwith.

If the defendant pleads guilty to a misdemeanor, the court can sentence immediately. If the defendant pleads guilty to a felony charge, the case is referred to a higher court.

City and State Courts

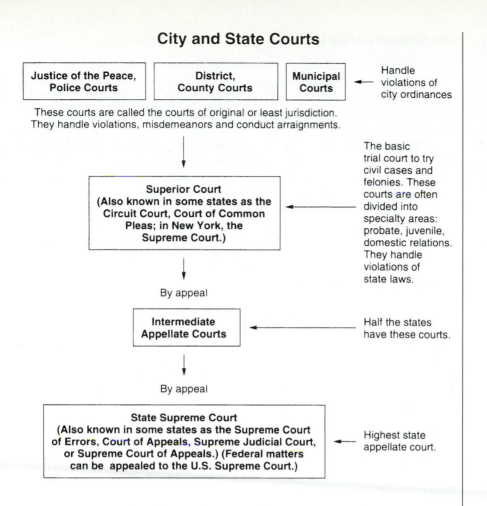

Justice of the Peace, Police Courts	District, County Courts	Municipal Courts

Handle violations of city ordinances ←

These courts are called the courts of original or least jurisdiction. They handle violations, misdemeanors and conduct arraignments.

↓

Superior Court
(Also known in some states as the Circuit Court, Court of Common Pleas; in New York, the Supreme Court.)

The basic trial court to try civil cases and felonies. These courts are often divided into specialty areas: probate, juvenile, domestic relations. They handle violations of state laws. →

↓

By appeal

Intermediate Appellate Courts

Half the states have these courts. →

↓

By appeal

State Supreme Court
(Also known in some states as the Supreme Court of Errors, Court of Appeals, Supreme Judicial Court, or Supreme Court of Appeals.) (Federal matters can be appealed to the U.S. Supreme Court.)

Highest state appellate court. →

If a plea of not guilty is entered to a misdemeanor, the judge can then conduct a trial or preliminary hearing. For felony not-guilty pleas, the case is referred to the appropriate court for a preliminary hearing. If the preliminary hearing is waived, the defendant is then bound over to the grand jury for action. Felonies are handled by courts which are variously called district, superior or circuit courts, depending on the state.

Checklist: Arraignments

___ Formal charge.

___ Plea.

___ Bail (higher, lower than requested; conditional release).

___ Behavior, statements of defendant.

___ Presentation, remarks of prosecutor, defense lawyer, judge.

___ Summary of crime.

Preliminary Hearing

At a preliminary hearing, determination is made whether there are reasonable grounds, or probable cause, to believe the accused committed the offense and whether there is sufficient evidence for the case to be bound over to the grand jury. If the presiding judge considers the evidence insufficient, he or she can dismiss the charge. Also, bail can be increased, eliminated or reduced at the hearing.

The defendant has another opportunity to seek to have the charge lowered through plea bargaining at this point in the process. Some attorneys handling criminal cases prefer to have their clients plead guilty and receive probation or a light sentence rather than risk a trial and a lengthy sentence.

The prosecutor usually goes along with plea bargaining, but if the crime is serious, the defendant has a long record or the presiding judge is convinced there is reason to believe a serious crime was committed, the case will be sent to a grand jury to decide whether the defendant should be indicted.

Here is the beginning of a story of a preliminary hearing in the federal system:

BOSTON, Dec. 24—A Harvard Law School student, who allegedly enrolled under separate identities twice in the last seven years, was ordered yesterday bound over to a United States grand jury on charges that he had falsified a federal student loan application. . . .

United States Magistrate Peter Princi found probable cause yesterday that the student falsified applications for $6,000 in federally insured loans, which helped to see him through 2½ years of law school. . . .

Grand Jury Action

Criminal defendants can be brought to trial in three ways, depending on the state. In half the states, a grand jury indicts. A jury of citizens, usually 23 (of which 16 make a quorum), decides whether the evidence is sufficient for a trial on the charges brought. If 12 jurors so decide, an indictment, known as a *true bill,* is voted. If not, dismissal, known as a *no bill,* is voted. Only the state's evidence is presented to the jury.

In 20 states, the prosecutor files a charge called an *information* and a judge decides at a preliminary hearing at which witnesses testify whether there is cause for a trial. In a few states, the prosecutor files affidavits to support the charge and the judge decides whether to move to trial.

Here are leads to grand jury indictments, the first by an Indiana state grand jury, the other by a federal grand jury:

INDIANAPOLIS—Former heavyweight champion Mike Tyson was indicted here today on a charge of raping an 18-year-old Miss Black America beauty pageant contestant and on three other criminal counts.

OKLAHOMA CITY—Timothy J. McVeigh and Terry L. Nichols, former army buddies who shared a hatred for the government, were indicted by a federal grand jury today on charges of blowing up a federal building here in April with a rented truck packed with 4,800 pounds of homemade explosives.

What Happens to the Defendant After Indictment

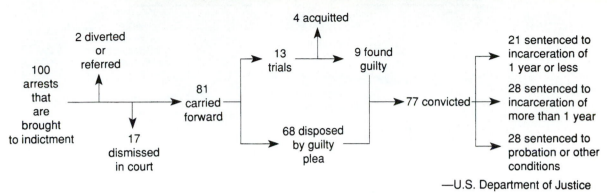

—U.S. Department of Justice

Rearraignment

After the indictment, the defendant is again arraigned, this time before a judge empowered to try felony cases. If the defendant pleads not guilty, a date for trial is set and bail is set. For example:

INDIANAPOLIS—Mike Tyson pleaded not guilty to charges he raped a beauty pageant contestant and was released on $30,000 bail.

In a 10-minute court appearance, Marion Superior Court Judge Patricia Gifford read Tyson the rape, criminal deviate conduct and confinement charges against him. If found guilty on all those charges, Tyson could face up to 63 years in prison. A trial date of Jan. 27 was set.

Plea bargaining continues at the rearraignment following grand jury indictment. Felonies, which usually are classified by degree—Class A, B, C, D and E—can be adjusted downward, a Class A felony moving down to a C or D, a Class C or D being negotiated down to a Class E felony or a misdemeanor.

Plea Bargaining

If every arrest were to be followed by a plea of not guilty and the accused granted the speedy trial promised by the Bill of Rights, the court system in every large city would collapse. The only way the courts can cope with the crush is to permit or to encourage arrangements whereby the defendant and the prosecutor agree that, in return for a lowered charge, the defendant will plead guilty. The nature of the sentence is often explicitly promised by the judge as a condition to the defendant's agreement to plead guilty.

Even serious crimes such as murder and rape are the subject of plea bargaining. In New York City, three-fourths of all murder arrests are plea bargained, and in Philadelphia three-fifths are plea bargained. Prosecutors defend the practice by saying that plea bargaining is necessary to cut down the backlog of cases in the courts. In Philadelphia, the backlog was cut from 20,000 to 13,000 through plea bargaining.

Avoiding a Trial

LOS ANGELES— A former respiratory therapist who once confessed to killing more than 40 elderly hospital patients pleaded guilty to murdering six people in an agreement with prosecutors.

Instead of engaging in what they said would probably be a long and costly trial, the district attorney's office agreed to allow Efren Saldivar, 32, to enter guilty pleas that will lead to six consecutive sentences of life without parole.

The victims, investigators found, were injected with a muscle relaxant that suppresses natural breathing. At one time, Saldivar said he had killed "anywhere from 100 to 200" patients in various hospitals in which he had worked. He later recanted, but investigators found enough evidence to bring charges of 40 deaths.

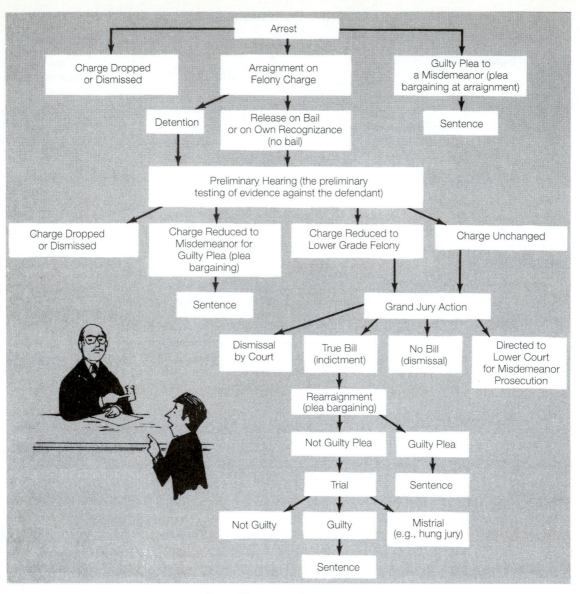

Court Process for a Felony

When the Bronx district attorney announced he would no longer allow plea bargaining in felony cases, legal experts said the move "could cripple the borough's criminal-justice system by overburdening judges, crowding jails and allowing some suspects to go free," *The New York Times* reported. The newspaper described the system as "a necessary evil in an overwhelmed court system," and said it is the "leading way criminal cases are decided in New York City and around the nation." Almost 85 percent of all city cases are plea bargained.

Interrupted Trial Plea bargaining continues even as the criminal trial is underway. Here is the beginning of a court story that involves plea bargaining. It was written by Joseph P. Fried of *The New York Times:*

The last defendant in the St. John's University sexual-assault case interrupted his trial yesterday to plead guilty to sharply reduced charges, then admitted he had done virtually everything he had originally been accused of.

The wrenching case came to an end in an emotional scene in a Queens courtroom in which a female spectator yelled out that the 22-year-old defendant was a "rapist" and his mother responded with screaming vituperation.

The plea bargain allowed the defendant, a student at the largest Roman Catholic university in the country who was accused with five others of what is known as acquaintance rape, to be given three years' probation. They were accused of sodomizing the victim and sexually abusing her in other ways.

Offer Spurned Sometimes the bargaining is unsuccessful. Here is the beginning of a story from *The Humboldt Beacon* by Nancy Brands Ward:

EUREKA—The case of three Headwaters activists arrested in Rep. Frank Riggs' Eureka office on Oct. 16 moved one step closer to trial this week as attorneys failed to reach a deal on a plea bargain.

After Judge Marilyn Miles asked during a pretrial hearing Monday if the case could be settled short of going to court, Deputy District Attorney Andrew Isaac offered to let the three women plead guilty to trespass and resisting arrest. In exchange, vandalism charges would be dropped, though the prosecution would reserve the right to bring them to the court's attention during sentencing.

"It was no offer," said Mark Harris, who represents Terri Slanetz, Jennifer Schneider and Lisa Sanderson-Fox, who'd locked themselves in Riggs' office in an October protest.

Pretrial Motions

After the defendant has been formally accused, several kinds of motions can be filed:

• **Motion to quash the indictment:** The defendant can challenge the legality of the indictment. If the motion to dismiss is granted, the indictment is quashed. The prosecutor can appeal the quashing. He or she also can draw up another indictment if the grand jury again hands up a true bill, even if the first has been quashed, because the constitutional protection against double jeopardy does not apply.

• **Motion for a bill of particulars:** When the defense attorney wants more details about the allegations against the accused, such a motion is filed.

• **Motion to suppress the evidence:** Evidence shown to be seized or obtained illegally may not be used in the trial if the court grants such a motion.

• **Motion for a change of venue:** A defendant who believes he or she cannot receive a fair trial in the city or judicial area where the crime took place may ask that it be transferred elsewhere. Such motions also are filed to avoid trials presided over by particular judges.

Motions Prepared

LOS ANGELES—Attorneys for O. J. Simpson are laying out a battery of motions to try to undermine the case against the former football star, Simpson's lead attorney said in an interview today.

During the pretrial stage of the Tyson rape case, the boxer's defense team made a motion to exclude a videotape on which Tyson was supposed to have made a disparaging remark about his accuser at a news conference following his arraignment. The defense motion was upheld when the judge later ruled the tape inadmissible at the trial.

Jury Selection

When a case emerges from the pretrial process and has been set for trial, a jury is usually empaneled. (The accused may waive the right to jury trial, in which case the judge hears the evidence in what is called a *bench trial.*)

Jurors' names are drawn from a wheel or jury box in which the names of all jurors on a jury list were placed. The list is made up of names drawn from the tax rolls, voting lists, driver's license files and so on.

Twelve jurors and several alternates are selected in a procedure during which the defense attorney and prosecutor are permitted to challenge the selection of jurors. There are two types of challenges: *peremptory,* when no reason need be given for wanting a person off the jury, and *for cause,* when a specific disqualification must be demonstrated. The number of peremptory challenges allotted each side is set by statute, usually 10 per side. A judge can set any number of challenges for cause.

Klansman's Jury　In the case of a former Klansman accused of a 1963 church bombing in which four black girls died, federal prosecutors used their peremptory challenges to remove 10 white men and 6 white women. The defense used 12 of its 16 challenges to strike blacks. The prosecutors relied on the advice of a jury consultant who organized two focus groups and polled nearly 500 Birmingham area residents to find out about attitudes toward racial issues and the church bombing 38 years before.

The jury took two hours to convict Thomas E. Blanton. It then sentenced him to life in prison. (The U.S. Supreme Court has ruled that peremptory challenges cannot be used to exclude people from juries on the basis of sex or race.)

Selection a Key　"Most trials are won or lost in jury selection," says Larry Scalise, a trial lawyer. In the trial of a woman accused of murdering her abusive husband, her lawyer said he concentrated on selecting a jury that was well-educated and sensitive to the victims of domestic violence. His client was acquitted.

Jury selection was a key factor in O. J. Simpson's acquittal at his criminal trial, court observers say. Through the use of surveys and focus groups, Simpson's lawyers learned that black men were three times more likely than black women to believe Simpson was guilty and that the more educated black men and women also considered him guilty.

In focus groups, Simpson's lawyers found, "Virtually every middle-aged African-American woman supported Simpson and resented the murder victim (Nicole Simpson)," says Jeffrey Toobin, the author of *The Run of His Life: The People v. O. J. Simpson.*

Toobin adds that the lead prosecutor Marcia Clark seriously compromised her chance of winning a conviction by not following the advice of jury consultants who told her that black women were hostile to the prosecution.

The criminal trial jury in the Simpson case included eight black women. The only whites were two women.

In the civil trial that found Simpson liable for the deaths, there was not a single black juror.

"No one wanted to tell what I regard as the truth about the Simpson case—that race was always at the heart of it," says Toobin.

Jury selection is so important it has spawned an industry—jury consultancy. Behavioral consultants advise attorneys how to select sympathetic jurors and how to use psychological techniques to persuade juries.

Jury Consultants   Jo-Ellan Dimitrius, one of about 250 jury consultants in the country, says that in assessing prospective jurors, she seeks clues from what they take to court—their reading matter, their body language and their responses to the questions lawyers ask.

Robert B. Hirschhorn, a consultant, advised lawyers defending a young man accused of murdering a 16-year-old girl to ask potential jurors, "Can you look Kevin in the eye and say, 'Kevin, I can give you a fair trial'?"

Those who replied, "I think I can" were dismissed by the defense. Those who said yes and then "looked at their shoes, we got rid of," Hirschhorn said. Those who gave an unequivocal "yes" were accepted by the defense.

The jury acquitted Kevin.

Consultants advise their clients on everything from the clothing to wear at a trial to whether men should wear their hairpieces. San Antonio attorney and trial consultant Harry Munsinger says that if he had been advising Mike Tyson at Tyson's rape trial he would have played down the boxer's size and strength by dressing him in pastels and looser-fitting suits.

Reporter's Fare

All of this is fair game for the court reporter. A careful eye to jury selection will indicate the strategy of prosecutor and defense attorney. Does the defense attorney want women on the jury because he believes they will be sympathetic to the abused wife who shot her husband? Is the prosecutor asking questions about the television shows and movies the jury panelists watch? Does she prefer those who like westerns and police dramas? If so, what does that tell you?

Are jury consultants in the courtroom? On whose side? What can they tell you?

We are ready to examine the procedure for trials, which the court reporter must master to do his or her job properly. But first a suggestion from the dean of court reporters, Theo Wilson of the New York *Daily News:* "Take the reader into the courtroom with you."

Jury Advisory

An assistant district attorney in Philadelphia made a training videotape for new prosecutors about jury selection:

In my experience, you look at how people are dressed. If you take middle-class people who are well dressed, you're going to do well. . . . You don't want smart people, because smart people will analyze the hell out of your case. They hold the courts up to higher standards. . . . You don't want people who are going to think it out. . . . If you're going to take blacks, you want older black men and women, particularly men. Older black men are very good. Guys seventy, seventy-five years old are from a different era; they have a different respect for the law. . . .

The Trial

A reporter cannot attend all the trials conducted in the courthouse that he or she covers. A reporter may sit through opening and closing statements and key testimony, but only the most celebrated cases are covered from opening statement to verdict and sentence. Reporters cover most trials by checking with the court clerk, the prosecutor and the defense attorney.

Because the reporter is dependent on sources who often have a stake in the trial, court transcripts are used in important trials if they can be obtained in time for broadcast or publication. A friendly court stenographer can quickly run off key testimony in an emergency.

Trial Process

The trial procedure follows this pattern:

Opening Statements

1. Opening statements by prosecuting attorney and the defense attorney outline the state's case and the defense or alibi of the defendant and give a general preview of the evidence.

"The opening statement is the single most important part of the trial," says Joseph W. Cotchett, a Burlingame, Calif., lawyer. "This is the time you win your case. It's the rule of primacy; the jurors hear the details of the case for the first time. You give them the critical facts you're going to prove."

Direct Examination

2. The prosecution presents its case through testimony of witnesses and evidence. At the end of the presentation, a judge can direct a verdict of acquittal if he or she finds that the state has not established what is called a *prima facie* case, failing to present sufficient proof of the crime that is charged. The questioning by the prosecutor of his or her witness is called *direct examination.*

In direct examination of the woman who accused Tyson of raping her, the prosecutor led her to describe the event after her introductory statement: "If I was a quitter I wouldn't be here. I start what I finish," she told the jury. Then she described in three and a half hours of testimony what had happened. She said, "I was terrified. I was begging him, trying anything that would work. It just felt like someone was ripping me apart."

The story in the *Daily News* began:

INDIANAPOLIS—Mike Tyson's 18-year-old accuser testified yesterday that the former champ laughed while she wept in agony as he raped her in his hotel suite here last July.

"Don't fight me," Tyson growled menacingly during the attack as he grabbed her, pulled her clothing off and pinned her while she feebly pushed his heavyweight arms and back, she testified.

Spin Doctors. Lawyers and others associated with a trial offer comments on the courtroom steps. "It takes a careful eye to separate the spin from the substance," says the AP's Linda Deutsch. Tips also are greeted with some skepticism. "When it comes out in court I assure you it will be my lead that day," Theo Wilson would tell tipsters at trials.

Nancy Stone, *The Plain Dealer*

Witness to His Mother's Murder

Here is the beginning of the story by Katherine L. Siemon and Eric Stringfellow of *The Plain Dealer* that accompanied this dramatic photograph by Nancy Stone:

Five-year-old DeVon Stapleton vividly remembers the night last spring when a stranger bludgeoned his mother to death while he watched from the back of a van.

Yesterday he spent about an hour trying to recount for a three-judge panel in Common Pleas Court what happened that night in April, how he and his mother tried to escape, and how he was left standing alone on a dark street corner after his mother was killed.

Barely tall enough to see over the witness stand and with a voice barely loud enough to be heard without a mi-crophone, DeVon pointed to the man who is on trial for the death of Ruby Stapleton.

"There, he's right there," DeVon said, shaking his finger at Reginald Jells when Assistant County Prosecutor Carmen Marino asked the boy if he saw the stranger in the courtroom.

Jells, 21, faces the death penalty for Stapleton's killing last April 18. He also is charged with kidnapping and aggravated robbery. During opening arguments yesterday, Marino said Stapleton's blood was found inside Jells' van and a footprint matching Jells' was found near the body.

Jells has denied the killing.

(Jells was convicted and sentenced to death.)

"I was telling him, 'Get off me, please stop.' I didn't know what to do," the woman said, her almost childlike voice captivating the hushed courtroom as she recounted the incident.

The prosecution calls other witnesses to support the contention of its major witnesses. In the Tyson case, the prosecutor drew from Tyson's chauffeur the statement that, when the woman left the hotel and returned to the limousine, "she looked like she may have been in a state of shock. Dazed. Disoriented. She seemed scared."

Cross-Examination

LOS ANGELES—A population geneticist acknowledged today that he made mistakes when he compiled statistics that linked O. J. Simpson to the killings of his former wife and her friend.

Under cross-examination, the geneticist said he was "sincerely sorry" and "embarrassed" by his errors.

Cross-Examination by Defense

3. The defense attorney may cross-examine the state's witnesses.

In a criminal defense trial, says Cornelius Pitts, a defense lawyer in Detroit, "relentless cross-examination is necessary. The objective is to prevent the prosecution from winning and to do what you have to do to attack the complainant and the complainant's witnesses to the extent their testimony is no longer credible to the jury."

Tyson's attorney spent three hours cross-examining the boxer's accuser: "Do you recall telling Tanya St. Clair that (Tyson) has the money and the build that you like? . . . Do you recall saying you like men with 'something you can hold on to'?"

In cross-examining the chauffeur, the defense attorney's questions sought to suggest that the driver was exhausted from overwork and could not have seen the woman clearly.

INDIANAPOLIS—The attorney defending Mike Tyson failed to shake his accuser from her story in more than three hours of cross-examination yesterday, but he did set the stage for other witnesses to discredit her account of what happened that night in Tyson's hotel suite.

In a rapid-fire series of questions, attorney Vincent Fuller questioned the accuser about statements she allegedly made to other contestants in the Miss Black America Pageant and to pageant participants in the days immediately preceding and following the July 19 incident in which she says she was raped by the former heavyweight boxing champion.

—New York Post

Redirect Examination

4. Redirect examination is permitted the prosecutor should he or she want to re-establish the credibility of evidence or testimony that the defense's cross-examination has threatened.

Motions

5. The defense may make a motion for a directed verdict of acquittal or of dismissal based on its contention the state did not prove its case.

Rebuttal

6. The defense may call witnesses to rebut the state's case. The defendant may or may not be called, depending on the defense attorney's strategy. The prosecutor is not permitted to comment on the defendant's failure to take the stand.

Tyson's attorneys called beauty pageant contestants to testify that his accuser had flirted with him and repeatedly talked about his money. Tyson did take the stand and under questioning by his attorney said he and his accuser had engaged in consensual sex. "No, she never told me to stop. She never said I was hurting her. She never said no. Nothing."

Cross-Examination by Prosecutor

7. The prosecutor may cross-examine the defense witnesses.

In cross-examination of the contestants, the prosecution elicited testimony that the plaintiff was naive and "not streetwise" about a date with Tyson. Tyson also was cross-examined:

INDIANAPOLIS—A visibly rattled and slightly peevish Mike Tyson, after an hour of intense cross-examination, left the stand yesterday having had some inconsistencies in his testimony high-lighted but with his basic story intact.

Attacking less with a sledgehammer than with a chisel, special prosecutor J. Gregory Garrison chipped away at Tyson's testimony but refrained from grilling Tyson about precisely what went on in Room 606 of the Canterbury Hotel on the morning of July 19, when an 18-year-old beauty pageant contestant says she was raped.

—*New York Post*

In the Simpson trial, the defense introduced an expert witness who said that the killings took too long for Simpson to have committed them. On cross-examination by the prosecutor, the witness stood fast:

LOS ANGELES—The prosecution today attacked the theory of an expert witness for O. J. Simpson that the two victims fought long and hard for their lives. But the expert, the former chief medical examiner for New York, fended off the attack and cited his long experience with murder cases.

Redirect Examination by Defense

8. Should the state seem to weaken the defense's case through its cross-examination, the defense may engage in redirect examination of its witnesses.

Rebuttals

9. Rebuttals are offered on both sides. Witnesses may be recalled. New rebuttal witnesses may be called, but new witnesses ordinarily cannot be presented without the judge's permission after a side has rested its case.

Note: At any time during the trial, the defense may move for a *mistrial*, usually on the basis that some irregularity has made a fair verdict by the jury impossible. If the judge grants the motion, the jury is discharged and the trial is stopped. Because double jeopardy does not apply in such situations, the defendant can be tried again.

Murder Jury

Jurors in the trial of a man accused of murdering a woman and her daughters listen as the evidence is summed up. The jury was sequestered for the trial that was widely covered because of the heinous nature of the crime and the dogged police work that resulted in the arrest of the accused murderer. The jury convicted him.

Summations

10. The defense and the state offer closing arguments in which they summarize the case for the jurors. These presentations, known as *summations,* provide reporters with considerable news. Attorneys sometimes make dramatic summations before the jury.

Charge to Jury

11. The judge charges or instructs jurors before they retire for deliberations. The judge may review the evidence, explain the law that should be applied to the facts of the case and explain the verdicts that can be reached. The jury must accept the judge's explanation of the law but is the sole judge of the facts in the case.

Jury Deliberation

12. Jury deliberations may be short or extended. In important trials, the reporter may want to stay with the jury until deadline because verdicts make headlines. A jury may ask for further instructions on the law, or it may wish to review certain material from the trial. Stories can be written speculating on the meaning of lengthy deliberations or the questions the jury asks the judge.

Trials of the Century

The O. J. Simpson murder trial was described by some journalists as "the trial of the century."

The same descriptive term was used for the trial in 1935 of Bruno Hauptmann for the kidnapping of Charles Lindbergh's son and for the 1970 murder trial of Charles Manson who, with his cult followers, murdered seven people.

AP court reporter Linda Deutsch lists other key trials: "The Pentagon Papers trial of Daniel Ellsberg that told us about the Vietnam War. . . . The Rodney King trials reflected racism in the ranks of the police department. And the Simpson trial, of course, focused on celebrity justice and racism in the courts."

Verdict

13. The verdict in a criminal trial must be unanimous—guilty or not guilty. If the jury reports it is deadlocked and has little chance of reaching a verdict, the judge declares a *mistrial* because of the *hung jury*. After a verdict of guilty, the defense may move to set aside the verdict or file a motion for a new trial. Such motions usually are denied, but the decision may be appealed.

After the jurors are discharged they are free to discuss their deliberations unless the judge gags the jury. In most states, the judge does not have that right. Following major trials, the reporter will interview jurors about their deliberations.

Verdict Essentials The time the jury deliberated, the counts on which the jury convicted and the possible length of the sentence(s) must be included in the verdict story.

INDIANAPOLIS, Feb. 10—Mike Tyson, the former heavyweight champion and one of the world's most recognized figures in and out of boxing, was found guilty tonight of raping an 18-year-old beauty pageant contestant last July.

In a verdict handed down almost 10 hours after it went to the jury, Mr. Tyson was found guilty on one count of rape and two counts of criminal deviate conduct.

Sentencing is set for March 6. Each of the counts carries a maximum sentence of six to 20 years. Under Indiana law, Mr. Tyson will likely receive an eight to 12 year sentence as a first-time offender with a juvenile record, Reuters reported.

In the case of an acquittal, the time of deliberation, the charge and the length of the trial usually go into the lead. In some cases, the makeup of the jury is considered relevant:

> LOS ANGELES—O. J. Simpson was found not guilty of the murders of his ex-wife and her friend after a year-long trial that attracted worldwide attention.

Theater. "I have always compared big courtroom trials to great theater filled as those trials are with revelations of human weakness and folly, with violence and sorrow and humor and pity and passion, all the more fascinating because these are real people, real life."

—*Theo Wilson*

The jury of eight blacks, two whites and one Hispanic reached their verdict yesterday after less than four hours of deliberation. The verdict was announced today in Superior Court by Judge Lance Ito.

The AP blended several elements in its lead when Timothy McVeigh was convicted of the Oklahoma City courthouse bombing:

DENVER (AP)—Timothy McVeigh was convicted Monday of the deadliest act of terror on U.S. soil, a verdict that brought jubilation and bitter tears to relatives of the 168 people killed in the Oklahoma City bombing. The jury will now decide whether he should pay with his life.

Sentence

14. The sentence may be pronounced immediately after the verdict or later, pending a probation report. State laws usually set ranges—minimum and maximum sentences—that may be imposed. Always include the probable time the defendant will serve.

INDIANAPOLIS, March 26—Mike Tyson, the former heavyweight champion who was convicted of rape last month, was sentenced to 10 years in prison today. But the judge suspended the last four years, meaning he will spend no more than six years behind bars.

In a rape case that has attracted worldwide attention and prompted debate about sexual roles and racial attitudes in the criminal justice system, Mr. Tyson is likely to be freed in three years with time off for good behavior.

—*The New York Times*

The AP lead to the sentencing of Timothy McVeigh centered on McVeigh's cryptic brief statement to the court. Here is how the story begins. Notice the inclusion of the reaction of the spectators:

DENVER (AP)—Making no apologies and no plea for mercy, Timothy McVeigh was formally sentenced to death Thursday after borrowing the words of a Supreme Court justice to suggest the blame for the Oklahoma City bombing rests with the government itself.

"Our government is the potent, the omnipresent teacher. For good or for ill, it teaches the whole people by its example," McVeigh said, quoting from a 1928 opinion written by Justice Louis Brandeis in a wiretapping case.

McVeigh, standing before the judge in khakis, a tan shirt and orange prison shoes, spoke for less than a minute in clipped, rapid-fire tones, ending: "That's all I have, Your Honor."

It was the first time he had spoken at any length in court.

Across the courtroom, some of his living victims and relatives of the 168 people killed in the April 19, 1995, blast at the Oklahoma City federal building sat stone-faced. Others stared angrily. They heard no admission of wrongdoing, no remorse.

Convictions on more than one count can lead to concurrent or consecutive sentences. A judge also may issue a suspended sentence, place the defendant on probation or levy a fine.

A majority of offenders in all states are placed under community supervision of some kind rather than incarcerated.

In some states, in trials involving the possibility of a death sentence, the jury decides the sentence following conviction, or a new jury is empaneled to decide.

Tougher Sentences   An increasing number of states are turning from the indefinite sentence to definite or determinate sentences which are fixed by law with no judicial latitude and no parole. This is a response to the public demand that the justice system be tougher with those committing violent crimes.

Studies indicate that only 15 percent of those arrested are first-time offenders, that 60 percent are recidivists—criminals who already have served prison terms—and 25 percent have been convicted but were given probation. These findings have led to the "three strikes and you're out" laws—life sentences for three-time offenders.

Checklist: Criminal Trials

A story written at any one of the 14 stages outlined here should include the current developments and the following basic information:

___ Formal charge.

___ Full identification of defendant.

___ Circumstances surrounding criminal act.

___ Summary of preceding developments.

___ Likely next stage.

Sources

Private attorneys; prosecutor's office, which includes assistant prosecutors, investigators and bureau heads; legal aid attorneys; law clerks of the judges; clerks of the court; court stenographers; bailiffs and security guards; police officers; probation department; state parole office; trial judges, many of whom like to chat with reporters. Clerks also can tip off reporters to important motions, hearings and trial dates.

Look for Color, Strategy, Tactics

Material that gives the trial individuality may include the behavior of the defendant or unusual testimony. Drama is enhanced by describing the setting, the reactions of spectators and the reactions of jurors.

The Full Story. It's not enough to give the sentence in the story. Tell the reader when the convicted person could be paroled. Except for sentences that specify no parole is possible, most criminals are let out of jail long before their full sentences, even for murder. For example:

He will be sentenced Feb. 6 to a mandatory life term with a possibility of parole after 9½ years.

Stories about testimony can be dramatized by using the question-and-answer technique for crucial testimony:

Q. Can you identify the man you say attacked you?
A. Yes, I can. He is sitting there, to your right at the other table where I'm pointing.

Material for the Q and A usually is taken from the court transcript to ensure accuracy.

Reporters understand the necessity of finding patterns of strategy and tactics during a trial. Every prosecutor has a plan, and every defense attorney keys his or her presentation to a theme. Each witness, every bit of evidence is presented with a purpose. The reporter's job is to discover the design of each side in this adversary proceeding. Strategy and tactics shift with the evidence, requiring the reporter to be alert during each day's testimony. The reporter asks himself or herself: What is the purpose of this line of questioning, this witness, this piece of evidence?

This kind of coverage gives the reader, listener or viewer a sense of the movement and direction of the trial. All other coverage is episodic.

Appeals

Convictions may be appealed to a higher court. In criminal cases, the appeal usually concerns errors or improper actions by the presiding judge. Sometimes, jury selection is appealed. Here is how the *Chicago Tribune* handled the disposition of Mike Tyson's appeal:

Boxer Mike Tyson's rape conviction and six-year sentence was upheld Friday by a state appeals court, which rejected arguments that a judge improperly limited defense testimony.

In a 2–1 decision, the Indiana Court of Appeals ruled that the trial court acted within its authority in blocking the testimony of three witnesses who would have contradicted the woman who accused the former world heavyweight boxing champion of raping her in a hotel room in 1991.

Stories about the System

Courthouse reporters are increasingly being asked to take an overview of their beats. Editors want stories about trends in the handling of criminal cases, how Supreme Court decisions affect the local judicial system, plea bargaining, new investigative techniques by the prosecutor's office, politics and the courts. Some editors want their reporters to do accountability pieces: Does the system work; are judges efficient in clearing caseloads; are white-collar criminals being treated leniently; are sentences for drug possession too severe?

One of the most sensitive issues in setting crime control policy is pretrial detention. Denial of bail resulting in detention deprives the defendant, presumed not guilty, of freedom, limits his or her participation in preparing a defense and deprives the person of earnings. Pretrial release, however, makes it possible for the defendant to commit crimes or to flee.

Court Records. With the docket number, records may be obtained, such as the police complaint, the affidavit filed by the complainant, the felony complaint, the disposition if a plea was made at the arraignment or preliminary hearing, the amount of bail. If a trial has been held, the trial record may be kept in another file, again by docket number.

Capital Punishment   Many stations and newspapers have examined the death penalty, which is authorized by 38 states and the federal government. Although more than 3,500 prisoners are under sentence of death, executions average 40 to 50 a year with an average wait of almost 11 years from sentence to execution. California, Texas and Florida alone have 40 percent of those awaiting execution. Over the past 25 years one-fourth of those executed were put to death in Texas.

The disproportionate number of black men on death row has spurred an examination of the judicial process. Although blacks make up about 12 percent of the population they constitute 43 percent of those sentenced to death.

A recent study has shown that people convicted of killing whites were 11 times more likely to be given the death penalty than were those convicted of killing blacks.

Sentencing Blacks   The state prison population is mostly male, young and minority. Data show that almost half (48 percent) of all prison inmates are black. The Sentencing Project in Washington, D.C., reports that "on any given day one in four black men between the ages of 20 and 29 is in prison or on probation or parole."

In some cities, the figures are staggering: 42 percent of the black men in Washington, D.C., aged 18 to 35 are in prison; for Baltimore, the figure is 57 percent.

Does this mean that the law enforcement and judicial systems have a bias that makes for these statistics?

Donna Wasiczko of the *Contra Costa Times* tried to answer this question. She looked at the local situation, and although she found no definitive answers she did find some troubling indicators.

She quotes lawyers for minority defendants who do say there is bias. For example, there is a greater tendency to deny bail to black defendants, who are therefore confined while awaiting trial. All but one of the local judges (the exception is a Hispanic woman judge) are white. Most of the juries are all white.

In the county, 9 percent of the population is black. Of inmates in the state prison from Contra Costa County, 51 percent are black.

Underage Drinkers Tom Puleo of *The Hartford Courant* examined the practice of arresting and trying the owners of bars for serving underage drinkers but not prosecuting the customers who had used forged and faked drivers' licenses. He found 95 percent of the underage drinkers were not arrested. After two months of stories, the state liquor control division issued a new set of guidelines calling for the arrest of the underage customers.

Deadbeat Dads Bonnie Britt of the *Asbury* (N.J.) *Park Press* found that some parents—most of them fathers—were avoiding child support ordered by the courts. More than $650 million was owed in the state, but law enforcement officers did nothing. Some mothers who were owed child support, she wrote, were evicted from their homes when they could not pay rent.

Aggressive Dads Monica Rohr of the *Sun-Sentinel*'s Miami bureau described a new factor in child-custody cases. Fathers are becoming more aggressive:

In the child custody war, the stakes are high, the strategies sometimes ruthless. Everything can become a weapon—child support, visitation, accusations of child molestation.

Now, something new is happening: Dads are fighting back. They're forming support groups and lobbying for legal reform.

They say child custody procedures often push fathers out of the family picture, leaving them to pay excessive child support while being isolated from their children.

These dads say the family court system is skewed against non-custodial parents—who in 90 percent of cases are men, legal experts say.

Inequities in family court do exist, with many older judges unwilling to give fathers the same rights as mothers, says Nancy Palmer, an Orlando lawyer who is chairman of The Florida Bar's legislative committee on family law. . . .

Doing Time Few reporters bother with life behind bars. Once the man or woman is sentenced, coverage concludes. The work of David Ward, professor of sociology at the University of Minnesota and a four-decade student of prisoners and prisons, points the way to a trove of stories about prison life. From his research in maximum security prisons he has concluded:

• Most prisoners advocate harsh measures to deter crime. "They are as concerned about what's happening in our society as everybody else. They are disgusted by child molesters and rapists and drive-by shooters. If anything, their remedies for crime are harsher than the general public's."

- Maximum security prisons, which some civil libertarians condemn, provide protection for inmates who, Ward says, told him that they "are concerned about personal safety. They're willing to give up some of the freedoms of a more open environment to feel safer."
- The general prison population is treated too leniently. "As far as I'm concerned inmates are living in hotels with amenities and people to wait on them. The staff takes care of their every need. There is not enough time for reflection."

Ward supports mandatory sentences and has little confidence in psychological counseling. He finds "not a shred of evidence that psychological treatments work."

Juvenile Defendants   State law closes the doors of juvenile hearings to the public. The theory is that rehabilitation is enhanced without publicity. But changes are being made in the system:

- More juveniles are being tried as adults, and the hearings and trials are open.
- Because of the heinous nature of some crimes, the media are using names of juveniles.
- In states where laws are stringent, the media are seeking access to the judicial process.

When a teen-ager was accused of murder in Sioux Falls, S.D., the *Argus Leader* asked for public hearings for the defendant. By law, juvenile proceedings are closed in South Dakota unless a judge decides there are compelling reasons to open them. In response to the paper's request, the judge proposed a contract with the newspaper in which the newspaper would agree not to publish certain material such as names, photographs and addresses of witnesses or those involved in the slaying. The *Argus Leader* declined to compromise.

Note: The prohibition against disclosing the names of juvenile offenders usually applies to officials, not the media, which means that if a reporter obtains a name, he or she is not prohibited from using it.

In reply to the judge's request that the newspaper limit coverage, Jack Marsh, executive editor of the *Argus Leader,* said, "Our request is that this court case be conducted in the public's full view. It would not be appropriate, nor practical, for us to be admitted to the courtroom and then be restricted in the information we publish. As the public's eyes and ears, the *Argus Leader* needs to be free to report fully what we observe."

Politics and the Courts

Elected or appointed, the judiciary has a deep involvement in politics. Mayors, governors, senators and the president reward party members and campaign supporters, despite their campaign promises of appointments to the bench on the basis of merit. Nominations to the federal judiciary are made by the president, approved by the Senate.

In many areas, the path to the bench begins with a political apprenticeship, either in a campaign or in a party post. Or it may be paved with contributions to a campaign.

During the Clinton presidency, the Republican-controlled Senate refused to confirm two-thirds of the president's nominees to federal appeals courts, and during the administration of George W. Bush, the Democratic-controlled Senate moved at snail's pace on the nominees of President Bush. Political ideology was involved, Clinton wanting activist judges, Bush nominating strict constructionists.

President Bush is a follower of the theory of original intent, the idea that the law must be found, not made. It is also described as the theory of strict interpretation of the Constitution. Critics of this conservative theory ask: "What was the intent of the men who composed the Constitution about cameras in the courtroom or the protection of endangered species?"

Elected Judges   In 39 states, judicial candidates must run for office or run to retain their posts. Many of these races have become costly and have descended to mudslinging. In Ohio, the race for two Supreme Court seats cost $9 million, and elections in Michigan for three Supreme Court seats cost the candidates $16 million.

As a result of these costly and sometimes pugnacious campaigns, efforts have been made in several states to limit campaign politics in the selection of judges. Some of the suggested reforms include replacing elective systems with appointive for major judicial posts; full public campaign support to replace fundraising; the appointment of "fair campaign" panels to monitor judicial races.

Good judges have come out of the political system. Some of the great justices on the Supreme Court of the United States owed their appointments to political considerations. The reporter who examines the system of election and appointment to the bench must be careful not to predict performance.

The Grand Jury

The grand jury may initiate investigations as well as act on charges brought by a prosecutor. It can look into the administration of public institutions and the conduct of local and state officials and investigate crime. In some states, grand juries must be empaneled to make periodic examinations of specific state institutions and official bodies.

Special grand juries can be appointed to look into matters such as mistreatment of patients in a state hospital or a tie-in between the police vice squad and organized crime. The district attorney or the attorney general's office directs the inquiry, although the governor may appoint a special prosecutor to direct the investigation.

When a grand jury initiates action on its own and hands up a report on offenses, the report is known as a *presentment*. A presentment may be a statement of the jury's findings or it can charge a person with a crime.

Grand jury deliberations are secret and any publication of the discussions is treated severely by the courts. However, reporters are free to write about the area of investigation, and witnesses can talk to the press about their testimony in most states. Reporters often will try to learn who is testifying by stationing themselves near the jury room. Knowing the identity of witnesses, reporters are free to speculate. But the morality of publishing the names of witnesses is questionable because the grand jury may question witnesses not directly involved in wrongdoing, and even those under suspicion are not to be considered guilty.

One way reporters have learned about witnesses is by watching for motions to dismiss subpoenas issued to require witnesses to appear before the grand jury. Such motions are usually part of the public record and thereby provide the reporter with a document that can be reported.

In covering grand jury matters, as any pretrial proceeding, the danger is that publicity may harm innocent people or impair a defendant's right to a fair trial. Several verdicts have been reversed because of newspaper and broadcast coverage. The reporter must balance the right of the individual with the public's need to know what its official bodies are doing. Once the grand jury takes formal action, the report can be publicized.

Trouble Areas   Some reporters knowingly violate or skirt the laws to obtain information about grand jury investigations. They act in the belief that there will be no prosecution of their deeds. Sometimes they are mistaken, as the managing editor, city editor and two reporters for *The Fresno Bee* learned after their newspaper published material from a sealed grand jury transcript. They refused to reveal their source and were charged with contempt of court.

The reporter should check local and state laws, particularly when assigned to the police or court beats. Here are some actions that violate the laws of many states:

• Publishing confidential grand jury information leaked by someone in the prosecutor's office. (It is legal to use information provided by a witness about what he or she told the grand jury.)
   • Using documents or property stolen from the police or an individual.
   • Using confidential records transmitted or sold by the police.

In these instances, the reporter becomes an accomplice to a criminal act and can be prosecuted.

Time Out for a Good Laugh

Court coverage is usually serious, sometimes high tension. But courtrooms sometimes ring with laughter. Attorneys do crack jokes, judges deign to comment sarcastically on cases and witnesses unwittingly provide laughs:

• A reporter heard this aside in a South Dakota federal district court from a man charged with theft of livestock when the jury returned a not-guilty verdict: "Does this mean I get to keep the cows?"

• In his summation before a state district court in the Midwest, the lawyer for a man charged with armed robbery pleaded, "I ask you, ladies and gentlemen of the jury, to give the defendant your best shot."

• When a Minnesota county court judge was asked to perform a marriage for two men, the judge turned to one of them and asked, "Which one of you has the menstrual cycle?"

"Not me," said one of the men. "I got a Harley-Davidson."

• The judge in a New York case looked at the divorcing couple and announced, "I am going to give Mrs. Sheldon $3,000 a month."

"Great," her husband said. "And I'll toss in a few bucks myself."

Further Reading

Alexander, S. L. *Covering the Courts: A Handbook for Journalists.* Lanham, Md.: University Press of America, 1998.

Chiason, Lloyd Jr., ed. *The Press on Trial: Crimes and Trials as Media Events.* Westport, Conn.: Greenwood Press, 1997.
(A study of 16 major criminal trials from the 1735 trial of colonial printer Peter Zenger through the trials of John Brown, Lizzie Borden and Bruno Hauptmann to the O. J. Simpson murder trial and how they reflected the concept of justice at the time of the trials.)

Thaler, Paul. *The Spectacle Media and the Making of the O. J. Simpson Story.* Westport, Conn.: Praeger Publishers, 1997.

Toobin, Jeffrey. *The Run of His Life: The People v. O. J. Simpson.* New York: Random House, 1996.

Two issues of the *Media Studies Journal* published by The Freedom Forum Media Studies Center are useful:

"Crime Story," a selection of articles about the police and courts by a variety of authors that include judges and reporters: Winter 1992 issue.

"Covering the Courts," articles about cameras in the courtroom, the Simpson and McVeigh trials and legal aspects of court coverage: Winter 1998 issue.

Bob Zellar, *The Billings Gazette*

**There is always a story
behind the result.**

Preview

The most heavily read section of the newspaper after local and entertainment news is sports news. Television coverage draws millions of viewers. The nation is made up of fans, many of them experts on the sports they follow.

The sports reporter handles:

• **Game stories:** Coverage requires the score, key plays and players, effect of the game on standings, turning point of the game and post-game interviews.

• **Profiles:** Personality stories on new players, athletes having outstanding seasons, game stars, coaches. Profiles require background, plenty of quotations, the individual in action.

• **Illegal and improper activities:** Payoffs to college players, drug use, racism, academic violations by coaches and schools, penalties to colleges.

• **Also:** Recruiting, salaries, personal lives of athletes, recollections.

When Susan V. Hands went to her first job to cover sports for *The Charlotte Observer,* she was anxious to investigate the growth of participant sports and to promote the development of women's athletics. Hands quickly shifted gears.

"I learned that people buy the morning paper to find out what happened in last night's football or basketball game. And our readers would be angry if, instead of finding the highlights and statistics of yesterday's North Carolina State basketball game, there was an investigative piece on the lack of athletic training available to girls in Charlotte high schools," she says.

Readers want to read about the game. They want to savor the important plays again, despite having seen some of them twice—once as they unfolded on TV and once again, courtesy of instant replay. But the assumption that readers have seen the game on television may no longer be valid, says Frank Barrows, managing editor of the *Observer.* With so many games available to television viewers, the reporter cannot presume that the reader saw any particular game.

"Game results sell newspapers," says Hands.

Fans also want to know what goes on off the court and the field. "We take you behind the scenes," says Mark Mulvoy, the publisher of *Sports Illustrated,* whose circulation of 3 million is said to reach 16 million men and 5 million women for each issue. And that is with a subscription cost of $70 a year, one of the highest among magazines.

Insatiable Demand

The appetite for sports is voracious. The Super Bowl draws 150 million viewers, and advertisers line up to spend more than a million dollars for a brief commercial. The Associated Press assigns 100 writers to cover sports, and these writers send out more than 150,000 words a day plus statistics—enough to fill 20 pages of an eight-column newspaper. The local sports staffs of most newspapers are larger than business, education and municipal government staffs combined.

All-news radio broadcasts sports briefs every 15 or 30 minutes, and all-sports radio stations offer 24 hours a day of sports talk. Then there are the sports cable TV stations, ESPN and Fox Sports, as well as numerous sports Web sites.

Sports is so pervasive that the language and personalities of sports have become part of our common vocabulary and metaphor. We say of someone who has failed in an enterprise that he "struck out." When someone does a great job, we say he "hit a home run."

Public interest in games goes back a long way, and just about every culture and country has a history of sports. In modern times, Hearst and Pulitzer recognized the interest in sports when they waged their circulation battles a hundred years ago. But the plunge into sports mania, historians say, began with a boxing match in 1926.

The Fight That Did It

When the Manassa Mauler, Jack Dempsey, met the erudite Gene Tunney for the heavyweight championship, the nation—and parts of the world—stood still. Publishers who had paid sports scant attention now found that "it is impossible to print too much," reported Will Owen Jones, the editor of the *Nebraska State Journal.* Jones had been asked by the American Society of Newspaper Editors to look into the "national obsession for sporting intelligence" because the serious editors were alarmed by the interest in what they considered entertainment.

Seven hundred reporters covered the fight. They dispatched two million words to an enthralled public, says Bruce J. Evensen of DePaul University in his article in the *Journalism Quarterly.* " 'Cave Man' Meets 'Student Champion': Sports Page Storytelling for a Nervous Generation During America's Jazz Age." Evensen writes, "Press coverage of the Dempsey-Tunney 1926 title fight signaled the arrival of the modern sports page as a major player in the struggle for circulation."

The Long Count Tunney won that match, dethroning the mighty Dempsey who had reigned as champion for seven years. The rematch the following year generated even more print, and it is still discussed on the sports pages. In the seventh round, Dempsey knocked Tunney down. But the referee did not begin to count over the downed new champ, because Dempsey failed to go to a neutral corner. Sportswriter Roger Kahn says that Tunney was on the canvas for a full 18 seconds. Later, when Tunney floored Dempsey with a sharp right hand to the jaw, the referee began the 10-count immediately, not pressing Tunney to go to a corner of the ring. Dempsey was counted out in what Kahn says was eight seconds. Kahn says there was much talk at the time of the interest of the mob in finding a referee.

To test prospective hires, some sports editors ask the applicants: "What's the 'long count?'" Those who answer, "Dempsey-Tunney, 1927" get the job.

Game Coverage

All aspects of sports interest fans, but the most pressing question they want answered is, "Who won?" Radio and television answer that question quickly enough for most games. Still, fans want to know more—how the key play came about, why the star failed in the clutch, what the coach thinks of the team's performance. Fans will read about the game, already knowing the score, and they will watch replays on TV and listen to recaps on radio.

For those games that do not make it to radio and TV, the newspaper will carry straight game stories, the result of the game in the first paragraph. But for most major sports, the news story is featurized in newspaper and sports magazine accounts.

Featurizing the Game Story

When the Green Bay Packers went into the Metrodome to play Minnesota, they carried a heavy burden, though the Packers were in first place in the National Football League and were favored to win the game. Instead of winning, they were demolished 35–13 . . . which just about everyone who follows the sport knew as the game was on national television.

So most stories began with a reference to the jinx that followed the Packers into the Minnesota home territory:

Mike Roemer

Losing Effort

Brett Favre was expected to direct his team to an easy victory over the Minnesota Vikings. But the game turned out to be a 60-minute exercise in frustration for the Packers' quarterback.

No matter how good the Green Bay Packers are they just do not play well in the Metrodome.

The Packers' star quarterback Brett Favre threw for only 169 yards against Minnesota's usually porous pass defense.

Before the game, it was ranked 28th in the league against the pass. But in stifling Favre on the way to a 35–13 win, they notched their eighth victory against Green Bay in the Packers' 10 visits to the Metrodome.

This story works for a national audience. Rewritten for broadcast, it went out on the network and cable stations. But for Minnesota papers and stations, the lead emphasized the Minnesota victory angle:

Minnesota quarterback Dante Culpepper outran, outpassed and outplayed Brett Favre in a runaway victory at the Metrodome yesterday.

The score is in the third paragraph of the story since there was hardly a soul among Minnesota fans who did not know that their team had trounced the Packers.

Baseball Playoff The National League playoff games were also televised nationally, and few baseball fans were unaware that the Arizona Diamondbacks had defeated the Atlanta Braves in the fifth game to win the playoff series 4 games to 1.

Fans look to some interesting sidelight, a key play, a rising star to lure them into reading about a game they had followed so closely the day or night before. Here's how one sportswriter handled the fifth and deciding game:

A couple of unknowns took center stage to propel the Arizona Diamondbacks into the World Series.

The Diamondbacks greatest strength, Randy Johnson, pitched seven innings and began to tire from a rising pitch count with his team a run ahead. Enter young Byung Hyun Kim, whose submarining pitches kept the Braves at bay over the eighth and ninth innings to preserve a 3–2 victory.

The deciding runs came from the bat of pinch-hitter Erubiel Durazo, who had not hit a home run off a left-handed pitcher since Sept. 9, 1999. His two-run homer came in the fifth inning on a 2–2 pitch from Braves pitcher Tom Glavine. The ball barely cleared the left-field wall.

Notice the details, the specifics in these three paragraphs. The task of the writer is to try to make the game come alive again. for those who have seen or heard the game and who know the score.

Lead Elements

Notice that in the football and baseball game stories key players were featured. When Michael Jordan returned to the basketball court and played in the opening game of the season, he was the center of the story, although his team lost:

> He did not have the rise in his legs, the
> touch on his jump shot, or his court savvy.
> Michael Jordan came up short in his come-
> back with the Washington Wizards in its
> loss to the Knicks last night.

As the season progressed, Jordan regained his touch and savvy. In three successive games, he scored 51, 45 and 29 points to become the fourth NBA player to reach 30,000 points, behind Kareem Abdul-Jabbar, Karl Malone and Wilt Chamberlain.

Most game stories focus on one of the following: a key player, a pivotal play, a change in the standings or a record set in the game.

See **Serena Wins** in *NRW Plus* for how a reporter handled a tennis match that most fans had seen on TV.

Andrew D. Bernstein,
NBA photo

Michael Jordan

"High in the air, his legs splayed, his tongue flopping out of his mouth, he seems weirdly relaxed, calm, as if there were no one special around and plenty of time to think through his next move, floating all the while. Faced with double coverage, as he almost always is, Jordan finds a way to wedge between defenders, elevate as if on an invisible forklift, his legs dangling, and then drop the ball through the hoop. The ease of his game makes the rest of the players, all of them stars in college, look rough, somehow—clumsy, a step slow."

—David Remnick

From the Players' Perspective

To see the game the right way, look at it the way the players do. The advice is given by Thomas Boswell, a sportswriter for *The Washington Post,* in his book *Why Time Begins on Opening Day* (New York: Doubleday, 1984). Boswell writes about baseball, but his suggestions apply to most sports that reporters cover:

Judge slowly. "Never judge a player over a unit of time shorter than a month . . . you must see a player hot, cold, and in between before you can put the whole package together."

Assume everybody is trying reasonably hard. ". . . giving 110 percent . . . would be counterproductive for most players. . . . Usually something on the order of 80 percent effort is about right."

Forgive even the most grotesque physical errors. "It's assumed that every player is physically capable of performing every task asked of him. If he doesn't it's never his fault. His mistake is simply regarded as part of a professional's natural margin of error."

Judge mental errors harshly. "The distinction as to whether a mistake has been made 'from the neck up or the neck down' is always drawn."

Pay more attention to the mundane than to the spectacular. "The necessity for consistency usually outweighs the need for the inspired."

Pay more attention to the theory of the game than to the outcome of the game. Don't let your evaluations be swayed too greatly by the final score. "If a team loses a game but has used its resources properly . . . then that team is often able to ignore defeat utterly. Players say, 'We did everything right but win.' "

Keep in mind that players always know best how they're playing. "At the technical level, they seldom fool themselves—the stakes are too high."

Stay ahead of the action, not behind it or even neck and neck with it. "Remember that the immediate past is almost always prelude."

Checklist: Games

___ Result: final score, names of teams, type of sport (if necessary, explain that it is high school, college, professional); league (NFL, AFC, Ivy League, Western Conference).

___ Where and when game took place.

___ Turning point of game; winning play; key strategy.

___ Outstanding players.

___ Effect on standings, rankings, individual records.

___ Scoring; details of important baskets, goals, runs, etc.; summaries of others.

___ Streaks, records involved, by team or player.

___ Postgame comments.

___ External factors: weather, spectators.

___ Size of crowd.

___Injuries and subsequent condition of athletes.

___Statistics.

___ Duration of game when relevant.

Game Details

Unless a game is exciting or important, sportswriter Ron Rapoport says he tends not to include much detail.

"Usually a couple of paragraphs are enough to sum up the key plays. I prefer to use the space to concentrate on one or two or three of the most interesting things that happened and to tell what the players involved or the manager thought about them.

"Often, a game story will be built around somebody who had a large effect—positive or negative—on the outcome," Rapoport says. "It is almost mandatory that we hear from this key player and, though there are some spontaneous talkers who begin at the sight of a notebook, it is almost always better to have a question in mind. This sounds simple enough, but often takes some thought. The right question will often do wonders.

"I also like to listen to what's being said by the players—not to reporters—but to each other. They often have funny conversations when they've won, sympathetic ones when they've lost. Good dialogue can dress up a story."

Listen to Edd Roush, who played for the Cincinnati Reds from 1916 to 1931 and had a lifetime .323 average. He is talking about today's ballplayers: "Don't ask me about these modern players. If they had come out to the park when I was playing we'd have run them out of town. These fellers bat .265 and think they're hitters. Their gloves are as big as two of ours and they still can't catch the ball. And they're millionaires." (From "A Visit to Edd Roush," by William Zinsser, *The American Scholar,* Winter 1989.)

Actions sometimes are as revealing as words. The small moves, the slight shift in the linebacker's position, a change in the way a guard plays his man—these details that the observant reporter picks up often mean the difference between victory and defeat. Watch a center fielder play each batter differently. Keep an eye on the way a forward moves to the basket in the second period after he missed all his shots in the first period.

For more advice on how to prepare for game coverage and how to keep statistics see **Coverage Preparation and Keeping Statistics** in *NRW Plus.*

Expanded Coverage

Todays sports reporters do more than just cover games. They handle labor negotiations, the commercialization and sometimes corruption of intercollegiate athletics, the off-field and off-court activities of athletes and their personal lives. Sports editors want enterprise, investigative stories: Is fan support strong or waning? What's the role of player agents? Who goes out for lacrosse, wrestling, fencing? What happens when a high school boy decides to play for the girls' lacrosse team? Are sports-conscious parents pressing their children too hard? (A

TV documentary reported that 70 percent of youngsters who are pushed into sports burn out by age 13 and that fewer than 1 percent of high school athletes qualify for any sort of college scholarship.)

Personal Lives

At one time, what athletes did off the field was their business, even if it affected their play. No one tried to find out why Hank Thompson played third base so strangely for the New York Giants. "I had always supposed it was simply Thompson's way to scoop up a grounder along with the bag and whatever bits of grass and gravel were in the area and hurl the entire package across the diamond, leaving the first baseman to sort it out as best he could," said Peter Andrews of the days he covered the team.

Today, he would find out and probably report that Thompson often played third base drunk.

Alan Robinson, an AP sportswriter, says, "We're people writing about people instead of people writing about heroes. That's healthy."

Athletes as Models

When Charles Barkley threw a man through a plate glass window in a bar, he received a call from Michael Jordan.

"Charles, I love you like a brother," Jordan said he told Barkley, "but you can't do that kind of thing. It's stupid. And you have to stay out of bars. They're only trouble."

Jordan is considered by many sportswriters to be the greatest of all basketball players. With that came close scrutiny of his successes and failures off the court as well as on. Asked about his refusal to endorse an African-American candidate for the U.S. Senate from his home state of North Carolina who was running against a candidate with a deeply conservative stance on race relations, Jordan replied, "Republicans buy shoes, too." As the major sports figure for Nike, Jordan also never spoke out when it was disclosed that Nike exploited its workers in foreign countries.

A sports columnist wrote of athletes in general, though he obviously had Jordan in mind, "The times have produced a remarkable chemical reaction in some players; it has fattened their wallets and bankrupted their wits."

A Different Score *Sports Illustrated* checked on the extracurricular activities of players in the National Basketball Association and came up with the report that many NBA players have fathered illegitimate children, one with seven by six different women. Another player has five illegitimate children to add to the two by his wife.

The detailed disclosure named several players on its "NBA All-Paternity Team." They include Patrick Ewing, Juwan Howard, Shawn Kemp, Jason Kidd, Stephon Marbury, Hakeem Olajuwon, Gary Payton and Scottie Pippen. Kemp pays an average of $6,000 a month for each of his seven children. Not to worry. He has a seven-year contract for $107 million.

No Story. The veteran sportswriter Robert Lipsyte says many sports reporters would not write about some of Muhammad Ali's antics. "They figured it would deny them access if they did," he says. Lipsyte adds, "A lot of athletes tend to be ordinary people with extraordinary skills. He was an extraordinary person. He was beautiful. He was a genius at what he was."

But reporters covered for Ali, he says. "He's not really being covered. He's being beatified. Access is carefully given."

One of the major basketball agents told the magazine, "I'd say there might be more kids out of wedlock than there are players in the NBA." He said he spends more time "dealing with paternity claims than negotiating contracts," *Sports Illustrated* reported. Fans do not take kindly to negative stories about their favorite players. For their reactions, see **Outraged Fans**, *NRW Plus*.

Fans prefer the brighter side of sports, and there are plenty of stories about athletes' overcoming adversity.

A Tragic Childhood   When Terry Glenn of the New England Patriots set an NFL record of 90 catches as a rookie, Thomas George of *The New York Times* interviewed him and told of Glenn's childhood:

> Glenn's mother was murdered in his hometown, Columbus, Ohio, when he was 13. His father lives somewhere in Columbus and Glenn has never met or seen him. Glenn grew up in his earliest years on welfare and wearing goodwill clothes. There were days when there was no electricity in his home.

A Dream Realized   Jerry Tipton of the *Herald-Leader* in Lexington, Ky., wrote a moving profile of George Adams, a University of Kentucky tail-back, from interviews with the football player and his friends and family. Tipton begins:

> When Ruth Adams, mother of nine, sits in the living room of her Lexington home, she can look at nine photographs of her children. Five of them are of her younger son, George.
>
> "The others get on me for having so much about George," she said. "I love them all, the grandchildren, too. But George has a special place."

Tipton develops his story slowly, and the picture that emerges is of a family with many difficulties. Adams' father drank. A brother and a sister have served time in jail. Another son, the mother said, is "in trouble."

"George never gave me no kind of trouble," she said, breaking a long pause. "He always brought good things home from school. He made me happy."

When others caused so much trouble, why didn't George?

"He saw so much pain in his mother's eyes," said Donnie Harville, who coached Adams in basketball at Lafayette High. "And he decided he wouldn't make his mother suffer more."

Tipton delves into the family's problems:

> Adams can remember seeing his father walking unsteadily down a street. The son would cross to the other side to avoid a face-to-face meeting. . . .

"When I was young, it hurt a lot," Adams said. "I mean a whole lot. I told myself I'm not going to be like that."

Adams had a dream. "If I can play pro football, the first thing I want to do with my first contract is buy my mother a house," he told Tipton.

Adams was selected in the first round of the professional football draft. He signed a four-year contract for $1.5 million, and he did buy a house for his mother.

Little Leaguers   A stroll over to the local fields some weekend to watch the youngsters playing Little League baseball can pay off with fascinating features. So can recollections of Little League graduates in the major leagues.

"I still remember it like it was yesterday," Paul O'Neill, a New York Yankee outfielder, told a reporter about his Little League days in Columbus, Ohio. "I pitched the championship game and struck out a kid named Darren Waugh to end it. I remember every detail. The games then meant as much to you as these games do now. And you got to go to Dairy Queen afterward."

Four of five of the major leaguers played Little League baseball. Ten-year-old Mark McGwire in his first at-bat in Southern California hit a home run, he recalls.

Looking back on a career with more strikeouts than any pitcher and more no-hit games, Nolan Ryan told Alan Schwarz of *The New York Times* his happiest memories of baseball were playing Little League in Alvin, Tex. "We played for the love of the game and the camaraderie. Little League was the first opportunity for children in Alvin to get involved in any organized activity. It was one of the biggest events in our lives," Ryan said.

Tomorrow's Major Leaguers

The Beat

In addition to covering games, the sports reporter attends sports banquets, drops by the pro shops at the golf and tennis courts, chats with the unsung athletes on the high school swimming, soccer, wrestling and track teams. The high school and college athletes who may go through a season never playing before more than a handful of spectators make for good stories. Not many readers understand why a youngster will run 10 to 20 miles a day to prepare for a cross-country meet, what it is like to engage in a noncontact sport in which the only adversary is the athlete's own mind and body. The runners, the javelin throwers, the swimmers, the gymnasts, the fencers and the wrestlers should not be overwhelmed by the glut of basketball and football coverage.

Sports Writing

Some of the best as well as some of the worst writing appears on the sports pages and is heard on sports broadcasts and telecasts. Perhaps it is the excitement of conflict that encourages these extremes. A team wins; a team loses. An athlete overcomes adversity; an athlete fails miserably when he or she is called on.

Tough Beat. Professional basketball writers say theirs is the most grueling of all sports beats. Covering games in so many cities requires frequent travel, sometimes coast-to-coast twice in a week. "I take care of my body as if I were a player," says David DuPree of *USA Today*. "I don't drink or smoke." Jackie MacMullan of *The Boston Globe* says she works out daily on road trips.

Consider this gem by John Updike about the last at-bat of the Boston Red Sox outfielder, Ted Williams. Williams, one of the greatest hitters in baseball, had done the unbelievable—hit a home run:

Though we thumped, wept, and chanted "We want Ted" for minutes after he hid in the dugout, he did not come back. Our noise for some seconds passed beyond excitement into a kind of immense open anguish, a wailing, a cry to be saved. But immortality is not transferable. The papers said that other players, and even the umpires on the field, begged him to come out and acknowledge us in some way, but he never had and did not now. God does not answer letters.

Now look at this not-so lustrous lead:

Coach Paul Bergen tried his hardest, but neither starters nor subs could stem the avalanche of baskets tossed through the hoops by a tide of Mustang players last night as the Cougars took a 86–42 drubbing from their crosstown rivals.

The sportswriter is trying hard, and that was his undoing. We have an "avalanche" caused by a "tide," and we have one of basketball writer's forbidden words up there in the lead, "hoops."

Let's look at a neat bit of writing at once as an antidote:

When the New York Yankees were winning pennant after pennant and Mickey Mantle was the home run king, Jim Murray of the *Los Angeles Times* wrote, "Rooting for the New York Yankees is like rooting for U.S. Steel."

Let 'em Talk

The experts on sports are the athletes themselves, and listening to them talk about their trade leads to good stories. The material can come in a locker room chat or a more formal interview.

In a piece about Billy Williams, a Chicago Cubs outfielder for many years and later its batting coach, Frederick C. Klein of *The Wall Street Journal* quotes him on hitting:

"You hear fans saying that this star or that one was a 'natural,' but 99 percent of the time they're wrong. Sure, you gotta have ability, but you also gotta work, and every good hitter I knew worked hard to get that way. You have to practice your swing all the time, just like a golf pro. And if you think golf's hard, try it sometime with a guy throwing the ball at you."

One of the best places to listen to athletes, and to ask talk-inducing questions, is the locker room.

"Right after a game when you're talking with athletes . . . that's when they're at their most vulnerable, and that's when you get the most out of a player," says Suzyn Waldman, whose beat includes the New York Yankees and the Knicks. She says, "Sports is flesh and blood, people and stories, and so much humanity."

Enduring Quotes   Some of the best lines of sportswriters are not of their making. All they have done is to quote their source:

A North Carolina State basketball player explaining why he was nervous at practice: "My sister's expecting a baby and I don't know whether I'm going to be an aunt or an uncle."

Shaquille O'Neal, after returning from Greece, was asked whether he had seen the Parthenon. His answer: "I really can't remember the names of the clubs we went to."

A Florida State football coach to his players: "You guys line up alphabetically by height."

Joe Theismann, former football player, then sports announcer: "Nobody in football should be called a genius. A genius is a guy like Norman Einstein."

Steve Spurrier, when University of Florida football coach, after hearing that a fire at Auburn's football dormitory had destroyed 20 books: "The real tragedy is that 15 of them hadn't been colored yet."

A Texas A&M basketball coach to one of his players who had received a D and four F's: "Son, looks to me like you're spending too much time on one subject."

Details, Specifics

Some of the finest writers in journalism toiled in the sports department. Their work is worth reading. Jimmy Cannon was one of the best.

Cannon, who worked for New York newspapers, spent a lot of time with athletes. They felt at ease talking to him, and they liked his respect for them and their sports.

Cannon knew the tedium of their lives on the road, and he occasionally wrote about it. When the Boston Celtics were in New York for a game with the Knicks, Cannon spent the day with Bob Cousy, regarded then as the best basketball player on the court.

The piece begins with the arrival of the Celtics:

> The Celtics arrived here Monday at
> 1:30 in the afternoon and checked into the
> Paramount Hotel where Cousy roomed
> with Tommy Heinsohn. He took a shower
> and put on fresh clothes and talked a
> while with Heinsohn. The topics were

Go Ahead. Some coaches warn their players not to talk to the press. Not basketball coach Gary Williams, who says, "College basketball players are going to meet a lot of weirdos in the real world, so why not let them talk to the press?"

Goodbye

Dick Young of the *Daily News* in New York took a strong personal approach to his coverage. When the Brooklyn Dodgers owner Walter O'Malley decided to move the team to Los Angeles in 1957, Young wrote in his column the following farewell:

> This is called an obit, which is short for obituary. An obit tells of a person who has died, how he lived, and of those who live after him. This is the obit on the Brooklyn Dodgers.
>
> Preliminary diagnosis indicates that the cause of death was an acute case of greed, followed by severe political implications. . . . and, now, Walter O'Malley leaves Brooklyn a rich man and a despised man.

unimportant but occasionally basketball intruded and they recalled fragments of games they had played.

They go to lunch, and Cannon writes: "Cousy ate pea soup, roast beef, potatoes, salad, ice cream and milk. He is a few pounds underweight and his face is lined." Notice the details in Cannon's account.

He accompanies Cousy on a visit to an agent. "He took the subway back to the hotel. He didn't feel tense or nervous but what would happen in the game was always on the rim of his consciousness. It seemed his body was tired in a heavy way."

They chat in the hotel, and Cousy talks about an opposing player he respects who is not given much credit for his playing, Cousy says.

The piece ends with two sentences about the game that night: "Cousy made 35 points, but the Celtics lost 110–99. They caught a late plane to Boston."

The Losers

Pete Hamill, a veteran journalist, wrote these lines to introduce his comments on a book about a baseball pitcher in the twilight of his career:

All good sports reporters know that the best stories are in the loser's locker room. Winners are bores—assuming a false modesty or performing a winner's strut while thanking their mothers, their agents or God. Losers are more like the rest of us. They make mistakes that they can't take back. They are imperfect when perfection is demanded, and thus suffer the sometimes permanent stain of humiliation. If organized sports teach any lessons about life, the most important is about accepting defeat with grace.

Straight Talk Best

Good writing means retaining the colorful language of sports, not falling into the homogeneous prose that infects too much of newspaper and television writing. Russell Baker, a columnist on *The New York Times* editorial page and a die-hard sports fan, bemoaned the decline of baseball talk that, he wrote, once "crackled with terseness, vibrancy and metaphor."

Baker had heard a television sportscaster say, "Ryan has good velocity and excellent location." He meant, Baker wrote, that "Ryan is throwing very fast and putting the ball where he wants to."

Great Lines Sportswriters have written some memorable lines, such as this one about a midwestern quarterback who was a wizard on the field, a dunce in the classroom: "He could do anything with a football but autograph it." (The line came back to some sportswriters when they wrote about a football player at UCLA who was arrested for killing his drug dealer. The player, it turned out, could not read—the product of the win-at-any-price philosophy of big-time sports.)

Nonarguable In 1931 when Babe Ruth was negotiating for a salary significantly greater than what President Herbert Hoover was earning, the Yankees balked. Ruth responded, "I had a better year than he did."

Lasting. The lead that Grantland Rice wrote to the 1924 Notre Dame–Army football game is considered the most famous in sports-writing history:

Outlined against a blue-gray October sky, the Four Horsemen rode again. In dramatic lore they are known as Famine, Pestilence, Destruction, and Death. These are only aliases. Their real names are Stuhldreher, Miller, Crowley and Layden.

Rice thus gave lasting fame to the Notre Dame backfield that won the game that day.

Defeated Warrior

This is one of the most famous of all sports photographs. It shows not a winner but a loser, a quarterback tackled behind his goal line and in his daze comes the realization that his career is about over. This photograph by Morris Berman of New York Giants quarterback Y. A. Tittle was almost tossed out by Berman's editors at the *Pittsburgh Post-Gazette* because it depicted a player on the losing team instead of a winning play or players.

Red Smith was a master writer. Of a notorious spitball pitcher, he wrote that "papers needed three columns for his pitching record: won, lost and relative humidity." Look at this lead he wrote about Buck Leonard, a black first baseman whose career ended before baseball was integrated:

> Wearing a store suit, horn-rimmed glasses, and a smile that could light up Yankee Stadium, a sunny gentleman of 64 revisited his past yesterday and recalled what it was like to be the black Lou Gehrig on a food allowance of 60 cents a day.

The last few words chill an otherwise warm recollection. They sum up a period of American life in a phrase.

Dizzy and Yogi The stilted writing of some reporters makes a sports fan long for Dizzy Dean, the St. Louis Cardinals pitcher and later a sports announcer who was known for his picturesque language. Once he was struck on the toe while pitching and a doctor examined him on the mound. "This toe is fractured," the doctor said. To which Dean replied, "Fractured hell. The damn thing's broken."

Pleased Packer. In his book *Instant Replay* about the fabled Green Bay Packers teams under Coach Vince Lombardi, the author, Dick Schapp, says that the team's fullback Jimmy Taylor spent four years in college "unscarred by education." Lombardi and fans were outraged. As for Taylor, Schapp said, "I was told that he liked it when it was read to him."

Sportswriters carry stories such as the Dizzy Dean incident in their hip pockets. They also have a collection of Yogi Berra's comments handy for use when appropriate:

- It's not over 'til it's over.
- It gets late early at Yankee Stadium.
- That place is too crowded; nobody goes there anymore.
- Ninety percent of baseball is half-mental.
- It's déjà vu all over again.
- When you come to a fork in the road, take it.
- If people don't want to come out to the ballpark, nobody's going to stop them.
- Slump? I ain't in no slump. I just ain't hitting.

Did Berra, former catcher for the New York Yankees and manager of a couple of major league teams, really say that, or are they creations of baseball writers who needed to brighten their copy? No one is talking.

Replenishment   Sportswriters are constantly adding to their storehouse of anecdotes and one-liners. Asked what his most difficult adjustment had been, Ichiro Suzuki, a Japanese baseball player on the Seattle Mariners team, answered, "I can't think of anything, so there must not be anything." Well, that may not rank with Berra's response to a writer who asked how the Yankees would do the coming season. He replied, "It's difficult to make predictions, especially about the future."

But how about this one from Suzuki? When asked his dog's name, he replied, "I would not wish to say without first asking its permission."

Anecdotes

Sportswriters are insatiable collectors of anecdotes they tuck away for use at the appropriate moment.

When an imaginative boxing promoter was trying to schedule a match between Muhammad Ali, who had made a friendly visit to Arab countries, and Mike Rossman, who carried the nicknames the Jewish Bomber and the Kosher Butcher, James Tuite of *The New York Times* recalled in his story a similar ethnic promotion. Years before, Irish Eddy Kelly and Benny Leonard, a Jewish fighter, were in the ring. Leonard was battering Kelly. Finally, in a clinch, Kelly whispered to Leonard, "Hub rachmones. [Yiddish for "take pity."] I'm really Bernie Schwartz."

Rossman, Tuite pointed out, was born Mike DePuano and took to wearing the Star of David on his trunks along with his new name to help sell tickets. The Ali-Rossman match was laughed out of the ring by pieces such as Tuite's.

When Reggie Jackson was elected to the Baseball Hall of Fame, sportswriters trundled out a battery of anecdotes about Jackson, who once referred to "the magnitude of me."

Jackson, who played with the Oakland Athletics, California Angels and New York Yankees, was a massive presence on the field: He hit 563 home runs in his 12 seasons, the sixth highest total in the history of the game, and led his teams to 11 division championships. He struck out more often (2,597) than any other player. And he was as large a force off the field as on, bragging, "I'm the straw that stirs the drink," to one reporter and to another, "I help intimidate the opposition just because I'm here."

He bragged to fellow players that he had an IQ of 160, to which Mickey Rivers, a Yankee teammate, replied, "You don't even know how to spell IQ."

Rivers was a man of plain talk and said to Jackson one day as Jackson—whose full name is Reginald Martinez Jackson—was rattling on about his greatness: "You got a white man's first name, a Puerto Rican's middle name and a black man's last name. No wonder you're so screwed up."

Myth Exploded   The story is one of baseball's most often told—of how the New York Giants came from way behind to snatch the National League pennant from the Brooklyn Dodgers in 1951 with a game-winning, pennant-winning home run by Bobby Thomson. It was, legend says, "the shot heard 'round the world."

The story lasted 50 years, its undoing the result of digging reporting by Joshua Harris Prager of *The Wall Street Journal*.

"I was talking to a friend," Prager says, "and he mentioned hearing a rumor that the Giants were stealing the Dodgers signs." (These are the hand signals a catcher sends out to the pitcher's mound telling the pitcher what kind of delivery to make.) His friend said he didn't believe it. But Prager decided to check the story and interviewed all 21 living members of the 1951 Giants.

"I was surprised so many didn't want to talk about it," Prager said. "Many of them were not happy I was doing it." Thomson broke down and cried. Some were furious. But some, Prager said, "wanted to talk about it."

Prager even located the telescope that was used in centerfield to spy on the catcher's signals. And he tracked down the family of the electrician who set up the buzzer system to relay the stolen signals to the Giants dugout, where they were sent out to Thomson at the plate.

Reporting Is the Key

As Yogi Berra put it, "You can see a lot just by observing." And that's the basis of good sportswriting, of all journalism, for that matter.

The game trophy may seem to go to the writers of the trade. But that's a superficial assessment. Roger Angell, who covers baseball for *The New Yorker* and is called the laureate of the sport because of the high quality of his writing, calls himself a journalist, a working reporter.

Joel Sartore,
The Wichita Eagle-Beacon

Turning Point

The end-zone catch, the successful goal-line stand, the last-second missed three-point attempt, the ninth-inning double play—these turning points in the game usually are the ingredients of the game story lead.

He says that his reporting, his insistence on using carefully observed details in his writing, gives his work authenticity. He also knows his trade. He knows, for example, whom to interview.

Pick the wrong player, Angell says, and you get clichés.

The reporters who spend time on their beats know who the right players are, and they realize that, no matter how much they think they know about the sports they cover, there is always an insightful athlete who can add to their understanding. They seek out these players.

They also know the way games are won and lost. How, for example, pulling the starting pitcher one batter too late led to the winning run. Why calling a run instead of a pass in the last minute of the game crossed up the opposition and led to a victory. They know why players fouled the star center at the end of a close basketball game, and not the guard who carried the ball downcourt.

They can examine data for a story on the disparity in salaries for men and women coaches, and they can track the graduation records of white and black athletes. They realize that there is as much going on off the field as on, and in the long run it may well be more important than this game or that one.

Sportscasters   Bob Costas, considered one of the best sports broadcasters in the business, sees a decline in his trade, the result of bad journalism. Most sports broadcasting, he says, is "bland shilling and repetition of clichés—not just clichéd expressions but clichéd takes on situations—broadcasting without any element of journalism or a fresh eye."

The essence of sports broadcasting, he says, is solid reporting of the sport and the event.

Starting Out

Many sports reporters learn the basics covering high school sports. Cathy Henkel, sports editor of *The Seattle Times,* began her career covering high school football games for *The Register-Guard* in Eugene, Ore.

"It was the best start I could have gotten," she says.

Some aspiring sportswriters begin in high school as stringers for local and regional newspapers and stations. Then they go on to cover college sports. Sam Smith, who covers the Chicago Bulls for the *Chicago Tribune,* was an accounting major at Pace College in New York. He liked sports and decided to cover it for the college weekly newspaper, the *Pace Press.*

The newspaper adviser spotted Smith's talent and suggested he add journalism to his studies. He did, found it a close fit with his interests and abilities and sold his accounting textbooks.

To the young reporter who can quote the pass completion records of the quarterbacks in the National Football League, being assigned to cover a high school football game may seem a letdown, if not a putdown. Not so.

High School Sports

A veteran sports reporter remarked that despite the attraction of professional football, major league baseball and skilled professional basketball players, local high school sports remains a dominant factor in many cities. "An American may not be too familiar with the workings of his city hall, but he knows his high school football team lineup."

A journalism instructor with years of reporting experience was astonished one Friday night early in his job at a midwestern state university to hear roars in the distance. They were persistent and sometimes advanced on him like a tidal wave. Concerned, he asked a neighbor what was going on.

"That's the Tigers game," he was told. The local high school football team was playing a team from the western part of the state. The instructor learned that some of the high school games outdrew the university's football games.

Big Draw   In many cities, high school sports are the only local spectator sports available to fans. For every Ohio State enthusiast, there are a dozen high school fans in the state.

"It's not uncommon in North and South Carolina for 10,000 people to watch a regular season high school football game," says *The Charlotte Observer*'s Susan Hands. "And every one of those 10,000 is a potential reader of the sports page, if his or her hometown high school hero's name is in the paper."

In fact, Hands says, the most widely read stories in the *Observer* are high school sports. Hands was responsible for covering 116 high school teams in the Carolinas. She handled most of the coverage by telephone and covered one game a week.

In Danville, Ill., the *Commercial-News* covers two local high schools and 30 area high schools as well as a local junior college and Big Ten sports at the University of Illinois and Purdue. The paper covers all home and away games of the local teams and covers each of the other 30 schools at least once. If an area team is in contention for the state playoffs, the *Commercial-News* will cover its games several times.

Readers cannot get high school coverage elsewhere, says Dave Smith, sports editor of *The Dallas Morning News*. He has added 25 reporters since 1995 to cover high school and local sports. A similar boost in high school coverage was made at *The Washington Post*. The *Daily News* in New York gives an entire page to high school coverage daily.

Don't Push

Young sportswriters sometimes try too hard. They push the language, reach too hard for words and phrases. When this happens, the result is sawdust and shavings.

Direct, slender, purposive prose flows naturally from the event. Sports has the built-in essentials of drama—conflict, leading characters, dramatic resolution. There are enough incidents and examples to highlight the event, anecdotes that illustrate the situation; high-quality quotations that reveal the nature of the individual and the event.

Good sportswriting is not confined to the big newspapers covering major teams. Jack Schlottman of *The Globe-Times* of Bethlehem, Pa., learned just before game time that the coach of a high school football team had benched 22 of his players for the season-ending traditional game with an intracity rival. The players had been told to go directly to their homeroom, not to stop for breakfast the morning of the game. Instead, they stopped off at a restaurant and started a food fight that led to a disturbance.

After the game that night, which the team with the benched players lost 43–0, Schlottman interviewed the coach, whose comment ended the piece:

"I'm still in the boy business and I hurt some boys tonight," the coach said. "Hopefully, I made some men."

Imitate, Then Innovate

Red Smith, acknowledged as one of the best sportswriters, said that his goal as he developed his craft was to purify and clarify his writing. "I have sought to become simpler, straighter and purer in my handling of the language," he said. "When I was very young I knowingly and unashamedly imitated others. I had a series of heroes who would delight me for a while and I'd imitate them.

"But slowly, by what process I have no idea, your own writing tends to crystallize, to take shape. Yet you have learned from all these guys and they are somehow incorporated into your own style. Pretty soon you're not imitating any longer."

In talking about his writing, Smith would recall the words of his teacher at Notre Dame, John Michael Cooney, who taught journalism in a basement room of the library. Cooney told his students he wanted clear sentences, "so definite they would cast a shadow."

The secret of Smith's writing is twofold—simplicity and good reporting. "The essential thing," Smith said, "is to report the facts."

Learn and Keep Learning

Because many fans are experts in the sports they follow, sports reporters have to know as much and probably more than their viewers or readers. Preparation is the key, and this includes mastering the elements of the sport being covered and its details. It means knowing the sports' history as well as the strengths and weaknesses of current athletes.

Baseball reporters know the names Willie Mays and Lou Gehrig, Jackie Robinson and Larry Doby. Basketball reporters know about Bob Cousy and Kareem Abdul-Jabbar. Football reporters know Bart Starr, Vince Lombardi and Joe Montana. They can place Sandy Koufax, Hank Aaron, Joe Louis,

Vocabulary. Sportswriters toss the word *hero* around indiscriminately. A last-second basket, a ninth-inning home run, a 75-yard pass and the athlete is called a hero or performed a heroic act. Hardly. As a letter writer to a local newspaper pointed out when the word appeared once too often for her, "Sportswriters should keep in mind the power of words and use them appropriately. The word *hero* should be used for those who truly are—those who help others in time of need, who make sacrifices for others. This is not to diminish athletes. Some are really great. But heroes are another matter entirely."

Advice from a Pro: Try Again, and Again

Red Smith was always helpful to young writers. When a college student sent Smith columns he had written for his school newspaper, Smith replied:

> When I was a cub in Milwaukee I had a city editor who'd stroll over and read across a guy's shoulder when he was writing a lead. Sometimes he would approve and sometimes say gently, "Try again," and walk away.
>
> My best advice is, try again. And then again. If you're for this racket, and not many really are, then you've got an eternity of sweat and tears ahead. I don't mean just you; I mean anybody.

Charles McCabe of the San Francisco *Chronicle* wrote a column shortly after Smith's death in which he said:

> Red was nearly always the last man to leave the press room. Like Westbrook Pegler, he was a bleeder. I well remember him at the Olympic Games in Squaw Valley. When everyone else left and was up at the bar, Red sat sweating, piles of rejected leads surrounding him. He hadn't really even started his story yet. But when the lead came he wrote fluently and always met his deadline.

Smith once remarked, "The English language, if handled with respect, scarcely ever poisoned the user."

Dale Earnhardt, Billie Jean King, Bobby Jones, Jesse Owens, Wilma Rudolph, Whirlaway and Eddie Arcaro without having to resort to reference books.

Breaking the Barriers   Some of these athletes established records. Gehrig, known as the Iron Man of baseball, held the record for playing in consecutive games until it was broken by Cal Ripken. Vince Lombardi was the greatest professional football coach of his time, leading the Green Bay Packers to spectacular successes. Whirlaway was one of the few horses to win the Kentucky Derby, the Preakness and the Belmont Stakes, horse racing's greatest triumph, the Triple Crown.

Jackie Robinson and Larry Doby set records of a different kind. They broke the race barriers in baseball, Robinson in the National League, Doby in the American League. See **Breaking the Barriers** in *NRW Plus* for their stories and how women established themselves as sports reporters despite opposition.

A Day at the Races   When they aren't sure of a new field they are assigned to, they do their homework. Andrea Sachs, a journalism student, learned how to learn when she was assigned to interview a jockey at a racetrack. Sachs had never seen a horse race. As she put it, "I didn't know the difference between a horse and a goat."

But she learned fast. To follow Sachs as she went about doing homework and then doing her interview, see **Quick Learner,** *NRW Plus.*

Two Developments

As sports attracted more and more fans, two aspects emerged that concern the sportswriter. One is the tug of partisanship, the pressure by fans on the journalist to become a rooter as well as a reporter. The other is the role of money in sports and its pervasive and sometimes corrupting influence.

Partisanship

Sports reporters by and large are closer to the teams and the players that they cover than other beat reporters are to their sources. Out of this relationship there are positive and negative consequences, says Rapoport.

"If you are around a group of people a lot you are going to learn a great deal about them and this can only help your reporting," he says. "The flip side of this, of course, is that familiarity breeds both admiration and contempt. Some sports personalities are delightful human beings; others are selfish creeps. Yet you cannot—must not—play favorites in your coverage even while you are expressing your opinion. Likewise, the team must not become 'we.' You must guard against letting your prejudices show."

Ahmad and Michael   On the other side of the equation is the cozy relationship some sportswriters cultivate with athletes. Ahmad Rashad, an NBC sports reporter, began an account of a Chicago-Orlando basketball game this way: "Here in Chicago, Michael Jordan and I have a ritual. We ride to the game together."

This angered Richard Sandomir, who reports on media sports coverage for *The New York Times.* Sandomir wrote in his column, "Isn't Rashad labeled a *reporter?* Or is he just a celebrity pal, whose friendship with Jordan can flout journalism's rules?"

In response, the executive producer of NBC sports said he was happy with their "great relationship. It accentuates his (Ahmad's) believability that they're friends. They often have dinner together. They drive to the games. Ahmad stays at Michael's house when he's in Chicago."

Distance Best   "Reporters and players should not have a game day 'ritual.' If they do, the journalist is compromised, his reporting rendered suspect for what is not revealed from their private rituals," says Sandomir.

The sportswriter Jimmy Cannon wrote, "Sportswriting has survived because of the guys who don't cheer." He was friendly with some of the players whose teams he covered but never a cheerleader.

Stanley Woodward, the legendary city editor of *The New York Herald Tribune,* remarked when he was its sports editor and read stories in which his reporters idolized athletes, "Will you please stop godding up these ball players."

Red Barber, radio's great baseball announcer, described the Brooklyn Dodgers in his warm southern drawl with affection, but it was no greater than his feeling for the Giants or Cubs. His love was for the game, not the team.

His calling the game impartially probably cost Barber his job when baseball coverage on television came under the control of team owners.

Bob Thayer,
The Journal Bulletin

**Fans Cheer,
Reporters Observe**

Team Control   "Every radio and television broadcaster for the 30 major league baseball teams is either paid by the club he or she covers or is hired with that club's approval," writes Ted Rose in the media review *Brill's Content.*

"As a practical matter, these broadcasters are not independent journalists but conduits to the public for the team that directly or indirectly employs them."

Costs of Independence   Many athletes are accustomed to being idolized, but when "the media want to show some perspective about sports or get behind something more important than who won or lost, the athletes generally dislike them," says former pitcher Jim Bouton. "Generally speaking, athletes dislike the media in direct proportion to the extent that reporters exercise their journalistic responsibilities."

Albert Belle of the Cleveland Indians may be the classic angry athlete. He doesn't like reporters and demonstrates his animosity. He was fined $50,000 for swearing at TV reporter Hannah Storm, and after he threw a baseball at *Sports Illustrated* photographer Tony Tomsic the American League ordered him to undergo counseling.

Some sportswriters have been such "homers"—rooters for the home teams—that they have ignored or downplayed NCAA violations, criminal acts by athletes and the mockery of sportsmanship.

A former basketball coach at Clemson says sports reporters must have known of the corruption and sleaziness in collegiate sports. "When I say, 'What's going on?' and you reply, 'I don't know. I didn't seen anything,' that's a lie. You see what kind of clothes he wears, you see his car, you've been to his room. And he comes from the Pulpwood city limits—you gotta be kidding."

Money

Sports is big business. The 100 major sports universities have revenues of more than $1 billion. The professional leagues continue to expand to tap new markets. Teams that were bought for a few million dollars 30 years ago sell for more than $100 million today.

Multimillion dollar signings are no longer news unless they approach $100 million. The top basketball and baseball players make $5 to $10 million a year in salaries, and endorsements can double that. In 1996, Michael Jordan's salary and endorsements amounted to $78 million.

Fans like a winner, and so the bidding for top athletes goes higher and higher, and the star player who at one time spent his career playing with one team—a Ted Williams, Joe DiMaggio, Bob Cousy—now is available to the highest bidder. Teams, too, shift locations, moving from market to market.

Cash Conscious

The historian Henry Steele Commager commented about the consequence of player and team mobility, "We have nothing to be loyal to."

Honesty's Reward. After 16 years as a TV analyst for the New York Mets baseball team, Tim McCarver was fired and a former Mets pitcher, Tom Seaver, was hired as McCarver's replacement. Sandomir described McCarver as "one of baseball's best and most outspoken analysts," which, baseball insiders said, was what cost McCarver his job. "I always tried to give fans the honest truth," McCarver said. Seaver will also be the Mets' pitching adviser and serve as a marketer and in promotion activities, hardly roles that indicate a middle-of-the-road approach to calling games. Sandomir wrote, "It's hard to see how a person would not find conflict in these multiple roles."

Multimillionaires. Coaching an NBA team these days, said a coach, is like dealing with 12 corporations rather than 12 players. Miami Heat Coach Pat Riley said the new ethic of team sports is "the disease of more."

Hank Aaron, the Hall of Fame baseball player and baseball executive, says money has corroded sports. "Today's players have lost all concept of history. Their collective mission is greed. Nothing means much of anything to them. As a group, there's no discernible social conscience among them; certainly no sense of self-sacrifice, which is what Jackie Robinson's legacy is based on. Where there is no conscience, there are no heroes."

Money is the name of the game in collegiate sports as well. Despite the crowded college stadiums and field houses, few universities make money from their teams. Only 10 to 20 schools take in more than they spend. Deficits can hit a million dollars a year, the losses made up by donations and tax revenues. Even college bowl games need money, and get it from states or cities. *USA Today* revealed that 11 of the 25 postseason games one year drew on various public funds, and officials of eight other bowls said they expected to ask state legislators to provide money.

The Goal: Win at Any Cost

The drive to build winning teams has led to lying, cheating and hypocrisy, some of which sports reporters have documented. They have shown that teams have recruited semiliterate athletes and that some schools have gone out of their way to keep the players eligible by having school work done for them, allowing them to take courses from professors who are known to pass athletes despite failing performance, and covering up infractions they commit.

For a record of infractions and illegal practices see **A Miscellany of Misdeeds** in *NRW Plus*.

Black athletes have been recruited for basketball who have little chance of graduating. A study by the NCAA shows low graduation rates of black basketball players at the University of Arizona (14 percent); University of Georgia (20 percent); Georgia Tech (33 percent); University of Kentucky (22 percent); Louisville University (8 percent); University of Minnesota (20 percent); Seton Hall (13 percent). The figures for Syracuse University for black athletes who enrolled from 1987–91 show none graduated.

Among the institutions that regularly graduate more than half their black basketball players are Duke, Georgetown, North Carolina, Providence, Stanford, Villanova and Virginia. Stanford graduated 100 percent in a recent period, Providence 92 percent.

For further material on graduation rates, see **Graduation Rates**, Academic Records *NRW Plus*.

Varied Recruits

The demand for winning teams by boosters, fans and television is intense, so much so that many colleges accept high school athletes with grade-school-level academic scores. They even take criminals.

Sports Isn't the Way out of the Ghetto

And the question arises: Can sports in fact help change the despair, and rebuild the community?

It hasn't. Once many more of us believed that sports and sports figures as models could lead us to the promised land. . . .

But today's life in the inner cities demonstrates that sports as a vehicle for change is not nearly as vital as it once was, or as we had once hoped, or expected.

It was Arthur Ashe who said, rightly, that minority kids spend too much time on the playing fields and not enough time in the libraries. There has simply been too much exploitation and offerings of false or miniscule hope in regard to minority youths in athletics. . . .

—Ira Berkow, *The New York Times* columnist

Seton Hall University in New Jersey grabbed one of the country's leading high school basketball players although he did not earn more than a combined score of 700 on his SAT test. The university kept its offer open to the youth even after he pleaded guilty to sexual abuse in a plea bargain. He had sodomized a young woman on the high school stairway.

When journalists wrote about the incident, the university grudgingly rescinded its scholarship offer. Two weeks later, a major basketball power in Utah made the student an offer but he accepted a full basketball scholarship to a Long Island university.

A leading schoolboy basketball player in Hampton, Va., was convicted on three felony counts of malicious wounding by a mob. Would that affect his chances to play college ball? "Every school in the country wants him," Bob Gibbons, a top scout of high school basketball players, told *USA Today.* "If he was John Dillinger, they'd take him."

Why stop with recruiting high school players for college? High school sports is, as we've seen, a major attraction in hundreds of cities. High schools are recruiting. "Now the college fan is wanting to follow the kids," says Mike Lardner of Sports Channel. "Teen-agers are part of a $10 billion market."

The lengths to which coaches will go to lure promising athletes to their campuses can provide the makings of good stories. To see how one sportswriter handled the recruiting of a high school basketball player see **Recruiting a High School Player** in *NRW Plus.*

A Case Study

In a two-part series, Sam Roe of *The Blade* described how some Toledo high schools were violating state high school athletic association rules by recruiting athletes from other high schools and from junior high schools. More than half the players on one nationally ranked basketball team were transfers. Roe quoted the mother of one transfer as saying that the coach had pressured her to lie about her residence. At another basketball powerhouse, a player's mother said the coach and his aides found an apartment for her family within the school district and paid the security deposit and two months' rent.

Some parents transferred "legal custody of their children to relatives in other school districts so the students can be eligible to play for the best teams," Roe wrote.

The reaction to the series was immediate. The state high school athletic association announced an inquiry, and a coalition of ministers held a rally at which Roe was denounced. More than 500 people at the rally condemned Roe, chanting, "In the South, they had Jim Crow. In Toledo, we have Sam Roe."

The group demanded a front-page retraction of the series and Roe's dismissal.

Six months later, the high school athletic association completed its investigation and placed the two high schools Roe wrote about on probation for two years and fined them $1,000 each for recruiting violations for their basketball teams.

An Overview

Roger Kahn—who wrote a fine book about baseball, *The Boys of Summer*—has a basic approach to his reporting. Most good sportswriters do. Here, from one of Kahn's columns in *Esquire,* is how he describes his approach to his beat:

> Sports tells anyone who watches intelligently about the times in which we live: about managed news and corporate policies, about race and terror and what the process of aging does to strong men. If that sounds grim, there is courage and high humor, too. . . .
>
> . . . I find sport a better area than most to look for truth. A great hockey goalie, describing his life on ice, once said, "That puck comes so hard, it could take an eye. I've had 250 stitches and I don't like pain. I get so nervous before every game, I lose my lunch."
>
> "Some football players," I said to the goalie, whose name is Glenn Hall, "say that when they're badly scared, they pray."
>
> Hall looked disgusted, "If there is a God," he said, "let's hope he's doing something more important than watching hockey games." Offhand I can't recall a better sermon.

Red Smith, who was writing his sports column for *The New York Times* until a few days before he died in 1982, said of sports:

> Sports is not really a play world. I think it's the real world. The people we're writing about in professional sports, they're suffering and living and dying and loving and trying to make their way through life just as the bricklayers and politicians are.
>
> This may sound defensive—I don't think it is—but I'm aware that games are a part of every culture we know anything about. And often taken seriously. It's no accident that of all the monuments left of the Greco-Roman culture, the biggest is the ball park, the Colosseum, the Yankee Stadium of ancient times. The man who reports on these games contributes his small bit to the history of his times.

Rapoport takes what he calls a practical view of sports coverage. "If you can't find something light or something that will make the reader smile or laugh, at least remember and try to show, in style or substance, that these are games these people are involved in, not foreign policy discussions," he says.

However, says Rapoport, "intensely dramatic and emotional things do happen, and when they do the reporter should not be afraid to haul out the heavy artillery.

"Just remember that in such cases the facts are usually enough."

For additional suggestions on covering sports, see **Post Scripts** in *NRW Plus.*

Further Reading

Anderson, David, ed. *The Red Smith Reader.* New York: Random House, 1983.

Angell, Roger. *A Pitcher's Story: Innings with David Cone.* New York: Warner Books, 2001.

Berkow, Ira. *A Biography of Red Smith.* New York: Times Books, 1986.

Bouton, Jim. *Ball Four: The Final Pitch.* Champaign, Ill.: Sports Publications Inc., 2000. The American Library Association selected this book by a former pitcher for the New York Yankees as the best sports book of the 20th century.

Cramer, Richard Ben. *Joe DiMaggio: The Hero's Life.* New York: Simon & Schuster, 2000.

Kahn, Roger. *The Boys of Summer.* New York: New American Library, 1973.

Kahn, Roger. *The Head Game: Baseball Seen from the Pitcher's Mound.* New York: Harcourt, Inc., 2000.

Mantle, Mickey, and Phil Pepe. *My Favorite Summer 1956.* New York: Doubleday, 1991.

Miller, Marvin. *A Whole Different Ball Game: The Sport and Business of Baseball.* Secaucus, N.J.: Birch Lane Press, 1991.

Montville, Leigh. *At the Altar of Speed: The Fast Life and Tragic Death of Dale Earnhardt.* New York: Doubleday, 2001.

Remnick, David. *King of the World: Muhammad Ali and the Rise of an American Hero.* New York: Random House, 1998.

Shulman, James I., and William G. Bowen. *The Game of Life: College Sports and Educational Values.* Princeton, N.J.: Princeton University Press, 2001.

Note: Cramer's book about Joe DiMaggio was greeted with mixed reviews. Some reviewers said it drew too dark a picture of DiMaggio. But most said the book was long overdue. One reviewer said the biography "of one of the greatest of American heroes will tarnish more than just an idol. It will tarnish the American myth, make it appear a manufactured product of wishful thinking and commercialism." In his review, Russell Baker remarked, "Heroes age best by dying young."

Josh Estey, *The Register-Guard*
(Eugene, Ore.)

Local businesses are covered.

Preview

Business and economic activity affects the cost and quality of the goods we buy; whether people buy or rent a home; the kind of car a person buys; even the college a high school graduate attends.

The business reporter handles:

- **Local spot news stories:** Store openings and closings, company personnel changes, new construction, changes in the business climate, annual reports of local companies.
- **Features:** New products developed by local enterprises, profiles of company officials and workers.
- **Interpretative stories:** Effects of national and international economic activity on local business, the influence of local business leaders on municipal policies and the budget.

Good Writing. Business stories need not be dull:

BURBANK, Calif.—After a year and a half of courtship, Mickey Mouse left Miss Piggy at the altar.

This *Wall Street Journal* lead began a story of the breakdown in plans by Walt Disney Co. to acquire the Muppet characters.

News about business and economics has become everybody's personal business. People want to know about the cost of living, job possibilities, how high or low interest rates may go, whether layoffs are imminent in local industries and the value of a bond or stock that they own.

Our food, clothing and shelter are produced by business enterprises, and their quality and the prices we pay for them are largely a result of business decisions. Even the quality of the air we breathe and the water we drink is affected by decisions made by the business community. We have a large stake in those decisions, and we want to be informed of them and to know how they are made.

News about commerce is as old as the newspaper itself. The gazettes and newsletters of the 17th century were established in the business centers of Europe for the emerging commercial class. Though it seems obvious that everyone would have a great interest in pocketbook news—news of the economy—editors came late to the realization and, until recently, business news was a minor part of the newspaper.

One cause of the awakening was the consumer movement in the 1970s that resulted in a new kind of coverage for television and for many newspapers—consumer journalism. Reacting to what appeared to be an attitude of *caveat emptor* (let the buyer beware) among U.S. businesses, newspapers and broadcast stations went into the marketplace to find out why the quality of goods and services was declining while prices were steadily rising.

Curiosity, if not skepticism, about business was strong. Consumers were irritated by products that fell apart too soon and too often, and they were infuriated by the indifference of manufacturers, sellers, repair people and mechanics.

The environmental movement also turned public attention, and then media attention, to the boardrooms of corporations. Journalists decided that their job was to make corporate power accountable. Tom Johnson, publisher of the *Los Angeles Times,* said, "Business news has become page one news because of the emergence of highly controversial issues in which there is an obvious potential for conflict between the corporate and the public interest." In 1968, the *Times* business staff had eight reporters. Today, there are 10 times as many.

Ample Opportunities

Business and economic reporting has exploded, making a wide range of opportunities for those who master the basics of the field. Newspapers publish business sections and have large reporting and editing staffs devoted to the subject. Television has grown from the nightly reading of the Dow Jones closing averages to full-scale coverage with several reporters assigned to the half-hour programs on the subject. Cable offers 24-hour business news. More than 12,000 men and women cover business.

Specialized business publications from *NursingLife* magazine and *Computer Design* to *Food Management* and *Construction Equipment* examine their fields in depth. Sal F. Marino, president of Penton Publishing, Inc., which publishes 30 business magazines says, "The business press is one of the best-kept secrets." He says there are "tremendous opportunities and rewards for the average journalist in the business press." There are more than 4,000 magazines, newsletters and newspapers of the business press.

Online information providers also have business journalists on their staffs. In Silicon Valley—the heart of the computer industry south of San Francisco—business reporters prowl the companies looking for news for news servers like CNET's NEWS.COM (www.news.com).

The Scope of Business News

On Friday night, Tom and Ann Ryan sit down after dinner to make a decision. The birth of their second child means they will need another bedroom. They must decide whether to rent a larger apartment or buy a house.

Tom Ryan spreads out a page of the local newspaper on the dining room table. He points to an article with a headline, "Mortgage Shopping." It begins:

> New York (AP)—Attention mortgage shoppers: Today's specials are 30-year conventional loans—just a 7.5 percent rate and no points if you buy your home now.

The story says that "at no time have there been so many loan options available for those looking to buy or refinance a home. Not since nearly 20 years ago have rates been so low and home prices so stable."

That clinches it for the Ryans. They decide to buy a new home.

Interest rates also are a concern of the Goldensohn family. Robert, a high school senior, wants to attend a private college. The tuition is high and he must have a student loan. The family income meets the necessities and little more. Robert may have to borrow at least $10,000 a year.

If they cannot handle the loan, Robert will have to attend a community college. Their newspaper carries a story on the latest information about student loans and interest rates. The Goldensohns decide they can afford a loan. Robert will go to a private college.

From Cattle Prices to Exchange Rates

In homes in every part of the city, people look to business stories for information. Workers whose contracts are tied to the cost of living watch the papers and television to see how their paychecks will be affected by the latest figures from Washington. Farmers follow the livestock and commodity markets. Vacationers search through the list of foreign exchange rates to see what the dollar is worth abroad before deciding where to spend their vacations. Residents north of the city hear that a new shopping center will be built there; they look through the business pages to find out more about it.

When the interest rates on savings accounts and certificates of deposit sank below 3 percent in the early 1990s, people began to look for higher-interest investments and were lured by advertisements: "Good News for C.D. Holders." What the ads did not point out is that unlike the certificates of deposit, whose principal is guaranteed by the Federal Deposit Insurance Corporation, the touted new investments had high risk.

Business reporters warned their readers of the risk, as they did when investment firms pushed closed-end government bond funds. Investing in such funds, wrote a *Wall Street Journal* reporter, was like paying $1.10 for a roll of 100 pennies.

And More   The Associated Press reports that the giant Merrill Lynch & Co. agreed to pay Orange County $400 million for giving the county "bad investment advice that led to the county's bankruptcy." The county had sought $2 billion.

The Gannett News Service in Washington reports a panel of experts recommends that people should be allowed to put their Social Security payments into private investments.

The *Los Angeles Times* reports that House and Senate committees want to make it harder for people with family incomes of more than $50,000 to wipe out their debts by filing for bankruptcy.

NEWS.COM reveals that some telephone companies are planning to include e-mail addresses in the white pages of their directories.

In its Personal Business page, *The New York Times* surveys the available digital cameras for average folks and includes Web sites for those seeking more information, including product reviews.

Two of *Commercial Carrier Journal*'s editors pose as businessmen and travel thousands of miles from Chinatowns in the United States to Hong Kong, Singapore and Taiwan to expose "the flood of counterfeit merchandise pouring into the United States from the Far East."

The *Argus Leader* in Sioux Falls, S.D., reports that a new pizza place, Papa Murphy's Take-N-Bake, will sell "fresh-made pizzas that can be baked at home." A pepperoni pizza sells for $6.

A business reporter for *The New York Times* watched a recruiter lecturing potential insurance sales personnel for Primerica Financial Services and heard what he later wrote was "a mix of fact and half-truths." Then the reporter, Michael Quint, widened his scope to describe "a companywide pattern of exaggerations in the recruitment of agents and the selling of policies to hundreds of thousands of Americans."

He pointed out that the company has 110,000 agents, "more than 90 percent of them part-timers with little training but a need for extra income." The sales tactics, Quint found by firsthand reporting, "are often misleading and sometimes dangerous to a customer's financial security."

Mike Roemer

Entrepreneurs

The enterprising reporter will pull up alongside the two girls and will stop on a lunchtime stroll when the street vendor is spotted. The perennial question: How's business?

The Human Element

Because business stories can be complicated, writers try to introduce human interest whenever possible in their copy. Vivian Marino—the AP business writer whose story on mortgage rates influenced the Ryans to buy a home rather than rent—says, "I try to keep my stories as interesting and memorable as possible, often by using anecdotal examples to which readers can relate."

In a story about the financial problems of some retirees, she began with a retired worker trying to get by on his pension:

NEW YORK (AP)—After three decades laboring in the grimy steel mills around Pittsburgh, Richard L. Walters thought he earned a clean retirement.

But since taking early leave from LTV Corp., Walters, 60, and his wife Audrey, 54, have been barely getting by. His $922 monthly pension check isn't enough for the loan payments on the couple's New Brighton, Pa., Victorian, along with food bills and other escalating expenses.

So he's trying to go back to work. "Right now, it's pretty hard to get a job around here. I've been tinkering around on people's cars, making a couple of dollars here and there. I would like to just stay retired, but the way things are now I can't."

Marino ranges widely. She has written pieces about compulsive credit card spenders, growing numbers of auto repossessions, how to obtain a credit file and how to challenge inaccurate information. For her New Frugality series, she described what happened to Yuppies, the free-spending generation of professionals. Some have now become Grumpies, she writes—grown-up mature professionals—who skimp along on reduced incomes.

For a piece on college scholarships, her reporting turned up the availability of thousands of scholarships offering billions of dollars. In fact, she writes, nearly "$7 billion in college money goes unclaimed each year, or about $600 for every student in the United States." Her piece begins:

NEW YORK (AP)—Short of cash for college? Billions of dollars are waiting for the right students to come along.

The Two-Ten International Footwear Foundation, for instance, provides up to $2,000 for undergrads with parents in the shoe business. Post-graduate students can get $12,500 from the International Union

for Vacuum Science, provided they study—you guessed it—vacuum science.

Even comedian David Letterman has gotten into the act, offering scholarships for telecommunications majors at alma mater Ball State University in Muncie, Ind. Grades aren't important.

Personal Finance

The Ryan and Goldensohn examples and Marino's story about Walters' retirement are called personal finance stories. A survey of readers found that personal finance is the most sought-after material on the business page. Readers—and listeners, too, stations have learned—seek information about solving credit problems, making decisions on investments, deciding whether to buy or lease.

Business Writer

When Vivian Marino joined the Miami bureau of the AP, she was assigned to do a series on the labor problems of Eastern Airlines. When she had done that, she was given more business assignments.

"I decided to carve out my own niche by concentrating on business and finance." Soon she was appointed regional business writer.

Then she was transferred to New York. "I had to learn about the markets and more complicated business and financial issues. I learned from my colleagues and from many of my sources. I also read a lot."

Marino writes a column on consumer affairs and personal finance for the AP.

The *Atlanta Journal-Constitution* carries a page weekly on personal finance. For the page, individuals open their checkbooks and bank books to reporters. The *Journal*'s business page feature "Money Makeover" deals with subjects such as planning for retirement and recovering from bankruptcy.

For a personal finance story about saving for college despite the downturn in the economy see **College Savings** in *NRW Plus.*

The Beat

The business reporter ranges widely. In the morning, she interviews local service station dealers about their price war, and that afternoon she localizes a story about the new prime rate and the effects of the failure of the coffee crop in Brazil.

Local stories she has covered include:

- Store openings, expansions and closings.
- Real estate transactions. New products from local enterprises. Construction projects planned.
- Plants opened, expanded, closed. Personnel changes, awards, retirements. Layoffs, bankruptcies.
- Annual and quarterly business reports. Annual meetings.
- Bond offerings by local government units.

If the newspaper or station has no labor reporter, the business reporter covers labor-management relations and the activities of labor unions.

In addition to these spot news stories, the business reporter is aware of trends and developments in the community and area. The business reporter knows the relationship between the prime rate and the local housing market and understands how the city's parking policies affect downtown merchants.

Local Stories

Here is how Bob Freund of *The Times-News* in Twin Falls, Idaho, began a roundup that blended local and national business and economic activity with area trends:

TWIN FALLS—As spring turned into summer, the brightest news for the Magic Valley economy was coming from consumers.

They climbed into new cars at an accelerated pace, and sought credit both to pay for the new wheels and for improvements at home.

They benefited from a vicious war of price cutting and couponing among area grocery stores.

Indicators compiled by *The Times-News* for the second quarter ending June 30 show some momentum in the Magic Valley economy, but also some significant drags.

Despite lower mortgage rates and a national surge in homebuying, the biggest consumer of all, the home buyer, still is not pounding down the doors at Magic Valley real estate agencies.

Josh Estey,
The Register-Guard

Ready to Go

Agriculture, the underlying financial pump for the valley economy, remains grounded by low commodity prices.

Of course, the Magic Valley is not alone in these problems. Idaho's economy generally is weak, and with trade imbalances pressing more and more on manufacturing, the U.S. is wavering in a twilight zone between recession and growth.

Nationally, economists are calling the situation a growth recession. The economy is growing, but it is not gaining enough strength to cut unemployment substantially.

A Drugstore Opening

In small communities the line between news and free advertising is so narrow it approaches invisibility. A large department store opening will be reported by the biggest newspapers. But a drugstore opening will not. The smaller newspaper or station will carry the drugstore opening and might cover the enlargement of a hardware store.

Here is the beginning of an 11-paragraph story that appeared in a newspaper in Massachusetts:

For 10 years, tailor Frank Saporito plied his trade with Davis & Norton Inc. on North Street here, where he was in charge of all alterations. When that business closed last month, Saporito was out of work—but not for long.

Saporito landed on his feet and decided to go into business for himself at 251 Fenn St., just across the street from the post office. He's been open there a little more than a week.

"I wanted to try it by myself," Saporito said. "I think it's a good move. I sure hope so."

Chain Store Alert

Business reporters keep an eye open for any moves into town by the major chain stores. Such moves can have a major impact on local business.

When Wal-Mart started building a store two miles outside Hudson, N.Y., local store owners took notice. The massive chain, the nation's largest retailer, has in other areas driven out local businesses because of its pricing policies. In Hudson, which marked a move into the northeast for the chain, local businesses spruced up their stores and decided that they will profit from the new shoppers who will be attracted to the area.

In other areas, the mood has been pessimistic. In Greenfield, Mass., local residents voted to bar Wal-Mart from moving into town.

Among the story possibilities: Sale of land for the new store; new employment; new tax revenues; impact on local business now, a year later, five years later.

Coffee Beans and Burritos

The photo on the left accompanied an article by Sherri Buri in the Sunday business section of *The Register-Guard* in Eugene, Ore., that begins:

Before Sony opened its compact disc factory in Springfield, it held a coffee tasting to decide which brand would flow through the company cafeteria's espresso machine.

One morning about two years ago, several local vendors set up shop at Sony's temporary offices in the Delta Oaks shopping center in Eugene. Nearly two hours and three gallons of coffee later, Eugene-based Full City Coffee walked away the winner.

"Money was never a question," recalled Michael Phinney, who owns Full City with his wife, Terril. "In fact, they never asked me how much we charge."

The 6-year-old coffee roasting company is just one of a huge network of local businesses that supply everything from coffee to custom steel work to the 375-employee high-tech company. These local suppliers demonstrate how high-tech giants, such as Sony and Hyundai, send out economic ripples far beyond the factory's payroll when they enter Lane County. . . .

In another article in the section, Jim Boyd profiles a local woman who decided to expand her weekend business:

It wasn't getting the financing. It wasn't finding a location. It wasn't recruiting good workers. The biggest obstacle that Ritta Dreier had to overcome when she recently expanded her business was simply deciding to do it.

For 19 years, Dreier has operated the 10-by-10-foot Ritta's Burritos booth at Saturday Market and other regional events. Despite its nomadic nature, the booth has been a money-maker.

"I can say there's some booths down at Saturday Market—food booths—that are probably happy to make $400 on a Saturday, and I would say there's several Saturday Market vendors that can—on a really, really busy day—can reach probably $1,800 dollars on a Saturday," she said. "And I'm one of the top-grossing vendors at Saturday Market and always have been."

On April 1, Dreier expanded her food service operation by opening Ritta's Burritos Home Cafe, a 29-seat restaurant at 755 Monroe St. that will serve as a permanent home for her business. It's in the same Blair Boulevard neighborhood as the Bagel Bakery, Taco Loco, Pacific Winds Music and Fisherman's Market.

She chose Home Cafe as the name because she has a great affection for her homes—her family home in Cedar Falls, Iowa; her own home on Polk Street; and now the Home Cafe.

Dreier, 41, was born in Cedar Falls and earned a degree in theater and speech in 1977 from Morningside College in Sioux City, Iowa. After graduation, she wanted to get out on her own so she joined her brother, Dan Dreier, and his first wife, Roberta, who were living in rural Eugene. . . .

Josh Estey,
The Register-Guard
New Business

Puff Pieces

Advertising salespeople sometimes promise an advertiser a story about a store expansion or about the cashier who has spent 25 years behind the Hamburger Heaven checkout counter. When the publisher orders a story, the piece is known as a BOM (business office must).

These stories are considered free advertising. Still, it could be argued that some of these events can make good stories. The perceptive business reporter sent to interview the hardware merchant who is enlarging his store might find that the store owner is staking his last dime on this gamble to keep from losing business to the Kmart outside town. And the Hamburger Heaven cashier could become a human interest story.

The Reporter's Requirements

The business reporter is a specialist who feels at home with numbers and is not frightened by lengthy reports and press releases, many of which contain rates, percentages, business and consumer indexes and the jargon of the business world.

Among the skills and attitudes the business reporter takes to the job is the recognition of the power business exerts. Along with this, the reporter has a healthy skepticism that keeps him or her from being awed by the muscle and money that business power generates.

Corporate Raider   The business reporter approaches the money managers and manipulators with the same objectivity and distance that any reporter takes on an assignment. In his profile of a corporate raider, Michael A. Hiltzik of the *Los Angeles Times* was able to find sources and anecdotes to get to the heart of his subject, Irwin L. Jacobs of Minneapolis. Jacobs acquires and merges companies, usually at great profit.

Jacobs usually would pledge to operate rather than to dismantle the firms "on the insight that Americans lionize industrialists and not liquidators," Hiltzik says. For his piece, Hiltzik was able to show that Jacobs dismantled one firm in 17 days, despite his promise to operate Mid American Bancorporation of Minnesota "for his children and his children's children," the story said. Jacobs' profit: an estimated $4 million.

Sour Investment   Specialist though he or she may be, the business reporter must know much more than the world of finance. When Hiltzik was assigned to cover the tribulations of a precious metals investment firm, he had to look through court documents with the same scrupulous and knowledgeable attention a courthouse reporter gives the records. In fact, Hiltzik found in one of the documents a human interest lead to his story about the complicated activities of the firm.

He began his lengthy account of Monex International Ltd. with the story of Kathleen Ann Mahoney, a professional singer who was living in Newport Beach, Calif., when she bought $10,000 worth of silver through Monex. The price of silver went up, and Hiltzik reports, she "invested another $12,000, then another $10,000, and then her last $13,000, relying on what she says was a Monex salesman's pitch that silver prices were rising so fast they might earn $100,000 for her over a year's time." The price of silver reached $50 an ounce.

"Four days later, Mahoney was wiped out. Silver had plunged to $28, and the crash had taken most of her investment with it." Hiltzik wrote.

Sources of Information

The business reporter has a harder job digging for information than most journalists do. Most reporters deal with public officials who live in goldfish bowls. Laws and a long tradition have made the public sector public.

The business world, however, is generally private, secretive and authoritarian. The head of a company can order his or her employees not to talk to reporters. Because businesspeople usually are in competition, secrecy is a natural part of business life. True, businesses are required to file many kinds of reports with various governmental agencies, and these are excellent sources of information. But in the day-to-day coverage of the beat, the business reporter must rely on human sources. Good sources can break the code of silence and secrecy.

Human Sources

Good contacts and sources can be made among the following:

- Bank officers, tellers.
- Savings and loan officials.
- Chamber of Commerce secretaries.
- Union leaders and working people.
- Securities dealers.
- Financial analysts.
- Real estate brokers.
- Trade organization officials.
- Teachers of business, economics.
- Transportation company officials.
- Federal and state officials in agencies such as the Small Business Administration, Commerce Department, various regulatory agencies.

Local Sources

Brenda Schmidt, business editor of the *Argus Leader* in Sioux Falls, S.D., writes the "Eye on Business" column. Usually, she has four or five items about the local business scene. On the next page is a typical column with Schmidt's comments about her sources alongside.

Close-Mouthed. The owners of small businesses are the most reluctant to reveal profits and losses to reporters. Small business is the riskiest commercial enterprise, says Karen Hallows of George Mason University, and shows the largest numbers of bankruptcies as well as the highest returns. Few owners want to reveal that they are going down the drain or making a pot of money.

Comments

■ I saw a sign saying a new grocery store was coming soon. New store owners love to talk about their businesses. I try to make it somewhat personal or give the column that "small town/heard-over-the-fence" feel. I always ask, "Why?"

■ This is another example of watching for signs on stores that have been vacant.

■ The owner sent a press release. Another section of the paper followed this item up with a feature.

■ I knew from covering the company it is expanding fast and likely would move its outlet from an industrial location to a retail site.

Grocery Will Feature Ethnic Twist

■ When Matt Sapari was deciding on a name for his new specialty grocery store, he chose something that reminds him of a popular Middle Eastern dish — stuffed grape leaves.

The Grape Vine, at 1921 S. Minnesota Ave., will sell Mediterranean sweets, cheese, olives, coffees, spices, Middle Eastern breads and groceries. Sapari said the store will be similar to the Olive Branch, which opened a few years ago on East 10th Street.

He hopes to be open by the end of March. The fresh baked products, such as baklava, will be shipped in from Detroit.

"There was a demand for something like that in South Dakota," Sapari said.

Sapari, who moved here from Kuwait seven years ago, has been in the construction business the last two years. His wife and a brother will operate the store.

■ Walt and Nancy Landry open Mind Games at noon today at 2012 S. Minnesota Ave.

The store will sell board games that have been tough to find in Sioux Falls and will rent game rooms to players who want to gather a group to play at the store. Popcorn is free.

"We think we'll appeal to a crowd that goes from 10-year-olds all the way up to kids of 60," he said.

The Landrys decided to start their business after they noticed friends going to Omaha, Neb., and Minneapolis to shop for games. With a little research, they found out Sioux City, Iowa, has three game businesses.

BRENDA SCHMIDT
EYE ON BUSINESS

"If Sioux City can support three stores at 75,000, surely Sioux Falls at 120,000 could support one store," he said.

Mind Games will sell strategic and tactical games such as Dungeons and Dragons, Wild West and Micro Armor, a game that uses mini tanks and recreates famous wars.

"You actually play against other people vs. playing against a computer," he said.

■ Dan Winkler of Sioux Falls has opened The Next Dimension, stand-up virtual reality games in the Dayton's wing at The Empire mall. A game is $5 for about five minutes.

Players also can join forces with other players to meet the computer challenges. Participants wear headsets, see texture mapped 3-D color graphics and hear stereo sound.

"You don't just play the game, you are the game," Winkler said.

■ Gateway 2000 opened its factory outlet this week at 3109 W. 41st St., Suite 4. The outlet is open from 9 a.m. to 9 p.m. Monday through Friday, 9 a.m. to 5 p.m. Saturday and noon to 4 p.m. Sunday.

The personal computer manufacturer's previous outlet was at 700 E. 54th St. N.

Schmidt's co-workers pass along information. An *Argus Leader* employee saw a sign that The Keg on East 10th Street was moving. Schmidt called the owner of the neighborhood bar known for its deep-fried chicken, and he told her, "We've just kind of outgrown the place."

Friends pass along tips. One said a piece of ground in The Empire mall parking lot would be used by Burger King, making it the city's ninth outlet for the fast-food chain.

Mike Kuehl called Schmidt to tell her his Powerhouse Gym, Fitness and Rehabilitation Center would open in three weeks. Sharon Busch called to say her Toys & Treasures store would be honored at the national toy fair in New York "for sponsoring a Goetz doll signing in October."

Even her husband pitches in. He told her about a longtime downtown fixture, 3 & Co. Antiques, leaving for a nearby town. Schmidt checked and a co-owner told her parking was the problem. Customers, he said, "are not going to concentrate on a $1,000 piece of furniture if they're worried about a $3 parking ticket."

Cultivating Sources

On first contact with a reporter, the business source is likely to be wary, says James L. Rowe Jr., New York financial correspondent of *The Washington Post.* "As a result, it is often difficult to gain the source's trust.

"But if the reporter does his or her homework, learns what motivates business people, is not afraid to ask the intelligent questions but doesn't have to ask the dumb one, more than enough sources will break down."

In developing sources for background material, the reporter will want to find people who can put events into perspective and who can clarify some of the complexities the reporter cannot. Caution is important. Not only must the sources be dependable, they must be independent of compromising connections and affiliations. Obviously, such sources are hard to find. The traditional independent source was the academician, the cloistered professor who had no financial stake in the matters he would comment about. But no more. Academicians now serve on the boards of banks, chemical companies and pesticide manufacturers. The alert reporter makes certain that background information from such sources is neither biased nor self-serving.

When quoting a source, note all of the person's business affiliations relevant to the story. In a banking story, it's not enough to say that Professor Thomas Graham teaches economics at the state university. His membership on the board of directors of the First National Bank should also be included.

Background Source The background source is infrequently quoted, and so readers and viewers cannot assess the information in terms of the source's affiliations. Because background sources influence reporters by providing perspective, the independence of these sources is essential. Good background sources can be found without leaving the office. The accountants, marketing people and the legal adviser to the newspaper or station can figure out some of the complexities of reports and documents. They also are close to the business community.

The business office has access to the local credit bureau and the facilities of Dun and Bradstreet, which can provide confidential information. These are helpful in running a check on a local business.

Reporter Check. Before he will arrange an interview with a Securities and Exchange official, Chris Ullman, SEC spokesman, makes sure the reporter has some background knowledge. "There's been an increase in the number of journalists who expect to be spoon-fed on complex issues without having done their homework," he says. "We've got to make sure there's a base level of understanding."

Chris Welles, a veteran business writer, says, "By far the most important sources on company stories are former executives. Unconstrained by the fear of being fired if word gets out that they talked to you, they can be extremely forthcoming about their former employer." Competitors are another good source, as are suppliers, the managers of investment portfolios, bankers and others who are likely to know the company's financial situation, such as the financial analysts who prepare reports on public corporations.

In interviews, Welles will share his problems in obtaining material. "Most people are predisposed to respond favorably to someone who, in a non-threatening way, asks for a little help." Welles says he listens "with great interest and sympathy." He says that "sources have a great deal of trouble terminating a conversation with someone who seems to be hanging on their every word."

Physical Sources

At the local level, reporters know how to use city and county tax records. The city and county keep excellent records of real estate transfers, and the assessor's office has the valuation of real property and of the physical plant and equipment—whatever is taxed. The sales tax shows how much business a firm is doing. Many local governments issue business licenses on which the principals involved are named and other information is given.

State governments also issue business licenses. There are scores of state boards; they license barbers, engineers, cosmetologists, doctors, morticians, lawyers, accountants and others. These agencies usually keep basic information about the businesses they oversee.

Exceptions. "My general practice when examining a financial document is to look for the exceptions, the deviations. Few journalists are trained accountants or can know much about every single industry they cover, so the trick is to look for numbers that stand out. If the debt a company is carrying goes each year: $80 million, $75 million, $85 million, $300 million; if companies A, B, and C in the cosmetics industry record profit margins of about 8 percent and company D is 4 percent, or 15 percent, there's a story."

—Michael Hiltzik,
Los Angeles Times

The state corporation commission or the secretary of state will have the names, addresses and sometimes the stock held by directors of corporations incorporated in the state and of firms that do a large amount of business in the state. The company's articles of incorporation and bylaws are also on file.

Digging into Records   Floyd Norris, chief financial correspondent for *The New York Times,* praises Carol Loomis of *Fortune:*

> She disclosed in Fortune that American Express had manufactured profits at its Fireman's Fund insurance subsidiary by engaging in a transaction that had no economic reality, but that enabled the company to report decent results when the company business was under great strain. . . . The company had avoided disclosing it in its filings with the Securities and Exchange Commission. . . . Loomis had gone through the reports that insurance companies must file with state insurance commissioners.

Loomis also noticed a footnote in the annual report of Aetna that the SEC had overlooked. After Loomis reported the aggressive accounting the SEC went after Aetna.

> What struck me was that Loomis was not simply reporting what others had said, or amplifying a corporate press release. The information she relied upon was public, but to get at it someone had to read the documents carefully and understand them.

One of the records available to reporters but routinely handled is the file of bankruptcies. Too many reporters are content to make a quick sweep of the file to see whether any big firms have gone bust. Lacking a prominent name or firm, the reporter settles for the total number filed this month, last month and last year. But behind each filing is a story. All the figures are public records. The story is in the interview with the person filing.

Bankruptcies

The commercial on the all-news radio station is friendly, helpful. "Deep in debt? Let us help you with your bankruptcy filing." The commercial goes on to tell the listener that bankruptcy is benign, no headaches afterward. The soothing voice of the announcer indicates everyone is doing it. Well, not exactly. But a lot of people in debt are: In 20 years, bankruptcy filings went from 200,000 to more than 1.3 million a year.

It's true that people seemingly with plenty of money are filing. Toni Braxton filed for bankruptcy under federal law, and news reports said she owned a Porsche, Lexus and baby grand piano. "I'm gonna go out and enjoy myself," she told a reporter as she left the federal building. Also filing: M. C. Hammer, Burt Reynolds and Kim Basinger.

But most people who file are really in trouble, and this is where there are stories. A local merchant opens a jewelry store with high hopes, and within a year he files. Why? Was it a poor location? Did he fail to have sufficient funds for a varied stock? Did a chain store open and undercut his prices?

Looking Locally. As the Argentine economy nosedived in 2001, Gilbert LeGras, a Reuters business reporter assigned to the South American country, decided to look beyond the country's public debt. Trained in a U.S. journalism school, LeGras knew that local governments as well as national governments issue bonds and go into debt.

He discovered a link to the debts of Argentina's 23 provinces. The debts, he found, were what a financial analyst later described as "terrifying." The day after LeGras's story appeared on the Reuters news wire, the central government closed the link.

Soon thereafter, Argentina declared default and the peso was devalued.

Credit Card Debts   There are personal bankruptcies as well, many of them the result of credit card debt that finally overwhelms the cardholders. It's estimated that almost 60 million households carry a credit card debt of more than $7,000 from month to month. Interest on credit cards can average 18 percent.

College students are big on credit cards, and there are stories there, too. Many students carry three, four, five cards so that when they reach the maximum credit allowance on one they use another, and then another.

Many credit card issuers make no check of applicants' ability to pay. A fourth of households with less than $10,000 annual income have credit card debt as do more than 40 percent of those with income from $10,000 to $25,000.

For more about covering bankruptcy proceedings, see **Bankruptcy** in *NRW PLUS.*

Reading

Daily reading of *The Wall Street Journal* is necessary for the business reporter. Written for businesspeople and those with some involvement in financial matters, the stories nevertheless are written in everyday language. The newspaper is both record keeper for the business community and its watchdog. Its investigative reporting is among the best in the country.

Business Week, a weekly business newsmagazine, is staffed by journalists with a good command of business, finance and economics. The magazine concentrates on the major industries and companies. Its long articles are aimed at the men and women who are in executive posts in business.

Forbes is addressed to investors, people who own stock in companies. The *Journal, Business Week,* and *Forbes* are pro-business. Although they do go after the bad apples in the barrel, they never question the barrel, the system itself, as former *Journal* staffer Kent MacDougall puts it. The most pro-business publication is *Nation's Business,* which is published by the U.S. Chamber of Commerce and the National Association of Manufacturers.

Many publications have online versions of their newspapers and magazines.

References

A good local library or any business school library at a college or university will have the following references that business reporters find useful:

- **Dun and Bradstreet directories:** One covers companies with capital under $1 million; another is for those whose capital exceeds $1 million. (Provides address, corporate officers, sales, number of employees.)
- **Who Owns Whom:** To find the parent company of a firm you are checking.
- **Standard & Poor's Register of Corporations, Directors and Executives.**
- **Moody's Manuals.**
- **Standard & Poor's Corporation Record:** Seven volumes of basic information on almost every publicly traded stock.

Most of these references are available online.

Regulatory Agencies

All levels of government regulate business. Local laws prescribe health, fire and safety regulations to which businesses must adhere. The city grants franchises and checks to see that the provisions are followed, such as those requiring public access to the local cable television company. Regional and county governments set standards for factory emissions.

The state regulates some banks, savings and loan institutions, insurance companies and public utilities. State agencies handle rate applications and oversee operational procedures of utilities. Basic information about these businesses is available to the journalist.

State licensing boards also regulate the trades and professions they license. Usually, they have the power to investigate complaints and to hold hearings. Although many of these boards are creatures of the businesses and professions they regulate, occasionally a board will act independently. Failure to take action is an even better story, as one reporter learned when the board regulating veterinarians failed to hold a hearing for a veterinarian who was the subject of a number of complaints by pet owners whose dogs and cats had died in his care.

Although most federal regulatory agencies are in Washington and too distant for personal checking, a local business reporter can ask the newspaper's Washington bureau or the AP to run something down. Federal agencies compile considerable material about companies and individuals seeking permission to operate interstate. Some agencies:

• **Federal Communications Commission (FCC):** Regulates radio and television stations. Ownership and stock information are available.
• **National Labor Relations Board (NLRB):** Concerned with labor disputes.

Developing sources on the beat, wide reading and a knowledge of how business works and is regulated allow the journalist to develop stories, to enterprise interesting and significant articles for readers and viewers and listeners.

Enterprise

Don Moffitt, a *Wall Street Journal* editor, says that business reporters "should consider that they have a license to inquire into the nuts and bolts of how people make a living and secure their well-being.

"For a local paper, the fortunes of the community's barbers, auto mechanics, bankers and public servants are business stories. Business is how people survive.

"If people are falling behind in their mortgage payments, show how and why they are falling behind, how they feel about it and what they're trying to do about it," he says.

"Local government financing and spending is, in part, a business story. Who's making money off the local bond issues, and why? Is the bank keeping the county's low-interest deposits and using the cash to buy the county's high-yielding paper? Who suffers when the township cuts the budget, or can't increase it? Show how they suffer."

Always go beyond the press release, business reporters say. When a $69 million reconstruction job at a shopping center was announced, the developers sent out stacks of press releases. By asking why so much money was being spent on releases, a reporter learned that sales at the center had sharply declined recently—a fact not mentioned in any of the releases.

Steve Lipson, business news writer for *The Times-News,* develops ideas for stories by a simple technique—keeping his eyes open. "I read ads, I notice changes in the businesses where I shop. I count the number of cars in a car dealer's lot, and I look at what people wear, eat and drink," Lipson says.

"I look for unique stories," he says. He did one on the growing popularity of potato-skin appetizers. "This big boost to potato consumption would land someone in the Idaho Hall of Fame if anyone knew who was responsible. Alas, my story found no one really knows."

Ideas can turn up anywhere, even in the small print in the back of the business section under "Foreign Exchange." The figures show how much the U.S. dollar is worth abroad. The exchange rates affect business. To see how, consult **The Dollar's Value Abroad** in *NRW Plus*.

Municipal Bonds

The school system and the city, county and state often decide on major construction projects. To finance them, large amounts of money have to be raised by selling bonds.

The bond story involves interest rates, the financial standing or rating of the local government and related matters that may seem complex for readers but that can be simplified with good reporting. First, check the rating of the governmental unit.

If the local government is not rated financially healthy, the bonds would not be seen as a good investment. To attract buyers of the bonds, the interest rate then would have to be set high. Just half of 1 percent more in interest could mean millions of dollars more that the taxpayers will have to pay in interest over the life of the bonds.

Reporters can learn about the health of the local government by examining two kinds of documents, the bond prospectus and the analysis by the rating agencies:

Prospectus: This document is required by law for the information of potential investors. It contains considerable information about the government entity offering the bonds.

Rating: The government entity's debt (which is what a bond is) is rated by organizations such as Moody's and Standard & Poor's. The lower the rating, the higher the interest rate on the bonds and the greater the cost to taxpayers. Reporters can obtain these ratings.

University Bonds

Almost all governments issue bonds and so do many private entities. Your university probably has issued bonds for a dormitory or classroom construction, possibly for building a stadium or field house. Just as governments that issue bonds are rated, so are colleges and universities. Some are given high ratings, others less than the best. Here is a story about a rating one university was given:

Standard & Poor's today announced it has upgraded Columbia University's debt rating from AA+ to AAA.

Only eight other universities are in the rating agency's top bracket: California Institute of Technology, Grinnell, Harvard, MIT, Princeton, Rockefeller University, Stanford and Yale.

Standard & Poor's upgraded Columbia's rating on the basis of a successful fund-raising campaign, effective financial strategies and the selectivity of the undergraduate and graduate programs.

Hospitals, Too. "Standard & Poor's today announced it has lowered from BBB to BBB– Englewood Hospital and Pascack Valley Hospital bond ratings because the market has become so competitive that hospitals are trying to gain market share by providing a wider range of costly services and specialty care."

In good times, these bonds can be easily repaid, says Thomas E. Calibeo, a senior vice president in the higher-education ratings group of Moody's Investors Service. But when the stock market declines, revenue sources for universities—earnings from endowments, gifts and tuition—are pinched and it is more difficult to meet interest payments

Skepticism and Doubt

"The business page is singularly marked by credulity," says Bernard Nossiter, a veteran business reporter. "Corporate and even Treasury pronouncements are treated as holy writ. Corporate officials are likely to be regarded with awe, at least until they are indicted."

One reason, he says, is that "reporters are literate rather than numerate," more at home with words than with figures.

One of the stories business interests find reporters eager to write is the new business or development piece. Anything that promises new jobs or an expanding economy in town is snapped up, even when the venture is speculative. In Alexandria, Va., a developer put up a huge sign announcing an 800,000-square-foot office building, and *The Washington Post* ran a picture and story. No tenant was ever signed up. Reporters need to dig deeper:

- **Questions for new ventures:** What evidence is there of secure financing? Who are the lenders?
- **Questions for developers:** What tenants have signed leases? Are they being given free rent? Have building permits been issued?

Morton Mintz, for many years a digging reporter at *The Washington Post* who exposed corporate greed that resulted in danger and death to the public, says that the press has failed to audit "impersonal crime committed by the large corporation." He recalls the response of Alfred P. Sloan Jr., head of General Motors, when GM was urged to use safety glass for windshields, as Ford had been doing for years.

GM was using ordinary flat glass, which, Mintz says, "breaks into shards, disfiguring, slashing, killing." Sloan's response:

Accidents or no accidents, my concern on this matter is a matter of profit and loss. . . . I am trying to protect the stockholders of General Motors and the Corporation's operating position—it is not my responsibility to sell safety glass. . . . You can say, perhaps, that I am selfish, but business is selfish. We are not a charitable institution—we are trying to make a profit for our stockholders.

Checking the Ladies   The women were fantastic investors. The feature stories about their investment group said they were getting better than 23 percent for their stock market purchases. Their books became best sellers. Their first book, in which they claimed their investment club had an annual return of 23.4 percent from 1984 through 1993, sold 800,000 copies. They were popular speakers, these Beardstown Ladies.

Handout Watchout

Here are the beginnings of three press releases. What do they have in common?

Unites States Steel Corp. today announced a series of moves designed to ensure that its steel sector will continue as a major force in world steel markets for the balance of the century and beyond. . . .

Greenbelt Cooperative Inc.'s Board of Directors unanimously approved a plan to strengthen the organization's financial position and continue expansion. . . .

W & J Sloane, the retail furniture company long noted for its reputation for quality, style and trend-setting furniture, is once again taking the lead in the furniture industry. . . .

If you found the companies are about to report high earnings or an expansion, go to the rear of the class. The firms were all announcing bad news. U.S. Steel cut 15,600 jobs and closed plants in several cities. Greenbelt closed its cooperative supermarkets and gas stations. And W & J Sloane closed a store and sharply reduced its range of furniture in other stores. All this was in the releases—buried.

Assigned to do a piece on the Ladies by *Chicago* magazine, Shane Tritsch was hardly moved by the prospect. "I wasn't all that excited about doing the 500th fawning story on the Beardstown Ladies," he told *Brill's Content* writer Elizabeth Lesly Stevens. "What in the world was left to say?"

He started to browse through the Ladies' famous *Investment Guide.* A small note on the copyright page said the Ladies included monthly dues when adding up their returns. Another glitch caught his eye, and this time he dug into the book. He came up with a return of 12.2 percent, a bit over half the Ladies' claim.

The Wall Street Journal picked up Tritsch's story and it became headline news. This story sparked a Price Waterhouse audit that found the actual return to be 9.1 percent annualized return over the decade.

To learn how to read stock tables, see **Stock Tables** in *NRW Plus.*

Checking the Banks   Banks spend lots of money trying to cultivate an image of friendliness, no doubt to counter their reputation as cold hearted. "For some time," says Michael Selz of *The Wall Street Journal,* "the nation's largest commercial banks claimed in advertisements and corporate promotions that they were lending aggressively to small businesses." He and Edward R. Foldessey, the *Journal's* computer-assisted reporting expert decided to test the claims.

They had access to 12,000 bank reports filed with federal regulators. Banks are required to disclose the amount and number of commercial and industrial loans of less than $1 million as well as mortgage loans. The *Journal* examined the loans of the big banks.

"The study contradicted many of the big banks' claims about serving the small business market," Selz says, despite claims such as that of one bank that it is the "market leader" in such loans. The big banks, the figures showed, were lending less to small businesses than much smaller banks were. Here is the beginning of Selz's story:

To prove its commitment to small-business lending, New York's Chemical Banking Corp. annually stages what it calls the "biggest blitz in banking history."

In each of the past three years, more than 1,000 officers of the nation's third largest bank holding company—including its chairman and chief executive, Walter V. Shipley—go "knocking on the doors" of prospective small-business borrowers in five states to make clear that Chemical wants to lend them money.

When it comes to small-business lending in the New York area, "we're the market leader," says Frank Lourenso, an executive vice president for Chemical's New York bank.

There's one problem with that claim: Federal banking reports show it isn't true.

Numbers Count

Many students are attracted to journalism because they like to write and because journalism is concerned with how people get along with each other. These students are interested in the qualitative aspect of life. Journalism, with its feature stories and its emphasis on human interest, can use the talents these students take to the job. But much of what we know about the world—and people—is derived from quantitative studies.

The student who is thinking about a career in business journalism—and this is one area of journalism that never seems to have enough reporters and editors—cannot manage without an ability to deal with numbers. If business is the bottom line on a balance sheet, then the student thinking of becoming a business reporter has to know what to make of the numbers on the line.

Checking on Numbers

Pauline Tai, former director of the Knight-Bagehot Fellowship Program in business journalism at Columbia University, says business reporters must be able to "analyze numbers. You can't just accept what a CEO tells you. You should be able to calculate. You have to know how the CEO came to a figure and what it means. You just don't take what you are being told as the truth. You have to look into it, and sometimes you have to stick your neck out and make judgments."

Note: More than a third of business executives polled by the Freedom Forum First Amendment Center said they regularly lie to the media. See *The Headline vs. The Bottom Line* by Mike Haggerty and Wallace Rasmussen, available from the Center at Vanderbilt University, 1207 18th Avenue, Nashville, TN 37212, (615) 321-9588.

The ability to blend the qualitative and the quantitative is essential to the business journalist. Numbers alone do say a lot, but when these barometers are matched with human beings, they take on dramatic significance. When home loan applications increase (quantitative), the reporter finds a family like the Ryans we met a while back and shows why this family decided to buy rather than to rent (qualitative).

To examine a business story that is essentially concerned with numbers, see **Annual Report** and **Stories about Earnings** in *NRW Plus*.

The CD also includes a section on the important documents large business must file with the federal government. These records are often used by business reporters for stories. See **Federal Records** in *NRW Plus*.

Depth Reporting

The Founding Fathers were concerned about the dangers of a strong central government. They could not have imagined the power that business would acquire. International banks and the conglomerates exercise enormous influence over the lives of people everywhere, and this power is worthy of scrutiny by the press in its role as watchdog.

Such examination starts at the local level. How much power do local real estate dealers and contractors have over planning and zoning decisions? What role does money play in elections? Does local government really have to give businesses and developers tax write-offs and abatements as an incentive? Is the tax structure equitable or does it fall too heavily on families, working people, home owners? In states with natural resources, is the severance tax properly balanced with other taxes, or are the extractive industries penalized or given preferential treatment?

Business reporters who dig deeply can come up with answers to some of these questions. Their articles are called public service journalism, journalism that gives people insights into the deep currents that swirl about us and are, to most of us, impenetrable.

Temptation

In her assessment of today's business writers, Diana B. Henriques of *The New York Times* finds the best "far more savvy about the modern machinery of business journalism" than she was when she began covering the beat in 1982. But she thinks them "far more naive about its age-old temptations." She writes in the *Columbia Journalism Review* (November/December 2000):

> Those covering the "new economy" for the "new media" seem especially mystified why it's such a big deal if they invest directly in industries they cover, or accept cheap insider stock in some industry pal's IPO, or do consulting work on the side for technology companies. . . .
>
> A technology journalist can avoid unseemly conflicts simply by investing only in broad-based mutual funds. . . .

This material was prepared by Jim O'Shea for *The Des Moines Register*.

Deficit: The difference between expenditures and revenues.

Debt: The total of all deficits. It is covered by debt obligations such as Treasury bonds and bills.

Business Terms

assets These are anything of value the company owns or has an interest in. Assets usually are expressed in dollar value.

balance sheet A financial statement that lists the company's assets, liabilities and stockholders' equity. It usually includes an *Earnings* or *Income Statement* that details the company's source of income and its expenses.

calendar or **fiscal year** Some companies report their income or do business on the regular calendar year. Others do it on a fiscal year that could run from any one month to the same month a year later. Always ask if the companies do business on a fiscal or calendar year. If the answer is fiscal, ask the dates and why. You might find out something unusual about the company.

capital expenditures This is the amount of money a company spends on major projects, such as plant expansions or capacity additions. It is important to the company and the community as well. If the company is expanding, include it in the story. Frequently, such plans are disclosed in stock prospectuses and other SEC reports long before the local paper gets its press release.

earnings Used synonymously with *profit*. Earnings can be expressed in dollar terms (XYZ earned $40) or on a per-share basis (XYZ earned $1 per share for each of its 40 shares of stock). When used as an earnings figure, always compare it to the earnings for the same period in the prior year. For example, if you want to say XYZ earned $1 a share during the first quarter, half

or nine months of 1993, compare that with the 50 cents per share the company earned in the first quarter, half or nine months of 1992. That would be a 100 percent increase in profit.

liabilities These are any debts of any kind. There are two types of liabilities: short term and long term. Companies consider anything that has to be paid off within a year a short-term liability and anything over a year a long-term liability.

sales or **revenues** These terms are used synonymously in many companies. A bank, for example, doesn't have sales. It has revenues. A manufacturer's sales and revenues frequently are the same thing, unless the company has some income from investments it made. Always include the company's sales in a story with its earnings. If you say a company earned $40 in 2001 compared to $30 in 2002, you also should tell the reader that the profit was the result of a 100 percent increase in the company's sales, from $100 in 2001 to $200 in 2002. Use both sales and earnings figures. Don't use one and not the other.

stockholders' equity This is the financial interest the stockholders have in the company once all of its debts are paid. For example, say XYZ company has assets of $1,000 and total debts of $600. The company's stockholders' equity is $400. If that figure is expressed on a per-share basis, it is called *book value*. (If XYZ had issued 40 shares of stock, each share would have a book value of $10.)

She writes that the editor of *Online Journalism Review* told her that a Silicon Valley gossip columnist had received cheap pre-IPO (initial public offering) shares from a local technology mogul and that when it was revealed "many supposedly sensible professionals wondered aloud whether she had done anything wrong."

Further Reading

Daniells, Lorna. *Business Information Sources,* 2d ed. Berkeley, Calif.: University of California Press, 1985.

Galbraith, J. Kenneth. *The Affluent Society.* Boston: Houghton Mifflin, 1958.

Kluge, Pamela Hollie. *Guide to Business and Economics Journalism.* New York: Columbia University Press, 1991.

Mintz, Morton. *At Any Cost.* New York: Pantheon Books, 1985.

Moffitt, Donald, ed. *Swindled: Classic Business Frauds of the Seventies.* Princeton, N.J.: Dow Jones Books, 1976.

Silk, Leonard. *Economics in the Real World.* New York: Simon & Schuster, 1985.

Smith, Adam. *The Money Game.* New York: Random House, 1976.

Thompson, Terri, ed. *Writing about Business: The New Columbia Knight-Bagehot Guide to Economics and Business Journalism.* New York: Columbia University Press, 2001.

24 Local Government and Education

Mike Roemer

**City planning and zoning—
part of the beat.**

Preview

Local government reporters cover the actions of municipal agencies and departments and the interplay of citizens, interest groups and local government in making policy. Some areas of coverage are:

- Budgets, taxes, bond issues.
- Politics.
- Zoning and planning.
- Education.

Reporters check on whether city agencies and departments are carrying out their responsibilities efficiently, effectively and economically.

People are more interested in local events than in any other kind of news. They want to know what the city council did about the proposal for free downtown parking, why the principal of the Walt Whitman High School was dismissed and how the new city manager feels about lowering the property tax.

Newspapers and stations respond to this interest by assigning their best reporters to key local beats, and usually the best of the best is assigned to city hall, the nerve center of local government. From city hall, elected and appointed officials direct the affairs of the community—from the preparation of absentee ballots to the adoption of zoning regulations. They supervise street maintenance and construction, issue birth and death certificates, conduct restaurant inspections, collect and dispose of waste and collect parking meter coins.

The city hall reporter is expected to cover all these activities. To do this, the reporter knows how local government works—the processes and procedures of agencies and departments, the relationship of the mayor's office to the city council, how the city auditor or comptroller checks on the financial activities of city offices.

City Government Activities

The city government engages in many essential activities that the reporter scrutinizes:

1. Authorization of public improvements such as streets, new buildings, bridges, viaducts.
2. Submission to the public of bond issues to finance these improvements.
3. Adoption of various codes, such as building, sanitation, zoning.
4. Issuance of regulations affecting public health, welfare and safety. Traffic regulations come under this category.
5. Consideration of appeals from planning and zoning bodies.
6. Appointment and removal of city officials.
7. Authorization of land purchases and sales.
8. Awarding of franchises.
9. Adoption of the expense and capital budgets.

The city is a major buyer of goods and services and is usually one of the city's largest employers. Its decisions can enrich some businesses, as indicated in the beginning of this story by Josh Getlin of the *Los Angeles Times:*

During the last year, Los Angeles Councilman Howard Finn and his wife enjoyed a free weekend in Newport Beach and Councilwoman Peggy Stevenson was wined and dined at some of New York's finer restaurants.

In both cases, Group W Cable TV officials were wooing council members to round up votes for the East San Fernando Valley franchise that could be worth $75 million.

Lavish entertaining is just part of a multimillion dollar campaign by six firms to win the city's last major cable franchise. . . .

Three Branches   The city is the creature of the state. The state assigns certain of its powers to the city, enabling the city to govern itself. The city has the three traditional branches of government—a judicial system and executive and legislative arms. In some cities, the executive is a powerful mayor who has control over much of the municipal machinery. In others, the mayor's job is largely ceremonial and the mayor may not even have a vote on the city council.

Legislative branches differ, too. But for the most part, the city council or commission has the power to act in the nine areas outlined above. The council or commission takes action in the form of ordinances and resolutions. An *ordinance* is a law. A *resolution* is a declaration or an advisory that indicates the intention or opinion of the legislative branch.

An ordinance is *enacted:* "The city council last night enacted an ordinance requiring dog owners to have their pets innoculated against rabies." A resolution is *adopted:* "City commission members last night adopted a resolution to make June 18 Frances Osmond Day in honor of the longtime city clerk who died last Tuesday."

Forms of Local Government

The city council–mayor system is the most common form of local government. In large cities, the mayor is usually a powerful figure in city government, the centerpiece of what is called the strong mayor system. In this system, the mayor appoints the heads of departments and all other officials not directly elected. This system enables the mayor to select the people he or she wants to carry out executive policies.

One way to classify local government is by the strength of the office of the mayor, the power the chief executive has to initiate and carry out programs and policies. The two systems have variations:

Weak Mayor	**Strong Mayor**
Commission	Council-mayor
Commission-manager	Mayor-manager
Council-manager	

Strong to Weak, Back to Strong

The weak mayor systems and the creation of the post of city manager were reactions to the misuse of power by strong mayors and their inability to manage the bureaucracy. To be elected and to hold office, the mayor had to be an astute politician, not necessarily an able administrator. The wheelings and dealings of the strong mayors—exposed by such muckrakers as Lincoln Steffens—led people to reject a system that some critics said encouraged corruption. A movement toward less-politicized and more efficient local government developed early in the 20th century. It took the form of the council-manager system.

The manager, who is hired by the council, is a professionally trained public administrator who attends to the technical tasks of running the city government—preparing the budget, hiring, administering departments and agencies. Although the manager does increase the managerial efficiency of local government, the system has been criticized as insulating government from the electorate by dispersing responsibility and accountability. Several cities have returned to the strong mayor system in an effort to place responsibility in the hands of an identifiable, elected official.

An offshoot of the council-manager system is the mayor-manager plan, the most prevalent system today. This combines the strong mayor, politically responsive to the electorate, with the trained technician who carries out executive policies and handles day-to-day governmental activities.

In weak mayor systems, elected commissioners serve as the legislative branch and the executive branch. The commissioners are legislators and also head various municipal departments—finance, public works, public safety, planning, personnel. Often, the commissioner of public safety also serves as mayor, a largely ceremonial post in this system. The commission form has been criticized for blurring the separation of powers between the legislative and executive branches. In the commission system, there is no single official that the electorate can hold responsible for the conduct of local affairs.

Governing the City

Mayor-Manager Form

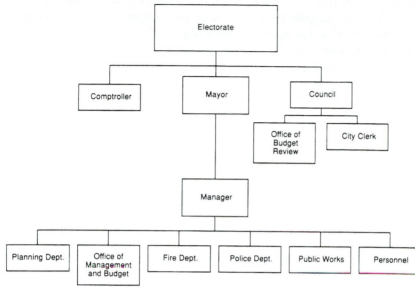

Council-Manager Form

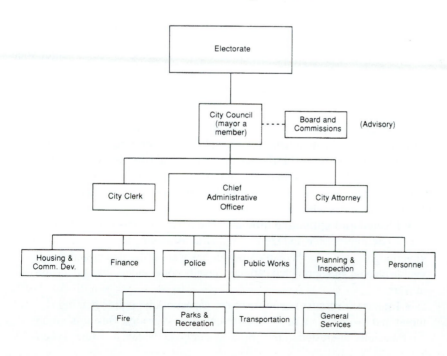

The Public Interest

As we saw, the city manager plan was initiated during a period of reform as a means of taking politics out of local government. Other means have been advanced: the nonpartisan ballot, extension of the merit system and career services to protect city jobs from being used for patronage, the payment of low salaries to mayors and council or commission members to take the profit out of public service. Many cities have been the battlegrounds between the good government groups and their opponents, who contend that the result of taking power from party leaders and elected officials is its transfer to nongovernmental groups and bureaucracies that are not answerable to the public.

There are few identifiable public interests that most people agree upon. There can be a public consensus on such matters as public safety and good roads. But the majority of issues resolve into a contest among differing special interests. The political process involves much more than the nomination and election of candidates. We can define the political process as the daily interaction of government, interest groups and the citizenry.

Participants in the Political Process

Professors Wallace S. Sayre of Columbia University and Herbert Kaufman of Yale put the political process in terms useful to the government reporter. They describe the participants as actors in a contest for a variety of goals, stakes, rewards and prizes. The police officer on the beat whose union is seeking to fend off reductions in the police force is an actor in the contest, as is the mother of three who is urging her school's Parents Association to speak out for more crossing guards at the elementary school. They are as much a part of the political process as the mayor who journeys to the state capital to seek a larger slice of state funds for welfare and health or who decides to seek re-election and lines up backing from unions and ethnic groups.

We can group the participants in the city's political process as follows:

- **The political party leaders:** The leaders and their organizations have a strong hand in the nominating process, but the other participants have increased their power and influence as the political party has declined in importance. Insurgents sometimes capture nominations, and the leaders must compromise their choices for the highest offices in the interest of finding candidates who can win.

- **Elected and appointed officials:** The mayor, members of the city council or commission and their administrators occupy key roles in governing the city. As the party's power has waned, the mayor and the visible elected and appointed officials have become independent decision makers.

- **Interest (pressure) groups:** Every aspect of city policy making is monitored by one or more of the political interest groups. Business groups are especially interested in the school system and the tax structure. When a school district reported that 66 percent of third-graders were reading at grade level compared to 88 percent in other districts, parents were concerned. So were real estate agents. Their reason: Poor schools would make it harder to sell homes in the district.

As for the city's tax structure, real estate interests will want a low property tax so that the cost of homes will be affordable. They will also want large and efficient police and fire departments because these keep insurance premiums low.

The banks are interested in policies about the city's indebtedness because they are the buyers of the bonds and notes the city issues to pay for large-scale construction projects such as roads and schools. Contractors push for public improvements. The bar association checks on law enforcement and the judiciary.

Religious groups and educational organizations keep track of school policies. Medical and health professions examine the activities of the health department. The nominating process and the election campaigns attract ethnic and labor groups as well as the good government groups.

Interest groups compete with each other to influence the city leadership and its bureaucracy, and this limits their influence. An interest group may control the decision making of a department or agency, as when, for example, the real estate interests take over the planning and zoning department or the banks and bond market control decisions about the sale of bonds.

• **Organized and professional bureaucracies:** City employees became independent of the party organization with the merit system, unionization and the professionalization of city services. Police, firefighters and teachers have been among the most active in influencing the political process.

• **Other governments:** The city government is in daily contact with a variety of other governmental units: the county, the state, the federal government, public authorities and special assessment districts. These governments are linked by a complex web of legal and financial involvements. State approval is often necessary for certain actions by the city. State and federal governments appropriate funds for such city services as education, health and welfare. City officials are almost always bargaining with other governmental units.

• **The press:** "The communication media provide the larger stage upon which the other participants in the city's political contest play their parts with the general public as an audience," says Kaufman. But, he continues, the media "do more than merely provide the public stage." They also take a direct part in the process. Having its own values, emphasis, stereotypes and preoccupations, the press is not an exact mirror or reporter, he says. The media highlight personalities, are fond of exposés, are too zealous in looking for stories about patronage crumbs—and are too skeptical of officials and party leaders, he says.

Lewis W. Wolfson of American University says that the press too often depicts government "not as a process, but as a succession of events, many of them in fact staged for the media." He suggests that the press "tell people more about how government works, how it affects them, and how they can influence it."

Auditing the Community

Along with covering the nine governmental activities listed at the beginning of this chapter, the local government reporter keeps tabs on the city's economic and social conditions.

The Economy

Much of the community's health depends on its economy—the availability of jobs, the ability of the city to meet its bonded indebtedness and to support first-rate schools and services. Reporters use several measuring sticks to gauge the local economy:

- Employment and unemployment rates.
- Housing construction and sales.
- Telephone and utility connections.
- Automobile sales.
- Hotel and motel occupancy rates.
- Sales tax revenues.

These factors also are considered by the agencies that rate the city's credit. A high rating means the city will be able to sell bonds at a low interest rate. A low rating means the city is in poor financial condition and will have to offer high interest rates as an inducement to buy its bonds, which furthers the city's tight financial condition. The local reporter regularly checks the city's credit rating.

Job Search   The Bureau of Labor Statistics makes monthly checks on employment in every state and for large metropolitan areas. It calls people at their homes and asks if they are working; if not, whether they are looking for work. The BLS also questions employers about their payrolls. Are they growing, shrinking? It asks about wages. The results of these surveys provide reporters with what *Baltimore Sun* business reporter Jay Hancock says is "the single best piece of current, state-based economic information you can get."

The data for states and large cities are available from the BLS home page: www.stats.bls.gov. Click *Data* on the main menu. Then click *Most Requested Series,* which gives you another menu. Go down to the *Employment and Unemployment* heading and click *State and Area Employment, Hours and Earnings* under the category *Nonfarm Payroll Statistics from the Current Employment Statistics.*

Click in your state and zero in on *Total Nonfarm Employment.* Hancock says not to base stories on a single month but to look for trends. Or take several months and strike an average. Then compare this current average with the same months from a year and five years ago.

The Schools

Good schools help make the city financially secure because industry and business are attracted to communities with an educated work force. Telemarketing has created new business centers around the country to handle catalog orders, to make hotel reservations, to plan vacations, even to help computer owners get back on track. These businesses look for pockets of hard-working, well-educated people to do their work.

The "toll-free capital of the U.S." is located in Omaha where tens of thousands of people work in telemarketing. South Dakota's major industry is processing credit card transactions. North Dakota workers handle half the reservations of the big Rosenbluth International travel company of Philadelphia. These areas are marked by above-average national test scores and high graduation rates for their high school students.

Dismal Showing   The national picture is, however, far from bright. Tests of high school seniors show that one-fourth are in effect functionally illiterate. A third of the others are barely proficient.

Education is not keeping pace with the skill requirements for a good job. Half the nation's 17-year-olds cannot read or do math well enough to do production work in an automobile plant.

Employers hire college graduates because they know that a high school diploma does not guarantee literacy or mathematical competence.

Some measures of the quality of education include dropout rate; high school graduation rate; percentage of graduates going on to college; SAT and ACT scores; pupil-teacher ratio; average teacher salary.

We will look in greater detail at education later in this chapter.

Additional Checkpoints

Journalists also keep track of other facets of community life that are indicators of how the city is meeting its obligations to all its residents, how the people get along with each other, whether problems are being solved.

These other measures of a community's well-being include:

Health: Reporters look at the children's immunization rate; infant and maternal death rates; suicide rate; availability of child health and prenatal clinics; health-information programs.

Social conditions: Percentage of children in single-parent homes living in poverty; teen-age motherhood rates; divorce rate; racial harmony; crime rates.

One of the most important indicators of a community's health is its social harmony. Is diversity a community goal? Here, the reporter relies on sources among the community's religious, political and economic leaders; teachers and students; working people.

From Idyllic Village to Urban Nightmare

". . . Not only are the streets dominated by the criminal element, but the schools and the housing projects as well. One's life is up for grabs, one's children will either be victimized by the criminal element or recruited into criminal enterprise. Almost nothing can be done to help the law-abiding majority of the ghetto unless and until crime and the drug trade are brought under control. . . ."
—Irving Kristol, *The Wall Street Journal.*
Right, Mel Finkelstein,
© *New York Daily News,* Inc.
Above right, Larry C. Price,
The Philadelphia Inquirer Magazine.
Above left, The Plumas County Museum.

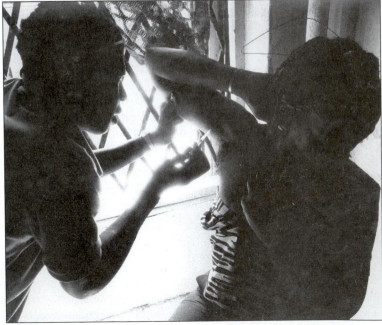

The larger the city, the more pressing the problems of race. But race is entwined with class—that is, minority groups are poor: 46 percent of black and 40 percent of Hispanic children live in poverty.

Another indicator of social conditions is teen-age motherhood. The United States has the highest rate of unwed teen-age childbearing. More than 1 million adolescent girls become pregnant every year, and half give birth. The likelihood of these young women finishing high school diminishes by 50 percent. More than 70 percent of the men in prisons and jails were born to teen-age mothers. A third of the children in the United States are born to unmarried women.

In most communities, these indicators point to pockets where the problems are magnified. These areas are marked by drugs, crime, poverty, poor health, high infant mortality rates, low educational attainment and unemployment.

For a closer look at these problems, see **Inner-City Problems,** *NRW Plus.*

The Demographics

Who lives in the city? What's the average age of the population, the male-female ratio, the income brackets, the educational attainment, the racial and ethnic makeup? What's the birthrate, the deathrate? Is the infant mortality rate higher than the state or national average? What is killing people in the community, heart attacks, cancer, AIDS, accidents?

Reporters who seek the answers to these and related questions give the public an insight into the changing nature of their communities and the consequences of these changes. As the Hispanic population grew in many states, political tensions developed, among these a battle for power between African-American and Hispanic blocs. Though both are minority groups, each has a distinct political agenda.

Out of these changing demographics a new beat emerged, covering race and ethnicity. To some of the reporters covering this beat, finding their way in these groups was difficult. Stephen Magagnini of *The Sacramento Bee* says doors in the American Indian community opened to him after he went to a sweatlodge in San Diego County.

"It was the most intense experience of my life," he said. "And it was a threshold crossing, proof that I was willing to sacrifice to gain truth and wisdom. Many doors opened after that".

Auditing the Community

In addition to covering the breaking news in the community—city council meetings, school board decisions, zoning actions—what should the local reporter look for so that citizens can tell whether the community is meeting their needs? What guidelines can we establish?

An African proverb states, "It takes a whole village to raise a child." This can be our starting point: How well is the community protecting, nurturing, educating and caring for its children? Are there indexes that help us establish quality of life guidelines for children?

Changed Complexion. Nearly half the nation's 100 largest cities have a majority of minorities. Blacks (24.1) percent), Hispanics (22.5 percent), Asians (6.6 percent) and others (3 percent) constitute 56.2 percent of the population of these cities.

The non-Hispanic white population shrank from 52.1 percent in the 1990 census to 43.8 percent in the 2000 census. the most striking change was the growth of the Hispanic population in the largest cities, from 17.2 percent to 22.5 percent.

Suggested Guidelines

One guideline is offered by the organization Zero Population Growth which every two years examines dozens of studies and reports for its "Children's Environmental Index."

How well, ZPG asks, do the cities it studies provide the means by which all the children can grow into healthy, happy adults? ZPG studies 219 cities for its report. Let's look at the measures it uses to reach its conclusions:

Health: infant mortality rate, percentage of low-birth-weight infants, percentage of births to teens, number of physicians per 10,000 population.

Economics: unemployment rate, percentage of children in poverty, median family income.

Crime: violent crimes per 1,000 population, property crimes per 1,000, juvenile arrests.

Education: student-teacher ratio, dropout rate.

Physical environment: number of bad air days, pounds of toxic releases per 1,000 population, hazard ranking (toxic wastes).

All of these figures are available to the journalist, many of them from on-line sources.

For a rundown of the ZPG's findings, see **The Good and the Not So Good,** *NRW Plus.* The CD also includes The Most Livable State Award in **State Rankings,** a list of the most and least livable states based on data in 43 categories.

Politics

Many of the most important issues that face communities are settled in elections. Candidates and their parties differ in the solutions they offer, and it is the task of the reporter covering politics to make clear the positions that define and differentiate the candidates so that an informed choice can be made.

Politics has been given a bad name over the years, and some reporters approach coverage with a disdain for the whole affair. Given the incessant attack on government, this distaste is understandable. But it's no way to approach the job. Not only that, but the assumption is wrong, the assumption that government is the enemy.

When confronted with this sort of attitude—President Clinton had remarked, "Government is not the solution"—the historian Stephen Ambrose responded, "The government surely was the solution to the Depression and in World War II and on the civil-rights front and on providing a decent life for old folks in this country."

Politics culminating in elections is democracy's means for allowing its citizens to choose who will govern. However, a lot gets in the way of the reporters doing their job properly.

Suburban Growth. Almost half the country's population lives in suburbs; 14 states have a majority suburban population. Some effects: political strength (majority Republican) shifting to the suburbs; a hostility to central-city government; greater concern for security and privacy; less concern for inner-city problems of race and class.

With the Bush Campaign   Jena Heath covered the Bush campaign in 2000 for the *Austin American-Statesman* from her base in Washington. She describes political reporting as the "push and pull between the candidate's need to control the message and our need to tell the real story." She found the Bush campaign aimed to "the TV folks, the real power in a business where beaming a neatly packaged candidate into voters' living rooms is the bottom line."

It is, of course, the reporter's job to shave away the fluff and get behind the camouflage.

Self Study   It is also the reporter's job to look within to see whether attitudes and biases obstruct his or her coverage. Everyone carries preferences, sympathies, likes and dislikes through life. For the reporter covering politics and issues involving conflicting ideas, personal feelings cannot be allowed to influence coverage. If a proposed state income tax schedule reduces the tax on high income earners and leaves the same tax levy on middle and low-income taxpayers, the reporter will carry the statements of the supporters of the bill that the new schedule will act as a stimulant to business, and the reporter will report the objections of opponents that the bill is a giveaway to the rich and further separates the well-to-do from the rest of the population.

For guidelines to covering politics and political campaigns, see **Some Tips on Campaign Coverage** *NRW Plus*.

Money Talk

The city school system needs teachers for the new high school west of town—money has to be budgeted by the school board. The health department needs special equipment to test for biological agents—it is asking the city council to increase its appropriation. Whether these expenditures are necessary, and if so whether the amount sought should be allocated—these determinations are made in a political context.

We next turn to how budgets are made.

Vern Herschberger,
Waco Tribune-Herald

The Budget

Covering local government—indeed, covering all levels of government—requires a knowledge of how money is raised and how it is spent. Money fuels the system.

"I've had to learn how to cover five governmental units, and I find the single best way to learn what they are doing is to attend budget hearings," says David Yepsen, political reporter for *The Des Moines Register*. "They let you know the current situation, what the problems are, the proposed solutions and where government is headed."

"Follow the buck," says the experienced reporter. The city hall reporter follows the path of the parking meter dime and the property tax dollar as they make their way through government. The path of these dimes and dollars is set by the budget.

The budget is a forecast or estimate of expenditures that a government will make during the year and the revenues needed to meet those expenses. It is, in short, a balance sheet. Budgets are made for the fiscal year, which may be the calendar year or may run from July 1 through June 30 or other dates. The budget is made by the executive branch (mayor, governor, president, school superintendent) and then submitted to the legislative body (city council, state legislature, Congress, board of education) for adoption.

A Compromise   The budget is the final resolution of the conflicting claims of individuals and groups to public monies. This means that the conscientious reporter watches the budgeting process as carefully as he or she examines the finished document. Aaron Wildavsky of the University of California at Berkeley describes the budget as "a series of goals with price tags attached." If it is followed, he says, things happen, certain policy objectives are accomplished.

The budget is a sociological and political document. As Prime Minister William Ewart Gladstone of Britain remarked more than 100 years ago, the budget "in a thousand ways goes to the root of the prosperity of the individuals and relation of classes and the strength of kingdoms."

The budget can determine how long a pregnant woman waits to see a doctor in a well-baby clinic, how many children are in a grade school class, whether city workers will seek to defeat the mayor in the next election.

Here is the beginning of a budget story by Paul Rilling of *The Anniston* (Ala.) *Star:*

A city budget may look like a gray mass of dull and incomprehensible statistics, but it is the best guide there is to the plans and priorities of city government.

Rhetoric and promises aside, the budget says what the city council really sees as the city's top priorities.

Tuesday, the Anniston City Council will consider for formal adoption the proposed city budget for fiscal . . .

Cover the Whole Process

City hall, education, county and state legislative reporters handle budget stories on a regular basis. Reporters on these beats begin to write stories several months before the budget is adopted so that the public can be informed of the give-and-take of the process and participate early in the decision making. In a six-week span, Bill Mertens, city hall reporter for *The Hawk Eye,* wrote more than a dozen stories. Here are the beginning paragraphs of two of them:

School crossing guards may be one of the programs lost if Burlington city councilmen intend to hold the new budget close to the existing one.

The city council has asked Burlington fire department heads to cut $30,000 from their budget request.

Income

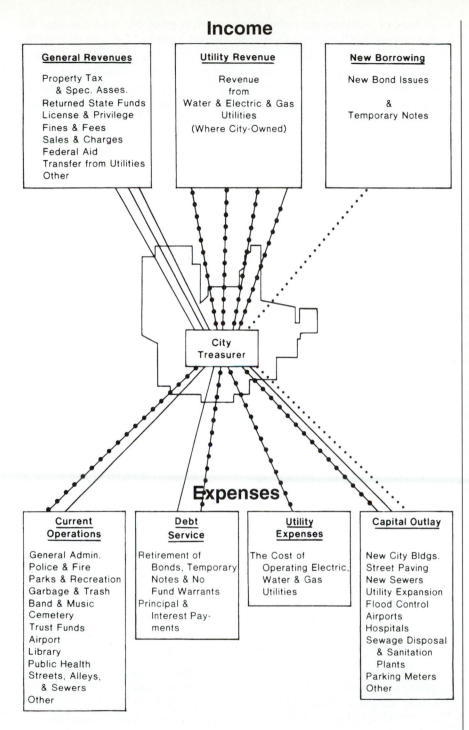

General Revenues

Property Tax
& Spec. Asses.
Returned State Funds
License & Privilege
Fines & Fees
Sales & Charges
Federal Aid
Transfer from Utilities
Other

Utility Revenue

Revenue
from
Water & Electric & Gas
Utilities
(Where City-Owned)

New Borrowing

New Bond Issues

&

Temporary Notes

City
Treasurer

Expenses

Current Operations

General Admin.
Police & Fire
Parks & Recreation
Garbage & Trash
Band & Music
Cemetery
Trust Funds
Airport
Library
Public Health
Streets, Alleys,
& Sewers
Other

Debt Service

Retirement of
Bonds, Temporary
Notes & No
Fund Warrants
Principal &
Interest Pay-
ments

Utility Expenses

The Cost of
Operating Electric,
Water & Gas
Utilities

Capital Outlay

New City Bldgs.
Street Paving
New Sewers
Utility Expansion
Flood Control
Airports
Hospitals
Sewage Disposal
& Sanitation
Plants
Parking Meters
Other

City's Money Flow

This chart shows the major sources of revenues and the major outlets for expenditures of a city.

By following the lines, you can see that general revenues are used for general purposes, except for utility expenses in cities in which the utilities are municipally owned. Utility revenue is used for all types of expenditures, but new borrowing is used for capital outlays for the most part.

Occasionally, temporary notes are issued in the form of anticipation notes sold to banks to pay for bills due immediately. These are short-term loans.

The anticipation notes take the following forms:

RANS—Revenue Anticipation Notes. Paid off when anticipated revenues develop.

TANS—Tax Anticipation Notes. Paid back when taxes are collected.

BANS—Bond Anticipation Notes. Paid off when bonds are sold.

Most of the dozen-plus stories were enterprised by Mertens. Knowing the budget process and having good sources, Mertens was able to keep a steady flow of interesting and important copy moving to the city desk. In his stories, Mertens was always conscious of the human consequences of the belt tightening. By writing about possible cuts in such areas as school crossing guards and the fire department, Mertens alerted the public. Residents could, if they wished, inform their council members of their opposition to the cuts.

Types of Budgets

Two types of governmental expenditures are budgeted—funds for daily expenses and funds for long-range projects. At the local governmental level, these spending decisions are included in two kinds of budgets: expense budgets and capital budgets.

Expense Budgets The expense or executive budget covers costs of daily expenses, which include salaries, debt service and the purchase of goods and services. Expense budget revenues are gathered from three major sources:

- Taxes on real estate—the property tax—usually the single largest source of income.
- General fund receipts, which include revenues from fines, permits, licenses, and taxes such as income, corporation, sales and luxury taxes. (States must give cities permission to levy taxes.)
- Grants-in-aid from the federal and state governments.

Capital Budgets The capital or construction budget lists the costs of capital projects to be built, such as roads and schools, and major equipment and products to be purchased. Capital budget funds are raised by borrowing, usually through the sale of bonds pledged against the assessed valuation of real estate in the governmental unit. Bonds are approved by the voters and then sold to security firms through bidding. The firms then offer them for public sale. The loan is paid back, much like a home owner's payments on a mortgage, over an extended period, 10, 20 or 30 years. Principal and interest are paid out of current revenues and are listed in the expenditures column of the expense budget as "debt service," which should run under 10 percent of the total budget for the city to be on safe economic footing.

Making the Budget

Most budgets are adopted in this series of steps:

1. Budget request forms go out to all department heads, who must decide on priorities for the coming year and submit them to the budget officer, mayor or school superintendent.
2. Meetings are held between the budget officer and department heads to adjust requests and formulate a single balanced program.

3. The budget is submitted to the city council or commission, the board of education or other legislative arm of the governmental unit. The budget is sometimes accompanied by a narrative explaining the requests.

4. The legislative body examines budget items for each department and agrees on allocations for each.

5. Public hearings are held.

6. The budget is adopted.

The reporter covers each stage of this process, the behind-the-scenes bickering, dickering and politicking as well as the formal activities of the various department heads, executives and legislators. All sorts of pressures are brought to bear on the budget makers. Property owners and real estate interests want the budget held down, for increased expenditures usually mean higher property taxes. The businessmen and -women who rely on selling goods and services to the city seek hefty budgets for the departments and agencies they serve. Employees want salary increases, generous fringe benefits and more lines in the budget for promotions. Politicians seek to reward constituencies and to fulfill campaign promises.

The Aftermath   After the budget is adopted, the reporter watches the consequences. Few, if any, agencies and departments are given what they request, which usually does no harm as most units purposely hike up their requests. But, sometimes, damage is done. In Ohio, the *Akron Beacon Journal* investigated school finances and found that "legislators and governors have siphoned hundreds of millions of dollars from education for other purposes." The result: "High school seniors in tears when their football season and marching band are canceled . . . elementary school children have to wait after school because there are not enough buses in working condition to take them home."

Checklist: Budgets

Adoption

___ Amount to be spent.

___ New or increased taxes, higher license and permit fees and other income that will be necessary to meet expenditures.

___ Cuts, if any, to be made in such taxes, fees or fines.

___ Comparison with preceding year(s) in dollars and in percentage increase or decrease. How much will an increase cost the typical home owner?

___ Justification for increases sought, cuts made.

___ Rate of current spending, under or over budget of previous year.

___ Patterns behind submission and subsequent adjustments, such as political motives, pressure groups, history.

___ Consequences of budget for agencies, departments, businesses, public. Which had significant cuts, increases.

Follow-Up

___ Per-person comparison of costs for specific services with other cities or school districts of same size.

___ Check of one or more departments to see how funds are used, whether all funds were necessary.

Sources

There are five major interest groups that seek to influence budget making and constitute the reporter's sources:

1. **Government:** chief executive, who submits the budget; mayor, governor, school superintendent, president; city manager; head of budget bureau or budget director; department heads; finance and taxation committees of the city council or commission; council members. (Party leaders outside government are sometimes helpful.)

2. **Money-providing constituencies:** local real estate association; property owners' association; chamber of commerce; taxpayer organizations; merchant and business groups; banks; savings and loan associations.

3. **Service-demanding groups:** lobbyists for education, health, welfare and other services.

4. **Organized bureaucracies:** public employees; municipal unions; civil service associations; the public employees' retirement fund manager.

5. **Independent groups:** League of Women Voters; National Municipal League; National League of Cities; U.S. Conference of Mayors; Advisory Commission on Intergovernmental Relations.

Compulsory Costs

Promises to cut spending and therefore lower taxes make for political rhetoric that entices voters, but the truth is that many items in the budget are mandated costs that cannot be shifted or eliminated without massive political changes. The mandated funds include salaries, debt service, pensions and matching funds that localities must produce to meet state and federal grants, particularly for such services as health, welfare and education. When the city accepts grants from the state or federal government, it must abide by rules and regulations that often require local expenditures.

The actual maneuvering room in most budgets is not great, especially because salaries, which represent the largest single expense item, are set by contract in many cities. Because of mandated costs, less than 10 percent of the budgets for most large cities is discretionary.

Costs can be reduced if commitments to the poor, the elderly and the ill are cut back. This, however, would antagonize the service-demanding constituencies. Maneuvering room could be created by changing earmarked funds, such as those for education, to general funds. Again, groups that benefit from the status quo would object. In tight times, city employees are pressed to forego wage increases.

Trade-Offs and Rewards   The competition for free-floating general funds is always intense, and the perceptive reporter will examine this contest during the budgetary process. In this competition, the administrator finds it necessary to trade off the demands of various groups. The trade-offs make good stories.

Some aspects of the process are hidden from view. The reporter must dig them out and learn which constituencies are involved, the motives of the participants. Are political debts being paid by building a school in one section of the city or by increasing salaries in a particular agency? Have cuts been made in the department of a critical or independent administrator?

Budget Politics

During a legislative session, the Republican governor of New York proposed a new formula for the distribution of state aid to local school districts that reflected the demands of big-city school officials. A few days later, a group of Republican state senators and assembly members from Long Island met with the governor, who was facing re-election. Following the meeting, the governor's aid formula was changed to give more aid to suburban school districts.

"What happened at the gathering," reported *The New York Times,* "was summed up later by Joseph M. Margiotta of Uniondale, the powerful Nassau County Republican leader, who related that the Long Island delegation had simply delivered to the governor the stern message that without more state education aid, Long Island property taxes would skyrocket in September and the governor's campaign would sink in October."

When Mayor John Lindsay of New York "dropped the broom and picked up the nightstick"—the graphic phrase the *Daily News* used to describe the shift in budget priorities from clean streets to public safety—it was widely interpreted as Lindsay's recognition that law and order would make a more attractive national issue than sanitation. Lindsay has presidential ambitions.

As the recession took hold in 2000 and continued in following years, cities and states had to take drastic measures to balance their budgets. The consequences were often dramatic: student protests against tuition increases at tax-supported colleges and universities, homeless people sleeping in welfare offices, oversized classes and school closings leading to parent protests.

Property Tax

The property tax is the largest single source of income for municipalities, counties, special districts and school systems. It affects more people than any other local tax but the sales tax. Considerable local, county and school coverage centers on the action of the council, commission or board in setting the property tax.

The tax is formally known as the *mill levy.* A mill is .1 cent (1/10¢), and the property tax technically is expressed in terms of mills levied for each dollar of assessed valuation of property. One-tenth of a mill per dollar works out to 10 cents per $100 in assessed valuation, or $1 per $1,000 in valuation.

Here is the formula for figuring the property tax or mill levy:

Mill levy = taxes to be collected ÷ assessed valuation

Let us assume budget officials estimate that $1 million will have to be collected from the property tax and that the assessed valuation of real estate in the city or school district is $80 million. Here is how the tax is figured:

Mill levy = $1 million ÷ $80 million
Mill levy = $1 ÷ $80 = $.0125
Mill levy = 1.25 cents on each $1 of assessed valuation

Because mill levies are usually expressed against $100 or $1,000 in assessed valuation, the levy in this community would be $1.25 for each $100 in valuation, or $12.50 for each $1,000 in valuation.

Note that the mill levy is applied to assessed valuations, not to actual value as determined in the marketplace. Assessed value is usually a percentage of market value.

Budget Adoption   Here is the beginning of a story about the adoption of the city budget:

The Mt. Pleasant City Council adopted a $217 million budget last night and set a tax rate of $108.50 for each $1,000 in assessed valuation.

The rate represents a $6 increase in the tax rate for property owners for next year.

Those owning homes assessed at $50,000, which is the average Mt. Pleasant assessment, will pay $5,425 a year in city property taxes. The current bill for a $50,000 home is $5,125.

Many Other Taxes   Remember that the property tax is a major source of revenue for several governmental units—city, county, school, special assessment districts, each of which sets its own tax levy on property. When covering the action of one unit in setting a tax rate, it is necessary to inform the reader that this particular property tax is not the only one the property owner will pay.

Property taxes levied by special assessment districts can add a large chunk to the tax bill. These special districts construct and maintain services such as power and water lines, hospitals, sewage systems and community development projects. Each district has the power to levy taxes on property within the district.

Property valuations are made by the tax assessor and are public record. The tax rate is set each year, but valuations on individual pieces of property are not changed often. Total assessed valuation does change each year because of new construction and shutdowns that add to or subtract from the tax rolls. The taxing district must establish the total assessed valuation each year before a new tax rate can be set.

See **Assessment Districts** in *NRW Plus.*

Reassessments

When the assessor does make new valuations, the intensity of feeling is considerable, as revealed in this story:

SPRING VALLEY, N.Y., Dec. 12—Listening to people here, a visitor would almost think that someone was stalking the streets, sowing horror and destruction.

But it is only the tax assessor, equipped with a collapsible 10-foot measuring stick, a set of appraisal cards, a practiced eye that can tell the difference between a toilet and a water closet and experience that tells him which adds more value to a house.

This village of 22,450 persons, 2,219 dwellings and 109 commercial properties is nearing the end of a year-long reappraisal. . . .

The purpose of a reassessment is to bring valuations up to date and to attempt to distribute the tax burden fairly. Generally, reassessments result in increased revenues from the property tax since assessors will often use the current market value of property as the guideline, not the original cost of the property.

When a community decides it must raise more revenue through the property tax, it has two alternatives: It can raise the property tax or it can raise property valuations. A reassessment is considered more equitable as the heaviest burden falls on those with the greater ability to carry the increase.

Politics   The assessor sometimes is politically motivated in establishing assessments. In some cities, residential properties are consistently underassessed in order to placate home owners. In Philadelphia, tax officials assessed residences at 40 percent of market value, whereas commercial property was assessed at 54 percent and industrial property at 59 percent. In Chicago, the political machine of Mayor Richard J. Daley underassessed large corporations and industries. At election time, these beneficiaries of the assessor could be counted on for large campaign contributions.

Borrowing

Most cities need seasonal funds to tide them over while waiting for income from taxes or grants to arrive. They also need money to finance major construction projects.

Anticipation Notes

For seasonal borrowing or for emergencies when small amounts are needed, the city may issue and sell anticipation notes to banks. Future tax collections and anticipated grants-in-aid are pledged as security. Usually, the state must approve.

Short-term low-interest borrowing consists of three types of anticipation notes—revenue, tax and bond. All notes must be repaid in a year.

Bonds

The idea behind the sale of bonds is that the costs of such long-range projects as schools, hospitals, streets, sewage plants and mass transit should be borne by those who use them over the anticipated lives of the projects.

There are three major types of bonds. They differ as to the type of security pledged to repay them:

- **General obligation:** Most frequently issued. Security is the general taxing power of the city. Bonds are retired by taxes on all property in the city.
- **Special improvement:** For construction of sidewalks, sewers and similar public works. Taxes are levied on the property owners who will benefit from the construction. Charges levied on the property are called *special assessments*. Special assessment districts are set up to levy and collect the taxes.
- **Revenue bonds:** To pay for the acquisition, construction and improvement of such properties as college dormitories and public utilities. The pledge is a lien on earnings, which are used to redeem the bonds. These earnings come from room charges in dormitories; water, gas and electric collections from utility customers; toll charges on bridges and highways.

Bonds are paid off in two ways:

- **Term bonds:** The securities are retired at the end of the specified term, 10, 15, 20 years. Meanwhile, money is set aside regularly in a sinking fund and invested to be used to retire the bonds at the end of the term.
- **Serial bonds:** Most common. A portion is retired each year.

Give Total Cost   In writing bond stories, the reporter should make sure to include the cost of the bonds to taxpayers. Some readers will be astonished to learn how much a seemingly small rate of interest can add to the principal.

When Nassau County in New York sold $103 million in bonds for roads, land purchases and new sewers, officials estimated that interest would cost about $50 million over the life of the bonds. One reason for the high cost of debt was the downgrading of the county by bond-rating agencies as a result of the county's financial problems. The downgrading resulted in the county having to offer higher interest rates to attract investors worried about the lowered rating of the bonds.

Here is the beginning of a story about a credit downgrading:

> TROY, N.Y. (AP)—The City of Troy, which continues to struggle with a four-year-old financial crisis, had its credit rating reduced below investment grade Friday by Moody's Investors Service.
>
> Moody's said it had cut Troy's credit rating from B-aa to B-a, one step below investment grade. . . .

Checking Up

Wherever public money is involved, audits are made to see that the money is spent properly. Most governmental units undergo internal checks made by their own auditors, and these make good stories. Here is the beginning of a story by Jayne Garrison of the *San Francisco Examiner:*

> OAKLAND—A Social Services Department audit says mismanagement and internal squabbling are so severe that clients would be better off if the agency were dismantled.

In addition, checks are made by an independent government agency or office. Cities, states and the federal government have a department or office independent of the executive that checks the financial activities of all agencies within government. At the federal level, the Government Accounting Office does this work. At the state level, the state auditor or comptroller is the watchdog, and at the city level an elected official, also known as the auditor or comptroller, examines the financial records of city offices.

A regular or preaudit examination determines whether there is money to pay for the goods, whether there are certified receipts for the delivered goods, whether there has been competitive bidding when required by law and whether the prices are reasonable.

Increasingly, auditors and comptrollers are conducting performance audits, which check the efficiency of the services, the quality of the goods and the necessity for purchasing them.

Preaudit example: A state official claims travel reimbursement for an official trip between Boulder and Denver. The auditor will determine whether the 39 miles claimed on the official's expense account attached to a pay order is the actual distance and will see whether the 29 cents a mile claimed is the standard state payment.

Performance audit example: The comptroller has decided to make a check of welfare rolls to see whether money is going out to ineligible people. The office makes a computer check of the welfare rolls against (a) death lists; (b) marriage certificates (if a person receiving aid to dependent children has married, the working spouse is obligated to support the children); (c) children in foster care homes still listed as at the residence; (d) city and state payrolls to determine if any employed people are receiving welfare.

Looking at the Files

Journalists make their own checks. They regularly look through vouchers and pay orders in the auditor's office, and they look at the canceled checks in the treasurer's office.

When a governmental unit wants to buy something, it sends a purchase order to the comptroller's or auditor's office, which makes a preaudit. Records are kept by the number of the purchase order, by the agency involved and often by the name of the vendor.

On delivery of the goods or services, a voucher is made up with the accompanying bill, and this starts the payment to the vendor. The payment is made in the form of a check, a warrant.

Dining Out   When Christopher Scanlan of *The Providence Journal* was examining vouchers of the Providence Housing Authority, he came upon payments of $3,319.59 made to restaurants in Providence and Warwick for "authority meetings." On checking, he learned that members of the authority had been meeting over meals for years. "The restaurant tabs were paid from authority funds, the majority of which are derived from rents paid by low income tenants at the city's 14 public housing projects and from federal subsidies," Scanlan wrote. After the story ran, the authority members agreed to hold meetings in the housing projects it manages.

High-Level Thievery   An examination of vouchers and warrants enabled George Thiem, a reporter for *The Chicago Daily News,* to expose a multimillion-dollar corruption scheme by the Illinois state treasurer. Thiem could see that a number of checks were endorsed by typewriter. Interviewing some of those who supposedly were paid by these checks for work done for the state, he learned that the people listed on the checks had never done state work; nor had they received the checks. The treasurer went to prison as a result of Thiem's investigation.

For more information on how to check government, see **Investigating Government** *NRW Plus.*

Zoning and Planning

For centuries, the mentally ill were locked up. The reasons seemed logical: Isolated, the mentally ill could be healed more rapidly; free in society, their conditions worsened; they were a danger to others and to themselves. Gradually, the truth seeped out. Journalists showed that institutions for the mentally ill were snake pits where the patients were treated inhumanely. Few were cured, and many were made worse. With the development of tranquilizing drugs and other treatment, it became possible to offer outpatient care. But there had to be a transition, a halfway house to help the patient adjust after institutionalization.

In New Jersey, the Catholic Diocese of Trenton decided to administer several such houses. The state intended to deinstitutionalize its mental patients, and the diocese sought to help. The diocese found a structure in Willingboro that fit its needs. But permission was required from the zoning board because the building was in a residential area.

The Willingboro zoning board, like thousands of other such boards, carries out the community's planning goals, which are usually set by the planning commission. The zoning boards divide an area into zones or districts and designate them residential, commercial or industrial. The boards then grant building and construction permits consistent with these designations.

The boards also regulate the height of buildings, lot size, yard dimensions and other aspects of construction. City councils enact the ordinances that the zoning boards enforce.

Zoning can be restrictive, a way of keeping certain people out of an area. By requiring that new construction be of single-residence homes on one-acre lots, a zoning regulation will effectively keep out of the area all but the well-to-do. When Laura King, who covered Willingboro on her suburban beat, attended the zoning board meeting at which the diocese requested a variance for its halfway house, she was struck by the hostility of the spectators. King decided that the opposition to the house was the story.

Neighborhood Stories

City hall reporters spend too much of their time in city hall, says a veteran municipal government reporter. He recommends that they make regular trips out of the protected environs of the municipal building and into the neighborhoods of the community to see what is on the minds of people, to check how city programs and policies have been carried out. Here is the beginning of a neighborhood story by Jayne Garrison of the *San Francisco Examiner:*

OAKLAND—In the heart of the Oakland flatlands, the moms and pops of small business are plotting to sweep out the rubble: dope, litter and boarded buildings.

About 35 merchants meeting in churches and stores the last few weeks have organized a voice they hope will boom across town to City Hall—the Central East Oakland Merchants Association.

This is the first time in more than a decade that merchants along central East 14th Street have tried to wield clout together. The odds against them are steep.

They have little political pull and even less money. They face absentee landlords who own some boarded storefronts, and youths who have no work outside the drug trade.

But they do have determination.

"You see that red church down there?" said Al Parham, nodding toward a tall brick steeple half a block past Seminary Avenue on East 14th Street. "They just built that. So people are coming back into the community. And they're going to church. They care."

CAR   A lot of local reporting is based on records and files that are kept online. For an examination of how these records are put to use by reporters see **Computer-Assisted Reporting** *NRW Plus.*

Covering the Schools

Communities spend more money on public education than on any other single tax-supported activity. Free public education has a long history in the United States. In 1642, the Massachusetts Bay Colony made education compulsory in the

James Woodcock,
The Billings Gazette

Crowded

Bonnie Olson tries to cope with the 26 children in her Billings, Mont., classroom. The state sets 20 as the classroom limit, but the school district did not have money to hire enough teachers.

primary grades and required towns to establish public schools. The cost is borne by all in the community, whether the individual has children in the public school or not. The reason was given succinctly by Thaddeus Stevens to the Pennsylvania state legislature in 1835 when some legislators objected to the general financing of the schools.

"Many complain of the school tax," Stevens said, "not so much on account of its amount, as because it is for the benefit of others and not themselves. This is a mistake. It is for their own benefit, inasmuch as it perpetuates the government and ensures the due administration of the laws under which they live, and by which their lives and property are protected."

The faith in education as the underpinning of democracy is a constant theme in American life, along with the belief that a good education can pave the way to a good job, if not to the good life. Education pervades the life of most families because they have children in school.

The interest in schools—which really means a concern for the community's children—led *The Fincastle Herald* in Virginia to run a banner across page 1 when the Scholastic Aptitude Test (SAT) scores for the county were made public. "Low SAT scores surprise school officials," read the headline. The story was accompanied by a large box comparing county scores with those in Virginia, southern states and the nation. The story by Edwin McCoy begins:

> Botetourt County students scored at least 20 points below the state and national averages on both parts of the Scholastic Aptitude Test (SAT), according to figures provided by the county school system this week.

McCoy described education as the "focal point in the community" in an editorial accompanying the news story. "The quality of education is important to industrial or commercial development because developers are interested in the quality of life in any area they choose to expand in or move to."

Structure of the System

The school system is based in school districts. The schools are independent of municipal government and are subject to state regulations through a state board of education. School boards, usually with five to seven members, are elected in nonpartisan elections, although in some cities board members are appointed by the mayor. The board hires a superintendent of schools who is responsible to the board.

Stories from the board and the superintendent's office involve such subjects as changes in the curriculum and personnel, teacher contracts, the purchase of new equipment, aid to education, teacher certification, school dates for opening, closing and holidays and the vast area of school financing that includes budgeting and the issuance of bonds.

The school administration can provide material for assessing the performance of the system and its schools. Dropout and truancy records are kept, as are the results of standardized tests. Reporters can compare the scores in their communities with those of other cities. Comparisons also can be made of schools within the system. Do the students in the low-scoring schools come from economically depressed areas with serious social and economic problems? Is there a correlation between income and achievement?

A check of high school graduates would indicate what percentage is going to college from each school. Interviews with the students may uncover information just as revealing as the students' test scores.

Financing Schools

Schools are financed by several sources. The averages work out to 48 percent from the state, 45 percent from local taxes and 7 percent from the federal government. In the Northeast, most states rely on 55 percent or more of their support from local property taxes, which favors students in well-to-do areas. In an attempt to equalize support for schools, several states have altered their school-financing formulas to make the state the major provider. In New Mexico, for example, 90 percent of school operating funds are provided by the state.

In the Classroom

The education reporter's responsibility is to hold the school system accountable to parents and to the community. The United States has committed itself to an educational system that will turn out large numbers of people educated beyond the level that the country demanded only of its educated elite a century ago. How well is it doing this?

The best way to begin to find out is to visit the classroom, to look at what is happening day after day and to check your observations against test scores and the assessments of parents and educators. When Bob Frazier of the *Register-Guard* in Eugene, Ore., covered education, he would scrunch all 6' 4" into a grade-schooler's chair and sit in class. The stories he wrote were much more significant than any release from the superintendent's office.

School visits will tell the reporter whether the principal has a sense of mission and exerts strong leadership. They will reveal the professional level of teachers, whether they are given respect and whether they, in turn, give students respect and attention. The school environment is checked: Is the school safe? Is there a strong code of behavior, and are violators punished? Is truancy increasing or declining? Records can be examined for the frequency, number and type of discipline problems and vandalism.

Does the high school have various tracks for its students, such as academic, vocational and general, and, if so, what percentage of students is in each? In the early 1960s, one of 10 students nationally was in the general track; by 1990, almost half were. (The general track usually gives credit for physical

To the Rescue. Private industry is making overtures to schools short of money. The most widely used source is Channel One, which provides television sets and audio equipment for the right to broadcast its TV newscast, with advertisers, in classrooms. Coca-Cola and Pepsi are signing up school districts for exclusive rights to sell their products. A school district in New York received $1.53 million for a 10-year deal from Coca-Cola, and in Colorado Springs a school official urged administrators to push Coca-Cola sales, even in classrooms.

Most of these deals are negotiated without public notice or meetings.

SAT Scores. Eight states among those with large numbers of students taking the SAT tests report scores of the combined verbal and math tests under 1,000: Florida, Georgia, Indiana, New York, North Carolina, Pennsylvania, South Carolina and Texas.

Maurice Rivenbank,
St. Petersburg Times

Inside Largo High

"I wore my Nikes and stayed away from ties," says Thomas French. Students talked openly with him.

and health education, work experience outside school, remedial English and mathematics and developmental courses such as training for adulthood and marriage.)

How much homework is given? A national survey of eighth-graders found youngsters spent 5½ hours a week on homework, 21 hours a week watching television. *The Raleigh Times* put at the top of page 1 its education reporter's story that half the state's students in the sixth and ninth grades do less than three hours of homework a week.

The School Budget

The allocation of federal, state and school district funds is made in the following process:

A budget for the following year is drafted by the schools superintendent and then submitted to the school board. The board holds hearings at which the superintendent defends his or her budget. Parents groups are heard, and if the teachers are organized into a union, the union speaks for raises for teachers.

Usually, the schools seek as much as possible and the board attempts to cut back to keep the mill levy (property tax) as low as possible. The board members have mixed motives. Although sensitive to the needs of the school system, they also reflect the larger community, which includes real estate interests that push to keep property taxes down.

The board then adopts a budget. In some states, the voters must approve this budget.

Hanging Out

Student life outside the classroom is worth covering, too. Thomas French of the *St. Petersburg Times* spent a year at Largo High School, listening to students talk about music, their sexual activity, their studies. He watched them sport chunks of gold jewelry, beepers and speed by the school in their late-model cars, "monster stereos with up to 1,000 watts" blaring.

The student culture is, some educators say, more important than the influence of the schools and of parents. Reporters have found a culture that pressures students to do the minimum work or be called "nerds." Students say they purposely do not do well because they want to avoid being ostracized. Many don't bother to do the homework, with no punishment by their instructors.

Asked what their parents think of their schoolwork, the little time they spend on homework, their C or worse grades, students say their parents are indifferent. French pointed out that student performance cannot be separated from the problems students take to the classroom.

"It was startling to learn from students how many of their families are disintegrating, no matter what their background," French said. "No one is immune any more. The sense of loss and emptiness and deep-seated anger is palpable in virtually every classroom I visit, from kindergarten through high school."

For French's description of how he went about reporting life inside and outside Largo High School see **A Year at School** in *NRW Plus*.

Widening Scope

Some education reporters consider themselves consumer reporters whose job it is to check on the quality of the teachers, the textbooks and the product. They also understand that the schools have become the focus of an intense political battle that ranges from what students should be allowed to read to how the schools should be financed. Every week seems to see battle lines forming in the community over a school issue. Let's start with one of the most contentious—textbooks.

What Can Jane and John Read?

For many years the answer in Texas was that they could read only the textbooks approved by a conservative religious majority on the state textbook adoption agency. The result was that Darwin was a nonperson in biology textbooks, evolution barely mentioned, creation science a plausible explanation of the origin of the universe and its species.

Because the state adopted few textbooks in each subject, it ordered vast quantities of the few approved books. Textbook publishers, like any business, played to the market. So the Texas approach to science, for example, became the norm for books used everywhere.

The Texas board would not use certain dictionaries because they contained profane and obscene words, and textbooks on health were especially vulnerable if they discussed sexuality, AIDS and breast self-examination techniques.

Reaction As journalists called attention to the board's actions, voters sent less zealous guardians to serve on it and publishers stiffened. When antiabortion and other groups demanded scores of changes in the health textbook, one publisher pulled out of the bidding.

"We simply cannot produce a product that does not provide children with adequate instruction on life-threatening issues," the publisher stated. An official of the Association of American Publishers said the requested changes were made "for political reasons. This was another case in which factions of the religious right are getting more involved in boards of education all over the country."

But the protectors of student morality have resources to thwart publishers—scissors, gluepots and volunteers to wield them.

The Franklin County, N.C., school board tore out three chapters from textbooks on student health. The chapters concerned the transmission of sexual diseases, contraception, pairing, marriage and parenting. The board said the chapters do not conform to its policy of abstinence. "Shades of 1936 Germany," Wayne Wilbourne, principal of Bunn High School, told *The News & Observer* of Raleigh.

Creation Science Although the courts have ruled that creation science is a religious tenet and has no place in the public school curriculum, the battle to include it rages on. Creation science is the belief that a divine being created life

---

Media Generation. The Henry J. Kaiser Family Foundation found children 8 to 18 years old are massive media consumers. On an average day, their media time is:

Watching TV	3:16
Listening to CD's or tapes	1:05
Listening to the radio	:48
Reading	:44
Using the computer	:31
Playing video games	:27
Using the Internet	:13

Hard. "Mathematics cannot be made easy. Nor, equally, can any school subjects which stretch the mind. That is because the life of the mind is not easy."

—John Casey, Fellow, Gonville and Caius College, Cambridge University

about 10,000 years ago, a literal reading of the Bible. Close to 50 percent of Americans agree: "God created humankind in its present form about 10,000 years ago."

In Kentucky, a public school superintendent was so offended by a science textbook's discussion of the Big Bang theory of the origin of the universe that he glued together the pages of hundreds of books. He was angry that the creationist theory was not in the textbook. "We're in a conservative area and a conservative county, and we want to maintain the relationship with our local churches and community," he said. "It has nothing to do with censorship or anything like that."

Bills are regularly introduced in state legislatures, and school board members persistent in trying to introduce creation science as a viable alternative to evolution. New Mexico, Kansas, Louisiana, Alabama and Tennessee are among the states in which the battles have been waged. In Alabama, stickers were pasted on 40,000 biology textbooks that state that evolution is a "controversial theory" students should question. The same instruction was given to teachers. The Christian Coalition and Eagle Forum, which support more religious activity in public schools, pushed the action.

Science instructors from these states' universities have been pulled into the politics of the situation, and in Kansas they succeeded in limiting the state board's anti-evolution action.

Dumbed Down Textbooks   A study of textbooks by the U.S. Department of Education found that many have decreased in difficulty by two grade levels since the mid-1970s. Few, if any, publishers aim their books at above-average students, the federal study found.

In one Massachusetts school district, the board dropped books by Mark Twain, John Steinbeck, Charles Dickens and others because they feared the authors' books might bore students. Among the books tossed out: *Tom Sawyer* and *A Tale of Two Cities.*

In *The New York Review of Books,* Alexander Stille writes, "The most recent textbooks appear to be designed on the debatable premise that they must compete with Nintendo games and MTV." Such books, he continues, "appeal to the lazier teachers who want both to keep the class busy and to avoid working with longer and more detailed texts."

Dumb Textbooks   Not only have textbooks become less rigorous, but they seem to be seriously flawed. "It is common nowadays to see schoolbooks that are packed, from cover to cover, with blatant factual and conceptual errors," says William F. Benetta who heads a textbook watchdog organization and is editor of its *Textbook Letter.*

The Sun of Baltimore examined the textbook situation in a lengthy article and found U.S. publishers wanting. It pointed out that a middle school physical science textbook mixed up velocity and acceleration, made two elements liquids that are solids and had grammatical as well as many factual blunders—foots for feet.

It quoted an education official as saying that she was told "by the best mathematicians in the country that the U.S. does not produce a textbook of the caliber we were looking for."

The editor of a major publisher's English composition textbook told prospective authors that they had to anchor their works "in the pop culture" in order to appeal to students.

Library Books Periodic attempts are made to purge books from school libraries, especially the books that deal with sex, race and sensitive contemporary subjects. Sometimes even the librarian is purged. The West Valley School Board of Kalispell, Mont., fired its grade school librarian after she had helped two seventh-grade students with their research for a class report on witchcraft in the middle ages.

In Ouachita Parish, La., more than 200 books were removed from a high school library after the principal ordered the librarians to get rid of anything having to do with sex.

In Georgia, a minister asked for the removal of art books from an elementary school library because they contained nudity. He was especially offended by reproductions of Michelangelo's Sistine Chapel and his statue of David.

For additional areas that education reporters look into see **Subjects for Coverage** *NRW Plus.*

> **Most Often Banned.** *Of Mice and Men,* John Steinbeck; *The Catcher in the Rye,* J. D. Salinger; *The Adventures of Huckleberry Finn,* Mark Twain; *I Know Why the Caged Bird Sings,* Maya Angelou; *The Color Purple,* Alice Walker.

Politics and Education

The conventional wisdom is that education is "above politics." The proof: The administration of the schools is separated from city government and placed in an independent board whose members are chosen without regard to party affiliation, usually in elections set apart from the partisan campaigning of the regular local election.

The truth is that education is inextricably bound up with politics. Politics enters the scene because, to put it simply, people differ in their notions of how youth should be trained, who should pay for it, who should control it. These differences are resolved in a political context. The conflict and its resolution should be at the heart of much of the reporter's coverage. The political debate runs from the White House to the local school board that meets in the little red schoolhouse.

Patronage Politics of a lower sort sometimes invades the school system. Its large instructional and administrative staffs are a plum for politicians seeking to reward friends and campaign contributors. Sean Patrick Lyons and the staff of the *Waterbury Republican-American* found that patronage had sunk its teeth deeply into the city's schools.

"We quickly found that teaching positions were the largest block of jobs not controlled by the civil service rules of the city," Lyons said. These jobs, among the highest-paid in the country, were not being advertised. Lyons found that a few relatives of school board members had been hired. "It all began to snowball from there," he said.

The staff found the system had doled out dozens of jobs to friends, relatives and donors to the campaigns of the mayor and school board members. "Some of the people who couldn't get interviews had far more experience and advanced degrees than those who were hired," Lyons said.

The team created a database of all the mayor's contributors and matched it with the list of employees. Relatives and friends were checked as well.

The result: The hiring system opened up and the state decided to monitor the city's hiring practices. "The political culture in the city has begun to shift dramatically," said Lyons.

Pleased Parents, Disturbing Data

Surveys have shown that a majority of parents are pleased with their children's education. Yet every measure of school achievement contains alarming material about students in many states.

The education reporter who consults the National Assessment of Educational Progress conducted by the U.S. Department of Education has available an unbiased insight into his or her state's schools. A recent NAEP survey found that fourth-graders in 13 states could not read at the "basic" level, defined as "partial mastery" of the knowledge and skills in reading that are expected of a fourth-grader.

These states are Alabama, Arizona, Arkansas, California, Delaware, Florida, Georgia, Hawaii, Louisiana, Maryland, Mississippi, New Mexico and South Carolina.

Nationally, 42 percent of fourth-graders score below the basic level. If we divide this overall figure into ethnic and racial groups, we find these percentages of low-scoring students:

White	32 percent
Black	72
Hispanic	67
Asian	23

The 10 states with the highest scoring fourth-graders in the NAEP test were Connecticut, Indiana, Iowa, Maine, Massachusetts, Montana, Nebraska, New Hampshire, North Dakota and Wisconsin.

The enterprising reporter will try to find causes for these figures. Among the factors that educators consider to affect academic performance are class size and pupil-teacher ratio. The better performing states showed a much higher overall percentage of classes with fewer than 25 students than did the states with poorly performing students. Also, the highest pupil-teacher ratio in the better states was 15.8 whereas the lowest ratio in the poor-performing states was 16.6. The median class size for the high-scoring states was 15.3; the median class size for the low-scoring states was 17.3.

Maine's class size averaged 14.1, California's 24.1.

The NAEP describes itself as "the only nationally representative and continuous assessment of what America's students know and can do in various subject areas." It issues "Report Cards" frequently. They are available to the public at this address: National Library of Education, Office of Educational Research and Improvement, U.S. Department of Education, 555 New Jersey Avenue, NW, Washington, DC 20208-5641, (202) 219-1651.

Covering a School Board Election

Increasingly, school board elections have become the focus of community tensions. As special-interest groups with a conservative agenda put candidates on the ballot, the lines dividing residents grow sharper.

In Sioux Falls, S.D., in a recent school board election, two conservative candidates challenged two incumbents seeking re-election. The incumbents were part of a 3–2 liberal majority, and the local newspaper made it clear that much was at stake in the election: What values shall the community's children be taught, and how would the school board respond to property tax concerns?

Early in the campaign, the *Argus Leader* asked the candidates about these two issues, and it ran their replies along with biographical information about the four candidates. The newspaper was stating what it believed were key issues the candidates should speak about so that voters would have relevant material on which to base their votes.

One of the candidates said that to save money he would eliminate sex education and "social agenda items not academic." As for teaching of values, this candidate stated, "We need Bible reading back in the school, not interpretation, but reading."

In her coverage of the election campaign, Corrine Olson, explored the candidates' approaches to the teaching of "values." The challengers were quoted as emphasizing "values in the instruction and discipline of children." The incumbents contended that the schools in Sioux Falls have been teaching values and stressed the importance of "tolerance" as "one of the values that should be embraced." One challenger said that Christian teachers should be able to practice their faith in their instruction in the schools.

Paralleling the news coverage, the editorial page set the issues out early. Rob Swenson, the editorial page editor, wrote a month before the election, "Voters will determine whether the board stays the present course or turns further to the right." In a final editorial before the vote, Swenson wrote that voters faced a choice between "ideologues of the radical, religious-tinged right" and the incumbents, described as "moderates" who would join with a liberal member to form a majority of three on the five-member board. The other two incumbents were described as having "reactionary views on issues such as patriotism and sex."

Olson's story of the election results begins:

> Sioux Falls voters decided Tuesday to stick with incumbents just one year after they supported a new direction for the school board.
>
> The incumbents won by a vote of almost two to one.

Depressing Data. Studies have shown:

- Fewer than a fifth of 11th graders can write a note applying for a summer job at a swimming pool.
- Of 21- to 25-year-olds, only 38 percent could figure their change from $3 if they had a 60-cent cup of soup and a $1.95 sandwich. One of five young adults can read a schedule well enough to tell when a bus will reach a terminal.
- Among college seniors, 58 percent could not identify Plato as the author of *The Republic;* 60 percent could not recognize the definition of Reconstruction; 58 percent knew that the Civil War was fought between 1850 and 1900; 25 percent did not know that Columbus landed in the New World before 1500.

'Control Spending, Emphasize Values'

A candidate in a school board election in Sioux Falls, S.D., outlines her program for the local schools. She wants administrative cutbacks to protect teaching positions and calls for a return to "basics" in instruction, along with an emphasis on "values."

Board of Education Meetings

School board meetings are often political battlegrounds on which important issues are fought out. The well-prepared reporter is able to provide depth coverage of these issues. The reporter is aware of the positions of the key players on some of the important matters that have come before the board and has kept track of developing issues. Here is a guide to covering board meetings.

Meetings Checklist

__ Actions taken.

__ How each member voted. If no formal vote but an informal consensus, get nods of heads or any other signs of approval or disapproval. Ask if uncertain.

__ Size and makeup of audience.

__ Reaction of audience to proposal(s).

___ Position of groups or organizations with a position on issue. (Obtain beforehand, if possible.)

___ Arguments on all sides.

___ Statements from those for and against proposal on what decision of board means.

New Educational Programs

Many meetings of school boards are concerned with new programs. Here is a checklist of items for the reporter:

Checklist

___ Source of idea.

___ Superiority to present program as claimed by sponsors.

___ Cost and source of funding program.

___ Basic philosophy or idea of program.

___ Other places it has been tried and results there. (Make independent check of this, if possible. How well is it working there? What is cost?)

___ Whether it has been tried before and discarded.

___ How does it fit in with what system is doing now? How it fits with trends in area, state, nation.

___ If someone is suggested to head it, who?

___ Arguments pro and con, naming those involved.

Knowing the Community

In this chapter, we have looked at how local government works, the role of money in the community, politics and education. There's much more to covering a community, of course, and the following 20 questions touch on some of these areas of community life the reporter should know about. The list was compiled by Gloria Brown Anderson, executive editor of *The New York Times* news service:

1. How is your community different from others in your state? How did it come to be established where it is?

2. Who are the major employers? What's the unemployment rate?

3. What are the most popular entertainment activities? What single event in the past year drew the biggest crowd?

4. What are the major institutional assets (museums, colleges, tourist attractions, sports teams, etc)?

5. Who are the town characters? Who's the most powerful person in town (politics, business, sports, education, etc)?

6. Who are your experts and what are their fields of expertise?

7. What's the dominant religion/philosophy? How are people treated who are not part of it?

8. What's driving the economy? (May not be the same as dominant employers.)

9. What are the major social problems?

10. Who are the most creative people in town (business, the arts, education, social scene, etc.)?

11. How many people move into your community every week? How many people leave? Why are they coming and going?

12. What's been the biggest change in the nature of the community in the past 10 years?

13. What's the high school dropout rate? Do most high school students go to college?

14. What legends or true stories do old-timers tell and retell?

15. How old is the oldest business and what is it?

16. What famous/accomplished people have roots in the community?

17. What kinds of books have been your community's best-sellers over the past five years?

18. What are the most popular TV shows? How many people have cable?

19. What happens in your community that has a significant impact on people elsewhere?

20. What's the demographic profile of your town? How does it compare with nearby communities?

Further Reading

Cremin, Lawrence A. *Transformation of the School: Progressivism in American Education.* New York: Random House, 1964.

French, Thomas. *South of Heaven: Welcome to High School at the End of the Twentieth Century.* New York: Doubleday, 1993.

Hewlett, Sylvia Ann. *When the Bough Breaks: The Cost of Neglecting Our Children.* New York: Basic Books, 1991.

Kidder, Tracy. *Among Schoolchildren.* Boston: Houghton Mifflin, 1989.

Rathbone, Cristina. *On the Outside Looking In.* Boston: Atlantic Monthly Press, 1998. (The author spent a year in a high school for rejects.)

Sayre, Wallace S., and Herbert Kaufman. *Governing New York City.* New York: Norton, 1965.

Shefter, Martin. *Political Crisis/Fiscal Crisis: The Collapse and Revival of New York City.* New York: Basic Books, 1985.

Wildavsky, Aaron. *The Politics of the Budgetary Process,* 2nd ed. Boston: Little, Brown, 1974.

PART SIX: Laws, Taste and Taboos, Codes and Ethics

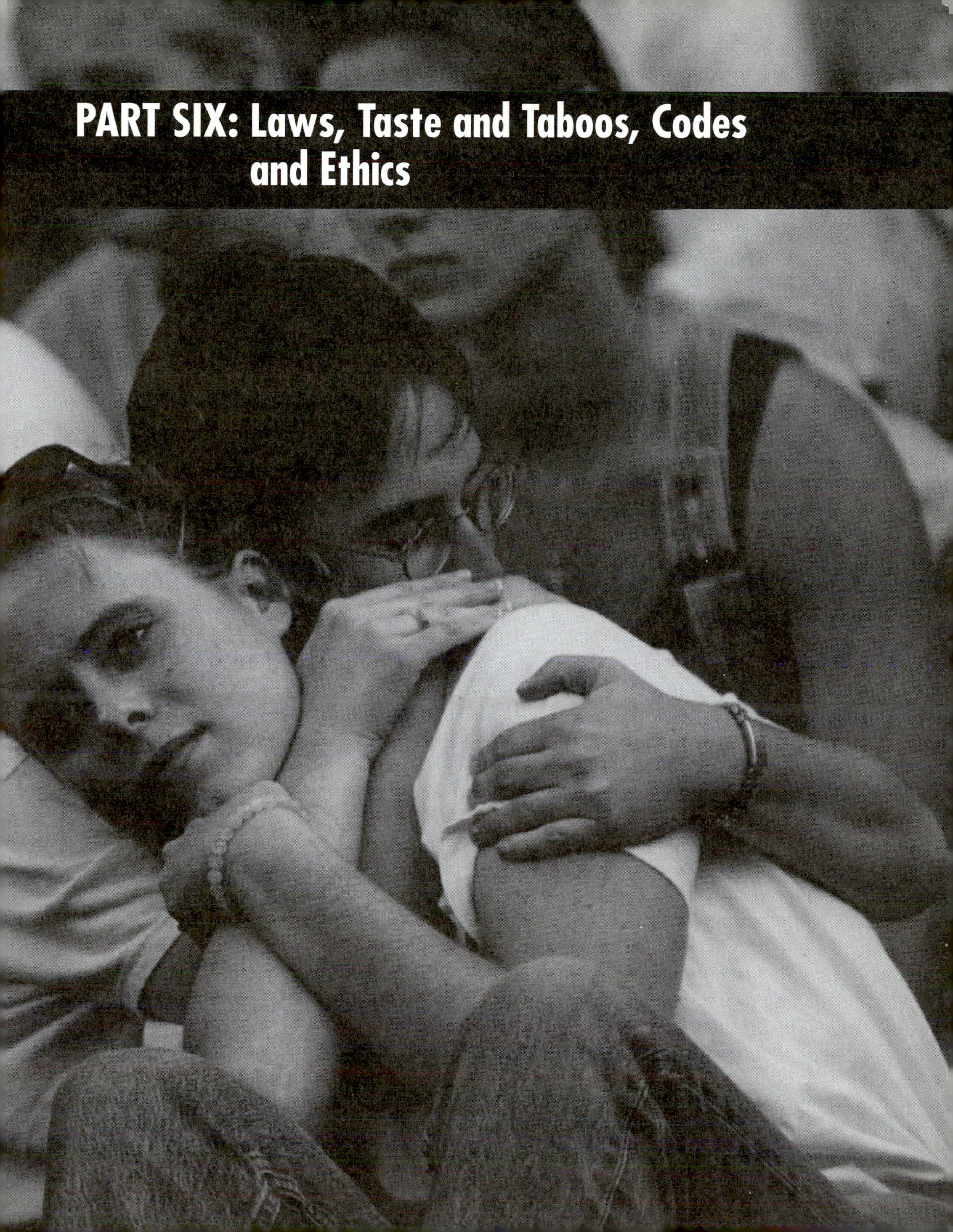

Part Six: Introduction

The final three chapters concern general guidelines for the journalist. As in most of journalism, there are few absolutes in these areas, and even those we tend to think of as unchanging do shift in time. Take libel law: Before 1964, libel was state law and wire service journalists had to exercise special care, for what was acceptable in one state could be the basis of a lawsuit in another. But with the Supreme Court decision in *The New York Times v. Sullivan* everything changed. In Chapter 25, we will examine the wide latitude this decision has given journalists.

Perhaps the greatest changes have occurred in the area of taste, where once journalists were hemmed in by a long list of taboos and agreed-upon prohibitions. In this Age of Candor, little seems off-limits, as we shall see in Chapter 26.

The last Chapter, 27, takes us to the area of ethics, and here, too, journalism has changed. Once-acceptable practices are now considered unethical, such as racial and religious identifications.

The areas overlap, as the photo of a family's grief on page 617 illustrates. It was legal for the photographer to snap this public scene at a California beach. But is it so wrenching that it approaches bad taste to spread the photo across the page of a newspaper? Another question: Is it an invasion of this family's privacy to show them grieving moments after the child's body was recovered? This is a matter of ethics, the morality of journalism. The newspaper apologized later, but the photographer said use of the photo was a public service in that it illustrates what can happen when water safety rules are not observed.

25 Reporters and the Law

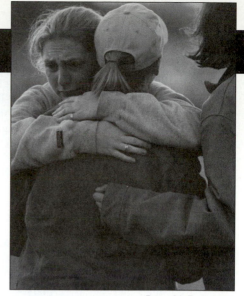

Dave McDermand,
The Bryan-College Station Eagle

**Mourning students' deaths—
an intrusion of privacy?**

Preview

The laws of libel and privacy limit what reporters may write. Stories that damage a person's reputation can be libelous, unless the material is privileged or can be proved to be true. Stories about an individual's personal life can invade the person's right to privacy.

- **Libel:** Most libelous stories are the result of careless reporting. Material that might injure someone is double-checked. The courts have made it more difficult for public figures or public officials to prove libel; but recent court decisions have limited these exceptions.
- **Privacy:** The right to privacy is protected by law. The personal activities of an individual can be reported if the material is about a newsworthy person and is not highly offensive.

One of the most dangerous areas for the journalist is libel. To the beginner, the region of libel is a land of mystery in which all the guideposts read, "Don't." To the experienced reporter, danger of libel is a cautionary presence in the newsroom.

Libel is published defamation of character. It is writing or pictures that:

- Expose a person to hatred, shame, disgrace, contempt or ridicule.
- Injure a person's reputation or cause the person to be shunned or avoided.
- Injure the person in his or her occupation.

Of course, many articles and pictures do libel individuals. In most cases, the defamatory material may be safe for publication if it is *privileged*. By privileged, we mean that the article is a fair and accurate report of a judicial, legislative or other public official proceeding or of anything said in the course of such sessions, trials or proceedings. The contents of most public records are privileged. Those who made our laws recognized that open debate of serious issues would be impeded unless the public had full access to official actions.

Another defense against libel is *truth*. No matter how serious the defamation may be, if the statement can be proved to be true and to have been made without malice, the defamed individual cannot successfully bring legal action.

A third defense, *fair comment and criticism,* most often involves editorial writers and reviewers. As long as the comment or criticism is directed at the work and not at the individual, the writing is safe.

In summary, the libel laws hold that a reporter is not in danger if the material is from a privileged proceeding (public *and* official) or if the material is substantially accurate or constitutes fair comment.

For broadcast journalists, defamatory statements made from a prepared script fall under libel, whereas extemporaneous defamatory remarks are treated as *slander,* which is defined as oral or uttered defamation.

Grounds for Libel Suits

Matter that might be held libelous by a court would have to:

1. Imply commission of a crime.
2. Tend to injure a person in his or her profession or job.
3. Imply a person has a disease, usually a loathsome disease that might lead to the individual's ostracism.
4. Damage a person's credit.
5. Imply unchaste behavior.
6. Indicate a lack of mental capacity.
7. Incite public ridicule or contempt.

For years, libel was a great weight on the shoulders of the press, particularly for newspapers that handled controversy and emphasized investigative reporting. The press associations had special concerns, for libel law was state law and was beyond the protection of the Constitution. What was legal in one state might have been libelous in another.

In effect, libel laws restrained the press, as the Supreme Court recognized in an epochal decision in 1964 that was to lighten the burden on the press. The court ruled that defamatory statements could have First Amendment protection. Our seven danger points are still to be watched, but the press now has much stronger defenses, thanks to the Supreme Court. To understand that decision—and to understand the organic nature of the law—we must travel back in time to Montgomery, Ala.

An Incident on a Bus

When Rosa Parks boarded the Cleveland Avenue bus in December 1955, she spotted an empty seat just behind the section reserved for whites. Tired from a day's work in a downtown department store, she eased into the space, only to be ordered to move. Seats were for white passengers only.

Mrs. Parks, a quiet, reserved woman, refused to give up her seat. She was taken off the bus and arrested. That weekend, plans were made by the black community to boycott Montgomery's buses.

Martin Luther King Jr., a black minister who helped plan the boycott, recalled how he awoke early Monday morning to see whether Montgomery's black residents would heed the word that it was better to walk in dignity than to ride in shame. The bus line that passed by the King home carried more blacks than any other line in the city. The first bus went by at 6 A.M. It was empty. Another, 15 minutes later, was empty, too.

That was the beginning of the boycott. Some 42,000 Montgomery blacks said they would walk to and from work or use volunteer vehicles and black-owned taxis until the bus system altered its seating arrangements and hired black drivers for buses along the predominantly black routes.

For 381 days, they stayed off the buses rather than be told to move to the back. Many people went to jail for violating the state's anti-boycott laws, including Mrs. Parks and Dr. King. Finally, the Supreme Court ruled bus segregation illegal.

Tension Mounts

Tensions mounted. In 1963, Medgar Evers, a black civil rights worker, was murdered in the doorway of his home in Jackson, Miss. The following year, three young civil rights workers were murdered in Philadelphia, Miss.

Newspapers and television stations sent waves of reporters to the South to report the conflict. Viewers saw fire hoses, police dogs and cattle prods used on blacks in Birmingham, and they saw the clubs of state troopers in Selma. The press reported the cry of blacks for an end to humiliation, economic exploitation, segregation in schools and discrimination at the polls.

It was also obvious the South was hardly budging. The border areas, portions of Tennessee and Kentucky and metropolitan communities such as Atlanta and Richmond accommodated. But not the towns and parishes of the Black Belt—Selma, Plaquemines, Yazoo City. Here, nonviolence met intractable resistance. Blacks might wait patiently outside the courthouse in Selma to register to vote. But the doors would stay closed to them, unless they were broken down by the federal government and the courts.

Press Coverage Increases

Because of the intensive coverage in the press, a consensus was developing outside the Black Belt. Most of the nation saw the anguish of the blacks who were hurling themselves against the wall of segregation, and some believed the nation was heading toward a race war.

In 1963, President Kennedy, aware of the developing conflict, declared that the struggle of blacks for civil rights was a "moral issue." Then four girls attending Sunday school in the black Sixteenth Street Baptist Church in Birmingham died in a bomb blast at the church.

The press stepped up its coverage. In some northern newspapers and on network television, the South was presented as a forbidding region of racism, its law officers openly defiant of the law, its white citizens unwilling to adjust to the changing times. Some southerners were angered by the coverage and some assaulted reporters covering civil rights demonstrations. The retaliation also took the form of suits against the press and television.

A Legal Club

Millions of dollars in damages were claimed by officials, who asserted they had been defamed by press and television. By 1964, libel suits seeking $300 million were pending against news organizations covering the racial story. One of the largest suits was brought against *The New York Times* by five officials in Alabama who contended that they had been inferentially damaged in an advertisement in the *Times* in 1960 that sought to raise funds for the civil rights movement. The advertisement, headlined "Heed Their Rising Voices," described the treatment of black schoolchildren by the Alabama police. The five officials brought suit for a total of $3 million.

Sullivan Case The first case to be tried involved L. B. Sullivan, a Montgomery city commissioner responsible for the police department. The judge in the case ordered segregated seating in the courtroom, and after he praised the "white man's justice" that had been brought to the country by the "Anglo-Saxon race," the all-white jury heard testimony. The jurors, whose names and photographs were printed in the local press, were told that although Sullivan's name had not been mentioned in the advertisement, his reputation had been damaged by the erroneous statements about the police.

During the trial, it was evident that the advertisement contained errors. It stated that Montgomery students had been expelled from school after singing "My Country 'Tis of Thee" on the steps of the state capitol. Actually, they were expelled for a sit-in in the courthouse grill. The advertisement also said students had been locked out of their lunchroom to "starve them into submission," which was false.

The jury agreed that Sullivan had been libeled and awarded him $500,000 in compensatory and punitive damages from the *Times*.

In a headline over the story about the suits against the *Times,* a Montgomery newspaper seemed to reveal the motives behind the libel suits: "State Finds Formidable Legal Club to Swing at Out-of-State Press."

The Court Acts

It was in this atmosphere that the Supreme Court considered the appeal of the *Times* from the state court decision. The case of *The New York Times v. Sullivan* (376 US 254) in 1964 was to mark a major change in the libel laws. But more important, by granting the press wider latitude in covering and commenting on the actions of public officials, the decision gave the press greater freedom to present issues of public concern, like the racial conflict that was tearing the country apart.

The Supreme Court understood the unique nature of the appeal. The Court commented, "We are required for the first time in this case to determine the extent to which the Constitutional protections for speech and press limit a state's power to award damages in a libel action brought by a public official against the critics of his official conduct."

In its decision, the Supreme Court took from the states their power to award damages for libel "in actions brought by public officials against critics of their official conduct." The Constitutional protections for free speech and free press would be seriously limited by state actions of the kind the Alabama court took, the Court said.

Brennan's Opinion

Justice William J. Brennan wrote, "The Constitutional guarantees require, we think, a federal rule that prohibits a public official from recovering damages for a defamatory falsehood relating to his official conduct unless he proves that the statement was made with 'actual malice'—that is, with knowledge that it was false or with reckless disregard to whether it was false or not."

The Court apparently agreed with the argument of Herbert F. Wechsler, who wrote in a brief for the *Times,* "This is not a time—there never was a time—when it would serve the values enshrined in the Constitution to force the press to curtail its attention to the tensest issues that confront the country or to forgo the dissemination of its publications in the areas where tension is extreme."

Justice Brennan noted in his opinion that the Supreme Court had seen in the use of such legal concepts as "insurrection," "contempt," "breach of the peace," "obscenity" and "solicitation of legal business" attempts to suppress the open discussion of public issues. Now it was libel.

In the Sullivan libel case, the Court extended the First Amendment in order to accomplish a social-political purpose—the protection of dissident voices in a repressive atmosphere. The right to criticize government, Brennan wrote, is "the central meaning of the First Amendment."

The decision, establishing what became known as the Times Doctrine, noted that the "Constitutional safeguard was fashioned to assure unfettered interchange of ideas for the bringing about of political and social changes desired by the people." To accomplish this, there must be "maintenance of the opportunity for free political discussion to the end that government may be responsive to the will of the people and that changes may be obtained by lawful means, an opportunity essential to the security of the Republic. . . ."

"Erroneous statement is inevitable in free debate," Brennan said. Running through the decision is the belief that free discussion will lead to a peaceful settlement of issues. Free expression, he was saying, has social utility. The Court seemed to be addressing itself to the millions of Americans in trauma because of the racial conflict.

"Actual Malice" In summary, the decision in the case makes it clear that, under the Constitution, no public official can recover damages for

Politic Action. The Sullivan case, like the school desegregation case 10 years before and the Nixon tapes decision 10 years later, reflected the need for a unanimous court decision in order to show the nation that certain issues were beyond debate.

The Sullivan decision supported a searching, vigorous and free press. *Brown v. Board of Education, Topeka,* said the 14th Amendment guaranteeing equal protection under the laws made school segregation unconstitutional.

The Watergate tape decision came at a time the president was under grave suspicion and a crisis of leadership threatened the nation.

"Throughout history," said an editorial writer for *The New York Times,* "the Court has been a vital factor on the political scene, even when trying to float majestically above it."

defamation in a newspaper article or "editorial advertisement" concerning his or her official conduct unless he or she can prove the article is defamatory and false and also show that:

1. The publication was made with the knowledge that it was false; or
2. The statement was made with reckless disregard of whether or not it was false.

Items 1 and 2 constitute the Court's concept of "actual malice."

The decision is the law in every state and takes precedence over federal and state laws, state constitutions and all previous state and federal court decisions.

Extension and Contraction of Times Doctrine

In the decade following the enunciation of the Times Doctrine, the Court went beyond applying it to public officials and included public figures and then private individuals involved in matters of public concern.

In a significant case, a businessman lost a libel suit that involved a clear case of error by a radio station. A distributor of nudist magazines was arrested while delivering magazines to a newsstand. The Philadelphia, Pa., police reported the incident to a local radio station, which broadcast an item about the distributor's arrest on a charge of selling obscene materials. Further, the station stated that the magazines were obscene. In a subsequent trial, the distributor was acquitted. The distributor said he had been defamed by the radio station and sued. A jury awarded him general and punitive damages.

The radio newsman had violated one of the first rules a beginner learns: Never state as fact what is only charged and therefore subject to determination in the courts.

Lucky Reporter The reporter and his station were fortunate, however. The Court of Appeals reversed the lower court verdict, and in 1971 the Supreme Court upheld the reversal on the distributor's appeal (*Rosenbloom v. Metromedia, Inc.*, 403 US 29). The Court ruled:

> We thus hold that a libel action, as here by a private individual against a licensed radio station for a defamatory falsehood in a newscast relating to his involvement in an event of public or general concern may be sustained only upon clear and convincing proof that the defamatory falsehood was published with knowledge that it was false or with reckless disregard of whether it was false or not.
>
> Calculated falsehood, of course, falls outside the "fruitful exercise of the right of free speech."

Rosenbloom was neither a public official nor a public figure. But he was involved in an event of "public or general concern," and ordinary citizens so involved can successfully bring a libel action only by a showing of actual malice, the Court stated.

Rosenbloom might have been luckier had his troubles occurred later, for the Supreme Court in 1974 reversed directions and did so again in 1976 and 1979. These rulings made it possible for many more libel plaintiffs to collect damages for defamatory falsehoods because for private citizens the proof of defamation may be negligence or carelessness, not the more difficult actual malice public figures are required to prove.

Public or Private Figure?

In the 1974 case of *Gertz v. Robert Welch, Inc.* (418 US 323), the Supreme Court suddenly ceased the steady expansion of First Amendment protection to publications in libel actions. Elmer Gertz, a civil rights lawyer in Chicago, had been defamed by *American Opinion*, a monthly magazine published by the John Birch Society. The magazine described Gertz, who was representing a client in a case, as a "Communist-fronter" and said he had designed a national campaign to discredit the police. Although the trial judge had found no evidence the magazine had published recklessly, a jury awarded Gertz $50,000. The magazine appealed.

The Supreme Court ruled that as a private citizen "who had achieved no general fame or notoriety in the community" Gertz did not have to show "actual malice" but was entitled to damages if he could prove the material was false and defamatory and that it had been the result of negligence or carelessness by the publication. The Court returned to an emphasis on the plaintiff's status rather than the subject matter.

Courts Differ

Just where is the line that divides a public figure from a private figure? The Supreme Court has not clarified the point. Lower courts have differed.

The Washington Post escaped a libel judgment when a federal district court ruled a police informant was a public figure and had to prove actual malice. The *Post* had incorrectly stated the informant was a drug user. But three months later, a federal judge in Maryland ruled that a police informant was a private individual and thus need only prove that a Baltimore newspaper was careless in mistakenly stating he had broken into a lawyer's office to steal documents for the police.

Public Officials and Public Figures

Public officials: Government employees who have responsibility for governmental activities—elected officials, candidates for political office, appointed officials such as judges, police officers and some others engaged in the criminal justice system. The Supreme Court has said that not all public employees are public officials.

Public figures: People who have considerable power and influence and those who "voluntarily thrust" themselves into public controversy. Newspaper columnists, television personalities and some celebrities who seek to influence the public are included. But not all prominent people are covered.

In state courts, a Kansas judge ruled that a lawyer appointed to defend a penniless criminal defendant was a public official. Two months later, a Michigan judge said that an attorney appointed to represent an impoverished defendant was neither public figure nor public official.

In Virginia, a circuit court ruled that a high school English teacher was a public figure. The teacher had sued the *Richmond Times-Dispatch* for a story that criticized her teaching. She appealed and the state Supreme Court concluded she was not a public figure because she was in no position to influence or control "any public affairs or school policy." The newspaper appealed to the U.S. Supreme Court and lost. The teacher was awarded $100,000.

Police Officers The Supreme Court may have clarified the status of police officers. In 1989, it ruled that an officer *The Danville* (Ill.) *Commercial News* had linked to a suspected burglary ring was a public official and would have to prove actual malice. A student newspaper at Cleveland State University profited from this decision when a suit in which a campus police officer sought $300,000 in damages was dismissed. The newspaper had stated in an editorial that the officer had a reputation for "excessive force, brutality and discrimination."

Caution: Events that are the subject of gossip or public curiosity and have no significant relation to public affairs usually do not confer on the persons involved in them the status of public figures. This means that no matter how public a person's marriage rift may be, that person is not necessarily a public figure.

If the reporter can prove that an event relates to public affairs or an important social issue, then the persons involved may be classified as public figures. For example, if a physician or a lawyer injects himself or herself into a controversy over a local bond issue, then the person has become a public figure for news about the bonds but not about his or her personal life.

Attributing a Libel Is No Defense

In a story about a development scheme in an area adjacent to the university, a student newspaper said that a member of the local planning board had received a "kickback" from the developer. (A kickback is an under-the-table payment for special treatment.) Asked whether he knew that such a charge is clearly libelous, the student replied, "But I attributed it."

His instructor could only shrug in exasperation. A reporter can be held liable if he or she repeats a libelous statement or quotes someone making such a statement unless the original material is privileged.

If the assertion had been made in court or at an official meeting, the statement—even if untrue—would be privileged and the privilege would be a defense against claims for damages, provided the report was fair and accurate.

Costly Attribution When the FBI zeroed in on a suspect in a deadly bombing at the Summer Olympics in Atlanta, the media identified the supposed bomber. Tom Brokaw on NBC said the investigators were close to "making the case" and that they "probably have enough to arrest him right now, probably enough to prosecute him, but you always want to have enough to convict him as well. There are still holes in the case."

Yes, there were holes in the case, holes so wide the FBI finally admitted it had spent two months investigating the wrong man, a security guard who had seen a suspicious backpack just before the explosion.

The *Atlanta Journal-Constitution* also used the FBI's identification: "Richard Jewell . . . fits the profile of the lone bomber."

When the media hunt was over, Jewell clearly had grounds for a libel suit. Rather than contest it, NBC settled for what was reported to be $500,000. The New York *Daily News* headlined the settlement story: BROKAW GOOFED AND NBC PAID.

Newspaper Wins   The Atlanta newspaper refused to settle, and in a lengthy and costly court process it prevailed. The court ruled that Jewell had become a public figure and this forced him to prove that the newspaper report was made with "actual malice." Jewell's suit collapsed when the newspaper showed that it had acted in good faith by quoting official sources.

Still, there is a lesson here. Reporters must make sure that charges have been filed or arrests made before naming suspects. What officials say they are doing or what they say they plan to do—these are not official acts and thus not free from libel suits by those named.

Conditional and Absolute Privilege

The privilege to those participating in court cases and legislative sessions is an "absolute privilege," meaning the participants—the judge, lawyers, witnesses—cannot be held legally accountable even for malicious and deliberately false statements that are made within the scope of their participation in the proceedings. A newspaper or station, however, cannot use absolute privilege as a defense in libel suits. Their protection is known as "conditional" or "qualified privilege." The newspaper must present full, fair and accurate reports that are free of actual malice in order to be granted privilege.

A candidate for re-election to Congress who says of his opponent, "That man is a swindler" on the floor of the House of Representatives can make the statement with impunity, and a reporter can publish the accusation. (Obviously, the reporter would also carry the accused's reply.) But should the congressman make the charge in a political rally and the reporter's newspaper print the allegation, both are in trouble, unless the reporter can prove the man is indeed a swindler, and this would require proof of the man's conviction on that charge.

Warning: These protections do not cover proceedings, meetings, or activities that are private in nature. They also do not cover records that are sealed by law or court order.

Jailed. Two reporters for the *Atlanta Journal-Constitution* who refused to reveal their source for the identification of Jewell in the libel case were ordered jailed by a state judge.

Hot News and Time Copy

The Supreme Court has been generous to reporters who make mistakes under pressure of deadline. But reporters who have time to check material may not fare so well under the Court's distinction between "hot news" and "time copy." The differences were spelled out in two companion cases decided in 1967, *Curtis Publishing Co. v. Butts* and *Associated Press v. Walker* (both 388 US 130), involving public figures.

Edwin Walker was a former Army general who had become involved in the civil rights disputes in the South and had taken a position against desegregation. He was on the campus of the University of Mississippi in September 1962 when it erupted over the enrollment of James Meredith, a black student.

The AP moved a story that Walker had taken command of a violent crowd and had personally led a charge against federal marshals on the campus. The AP said Walker had encouraged rioters to use violence and had instructed white students how to combat the effects of tear gas. He sued for $800,000 in damages. Walker testified that he had counseled restraint and peaceful protest and had not charged the marshals. The jury believed his account and awarded him the sum he sought. The trial judge cut out the $300,000 in punitive damages because he found no actual malice in the AP account.

Game Fix   Wally Butts was the athletic director of the University of Georgia in 1962. He was employed by the Georgia Athletic Association, a private corporation, and so, like Walker, he was a private citizen when, according to *The Saturday Evening Post,* he conspired to fix a football game between Georgia and Alabama in 1962. An article in the magazine said an Atlanta insurance salesman had overheard a conversation between Butts and Bear Bryant, coach of the Alabama football team, in which Butts outlined Georgia's offensive strategy in the coming game and advised Bryant about defending against the plays.

Butts sued for $5 million in compensatory damages and $5 million in punitive damages. The jury awarded him $60,000 on the first charge and $3 million on the second, which was subsequently reduced to $460,000.

Winner, Loser   The Curtis Publishing Co., publishers of *The Saturday Evening Post,* and the AP appealed to the Supreme Court. Butts won his appeal, but Walker lost. The Court ruled that the evidence showed that the Butts story was not "hot news," but that the Walker story was. The *Post*'s editors, the Court stated, "recognized the need for a thorough investigation of the serious charges" but failed to make the investigation.

In the Walker case, the Court noted, "In contrast to the Butts article, the dispatch which concerns us in *Walker* was news which required immediate dissemination. . . . Considering the necessity for rapid dissemination, nothing in this series of events gives the slightest hint of a severe departure from publishing standards. We therefore conclude that Walker should not be entitled to damages from the Associated Press."

All Speech Not Equal

In a decision that worried some journalists, the Supreme Court in 1985 ruled that punitive damages can be awarded without the plaintiff's proving actual malice if the libelous material is not a matter of "public concern." The case, decided in 1985 by a vote of five to four, arose from an erroneous credit report by Dun & Bradstreet about a firm, Greenmoss Builders. The court let stand a $300,000 award for punitive damages.

"We have long recognized that not all speech is of equal First Amendment importance," wrote Justice Lewis E. Powell in his opinion. "It is speech on 'matters of public concern' that is 'at the heart of the First Amendment's protection.' . . . Speech on matters of purely private concern is of less First Amendment concern."

The court did not define "public concern," and this worried journalists and their lawyers, who were also concerned by the Court's decision not to apply what is known as the Gertz rule, which prohibits the award of punitive damages when there is no showing of actual malice. The court said the Gertz rule does not apply on matters of nonpublic concern.

Accuracy the Best Route

Most libel cases originate in a reporter's error. The lesson is clear: Follow Joseph Pulitzer's three rules for journalism, "Accuracy, accuracy, accuracy," or risk trouble.

Well, you might say, look at how many cases the media won despite the mistakes. True, but in most of these cases the legal costs were ferocious. It can cost up to a million dollars for the average case, and *Time* estimated that had it not won its case quickly when the Scientology organization sued, its legal fees might have amounted to $10 to $15 million in a drawn-out case.

Accuracy means checking everything yourself, not accepting someone's word or work as fact. This lesson was hard-learned by the authors of an ethics handbook published by the Society of Professional Journalists and the Poynter Institute for Media Studies. An anchor at KXAS-TV in Dallas filed a libel suit alleging he was unfairly portrayed as having a conflict of interest in acting as a "master of ceremonies during rallies for [George W.] Bush at several campaign stops." The publishers apologized and paid the anchor's $18,000 legal fees. In its statement of apology, the publishers said a researcher had incorrectly summarized information that had been published in a Fort Worth newspaper.

Libel Online

The U.S. Supreme Court has given the Internet the same First Amendment protection as the print media, but the laws are being written about where responsibility lies for libel.

Matt Drudge, the Internet tipster-gossip who puts out The Drudge Report, carried an item that the communications adviser to President Clinton, Sidney Blumenthal, had beaten his wife. His sources were identified as "top GOP operatives" who told Drudge "there are court records" to prove their charge. Drudge did not produce the records, and the adviser sued.

Drudge retracted, saying he had been used "to broadcast dirty laundry. I think I've been had."

Who is liable? Not the carrier, AOL. Online service providers were immunized from libel suits in the Internet Decency statute. But Drudge is not exempt.

Next, to another cautionary area, that of privacy, an area that is increasingly troublesome to journalists because of the public's anger at the media for what it considers media intrusiveness.

Privacy

Whereas truth is the strongest defense against libel, it is the basis of invasion of privacy suits. Invasion of privacy is said to occur when an individual is exposed to public view and suffers mental distress as a consequence of the publicity. Unlike defamation, which has deep roots in the common law, the right to privacy is a fairly new legal development and one in which there is less certainty for the reporter than in the area of libel.

A balance must be struck by the courts between the public's right to know—a right commonly accepted though not in the Constitution—and the individual's right to privacy.

Three categories of privacy concern the reporter:

1. Publicity that places a person in a false light in the public eye. The Times Doctrine applies, provided the matter is of public interest.
2. Public disclosure of embarrassing private facts about an individual. If the facts are in an official document, they can be published, but not if they are private acts of no legitimate concern to the public.
3. Intrusion by the journalist into a private area for a story or a picture without permission—eavesdropping or trespassing. The use of electronic devices to invade a home or office is illegal. Newsworthiness is not a defense.

The Test: Newsworthiness

Except for intrusion, the newsworthiness of the event is a defense against invasion of privacy suits. A public event cannot have privacy grafted on it at the behest of the participants. However, the reporter cannot invade a person's home or office to seek out news and make public what is private. Nor can he or she misrepresent the purpose of reporting to gain access to home or office. There is no prohibition against following and watching a person in a public place, but the reporter cannot harass an individual.

Although the law of libel and the right of privacy are closely related, they involve distinctive legal principles and are fundamentally different. Libel law is designed to protect a person's character and reputation. The right of privacy protects a person's peace of mind, feelings, spirits and sensibilities. Generally, privacy guarantees an individual freedom from the unwarranted and unauthorized public exposure of the person or his or her affairs in which the public has no legitimate interest.

The right of privacy is the right of a person to be let alone unless he or she waives or relinquishes that right. Certain people, defined by the federal courts as "newsworthy," lose their right to privacy, but the material published about them cannot be "highly offensive."

In making rulings on the claim of invasion of privacy, the Supreme Court has applied the Times Doctrine. That is, even if the claimant could prove that the report was false, if it were a matter of public interest, the person bringing the action would have to show the error was made "with knowledge of its falsity or in reckless disregard of the truth."

"Calculated Falsehoods"

In one case, decided in 1974 by the Supreme Court, such disregard of the truth was proved by a claimant. The Court in *Cantrell v. Forest City Publishing Co.* (419 US 245) upheld an award against *The Plain Dealer* in Cleveland on the ground that a reporter's story about a visit to the home of the claimant "contained significant misrepresentations." Although the woman was not at home when the reporter visited, the article said she "will talk neither about what happened nor about how they were doing. . . ." He wrote that the widow "wears the same mask of nonexpression she wore at the funeral." A lower court jury awarded her $60,000 to compensate for the mental distress and shame the article caused. An appeals court reversed the verdict, and the woman appealed to the Supreme Court, which found the reporter's statements implying that the woman had been interviewed were "calculated falsehoods."

Rape Victims   The decision was eight to one. Some months later in another eight to one decision, the Supreme Court ruled on the second category involving privacy—the rights of private individuals to keep their personal affairs from public disclosure. In this case, the Court nullified a Georgia law that made it a misdemeanor to print or broadcast the name of a rape victim. The case involved the father of a young woman who had been raped and killed by a gang of teen-age boys. An Atlanta television station had used the victim's name, and the state court had ruled in favor of the father under the state law. The station appealed.

In setting aside the Georgia law, the Supreme Court stated that "once true information is disclosed in public court documents open to public inspection, the press cannot be sanctioned for publishing it." The Court stated (in *Cox Broadcasting Corp. v. Martin Cohn,* 420 US 469):

> The commission of crimes, prosecutions resulting therefrom, and judicial proceedings arising from the prosecutions are events of legitimate concern to the public and consequently fall within the press' responsibility to report the operations of government.

Pictures. The picture was stark and it led to a suit for invasion of privacy. The photo in *Today* of Cocoa, Fla., showed a woman covered only by a towel as she fled from a house where her estranged husband had kept her hostage. A lower court jury awarded her $10,000 in damages, but the state Supreme Court upheld an appeals court decision that overturned the verdict. The appeals court said the law is clear "that when one becomes an actor in an occurrence of public interest, it is not an invasion of privacy to publish her photograph with an account of such occurrence. . . . The published photograph is more a depiction of grief, fright, emotional tension and flight than it is an appeal to other sensual appetites."

In both cases, the Supreme Court cautioned against broad interpretations of its rulings. Nevertheless, the first case clearly indicates that the press must take care in publishing material about individuals that is false, and the second indicates the Court will not extend the right of privacy to private persons involved in actions described in official documents.

Privacy Guideline   Here is a useful guide from a federal appeals court ruling:

> A reporter or publication that gives publicity to the private life of a person is not subject to liability for unreasonable invasion of privacy if the material (1) is about a newsworthy person—who need not be an elected official or a celebrity—and (2) is not "highly offensive to a reasonable person, one of ordinary sensibilities and is of legitimate public concern."

Secret Taping

The courts are not sympathetic to the use of hidden electronic devices for newsgathering. When used, the courts have ruled, they can intrude on a person's right to privacy. In a 1998 decision, the California Supreme Court ruled that newspapers and television stations can be sued for intrusion if reporters or photographers are "unlawfully spying on them in the name of news gathering." And the following year, the Court ruled against an ABC News reporter who had secretly recorded an employee of a psychic hot line. The reporter had posed as a co-worker.

Hidden Camera   When *Life* had a reporter pose as someone needing help in the magazine's exposé of a man who claimed to heal people with herbs, clay and minerals, the healer sued. The reporter had a radio transmitter hidden in her pocketbook. Also, a photo was taken with a hidden camera.

In its defense, *Life* said investigative reporting would be difficult without such tactics. But the federal appeals court disagreed:

> We agree that newsgathering is an integral part of news dissemination. We strongly disagree, however, that the hidden mechanical contrivances are "indispensable tools" of newsgathering. Investigative reporting is an ancient art; its successful practice long antecedes the invention of miniature cameras and electronic devices. The First Amendment has never been construed to accord newsmen immunity from torts or crimes committed during the course of newsgathering. The First Amendment is not a license to trespass, to steal, or to intrude by electronic means into the precincts of another's home or office. . . .

Telephone Taping   Reporters routinely tape their telephone conversations with sources who are sensitive about being quoted accurately, and they tape when reporting sensitive issues. In most states, one-party consent (the reporter's) is all that is necessary. But in 10 states all parties involved must agree to the taping—California, Connecticut, Illinois, Maryland, Massachusetts, Montana, New Hampshire, Pennsylvania, South Dakota and Washington.

Monica Lewinsky's telephone conversations about her relationship with President Clinton were taped by her friend Linda Tripp, who lived in Maryland. Tripp did not inform Lewinsky she was being taped. A grand jury decided to look into the taping.

Food Lion   The ABC news magazine show "Primetime Live" infiltrated a supermarket with hidden cameras used by people the market chain had hired. The program charged that the store was selling old and tainted meat disguised to look fresh. Food Lion sued, and in his charge to the jury the judge told it to assume the story was correct but to consider Food Lion's allegation of fraud, trespass and breach of loyalty. The jury awarded Food Lion $5.5 million in punitive damages. But the U.S. Court of Appeals for the Fourth Circuit reversed the verdict, ruling that the charges Food Lion brought were an end run around the First Amendment requirements for libel suits.

Public Angry   People, polls show, are not happy with media intrusions. A poll conducted by the Scripps Howard News Service and the E. W. Scripps School of Journalism at Ohio University asked: How often do you think newspapers and television news programs violate the privacy rights of private citizens who are not celebrities?

The responses:

Often—33 percent

Sometimes—45 percent

Rarely—13 percent

Never—4 percent

Don't Know—5 percent

Another question: Should journalists be subject to criminal prosecution and even prison if they violate a person's privacy?

The responses are startling:

Yes—56 percent

No—27 percent

The Ethical Factor   There is an ethical as well as a legal aspect to privacy, which the polls hint at in reflecting the aversion the public has to the media's probing into the personal.

This repulsion was evident in the reaction to the lengthy videotape of President Clinton's grand jury testimony about his affair with Monica Lewinsky. In a CNN poll, 55 percent said they would not watch, and 15 percent said they would look only at what the news programs considered the important segments.

Clearly, many people see the media's interest in private lives as prying, feasting on the distasteful.

Avoiding the Dangers

The guide in libel and invasion of privacy suits seems fairly clear. Caution is necessary when the following are *not* involved—public officials, public figures, public events. When a private individual is drawn into the news, the news report must be full, fair and accurate. Of course, no journalist relies on the law for loopholes. He or she is always fair and accurate in coverage.

Libel suits usually result from:

- Carelessness.
- Exaggerated or enthusiastic writing.
- Opinions not based on facts.
- Statements of officials or informants made outside a privileged situation.
- Inadequate verification.
- Failure to check with the subject of the defamation.

When a libel has been committed, a retraction should be published. Although a retraction is not a defense, it serves to lessen damages and may deprive the plaintiff of punitive damages.

Rush + Inference = Libel Troubles

Most libel suits result from a reporter's rush to publish or broadcast the story. The usual care is not exercised in the speed-up. When the *New York Post* reported that Whitney Houston had been hospitalized in Miami after overdosing on diet pills, a $60 million libel suit was filed. The reporters handling the story would have learned it was a hoax had they called the hospital, which had no record of the singer's admission or treatment. The newspaper retracted the story the next day.

Libel suits also result from one of our old enemies—the inference, or jumping from the known to the unknown. A copy editor for an Indiana newspaper wrote this headline over the story of the closing of a restaurant: "Health board shuts doors at Bandido's; Investigators find rats, bugs at north-side eatery." The restaurant owner sued, contending the investigators did not find rats in his eatery. The copy editor testified in the trial: "When I saw the word 'rodent' or 'rodent droppings,' that said rats to me."

The jury awarded the restaurant owner $985,000.

The Reporter's Rights

The press carries a heavy burden. It has taken on the task of gathering and publishing the news, interpreting and commenting on the news and acting as watchdog in the public interest over wide areas of public concern. The burden of the press has been lightened by the foresight of the Founding Fathers through the guarantee in the First Amendment of the Constitution that Congress shall make no law abridging freedom of speech or of the press. This means that the press has the right to publish what it finds without prior restraint.

To journalists, it also means that they have the freedom to gather and prepare news and that the processes involved in these activities are shielded from a prying government and others. Also, journalists understood that their sources, their notes, their thoughts and their discussions with sources and their editors were protected.

Wide Protection

They had good reason to believe all this. State legislatures and the courts interpreted the concept of press freedom to cover these wide areas of news gathering and publication. In 1896, for example, the state of Maryland passed a law allowing reporters to conceal their sources from the courts and from other officials. The concern of the public traditionally has been that the press be free and strong enough to counterpose a powerful executive. This sensitivity to central government began with the revolution against the British Crown. It was reinforced by the generations of immigrants who fled czars, kings, dictators and tyrants.

Old as the story of the abuse of power may be, and as frequent as the exposures of its ruinous consequences have been by the press, the dangers implicit in centralized government are always present. This tendency of government to excessive use of its power was foreseen by the American revolutionaries who sought to make in the press a Fourth Estate outside government control and free to check on government.

But Not Absolute

There is, however, no clear-cut constitutional statement giving the press the privileges it came to consider immutable. Absolute freedom of the press has never been endorsed by a majority of the Supreme Court, but the federal courts usually have been sympathetic to the rights of the press. However, in the 1970s following Watergate, as the press started to dig and check with growing tenacity, a former ally in its battles with governmental power—the judiciary—began to render decisions the press found to be increasingly restricting. Many of these decisions—particularly those of the Supreme Court—convinced the press that its assumptions about its privileges were false. The press, the courts ruled, has no greater rights than any citizen of the land.

In its balancing of the public right to know against individual rights to privacy and the accused's rights to a fair trial, the courts denied the confidentiality of sources, the protection of unpublished material and the privacy of the editorial process. The courts gradually limited the press' access to information, and some newsgathering was specifically prohibited.

News Gathering

There are, of course, still wide areas of news gathering open to the press. Generally, the actions of official bodies are accessible to journalists. Judicial, legislative and executive activities can be freely covered—with some exceptions.

Worthwhile. "And always, long before falling asleep, I remember the wise words of an American judge who said—when he tried a newspaper for some disgusting slanders—'All the idiotic nonsense that all American newspapers write is a small, necessary and basically unimportant levy we pay for that immense, beautiful and vitally important gift that is the freedom of speech.'"
—*Václav Havel,
playwright
and president
of the Czech Republic*

Compliance. *The Hartford Courant* decided to abide by a judge's order to turn over nine negatives of unpublished photographs requested by a woman accused of a weapons charge. She wanted to show the court through the photos that she was not carrying a weapon when she entered a house. The newspaper went along with the order to avoid a court decision that might set a precedent, that would bind the media to turn over requested material in all future cases, the managing editor said.

A reporter has the right to cover a city council meeting, except for executive sessions. But the reporter has no legal right to sit in on a meeting of the board of the American Telephone & Telegraph Co., a private company.

Journalists have rights—along with all citizens—to vast areas of official activities. The Supreme Court has ruled *(Branzburg v. Hayes)* that the press has protection in some of its newsgathering activities. The Court stated that "without some protection for seeking out the news, freedom of the press would be eviscerated."

But the Court also ruled in *Branzburg* that a reporter cannot protect information a grand jury seeks, and that grand jury proceedings are closed to the press. When *The Fresno Bee* published material from a grand jury inquiry and its staff members refused to tell the court how they had obtained the information, they were sent to jail for contempt of court.

Executive sessions of public bodies may be closed to the press, but the reason for holding closed-door sessions must not be trivial. Usually, state laws define what constitutes an executive session. Reporters are free to dig up material discussed at these closed meetings.

Material of a confidential and personal nature held by such agencies as health and welfare departments is not available to the press. A reporter has no legal right to learn whether a certain high school student was treated for gonorrhea by a public health clinic. But the reporter is entitled to data on how many were treated last month or last year and at what cost, how many people the clinic has on its staff and so on. Nor are there prohibitions against a reporter interviewing a clinic user who is willing to talk about his or her treatment, just as a person who appears before a grand jury may tell reporters about the testimony he or she gave to the jury.

News Gathering Process Not Protected

The courts have allowed plaintiffs to examine how a story was obtained and written. When a copy editor at *The Washington Post* wrote a memo saying she found the thrust of an article "impossible to believe," the memo was admitted in the suit. The existence of e-mail records has complicated matters for the media as it has been difficult to remove e-mails from computers and servers, and these can be used in suits. This has given pause to some journalists who use the computer for e-mail interviews. The unedited, unused portions are available to plaintiffs.

Free Press—Fair Trial

Judges contend that some news can prejudice jurors and thus compromise a defendant's Sixth Amendment "right to an impartial jury," making a fair trial impossible. Criminal convictions have been set aside because of such publicity.

Judges do have ways to protect the defendant from damaging publicity that would compromise the defendant's right to a fair trial. In *Nebraska Press Association v. Stuart* (427 US 539), the Supreme Court discussed changing the location of the trial, adjourning the trial until pretrial publicity that may be prejudicial has dissipated, careful questioning of jurors during the voir dire (jury impaneling), sequestering the jury and other strategies.

Confidentiality Requires Protection

Many attacks on the press in the courts have concerned confidentiality. The courts have been determined to seek out the sources of information to assist law enforcement officers and defendants. The press has been equally determined to honor its promise of confidentiality to sources.

A Boston television reporter was sentenced to three months in jail for contempt of court for refusing to identify a source who told her he saw police officers loot a pharmacy. A grand jury was looking into the matter and a prosecutor told the judge his office was stymied without the testimony of the witness.

Journalists traditionally have honored the request for confidentiality, sometimes at a heavy price. In 17th-century England, a printer, John Twyn, refused to give the Star Chamber the name of the author of a pamphlet about justice that Twyn had published. The Chamber called the pamphlet treasonous, and when Twyn would not speak, it passed the following sentence:

> (You will be) . . . drawn upon an hurdle to the place of execution; and there you shall be hanged by the neck, and being alive, shall be cut down, and your privy members shall be cut off, your entrails shall be taken out of your body, the same to be burnt before your eyes; your head to be cut off, your body to be divided into four quarters, and your head and quarters to be disposed of at the pleasure of the King's Majesty.

Shield Laws

One effect of the attack on confidentiality was the enactment of state shield laws, in effect in most states. These laws provide varying degrees of confidentiality for sources and materials.

Reporters contend that their notes—which may include the names of confidential sources as well as the reporters' own investigative work—should be treated as confidential. State shield laws grant the reporter this protection unless in a criminal case the defense can prove that the notes are relevant and that alternative sources of information have been exhausted.

Shield laws are important. When the highest state court rules on matters covered by the state constitution, the issue cannot be reviewed by the U.S. Supreme Court because the state court is the final authority on the meaning of the state's constitutional guarantees. Some state constitutions have even broader protections than the U.S. Constitution.

The shield law is a helpful successor to the sunshine law, which requires public bodies to meet in public unless there is a compelling reason for privacy.

Newspapers and broadcast stations contend that confidentiality is essential to freedom of the press. The press points out that the power of the government to punish people involved in unpopular causes led the courts to safeguard anonymity in many areas. The courts recognize the doctor-patient and lawyer-client relationship as generally beyond legal inquiry. Journalists have sought the same protection for their sources.

If the press is to be the watchdog of government, as the press believes the framers of the Constitution intended, then the press must be free to discover what public officials are doing, not limited to publishing what officials say they are doing. In order to ferret out the activities of public officials, insiders and informants are necessary. These informants usually must be promised anonymity. The courts, however, have not been sympathetic to reporters who seek to honor confidentiality in the face of court demands for disclosure.

Keep the Promise Once a reporter promises confidentiality, he or she must honor that pledge, the Supreme Court ruled in *Cohen v. Cowles Media* in a 1991 decision. St. Paul and Minneapolis newspapers promised a source that damaging information he gave them about a candidate would not carry his name.

After the newspapers decided to use the source's name, he was fired from his job. The source sued, and the court ruled that First Amendment protections do not prevent a newspaper from being held liable for violating a promise of confidentiality. The state law on an implied contract was violated, the court ruled.

Tips and Tidbits

Here is some useful advice taken from court decisions, laws and the experience of journalists:

Interviewing Jurors Jurors are free to talk about their experiences once a trial ends. But contact with jurors while they are deliberating can lead to contempt-of-court charges.

The same general rule applies to those serving on grand juries. The laws affecting witnesses appearing before grand juries vary from state to state. Some allow witnesses to talk about their testimony, but others forbid it until the grand jury inquiry is over.

Taping The courts have ruled that it is illegal to use a tape recorder secretly while posing as someone else. This is invasion of privacy through *intrusion*.

Don R. Pember of the University of Washington, author of a mass media law textbook, advises his students to turn on the tape recorder and to ask permission. Then the consent is recorded. Generally, he says, be "up-front with recorders."

Wire Service Defense Newspapers that publish wire service stories with libelous material have been protected by the "wire service defense." This legal concept holds that if the newspaper was not aware of the defamatory material in the story, could not reasonably have been expected to detect such material and reprinted the material without substantial changes, then the publication will not be held liable, whether private or public figures are defamed by the article.

Altering Quotes   The U.S. Supreme Court has ruled that changing a quote does not necessarily constitute libel unless the change gives a different meaning than the source intended. The Court stated:

> If every alteration constituted the falsity required to prove actual malice, the practice of journalism, which the First Amendment standard is designed to protect, would require a radical change, one inconsistent with our precedents and First Amendment principles.

Illegal-Legal.   The Supreme Court ruled that the First Amendment protects journalists who use material that was improperly obtained and passed along to them. This covers such material as telephone conversations, corporate documents and government memos. The Court stated: "A stranger's illegal conduct does not suffice to remove the First Amendment shield from speech about a matter of public concern."

Press Disclosures Affect Freedoms

The press considers itself a critic not only of sacred cows, but also of sacred institutions. This disturbs those who want and need ideals and heroes, men and women to look up to, to be loyal to. Few individuals or institutions can stand up under the scrutiny to which the press subjects them.

The public reaction has been to resort to the ancient technique of blaming the messenger.

Tyrone Brown, a law clerk to Chief Justice Earl Warren in the 1960s, then general counsel for Post-Newsweek Broadcasting and later a member of the Federal Communications Commission, said the Court's rulings reflect attitudes toward the press.

"All those so-called absolute principles like the First Amendment are functions of the time when they're decided," Brown says. "The Justices' role is a process role—making accommodations between various power groups in the country at various times."

In several decisions affecting the press, some justices have suggested that the Times Doctrine be re-examined. They have asserted that subsequent rulings favorable to the press have permitted the press to abuse privacy and to be held exempt from responsibility for its coverage.

The courts have been more willing to close judicial proceedings and to gag those involved in civil and criminal trials. And countless officials are more reluctant to allow reporters access to public records and entrance to meetings.

"There is an attitude of too many public officials that the material they are caretakers for belongs to them and not to the public," said Paul K. McMasters, the deputy editorial director of *USA Today*.

Although every state and the District of Columbia have open records and open meetings laws, "many newspapers ranging in size from the smallest to the largest national dailies find themselves almost continually snarled in disputes over one of our most basic democratic rights: To find out what branches of the government and its agencies are doing," reported the American Society of Newspaper Editors.

Summing Up

- The police cannot arbitrarily deny a press pass to a reporter.
- Except for placing reasonable restrictions on access to events behind police lines, the police cannot interfere with a reporter engaged in newsgathering activities in public places.
- Reporters cannot be denied access to open meetings of legislative or executive bodies.
- The reporter can try to use state law to open certain hearings of public bodies that have been closed as "executive sessions." But there is no constitutional right to attend. Several states have adopted "sunshine laws" that require public agencies to have open meetings and open records.
- Reporters do not have a constitutional right to documents and reports not available to the general public. (The Supreme Court has equated the press' right to access with the right of access of the public.)
- Reporters cannot guarantee a source confidentiality, should be careful about what they print about the criminal past of defendants, may be required to surrender documents to a grand jury or testify before it, should be careful about assuring sources they are protected by a state shield law.

Further Reading

Chaffee, Zechariah Jr. *Free Speech in the United States.* Cambridge, Mass.: Harvard, 1948.

Denniston, Lyle. *The Reporter and the Law.* New York: Hastings House, 1980.

Hand, Learned. *Liberty.* Stamford, Conn.: Overbrook Press, 1941.

Lewis, Anthony. *Make No Law: The Sullivan Case and the First Amendment.* New York: Random House, 1992.

Oran, Daniel. *Law Dictionary for Non-Lawyers.* St. Paul, Minn.: West, 1975.

Pember, Don R. *Mass Media Law,* 11th ed. New York: McGraw Hill Companies, 1999.

Sanford, Bruce W. *Synopsis of the Law of Libel and the Right of Privacy.* New York: World Almanac Publications, 1984.

26 Taste—Defining the Appropriate

Susan Watts, *Daily News*

Pictures cause most complaints.

Preview

Material that is obscene, vulgar or profane can offend readers and listeners. But it also can be informative, and sometimes the reporter risks offending to move closer to the truth.

Decisions to use such material depend on:

• **Context:** If the event is significant and the material is essential to describing the event, offensive material may be used.
• **Nature of the audience:** A publication for adults or a special-interest group will contain material that a mass medium might not.
• **Prominence of those involved:** Public officials and public figures lead public lives. What would constitute prying into the life of a private individual may be necessary reporting of the activities of those in public life.

The *Daily News* in New York published the above photo the day after the terror bombers had struck the World Trade Center towers. It also printed what some have called the most horrific picture ever published in America—the photo of a severed hand found on a sidewalk near the towers. In response to complaints about the photos, Editor in Chief Ed Kosner said, "It's no time to be squeamish."

Readers of *The New York Times* and *The Washington Post* also complained about photos the newspapers published of people jumping from the towers. In Tucson, the *Arizona Daily Star* ran the same photo on its Web site and then removed it after protests. More than 60 people complained to *The Morning Call* in Allentown, Pa. Naomi Halperin, the newspaper's director of photography, conceded that the photo may have been too large for many readers' taste. "But one compelling reason to publish it kept coming forward: It was the truth. The most horrific part of this tragedy is the loss of life," she said.

Questions of taste have bedeviled the media for years—for a few centuries, for that matter. Listen to Benjamin Franklin respond to complaints he was hearing about the material he published when he was a colonial printer: "If all printers were determined not to print anything till they were sure it would offend nobody, there would be very little printed."

Actually, the standards that determine what is acceptable and what is offensive are constantly changing. They vary with time and with place, and they depend on the context in which the material is used.

Changing Guidelines

R. W. Apple recalls his editor at *The New York Times* telling him to stake out President Kennedy's hotel room during Kennedy's overnight stay in New York City. Apple said he watched "a well-known actress take the back elevator to his suite." Apple eagerly reported his find to the paper. "I was told to forget my 'scoop.' The *Times* was interested in visitors with affairs of state on their mind, not the other kind."

Today, the *Times* carries material like the following in a wedding story:

> It's hard to imagine a couple more excited about having a baby than Wendy Cohen and Craig Teper. They are expecting a girl in May and have already built a tiny, bright nursery for her in their one-bedroom apartment in Manhattan, and given her a name—Zoe. While some couples might be encouraged to downplay a pregnancy at their wedding, Ms. Cohen and Mr. Teper, who call Zoe "the icing on our cake of life," chose to do the opposite and built their celebration around her.

From Goldwater to Clinton   In 1981, when Sandra Day O'Connor was nominated to the Supreme Court, some conservative leaders questioned her conservative credentials. They thought she might be liberal on abortion and other social issues. Jerry Falwell, founder of the Moral Majority, told reporters that "every good Christian should be concerned" about the nomination.

To which Barry Goldwater, whose conservative credentials landed him the Republican Party's 1964 presidential nomination, replied, "Every good Christian should line up and kick Jerry Falwell's ass." A few newspapers printed Goldwater's remark. Most paraphrased it, and broadcast stations took a pass on the Arizona senator's remark.

But few media outlets avoided the explicit details that emerged in 1998 from the investigation of President Clinton's affair with Monica Lewinsky. There were references to oral sex and to Clinton's kissing Lewinsky's breasts. Newspapers printed explicit sexual details and four-letter words from the Starr report.

No one wants to offend readers or viewers. Nor—in the case of broadcast journalists—is there sense in offending the Federal Communications Commission, which has rules about obscenity, indecency and profanity. But how does a reporter or an editor decide when to risk giving offense in order to provide essential information? Just what is the "good taste" that journalists are supposed to exercise? Let's try to establish some guidelines.

Freud on Language
"Anyone who considers sex as something mortifying and humiliating to human nature is at liberty to make use of the more genteel expressions 'Eros' and 'erotic.' I might have done so myself from the first and spared myself much opposition. But I did not want to, for I like to avoid concessions to faintheartedness. One can never tell where that road may lead; one gives way first in words, and then little by little in substance too. I cannot see any merit in being ashamed of sex. . . ."
—Sigmund Freud, Group Psychology and the Analysis of the Ego (1921)

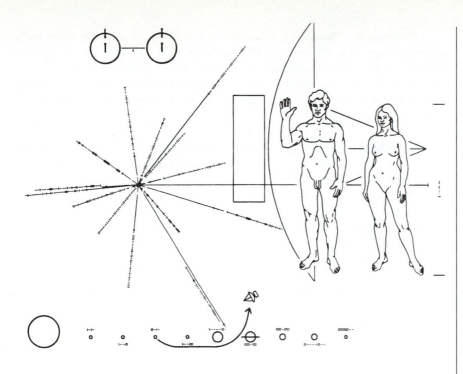

Taste Is Relative

Taste is usually defined as a set of value judgments in behavior, manners, or the arts held in common by a group or class of people. Generally, these values help keep society stable and insulate it from sudden and possibly destructive change. Those who advocate strict controls on pornography, for example, argue that such material stimulates anti-social behavior.

These values are not absolute. Several factors are involved in setting standards. First, to a history lesson that shows us that what was once deemed offensive is now yawned at. We go back 30 years to a space shoot.

Time

Two Cornell University astronomers had an idea for the Pioneer 10 spacecraft flight. For its journey beyond our solar system it would carry a drawing of a man and a woman as well as information about the planet Earth. Should the spacecraft then nuzzle down on some distant civilization the inhabitants could visualize what Earth man and woman look like.

The National Aeronautics and Space Administration accepted the suggestion, and when Pioneer 10 was launched, a gold-plated aluminum plaque engraved with a sketch of the Earth and its solar system and a drawing of a naked man and woman standing next to each other was aboard. NASA released the drawing to newspapers, thereupon confronting many editors with a dilemma. The picture was newsworthy, but would its publication be in bad taste?

Castrated   The *Chicago Sun-Times* published the drawing in an early edition after an artist had removed the man's testicles. In a later edition, the rest of the genitals were erased. *The Philadelphia Inquirer* did even more brushwork: The male had no genitals and the nipples had been removed from the woman's breasts. The *Los Angeles Times* ran the drawing untouched. "Filth," a reader wrote in protest.

Shocked   In 1939, people were scandalized when in the movie *Gone with the Wind,* Rhett Butler turned to Scarlett O'Hara and said, "Frankly, my dear, I don't give a damn." The word *rape* was taboo in many newspapers until the 1950s.

Today, movies, theater, books and magazines leave little to the imagination. For those with exotic tastes, a $7 billion a year pornography industry caters to every conceivable fantasy, with not much legal interference. In time, journalism dropped many of its taboos, too.

Let's track some of these changes. First, we'll look at language, to the use of words that have been taboo but with the years have become acceptable.

Offensive Words

The story that appeared in the April 18, 1966, issue of *The New York Times* about the Masters-Johnson study used words such as *vagina, vaginal lubrication, intravaginal diaphragms* and *orgasm.* As the story was being edited, a problem came up on the copy desk.

As the event is recounted by a *Times* copy editor, the desk noticed the frequent and explicit references to the female sex organ (six) and only euphemistic references (two) to the penis—"genital organ" and "the organ." The question was referred to an assistant managing editor who served as the arbiter of language and taste at the *Times.* He decreed *vagina* for the woman and *organ* for the man as proper.

Two years later, the *Times* was more forthcoming in its use of explicit language. Reporting the changes *The Washington Post* and *Chicago Tribune* had made in a review appearing in their Sunday book review supplement, "Book World," the *Times* reported that the newspapers had called back a press run of the supplement to delete a section that "consisted of a paragraph containing reference to the penis in a discussion of the sexual behavior of primates."

Here is the paragraph that so offended the sensibilities of decision makers at the *Post* and *Tribune* that they called back a million copies of the press run at a cost of $100,000:

> Many a cocktail party this winter will
> be kept in motion by this provocative chit
> chat; man is the sexiest primate alive; the
> human male and not the gorilla possesses
> the largest penis of all primates. . . .

The *Post* and *Tribune* were clinging to the concept of the newspaper as family reading, although *Life* and *Newsweek* had used the word in their stories about the book, *The Naked Ape* by Desmond Morris, and although it was commonplace among millions of nursery school children who had been instructed to call a penis a penis.

Integration Battles In 1960, during a school integration demonstration in New Orleans, the AP quoted some of the women who were shouting at the leader of the school sit-ins: "Jew bastard, nigger lover." In answer to many protests that the use of such words was in bad taste, the AP said it "judged them essential to establishing the temper and the mood of the demonstrators."

Gradually, pertinence or significance was becoming the guideline in determining whether an obscenity or profanity should be included in news accounts.

Watergate Tapes A major turning point was reached during Watergate when the tapes of the White House conversations revealed a profusion of vulgarities and profanities. As the West Coast journalism review *feed/back* put it, the "Nixon administration made inoperative the detente that existed in the daily press against words once excised by editors."

The words *shit* and *fuck,* used in the White House, appeared in such papers as *The Washington Post*, the *St. Paul Pioneer Press*, the *Atlanta Journal*, the *Kansas City Star* and *The Seattle Times.*

It would have been impossible, many editors felt, to have changed the emphatic language of a statement by President Nixon from the key tape of March 22, 1973:

> I don't give a shit what happens. I want you all to stonewall it, let them plead the
> Fifth Amendment, cover up or anything else if it'll save the plan. That's the whole point.

The AP made a survey of newspapers using the Watergate material and found nearly a third of them printed all or nearly all of the obscenities without alteration. Slightly more than half sanitized the word *shit* or other words, and 15 percent of the papers completely edited out the vulgarities and profanities by paraphrase or deletion.

One of the newspapers that did not use Nixon's language was the Huntington (W. Va.) *Herald-Dispatch* and *Advertiser,* whose executive editor said, "In this very Fundamentalist market, we came to the conclusion that there was no reason to offend unnecessarily."

Hypocrisy Turning away from some kinds of reality while daily parading humanity's most obscene acts—murder, torture, terrorism—seems an act of hypocrisy to some editors. Another kind of hypocrisy—the discrepancy between private and public morality—is revealed by an incident involving television station WGBH in Boston. The station decided to do a program a few days after the 1968 student demonstrations on the Harvard campus. It invited people from the community to have their say. One of those who showed up took the microphone at the beginning of the program and shouted, "What I have to say is fuck Harvard and fuck Pusey [Harvard's president] and fuck everybody." David Ives, the president of the public TV station recalled, "I was upstairs, and you have never seen so many telephone calls. The most interesting thing about them was the quality of what they said.

"One woman said, 'I just want you to know that no language like that has ever been permitted in this house.' And in the background you could hear a man saying, 'You know God damn well it has.' Another protest came from a man who called and said, 'I'm just not going to have any of that kind of shit in my living room.' "

Profanity-Obscenity   In a story about the decline of classroom decorum, *The Chronicle of Higher Education* quoted a student's *goddamned* but used hyphens for another student's *shit* and *fuck.* The senior editor for copy explains:

We try to keep all tasteless and offensive language out of the paper. However, we see the need for flexibility when specificity seems called for, as it did . . . we felt that there was no way around quoting at least a couple of examples of the offensive language of some students in the classroom.

So we made a series of judgment calls, which are certainly subjective decisions. "Shit" is a word we are simply unwilling to publish, and so it got the hyphens. So is "fuck," in a subsequent passage. By comparison, "goddamned" seemed like a milder imprecation, and so we spelled it out.

The editor cites *The New York Times Manual of Style and Usage,* which advises "obscenity and offensive vulgarity . . . should not appear in the paper . . . but profanity in its milder forms can on some occasions be justified." (In its new stylebook, the *Times* warns that use of profanity "will enrage some readers.")

Air It. "Therefore whatever you have said in the dark shall be heard in the light, and what you have whispered in private rooms shall be proclaimed from the housetops."
—*Luke 12:3*

AIDS   At first reluctant to use direct language and graphic descriptions, television, radio and newspapers finally faced the reality of AIDS reporting. They dropped the euphemism *safe sex* and spoke and wrote about *condoms*. They replaced vague allusions to *sexual practices* and used *anal* and *oral intercourse* in describing how the disease can be transmitted.

The New York Times, hardly an innovator among newspapers, ran a story in 1987 headlined, "Among Women, the Talk Is of Condoms." Here is an excerpt from the piece:

"I keep them with me," said Rebecca Pailes, a 25-year-old fashion designer. "I have them in my house. I won't have sex without them."

She uses a diaphragm also for birth control. "I use condoms," she said, "just to prevent disease."

"I don't trust anybody," said Judith, the 37-year-old owner of a small employment agency, who asked that her last name not be used. "I'm cynical about men. Nobody's worth the risk. Who knows who the people they've been with have been with? But I'm not going to give up sex."

Judith, who described herself as alternating between celibacy and promiscuity, keeps a drawerful of condoms in her kitchen.

"I give them to my friends who are celibate and say 'Here, now you can have sex,' " she said.

This was quite a change from the guarded coverage of the death from AIDS of the movie star Rock Hudson in 1985. Although many publications used the death to illustrate the danger of unsafe sex, only *Time* used the word *condom.*

Offensive Subjects

Disease and Disability   For reasons now difficult to understand, mentioning certain diseases and disabilities was considered poor taste in days past. It was considered improper to call attention to the fact that President Franklin D. Roosevelt used a wheelchair and that he could not stand unaided. No one wrote about his physical condition—the result of polio—and no one photographed FDR in ways that would reveal his disability.

When President Eisenhower had a heart attack in 1955, the press did follow that closely. But two years later when his wife underwent a hysterectomy reporters were satisfied with the explanation that she had undergone a "two-hour operation . . . similar to those many women undergo in middle age."

Gradually, good sense took over. When Betty Ford, wife of President Ford, underwent a mastectomy in 1977, the press reports were explicit.

But some frank language remained taboo longer.

> **STD.** The incidence of sexually transmitted diseases—chlamydia, gonorrhea and syphilis—is highest in Baltimore, Newark, St. Louis, New Orleans and Washington, D.C. STD, which is described as the pathway for infertility among women and AIDS among both sexes and children, receives little or no attention in the media, according to those in the health field.

Sexuality   The taboos against explicit reference to intercourse and other sexual activities were broken by news events that made it impossible to avoid the specifics. We've seen how the AIDS epidemic was one of these events. President Clinton's sexual liaisons were another. If journalism is the mirror held to life, then a journalism prohibited from chronicling important events in our lives offers a distorted image.

With the understanding that the media lagged in informing the public on such issues as sex education, venereal disease and how sex influences our behavior, journalists have come to report more fully the area of sex. Although cable TV, fiction, the movies and magazines flung off the fig leaf and discarded the asterisk and dash years ago, the networks and newspapers are slowly moving toward being more candid about sexuality.

The early breakthroughs came as the result of two studies of human sexual behavior. Alfred C. Kinsey's *Sexual Behavior in the Human Male,* was treated gingerly by the mass media when it was published in 1948. In 1966, another important work on sexual activity, *Human Sexual Response,* by Dr. William H. Masters and Virginia E. Johnson, was published. The result of a detailed 11-year study of sexual physiology, the work was too important to be ignored.

A related subject, homosexuality, was taboo for years until AIDS came on the scene and required frank discussion of one of its transmission routes. Given this opening and the increased activity of gay and lesbian groups, the opening was widened.

Gay Activities   Movies, even a TV sitcom, openly discussed single-sex relationships. Slowly, and despite complaints from some religious groups, newspapers are acknowledging gay and lesbian activities, public and personal. In 1993, *The Salina Journal* published the first gay or lesbian wedding announcement ever printed in a Kansas daily newspaper. The announcement was carried in a full-page story in the Lifestyles section under the headline "Out of the Closet."

The reaction: A handful wrote to support the newspaper. Most wrote that they were shocked and appalled, and 116 readers canceled subscriptions. But for the first time in anyone's recollection at the paper, the Sunday issue sold out.

The *Journal*'s editor, George Pyle, said, "Our editorial policy has always been in favor of equal rights. It would be kind of hypocritical to say that on the editorial page and then to say on the lifestyle pages that 'We're not going to include you.' "

In an editorial follow-up, Pyle recommended that Kansas legalize gay and lesbian marriages: "It's time for America to get out of this massive state of denial. They're queer. They're here. Get used to it."

Rape   Almost as incendiary in the area of taste is the subject of rape. Is it offensive to name the victim? Generally, newspapers do not print the names of women who allege that they have been raped, even when they testify at trials. Some reasons:

• The victim risks being blamed. Some people believe the victims want to be raped.
• Publication would stigmatize the woman.

When she was editor of *The Des Moines Register,* Geneva Overholser said that although her newspaper did not run the names of rape victims she favored their publication because it would help erase the stigma and focus attention on the crime which is one of "brutal violence" rather than a "crime of sex."

Rape, she said, is "an American shame. Our society needs to see that and to attend to it, not hide it or hush it up. As long as rape is deemed unspeakable—and is therefore not fully and honestly spoken of—the public outrage will be muted as well."

Personal Behavior   For years, reporters turned a blind eye to the personal misbehavior of candidates and officeholders. They ignored senators who careened toward their desks in the U.S. Senate after their morning's pick-me-ups. They took a pass on the congressmen who were sleeping with their secretaries. In 1987, matters changed when *The Miami Herald* staked out an apartment building to demonstrate Gary Hart's infidelities. A few days later, a *Washington Post* reporter asked Hart, who was considered a Democratic presidential candidate, "Have you ever committed adultery?"

As we see, our guidelines for the line between the acceptable and the unacceptable have changed with the passage of time. As events of considerable magnitude affected society, journalists had to describe them, and to do so fully they had to loosen the bindings that the arbiters of good taste had placed on language and subject matter.

But the changes are not, have not been, absolute. Taste varies with place and context, our next subject.

Place and Context

We know that communities differ. Some are more easy-going, cosmopolitan, more accepting of the different, the unique, the unusual. Language inoffensive in a newspaper or on a station in San Francisco would be tasteless to many residents of Salt Lake City.

Taste also is a function of the context in which the material is used. A story in *Rolling Stone* would contain language and references abhorrent to a reader of *The Christian Science Monitor*. Here is a sidebar to an article by Karen Rothmyer in the *Columbia Journalism Review*:

Meeting Mr. Scaife

Richard Scaife rarely speaks to the press. After several unsuccessful efforts to obtain an interview, this reporter decided to make one last attempt in Boston, where Scaife was scheduled to attend the annual meeting of the First Boston Corporation.

Scaife, a company director, did not show up while the meeting was in progress. Reached eventually by telephone as he dined with the other directors at the exclusive Union Club, he hung up the moment he heard the caller's name. A few minutes later he appeared at the top of the Club steps. At the bottom of the stairs, the following exchange occurred:

"Mr. Scaife, could you explain why you give so much money to the New Right?"

"You fucking Communist cunt, get out of here."

Well. The rest of the five-minute interview was conducted at a rapid trot down Park Street, during which Scaife tried to hail a taxi. Scaife volunteered two statements of opinion regarding his questioner's personal appearance—he said she was ugly

Taboo No Longer. *The New York Times*, facing a severe decline in advertising, decided to accept personal ads from readers seeking romance. Many publications had long accepted such ads before *The Times* acted in 2001. A company spokeswoman said, "Any language or phrasing that is suggestive or in questionable taste in the opinion of *The Times* will be declined."

Cleansed. But another journalism review found the language too strong. In its profile of Scaife, *Brill's Content* quoted the *Columbia Journalism Review's* reference to Rothmyer: ". . . he called her 'a f——ing Communist c——.' "

and that her teeth were "terrible"—and also the comment that she was engaged in "hatchet journalism." His questioner thanked Scaife for his time.

"Don't look behind you." Scaife offered by way of a goodbye.

Not quite sure what this remark meant, the reporter suggested that if someone were approaching it was probably her mother, whom she had arranged to meet nearby. "She's ugly, too," Scaife said, and strode off.

The *Review*'s editors wanted to show its readers the full dimension of Scaife's personality. Because most of the readers are journalists, the editors knew this brief exchange would enlighten rather than offend them.

Reactions

The steady lifting of taboos has not gone unnoticed by those in society who describe themselves as having traditional values. They are convinced that a liberal approach to matters of taste is really a corruption of our value system, and their organizations pepper broadcast stations and publications with complaints.

Ignored at first as the grousing of a small segment of the public, the protests found widening support in the 1990s. So much support, that politicians—whose sensitivities to public sentiment are finely tuned—made "values" a political issue. They could tell a mood change was in the air. Violence in films, mayhem on television, rap lyrics that glorified killing the police and described women as whores . . . many people were beginning to wonder whether the media were going too far.

The Religious Right has led some of these counterstruggles on the battleground of decorum and taste, sometimes with the weapon of censorship, and this has alerted organizations like the American Civil Liberties Union. The ACLU has defended the publication of pornography as a First Amendment issue.

Obscenity and the Law

On matters of obscenity, indecency and profanity, *Miller v. California* in 1973 (413 US 15) is the standard for determining whether a printed work is obscene. The Court set state rather than national standards. It asserted, "Diversity is not to be strangled by the absolutism of imposed uniformity."

The Four-Letter Word. In a case before the Supreme Court over a "particular four-letter word," Justice John Marshall Harlan wrote that although the word is "perhaps more distasteful than most others of its genre, it is nevertheless true that one man's vulgarity is another's lyric."

The test is whether the work, taken as a whole, (a) appeals to the prurient interest as decided by "an average person applying contemporary community standards," (b) depicts or describes in a patently offensive way sexual conduct specifically defined by the applicable state law, and (c) lacks to a reasonable person any serious literary, artistic, political or scientific value.

For the work to be ruled obscene, all three elements must be present.

Although the courts have ruled that obscenity is not constitutionally protected, they have been reluctant to rule against printed material, even the pornographic publications that are sold at newsstands.

Limits on Broadcasting

The Federal Communications Commission is empowered to enforce federal statutes and the decisions of the courts in the areas of obscenity, indecency and profanity. The FCC can fine a station or revoke its license if it finds that it violated section 1464 of the federal Criminal Code, which provides for penalties for uttering "any obscene, indecent or profane language by means of radio communication." ("Radio" includes television.)

But even broadcasters and the FCC have changed with the times. In 1960, NBC censored the use of the initials *W.C.* on a nightly televised network talk program. *W.C.* stands for *water closet,* which in Britain means *toilet.* A dozen years later, the Public Broadcasting Service showed an "education entertainment" called the "V.D. Blues." There were no protests about the initials, and there were surprisingly few objections to some of the language in such songs as "Don't Give a Dose to the One You Love Most" and "Even Dr. Pepper Won't Help You," which was about the futility of douching as a contraceptive practice.

Although some stations made cuts, and stations in Arkansas and Mississippi did not carry the program, the majority of public broadcast stations decided that the program was a public service. When "V.D. Blues" was followed by a 2½ hour hotline on a New York City station, 15,000 people called with questions about venereal disease. One of the city's V.D. clinics reported the next day that the number of persons seeking blood tests went up by a third.

The program obviously was aimed at teen-agers, whose venereal disease rate is epidemic. But stations must be aware of children in the audience, as the FCC and Congress have indicated.

The Case of the "Filthy Words"

In 1973, in a broadcast in the early afternoon over station WBAI (FM) in New York City, George Carlin gave a comedy monologue entitled "The Seven Words You Can't Say on Radio and Television." Carlin said his intent was to show that the language of ordinary people is not threatening or obscene. The station later said in its defense that the broadcast was in the tradition of satire. In the broadcasts Carlin had said:

> I was thinking one night about the words you couldn't say on the public airwaves . . . and it came down to seven but the list is open to amendment and in fact has been changed. . . . The original seven words were shit, piss, fuck, cunt, cocksucker, motherfucker and tits. . . .

He repeated the tabooed words several times in what he said later was a purposeful "verbal shock treatment."

There was one complaint, and the FCC investigated. In 1975, it issued a declaratory order finding that the words were "patently offensive by contemporary community standards for the broadcast medium and are accordingly 'indecent' when broadcast by radio or television. These words were broadcast at a time when children were undoubtedly in the audience."

FCC Rules. The FCC has stated that no words as such are indecent, but case studies show that the Commission has acted when there are *expletives,* as in the Carlin case, when *sexual innuendo* is clear and when sexual or excretory activities are described.

The station was not prosecuted. The finding, however, was made part of the station's file. In effect, the station was put on probation.

Limited Protection The station appealed to the federal courts, and many stations and civil rights advocates joined the appeal against what was seen as a threat to freedom of expression. The case—which became known as the "Filthy Words Case"—reached the United States Supreme Court, and in 1978 in *FCC v. Pacifica,* the Court ruled five to four that radio and television stations do not have the constitutional right to broadcast indecent words. It said that the government has the right to forbid such words because of the broadcast medium's "uniquely pervasive presence in the lives of all Americans." The Court stated that "of all forms of communication, it is broadcasting that has received the most limited First Amendment protection."

The Supreme Court emphasized the limits of its ruling:

> It is appropriate, in conclusion, to emphasize the narrowness of our ruling. . . . The Commission's (FCC) decision rested entirely on a nuisance rationale under which context is all important. . . . The time of day was emphasized by the Commission. . . .

Since the court ruling, the FCC and Congress have tried to find the fine line between First Amendment freedom for broadcasters and regulation of what it considers indecent material. In 1987 it established a "safe harbor," the six hours between midnight and 6 A.M. when children ostensibly would be asleep and stations could broadcast so-called indecent programming.

Two years later, Congress imposed a 'round-the-clock ban on such material, but a federal Court of Appeals found the law unconstitutionally broad. In 1992, as a warning to commercial broadcasters, the FCC fined shock-jock Howard Stern $600,000 for broadcasting indecent material. But that did not stop him, nor his imitators. At last count, Infinity Broadcasting, Stern's boss, had paid $1.7 million. Much of the material broadcast today that is not considered indecent would have shocked the FCC a few years ago. The boundaries of taste are elastic.

Political Pressure

Fines and other pressures on broadcasters do not arise spontaneously. Like much else involving the government, FCC actions are touched by politics. During the 1980s and into the 1990s, pressures from the American Family Association, the Religious Roundtable and other religious and so-called family-values organizations led Congress to confirm FCC nominees who took a hard line in enforcing the rules against indecency.

Toward the end of the decade, with a less strict agenda, the FCC issued far fewer fines. Milagros Rivera-Sanchez and Michelle Ballard of the University of Florida tell the story of FCC enforcement in the Spring 1998 issue of *Journalism and Mass Communication Quarterly.*

'Too Horrible'

Graphic photos arouse greater anger than printed or spoken words. These stark photos of a cyclist dying and a despondent Bosnian woman's suicide provoked heavy reader response critical of their use.

The cyclist, bleeding from the head and curled in a fetal position, had just hit a rock wall at 55 miles an hour.

The woman apparently hanged herself in fear of Serbian atrocities during the civil strife in the former Yugoslavia.

Top: AP photo
by Pascal Pavani

Bottom: AP photo
by Darko Bandic

Pictures

The front-page color photograph of the dying racing bicyclist infuriated many readers of *The Sacramento Bee* as did the equally graphic photo on page 1 in *The Press-Enterprise* of Riverside, Calif., of a woman who had hanged herself in Bosnia.

The *Bee*'s ombudsman, Art Nauman, said, "Only a few times in my 15-year tenure as an ombudsman have I had as an intense outpouring of negative reader comments as I had on this picture."

Readers, says the Reader Representative of *The Hartford Courant,* may be appalled at a news story, but they are shocked and outraged at a news photo."

The Defense

In response, editors are equally vehement. Managing Editor Mel Optowsky of *The Press-Enterprise,* responded: "The story that picture tells is a horror. What is going on in Bosnia is a horror. It is a holocaust, the destruction of a people's body, mind, spirit and their worldly goods.

"The picture tells the story of the holocaust in a way that tens of thousands of words cannot."

Optowsky said the staff had a long discussion about using the photo.

"We discussed, for instance, the failure of much of the American press 60 years ago to adequately describe another holocaust and the consequent failure of a good people, the American people, to do something about it."

The Flint (Mich.) *Journal* published a photo of a Somali mother mourning the death of her young son whose emaciated body is clearly visible in the photo. Readers complained and in an editorial, the newspaper responded:

Good. It should.

It should offend all of us.

We should be outraged and incensed—not that newspapers would publish such a graphic and tragic image, but that the world would allow such suffering, such violence to continue.

Yes, the picture was horrifying. It made people uncomfortable. That was the point in publishing it. It was to open people's eyes to the catastrophe that continues to unfold there.

Photo Guidelines

Claude Cookman, who worked as a picture editor for newspapers, says that these questions must be resolved:

1. What do the pictures really show?
2. What are the readers likely to add to or read into their interpretation of the photos' content?
3. What are the circumstances under which the photographs were obtained?
4. How compelling is the news situation out of which the photos arose?

Shocking. The cover of the Aug. 15, 1993, *New York Times Magazine* brought gasps from its 1.8 million readers—and shock, anger and applause. The cover was a full-page color photograph of a woman in a white dress displaying her scarred chest, the result of her mastectomy that removed a breast. It was used to illustrate an article about breast cancer, "You Can't Look Away Any More."

The photograph drew 500 letters, about two-thirds favorable. The woman in the photograph, the model Matuschka, who took the photo herself, said she has tried to use her own experience to make people confront the growing problem of breast cancer. She said the magazine editor accepted her photo "without a lot of hemming and hawing . . . it took a lot of guts."

5. How compelling or significant are the photos in terms of what they teach us about the human experience?

6. Do the positive reasons for publishing the photos outweigh the almost certain negative reaction they will elicit from a sizable portion of the readership?

Application

The photo of a family crying over the body of the drowned child below remains one of the most disputed photographs published. Many readers

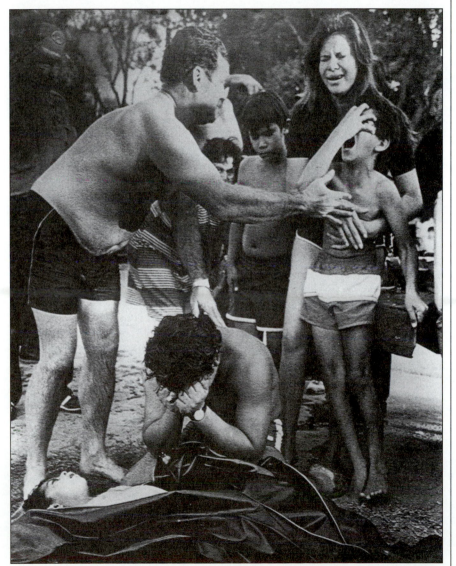

John Harte, *The Bakersfield Californian*

protested its use in *The Bakersfield Californian* as an invasion of the family's privacy. The managing editor apologized: "We make mistakes—and this clearly was a big one."

The photographer, John Harte, did not apologize for taking it or for his newspaper's using it:

> Our area is plagued by an unusually high number of drownings annually. During the week this photo was taken, there were four drownings, two that day, in our area's public waters. . . . We hoped that by running this one our readers would have gotten the message that we felt it was important they witness the horror that can result when water safety is taken lightly.

Harte was applying No. 6 in Cookman's list. Is this sufficient to defend the use of the photograph?

Christopher Meyers, a member of the philosophy department at the California State University at Bakersfield, wrote that the basic defense for use of the photograph was its journalistic merit: "It was timely; the 'story' was relevant to *Californian* readers; the photograph is both artistically compelling and emotionally gripping. . . ."

But he finds its use morally indefensible. It was an invasion of the family's privacy and it reduced the family to objects of our interest, denying them their status as "part of the human family." As for the argument the photographer presents, Meyers says that it would be impossible to determine that the photograph did indeed save any lives. This use of utilitarian ethics as a defense might "justify some use of the photo," he said, but not the way it was used.

There was in this case, he says, "too much emphasis on journalistic values and not enough on moral values."

Death

Nora Ephron, a media critic, says of pictures of death: "I recognize that printing pictures of corpses raises all sorts of problems about taste and titillation and sensationalism; the fact is, however, that people die. Death happens to be one of life's main events. And it is irresponsible—and more than that, inaccurate—for newspapers to fail to show it."

A sensitivity to personal feelings is essential to the journalist, not because invasions of privacy are illegal but because compassion is a compelling moral demand on the journalist. The photograph can be as callously intrusive as the television crew at the scene of a disaster poking camera and microphone in the faces of the bereaved. Yet death is part of reality, and it is possible to be overly sensitive to it.

Death has provided the press with almost as many problems as has sexual material. We cringe at confrontation with our mortality. Morticians try to make death resemble life. Wakes are no longer fashionable. Black for the bereaved is a past practice. Children are kept from funerals by solicitous relatives. Death is said to be our last taboo.

Young reporters sometimes go to the other extreme. Carried away by the drama of violence, they may chronicle the details of death—the conditions of bodies strewn alongside the airliner, the mutilated homicide victim, the precise plans of the youngster who committed suicide in the family's garage.

This enthusiasm is as tasteless as prurient sexual interest, for it uses the tabooed subject as the means to shock readers, to call attention to the reporting rather than to the subject. Death can be terrible and horrifying. But its terror and horror are best made known through understatement. In sensitive areas, the whisper speaks louder than the shout.

Summing Up

Standards of taste traditionally were set by the upper class and the elders of the community. This held on, more or less, until the Depression of the 1930s, World War II and the postwar social upheavals.

With the economic collapse of the Depression came a questioning of the old ways, an unwillingness to accept edicts from authorities and a willingness to experiment with new, daring and different ideas. The old ways had given the country malnourished children, had uprooted families and had forced poor but proud men and women to seek welfare.

Social Ferment   World War II thrust an isolationist nation into a maelstrom. Not only did the shrinking of the protective oceans force the country to change its geopolitical assumptions, the war caused massive social disruption: Millions of young men were uprooted, hundreds of thousands of women were enlisted in the work force, blacks migrated from the agrarian south to the industrialized Midwest and Northeast. Classes, sexes and races mixed and mingled.

At the same time, unspeakable atrocities occurred over Europe and Asia. The Nazi brutalities, at first disbelieved as too vile, too incomprehensible to be true, were verified. Murder of the children, the disabled and the different had become German state policy. A nation that had given the world Beethoven and Goethe had acquiesced in the state's policy of slaughter.

The pictures of stacks of dead, Edward R. Murrow's broadcast from Buchenwald, the testimony of the killers at their trials could not be overlooked.

Nor could the changes at home.

Old Balances Upset   The civil rights struggles of the 1950s and the liberation movements of the 1960s involved actions and language the old rules of taste would have deemed improper. But journalists knew that they had to be reported. The profanities and obscene acts that accompanied the country's crises were symbols of the collapse of the old order. The battles and the new balances—the young, for example, were exerting greater social and political power—had to be reported.

Although some of the more conservative members of the community considered the young to be the modern counterparts of the barbarians at the gates, the young unquestionably were causing significant changes in society. But to report the full dimensions of these activities—the language and slogans—the press would risk censure by the upholders of order in the community, the very people upon whom the newspaper depends for its survival. Radio and television station managers had less leeway. The FCC, they said, required them to conform to contemporary community standards.

But new technology widened the gap between those who tried to uphold the old rules and those who were offering words and pictures. Cable TV moved a wide variety of experiences, including explicit sexual material, into the home.

But taste is not a free-for-all for journalists. Those who work for the standard media need guidelines.

General Guidelines

First, some personal rules of the road. Although journalists are told that decisions on matters of taste are made by their editors, individual criteria are helpful.

Obviously, what and how a reporter sees are influenced by his or her attitudes and values. A censorious reporter may block out relevant material. A prurient reporter may overindulge his or her fantasies. An open attitude toward these issues is a corrective to the natural propensity to be guided, and consequently victimized, by impulse and sentiment.

By their nature, editors are conservative. Like libel lawyers, when they are in doubt they tend to throw out questionable material. Reporters learn early in their careers to fight for stories. The reporter who has a set of standards from which to argue his or her story past the desk will be better able to do a good job of presenting to readers and listeners the world of reality.

The self-appointed guardians of good taste no longer have the power to issue dicta. Now, it's the journalist who decides what is essential and what is offensive and unnecessary. Guidelines are essential for responsible use of this power. Here are some:

1. Is the questionable material essential to a story of significance? If so, there is compelling reason to use it.
2. Use depends on the nature of the publication's readers and the station's listeners. But care should be taken to see to it that all are considered, not just those who are most vociferous.
3. The tradition of the publication or station is a consideration.
4. The private as well as the public actions of public officials and public figures are the subject of journalism if they bear on matters of public concern.

27 The Morality of Journalism

Preview

Journalism ethics has developed in two directions:

1. News organizations have adopted codes of ethics and guidelines that:
- Prohibit journalists from accepting anything of value from sources.
- Limit activities that may pose conflicts of interest.
- Stress the journalist's responsibility to society and the obligation to be accurate, impartial and independent.

2. Reporters have adopted a personal code that stresses:
- Compassion for the poor, the disabled, the different.
- Moral indignation when the powerless are victimized.
- Willingness to place responsibility for the failures of policies on those who made them.
- Commitment to the improvement of their skills.

Joseph Pulitzer's Credo

Above knowledge, and above news, above intelligence, the heart and soul of a newspaper lie in its moral sense, in its courage, its integrity, its humanity, its sympathy for the oppressed, its independence, its devotion to the public welfare, its anxiety to render public service.

"I don't mean to seem unfriendly," the fragile old man said, "but I just don't want people to see any stories about me." He looked down for a moment and then back to his visitor, Kevin Krajick, a reporter for *Corrections* magazine. Krajick was on assignment to interview elderly prisoners, and during his stop at the Fishkill, N.Y., state penitentiary, he had been told about one of the oldest, Paul Geidel, 84 years old and in his 68th year behind bars for murder.

Geidel offered to make toast and tea for Krajick, and he accepted. Geidel had turned away many reporters before, but a guard had suggested Krajick try anyway, and he had led the young reporter to Geidel's 10×10 room in the prison infirmary.

With the gentleness of his age, Geidel said he understood that Krajick's job was "to get a story." He respected that calling, he said, but he really didn't want to talk about himself.

"I began slipping in questions about his past, his feelings about his life," Krajick recalled, "He answered several of them, but he said several times, he did not want 'any story.' "

The Dilemma

"He had tried to live in solitude and repentance, he said, and any notoriety upset him. He wanted to die in obscurity," Krajick said. A reporter had visited Geidel a few years before and had promised that no story would come out of their conversation, Geidel told Krajick.

"I thought they would leave me alone, but then one day I pick up the paper, and oh, there's my name and my picture splattered all over the front page."

Geidel, the son of an alcoholic saloon keeper, was put in an orphanage at seven. At 14, he quit school and worked at menial jobs. When he was 17, he broke into a hotel room in New York, stuffed a chloroformed gag in a guest's mouth, grabbed a few dollars and fled in a panic. The victim suffocated. Geidel was sentenced to life in prison for second-degree murder.

It was all in the newspaper, again, 60 years later.

"It was terrible, just terrible," Geidel said.

No Story . . .

"I had decided at that point that I would not put him through the pain of printing a story about him," Krajick said. "I told him that I would not. I figured there were plenty of interesting elderly prisoners who wouldn't mind being written about."

The two drank their tea, chatted about an hour and parted good friends.

"Then I learned that Mr. Geidel had served the longest prison term in U.S. history. I started to waver. I checked the files and found that several magazines and television stations had run stories on him when he refused parole at the age of 81. I then called the state corrections and parole authorities to find out how Geidel had been held for such an incredible term—a point that had not been made clear in the previous articles.

"It turned out that he had been classified as criminally insane on what turned out to be a pretty flimsy basis and then totally forgotten about. He had not stood up for himself during all those years and had no one on the outside to do it for him."

. . . or a Story of Significance?

"This obviously was a story of more significance than I had first thought. It was the most dramatic demonstration possible of the abuse of power under the boundless mental commitment statutes that most states have. What could be more moving than the story of the man who had spent the longest term ever, whom everyone acknowledged as meek and repentant and who, under other circumstances, would have been released before he reached the age of 40?

"The public clearly had reason to know about this man's life. It would be difficult to justify leaving him out since I was writing what was supposed to be a definitive article on elderly prisoners for the definitive publication on prisons."

Krajick faced a moral dilemma. Were the reasons for publishing his story sufficiently compelling to outweigh his promise to Geidel and the pain that the article would certainly inflict on the old man?

"I was anxious not to hurt a man who had, as prison records and he himself said, spent his life in mental anguish. I was sympathetic with his wish to remain obscure."

In his work, Krajick had faced situations in which people had been imprudently frank with him and had asked to be spared publicity. Those decisions had not been hard to make. He had reasoned that those who are hurt or embarrassed by the truth usually deserve to be. But Geidel deserved neither society's curiosity nor its condemnation. He had paid his debt to society.

Balancing Values

In the balance Krajick was striking—a balance of conflicting values—were two other factors: Articles had already been written about Geidel and he had become a statistic in the *Guinness Book of World Records,* which would soon draw other reporters whose articles, Krajick felt, would be more flamboyant and less accurate than his.

"On this basis, I decided to print the article, though not without misgivings," Krajick said. "I realized that if Mr. Geidel were to see the article he would be distressed, and he would feel betrayed by the young man who was nice to him but ended up lying. I only hope those around him have the sense not to show him the article. That would be the only escape for my conscience."

The piece appeared in the magazine under the title, "The Longest Term Ever Served: 'Forget Me.' " The concluding paragraph of the article reads:

> As his visitor left, he offered to write to Geidel. "Oh, no, please," he said. "Please. I don't mean to seem unfriendly. But please don't write. Forget me. Forget all about me." A distressed look crossed his face and he turned and hobbled down the hall to clean the teapot.

For a description of another ethical dilemma and its resolution by a photographer of domestic abuse see **Privacy Invasion or Public Service?** in *NRW Plus.*

Guiding Values

As we have just seen, journalists make choices about what they write. They and their editors are constantly making decisions about what to cover, what to include in the story and what to leave out. Selection is at the heart of journalism, and it is guided by values established by journalistic practice and the society at large.

These values are especially helpful to journalists when the choice is between alternative actions, each of which has some claim to principle. This is no different from the decision making most of us face almost daily. "We are doomed to choose," says the philosopher Isaiah Berlin, "and every choice may entail an irreparable loss. The world we encounter in ordinary experience is one in which we are faced with choices between ends equally ultimate and claims equally absolute, the realization of some of which must inevitably involve the sacrifice of others. . . . If, as I believe, the ends of men are many, and not all of them are in principle compatible with each other, then the possibility of conflict—and of tragedy—can never be wholly eliminated from human life, either personal or social. The necessity of choosing between absolute claims is then an inescapable characteristic of the human condition."

Journalists, then, must choose, just as we watched Kevin Krajick choose between keeping his word to an aged convict or exposing a system that had unjustly confined him for too many years. Was he wrong? Berlin would say, no, and he would add that yes, Krajick did harm the elderly prisoner.

Life as Referent

Can the journalist refer to some universal values as guides to choice, or is decision subject to particular circumstances—what the philosophers call a *situational ethic?* Traditionally—perhaps instinctively—people have sought absolutes as guides. And as often as the priest or the guru has supplied them, they have been found to be impractical. Or they have been discovered to be a way of keeping a religious, political, economic or social system in power.

Even so, we may find in these searches for an ethic to live by some suggestions for a useful journalistic morality. The concern for the good life, the properly led life, is almost as powerful as the need for sustenance. We may find some guides from religion and philosophy, from the Prophets and Plato, from the guru who traces his ethic to the Bhagavad-Gita and from contemporary philosophers.

"Life is the referent of value," says Allen Wheelis, a psychiatrist, who writes about ethics. "What enlarges and enriches life is good; what diminishes and endangers life is evil." If we start our search for an ethic by first defining life as physical survival and apply Wheelis' referent to one of the immediate problems of industrial societies, we see that what poisons the air, water and earth is bad. To preserve an atmosphere we can breathe is good. Industries that endanger the lives of their workers or nearby residents are bad. Safety procedures—or plant closures if this cannot be accomplished—are good.

But some factory owners and some automobile manufacturers have opposed strict environmental protection standards. To clean up a plant, to make a car that does not emit pollutants, to make a process safe in the factory would increase the price of the car or make operating the plant so expensive it might have to be shut down, owners have said. This means unemployment, a loss of taxes to the local community, a decline in business where the plant or factory is located. No wonder that workers and politicians often join industrialists to oppose proposals for safety, clean air and clean water.

A Journalist's Moral Framework

• **Loyalty to the facts.** "You inevitably develop an intense sense of revulsion or a mild attachment for one candidate or the other," said Joseph Alsop, Jr., a political writer. "But you have to be loyal to the facts or lose your reputation." John Dewey put it this way: "Devotion to fact, to truth, is a necessary moral demand."

• **An involvement in the affairs of men and women** that requires experiencing or witnessing directly the lives of human beings. Involvement generates compassion, accuracy and fairness, which are the foundations of an ethical journalism.

• **The ability to distance one's self from experience** to generate understanding. Antonio Gramsci, an Italian writer imprisoned by Mussolini for his commitment to freedom, said he had to learn the necessity of being "above the surroundings within which one lives, but without despising them or believing one's self superior to them."

• **A detached curiosity,** an exploratory attitude toward events and ideas. Detachment requires the journalist to be bound by evidence and reasonable deductions. Detachment is not indifference, which develops when, as Northrop Frye puts it, the person "ceases to think of himself as participating in the life of society. . . ."

• **A reverence for shared values, rules, codes, laws and arrangements** that give a sense of community. Such concern causes the journalist to keep careful watch for any action that can divide people by groups, classes or races.

• **Faith in experience** when intelligently used as a means of disclosing some truths.

• **An avoidance of a valueless objectivity.** This kind of objectivity can lead to what philosopher Stuart Hampshire describes as a "ice age of not caring." He writes that such an attitude can mean the end of civilization "not in a flurry of egotism and appetite leading to conflict . . . but in passivity and non-attachment, in a general spreading coldness. . . ."

• **A willingness "to hold belief in suspense,"** to doubt until evidence is obtained, to go where the evidence points instead of putting first a personally preferred conclusion; "to hold ideas in solution and use them as hypotheses instead of dogmas to be asserted: and (possibly the most distinctive of all) enjoyment of new fields for inquiry and of new problems." (John Dewey.)

• **An awareness of our limitations and responsibilities.** The story can never equal the whole truth. A concern for the consequences, the impact of what we write. A firm understanding of the line between fact and fiction.

• **Belief in the methods of journalism**—the conviction that this method will lead to some kind of truth worth sharing.

• **A moral vision of the future.** "If you don't have that vision," says the Indian writer Ved Mehta, "sooner or later the system will collapse." Without a moral vision, the journalist's compulsion may be power, profit and place in society.

• **An understanding that our words have consequences** and that we have some responsibility for the consequences.

• **To be active rather than reactive.** Walter Karp, a contributing editor of *Harper's Magazine,* writes: "The first fact of American journalism is its overwhelming dependence on sources, mostly official, usually powerful." The reporter who develops his or her own agenda for coverage is not source driven. This reporter goes into the community to help define the issues.

The Journalist. "A journalist, in any effort to render truth, has three responsibilities: to his reader, to his conscience and to his human subjects."
—*John Hersey,*
New Yorker *writer*

The reporter's obligation is to "serve the public—not the profession of journalism, not a particular newspaper, not the government, but the public. . . ."
—*Clifton Daniel, former managing editor of* The New York Times

Is it the responsibility of the journalist to continue to point out that the factory is poisoning the air? Or does the reporter turn away? If he or she does, jobs may be saved, the profits of the company assured and taxes kept low, surely good ends.

Timeless Dilemma   The dilemma is not new. The playwright Henrik Ibsen describes it in his play *An Enemy of the People.* Dr. Thomas Stockman, medical officer of the municipal baths, a considerable tourist attraction, discovers that the baths—the source of the town's economic resurgence—are being poisoned by the nearby tanneries. He wants to close them as a menace to public health.

But any revelation about the pollution will lead people to shun the baths, and this will cause economic problems, among them unemployment and higher tax rates for property owners. Dr. Stockman is reviled as an enemy of the people.

The practical concerns of a money-based society have occupied many writers. Dickens' novels cry out against the "cash-nexus" as the "only bond between man and man," as one literary critic put it.

"Breathe the polluted air," Dickens says in *Dombey and Son.* "And then, calling up some ghastly child, with stunted form and wicked face, hold forth on its unnatural sinfulness, and lament its being, so early, far away from Heaven—but think a little of its being conceived, and born, and bred, in Hell!"

No Choice   If "life is the referent of value," what other choice has the professional, whose reason for being is service to the public, than to see and to speak out so that others may see and understand? In the calculus of values, life means more than the bottom line on a ledger sheet. Joseph Conrad said, "My task which I am trying to achieve is, by the power of the written word, to make you hear, make you feel—it is, before all, to make you see. That—and no more, and it is everything."

Harold Fruchtbaum, a Columbia University social scientist, describes as "one of the intellectual's primary functions" the task of placing "responsibility for the failures of our society on the people and the institutions that control the society." Translated into a moral concern for the journalist, this is the task of holding power accountable, whether the power be held by a nation's president or a school superintendent.

Communal Life

In holding the powerful accountable to the people, the journalist takes to his or her job a sense of communal life. That is, the reporter has a set of values that reveal when power is being abused to the point that the quality of life in the community suffers. Philosophers through the ages have talked about the "good life," which has its starting point in a communal life whose underpinnings are freedom, tolerance and fairness. In such a society, individuals have basic rights that neither the state nor other individuals may violate, and the individual has, in turn, obligations to the community.

Worthwhile. In addressing the graduating class at Rice University, the novelist Kurt Vonnegut said most of the graduates "will find themselves building or strengthening their communities. Please love such a destiny, if it turns out to be yours, for communities are all that is substantial about what we create or defend or maintain in this world."

"All the rest is hoopla."

In writing about the American philosopher John Dewey, Sidney Hook said that Dewey believed

> . . . the logic of democracy requires the elimination of economic, ethnic, religious and educational injustices if the freedom of choice presupposed by the ethos of democracy is to be realized.
>
> One man, one vote is not enough—if one man can arbitrarily determine the livelihood of many others, determine where and under what conditions they can live, determine what they can read in the press or hear on the air.

Dewey believed that the community has the responsibility for eliminating hunger and poverty, that political power must be harnessed to solve the problems of group and individual welfare. Economic conditions must be such, he wrote, that the equal right of all to free choice and free action is achieved.

Communal life is an unfolding process in which the experienced past and the desired and anticipated future are considered in making the present. The journalist plays a key role in this process. Every day, the reporter describes the immediate and the past while showing the possible future in his or her work.

The Good Life as Guide

When moral philosophers speak of the good life they mean a life in which people can read, speak and choose freely; that they need not live in fear of want; that they can count on shared values such as the desirability of equal opportunity and the undesirability of crime.

Journalists enrich and promote these activities through the values that they take to the job. For example, a journalist is told that at the local university the political science department is promoting socialism, that instructors are doing more than describing the ideology; they are endorsing it. To check on the charge, the reporter disguises herself as a student and sits in on lectures. In her story, she describes her experiences, quoting class lectures and discussions, using the names of students and instructors. The charge is found to be groundless.

We do know that posing and using disguises are generally not acceptable in society. Let us strike a balance in deciding whether the use of a disguise by the reporter was ethical:

- **The benefits:** An irresponsible allegation was proved false. The reporter was able to do firsthand reporting, which is more persuasive and closer to truth than transcribing the instructors' denials.
- **The costs:** Deception was used as a journalistic method. Privacy was violated.

We can say that the costs of some of these actions—no matter how well intended—outweigh the benefits if we keep in mind that the good life is the healthy communal life. What kind of campus community will we have if we cannot speak freely and openly to one another in class because we fear our words may be broadcast or published? What kind of community will we have when we fear peering eyes so much that we must shred our garbage or fear our telephone conversation is being taped?

Actions that hurt people or disrupt the community are immoral, unless justified by powerful moral considerations, we all agree. A story about a convicted rapist will hurt the rapist; but we justify the story because punishment of those who commit crimes shows the community that society does not tolerate and will punish crimes. Crime unpunished can lead to the breakdown of the community.

Survival and the good communal life—are there additional guidelines, more specific guidelines that we can find that are of use to the journalist in helping him or her to make choices? Through an examination of a few of the practical problems reporters face, we may find some.

Some Case Studies

First Incident   Seymour Hersh, who won the Pulitzer Prize in 1970 for his disclosures about the My Lai massacre in Vietnam and more than a dozen other major journalism awards, told a gathering of journalists at the Nieman Foundation at Harvard that he found out "some pretty horrible stuff" about a former president. "There was a serious empirical basis for believing he was a wife beater, and had done so—at least hospitalized her a number of times. I had access to some records. Okay? I'm talking about trauma, and three different cases," Hersh said.

Second Incident   A prominent businessman died and in preparing the obituary it was learned that 30 years before when he was a county official he was sentenced to prison for embezzling funds from his office. Since then, he had led an exemplary life. Does the conviction go into the obituary?

Third Incident   Shortly after a rape charge was filed against a young member of the Kennedy family, a London newspaper and then a U.S. tabloid, NBC and *The New York Times* used the victim's name. Was it right to use her name?

Fourth Incident   The news shocked the people of Missoula. The 21-year-old daughter of a well-known couple had been stabbed to death outside her Washington, D.C., apartment house. She had been a high school honor student and an accomplished musician and had won a scholarship to Radcliffe.

Less than a week later, Rod Deckert, the managing editor of *The Missoulian,* a 32,500 circulation daily in the city, had an even more shocking story on his desk: The young woman had been a streetwalker in Washington, "a $50-a-trick prostitute" who "used to talk freely about her work and bragged about being 'a pro,'" according to a story *The Washington Post* planned to run the next day under the headline, "A Life of Promise That Took a Strange and Fatal Turn." The *Post* had learned she had returned to Missoula after dropping out of Radcliffe and one night in a bar she had been approached by a man who asked her to return with him to the East. He was a pimp who recruited young women around the country.

Deckert was confronted with a difficult decision. If he ran the story, the family would suffer new anguish. If he did not, he would be suppressing news that was bound to be known because papers distributed in Missoula and nearby might carry the dramatic story of a small-town girl who came to a sordid end in the East. It was, Deckert said, "the most painful day in my 11 years of life in the newsroom."

The Decisions

1. **Wife Beater**   No, Hersh said, he did not write the story. He decided not to because he said he could not "find any connection between what he did in his private life" with his public life as president.

But today, he continued, he would write the story, name the former president. "It's a different world now," he said. "If I didn't write it, the sources would tell it anyway." In other words, he said, the story could not be kept out of circulation.

2. **Obituary**   The newspaper did include the embezzlement conviction, and after readers complained the newspaper apologized in an editor's note.

3. **Rape**   NBC and the *Times* defended their breaking the practice of not naming rape victims by pointing out that her name was already in circulation. However, at the *Times,* dozens of staff members protested the decision.

4. **Murder**   Deckert reasoned that the young woman's experience could be a warning to other young women in the university community. However, he had to weigh this against the pain it would cause the family and friends.

Deckert decided to run an edited version of *The Washington Post* story with some locally gathered inserts. Deckert played the story on page 12 with no art under an eight-column headline.

Right or Wrong?

We cannot say with absolute certainty that the decisions made in each of these incidents was morally correct or incorrect. We can, however, examine them with some guidelines in mind and reach some reasonable conclusions.

1. Hersh was acting responsibly in not using the material if, as he said, he could see no connection between the president's behavior in his personal life and his behavior in his public office. Today, though, he says he would use it on the assumption that the story would get out anyway. What he is saying is that he would use it so that he would be the first with the revelation. Presumably, his sources leaked the information to him so that he would use it, and when he did not, they would give it to someone else. Somewhere along the line, the material would be used, Hersh reasoned.

A reporter's instincts are to score exclusives, not to be beaten by a competitor. This, of course, leads to a kind of journalism that short-circuits verification and emphasizes revelation. This kind of journalism is clearly immoral. But in this situation, Hersh had what he considers proof of the president's wife beating.

Nevertheless, making the decision on the basis of scoring a beat is questionable. There is, however, a deeper rationale for using such material, and it was made by the reporters who delved deeply into President Clinton's personal life to reveal his sexual escapades. Their contention was that the disclosures revealed the kind of person he is, and that his infidelities showed a duplicity that could affect his performance in office.

Journalists were, and remain, deeply divided over the relevance of personal behavior to public office. In Clinton's case, the extensive revelations made by the investigation in his impeachment made news of much of Clinton's personal life, and that material had to be reported.

Clearly, a person whose behavior in office is so erratic that he cannot perform his duties surrenders his or her right to privacy. But no one accused the president Hersh knew about or Clinton of being unable to perform their presidential duties because of personal misbehavior.

2. Disclosure of a minor crime committed 30 years before by a person who is dead seems to serve no end but the purpose—often sound enough—of full disclosure. If truth is served by presenting all the facts, then certainly we are on sound moral ground if we include this unsavory but factual detail in the obituary. But the journalist knows that he or she is forced to select for use from a limited stockpile of information the few facts that can be fitted into the restricted time and space allocations. In this selection process, the journalist applies to the material the tests of utility, relevance and significance within a value system.

Had the crime been well-known at the time of the man's death, the journalist could not ignore it. What the public knows the press cannot skip over without risking charges of covering up information.

3. The defense is based on an old journalistic maxim: If my competition has it, I will use it. In the rough-and-tumble of competition in the media market, the use of the name passes the reality test. But it doesn't pass the ethical test. Without having their permission, we generally avoid using the names of victims of sex crimes.

But suppose she were well-known, someone whose name is in the media often. Can we justify holding back and risking the accusation that we are protecting the person in order to curry favor? Reality again intrudes: People who live in the public eye pay a price for their fame.

4. The Missoula situation resembles Incident 3 in that the identification of the victim was known. There was no way the community would remain ignorant of the death of the young woman. Had the newspaper failed to run some story, accusations could have been made that the newspaper showed partiality to a middle-class family, whereas day after day it chronicles the troubles of others less affluent and influential. The newspaper could have handled the story with an editor's note admitting its dilemma, which might have alleviated the violent reaction to publication—the newspaper's editorial writer condemned the story and scores of people protested with calls and cancellations. (Krajick's dilemma might have been less intense had he considered an editor's note. Although readers usually need not be told the reporter's problems, situations such as these can be less troublesome with full disclosure.)

Suppose the Missoula newspaper alone had learned that the young woman died a prostitute. Should it have included the fact in its story? If her work had been an inextricable part of the crime, there would have been no way to avoid it. But she had been found dead near her apartment house, the victim of an unknown assailant. No newspaper dredges up every aspect of an individual's past, whether for an obituary or a straight news story.

However, as it turned out later, her work was part of her death, for the man charged with her murder was her pimp. The sordid affair would have to have been told when her murderer was arrested and charged.

Postscript: Eight months after the *Missoulian* published the story of the young woman's murder, a late model Chrysler New Yorker rolled into Missoula and the four occupants went to work. Two cruised bars, and two went to the high schools. Within hours, the police were informed by an alerted public. The four men were arrested and convicted of criminal trespass and soliciting for prostitution.

The Author's Problem The Missoula incident posed an ethical problem for me. In the first draft of this section, I used the young woman's name, following the instinctive reaction of a journalist to supply basic information. Surely, in a book that seeks to examine a subject in detail, the name would seem to be relevant. But is it? What does it add to the information necessary to understand the situation? Nothing. It would appear to be information for the sake of information, which has some merit. Balance this against the damage revelation could cause.

> **A Calling.** "At its best, journalism is a calling for people, just like it is for academics. People often sacrifice much larger incomes to pursue this vocation. Journalism is also imbued with this sense of autonomy and independence, along with a spirit of public responsibility. That is the sense of journalism I picked up while working on my father's paper."
> —*Lee C. Bollinger, president, University of Michigan*

This textbook is used in Montana and it could cause grief to the family. Still, there is a principle no journalist can turn from: What the public knows or will learn, the journalist cannot ignore. Surely, after the newspaper ran the story, most people in town knew the identity of the young woman. But the story is now several years old.

The argument can continue indefinitely. Unlike the philosopher, who may spin out syllogisms for a lifetime, the journalist must act quickly. The decision in this case was against disclosure. What would you have done?

Something New

The concern for the people involved in news events is fairly new to journalism. For many years, outsiders had urged on the media a sense of responsibility, a caution that the First Amendment was not a license for sensation mongering in pursuit of unconscionable money making.

As the criticism grew and as journalism aspired to status as a profession, journalists paused and examined their practices. A study showed that four of five newspapers accepted free travel. Gifts were seen to flow into the newsroom from those who sought special treatment. Some reporters had side jobs as publicists for the people they covered.

The situation cried out for change, and one route seemed the adoption of rules, codes of acceptable conduct. But these were slow to catch on. In 1974, one of ten newspapers had such a code. Within a decade, three of four had codes that called for accuracy, impartiality, the avoidance of conflicts of interest. They proscribed activities such as the acceptance of gifts from sources.

Journalists began to realize that without some kind of moral framework the practice of journalism could not lay claim to its privileged status under the First Amendment.

Codes of Conduct

These codes were modeled on general codes of ethics such as the one adopted in 1923 by Sigma Delta Chi, a journalism fraternity. The codes not only prohibited specific practices, they sought to establish ethical norms. They were a reaction to an outlook and to practices that had tainted journalism with a grubbiness inconsistent with the standards of professional conduct.

The renewed interest in establishing journalism as a profession found a base on which to build in the report of the Commission on Freedom of the Press. The study, issued in 1947, was a response to criticism of the U.S. press as insular, often sensational and sometimes irresponsible. The members of the Commission—most of them prestigious faculty members at leading universities—concluded that the press had not been "adequate to the needs of society."

(**The Code of Ethics of the Society of Professional Journalists** is in Appendix D in *NRW Plus.*)

One finding was particularly pertinent—that the press had failed to give "a representative picture of the constituent groups in the society." Vast segments of society had been ignored by the press, particularly the young and the aged, racial minorities, the poor and women.

Gradually, the press became more responsive to external criticism. Journalists themselves became outspoken about practices they considered compromising, and their criticisms began to appear in the various press reviews that sprang up around the country. Journalists began to take their trade more seriously— possibly because of the steady infusion of college-trained reporters who were questioning some of the assumptions of the craft. The climate was established for journalists to codify good practices, to set lines between the acceptable and the morally indefensible.

For an examination of some of the practices the codes discuss see **Sins of Commission** in *NRW Plus*.

Limitations of the Codes

Although the codes establish boundaries and describe acceptable practices, they are only a beginning. They cannot assist journalists in resolving some of their most difficult problems. These involve dilemmas in which the choice is between conflicting moral or ethical actions.

Krajick had to choose between what he saw as two positive ends. To print the story would reveal some truths about a system that crushed one prisoner and might still be affecting others. It would be morally right to use Geidel to illustrate the inadequacy of the mental competency process, he believed. Not writing about Geidel would also be a moral action because then Geidel would be spared the agony of the exposure. Surely, a man who has spent 68 years behind bars deserves our compassion. Moreover, there was Krajick's promise not to use the material. Can a public need justify the reporter's going back on his or her word?

Looking to codes for guidance, we find in one of them, that of the Society of Professional Journalists, that the journalist should "serve the general welfare." Krajick would serve the general welfare with publication. The same code stresses "respect for the dignity, privacy, rights and well-being of people encountered in the course of gathering and presenting the news." Clearly, respect for Geidel would mean heeding his plea not to write about him. The codes are no help here beyond identifying the clear moral choices.

No code can make a journalist a person of good conscience. Only a personal commitment to a journalistic morality can do so. Also, most codes emphasize prohibitions, actions not to take, practices not to undertake.

But the great failure of the press, as the Commission on Freedom of the Press stressed, is not its sins of commission, but rather its sins of omission, its failure to look into the significant actions of the powerful and the travails and the longings of the powerless.

Sins of Omission

No code led *The Charlotte Observer* to point out that North Carolina's leading income producer, its tobacco crop, is the single greatest cause of lung cancer, which is responsible, health authorities say, for 1,000 deaths a day. It was the conscience of the *Observer*'s management and editors that led the newspaper to examine the issue in detail in a special section.

". . . the duty of journalists is to serve the truth."

The Wall

"When journalism students arrive at my door to ask what they should know about being reporters, I give them the same spiel again and again. I'm sure some consider it a rant:

Being a reporter is a privilege. For that privilege, you have to give up some of your rights as a citizen. You're no longer a Democrat or a Republican, no longer a public proponent of any social issue, a protester in demonstrations, a signer of petitions, an advocate of good causes, a fundraiser for charities, or an advocate on behalf of any constituency. Whether objectivity is achievable in the absolute sense, a reporter has, above all else, to be fair. Prepare to be unpopular. Finally, get ready to be fired for the wrong reason or quit on principle.

—Carol Marin,
CBS News

Nor did any code stimulate the *Atlanta Journal-Constitution* to investigate racial discrimination practiced by lending institutions in Atlanta. Bill Dedman took on the task of proving that banks and other lenders were systematically denying loans to blacks. His reporting led to significant reforms. (Dedman won the Pulitzer Prize for investigative reporting.)

Sins of omission occur when the journalist refuses to act in situations in which revelation is required. The philosopher Jeremy Bentham described this immoral act as "Keeping at rest; that is, forebearing."

We will be looking at other examples of journalists who refused to forbear. Before we do that, first a fact of life about journalism and next some reassurance.

Money The fact of life is that journalism is a business. Most of the media operate to make a profit, and the trend clearly today is to maximize profit, sometimes at the expense of good journalism. One of the ways the media are working at keeping their profit margins acceptable to stockholders is by converging print, broadcasting and the Internet. For an explanation of the reasons for this trend, see **Convergence** in *NRW Plus*.

For a more reassuring insight into the currents that have grown into a strong stream of activist journalism, let's step back and survey what is known as public service journalism.

Morality Underlies Journalism

Morality is basic to the theory and practice of journalism. The press justifies its freedom in terms of moral imperatives; it rationalizes much of its behavior with moral declarations.

If public consent freely given is essential to the proper functioning of a democracy, then for the consent to be meaningful the public must be adequately informed by a press free of government or any other control. Thomas Jefferson expressed this simply: "Where the press is free and every man able to read, all is safe." The First Amendment makes this consensual system possible. Although neither the Constitution nor any laws require that the press carry out its essential role in the system, the press takes on the responsibility for setting before the public the issues it considers important so that they can be openly discussed. The cultural historian Christopher Lasch says, "The job of the press is to encourage debate."

See **The Democratic Commitment** in *NRW Plus*.

Recorders and Activists

Journalists differ in their interpretation of their role as suppliers of information. Some contend that it is sufficient for journalism to create a record, to report the deeds and declarations of those in power. Others go further. They would initiate coverage, make searching examinations of power, practice what some of them describe as an activist or watchdog journalism.

The first group believes that journalists are called upon to present matters that readers are interested in, and some of these editors conduct focus groups and have reader-advisory panels to inform them of their readers' concerns.

The second group prefers to lead from its own conception of community needs, its own insight into what constitutes community misdeeds that require attention and correction. These are activist journalists like David Willman of *The Washington Post* who took it upon himself to expose laxity in the Federal Drug Administration in allowing a drug to be sold that was killing people. Thomas Winship, former editor of *The Boston Globe,* was labeled an "activist editor" by colleagues, a label he bore proudly, he said. He learned about this kind of journalism when he was breaking in as a reporter at *The Washington Post*. The publisher, Philip L. Graham, "burned into my young, impressionistic head the idea that the license to print carried with it the obligation to give something back to the community," Winship says.

Activist and watchdog journalism go back to the work of the colonial printers in a tradition that has taken journalism to its most notable achievements in rendering public service.

This tradition embraces a skepticism (see **A College Education,** *NRW Plus*) and the practice of **Adversary Journalism,** *NRW Plus*.

Past and Present

During the American colonial period, journalists in the 13 colonies vigorously opposed what they termed "onerous taxes" and the lack of representation in decision making. These journalists became a major force in the struggle for independence. The colonial journalist had a point of view and expressed it.

Before the Civil War, an outspoken and active abolitionist press called for the emancipation of the slaves. And after the abolition of slavery, as Jim Crow laws and practices became commonplace in some parts of the country, journalists spoke out. Ida B. Wells, for example, exposed lynch law and mob rule at great personal risk.

As people moved to the cities and the country grew from an agrarian economy to become an industrial behemoth, exploitation and abuses proliferated. Industrialists—some described as "robber barons" because of their ruthless practices—took control of major industries. Workers were exploited and prevented from forming unions, sometimes at the point of a gun. Crooked politicians ran many large cities. In response, a group of journalists began to tell the story as the 20th century opened.

The Muckrakers

As the century began, four-fifths of the people in the United States were living in poverty. People were commodities. The mines and mills exploited child labor. Blacks were treated as chattel.

At first derisively described as *muckrakers,* this group of brilliant men and women took on the robber barons, the labor exploiters and the political hacks. They became known as the nation's voices of conscience. Some wrote books and others magazine articles, several took photographs and some worked for the daily press.

Racism

Ray Stannard Baker in 1908 described racism in Southern courts.

> One thing impressed me especially, not only in this court but in all others I have visited: a Negro brought in for drunkenness, for example, was punished much more severely than a white man arrested for the same offense. . . . The white man sometimes escaped with a reprimand, he was sometimes fined three dollars and costs, but the Negro, especially if he had no white man to intercede for him, was usually punished with a ten or fifteen dollar fine, which often meant he had to go to the chain-gang.

Chain Gangs   Baker points out that one reason for the large number of arrests is the profit to the counties and state in hiring out convicts to private contractors. "Last year the net profit to Georgia from chain-gangs, to which the commission refers with pride, reached the great sum of $354,853.55. . . . The natural tendency is to convict as many men as possible—it furnishes steady, cheap labour to the contractors and profit to the state. . . ."

These journalists did not condemn some vague system. They named names and held individuals responsible for their actions. Baker wrote that "some of the large fortunes in Atlanta have come chiefly from the labour of chain-gangs of convicts leased from the state." He described a banker who was also a member of the city police board and the owner of brickyards where many convicts were used on lease from the state at cheap rates.

Like the other muckrakers, Baker was adept at using files and records:

> From the records I find that in 1906, one boy 6-years-old, seven of 7 years, 33 of 8 years, 69 of 9 years, 107 of 10 years, 142 of 11 years, and 219 of 12 years were arrested and brought into court, 578 boys and girls, mostly Negroes, under 12 years of age.

Pulitzer's Journalism

One of the major practitioners of muckraking journalism was Joseph Pulitzer, the owner of the *St. Louis Post-Dispatch* and the New York *World.* Pulitzer's editors conducted crusades, newspaper campaigns to expose and remedy practices they considered wrong, unfair, unjust. They took their cue from Pulitzer's edict that the newspapers should never be content with "merely printing the news."

Instead, he said, his newspapers should be concerned "with the things that ought to happen tomorrow, or the next month, or the next year," and that they "will seek to make what ought to be come to pass." The "highest mission of the press," he said, "is to render public service."

His legacy continued under editors who were committed to using the press as an instrument of justice, reform and change. One Pulitzer reporter, Paul Y. Anderson, doggedly followed a paper trail that led to the exposure of the collusion of two of President Harding's cabinet members with oil interests that corruptly leased federal oil field reserves.

Making Journalism of Injustice

Pulitzer's edict to his editors to seek out issues, to make news of injustice and wrongdoing could be described as an instruction to journalists to establish agendas for their communities. This is an approach to journalism that has no borders.

Deformed Children   Harold Evans, editor of London's *Sunday Times,* said the "real power" of the press consists of its ability "to create an agenda for society."

Fair play was on Evans' mind when he heard that the manufacturers of the drug thalidomide had pressured parents of children deformed by the drug to accept a pittance in damages. Through its coverage of the issue, Evans said, the *Times* forced the crippled children "into the conscience of the country." The stories led to settlements 50 times greater than the original stipend.

Terror in Argentina   When Argentina was in the grip of a murderous dictatorship in the 1970s and 1980s, few protested the arrests, torture and killing of schoolchildren, pregnant women, college students . . . anyone who spoke out against the tyranny. People were snatched from their homes, grabbed on the streets. Tortured, never given a trial, many were drugged, their stomachs slit and then were tossed out of navy planes over the ocean.

Some risked death to speak out despite what an army chief of state later described as an atmosphere of guilt by "commission or omission, by our presence or our absence, by recommending or passively allowing it to happen."

Robert Cox, an American who was editor of the English-language *Buenos Aires Herald,* published lists of the missing on the front page. Death threats flooded his office. He was arrested, taken to a cell past a huge Nazi flag on the wall, briefly imprisoned and then forced to leave the country.

The journalist Rodolfo Walsh could not remain silent. He wrote a public indictment of "the most savage reign of terror Argentina has ever known"; that its rulers had created "virtual concentration camps in all the principal military bases"; that the torturers felt a "need to utterly destroy their victims, depriving them of all human dignity. . . ."

Walsh knew he was signing his own death warrant through his reporting. He closed his indictment by saying that he had to speak out to be "faithful to the commitment I made a long time ago to be a witness in difficult times." The day after his statement was released, he was abducted. His body has never been found.

> **Democracy's Base.** "Representative democracy is inconceivable without forms of mass communication—to create awareness of public issues that face a society whose members are not personally in touch with each other, who lack common geographic reference points, and whose central institutions are remote from the people they serve or exploit."
>
> —*Leo Bogart*

Two Courageous Women

In the United States, racial justice has been a pursuit of activist journalists. Courageous editors and publishers have bucked community traditions—and advertisers—to expose racism.

In Florida "Perhaps I'd have had the time to enjoy my growing daughter, my home and community life if I had concentrated on the till, and not worried about the word 'justice.' I am certain, now, that my concern over justice interfered with the cash register.

"I was advised time and again by wiser heads than mine to watch out for the pitfalls of 'taking a stand'—that to mount a high platform of principle was taking a downward plunge economically. I refused to listen, and so I am badly bruised by all the plunges I have taken.

"But I could not have done it any any other way."

This is Mabel Norris Reese looking back on her turbulent years as publisher of the Mount Dora, Fla., *Topic*.

When the county sheriff shot and killed one Negro prisoner and wounded another while returning them from the state prison for retrial, Reese said she "opened both barrels."

Costly Coverage "I covered the inquest in which the sheriff contended that the Negroes had tried to escape, and I used all the language at my command to describe the wounded Negro and relate his account of the shooting."

The result: "Our printing plant began to suffer from lost revenue."

When the Supreme Court ordered the desegregation of public schools, Reese defended the ruling. "I pleaded for tolerance, for cool heads to guide the transition."

The result: "There was an explosion of fire in my yard soon after this— flames licked at a great, gasoline soaked wooden cross that had been planted there. Two nights later, the *Topic*'s office windows were smeared with big red crosses and beneath them were the initials 'KKK'."

Next, the sheriff ordered five children out of the public school because, he said, they looked like Negroes. Reese condemned the sheriff. Advertising declined, and the business community financed the installation in town of a competing newspaper. More seriously, an attempt was made to burn down the home of the children and bombs were tossed into Reese's yard.

Communal Silence By 1960, a new sheriff was in office. But things had not changed. "Here the sheriff is regarded as the one man who can 'protect' the white people from integration. And he's considered the one man who can keep the labor unions from doing anything about the low wages in the citrus industry. So he is backed blindly by the powers that be." The churches, she said, "were silent," and "the average merchant feels it is a matter of life and death to mind his own business. His mind works to the tune of the cash register, not to the beat of his heart."

Truth Telling

Speak truth to power.

— *Milan Kundera*

Let us say that truth is meant to imply a devotion to the human being. . . . It is not to be confused with a devotion to a Cause; and Causes, as we know, are notoriously bloodthirsty.

— *James Baldwin*

My obligation is not to solve problems but simply to present them correctly.

— *Anton Chekhov*

The true artist must shun power, because power systems are not instruments of truth.

— *Robert Brustein*

Truth is a scarce and slippery commodity. There are not two sides to every problem but maybe ten, held with genuine conviction by serious people who probably know more about the facts than does the reporter.

— *James Reston*

Every time I paint a portrait I lose a friend.

— *John Singer Sargent*

The hottest places in Hell are reserved for those who, in a time of great moral crisis, maintain their neutrality.

— *Dante*

The smallest atom of truth represents someone's bitter toil and agony; for every ponderable chunk of it there is a brave truth-seeker's grave upon some lonely ash dump. . . .

— *H.L. Mencken*

Despite the attacks and the coolness of the business class, Reese's paper survived. Not so lucky was another courageous woman editor.

In Mississippi   Hazel Brannon Smith, the editor of two weekly newspapers in the Mississippi Delta country, would not forbear. She refused to be silent in the face of injustice. In 1946, she was found guilty of contempt of court for interviewing the widow of a black man who was whipped to death.

In an editorial she wrote in 1954, she accused the sheriff who had shot a young black man in the back of "violating every concept of justice, decency and right." The sheriff sued for libel and was awarded $10,000. The state supreme court overturned the ruling.

That year, Smith was invited to join "something called a 'Citizens' Council," she said, by "a local prominent man." The idea was to maintain segregation in the schools. Legal, nonviolent tactics would be used, she was told. "If a Nigra won't go along with our thinking on what's best for the community as a whole," Smith said the man told her, "he'll simply have his credit cut off." The idea was to use fear, he told her. Smith refused to go along. Her refusal cost her dearly.

Scripps Howard Awards

Abuse, Neglect

Alison Young went through stacks of nursing home inspection reports and found needless suffering, poor care, bad hygiene, physical abuse, affronts to human dignity. Her five-part series for the *Detroit Free Press* was based on public records. "I got into this business to give voice to the voiceless and to effect change," she says.

Communal Silence   She said the community became a battleground with intimidation the weapon, not only against blacks but against those who opposed the Council. "It finally got to the point where bank presidents and leading physicians were afraid to speak their honest opinions because of the monster among us," she said. "The idea was that 'we' would present a solid, united stand.

"I dissented by presuming to say that the truth had to be printed."

She was one of the few who dissented, and the pressure grew.

"My newspapers were boycotted, bombed and burned, a new newspaper was organized in Lexington to put me out of business, my life was threatened, and my husband lost his job as county hospital administrator—all because of pressure brought by this professional hate-peddling organization," she said.

She and her husband managed to keep going, but the income was never enough and she had to mortgage her home to pay her bills. Finally, in 1985, she gave up. The bank took her home. Soon thereafter she died, penniless.

For more about journalists who stood up to protest racial injustice, see **Standing Strong . . . and Alone** *NRW Plus.*

Next, let's look at some examples of activist journalism, which is another way of describing public service journalism. This kind of journalism has long been considered the moral justification for journalism's privileges, which range from the First Amendment in the Bill of Rights to the most recent court decisions granting journalism rights no other enterprise can claim.

Activist Journalism

• *The Los Angeles Times:* Reporter T. Christian Miller's computer-assisted analysis of records revealed that Los Angeles county officials repeatedly manipulated a growth plan for one of the region's precious natural resources, the Santa Monica Mountains. The manipulation favored developers and in one case officials approved construction of 204 homes on space earmarked for 37.

• *The Courier-Journal:* A yearlong investigation found that coal mine operators routinely ignored safety rules and faked air-quality tests.

• **ABC News' 20/20:** "Made in America" showed oppressed Chinese workers housed in crowded, rat-infested barracks were making clothing in U.S. territory Saipan for Ralph Lauren, Gap and other firms.

• **Pacific Radio:** Revealed the complicity of Chevron in the death of two Nigerian environmental activists.

• *The Philadelphia Inquirer:* Showed that city police dogs had attacked 350 innocent people.

• *The Albuquerque Tribune:* Showed that drunk drivers are allowed to keep driving despite many convictions. Uncovered extensive dumping of dangerous wastes in New Mexico.

• *The Ledger,* **Lakeland, Fla.:** Revealed that a fungicide caused crop and nursery damage and that the manufacturer, DuPont Co., knew that the fungicide had the potential to cause harm but was silent.

- *Star Tribune,* **Minneapolis:** Revealed that the state's foster care system allowed known criminals and sex offenders to become foster parents.
- *The Muskegon* **(Mich.)** *Chronicle:* Showed that the founder of a chemical plant made huge profits while knowingly exposing his workers to a cancer-causing chemical.
- *Fort Worth Star-Telegram:* Reported that 250 U.S. servicemen had lost their lives as a result of a design problem in helicopters.

An activist journalism calls on the community to act: To see that city officials rid the local water supply of carcinogens (*The Washington* (N.C.) *Daily News*); to make the government regulate the American blood industry (*The Philadelphia Inquirer*); to force the Federal Aviation Administration to do a better job of the medical screening of airline pilots (*The Pittsburgh Press*); to require the county child-welfare agency to protect neglected and abused children (*The Blade*).

Results This activist journalism does achieve results. After the *Winston-Salem Journal* series that showed that the county's high infant mortality rate had not changed in 10 years although the state's rate steadily declined during the decade, the county hired an infant-mortality coordinator and community leaders pledged to undertake a forceful program.

Sam Roe of *The Blade* in Toledo, Ohio, went beyond "merely printing the news" to expose problems with tragic consequences in a county children's service. See "**Abused by the System**" *NRW Plus.*

A Personal Guide

Some of the practices that have made journalism a powerful force in communities have changed through the years. One is the taboo against reading copy back to a source before publishing or airing it. No longer. For a rationale for the change, see **Checking Back** in *NRW Plus.*

Still, some practices and guidelines have persisted. Young journalists might consider these as guidelines for the practice of their journalism. From a variety of sources—from the Greek philosophers to today's police and White House reporters—the following emerge as suggestions for your consideration:

- A belief in and a commitment to a political culture in which the cornerstone is restraint in the use of power.
- Moderation in life and behavior.
- A secular, scientific attitude toward the work at hand. Knowledge is allowed to speak for itself. The professional does not believe on the basis of hope but of evidence.
- An openmindedness that seeks out and tries to comprehend various points of view, including those in conflict with those the reporter holds.

• Responsibility to one's abilities and talent. To leave them fallow, to fail to labor to develop them through indolence or want of seriousness of purpose demeans the self and punishes the society whose betterment depends on new ideas vigorously pursued. For Homer, the good was the fulfillment of function. For Aristotle, the good was living up to one's potential, and for Kant the development of one's talents was a duty, and adherence to "duties" constituted the moral life. The reporter who fails to report and write to his or her potential is immoral.

• An understanding of and a tolerance for the ambiguities involved in most important issues and the ability to act despite these uncertainties and doubts. The willingness to take responsibility for these actions.

• The willingness to admit errors.

• A capacity to endure solitude and criticism, the price of independence.

• A reluctance to create heroes and villains to the rhythm of the deadline.

• A knowledge of the pathfinders in fields of knowledge, including journalism.

• A commitment to work.

• A sense of the past. W. H. Auden said, "Let us remember that though great artists of the past could not change the course of history, it is only through their work that we are able to break bread with the dead, and without communion with the dead, a fully human life is impossible."

• Resistance to praise. Humility. "You have to fight against the praise of people who like you," says I. F. Stone, the crusading journalist. "Because you know darn well it wasn't good enough." He tells the story of the great conductor Arturo Toscanini who was engulfed by admirers after a concert. "Maestro, you were wonderful," one said. Toscanini knew the oboe had not come in at the right point and that the violins were off. And Toscanini burst into tears because he knew it had not been good enough.

• Duty. John Dewey said, "If a man is burdened with an idea, he not only desires to express it; he ought to express it. He owes it to his conscience and the common good. The indispensable function of expressing ideas is one of obligation—to the community and also to something beyond the community, let us say to truth."

• Avoidance of the desire to please. Self-censorship is a greater enemy than outside censorship. Pleasing an editor, the publisher or the source is commonplace. Setting one's values to the "pragmatic level of the newsroom group," as Warren Breed puts it, can lead to timid, status-quo journalism.

• A wariness about making words an end in themselves. André Maurois, the French writer and political activist, writes:

Power, Glory and Money are only secondary objects for the writer. No man can be a great writer without having a great philosophy, though it may often be unexpressed. A great writer has respect for *values*. His essential function is to raise life to the dignity of thought, and he does this by giving it a shape. If he refuses to perform this function he can be a clever juggler and play tricks with words such as his fellow writers may admire, but his books will be of little interest to anybody else. If, on the contrary, he fulfills it, he will be happy in his writing. Borne aloft by the world as reflected in himself, and producing a sound echo in his times, he helps to shape it by showing to men an image of themselves which is at once true and disciplined.

Summing Up

Reporters should seek to give voice to all groups in society, not to report solely those who hold power.

The public's need to know is an immanent value.

In determining what shall be reported and what shall be included in a news story, the reporter should consider the relevance of the material to the real needs of the audience.

If the reporter cannot disclose in the story the tactics and techniques used to gather information for the story, such tactics should not be used.

The reporter should:

- Be wary of treating people as a means.
- Believe on the basis of facts, not hope.
- Be committed to a value system but be free from ideologies and commitments that limit thought.
- Be wary of promising to help a source in return for material.

In balancing moral alternatives, the choice can be made on the basis of:

- The importance of the possible actions to life. (Life is the referent of value.)
- The public interest as against the private interest.
- The extent of knowledge of the event. If it is public knowledge or is likely to become so and the material is significant and relevant, the information should be used.
- Serving the needs of society. If the material assists people in participating justly, equally and freely in a meaningful community life, then it should be used.

Further Reading

The Adversary Press. St. Petersburg, Fla.: The Poynter Institute for Media Studies, 1983. (A discussion of ethics by 19 editors, publishers and scholars at an Institute seminar.)

Bagdikian, Ben H. *The Effete Conspiracy and Other Crimes by the Press*. New York: Harper & Row, 1972.

Benjamin, Burton. *Fair Play*. New York: Harper & Row, 1988.

Black, Max, ed. *The Morality of Scholarship*. Ithaca, N.Y.: Cornell University Press, 1967.

Commission on Freedom of the Press. *A Free and Responsible Press*. Chicago: University of Chicago Press, 1947.

Downie, Leonard Jr., and Robert G. Kaiser. *The News About the News: American Journalism in Peril.* New York: Alfred A. Knopf, 2002.

Fallows, James. *Breaking the News: How the Media Undermine American Democracy.* New York: Pantheon Books, 1996.

Gerald, J. Edward. *The Social Responsibility of the Press.* Minneapolis: University of Minnesota Press, 1963.

Hulteng, John. *Playing It Straight.* Chester, Conn.: The Globe Pequot Press, 1981.

Ibsen, Henrik. *An Enemy of the People.* 1882. (Available in many anthologies and collections.)

Kovach, Bill, and Tom Rosenstiel. *Warp Speed: America in the Age of Mixed Media.* New York: The Century Foundation Press, 1999.

McChesney, Robert. *Rich Media, Poor Democracy: Communication Politics in Dubious Times.* Champaign, Ill., 1999.

McCulloch, Frank, ed. *Drawing the Line.* St. Petersburg, Fla.: The Poynter Institute for Media Studies, 1984.

Pierce, Robert N. *A Sacred Trust. Nelson Poynter and the St. Petersburg Times.* Gainesville, Fla.: University Press of Florida, 1994.

Reston, James. *The Artillery of the Press.* New York: Harper & Row, 1960.

Smith, Z. N., and Pamela Zekman. *The Mirage.* New York: Random House, 1979.

Swados, Harvey. *Years of Conscience: The Muckrakers.* New York:, World Publishing, 1962.

Waldron, Ann. *Hodding Carter: The Reconstruction of a Racist.* Chapel Hill, N.C.: Algonquin Books of Chapel Hill, 1993.

In their book *The Elements of Journalism,* Kovach and Rosenstiel list principles in the practice of journalism. The nine principles and other material concerning journalism ethics are included in the CD *NRW Plus,* Chapter 27. See **Nine Core Principles.**

Glossary

These definitions were provided by the press associations and working reporters and editors. Most of the brief entries are from the *New England Daily Newspaper Study,* an examination of 105 daily newspapers, edited by Loren Ghiglione (Southbridge, Mass.: Southbridge Evening News Inc., 1973).

Print Terms

add An addition to a story already written or in the process of being written.

assignment Instruction to a reporter to cover an event. An editor keeps an assignment book that contains notations for reporters such as the following:

Jacobs—10 a.m.: Health officials tour new sewage treatment plant.

Klaren—11 a.m.: Interview Ben Wastersen, possible Democratic congressional candidate.

Mannen—Noon: Rotary Club luncheon speaker, Horlan, the numerologist. A feature?

attribution Designation of the person being quoted. Also, the source of information in a story. Sometimes, information is given on a not-for-attribution basis.

background Material in a story that gives the circumstances surrounding or preceding the event.

banger An exclamation point. Avoid. Let the reader do the exclaiming.

banner Headline across or near the top of all or most of a newspaper page. Also called a *line, ribbon, streamer, screamer.*

B copy Bottom section of a story written ahead of an event that will occur too close to deadline for the entire story to be processed. The B copy usually consists of background material.

beat Area assigned to a reporter for regular coverage—for example, police or city hall. Also, an exclusive story.

body type Type in which most of a newspaper is set, usually 8- or 9-point type.

boldface Heavy, black typeface; type that is blacker than the text with which it is used. Abbreviated *bf.*

break When a news development becomes known and available. Also, the point of interruption in a story continued from one page to another.

bright Short, amusing story.

bulldog Early edition, usually the first of a newspaper.

byline Name of the reporter who wrote the story, placed atop the published article. An old-timer comments on the current use of bylines: "In the old days, a reporter was given a byline if he or she personally covered an important or unusual story, or the story was an

Joel Sartore,
Wichita Eagle-Beacon

exclusive. Sometimes if the writing was superior, a byline was given. Nowadays, everyone gets a byline, even if the story is a rewrite and the reporter never saw the event described in the story."

caps Capital letters; same as *uppercase.*

caps and lowercase Initial capital in a word followed by small letters. See **lowercase.**

caption See **cutline.**

clip News story clipped from a newspaper, usually for future reference.

cold type In composition, type set photographically or by pasting up letters and pictures on acetate or paper.

column The vertical division of the news page. A standard-size newspaper is divided into five to eight columns. Also, a signed article of opinion or strong personal expression, frequently by an authority or expert—a sports column, a medical column, political or social commentary.

copy Written form in which a news story or other material is prepared.

copy flow After a reporter finishes a story, it moves to the city desk where the city editor reads it for major errors or problems. If it does not need further work, the story is moved to the copy desk for final editing and a headline. It then moves to the mechanical department.

correction Errors that reach publication are retracted or corrected if they are serious or someone demands a correction. Libelous matter is always corrected immediately, often in a separate news story rather than in the standard box assigned to corrections.

correspondent Reporter who sends news from outside a newspaper office. On smaller papers, often not a regular full-time staff member.

crony journalism Reporting that ignores or treats lightly negative news about friends of a reporter. Beat reporters sometimes have a tendency to protect their informants in order to retain them as sources.

crop To cut or mask the unwanted portions, usually of a photograph.

cut Printed picture or illustration. Also, to eliminate material from a story. See **trim.**

cutline Any descriptive or explanatory material under a picture.

dateline Name of the city or town and sometimes the date at the start of a story that is not of local origin.

deadline Time at which the copy for an edition must be ready.

edition One version of a newspaper. Some papers have one edition a day, some several. Not to be confused with *issue,* which usually refers to all editions under a single date.

editorial Article of comment or opinion, usually on the editorial page.

editorial material All material in the newspaper that is not advertising.

enterprise copy Story, often initiated by a reporter, that digs deeper than the usual news story.

exclusive Story a reporter has obtained to the exclusion of the competition. Popularly known as a *scoop,* a term never used in the newsroom.

feature Story emphasizing the human or entertaining aspects of a situation. A news story or other material differentiated from straight news. As a verb, it means to give prominence to a story.

file To send a story to the office, usually by wire or telephone or to put news service stories on the wire.

filler Material used to fill space. Small items used to fill out columns where needed. Also called *column closers* and *shorts.*

flag Printed title of a newspaper on page 1. Also known as *logotype* or *nameplate.*

folo Story that follows up on a theme in a news story. When a fire destroyed a parochial school in Chicago, newspapers followed up the fire coverage with stories about fire safety precautions in the Chicago schools.

free advertising Use of the names of businesses and products not essential to the story. Instead of the brand name, use the broad term *camera* for Leica or Kodak.

futures calendar Date book in which story ideas, meetings and activities scheduled for a later occurrence are listed. Also known as a *futures book.* Kept by city and assignment editors and by careful reporters.

good night An expression meaning there is nothing further for the reporter from the desk for the day. Reporters call in when they take a break. Desks need to know where their reporters are in case of breaking stories.

graf Abbreviation for *paragraph.*

Guild Newspaper Guild, an international union to which reporters and other newspaper workers belong. Newspapers that have contracts with the Guild are said to be "organized."

handout Term for written publicity or special-interest news sent to a newspaper for publication.

hard news Spot news; live and current news in contrast to **features.**

head or **headline** The display type over a printed news story.

head shot Picture featuring little more than the head and shoulders of the person shown.

HFR Abbreviation for "hold for release." Material that cannot be used until it is released by the source or at a designated time. Also known as *embargoed material.*

insert Material placed between copy in a story. Usually, a paragraph or more to be placed in material already sent to the desk.

investigative reporting Technique used to unearth information that sources often want hidden. This type of reporting involves examination of documents and records, the cultivation of informants, painstaking and extended research. Investigative reporting usually seeks to expose wrongdoing and has concentrated on public officials and their activities.

In recent years, industry and business have been scrutinized. Some journalists contend that the term is redundant, that all good reporting is investigative, that behind every surface fact is the real story that a resourceful, curious and persistent reporter can dig up.

italics Type in which letters and characters slant to the right.

jump Continuation of a story from one page to another. As a verb, to continue material. Also called *runover.*

kill To delete a section from copy or to discard the entire story; also, to *spike* a story.

lead (pronounced *leed*) First paragraph in a news story. In a direct or straight news lead, it summarizes the main facts.

In a delayed lead, usually used on feature stories, it evokes a scene or sets a mood.

Also used to refer to the main idea of a story: An editor will ask a reporter, "What's the lead on the piece?" expecting a quick summary of the main facts.

Also, a tip on a story; an idea for a story. A source will tell a reporter, "I have a lead on a story for you."

localize To emphasize the names of persons from the local community who are involved in events outside the city or region: A local couple rescued in a Paris hotel fire; the city police chief who speaks at a national conference.

lowercase Small letters, as contrasted with capitals.

LTK Designation on copy for "lead to come." Usually placed after the **slug.** Indicates the written material will be given a lead later.

makeup Layout or design. The arrangement of body type, headlines and illustrations into pages.

masthead Formal statement of a newspaper's name, officers, place of publication and other descriptive information, usually on the editorial page. Sometimes confused with *flag* or *nameplate.*

morgue Newspaper library.

mug shot See **head shot.**

new lead See **running story.**

news hole Space in a newspaper allotted to news, illustrations and other nonadvertising material.

obituary Account of a person's death; also called *obit.*

offset Printing process in which an image is transferred from a printing plate to a rubber roller and then set off on paper.

off-the-record Describes material offered the reporter in confidence. If the reporter accepts the material with this understanding, it cannot be used except as general background in a later story. Some reporters never accept off-the-record material. Some reporters will

accept the material with the provision that if they can obtain the information elsewhere, they will use it. Reporters who learn of off-the-record material from other than the original source can use it.

No public, official meeting can be off-the-record, and almost all official documents (court records, police information) are public information. Private groups can ask that their meetings be kept off-the-record, but reporters frequently ignore such requests when the meeting is public or large numbers of people are present.

op-ed page Abbreviation for the page opposite the editorial page. The page usually is devoted to opinion columns and related illustrations.

overnight Story usually written late at night for the afternoon newspapers of the next day. Most often used by the press services. The overnight, or *overnighter,* usually has little new information in it but is cleverly written so that the reader thinks the story is new. Also known as *second-day stories.*

play Emphasis given to a news story or picture—size and place in the newspaper of the story; typeface and size of headline.

P.M. Afternoon or evening newspaper.

pool Arrangement whereby limited numbers of reporters and photographers are selected to represent all those assigned to the story. Pooling is adopted when a large number of people would overwhelm the event or alter its nature. The news and film are shared with the rest of the press corps.

precede Story written prior to an event; also, the section of a story preceding the lead, sometimes set in italic.

press release Publicity handout, or a story given to the news media for publication.

proof Reproduction of type on paper for the purpose of making corrections or alterations.

puff piece or **puffery** Publicity story or a story that contains unwarranted superlatives.

quotes Quotation marks; also a part of a story in which someone is directly quoted.

rewrite To write for a second time to strengthen a story or to condense it.

rewriteman Person who takes the facts of stories over the telephone and then puts them together into a story and who may rewrite reporters' stories.

roundup A story that joins two or more events with a common theme, such as traffic accidents, weather, police reports. When the events occur in different cities and are wrapped up in one story, the story is known as an *undated roundup.*

rowback A story that attempts to correct a previous story without indicating that the prior story had been in error or without taking responsibility for the error.

running story Event that develops and is covered over a period of time. For an event covered in subsequent editions of a newspaper or on a single cycle of a wire service, additional material is handled as follows:

New lead—important new information; Adds and inserts—less important information; Sub—material that replaces dated material, which is removed.

sell Presentation a reporter makes to impress the editor with the importance of his or her story; also, editors sell stories to their superiors at news conferences.

shirttail Short, related story added to the end of a longer one.

short Filler, generally of some current news value.

sidebar Story that emphasizes and elaborates on one part of another nearby story.

situationer Story that pulls together a continuing event for the reader who may not have kept track as it unfolded. The situationer is helpful with complex or technical developments or on stories with varied datelines and participants.

slant To write a story so as to influence the reader's thinking. To editorialize: to color or misrepresent.

slug Word or words placed on all copy to identify the story.

source Person, record, document or event that provides the information for the story.

sourcebook Alphabetical listing, by name and by title, of the addresses and the office and home telephone numbers of people on the reporter's beat and some general numbers—FBI agent in charge in town, police and fire department spokesperson, hospital information, weather bureau.

split page Front page of an inside section; also known as the *break page, second front page.*

stringer Correspondent, not a regular staff member, who is paid by the story or by the number of words written.

style Rules for capitalization, punctuation and spelling that standardize usage so that the material presented is uniform. Most newspapers and stations have stylebooks. The most frequently used is the common stylebook of the Associated Press. Some newspapers stress the "down" or "lowercase" style in their titles. Some newspapers capitalize (uppercase) frequently. Also, the unique characteristics of a reporter's writing or news delivery.

stylebook Specific listing of the conventions of spelling, abbreviation, punctuation and capitalization used by a particular newspaper or wire service. Broadcast stylebooks include pronunciations.

sub See **running story.**

subhead One-line and sometimes two-line head (usually in boldface body type) inserted in a long story at intervals for emphasis or to break up a long column of type.

text Verbatim report of a speech or public statement.

tight Refers to a paper so crowded with ads that the news space must be reduced. It is the opposite of the *wide open paper.*

tip Information passed to a reporter, often in confidence. The material usually requires further fact gathering. Occasionally, verification is impossible

and the reporter must decide whether to go with the tip on the strength of the insider's knowledge.

trim To reduce or condense copy carefully.

update Story that brings the reader up-to-date on a situation or personality previously in the news. If the state legislature appropriated additional funds for five new criminal court judges to meet the increased number of cases in the courts, an update might be written some months later about how many more cases were handled after the judges went to work. An update usually has no hard news angle.

verification Determination of the truth of the material the reporter gathers or is given. The assertions, sometimes even the actual observations, do not necessarily mean the information is accurate or true. Some of the basic tools of verification are the telephone book, for names and addresses; the city directory, for occupations; *Who's Who,* for biographical information. For verification of more complex material, the procedure of Thucydides, the Greek historian and author of the *History of the Peloponnesian War,* is good advice for the journalist:

"As to the deeds done in the war, I have not thought myself at liberty to record them on hearsay from the first informant or on arbitrary conjecture. My account rests either on personal knowledge or on the closest possible scrutiny of each statement made by others. The process of research was laborious, because the conflicting accounts were given by those who had witnessed the several events, as partiality swayed or memory served them."

wire services Synonym for *press associations,* the Associated Press and United Press International. There are foreign-owned press services to which some newspapers subscribe: Reuters, Agence France-Presse.

Broadcast Terms

actuality An on-the-scene report.

audio Sound.

close-up Shot of the face of the subject that dominates the frame so that little background is visible.

cover shot A long shot usually cut in at the beginning of a sequence to establish place or location.

cue A signal in script or by word or gesture to begin or to stop. Two types: incue and outcue.

cut Quick transition from one type of picture to another. Radio: A portion of an actuality on tape used on broadcast.

cutaway Transition shot—usually short—from one theme to another; used to avoid **jump cut.** Often, a shot of the interviewer listening.

dissolve Smooth fading of one picture for another. As the second shot becomes distinct, the first slowly disappears.

dolly Camera platform. Dolly-in: Move platform toward subject. Dolly-out: Move platform away.

dub The transfer of one videotape to another.

establishing shot Frequently a wide shot; used to give the viewer a sense of the scene of action.

FI or **fade in** A scene that begins without full brilliance and gradually assumes full brightness. **FO** or **fade out** is the opposite.

freeze frame A single frame that is frozen into position.

graphics All visual displays, such as artwork, maps, charts and still photos.

jump cut Transition from one subject to a different subject in an abrupt manner. Avoided with **cutaway** shot between the scenes.

lead-in Introductory statements to film or tape of actual event. The lead-in sets up the actuality by giving the context of the event.

lead-out Copy that comes immediately after tape or film of an actuality. The lead-out identifies the newsmaker again so listeners and viewers will know whom they just heard or saw. Used more often in radio. Also known as *tag lines.*

long shot Framing that takes in the scene of the event.

medium shot Framing of one person from head to waist or of a small group seated at a table. Known as *MS*.

mix Combining two or more sound elements into one.

montage A series of brief shots of various subjects to give a single impression or communicate one idea.

O/C On camera. A reporter delivering copy directly to the camera without covering pictures.

outtakes Scenes that are discarded for the final story.

panning or **pan shot** Moving the camera from left to right or right to left.

remote A taped or live broadcast from a location outside the studio; also, the unit that originates such a broadcast.

segue An uninterrupted transition from one sound to another; a sound dissolve. (Pronounced *seg-way*.)

SOF Sound on film. Recorded simultaneously with the picture.

SOT Sound on tape. Recorded simultaneously with picture on tape.

trim To eliminate material.

V/O Reporter's voice over pictures.

VTR Videotape recording.

zooming Use of a variable focus lens to take close-ups and wide angle shots from a stationary position. By using a zoom lens, a camera operator can give the impression of moving closer to or farther from the subject.

Internet Terms

chat To talk in real time with others online through a commercial service such as America Online or CompuServe.

content provider Firm or organization that creates content, such as Salon or CNET.

flaming Hostile chat, commentary or e-mail.

hit Request by a Web user to a server for an image or a file. Hits are used to measure the frequency or popularity of a site. Most sites now use *page views* as the more reliable measure of how many people visit a site.

home page Online site or home for a multitude of information—about movie stars, athletes, pets or commercial messages. Can be in the form of text, graphics, sound, animation.

HTML Abbreviation for Hypertext Markup Language, the language used to create World Wide Web documents.

Hyperlink Location on the Internet that takes the user to another site. Using the mouse, a user *clicks on* the link to be carried to the other document. Hyperlinks are indicated often by highlighting or boldface type.

Hypertext System of coding text to link electronic documents with one another. Elements in a hypertext document are linked to elements in other documents.

instant message Programs that allow users to send real-time messages across the Net. Popular versions are AOL's IM and icq.com.

Internet Global network of computers communicating in a common language or protocol (TCP/IP, Transmission Control Protocol/Internet Protocol) over telephone lines or microwave links. Home to the World Wide Web, newsgroups and online forums. Always preceded by "the" unless used as a modifier. The "i" is always capped. Synonymous with the Net.

listserv Mail-handling software that allows people to subscribe to mailing lists. The lists consist of e-mail addresses. Subscribers receive the messages posted to the central mail-handling address.

log on The process of identifying oneself on the computer to gain access to a network.

mailing list Ongoing e-mail discussion devoted to a specific topic. Lists can be public or private, moderated or unmoderated. Also, a group of people (subscribers) with a common interest. The Internet has 15,000 mailing lists.

search engine Way to locate information on the Internet by keyword(s) or concept. With Web access, search engines are free.

snail mail Postal mail.

spam Electronic litter. Unwanted advertisements, junk postings. Similar to junk mail. Spamming is the act of sending spam.

Usenet newsgroups Collection of informal forums, bulletin boards or newsgroups distributed over the Internet and devoted to a variety of interests and topics. More than 16,000 exist.

Web Short for the World Wide Web, part of the Internet that allows users to access text, pictures, charts, documents, graphics, sounds and video.

Web site Collection of pages on the Web that can be accessed through a main title or contents page, which is called a *front door*. A site can be likened to a TV network or a publishing house.

Appendixes

The following appendixes are included in the CD *NRW Plus* that is wrapped with the textbook:

A—Grammar
B—Public Opinion Polling Checklist
C—How to Use the FOIA—Freedom of Information Act
D—Code of Ethics
E—Sources Online
F—Copy Editing Symbols
G—The Journalism Job Hunt

Stylebook

addresses Abbreviate *Avenue, Boulevard, Street* with specific address: *1314 Kentucky St.* Spell out without specific address: *construction on Fifth Avenue.*

Use figures for the address number: *3 Third Ave.; 45 Main St.* Spell out numbers under 10 as street names: *21 Fourth Ave.; 450 11th St.*

age Use figures. To express age as an adjective, use hyphens: *a 3-year-old girl.* Also use hyphens when age is expressed as a noun as in: *a 10-year-old.* Unless otherwise stated, the figure is presumed to indicate years: *a boy, 4, and his sister, 6 months.*

Infant: under one year of age; *child:* someone in the period between infancy and youth, ages 1 to 13; *girl, boy:* under 18; *youth:* 13–18; *man, woman:* over 18; *adult:* over 18, unless used in specific legal context for crimes such as drinking; *middle-aged:* 35–55; *elderly:* over 65. Avoid *elderly* when describing individuals.

a.m., p.m. Lowercase with periods.

amendment Capitalize when referring to specific amendments to the U.S. Constitution. Spell out for the first through ninth; use figures for 10th and above: *First Amendment, 10th Amendment.*

anti- Hyphenate all but words that have their own meanings: *antibiotic, antibody, anticlimax, antidote, antifreeze, antihistamine, antiknock, antimatter, antiparticle, antipasto, antiperspirant, antiseptic, antiserum, antithesis, antitoxin, antitrust.*

bi, semi When used with periods of time, the prefix *bi* means every other; *semi* means twice. A biannual conference meets every other year. A semiweekly newspaper comes out twice a week. No hyphens.

brand name A nonlegal term for a trademark. Do not use as generic terms or as verbs: make it *soft drink* instead of *Coke* or *coke; photocopy* instead of *Xerox.*

capitalization Generally, follow a down style.

Proper nouns: Use capitals for names of persons, places, trademarks; titles when used with names; nicknames of people, states, teams; titles of books, plays, movies.

century Lowercase, spelling out numbers less than 10, except when used in proper nouns—*the fifth century, 18th century,* but *20th Century-Fox* and *Nineteenth Century Society*—following the organization's practice.

chairman, chairwoman Use *chairman* or *chairwoman* instead of *chair* or *chairperson; spokesman* or *spokeswoman* instead of *spokesperson* and similar constructions unless the *-person* construction is a formal title.

Use *chairman* or *spokesman* when referring to the office in general. A neutral word such as *representative* often may be the best choice.

co- Use a hyphen when forming nouns, adjectives and verbs that indicate occupation or status: *co-star, co-written.* No hyphen for other constructions: *coeducation, coexist.*

Congress Capitalize when referring to the U.S. Senate and House of Representatives. The term is correctly used only in reference to the two legislative branches together. Capitalize also when referring to foreign governments that use the term or its equivalent.

Do not capitalize *congressional* unless it is part of a proper name.

Constitution, constitutional Capitalize when referring to the U.S. Constitution, with or without the *U.S.* modifier. When referring to other constitutions, capitalize only when preceded by the name of a nation or state. Lowercase *constitutional.*

court names Capitalize the full proper names of courts at all levels. Retain capitalization if *U.S.* or a state name is dropped.

dates *July 6, 1957, was her birth date.* (Use commas.) *She was born in July 1957.* (No comma between the month and year.)

Abbreviate the month with a specific date: *Feb. 19.* Spell out all months when standing alone. With dates, use abbreviations: *Jan., Feb., Aug., Sept., Oct., Nov., Dec.* Spell out *March, April, May, June, July.*

directions and regions Lowercase *north, south, northeast,* etc. when they indicate compass direction: *Police followed the car south on Route 22.*

Capitalize when they refer to regions: *Southern accent; Northeastern industry.*

With names of nations, lowercase except when they are part of a proper name or are used to designate a politically divided nation: *tourism in southern France,* but *South Korea* and *Northern Ireland.*

Lowercase compass points when they describe a section of a state or city except when they are part of a proper name (*South Dakota*) or when they refer to a widely known region (*Southern California; the East Side of New York*).

Capitalize them when combining them with a common noun to form a proper noun: *the Eastern Hemisphere; the North Woods.*

entitled Does not mean *titled. Citizens 18 and older are entitled to vote,* but *the book is titled "News Reporting and Writing."*

ex- No hyphen for words that use *ex* in the sense of *out of: excommunicate, expropriate.* Hyphenate when using in the sense of *former: ex-husband, ex-convict. Former* is preferred with titles: *Former President Gerald R. Ford.*

fireman Use *firefighter* because some women hold this job.

fractions Spell out amounts less than 1, using hyphens: *one-half, two-thirds.* Use figures for amounts larger than 1, converting to decimals whenever possible: *3.5* instead of *three and one-half or 3 1/2.*

Figures are preferred in tabular material and in stories about stocks.

gay Acceptable as a popular synonym for *homosexual.* May be used as a noun and an adjective.

handicapped, disabled, impaired Avoid describing an individual as *disabled* or *handicapped* unless it is essential to the story. If necessary to use, make clear what the handicap is and how it affects the person's mental or physical activity. *Disabled* refers to a condition that interferes with a person's ability to do something independently. *Handicap* should be avoided in describing a disability. *Blind* means complete loss of sight. For others, use *partially blind. Deaf* means complete loss of hearing. For others, use *partial hearing loss* or *partially deaf. Mute* refers to people who physically cannot speak. For others, use *speech impaired.* Do not use *wheelchair-bound* unless necessary, and then say why.

Do not identify someone as having a disability unless the disability is relevant, and the relevance is clear. People with disabilities should not be described as heroes or victims. Describe the symptoms or difficulties the person encounters and let the reader reach conclusions.

historical periods and events Capitalize widely recognized periods and events in anthropology, archaeology, geology and history: *the Bronze Age, the Ice Age, the Renaissance.*

Capitalize widely recognized popular names for eras and events: *the Glorious Revolution, the Roaring '20s.*

holidays and holy days Capitalize them. In federal law, the legal holidays are New Year's, Martin Luther King's Birthday, President's Day, Memorial Day, Independence Day, Labor Day, Columbus Day, Veterans Day, Thanksgiving and Christmas.

States are not required to follow the federal lead in designating holidays, except that federal employees must receive the day off or must be paid overtime if they work.

Jewish holy days: Hanukkah, Passover, Purim, Rosh Hashana, Shavuot, Sukkot and Yom Kippur.

in- No hyphen when it means *not: invalid; inaccurate.* Mostly used without the hyphen in other combinations, but there are a few exceptions: *in-house; in-depth.* Consult a dictionary when in doubt.

-in Always precede with a hyphen: *break-in; sit-in; write-in.*

initials Use periods and no space: *H.L. Mencken; C.S. Lewis.* This practice has been adopted to ensure that initials will be set on the same line.

like- Follow with a hyphen when used to mean *similar to: like-minded; like-natured.*

-like No hyphen unless the *l* would be tripled: *lifelike,* but *shell-like.*

mailman Use the term *letter carrier* or *mail carrier* because many women work for the Postal Service.

man, mankind *Humanity* is preferred for the plural form. Use *a person* or *an individual* in the singular. A phrase or sentence usually can be reconstructed to eliminate any awkwardness.

National Organization for Women. Not *National Organization of Women.*

nationalities and races Capitalize the proper names of nationalities, peoples, races, tribes, etc. Lowercase *black* and *white.* Lowercase derogatory terms such as *honky* and *nigger.* Use them only in direct quotations.

  See **race** for guidelines on when racial identification is pertinent in a story.

nobility Capitalize *king, queen, duke* and other titles when they precede the individual's name. Lowercase when standing alone: *King Juan Carlos,* but *the king of Spain.*

non- In general, do not hyphenate if *not* could be used before the root word. Hyphenate before proper nouns or in awkward combinations: *non-nuclear.*

numerals Spell out *one* through *nine,* except when used to indicate age, votes, building numbers, scores. Use figures for *10* and above.

  Spell out a number when it begins a sentence: *Fifteen members voted against the bill.* Use figures when a year begins a sentence: *1999 began auspiciously.*

  Use figures for time, temperature, dimensions, percentages, percents and money: *$5,* but *a dollar.*

  If a series has mixed numbers, use all numbers: *His table had scattered on it 6 magazines, 13 books and 11 newspapers.*

  For amounts of $1 million and more, use the *$* sign and figures up to two decimal places with the *million, billion, trillion* spelled out: *$1.65 million.* Exact amounts are given in figures: *$1,650,398.*

  When spelling out large numbers, separate numbers ending in *y* from the next number with a hyphen: *seventy-nine; one hundred seventy-nine.*

people, persons Use *person* when referring to an individual. *People* is preferred to *persons* in all plural uses.

  People also is a collective noun that takes a plural verb when used to refer to a single race or nation: *The Philippine people are awaiting the president's decision on the offer of aid.* In this sense, *peoples* is the plural form: *The peoples of Western Europe do not always agree on East-West issues.*

percentages Use figures—decimals, not fractions—and the word *percent,* not the symbol: *2.5 percent; 10 percent.* For amounts less than 1 percent, place a zero before the decimal: *0.6 percent.*

When presenting a range, repeat *percent* after each figure: *2 percent to 5 percent.*

policeman Use *police officer* instead.

political parties and philosophies Capitalize the name of the party and the word *party* when it is used as part of the organization's proper name: *the Democratic Party.*

Capitalize *Communist, Conservative, Democrat, Liberal,* etc., when they refer to the activities of a specific party or to individual members.

Lowercase the name of a philosophy in noun and adjective forms unless it is derived from a proper name: *communism; fascist,* but *Marxism; Nazi.*

In general, avoid the terms *conservative, radical, leftist* and *rightist.* In casual and popular usage, the meanings of these terms vary, depending on the user and the situation being discussed. A more precise description of an individual's or a group's political views is preferred.

post office Should not be capitalized. The agency is the U.S. Postal Service.

prefixes See entries for specific prefixes. Generally, do not hyphenate when using a prefix with a word starting with a consonant.

Except for *cooperate* and *coordinate,* use a hyphen if the prefix ends in the same vowel that begins the following word: *re-elect,* not *reelect.*

Use a hyphen if the word that follows is capitalized: *pan-American; anti-Catholic.*

Use a hyphen to join doubled prefixes: *sub-subclause.*

presidency Always lowercase.

president Capitalized only as a title before an individual's name: *President George W. Bush,* but *the president said he would spend New Year's in Houston.*

presidential Lowercase unless part of a proper name: *presidential approval,* but *Presidential Medal of Freedom.*

race Race, religion and national origin are sometimes essential to a story but too often are injected when they are not pertinent. When in doubt about relevance, substitute descriptions such as *white, Baptist, French.* If one of these descriptions would be pertinent, use the original term.

religious references
DEITIES: Capitalize the proper names of monotheistic deities, pagan and mythological gods and goddesses: *Allah, the Father, Zeus.* Lowercase pronouns that refer to the deity: *he, him, thee, who,* etc.

Lowercase *gods* when referring to the deities of polytheistic religions. Lowercase such words as *god-awful, godlike, godsend.*

LIFE OF JESUS CHRIST: Capitalize the names of major events in the life of Jesus Christ in references that do not use his name: *the Last Supper; the Resurrection.* Lowercase when the words are used with his name: *the ascension of Christ.* Apply the same principle to events in the life of his mother, Mary.

RITES: Capitalize proper names for rites that commemorate the Last Supper or signify a belief in Jesus Christ's presence: *the Lord's Supper; Holy Eucharist.* Lowercase the names of other sacraments.

HOLY DAYS: Capitalize the names of holy days: *Hanukkah.*

OTHER WORDS: Lowercase *heaven, hell, devil, angel, cherub, apostle, priest,* etc.

rock 'n' roll Not *rock and roll.*

room numbers Use figures and capitalize *room:* The faculty met in Room 516. Capitalize the names of specially designated rooms: *Oval Office; Blue Room.*

saint Abbreviate as *St.* in the names of saints, cities and other places except *Saint John* (New Brunswick), to distinguish it from St. John's, Newfoundland, and *Sault Ste. Marie.*

seasons Lowercase *spring, summer, fall, winter* and their derivatives. Capitalize when part of a formal name: *St. Paul Winter Carnival; Summer Olympics.*

self- Always hyphenate: *self-motivated; self-taught.*

senate, senatorial Capitalize all references to specific legislative bodies, regardless of whether the name of the nation or state is used: *U.S. Senate; the state Senate.*

Lowercase plural uses: *the Iowa and Kansas state senates.* Lowercase references to nongovernmental bodies: *the student-faculty senate.*

Always lowercase *senatorial.*

sexism Avoid stereotyping women or men. Be conscious of equality in treatment of both sexes.

When writing of careers and jobs, avoid presuming that the wage earner is a man and that the woman is a homemaker: *the average family of five* instead of *the average worker with a wife and three children.*

Avoid physical descriptions of women or men when not absolutely relevant to the story.

Use parallel references to both sexes: *the men and the women,* not *the men and the ladies; husband and wife,* not *man and wife.*

Do not use nouns and pronouns to indicate sex unless the sex difference is basic to understanding or there is no suitable substitute. One way to avoid such subtle sexism is to change the noun to the plural, eliminating the masculine pronoun: *Drivers should carry their licenses,* not *Every driver should carry his license.*

Personal appearance and marital and family relationships should be used only when relevant to the story.

state names Spell out names of the 50 U.S. states when they stand alone in textual matter.

The names of eight states are never abbreviated: *Alaska, Hawaii, Idaho, Iowa, Maine, Ohio, Texas, Utah.*

Abbreviate other state names when used with a city, in a dateline or with party affiliation. Do not use Postal Service abbreviations.

Ala.	*Fla.*	*Md.*	*Neb.*	*N.D.*	*Tenn.*
Ariz.	*Ga.*	*Mass.*	*Nev.*	*Okla.*	*Vt.*
Ark.	*Ill.*	*Mich.*	*N.H.*	*Ore.*	*Va.*
Calif.	*Ind.*	*Minn.*	*N.J.*	*Pa.*	*Wash.*
Colo.	*Kan.*	*Miss.*	*N.M.*	*R.I.*	*W.Va*
Conn.	*Ky.*	*Mo.*	*N.Y.*	*S.C.*	*Wis.*
Del.	*La.*	*Mont.*	*N.C.*	*S.D.*	*Wyo.*

statehouse Capitalize all references to a specific statehouse, with or without the state name. But lowercase in all plural uses: *the New Mexico Statehouse; the Arizona and New Mexico statehouses.*

suspensive hyphenation Use as follows: *The 19- and 20-year-olds were not served alcoholic beverages.* Use in all similar cases.

Although the form looks somewhat awkward, it guides readers, who may otherwise except a noun to follow the first figure.

syllabus, syllabuses Also: *memorandum, memorandums.*

teen, teen-ager (noun), **teen-age** (adjective) Do not use *teen-aged.*

telecast (noun), **televise** (verb)

temperatures Use figures for all except *zero.* Use the word *minus,* not a minus sign, to indicate temperatures below zero. *The day's high was 9; the day's low was minus 9.*

Temperatures are higher and lower and they rise and fall but they do not become warmer or cooler.

Third World The economically developing nations of Africa, Asia and Latin America.

time Exact times often are unnecessary. *Last night* and *this morning* are acceptable substitutes for *yesterday* and *today.* Use exact time when pertinent but avoid redundancies: *8 a.m. this morning* should be *8 a.m. today* or *8 o'clock this morning.*

Use figures except for *noon* and *midnight: 12 noon* is redundant.

Separate hours from minutes with a colon: *3:15 p.m.*

titles

ACADEMIC TITLES: Capitalize and spell out formal titles such as *professor, dean, president, chancellor and chairman* when they precede a name. Lowercase elsewhere. Do not abbreviate *Professor* as *Prof.*

Lowercase modifiers such as *journalism* in *journalism Professor John Rist* or *department* in *department chairwoman Kim Power,* unless the modifier is a proper name: *French Professor Jeannette Spear.*

COURTESY TITLES: Do not use the courtesy titles *Miss, Mr., Mrs.* or *Ms.* on first reference. Instead, use the person's first and last names. Do not use *Mr.* unless it is combined with *Mrs.: Kyle Scott Hotsenpiller; Mr. and Mrs. Kyle Scott Hotsenpiller.*

Courtesy titles may be used on second reference for women, according to the woman's preference and these guidelines:

• Married women: On first reference, identify a woman by her own first name and her husband's last name, if she uses it: *Betty Phillips.* Use *Mrs.* on first reference only if a woman requests that her husband's first name be used or her own first name cannot be determined: *Mrs. Steven A. Phillips.*

On second reference, use *Mrs.* unless a woman initially identified by her own first name prefers *Ms.: Rachel Finch; Mrs. Finch; Ms. Finch.* Or use no title: *Finch; Rachel Finch.*

If a married woman is known by her maiden name, precede it by *Miss* on second reference unless she prefers *Ms.: Sarah Wilson; Miss Wilson* or *Ms. Wilson.*

• Unmarried women: Use *Miss, Ms.* or no title on second reference, according to the woman's preference.

For divorced and widowed women, the normal practice is to use *Mrs.* or no title on second reference, according to the woman's preference. Use *Miss, Ms.* or no title, according to the woman's preference, if the woman returns to her maiden name.

If a woman prefers *Ms.* or no title, do not include her marital status in a story unless it is pertinent.

GOVERNMENTAL TITLES: Capitalize when used as a formal title in front of a person's name. It is not necessary to use a title on second reference: *Gov. Fred Florence; Florence.* For women who hold official positions, use the courtesy title on second reference, according to the guidelines for courtesy titles: *Gov. Ruth Arnold; Miss Arnold, Mrs. Arnold, Ms. Arnold, Arnold.* (Some newspapers do not use the courtesy title on second reference.)

Abbreviate *Governor* as *Gov., Lieutenant Governor* as *Lt. Gov.* when used as a formal title before a name.

Congressional titles: Before names, abbreviate *Senator* as *Sen.* and *Representative* as *Rep.* Add *U.S.* or *state* if necessary to avoid confusion.

Short form punctuation for party affiliation: Use abbreviations listed under **state names** and set them off from the person's name with commas: *Sen. Bob Graham, D-Fla., and Rep. Barney Frank, D-Mass., attended the ceremony.*

Capitalize and spell out other formal government titles before a person's name. Do not use titles on second references: *Attorney General Jay Craven spoke. Craven said . . .*

Capitalize and spell out formal titles instead of abbreviating before the person's name in direct quotations only. Lowercase in all uses not mentioned already.

OCCUPATIONAL TITLES: They are always lowercase: *senior vice president Nancy Harden.* Avoid false titles: *bridge champion Helen P. George* should be: *Helen P. George, Sioux Falls bridge tourney winner.*

RELIGIOUS TITLES: The first reference to a clergyman, clergywoman or nun should include a capitalized title before the person's name.

On second reference: for men, use only a last name if he uses a surname. If a man is known only by a religious name, repeat the title: *Pope Paul VI* or *Pope Paul* on first reference; *the pope* or *the pontiff* on second reference. For women, use *Miss, Mrs., Ms.* or no title, according to the woman's preference.

Cardinals, archbishops, bishops: On first reference, use the title before the person's first and last name. On second reference, use the last name only or the title.

Ministers and priests: Use *the Rev.* before a name on first reference. Substitute *Monsignor* before the name of a Roman Catholic priest who has received this honor.

Rabbis: Use *Rabbi* before a name on first reference. On second reference, use only the last name of a man; use *Miss, Mrs., Ms.* or no title before a woman's last name, according to her preference.

Nuns: Always use *Sister* or *Mother: Sister Agnes Mary* in all references if the nun uses only a religious name; *Sister Ann Marie Graham* on first reference if she uses a surname. *Sister Graham* on second.

TITLES OF WORKS: For titles of books, movies, operas, plays, poems, songs, television programs and lectures, speeches and works of art, apply the following guidelines:

Capitalize the principal words, including prepositions and conjunctions of four or more letters.

Capitalize an article or word of fewer than four letters if it is the first or last word in a title.

Place quotation marks around the names of all such works except the Bible and books that are primarily catalogs of reference material, including almanacs, directories, dictionaries, encyclopedias, handbooks and similar publications.

Translate a foreign title into English unless a work is known to the American public by its foreign name.

Do not use quotation marks or italics with the names of newspapers and magazines.

TV Acceptable as an adjective but should not be used as a noun.

upstate, downstate Always lowercase.

venereal disease *VD* is acceptable on second reference.

versus Abbreviate as *vs.* in all uses.

vice Use two words, no hyphen.

vice president Follow the guidelines for **president.**

war Capitalize when part of the name for a particular conflict: *World War II; the Cold War.*

well- Hyphenate as part of a compound modifier: *a well-dressed man.*

wide- Usually hyphenated: *wide-eyed.* Exception: *widespread.*

words as words When italics are available, italicize them. Otherwise, place in quotation marks: *Rep. Ellen Jacobson asked journalists to address her as "congresswoman."*

years Use figures. Us an *s* without the apostrophe to indicate spans of centuries: *the 1800s.* Use an apostrophe to indicate omitted numerals and an *s* to indicate decades: *the '80s.*

Years are the only figures that may be placed at the start of a sentence: *1959 was a year of rapid city growth.*

Punctuation

Keep a good grammar book handy. No stylebook can adequately cover the complexities of the 13 punctuation marks: apostrophe, bracket, colon, comma, dash, ellipsis, exclamation point, hyphen, parenthesis, period, question mark, quotation mark, semicolon. The following is a guide to frequent problems and usages:

Apostrophe Use (1) for possessives, (2) to indicate omitted figures or letters and (3) to form some plurals.

1. **Possessives.** Add apostrophe and *s ('s)* to the end of singular and plural nouns or the indefinite pronoun unless it has an *s* or *z* sound.

> *The woman's coat. The women's coats.*
> *The child's toy. The children's toys.*
> *Someone's pistol. One's hopes.*

If the word is plural and ends in an *s* or *z* sound, add an apostrophe only:

> *Boys' books. Joneses' farm.*

For singular common nouns ending in *s,* add an apostrophe and *s ('s)* unless the next word begins with s:

> *The witness's testimony. The witness' story.*

For singular proper nouns, add only an apostrophe:

> *Dickens' novels. James' hat.*

2. **Omitted figures or letters.** Use in contractions: *Don't, can't.* Put in place of omitted figures: *Class of '88.*

3. **To form some plurals.** When figures, letters, symbols and words are referred to as words, use the apostrophe and *s.*

> a. Figures: *He skated perfect 8's.*
> b. Letters: *She received all A's in her finals.*
> c. Symbols: *Journalists never use **&**'s to substitute for the **and**s in their copy.*

Caution: The pronouns *ours, yours, theirs, his, hers, whose* do not take the apostrophe. *Its* is the possessive pronoun. *It's* is the contraction of *it is*.

Note: Compound words and nouns in joint possession use the possessive in the last word:

- Everybody else's homes.
- His sister-in-law's book.
- Clinton and Gore's party.

If there is separate possession, each noun takes the possessive form: *Clinton's and Bush's opinions differ.*

Brackets Check whether the newspaper can set them. Use to enclose a word or words within a quote that the writer inserts: *"Happiness [his note read] is a state of mind."* Try to avoid the need for such an insertion. Use for paragraphs within a story that refer to an event separate from the datelined material.

Colon The colon is usually used at the end of a sentence to call attention to what follows. It introduces lists, tabulations, texts and quotations of more than one sentence.

It also can be used to mark a full stop before a dramatic word or statement: *She had only one goal in life: work.* The colon is used in the time of day: *7:45 p.m.;* elapsed time of an event: *4:01.1;* in dialogue in question and answer, as from a trial.

Comma The best general guide for the use of the comma is the human voice as it pauses, stops and varies in tone. The comma marks the pause, the short stop:

1. He looked into the hospital room, but he was unable to find the patient.
2. Although he continued his search on the floor for another 20 minutes, he was unable to find anyone to help him.
3. He decided that he would go downstairs, ask at the desk and then telephone the police.
4. If that also failed, he thought to himself, he would have to give up the search.

Note that when reading these sentences aloud, the commas are natural resting points for pauses. The four sentences also illustrate the four principles governing the use of commas:

1. The comma is used to separate main clauses when they are joined by a coordinating conjunction. (The coordinating conjunctions are *for, nor, and, but, or*). The comma can be eliminated if the main clauses are short: *He looked into the room and he froze.*
2. Use the comma after an introductory element: a clause, long phrase, transitional expression or interjection.
3. Use the comma to separate words, phrases or clauses in a series. Also, use it in a series of coordinate adjectives: *He was wearing a long, full cape.*

4. Set off nonessential material in a sentence with comma(s). When the parenthetical or interrupting nonrestrictive clauses and phrases are in the middle of a sentence, two commas are needed: *The country, he was told, needed his assistance.*

Other uses of the comma:

- With full sentence quotes, not with partial quotes: *He asked, "Where are you going?" The man replied that he was "blindly groping" his way home.*
- To separate city and county, city and state. In place of the word *of* between a name and city: *Jimmy Carter, Plains, Ga.*
- To set off a person's age: *Orville Sterb, 19, of Fullerton, Calif.*
- In dates: *March 19, 1940, was the date he entered the army.*
- In party affiliations: *Jim Bunning, R-Ky., spoke.*

Caution: The comma is frequently misused by placing it instead of the period or semicolon between two main clauses. This is called *comma splice:*

WRONG: The computer was jammed, he could not write his assignment.
RIGHT: The computer was jammed. He could not write his assignment.
The computer was jammed; he could not write his assignment.

Dash Use a dash (1) to indicate a sudden or dramatic shift in thought within a sentence, (2) to set off a series of words that contains commas and (3) to introduce sections of a list or a summary.

The dash is a call for a short pause, just as are the comma and the parentheses. The comma is the most often used and is the least dramatic of the separators. The parentheses set off unimportant elements. The dash tends to emphasize materials. It has this quality because it is used sparingly.

1. He stared at the picture—and he was startled to find himself thinking of her face. The man stood up—painfully and awkwardly—and extended his hand in greeting.

2. There were three people watching them—an elderly woman, a youth with a crutch at his side and a young woman in jeans holding a paperback—and he pulled her aside out of their view.

3. He gave her his reasons for being there:
   —He wanted to apologize;
   —He needed to give her some material;
   —He was leaving on a long trip.

Note: This third form should be used infrequently, usually when the listing will be followed by an elaboration.

The dash is also used in datelines.

Ellipsis Use the ellipsis to indicate material omitted from a quoted passage from a text, transcript, play, etc.: *The minutes stated that Breen had asked, "How many gallons of paint . . . were used in the project?* Put one space before and one space after each of the three periods. If the sentence preceding the omission ends with a period, use four periods, one to mark the end of the sentence (without space, as a regular period), three more for the ellipsis.

The ellipsis is also used by some columnists to separate short items in a paragraph.

Do not use to mark pauses or shifts in thought or for emphasis.

Exclamation point Much overused. There are reporters who have gone through a lifetime of writing and have never used the exclamation point, except when copying material in which it is used. The exclamation point is used to indicate powerful feelings, surprise, wonder. Most good writers prefer to let the material move the reader to provide his or her own exclamation.

When using, do not place a comma or period after the exclamation point. Place inside quotation marks if it is part of the quoted material.

Hyphen The hyphen is used (1) to join words to express a single idea or (2) to avoid confusion or ambiguity.

1. Use the hyphen to join two or more words that serve as a single adjective before a noun: *A well-known movie is on television tonight. He had a know-it-all expression.*

Caution: Do not use the hyphen when the first word of the compound ends in *-ly* or when the words follow the noun: *She is an easily recognized person. His hair was blond black.*

2. Avoid (a) ambiguity or (b) an awkward joining of letters or syllables by putting a hyphen between prefixes or suffixes and the root word.

a. He recovered the chair. He re-covered the chair.

b. Re-enter, macro-economics, shell-like.

Parentheses Generally, avoid. It may be necessary for the insertion of background or to set off supplementary or illustrative material.

Use a period inside a closing parenthesis if the matter begins with a capital letter.

Period Use the period at the end of declarative sentences, indirect questions, most imperative sentences and most abbreviations. Place the period inside quotation marks.

Question mark The question mark is used for direct questions, not indirect questions.

DIRECT: Where are you going?

INDIRECT: He asked where she was going.

The question mark goes inside quotation marks if it applies to the quoted material: *He asked, "Have you seen the movie?"* Put it outside if it applies to the entire sentence: *Have you seen "Guys and Dolls"?*

> **Terse.** "Our composing room has an unlimited supply of periods available to terminate short, simple sentences."
> —*Turner Catledge, managing editor,* The New York Times

Quotation marks Quotation marks set off (1) direct quotations, (2) some titles and nicknames and (3) words used in a special way.

    1. Set off the exact words of the speaker: *"He walked like a duck,"* she *said. He replied that he walked "more like an alley cat on the prowl."*

    2. Use for titles of books, movies, short stories, poems, songs, articles from magazines and plays. Some nicknames take quotation marks. Do not use for nicknames of sports figures.

    3. For words used in a special sense: *"Indian giver" and similar phrases are considered to be ethnic slurs.*

    Punctuation with quotation marks:

The comma: Use it outside the quotation marks when setting off the speaker at the beginning of a sentence: *He said, "You care too much for money."* Use inside the quotation marks when the speaker ends the sentence: *"I just want to be careful," he replied.*

The colon and semicolon: Always place outside the quotation marks: *She said she wanted no help from him: "I can handle the assignment myself." He mentioned her "incredible desire for work"; he meant her "insatiable desire for work."*

The dash, question mark and exclamation point: Place them inside when they apply to quoted matter only; outside when they refer to the whole sentence: *She asked, "How do you know so much?" Did she really wonder why he knew "so much"?*

For quotes within quotes, use a single quote mark for the inner quotation: *"Have you read 'War and Peace'?" he asked.* Note, no comma is used after the question mark.

Semicolon Usually overused by beginning reporters. Unless there is a special reason to use the semicolon, use the period.

    Use the semicolon to separate a series of equal elements when the individual segments contain material that is set off by commas. This makes for clarity in the series: *She suggested that he spend his allowance on the new series at the opera, "Operas of the Present"; books of plays by Shaw, Ibsen and Aristophanes; and novels by Tolstoy, Dickens and F. Scott Fitzgerald.*

Classy. "I think one reason the critics have been slow, even up to this moment, in acknowledging me as a serious writer is that I don't use semicolons. I never understood them. They don't really stand for anything. I think it's a way of just showing off you've been to college."

—*Kurt Vonnegut*

Credits

Text

Chapter 1
p. 7: David Kranz and Rob Swenson; **p. 9:** David Kissel; **p. 21:** Jack Kelley, *USA Today.*

Chapter 2
p. 44-45: News stories from the Associated Press. Used with Permission.

Chapter 3
p. 80: Map reproduced with permission of the American Society of Newspaper Editors.

Chapter 5
p. 123: Excerpt from news story used with permission of the *St. Petersburg Times;* **p. 124:** Excerpt from news story used with permission of the *El Paso Herald-Post;* **p. 127:** Excerpt from news story used with permission of *The Wall Street Journal.*

Chapter 6
p. 141: News story from the *Daily News.* Used with permission. *p. 141–142:* News story from *The New York Times.* Used with permission.

Chapter 7
p. 178: News story from *The Charlotte Observer.* Used with permission. **p. 178:** Front page of the **Daily News.** Used with permission. **p. 180:** News story from *The State Journal* (Topeka, Kan.) Used with permission. **p. 180–181:** News story from *The Fresno Bee.* Used with permission.

Chapter 8
p. 195: Excerpts from news story used with permission of the *Lexington* (Ky.) *Herald-Leader.* **p. 195–196:** Elizabeth Leland, *The Charlotte Observer;* **p. 197:** Excerpts from news story used with permission of the *Houston Chronicle;* **p. 200–201:** Excerpts from news story used with permission of *The Evening Sun* (Baltimore); **p. 201:** Carl Hiassen, *Miami Herald;* **p. 206:** Jeffrey A. Tannenbaum of *The Wall Street Journal;* **p. 212:** Script of "This Neighborhood is Obsolete;" **p. 214–215:** Sam Roe, *The Blade;* **p. 216:** Copyright *St. Petersburg Times* 1999.

Chapter 9
p. 220–224, 227: Excerpts from Associated Press stories. Used with permission. **p. 231:** Adapted from *Writing Broadcast News,* 2/e by Mervin Block (Bonus Books, 1998); **p. 234–235:** Excerpts from WSMV-TV script. Used with permission. **p. 236:** Excerpts from "The CBS Evening News." Used with permission. **p. 237:** Excerpt from story aired on KTRH NewsRadio in Houston, reported by Stephen Dean; **p. 239:** Adapted from *Writing Broadcast News* by Mervin Block. Used with permission. (Bonus Books, 1987).

Chapter 11
p. 271: Excerpt from news story used with the permission of *The St. Petersburg Times.* **p. 283:** Excerpt from story in the *Winston-Salem Journal.* Used with permission. **p. 287–289:** By Charles M. Young. From *Rolling Stone Magazine,* June 1, 1978. By Straight Arrow Publishers, Inc., © 1978. All rights reserved. Reprinted by permission.

Chapter 12
p. 300–301: Excerpt from news story in *The New York Times.* Used with Permission.

Chapter 13
p. 306: Excerpts from news story in *The St. Petersburg Times.* Used with Permission. **p. 322:** Portion of front page of *The Wall Street Journal.* Used with permission.

Chapter 14
p. 329: Page excerpt from the *Winston-Salem Journal.* Used with permission. **p. 338:** Excerpt from news story in *USA Today.* Used with permission. **p. 344–345:** Excerpts from news stories in *The Providence Journal-Bulletin.* Used with permission. **p. 346:** Excerpt from a news story in the *Fort Worth Star-Telegram.* Used with permission.

Chapter 18

Opener: Ted S. Warren, Austin American-Statesman; **p. 407:** Ricardo Ferro, *St. Petersburg Times;* **p. 412:** Christobal Perez, *The News & Observer;* **p. 414:** Lloyd B. Cunningham, *Argus Leader.*

Chapter 19

Opener: Dave McDermand, *The Bryan-College Station Eagle;* **p. 431:** R. L. Chambers.

Chapter 20

Opener: Richard Green, *The Californian;* **p. 438:** Rodolfo Gonzales, *San Antonio Light;* **p. 440:** Diana K. Sugg; **p. 443:** Rodger Mallison, *Fort Worth Star-Telegram;* **p. 449:** O. Gordon Williamson Jr., *The Orlando Sentinel;* **p. 456:** Donna Ferrato, Domestic Abuse Awareness Project; **p. 462:** Jeff Widener, *Evansville Press.*

Chapter 21

Opener: Philip Kamrass, *Times Union;* **p. 481:** Nancy Stone, *The Plain Dealer;* **p. 484:** Maurice Rivenbank, *St. Petersburg Times.*

Chapter 22

Opener: Bob Zellar, The Billings Gazette; **p. 497:** Mike Roemer; **p. 498:** Andrew D. Bernstein, NBA photo; **p. 507:** Morris Berman, Pittsburgh Post-Gazette; **p. 510:** Joel Sartore, The Wichita Eagle Beacon; **p. 514:** Bob Thayer, The Journal Bulletin.

Chapter 23

Opener: Mike Roemer; **p. 523:** Mike Roemer; **p. 524:** Vivian Marino; **p. 527 (top and bottom):** Josh Estey, *The Register Guard.*

Chapter 24

Opener: Mike Roemer; **p. 552 (upper left):** The Plumas County Museum; **p. 552 (upper right):** Larry C. Price, *The Philadelphia Inquirer Magazine;* **p. 552 (bottom):** Mel Finkelstein, © *New York Daily News, Inc.;* **p. 570:** Maurice Rivenbank, *St. Petersburg Times;* **p. 574:** James Woodcock, *The Billings Gazette;* **p. 576:** Mike Roemer, *Argus Leader.*

Chapter 25

Opener: Dave McDermand, *The Bryan-College Station Eagle.*

Chapter 26

Opener: Susan Watts, *Daily News;* **p. 615 (top):** Pascal Pavani, Associated Press; **p. 615 (bottom):** Darko Bandic, Associated Press; **p. 617:** John Harte, *The Bakersfield Californian.*

Chapter 27

p. 640: Scripps Howard Awards.

Name Index

A

Aaron, Hank, 512, 516
ABC, 3, 20, 31, 64, 71, 230, 334
ABC News, xvii, 401, 594, 595, 640
Abdul-Jabbar, Kareem, 498, 512
Abel, Elie, 325
Abilene Reporter-News, xxiii
Acta Diurna, 65, 67
Adams, George, 502–503
Adams, John Quincy, 165
The Adventures of Huckleberry Finn,
        33–35, 573
The Adversary Press, 643
Advisory Commission on
        Intergovernmental Relations, 560
The Affluent Society, 543
Afghanistan, 32, 42, 102
Agee, James, 290, 292
Agnew, Spiro, 387
AIDS, 3, 5, 24, 609, 610, 629
Akron (Ohio) *Beacon Journa*l, xx, 559
Alabama, 71, 572, 574
The Alabama Journal (Montgomery), xx
Alabiso, Vincent, 36
Alberts, James, 33
Albom, Mitch, 513
The Albuquerque (N.M.) *Tribune,*
        xx, 640
Alexander, Ames, 83
Alexander, Jack, 366
Alexander, Jan, 314
Alexander, S. L., 494
The Algiers Motel Incident, 267
Ali, Muhammad, 333, 501, 508
Alice's Adventures in Wonderland, 161
Alkofer, Bill, xxii

All the President's Men, 36
Allen, Everett, 151
Allen, Glenna, 195
Allport, Gordon, 393
Almond, Steven, 290–291
Alonso, Luis Minguel, 260
Alsop, Joseph, Jr., 625
AltaVista, 94
Alvarez, Maria T., xx
Ambrose, Stephen, 240, 554
American, 389
American Bankruptcy Institute, 532
        www.abiworld.org, 532
American Business Editors and
        Writers, 534
*The American Character: Views of
        America from The Wall Street
        Journal,* 218
American Civil Liberties Union,
        227, 612
*The American Conversation and the
        Language of Journalism,* 188
American Express, 533
American Family Association, 614
American Heritage Center, 217
The American Medical Association, 456
American Mercury, 294–295
American Opinion, 587
*The American Press and the Covering of
        the Holocaust,* 279, 292
American Red Cross, 8, 54
*The American Schola*r, 500
American Society of Newspaper Editors,
        278, 496, 601–602
American Urban Radio Network, 71
The American Way of Death, 434
Ames (Iowa) *Daily Tribune,* 369

Among Schoolchildren, 578
Amsterdam News, 71
Anchorage Daily News, xx
*And So It Goes: Adventures in
        Television,* 243
Anderson, Daniel, 32
Anderson, David, 519
Anderson, Gloria Brown, 577
Anderson, Paul Y., 390, 637
Anderson, Walter, 52
Andrews, Peter, 501
Angell, Roger, 509–510, 519
Angelou, Maya, 573
The Anniston (Ala.) *Star,* xx, 83, 261,
        323, 461–462, 556
Anti-Defamation League, 572
Antonen, Mel, 358
The APF Reporter, 260
Apple, R.W., 604
Arcaro, Eddie, 350, 513
*Areopagitica, A Speech for the Liberty of
        Unlicensed Printing,* 98
Argentina, 533, 637
Argus Leader (Sioux Falls, S.D.), xvii,
        xxii, 5–9, 25, 70–71, 317, 414,
        442, 491, 523, 529–531, 575–576
Aristophanes, 192, 295
Aristotle, 41, 642
Arizona, 574
Arizona Daily Star (Tucson), 603
The Arizona Republic, xvii, 183
Arkansas, 9, 574
Arlen, Michael J., 243
Armour, Stephanie, 148–149
Armstrong, Ken, 74
Arnett, Peter, 41
Arnold, Marjorie, xvi

I

Boyden, Helen Childs, 425
Boyle, Hal, 154
The Boys of Summer, 518, 519
The Boys on the Bus, 267
Bradlee, Benjamin C., xiii, xix, 80, 259
Bradley, Joseph B., 394
Bragg, Rick, 120–121, 155–157, 181, 469–470
Brandeis, Louis, 486
Branzburg v. Hayes, 598
The Brattleboro (Vt.) *Reformer,* 378
Braxton, Toni, 533
Breaking the News: How the Media Undermine American Democracy, 644
Brecher, Elinor J., 457
Breckenridge, Patti, 94
Breed, Warren, 642
Brennan, William J., 585, 586, 598
Bridgeman, P.W., 162
Brill's Content, 82, 515, 539, 611
Brink, William, 178–179
Brisbane, Arthur, 172
Britt, Bonnie, 490
Broadcast Newswriting: The RTNDA Reference Guide, 243
Broadcasting, xxi
Brody, Jane E., 141–142
Brokaw, Tom, 588–589
Brookings Institution, 309
Brown v. Board of Education, Topeka, 296, 585
Brown, Anne Wiggins, 341
Brown, Cailin, 18–19
Brown, Heather, 13
Brown, Kevin, 516
Brown, Les, 342
Brown, Peter, 627
Brown, Tyrone, 601
Browne, Malcolm W., 41, 185
Brubaker, Herb, 230
Brustein, Robert, 639
Bryan, D. Tennant, 430–431
Bryant, Bear, 590
Buchanan, Charles, 283
Buchanan, Edna, 57, 121, 129, 159, 173, 435, 444, 457, 458, 464
Buchanan, Pat, 340
Buchwald, Art, 218
Buckingham, Jane Rinzler, 84
Buckley, Priscilla, 394
Buckowski, Paul, xxiii
Bucks County (Pa.) *Courier Times,* xvi, 469
Buenos Aires Herald, 637

Buri, Sherri, 526–527
Burnham, David, 76
Burroughs, William, 164
Buruma, Ian, 72
Bush, George, 50, 368
Bush, George W., 42, 49, 82, 264, 298, 368, 492, 555, 591, 608, 634
Business Information Sources, 543
Business Week, 535
But We Were Born Free, 54
Butts, Wally, 590

C

Calibeo, Thomas E., 538
California, 574
The Californian, 435
Calley, William, 277
Callison, Jill, 7
The Camera Age: Essays on Television, 243
Campbell, Carroll A., 277
Campbell, Cole C., 126–127
Campbell, Steve, 199
Campbell, Will, 627
Camus, Albert, xii
Cannon, Jimmy, 505–506, 514
Cantrell v. Forest City Publishing Co., 593
Capote, Truman, 349, 364, 464
Cappiello, Dina, 77
Cappon, Jack, 173
Carey, Art, xvi, 209, 409
Carlin, George, 613
Carrel, Todd, 31
Carrol, Lewis, 138
Carson, Rachel, 238
Carswell, Harrold, 340
Carter, Bill, 44
Carter, Shawn, 468
Casey, John, 571
Cassidy, John, 151
Caster, Alfred, 229
Castro, Fidel, 278–279
Cataffo, Linda, 2
The Catcher in the Rye, 113, 573
Catledge, Turner, S-13
Cato Institute, 309
" 'Cave Man' Meets 'Student Champion': Sports Page Storytelling for a Nervous Generation During America's Jazz Age.", 496
CBS, 22, 32, 71, 102, 222, 226, 240, 242, 301, 633

"CBS Evening News", 223, 236, 242, 331
Center for New Media, 89
Cenziper, Debbie, 76, 93, 210
Cerf, Bennett, 364–365
Chaffee, Zechariah Jr., 602
Challenger, 71, 163
Chamberlain, Wilt, 498
Chambers, Marcia, xvi, 299–301, 382
Chambers, R.L., 165, 431
Chancellor, John W., 60, 113, 116
Channel 4000, xxi
  wcco.com, xxi
Channel One, 569
Charkins, Ralph James, 522
The Charleston (W. Va.) *Gazette,* xx, 83
The Charlotte (N.C.) *Observer,* xvi, xvii, xix, 72, 76, 83, 84, 85–86, 93, 114, 149–150, 193–194, 195–196, 210, 405, 413, 495, 511, 633
Chekhov, Anton, 162, 285–286, 639
Chemical Banking Corp., 540
Cheney, Dick, 342, 608
Cheney, Lynn, 342
Chevron, 640
Chiason, Lloyd Jr., 494
Chicago, 539
Chicago American, 253–254
The Chicago Daily News, 566
Chicago, Ill., 28, 74
Chicago Sun-Times, xvii, 606
Chicago Tribune, xi, xx, xxi, 67, 74, 83, 97, 132, 155, 172, 310, 488, 510, 606–607
Chicago Tribune Press Service, 91
The Chief: The Life of William Randolph Hearst, 218
"Children: The Forgotten Farmworkers", 390–391
China, 56, 65, 72
China Misperceived: American Illusions and Chinese Reality, 250
The Christian Science Monitor, 134, 303, 333, 611
Chronicle (San Francisco), 513
The Chronicle of Higher Education, 340, 608
Chung, Connie, 331
Churchill, Winston, 319
Chusmir, Janet, xix
Ciardi, John, 131, 157, 187
Cicero, 177–178
Cincotta, Gale, 211
Citizen Hearst, 191
Civil War, 191, 635

KGUN-TV (Tucson), xviii, 242
KHOU-TV, xxi
Kidd, Jason, 501
Kidder, Tracy, 578
Kidnapped, 188
Kilgore, Barney, 525
Kim, Byung Hyun, 498
Kimball, Penn, 243
King Lear, 241
King of the World: Muhammad Ali and the Rise of an American Hero, 519
King, Billie Jean, 513
King, John, 634
King, Joseph Jr., 354–355
King, Larry, 634
King, Laura, 567
King, Martin Luther, Jr., 583, 610
King, Rodney, 485
King, Stephen, 154, 164
King, Wayne, 131
KING-TV (Seattle), xxi
The Kingdom and the Power, 36
Kinsey, Alfred C., 610
Kissel, Kelly P., 5, 9–11
Kissinger, Henry, 333
KIVA-TV (El Paso), 184
Klein, Frederick C., 504
Kline, Joel, 337
Klinkenberg, Jeff, xvii, 306
Klotzbach, Ken, 6, 8
Kluge, Pamela Hollie, 543
Kluger, Richard, 189
Kmart, 527
KMOV (St. Louis), xxi
KMTW-TV (Auburn, Maine), xxi
KNAU-FM (Flagstaff, Ariz.), 238
Kneeland, Carole Kent, 241–242
Knight-Ridder, 78, 83, 149, 218
The Knoxville News-Sentinel, 68, 254
KNX-AM, xxi
KNXT-TV (Los Angeles), xxi
Koch, Edward, 49, 208
Kolata, Gina, 297–298
KOTV (Tulsa), xviii, 237–238
Koufax, Sandy, 512
Kovach, Bill, 28, 48, 99, 267, 325, 635, 644
KPIX-TV (San Francisco), xxi
KPNX-TV (Phoenix, Ariz.), 235–236
KPRC-TV, xviii
Krajicek, David J., 457, 464
Krajick, Kevin, 312–313, 621–624, 631, 633
Kramer, Joel, 369

Kranz, David, 6–7, 9
Kretchmer, Stanley, 45
Kristol, Irving, 273, 296, 552
KRLD-AM (Dallas), xviii
Kroeger, Brooke, 36
KRON-TV (San Francisco), xviii, xxi, 256
KSBW-TV (Salinas, Calif.), xviii
KSEE-TV (Fresno, Calif.), xviii
KSL-TV, xviii
KTRH-AM (Houston), xviii, 237
KTUL-TV (Tulsa), xviii
KTUX-TV (Salt Lake City), xviii
KTVK-TV (Phoenix, Ariz.), 242
KTVS-TV (Detroit), xviii
Ku Klux Klan, 3, 108, 257, 302, 353, 478, 638
Kumar, Stanley, 51
Kundera, Milan, 639
Kunkel, Thomas, 83, 87
Kuralt, Charles, 226, 241
KVUE-TV (Austin, Tex.), xviii, 241, 242, 445
KWWL-TV (Waterloo, Iowa), xviii
KWY-TV, xviii
KXAS-TV (Dallas), 591
KXLY-TV (Spokane), xviii
KXTV (Sacramento), xviii

L

Labistida, Francisco, 303
Lack, Andrew, 242
Lahser, Robert, 150
Landauer, Jerry, 387
Landers, Ann, 203
Landi, Joe, 370
Lange, Dorothea, 293, 642
Language in Thought and Action, 402
The Language of Prejudice, 393
LaPeter, Leonora Bohen, 122–123
Lardner, Mike, 517
Lardner, Ring, 164, 389
Las Vegas, Nev., 26
Lasch, Christopher, 252, 634
Lass, Abraham H., 426
Late City Edition, 192
Latza, Greg, xxii
Law Dictionary for Non-Lawyers, 590, 602
Lawlor, Eric, xvii, 197, 199, 205
Lazio, Rick, 251–252
Le Carré, John, 319–320
Leach, John, xvii, 183
League of Women Voters, 560

Leaving Readers Behind: The Age of Corporate Journalism, 83, 87
The Ledger, (Lakeland, Fla.), 640
Lee, Irving, 393
Lee, Patrick, 98
Lee, Spike, 171
Leinwand, Donna, 432
Leland, Elizabeth, xvii, 195–196
Lennon, John, 332
"Leonore No. 3", 56
Leonard, Benny, 508
Leonard, Buck, 507
Leonard, Elmore, 340
Lester, Will, 42
"Let Us Now Appraise Famous Writers":, 364
Let Us Now Praise Famous Men, 290, 292
Letterman, David, 524
Levi, Primo, 180
Lewinsky, Monica, 44, 81, 369, 401, 595, 604
Lewis, Anthony, 304, 602
Lewis, Oscar, 286, 362
Lewis, Tony, 259
Lexington (Ky.) *Herald-Leader,* 194–195, 319–320, 588
Lexis-Nexis, 95
Libel Manual, 607
Liberty, 602
Liddy, Chuck, xxiii
Liebling, A. J., 39, 61, 330, 350
Liebling, Joe, 82
Life, 594, 607
Lilienfield, Robert, 60, 252
Lincoln, Rosemary, 465
Lindbergh, Charles, 485
Lindsay, John, 112, 561
Lino, Pat, 247
Lippmann, Walter, 57, 251, 281, 310, 393, 402
Lipson, Steve, 536
Lipstadt, Deborah E., 279, 292
Lipsyte, Robert, 501
Little Rock, Ark., 335–336
Little, Carl Victor, 111
Lockhart, Michael, 355
Loercher, Diana, 333
Loh, Jules, 192, 372
Lombardi, Vince, 507, 512, 513
Long, Earl K., 336, 340
Loomis, Carol, 533
Lorentz, Pare, 642
Los Alamos, 40
Los Angeles, 28

Subject Index

D

E

F

G

H

M

Magazine-story formula, 209
Magazines, 84, 124, 305, 315
Malice, actual, 585–586, 590
Mascots, 394–395
Math skills, 101–104, 540–541
Means/modes/medians, 105–106
Media events, 250
Media manipulation, 251–254
Meeting stories, 374, 377
    checklists, 377–378
Memory, 364, 387
Metaphors, 228
Mill levy, 562
Miranda warning, 446–447
Misspelling, 60, 91, 165–166, 187,
    249, 266
Mistakes, 35, 39–40, 49, 60, 165, 187,
    269, 429, 586, 590
Mobile workstation, 90
Morgue (newspaper), 254
Movement, 171
Muckrakers, 389–390, 635–636
Mug shots, 451
Multiple-element stories, 134, 140–142
Municipal Bonds, 537, 545, 564
Murder stories, 14–16, 31, 271, 437,
    438, 448–449

N

Names, 145, 295, 319, 408–409, 416,
    418, 458
Narrative style, 129
Native Americans, 394–395
Necessity, 64, 74
Neighborhood stories, 567
New Journalism, 176, 182
New media, 89–91
News, 66
    as a business, 78–81, 81–83, 634
    as entertainment, x, 39, 66–67,
        190, 242
    guidelines, 68
    nature of, 3
    ownership, 81–83, 192
    relative, 77–86
    serious, 20
News conference stories, 248, 374,
    380–383, 384
    checklists, 383
News element, 145
News events, 293, 305
News features, 125, 190, 201–206
    broadcast, 232
    delayed leads, 122, 125, 190

News Filters, 41–42, 43
News gathering, 65
News groups, 96
News interviews, 326–327, 337–339
News library, 34, 49, 254, 266, 301, 305,
    319, 330, 416
News peg, 163, 190, 326
News point, 124–125, 129
News values, 64–87
    conflict, 64, 71–72
    currency, 64, 73–74
    impact, 64, 69–70
    necessity , 64, 74–77
    prominence , 64, 70
    proximity, 64, 70–71
    timeliness, 64, 68–69
    unusual events, 64, 72
Newsbook, 65
Newsletters, 65
Newsreaders, 229
Newsworthiness, 64, 74, 291,
    592–593, 629
No bill, 474
No comment, 349
Notes, 363
Nouns, 136, 166, 168, 179, 187
Number crunching, 96–97
Nut graph, 143, 209

O

Obituaries, 132–133, 145, 416–434, 629
    advanced, 429
    causes of death, 432–433
    checklists, 418
    embarrassing material, 430–431
    frequently asked questions,
        429–434
    humor , 425
    leads, 132–133, 429, 433
    localizing, 433
    online, 418
    paid, 427
    sources, 419–421
    suicide, 433
    verification, 430
Objectivity, 38, 53–55, 64, 180, 204, 528
Obscenity, 603, 608–609
    laws, 612
Observation, 43, 268–292, 360–361,
    397, 510
    direct/firsthand, 38, 41, 43, 44–45,
        172, 246, 248
    participant, 283–286
    second-and thirdhand accounts, 42–44
    unobtrusive, 282

Occupation, 145, 319, 332, 416, 418, 458
Offensive language, 603, 612
Ombudsman, 616
Omission, 56–57, 633–634
On/off the record, 47, 253, 364–365
Online evaluation, 315
Online journalism, xvi, 48, 68, 183
    libel, 591–592
Online leads, 121
Opinion, 50, 596
Opportunities, 521
Ordinances, 545
Overwriting, 205
Ownership, 81–83

P

Panel discussions, 383–384
Paper trail, 316
Parallel structure, 169
Paraphrasing, 175, 204, 366, 368,
    379, 604
Participant observation, 283–286
Penny papers, 65, 191
Percentages, 102, 528, S-5
Peremptory challenge, 478
Persistence, 28
Photojournalism, 603, 616–619, 623, 642
Place, 169
Plea bargaining, 465, 475–477
Polar alternatives, 399
Police reporting, 9–11, 14–16, 241–242,
    435–464
    arrest process, 446–449
    burglary and robbery, 452
    campus crime, 459–461
    cautions and warnings, 458–459
    checklists, 451–452
    crime classification, 449
    databases, 453–454
    domestic violence, 456–457
    felonies, 444
    juvenile, 236, 438, 458
    leads, 129
    murder, 450–451, 454–455
    police, 439–442
    rape, 455
    rates, 436–437, 442, 450, 455,
        459–460
    sources, 444
    victims, 454–455
Political stories, 544–565
Polling, 88, 107–110, 252, 595
Pornography, 605
Predictions, 401
Prepositions, 166

Present tense, 219
Press kit, 249
Press releases, 33–34, 246, 250, 381, 382, 539, 541, 542
Pressure groups, 548–549
Privacy, 581, 592–595, 600, 623, 629
   calculated falsehoods, 593
   difference from libel, 592–593
   guidelines, 594, 596
   hidden devices, 594–595
   Times Doctrine, 592
Private figures, 587–588
Privilege, 581, 589, 596
Prizes and awards, xii, xiii, xx–xxi, 75, 238, 257
   Pulitzer Prizes, xii, xiii, xx–xxi, 24, 28, 75, 99, 129, 151, 169, 182, 192, 193, 262, 272, 277, 279, 316, 325, 424, 453, 628, 634, 636–637
Profanity, 603, 608–609, 613
Profiles, 205, 435, 440, 495
   interviewing, 326, 328, 339–346
   miniprofile, 343–346
Prominence, 64, 85, 419, 427, 603
Pronouncers, 228
Pronouns, 166, 168
Proximity, 64, 70–71
Pseudo-events, 250–251
Pseudo-sources, 309
Public officials, 587
Public records, 25, 41, 48–49, 88, 98, 305–306, 316, 601
Public relations, 252
Public service journalism, xi–xii, 83, 623, 634, 635, 636
Puff pieces, 527
Punctuation, 91, 167

Q

Questions, asking, 28, 326, 328, 331–335, 358–360, 405
Quotations, 38, 47, 140, 153, 158–160, 163, 172, 174–176, 199–200, 204, 209, 309, 323, 331, 335, 338–339, 340–342, 363, 365–368, 407, 426, 495, 505, 601, 608
   guidelines, 366
   literal, 367–368
Quote lead, 119, 158

R

Race, S-5
Racism, 97, 211–213, 302, 392, 394–395, 489–490, 636, 638–640

Radio, 68, 183, 229
Rap sheet, 301
Rape, 475, 593, 610–611, 629
Rapport, 330
Rates, 103–104, 516, 528, 629
   crime, 436–437, 442, 450, 455, 459–460
   education, 574
   gangs, 438
   infant mortality, 100–101
   murder, 104, 450, 454–455
   pedestrian accidents, 408
   rape, 453, 455–456
Readability, 111, 168
   leads, 133–134, 134–135
Readers, 2, 206, 268, 324
Reading, 35, 184, 293, 324, 505
   recommended books, 35–36, 60–61, 87, 109–110, 136, 152, 188–189, 218, 243, 267, 292, 304, 325, 349, 373, 402, 434, 464, 494, 519, 543, 578, 602, 643–644
   recommended business publications, 534–535
Records, public, 25, 41, 48–49, 88, 98, 305–306, 309, 316, 601
Redlining, 211–213
Reference books, 88, 91–93, 305, 330, 416, 535
Regulatory agencies, 535–536
Religion reporting, 149–150
Reporters
   and the law, 581
   appearance and behavior, 352–353
   beats, 57, 77, 85, 293, 308–309, 404–405
   characteristics, xii–xiii, 2, 27–29
   computer-assisted, 313
   environmental, 75–76
   in-depth, 55
   investigative, 385
   math skills, 101–104, 295, 303, 540–541
   skills for covering business, 528–529
Reporting, 246–267, 339
   accidents, 406–415
   broadcast, 183–184, 219–232, 250–251
   computer-assisted, 25–26, 27, 96–97, 258, 263, 567
   court, 465–494
   crime/police, 9–11, 14–16, 241–242, 249, 435–464
   depth, 541
   disaster stories, 3–4, 6–9, 31, 410–414

   education, 146–147, 544, 551, 567–578
   environmental, 237–238
   fires, 435
   government, 544–565
   interpretive, 248, 520
   investigative, 22–23, 30, 246, 260–263, 435, 634
   Layer I, 247–254, 255
   Layer II, 247–249, 250, 255–260
   Layer III, 247–249, 263–265
   Live In, 286–289, 290
   meetings, 374, 377–380
   news conferences, 248, 374, 380–383, 384
   obituaries, 145, 416–434, 629
   religion, 149–150
   sports, 495–519
   war, 31–32
   weather, 112, 128
Reportorial enterprise, 246, 248
Resolutions, 545
Responsibility, 59, 64, 630
Reverse directory, 91
Rewriting, 186–187
Riots, 42–44
Roundup, 134

S

S-V-O sentence structure, 111, 131–133, 136
Said, 164
Scandals, 65
Scoops, 30, 66
Scope, 521–522
   business news, 521–522
Scripts , 222–225, 234–235, 236–237
Search engines, 94–95, 305
Secondhand account observation, 41–42, 44
Segregation, 582–584, 607
Selectivity, 57
Sentences, 187
   compound, 133
   length, 133–134, 167–168, 169
   S-V-O structure, 111, 131–133, 136, 225, 231, 243
Series, 190, 213–216, 317
   investigative, 216–218, 317
Serious news, 20
Sexism, 395–396, S-6
Sexual harassment, 237
Sexuality, 609–610
Shadow reality, 392–393
Shield laws, 599–600, 602

tive inertial forces were present (conversion plant, autocratic plant manager), participation between leaders and constituents as equals was less (e.g., fewer challenges by constituents, more leader-led discussion, and more constituent approval-seeking). When these inertial forces were absent (STS since start-up, participative plant manager), constituents assumed a more assertive and equal role in communication (e.g., more constituent-led discussion and challenges of leader assertions and fewer leader control attempts).

Using the Ellis (1979) coding scheme, Dugan (1989) used relational control analysis to study control patterns in performance feedback sessions. As indicated in the feedback section, she found that when attributions were based on a lack of constituent ability, leaders resisted and constituents complied with their partners' attempts to control. When attributions were based in constituents' lack of effort, leaders and constituents alternated in their attempts to control the relationship and were significantly more likely to comply with the other's structuring attempts. Attributional shifts, agreements about performance, and salary increases were associated with the more negotiated lack of effort condition.

Operant Models of Effective Supervision

A second line of interactional research is grounded in the theory of operant conditioning (Honig & Stadden, 1977; Skinner, 1974). Komaki and her colleagues have developed an operant model of effective supervision to explain what leaders do to motivate their constituents to perform consistently especially for tasks requiring coordination (Komaki, 1986, 1998; Komaki, Zlotnick, & Jensen, 1986). Komaki makes a tripartite distinction between three categories of supervisory communication. Performance antecedents occur before performance and involve the communication of expectations via instructions, rules, training, or goals. Performance monitoring occurs during or after performance and involves the

gathering of performance information through work sampling and inquiries. Performance consequences occur during or after performance and involve communicating knowledge about performance in the form of feedback, recognition, or corrections. Central to this model is the notion that effective leaders go beyond providing performance antecedents to both monitor and provide consequences in a timely fashion.

Komaki (1998) reviewed 18 studies conducted over the past several years that test various aspects of her model. This review reports on a triangulation between field and laboratory studies, intercultural studies, and field sites as diverse as sailboat competitions, police organizations, insurance firms, newspapers, construction sites, and government offices. Tests of the model reveal that effective leaders spend more time monitoring and providing consequences than their lackluster counterparts (Brewer, Wilson, & Beck, 1994; Komaki, 1986; Komaki, Desselles, & Bowman, 1989). Work sampling is the most frequent type of performance monitoring used, and a variety of reinforcers (positive, negative, and neutral) form the consequences. Moreover, it is monitoring combined with consequences that is crucial to effectiveness (Brewer, 1995; Larson & Callahan, 1990). Lackluster leaders not only spend less time monitoring and providing consequences, but they are more likely to spend time alone or be passive participants by failing to steer the conversation toward performance-related discussion (Komaki, 1998).

More recent tests of the model have focused on the timing of the antecedent-monitoring-consequence (AMC) sequence where effective leaders have been found to deliver the AMC sequence quickly (Komaki, 1998). In contrast, lackluster leaders belabor their instructions, become distracted by discussions of work minutia, fail to participate fully in work discussions, or leave the scene to do their own work. Addressing the issue of why performance monitoring and consequences are effective, Komaki and colleagues (Goltz, 1993; Komaki, 1998; Komaki & Citera, 1990) found that monitoring stimulated constituents to talk about their own performance. This prompted leaders to continue monitoring or provide consequences. In contrast to providing performance antecedents to constituents, performance monitoring increases the likelihood that discussions of the constituents' performance were specific and focused rather than vague and general.

New Directions: Individual Concerns and Cognitive Outcomes

Systems-interactional research is carefully designed and uses sophisticated methods to study communication (Schnell & Sims, 1993). However, relational control and performance-monitoring studies can be a narrow basis on which to understand leadership communication. With respect to Komaki's work, Schnell and Sims (1993) note some potential confusion between the three categories of supervisory communication (antecedents, monitors, and consequences). For example, asking questions about how work is done or why it was done in a particular way (performance monitor) could be perceived as an evaluation (consequence) especially if the work is highly autonomous and involves singular outcomes.

Similar validity questions have been raised about relational coding (Folger, Hewes, & Poole, 1984) where the issue boils down to a simple question: Would a participant in the interaction code an utterance the same way that an observer would? Research in this area distinguishes between construct validity based on the culturally recognized functions of language versus validity based on private and idiosyncratic meanings (Folger et al., 1984). Systems-interactional research employs the former since cultural meanings often prefigure private interpretations (Sigman, 1987, 1992), and queries are not made about individual interpretations (Folger, 1991; Newell & Stutman, 1991).

Nevertheless, systems-interactional research neglects the private experiential side of discourse and its threefold impact. First, personal and cultural interpretations of discourse may diverge. However, coding across numerous messages and attention to how the coding scheme might play out in specific organizational contexts could minimize this problem. For example, Fairhurst (1990) modified the "backchannel" code from Courtright et al. (1989) to Fairhurst et al. (1995) for precisely this reason. Komaki's (1998) attention to context is most apparent in the evolution of her coding of consequences, particularly those delivered directly versus indirectly and the range of effectiveness measures that she employs. Second is the even more damaging fact that a focus on individual interpretations will reveal some segments of discourse as more important than others. This runs counter to the systems-interactional assumption that every message is like every other message and given equal weight. Third, prospective and retrospective summaries and judgments of discourse are the self-conscious, social cognitive basis of action. As argued, much can be learned about why people act as they do based on how they interpret the behaviors of the interactional systems of which they are a part. Although systems-interactional coding schemes must continue their coding of language at a culturally recognizable level to retain a measure of efficiency in the coding process (thereby accepting the first two points as limitations), more research such as by Dugan (1989), Fairhurst et al. (1987), and Komaki (1998) would address the much needed focus on systems-interactional patterns and their cognitive outcomes.

CONCLUSION

This chapter is premised on a dualistic reframing of the leadership communication literature. Wherever possible, I have sought to represent the complexities of the dualisms and the nuanced positions that may reflect this. For example, multiple operationalizations of system characterize the individual-system dualism. A meaning-centered view of communication is represented as surface and deep-structure systems of meaning such as in the discussion of influence tactics. Early symbolic views of leadership (Bennis & Nanus, 1985; Pfeffer, 1981; Pondy, 1978) are characterized as both transmissional and meaning centered because managers are the primary symbolizing agents. These are just a few examples.

Because "either-or" thinking about key dualisms often surfaces in research, this style of thinking mitigates against adopting a "both-and" orientation.[11] However, both the individual and the system are constitutive elements of leadership. Both transmission and meaning are necessary elements of the communication process. Likewise, both cognitive outcomes and conversational practices must be studied to understand the communicative management of leadership fully.

Each of the five research programs reviewed tends to favor one side of the dualism; its counterpart was used to push the research agenda toward a more complex view of the subject. This analysis revealed that there is still much to learn about leader-constituent influence, feedback processes, charisma and vision, leader-member exchange, and systems-interactional functioning.

And it is here that this review of the leadership communication literature ends with a call not to abandon individualistic, psychological approaches in the study of influence tactics, feedback, or charisma, but to embrace more fully systemic approaches. Alternatively, leader-member exchange and systems-interactional leadership research should not be satisfied with its relational systems orientation, but should more fully embrace wider systems and individualistic concerns. When this is done, and when communication is conceived of more complexly (as both transmission and meaning) and studied more complexly (as both cognitive outcomes and conversational

practices), there will be even greater strides in our understanding of the communication between leaders and their constituents.

NOTES

1. The terms *dualism, duality, dialectic,* and *dichotomy* appear to be used differently by different scholars (e.g., Giddens, 1984; Werner & Baxter, 1994). My use of the term dualism is necessarily very broad to capture wide-ranging tensions within the literature (e.g., both epistemological and ontological). I use the term dualism to characterize two opposing influences making no generalizable assumptions about independence, simultaneity, or possible unification.

2. Jacques Derrida (1976) and other postmodernists offer several criticisms of oppositional or dualistic thinking. First, language creates meaning, and because interpretations of language are highly context sensitive, meaning should be endlessly deferred (hence Derrida's notion of *différance*). Second, positions that reflect mixed or compromise stances between opposites are often ignored, effectively removing the ambiguities and complexities that exist in the space between dichotomous ends. Third, dualistic thinking is inevitably hierarchical where one end is defined only in terms of the dimensions salient to the dominant end (Collins, 1986). However, postmodernists also use dualistic thinking as a heuristic—as a form of deconstruction rather than as presumed sedimented oppositional forms.

3. The work of Leslie Baxter and colleagues (Baxter & Montgomery, 1996; Werner & Baxter, 1994) was a significant influence in this regard.

4. Some programs of research are moving beyond the dyadic level of analysis to focus on group and organization levels (e.g., charisma, leader-member exchange).

5. See Barge (1994a), Rost (1991), and Smith and Peterson (1988) for discussions that analyze and critique these assumptions.

6. Other dualisms can certainly be named including the tension between theory and practice, a tension born of the view that much of what we know about leadership is not easily operationalized in practical settings (House & Aditya, 1997). There is also a tension between the study of leadership and management, and a tension that is based on the large number of studies (especially through the 1970s) that ignores senior-level leadership while focusing on lower- and middle-level managers whose only concern appears to be direct supervision of their immediate constituents (House & Aditya, 1997). While these and other dualisms can certainly be named, for purposes of this review (which is biased toward the dyadic) they play a less central role.

7. Bopp and Weeks (1984) made a related argument in family therapy.

8. As will become apparent, leader-member exchange is a notable exception. LMX takes a systems view, typically from a social cognitive perspective.

9. Though it may be argued that in the case of social desirability, the cultural is clearly at work. Unfortunately, there is often no way to know for sure because there is so little testing for social desirability.

10. Although I use the term *charismatic and visionary leadership,* Bryman (1993) refers to the charisma theories as "the new leadership theories," while House and Aditya (1997) use the term "neocharismatic theory." All generally refer to the same body of work beginning with House (1977) and Bass (1985).

11. Baxter and Montgomery (1996), among others, discuss a "both-and" orientation.

REFERENCES

Albright, M. D., & Levy, P. E. (1995). The effects of source credibility and performance rating discrepancy on reactions to multiple raters. *Journal of Applied Social Psychology, 25,* 577-600.

Altman, I., Vinsel, A., & Brown, B. B. (1981). Dialectic conceptions in social psychology: An application to social penetration and privacy regulation. In L. Berkowitz (Ed.), *Advances in experimental social psychology* (pp. 107-160). New York: Academic Press.

Ammons, R. B. (1956). Effects of knowledge of performance: A survey and tentative theoretical formulation. *Journal of General Psychology, 54,* 279-299.

Ansari, M. A., & Kapoor, A. (1987). Organizational context and upward influence tactics. *Organizational Behavior and Human Decision Processes, 40,* 39-49.

Antonioni, D. (1994). The effects of feedback accountability on upward appraisal ratings. *Personnel Psychology, 47,* 349-356.

Arkin, R. M., & Sheppard, J. A. (1990). Strategic self-presentation: An overview. In M. J. Cody & M. L. McLaughlin (Eds.), *The psychology of tactical communication* (pp. 175-193). Clevedon, UK: Multilingual Matters.

Ashford, S. J. (1986). Feedback-seeking in individual adaptation: A resource perspective. *Academy of Management Journal, 29,* 465-487.

Ashford, S. J., & Cummings. L. L. (1983). Feedback as an individual resource: Personal strategies of creating information. *Organizational Behavior and Human Performance, 32,* 370-398.

Ashford, S. J., & Northcraft, G. B. (1992). Conveying more (or less) than we realize: The role of impression-management in feedback seeking. *Organizational Behavior and Human Decision Processes, 53,* 310-334.

Ashford, S. J., & Tsui, A. S. (1991). Self-regulation for managerial effectiveness: The role of active feedback seeking. *Academy of Management Journal, 34,* 251-280.

Atwater, L. E., Roush, P., & Fischthal, A. (1995). The influence of upward feedback on self- and follower ratings of leadership. *Personnel Psychology, 48,* 35-59.

Atwater, L. E., & Waldman, D. A. (1998). Introduction: 360-degree feedback and leadership development. *Leadership Quarterly, 9,* 423-426.

Avolio, B. J., & Bass, B. M. (1988). Transformational leadership, charisma and beyond. In J. G. Hunt, B. R. Baglia, H. P. Dachler, & C. A. Schriesheim (Eds.), *Emerging leadership vistas* (pp. 29-50). Lexington, MA: Lexington Books.

Avolio, B. J., & Bass, B. M. (1995). Individual consideration viewed at multiple levels of analysis: A multi-level framework for examining the diffusion of transformational leadership. *Leadership Quarterly, 6,* 183-198.

Avolio, B. J., Howell, J. M., & Sosik, J. J. (1999). A funny thing happened on the way to the bottom line: Humor as a moderator of leadership style effects. *Academy of Management Journal, 42,* 219-227.

Avolio, B. J., Waldman, D. A., & Einstein, W. O. (1988). Transformational leadership in a management game simulation: Impacting the bottom line. *Group and Organization Studies, 13,* 59-80.

Awamleh, R., & Gardner, W. L. (1999). Perceptions of leader charisma and effectiveness: The effects of vision content, delivery, and organizational performance. *Leadership Quarterly, 10,* 345-374.

Baker, D. D., & Ganster, D. C. (1985). Leader communication style: A test of average versus vertical dyad linkage models. *Group and Organization Studies, 10,* 242-259.

Bandura, A. (1982). Self-efficacy: Mechanism in human agency. *American Psychologist, 37,* 122-147.

Bandura, A. (1986). *Social foundations of thought and action: A social cognitive theory.* Englewood Cliffs, NJ: Prentice Hall.

Bandura, A. (1991). Social cognitive theory of self-regulation. *Organizational Behavior and Human Decision Processes, 50,* 248-287.

Bandura, A., & Cervone, D. (1983). Self-evaluative and self-efficacy mechanisms governing the motivational effects of goal systems. *Journal of Personality and Social Psychology, 45,* 1017-1028.

Barclay, J. H., & Harland, L. K. (1995). Peer performance appraisals: The impact of rater competence, rater location, and rater correctability on fairness perceptions. *Group & Organization Management, 20,* 39-60.

Barge, J. K. (1994a). *Leadership: Communication skills for organizations and groups.* New York: St. Martin's.

Barge, J. K. (1994b). Putting leadership back to work. *Management Communication Quarterly, 8,* 95-109.

Barge, J. K., Downs, C. W., & Johnson, K. M. (1989). An analysis of effective and ineffective leader conversation. *Management Communication Quarterly, 2,* 357-386.

Barge, J. K., & Schleuter, D. W. (1991). Leadership as organizing: A critique of leadership instruments. *Management Communication Quarterly, 4,* 541-570.

Bargh, J. A. (1989). Conditional automasticity: Varieties of automatic influence in social perception and cognition. In J. S. Uleman & J. A. Bargh (Eds.), *Unintended thought* (pp. 3-51). New York: Guilford.

Baron, R. A. (1988). Negative effects of destructive criticism: Impact on conflict, self-efficacy, and task performance. *Journal of Applied Psychology, 73,* 199-207.

Baron, R. A. (1990). Countering the effects of destructive criticism: The relative efficacy of four interventions. *Journal of Applied Psychology, 75,* 235-245.

Barry, B., & Watson, M. R. (1996). Communication aspects of dyadic social influence: A review and integration of conceptual and empirical developments. In B. R. Burleson (Ed.), *Communication yearbook 19* (pp. 269-318). Thousand Oaks, CA: Sage.

Bartlett, C. A., & Ghoshal, S. (1994). Changing the role of top management: Beyond strategy to purpose. *Harvard Business Review, 72*(6), 79-88.

Bass, B. M. (1981). *Stogdill's handbook of leadership.* New York: Free Press.

Bass, B. M. (1985). *Leadership and performance: Beyond expectations.* New York: Free Press.

Bass, B. M. (1988). Evolving perspectives on charismatic leadership. In J. A. Conger & R. N. Kanungo (Eds.), *Charismatic leadership* (pp. 40-77). San Francisco: Jossey-Bass.

Bateson, G. (1972). *Steps to an ecology of the mind.* New York: Ballantine.

Bauer, T., & Green, S. G. (1996). The development of leader-member exchange: A longitudinal test. *Academy of Management Journal, 39,* 1538-1567.

Baum, J. R., Locke, E. A., & Kirkpatrick, S. A. (1998). A longitudinal study of the relation of vision and vision communication to venture growth in entrepreneurial firms. *Journal of Applied Psychology, 83,* 43-54.

Baxter, L. (1988). A dialectical perspective on communication strategies in relationship development. In S. Duck, D. Hay, S. Jobfoll, W. Ickes, & B. Montgomery (Eds.), *Handbook of personal relationships: Theory research, and interventions* (pp. 257-274). Chichester, UK: Wiley.

Baxter, L. (1990). Dialectical contradictions in relationship development. *Journal of Personal and Social Relationships, 7,* 69-88.

Baxter, L. (1992). Interpersonal communication as a dialogue: A response to the "social approaches" forum. *Communication Theory, 2,* 330-336.

Baxter, L. A., & Goldsmith, D. (1990). Cultural terms for communication events among some American high school adolescents. *Western Journal of Speech Communication, 54,* 377-394.

Baxter, L. A., & Montgomery, B. M. (1996). *Relating: Dialogue and dialectics.* New York: Guilford.

Baxter, L. A., & Willmott, W. (1984). Secret tests: Social strategies for acquiring information about the state of the relationship. *Human Communication Research, 11,* 171-201.

Becker, T. E., & Klimoski, R. J. (1989). A field study of the relationship between the organizational feedback environment and performance. *Personnel Psychology, 42,* 343-358.

Bennett, N., Herold, D. M., & Ashford, S. J. (1990). The effects of tolerance for ambiguity on feedback seeking behavior. *Journal of Occupational Psychology, 63,* 343-348.

Bennis, W. G., & Nanus, B. (1985). *Leaders: Strategies for taking charge.* New York: Harper & Row.

Benson, J. K. (1977). Organizations: A dialectical view. *Administrative Science Quarterly, 22,* 1-20.

Berger, P., & Luckmann, T. (1966). *The social construction of reality.* Garden City, NY: Anchor.

Bernardin, H. J., Dahmus, S. A., & Redmon, G. (1993). Attitudes of first-line supervisors toward subordinate appraisals. *Human Resource Management, 32,* 315-324.

Beyer, J. M. (1999). Taming and promoting charisma to change organizations. *Leadership Quarterly, 10,* 307-330.

Beyer, J. M., & Browning, L. D. (1999). Transforming an industry in crisis: Charisma, routinization, and supportive cultural leadership. *Leadership Quarterly, 10,* 483-520.

Bies, R. J., & Sitkin, S. B. (1992). Excuse-making in organizations: Explanation as legitimation. In M. L. McLaughlin, M. J. Cody, & S. Read (Eds.), *Explaining oneself to others: Reason giving in a social context* (pp. 183-198). Hillsdale, NJ: Lawrence Erlbaum.

Bizzell, P., & Herzberg, B. (Eds.). (1990). *The rhetorical tradition: Readings from classical times to the present.* Boston: Bedford/St. Martin's.

Bopp, M. J., & Weeks, G. R. (1984). Dialectical metatheory in family therapy. *Family Process, 23,* 49-61.

Borchgrevink, C. P., & Boster, F. J. (1994). Leader-member exchange: A test of the measurement model. *Hospitality Research Journal, 17,* 75-100.

Borchgrevink, C. P., & Donohue, W. A. (1991). *Leader-member exchange and power distance reduction theory.* Unpublished manuscript, Michigan State University.

Boyd, N. G., & Taylor, R. R. (1998). A developmental approach to the examination of friendship in leader-follower relationships. *Leadership Quarterly, 9,* 1-26.

Braaten, D. O., Cody, M. J., & DeTienne, K. B. (1993). Account episodes in organizations: Remedial work and impression management. *Management Communication Quarterly, 6,* 219-250.

Bradford, D. L., & Cohen, A. R. (1984). *Managing for excellence: The guide to developing high performance in contemporary organizations.* New York: John Wiley.

Brewer, N. (1995). The effects of monitoring individual and group performance on the distribution of effort across tasks. *Journal of Applied Social Psychology, 25,* 760-777.

Brewer, N., Wilson, C., & Beck, K. (1994). Supervisory behavior and team performance amongst police patrol sergeants. *Journal of Occupational and Organizational Psychology, 67,* 69-78.

Brook, P. (1968). *The empty space.* Markham, Ontario: Penguin.

Brown, D. J., & Lord, R. G. (1999). The utility of experimental research in the study of transformational/ charismatic leadership. *Leadership Quarterly, 10,* 531-540.

Brown, P., & Levinson, S. (1978). Universals in language usage: Politeness phenomena. In E. N. Goody (Ed.), *Questions and politeness: Strategies in social interactions* (pp. 56-289). Cambridge, UK: Cambridge University Press.

Bryman, A. (1992). *Charisma and leadership in organizations.* London: Sage.

Bryman, A. (1993). Charismatic leadership in business organizations: Some neglected issues. *Leadership Quarterly, 4,* 289-304.

Burke, K. (1954). Fact, inference, and proof in the analysis of literary symbolism. In L. Bryson (Ed.), *Symbols and values: An initial study* (Thirteenth Symposium of the Conference on Science, Philosophy, and Religion, pp. 283-306). New York: Harper.

Burke, K. (1957). *The philosophy of literary form.* New York: Vintage.

Burke, K. (1962). *A rhetoric of motives.* Berkeley: University of California Press.

Burns, J. M. (1978). *Leadership.* New York: Harper & Row.

Burns, T., & Stalker, G. M. (1961). *The management of innovation.* London: Tavistock.

Calás, M. B. (1993). Deconstructing charismatic leadership: Re-reading Weber from the darker side. *Leadership Quarterly, 4,* 305-328.

Callister, R. R., Kramer, M. W., & Turban, D. B. (1999). Feedback seeking following career transitions. *Academy of Management Journal, 42,* 429-438.

Case, T., Dosier, L., Murkison, G., & Keys, B. (1988). How managers influence superiors: A study of upward influence tactics. *Leadership and Organizational Development Journal, 9,* 25-31.

Cashman, J., Dansereau, F., Graen, G., & Haga, W. (1976). Organizational understructure and leadership: A longitudinal investigation of the managerial role-making process. *Organizational Behavior and Human Performance, 15,* 278-296.

Chacko, H. E. (1990). Methods of upward influence, motivational needs, and administrators' perceptions of their supervisors' leadership styles. *Group and Organization Studies, 15,* 253-265.

Cheng, J. L. C. (1983). Organizational context and upward influence: An experimental study of the use of power tactics. *Group and Organization Studies, 8,* 337-355.

Chiles, A. M., & Zorn, T. E. (1995). Empowerment in organizations: Employees' perceptions of the influences of empowerment. *Journal of Applied Communication Research, 23,* 1-25.

Church, A. H., & Bracken, D. W. (1997). Advancing the state of the art of 360-degree feedback. *Group & Organization Management, 22,* 149-161.

Clegg, S. (1975). *Power, rule, and domination: A critical and empirical understanding of power in sociological theory and organizational life.* London: Routledge and Kegan Paul.

Clegg, S. (1979). *The theory of power and organization.* London: Routledge and Kegan Paul.

Collins, J. C., & Porras, J. I. (1996). Building your company's vision. *Harvard Business Review, 74,* 65-77.

Collins, P. (1986). Learning from the outsider within: The sociological significance of black feminist thought. *Social Problems, 33,* S14-S32.

Conger, J. A. (1989). *The charismatic leader.* San Francisco: Jossey-Bass.

Conger, J. A. (1991). Inspiring others: The language of leadership. *The Executive, 5,* 31-45.

Conger, J. A. (1993). Max Weber's conceptualization of charismatic authority: Its influence on organizational research. *Leadership Quarterly, 4,* 277-288.

Conger, J. A. (1999). Charismatic and transformational leadership in organizations: An insider's perspective on these developing streams of research. *Leadership Quarterly, 10,* 145-180.

Conger, J. A., & Hunt, J. G. (1999). Charismatic and transformational leadership: Taking stock of the present and future. *Leadership Quarterly, 10,* 121-128.

Conger, J. A., & Kanungo, R. N. (1987). Toward a behavioral theory of charismatic leadership in organizational settings. *Academy of Management Review, 12,* 637-647.

Conger, J. A., & Kanungo, R. N. (1988). The empowerment process: Integrating theory and practice. *Academy of Management Review, 13,* 471-482.

Conger, J. A., & Kanungo, R. N. (1993, August). *A behavioral attribute measure of charismatic leadership in organizations.* Paper presented at the annual meeting of the Academy of Management, Atlanta, GA.

Conger, J. A., & Kanungo, R. N. (1998). *Charismatic leadership in organizations.* Thousand Oaks, CA: Sage.

Connell, I., & Galasinski, D. (1996, May). *Missioning democracy.* Paper presented at the annual meeting of the International Communication Association, Chicago.

Conrad, C. (1983). Organizational power: Faces and symbolic forms. In L. L. Putnam & M. E. Pacanowsky (Eds.), *Communication and organizations: An interpretive approach* (pp. 173-194). Beverly Hills, CA: Sage.

Cooperrider, D., Barrett, F., & Srivastva, S. (1995). Social construction and appreciative inquiry: A journey in organizational theory. In D. Hosking, P. Dachler, & K. Gergen (Eds.), *Management and organization: Relational alternatives to individualism* (pp. 157-200). Aldershot, UK: Avebury.

Corman, S. R., & Krizek, R. L. (1993). Accounting resources for organizational communication and individual differences in their use. *Management Communication Quarterly, 7*, 5-35.

Couch, C. J. (1989). From hell to utopia and back to hell. *Symbolic Interaction, 12*, 265-279.

Courtright, J. A., Fairhurst, G. T., & Rogers, L. E. (1989). Interaction patterns in organic and mechanistic systems. *Academy of Management Journal, 32*, 773-802.

Courtright, J. A., Millar, F. E., & Rogers-Millar, L. E. (1979). Domineeringness and dominance: A replication and expansion. *Communication Monographs, 46*, 179-192.

Cronen, V. E., Pearce, W. B., & Harris, L. M. (1982). The coordinated management of meaning: A theory of communication. In F. E. X. Dance (Ed.), *Human communication theory* (pp. 61-89). New York: Harper & Row.

Cusella, L. P. (1987). Feedback, motivation, and performance. In F. M. Jablin, L. L. Putnam, K. H. Roberts, & L. W. Porter (Eds.), *Handbook of organizational communication: An interdisciplinary perspective* (pp. 624-678). Newbury Park, CA: Sage.

Dansereau, F. (1995a). Leadership: The multiple-level approaches, Part 1. *Leadership Quarterly, 6*(2), 97-247.

Dansereau, F. (1995b). Leadership: The multiple-level approaches, Part 2. *Leadership Quarterly, 6*(3), 249-450.

Dansereau, F., Graen, G., & Haga, W. (1975). A vertical dyad linkage approach to leadership in formal organizations. *Organizational Behavior and Human Performance, 13*, 380-397.

Dansereau, F., Yammarino, F. J., & Markham, S. E. (1995). Leadership: The multiple-level approaches. *Leadership Quarterly, 6*, 97-109.

Davis-Blake, A., & Pfeffer, J. (1989). Just a mirage: The search for dispositional effects in organizational research. *Academy of Management Review, 14*, 385-400.

Deci, E. L. (1975). *Intrinsic motivation.* New York: Plenum.

Deetz, S. A. (1985). Critical-cultural research: New sensibilities and old realities. *Journal of Management, 11*, 121-136.

Deetz, S. A., & Kersten, A. (1983). Critical models of interpretive research. In L. L. Putnam & M. E. Pacanowsky (Eds.), *Communication and organizations: An interpretive approach* (pp. 147-171). Beverly Hills, CA: Sage.

Deluga, R. J. (1991a). The relationship of subordinate upward influence behavior, health care manager interpersonal stress, and performance. *Journal of Applied Psychology, 21*, 78-88.

Deluga, R. J. (1991b). The relationship of upward-influencing behavior with subordinate-impression management characteristics. *Journal of Applied Social Psychology, 21*, 1145-1160.

Deluga, R. J., & Perry, J. T. (1991). The relationship of subordinate upward influencing behavior, satisfaction, and perceived superior effectiveness with leader-member exchanges. *Journal of Occupational Psychology, 64*, 239-252.

Deming, W. E. (1982). *Out of the crisis.* Cambridge, UK: Cambridge University Press.

Den Hartog, D. N., & Verburg, R. M. (1997). Charisma and rhetoric: Communicative techniques of international business leaders. *Leadership Quarterly, 8*, 355-392.

DePree, M. (1993). *Leadership jazz.* New York: Doubleday.

Derrida, J. (1976). *Grammatolgie* (G. C. Spivak, Trans.). Baltimore: Johns Hopkins University Press.

DiTomaso, N. (1993). Weber's social history and Etzioni's structural theory of charisma in organizations: Implications for thinking about charismatic leadership. *Leadership Quarterly, 4*, 257-276.

Dienesch, R. M., & Liden, R. C. (1986). Leader-member exchange model of leadership: A critique and further development. *Academy of Management Review, 11*, 618-634.

Dockery, T. M., & Steiner, D. D. (1990). The role of the initial interaction in leader-member exchange. *Group and Organization Studies, 15*, 395-413.

Dosier, L., Case, T., & Keys, B. (1988). How managers influence subordinates: An empirical study of downward influence tactics. *Leadership and Organizational Development Journal, 9*, 22-28.

Dow, T. E., Jr. (1969). The theory of charisma. *Sociological Quarterly, 10*, 306-318.

Doz, Y. L., & Prahalad, C. K. (1987). A process model of strategic redirection in large complex firms: The case of multinational corporations. In A. Pettigrew (Ed.), *The management of strategic change* (pp. 63-83). Oxford, UK: Basil Blackwell.

Drake, B. H., & Moberg, D. J. (1986). Communicating influence attempts in dyads: Linguistic sedatives and palliatives. *Academy of Management Review, 11*, 567-584.

Drecksel, G. L. (1991). Leadership research: Some issues. In J. A. Anderson (Ed.), *Communication yearbook 14* (pp. 535-546). Newbury Park, CA: Sage.

Duchon, D., Green, S., & Taber, T. (1986). Vertical dyad linkage: A longitudinal assessment of antecedents, measures, and consequences. *Journal of Applied Psychology, 71,* 56-60.

Dugan, K. W. (1989). Ability and effort attributions: Do they affect how managers communicate performance feedback information? *Academy of Management Journal, 32,* 87-114.

Dulebohn, J. H., & Ferris, G. R. (1999). The role of influence tactics in perceptions of performance evaluations' fairness. *Academy of Management Journal, 42,* 288-303.

Earley, P. C., Northcraft, G. B., Lee, C., & Lituchy, T. R. (1989). Impact of process and outcome feedback on the relation of goal-setting to task performance. *Academy of Management Journal, 33,* 87-105.

Ehrlich, S. B., Meindl, J. R., & Viellieu, B. (1990). The charismatic appeal of a transformational leader: An empirical case study of a small high-technology contractor. *Leadership Quarterly, 1,* 229-248.

Eisenberg, E. M. (1990). Jamming: Transcendence through organizing. *Communication Research, 17,* 139-164.

Ellis, D. (1979). Relational control in two group systems. *Communication Monographs, 46,* 245-267.

Erez, M., Rim, Y., & Keider, I. (1986). The two sides of the tactics of influence: Agent vs. target. *Journal of Occupational Psychology, 59,* 25-39.

Facteau, C. L., Facteau, J. D., Schoel, L. C., Russell, J. E. A., & Poteet, M. L. (1998). Reactions of leaders to 360-degree feedback from subordinates and peers. *Leadership Quarterly, 9,* 427-448.

Fairhurst, G. T. (1990). *Supplemental coding rules and modification of the relational control coding scheme.* Unpublished manuscript, University of Cincinnati, Cincinnati, OH.

Fairhurst, G. T. (1991). *The leader-member exchange patterns of women leaders in industry.* Paper presented at the Society for Organizational Behavior, Albany, NY.

Fairhurst, G. T. (1993a). Echoes of the vision: When the rest of the organization talks Total Quality. *Management Communication Quarterly, 6,* 331-371.

Fairhurst, G. T. (1993b). The leader-member exchange patterns of women leaders in industry: A discourse analysis. *Communication Monographs, 60,* 321-351.

Fairhurst, G. T. (1996, May). *"Governing ideas" that really govern.* Paper presented at the annual meeting of the International Communication Association, Chicago.

Fairhurst, G. T., & Chandler, T. A. (1989). Social structure in leader-member interaction. *Communication Monographs, 56,* 215-239.

Fairhurst, G. T., Cooren, F., & Cahill, D. (2000). *A structuration approach to management policy in successive downsizings.* Paper presented at the National Communication Association Conference, Seattle, WA.

Fairhurst, G. T., Green, S. G., & Courtright, J. A. (1995). Inertial forces and the implementation of a sociotechnical systems approach: A communication study. *Organization Science, 6,* 168-185.

Fairhurst, G. T., Green, S. G., & Snavely, B. K. (1984a). Face support in controlling poor performance. *Human Communication Research, 11,* 272-295.

Fairhurst, G. T., Green, S. G., & Snavely, B. K. (1984b). Managerial control and discipline: Whips and chains. In R. Bostrom (Ed.), *Communication yearbook 8* (pp. 558-593). Beverly Hills, CA: Sage.

Fairhurst, G. T., Jordan, J. M., & Neuwirth, K. (1997). Why are we here? Managing the meaning of an organizational mission. *Journal of Applied Communication Research, 25,* 243-263.

Fairhurst, G. T., Rogers, L. E., & Sarr, R. A. (1987). Manager-subordinate control patterns and judgments about the relationship. In M. McLaughlin (Ed.), *Communication yearbook 10* (pp. 395-415). Newbury Park, CA: Sage.

Fairhurst, G. T., & Sarr, R. A. (1996). *The art of framing: Managing the language of leadership.* San Francisco: Jossey-Bass.

Falbe, C. M., & Yukl, G. (1992). Consequences for managers of using single influence tactics and combinations of tactics. *Academy of Management Journal, 35,* 638-652.

Farmer, S. M., Maslyn, J. M., Fedor, D. B., & Goodman, J. S. (1997). Putting upward influence strategies in context. *Journal of Organizational Behavior, 18,* 17-42.

Fedor, D. B. (1990). *Feedback recipients' responses to negative feedback: Investigating the role of uncertainty.* Paper presented at the fifth annual conference of the Society for Industrial and Organizational Psychology, Miami, FL.

Fedor, D. B. (1991). Recipient responses to performance feedback: A proposed model and its implications. In G. R. Ferris & K. M. Rowland (Eds.), *Research in personnel and human resources management* (Vol. 9, pp. 73-120). Greenwich, CT: JAI.

Fedor, D. B., Rensvold, R. G., & Adams, S. M. (1992). An investigation of factors expected to affect feedback seeking: A longitudinal field study. *Personnel Psychology, 45,* 779-805.

Ferris, G. R., Judge, T. A., Rowland, K. M., & Fitzgibbons, D. E. (1994). Subordinate influence and the performance evaluation process: Test of a model. *Organizational Behavior and Human Decision Processes, 58,* 101-135.

Fine, G. (1992). Agency, structure, and comparative contexts: Toward a synthetic interactionism. *Symbolic Interaction, 15,* 87-107.

Fiol, C. M., Harris, D., & House, R. (1999). Charismatic leadership: Strategies for effecting social change. *Leadership Quarterly, 10,* 449-482.

Fisher, B. A. (1978). *Perspectives on human communication.* New York: Macmillan.

Fisher, B. A. (1985). Leadership as medium: Treating complexity in group communication research. *Small Group Behavior, 16,* 167-196.

Fisher, B. A. (1986). Leadership: When does the difference make a difference? In R. Hirokawa & M. S. Poole (Eds.), *Communication and group decision-making* (pp. 197-215). Beverly Hills, CA: Sage.

Fiske, S. T., & Taylor, S. E. (1991). *Social cognition.* New York: McGraw-Hill.

Fleishman, E. A. (1953). The description of supervisory behavior. *Journal of Applied Psychology, 37,* 1-6.

Florin-Thuma, B. C., & Boudreau, J. W. (1987). Performance feedback utility in a small organization: Effects on organizational outcomes and managerial decision processes. *Personnel Psychology, 40,* 693-713.

Folger, J. P. (1991). Interpretive and structural claims about confrontations. In J. A. Anderson (Ed.), *Communication yearbook 14* (pp. 393-402). Newbury Park, CA: Sage.

Folger, J. P., Hewes, D., & Poole, M. S. (1984). Coding social interaction. In B. Dervin & M. J. Voight (Eds.), *Progress in communication sciences* (Vol. 4, pp. 115-161). Norwood, NJ: Ablex.

Frost, P. J. (1987). Power, politics, and influence. In F. M. Jablin, L. L. Putnam, K. H. Roberts, & L. W. Porter (Eds.), *Handbook of organizational communication: An interdisciplinary perspective* (pp. 503-548). Newbury Park, CA: Sage.

Frost, P. J., Moore, L. F., Louis, M. R., Lundberg, C. C., & Martin, J. (1991). *Reframing organizational culture.* Newbury Park, CA: Sage.

Funderburg, S. A., & Levy, P. E. (1997). The influence of individual and contextual variables on 360-degree feedback system attitudes. *Group & Organization Management, 22,* 210-235.

Gardner, W. L., & Avolio, B. J. (1998). The charismatic relationship: A dramaturgical perspective. *Academy of Management Review, 23,* 32-58.

Garko, M. G. (1992). Persuading subordinates who communicate in attractive and unattractive styles. *Management Communication Quarterly, 5,* 289-315.

Gavin, M. B., Green, S. G., & Fairhurst, G. T. (1995). Managerial control strategies for poor performance over time and the impact on subordinate and manager reactions. *Organizational Behavior and Human Decision Processes, 63,* 207-221.

Geddes, D. (1993). Examining the dimensionality of performance feedback messages: Source and recipient perceptions of influence attempts. *Communication Studies, 44,* 200-215.

Geddes, D., & Baron, R. A. (1997). Workplace aggression as a consequence of negative performance feedback. *Management Communication Quarterly, 10,* 433-454.

Geddes, D., & Linnehan, F. (1998). Exploring the dimensionality of positive and negative performance feedback. *Communication Quarterly, 44,* 326-344.

Gergen, K. J. (1985). The social constructionist movement in modern psychology. *American Psychologist, 40,* 266-275.

Gerstner, C. R., & Day, D. V. (1997). Meta-analytic review of leader-member exchange theory: Correlates and construct issues. *Journal of Applied Psychology, 82,* 827-844.

Giddens, A. (1979). *Central problems in social theory: Action, structure, and contradiction in social analysis.* London: Macmillan.

Giddens, A. (1984). *The constitution of society.* Berkeley: University of California Press.

Gioia, D. A., & Longenecker, C. O. (1994). Delving into the dark side: The politics of executive appraisal. *Organizational Dynamics, 22,* 47-58.

Gioia, D. A., & Sims, H. P., Jr. (1986). Cognition-behavior connections: Attribution and verbal behavior in leader-subordinate interactions. *Organizational Behavior and Human Decision Processes, 37,* 197-229.

Goltz, S. M. (1993). Dynamics of leaders' and subordinates' performance-related discussions following monitoring by leaders in group meetings. *Leadership Quarterly, 4,* 173-187.

Graen, G. B. (1989). *Unwritten rules for your career: 15 secrets for fast-track success.* New York: John Wiley.

Graen, G. B., & Cashman, J. (1975). A role-making model of leadership in formal organizations: A developmental approach. In J. G. Hunt & L. L. Larson (Eds.), *Leadership frontiers* (pp. 143-166). Kent, OH: Kent State University Press.

Graen, G., Cashman, J. F., Ginsburg, S., & Schiemann, W. (1977). Effects of linking-pin quality on the quality of working life of lower participants. *Administrative Science Quarterly, 22,* 491-504.

Graen, G. B., Novak, M., & Sommerkamp, P. (1982). The effects of leader-member exchange and job design on productivity and satisfaction: Testing a dual attachment model. *Organizational Behavior and Human Performance, 30,* 109-131.

Graen, G. B., & Scandura, T. (1987). Toward a psychology of dyadic organizing. In B. Staw & L. L. Cummings (Eds.), *Research in organizational behavior* (Vol. 9, pp. 175-208). Greenwich, CT: JAI.

Graen, G. B., Scandura, T. A., & Graen, M. R. (1986). A field experimental test of the moderating effects of growth need strength on productivity. *Journal of Applied Psychology, 71,* 484-491.

Graen, G. B., & Uhl-Bien, M. (1991). The transformation of professionals into self-managing and partially self-designing contributors: Towards a theory of leadership making. *Journal of Management Systems, 3,* 33-48.

Graen, G. B., & Uhl-Bien, M. (1995). Relationship-based approach to leadership: Development of a leader-member exchange (LMX) theory of leadership over 25 years—Applying a multi-level multi-domain perspective. *Leadership Quarterly, 6,* 219-247.

Graen, G. B., & Wakabayashi, M. (1994). Cross-cultural leadership-making: Bridging American and Japanese diversity for team advantage. In H. C. Triandis, M. D. Dunnette, & L. M. Hough (Eds.), *Handbook of industrial and organizational psychology* (Vol. 4, pp. 415-446). New York: Consulting Psychologists Press.

Graen, G. B., Wakabayashi, M., Graen, M. R., & Graen, M. G. (1990). International generalizability of American hypothesis about Japanese management progress: A strong inference investigation. *Leadership Quarterly, 1,* 1-11.

Graham, J. W. (1991). Servant-leadership in organizations: Inspirational and moral. *Leadership Quarterly, 2,* 105-119.

Green, S. G., Fairhurst, G. T., & Snavely, B. K. (1986). Chains of poor performance and supervisory control. *Organizational Behavior and Human Decision Processes, 38,* 7-27.

Greguras, G. J., & Robie, C. (1998). A new look at within-source interrater reliability of 360-degree feedback ratings. *Journal of Applied Psychology, 83,* 960-968.

Greller, M. M., & Herold, D. M. (1975). Sources of feedback: A preliminary investigation. *Organizational Behavior and Human Performance, 13,* 244-256.

Hanser, L. M., & Muchinsky, P. M. (1978). Work as an information environment. *Organizational Behavior and Human Performance, 21,* 47-60.

Harper, N. L., & Hirokawa, R. Y. (1988). A comparison of persuasive strategies used by female and male managers: An examination of downward influence. *Communication Quarterly, 36,* 157-168.

Haslett, B. J. (1987). *Communication: Strategic action in context.* Hillsdale, NJ: Lawrence Erlbaum.

Hater, J. J., & Bass, B. M. (1988). Superiors' evaluations and subordinates' perceptions of transformational and transactional leadership. *Journal of Applied Psychology, 73,* 695-702.

Hazucha, J. F., Hezlett, S. A., & Schneider, R. J. (1993). The impact of 360-degree feedback on management skills development. *Human Resource Management, 32,* 325-351.

Hemphill, J. K., & Coons, A. E. (1957). Development of the Leader Behavior Description Questionnaire. In R. M. Stogdill & A. E. Coons (Eds.), *Leader behavior: Its description and measurement.* Columbus: Ohio State University, Bureau of Business Research.

Herold, D. M., & Greller, M. M. (1977). Feedback: The development of a construct. *Academy of Management Journal, 20,* 142-147.

Herold, D. M., Liden, R. C., & Leatherwood, M. L. (1987). Using multiple attributes to assess source of performance feedback. *Academy of Management Journal, 30,* 826-835.

Hewes, D. E., & Planalp, S. (1987). The individual's place in communication science. In C. R. Berger & S. H. Chaffee (Eds.), *Handbook of communication science* (pp. 146-183). Newbury Park, CA: Sage.

Hirokawa, R. Y., Kodama, R. A., & Harper, N. L. (1990). Impact of managerial power on persuasive strategy selection by female and male managers. *Management Communication Quarterly, 4,* 30-50.

Hirokawa, R. Y., & Miyahara, A. (1986). A comparison of influence strategies utilized by managers in American and Japanese Organizations. *Communication Quarterly, 34,* 250-265.

Hofstede, G. (1981). *Culture's consequences: International differences in work-related values.* Beverly Hills, CA: Sage.

Holladay, S. J., & Coombs, W. T. (1993). Communicating visions: An exploration of the role of delivery in the creation of leader charisma. *Management Communication Quarterly, 6,* 405-427.

Holladay, S. J., & Coombs, W. T. (1994). Speaking of visions and visions being spoken: An exploration of the effects of content and delivery on perceptions of leader charisma. *Management Communication Quarterly, 8,* 165-189.

Honig, W. K., & Stadden, J. E. R. (1977). *Handbook of operant behavior.* Englewood Cliffs, NJ: Prentice Hall.

Hosking, D. M., & Morley, I. E. (1988). The skills of leadership. In J. G. Hunt, B. R. Baglia, H. P. Dachler, & C. A. Schriesheim (Eds.), *Emerging leadership vistas* (pp. 89-106). Lexington, MA: Lexington Books.

House, R. J. (1977). A 1976 theory of charismatic leadership. In J. G. Hunt & L. L. Larson (Eds.), *Leadership: The cutting edge* (pp. 189-207). Carbondale: Southern Illinois University Press.

House, R. J., & Aditya, R. (1997). The social scientific study of leadership: Quo vadis? *Journal of Management, 23,* 409-473.

House, R. J., & Howell, J. M. (1992). Personality and charismatic leadership. *Leadership Quarterly, 3,* 81-108.

House, R. J., Spangler, W. D., & Woycke, J. (1991). Personality and charisma in the U.S. presidency: A psychological theory of leader effectiveness. *Administrative Science Quarterly, 36,* 364-396.

Howell, J. M., & Frost, P. J. (1989). A laboratory study of charismatic leadership. *Organizational Behavior and Human Decision Processes, 43,* 243-269.

Howell, J. M., & Higgins, C. A. (1990a). Champions of technological innovation. *Administrative Science Quarterly, 35,* 317-341.

Howell, J. M., & Higgins, C. A. (1990b). Leadership behaviors, influence tactics, and career experiences of champions of technological innovation. *Leadership Quarterly, 1,* 249-264.

Hui, C., & Graen, G. (1997). Guanxi and professional leadership in contemporary Sino-American joint ventures in Mainland China. *Leadership Quarterly, 8,* 451-466.

Hunt, J. G. (1999). Transformational/charismatic leadership's transformation of the field: An historical essay. *Leadership Quarterly, 10,* 129-143.

Hunt, J. G., Boal, K. B., & Dodge, G. E. (1999). The effects of visionary and crisis-responsive charisma on followers: An experimental examination of two kinds of charismatic leadership. *Leadership Quarterly, 10,* 423-448.

Hunt, J. G., & Conger, J. A. (1999). From where we sit: An assessment of transformational and charismatic leadership research. *Leadership Quarterly, 10,* 335-344.

Huspek, M., & Kendall, K. E. (1991). On withholding political voice: An analysis of the political vocabulary of a "nonpolitical" speech community. *Quarterly Journal of Speech, 77,* 1-19.

Ilgen, D. R., Fisher, C. D., & Taylor, M. S. (1979). Consequences of individual feedback on behavior in organizations. *Journal of Applied Psychology, 64,* 359-371.

Isaacs, W. N. (1993). Taking flight: Dialogue, collective thinking, and organizational learning. *Organizational Dynamics, 22,* 24-39.

Isaacs, W. N. (1999). *Dialogue: The art of thinking together.* New York: Currency.

Jablin, F. M. (1987). Organizational entry, assimilation, and exit. In F. M. Jablin, L. L. Putnam, K. H. Roberts, & L. W. Porter (Eds.), *Handbook of organizational communication: An interdisciplinary perspective* (pp. 679-740). Newbury Park, CA: Sage.

Jacobs, T. (1971). *Leadership and exchange in formal organizations.* Alexandria, VA: Human Resources Research Organization.

Jermier, J. M. (1993). Charismatic leadership: Neo-Weberian perspectives. *Leadership Quarterly, 4,* 217-412.

Jermier, J. M., Knights, D., & Nord, W. R. (1994). *Resistance and power in organizations.* London: Routledge.

Katz, D., & Kahn, R. L. (1978). *The social psychology of organizations* (2nd ed.). New York: John Wiley.

Keller, T., & Dansereau, F. (1995). Leadership and empowerment: A social exchange perspective. *Human Relations, 48,* 127-145.

Kellermann, K., & Cole, T. (1994). Classifying compliance messages: Taxonomic disorder and strategic confusion. *Communication Theory, 4,* 3-60.

Kerr, S., & Jermier, J. M. (1978). Substitutes for leadership: Their meaning and measurement. *Organizational Behavior and Human Performance, 22,* 375-403.

Kim, Y. Y., & Miller, K. I. (1990). The effects of attributions and feedback goals on the generation of supervisory feedback message strategies. *Management Communication Quarterly, 4,* 6-29.

Kipnis, D., & Schmidt, S. M. (1982). *Profiles of organizational influence strategies.* Toronto, Canada: University Associates.

Kipnis, D., & Schmidt, S. M. (1985). The language of persuasion. *Psychology Today, 42,* 40-46.

Kipnis, D., & Schmidt, S. M. (1988). Upward-influence styles: Relationship with performance evaluations, salary, and stress. *Administrative Science Quarterly, 33,* 528-542.

Kipnis, D., Schmidt, S. M., Swaffin-Smith, C., & Wilkinson, L. (1984). Patterns of managerial influence strategies: Shotgun managers, tacticians, and bystanders. *Organizational Dynamics, 12,* 58-67.

Kipnis, D., Schmidt, S. M., & Wilkinson, I. (1980). Intra-organizational influence tactics: Explorations in getting one's way. *Journal of Applied Psychology, 65,* 440-452.

Kirkpatrick, S. A., & Locke, E. A. (1996). Direct and indirect effects of three core charismatic leadership components on performance and attitudes. *Journal of Applied Psychology, 81,* 36-51.

Klein, K. J., & House, R. J. (1995). On fire: Charismatic leadership and levels of analysis. *Leadership Quarterly, 6,* 183-198.

Kluger, A. N., & DeNisi, A. (1996). The effects of feedback interventions on performance: A historical review, a meta-analysis, and a preliminary feedback intervention theory. *Psychological Bulletin, 119,* 254-284.

Kluger, A. N., Lewinsohn, S., & Aiello, J. R. (1994). The influence of feedback on mood: Linear effects on pleasantness and curvilinear effects on arousal. *Organizational Behavior and Human Decision Processes, 60,* 276-299.

Knapp, M. L., Miller, G. R., & Fudge, K. (1994). Background and current trends in the study of interpersonal communication. In M. L. Knapp & G. R. Miller (Eds.), *Handbook of interpersonal communication* (2nd ed., pp. 3-20). Thousand Oaks, CA: Sage.

Kolb, D. M., & Putnam, L. L. (1992). The dialectics of disputing. In D. M. Kolb & J. M. Bartunek (Eds.), *Hidden conflicts in organizations* (pp. 1-31). Newbury Park, CA: Sage.

Komaki, J. L. (1986). Toward effective supervision: An operant analysis and comparison of managers at work. *Journal of Applied Psychology, 71,* 270-278.

Komaki, J. L. (1998). *Leadership from an operant perspective.* London: Routledge.

Komaki, J. L., & Citera, M. (1990). Beyond effective supervision: Identifying key interactions between superior and subordinate. *Leadership Quarterly, 1,* 91-106.

Komaki, J. L., Desselles, M. L., & Bowman, E. D. (1989). Definitely not a breeze: Extending an operant model of effective supervision to teams. *Journal of Applied Psychology, 74*, 522-529.

Komaki, J. L., Zlotnick, S., & Jensen, M. J. (1986). Development of an operant-based taxonomy and observational index. *Journal of Applied Psychology, 71*, 260-269.

Korsgaard, M. A., Meglino, B. M., & Lester, S. W. (1997). Beyond helping: Do other-oriented values have broader implications in organizations? *Journal of Applied Psychology, 82*, 160-177.

Kotter, J. P. (1990). *A force for change: How leadership differs from management.* New York: Free Press.

Kouzes, J. M., & Posner, B. Z. (1993). *Credibility: How leaders gain and lose it, why people demand it.* San Francisco: Jossey-Bass.

Kouzes, J. M., & Posner, B. Z. (1995). *The leadership challenge.* San Francisco: Jossey-Bass.

Kramer, M. W. (1995). A longitudinal study of superior-subordinate communication during job transfers. *Human Communication Research, 22*, 39-64.

Krone, K. J. (1991). Effects of leader-member exchange on subordinates' upward influence attempts. *Communication Research Reports, 8*, 9-18.

Kuhnert, K. W., & Lewis, P. (1987). Transactional and transformational leadership: A constructive/developmental analysis. *Academy of Management Review, 12*, 648-657.

Lannamann, J. W. (1991). Interpersonal communication research as ideological practice. *Communication Theory, 1*, 179-203.

Larson, J. R., Jr. (1989). The dynamic interplay between employees' feedback-seeking strategies and supervisors' delivery of performance feedback. *Academy of Management Review, 14*, 408-422.

Larson, J. R., Jr., & Callahan, C. (1990). Performance monitoring: How it affects work productivity. *Journal of Applied Psychology, 75*, 530-538.

Larson, J. R., Jr., Glynn, M. A., Fleenor, C. P., & Scontrino, M. P. (1987). Exploring the dimensionality of managers' performance feedback to subordinates. *Human Relations, 39*, 1083-1102.

Larwood, L., Falbe, C. M., Kriger, M. P., & Miesing, P. (1995). Structure and meaning of organizational vision. *Academy of Management Journal, 38*, 740-769.

Larwood, L., Kriger, M. P., & Falbe, C. M. (1993). Organizational vision: An investigation of the vision construct-in-use of AACSB Business School deans. *Group & Organization Management, 18*, 214-236.

Latham, G. P., & Locke, E. A. (1991). Self-regulation through goal-setting. *Organizational Behavior and Human Decision Processes, 50*, 212-247.

Lauterbach, K. E., & Weiner, B. J. (1996). Dynamics of upward influence: How male and female managers get their way. *Leadership Quarterly, 7*, 87-108.

Lee, J. (1997). Leader-member exchange, the "Pelz effect," and cooperative communication between group members. *Management Communication Quarterly, 11*, 266-287.

Lee, J., & Jablin, F. M. (1995). Maintenance communication in superior-subordinate work relationships. *Human Communication Research, 22*, 220-257.

Ledford, G. E., Jr., Wendenhof, J. R., & Strahley, J. T. (1995). Realizing a corporate philosophy. *Organizational Dynamics, 23*, 5-19.

Leont'ev, A. N. (1978). *Activity, consciousness and personality.* Englewood Cliffs, NJ: Prentice Hall.

Levine, S. (1949). An approach of constructive leadership. *Journal of Social Issues, 5*, 46-53.

Levy, P. E., Albright, M. D., Cawley, B. D., & Williams, J. R. (1995). Situational and individual determinants of feedback seeking: A closer look at the process. *Organizational Behavior and Human Decision Processes, 62*, 23-37.

Liden, R. C., & Maslyn, J. M. (1998). Multidimensionality of leader-member exchange: An empirical assessment through scale development. *Journal of Management, 24*, 43-72.

Liden, R. C., & Mitchell, T. R. (1989). Ingratiation in the development of leader-member exchanges. In R. A. Giacalone & P. Rosenfeld (Eds.), *Impression management in the organization* (pp. 343-361). Hillsdale, NJ: Lawrence Erlbaum.

Liden, R. C., Sparrowe, R. T., & Wayne, S. J. (1997). Leader-member exchange theory: The past and potential for the future. In G. R. Ferris (Ed.), *Research in personnel and human resources management* (Vol. 15, pp. 47-119). Greenwich, CT: JAI.

Liden, R. C., Wayne, S. J., & Stilwell, D. (1993). A longitudinal study on the early development of leader-member exchange. *Journal of Applied Psychology, 78*, 662-674.

Likert, R. (1961). *New patterns of management.* New York: McGraw-Hill.

Littlejohn, S. W. (1983). *Theories of human communication* (2nd ed.). Belmont, CA: Wadsworth.

Locke, E. A., Frederick, E., Lee, C., & Bobko, P. (1984). Effect of self-efficacy, goals, and task strategies on task performance. *Journal of Applied Psychology, 69*, 694-699.

Locke, E. A., & Latham, G. P. (1990). *A theory of goal-setting and task performance.* Englewood Cliffs, NJ: Prentice Hall.

London, M., Smither, J. W., & Adsit, D. J. (1997). Accountability: The Achilles' heel of multisource feedback. *Group & Organization Management, 22*, 162-184.

Louie, T. A. (1999). Decision makers' hindsight bias after receiving favorable and unfavorable feedback. *Journal of Applied Psychology, 84*, 29-41.

Lowe, K. B., Kroeck, K. G., & Sivasubramaniam, N. (1996). Effectiveness correlates of transformational and transactional leadership: A meta-analytic review of the MLQ. *Leadership Quarterly, 7*, 385-425.

Mainiero, L. A. (1986). Coping with powerlessness: The relationship of gender and job dependency to empowerment strategy usage. *Administrative Science Quarterly, 31,* 633-653.

Manz, C. C., & Sims, H. P. (1987). Leading workers to lead themselves: The external leadership of self-managing work teams. *Administrative Science Quarterly, 32,* 106-128.

Manz, C. C., & Sims, H. P. (1989). *Super-leadership: Leading others to lead themselves.* New York: Prentice Hall.

Martin, J. (1992). *Cultures in organizations: Three perspectives.* Oxford, UK: Oxford University Press.

Martocchio, J. J., & Webster, J. (1992). Effects of feedback and cognitive playfulness on performance in microcomputer software training. *Personnel Psychology, 45,* 553-578.

Maslyn, J. M., Farmer, S. M., & Fedor, D. B. (1996). Failed upward influence attempts: Predicting the nature of subordinate persistence in pursuit of organizational goals. *Group & Organization Management, 21,* 461-480.

McPhee, R. D. (1988). Vertical communication changes: Toward an integrated approach. *Management Communication Quarterly, 1,* 455-493.

Meindl, J. R. (1990). On leadership: An alternative to conventional wisdom. In B. M. Staw & L. L. Cummings (Eds.), *Research in organizational behavior* (Vol. 12, pp. 159-203). Greenwich, CT: JAI.

Meindl, J. R., Ehrlich, S. B., & Dukerich, J. M. (1985). The romance of leadership. *Administrative Science Quarterly, 30,* 78-102.

Mento, A. J., Steel, R. P., & Karren, R. J. (1987). A meta-analytic study of the effects of goal-setting on task performance: 1966-1984. *Organizational Behavior and Human Decision Processes, 39,* 52-83.

Middleton, D., & Edwards, D. (1990). Introduction. In D. Middleton & D. Edwards (Eds.), *Collective remembering* (pp. 1-22). Newbury Park, CA: Sage.

Mintzberg, H. (1987, July-August). Crafting strategy. *Harvard Business Review, 65,* 66-75.

Montgomery, B. M. (1992). Communication as the interface between couples and culture. In S. A. Deetz (Ed.), *Communication yearbook 15* (pp. 475-507). Newbury Park, CA: Sage.

Morgan, G. (1986). *Images of organization.* Beverly Hills, CA: Sage.

Morris, G. H., & Coursey, M. (1989). Negotiating the meaning of employees' conduct: How managers evaluate employees' accounts. *Southern Communication Journal, 54,* 185-205.

Morris, G. H., Gaveras, S. C., Baker, W. L., & Coursey, M. L. (1990). Aligning actions at work: How managers confront problems of employee performance. *Management Communication Quarterly, 3,* 303-333.

Morrison, E. W., & Bies, R. J. (1991). Impression management in the feedback-seeking process: A literature review and research agenda. *Academy of Management Review, 16,* 522-541.

Nadler, D. A. (1988). Organizational frame bending: Types of change in complex organizations. In R. Kilmann & T. Covin (Eds.), *Corporate transformation: Revitalizing organizations for a competitive world* (pp. 66-84). San Francisco: Jossey-Bass.

Nanus, B. (1992). *Visionary leadership.* San Francisco: Jossey-Bass.

Newell, S. E., & Stutman, R. K. (1991, May). *Stalking culturally shared interpretations and restricted meanings in conflict episodes.* Paper presented at the International Communication Association Convention, Chicago.

Niehoff, B. P., & Moorman, R. H. (1993). Justice as a mediator of the relationship between methods of monitoring and organizational citizenship behavior. *Academy of Management Journal, 63,* 527-556.

Nisbett, R. E., & Wilson, T. (1977). Telling more than we can know: Verbal reports on mental processes. *Psychological Review, 84,* 231-259.

Northcraft, G. B., & Ashford, S. J. (1990). The preservation of self in everyday life: The effects of performance expectations and feedback context on feedback inquiry. *Organizational Behavior and Human Decision Processes, 47,* 42-64.

Northcraft, G. B., & Earley, P. C. (1989). Technology, credibility, and feedback use. *Organizational Behavior and Human Decision Processes, 44,* 83-96.

Nussbaum, B., Moskowitz, D. B., & Beam, A. (1985, January 12). The new corporate elite. *Business Week,* pp. 62-81.

O'Keefe, D. J. (1994). From strategy-based to feature-based analyses of compliance gaining message classification and production. *Communication Theory, 4,* 61-68.

Pawar, B. S., & Eastman, K. K. (1997). The nature and implications of contextual influences on transformational leadership: A conceptual examination. *Academy of Management Review, 22,* 80-109.

Peterson, M. F., & Sorenson, R. L. (1991). Cognitive processes in leadership: Interpreting and handling events in an organizational context. In J. A. Anderson (Ed.), *Communication yearbook 14* (pp. 501-534). Newbury Park, CA: Sage.

Pettigrew, A. M. (1979). On studying organizational cultures. *Administrative Science Quarterly, 24,* 570-581.

Pfeffer, J. (1981). Management as symbolic action: The creation and maintenance of organizational paradigms. In L. L. Cummings & B. M. Staw (Eds.), *Research in organizational behavior* (Vol. 3, pp. 1-52). Greenwich, CT: JAI.

Phillips, E. T. (1996). *Life cycle of project team effectiveness, from creation to conclusion, as a function of dyadic team composition: A naturally occurring field simulation.* Unpublished doctoral dissertation, University of Cincinnati, Cincinnati, OH.

Phillips, N. (1997). Bringing the organization back in: A comment on conceptualizations of power in upward influence research. *Journal of Organizational Behavior, 18,* 43-47.

Podsakoff, P. M., & Farh, J. L. (1989). Effects of feedback sign and credibility on goal-setting and task performance. *Organizational Behavior and Human Decision Processes, 44,* 45-67.

Pondy, L. R. (1978). Leadership is a language game. In M. W. McCall, Jr. & M. M. Lombardo (Eds.), *Leadership: Where else can we go?* (pp. 88-99). Durham, NC: Duke University Press.

Prasad, P. (1993). Symbolic processes in the implementation of technological change: A symbolic interactionist study of work computerization. *Academy of Management Journal, 36,* 1400-1429.

Putnam, L. L. (1983). An interpretive perspective: An alternative to functionalism. In L. L. Putnam & M. E. Pacanowsky (Eds.), *Communication and organizations: An interpretive approach* (pp. 31-54). Beverly Hills, CA: Sage.

Putnam, L. L., Phillips, N., & Chapman, P. (1996). Metaphors of communication and organization. In S. R. Clegg, C. Hardy, & W. R. Nord (Eds.), *Handbook of organization studies* (pp. 375-408). London: Sage.

Rawlins, W. K. (1992). *Friendship matters: Communication, dialectics, and the life course.* New York: Aldine.

Reilly, K. R., Smither, J. W., & Vasilopoulos, N. C. (1996). A longitudinal study of upward feedback. *Personnel Psychology, 49,* 599-612.

Ricoeur, P. (1971). The model of the text: Meaningful action considered as text. *Social Research, 38,* 529-562.

Riggio, R. E. (1987). *The charisma quotient: What it is, how to get it, and how to use it.* New York: Dodd, Mead and Company.

Riley, P. (1988). Chapter 4 commentary: The merger of macro and micro levels of leadership. In J. G. Hunt, B. R. Baglia, H. P. Dachler, & C. A. Schriesheim (Eds.), *Emerging leadership vistas* (pp. 80-83). Lexington, MA: Lexington Books.

Rogers, L. E., & Farace, R. V. (1975). Relational communication analysis: New measurement procedures. *Human Communication Research, 1,* 222-239.

Rogers, L. E., & Millar, F. E., & Bavelas, J. B. (1985). Methods for analyzing marital conflict discourse: Implications of a systems approach. *Family Process, 24,* 175-187.

Rogers-Millar, L. E., & Millar, F. E. (1979). Domineeringness and dominance: A transactional view. *Human Communication Research, 5,* 238-246.

Rogers, P. S., & Swales, J. M. (1990). We the people? An analysis of the Dana Corporation policies document. *Journal of Business Communication, 27,* 293-314.

Rost, J. C. (1991). *Leadership for the twenty-first century.* New York: Praeger.

Rychlak, J. F. (1977). *The psychology of rigorous humanism.* New York: John Wiley.

Salancik, G. R., & Pfeffer, J. (1977). Constraints on administrative discretion: The limited influence of mayors on city budgets. *Urban Affairs Quarterly, 12,* 485-498.

Sashkin, M., & Fulmer, R. (1988). Toward an organizational leadership theory. In J. G. Hunt, B. R. Baglia, H. P. Dachler, & C. A. Schriesheim (Eds.), *Emerging leadership vistas* (pp. 51-60). Lexington, MA: Lexington Books.

Scandura, T. (1995). *Leader-member exchange model of leadership and fairness issues.* Unpublished manuscript, University of Miami, Miami, FL.

Scandura, T. A., & Graen, G. B. (1984). Moderating effects of initial leader-member exchange status on the effects of a leadership intervention. *Journal of Applied Psychology, 69,* 428-436.

Scandura, T. A., Graen, G. B., & Novak, M. (1986). When managers decide not to decide autocratically. *Journal of Applied Psychology, 69,* 428-436.

Scheflen, A. E. (1974). *How behavior means.* Garden City, NY: Anchor.

Schein, E. H. (1992). *Organizational culture and leadership* (2nd ed.). San Francisco: Jossey-Bass.

Schiemann, W. A., & Graen, G. B. (1984). *Structural and interpersonal effects in patterns of managerial communication.* Unpublished manuscript, University of Cincinnati, Cincinnati, OH.

Schilit, W. K. (1987). Upward influence activity in strategic decision-making. *Group and Organization Studies, 12,* 343-368.

Schlenker, B. R. (1980). *Impression management: The self-concept, social identity, and interpersonal relations.* New York: Brooks/Cole.

Schmidt, S. M., & Kipnis, D. (1984). Managers' pursuit of individual and organizational goals. *Human Relations, 37,* 781-794.

Schnell, E. R., & Sims, H. P., Jr. (1993, August). *The language of leadership: A review of observational studies of leader verbal behavior.* Paper presented at the annual meeting of the Academy of Management Association, Atlanta, GA.

Schonbach, P. (1990). *Account episodes: The management or escalation of conflict.* Cambridge, UK: Cambridge University Press.

Schriesheim, C. A., Castro, S. L., & Cogliser, C. C. (1999). Leader-member exchange (LMX) research: A comprehensive review of theory, measurement, and data-analytic practices. *Leadership Quarterly, 10,* 63-114.

Schriesheim, C. A., Cogliser, C. C., & Neider, L. L. (1995). "Is it trustworthy?" A multiple levels-of-analysis reexamination of an Ohio State leadership study with implications for future research. *Leadership Quarterly, 6,* 111-145.

Schriesheim, C. A., & Hinkin, T. R. (1990). Influence tactics used by subordinates: A theoretical and empirical analysis and refinement of the Kipnis, Schmidt, and Wilkinson subscales. *Journal of Applied Psychology, 75,* 246-257.

Schriesheim, C. A., Neider, L. L., Scandura, T. A., & Tepper, B. J. (1992). Development and preliminary validation of a new scale (LMX-6) to measure leader-member exchange in organizations. *Educational and Psychological Measurement, 52,* 135-147.

Seeger, M. W. (Ed.). (1994). *"I gotta tell you": Speeches of Lee Iacocca.* Detroit, MI: Wayne State University Press.

Seers, A. (1989). Team-member exchange quality: A new construct for role-making research. *Organizational Behavior and Human Decision Processes, 43,* 118-135.

Senge, P. (1990). *The fifth discipline.* New York: Doubleday.

Senge, P., Kleiner, A., Roberts, C., Ross, R., Roth, G., & Smith, B. (1999). *The dance of change: The challenge to sustaining momentum in learning organizations.* New York: Doubleday.

Shamir, B., Arthur, M. B., & House, R. J. (1994). The rhetoric of charismatic leadership: A theoretical extension, a case study, and implications for research. *Leadership Quarterly, 5,* 25-42.

Shamir, B., House, R. J., & Arthur, M. B. (1993). The motivational effects of charismatic leadership: A self-concept based theory. *Organization Science, 4,* 577-594.

Shamir, B., & Howell, J. M. (1999). Organizational and contextual influences on the emergence and effectiveness of charismatic leadership. *Leadership Quarterly, 10,* 257-284.

Shea, C. M., & Howell, J. M. (1999). Charismatic leadership and task feedback: A laboratory study of their effects on self-efficacy and task performance. *Leadership Quarterly, 10,* 375-396.

Shotter, J. (1993). *Conversational realities: Constructing life through language.* London: Sage.

Sias, P. M. (1996). Constructing perceptions of differential treatment: An analysis of coworker discourse. *Communication Monographs, 63,* 171-187.

Sias, P. M., & Jablin, F. M. (1995). Differential superior-subordinate relations, perceptions of fairness, and coworker communication. *Human Communication Research, 22,* 5-38.

Siehl, C. (1985). After the founder: An opportunity to manage culture. In P. Frost, L. Moore, M. Louis, C. Lundberg, & J. Martin (Eds.), *Organizational culture* (pp. 125-140). Beverly Hills, CA: Sage.

Siehl, C., & Martin, J. (1984). The role of symbolic management: How can managers effectively transmit organizational culture? In J. G. Hunt, D. M. Hosking, C. A. Schriesheim, & R. Stewart (Eds.), *Leaders and managers: International perspectives on managerial behavior and leadership* (pp. 227-239). Elmsford, NY: Pergamon.

Sigman, S. J. (1987). *A perspective on social communication.* Lexington, MA: Lexington Books.

Sigman, S. J. (1992, May). *A social communication contribution to the micro-macro question.* Paper presented at the International Communication Association Convention, Miami, Miami, FL.

Sillars, S., & Scott, M. (1983). Interpersonal perception between intimates: An integrative review. *Human Communication Research, 10,* 153-176.

Skarlicki, D. P., & Folger, R. (1997). Retaliation in the workplace: The roles of distributive, procedural, and interactional justice. *Journal of Applied Psychology, 82,* 434-443.

Skinner, B. F. (1974). *About behaviorism.* New York: Vintage.

Smircich, L. (1983). Organizations as shared meanings. In L. Pondy, P. Frost, G. Morgan, & T. Dandridge (Eds.), *Organizational symbolism* (pp. 55-65). Greenwich, CT: JAI.

Smircich, L., & Morgan, G. (1982). Leadership: The management of meaning. *Journal of Applied Behavioral Science, 18,* 257-273.

Smith, P. B., & Peterson, M. F. (1988). *Leadership, organizations, and culture.* London: Sage.

Smither, J. W., London, M., Vasilopoulos, N. L., Reilly, R. R., Millsap, R. E., & Salvemini, N. (1995). An examination of the effects of an upward feedback program over time. *Personnel Psychology, 48,* 1-34.

Smither, J. W., Wohlers, A. J., & London, M. (1995). A field study of reactions to normative versus individualized upward feedback. *Group & Organization Management, 20,* 61-89.

Sparrowe, R. T. (1994). Empowerment in the hospitality industry: An exploration of antecedents and outcomes. *Hospitality Research Journal, 17,* 51-73.

Sparrowe, R. T., & Liden, R. C. (1997). Process and structure in leader-member exchange. *Academy of Management Review, 22,* 522-564.

Sullivan, J., & Taylor, S. (1991). A cross-cultural test of compliance-gaining theory. *Management Communication Quarterly, 5,* 220-239.

Sullivan, J. J., Albrecht, T. L., & Taylor, S. (1990). Process, organizational, relational, and personal determinants of managerial compliance-gaining communication strategies. *Journal of Business Communication, 4,* 331-355.

Swales, J. M., & Rogers, P. S. (1995). Discourse and the projection of corporate culture: The mission statement. *Discourse & Society, 6,* 223-242.

Swanson, E. B., & Ramiller, N. C. (1997). The organizing vision in information systems innovation. *Organization Science, 8,* 458-474.

Sypher, B. D. (1991). A message-centered approach to leadership. In J. A. Anderson (Ed.), *Communication yearbook 14* (pp. 547-559). Newbury Park, CA: Sage.

Tannenbaum, R., & Schmidt, W. H. (1958). How to choose a leadership pattern. *Harvard Business Review, 36,* 95-101.

Tedeschi, J. (1990). Self-presentation and social influence: An interactionist perspective. In M. J. Cody & M. L. McLaughlin (Eds.), *The psychology of tactical communication* (pp. 299-323). Clevedon, UK: Multilingual Matters.

Tepper, B. J. (1993). Patterns of downward influence and follower conformity in transactional and transformational leadership. In D. P. Moore (Ed.), *Academy of Management best papers proceedings* (pp. 267-271). Madison, WI: Omni.

Tepper, B. J., Eisenbach, R. J., Kirby, S. L., & Potter, P. W. (1998). Test of a justice-based model of subordinates' resistance to downward influence attempts. *Group & Organization Management, 23,* 144-160.

Thacker, R. A., & Wayne, S. J. (1995). An examination of the relationship of upward influence tactics and assessments of promotability. *Journal of Management, 21,* 739-756.

Tichy, N., & DeVanna, M. (1986). *The transformational leader.* New York: John Wiley.

Tjosvold, D. (1985). The effects of attribution and social context on superiors' influence and interaction with low performing subordinates. *Personnel Psychology, 38,* 361-376.

Tompkins, P. K., & Cheney, G. (1983). Account analysis of organizations: Decision-making and identification. In L. L. Putnam & M. E. Pacanowsky (Eds.), *Communication and organizations: An interpretive approach* (pp. 123-146). Beverly Hills, CA: Sage.

Trice, H. M., & Beyer, J. M. (1986). Charisma and its routinization in two social movement organizations. In B. M. Staw & L. L. Cummings (Eds.), *Research in organizational behavior* (Vol. 8, pp. 113-164). Greenwich, CT: JAI.

Trice, H. M., & Beyer, J. M. (1991). Cultural leadership in organizations. *Organization Science, 2,* 149-169.

Uhl-Bien, M., & Graen, G. B. (1992). Self-management and team-making in cross-functional work teams: Discovering the keys to becoming an integrated team. *Journal of High Technology Management, 3,* 225-241.

Uhl-Bien, M., & Graen, G. B. (1993). Leadership-making in self-managing professional work teams: An empirical investigation. In K. E. Clark, M. B. Clark, & D. P. Campbell (Eds.), *The impact of leadership* (pp. 379-387). West Orange, NJ: Leadership Library of America.

VandeWalle, D., & Cummings, L. L. (1997). A test of the influence of goal orientation on the feedback seeking process. *Journal of Applied Psychology, 82,* 390-400.

Vecchio, R. P., & Sussman, M. (1991). Choice of influence tactics: Individual and organizational determinants. *Journal of Organizational Behavior, 12,* 73-80.

Wakabayashi, M., & Graen, G. B. (1984). The Japanese career progress study: A 7-year follow-up. *Journal of Applied Psychology, 69,* 603-614.

Waldron, V. R. (1991). Achieving communication goals in superior-subordinate relationships: The multifunctionality of upward maintenance tactics. *Communication Monographs, 58,* 289-306.

Waldron, V. R., Hunt, M. D., & Dsilva, M. (1993). Towards a threat management model of upward communication: A study of influence and maintenance tactics in the leader-member dyad. *Communication Studies, 44,* 254-272.

Walsh, J., Ashford, S., & Hill, T. (1985). Feedback obstruction: The influence of information environment on employee turnover intentions. *Human Relations, 38,* 23-46.

Wasielewski, P. L. (1985). The emotional basis of charisma. *Symbolic Interaction, 8,* 207-222.

Watson, K. M. (1982a). An analysis of communication patterns: A method for discriminating leader and subordinate roles. *Academy of Management Journal, 25,* 107-120.

Watson, K. M. (1982b). A methodology for the study of organizational behavior at the interpersonal level of analysis. *Academy of Management Review, 7,* 392-403.

Watzlawick, P., Beavin, J. H., & Jackson, D. D. (1967). *Pragmatics of human communication.* New York: Norton.

Wayne, S. J., & Ferris, G. R. (1990). Influence tactics, affect, and exchange quality in supervisor-subordinate interactions: A laboratory experiment and field study. *Journal of Applied Psychology, 75,* 487-499.

Wayne, S. J., & Green, S. A. (1993). The effects of leader-member exchange on employee citizenship and impression management behavior. *Human Relations, 46,* 1431-1440.

Wayne, S. J., Liden, R. C., Graf, I. K., & Ferris, G. R. (1997). The role of upward influence tactics in human resource decisions. *Personnel Psychology, 50,* 979-1006.

Wayne, S. J., Liden, R. C., & Sparrowe, R. T. (1994). Developing leader-member exchanges. *American Behavioral Scientist, 37,* 697-714.

Weaver, R. (1953). *The ethics of rhetoric.* South Bend, IN: Gateway Editions.

Weber, M. (1968). *Economy and society* (3 vols., G. Roth & C. Wittich, Eds.). New York: Bedminister. (Original work published 1925)

Weeks, G. R. (1986). Individual-system dialectic. *American Journal of Family Therapy, 14,* 5-12.

Weick, K. E. (1969). *The social psychology of organizing.* Reading, MA: Addison-Wesley.

Weick, K. E. (1987). Theorizing about organizational communication. In F. M. Jablin, L. L. Putnam, K. H. Roberts, & L. W. Porter (Eds.), *Handbook of organizational communication: An interdisciplinary perspective* (pp. 97-122). Newbury Park, CA: Sage.

Weick, K. E., & Roberts, K. H. (1993). Collective mind in organizations: Heedful interrelating on flight decks. *Administrative Science Quarterly, 38,* 357-381.

Weierter, S. J. M. (1997). Who wants to play "follow the leader"? A theory of charismatic relationships based on routinized charisma and follower characteristics. *Leadership Quarterly, 8,* 171-193.

Wendt, R., & Fairhurst, G. T. (1994). Looking for "the vision thing": The rhetoric of leadership in the 1992 presidential election. *Communication Quarterly, 42,* 180-195.

Werner, C. M., & Baxter, L. A. (1994). Temporal qualities of relationships: Organismic, transactional, and dialectical views. In M. L. Knapp & G. R. Miller (Eds.), *Handbook of interpersonal communication* (2nd ed., pp. 323-379). Thousand Oaks, CA: Sage.

Westley, F., & Mintzberg, H. (1989). Visionary leadership and strategic management. *Strategic Management Journal, 10,* 17-32.

Wheatley, M. J. (1992). *Leadership and the new science: Learning about organization from an orderly universe.* San Francisco: Berrett-Koehler.

Wiener, N. (1948). *Cybernetics: On control and communication in the animal and the machine.* New York: John Wiley.

Wiener, N. (1954). *The human use of human beings: Cybernetics and society.* Garden City, NY: Doubleday Anchor.

Williams, J. R., Miller, C. E., Steelman, L. A., & Levy, P. E. (1999). Increasing feedback seeking in public contexts: It takes two (or more) to tango. *Journal of Applied Psychology, 84,* 969-976.

Wofford, J. C. (1999). Laboratory research on charismatic leadership: Fruitful or futile? *Leadership Quarterly, 10,* 523-530.

Wood, R. E., & Bandura, A. (1989). Impact of conceptions of ability on self-regulatory mechanisms and complex decision-making. *Journal of Personality and Social Psychology, 56,* 407-415.

Wyer, R. S., Jr., & Srull, T. K. (1980). The processing of social stimulus information: A conceptual integration. In R. Hatie, T. M. Ostrom, E. B. Ebbesen, R. S. Wyer, Jr., D. L. Hamilton, & D. E. Carlston (Eds.), *Person memory: The cognitive basis of social perception* (pp. 227-300). Hillsdale, NJ: Lawrence Erlbaum.

Wyer, R. S., Jr., & Srull, T. K. (1986). Human cognition in its social context. *Psychological Review, 93,* 322-359.

Xin K. R., & Tsui, A. S. (1996). Different strokes for different folks? Influence tactics by Asian-American and Caucasian-American managers. *Leadership Quarterly, 7,* 109-132.

Yagil, D. (1998). Charismatic leadership and organizational hierarchy: Attributions of charisma to close and distant leaders. *Leadership Quarterly, 9,* 161-176.

Yammarino, F. J., & Bass, B. M. (1990). Long-term forecasting of transformational leadership and its effects among Naval officers. In K. E. Clark & M. B. Clark (Eds.), *Measures of leadership* (pp. 151-169). West Orange, NJ: Leadership Library of America.

Yammarino, F. J., Spangler, W. D., & Bass, B. M. (1993). Transformational leadership and performance: A longitudinal investigation. *Leadership Quarterly, 4,* 81-102.

Yukl, G. (1994). *Leadership in organizations* (3rd ed.). Englewood Cliffs, NJ: Prentice Hall.

Yukl, G., & Falbe, C. M. (1990). Influence tactics and objectives in upward, downward, and lateral influence attempts. *Journal of Applied Psychology, 75,* 132-140.

Yukl, G., Falbe, C. M., & Youn, J. Y. (1993). Patterns of influence behavior for managers. *Group & Organization Management, 18,* 5-28.

Yukl, G., Guinan, P. J., & Sottolano, D. (1995). Influence tactics used for different objectives with subordinates, peers, and superiors. *Group & Organization Management, 20,* 272-296.

Yukl, G., Kim, H., & Chavez, C. (1999). Task importance, feasibility, and agent influence behavior as determinants of target commitment. *Journal of Applied Psychology, 84,* 137-143.

Yukl, G., & Tracey, B. (1992). Consequences of influence tactics used with subordinates, peers, and the boss. *Journal of Applied Psychology, 77,* 525-535.

Zaleznik, A. (1977). Managers and leaders: Are they different? *Harvard Business Review, 55*(5), 67-78.

Zhou, J. (1998). Feedback valence, feedback style, task autonomy, and achievement orientation: Interactive effects on creative performance. *Journal of Applied Psychology, 83,* 261-176.

Zorn, T. E. (1991). Construct system development, transformational leadership, and leadership messages. *Southern Communication Journal, 56,* 178-193.

Zorn, T. E. (1995). Bosses and buddies: Constructing and performing simultaneously hierarchical and close friendship relationships. In J. T. Wood & S. Duck (Eds.), *Understudied relationships: Off the beaten path* (pp. 122-145). Thousand Oaks, CA: Sage.

Zorn, T. E., & Leichty, G. B. (1991). Leadership and identity: A reinterpretation of situational leadership theory. *Southern Communication Journal, 57,* 11-24.

12

Emergence of Communication Networks

PETER R. MONGE
University of Southern California

NOSHIR S. CONTRACTOR
University of Illinois

Communication networks are the patterns of contact between communication partners that are created by transmitting and exchanging messages through time and space. These networks take many forms in contemporary organizations, including personal contact networks, flows of information within and between groups, strategic alliances between firms, and global network organizations, to name but a few. This chapter examines the theoretical mechanisms that theorists and researchers have proposed to explain the creation, maintenance, and dissolution of these diverse and complex intra- and interorganizational networks. This focus provides an important complement to other reviews of the literature that have been organized on the basis of antecedents and outcomes (Monge & Eisenberg, 1987) or research themes within organizational behavior (Brass & Krackhardt, in press; Krackhardt & Brass, 1994).

AUTHORS' NOTE: National Science Foundation Grants ECS-94-27730, SBR-9602055, and IIS-9980109 supported preparation of this chapter. We wish to express our appreciation to George Barnett, Steve Corman, Marya Doerfel, Andrew Flanagin, Janet Fulk, Caroline Haythornthwaite, Maureen Heald, Fred Jablin, David Johnson, David Krackhardt, Leigh Moody, Linda Putnam, Heidi Saltenberger, Stan Wasserman, Rob Whitbred, and Evelien Zeggelink for helpful comments on earlier drafts of this chapter.

The chapter begins with a brief overview of network analysis, an examination of the relationship between formal and emergent networks, and a brief discussion of organizational forms. The core of the chapter focuses on ten families of theories and their respective theoretical mechanisms that have been used to explain the emergence, maintenance, and dissolution of communication networks in organizational research. These are (a) theories of self-interest (social capital theory and transaction cost economics), (b) theories of mutual self-interest and collective action, (c) exchange and dependency theories (social exchange, resource dependency, and network organizational forms), (d) contagion theories (social information processing, social cognitive theory, institutional theory, structural theory of action), (e) cognitive theories (semantic networks, knowledge structures, cognitive social structures, cognitive consistency), (f) theories of homophily (social comparison theory, social identity theory), (g) theories of proximity (physical and electronic propinquity), (h) uncertainty reduction and contingency theories, (i) social support theories, and (j) evolutionary theories. The chapter concludes with a discussion of an agenda for future research on the emergence and evolution of organizational communication networks.

NETWORK ANALYSIS

Network analysis consists of applying a set of relations to an identified set of entities. In the context of organizational communication, network analysts often identify the entities as people who belong to one or more organizations and to which are applied one or more communication relations, such as "provides information to," "gets information from," and "communicates with." It is also common to use work groups, divisions, and entire organizations as the set of entities and to explore a variety of relations such as "collaborates with," "subcontracts with," and "joint ventures with."

Relations in a World of Attributes

Relations are central to network analysis because they define the nature of the communication connections between people, groups, and organizations. This focus stands in sharp contrast to other areas of the social sciences, which have tended to study *attributes,* the characteristics of people, groups, and organizations rather than the relations between them. Relations possess a number of important properties, including the number of entities involved, strength, symmetry, transitivity, reciprocity, and multiplexity. A large literature exists that describes these properties and other fundamentals of network analysis, including network concepts, measures, methods, and applications (see, e.g., Haythornthwaite, 1996; Marsden, 1990; Monge, 1987; Monge & Contractor, 1988; Scott, 1988, 1992; Stohl, 1995; Wasserman & Faust, 1994; Wigand, 1988). Since the focus of this chapter is on theory and research results, it is not feasible to further explore the details of network analysis. However, in addition to the references cited above, Tables 12.1, 12.2, and 12.3 (from Brass, 1995b) summarize major network concepts. These tables describe measures of network ties, measures assigned to individuals, and measures used to describe entire networks.

Network linkages

Network linkages are created when one or more communication relations are applied to a set of people, groups, or organizations. For example, in organizational contexts Farace, Monge, and Russell (1977) identified three distinct important communication networks in terms of production, maintenance, and innovation linkages.

Other kinds of communication linkages are possible. For example, Badaracco (1991) distinguished two types of knowledge, which he called migratory and embedded, each associated with a different type of linkage. Migra-

TABLE 12.1 Typical Social Network Measures of Ties

Measure	Definition	Example
Indirect links	Path between two actors is mediated by one or the other	A is linked to B, B is linked to C; thus A is indirectly linked to C through B
Frequency	How many times, or how often the link occurs	A talks to B 10 times per week
Stability	Existence of link over time	A has been friends with B for 5 years
Multiplexity	Extent to which two actors are linked together by more than one relationship	A and B are friends, they seek out each other for advice, and work together
Strength	Amount of time, emotional intensity, intimacy, or reciprocal services (frequency or multiplexity often used as measure of strength of tie)	A and B are close friends, or spend much time together
Direction	Extent to which link is from one actor to another	Work flows from A to B, but not from B to A
Symmetry	Extent to which relationship is bi-directional	A asks B for advice, and B asks A for advice

SOURCE: Reprinted from D. J. Brass. "A Social Network Perspective on Human Resources Management," in G. R. Ferris (Ed.), *Research in Personnel and Human Resources Management*, Vol. 13. Copyright 1995, p. 44, with permission from Elsevier Science.

tory knowledge is that information that exists in forms that are easily moved from one location, person, group, or firm to another. Migratory knowledge tends to be contained in books, designs, machines, blueprints, computer programs, and individual minds, all of which encapsulate the knowledge that went into its creation. Embedded knowledge is more difficult to transfer. It "resides primarily in specialized relationships among individuals and groups and in the particular norms, attitudes, information flows, and ways of making decisions that shape their dealings with each other" (Badaracco, 1991, p. 79). Craftsmanship, unique talents and skills, accumulated know-how, and group expertise and synergy are all difficult to transfer from one place to another and particularly difficult to transfer across organizational or even divisional boundaries.

The two types of network linkages Badaracco (1991) identified were the product link, associated with migratory knowledge, and the knowledge link, associated with embedded knowledge. In the interfirm context, a product link is an arrangement whereby a company relies on "an outside ally to manufacture part of its product line or to build complex components that the company had previously made for itself" (p. 11). Knowledge links are alliances whereby companies seek "to learn or jointly create new knowledge and capabilities" (p. 12). These "alliances are organizational arrangements and operating poli-

TABLE 12.2   Typical Social Network Measures Assigned to Individual Actors

Measure	Definition
Degree	Number of direct links with other actors
In-degree	Number of directional links to the actor from other actors (in-coming links)
Out-degree	Number of directional links from the actor to other actors (out-coming links)
Range (diversity)	Number of links to different others (others are defined as different to the extent that they are not themselves linked to each other, or represent different groups or statuses)
Closeness	Extent to which an actor is close to, or can easily reach all the other actors in the network. Usually measured by averaging the path distances (direct and indirect links) to all others. A direct link is counted as 1, indirect links receive proportionately less weight
Betweenness	Extent to which an actor mediates, or falls between any other two actors on the shortest path between those actors. Usually averaged across all possible pairs in the network
Centrality	Extent to which an actor is central to a network. Various measures (including degree, closeness, and betweenness) have been used as indicators of centrality. Some measures of centrality weight an actor's links to others by centrality of those others
Prestige	Based on asymmetric relationships, prestigious actors are the object rather than the source of relations. Measures similar to centrality are calculated by accounting for the direction of the relationship (i.e., in-degree)
Role	
Star	An actor who is highly central to the network
Liaison	An actor who has links to two or more groups that would otherwise not be linked, but is not a member of either group
Bridge	An actor who is a member of two or more groups
Gatekeeper	An actor who mediates or controls the flow (is the single link) between one part of the network and another
Isolate	An actor who has no links, or relatively few links to others

SOURCE: Reprinted from D. J. Brass. "A Social Network Perspective on Human Resources Management," in G. R. Ferris (Ed.), *Research in Personnel and Human Resources Management*, Vol. 13. Copyright 1995, p. 45, with permission from Elsevier Science.

cies through which separate organizations share administrative authority, form social links, and accept joint ownership, and in which looser, more open-ended contractual arrangements replace highly specific, arm's length contracts" (Badaracco, 1991, p. 4).

Research on interorganizational linkages began almost 40 years ago with the work of Levine and White (1961) and Litwak and Hylton (1962), which spawned a quarter century's worth of interest on the exchange of goods and material resources (see, e.g.,

TABLE 12.3   Typical Social Network Measures Used to Describe Networks

Measure	Definition
Size	Number of actors in the network
Inclusiveness	Total number of actors in a network minus the number of isolated actors (not connected to any other actors). Also measured as the ratio of connected actors to the total number of actors
Component	Largest connected subset of network nodes and links. All nodes in the component are connected (either direct or indirect links) and no nodes have links to nodes outside the component
Connectivity (reachability)	Extent to which actors in the network are linked to one another by direct or indirect ties. Sometimes measured by the maximum, or average, path distance between any two actors in the network
Connectedness	Ratio of pairs of nodes that are mutually reachable to total number of pairs o nodes
Density	Ratio of the number of actual links to the number of possible links in the network
Centralization	Difference between the centrality scores of the most central actor and those of all other actors in a network is calculated, and used to form ratio of the actual sum of the differences to the maximum sum of the differences
Symmetry	Ratio of number of symmetric to asymmetric links (or to total number of links) in a network
Transitivity	Three actors (A, B, C) are transitive if whenever A is linked to B and B is linked to C, then C is linked to A. Transitivity is the number of transitive triples divided by the number of potential transitive triples (number of paths of length 2)

SOURCE: Reprinted from D. J. Brass. "A Social Network Perspective on Human Resources Management," in G. R. Ferris (Ed.), *Research in Personnel and Human Resources Management*, Vol. 13. Copyright 1995, p. 44, with permission from Elsevier Science.

Mitchell, 1973; Warren, 1967). More recent work has focused on communication, information, and knowledge linkages (Gulati, 1995). Eisenberg et al. (1985) developed a two-dimensional typology of interorganizational linkages based on linkage content and linkage level. The content dimension separated material content from symbolic or informational content. The level dimension distinguished three forms of exchange. Eisenberg et al. (1985) state:

An *institutional* linkage occurs when information or materials are exchanged between orga-

nizations without the involvement of specific organizational roles or personalities (e.g., routine data transfers between banks). A *representative* linkage occurs when a role occupant who officially represents an organization within the system has contact with a representative of another organization (e.g., an interagency committee to formulate joint policies). The emphasis here is on the official nature of the transaction and the representative capacities of the individuals. Finally, a *personal* linkage occurs when an individual from one organization exchanges information or material with an individual in another organization, but in a nonrepresentative or private capacity (i.e., via friendship or "old school" ties). (p. 237, emphasis in the original).

Formal Versus Emergent Networks

Historically, organizational communication scholars have made important theoretical and empirical distinctions between formal and emergent networks. Theoretically, the notion of "emergent network" was a designation that originally differentiated informal, naturally occurring networks from formal, imposed, or "mandated" networks (Aldrich, 1976), the latter of which represented the legitimate authority of the organization and were typically reflected by the organizational chart. The formal networks were presumed to also represent the channels of communication through which orders were transmitted downward and information was transmitted upward (Weber, 1947). Early organizational theorists were aware that the formal organizational structure failed to capture many of the important aspects of communication in organizations and discussed the importance of informal communication and the grapevine (Barnard, 1938; Follett, 1924). Several scholars developed ways to study the grapevine and informal networks such as Davis's (1953) episodic communication in channels of organizations (ECCO) analysis, a technique for tracing the person-to-person diffusion of rumors or other items of information in an organization.

Researchers have provided considerable evidence over the years for the coexistence of the two networks. For example, using a variant of ECCO analysis, Stevenson and Gilly (1991) found that managers tended to forward problems to personal contacts rather than to formally designated problem solvers, thus bypassing the formal network. Similarly, Albrecht and Ropp (1984) discovered that "workers were more likely to report talking about new ideas with those colleagues with whom they also discussed work and personal matters, rather than necessarily following prescribed channels based upon hierarchical role relationships" (p. 3). Stevenson (1990) argued

that the influence of formal organizational structure on the emergent structure could be best understood on the basis of a status differential model. In a study of a public transit agency, he found evidence that the social distance across the hierarchy reduced the level of communication between higher- and lower-level employees, with middle-level employees serving as a buffer.

An important rationale for studying emergent communication networks has evolved out of the inconclusive findings relating formal organizational structure to organizational behavior (Johnson, 1992, 1993; see also McPhee & Poole, Chapter 13, this volume). Jablin's (1987) review of the empirical research on formal organizational structures pointed to the inconclusive nature of studies involving structural variables such as hierarchy, size, differentiation, and formalization. More recently, a series of meta-analytic studies has concluded that the relationships between formal structure, organizational effectiveness (Doty, Glick, & Huber, 1993; Huber, Miller, & Glick, 1990), and technology (Miller, Glick, Wang, & Huber, 1991) are largely an artifact of methodological designs. The fact that formal structural variables have failed to provide much explanatory power has led several scholars to argue that emergent structures are more important to study than formal structures because they better contribute to our understanding of organizational behavior (Bacharach & Lawler, 1980; Krackhardt & Hanson, 1993; Krikorian, Seibold, & Goode, 1997; Roberts & O'Reilly, 1978; Roethlisberger & Dickson, 1939).

These problems with formal structures and the recent priority given to emergent structure have prompted scholars to develop network measures that capture in emergent networks the key concepts used to describe formal organizational structure. For example, Krackhardt (1994) has developed four measures of informal structure—connectedness, hierarchy, efficiency, and least-upper-boundedness (unity-of-command)—that map onto theories of an organization's formal organizational structure.

Further, the increased use of new computer-mediated communication systems has spawned research that uses formal organizational structure as a benchmark against which to compare communication networks that emerge in an electronic medium. Several interesting, though somewhat conflicting, findings have emerged. In a two-year study of over 800 members of an R&D organization, Eveland and Bikson (1987) found that electronic mail served to augment, and in some cases complement, formal structures. On the other hand, Bizot, Smith, and Hill (1991) found that electronic communication patterns corresponded closely to the formal organizational structures in a traditionally hierarchical R&D organization. Lievrouw and Carley (1991) argued that new communication technologies might usher in a new era of "telescience" by offering alternatives to the traditional organizational structures in universities and industry. However, Rice (1994b) found that the electronic communication structures initially mirrored formal organizational structures, but these similarities diminished over time. Hinds and Kiesler (1995) explored the relationship between formal and informal networks in a telecommunications company. They found that communication technologies were increasingly used as a tool for lateral communication across formal organizational boundaries; this finding was most pronounced for technical workers.

The literature comparing face-to-face or mediated emergent communication structures with formal structures generally demonstrates a "pro-emergent bias." That is, the theory and empirical evidence focus on the advantages of informal communication to individuals and organizations. However, Kadushin and Brimm (1990) challenged the assumption that three types of emergent networks, (a) the shadow networks (the "real" way things get done), (b) the social interaction networks, and (c) the career networks (the venue for so-called networking) always serve to augment the limitations of the organization's formal network. Instead, they argued that these three informal networks frequently work at

cross-purposes, thereby restricting rather than promoting the organization's interests. In a study of senior executives in a large, international high-technology company, they found that by saying, "Please network, but don't you dare bypass authority," organizations create what Bateson (1972) called a "double bind," a choice situation where each alternative conflicts with the others. They argued that "an important first step is to recognize the incompatibilities between emergent network structures and corporate authority structures and to move this inconsistency from the realm of double bind to the domain of paradox" (Kadushin & Brimm, 1990, p. 15).

Clearly, there is continuing scholarly interest in the study of the differences between formal and emergent networks in organizations. Ironically, however, the distinction between formal and informal structures in organizations has diminished significantly in recent years and may become increasingly irrelevant in the coming decade. Reasons for this center on shifts in organizational structure and management philosophy. Prominent among these are changes to more team-based forms of organizing, the adoption of matrix forms of organizational structure (Burns & Wholey, 1993), and shifts to network forms of organizing (Miles & Snow, 1986, 1992, 1995; Monge, 1995). At the core of these changes has been the explosion of lateral forms of communication (Galbraith, 1977, 1995) made possible by new information technologies that facilitate considerable point-to-point and broadcast communication without regard for traditional hierarchy.

These developments have eroded the distinction between prior structural categories used to characterize organizations, specifically, between formal and informal and/or between formal and emergent. Contrary to traditional views, contemporary organizations are increasingly constructed out of emergent communication linkages, linkages that are ephemeral in that they are formed, maintained, broken, and reformed with considerable ease (Palmer, Friedland, & Singh, 1986). As Krackhardt (1994) says,

An inherent principle of the interactive form is that networks of relations span across the entire organization, unimpeded by preordained formal structures and fluid enough to adapt to immediate technological demands. These relations can be multiple and complex. But one characteristic they share is that they *emerge* in the organization, they are not preplanned. (p. 218, emphasis in the original)

The networks that emerge by these processes and the organizations they create are called network and organizational forms. Both are reviewed in the following section.

Network and Organizational Forms

Communication network patterns that recur in multiple settings are called *network forms*. An early theoretical article by Bavelas (1948) based on Lewin's (1936) psychological field theory identified a number of small-group communication network forms in organizations, including the chain, circle, wheel, and comcon (*com*pletely *con*nected), and theorized about how the different forms processed information. These network forms varied in the degree to which they were centralized, with the wheel being the most centralized and the comcon the least centralized.

This theoretical article and an imaginative experimental design created by Leavitt (1951) generated hundreds of published articles over some 25 years. The primary focus of these efforts was the impact of information processing via the different network forms on productivity and satisfaction (see Shaw, 1964, for a review of this literature). Two prominent findings emerged from this research. First, centralized organizations were more efficient for routine tasks, while decentralized networks were more efficient for tasks that required creativity and collaborative problem solving. Second, people in decentralized organizations were more satisfied with the work processes than people in centralized organizations, with the exception in the latter case that the central

person in centralized networks was extremely satisfied. Unfortunately, little further theoretical development accompanied this plethora of empirical research. As a result, this line of inquiry has essentially died; almost no articles have been published on small-group network forms in organizations during the past 20 years.

Organizational structures, including communication networks, that share common features or patterns across a large number of organizations are called *organizational forms* (McKelvey, 1982). Weber (1947) argued that bureaucracy was the universal organizational form. Three principal theoretical mechanisms that created bureaucracy were rationalization, differentiation, and integration. Rationalization occurred by specifying legitimating instructions that produced standard operating procedures, thus leaving little opportunity for individual autonomy. Rationalizing the network meant specifying who could say what to whom, often summarized by the injunction that commands should flow downward and information upward in the bureaucracy. Differentiation was the process of breaking work up into its various components. This often led to job specialization particularly as production processes proliferated and increased in size and complexity. As work became differentiated, the various parts needed to be coordinated, and thus processes of integration came into operation. Weber argued that bureaucracy differentiated along vertical organizational lines and primarily integrated that way as well. Bureaucracy allowed little room for lateral, cross-level, or cross-boundary communication networks, that is, informal or emergent networks, a feature for which it has been frequently criticized (Heckscher, 1994).

Miles and Snow (1986, 1992) identified four major organizational forms that have developed over the past century: (a) the traditional functional form, which emerged during the early part of the century; (b) the divisional (or multidivisional) form, which was begun by Alfred P. Sloan at General Motors in the 1940s (see Chandler, 1977); (c) the matrix form, which evolved during the 1960s and

1970s; and (d) the network form, which has emerged over the past decade. Miles and Snow (1992) argue that each of these forms contains its own operating logic, or in terms of this chapter, theoretical mechanism. The functional form uses a logic of "centrally coordinated specialization" (p. 58), which enables it to efficiently produce a limited set of standardized goods or services for a stable, relatively unchanging market. The divisional form operates by a logic of "divisional autonomy with centrally controlled performance evaluation and resource allocation" (p. 60). Divisions produce separate products or focus on separate markets but are collectively accountable to centralized authority through their communication networks. The ability to develop new divisions enables the multidivisional form to pursue new opportunities in changing markets. The matrix form combines the operating logic of functional and multidivisional forms, using the functional form to produce standardized goods and services and the shared resources of the multidivisional form to explore new opportunities via project groups or teams. The network form uses flexible, dynamic communication linkages to connect multiple organizations into new entities that can create products or services.

THEORETICAL MECHANISMS TO EXPLAIN THE EMERGENCE OF NETWORKS

Communication network analysis falls within the intellectual lineage of structural analysis, which has had a long and distinguished history. In sociology, Herbert Spencer (1982) and Émile Durkheim (1895/1964) are often credited with introducing structural concepts into sociological thinking. In anthropology, Radcliffe-Brown (1952/1959) incorporated structural-functionalist ideas into his watershed analysis of cultures. And in linguistics, structural thinking can be traced to the pio-

neering work of de Saussure (1916/1966). Most structural analyses of organizations and communication can be located in one of three traditions: positional, relational, and cultural.

The *positional* tradition is rooted in the classical work of Max Weber (1947), Talcott Parsons (1951), and George Homans (1958). Organizational structure is viewed as a pattern of relations among positions. Sets of organizational roles are associated with positions and specify designated behaviors and obligatory relations incumbent on the people who assume the positions. The positions and attached roles constitute the relatively stable and enduring structure of the organization independent of the people who fulfill the roles. This tradition leads to the view that positions and roles determine who communicates with whom, and consequently, the communication structure of the organization. White, Boorman, and Breiger (1976) and Burt (1982) have developed the most significant recent positional theories applicable to organizational communication under the rubric of structural equivalence. This theory argues that people maintain attitudes, values, and beliefs consistent with their organizational positions irrespective of the amount of communication that they have with others in their organizational networks. The positional tradition has been criticized for its inability to take into account the active part individuals play in creating and shaping organizational structure (Coleman, 1973; Nadel, 1957; White et al., 1976).

The *relational* tradition focuses primarily on the direct communication that establishes and maintains communication linkages. Taken collectively, these linkages create an emergent communication structure that connects different people and groups in the organization irrespective of their formal positions or roles. Rooted in systems theory (Bateson, 1972; Buckley, 1967; Watzlawick, Beavin, & Jackson, 1967), the relational tradition emphasizes the dynamic, constantly changing, enacted nature of structure created by repetitive patterns of person-to-person message flow. Rogers and Kincaid (1981) claim that it is the dominant tradition in organizational communication.

The *cultural* tradition examines symbols, meanings, and interpretations of messages transmitted through communication networks. As part of the resurgence of interest in organizational culture (Frost, Moore, Louis, Lundberg, & Martin, 1985), much of the work has been based on Giddens's (1976, 1984) writings on structuration, which attempt to account for both the creative and constraining aspects of social structure. These studies are characterized by an explicit concern for the continual production and reproduction of meaning through communication, examining simultaneously how meanings emerge from interaction and how they act to constrain subsequent interaction. The cultural tradition has spawned recent work on semantic networks (Monge & Eisenberg, 1987) described later in this chapter. These three traditions are discussed in greater detail in Monge and Eisenberg (1987).

Although interesting and useful, these network traditions focus attention at a metatheoretical level and fail to specify the *theoretical mechanisms* that describe how people, groups, and organizations forge, maintain, and dissolve linkages. Further, while a number of scholars over the past decade have called for greater explication of network theory (e.g., Rogers, 1987; Salancik, 1995; Wellman, 1988), almost none have provided it. Finally, while several reviewers have identified theories that are applicable to network research within and between organizations (Brass & Krackhardt, in press; Galaskiewicz, 1985; Grandori & Soda, 1995; Mizruchi & Galaskiewicz, 1994; Smith, Carroll, & Ashford, 1995), none have systematically explored the theories and their theoretical mechanisms.

This chapter addresses these omissions in the organizational communication network literature by focusing on the role of theory and theoretical mechanisms in explaining the emergence of communication networks. More specifically, it examines the extant organiza-tional literature using a network perspective with special attention to the mechanisms that help explain the *emergence* of networks. This review will demonstrate that a wide array of theories is amenable to network formulations. In some cases, different theories, some using similar theoretical mechanisms, offer similar explanations but at different levels of analysis. The review will also underscore the considerable variation in the depth of conceptual development and empirical research across the different theories and theoretical mechanisms. Since the chapter focuses on theoretical mechanisms, many other interesting network articles that have little or no bearing on these issues have not been included. The theories and their theoretical mechanisms are summarized in Table 12.4.

Theories of Self-Interest

Social theorists have long been fascinated by self-interest as a motivation for economic and other forms of social action (Coleman, 1986). Theories of self-interest postulate that people make what they believe to be rational choices in order to acquire personal benefits. The strong form of this theoretical mechanism stipulates that people attempt to maximize their gains (or minimize their losses). The weaker theoretical form says that people "satisfice" rather than maximize, which means that people choose the first good alternative they find rather than exploring all alternatives and selecting the best. Two theories of self-interest that have been used to explore communication network issues are examined in this section: the theory of social capital and transaction cost economics theory.

Theory of Social Capital

The deployment of social capital (Coleman, 1988) in networks is best represented in Burt's (1992) theory of structural holes. This theory argues that people accumulate social resources, or "social capital," which they in-

TABLE 12.4 Ten Families of Theories and Their Theoretical Mechanisms to Explain the Emergence of Networks

Theories	Theoretical Mechanisms	Relevant Organizational Variables
1. Theories of self-interest Theory of Social Capital Theory of Structural Holes Transaction Cost Economics Theory	Investments in opportunities Control of information flow Cost minimization	Employee autonomy, flexibility Employee effectiveness Employee efficiency Organizational innovation Coordination by markets and hierarchies
2. Theories of mutual self-interest and collective action Public Goods Theory Critical Mass Theory	Joint value maximization Inducements to contribute Number of people with resources and interests	Contributions to collective good Mobilization of resources Adoption of innovations
3. Exchange and dependency theories Social Exchange Theory Resource Dependency Theory Network Organizations	Exchange of valued resources (material or information)	Power, leadership Trust and ethical behavior Interorganizational linkages Coordination by networks Virtual organizing
4. Contagion theories Social Information Processing Theory Social Learning Theory Institutional Theory Structural Theory of Action	Exposure or contact leading to: Social influence Imitation, modeling Mimetic behavior Similar positions in structure and roles	General workplace attitudes Attitudes toward technologies Behavior through contagion Interorganizational contagion
5. Cognitive theories Semetic and Knowledge Networks Cognitive Social Structures Cognitive Consistency theories Balance Theory Theory of Cognitive Dissonance	Cognitive mechanisms leading to: Shared interpretations Similarity in perceptual structures Drive to restore balance Drive to reduce dissonance	Shared interpretations on key organizational concepts Shared attributions of other individuals Shared perceptions of the social structure Workplace attitudes such as satisfaction Workplace behaviors such as turnover

Theory	Mechanism	Application
6. Homophily theories Social Comparison Theory Social Identity Theory	Choose similar others as basis of comparison Choose categories to define one's own group identity	Demographic variables such as age, tenure, gender, and race
7. Theories of physical and electronic proximity Physical Proximity Electronic Proximity	Influence of distance Influence of accessibility	Workplace attitudes
8. Uncertainty reduction and contingency theories Uncertainty Reduction Theory Contingency Theory	Choose communication links to reduce uncertainty	Communication about innovation Organizational structural characteristics Introduction of new technologies Market exchanges Interorganizational conflict
9. Social support theories	Choose communication links to gain or mobilize social resources	Buffer social and psychological stress Coping with stress General workplace attitudes
10. Theories of network evolution Structuration Theory Computation and Mathematical Organizational Theory Organizational Life Cycle and Developmental Theories	Selection and retention Duality of structure Nomothetic non-linear generative mechanisms Evolution of structures as a function of life-cycle stages	Foundings and extinctions Change in network configurations, role configurations, appropriation of new structures and media

vest in social opportunities from which they expect to profit. These investments are largely motivated by self-interest, defined as the return people expect to get on the social capital they invest. Network "holes" are those places in a network where people are unconnected. Consequently, holes provide opportunities where people can invest their social capital. To invest in, fill, or exploit these holes, people link directly to two or more unconnected others, thus creating indirect ties between the people to whom they link. People who link others by filling structural holes also enhance their own structural autonomy because they can control the information that flows between others. Consequently, Burt (1992) argues that the diversity of individuals' networks is a better predictor of their social capital than network size. Researchers have examined the relationships between social capital and organizational effectiveness, efficiency, and innovation. Each area is reviewed below.

Social capital and effectiveness. Researchers (Benassi & Gargiulo, 1993; Burt, 1992) have argued that network linkages enable and constrain the flexibility, autonomy, and therefore, the effectiveness of organizational members. Consistent with Burt's (1992) argument, Papa (1990) found that organization members with diverse networks across departments and hierarchical levels were significantly more likely to both increase productivity and hasten the speed with which this change occurred. Similarly, Burt (1992) found that the occurrence of structural holes in managers' networks was positively correlated with managerial effectiveness. However, he notes that this finding was not supported among female managers and recent recruits, where effectiveness was correlated with strong ties to others. Ibarra and Andrews's (1993) research showed that individuals who were central in the advice and friendship networks were more likely to perceive autonomy in their work. Benassi and Gargiulo (1993) found that the flexibility of managers in an Italian subsidiary of a multi-

national computer manufacturer significantly affected their likelihood of success in coordinating critical interdependencies. Managers were rated as having high flexibility if (a) their communication networks were constrained by a low level of aggregate interdependencies and consultations with others in their network, and (b) their communication network had structural holes among the people imposing these constraints. More recently, Burt (1997) reports that social capital is especially valuable for managers with few peers because such managers do not have the guiding frame of reference provided by numerous competitors, or the legitimacy provided by numerous people doing the same kind of work (p. 356). In addition, Burt (1991) has developed computational measures of "structural autonomy" to assess the level and distribution of constraints affecting individuals in a network.

Walker, Kogut, and Shan (1997) tested Burt's theory of structural holes at the interorganizational level. Their research showed that developing and nurturing social capital in the biotechnology industry was a significant factor in "network formation and industry growth" (p. 109). In the development of enduring relationships, firms choose to increase social capital rather than exploit structural holes. However, they argue that "structural hole theory may apply more to networks of market transactions than to networks of cooperative relations" (p. 109). In the case of market transactions, firms are not bound by the structural constraint to cooperate over time and may therefore be more inclined to exploit structural holes.

In related research, Baker (1987) found that organizations with low levels of debt improved their autonomy in managing transactions by establishing communication relationships with many, rather than one or a few, investment banks. Kosnik (1987) found that companies who had more outside directors, especially directors from firms that had transactions with the focal firm, had less autonomy in engaging in "greenmail," the private repurchase of company stock. In contrast, the

CEOs of firms that had more outside directors had greater autonomy in negotiating "golden parachute" policies for the firms' top executives (Cochran, Wood, & Jones, 1985; Singh & Harianto, 1989; Wade, O'Reilly, & Chandratat, 1990).

Social capital and efficiency. Granovetter's (1982) theory of the "strength of weak ties" was also based on the premise that the people with whom a person has weak ties are less likely to be connected to one another; that is, the person is embedded in a structural hole. Consequently, the information obtained from these weak ties is less likely to be redundant and more likely to be unique, thereby making weak ties "information rich." Burt (1992) argued that being embedded in a structural hole allows actors to be more efficient in obtaining information. Using data from the 1985 and 1987 General Social Survey, Carroll and Teo (1996) found that the members of managers' core discussion networks were less likely to be connected to one another than members of nonmanagers' networks; consequently, nonmanagers' core discussion networks were less efficient in obtaining information. Contrary to conventional wisdom, Granovetter (1982) found that individuals were more likely to find jobs through their weak ties than through strong ties or formal listings. However, Lin, Ensel, and Vaughn's (1981) research showed that weak ties were effective only if they connected individuals to diverse others who could provide nonredundant information.

Social capital and innovation. The diversity of information obtained from ties has also been used to explain the introduction of innovations in organizations. Rogers (1971) noted that innovations were more likely to be introduced to an organization by cosmopolites, that is, people with diverse networks, including several external to the organization. In a study of the inventory and control systems of manufacturing industries, Newell and Clark (1990) reported that British firms were less innovative than their U.S. counterparts in part because they were less central in their interorganizational communication networks. More recently, Burns and Wholey (1993) found that hospitals that were centrally located in an interorganizational network were more likely to be early adopters of an innovation (the matrix form of management) than other hospitals in their network. Brass (1995a) suggested that being embedded in networks with structural holes can also enhance employees' ability to provide creative solutions to organizational problems.

Extensions to social capital. Since the introduction of the "social capital" concept in 1988 by Coleman, an impressive body of theoretical and empirical evidence has demonstrated its relevance. It was developed as a concept distinct from "human capital," which focuses on the attributes of individuals, such as seniority, intelligence, and education. Many of the informal means by which individuals accrue social capital rely on their knowledge of the existing communication networks. However, as the workforce moves from being physically co-located to "virtual environments," it is unclear whether electronic forms of communication such as email, which provide such things as distribution lists and records of messages, make it easier or more difficult for individuals to assess the existing social structure. Hence, as scholars examine the workforce of the 21st century, there is a pressing need for research that examines the distinctive strategies by which individuals can identify structural holes and thereby accumulate social capital in virtual organizations.

Transaction Cost Economics Theory

From the viewpoint of traditional economic theory, the market was the classical organizational form, where buyers and sellers communicated their intentions to each other, and where supply and demand were presumed to determine prices for goods. This is the purest form of self-interest theory. By contrast, neoclassical economics examined the development of hierarchical and vertically integrated forms as a more efficient alternative to markets (Coase, 1937), though one that is equally self-interested. However, over the past decade important changes in theories and views of organizational structuring have been occurring. A new organizational form, the network organization, is emerging as an alternative to both markets and vertically integrated organizations. This section examines these two traditional organizational forms, the market and hierarchies; the following section explores the development of the new alternative, the network form.

Williamson (1975, 1985) developed transaction cost economics to explain the organization of economic activity. All organizations require raw materials or components to manufacture their own goods or services. Thus, Williamson argued, organizations face a choice between buying resources from other firms or acquiring other firms in order to make the suppliers' goods or services at lower costs than what they could buy them, what is frequently called the buy-or-make decision. (It is also possible to develop internal capabilities, but this is generally seen as a more expensive option.) Williamson viewed the first alternative as governed by market mechanisms, where an organization hunts for the best prices among the alternative supplier firms. "Transaction costs" are the expenses associated with finding information about prices and quality from the available firms and negotiating contracts. He saw the second alternative, vertical integration, as governed by hierarchical forces, the administrative costs, including communication, associated with managing the internal production of acquired supplier firms. Economic organizations, Williamson argued, attempt to minimize transaction costs by making a choice between markets and hierarchies. Vertical integration, he said, is the efficient alternative when the transaction costs for markets are greater than the administrative costs of production through hierarchical ownership (Zajac & Olsen, 1993, p. 133). Clearly, the theoretical mechanism in Williamson's

theory is efficient self-interest. Organizations make self-interested choices among alternative organizational forms by attempting to minimize the communication, information search, and decision-making costs associated with finding sellers in the market or acquiring suppliers. It should be clear that this mechanism is centered very much in the decision framework of individual firms. The alternative forms generated by this mechanism differ considerably in the nature of their communication networks.

Gupta and Govindarajan (1991) have extended Williamson's theory to the arena of multinational corporations. They argued that governance in multinational corporations can be viewed as a network of transaction cost exchanges. Home offices govern subsidiaries by regulating three critical transaction flows: capital, product, and knowledge. The fact that subsidiaries are located in different countries creates different strategic contexts and communication problems that determine the magnitude and direction of transaction flows.

A number of criticisms have been leveled against transaction cost economics. Granovetter (1985) observes that analyses of human and organizational economic behavior generally cluster at two ends of a continuum. Traditional neoeconomics treats human behavior and institutional action independent of social relations and interpersonal communication, a view that Granovetter calls an undersocialized viewpoint. More reformist economists and sociologists (e.g., Piore, 1975) tend to see economic action as severely constrained by social influences, a position he calls an oversocialized view. By contrast, Granovetter argues for a third alternative, that economic behavior of both individuals and organizations occurs within existing communication structures and ongoing social relations, a position he calls the embedded view. "The embeddedness argument," he says, "stresses instead the role of concrete personal relations and structures (or 'networks') of such relations" (p. 490). This view was supported by Uzzi's (1996) study of New York dress apparel firms, which showed that "embeddedness is an exchange system with unique opportunities relative to markets and that firms organized in networks have higher survival chances than do firms which maintain arm's-length market relationships" (p. 674).

Of course, there are drawbacks to embeddedness. Just as theory about the behavior of individual people or organizations can be over- or undersocialized, so can organizations be overembedded or underembedded. As Grabher (1993) says, "Too little embeddedness may expose networks to an erosion of their supportive tissue of social practices and institutions. Too much embeddedness, however, may promote a petrifaction of this supportive tissue and, hence, may pervert networks into cohesive coalitions against more radical innovations" (pp. 25-26). Similarly, Uzzi (1997), recognizing the paradox of embeddedness in the New York apparel economy, identified three conditions that turn embeddedness into a liability: "(1) There is an unforeseeable exit of a core network player, (2) institutional forces rationalize markets, or (3) overembeddedness characterizes the network" (p. 57).

Another criticism developed by Granovetter (1985) and Powell (1990) is that the dichotomy between markets and hierarchies does not exhaust all of the important organizational forms. Lazerson (1993) claims that "the false promises of vertical integration have stimulated interest in alternative organizational forms that are neither hierarchies nor markets" (p. 203). Williamson (1985, 1991) acknowledged this possibility in his discussion of alliances as hybrid forms. These, he said, exist between the other two and occur when the transaction costs associated with market exchange are too high but not high enough to justify vertical integration. However, a number of scholars, including Powell (1990), have argued that at least one alternative, the network organization, is neither market nor hierarchy in form. This issue is discussed in a later section of the chapter.

Zajac and Olsen (1993) critiqued Williamson's perspective on two accounts. First, they pointed out that Williamson's analysis fails to account for communication and other processes encountered in the transaction costs analysis. Instead, they proposed an alternative three-stage process that they argue enables firms to determine whether they should enter into the relation. These three are the initializing stage, the processing stage, and the reconfiguring stage. During the first stage each potential partner to the relation determines its own objectives, reviews exchange alternatives, and begins exploratory contacts to examine the feasibility of the relationships. Here, Zajac and Olsen (1993) contend, the first rounds of exchange "often take the form of preliminary communication and negotiation concerning mutual and individual firm interests, and/or feasibility studies and general information exchange" (p. 139). During the second stage firms engage in both serial and parallel information processing, "interfirm communications . . . occurring between individuals at multiple organizational levels and multiple functional areas" (p. 140). The third stage, reconfiguration, consists of evaluation of the relationship followed by a return to either of the previous two stages to (a) seek relational changes or (b) reaffirm the status quo. In essence, this stage affirms the information and communication network linkages on which the organizational relations can be established.

The second problem they identified is that Williamson's view of transaction cost minimization takes the perspective of only one organization. This is an error, they claimed, because a relationship has two sides, both of which should be included in any comprehensive account. Thus, they argued that transaction cost minimization from the perspective of one firm be replace by a "joint value maximization principle" that focuses on the benefits to both (or multiple) firms. More specifically, they propose that "value estimations of interorganizational strategies require that a focal firm consider the value sought by that firm's exchange partner. By taking the partner's perspective, the focal firm can better estimate the value and duration of the interorganizational strategy, given that value and duration are determined interdependently by other firms" (p. 137).

It is worth noting that Zajac and Olsen's critique transforms the self-interest theoretical mechanism for creating organizational communication networks into one that is jointly rather than individually self-interested. Further, it attempts to maximize collective value rather than minimize individual costs. This theoretical mechanism to account for the emergence of communication networks, mutual self-interest, is reviewed more fully in the following section.

Theories of Mutual Self-Interest and Collective Action

Collective action is a term that has been broadly applied to a wide range of phenomena in the social sciences, including organizational communication (Coleman, 1973). Its main focus is on "mutual interests and the possibility of benefits from coordinated action" (Marwell & Oliver, 1993, p. 2) rather than on individual self-interests. Samuelson (1954) first articulated public goods theory to explain how people could be induced to contribute to collective goods in the public domain such as bridges, parks, and libraries. Applications of this perspective to the interactive communication public goods of connectivity and communality have been made recently by Fulk, Flanagin, Kalman, Monge, and Ryan (1996).

The logic of collective action is based on the assumption that individuals motivated by self-interest will avoid investing resources in a joint endeavor whenever possible, leaving others to contribute their share even though all will benefit (Olson, 1965). This phenomenon is known as "free riding." Peer pressure is often applied to overcome this tendency to free ride and serves to make individuals comply with the need to contribute their fair share, thus facilitating collective action. Original formulations treated individuals as if they were isolated and independent of others making similar decisions. Oliver (1993), Markus (1990), and Marwell and Oliver (1993) have criticized this view and emphasized the importance of the network of relations in which people are embedded. Computer simulation experiments by Marwell and Oliver (1993) showed that the extent to which people are interconnected in communication networks increases their willingness to support the collective good. Using a similar research strategy, Marwell, Oliver, and Prahl (1988) showed that centralization and resource heterogeneity in the network influenced aggregate contributions to a collective good.

Empirical studies using collective action as an explanatory mechanism fall into two categories: the group's mobilization as indexed by its level of involvement, and the adoption of innovations. Research using a collective action mechanism has focused on the effect of the network on mobilization, as well as more specifically the adoption of innovations. Each of these two areas is discussed below.

Collective Action and Mobilization

In a retrospective study of the insurgency in the Paris Commune of 1871, Gould (1991) underscored the importance of examining multiple, partially overlapping networks in explaining the insurgents' solidarity and commitment. He found that the

> importance of neighborhood identity and the patterns of arrests showed that preexisting social ties among neighbors and organizational ties formed by the National Guard worked together to maintain solidarity in the insurgent ranks. . . . Cross-neighborhood solidarity could not have emerged in the absence of enlistment overlaps that linked each residential area with Guard units in other areas. (p. 727)

Applied to organizational contexts, Gould's findings suggest that collective action is less likely to succeed if the informal networks are structured so as to be either isomorphic with preexisting formal ties, or if they "completely cut across preexisting networks" (p. 728).

Knoke (1990, p. 5) examined the determinants of member participation and commitment among 8,746 respondents from 35 "collective action organizations," professional associations, recreational clubs, and women's associations. He discovered that "members' involvements in their collective action organizations are enhanced by extensive communication networks that plug them into the thick of policy discussions, apart from whatever degree of interest they may have in particular policy issues" (p. 185). At the interorganizational level, Laumann, Knoke, and Kim (1985) found that health organizations central in their industry's communication networks were more involved in mobilizing efforts on national policy issues affecting their domain. However, this relationship did not hold up among organizations in the energy industry. Laumann et al. (1985) concluded that centrality in a communication network was more important in predicting collective action in industries that were less institutionalized.

Collective Action and the Adoption of Innovations

Theories of collective action have also been used to examine the adoption of new interactive communication technologies (Markus, 1990; Rafaeli & LaRose, 1993). Valente (1995, 1996) has examined the effect of "threshold" (Granovetter, 1978) on adoption behavior. The *threshold* is defined as the number of other adopters that must be present in a person's network before the person decides to adopt. The threshold levels of individuals determine whether the group as a whole can achieve the critical mass necessary for rapid and widespread collective action. Rice, Grant, Schmitz, and Torobin (1990) examined the role of critical mass in predicting the adoption of an electronic mail system at a decentralized federal agency. They found that individuals' decisions to adopt the system were contingent on the decisions of others with whom they reported high levels of task interdependence.

Further, individuals' adoption decisions were influenced by the extent to which they valued the potential communication with others who were likely to be accessible via the new system. Gurbaxani (1990) used an adoption model based on critical mass theory to predict with considerable accuracy university adoption of the Bitnet computer network. At the interorganizational level, studies on governmental and nonprofit organizations have examined the role of network ties in overcoming obstacles to collective action (Mizruchi & Galaskiewicz, 1994; Rogers & Whetten, 1982; Turk, 1977).

Extensions to Collective Action Theory

The interest in examining the emergence of networks from a collective action perspective is relatively recent. It has been used persuasively to address issues of mobilization and the adoption of innovation. However, unlike some other mechanisms discussed in this chapter, the theoretical developments in this area have not been well complemented by empirical evidence. Scholars have proposed mathematical models, and some have carried out simulations. However, few of these efforts have been empirically validated.

In addition to the need for more empirical research, there are also some conceptual issues that continue to be advanced. First, the conceptualization of information technologies, such as discretionary databases, as "public goods" (Fulk et al., 1996), suggests that collective action theories can offer a more sophisticated explanation of the emergence of organizational networks, extending their present use to study the adoption of technologies in organizations. Discretionary databases are the message repositories that link knowledge suppliers and consumers, thereby creating connective and communal networks of individuals who share knowledge domains.

Second, there is potential for the application of network approaches to the conceptualization of free riding and its role in collective action. Collective action by groups is based on an underlying premise of social control. Homans's (1974) cohesion-compliance hypothesis predicts that group members are able to enforce social control on one another by exchanging peer approval for compliance with group obligations. Flache and Macy (1996) argue that under some circumstances members may choose to offer peer approval in exchange for peer approval rather than compliance from others. Using computer simulations of groups' networks, they observed that in these situations groups may reach a high level of cohesion that is not accompanied by a higher level of compliance or better group performance. Contrary to Homans's cohesion-compliance hypothesis, Flache and Macy (1996) concluded that "peer pressure can be an effective instrument for blocking compliance, especially in groups in which the cost of compliance is high relative to the value of approval" (p. 29). Oliver (1980) describes this phenomenon, where social control is directed toward the maintenance of interpersonal relationships at the expense of compliance with group obligations, as the "second-order free-rider problem."

Exchange and Dependency Theories

Extensive research has been conducted that seeks to explain the emergence of networks based on exchange and dependency mechanisms. Social exchange theory, originally developed by Homans (1950, 1974) and Blau (1964), seeks to explain human action by a calculus of exchange of material or information resources. In its original formulation, social exchange theory attempted to explain the likelihood of a dyadic relationship based on the supply and demand of resources that each member of the dyad had to offer. Emerson (1962, 1972a, 1972b) extended this original formulation beyond the dyad, arguing that to examine the potential of exchange and power-dependence relationships, it was critical to examine the larger network within

which the dyad was embedded. Since then, several scholars have developed this perspective into what is now commonly referred to as network exchange theory (Bienenstock & Bonacich, 1992, 1997; Cook, 1977, 1982; Cook & Whitmeyer, 1992; Cook & Yamagishi, 1992; Markovsky, Willer, & Patton, 1988; Skvoretz & Willer, 1993; Willer & Skvoretz, 1997; Yamagishi, Gillmore, & Cook, 1988).

Network exchange theory posits that individuals' power to bargain is a function of the extent to which they are vulnerable to exclusion from communication and other exchanges within the network. The argument is that individuals forge network links on the basis of their analysis of the relative costs and returns on investments. Likewise, individuals maintain links based on the frequency, the uncertainty, and the continuing investments to sustain the interaction. Location in the network may confer on some people an advantage over others in engaging in exchange relationships. Aldrich (1982) notes that this argument is at the core of several theories dealing with social exchange as well as resource dependency theories. Within organizations, network researchers have proposed a social exchange mechanism for the study of (a) power, (b) leadership, and (c) trust and ethical behavior. At the interorganizational level, researchers have (a) tested resource dependency theory, (b) examined the composition of corporate elites and interlocking board of directorates, and (c) sought to explain the creation, maintenance, and dissolution of interorganizational links. Each area is examined in greater detail below. The section concludes with proposed extensions to the study of organizational networks from a social exchange perspective.

Power

Social exchange theory has been used to examine the power that ensues from a structural position. In terms of exchange theory, power is defined as a function of dependence on others in the network. Location in the communication network is associated with greater power to the extent it offers greater access to valued material and informational resources. Specifically, people, groups, and organizations have power to the extent that they have access to alternate sources of a valued resource, and the extent to which they control resources valued by others in the network (Emerson, 1962). In a series of experimental and simulation studies, Cook and her colleagues (Cook & Emerson, 1978; Cook, Emerson, Gillmore, & Yamagishi, 1983) found evidence to support a power-dependence relationship. Carroll and Teo (1996) found that to increase their resources, organizational managers were more motivated than nonmanagers to have larger core discussion networks and to create more communication links outside the organization by memberships in clubs and societies. In her study of interorganizational social services, Alter (1990) found that the existence of a centralized, dominant core agency reduced the level of conflict and competition between service organizations and improved their level of cooperation. However, Hoffman, Stearns, and Shrader (1990) found that organizational centrality in four multiplex interorganizational networks depended on the nature of the network.

Several studies have equated network centrality with different sources of power. Brass (1984) suggested two measures of centrality that reflect different dimensions of power. Closeness, the extent to which people, groups, and organizations can reach all others in a network through a minimum of intermediaries, corresponds to the "access of resources" dimension of power (Sabidussi, 1966). Betweenness, the extent to which a network member lies between others not directly connected, corresponds to the "control of resources" dimension of power (Freeman, 1977, 1979). Brass (1984, 1985b) showed that both measures of centrality correlated with reputational measures of power. Further, Brass (1984, 1985b) found that employees with high scores on network indicators of power were more likely to be promoted to supervisory positions, and Burkhardt and Brass (1990) discovered that early adopters of a new technology increased their power. Ibarra (1993a) found that centrality in the informal network was at least as important as the formal hierarchical network in predicting power; Krackhardt (1990) reported similar results for advice and friendship networks. Interestingly, Brass and Burkhardt's (1992) research revealed that measures of centrality at the departmental level were more strongly related to several indexes of power than measures at the subunit or the organizational levels.

Leadership

The success of network formulations to predict power has prompted some scholars to suggest its use in extending theories of leadership such as Graen's (1976) leader-member exchange theory (Krackhardt & Brass, 1994) and attribution theories of leadership (McElroy & Shrader, 1986). Fernandez (1991) found that the effects of informal communication networks on perceptions of leadership were different in three types of organizations. Specifically, he found that informal communication predicted perceptions of leadership most strongly in the participatory organization, a telephone-counseling center; only weakly in the professional organization, a public finance department of a large investment bank; and not at all in the hierarchical organization, a metallurgical firm.

Trust and Ethical Behavior

Researchers have also used social exchange theory to study the development and utility of trust in organizational and interorganizational networks. As Burt and Knez (1996) note, "Trust is committing to an exchange before you know how the other person will reciprocate" (p. 69). In a study of managers in a large high-technology firm, they found that the communication networks in which two individuals were embedded predicted the probability of a trust relationship between them. In particular, the trust between two individuals in close contact was high if other members in the organizations indirectly connected the two members to one another. Further, the *dis*trust between two individuals who were not in close contact was further attenuated if other members in the organization indirectly connected them to one another. This research indicates that indirect communication linkages reinforce trust and distrust relations between people. Labianca, Brass, and Gray (1998) also reported a similar amplification effect. They suggest that the amplification effect occurs because the secondhand information transmitted by indirect communication linkages "may be more polarized or exaggerated (either positively or negatively) than firsthand information" (p. 64), as grapevine (rumor) studies have found (e.g., DeFleur & Cronin, 1991; Schachter & Burdick, 1955).

In a study involving trust as measured via friendship networks, Krackhardt and Stern (1988) found that a relatively higher proportion of interunit (as compared to intraunit) friendship ties was particularly helpful to organizations coping with crisis conditions. In this case, the high level of trust was seen as a prerequisite for the increased interunit coordination required during a period of high uncertainty and the ensuing potential conflict. Larson's (1992) study of entrepreneurial firms indicated that trust as well as shared reciprocity norms, close personal relations, and reputation determined with whom and how exchanges occurred.

Researchers examining ethical behavior in organizations also deploy the exchange mechanism. Brass, Butterfield, and Skaggs (1995) suggest that networks could also offer an explanation for the likelihood of unethical behavior in a dyad since the connectedness of people is highly related to their observability. Brass et al. (1995) propose that "the strength of the relationship between two actors will be positively related to the opportunity to act in an unethical manner, but negatively related to the motivation to act unethically. Frequency and trust provide increased opportunity, but

intimacy and empathy decrease the motivation" (p. 6).

Resource Dependency Theory and Power in Interorganizational Networks

In his now classic article, Benson (1975) defined interorganizational networks as a political economy. By this he meant that interorganizational communication and exchange networks were the mechanisms by which organizations acquired and dispensed scarce resources, thus creating and perpetuating a system of power relations. Organizations were viewed as dependent on their positions in the network, which subsequently influenced their ability to control the flow of scarce resources.

Pfeffer and Salancik (1978) drew on Benson's work on political economy and social exchange mechanisms (Emerson, 1962, 1972a, 1972b) to formulate resource dependency theory. This theory argues that organizations structure their resource linkages to buffer themselves from the organization's environment (Pfeffer & Salancik, 1978). In particular, they identify two mechanisms that organizations can use toward this end. First, by network extension, organizations can seek to increase the number of exchange alternatives by creating new network links. Second, by network consolidation, they can decrease the number of exchange alternatives for others by forming a coalition with other resource providers. These counterbalancing mechanisms provide an explanation for the stability of exchange relationships and potential redistribution of power among the individuals. Burt (1991) developed a measure of equilibrium to assess the likelihood that network members have the resources to reconfigure their exchange networks and thereby the distribution of power.

A major tenet of resource dependency theory is that organizations tend to avoid interorganizational linkages that limit their decision making and other forms of autonomy. Oliver (1991; see also Oliver, 1990) tested this assumption across five relational types that ranged from highest to lowest levels of autonomy: personal meetings, resource transfers, board interlocks, joint programs, and written contracts. Surprisingly, she found no evidence that linkages that implied greater loss of autonomy led to lower likelihood of establishing the relationship.

A substantial body of empirical research draws on a resource dependency framework to study the pattern of interorganizational networks. These studies examine a wide variety of resource relationships, including money, material, information, and messages. However, the focus of these relationships is more concerned with the pattern of relationships than their content; thus, the majority of resource dependency research is conducted from a positional perspective. In some of the earlier studies in this area, Laumann and Pappi (1976) and Galaskiewicz (1979) reported that organizations that were more central in their networks had greater reputational influence. In a broad-based study assessing the power of the U.S. labor force, Wallace, Griffin, and Rubin (1989) discovered that the labor force in industries that were more central in the network of interindustry transactions were more likely to receive higher wages than the labor force in peripheral industries. Gerlach's (1992) study of the Japanese corporate network, including intercorporate *keiretsu* groupings, found strong evidence of the centrality of financial institutions in these networks and their resultant ability to control the capital allocation process (see also Lincoln, Gerlach, & Takahashi, 1992). However, in a study of health systems, Oliver and Montgomery (1996) observed that "the organization with greatest influence within the system (because of its ability to allocate funds) may not be the organization that takes the largest role in terms of coordinating routine contacts" (p. 771), such as client referrals.

Two studies show the impact of resource exchange on effectiveness. Miner, Amburgey, and Stearns's (1990) research on 1,011 newspaper publishers in Finland from 1771 to 1963 found that publishers with a greater number of interorganizational resource linkages, typically to political parties, had a higher overall success rate. Goes and Park (1997) found that "a greater volume of [resource] exchanges between hospitals increases the likelihood that innovation will spread between them" (p. 771).

Provan and Milward (1995) reported research designed to extend resource dependency theory by focusing on the effectiveness of the entire interorganizational network (see also Provan, 1983) rather than the antecedents and outcomes of individual organizations. Further, they pointed out that how well individual organizations perform is less important than how the interorganizational network as a whole performs. Studying the mental health care delivery system in four cities, they found that networks with a centralized decision-making agency were more effective than networks in which decision making was widely dispersed across agencies. Their data also suggested that the relationship between network structure and network effectiveness is influenced by the existence of a relatively munificent environment and the degree to which the overall network is stable.

Corporate Elites and Interlocking Boards of Directors

Corporate elites and networks created by linkages among people who serve on multiple corporate boards are areas that have received considerable research attention in interorganizational relations. As Knoke (1993) indicated, "A power elite is established at the intersection of three social formations: a class-conscious upper social class of wealth-holders, interlocked directors of major corporations, and a policy-planning network of foundations, research institutes, and nonpartisan organizations" (p. 26). Useem's (1984) classic study argued that these overlapping networks of friendship, ownership, membership, and directorship produced a core set of individuals, or "inner circle," which wields enormous power. Knoke (1993) explained that "because its members simultaneously hold multiple directorships, the core can act politically in the interests of the class, which transcend the parochial concerns of its individual firms" (p. 26). Consistent with this view, Romo and Anheier (1996) found evidence that a core group of elites explained the emergence and institutionalization of consortia for private development organizations in Nigeria and Senegal. Studies have also shown that individuals who were more centrally located in the interlocking board of directors were also more likely to play a leadership role in cultural, philanthropic, and policy-making organizations (Domhoff, 1983; Mizruchi & Galaskiewicz, 1994; Ogliastri & Davila, 1987; Ratcliff, Gallagher, & Ratcliff, 1979; Useem, 1980).

Historically, the focus of interlocking directorate research has been on corporate control. However, Minz and Schwartz (1985) argued that "the most compelling interpretation of the overall network created by the collection of individual reasons for and response to director recruitment is a general communication system" (p. 141). In fact, as Mizruchi (1996) contends, "the emphasis on interlocks has moved increasingly toward their value as a communication mechanism rather than as a mechanism of control" (p. 284).

Creation, Maintenance, Dissolution, and Reconstitution of Interfirm Links

Studies have also deployed a resource dependency framework to explain the creation of links in interorganizational networks. Mizruchi and Stearns (1988) found two general factors that explained the addition of new financial members to an organization's board of directors. Under favorable economic conditions, when capital demand and supply are increasing, organizations initiate links with financial institutions through their board of directors to co-opt these institutions' financial and informational resources. However, during unfavorable economic conditions, including contractions in the business cycle, lower solvency, and lower profitability, it is the financial institutions that infiltrate companies' boards of directors to protect their investments. This finding is qualified by Boyd's (1990) research that showed high-performing firms responded to resource scarcity and competitive uncertainty by decreasing the number of their directors but increasing the density of their linkages with other firms. Mizruchi (1996) argued that a number of other factors also affect the creation of interlocking directorates. These include creating legitimacy for the firm, advancing the careers of those who serve as directors, and fostering the social cohesion of the corporate upper class.

Palmer et al. (1986) used resource dependency theory to hypothesize the conditions under which a broken interlock tie between two organizations (due to death, retirement, etc.) would be reconstituted. They found that interlock ties were likely to be reconstituted if the departing member represented an organization with which the focal organization had (a) formal coordination, such as long-term contracts or joint ventures; (b) direct business ties; or (c) headquarters that were physically proximate.

Larson (1992) demonstrated that firms tend to enter repeated alliances with each other; thus, dependencies tend to generate further dependencies. Gulati's (1995) research showed that the information provided by both direct and indirect ties of prior alliances established the basis for the formation of additional alliances. However, his research also showed that as the benefits of linking with specific others declined over time organizations looked for new alliances. Of course, as Baum and Oliver (1992) noted, there is a carrying capacity to alliances in that most organizations can successfully support only a limited number of connections, and many firms fear the overdependence that too many ties might bring.

Seabright, Levinthal, and Fichman (1992) theorized that reductions in the resource fit between organizations would lead to pressures to dissolve interorganizational relations while increases in personal and structural attachments would counter those pressures and lead to continued relations. Their results supported the hypotheses but also showed that personal and structural attachments attenuated the firms' likelihood of dissolving ties under conditions of reduced fit. This finding underscores the importance of established communication and social attachments in maintaining interorganizational relations beyond the point where a strict exchange or resource dependency perspective would predict that they would dissolve, even at times when it might be disadvantageous to maintain them. Overall, however, Mizruchi's (1996) review of the research literature on corporate interlocks led him to conclude that "although the findings have been mixed, on balance they support the view that interlocks are associated with interfirm resource dependence" (p. 274).

The research on interlocking directorates assumes that each organization is a separate entity tied together at the top by corporate elites. While interest continues in interlocking directorates, a new field of research has developed over the past decade that focuses on an emergent organizational form, network organizations. This perspective relaxes these two assumptions of separate entities and executive ties only. We explore this new area in the next section.

Network Organizations

Network organizations are composed of a collection of organizations along with the linkages that tie them to each other, often organized around a focal organization. There are numerous variations on the network organizational form including joint partnerships, strategic alliances, cartels, R&D consortia, and a host of others.

The theoretical mechanisms that generate most network organizations are exchange and dependency relations. Rather than being organized around market or hierarchical principles, network organizations are created out of complex webs of exchange and dependency relations among multiple organizations. In a sense, the network organization becomes a supraorganization whose primary function is linking many organizations together and coordinating their activities. Unlike interlocking directorates, the network ties usually occur throughout the entire organization rather than only at the top, and the separate organizations often give up some or all of their individual autonomy to become a part of the new network organization.

Miles and Snow (1992) observe that network organizations differ from their predecessors (functional, multidivisional, and matrix forms) in four important ways. First, rather than subsume all aspects of production within a single hierarchical organization they attempt to create a set of relations and communication networks among several firms, each of which contributes to the value of the product or service. Second, networks are based on a combination of market mechanisms and informal communication relations. As they say, "The various components of the network recognize their interdependence and are willing to share information, cooperate with each other, and customize their product or service—all to maintain their position within the network" (p. 55). Third, members of networks are often assumed to take a proactive role in improving the final product or service, rather than merely fulfilling contractual obligations. Finally, a number of industries are beginning to form network organizations along the lines of the Japanese keiretsu, which links together producers, suppliers, and financial institutions into fairly stable patterns of relations.

Poole (in press) argues that new organizational forms, including network organizations, are constituted out of six essential qualities:

1. The use of information technology to integrate across organizational functions
2. Flexible, modular organizational structures that can be readily reconfigured as new projects, demands, or problems arise
3. Use of information technology to coordinate geographically dispersed units and members

4. Team-based work organization, which emphasizes autonomy and self-management
5. Relatively flat hierarchies and reliance on horizontal coordination among units and personnel
6. Use of intra- and interorganizational markets to mediate transactions such as the assignment and hiring of personnel for projects and the formation of interorganizational networks.

In today's world, nearly all organizations are embedded to some extent in an emergent interorganizational communication network. For example, most economic institutions are linked together in "value chains" (Porter, 1980) or "value constellations" (Norman & Ramirez, 1993) where each receives a partially finished product from an "upstream organization," adds its contribution, and then delivers it to the next "downstream organization" for its contribution. Similarly, educational institutions typically relate to other educational institutions in a chain from preschool to postgraduate education. And religious organizations are frequently affiliated with coalitions of other like-minded religious groups. Of course, all must deal with the taxation authorities of federal, state, and local governments.

In one sense, network organizations create what have come to be called "boundaryless organizations" (Nohria & Berkley, 1994). Where one organization begins and the other ends is no longer clear. Organizations come to share knowledge, goals, resources, personnel, and finances, usually with highly sophisticated communication technology (Monge & Fulk, 1999). To accomplish this they must establish collaborative work arrangements, since that is the only way to transfer embedded knowledge.

Ghoshal and Bartlett (1990) argued that multinational corporations (MNCs) have traditionally been viewed as an intraorganizational network, in many ways not different from traditional national companies. Each satellite, subsidiary, or foreign partner has been seen as directly connected to the home corporate office, thus tying the MNC into an integrated hub-and-spoke structural whole. However, they point out that this view of the MNC fails to take into account the extended networks in which each of the subsidiaries is embedded. These national, regional, and competing global networks require a reconceptualization of MNCs as network organizations.

Limitations of Network Organizations

Several authors have pointed out that network organizations have a number of limitations. Miles and Snow (1992) observe that network organizations contain the vestigial weaknesses of their predecessors, the functional, multidivisional, and matrix forms. To the extent that parts of these prior forms remain in the network organization, the new form retains their prior limitations. Krackhardt (1994) identifies four potential constraints on communication and other networks. The first he calls the "law of N-squared," which simply notes that the number of potential links in a network organization increases geometrically with the number of people. In fact, it grows so quickly that the number of people to which each person could be linked quickly exceeds everyone's communication capacity. The second constraint is the "law of propinquity," a rather consistent empirical finding that "the probability of two people communicating is inversely proportional to the distance between them" (p. 213). Though numerous communication technologies have been designed to overcome this phenomenon, Krackhardt argues that the tendency remains and is difficult for people to overcome. The third constraint he identifies is the "iron law of oligarchy," which is the tendency for groups and social systems, even fervently democratic ones, to end up under the control of a few people. Finally, Krackhardt (1994) notes the potential problem of overembeddedness. He observes that "people as a matter of habit and preference are likely to seek out their old standbys, the people they have grown to trust, the people they always go to and depend on, to deal with new problems, even though they may not be the ones best able to address these problems" (p. 220).

Poole (in press) also points to several human problems that stem from the tightly coupled technology but fluid management philosophies on which most network organizations are built. Foremost among these are maintaining a sense of mission, commitment, loyalty, and trust, and dealing with increased levels of work stress and burnout.

Extensions to Exchange and Dependency Theories

While some variation exists across different studies, the preponderance of evidence suggests that many inter- and intraorganizational communication networks are created and maintained on the basis of exchange mechanisms. Further, as people and organizations find their exchanges no longer rewarding or as new or competitive others offer better bargains in the exchange, linkages begin to dissolve.

Despite its intellectual roots in the study of interpersonal relationships, exchange and dependency theories have been more extensively deployed in the study of interorganizational networks, often within the context of resource dependency theory, rather than intraorganizational networks. Much of the intraorganizational research reviewed above, while premised in a social exchange perspective, does not invoke the theory explicitly. Further, in areas such as leadership, trust, and ethical behavior, the studies so far are more illustrative then programmatic attempts at applying social exchange theory. X-Net, a computer simulation tool developed by Markovsky (1995), should help researchers explore the emergence of networks in terms of different rules of exchange and varied resources. Researchers have also proposed integrating net-

work exchange theory with rational choice theory (Markovsky, 1997) and identity theory (Burke, 1997), and a general theoretical method called E-state structuralism (Skvoretz & Fararo, 1996; Skvoretz & Faust, 1996), which integrates research on expectation states theory (Berger, Cohen, & Zelditch, 1966) with network exchange theory. Expectation states theory argues that a person's "behavior towards social objects depends on postulated and unobservable states of relational orientations to objects, E-states for short" (Skvoretz & Fararo, 1996, p. 1370). The social objects toward which individuals orient are the networks of ties among the individuals. E-state models specify "how the state of this network, i.e., the number and nature of the ties linking actors, changes over time as individuals interact" (Skvoretz & Fararo, 1996, p. 1370).

Contagion Theories

Contagion theories are based on the assumption that communication networks in organizations serve as a mechanism that exposes people, groups, and organizations to information, attitudinal messages, and the behavior of others (Burt, 1980, 1987; Contractor & Eisenberg, 1990). This exposure increases the likelihood that network members will develop beliefs, assumptions, and attitudes that are similar to those of others in their network (Carley, 1991; Carley & Kaufer, 1993). The contagion approach seeks to explain organizational members' knowledge, attitudes, and behavior on the basis of information, attitudes, and behavior of others in the network to whom they are linked. Rogers and Kincaid (1981) refers to this as the *convergence* model of communication.

Theories that are premised on a contagion model, at least in part, include social information processing theory (Fulk, Steinfield, Schmitz, & Power, 1987; Salancik & Pfeffer, 1978), social influence theory (Fulk, Schmitz, & Steinfield, 1990; see also Marsden &

Friedkin, 1994), structural theory of action (Burt, 1982), symbolic interactionist perspectives (Trevino, Lengel, & Daft, 1987), mimetic processes exemplified by institutional theories (DiMaggio & Powell, 1983; Meyer & Rowan, 1977), and social cognitive theory (Bandura, 1986). Fulk (1993) notes that these constructivist perspectives "share the core proposition that social and symbolic processes produce patterns of shared cognitions and behaviors that arise from forces well beyond the demands of the straightforward task of information processing in organizations" (p. 924). She also points out that the mechanisms offered by these theories differ not so much because of conflicting premises as because the theories focus on different aspects of the social construction process.

The contagion mechanism has been used to explain network members' attitudes as well as behavior. Erickson (1988) offers a comprehensive overview of the various theories that address the "relational basis of attitudes" (p. 99). She describes how various network dyadic measures such as frequency, multiplexity, strength, and asymmetry can shape the extent to which others influence individuals in their networks. Moving beyond the dyadic level of network contagion, she also describes cohesion and structural equivalence models that offer alternative, and in some cases complementary, explanations of the contagion process. Contagion by cohesion implies that the attitudes and behaviors of the others with whom they are directly connected influence network members. Contagion by structural equivalence implies that others who have similar structural patterns of relationships within the network influence people.

An impressive body of empirical research at both the intraorganizational and interorganizational levels is based on the contagion mechanism. At the intraorganizational level, studies have proposed a contagion mechanism to explain (a) general workplace attitudes, (b) attitudes toward technologies, and (c) organizational behavior such as turnover and absenteeism. Researchers have also used contagion

to explain interorganizational behavior. Each of these topics is reviewed on the following pages. The section concludes with suggestions for extensions of organizational research based on a contagion mechanism.

General Workplace Attitudes

Several studies have examined the extent to which contagion explains individual attitudes in the workplace. Friedkin's (1984) early research showed that educational policy makers were more likely to perceive agreement with others who were either in the same cohesive social circle or were structurally equivalent. Walker (1985) discovered that members of a computer firm who were structurally equivalent were more likely to report similar cognitions about means-ends relationships of product development. And Rentsch (1990) found that members of an accounting firm who communicated with one another were more likely to share similar interpretations of organizational events.

Goodell, Brown, and Poole (1989) use a structurational argument (Poole & McPhee, 1983) to examine the relationship between communication network links and shared perceptions of organizational climate. Using four waves of observation over a ten-week period from an organizational simulation, they found that members' communication networks were significantly associated with shared perceptions of the organizational climate only at the early stages of organizing (weeks two and four). In another study comparing the cohesion and structural equivalence mechanisms of contagion, Hartman and Johnson (1989, 1990) found that members who were cohesively linked were more likely to have similar levels of commitment to the organization. However, those who were structurally equivalent were more likely to have similar perceptions of role ambiguity in the workplace. Pollock, Whitbred, and Contractor (1996) compared the relative efficacy of three models that seek to explain an individual's satisfaction in the workplace: the job characteristics model (Hackman & Oldham, 1976), the individual dispositions model (Staw & Ross, 1985), and the social information processing model (Salancik & Pfeffer, 1978). Using data from the public works division of a military installation, Pollock et al. (1996) found that employees' satisfaction was significantly predicted only by the social information processing model, that is, by the satisfaction of friends and communication partners in their social networks, but not by the characteristics of their jobs or their individual dispositions.

Attitudes Toward Technologies

Several researchers have examined the extent to which contagion explains organizational members' attitudes toward technologies. Drawing on social information processing theory (Salancik & Pfeffer, 1978) and social cognitive theory (Bandura, 1986), Fulk and her colleagues (Fulk, Schmitz, & Ryu, 1995; Schmitz & Fulk, 1991) found that organizational members' perceptions and use of an electronic mail system were significantly influenced by the attitudes and use of the members' supervisors and five closest coworkers. Further, Fulk (1993) found that social influence was even more pronounced in more cohesive groups. The attitudes and use of other members in their communication networks significantly influenced individuals' attitudes and use of an electronic mail system. This effect was attenuated, but persisted, even after she controlled for the effect of the work group's attitudes and use on each group member.

Rice and Aydin's (1991) research showed that hospital employees who communicated with one another or shared supervisory-subordinate relationships were more likely to share similar attitudes about a recently introduced information technology. Rice et al. (1990) found that individuals' use of email in a decentralized federal agency was predicted by the use of the technology by others in their communication network. Further, groups of individuals who communicated more strongly

with one another were more likely to share similar distinct email usage patterns.

Using longitudinal data from a federal government agency, Burkhardt (1994) found that individuals' attitudes and use of a recently implemented distributed data-processing computer network were significantly influenced by the attitudes and use of others in their communication network. She found that individuals' perceptions of their self-efficacy with (or mastery of) the new technology were significantly influenced by those with whom they had direct communication, which is the theoretical mechanism of contagion by cohesion. However, individuals' general attitudes and use of the technology itself were more influenced by the attitudes and behaviors of those with whom they shared similar communication patterns, that is, contagion by structural equivalence. Burkhardt also found that the contagion effect was higher for individuals who scored higher on a self-monitoring scale.

Extending this line of longitudinal research on contagion effects, Contractor, Seibold, and Heller (1996) conducted a study comparing the evolution of the social influence process in face-to-face and computer-augmented groups. They found that group members initial influence on each others' perceptions of the structures-in-use (i.e., the interaction norms enacted during the meeting) was high in the face-to-face condition, while group members using group decision support systems (GDSSs) started out with low levels of social influence on one another. However, the difference between face-to-face and technologically augmented groups was only transient. By their third meeting, members in all groups heavily influenced each other's perceptions of the structures-in-use. While the preponderance of research has focused on similarity in attitudes based on contagion, Bovasso (1995) reports results from a process he calls "anticontagion." In a study of managers at a large, multinational high-tech firm, Bovasso found that "individuals who perceive themselves as strong leaders are influenced by peers who do not perceive themselves as strong leaders" (pp. 1430-1431) and vice versa.

Behavior Through Contagion

Several network studies have used a contagion explanation for organizational members' behaviors, including voluntary turnover, absenteeism, job-seeking, socialization, and unethical behavior. Krackhardt and Porter (1986) found that employees voluntarily quitting their jobs were more likely to be structurally equivalent to one another than those who remained. However, they found that employees who were absent were more likely to be cohesively connected with one another through friendship ties. They suggested that decisions about turnover were more closely related to individuals' roles in the organization and hence, members were more influenced by others in similar roles. On the other hand, decisions about absenteeism reflected norms in the organizations that were communicated through cohesive friendship ties. In a more recent study, Feeley and Barnett (1996) examined employee turnover at a supermarket and found that both social influence and structural equivalence networks predicted the likelihood of employees leaving the organization. Kilduff (1992) studied graduate business students' job-seeking behavior and found that students' decisions to interview with particular organizations were influenced by the opinions communicated to them by others in their friendship networks. The contagion effect was more pronounced for students who reported being high self-monitors. Zey-Ferrell and Ferrell (1982) reported that employees' self-reported unethical behavior was better predicted by their perceptions of their peer behavior than either their own beliefs or those of top management. Research on organizational socialization (Jablin & Krone, 1987; Sherman, Smith, & Mansfield, 1986) has also identified newcomers' positions in their new communication networks as a predictor of their assimilation into the organization.

Interorganizational Contagion

The contagion mechanism has also been used to explain behavior at the interorganizational level. Organizations can link to other organizations in many ways. Useem (1984) describes how organizations use director interlocks as a tool to scan their environment. These linkages are important because they provide the opportunity for communication and the exchange of ideas, practices, and values. Both the formal activities surrounding the board meetings and the informal activities and acquaintance ties that are created enable people to discover how things are done in other organizations. In these and similar interorganizational studies, the opportunity to communicate afforded by the existence of linkages is viewed as more important than specific message content.

Consistent with Useem's (1984) view, much of the more recent literature examines the mechanisms by which organizations use these linkages to transfer organizational practices and structural forms. Davis (1991) found that *Fortune* 500 corporations were more likely to adopt the "poison pill" strategy to defend against corporate takeovers if their boards had directors from organizations that had already adopted a similar strategy. Haunschild's (1993) research showed that the number and types of corporate acquisitions undertaken by their interlock partners significantly influenced the number and type of takeovers attempted by firms. Likewise, her 1994 research demonstrated that "acquisition premiums" (p. 406), the price that a firm pays to acquire another firm over the market value prior to the takeover announcement, are similar to those that their partner firms paid for their acquisitions. Other research by Palmer, Jennings, and Zhou (1993) has shown that firms are more likely to adopt a multidivisional form when they are linked to corporations that have already adopted that form. Similarly, Burns and Wholey (1993) found that a hospital's decision to adopt a matrix management program was significantly predicted by the adoption decision of other local hospitals with high prestige and visibility. Goes and Park (1997) found that hospitals that were structurally tied to other hospitals in a multihospital system were more likely to adopt innovations, and Westphal, Gulati, and Shortell (1997) found that contagion also explained the adoption of total quality management (TQM) practices in the organization. However, they observed that early adopters of TQM were more likely to use the other early adopters in their medical alliance network to clarify their functional understanding of TQM. The early adopters were therefore more likely to customize the program to their organizational needs. In contrast, late adopters were more likely to seek out other adopters in their alliance network to determine the legitimacy of using TQM. Hence, the late adopters were more likely to adopt the TQM program without any customization. Stearns and Mizruchi (1993) found that the type of financing used by a firm, short- versus long-term debt, was influenced by the types of financial institutions to which it was linked by its board of directors, commercial bankers versus representatives of insurance companies. However, the embeddedness of an organization's board of directors has a somewhat counterintuitive influence on the selection of its CEO. Khurana (1997) found that *Fortune* 500 companies whose boards of directors were well embedded into the system of interlocking directorates were *less* likely to choose an outsider as a CEO because "a high level of embeddedness is likely to constrain actions rather than facilitate them" (p. 17).

Interlocking directorates are only one of several possible mechanisms for linking organizations. Organizations are likely to be linked to bankers, attorneys, accountants, suppliers, and consultants, all of whom serve as conduits for the flow of information between organizations. Basing their arguments on the mimetic processes articulated by institutional theory (DiMaggio & Powell, 1983), Galaskiewicz and Burt (1991), and Galaskiewicz and Wasserman (1989) discovered that contribution officers who were structurally equivalent in an interorganizational corporate network were more likely to give charitable donations to the same nonprofit groups than those who were cohesively linked. Mizruchi (1989, 1992) found that organizations that were structurally equivalent in the interorganizational network were more likely to have similar patterns of political contributions. Baum and Oliver (1991) showed that increased ties to legitimating institutions significantly reduced the likelihood of failure among new organizations. And in a ten-year study, Goes and Park (1997) found that hospitals linked to their institutional environments through industry and trade associations were more likely to adopt innovations in an effort to gain legitimacy. This effect was even more pronounced when the hospital industry entered a turbulent phase after introduction of two regulatory events in 1983. Interestingly, these findings are similar to those obtained under predictions from exchange and resource dependency theories, though obviously generated by a different theoretical mechanism.

Extensions to Contagion Theories

Contagion theories offer by far the most common theoretical mechanisms for studying the emergence of networks. The notion of a network as labyrinth of conduits for information flow lends itself to theoretical mechanisms based on contagion. However, while network researchers frequently invoke contagion theories, they often fall short of articulating specific mechanisms and network models by which individuals, groups, and organizations influence each other's actions and behaviors (Contractor & Eisenberg, 1990; Marsden & Friedkin, 1994; Rice, 1993b). There are four recent attempts to articulate mechanisms that make the contagion process more theoretically specific and comprehensive for communication networks.

First, Krackhardt and Brass (1994) note that the contagion processes described by social information processing theory must over time lead to an equilibrium wherein everyone in the network will eventually converge in their attitudes or actions. They note that this conclusion undermines the very premise of social information processing theory, which seeks to explain the variation in people's attitudes based on their differential exposure to social information. Krackhardt and Brass (1994) suggest that the *principle of interaction* that is assumed by contagion theories needs to be augmented by a second contagion mechanism, the *principle of reflected exclusivity*. The principle of interaction states that greater interaction leads to greater similarity in attitudes. By contrast, the principle of reflected exclusivity states that "the degree of influence person j has on person i's evaluation . . . is inversely proportional to the amount of time person j spends with all others" (Krackhardt & Brass, 1994, p. 219).

Second, Krassa (1988) advocates the inclusion of members' threshold levels in a social influence model. In its simplest form, the threshold is the number of others that people must be influenced by before succumbing (Granovetter, 1978). Individuals' thresholds could be a function of the intensity of their opinion and their aversion to the risk of being socially isolated. Krassa (1988) uses computer simulations of a contagion model to demonstrate the effects of people's threshold distributions on their opinions.

Third, Rice (1993b) has argued that a network contagion model of social influence should also take into consideration the ambiguity of the situation. Drawing on research by Moscovici (1976), Rice (1993b) argues that people are more vulnerable to social influence by contagion when confronted with ambiguous, or novel, situations. Based on this argument, Contractor and Grant (1996) hypothesized that groups using new collaboration technologies (a novel situation) would be more likely to influence each other's perceptions of the medium than groups in a traditional face-to-face meeting. However, they found that social influence was actually greater in face-to-face groups, perhaps because the novelty in this case was associated with the very medium used to socially influence one another.

Finally, in an attempt to extend the current debate surrounding the relative efficacy of contagion via cohesion versus structural equivalence, Pattison (1994) argued for a closer examination of automorphic or regular equivalence in addition to mechanisms based on contagion by cohesion and structural equivalence. Unlike structural equivalence, which in its strict operationalization is defined as two individuals having identical network links to the same others, regular equivalence is defined as two people having similar patterns of relationships, but not necessarily with the same others (White & Reitz, 1989). Pattison (1994) argues that people who are regularly equivalent are more likely to have similar social cognitions because "cognitive processes may directly involve the individual's perceptions of his or her social locale" (p. 93). In a longitudinal study of students in an undergraduate class, Michaelson and Contractor (1992) found that students who were regularly equivalent were more likely to be perceived as similar by their classmates than those who were structurally equivalent.

Cognitive Theories

The contagion mechanisms discussed in the previous section focused on the extent to which others who were linked to individuals via cohesion or structural equivalence influenced their attitudes and actions. These studies explain attitudes and behavior based on individuals' actual interactions. Researchers have employed four concepts to gain insight into the structure of individuals' cognitions: semantic networks, knowledge structures, cognitive social structures, and cognitive consistency. These areas are discussed in greater detail below.

Semantic Networks

With an eye toward a more systematic treatment of message content, semantic networks were introduced into the organizational communication literature by Monge and Eisenberg (1987; see also Carley, 1986; Danowski's [1982] word network analysis; Dunn & Ginsberg, 1986; Fiol's [1989] semiotic analysis; Rogers & Kincaid's [1981] convergence theory of networks; Woelfel & Fink's [1980] Galileo system). The essential feature of this perspective was a focus on the shared meanings that people have for message content, particularly those messages that comprise important aspects of an organization's culture, such as corporate goals, slogans, myths, and stories. Monge and Eisenberg (1987) argued that asking people to provide their interpretations of one or more significant communication messages, events, or artifacts could create semantic networks. Content analysis of members' responses provides categories of interpretation. Linkages can then be created between people who share similar interpretations. The resultant network articulation provides a picture of the groups of people who share common understandings, those who have idiosyncratic meanings such as isolates, and those who serve as liaisons and boundary spanners between the various groups.

With respect to empirical studies of semantic networks Lievrouw, Rogers, Lowe, and Nadel (1987) used four methods to identify the invisible research colleges among biomedical scientists: (a) co-citation analysis, (b) coword occurrence, (c) interpretive thematic analysis, and (d) network analysis. They concluded that their focus on the content of the networks helped clarify the structure of the invisible colleges. On the basis of communication network patterns alone, all the scientists would have been clustered into one invisible college. However, a closer examination of content helped them identify several invisible colleges, "each of which represents a distinct and identifiable line of research" (p. 246).

In a study of a high-technology firm, a library, and a hospital, Contractor, Eisenberg, and Monge (1996) examined the semantic networks representing the extent to which em-

ployees shared interpretations of their organizations' missions. In addition to their actual agreement, employees were also asked to report their perceived agreement, that is, the extent to which they believed others shared their interpretations in the organization. They found that employees at higher levels in the hierarchy were more likely to perceive agreement, even in cases when there was no agreement. However, employees with more tenure in the organization were more likely to have actual agreement, even though they did not perceive that others shared their interpretations of the mission. Contrary to the accepted view that communication builds shared meaning, employees cohesively connected in the communication network were not more likely to agree with their colleagues' interpretations of the organizational mission, even though they perceived agreement. However, employees who were structurally equivalent were more likely to share actual agreement, even though they were not as likely to perceive agreement.

Krackhardt and Kilduff (1990) applied the notion of semantic networks to examine individuals' attributions about others in the network. They asked individuals in an organization to make cultural attributions on seven dimensions about the behaviors of each other member in the organization. They found that individuals who were friends were more likely than nonfriends to make similar attributions about other members in the organization. Rice and Danowski (1993) applied the notion of semantic networks to examine individuals' attributions of the appropriation of a voice mail system. They found that individuals who used the system for "voice processing" (i.e., routing and structuring the flow of messages among individuals) characterized their use of the technology in terms that were systematically distinct from those who used the voice mail technology as a substitute for traditional answering machines.

Two studies have used semantic networks to examine variations in national cultures. Jang and Barnett (1994) analyzed the chief operating officer's letter that 17 Japanese and 18 U.S. organizations published in the organization's annual report to stockholders. They found that the co-occurrence of words in these messages resulted in two distinct clusters for the Japanese and U.S. companies. Further, the words co-occurring in the Japanese annual reports focused on concepts related to organizational operations, while the U.S. documents focused on concepts related to organizational structure. In a study of 12 managers from five European countries, Stohl (1993) examined the cultural variations associated with managers' interpretation of a key communicative process, worker participation. She found that the semantic network based on shared interpretations of the concept reflected greater connectedness within countries than between countries. Further, similarities in interpretations about worker participation were systematically associated with three of Hofstede's (1984) dimensions of cultural variability across countries. These were (a) the power distance index, the extent to which less powerful people accept inequality in power; (b) the uncertainty avoidance index, the extent to which people avoid uncertainty by relying on strict codes of behavior; and (c) individualism, the extent to which citizens place primary importance on the needs of the individual rather than the collective.

Extensions to semantic networks. The theoretical mechanisms of contagion have also been used to explain the co-evolution of communication and semantic networks. Contractor and Grant (1996) developed a computer simulation of the effects of social contagion in communication and semantic networks that contained varying levels of initial network density and heterogeneity. They found that the time required for semantic convergence within groups was positively related to the density of the communication and semantic networks, inversely related to the heterogeneity of the communication network, and inversely related to the individual's inertia against being influenced socially. Significantly, the initial heterogeneity in the seman-

tic network, an indicator of initial variation in interpretations, was not a significant predictor of the time required for semantic convergence.

In a similar endeavor, Carley (1991) offered a "constructural" theory of group stability, modeling the parallel cultural and social evolution of a group. Social structure was defined as the distribution of interaction probabilities, and culture was defined as the distribution of distinct facts. Carley's (1991) model described a cycle of three events for each group member: "(1) action—exchange information with their partners; (2) adaptation—acquire the communicated information and update the probabilities of interaction; and then (3) motivation—choose new interaction partners on the basis of their new probabilities of interaction" (p. 336). Results of computer simulations showed that these groups did not evolve monotonically toward greater homogeneity. Instead they often oscillated through cycles of greater and lesser cohesiveness. Her simulations also indicated that groups with "simpler" cultures (i.e., fewer facts to be learned by group members) tended to stabilize more quickly. Further, those in less homogeneous groups (i.e., where facts were not equally distributed) were less likely to stabilize, since they could form enduring subcultures. One corollary of constructural theory is that the probabilities for two individuals to interact are not symmetric (Carley & Krackhardt, 1996).

Network Organizations as Knowledge Structures

A complementary view of semantic networks as meaning structures is provided by Kogut, Shan, and Walker (1993), who argued that it is interesting to view interorganizational networks as structures of knowledge. Organizations seek out other organizations because they want to establish some form of relationship. But to do so, they must first find at least some of the other organizations that are also interested in entering into the relationship with them and choose among the alternatives. This means they must acquire information about the other organization and compare it with information from other organizations. Often, in searching for partners, organizations begin close to home or on the basis of recommendations from others with whom they are already linked. Over time, this searching process builds up a knowledge base about the skills, competencies, trustworthiness, and other capabilities of the organizations.

Once organizations choose partners, however, they tend to spend less time seeking other partners. As Kogut et al. (1993) say, "Because information is determined by previous relations and in turn influences the subsequent propensity to do more relations, the structure of the network tends to replicate itself over time. The early history of cooperation tends to lock in subsequent cooperation" (p. 70). Further, they observe:

> The replication of the network is a statement of the tendency of learning to decline with time. The structure of the network is a limiting constraint on how much new learning can be achieved. . . . But when viewed from the perspective of the evolution of networks, there is a tendency for old lessons to be retaught. (p. 71)

Powell, Koput, and Smith-Doerr (1996) argue that learning networks are particularly important in industries where there is rapid technological development, knowledge is complex, and expertise is distributed around many organizations. Using data collected on 225 firms over four years, they found strong evidence for increasing levels of interorganizational communication and collaboration in the biotechnology industry, including increases in ties and network density. In a study of two new biotechnology firms (NBFs), Liebeskind, Oliver, Zucker, and Brewer (1996, p. 428) documented how they used social networks to "source their most critical input—scientific knowledge." They found that "almost none of the individual-level exchanges of knowledge through research collaboration involved organiza-

tions with which either NBF had a market agreement" (p. 439). The lack of market-based contractual arrangements increased their flexibility to create and dissolve networks as well as adapt strategically to evolving research interests.

Bovasso (1992) used four network measures of an organization's structure—density, range, prominence, and elitism—to examine the changes that resulted when three high-technology, knowledge-intensive firms on three continents were merged by the parent corporation to create a single networked organization. In the newly formed networked organization, Bovasso found support for the emergence of a structural convergence, with geographic divisions and hierarchical levels having a smaller impact on members' involvement in the influence of ideas and control of resources. More specifically, geographical and hierarchical differences in prominence, elitism, and density scores between middle and upper management in the three firms were reduced.

Cognitive Social Structures

Several researchers (Corman & Scott, 1994; Krackhardt, 1987) have sought to distinguish people's cognitions of social structures from their actual, observed communication networks. This line of research was precipitated by a series of studies in the early 1980s questioning the ability of informants to accurately report their own communication network patterns (Bernard, Killworth, & Sailer, 1980, 1982; Bernard, Killworth, & Cronenfeld, 1984; Freeman, Romney, & Freeman, 1987). Their results underscored the problematic nature of collecting self-report measures of communication network data if the underlying theory being tested was based on the assumption that individuals' attitudes and behavior were shaped by their actual communication networks. However, as Richards (1985) argued, the differences between self-reported and observed network data are problematic only if the underlying theoretical construct being measured was actual communication behavior (see also Marsden, 1990). In fact, Richards (1985) notes, many social and psychological theories are based on individuals' perceptions—an assertion well captured by W. I. Thomas's observation that "perceptions are real in their consequences even if they do not map one-to-one onto observed behaviors" (Krackhardt, 1987, p. 128; Pattison, 1994). For researchers drawing on such social and psychological theories, a discrepancy between observed and self-reported measures would suggest a measurement error in using data about observed communication.

Krackhardt (1987) developed the concept of cognitive social structures to characterize individuals' perceptions of the social networks. Cognitive social structures assume the status of socially shared, structural "taken-for-granted facts" (Barley, 1990, p. 67) by individuals about the predictable and recurrent interactions among individuals in the network, even if these cognitions are at variance with the actual communication. Krackhardt (1987) aggregated individuals' cognitive social structures to estimate a "consensual" cognitive social structure, in which a link existed between two individuals if others in the network perceived this tie, irrespective of whether it was acknowledged by either of the people in the dyad. As such, a link in the "consensual" cognitive social structure indexed a common adage: It is not who you know, but who others think you know.

Several empirical studies have demonstrated the explanatory power of the cognitive social structure concept. Krackhardt (1987) found that managers in a high-technology entrepreneurial firm who were deemed as highly central (betweenness) in the consensual cognitive social structure were significantly more likely to be able to reconstruct the "actual" advice network reported by the people involved. Krackhardt (1990) also found that the perceived influence of organizational members was significantly associated with their ability to accurately estimate the consensual cognitive social structure in terms of advice relationships. Krackhardt's (1992) research chronicled how a union's inability to accurately assess the organization's social structure led to its failure in organizing employees. Further, Kilduff and Krackhardt (1994) demonstrated that individuals' reputations in the organization were more closely associated with their centrality in the consensual cognitive structure than in the "actual" communication network based on the self-reports of the people involved. Finally, Heald, Contractor, Koehly, and Wasserman (1996) found that individuals of the same gender, in the same department, and in a supervisor-subordinate relationship were more likely to share similar cognitive social structures. Those individuals who were linked in acquaintance and communication networks were also more likely to share similar cognitive social structures.

Extensions to cognitive social structures. The conceptual and empirical work on cognitive social structures has moved the initial debate about differences between actual and perceived communication from the methodological and measurement domain to a substantive exploration of the ways in which actual and perceived communication enable and constrain each other. Corman and Scott (1994) deployed Giddens's (1984) structuration theory to argue that three modalities explain the recursive relationships between observable communication and cognitive social structures: reticulation, activation, and enactment. Reticulation denotes the duality in which perceived communication relationships are produced and reproduced in observable communication behavior. Activation represents the duality of activity foci in the structural domain with joint activity in the interaction domain. Enactment relates coding conventions in the structural domain to triggering events in the interaction domain (Corman, 1997, p. 69). They refer to this perspective as the latent network of perceived communication relationships.

Research on cognitive social structures has taken on additional currency with the advent of virtual organizations, supported by information and communication technologies. In traditional organizations, individuals who are physically co-located have several opportunities to observe face-to-face interactions, and thereby shape their perceptions and social cognitions (Brewer, 1995) of the organization's social structures. The pervasiveness of electronic communication media in virtual organizations makes it increasingly difficult for individuals to discern social structures. Consequently, organizational members have significant problems accurately determining "Who knows who?" and "Who knows who knows who?" Information technologies that are responsible for triggering this problem can also be used to overcome these obstacles. Because information transacted over electronic media such as the Web can be stored in digital form, a new generation of software called "collaborative filters" has emerged (Contractor, 1997; Contractor, O'Keefe, & Jones, 1997; Contractor, Zink, & Chan, 1998; Kautz, Selman, & Shah, 1997; Nishida, Takeda, Iwazume, Maeda, & Takaai, 1998). These filters can be used to make visible the organization's virtual social and knowledge structures. Collaborative filters process individuals' interests, relationships, and the structure and content of their electronically stored information (such as Web pages). They can assist individuals in searching the organization's databases to automatically answer questions about the organization's knowledge network, that is, "Who knows what?" as well as questions about the organization's cognitive knowledge networks, that is, "Who knows who knows what?" within the organization. The use of these kinds of tools is likely to have a leveling effect on the organization's cognitive social structure, because they can potentially undermine the perceived centrality of those individuals in the organization who are viewed as important resources about the organization's social and knowledge networks.

Cognitive Consistency

Like the semantic networks and cognitive social structures discussed above, consistency theories focus on members' cognitions. However, in this case the explanatory mechanism underscores individuals' aspirations for consistency in their cognitions. When applied to organizational communication networks, consistency theories seek to explain the extent to which a drive for consistency is manifest in people's networks and attitudes. That is, members' attitudes are viewed as a function of the balance in their networks rather than alternative mechanisms such as contagion. Heider's (1958) balance theory posited that if two individuals were friends, they should have similar evaluations of an object. This model was extended and mathematically formulated by Harary, Norman, and Cartwright (1965), and later by Davis and Leinhardt (1972), and Holland and Leinhardt (1975), who argued that the object could be a third person in a communication network. If the two individuals did not consistently evaluate the third person, they would experience a state of discomfort and would strive to reduce this cognitive inconsistency by altering their evaluations of either the third person or their own friendship. They extended this line of argument to all possible triads in a network. Researchers have examined the effects of cognitive consistency on both attitudes and behavior.

The effect of cognitive consistency on attitudes. Consistency theories have played an important role in clarifying an earlier debate about the relationship between involvement in communication networks and work attitudes such as job satisfaction and organizational commitment. Early studies (e.g., Brass, 1981; Eisenberg, Monge, & Miller, 1984; Roberts & O'Reilly, 1979) reported contradictory and inconsistent findings about the extent to which individuals who were well connected, integrated, or central in their communication networks were more likely to be satisfied and committed to their organizations. Consistency theories suggest that it is not the centrality or number of links in individuals' networks but the perceived balance within the network that influences level of satisfaction and commitment. Krackhardt and Kilduff (1990) found that individuals' job satisfaction scores were predicted by the extent to which they agreed with their friends on cultural attributions about other members in the network. Kilduff and Krackhardt (1993) found that individuals who were highly central in the friendship network were less satisfied than others who were less central; however, those who saw their friendship networks in balance (they call it "schema consistent") were more likely to be satisfied and committed. In a study of three organizations (described earlier in the Semantic Networks section), Contractor, Eisenberg, and Monge (1996) also found that the extent to which employees shared common interpretations of their organization's mission had no direct bearing on their level of satisfaction or organizational commitment. However, those who perceived greater agreement with others' interpretations were more likely to be satisfied and committed. Barnett and Jang (1994), while not explicitly invoking consistency theories, found that members of a police organization who were central and connected in their communication networks were more likely to perceive their views of salient organizational concepts as being consistent with those of others. Researchers have used network concepts of transitivity to operationalize the effect of balance in the network.

The effect of cognitive consistency on behavior. Consistency theories have also been related to the behavior of organizational members. Krackhardt and Porter (1985) found that friends of those who voluntarily left an organization were no longer exposed to their former coworkers' unhappiness and were therefore able to restore their previous perceived balance; as a result they reported greater levels of satisfaction following the departure of these friends from the organization. Brass et al. (1995) argued that the need for balance among three people can also influence the likelihood of unethical behavior. "The addition of the third party with strong ties to both other actors will act as a major constraint on unethical behavior when the two actors are only weakly connected" (p. 7). Further, they proposed that the likelihood of unethical behavior is least likely to occur when all three people are connected by strong ties (i.e., a Simmelian triad; Krackhardt, 1992).

Extensions to cognitive consistency theories. The deployment of consistency theories to explain organizational phenomena is relatively recent. Conceptually and analytically, it challenges network researchers to move from the dyad to the triad as the smallest unit of analysis. As the examples above indicate, it has the potential of resolving many of the inconsistent results in network studies that use the dyad as the primary unit of analysis.

Like the other cognitive theories discussed in the previous section, consistency theories have also been used to address the ongoing debate about differences between actual and perceived communication. Freeman (1992) suggested that consistency theories offer a systematic explanation for differences between actual and self-report data on communication. He argued that individuals' needs to perceive balance in observed communication networks help explain some of the errors they make in recalling communication patterns. Using experimental data collected by De Soto (1960), Freeman found that a large proportion of the errors in subjects' recall of networks could be attributed to their propensity to "correct" intransitivity, a network indicator of imbalance, in the observed network.

Theories of Homophily

Several researchers have attempted to explain communication networks on the basis of homophily, that is, the selection of others who are similar. Brass (1995b) notes that "similarity is thought to ease communication, increase predictability of behavior, and foster trust and reciprocity" (p. 51). Homophily has been studied on the basis of similarity in age, gender, education, prestige, social class, tenure, and occupation (Carley, 1991; Coleman, 1957; Ibarra, 1993b, 1995; Laumann, 1966; Marsden, 1988; McPherson & Smith-Lovin, 1987).

Several lines of reasoning support the homophily hypothesis. These fall into two general categories: the similarity-attraction hypothesis (Byrne, 1971) and the theory of self-categorization (Turner, 1987). The similarity-attraction hypothesis is exemplified in the work of Heider (1958), who posited that homophily reduces the psychological discomfort that may arise from cognitive or emotional inconsistency. Similarly, Sherif (1958) suggested that individuals were more likely to select similar others because by doing so they reduce the potential areas of conflict in the relationship. The theory of self-categorization (Turner & Oakes, 1986) suggests that individuals define their social identity through a process of self-categorization during which they classify themselves and others using categories such as age, race, gender. Schachter (1959) argued that similarity provided individuals with a basis for legitimizing their own social identity. The manner in which individuals categorize themselves influences the extent to which they associate with others who are seen as falling into the same category.

A substantial body of organizational demography research is premised on a homophily mechanism. In addition, several studies have focused specifically on gender homophily. Each area is reviewed below.

General Demographic Homophily

The increased workforce diversity in contemporary organizations has seen a rise in the creation of heterogeneous work groups that complicate individuals' desires for homophily. Several studies have examined the extent to which individuals' predilection for homophily structures organizational networks. Zenger and Lawrence (1989) found that technical communication among researchers in a high-technology firm was related to their age and tenure distribution. Studies by O'Reilly and colleagues (Tsui, Egan, & O'Reilly, 1992; Tsui & O'Reilly, 1989; Wagner, Pfeffer, & O'Reilly, 1984) found that differences in age among employees hindered communication and social integration and resulted in lower

commitment and greater turnover among employees.

Basing their arguments on the principle of homophily, Liedka (1991) studied the age and education distribution of members recruited to join voluntary organizations such as youth groups, farm organizations, and sports clubs. Using data collected in the 1985 and 1986 General Social Survey, he found results at the aggregate level, suggesting that members of voluntary organizations were more likely to persuade others similar to their age and education to join the organization. He also found that when people in the same age groups were more densely connected, they were more likely to be represented in voluntary organizations. At the interorganizational level, Galaskiewicz (1979) and Schermerhorn (1977) found that interorganizational links were more likely to occur among individuals who perceived similarity in religion, age, ethnicity, and professional affiliations.

Gender Homophily

Considerable research has examined the effect of gender homophily on organizational networks. Lincoln and Miller (1979) found that similarities in sex and race of organizational employees were significant predictors of their ties in a friendship network. Brass's (1985a) research indicated that communication networks in an organization were largely clustered by gender.

Several studies have examined the effects of gender homophily on friendship. For instance, Leenders (1996) discovered that gender was a more influential predictor of enduring friendship ties than proximity. In a study of 36 female and 45 male senior managers in two New York state government bureaucracies, Moore (1992) found that "half of the advice cliques and nearly that proportion of cliques in the friendship network contain men only" (p. 53). Ibarra's (1992) research of an advertising agency revealed that even though women reported task-related, communication, advice influence ties with men, they were more likely to select other women in their social support and friendship networks. Men, on the other hand, were more likely to have instrumental as well as noninstrumental ties with other men. She pointed out that the constraints of social exchange (see earlier section) and the resulting need to be connected with the organization's predominantly male power base often force women to forgo their propensity for homophily in terms of their instrumental relationships.

Some aspects of culture bear on the preceding results. For example, contrary to other findings, research by Crombie and Birley (1992) showed that the network of contacts among female entrepreneurs in Ireland was not different from that of men in terms of size, diversity, density, and effectiveness. Perhaps the reason for this result is that the people in this study were entrepreneurs. However, the women tended to be younger, owners of smaller businesses that had been established for shorter periods of time, and less involved in traditional exterior activities such as belonging to civic organizations. Women also tended to rely on men and women for advice while men consulted largely with other men. In similar fashion, Ethington, Johnson, Marshall, Meyer, and Chang (1996) studied two organizations with different gender ratios. They found that men and women were equally integrated into and prominent in each other's networks in an organization that had an equal ratio of men and women and an equal gender distribution in the power hierarchy. However, in an organization that had a 75%–25% female-to-male ratio, the networks were more segregated and women were more prominent.

Extensions to Theories of Homophily

Communication scholars have maintained an enduring interest in the principle of homophily as a theoretical mechanism to explain the emergence of networks. In response to the ongoing focus on workforce diversity, they have invoked this mechanism in the study of gender and race issues. The principle of homophily has also been suggested as a network mechanism that is relevant to researchers interested in the social comparison processes used by individuals to make assessments, for instance, about their perceptions of equity in the workplace. According to equity theory (Adams, 1965), individuals' motivations are a direct function of the extent to which their input (i.e., efforts) to output (i.e., rewards) ratios are commensurate with those of "relevant" others. Social comparison theory (Festinger, 1954) suggests that these relevant others are selected on the basis of being similar, or homophilous, in salient respects. Likewise, social identity theory (Turner & Oakes, 1989) proposes that these relevant others are those who are seen as sharing the same "social identity" as the focal person. Krackhardt and Brass (1994) suggest that the selection of relevant others is constrained and enabled by the networks in which individuals are embedded. Individuals could select as relevant others those with whom they have close communication ties (i.e., a cohesion mechanism) or with others who they see as having similar roles (i.e., a structurally equivalent mechanism).

Several scholars have urged that similarity of personality characteristics be used to explain involvement in communication networks (Brass, 1995b; Tosi, 1992). McPhee and Corman (1995) adopted a similar perspective in an article that drew on Feld's (1981) focus theory to argue that interaction is more likely to occur among individuals who share similar foci, including being involved in the same activities. They found limited support for their hypotheses in a study of church members, suggesting the need for further research.

Theories of Physical and Electronic Proximity

A number of researchers have sought to explain communication networks on the basis of physical or electronic propinquity (Corman, 1990; Johnson, 1992; Rice, 1993a). Proximity facilitates the likelihood of communication by increasing the probability that individuals will meet and interact (Festinger, Schachter, & Back, 1950; Korzenny & Bauer, 1981; Monge, Rothman, Eisenberg, Miller, & Kirste, 1985). If these interactions were to occur, they would allow individuals the opportunity to explore the extent to which they have common interests and shared beliefs (Homans, 1950). Early research in organizational settings indicated that the frequency of face-to-face dyadic communication drops precipitously after the first 75-100 feet (Allen, 1970; Conrath, 1973). Zahn's (1991) more recent research also demonstrated that increased physical distance between offices, chain of command, and status led to decreased probability of communication. Likewise, Van den Bulte and Moenaert (1997) found that communication among R&D teams was enhanced after they were co-located. Therefore, individuals who are not proximate are deprived of the opportunity to explore these common interests and are hence less likely to initiate communication links. As such, physical or electronic proximity is a necessary but not sufficient condition for enabling network links. Dramatic evidence of the influence of physical proximity involves the physical dislocation of 817 employees of the Olivetti factory in Naples following the 1983-1984 earthquakes. Bland et al. (1997) report that employees who were permanently relocated rather than evacuated only temporarily reported the highest distress levels due to the disruption in their social networks. Rice (1993b) notes that physical proximity may also facilitate contagion (see section above) by exposing spatially co-located individuals to the same ambient stimuli. Rice and Aydin (1991) found modest evidence of the role played by physical proximity on employees' attitudes toward a new information system. At the interorganizational level, Palmer et al. (1986) found that interlock ties were more likely to be reconstituted if departing members represented organizations whose headquarters were physically proximate to that of focal organizations.

The effects of new communication technologies on the creation and modification of social networks are well documented (Barnett & Salisbury, in press; Rice, 1994a; Wellman et al., 1996). Less intuitive, but just as evident, are the effects of new technologies in preserving old communication structures. In a study of three sectors of the UK publishing industry (the book trade, magazine and newspaper trade, and the newsprint suppliers), Spinardi, Graham, and Williams (1996) found that the introduction of electronic data interchange consolidated and further embedded existing interorganizational relationships, thereby preventing business process reengineering.

Extensions to Theories of Proximity

The proliferation of information technologies in the workplace capable of transcending geographical obstacles has renewed interest in the effects of physical and electronic proximity and their interaction on communication patterns (Kraut, Egido, & Galegher, 1990; Steinfield & Fulk, 1990). Fulk and Boyd (1991) underscored the potential of network analysis "to test the situational moderating effect of geographic distance on media choice" (p. 433). Corman (1996) suggested that cellular automata models are particularly appropriate for studying the effects of physical proximity on communication networks. Cellular automata models can be used to study the collective and dynamic effects of proximity on the overall communication network when individuals in the network apply theoretically derived rules about creating, maintaining, or dissolving links with their "local," that is, proximate, network neighbors.

Uncertainty Reduction and Contingency Theories

Uncertainty about individual and organizational environments has played an important role in explaining organizational processes. Two theories have incorporated communication network concepts to explain how people reduce this uncertainty. Uncertainty reduction theory (URT) and contingency theory are reviewed in this section.

Uncertainty Reduction Theory

URT (Berger, 1987; Berger & Bradac, 1982) suggests that people communicate to reduce uncertainty thereby making their environments more predictable (Weick, 1979). Researchers have examined how communication networks help manage and reduce the organization's uncertainty (Leblebici & Salancik, 1981; Miller & Monge, 1985). However, as Albrecht and Hall (1991) note, "innovation, and especially *talk* about innovation, is inherently an uncertainty-*producing* process" (p. 537). As a result, Albrecht and Ropp (1984) found that communication about innovation is most likely to occur among individuals who have strong multiplex ties (i.e., both work and social ties) that guarantee them a level of relational certainty and thereby greater perceived control in a potentially uncertain situation. Albrecht and Hall (1991) found evidence that the need to reduce uncertainty also explained the creation of dominant elites and coalitions in innovation networks. Burkhardt and Brass (1990) chronicled the changes in the communication network following the introduction of a new technology. They found that the uncertainty resulting from the introduction of the technology motivated employees to seek out new contacts and hence change their communication networks. Kramer (1996) found that the employees who had experienced job transfers were more likely to have positive attitudes about the adjustment if their reconstituted network offered the quality of communication that reduced their uncertainty.

At the interorganizational level, Granovetter (1985) argued that organizational decision makers use social networks to reduce uncertainty associated with market exchanges, thereby reducing their transaction costs (see earlier discussion). Picot (1993) suggested that network organizations were superior to markets and hierarchies when task uncertainty was high and task specificity was low. In a study of relationships between firms and their investment banks, Baker (1987) reported that the firms' financial officers often drew on their informal networks to reduce uncertainty surrounding the creation of a market tie. The reduction of uncertainty due to strong ties was also useful to explain the reduction of interorganizational conflict. Using data from intergroup networks in 20 organizations, Nelson (1989) found that organizations with strong ties between their groups were less likely to report high levels of conflict than those organizations that had groups that were connected by weak ties.

Contingency Theory

In the early 1960s, organizational scholars began to focus their attention on the environment and ways to reduce the uncertainty it created. Emery and Trist (1960) developed sociotechnical systems theory in which they argued that the nature of an organization's environment significantly influences its structure and operations (Emery & Trist, 1965). A contingency theory approach to formal organizational structures is based on the premise that an organization should structure itself in a manner that maximizes its ability to reduce the uncertainty in its environment. For example, Burns and Stalker (1961) contrasted "organic" with bureaucratic organizations, which they labeled "mechanistic." The defining feature of organic organizations was that their structures were internally adaptable to changing features of the environment while mechanistic organizations were not. Lawrence and Lorsch's (1967) contingency theory formalized this view and argued that all internal relations and structures were contingent on external conditions. Galbraith (1977) argued that organizations needed to develop slack resources and flexible, internal lateral communication networks to cope with environmental uncertainty. Thus, the theoretical mechanism in contingency theory that accounted for the formation, maintenance, and eventual dissolution of communication networks was the level of uncertainty in the organization's environment. Stable environments led organizations to create long-standing, entrenched networks, while turbulent environments led organizations to create flexible, changing networks.

In an empirical study of Burns and Stalker's distinction between mechanistic and organic organizations, Tichy and Fombrun (1979) found that the differences between the formal and informal communication networks were more pronounced in mechanistic organizations than they were in organic organizations. Barney's (1985) inductive blockmodeling, clustering, and scaling techniques identified the dimensions of informal communication structure in interaction data collected by Coleman (1961) from the entire student population of ten Midwestern high schools. One dimension identified was "analogous to Burns and Stalker's (1961) organic-mechanistic dimension of formal structure" (Barney, 1985, p. 35), which proved to be consistent with contingency theory's proposed relationship between environmental diversity and formal organizational structure (Miles, 1980).

Shrader, Lincoln, and Hoffman (1989) tested Burns and Stalker's argument that organic forms of organizational structure would result in informal organizational communication networks that were denser, more highly connected, and more multiplex than those found in mechanistic organizations. They found that organic "smaller organizations made up of educated staff applying nonroutine technologies have denser, more cohesive, and less-segmented networks consisting largely of symmetric or reciprocated ties" (p. 63). By contrast, vertically and horizontally differentiated, as well as formalized, mechanistic organizations were less densely connected, more segmented, and less likely to have symmetric and reciprocated communication ties.

Contingency theory's proposed relationship between technology and the organization's structure was examined in a study by Brass (1985b). Using network techniques to measure pooled, sequential, and reciprocal interdependencies in an organization's workflow, Brass (1985b) found that the relationship between interpersonal communication and performance was contingent on the extent of horizontal differentiation in the organization's structure and the coordination requirements of the task.

Extensions to Uncertainty Reduction and Contingency Theories

The review above suggests that the deployment of uncertainty reduction theory was more prevalent in the 1980s and has been on the decline lately. This decline corresponds, not coincidentally, with the increasing critique of the scope and operationalization of the "uncertainty" concept (Huber & Daft, 1987). Future network research from an uncertainty reduction perspective should respond to calls for a conceptual delineation between uncertainty reduction and equivocality reduction (Weick, 1979). The relative efficacy of networks to help reduce uncertainty and equivocality is a potentially useful but as yet untapped area of inquiry. Further, past network research based on uncertainty reduction theory has not distinguished between uncertainty reduction and uncertainty avoidance (March & Weissinger-Baylon, 1986). The use of communication networks to reduce uncertainty implies the presence or creation of links, while the avoidance of uncertainty may imply the absence or dissolution of links.

Although the research literature testing the validity of the contingency mechanism is sparse, it tends to support the importance of internal adaptability to external constraints. In fact, most theorists today accept the contingency thesis without significant empirical support because the enormous increase in the rates of environmental change in the contemporary world makes it seem intuitively obvious. No subsequent theory has argued against the contingency mechanism, and Galbraith's

(1977) extensive analysis of the development of slack resources and deployment of lateral communication linkages remains the clearest statement of how to develop communication networks to cope with rapidly changing environmental uncertainty.

Social Support Theories

Interest in social support networks can be traced back to Durkheim's (1897/1977) groundbreaking work on the impact of solidarity and social integration on mental health. A social support explanation focuses on the ways in which communication networks help organizational members to cope with stress. Wellman (1992) and others have adopted this framework in their study of social support networks. Their research is largely based on the premise that social networks play a "buffering" role in the effects of stress on mental well-being (Berkman & Syme, 1979; Hall & Wellman, 1985).

Two general mechanisms exist by which social networks buffer the effects of stress. First, an individual in a dense social support network is offered increased social support in the form of resources and sociability. Lin and Ensel's (1989) research produced evidence that strong ties in the support network provided social resources that helped buffer both social and psychological stress. Second, Kadushin (1983) argued that social support can also be provided by less dense social circles. Social circles (Simmel, 1955) are networks in which membership is based on common characteristics or interests. Membership in a social circle can help provide social support "by (1) conveying immunity through leading the members to a better understanding of their problems, (2) being a resource for help, or (3) mobilizing resources" (Kadushin, 1983, p. 191).

A substantial amount of research exists on the role of networks in providing social support in varying organizational contexts, such as families, communities, and neighborhoods (for reviews, see O'Reilly, 1988; Walker, Wasserman, & Wellman, 1994). In a classic longitudinal study of residents in a northern California county, Berkman and Syme (1979) found that respondents "who lacked social and community ties were more likely to die in the follow-up period than those with more extensive contacts" (p. 186). Berkman (1985) found that individuals with fewer social support contacts via marriage, friends, relatives, church memberships, and associations had a higher mortality rate.

Researchers (Barrera & Ainlay, 1983; Cutrona & Russell, 1990; Wellman & Wortley, 1989, 1990) have identified four dimensions of social support, including emotional aid, material aid (goods, money, and services), information, and companionship. Considerable empirical evidence demonstrates that individuals cannot rely on a single network link, except to their parents or children, to provide all four dimensions of social support. Studies by Wellman and Wortley (1989, 1990) of a community in southern Ontario, Canada, found that individuals' specific network ties provided either emotional aid or material aid, but not both. Additionally, studies have found that women are more likely to offer emotional aid than men (Campbell & Lee, 1990).

Remarkably few studies have examined networks of social support in organizational contexts even though several scholars have underscored the need for research in this area (Bass & Stein, 1997). For example, Langford, Bowsher, Maloney, and Lillis (1997) propose the examination of networks to study social support in nursing environments such as hospitals and nursing homes. A comparison of six hospital units by Albrecht and Ropp (1982) found that the volume and tone of interaction in the medical surgical unit's communication network improved their ability to cope with chronic pressures and stress. In one of the few studies of social support networks in organizations, Cummings (1997) found that individuals who reported receiving greater social support from their network were more likely to generate radical (i.e., "frame-breaking") innovation.

Hurlbert (1991) used ego-centric network data for a sample of respondents from the 1985 General Social Survey (the first national sample containing network data) to examine the effect of kin and coworker networks on stress, as measured by individuals' job satisfaction. She argued that individuals' networks may (a) provide resources to decrease the level of stress created by job conditions, or (b) provide support thereby helping the individual cope with job stress. She found that membership in a coworker social circle was positively associated with job satisfaction, even after controlling for other social and demographic variables. The effect on job satisfaction was even higher if the coworkers were highly educated, suggesting that they were able to offer additional instrumental resources. However, Hurlbert (1991) also found that for individuals who were in blue-collar jobs or those with low security, "kin-centered networks may exacerbate, rather than ameliorate, negative job conditions" (p. 426). Consistent with this latter finding, Ray (1991) and Ray and Miller (1990) found that individuals who were highly involved in networks offering social support to friends and coworkers were more likely to report high levels of emotional exhaustion. The negative effects of the network on individuals were also reported in a longitudinal study of relatively well-functioning older men and women. Seeman, Bruce, and McAvay (1996) found that men who had larger instrumental support networks were more likely to report the onset of activities of daily living disability. They speculated that these results may reflect "the consequences of greater reliance on others, a behavior pattern which may, over time, erode the recipient's confidence in their [sic] ability to do things independently" (pp. S197-S198).

At the interorganizational level, Eisenberg and Swanson (1996) noted that Connecticut's Healthy Start program served an important social support role for pregnant women by serving as referral to hospitals and agencies. Zinger, Blanco, Zanibbi, and Mount (1996) reported that Canadian small businesses relied more heavily on an informal support network than government programs. Paterniti, Chellini, Sacchetti, and Tognelli (1996) described how an Italian rehabilitation center for schizophrenic patients successfully created network links with other organizations to reflect "the social network that surrounds the patient and from which he [sic] has come" (p. 86).

Extensions to Social Support Theories

The amount of research on social support networks has increased substantially in the past few years. Some of these changes are perhaps motivated by changes in the organizational landscape, such as the increase in outsourcing, telecommuting, job retraining for displaced workers (Davies, 1996), and small business start-ups (Zinger et al., 1996). All of these activities often serve to isolate the individual worker from the institutional support structures of traditional organizations. Hence, there is greater salience today for improving our understanding of the role of social support mechanisms in the emergence of networks.

Early research on the role of networks in providing social support focused on structural characteristics of the networks, such as tie strength, frequency, reciprocity of the links, the size, and the density of the networks. Walker et al. (1994) noted that recent network research has abandoned the notion of social support as a unitary construct as well as the assumption that the presence of a tie can be equated with the provision of social support. Instead, they model social support as "a complex flow of resources among a wide range of actors rather than as just a transaction between two individuals" (p. 54). Indeed, in a study of low-income, immigrant women Vega, Kolody, Valle, and Weir (1991) found that the women's overall frequency of interaction with friends and family was not correlated with levels of depression. However, the quality of social support, measured as the frequency of specific social support messages, was the best predictor of low depression scores among the women.

Theories of Network Evolution: Emergent Versus Emergence

In a special issue of the *Journal of Mathematical Sociology*, "The Evolution of Networks," Stokman and Doreian (1996) examined the distinction between the terms *network dynamics* and *network evolution*. They argued that the study of network dynamics provides a quantitative or qualitative temporal characterization of change, stability, simultaneity, sequentiality, synchronicity, cyclicality, or randomness in the phenomena being observed (Monge & Kalman, 1996). The focus is on providing sophisticated descriptions of the manifest change in networks. In contrast, Stokman and Doreian define the study of network evolution to contain an important additional goal: an explicit, theoretically derived understanding of the mechanisms that determine the temporal changes in the phenomena being observed. While most of the longitudinal network studies reviewed in this chapter contain theoretical mechanisms to explain changes over time, many of them could be more explicit about this connection and move more in the direction of fully developed theories of network evolution.

In an early example, Fombrun (1986) theorized about evolution in terms of infrastructures, sociostructures, and superstructures that interacted dynamically with each other across organizational, population, and community levels. He identified two dynamically opposing forces that led both to conflict and to eventual resolution: processes of convergence and processes of contradiction. In a more recent example, Salancik (1995) critiqued the intellectual contributions of Burt's (1992) structural theory of holes. He noted that it was important to acknowledge Burt's finding that a person occupying a structural hole will gain political advantage, but he also asserted that "a more telling analysis might explain why the hole exists or why it was not filled before" (Salancik, 1995, p. 349). Salancik challenged network researchers to invest efforts in creating a more specific network theory. Such a theory does not take a network as given. Instead, it seeks to uncover the mechanisms that create network evolution.

Two of the more comprehensive reviews of network studies have called for greater attention to the evolution of networks (Brass, 1995b; Monge & Eisenberg, 1987). While both were organized around antecedents and outcomes of networks, they acknowledged that such distinctions are often nonexistent and potentially misleading. Monge and Eisenberg (1987, p. 310) offered a hypothetical scenario to illustrate the ongoing evolution of a network, a concept they term *reorganizing.* Brass (1995b) underscored the importance of articulating the dynamic nature of the relationships between networks, their antecedents, and outcomes.

Four lines of research emphasize the importance of this perspective. The first articulated a recursive model of communication networks and media (Contractor & Eisenberg, 1990). Drawing on structuration theory (Giddens, 1984) and the theory of structural action (Burt, 1982), they proposed that while networks influence individuals' adoptions, perceptions, and use of new media, this use has the potential for altering the very networks that precipitated their use in the first place. In some instances, this altered network has the potential of subverting individuals' continued use of the media. Hence, the coevolution of communication networks and the activities they shape are inextricably linked and must be examined as a duality.

Similarly, Barley (1990) and Haines (1988) have argued for the use of network analytic techniques to articulate and extend structuration theory. Barley (1990) used network analytic tools to describe the situated ways in which relatively small role differences in initial conditions reverberated through seemingly similar social systems, resulting over time in widely different social structures. Barley (1990) rejected contingency theories because they offer static predictions of a match between technologies and social structures. Instead, he argued for using networks as a way of making explicit the theory of negotiated order (Fine & Kleinman, 1983).

According to this theory, structures are by-products of a history of interactions and are subsequently perceived as fact by organizational members. However, he notes that theories such as structuration or negotiated order provide few analytic tools for explicating the links between the introduction of a technology, the interaction order, and the organization's structure. He offers network analytic tools as one way of explicating these links. Barley (1990) chronicled how the material attributes of a CT scanner recently adopted in two radiology departments affected the nonrelational elements of employees' work roles, including their skills and tasks; this, in turn, affected their immediate communication relationships and precipitated more widespread changes in the department's social network. Significantly, his analysis explains why the technology was appropriated differently in the two radiology departments. Barley's empirical work exemplifies several symbolic interactionists who argue for the importance of understanding the emergence of social order as a process of social construction (Berger & Luckmann, 1966; Giddens, 1976, 1984).

From Barley's (1990) standpoint, network techniques offer an opportunity to illustrate the ideographic and idiosyncratic nature of organizational phenomena. The ideographic assumption reflects an ontological viewpoint that rejects the nomothetic goal of seeking generalizable regularities in explaining organizational phenomena. Instead, the goal of the researcher with an ideographic viewpoint is to understand the processes that unfold in the particular organization being studied. Zack and McKenney (1995) offer a more recent example of work in this tradition. They examined the appropriation of the same group-authoring and -messaging computer system by the managing editorial groups of two morning newspapers owned by the same parent corporation. Drawing on Poole and DeSanctis' (1990) theory of adaptive structuration, they discovered that the two groups' appropriation of the technology, as indexed by their communication networks, differed in accordance with the different contexts at the two

locations. Further, they found evidence that the groups' performance outcomes for similar tasks were mediated by these interaction patterns.

A second line of research embraces the central precept of focusing attention on evolution of networks, but seeks nomothetic, that is, lawful and generalizable, underlying theoretical mechanisms to explain the appearance of seemingly ideographic, nongeneralizable, surface phenomena (Stokman & Doreian, 1996). These authors argue for the development of computational models that incorporate network mechanisms that both influence and are influenced by people in the social network. This line of research extends recent work in object-oriented modeling, cellular automata (CA), and neural networks to capture the ongoing, recursive, and nonlinear mechanisms by which organizational networks evolve over time (Abrahamson & Rosenkopf, 1997; Banks & Carley, 1996; Corman, 1996; McKelvey, 1997; Stokman & Zeggelink, 1996; Woelfel, 1993). Banks and Carley (1996) compared three mathematical models of network evolution based on social comparison theory (Heider, 1958), exchange theory (Blau, 1964), and constructuralism (Carley, 1990, 1991). They noted that the pattern of network evolution associated with the three models were not always distinct, thereby making it difficult to empirically validate one model over the other. They offer statistical tests that, at the very least, allow for the falsification of a particular model.

Corman (1996) suggested that multidimensional CA models offer insights into the unanticipated consequences of collective communication behavior. His computer simulations of a simplified CA model based, in part, on Giddens's structuration theory, suggested that integrationist strategies by individuals were, unintentionally and perversely, most responsible for segregation in communication structures.

Zeggelink, Stokman, and Van de Bunt (1996) modeled the likelihood of various configurations of friendship networks that may emerge among an initial set of mutual strangers. Their stochastic model deployed network mechanisms of selection and contagion to explain the creation, maintenance, and dissolution of friendship ties among the individuals. The complex specifications of such models make it impossible to mentally construe the long-term dynamics implied by the models. Further, given the nonlinearities implied by the mechanisms, these models are often analytically intractable. Hence, researchers use computer simulations to help assess the long-term evolutionary implications of the proposed network mechanisms. For instance, Stokman and Zeggelink (1996) developed simulations and then empirically tested the network configuration of policy makers charged with determining the fate of a large farming cooperative in the Netherlands. This research (see also Robinson, 1996) is based on the assumption that ideographic differences in the dynamics of friendship networks can be adequately explained and stochastically predicted by nomothetic underlying network mechanisms.

The use of computer simulations to study the evolution of networks requires considerable programming knowledge by researchers. To make these efforts more accessible to a larger community of researchers, Hyatt, Contractor, and Jones (1997) have developed an object-oriented simulation environment, called Blanche (available online at http://www.tec.spcomm.uiuc.edu/blanche.html). Blanche provides an easy user-interface to support the specification of mathematical models, execution simulations, and the dynamic analysis of the network evolution.

A third line of research examines the evolution of organizational networks as a function of the stage in an organization's life cycle. Monge and Eisenberg (1987) suggested that at early stages organizations are likely to have structures that are less stable and formal. Building on this suggestion, Brass (1995b) noted that structuration theory would suggest that these patterns would become more stable and formalized as organizations mature.

A fourth line of research focuses on the emergence of network organizations, such as strategic alliances, partnerships, and research consortia, in lieu of discrete market transactions or internal hierarchical arrangements. Ring and Van de Ven (1992, 1994) focused attention on the developmental processes of interorganizational relations: emergence, evolution, and dissolution. They proposed, as a framework for this process, "repetitive sequences of negotiation, commitment, and executions stages, each of which is assessed in terms of efficiency and equity" (p. 97). Drawing on much of the same literature, Larson and Starr (1993) proposed a model to explain the emergence of entrepreneurial organizations. Finally, Topper and Carley (1997) described the evolution of a multiorganization network organization in a hyperturbulent environment: the integrated crisis management unit network that responded to the Exxon *Valdez* disaster.

The four streams of research reviewed in this section share an intellectual commitment to a better understanding of the situational evolution of organizational networks. Future research that combines this commitment to situated evolution with the theoretical mechanisms reviewed in this chapter has the potential to significantly extend our knowledge of organizational communication networks and the explanatory power of our models and theories.

CONCLUSION

This chapter has focused on emergence of communication networks—their creation, maintenance, and dissolution—within and among organizations. Ten major families of theories were reviewed to explore the theoretical mechanisms that have been used by network scholars to examine these evolutionary processes in organizational communication networks. Six conclusions seem warranted from this review.

First, the literature reviewed in this chapter focuses much more on the creation of networks than their maintenance or dissolution. This imbalance reflects a serious shortcoming in current theoretical perspectives and empirical research. Theories that describe conditions under which the likelihood of creating network links is lower rather than higher must be examined more carefully to see if these conditions also predict the dissolution of network links. The Seabright et al. (1992) research, reviewed earlier, offers a notable example of such an attempt. Their study found evidence that reductions in the resource fit between organizations would lead to pressures to dissolve interorganizational network links.

Second, considerable additional work is required to reduce or eliminate the extensive redundancy that exists among the different theoretical perspectives. For example, as discussed earlier, the theoretical mechanisms in exchange theory and social support theory share a great deal in common with each other. Likewise, homophily, which is defined as similarity of individual characteristics, can be viewed as conceptually overlapping with proximity, which can be viewed as similarity of location. Other examples abound in this review. Some of this redundancy stems from conceptual vagueness, as was mentioned earlier with the notion of uncertainty. Other aspects of redundancy are attributable to the fact that the theories were developed in different contexts, as is the case for network organizational forms, which clearly use exchange mechanisms though they emerged out of interests in economic markets and transaction costs. Still another source of overlap is that different theories were developed in different disciplinary traditions, including communication, economics, political science, social work, and sociology, to name but a sample.

The third conclusion is that the time may have come to explore a more eclectic, multitheoretical approach to network theory in which several theories are used simultaneously to predict communication network behavior and outcomes. While elimination of conceptual and theoretical redundancy will be beneficial, it seems unlikely to produce a general, integrated theory (and there are those who argue in principle that such a feat is impossible). None of the theories reviewed in this chapter, by themselves, seem sufficiently powerful to explain large portions of the variance in network emergence. Nor do they individually seem capable of predicting the emergence, maintenance, and dissolution of communication networks with anything near a reasonable level of precision. Consequently, an integrative, multitheoretical alternative appears worth exploring. A multitheoretical approach would use different theories to account for different aspects of network phenomena or to account for the same aspects at different points in the evolutionary process. There is some precedence for this strategy in the public goods literature, which examines one set of mechanisms for the creation of public goods but an alternative set for their maintenance (Monge et al., 1998).

A fourth conclusion is that it is important to focus attention on uniquely network forms of communication network theory. This review has highlighted the fact that most theoretical explanations for communication networks, though not all, stem from nonnetwork theories applied to network phenomena. More theoretical effort is required like the work that helped to develop network exchange theories, structural holes theory, and network evolution theories. Wasserman and Pattison (1996) have recently made important contributions in this direction with the development of "p*" models, which explore how the various endogenous characteristics of a matrix of network relations, together with other exogenous explanatory variables, shape the outcomes of the network.

Fifth, much work needs to be done to develop network theories that bridge the expansive analytic levels covered by network analysis. In one sense, the fact that networks span such diverse phenomena and operate on so many levels underscores their importance in everyday life. On the other hand, these expansive and multilevel qualities make theoretical integration a very challenging task. Theories that range from internal cognitive social structures to global network organizations make formidable intellectual leaps that need careful examination and theoretical development.

Finding commonalities as well as disjunctures across levels will be an important part of building a more integrated theory of communication networks.

Finally, as the literature reviewed here demonstrates, the study of emergence in communication networks continues to be overwhelmingly influenced by structural perspectives. Of the three network traditions employed throughout this chapter, the positional and relational traditions continue to dominate, while the cultural tradition has struggled to bridge the gap between structure and the content of communication networks. The theoretical mechanisms used in network research invest greater currency in the structural relationships among people than on the types of network linkages (e.g., material vs. symbolic, product vs. knowledge; see the earlier discussion in this chapter) or the content of the messages within these networks. Wellman (1988) notes that the genesis for this bias goes back to Georg Simmel's influence on the pioneers of network research (e.g., Simmel, 1955). In fact, Wellman (1988) characterizes the early work of an influential minority of formalists (e.g., Fararo, 1973; Holland & Leinhardt, 1979; Lorrain & White, 1971) by asserting that in "concentrating on the form of network patterns rather than their content . . . they have shared a Simmelian sensibility that similar patterns of ties may have similar behavioral consequences no matter what the substantive context" (p. 25). Even the network studies based on the cultural tradition (e.g., semantic networks) are largely focused on structural explanations for the emergence of these networks, despite the fact that they are based on network linkages representing common interpretations. They seek to explain variation in the structure of the semantic networks rather than variation in the content (e.g., types of linkages or messages) within these networks. Missing from the network literature is any systematic theoretical or empirical work aimed at examining the relationship between the structure of networks and the content of messages, symbols, and interpreta-

tions that produce and reproduce them. Consequently, we know very little about the manner in which different network configurations (e.g., centralized networks, dense networks) are likely to facilitate the creation of certain types of messages (e.g., supportive, critical). Conversely, little is known about how the production and reproduction of certain types of messages or symbols are likely to influence the structural emergence of communication networks.

The field of organizational network analysis has grown exponentially since the original chapter on emergent communication networks was published in the *Handbook of Organizational Communication* more than a decade ago (Monge & Eisenberg, 1987). The diversity of scholars from various intellectual backgrounds who are currently developing theories of communication and other networks in organizations is truly impressive, as is the high quality of their work. Even more important, as this review has demonstrated, is the development and application of theories and theoretical mechanisms in what once was a very atheoretical field. There is, of course, a great deal remaining to be done. But continued work in these theoretical areas, with special attention to network evolution, promises to make the years ahead a very exciting time for organizational communication network scholars.

REFERENCES

Abrahamson, E., & Rosenkopf, L. (1997). Social network effects on the extent of innovation diffusion: A computer simulation. *Organization Science, 8,* 289-309.

Adams, J. S. (1965). Inequity in social exchange. In L. Berkowitz (Ed.), *Advances in experimental social psychology* (pp. 267-300). New York: Academic Press.

Albrecht, T., & Ropp, V. A. (1982). The study of network structuring in organizations through the use of method triangulation. *Western Journal of Speech Communication, 46,* 162-178.

Albrecht, T. L., & Hall, B. (1991). Relational and content differences between elites and outsiders in innovation networks. *Human Communication Research, 17,* 535-561.

Albrecht, T. L., & Ropp, V. A. (1984). Communicating about innovation in networks of three U.S. organizations. *Journal of Communication, 34,* 78-91.

Aldrich, H. (1976). Resource dependence and interorganizational relations: Relations between local employment service offices and social service sector organizations. *Administration & Society, 7,* 419-454.

Aldrich, H. (1982). The origins and persistence of social networks. In P. V. Marsden & N. Lin (Eds.), *Social structure and network analysis* (pp. 281-293): Beverly Hills, CA: Sage Press.

Allen, T. (1970). Communication networks in R&D laboratories. *R&D Management, 1,* 14-21.

Alter, C. (1990). An exploratory study of conflict and coordination in interorganizational service delivery systems. *Academy of Management Journal, 33,* 478-502.

Bacharach, S. B., & Lawler, E. J. (1980). *Power and politics in organizations.* San Francisco: Jossey-Bass.

Badaracco, J. L., Jr. (1991). *The knowledge link: How firms compete through strategic alliances.* Boston: Harvard Business School Press.

Baker, W. E. (1987). *Do corporations do business with the bankers on their boards? The consequences of investment bankers as directors.* Paper presented at the Nags Head Conference on Corporate Interlocks, Kill Devil Hills, NC.

Bandura, A. (1986). *Social foundations of thought and action.* Englewood Cliffs, NJ: Prentice Hall.

Banks, D. L., & Carley, K. M. (1996). Models for network evolution. *Journal of Mathematical Sociology, 21,* 173-196.

Barley, S. R. (1990). The alignment of technology and structure through roles and networks. *Administrative Science Quarterly, 35,* 61-103.

Barnard, C. I. (1938). *The functions of the executive.* Cambridge, MA: Harvard University Press.

Barnett, G. A., & Jang, H. (1994). *The relationship between network position and attitudes toward the job and organization in a police organization.* Paper presented at the annual meeting of the International Communication Association, Sydney, Australia.

Barnett, G. A., & Salisbury, J. G. T. (in press). Communication and globalization: A longitudinal analysis of the international telecommunication network. *Journal of World-Systems Research.*

Barney, J. B. (1985). Dimensions of informal social network structure: Toward a contingency theory of informal relations. *Social Networks, 7,* 1-46.

Barrera, M., Jr., & Ainlay, S. L., (1983). The structure of social support: A conceptual and empirical analysis. *Journal of Community Psychology, 11,* 133-143.

Bass, L. A., & Stein, C. H. (1997). Comparing the structure and stability of network ties using the social support questionnaire and the social network list. *Journal of Social and Personal Relationships, 14,* 123-132.

Bateson, G. (1972). Double bind, 1969. In G. Bateson (Ed.), *Steps to an ecology of mind* (pp. 271-278). New York: Ballantine.

Baum, J., & Oliver, C. (1991). Institutional linkages and organizational mortality. *Administrative Science Quarterly, 36,* 187-218.

Baum, J., & Oliver, C. (1992). Institutional embeddedness and the dynamics of organizational populations. *American Sociological Review, 57,* 540-559.

Bavelas, A. (1948). A mathematical model for group structure. *Applied Anthropology, 7,* 16-30.

Benassi, M., & Gargiulo, M. (1993, June). *Informal hierarchy and managerial flexibility in network organization.* Paper presented at the Third European Conference on Social Network Analysis, Munich, Germany.

Benson, J. K. (1975). The interorganizational network as a political economy. *Administrative Science Quarterly, 20,* 229-249.

Berger, C. R. (1987). Communicating under uncertainty. In M. E. Roloff & G. R. Miller (Eds.), *Interpersonal processes: New directions in communication research* (pp. 39-62). Newbury Park, CA: Sage.

Berger, C. R., & Bradac, J. J. (1982). *Language and social knowledge: Uncertainty in interpersonal relations.* London: Edward Arnold.

Berger, J., Cohen, B., & Zelditch, M., Jr. (1966). Status characteristics and expectation states. In J. Berger, M. Zelditch, Jr., & B. Anderson (Eds.), *Sociological theories in progress* (Vol. 1, pp. 29-46). Boston: Houghton Mifflin.

Berger, P., & Luckmann, T. (1966). *The social construction of reality.* Garden City, NY: Doubleday.

Berkman, L. (1985). The relationship of social networks and social support to morbidity and mortality. In S. Cohen & S. L. Syme (Eds.), *Social support and health* (pp. 241-262). Orlando, FL: Academic Press.

Berkman, L., & Syme, S. L. (1979). Social networks, host resistance, and mortality. *American Journal of Epidemiology, 109,* 186-204.

Bernard, H., Killworth, P., & Sailer, L. (1980). Informant accuracy in social network data IV: A comparison of clique-level structure in behavioral and cognitive network data. *Social Networks, 2,* 191-218.

Bernard, H., Killworth, P., & Sailer, L. (1982). Informant accuracy in social network data V. An experimental attempt to predict actual communication from recall data. *Social Science Research, 11,* 30-66.

Bernard, H. R., Killworth, P., & Cronenfeld, D. (1984). The problem of informant accuracy: The validity of retrospective data. *Annual Review of Anthropology, 13,* 495-517.

Bienenstock, E. J., & Bonacich, P. (1992). The core as solution to exclusionary networks. *Social Networks, 14,* 231-244.

Bienenstock, E. J., & Bonacich, P. (1997). Network exchange as a cooperative game. *Rationality and Society, 9,* 37-65.

Bizot, E., Smith, N., & Hill, T. (1991). Use of electronic mail in a research and development organization. In J. Morell & M. Fleischer (Eds.), *Advances in the implementation and impact of computer systems* (Vol. 1, pp. 65-92). Greenwich, CT: JAI.

Bland, S. H., O'Leary, E. S., Farinaro, E., Jossa, F., Krogh, V., Violanti, J. M., & Trevisan, M. (1997). Social network disturbances and psychological distress following earthquake evacuation. *Journal of Nervous and Mental Disease, 185,* 188-194.

Blau, P. M. (1964). *Exchange and power in social life.* New York: John Wiley.

Bovasso, G. (1992). A structural analysis of the formation of a network organization. *Group & Organization Management, 17,* 86-106.

Bovasso, G. (1995). A network analysis of social contagion processes in an organizational intervention. *Human Relations, 49,* 1419-1435.

Boyd, B. (1990). Corporate linkages and organizational environment: A test of the resource dependence model. *Strategic Management Journal, 11,* 419-430.

Brass. D. J. (1981). Structural relationships, job characteristics, and worker satisfaction and performance. *Administrative Science Quarterly, 26,* 331-348.

Brass, D. J. (1984). Being in the right place: A structural analysis of individual influence in an organization. *Administrative Science Quarterly, 29,* 518-539.

Brass, D. J. (1985a). Men's and women's networks: A study of interaction patterns and influence in organizations. *Academy of Management Journal, 28,* 327-343.

Brass, D. J. (1985b). Technology and the structuring of jobs: Employee satisfaction, performance, and influence. *Organizational Behavior and Human Decision Processes, 35,* 216-240.

Brass, D. J. (1995a). Creativity: It's all in your social network. In C. M. Ford & D. A. Gioia (Eds.), *Creative action in organizations* (pp. 94-99). London: Sage.

Brass, D. J. (1995b). A social network perspective on human resources management. *Research in Personnel and Human Resources Management, 13,* 39-79.

Brass, D. J., & Burkhardt, M. E. (1992). Centrality and power in organizations. In N. Nohria & R. G. Eccles (Eds.), *Networks and organizations: Structure, form, and action* (pp. 191-215). Boston: Harvard Business School Press.

Brass, D. J., Butterfield, K. D., & Skaggs, B. C. (1995, June). *The social network structure of unethical behavior.* Paper presented at the International Association of Business and Society, Vienna, Austria.

Brass, D. J., & Krackhardt, D. (in press). Communication networks and organizations: A meso approach. In H. L. Tosi (Ed.), *Extensions of the environment/or-*

ganization/person model (Vol. 2). Greenwich, CT: JAI.

Brewer, D. D. (1995). The social structural basis of the organization of persons in memory. *Human Nature, 6,* 379-403.

Buckley, W. (1967). *Sociology and modern systems theory.* Englewood Cliffs, NJ: Prentice Hall.

Burke, P. J. (1997). An identity model for network exchange. *American Sociological Review, 62,* 134-150.

Burkhardt, M. R. (1994). Social interaction effects following a technological change: A longitudinal investigation. *Academy of Management Journal, 37,* 869-896.

Burkhardt, M. E., & Brass, D. J. (1990). Changing patterns of patterns of change: The effects of a change in technology on social network structure and power. *Administrative Science Quarterly, 35,* 104-127.

Burns, T., & Stalker, G. M. (1961). *The management of innovation.* London: Tavistock.

Burns, L., & Wholey, D. R. (1993). Adoption and abandonment of matrix management programs: Effects of organizational characteristics and interorganizational networks. *Academy of Management Review, 36,* 106-138.

Burt, R. S. (1980). Models of network structure. *Annual Review of Sociology, 6,* 79-141.

Burt, R. S. (1982). *Toward a structural theory of action: Network models of stratification, perception and action.* New York: Academic Press.

Burt, R. S. (1987). Social contagion and innovation: Cohesion versus structural equivalence. *American Journal of Sociology, 92,* 1287-1335.

Burt, R. S. (1991). Contagion. In R. S. Burt, *Structure: A computer program.* New York.

Burt, R. S. (1992). *Structural holes: The social structure of competition.* Cambridge, MA: Harvard University Press.

Burt, R. S. (1997). The contingent value of social capital. *Administrative Science Quarterly, 42,* 339-365.

Burt, R. S., & Knez, M. (1996). Trust and third-party gossip. In R. M. Kramer & T. R. Tyler (Eds.), *Trust in organizations: Frontiers of theory and research* (pp. 68-89). Thousand Oaks, CA: Sage.

Byrne, D. E. (1971). *The attraction paradigm.* New York: Academic Press.

Campbell, K. E., & Lee, B. A. (1990). Gender differences in urban neighboring. *Sociological Quarterly, 31,* 495-512.

Carley, K. (1986). An approach for relating social structure to cognitive structure. *Journal of Mathematical Sociology, 12,* 137-189.

Carley, K. (1990). Group stability: A socio-cognitive approach. In L. E. B. Markovsky, C. Ridgeway, & H. Walker (Eds.), *Advances in group processes: Theory and research* (Vol. 7, pp. 1-44). Greenwich, CT: JAI.

Carley, K. (1991). A theory of group stability. *American Sociological Review, 56,* 331-354.

Carley, K. M., & Kaufer, D. S. (1993). Semantic connectivity: An approach for analyzing symbols in semantic networks. *Communication Theory, 3,* 183-213.

Carley, K. M., & Krackhardt, D. (1996). Cognitive inconsistencies and non-symmetric friendship. *Social Networks, 18,* 1-27.

Carroll, G. R., & Teo, A. C. (1996). On the social networks of managers. *Academy of Management Journal, 39,* 421-440.

Chandler, A. D. (1977). *The visible hand: The managerial revolution in American business.* Cambridge, MA: Harvard University Press.

Coase, R. H. (1937). The nature of the firm. *Economica, 4,* 386-405.

Cochran, P. L., Wood, R. A., & Jones, T. B. (1985). The composition of boards of directors and incidence of golden parachutes. *Academy of Management Journal, 28,* 664-671.

Coleman, J. S. (1957). *Community conflict.* New York: Free Press.

Coleman, J. S. (1961). *The adolescent society: The social life of the teenager and its impact on education.* New York: Free Press.

Coleman, J. S. (1973). *The mathematics of collective action.* Chicago: Aldine.

Coleman, J. S. (1986). *Individual interests and collective action: Selected essays.* New York: Cambridge University Press.

Coleman, J. S. (1988). Social capital in the creation of human capital. *American Journal of Sociology, 94,* 95-120.

Conrath, D. (1973). Communication environment and its relationship to organizational structure. *Management Science, 4,* 586-603.

Contractor, N., Zink, D., & Chan, M. (1998). IKNOW: A tool to assist and study the creation, maintenance, and dissolution of knowledge networks. In *Proceedings of the Kyoto Meeting on Social Interaction and Communityware* [Lecture Notes in Computer Science]. Berlin: Springer-Verlag

Contractor, N. S. (1997). *Inquiring knowledge networks on the Web. Conceptual overview.* Available: http://www.tec.spcomm.uiuc.edu/nosh/IKNOW/sld001.htm.

Contractor, N. S., & Eisenberg, E. M. (1990). Communication networks and new media in organizations. In J. Fulk & C. Steinfield (Eds.), *Organizations and communication technology* (pp. 143-172). Newbury Park, CA: Sage.

Contractor, N. S., Eisenberg, E. M., & Monge, P. R. (1996). *Antecedents and outcomes of interpretative diversity.* Unpublished manuscript.

Contractor, N. S., & Grant, S. (1996). The emergence of shared interpretations in organizations: A self-organizing systems perspective. In J. Watt & A. VanLear (Eds.), *Cycles and dynamic processes in communication processes* (pp. 216-230). Thousand Oaks, CA: Sage.

Contractor, N. S., O'Keefe, B. J., & Jones, P. M. (1997). *IKNOW: Inquiring knowledge networks on the Web* [Computer software]. University of Illinois. (http://iknow.spcomm.uiuc.edu)

Contractor, N. S., Seibold, D. R., & Heller, M. A. (1996). Interactional influence in the structuring of media use in groups: Influence of members' perceptions of group decision support system use. *Human Communication Research, 22,* 451-481.

Cook, K. S. (1977). Exchange and power in networks of interorganizational relations. *Sociological Quarterly, 18,* 62-82.

Cook, K. S. (1982). Network structures from an exchange perspective. In P. V. Marsden & N. Lin (Eds.), *Social structure and network analysis* (pp. 177-218). Beverly Hills, CA: Sage.

Cook, K. S., & Emerson, R. M. (1978). Power, equity, and commitment in exchange networks. *American Sociological Review, 43,* 721-739.

Cook, K. S., Emerson, R. M., Gillmore, M. R., & Yamagishi, T. (1983). The distribution of power in exchange networks: Theory and experimental results. *American Journal of Sociology, 89,* 275-305.

Cook, K. S., & Whitmeyer, J. M. (1992) Two approaches to social structure: Exchange theory and network analysis. *Annual Review of Sociology, 18,* 109-127.

Cook, K. S., & Yamagishi, T. (1992). Power in exchange networks: A power-dependence formulation. *Social Networks, 14,* 245-265.

Corman, S. R. (1990). A mode of perceived communication in collective networks. *Human Communication Research, 16,* 582-602.

Corman, S. R. (1996). Cellular automata as models of unintended consequences of organizational communication. In J. H. Watt & C. A. Van Lear (Eds.), *Dynamic patterns in communication processes* (pp. 191-212). Thousand Oaks, CA: Sage.

Corman, S. R. (1997). The reticulation of quasi-agents in systems of organizational communication. In G. A. Barnett & L. Thayer (Eds.), *Organization communication emerging perspectives V: The renaissance in systems thinking* (pp. 65-81). Greenwich, CT: Ablex.

Corman, S. R., & Scott, C. R. (1994). Perceived networks, activity, foci, and observable communication in social collectives. *Communication Theory, 4,* 171-190.

Crombie, S., & Birley, S. (1992). Networking by female business owners in Northern Ireland. *Journal of Business Venturing, 7,* 237-251.

Cummings, A. (1997). *The radicalness of employee ideas: An interactive model of co-worker networks and problem-solving styles.* Unpublished doctoral dissertation, University of Illinois, Champaign.

Cutrona, C. E., & Russell, D. W. (1990). Type of social support and specific stress: Toward a theory of optimal matching. In B. R. Sarason, I. G. Sarason, & G. R. Pierce (Eds.), *Social support: An interactional view* (pp. 319-366). New York: John Wiley.

Danowski, J. A. (1982). Computer-mediated communication: A network-based content analysis using a CBBS conference. In M. Burgoon (Ed.), *Communication yearbook 6* (pp. 905-924). Beverly Hills, CA: Sage.

Davies, G. (1996). The employment support network—An intervention to assist displaced works. *Journal of Employment Counseling, 33,* 146-154.

Davis, G. F. (1991). Agents without principles? The spread of the poison pill through the intercorporate network. *Administrative Science Quarterly, 36,* 583-613.

Davis, J., & Leinhardt, S. (1972). The structure of positive interpersonal relations in small groups. In J. Berger (Ed.), *Sociological theories in progress* (Vol. 2, pp. 218-251). Boston: Houghton Mifflin.

Davis, K. (1953). A method of studying communication patterns in organizations. *Personnel Psychology, 6,* 301-312.

DeFleur, M. L., & Cronin, M. M. (1991). Completeness and accuracy of recall in the diffusion of the news from a newspaper versus a television source. *Sociological Inquiry, 61,* 148-166.

DiMaggio, P. J., & Powell, W. W. (1983). The iron cage revisited: Institutional isomorphism and collective rationality in organizational fields. *American Sociological Review, 48,* 147-160.

de Saussure, R. (1966). *Course in general linguistics.* New York: McGraw-Hill. (Original work published 1916)

De Soto, C. B. (1960). Learning a social structure. *Journal of Abnormal and Social Psychology, 60,* 417-421.

Domhoff, G. W. (1983). *Who rules America now? A view of the '80s.* Englewood Cliffs, NJ: Prentice Hall.

Doty, D. H., Glick, W. H., & Huber, G. P. (1993). Fit, equifinality, and organizational effectiveness: A test of two configurational theories. *Academy of Management Journal, 36,* 1196-1250.

Dunn, W. N., & Ginsberg, A. (1986). A sociocognitive network approach to organizational analysis. *Human Relations, 39,* 955-976.

Durkheim, É. (1964). *The rules of sociological method.* London: Free Press. (Original work published 1895)

Durkheim, É. (1977). *Suicide: A study in sociology* (J. A. Spaulding & G. Simpson, Trans.). New York: Free Press. (Original work published 1897)

Eisenberg, E. M., Farace, R. V., Monge, P. R., Bettinghaus, E. P., Kurchner-Hawkins, R., Miller, K., & Rothman, L. (1985). Communication linkages in interorganizational systems. In B. Dervin & M. Voight (Eds.), *Progress in communication sciences* (Vol. 6, pp. 210-266). Norwood, NJ: Ablex.

Eisenberg, E. M., Monge, P. R., & Miller, K. I. (1984). Involvement in communication networks as a predictor of organizational commitment. *Human Communication Research, 10,* 179-201.

Eisenberg, E. M., & Swanson, N. (1996). Organizational network analysis as a tool for program evaluation. *Evaluation and the Health Professions, 19,* 488-507.

Emerson, R. M. (1962). Power-dependence relations. *American Sociological Review, 27,* 31-41.

Emerson, R. M. (1972a). Exchange theory, Part I: A psychological basis for social exchange. In J. Berger, M. Zelditch, & B. Anderson (Eds.), *Sociological theories in progress* (Vol. 2, pp. 38-57). Boston: Houghton Mifflin.

Emerson, R. M. (1972b). Exchange theory, Part II: Exchange relations and networks. In J. Berger, M. Zelditch, & B. Anderson (Eds.), *Sociological theories in progress* (Vol. 2, pp. 58-87). Boston: Houghton Mifflin.

Emery, F. E., & Trist, E. L. (1960). Sociotechnical systems. In C. W. Churchman & M. Verhulst (Eds.), *Management science, models and techniques* (pp. 83-97). New York: Pergamon.

Emery, F. E., & Trist, E. L. (1965). The causal texture of organizational environment. *Human Relations, 18,* 21-32.

Erickson, B. (1988). The relational basis of attitudes. In B. Wellman & S. D. Berkowitz (Eds.), *Social structures: A network approach* (pp. 99-121). Cambridge, UK: Cambridge University Press.

Ethington, E. T., Johnson, J. D., Marshall, A., Meyer, M., & Chang, H. J. (1996, May). *Gender ratios in organizations: A comparative study of two organizations.* Paper presented at the annual conference of the International Communication Association, Chicago.

Eveland, J. D., & Bikson, T. K. (1987). Evolving electronic communication networks: An empirical assessment. *Office: Technology and People, 3,* 103-128.

Farace, R. V., Monge, P. R., & Russell, H. M. (1977). *Communicating and organizing.* Reading, MA: Addison-Wesley.

Fararo, T. J. (1973). *Mathematical sociology: An introduction to fundamentals.* New York: John Wiley.

Feeley, T. H., & Barnett, G. A. (1996). Predicting employee turnover from communication networks. *Human Communication Research, 23,* 370-387.

Feld, S. (1981). The focused organization of social ties. *American Journal of Sociology, 86,* 1015-1035.

Fernandez, R. M. (1991). Structural bases of leadership in intraorganizational networks. *Social Psychology Quarterly, 54,* 36-53.

Festinger, L. (1954). A theory of social comparison processes. *Human Relations, 7,* 114-140.

Festinger, L., Schachter, S., & Back, K. (1950). *Social pressures in informal groups: A study of human factors in housing.* Palo Alto, CA: Stanford University Press.

Fine, G. A., & Kleinman, S. (1983). Network and meaning: An interactionist approach to structure. *Symbolic Interaction, 6,* 97-110.

Fiol, C. M. (1989). A semantic analysis of corporate language: Organizational boundaries and joint venturing. *Administrative Science Quarterly, 34,* 277-303.

Flache, A., & Macy, M. W. (1996). The weakness of strong ties: Collective action failure in a highly cohesive group. *Journal of Mathematical Sociology, 21,* 3-28.

Follett, M. P. (1924). *Creative experience.* New York: Longmans, Green.

Fombrun, C. J. (1986). Structural dynamics within and between organizations. *Administrative Science Quarterly, 31,* 403-421.

Freeman, L. (1977). A set of measures of centrality based on betweenness. *Sociometry, 40,* 35-41.

Freeman, L. (1979). Centrality in social networks: I. Conceptual clarification. *Social Networks, 1,* 215-239.

Freeman, L. C. (1992). Filling in the blanks: A theory of cognitive categories and the structure of social affiliation. *Social Psychology Quarterly, 55,* 118-127.

Freeman, L. C., Romney, A. K., & Freeman, S. C. (1987). Cognitive structure and informant accuracy. *American Anthropologist, 89,* 31-325.

Friedkin, N. E. (1984). Structural cohesion and equivalence explanations of social homogeneity. *Sociological Methods & Research, 12,* 235-261.

Frost, P., Moore, L., Louis, M. R., Lundberg, C., & Martin, J. (1985). *Organizational culture.* Beverly Hills, CA: Sage.

Fulk, J. (1993). Social construction of communication technology. *Academy of Management Journal, 36,* 921-950.

Fulk, J., & Boyd, B. (1991). Emerging theories of communication in organizations. *Yearly Review of the Journal of Management, 17,* 407-446.

Fulk, J., Flanagin, A. J., Kalman, M. E., Monge, P. R., & Ryan, T. (1996). Connective and communal public goods in interactive communication systems. *Communication Theory, 6,* 60-87.

Fulk, J., Schmitz, J., & Ryu, D. (1995). Cognitive elements in the social construction of communication technology. *Management Communication Quarterly, 8,* 259-288.

Fulk, J., Schmitz, J., & Steinfield, C. W. (1990). A social influence model of technology use. In J. Fulk & C. Steinfield (Eds.), *Organizations and communication technology* (pp. 117-140). Newbury Park, CA: Sage.

Fulk, J., Steinfield, C. W., Schmitz, J., & Power, J. G. (1987). A social information processing model of media use in organizations. *Communication Research, 14,* 529-552.

Galaskiewicz, J. (1979). *Exchange networks and community politics.* Beverly Hills, CA: Sage.

Galaskiewicz, J. (1985). Interorganizational relations. *Annual Review of Sociology, 11,* 281-304.

Galaskiewicz, J., & Burt, R. S. (1991). Interorganizational contagion in corporate philanthropy. *Administrative Science Quarterly, 36,* 88-105.

Galaskiewicz, J., & Wasserman, S. (1989). Mimetic and normative processes within an interorganizational field: An empirical test. *Administrative Science Quarterly, 34,* 454-479.

Galbraith, J. R. (1977). *Organization design.* Reading, MA: Addison-Wesley.

Galbraith, J. R. (1995). *Designing organizations: An executive briefing on strategy, structure, and process.* San Francisco: Jossey-Bass.

Gerlach, M. (1992). *Alliance capitalism.* Berkeley: University of California Press.

Ghoshal, S., & Bartlett, C. A. (1990). The multinational corporation as an interorganizational network. *Academy of Management Review, 15,* 603-625.

Giddens, A. (1976). *New rules of sociological method.* London: Hutchinson.

Giddens, A. (1979). *Central problems in social theory.* Cambridge, UK: Cambridge University Press.

Giddens, A. (1984). *The constitution of society: Outline of the theory of structuration.* Cambridge, UK: Polity.

Goes, J. B., & Park, S. H. (1997). Interorganizational links and innovation: The case of hospital services. *Academy of Management Journal, 40,* 673-696.

Goodell, A., Brown, J., & Poole, M. S. (1989). *Organizational networks and climate perceptions: A longitudinal analysis.* Unpublished manuscript.

Gould, R. V. (1991). Multiple networks and mobilization in the Paris Commune, 1871. *American Sociological Review, 56,* 716-729.

Grabher, G. (1993). Rediscovering the social in the economics of interfirm relations. In G. Grabher (Ed.), *The embedded firm: On the socioeconomics of industrial networks* (pp. 1-31). New York: Routledge.

Graen, G. (1976). Role making processes within complex organizations. In M. D. Dunnette (Ed.), *Handbook of industrial and organizational psychology* (pp. 1201-1245). Chicago: Rand McNally.

Grandori, A., & Soda, G. (1995). Inter-firm networks: Antecedents, mechanisms, and forms. *Organization Studies, 16,* 183-214.

Granovetter, M. (1978). Threshold models of diffusion and collective behavior. *Journal of Mathematical Sociology, 9,* 165-179.

Granovetter, M. (1982). The strength of weak ties: A network theory revisited. In P. Marsden & N. Lin (Eds.), *Social structure and network analysis* (pp. 105-130). Beverly Hills, CA: Sage.

Granovetter, M. S. (1985). Economic action and social structure: The problem of embeddedness. *American Journal of Sociology, 91,* 481-510.

Gulati, R. (1995). Social structure and alliance formation patterns: A longitudinal analysis. *Administrative Science Quarterly, 40,* 619-652.

Gupta, A. K., & Govindarajan, V. (1991). Knowledge flows and the structure of control within multinational corporations. *Academy of Management Review, 16,* 768-792.

Gurbaxani, V. (1990). Diffusion in computing networks: The case of Bitnet. *Communications of the ACM, 33,* 65-75.

Hackman, J. R., & Oldham, G. (1976). Motivation through the design of work: Test of a theory. *Organizational Behavior and Human Performance, 16,* 250-279.

Haines, V. A. (1988). Social network analysis, structuration theory and the holism-individualism debate. *Social Networks, 10,* 157-182.

Hall, A., & Wellman, B. (1985). Social networks and social support. In S. Cohen & S. L. Syme (Eds.), *Social support and health* (pp. 23-41). Orlando, FL: Academic Press.

Harary, F., Norman, R. Z., & Cartwright, D. (1965). *Structural models: An introduction to the theory of directed graphs.* New York: John Wiley.

Hartman, R. L., & Johnson, J. D. (1989). Social contagion and multiplexity: Communication networks as predictors of commitment and role ambiguity. *Human Communication Research, 15,* 523-548.

Hartman, R. L., & Johnson, J. D. (1990). Formal and informal group structures: An examination of their relationship to role ambiguity. *Social Networks, 12,* 127-151.

Haythornthwaite, C. (1996). Social network analysis: An approach and technique for the study of information exchange. *Library & Information Science Research, 18,* 323-342.

Haunschild, P. R. (1993). Interorganizational imitation: The impact of interlocks on corporate acquisition activity. *Administrative Science Quarterly, 38,* 564-592.

Haunschild, P. R. (1994). How much is that company worth? Interorganizational relationships, uncertainty, and acquisition premiums. *Administrative Science Quarterly, 39,* 391-411.

Heald, M. R., Contractor, N. S., Koehly, L., & Wasserman, S. (1996). *Formal and emergent predictors of coworkers' perceptual congruence on an organization's social structure.* Unpublished manuscript.

Heckscher, C. (1994). Defining the post-bureaucratic type. In C. Heckscher & A. Donnellon (Eds.), *The post-bureaucratic organization: New perspectives on organizational change* (pp. 14-62). Thousand Oaks, CA: Sage.

Heider, F. (1958). *The psychology of interpersonal relations.* New York: John Wiley.

Hinds, P., & Kiesler, S. (1995). Communication across boundaries: Work, structure, and use of communication technologies in a large organization. *Organization Science, 6,* 373-393.

Hoffman, A. N., Stearns, T. M., & Shrader, C. B. (1990). Structure, context, and centrality in interorganizational networks. *Journal of Business Research, 20,* 333-347.

Hofstede, G. (1984). *Culture's consequences: International differences in work-related values.* Beverly Hills, CA: Sage.

Holland, P. W., & Leinhardt, S. (1975). The statistical analysis of local structure in social networks. In D. R. Heise (Ed.), *Sociological methodology, 1976* (pp. 1-45). San Francisco: Jossey-Bass.

Holland, P. W., & Leinhardt, S. (1979). *Perspectives on social network research.* New York: Academic Press.

Homans, G. C. (1950). *The human group.* New York: Harcourt Brace.

Homans, G. C. (1958). Social behavior as exchange. *American Journal of Sociology, 63,* 597-606.

Homans, G. C. (1974). *Social behavior: Its elementary forms* (Rev. ed.). New York: Harcourt Brace.

Huber, G. P., & Daft, R. L. (1987). The information environments of organizations. In F. M. Jablin, L. L. Putnam, K. H. Roberts, & L. W. Porter (Eds.), *Handbook of organizational communication: An interdisciplinary perspective* (pp. 130-164): Newbury Park, CA: Sage.

Huber, G. P., Miller, C. C., & Glick, W. H. (1990). Developing more encompassing theories about organizations: The centralization-effectiveness relationship as an example. *Organization Science, 1,* 11-40.

Hurlbert, J. S. (1991). Social networks, social circles, and job satisfaction. *Work and Occupations, 18,* 415-430.

Hyatt, A., Contractor, N., & Jones, P. M. (1997). Computational organizational network modeling: Strategies and an example. *Computational and Mathematical Organizational Theory, 4,* 285-300.

Ibarra, H. (1992). Homophily and differential returns: Sex differences in network structure and access in an advertising firm. *Administrative Science Quarterly, 37,* 422-447.

Ibarra, H. (1993a). Network centrality, power, and innovation involvement: Determinants of technical and administrative roles. *Administrative Science Quarterly, 36,* 471-501.

Ibarra, H. (1993b). Personal networks of women and minorities in management: A conceptual framework. *Academy of Management Review, 18,* 56-87.

Ibarra, H. (1995). Race, opportunity, and diversity of social circles in managerial networks. *Academy of Management Journal, 38,* 673-703.

Ibarra, H., & Andrews, S. B. (1993). Power, social influence, and sense making: Effects of network centrality and proximity on employee perceptions. *Administrative Science Quarterly, 38,* 277-303.

Jablin, F. M. (1987). Formal organization structure. In F. M. Jablin, L. L. Putnam, K. H. Roberts, & L. W. Porter (Eds.), *Handbook of organizational communication: An interdisciplinary perspective* (pp. 389-419). Newbury Park, CA: Sage.

Jablin, F., & Krone, K. J. (1987). Organizational assimilation. In C. Berger & S. H. Chaffee (Eds.), *Hand-

book of communication science (pp. 711-746). Newbury Park, CA: Sage.

Jang, H., & Barnett, G. A. (1994). Cultural differences in organizational communication: A semantic network analysis. *Bulletin de Methodologie Sociologique, 44,* 31-59.

Johnson, J. D. (1992). Approaches to organizational communication structure. *Journal of Business Research, 25,* 99-113.

Johnson, J. D. (1993). *Organizational communication structure.* Norwood, NJ: Ablex.

Kadushin, C. (1983). Mental health and the interpersonal environment: A reexamination of some effects of social structure on mental health. *American Sociological Review, 48,* 188-198.

Kadushin, C., & Brimm, M. (1990). *Why networking fails: Double binds and the limitations of shadow networks.* Paper presented at the Tenth Annual International Social Networks Conference, San Diego, CA.

Kautz, H., Selman, B., & Shah, M. (1997). Combining social networks and collaborative filtering. *Communications of the ACM, 40,* 63-65.

Khurana, R. (1997). *Director interlocks and outsider CEO selection: A field and statistical examination of the Fortune 500 between 1990-1995.* Unpublished doctoral dissertation, Harvard University.

Kilduff, M. (1992). The friendship network as a decision-making resource: Disposition moderators of social influences on organizational choice. *Journal of Personality and Social Psychology, 62,* 168-180.

Kilduff, M., & Krackhardt, D. (1993). *Schemas at work: Making sense of organizational relationships.* Unpublished manuscript.

Kilduff, M., & Krackhardt, D. (1994). Bringing the individual back in: A structural analysis of the internal market for reputation in organizations. *Academy of Management Journal, 37,* 87-108.

Knoke, D. (1990). *Political networks: The structural perspective.* Cambridge, UK: Cambridge University Press.

Knoke, D. (1993). Networks of elite structure and decision making. *Sociological Methods & Research, 22,* 23-45.

Kogut, B., Shan, W., & Walker, G. (1993). Knowledge in the network and the network as knowledge: Structuring of new industries. In G. Grabher (Ed.), *The embedded firm: On the socioeconomics of industrial networks* (pp. 67-94). New York: Routledge.

Korzenny, F., & Bauer, C. (1981). Testing the theory of electronic propinquity: Organizational teleconferencing. *Communication Research, 8,* 479-498.

Kosnik, R. D. (1987). Greenmail: A study of board performance in corporate governance. *Administrative Science Quarterly, 32,* 163-185.

Krackhardt, D. (1987). Cognitive social structures. *Social Networks, 9,* 109-134.

Krackhardt, D. (1990). Assessing the political landscape: Structure, cognition, and power in organizations. *Administrative Science Quarterly, 35,* 342-369.

Krackhardt, D. (1992). The strength of strong ties: The importance of *philos* in organizations. In N. Nohria & R. Eccles (Eds.), *Networks and organizations: Structure, form and action* (pp. 216-239). Boston: Harvard Business School Press.

Krackhardt, D. (1994). Constraints on the interactive organization as an ideal type. In C. Heckscher & A. Donnellon (Eds.), *The post-bureaucratic organization: New perspectives on organizational change* (pp. 211-222). Thousand Oaks, CA: Sage.

Krackhardt, D., & Brass, D. J. (1994). Intra-organizational networks: The micro side. In S. Wasserman & J. Galaskiewicz (Eds.), *Advances in social network analysis: Research in the social and behavioral sciences* (pp. 207-229). Thousand Oaks, CA: Sage.

Krackhardt, D., & Hanson, J. R. (1993). Informal networks: The company behind the chart. *Harvard Business Review, 71,* 104-112.

Krackhardt, D., & Kilduff, M. (1990). Friendship patterns and culture: The control of organizational diversity. *American Anthropologist, 92,* 142-154.

Krackhardt, D., & Porter, L. (1985). When friends leave: A structural analysis of the relationship between turnover & stayers' attitudes. *Administrative Science Quarterly, 30,* 242-261.

Krackhardt, D., & Porter, L. (1986). The snowball effect: Turnover embedded in social networks. *Journal of Applied Psychology, 71,* 50-55.

Krackhardt, D., & Stern, R. N. (1988). Informal networks and organizational crises: An experimental situation. *Social Psychology Quarterly, 51,* 123-140.

Kramer, M. W. (1996). A longitudinal study of peer communication during job transfers: The impact of frequency, quality, and network multiplexity on adjustment. *Human Communication Research, 23,* 59-86.

Krassa, M. A. (1988). Social groups, selective perception, and behavioral contagion in public opinion. *Social Networks, 10,* 109-136.

Kraut, R. E., Egido, C., & Galegher, J. (1990). Patterns of contact and communication in scientific research collaboration. In J. Galegher, R. E. Kraut, & C. Egido (Eds.), *Intellectual teamwork: Social and technological foundations of cooperative work* (pp. 149-172). Hillsdale, NJ: Lawrence Erlbaum.

Krikorian, D. D., Seibold, D. R., & Goode, P. L. (1997). Reengineering at LAC: A case study of emergent network processes. In B. D. Sypher (Ed.), *Case studies in organizational communication: Vol. 2. Perspectives on contemporary work life* (pp. 129-144). New York: Guilford.

Labianca, G., Brass, D., & Gray, B. (1998). Social networks and the perceptions of intergroup conflict:

The role of negative relationships and third parties. *Academy of Management Journal, 41,* 55-67.

Langford, C. P. H., Bowsher, J., Maloney, J. P., & Lillis, P. P. (1997). Social support: A conceptual analysis. *Journal of Advanced Nursing, 25*(1), 95-100.

Larson, A. (1992). Network dyads in entrepreneurial settings: A study of the governance of exchange relations. *Administrative Science Quarterly, 37,* 76-104.

Larson, A., & Starr, J. A. (1993). A network model of organization formation. *Entrepreneurship: Theory and Practice, 17,* 5-15.

Laumann, E. O. (1966). *Prestige and association in an urban community.* Indianapolis, IN: Bobbs-Merrill.

Laumann, E. O., Knoke, D., & Kim, Y.-H. (1985). An organizational approach to state policymaking: A comparative study of energy and health domains. *American Sociological Review, 50,* 1-19.

Laumann, E. O., & Pappi, F. U. (1976). *Networks of collective action.* New York: Academic Press.

Lawrence, R. R., & Lorsch, J. W. (1967). *Organization and environment: Managing differentiation and integration.* Cambridge, MA: Harvard University Press.

Lazerson, M. (1993). Factory or putting out? Knitting networks in Modena. In G. Grabher (Ed.), *The embedded firm: On the socioeconomics of industrial networks* (pp. 203-226). New York: Routledge.

Leavitt, H. J. (1951). Some effects of certain communication patterns on group performance. *Journal of Abnormal and Social Psychology, 46,* 38-50.

Leblebici, H., & Salancik, G. R. (1981). Effects of environmental uncertainty on information and decision processes in banks. *Administrative Science Quarterly, 26,* 578-596.

Leenders, R. T. A. J. (1996). Evolution of friendship and best friendship choices. *Journal of Mathematical Sociology, 21,* 133-148.

Levine, J. H., & White, P. (1961). Exchange as a conceptual framework for the study of interorganizational relationships. *Administrative Science Quarterly, 5,* 583-601.

Lewin, K. (1936). *Principles of topological psychology* (F. Heider & G. Heider, Trans.). New York: McGraw-Hill.

Liebeskind, J. P., Oliver, A. L., Zucker, L., & Brewer, M. (1996). Social networks, learning, and flexibility: Sourcing scientific knowledge in new biotechnology firms. *Organization Science, 7,* 428-443.

Liedka, R. V. (1991). Who do you know in the group? Location of organizations in interpersonal networks. *Social Forces, 70,* 455-474.

Lievrouw, L. A., & Carley, K. (1991). Changing patterns of communication among scientists in an era of "telescience." *Technology in Society, 12,* 457-477.

Lievrouw, L. A., Rogers, E. M., Lowe, C. U., & Nadel, E. (1987). Triangulation as a research strategy for identifying invisible colleges among biomedical scientists. *Social Networks, 9,* 217-248.

Lin, N., & Ensel, W. M., (1989). Life stress and health: Stressors and resources. *American Sociological Review, 54,* 382-399.

Lin, N., Ensel, W. M., & Vaughn, J. C. (1981). Social resources and strength of ties: Structural factors in occupational status attainment. *American Sociological Review, 46,* 393-405.

Lincoln, J., & Miller, J. (1979). Work and friendship ties in organizations: A comparative analysis of relational networks. *Administrative Science Quarterly, 24,* 181-199.

Lincoln, J. R., Gerlach, M. L., & Takahashi, P. (1992). *Keiretsu* networks in the Japanese economy: A dyad analysis of intercorporate ties. *American Sociological Review, 57,* 561-585.

Litwak, E., & Hylton, L. F. (1962). Interorganizational analysis: A hypothesis on coordinating agencies. *Administrative Science Quarterly, 6,* 392-420.

Lorrain, F., & White, H. (1971). Structural equivalence of individuals in social networks. *Journal of Mathematical Sociology, 1,* 49-80.

March, J. G., & Weissinger-Baylon, R. (1986). *Ambiguity and command: Organizational perspectives on military decision making.* Marshfield, MA: Pitman.

Markovsky, B. (1995). Developing an exchange network simulator. *Sociological Perspectives, 38,* 519-545.

Markovsky, B. (1997). Network games. *Rationality and Society, 9,* 67-90.

Markovsky, B., Willer, D., & Patton, T. (1988). Power relations in exchange networks. *American Sociological Review, 53,* 220-236.

Markus, M. L. (1990). Toward a "critical mass" theory of interactive media. In J. Fulk & C. Steinfield (Eds.), *Organizations and communication technology* (pp. 194-218). Newbury Park, CA: Sage.

Marsden, P. V. (1988). Homogeneity in confiding relations. *Social Networks, 10,* 57-76.

Marsden, P. V. (1990). Network data and measurement. *Annual Review of Sociology, 16,* 435-463.

Marsden, P. V., & Friedkin, N. E. (1994). Network studies of social influence. In S. Wasserman & J. Galaskiewicz (Eds.), *Advances in social network analysis: Research in the social and behavioral sciences* (pp. 3-25). Thousand Oaks, CA: Sage.

Marwell, G., & Oliver, P. (1993). *The critical mass in collective action: A micro-social theory.* Cambridge, UK: Cambridge University Press.

Marwell, G., Oliver, P. E., & Prahl, R. (1988). Social networks and collective action: A theory of the critical mass, III. *American Journal of Sociology, 94,* 502-534.

McElroy, J. C., & Shrader, C. B. (1986). Attribution theories of leadership and network analysis. *Journal of Management, 12,* 351-362.

McKelvey, B. (1982). *Organizational systematics: Taxonomy, evolution, and classification.* Berkeley: University of California Press.

McKelvey, B. (1997). Quasi-natural organization science. *Organization Science, 8,* 352-380.

McPhee, R. D., & Corman, S. R. (1995). An activity-based theory of communication networks in organizations, applied to the case of a local church. *Communication Monographs, 62,* 132-151.

McPherson, J. M., & Smith-Lovin, L. (1987). Homophily in voluntary organizations: Status distance and the composition of face to face groups. *American Sociological Review, 52,* 370-379.

Meyer, J. W., & Rowan, B. (1977). Institutionalized organizations: Formal structure as myth and ceremony. *American Journal of Sociology, 83,* 340-363.

Michaelson, A., & Contractor, N. (1992). Comparison of relational and positional predictors of group members' perceptions. *Social Psychology Quarterly, 55,* 300-310.

Miles, R. E. (1980). *Macro organizational behavior.* Santa Monica, CA: Goodyear.

Miles, R. E., & Snow, C. C. (1986). Organizations: New concepts for new forms. *California Management Review, 28,* 62-73.

Miles, R. E., & Snow, C. C. (1992, Summer). Causes of failure in network organizations. *California Management Review, 11,* 53-72.

Miles, R. E., & Snow, C. C. (1995). The new network firm: A spherical structure built on a human investment philosophy. *Organizational Dynamics, 23,* 5-18.

Miller, C. C., Glick, W. H., Wang, Y. D., & Huber, G. P. (1991). Understanding technology-structure relationships: Theory development and meta-analytic theory testing. *Academy of Management Journal, 34,* 370-399.

Miller, K. I., & Monge, P. R. (1985). Social information and employee anxiety about organizational change. *Human Communication Research, 11,* 365-386.

Miner, A. S., Amburgey, T. L., & Stearns, T. M. (1990). Interorganizational linkages and population dynamics: Buffering and transformational shields. *Administrative Science Quarterly, 35,* 689-713.

Mintz, B., & Schwartz, M. (1985). *The power structure of American business.* Chicago: University of Chicago Press.

Mitchell, J. C. (1973). Networks, norms and institutions. In J. Boissevain & J. C. Mitchell (Eds.), *Network analysis* (pp. 15-35). The Hague, Netherlands: Mouton.

Mizruchi, M. S. (1989). Similarity of political behavior among large American corporations. *American Journal of Sociology, 95,* 401-424.

Mizruchi, M. S. (1992). *The structure of corporate political action.* Cambridge, MA: Harvard University Press.

Mizruchi, M. S. (1996). What do interlocks do? An analysis, critique, and assessment of research on interlocking directorates. *Annual Review of Sociology, 22,* 271-298.

Mizruchi, M. S., & Galaskiewicz, J. (1994). Networks of interorganizational relations. In S. Wasserman & J. Galaskiewicz (Eds.), *Advances in social network analysis: Research in the social and behavioral sciences* (pp. 230-253). Thousand Oaks, CA: Sage.

Mizruchi, M. S., & Stearns, L. B. (1988). A longitudinal study of the formation of interlocking directorates. *Administrative Science Quarterly, 33,* 194-210.

Monge, P. R. (1987). The network level of analysis. In C. R. Berger & S. H. Chaffee (Eds.), *Handbook of communication science* (pp. 239-270). Newbury Park, CA: Sage.

Monge, P. R. (1995). Global network organizations. In R. Cesaria & P. Shockley-Zalabak (Eds.), *Organization means communication* (pp. 135-151). Rome: Sipi Editore.

Monge, P. R., & Contractor, N. (1988). Communication networks: Measurement techniques. In C. H. Tardy (Ed.), *A handbook for the study of human communication* (pp. 107-138). Norwood, NJ: Ablex.

Monge, P. R., & Eisenberg, E. M. (1987). Emergent communication networks. In F. M. Jablin, L. L. Putnam, K. H. Roberts, & L. W. Porter (Eds.), *Handbook of organizational communication: An interdisciplinary perspective* (pp. 304-342). Newbury Park, CA: Sage.

Monge, P. R., & Fulk, J. (1999). Communication technology for global network organizations. In G. DeSanctis & J. Fulk (Eds.), *Shaping organizational form: Communication, connection, community* (pp. 71-100). Thousand Oaks, CA: Sage.

Monge, P. R., Fulk, J., Kalman, M., Flanagin, A. J., Parnassa, C., & Rumsey, S. (1998). Production of collective action in alliance-based interorganizational communication and information systems. *Organization Science, 9,* 411-433.

Monge, P. R., & Kalman, M. (1996). Sequentiality, simultaneity, and synchronicity in human communication. In J. Watt & A. Van Lear (Eds.), *Cycles and dynamic patterns in communication processes* (pp. 71-92). New York: Ablex.

Monge, P. R., Rothman, L. W., Eisenberg, E. M., Miller, K. I., & Kirste, K. K. (1985). The dynamics of organizational proximity. *Management Science, 31,* 1129-1141.

Moore, G. (1992). Gender and informal networks in state government. *Social Science Quarterly, 73,* 46-61.

Moscovici, S. (1976). *Social influence and social change.* London: Academic Press.

Nadel, S. F. (1957). *The theory of social structure.* New York: Free Press.

Nelson, R. E. (1989). The strength of strong ties: Social networks and intergroup conflict in organizations. *Academy of Management Journal, 32,* 377-401.

Newell, S., & Clark, P. (1990). The importance of extra-organizational networks in the diffusion and appropriation of new technologies. *Knowledge: Creation, Diffusion, Utilization, 12,* 199-212.

Nishida, T., Takeda, H., Iwazume, M., Maeda, H., & Takaai, M. (1998) The knowledge community: Facilitating human knowledge sharing. In T. Ishida (Ed.), *Community computing: Collaboration over global information networks* (pp. 127-164). Chichester, UK: Wiley.

Nohria, N., & Berkley, J. D. (1994). The virtual organization: Bureaucracy, technology, and the implosion of control. In C. Heckscher & A. Donnellon (Eds.), *The post-bureaucratic organization: New perspectives on organizational change* (pp. 108-128). Thousand Oaks, CA: Sage.

Norling, P. M. (1996). Network or not work: Harnessing technology networks in DuPont. *Research Technology Management, 39,* 42-48.

Norman, R., & Ramirez, R. (1993, July-August) From value chain to value constellation: Designing interactive strategy. *Harvard Business Review, 71,* 65-77.

Ogliastri, E., & Davila, C. (1987). The articulation of power and business structures: A study of Colombia. In M. Mizruchi & M. Schwartz (Eds.), *Intercorporate relations* (pp. 233-263). New York: Cambridge University Press.

Oliver, A. L., & Montgomery, K. (1996). A network approach to outpatient service delivery systems: Resources flow and system influence. *Health Services Research, 30,* 771-789.

Oliver, C. (1990). Determinants of interorganizational relationships: Integration and future directions. *Academy of Management Review, 15,* 241-265.

Oliver, C. (1991). Network relations and loss of organizational autonomy. *Human Relations, 44,* 943-961.

Oliver, P. E. (1980). Rewards and punishments as selective incentives for collective action: Theoretical investigations. *American Journal of Sociology, 8,* 1356-1375.

Oliver, P. E. (1993). Formal models of collective action. *Annual Review of Sociology, 19,* 271-300.

Olson, M., Jr. (1965). *The logic of collective action.* Cambridge, MA: Harvard University Press.

O'Reilly, P. (1988). Methodological issues in social support and social network research. *Social Science and Medicine, 26,* 863-873.

Palmer, D., Friedland, R., & Singh, J. V. (1986). The ties that bind: Organizational and class bases of stability in a corporate interlock network. *American Sociological Review, 51,* 781-796.

Palmer, D., Jennings, P. D., & Zhou, X. (1993). Late adoption of the multidivisional form by large U.S. corporations: Institutional, political and economic accounts. *Administrative Science Quarterly, 38,* 100-131.

Papa, M. J. (1990). Communication network patterns and employee performance with new technology. *Communication Research, 17,* 344-368.

Parsons, T. (1951). *The social system.* New York: Free Press.

Paterniti, R., Chellini, F., Sacchetti, & Tognelli, M. (1996). Psychiatric rehabilitation and its relation to the social network. *International Journal of Mental Health, 25,* 83-87.

Pattison, P. (1994). Social cognition in context: Some applications of social network analysis. In S. Wasserman & J. Galaskiewicz (Eds.), *Advances in social network analysis: Research in the social and behavioral sciences* (pp. 79-109). Thousand Oaks, CA: Sage.

Pfeffer, J., & Salancik, G. (1978). *The external control of organizations.* New York: Harper & Row.

Picot, A. (1993). Structures of industrial organization—Implications for information and communication technology. In W. Kaiser (Ed.), *Vision 2000: The evolution of information and communication technology for the information society* (pp. 278-293). Munich, Germany: Munchner Kreis.

Piore, M. J. (1975). Notes for a theory of labor market stratification. In R. Edwards, M. Reich, & D. Gordon (Eds.), *Labor market segmentation* (pp. 125-150). Lexington, MA: D. C. Heath.

Pollock, T., Whitbred, R., & Contractor, N. S. (1996, February). *Social information processing, job characteristics and disposition: A test and integration of competing theories of job satisfaction.* Paper presented at the Sunbelt XVI International Social Network Conference, Charleston, SC.

Poole, M. S. (in press). Organizational challenges for the new forms. In G. DeSanctis & J. Fulk (Eds.), *Shaping organization form: Communication, connection and community.* Thousand Oaks, CA: Sage.

Poole, M. S., & DeSanctis, G. (1990). Understanding the use of group decision support systems: The theory of adaptive structuration. In J. Fulk & C. Steinfield (Eds.), *Organizations and communication technology* (pp. 173-193). Newbury Park: Sage.

Poole, M. S., & McPhee, R. D. (1983). A structurational analysis of organizational climate. In L. L. Putnam & M. E. Pacanowsky (Eds.), *Communication and organizations: An interpretive approach* (pp. 195-220). Beverly Hills, CA: Sage.

Porter, M. E. (1980). *Competitive strategy: Techniques for analyzing industries and competitors.* New York: Free Press.

Powell, W. W. (1990). Neither market nor hierarchy: Network forms of organization. In L. L. Cummings & B. Staw (Eds.), *Research in organizational behavior* (Vol. 12, pp. 295-336). Greenwich, CT: JAI.

Powell, W. W., Koput, K. W., Smith-Doerr, L. (1996). Interorganizational collaboration and the locus of innovation: Networks of learning in biotechnology. *Administrative Science Quarterly, 41,* 116-145.

Provan, K. G. (1983). The federation as an interorganizational linkage network. *Academy of Management Review, 8,* 79-89.

Provan, K. G., & Milward, H. B. (1995). A preliminary theory of interorganizational network effectiveness: A comparative study of four community mental health systems. *Administrative Science Quarterly, 40*, 1-33.

Radcliffe-Brown, A. R. (1959). *Structure and function in primitive society.* New York: Free Press. (Original work published 1952)

Ratcliff, R. E., Gallagher, M. E., & Ratcliff, K. S. (1979). The civic involvement of bankers: An analysis of the influence of economic power and social prominence in the command of civic policy positions. *Social Problems, 26*, 298-313.

Rafaeli, S., & LaRose, R. J. (1993). Electronic bulletin boards and "public goods" explanations of collaborative mass media. *Communication Research, 20*, 277-297.

Ray, E. B. (1991). The relationship among communication network roles, job stress, and burnout in educational organizations. *Communication Quarterly, 39*, 91-102.

Ray, E. B., & Miller, K. I. (1990). Communication in health-care organizations. In E. B. Ray & L. Donohew (Eds.), *Communication and health: Systems and applications* (pp. 92-107). Hillsdale, NJ: Lawrence Erlbaum.

Rentsch, J. R. (1990). Climate and culture: Interaction and qualitative differences in organizational meanings. *Journal of Applied Psychology, 75*, 668-681.

Rice, R. E. (1993a). Media appropriateness: Using social presence theory to compare traditional and new organizational media. *Human Communication Research, 19*, 451-484.

Rice, R. E. (1993b). Using network concepts to clarify sources and mechanisms of social influence. In G. Barnett & W. Richards, Jr. (Eds.), *Advances in communication network analysis* (pp. 1-21). Norwood, NJ: Ablex.

Rice, R. E. (1994a). Network analysis and computer-mediated communication systems. In S. Wasserman & J. Galaskiewicz (Eds.), *Advances in social network analysis: Research in the social and behavioral sciences* (pp. 167-206). Thousand Oaks, CA: Sage.

Rice, R. E. (1994b). Relating electronic mail use and network structure to R&D work networks and performance. *Journal of Management Information Systems, 11*(1), 9-20.

Rice, R. E., & Aydin, C. (1991). Attitudes toward new organizational technology: Network proximity as a mechanism for social information processing. *Administrative Science Quarterly, 36*, 219-244.

Rice, R. E., & Danowski, J. (1993). Is it really just like a fancy answering machine? Comparing semantic networks of different types of voice mail users. *Journal of Business Communication, 30*, 369-397.

Rice, R. E., Grant, A., Schmitz, J., & Torobin, J. (1990). Individual and network influences on the adoption of perceived outcomes of electronic messaging. *Social Networks, 12*, 27-55.

Richards, W. D. (1985). Data, models, and assumptions in network analysis. In R. D. McPhee & P. K. Tompkins (Eds.), *Organizational communication: Traditional themes and new directions* (pp. 109-147). Newbury Park, CA: Sage.

Ring, P. S., & Van de Ven, A. H. (1992). Structuring cooperative relationships between organizations. *Strategic Management Journal, 13*, 48-498.

Ring, P. S., & Van de Ven, A. H. (1994). Developmental processes of cooperative interorganizational relationships. *Academy of Management Review, 19*, 90-118.

Roberts, K. H., & O'Reilly, C. A. (1978). Organizations as communication structures: An empirical approach. *Human Communication Research, 4*, 283-293.

Roberts, K. H., & O'Reilly, C. A. (1979). Some correlates of communication roles in organizations. *Academy of Management Journal, 22*, 42-57.

Robinson, D. T. (1996). Identity and friendship: Affective dynamics and network formation. *Advances in Group Processes, 13*, 91-111.

Roethlisberger, F., & Dickson, W. (1939). *Management and the worker.* New York: John Wiley.

Rogers, D. O., & Whetten, D. A. (1982). *Interorganizational coordination.* Ames: Iowa State University Press.

Rogers, E. M. (1971). *Communication of innovations.* New York: Free Press.

Rogers, E. M. (1987). Progress, problems, & prospects for network research. *Social Networks, 9*, 285-310.

Rogers, E. M., & Kincaid, D. L. (1981). *Communication networks: Toward a new paradigm for research.* New York: Free Press.

Romo, F. P., & Anheier, H. K. (1996). Success and failure in institutional development—A network approach. *American Behavioral Scientist, 39*, 1057-1079.

Sabidussi, G. (1966). The centrality index of a graph. *Psychometrika, 31*, 581-603.

Salancik, G. R. (1995). Wanted: A good network theory of organization. *Administrative Science Quarterly, 40*, 345-349.

Salancik, G. R., & Pfeffer, J. (1978). A social information processing approach to job attitudes and task design. *Administrative Science Quarterly, 23*, 224-253.

Samuelson, P. (1954). The pure theory of public expenditure. *Review of Economics and Statistics, 36*, 387-389.

Schachter, S. (1959). *The psychology of affiliation.* Stanford, CA: Stanford University Press.

Schachter, S., & Burdick, H. (1955). A field experiment on rumor transmission and distortion. *Journal of Abnormal and Social Psychology, 50*, 363-371.

Schermerhorn, J. R. (1977). Information sharing as an interorganizational activity. *Academy of Management Journal, 20,* 148-153.

Schmitz, J., & Fulk, J. (1991). Organizational colleagues, information richness, and electronic mail: A test of the social influence model of technology use. *Communication Research, 18,* 487-523.

Scott, J. (1988). Trend report: Social network analysis. *Sociology, 22,* 109-127.

Scott, J. (1992). *Social network analysis.* Newbury Park, CA: Sage.

Seabright, M. A., Levinthal, D. A., & Fichman, M. (1992). Role of individual attachments in the dissolution of interorganizational relationships. *Academy of Management Journal, 35,* 122-160.

Seeman, T. E., Bruce, M. L., McAvay, G. J. (1996). Social network characteristics and onset of ADL disability: MacArthur studies of successful aging. *Journal of Gerontology, 51B,* S191-S200.

Shaw, M. (1964). Communication networks. In L. Berkowitz (Ed.), *Advances in experimental psychology* (Vol. 1, pp. 111-147). New York: Academic Press.

Sherif, M. (1958). Superordinate goals in the reduction of intergroup conflicts. *American Journal of Sociology, 63,* 349-356.

Sherman, J. D., Smith, H., & Mansfield, E. R. (1986). The impact of emergent network structure on organizational socialization. *Journal of Applied Behavioral Science, 22,* 53-63.

Shrader, C. B., Lincoln, J. R., & Hoffman, A. N. (1989). The network structures of organizations: Effects of task contingencies and distributional form. *Human Relations, 42,* 43-66.

Simmel, G. (1955). *Conflict and the web of group affiliations.* Glencoe, IL: Free Press.

Singh, H., & Harianto, F. (1989). Management-board relationships, takeover risk, and the adoption of golden parachutes. *Academy of Management Journal, 32,* 7-24.

Skvoretz, J., & Fararo, T. J. (1996). Status and participation in task groups: A dynamic network model. *American Journal of Sociology, 101,* 1366-1414.

Skvoretz, J., & Faust, K. (1996). Social structure, networks, and E-state structuralism models. *Journal of Mathematical Sociology, 21,* 57-76.

Skvoretz, J., & Willer, D. (1993). Exclusion and power: A test of four theories of power in exchange networks. *American Sociological Review, 58,* 801-818.

Smith, K. G., Carroll, S. J., & Ashford, S. J. (1995). Intra- and interorganizational cooperation: Toward a research agenda. *Academy of Management Journal, 38,* 7-23.

Spencer, H. (1982). *Principles of sociology* (Vol. 2, Pt. 2). New York: Appleton-Century-Crofts.

Spinardi, G., Graham, I., & Williams, R. (1996). EDI and business network redesign: Why the two don't go together. *New Technology, Work and Employment, 11,* 16-27.

Staw, B., & Ross, J. (1985). Stability in the midst of change. *Journal of Applied Psychology, 70,* 469-480.

Stevenson, W. B. (1990). Formal structure and networks of interaction within organizations. *Social Science Research, 19,* 113-131.

Stearns, L. B., & Mizruchi, M. S. (1993). Board composition and corporate financing: The impact of financial institution representation on borrowing. *Academy of Management Journal, 36,* 603-618.

Steinfield, C. W., & Fulk, J. (1990). The theory imperative. In J. Fulk & C. Steinfield (Eds.), *Organizations and communication technology* (pp. 13-25). Newbury Park, CA: Sage.

Stevenson, W. B., & Gilly, M. C. (1991). Information processing and problem solving: The migration of problems through formal positions and networks of ties. *Academy of Management Journal, 34,* 918-928.

Stohl, C. (1993). European managers' interpretations of participation: A semantic network analysis. *Human Communication Research, 20,* 97-117.

Stohl, C. (1995). *Organizational communication: Connectedness in action.* Thousand Oaks, CA: Sage.

Stokman, F. N., & Doreian, P. (1996). Concluding remarks. *Journal of Mathematical Sociology, 21,* 197-199.

Stokman, F. N., & Zeggelink, E. P. H. (1996). Is politics power or policy oriented? A comparative analysis of dynamic access models in policy networks. *Journal of Mathematical Sociology, 21,* 77-111.

Tichy, N. M., & Fombrun, C. (1979). Network analysis in organizational settings. *Human Relations, 32,* 923-965.

Topper, C. M., & Carley, K. M. (1997, January). *A structural perspective on the emergence of network organizations.* Paper presented at the International Sunbelt Social Networks Conference, San Diego, CA.

Tosi, H. L. (1992). *The environment/organization/person contingency model: A meso approach to the study of organizations.* Greenwich, CT: JAI.

Trevino, L., Lengel, R., & Daft, R. (1987). Media symbolism, media richness and media choice in organizations: A symbolic interactionist perspective. *Communication Research, 14,* 553-575.

Tsui, A. S., Egan, T. D., & O'Reilly, C. A. (1992). Being different: Relational demography and organizational attachment. *Administrative Science Quarterly, 37,* 549-579.

Tsui, A. E., & O'Reilly, C. A., III. (1989). Beyond simple demographic effects: The importance of relational demography in superior-subordinate dyads. *Academy of Management Journal, 32,* 402-423.

Turk, H. (1977). Interorganizational networks in urban society: Initial perspectives and comparative research. *American Sociological Review, 35,* 1-20.

Turner, J. C. (1987). *Rediscovering the social group: A self-categorization theory.* Oxford, UK: Basil Blackwell.

Turner, J. C., & Oakes, P. J. (1986). The significance of the social identity concept for social psychology with reference to individualism, interactionism, and social influence. *British Journal of Social Psychology, 25,* 237-252.

Turner, J. C., & Oakes, P. J. (1989). Self-categorization theory and social influence. In P. B. Paulus (Ed.), *Psychology of group influence* (pp. 233-275). Hillsdale, NJ: Lawrence Erlbaum.

Useem, M. (1980). Corporations and the corporate elite. *Annual Review of Sociology, 6,* 41-77.

Useem, M. (1984). *The inner circle: Large corporations and business politics in the U.S. and UK.* New York: Oxford University Press.

Uzzi, B. (1996). The sources and consequences of embeddedness for the economic performance of organizations: The network effect. *American Sociological Review, 61,* 674-698.

Uzzi, B. (1997). Social structure and competition in interfirm networks: The paradox of embeddedness. *Administrative Science Quarterly, 42,* 35-67.

Valente, T. W. (1995). *Network models of the diffusion of innovations.* Cresskill, NJ: Hampton.

Valente, T. W. (1996). Social network thresholds in the diffusion of innovations. *Social Networks, 18,* 69-89.

Van den Bulte, C., & Moenaert, R. K. (1997). *The effects of R&D team co-location on communication patterns among R&D marketing, and manufacturing.* ISBM Report 7-1997. University Park: Pennsylvania State University, Institute for the Study of Business Markets.

Vega, W. A., Kolody, B., Valle, R., & Weir, J. (1991). Social networks, social support and their relationship to depression among immigrant Mexican women. *Human Organization, 50,* 154-162.

Wade, J., O'Reilly, C. A., III, & Chandratat, I. (1990). Golden parachutes: CEOs and the exercise of social influence. *Administrative Science Quarterly, 35,* 587-603.

Wagner, W. G., Pfeffer, J., & O'Reilly, C. A. (1984). Organizational demography and turnover in top management groups. *Administrative Science Quarterly, 29,* 74-92.

Walker, G. (1985). Network position and cognition in computer software firm. *Administrative Science Quarterly, 30,* 103-130.

Walker, G., Kogut, B., & Shan, W. (1997). Social capital, structural holes and the formation of an industry network. *Organization Science, 8,* 109-125.

Walker, M. E., Wasserman, S., & Wellman, B. (1994). Statistical models for social support networks. In S. Wasserman & J. Galaskiewicz (Eds.), *Advances in social network analysis: Research in the social and behavioral sciences* (pp. 53-78). Thousand Oaks, CA: Sage.

Wallace, M., Griffin, L. J., & Rubin, B. A. (1989). The positional power of American labor, 1963-1977. *American Sociological Review, 54,* 197-214.

Warren, R. (1967). The interorganizational field as a focus for investigation. *Administrative Science Quarterly, 12,* 396-419.

Wasserman, S., & Faust, K. (1994). *Social network analysis: Methods and applications.* New York: Cambridge University Press.

Wasserman, S., & Pattison, P. (1996). Logit models and logistic regressions for social networks: I. An introduction to Markov graphs and p*. *Psychometrika, 61,* 401-425.

Watzlawick, P., Beavin, J., & Jackson, D. (1967). *Pragmatics of human communication.* New York: Norton.

Weber, M. (1947). *The theory of social and economic organization* (A. H. Henderson & T. Parsons, Eds. & Trans.). Glencoe, IL: Free Press.

Weick, K. E. (1979). *The social psychology of organizing* (2nd ed.). Reading, MA: Addison-Wesley.

Wellman, B. (1988). Structural analysis: From method and metaphor to theory and substance. In B. Wellman & S. D. Berkowitz (Eds.), *Social structures: A network approach* (pp. 19-61). Cambridge, UK: Cambridge University Press.

Wellman, B. (1992). Which types of ties and networks provide what kinds of social support? In E. J. Lawler (Ed.), *Advances in group processes* (Vol. 9, pp. 207-235). Greenwich, CT: JAI.

Wellman, B., Salaff, J., Dimitrova, D., Garton, L., Gulia, M., & Haythornthwaite, C. (1996). Computer networks as social networks: Collaborative work, telework, and virtual community. *Annual Review of Sociology, 22,* 213-238.

Wellman, B., & Wortley, S. (1989). Brothers' keepers: Situating kinship relations in broader networks of social support. *Sociological Perspectives, 32,* 273-306.

Wellman, B., & Wortley, S. (1990). Different strokes from different folks: Community ties and social support. *American Journal of Sociology, 96,* 558-588.

Westphal, J. D., Gulati, R., & Shortell, S. M. (1997). Customization or conformity? An institutional and network perspective on the content and consequences of TQM adoption. *Administrative Science Quarterly, 42,* 366-394.

White, D. R., & Reitz, K. P. (1989). Rethinking the role concept: Homomorphisms on social networks. In L. C. Freeman, D. R. White, & A. K. Romney (Eds.), *Research methods in social network analysis* (pp. 429-488). Fairfax, VA: George Mason University Press.

White, H. C., Boorman, S. A., & Breiger, R. L. (1976). Social structure from multiple networks: I. Block-models of roles and positions. *American Journal of Sociology, 81,* 730-780.

Wigand, R. T. (1988). Communication network analysis: History and overview. In G. Goldhaber & G. Barnett

(Eds.), *Handbook of organizational communication* (pp. 319-359). Norwood, NJ: Ablex.

Willer, D., & Skvoretz, J. (1997). Network connection and exchange ratios: Theory, predictions, and experimental tests. In E. J. Lawler (Ed.), *Advances in group processes* (Vol. 14, pp. 199-234). Greenwich, CT: JAI.

Williamson, O. E. (1975). *Markets and hierarchies: Analysis and antitrust implications, a study of the economics of internal organization.* New York: Free Press.

Williamson, O. E. (1985). *The economic institutions of capitalism: Firms, markets, relational contracting.* New York: Free Press.

Williamson, O. E. (1991). Comparative economic organization: The analysis of discrete structural alternatives. *Administrative Science Quarterly, 36,* 269-296.

Woelfel, J. (1993). Artificial neural networks in policy research: A current assessment. *Journal of Communication, 43,* 62-80.

Woelfel, J., & Fink, E. L. (1980). *The Galileo system: A theory of social measurement and its application.* New York: Academic Press.

Yamagishi, T., Gillmore, M. R., & Cook, K. S. (1988). Network connections and the distribution of power in exchange networks. *American Journal of Sociology, 93,* 833-851.

Zack, M. H., & McKenney, J. L. (1995). Social context and interaction in ongoing computer-supported management groups. *Organization Science, 6,* 394-422.

Zahn, G. L. (1991). Face-to-face communication in an office setting: The effects of position, proximity, and exposure. *Communication Research, 18,* 737-754.

Zajac, E. J., & Olsen, C. P. (1993). From transaction cost to transactional value analysis: Implications for the study of interorganizational strategies. *Journal of Management Studies, 30,* 131-145.

Zeggelink, E. P. H., Stokman, F. N., & Van de Bunt, G. G. (1996). The emergence of groups in the evolution of friendship networks. *Journal of Mathematical Sociology, 21,* 29-55.

Zenger, T. R., & Lawrence, B. S. (1989). Organizational demography: The differential effects of age and tenure distributions on technical communication. *Academy of Management Journal, 32,* 353-376.

Zey-Ferrell, M., & Ferrell, O. C. (1982). Role set configuration and opportunity as predictors of unethical behavior in organizations. *Human Relations, 35,* 587-604.

Zinger, J. T., Blanco, H., Zanibbi, L., & Mount, J. (1996). An empirical study of the small business support network—The entrepreneur's perspective. *Canadian Journal of Administrative Sciences, 13,* 347-357.

13

Organizational Structures and Configurations

ROBERT D. McPHEE
Arizona State University

MARSHALL SCOTT POOLE
Texas A&M University

Most theory and research in organizational communication must navigate between Scylla and Charybdis. The Scylla is the temptation to construe the adjective *organizational* too broadly, to argue that any system or process of interaction has some sort of organization, so that all communication becomes organizational communication and we are carried off to study pick-up ball games rather than the major leagues, parties rather than political parties. In avoiding this Scylla, we risk sailing into danger from the Charybdis of the "container metaphor" (Axley, 1984; Smith, 1993), assuming that *organizational communication* is encapsulated within the confines of an ontologically prior entity, the organization. Communication so situated is of course influenced if not determined by its preestablished, well-known wrapper.

The channel of safety is difficult to perceive. At one level, we must pay systematic attention to the "embeddedness" of organizational communication processes. Their relation to an unusually explicit and important large-scale structure marks processes of interaction in the conduct of work operations, supervision and leadership, decision making, and large-scale coordination and control. Typically, most members of an organization know what their jobs are, how they are related to other jobs, who the boss is, who has what organizational powers. Their communication, in broad content and in fine-detailed organization, depends on knowledge of these facts.

Studying that dependence is one major task of organizational communication. But as we study the relation of communication to its structured context, we must remember that *organizational structure* is not a physical object or ontological constant. It is a social "reality" partly constituted—and sometimes transformed—in real-time interaction. But only partly. Organizational structure endures and alters the course of events because it is "inscribed" in the memory stocks and the material setting of the organization, and because it is responsive to and legitimized by institutionalized expectations in society at large. As organizational communication scholars, we must be concerned to fashion our theories so that they respond adequately both to our common knowledge of organizations in our cultural life and to the theoretical demands of "organization" as a problematic concept. Life today is shaped by complex organizational forces and products. What is it about organizational structure that gives it influence over organizational communication processes? How does that influence work and with what results? And how does communication in turn enact and shape organizational structures?

In this essay, we will survey some answers offered by recent research to these and related questions. This chapter is the successor to Jablin's chapter "Formal Organization Structure," in the 1987 *Handbook of Organizational Communication.* A relatively small amount of space will be devoted to reviewing new literature along the lines Jablin surveyed, because there have not been many significant new findings in these areas and most findings reinforce his earlier conclusions. Most significant advances since Jablin's (1987) review have focused on different questions and explanatory modes. The study of organizational structures has been decisively influenced by arguments for nontraditional analyses of organizational configuration, by perspectives such as structuration theory and postmodernism, and by issues such as the controversy about the relation between macro- and microlevel theories and the relevance of typological constructs.

This chapter will build from the old to the new, as follows: In the first section, we review literature, which takes the traditional approach of decomposing structure into a set of dimensions or variables. In this perspective, communication structure and processes are cast up as variables that are related to other (noncommunicational) structural variables. Inquiry guided by this approach results in lists of propositions and findings. Those aligned with this stream of research would view these findings as a treasure trove of specifics about the variables that determine communication patterns and effectiveness, integrated by the theoretic tradition that stems from Weber's. To skeptics, they represent a pile of atomistic and fragmented ideas in need of organization. In general, the studies reviewed in this section assume, more or less consistently, the "container" metaphor, treating structure as prior to and different in kind from communication process (Axley, 1984).

The second section reviews a stream of research designed to unify these clusters of atomistic findings by offering configurational views of structure. The configurational approach defines organizational types that are composed of specific combinations of structural features. These types are wholes, and communication structures and processes are an integral part of each configuration. As a result, the configurational approach clarifies the relationship of communication to the other structural features and accords communication a more important place in organizational structure than does the traditional approach. Indeed, some types may be distinguished primarily on the basis of the communication that occurs within them. Configurational approaches also typically are concerned with how organizations evolve over time and in response to changes in their environments, and with how they develop from one type into another. The configurational perspective offers, from one perspective, an integrated, often communication-centered account and explanation of organizations' structural features, processes, overall character, and evolution. A more skeptical audience would challenge the mix of metaphors used to achieve this integration, noting the frequency of references to reified structure.

The third section of this review concentrates on approaches, which attempt to redefine organizational structure and its constitution in communicative terms or to replace reified-structure terms with communicative ones. We review theories and research that either (a) construe traditional structural dimensions in less reified communicative terms, (b) examine how information technology functionally displaces traditional structural options, (c) relate microlevel analyses to macrolevel structural categories, or (d) reanalyze in communication terms the traditional concept of structure itself. From one perspective, these approaches have the advantage of putting communication in the forefront and of emphasizing communication as the foundation of organizational structure. Traditionalists might argue, however, that they overemphasize process and interaction, treating organizations as fleeting and insubstantial and denying the very real material and institutionally sedimented specificity of organizations—a problem which many of these approaches themselves recognize and try to cope with.

We mean to convey a sense of progression from the first to the third approach to organizational structure. However, it is important to note that no historical progression is implied. Research on all three approaches continues to the present, and findings from one stream of research can be applied in the others.

TRADITIONAL DIMENSIONS OF STRUCTURE

The idea of organizational structure has traditionally been elaborated using concepts articulated by early formal theorists of administration: the overall organizational pattern, including the differentiation of work into distinct assignments or specialties and functional subunits and the hierarchical embedding of managers and subunits; formalization; and centralization. These characteristics are usually interpreted as properties of the whole organizational system, though they may also be applied to distinct subunits. Jablin (1987) has reviewed the empirical literature exploring the relations of these properties to organizational communication processes in the first edition of this handbook, and we will supplement his chapter with a discussion of research since his review.

The majority of research on organizational structure follows a pattern traced in the work of Weber and Taylor, and crystallized by Burns and Stalker. It presents structural properties such as differentiation, centralization, and formalization as elements of a bureaucratic or mechanistic style of organizing, opposed to a contrary, organismic style (Burns & Stalker, 1961). In the welter of theoretical argument and research findings, the major theme is that mechanistic elements involve more control over worker behavior and less flexibility than do organic structures. These consequences result partly from restricting and channeling internal organizational communication. Indeed, formal structures serve as a substitute for communication in organizations by providing the coordination that is otherwise achieved through communicating (McPhee, 1985; Perrow, 1986).

Organizational Pattern

This section will review literature concerning a variety of properties, which Jablin (1987) previously reviewed under the headings of "Configuration" and "Complexity." However, we use the term *configuration* in a different way in the next main section, so we will use the term *pattern* in this section. The properties discussed in this section describe the material "shape" of the organization's mandated relations of people and practices. The various constructs have common roots in scientific management theories, but are independent enough to stimulate their own autonomous research traditions.

Horizontal differentiation. This facet of organization, often called "division of labor," not only describes the organization, it also creates the problem for which organizational structure is the answer. Increasing differentiation means that work is divided up into ever-smaller sets of operations/skills and that each set of skills—job or occupation, of individual or work group—is more clearly and rigidly distinguished from others. The push toward greater differentiation was justified by advocates of scientific management as rational and necessary to the growth of knowledge about and control over work. More recently, the communication, cooperation, and conflict resolution problems created by rigid differentiation have been emphasized, and the "segmental" ideal has lost favor (Kanter, 1983; Mintzberg, 1989). The emphasis on "integration" (Lawrence & Lorsch, 1967) has been supplanted by an emphasis on overall and shared responsibility, especially in the popular literature (Peters & Waterman, 1982). In contrast, the argument by Karl Weick for loose coupling (the property of having fairly autonomous parts) and requisite variety (the requirement of having parts varied enough to respond appropriately to different parts of the environment) (1979; cf. Orton & Weick, 1990) seems to indicate that differentiation may have positive effects and be necessary for organizational adaptability.

Some studies on differentiation and organizational communication have supported the view that differentiation produces problems. Smith, Grimm, Gannon, and Chen (1991) found that complexity (which they viewed as an information-processing variable) deterred responses to external strategic initiatives among interdependent units. Shrader, Lincoln, and Hoffman (1989) found that differentiation led to more clustering and less density and reciprocity in interorganizational networks, resulting in greater fragmentation into isolated cliques. Souder and Moenaert (1992) argued that interfunctional convergence (which indicates lower differentiation) aids in uncertainty reduction and information

transfer during innovation. A common idea across these studies is that differentiation blocks proactive, innovative cooperation among distinct units.

Contrariwise, several authors found evidence for a less negative view of differentiation. Miller, Droje, and Toulouse (1988) found that differentiation of special control and liaison units increased the rationality of and interaction about strategy decisions. Alter (1990) found that functional differentiation among organizations in a network reduced conflict. Finally, Colling and Fermer (1992) uncovered several dramatically different models of decision making as differentiation among parties increased; these were not necessarily inferior to more integrative, rational models of decision making, and may be better adapted to the contingencies of highly differentiated organizations. The common benefit of differentiation in these studies seems to be coordinated action rooted in complementarity, the classic advantage touted for differentiation. The problem of optimizing the trade-off of differentiated diversity and unity seems to remain as pressing for organizations as for society.

Size. The presumption among theorists is that greater organizational size leads to more mechanistic organization, as the coordination burden overwhelms informal organizing processes. In his original review, Jablin (1987) focused on the question of whether size negatively affected organizational communication amount and quality. Succeeding research has also yielded mixed results, but has focused on breadth of participation and nature of decision making. On the one hand, increasing size has been found to result in greater and broader decision participation (Connor, 1992) and more comprehensiveness in decision making—more breadth in number of alternatives scanned, as well as more employees involved in the decision (Smith et al., 1991). On the other hand, Smeltzer and Fann (1989) found size leading to some restrictions on decision-making breadth. They found managers from large companies to be quite similar to ones from small companies in concern about communication. However, in comparison with small companies, large-company managers were more oriented to internal communication with subordinates and within the formal hierarchy, more concerned with such functions as monitoring and exchanging routine information, and less concerned with external communication and organizational politics. These studies point to mixed benefits of communication in larger organizations.

Vertical hierarchy. Jablin's (1987) review summarized two types of studies related to hierarchy: Some focused on the impacts of individual hierarchical level (e.g., superior-subordinate communication) while others concentrated on vertical complexity as a property of the organizational system as a whole. Since his review, nearly all the relevant literature falls in the first type.

Several studies have shown variations in communication behavior by hierarchical level. Level was positively related to time spent communicating (but not to reported autonomy) in research reported by Yammarino and Naughton (1988). MacLeod, Scriven, and Wayne (1992) similarly found that hierarchical level raised the frequency of oral communication episodes. Their research also revealed complex effects of level on the location where interaction occurred, the medium involved, and for external contacts, the functional category of the contact. They also found that level sometimes interacted with group size, with middle-level females involved especially often in small-group meetings and in formally scheduled meetings (perhaps to function as token members). In research with a result partially contrary to this pattern of level-interaction relationships, Zenger and Lawrence (1989) found that level was positively related to amount of technical communication outside, but not inside, an electronics firm. Rice and associates reported mixed results concerning the influence of level on

adoption (but not use) of computer-mediated communication, with Rice, Chang, and Torobin (1992) supporting a relationship, but not Rice and Shook (1990).

Level also influences problem-solving communication, with higher levels tending toward more ad hoc and innovative solution processes. Barnard (1991) found that higher-level employees exhibited greater reliance on peers for advice than did those at lower levels. Stevenson and Gilly (1991) also report that when managers (as opposed to nonmanagers) refer problem cases to other parts of an organizational network, they pass the problem case less often to the person formally assigned to deal with it, and more often to an acquaintance of theirs, perhaps because they see the problem as nonroutine and needing special attention.

Several studies were concerned with the effects of level on communicative influence. Brass and Burkhardt (1993) found that the higher the level, the greater the use of influence styles of assertiveness and exchange-offering, but not of ingratiation or rationality. In a study that limited communication to one-way choice proposals, Driskell and Salas (1991) found that status and stress level related to response to influence, with higher status leading to reduced openness to influence while higher stress increased influence acceptance. Ragins and Cotton (1991) found that higher level led to more influence in the special case of gaining a mentor. So as we would expect, level in the formal hierarchy does covary with various sorts of communicative influence.

Some research also suggests that differences in perspective about communication exist across hierarchical levels. For instance, Clampitt and Downs (1993) found that the perception that corporate information has an impact on productivity was widespread among managers, and especially executives, but not regular employees (but all levels agreed that feedback from one's boss affected productivity). In a study by Thomas, Shankster, and Mathieu (1994), rank affected the likelihood that one will view a problem as political, with higher ranks seeing things as less political. Finally, McCauley, Ruderman, Ohlcott, and Morrow (1994) found a relationship of rank to the challenges newcomers see in their jobs (including weak increases for such communication-related challenges as influencing without authority and proving oneself, and a moderate effect for developing new directions).

Overall, this research is compatible with a view of the upper strata of organizations as relatively organic. Insofar as high-level managers use face-to-face communication to solve nonroutine problems and make (verbally expressed) policies, their communication behaviors would exhibit the differences suggested by these studies.

Formalization

Formalization is typically defined as the extent to which rules and procedures mandated for work are explicitly stated, usually in writing and/or a ceremonial announcement. The construct obviously is linked to Weber's (1946) characterization of bureaucracy as involving processes including communication that proceed "according to calculable rules" (p. 215) One theoretical presumption is that inflexible rules can lead to ineffectiveness. Olson (1995) illustrates this effect in a study of a public clinic where record-keeping rules forced structured interviews that were very effective for collecting information, but too inflexible to optimally serve clients. Another theoretical presumption is that appropriate rules, systematically followed, can enhance the systematic rationality of decisions. This claim received some recent research support, as Miller (1987) and Miller et al. (1988) found that the perceived rationality of strategic decision making was associated with formal controls over the decision process. Miller (1987) advanced the construct of "formal integration," referring to specific provision for information-gathering specialists and liaisons, as a structural dimension with direct communicative implications that increased perceived rationality of decision making.

Souder and Moenaert (1992) argued that formalization is valuable in innovation if preceded by effective uncertainty-reducing procedures in planning. Gilsdorf (1992) showed a beneficial side of formalization in discussing evidence for the need for written corporate policies governing communication of sensitive information, crisis communication, and communication of corporate values, among other things.

As a defining property of bureaucracy, formalization is also theoretically opposed to organicity (ongoing dynamic adaptiveness through mutual adjustment). This negative relationship was supported by the research of Shrader et al. (1989), who found that formalization led to reduced interorganizational network organicity, especially for a network of social service client referrals. In contrast, Hoffman, Stearns, and Shrader (1990) found formalization leading to higher network centrality.

Finally, the use of formalization as a means for rational control is widely discussed in the literature. Its general development as a control instrumentality was clearly presented by Beniger (1986), who argued that formalization along with other means of control were invented to allow the growing complexity and the growing geographic spread of corporate operations. In another intensive historical survey, Yates (1989) concentrated on the development of early-19th-century communication technologies, media, and forms conducive to such a mode of control. Her detailed analyses displayed the concern for corporation-wide coordination and control that led corporate executives to fight for widespread use of general orders, procedure manuals, and performance graphs as formal communication vehicles. These justly praised books were major contributions to our understanding of evolving corporate communication modes.

Centralization

The interesting question about the centralization/decentralization dimension is not what communication variables it influences, but what it is itself and what its broader implications are for communication. What exactly is centralization? Mintzberg (1979) argues that complete centralization, which grants all decisions to the top decision maker, can be defined unambiguously. However, in cases where power is ceded to lower levels, many different types of decentralization are possible. Mintzberg distinguishes several different types of decentralization, including (1) vertical decentralization, dispersal of formal power down the chain of authority; (2) horizontal decentralization, dispersal of power to nonmanagers who are near the same level as the managers; and (3) geographical dispersion of the organization. Moreover, decentralization may be done selectively, to some parts of the organization rather than others, and some types of decisions can be centralized while others are decentralized.

Mintzberg defined five generic parts of the organization in which power may be vested: strategic apex, middle management, operating core, support staff, and technostructure. Which part or parts become more powerful and significant determines the nature of organizational structures with very different organizational consequences. Mintzberg's predictions regarding the outcomes of decentralization are not as straightforward as the studies summarized below imply. For example, the configuration that involves most power for the "ordinary worker," the *professional bureaucracy,* also leads to high worker autonomy and a consequent lack of cohesion, leading in turn to destructive mobilization of interest groups during political conflicts.

As for centralization's effects, recent research supports the pattern found by Jablin (1987): Decentralization is accompanied by increased communication on many dimensions. The first dimension is raw amount of communication; for instance, Miller (1987) found decentralization of strategic decision making to lead to more interaction (along with a greater tendency toward risk taking, and somewhat more future orientation, though not to greater rationality of decisions). Supporting

this relationship, Yammarino and Naughton (1988) reported that increased autonomy was accompanied by reports of more time spent communicating. In addition, according to Pearson (1992), decentralization through autonomous work groups led to growing feedback.

This finding touches on a second group of dimensions—communication effectiveness—that are enhanced by reduced centralization. For instance, Macey, Peterson, and Norton (1989) revealed that a participation program led to increased influence by members, group cohesiveness, organizational involvement, and clarity of decision making. Managerial consideration and role clarification covaried weakly with a second-order factor involving decentralized decision making and autonomy, in a study by Evans and Fischer (1992). Finally, Trombetta and Rogers (1988) found that participation led to communicative openness and adequacy (though not commitment).

Openness was explored in a series of publications by Krone (1992, 1994, cf. 1986), focused on the use of open versus manipulative upward persuasive strategies. Following the suggestion of Hage and Aiken (1967), Krone used two measures of (de)centralization, autonomous control over own work and participation in broader decisions. Participation led to choice of more open communication and empathic influence strategies, with the latter involving appeal to commonalities and values important to the manager. Both participation and autonomy predicted the likelihood of attempting upward influence, the perceived likelihood of success, and the level of upward trust. Higher values of both measures of centralization also led to higher perceived quality of leader-member exchange (LMX). Krone's use of two conceptually and empirically distinct indicators of centralization illustrates the problem of polysemy facing the concept.

To sum up, the literature on centralization suffers from two important problems. First, (de)centralization is used in many different ways, which apply to quite different organizational communication processes. Horizontal decentralization requires communication across professional boundaries, which presents one set of problems and requires specific types of communication devices, such as integrating managers and task forces. Vertical decentralization confronts the organization with the need to maintain communication through multiple layers, with the problems of distortion and control loss through vertical communication (e.g., Conrad & Poole, 1998), which require a different set of measures such as managerial communication programs and decision support systems. Second, different studies, which ostensibly focus on the same variable, (de)centralization, may apply to quite different organizational levels or subsystems and yield quite different effects. What seems to be a single variable is really a family of quite diverse concepts. When we take this into account, apparent inconsistencies in findings may evaporate, and apparent consistencies may prove puzzling.

In general, participation and decentralization as systemic organizational properties should be distinguished from the way organizational members perceive these properties. Measures such as perceived autonomy and decision participation do not tell us much about overall organizational structure, but rather tell us about immediate experiences of members. These experiences probably depend more on immediate supervisory and coworker behavior than anything else and have little reference to structural features in distant parts of the organization. Even high values of perceived participation may be invalid structural indicators, if the mass of workers is unaware of important decisions or if organizational structures and processes leave workers uninterested in issues that otherwise would draw their concern (Kanter, 1977).

Concluding Comments

One problem with breaking structure down into numerous dimensions is that possible structures increase exponentially with each new dimension considered. This proliferation makes predictions about communication problematic. Moreover, it runs counter to experience and research, which implies that there are a relatively small number of types of organizations, or at least not an infinitude of different varieties. To capture covariations among dimensions and to distill the unique character of organizations, researchers have attempted to define organizational types, reflected in structural configurations. As we will see, configurations are important because communication can be understood within an organized frame rather than within the relationship-by-relationship array resulting from the dimensional approach.

ORGANIZATIONAL CONFIGURATIONS

The configurational view of structure can be traced back to Weber's concept of bureaucracy, and perhaps even to Aristotle's analysis of types of government. A number of authors have recently revived configurational thinking with vigorous and intriguing arguments (McKelvey, 1982; Miller, 1990; Mintzberg, 1979, 1989). Some authors argue for systems of configurations, and such theories shall be our primary concern. Other scholars have advanced very interesting cases for new configurations, with such names as the "learning organization," the "postbureaucratic organization," or "excellent organizations." One advantage of the configurational approach for organizational communication research is that it offers a more holistic conception of structure that can highlight communicative implications better than reductionist arguments that dissolve the organization into a number of dimensions, most of which have limited relevance to communication per se. Communication is part and parcel of many configuration concepts and permeates the organization when it is considered as a whole. In this section, we review the nature of the configurational approach along with some key examples.

There is some disagreement about the nature of configurational constructs. Perhaps the most common view is that a configuration is a specific set of values on multiple dimensions that has special descriptive or other utility (Lammers, 1988; McKelvey, 1982; Stinchcombe, 1968). This nominalist view contrasts with two others: (1) the view of organizational types as generated and rendered consistent by an underlying (metaphorically genetic) determining characteristic or causal process, and (2) the view of organizational types as comprised by similarities in causes or effects. So one might call a cluster of organizations "adhocratic" because they happen to share certain features, or because they have features determined by the same underlying causes, or because they are similar in origin and the kind of "niche" they occupy in the organizational ecosystem.

A second difference in the literature concerns the treatment of types as "real" versus "ideal." On the one hand, types can be viewed as empirical existents, defined by a combination of values on empirically measurable dimensions. On the other hand, they can be viewed as ideal types, never realized in practice but representing idealizations that are useful for theoretical and prescriptive purposes. Finally, there is disagreement in the literature over the question of generality: Is a configuration always a description of units of only one sort (organizations, say, or work groups), or can the same typal description apply in numerous ways—to different levels of analysis, to parts of organizations rather than the whole, or as styles/features—clusters that can overlay or apply in combination to a single organization?

A resolution of the first issue has the potential to resolve the others: If a type or configuration has an underlying source or logic, that source or logic will determine whether the type should be treated as real or ideal, and whether it applies at multiple levels and in hybrids. The connection among these three aspects—the logic, the array of traits, and the range/realism of application—is reflected in the requirements for configurational theory.

Construction of Configurational Theories

Scholars often distinguish between typologies and taxonomies; the former begin with theoretical analysis to generate ideal configuration-descriptions, while the latter seek empirical clusters to infer types. Both approaches are used to construct configurational theories, with Mintzberg (1979) exemplifying the typological approach and McKelvey (1982) the taxonomical. Hence, there is no optimal sequence of steps for constructing typological theories; scholars can start with data that lead to theory or vice versa. Rather than itemize steps for the construction of configurational theories, we list some necessary tasks, as follows:

1. Identify structural (and other) variables, characteristics, or elements, which can be used to describe the surface structure of the configuration. These traits include communication features such as the properties of channels and networks, structurally sedimented dimensions of communication climate, and so on.

2. Determine the specific combinations of values on variables, characteristics, or elements belonging to each configuration.

3. Determine the situations or contexts in which the various configurations are possible, likely, or appropriate.

4. Determine the consequences of each configuration in the range of contexts in which it might appear. As contingency theorists would argue, such consequences often depend on the information-processing and decision-making constraints and supports involved in the configuration.

5. Discover or work out a logic underlying the configurations and distinguishing them—a dynamic, imperative, or process sufficient to unify various structural elements into coherent ensembles and to account for their differences. As in the first and fourth tasks above, this procedure typically shows how communication assumptions are intrinsic to organizational structural theory—the bind-

ing logic of a configuration is often a logic of information processing, coordination, control, or some other communication process (McPhee, 1985).

6. Determine the ways in which configurations might be combined or partially realized within a particular organization. Clear types may not always be apparent in specific cases.

7. Determine the principles of generation, deviation, and/or transformation of organizations from one configuration, perhaps to another. Again, communicative considerations may lead to such changes.

8. Find evidence of the consistency or mutual affinity of the combination of elements, the presence and operation of the underlying logic, and/or the evolution of one configuration into others.

Configurational approaches are not commonly employed in organizational communication research, in part because organizational communication researchers have focused mostly on dyadic or group communication and avoided considering larger units of analysis. As we will argue, we believe that the development of configurational typologies is a promising direction for understanding the relation of communication and structure. This contention can be illustrated by considering a prominent example of configurational theory.

Mintzberg's Configurational Array

Henry Mintzberg (1979, 1983a, 1983b, 1989) has developed an especially influential and appealing typological theory over the past 20 years. It has special relevance to organizational communication scholarship because of the ubiquity of communication processes and ideas in the theory.

Mintzberg's theory begins with the distinction among five coordination mechanisms —direct supervision, standardization of work processes, of outputs, and of skills, and mutual adjustment—to which standardization of

norms, plus politics (an anticoordination process) were later added. Such mechanisms are important because they fulfill a necessary and formative prerequisite for any organization, making the work of the various employees related and "organized."

Mintzberg also noted that various parts of the organization, empowered by specific coordination mechanisms, exerted pressure on or "pulled" the organization to emphasize those mechanisms. The mechanism plus the power wielded by one part of the organization provided the logic that Mintzberg used to deduce the characteristics of and contingencies that determined his seven fundamental configurations. In 1989, these types were labeled the *entrepreneurial, machine, professional, diversified, innovative, missionary,* and *political* forms. Many of Mintzberg's configurations are similar to those in earlier typologies: The machine form, for instance, is very similar to Burns and Stalker's mechanistic type and Perrow's engineering type (Lammers, 1988). One of the strengths of Mintzberg's theory is its extensive elaboration: He identifies nine structural dimensions (called "design parameters") and five contingency dimensions, which vary across the configurations, and he is able to display striking and insightful relations between ideas explicit or implicit in the literature about these dimensions and the distinctions on which his typology rests. Among the design parameters are several that reflect centralization and formalization. Mintzberg argues that these parameters, like the ones more obviously reflecting communication processes, are best explained either by the requirements of organizational work patterns and coordination (the coordination mechanisms) or by a process of overall adjustment consistent with one of his configurations. In short, his theory gives a deep account of, for example, why decentralization is related to increased vertical communication.

Communication figures prominently in Mintzberg's theory. It is the substance of two of his coordinating mechanisms, mutual adjustment and direct supervision, and it is implicitly required by the others as well. Two of his design parameters are liaison devices (ways to achieve coordination through direct or facilitated communication) and planning/control systems (featuring feedback and plan-implementation interactions); others involve training and indoctrination, decentralization through delegation and multilevel decision making, and other processes in which communication plays an important part. Formalization and other structural dimensions with communication significance (see the preceding and especially the next main sections) are also implicated in a number of design parameters. Even the "pulls" exerted by different parts of the organization surface as logics of organizational argument and decision making (McPhee, 1988)

In his 1989 book, Mintzberg gives explicit and innovative attention to the issue of overlapping configurations, as well as to change among configurations. He mentions a number of different ways configurations can overlap or be combined; he also mentions important issues that arise in these hybrid forms and notes that they are difficult to handle. For instance, "contradiction" is a mode of integration where two mechanisms are both needed in the organization, but they tend to develop a problematic dialectical opposition. He also introduces a "life-cycle model" of organizational transformation that indicates the most likely changes from one configuration to another, as well as forces leading to such changes.

Despite its influence, Mintzberg's theory has been directly tested only once, by Doty, Glick, and Huber (1993). Their test finds little support for the theory; only about 25% of their organizations fit Mintzberg's descriptions well (in his 1989 book, Mintzberg mentions that the student groups he assigns to study organizations find fit in about half the cases). Doty et al. mention several problems with the theoretical validity of their test, especially that it includes only five of Mintzberg's configurations; in addition, we note that they give no special weight to coordinating mechanisms, treat hybrids in ways not strictly compatible with Mintzberg's analysis, and rely

only on CEO perceptions as data. Despite these possible problems with the study, the lack of convincing support for the theory's central empirical claims is frustrating, given its interpretive appeal and ability to reconcile a large amount of prior research.

Advantages of Configurational Theories

Why is the configurational approach important? We can discern at least five reasons. First, configurational theories avoid the problems of ambiguity raised in the above discussion of centralization, since specific structural features are always embedded in a more multidimensional and holistic view of the organizational system. Configurations automatically supply a context for particular constructs.

Second, such theories simplify complex interrelations of multiple variables to a few clearer and more easily exemplified gestalts that are easy to remember and use in analysis. So configurational theories are valuable heuristically—especially compared to the buzzing, booming confusion of reality—even if they are not wholly consistent with empirical situations (Miller & Mintzberg, 1983; Mintzberg, 1979).

Third, communication is an integral part of configurational theories. The traditional dimensional approach defines communication in terms of separate constructs that may or may not be included in a given proposition or theory (e.g., the more levels in a hierarchy, the greater the distortion due to transmission). However, a configurational theory defines organizations as whole types, and communication is a critical aspect of each type, an inherent part of its description. So the organic organization not only implies decentralization but also dense, shifting communication networks and greater amounts of informal communication. Moreover, some types are defined primarily in terms of their communication structures and processes.

Fourth, theorizing about configurations tends to lead to integrative formulations. To develop a configurational theory, researchers must focus on issues such as the systematic interconnectedness of organizational parts or dimensions; the multiple causal directions linking structure, strategy, and environment (Child, 1972); or the multiple consequences of a single organizational determinant such as coordination mechanism (Mintzberg, 1979). Configurational thinking requires researchers to capture and summarize the insights of varied theories and research in a common frame that explains or interprets them in common terms. For example, Mintzberg's (1979) theory uses a highly systematic and insightful reading of a vast array of research literature to support his configurational theory, which offers an integrative explanation of how various configurations evolve into each other. His view is architectonic, in the sense used by Kant (1970)—it organizes the major ideas and issues of organizational theory.

Finally, configurational theories can be tested through the evaluation of three types of hypotheses. The first is a "consistency" hypothesis: that the system characteristics and values for each configuration, including communication characteristics, "belong together." This hypothesis often reduces to the claim that real organizations approximate the types or a space determined by them. For instance, as Doty and Glick (1994) argue, configurational theories may imply a clustering of organizations around specific (ideal-typic) profiles of values. Researchers can test whether the average observed distance from organizations to the closest configuration was significantly less than the average distance for randomly distributed organizations (though this is not a test employed by Doty et al., 1993). As another example, Burns and Stalker's (1961) claim that organizations are arrayed along a continuum between extremely bureaucratic and extremely organismic could be tested as the hypothesis that their structure of variables is unidimensional (cf. Hage, 1965; also Ostroff & Schmitt, 1993). This sort of hypothesis might be of special interest to communication researchers because communication either might exhibit ideal-typic consistency

with other traits (mechanistic communication for a mechanistic organization), or it might function as a supplement compensating for the weaknesses of the type (e.g., Barker, 1993, describes group discipline as compensating for a "loose" democratic structure).

The second type of hypothesis posited by contingency theory revolves around claims about the processes that generate certain configurations. For instance, DiMaggio and Powell (1983) discussed the pressures and advantages that motivate structural change to resemble dominant configurations within specific industries. Probably the most popular variant of configuration-explaining theory is a "fit" hypothesis: the claim that organizations facing specific environmental or other contingencies are likely to resemble a type that is especially called for by those contingencies. For instance, Doty et al. (1993) use an array of contingencies to predict which of Mintzberg's configurations their organizations would resemble, then assessed the correctness of these predictions. Since communication processes would be involved in strategic choice about the environment and the structure (Child, 1972), communication research would be vital to the establishment of such hypotheses.

The third type of hypothesis is the prediction of certain consequences such as effectiveness or survival as results of consistently resembling a configuration. For example, Doty and his colleagues tested relations between similarity to an ideal type and other variables such as effectiveness. Of course, to motivate acceptance of a configurational theory the hypotheses suggested above must accumulate enough support to be encouraging.

Problems With Configurational Theories

Configurational theorizing has a number of strengths, but these assets are complemented by some unique weaknesses. One problem stems from the lack of consensus on just what a configuration or type is. As a result there is no agreement on the necessary components of configurational theories. This issue makes it difficult for researchers to judge when a configurational theory is complete and satisfactory. Second, arriving at a typology may prematurely terminate efforts at explanation. Once researchers have a clear, concrete, well-labeled configuration, there is a temptation to assume that the task of theorizing is finished (Reynolds, 1971). Therefore researchers do not take things further to provide explanation of the origin of the configurational forms and the differences among them, or the whole range of processes producing consistency and fit. Configurational theories can deter the development of process theories, which might more fully reveal the determining or constitutive role of communication.

Third, most configurational theories are what Althusser (1972) called "expressive totalities"—they are supposed to be consistent because each part reflects the underlying logic of the whole. But a good theory would question: Isn't this total consistency too strong—if every quality of an organization was "bureaucratic," might that not result in excessive rigidity that counteracts the useful features of the type? A better configuration might balance off conflicting logics, or list the necessary conditions for success and make sure that the configuration meets them. A fourth problem is that configurations may be culture bound, even if they seem universal; Meyer (1995), for example, mentions how much better the concept of bureaucracy worked in Germany than in America. Finally, there is always the danger that theorists will react to deviations from a type by constantly adding new types. This multiplication may complicate the theory until it is unworkable.

New Organizational Configurations

In recent years, a number of new organizational forms have been identified, which nonetheless seem fundamentally different and important enough to avoid the dangers just mentioned. They have been given diverse names, such as the "dynamic network" (Miles & Snow, 1986), the "shamrock" (Handy, 1989), the "postbureaucratic organization" (Heckscher, 1994), and the "virtual organization" (Davidow & Malone, 1992; Lucas, 1996; Mowshowitz, 1994). They are described as configurations, but they seem irreducible to any of the standard configurations identified by Mintzberg or others. The argument is often made that new forms are motivated by a fundamental change in economics and society and that they are replacing "outmoded," older forms. However, some analyses have suggested that so-called new forms have actually been around for hundreds of years, but have only recently garnered the interest of a wide group of scholars and analysts (Lammers, 1988; Winter & Taylor, 1996). Several of these new forms may well be criticized on the grounds that they needlessly multiply the number of configurations, thus leading to unwieldy and unworkable theories.

These new configurations are particularly interesting because of their dependence on communication. Moreover, as we will note later, the increasing prominence of new (or previously marginalized) forms may signal a changing relationship between communication and organizational structure. We can review only a selection of forms and issues surrounding them here.

Drivers of New Organizational Forms

A common analysis is that new organizational forms have been evolving at an increasingly rapid rate due to several important changes in the organizational environment (see, e.g., Drucker, 1994; Huber, 1984). The trend toward global economic and social integration has engendered increased competition for both private and public organizations. Scholars have observed the emergence of "hypercompetition" in industry sectors such as health care and consumer products (Ilinitch, D'Aveni, & Lewin, 1996). Hypercompetition is characterized by increasingly fierce competition among organizations (even those allied in joint ventures and traditionally stable markets) and organizational strategies that attempt to redefine the "rules" of competition through the development of new products and delivery modes to gain advantage.

A second driver is the evolution of most economically advanced countries into "knowledge societies" (Drucker, 1994). In knowledge societies, the most important work involves the generation and application of abstract knowledge, such as scientific theory or law. Knowledge work organizes and reorganizes other types of work. It evolves as research and scholarship develop improved understanding of the natural and social worlds. And with over 90% of the scientists who have ever lived currently working, the rate of change in knowledge is increasing rapidly (Drucker, 1994).

The third driver is the emergence of information technology, the key enabler of new organizational forms. This communication-centered technology has enjoyed unprecedented growth, driven mostly by the rapid decrease in cost for functionality. Benjamin and Scott-Morton (1988) report that while traditional production technologies showed a 170% improvement in the ratio of capital to labor prices over the 30-year period 1950-1980, information technology had a 2500% improvement in the capital/labor price ratio over the same period. This cost advantage of technology over labor has resulted in rapid implementation of information technologies, resulting in organizational restructuring and displacement of workers.

These forces have created several new imperatives for organizations. First, the most important resource organizations now have is their members' knowledge and skills, and organizations must preserve this knowledge and develop it further. Member competence, more than any physical plant or information system, is the key to being able to adapt to changing circumstances and to take advantage of scientific and technological advances. These features place an imperative on the organization

to structure itself so that it can harness member competencies, develop them further, and keep members with critical competencies committed. Traditional organizational structures, based on division of labor, have paid remarkably little attention to capturing and exploiting the organization's knowledge base. For both new and traditional forms, this imperative is now a critical issue.

Another imperative that guides the new forms is the need to satisfy conflicting demands imposed by the "new order." Organizations must simultaneously respond to the need for flexibility, to find ways to address mounting exigencies and the need for control, to implement effectively the measures devised and to maintain coordinated action. Closely related is the need to institutionalize change and the capacity for evolutionary reorientation, which requires the organization to find a way of balancing stability and change. Organizations must also emphasize speed of product development and time to market, while at the same time maintaining high quality. The need to cope with these and other conflicting demands forces organizations to adopt forms that appear to be unusual hybrids of more traditional structures or that resemble networks and markets more than hierarchies.

Characteristics of New Forms

New forms are constituted by one or more of the following characteristics (Poole, 1999):

1. Use of information technology to integrate across organizational functions, to reengineer production and service processes, and to create tighter interdependence among activities. These characteristics speed up production and response time and enable the organization to adapt to customer needs and environmental demands in highly specific ways.

2. Flexible, modular organizational structures that can be readily reconfigured as new

projects, demands, or problems arise. These structures may be composed of units of a single larger organization, or they may be different organizations joined by brokers or through various types of interorganizational alliances. The accounting and information systems play important roles in the creation and maintenance of flexible structures, substituting for traditional hierarchical control (Child, 1987).

3. Use of information technology to coordinate geographically dispersed units and members. In the extreme case, there may be a virtual organization, whose dispersed members are linked primarily through telecommunications and information technology.

4. Team-based work organization, which emphasizes autonomy and self-management. This system is generally combined with high emphasis on quality and continuous improvement.

5. Relatively flat hierarchies and reliance on horizontal coordination among units and personnel. Power may be much more dispersed in such organizational arrangements.

6. Use of intra- and interorganizational markets to mediate transactions such as the assignment and hiring of personnel for projects and the formation of interorganizational networks. The market mechanism is used as an alternative to hierarchy when many comparable individual units or actors are involved.

These features include the modal qualities found in a range of descriptions of new organizations (Child, 1987; Eccles & Crane, 1987; Hammer & Champy, 1993; Heckscher, 1994; Jarvenppa & Ives, 1994; Konsynski & Sviokla, 1994; Lucas & Baroudi, 1994; Nohria & Berkley, 1994; Powell, 1990; Scott-Morton, 1991), though not every new organization embodies all six. To illustrate how these characteristics fit together, we will

now turn to descriptions of two of the most common new configurations, the network organization and the virtual organization.

Variants of New Forms

The *network organization* refers not to a single formal organization but to a more or less formal relationship among several different organizations (Powell, 1990; for reviews, see Grandori & Soda, 1995). Baker (1992) writes:

> A network organization is characterized by integration across formal boundaries of multiple types of socially important relations. Such "thick" network organizations are integrated over many types of communication and other relationships—strong and weak task-related communication, informal socializing, advice-giving and advice-getting, and so on. (p. 400)

The model for these organizations is drawn from social network theory (Monge & Contractor, Chapter 12, this volume; cf. Johnson, 1993). Several different types of network organizations can be distinguished. In some cases, a group of highly independent organizations takes on differentiated roles within an interdependent network organized by a broker (Miles & Snow, 1986). Miles and Snow referred to these organizations as "dynamic networks" because their component organizations were assembled and disassembled to meet specific needs for a limited period of time. Dynamic networks have long been used in industries such as construction, where contractors assemble various building functions from smaller, specialized firms. Most scholars considered such organizations marginal or unusual until recently, when this form spread through sectors traditionally dominated by integrated organizations. Network organizations may also be more permanently organized around one or more major firms, with the smaller organizations functioning as dependent satellites. One example of a satellite network is the agglomeration of large automobile manufacturers and their supplier networks. Another type of network organization evolves when firms enter into joint ventures or contract relationships (Ring & Van de Ven, 1994). The component organizations in such networks tend to have more equal power and status than those in dynamic networks or satellite networks.

Larson (1992) argues that network organizations are a distinctive configuration: "They are distinct from market or hierarchical arrangements in their heavy reliance on reciprocity, collaboration, complementary interdependence, a reputation and relationship basis for communication, and an informal climate oriented toward mutual gain" (p. 77). She joins a number of authors in pointing to trust and trust building as the fundamental necessity for network relationship growth and maintenance (Handy, 1989).

However, while trust is a foundation of some types of network organizations, it may also be supplemented by full disclosure information systems to sustain integration. A full disclosure information system includes an accounting information system and electronic communication systems (Child, 1987). The accounting information system is a set of open databases that shows participating units whether other units are meeting their responsibilities and contributing value to the organization, while the electronic communication system integrates workflow and coordinates activities.

A *virtual organization* is one that has no physical existence, but instead exists in whole or part across a computer network (Davidow & Malone, 1992; Lucas, 1996). What appears to be an integrated organization is in fact a virtual network comprised by a negotiated agreement among different organizations. Information technology and telecommunications enable these dispersed organizations to coordinate their activities and to maintain coherent work processes. Each part of the virtual organization is able to focus on its particular function. By staying small, the component organi-

zations keep their costs for management and overhead down, enhancing efficiency. Smallness also makes communication easier within the components, opening them up for fast development and testing of new ideas.

Virtual organizations generally evolve gradually, as organizations move one function, such as order handling, to an outside source that manages it using information technology. Hence, many organizations are at least partly "virtual." However, most descriptions of virtual organizations go much further, and depict them as primarily linked by information technology and highly flexible in joining different units into the working whole. As we will see below, taken to its extreme, the virtual organization implies a whole new logic of organizational design.

Mowshowitz (1994, 1997) gives a thoroughgoing definition of the virtual organization as one in which there are (a) multiple possible goals and requirements, (b) multiple structures and processes for achieving these goals and requirements, (c) the capacity to switch between different structures and processes as goals shift, and (d) the capacity to switch between different structures and processes for the same goal, as costs and benefits of the structures and processes shift. This definition of virtual organization implies extreme flexibility, because the switching is assumed to occur relatively rapidly, as it does in memory allocation in computers. The virtual organization takes design one step past traditional contingency theories: It posits that organizational structures not only change in response to different goals and requirements, but that there are multiple structural features that can be switched as the need arises. Of course, communication here is not merely a structural feature, but is basic to the switching process. It is unclear how many actual organizations could achieve this extreme degree of flexibility in practice. Mowshowitz cites global production organizations such as Shell and IBM as examples. Whether it is real or an ideal type, the virtual organization defined by Mowshowitz suggests a new logic of organizational design.

Implications of New Organizational Configurations

While the configurational view in general gives a more complete treatment of the structure-communication relationship than dimensional views, new organizational forms emphasize it still further. One interesting implication is that the organizing principle of the new forms is not the chain of command, but the network. New forms still have authority distributions, but higher authority is not logically associated with the "top" of the organization. In some cases, the broker or hub organization holds primary authority. In others, authority and power are distributed, with different parts of the network predominating at different contexts or times. In such configurations, power is influenced by network dynamics as well. For example, a network with many structural holes would be expected to have more dispersed power than one with few (see Monge & Contractor, this volume).

Second, structure and communication are more obviously related in new and looser configurations than traditional views of organizational structure allow. Sometimes communication requirements are the drivers of organizational structure, as when organizations form integrated engineering-production-marketing teams to handle product design to reduce reworking and redesign. In other cases, communication is driven by structural forces, as the traditional theories reviewed at the beginning of this chapter suggest. In the new forms, communication comes into the foreground as a major facet of structure rather than as a secondary variable that "comes with" or "is influenced by" structure. Studies of the new forms may have emphasized the communicative and coordinating functions of structure almost totally—the financial and external functions have received much less attention.

When communication was considered in traditional theories of structure, it was usually construed as information transmission. Discussions of new forms suggest that structures serve other communication-related functions in addition to information transfer, such as fostering trust and the creation and retention of knowledge. When trust is recognized as an essential underpinning of structure in the new configurations (Handy, 1989), then the role of structure in promoting (or hindering) the interactions that facilitate trust becomes important. When "knowledge management" requires structures that identify important knowledge, provide means for linking forms of knowledge, generate new knowledge, and retain valuable knowledge, it becomes apparent that "organizational cognition and learning" are more than information processing. Communication fostering organization-level learning must foster productive interactions among members that create higher-order learning and insight. When the dynamism of temporary, flexible forms puts jobs at risk and brings new opportunities to the best, structural designers must consider how to nurture valued employees. So some companies develop novel methods of reputational rating that gives employees credentials to move through their fluid, shifting unit compositions (Heckscher, 1994), while others try to develop egalitarian structures that make work meaningful and create a sense of shared ownership among employees. Theories of human relations and organizational culture have long emphasized these aspects of communication, but structural theories have only recently come to see them as important.

The importance of information technology in many new organizational forms has made it easier for theorists to acknowledge the communication-structure relationship. In a sense, information technology provides a material embodiment of communication processes that may have seemed too transitory and ephemeral to consider as structural variables in earlier research. Information technology also makes communication a commodity that can be stored, operated on, manipulated, and transferred. Somewhat paradoxically, this works against viewing communication as more than information transfer. So there are trends in studies of new forms that both promote and inhibit moving beyond the informational view of communication.

A final important implication of new configurations is the high emphasis they place on integration. With such fluid, unmappable forms, it is critical to have strong integration mechanisms. So methods of integration ranging from linking roles to teams to advanced information technology are crucial in new organizations, as well as in older communication-intensive forms such as the matrix and the adhocracy (see Conrad & Poole, 1998, chap. 5, for a review of integration forms). Cushman and King (1993, 1995) have described *high-speed management* as one logic of organizing that amalgamates aspects of the technological basis for new forms mentioned above, with a variety of other communication and governance features. The unifying logic of high-speed management is the contribution of the various design choices to integrate the organization to achieve proactivity in innovation, speed of diagnosis and response, mutually beneficial cooperation with complementary organizations, and constant adaptation to excellent standards.

Conclusion

It is unclear at this point in time how many of the "new forms" will stand the test of time. On further analysis, some may be reducible to previously defined forms. Others may well be unstable transitional forms. However, the issues raised by the new forms promise to redefine how the structure-communication relationship is conceptualized.

In this section, we have reviewed some of the literature on organizational configurations and its relationship to organizational communication. We believe this second current of literature has some unique strengths that organizational communication theories can take advantage of; however, we also believe that a theoretically adequate account must go beyond current versions of "configurationism" to cope with some problems raised by the issues surveyed in the next section.

NEW VIEWS OF STRUCTURE AND COMMUNICATION

The preceding review illustrates the tendency of structural research in sociology and management to treat communication as a supporting actor rather than as featured star. Communication research has, for the most part, returned the favor by largely neglecting formal structural variables in favor of emergent structures such as networks. We believe that part of the reason for this neglect is the recognition by communication researchers that traditional conceptions of structure are too narrow relative to the communication phenomena they are intended to explain. In this section, we discuss several emerging perspectives that conceptualize traditional structural ideas in communicational and process-oriented terms. These perspectives reveal both new implications and theoretical problems for future research.

New Social Theories Applying to Traditional Structural Dimensions

As the social-theoretic paradigm culminating in structural-functionalism has been challenged and superseded (Gouldner, 1970), conceptions of formal structure linked to functionalism have been transformed. We review here a number of developments in social and communication theory that deal with, but alter our view of, structure and pattern. These developments highlight major conceptual problems and suggest transformations in concepts that have important implications for communication.

Organizational Pattern and Hierarchy: The Problem of Relational Context

Studies of the influence of vertical rank on communication, as well as of superior-subordinate communication in general, rarely examine the overall relational context in which the manager's communication is embedded. This problem plagues configurational as well as traditional studies. Two theoretical positions argue that the neglect of such contextual phenomena may block the growth of insights into managerial communication.

Dansereau, Yammarino, and their colleagues have developed a theoretical and methodological basis for the detailed examination of the context effects on superior-subordinate communication processes (Yammarino & Dubinsky, 1992). They argue that any communication behavior by a manager may reflect the influence of several units of analysis—the individual (manager), the work group he or she manages, and/or a larger unit that he or she is part of. Those larger units can have two kinds of effects: They can determine the average level of behavior by managers (a between-groups effect), or they can be the sites of differential behavior by the manager, say, toward a specific employee (a within-groups effect). This model allows the study of multiple levels both of behavior and of covariation. For instance, Yammarino and Dubinsky (1992) find differences between retail and insurance supervision in the extent to which superiors and subordinates in dyads are similar in the relations among their attitudes—for example, in the extent to which they reason similarly. They attribute this difference to a contrast in the interaction environments of dyads in the two industries. In general, they argue that studies ignoring the possible impacts of different units of analysis may be deficient.

Another argument, influenced by the structuration perspective, is posed by McPhee (1988). He emphasizes the flow of influence, information, and empowerment in the vertical chains connecting the top of any organizational pyramid with bottom-level employees. The analysis starts with the premise that every manager except the top one is not an autonomous controller, but instead a person maneuvering "in the middle" (Roethlisberger, 1941), under pressure from both sides. Studies by Pettigrew (1973, 1985) nicely illustrate how

managers in a hierarchy maneuver strategically, while dealing with the constraint posed by countervailing commitments elsewhere in the hierarchy, to influence decisions or implement programs. As a result, managerial communication is affected by the overall patterns of "flow" of resources and problems through the vertical chain. McPhee summarizes three theoretical positions that imply different communication patterns in the vertical chain. One pattern, the homogeneous model, portrays dyadic links in the vertical chain as basically similar in function and process. A second pattern, the multiple strata model, suggests that there are several qualitatively distinct strata in any reasonably long vertical chain, each of which represents a different social milieu and perspective in the organization. A manager and his or her subordinate within a stratum will communicate easily and from a similar perspective; communication in dyads where a manager on one level has a subordinate on a distinctly lower level is more incongruous and may therefore involve less mutual understanding and support. In the latter case, we could say that a "gap" between the strata existed, due perhaps to different fundamental task concerns (Parsons, 1960). A final pattern, the multiple clusters model, assumes that superior-subordinate communication is strong (frequent, consensual, and cooperative rather than controlling) mainly when it involves considerable coinvolvement in activities and/or alliances.

A cross-organizational interview study of organizational vertical chains revealed most support for the multiple strata model (McPhee, 1998). The study found that the hierarchy typically divides into three sections or strata, each composed of relatively strong and multiplex relationships, but with the sections separated by relatively weak links revealing mutual autonomy of the strata. If the multiple strata model holds more generally in organizations, it would change the way we view many of the phenomena of vertical communication. For instance, a famous and quite well-confirmed pattern exhibited in organizational hierarchies is the Pelz effect (Pelz,

1952): The impact of managerial behavior on a subordinate's job satisfaction depends on the manager's upward influence. However, the multiple strata model would lead us to predict three possible patterns: If there is no stratum gap separating the manager from the superior or subordinate, the manager will tend to share an outlook with those above and below him or her, and the manager should be able to get resources that the subordinate would value. However, if a stratum gap separates the manager from his or her boss, the manager will tend to have trouble eliciting resources from above. Finally, if the gap separates the manager from the subordinate, the manager often will not perceive the need to elicit resources, leading again to dissatisfaction from the subordinate.

This argument asserts the communicative consequences of level, not in general, but for interaction within versus across strata boundaries. To explore it, researchers would have to identify, first, markers of strata and gaps, then discover the typical and exceptional results of gaps. For instance, across the same type of gap one manager might avoid the troublesome attempt to communicate more than perfunctorily, another might enter into full conflict with the subordinate, while a third might attempt to change the subordinate's perspective enough to allow confirming communication. One of these reactions (or another) might be most frequent, but all three are interpretative responses to a common condition of action, responses that all would confirm the existence and importance of the gap.

Centralization: The Problem of Fields of Control

The key issue facing research on centralization is the question of the relation of centralization to control. High centralization of power over broad classes of decisions is one mode of control, but control becomes increasingly difficult with the growing complexity and dynamism of organizations and their environments. Moreover, the lines of scholarship reviewed below suggest that a distribution of

decision power is not incompatible with a growth of overall control in line with the wishes and interests of a central authority.

One example of theory and research that separates centralization from control is Foucault's (1977). He is famous for reviving interest in Bentham's "Panopticon" and for suggesting that the design of modern office buildings often followed panoptic principles of allowing the constant observation of workers by superiors. But the main concept underlying Foucault's panoptic model is not provision for potentially constant visual observation, nor is it the idea that a central authority maintains surveillance, whether visually, through communication media, or through a pyramid of officials. "Although it is true that pyramidal organization gives it a 'head,' it is the apparatus as a whole that produces 'power' and distributes individuals in this permanent and continuous field" (Foucault, 1977, p. 177). It is the sense of being under scrutiny, inscribed into the very being of organization members, that changes them so as to give power to the center. One good example of this is Perin's (1991) study of telecommuting in the Internal Revenue Service (IRS). She found that her sample of professionals came into the office far more often than necessary, because they felt uncomfortable not being "provably working" in the way that on-site scrutiny guarantees. (For other discomforts of decentralization, see Colling & Ferner, 1992; for other analyses of centralized surveillance as embodied in organizational structure, see Dandeker, 1990.)

Two lines of work illustrate the implications of Foucault's ideas for the communicative study of organizational centralization and fields of control. One is Zuboff's (1988) application of Foucault's analysis to information technology, as described at some length below. Second is James Barker's (1993) work on concertive control, which explores decentralization from a different direction. His studies of self-managing work teams reveal not only the persuasive inculcation of decision premises from above but also the strikingly intense pressure exerted by teammates in the organization's interests. Such teams are commonly thought to be instruments of decentralization, but instead may bring increased control, through a process the workers themselves constitute.

The implication of this work is that decentralization is limited as a measure of worker autonomy and participation. Research is needed to clarify how communication interacts with structural moves to either increase or decrease power sharing in organizations.

Formalization: The Problem of Implications

Developing currents of scholarship are transforming the traditional literature on formalization by elaborating the nature and implications of the concept of formalization itself. Formalization certainly contributes to systematic rationality and to control (Dandeker, 1990), but perhaps more important is the sense of trust it fosters, since formalization clarifies commitments, gives a standard for procedural fairness, and provides recourse in case of violations (Breton & Wintrobe, 1982; Morand, 1995; Perrow, 1986). Moreover, since formalized rules or criteria promise systematic attention by the organization, they can be used to signal the interest of the organization. Peters (1980) notes the direct communicative functions of formalization. Meyer and Rowan (1977) began the analysis of the more covert use of formal organizational documents as signals to varied audiences that the organization is rational and conformable in other ways (cf. Jermier, Slocum, Fry, & Gaines, 1991). Langley (1990) notes four purposeful uses of formal analysis: for information, for communication, for direction/control, and for (political) symbolism. Her analysis indicates that the consequences of formalization vary with the combinations of these functions.

But the sense of formality as a resource for communication carries over into another important stream of ideas, focusing on formality as a quality of conduct or discourse. To act or

speak formally, argues Morand (1995), is to use a certain array of codes (often not formalized themselves) that mandate elaboration, finishing of acts, sobriety, consideration of others, and maintenance of attention (cf. Stohl & Redding, 1987). We might note that such codes include not only language, dress, and other surface attributes but also substantive codes of organizational evaluation, such as numerical systems for measuring productivity and cost. Behavior and talk that are formal, says Morand, have a variety of effects, including ratification of authority, routinization, a sense of detached impersonality, a sense of procedural fairness, and status differentiation. He argues that such codes are likely to arise in organizational structures that are bureaucratic, but this claim may be too limited. Formal codes of behavior, in more or less unrecognized organizational ceremonies, are part and parcel of the constitution of any formal order, as noted by Katovich (1985) and Golding (1991). Regular ceremonies, by marking the status claims of organizational authorities, dramatize the organization itself. As Baxter (1993) illustrates, "putting it in writing" can be a stylistic preference that reflects assumptions about personhood and social order that are quite different from those reflected in the stylistic preference for "talking things through" and relying on the word of all parties.

Recent scholarship on formalization also goes to a deeper level. Formalization is not simply a communication or control tool or ceremonial marker, it is a quality that helps constitute the subjectivity characteristic of the organizational domain. As Foucault (1977; cf. Fox, 1989) argues, the medium of information gathering, management, and use are correlated with a formalized type of knowledge that generates and represents disciplinary power. This power/knowledge complex cuts up and orders space and time to allow maximum regulation and creates a mode of subjectivity that makes us liable to such power. Giddens (1991) qualified this with the argument that capacities for surveillance, requiring formalization as a basis for recording information, are characteristic of modernity and are linked to the trust in abstract systems that we routinely grant to organizations today. Hassard (1991), like Giddens, notes how formalization recreates time as a medium of regulation vital to capitalism and implicit on the design of organizations (which are arranged to save time). Cooper (1992) distinguishes three aspects of formalized systems: their capacity as "communicable" to substitute for immediate presence and allow long-distance control; their capacity as representations to substitute for the thing itself in analysis and planning; and their capacity as symbolic representations to be abbreviated, compressed, and thereupon processed in ways impossible with the original referents. All these analyses place the tendency toward formality at the core of the phenomenon of organization, but we must also remember, as Cooper and Burrell (1988) argue, that formalization implies its opposite, the tendency toward informality (cf. Katz, 1965, for evidence that more formalized work leads organizations to grant a "sphere of informality" to workers). In all these ways "formalization" is conceptually close kin to "organization" itself and becomes a vehicle for understanding the influence of communication on organization.

The Challenge of the New Forms

Clearly, various features of organizational structure depended on communication. However, the advent of information technology as an important adjunct to traditional structural modes underscores the bond of structure and communication. Indeed, the improvements wrought by information technology suggest that insufficiency in communication and information processing is probably the critical factor that has kept structures from realizing their potential prior to the "information age." Information technology enables organizations to "perfect" classical structural parameters by providing rapid, accurate, and monitorable communication.

Centralization and "Informating"

We noted in the previous section how new research is transforming the concept of centralization into a broader sense of fields of control. As numerous commentators have noted, information technology seems foreordained to enable organization to realize Bentham's panoptic vision (see, e.g., Finlay, 1987; Garson, 1988; Mulgan, 1991; Poster, 1990; Zuboff, 1988). Information technology enables organizations to monitor the number of keystrokes per minute, time spent booking reservations, access to libraries, and adherence to budgets, all of which can be used to control members who know they are being watched. This situation changes the nature of work to make it more open to control than ever before. Yet by providing information at the points where work is done and decisions made, information technology can also enable lower members to enjoy a degree of flexibility and control. On one hand, information technology can reassure those in authority that they can always check on subordinates, and encourage them to delegate and empower. On the other hand, broader information access and power brings with it dangers of employee discretion that may tempt managers to exert control by limiting access to the system or by designing the information technology so that it allows only limited and prestructured sequences of operations.

As Zuboff (1988) has noted, firms that employ information technology to improve work processes may "informate" their work, allowing workers to use the information technology to study work processes and improve them even further. On the other side of the coin are those firms that use technology to further "post-Fordism," the tight control of management over work processes (Prechel, 1994). Somewhere in between are organizations that use information technology as a form of technical/bureaucratic control in which the technology is imbued with managerial values. Lower-echelon members are given apparent control over their jobs, while the main parameters are subtly set by managerial control over the design of the technology. Garson (1988), for example, discusses a case where investment advisers were given an expert system to help them in their decision making; they were given what appeared to be extensive control over investment decisions, subject to the parameters set by the expert system. In effect they were indirectly controlled by the system, while thinking they were making "their own" moves.

Zuboff (1988) also shows that information technology allows control of both ordinary employee work and the work of managers, even at fairly high levels, and also allows simultaneous control of work by prefabricated programs and multiple layers of managers. That information technology enables such different "flavors" of centralization to be enacted indicates the much finer degree of control over authority distributions possible when the communicative side of centralization is made more manageable.

Formalization and New Formal Parameters

Benjamin and Scott-Morton (1989) note several advances in integration that information technology makes possible, each of which is dependent on improvements in formalization:

1. Information technology makes it possible to integrate the forms and processes that govern several different transactions in one interface. This enables linkage of different formal processes, such as travel reservation services involving airline ticketing, car rental, and hotel reservations. Moreover, these forms can be linked so that information moves between them and the linkages and nature of the forms can be changed fairly easily and quickly.

2. Information technology also supports integration of multiple forms of representation into a single representation. For example, a design database might integrate and substitute for traditional engineering drawings, production specifications, bills of materials, and machine tool instructions. In this instance, four different representations of different aspects of a product are replaced by a single representation that translates them into common terms.

3. "The integration of expert knowledge to provide a standardized process for accomplishing or supporting tasks" (p. 94) is another advance in which knowledge as well as rules constitutes the formalizing mode.

These results of implementing information technology indicate a different side of organizational formalization, one highlighting positive empowerment rather than one relying on red tape and stultifying constraint. Information technology makes it easy to reconfigure formal structures, enabling the organization to be more flexible and responsive. Further, because it is an integral part of the work process, information technology makes formal structures much more "enforceable" than they are by human agents. Information technology also enables types of formalization that were not previously feasible, such as the incorporation of expert systems into organizational processes.

The potency of information technology in integrating the organization has been widely discussed. Integration of members through electronic mail, conferencing, and groupware systems enables geographically dispersed organizations to act and react as though they operated at a single site. But perhaps even more important is the growing use of information technology for knowledge integration. Information systems can be used to index important knowledge, create knowledge communities, and capture knowledge in the forms of expert systems and process analyses. What is easy to miss in the attention given to hardware and software is the critical role of communication and interaction in the creation and harnessing of knowledge in formal languages, databases, and other organization-constituting resources. While the technology makes knowledge communities possible, the interactions among the members of these communities are what actually create and apply knowledge.

A key dimension of information technology, *interactivity,* seems likely to become an increasingly important design parameter for organizations. Interactivity (Rice & Associates, 1984) refers to the extent to which a communication technology permits interaction between members that is similar to face-to-face communication in pacing and interchange. Information technologies permit transactions via forms and formal channels, which have traditionally been time-consuming and burdensome, to be conducted much more rapidly and interactively, often in real time. Information technology makes structured activities much more like interpersonal communication than routing through "channels." Traditionally, the reference points for structural design have been the flowchart and the rulebook; new configurations suggest that an additional reference point is the interpersonal interaction.

Theory and research on new configurations also suggest new structural models. Most models of organizational structure are premised on uncertainty reduction (e.g., Galbraith, 1973). Newer models are premised instead on the need to create uncertainty. Volberda (1996) develops a novel scheme for structuring organizations in hypercompetitive environments on the basis of their flexibility, which he defines as a function of the variety of capabilities they can employ and the speed with which they can employ them. Volberda defines four types of organizational structures based on their degree of flexibility: The rigid form has a few capabilities and can change them only slowly; the planned form has relatively more and more varied capabilities and can change them within the parameters of the plan, but is otherwise limited in what it can achieve; the flexible form has a large mix of capabilities and can flexibly adapt them to exigencies; finally, the chaotic form has an extensive and varied mix of capabilities, but cannot control the application as well as the flexible form can. The strength of the chaotic form is that it proliferates new ideas and adaptations; its weakness is that it cannot easily capitalize on them due to its lack of organization.

In all four forms, communication plays a central role. However, rather than reducing uncertainty or providing information, the focus is on enacting ambiguity and problematizing current arrangements. The nature of the organization's communication system influences its ability to marshal ideas and organizational capabilities. And communication is critical in maintaining members' commitment, which affects the pool of knowledge that determines flexibility.

Multilevel Analysis

The substantive theoretical advances described in the preceding two sections have been accompanied, especially over the past decade, by progress at the metatheoretical level. A large and growing literature addresses the issue of the relationship among "system levels," also termed the "macro-micro" or "meso" relationship. Of course, many of the theoretic currents discussed above implicitly or explicitly involve cross-level concepts and claims. Various scholars who have addressed the macro-micro and levels problems have challenged the validity of traditional theoretical approaches and offer new resources for theory development in organizational communication.

The macro-micro problem has a long history in sociology. Since the writings of Durkheim (1938) and Weber (1949), sociologists have been divided between those emphasizing explanation based on large-scale societal characteristics and those emphasizing explanation based on the individual experience, interpretive schemes, and actions of individuals. The revolt against Talcott Parsons's

(1960) functionalism by symbolic interactionists and exchange theorists exhibited their commitment to explaining social patterns as the result of processes of social interaction among individuals. Today, it is generally accepted that the problem is not whether both levels of phenomena should be recognized, but rather how to give each level its due and how to spell out coherent relationships among levels. Theories that seem perfectly good at one level are often found to be "weak" at the other (Giddens, 1976), either because they incorrectly reduce one level to an adjunct of the other, because they oversimplify one level, because they neglect to theorize one level (treating that level as transparent or common sense), or because they neglect relationships between levels.

For most organizational communication scholars, the macro-micro problem is often a question of how to avoid the temptation to overemphasize the microlevel. The general tendency is to concentrate on microsituations such as influence, superior-subordinate communication, or group communication, with macrolevel or structural variables entering in as context. The unit of analysis in most quantitative communication studies is either the individual or the episode, and such units are analyzed as batches, without much concern for their interrelationships.

Opponents of the microlevel reductionism have developed new conceptualizations of the nature of levels and how they relate to each other that promise to uncover different avenues of thinking in communication research. First, several theorists have discussed what differentiates levels. The most popular basis for level distinction is spatial and temporal extension, but Wiley (1988; cf. Weick, 1995) has argued persuasively that levels can be distinguished on several other dimensions as well. McPhee (1998) has adapted Wiley's scheme to array five dimensions:

1. *Abstractness*, ranging from knowledge and norms related only to a specific group of people and situations to knowledge/norms that have meaning independent of the social positions/roles of people involved (e.g., mathematics).

2. *Time-space*, with more macrophenomena involving interdependence across longer distances.

3. *Social differentiation*, in the straightforward sense of "differences." More macrophenomena involve people and mixed groups whose backgrounds, resource bases, and other characteristics are more diverse and varied, within the single unit involving them, than microphenomena.

4. *Reticular or network size/complexity*, ranging from one (or more) isolated individuals or relationships to increasing network extent and interconnectedness in macrolevel phenomena.

5. *Systemic/functional complexity*, with "macro" systems exhibiting more diverse tasks or operations that are more complexly interdependent with one another.

The first three dimensions are not essentially social—they can characterize sets of people who are almost completely oblivious of one another. In contrast, the fourth and especially the fifth dimensions imply social contact among parties. Each of these dimensions can underlie relations among smaller units that may constitute a larger unit, with emergent causal powers, at a higher level of analysis. Communication scholars can study the (often communicative) relations among smaller units, without assuming that the larger unit simply reduces to the smaller ones or that communication works the same way inside and outside such relational contexts.

The initial contribution of the macro-micro literature is that macro-micro axes can shed new light on traditional structural concepts. For instance, "formalization" can be a trait of a particular worker's job or of a corporate system. Formalization in the latter is more "macro" than the former because it describes (1) many different types of jobs, (2) of workers at different points geographically and perhaps historically, (3) probably involving a variety of individual-job formalization levels, (4) with formalization levels linked in various ways, and (5) with a variety of groups and practices involved in supporting formalization as a social enterprise. Such groups might include the consultants, governmental bodies, and professions that do so much to influence the level of formalization in American organizations. This example makes it evident that formalization is a complex phenomenon that cannot be satisfactorily characterized with a single variable. If formalization is characteristic of a society, the theoretical significance of individual-level formalization must be portrayed in the context of that social phenomenon, in relation to the distribution and connections of the social form, as supported by conformity or innovative resistance. This suggests that researchers must pay more attention to macro-oriented conceptual analysis.

The second contribution of this literature is its development of the idea of multiple "dynamics," "mechanisms," or "logics" that reproduce or condition the effects of social structure (Alexander, 1987; House, Rousseau, & Thomas-Hunt, 1995; Kontopoulos, 1993; Turner, 1988; cf. McPhee, 1985; Van de Ven & Poole, 1995). Some of these theories posit multiple, relatively simple processes that appear or combine only under partly specifiable conditions (including subjective choice). For the example of formalization, rather than assuming that rule writing/dissemination is a necessary managerial response to routine work, formalization could be a function of larger social imperatives that have been drilled into managers in business schools and exemplified in communicative genres such as policy-and-procedure manuals. Socialization and the influence of genre may well operate through different mechanisms, and the relationships among the two generative mechanisms must be specified to develop clear explanations. Other theories (such as the examples given in House et al., 1995) specify variables or situations that determine the causal power of a given level of analysis. For instance, House et al. note that the existence of "entrainment" (synchrony in the activity of subunits) implies an increase in the influence

of other higher-level units. Thus, if subunits work at synchronous rates, they find it easier to cooperate in adapting to new situations.

The micro-macro literature thus registers two main critiques of standard theory and research about organizational structure and communication. First is the problem of conceptualization: Structural and communication phenomena that primarily characterize groups must not be studied at the individual or dyadic levels. Second is the problem of explanation: Explanations involving macrolevel phenomena may require a more complex pattern than do relatively simple phenomena. Developing more complex, layered, and nuanced explanations for communication and its relationship to other structural features will increase our appreciation of how communication enters into the constitution of organizational structure in the larger sense.

Communication Concepts of Structure

One move toward more nuanced explanation is to give primacy to the discursive and communicative dimensions of organizations. This view implies that structure is inherently a communicative phenomenon and suggests a fundamentally different understanding of structure. However, it is hard to theorize how communication could constitute formal structure. Often communication researchers have fallen back on several lines of argument. One argument is that communication networks are the essence of structure, which results in placing informal structure in the primary position and giving formal structure a subsidiary role as a resource for generating networks or as a variable that influences their emergence. However, the research summarized to this point shows the importance of maintaining formal structure as a key term in our theories. A second line of argument is that communicative process generates formal structure, which is important only because it in turn affects process (see McPhee, Habbel, & Fordham-Habbel, 1987, for a survey of the major theories that elaborate this argument). In this work, formal structure also occupies a peripheral and epiphenomenal role: It is the dead chitin left behind as the insect of interest (process) emerges to live. But just as the skin was vital to the pupa, formal structure is useful to and distinctive of the organization—it is not just reproduced, but is drawn on in and constrains organizational processes. Researchers must face the question: What is it about formal structure that makes it efficacious, yet is fundamentally communicative or discursive? In recent years, several lines of work have shed insight on this question.

Formal Structure as Product/Feature of Communication

McPhee (1985, 1989) has argued that the formal structure of organizations is communicative in nature, but is the result of an analytically distinct communicative system in any particular organization. He labeled communication taking place within this system as "structure-communication." To simplify matters, we will use the acronym FSC (formal structural communication) for communication processes that are part of this system.

This theory of organizational structure is oriented toward the self-consciously organized systems that dominate economic, political, and civic life. Authors as different as Perrow (1986) and Giddens (1991) stress that organizations multiply both human productive effectiveness and social capacities for domination. This theory is meant to illuminate the distinctive features of organizational communication that help explain the proliferation of the complex organization as a social form; the effectiveness of complex, formalized organizations in concentrating power and producing goods and services; and the importance and functions of references to formal structure in organizational communication.

FSC is really an aspect of most communication in formal organizations. It is the meaning or property of organizational communication that establishes, explains, enforces, obeys, resists, or assumes the existence, power, and authority of an organization's structure. Prototypical examples of such communication take many forms, from an organizational charter, to company newspaper articles about a structural change, to a manager's explanation of the structure, to coworkers' explanations of what the manager really meant and how far the structure can be stretched. Obviously, such communication differs in quantity and quality across and within organizations, times, and contexts.

Formal structure itself, then, is produced and reproduced by FSC. McPhee's theory of FSC argued that the system of FSC prototypically centers on written documents and, more generally, that the medium of writing is primal for constituting organizations. The term *written* is meant to include all symbolic inscriptions on relatively permanent media, certainly including drawn organizational charts, and could extend in principle to cover memory formulations. Written orders and organization charts have two important qualities: They are (1) *enduring,* and so able to be stored, copied, and liable to be treated as real even if not immediately present in a situation; and (2) *abstract,* and so especially able to be interpreted and obeyed consistently in multiple settings.

These foundational qualities lead easily to some other typical ones. For instance, written structural documents can *reify and characterize* acts, practices, and relations. Once a statement such as "Al will report to Betty" is authoritatively announced and inscribed in official records, the abstract relation of superior to subordinate defines and conditions the human communicative relationship between Al and Betty, leading both of them, and outsiders as well, to see Betty as more important and properly commanding. (Obviously, this relation is just one element in any concrete setting, and it is interpreted and transformed as discussed below.) The enduring and abstract character of written structure formulations also makes *technical elaboration and manipulation* of practices and relations easy. Few things come as easily to an experienced boss as redrawing an organization chart. Finally, their existence "in writing" allows formal structural inscriptions to be *powerful though absent,* in a way characterized by Smith's (1990) concept of textually mediated social interaction, discussed below. Even if no one has a copy of a set of rules around, they still often argue about the content of the rules, then may go and check them—they rarely argue that the rules *should* say X, so we should do X.

Structure-communication has three important properties: First, structure-communication is a substitute for direct communication. For instance, instead of endless disputes about what new products to produce, executives will usually stipulate a hierarchy of officials responsible for deciding about new products, plus a decision-making procedure. The organization typically announces the structure, managers explain and enforce the structure, adjusting problems, and that's it. This one-way process deprives lower-level participants of a voice in establishing and negotiating the structure. And of course, plenty of communication remains, including that involved in making decisions, along with informal "sensemaking" on the part of employees, as they deal with the structure day-to-day, puzzle it out, and talk about it with colleagues. Members construct a meaning for the structure based on their own interpretation of available cues. Organizational structure is valuable only if it eliminates enough communication to yield efficiency without lowering decision quality and legitimacy too much. This property implies that decision discussions in a formal organization should refer to formal structure rather than carry out some of the functions that would be found in totally informal groups, and the references to formal structure should lead group decisions to contribute to organizational power.

Second, FSC is authoritative metacommunication about members' relationship to the organization. For instance, Yates (1989) reported that the Scoville Manufacturing Company required orders by supervisors to be written, and approved from above, to control downward relations and the conduct of those supervisors. It is commonplace to acknowledge that formal position in an organization signals responsibilities, status level, and power (Peters, 1980). Members' histories of position moves indicate the development of their place in the firm and whether they are rising, as well as the development of their competency. But there is also other, more subtle authoritative communication concerning relationships. Structures symbolize what the organization values and what kinds of people it wants its members to become. The fact that formal structure is part of organizations as an institutionalized form, elaborating property or political rights protected in contract and law, gives authority to the formal structural presuppositions of FSC. "Authoritative metacommunication," though, is probably different from the tacit, analogic metacommunication of Watzlawick, Beavin, and Jackson (1967), and their different processes deserve study.

In addition, the structure of the organization is itself the topic of member metacommunication. An important aspect of the member's relation to the organization is the attitude he or she has toward structures themselves. Are rules, procedures, hierarchies to be taken strictly seriously or can they be circumvented? Are structures a public trust, not to be altered or violated, or are they the "property" of the user, to be used for whatever ends he or she deems suitable? Communication about structures from managers, colleagues, and others informs members' use of structures, and therefore how the structure is reproduced and whether it is maintained or changed.

Third, FSC is differentiated—it does not work the same way everywhere in the organization. This is crucial to the "systemness" of organizations—their economic or political unity is "carried" in the abstract authority of their structural documents (cf. Yates, 1989). Giddens's (1984) concept of "distantiation" is important here—it refers to the fact that interaction such as FSC produces and reproduces, enacts and binds human presence (and absence) in space and time. The geography of the organization is elaborated along an axis of structural power—who has what powers in what parts of the organization, who can change the structure and who cannot. For instance, two structurally distinct parts of complex organizations occupy the process of "conception" where executive goals and basic structuring decisions are made, and of the "reception" stage where formal structure is renegotiated in the course of work practices. As complex structures have evolved, between those stages a stage of implementation has become common, where middle managers and staff members (most commonly) elaborate and inscribe an elaborated structure in the organization's official memory stocks.

During the stage called "implementation" in FSC theory, there are certain key communicators, including organizational designers, consultants, top executives, middle managers, and experts in the use of particular structures. These experts include industrial engineers, organizational development specialists, accountants, strategic planners, and MIS specialists, who all have highly specialized vocabularies and approaches that others must learn and live with if they are to use their structures effectively. The hitch is that others are not as facile at using specialists' concepts as are the specialists. This gives specialists a great deal of power, not just because they control important processes but because they can impose their vocabulary and views on other members. Others must work on unfamiliar ground and in many respects must simply accept the definition of the situation imposed by the specialists, and those not facile with the vocabulary and style of structure-communication will have two strikes against them from the start.

This specialization has both advantages and disadvantages for the organization. One advantage is that having these professional specialties makes it fairly easy for organizations in the same sector of the economy to work with each other. If one company, for example, is entering a joint venture with another, their financial people can negotiate fairly easily, because they have similar views of the world and share a common profession. It is also advantageous, because specialists can use esoterica to protect the firm from outsiders or impress outsiders (Meyer & Rowan, 1977). The problems the IRS has in interpreting a firm's records during audits illustrate this point clearly.

But specialized structural vocabularies may be used to silence nonspecialists. They may also unnecessarily limit the structural options the firm considers. Nonspecialist members may have good ideas about problems and possible solutions to structural problems. But if these ideas don't fit in the conceptual scheme of the experts, they may be disregarded. The specialized vocabulary may be a trap that keeps the organization from seeing new structural options. For example, Kanter (1983) observes that overemphasis on formal structures by designers and top management has limited their ability to see the usefulness of less formal organization forms, such as quality circles. Ironically, Kanter gave these forms a technical name, "parallel organizations," to make them more acceptable to organizational designers. The power of the specialized vocabulary of implementers, combined with the inaccessibility of structural conception decisions, makes it very difficult for ordinary organizational member experience to affect fundamental organizational structural attributes.

The specialist's expertise and control over the terms of discourse is a powerful resource in the structuring of organizations. But like all resources, this is produced and reproduced as the expert works with others. As others become more knowledgeable about theories of structure and terminology, the expert's power wanes. And an expert who throws his or her weight around unadvisedly may undermine faith in expertise, thus hastening his or her own eclipse. But after we join the chorus of criticism of middle management and staff,

FSC theory forces us to confront a major premise: These specialists are the most persistent enunciators of the stream of discourse crucial to the constitution of organizations.

The impact of FSC is tempered by other structural elements—technology, other professions, market competition, national culture, constructions of gender and race, for example. The efficacy of formal structure will depend on the transformative action of organizational agents. One structural element deserves special mention, as has been indicated above: information technology. Research described above, and popular images of information technology, portray the mediated communication network as the new medium for fundamental organizational structuring. We must emphasize the importance of maintaining a critical perspective toward the new hucksterism of information technology, by keeping three possibilities in mind. First, the new media may simply be new, better media for conveying the same old control relationships, reflecting the formal structure. Second, formal structure may remain in hidden control, determining information access or becoming apparent only during resource allocation or conflict resolution. Finally, the popular image may be correct, and formal structure may be much less important in organizations of the future. Only time and future research will tell.

FSC is the vehicle through which abstract structures are enacted in organizations. But between the inscribed structure and the immediate, practical control relations that guide work processes is a gap. The existence of this gap has led many to argue that formal structure is often ignored, and thus unimportant, and that it has been superseded by informal processes. Such views fail to recognize that cases of apparent inaccuracy and irrelevance of formal structure can be interpreted as cases of miscommunication, or more likely resistance as a typical part of the process of reception. More explicit attention to structure-communication and its various modalities may help bridge the gap between abstract conception and execution of organizational structures.

Textually Mediated Social Relations

In her attempt to characterize patriarchal relations of ruling, the feminist sociologist Dorothy Smith (1990) introduces the term *textually mediated social relations*. This term has important theoretical implications for understanding the communicative underpinnings of structure, and further elaborates some aspects of FSC.

Smith notes that texts are not dead objects for study; their life is refractive and involves "organizing a course of concerted social action."

> The appearance of meaning in the permanent material form of a text detaches meaning from the lived processes of its making. The text's capacity to transcend the essentially transitory character of social processes and to remain uniform across separate and diverse local settings is key to the distinctive social organization and relations they [*sic*] make possible. (p. 168)

Texts operating this way ideologically conceal the relations involved in their production and use; they constitute subjective positions, possibilities, and facts. Smith continues:

> A job description, for example, is misread by the sociologist if she expects to be able to treat it as an account of an actual work process. In fact, its organizational force is in part achieved precisely because it does not describe any particular work process but can enter a variety of settings and order the relations among them. (p. 218)

Smith gives the example of a female secretary whose work overlaps that of her boss considerably, but who is not a candidate for advancement because she receives no credit for executive experience due to the "systems of representations ordering the internal labor market of the organization" (p. 219). Her relations with other people at work are organized by her job description, no matter how inaccurate it may be, because it is one of the documents that patterns the organization and holds it together.

Smith's work suggests that formal organizational structure can be reconceptualized as the textually mediated social relational pattern of the organization. This definition is useful because it avoids situational solipsism. The text is not part of most social episodes, though it organizes them and its effects can be found. As argued in the section about FSC, this text stands outside the typical organizational communication process, so that an organization is not a communicative act or process, but a reflexive relationship among communications on varied levels. Thus, formalization is not merely a set of mandated rules, but the restricted possibilities for control of their own work emerging in the discourse of coworkers.

Conversation analysts and postmodernists are endeavoring to turn our attention to the practices and mechanisms underlying the communicative production of meaning and order. A shortcoming of this work is that it is not usually linked to long-term control decisions about organizational design and strategy. The notion of textually mediated organization offers the possibility of making this connection. Texts such as job descriptions or strategic plans are typically produced in the context of major managerial initiatives such as long-term planning or job reorganizations. Hence, they serve as the link between global managerial and control moves and local enactments of them.

Taylor's Textual/Conversational Theory of Organizations

James Taylor and his colleagues have discussed the constitution of organizations as communication in an extensive body of work (Taylor, 1993; Taylor, Cooren, Giroux, & Robichaud, 1996; Taylor & Van Every, 1993).

Responding to their studies of computerization in organizations, as well as to Ruth Smith's (1993) challenging exploration of alternative assumptions about the organization-communication relationship, Taylor and his colleagues have devoted themselves to integrating and adapting a varied list of philosophical and linguistic concepts so as to analyze "organization" as "communication." Thus, Taylor and Van Every (1993) write, "An organization, as we visualize it, is nothing but a fabric of communication: a collection of people in a process of talking, writing, and transacting with each other" (p. xiii). But they try to avoid a simple reductionist stance by identifying the specific features of communication that lead to the phenomenon of organization.

The array of communication concepts they have analyzed and marshaled is daunting, but two themes seem to persist through their work. One is the shift from a linear to a transactional model of communication. Taylor and his colleagues argue that a transactional model correctly elaborated can improve our understandings of agency and the subject/object dichotomy, which in turn allows a better understanding of seemingly linear processes like supervision, computerized information transmission, and speech act articulation. They note that the grammar of transactional forms includes relationships involved in formal organizational structure. The other, and more relevant, thread is the argument that communication is a dialogue of two modalities, conversation and text (where, to foreshadow, text will include phenomena like an organization's formal structure). The argument here is that two simultaneous processes occur in all communication. First is the "translation of text into conversation," as the content of remarks is given illocutionary force through the communicative action of speaker and hearer (Taylor et al., 1996, pp. 8-12). This force, which is what makes a locution by a boss into an order, is "precisely what we usually mean by *organization*" (p. 12). But a second process is also always present: "textuallization of the conversation" (p. 14). At its most basic, this is the process wherein conversation is bracketed, interpreted, and retained, even in the course of later conversational narrative. Taylor and his colleagues emphasize the framing, objectifying power and note that to preserve that power in writing is a matter of artistry (Taylor, 1993, p. 218; Taylor & Van Every, 1993, pp. 119, 130). Texts can be authoritative, but that property requires a "master conversation," a process that has or appropriates the responsibility "to write the text for the organization as a whole" (Taylor & Van Every, 1993, p. 126). This authority is a result of networking and consensual validation (Taylor et al., 1996, p. 16). The result is a "authentic text," comprising "the official organization," fixing its "macrostruc- ture" in a way that "specifies the organizational agents and their duties, . . . describes the activities and their expected outcomes," and allowing bosses to marshal illocutionary force (and have their writings be authoritative in turn) (Taylor & Van Every, 1993, p. 126). This text is the organizational structure.

In its application to organizational structure, this view of organizations as communication is similar in many ways to the view of organizational structure stated by McPhee in 1985. Similarities between the two approaches include the view that organization as an enduring system is "generated" by production of a text (Taylor & Van Every, 1993, p. 107) and the idea that organizational structure is "a fabrication of language" (p. 115). McPhee's concept of sites or stages is parallel to the idea of the disjunction between textually articulated structure and practical interactive relationships (p. 120, 136) and the view that "authorities" are specially privileged as authors of organization-generating texts (though the idea that top managers alone are "writers" of structure seems too limiting) (p. 126). The properties of FSC presaged the idea of structural text as "meta" to more mundane communication, informing its interpretation (p. 126, 122, 127), as well as the idea that the

constitution of organization by text involves distantiation.

Of course, there are also two important differences. One is the nature of Taylor and colleagues' project: They intend to show how organizational process is explicable directly from the nature and resources of communication in general, while FSC theory concentrates on formal structure, portraying it as constituted by a unique configuration of communication systems. Second, Taylor and his colleagues draw on a broad range of ideas from philosophy, linguistics, and social psychology, while FSC theory has focused on the elaboration of structuration theory to handle a notion of formal structure that is more circumscribed.

One limitation of Taylor et al.'s approach is that it attempts to use communication concepts that apply to all interaction, perhaps influenced by the idea that if organization and communication are equivalent, all communication should be organizational. Since these concepts must of necessity apply to marriages, mobs, and communities that intercommunicate, they are hindered from finding crucial explanatory concepts for specifically organizational communication. Thus, one member of a mob can give another orders ("Go that way"), but there are crucial differences between such "orders" and those given by a boss, and that difference must be central to a theory of organizational communication. Taylor and his colleagues analyze necessary conditions for the possibility of organization, and they argue that such conditions are important in practice, especially in the case of information technology. But an important remaining task is the determination of sufficient conditions for the kinds of organizations so important in the modern world.

A second issue arises because this position is structured along dichotomous lines. Thus, in Taylor (1993, p. 222), a dichotomy between the governors and the governed is portrayed as parallel to two rival texts and two rival conversations. However, it is likely that explaining

the possibility of organization inescapably requires a third standpoint or site (internal to the
system, not an external one such as "benefi-
ciary"; Taylor, 1993). Throughout history and
before, there have been power differences,
rulers and the ruled; organization appeared
when that relationship became recognized,
objectified, but above all, instrumentalized.
Once reified, a leadership position can be used
as a tool to motivate or to aid coordination. As
orders, promises, and other speech acts gain
the stability of text, they are no longer simply
subject to the will of the boss—the boss is
committed to a set of decisions once he or she
makes them, and an independent authority
(possibly external, such as the state, or internal, such as the specialists discussed by FSC)
is needed to validate and implement them. In
their most recent work, Taylor and colleagues
seem to be moving closer to this view through
such concepts as distantiation and mediation
(Cooren & Taylor, 1997; Taylor et al., 1996).

Comments

The three perspectives discussed in this
section all offer ways to "catch quicksilver."
They try to capture the (perhaps) fleeting moments in which structures are produced and
reproduced, enacted and carried forth through
communication and interaction. Years ago,
Herbert Simon (1976) argued that organizational structures were simply the sum total of
relationships among organizational members.
However, it is one thing to make this claim
and another to theorize it in a way amenable to
constructive research. One response to this
challenge has been to emphasize the informal,
emergent aspects of organizational structure,
and in communication research this has produced an efflorescence of research on communication networks. However, it is important to complement this important research
with analysis of how communication constitutes even the most permanent-seeming aspects of organizations, their formal structures.

Attacking this problem puts communication
firmly on its feet as the major instrument of
structure in organizations.

CONCLUSION

This review has presented multiple approaches to formal structure and communication. We highlight the differences and live issues involved in each major approach or
perspective in Table 13.1.

The traditional reductive *dimensional* approach differentiates various structural properties of organizations, some of which pertain
to or characterize communication. Structural
features are then related to communication
variables and to communication processes.
This approach considers communication to be
one variable among many and tends to rele-
gate it to a secondary position, behind more
substantial structural features as formalization
or centralization. The dimensional approach
illuminates structural causes and correlates of
particular types of communication or communication structures. This approach yields a
number of interesting and useful findings for
practitioners. However, it suffers from the disadvantage of endless multiplication of relationships and inability to see "the bigger picture" of how structural dimensions fit together
and how communication fits within the whole.
Its definitions seem hard to link to powerful
communication theories. And, since most
structural variables are construed as non-
communicative, the dimensional view has
paradoxically turned communication research
away from most types of structure.

The *configurational* view is intriguing but
inchoate. Most configurational theorizing explicitly considers communication as an important feature of organizational structure.
Studies of new organizational forms especially have emphasized the importance of
communication in organizational structuring.
However, there is some debate as to whether

TABLE 13.1 Approaches to the Structure–Communication Relationship

Approach	View of Formal Structure	Relation to Communication	Key Research Issues
Dimensional	Set of variables	It serves as an independent variable; also serves as a container/channel for processes	Mediating processes leading to the effects of structure
Configurational	Set of internally related elements constituting the organization	Totality that includes communication in an encompassing system	Identifying an adequate set of configurations; integrating configurations with organizational process theories; communication-based configurations; processes involved in inconsistent configurations
New views of structural dimensions	Structured processes embedded in multiple systemic levels	Communication as a medium of structuring processes	Relationship of new to old conceptions of dimensions
Structure/communication	A product of communication	Communication mediates structure in dialogue; is a metacommunication; is a reification of communication processes	Effects of context and other factors on communication and enactment of structures; relation of structuring processes to other organizational processes

so-called new forms are actually qualitatively different types of organizations. Moreover, new technologies offer the opportunity to enhance the operation of older structural forms. Configurational thinking is holistic, where dimensional thinking is reductionistic. The former has the advantage of providing a more complex view of structure and how communication figures in it. Configurational theories embrace the complexity of organizations and highlight the interconnected nature of structures and design choices. This very complexity, however, makes configurational theories daunting to construct and elaborate. A promising research avenue is to concentrate first on identifying processes that have the power to generate configurations and then derive the configurations and their relationships, as Mintzberg has attempted to do. This would provide a positive basis for explaining conditions of, interruptions in, or blockages of this configuring power. Several of the new views of structure and communication presented in this chapter derive process-based views of structure, though they do not explicitly address configuration.

Many of the most interesting insights into the structure-communication relationship have resulted from deeper analysis of traditional structural dimensions. By considering the *social system that embeds hierarchies,* we can illuminate the uneven nature of superior-subordinate relationships in any given hierarchy. Processes that create different strata or social groups in organizations play an important role in determining how formal structure controls member behavior. Reconceptualizations of formalization subordinate its rationalizing, instrumental character and consider it instead as a stylistic element, which emerges in discourse. Studies of new organizational forms suggest how information technology enables centralization and formalization to be enacted more effectively. However, they also highlight multiple new and effective modes of organizing that may "dissolve" these traditional dimensions by enabling structures that are decentralized but offer the possibility of reasserting centralized control

rapidly when the power center deems it necessary and that rewrite formalizations rapidly (removing the rigidity of formalization), in response to organizational learning and discursive changes. Multilevel analyses highlight the complexity of structural effects and call into question the assumptions that structural effects emerge from "one way" causal relations in which structures determine microlevel behavior or in which microlevel processes enact structures. Instead, multilevel research suggests that there is great variety in the causal fields set up by structures. Multilevel studies highlight the need to identify factors that influence the nature and strength of relationships across different levels. For example, in a strongly litigious environment, formalization of organizational policies and procedures may have a much stronger effect on member behavior than in organizations in a more benign environment, where there is greater room for slippage and transactional mistakes.

In recent years, several theories have emerged that consider *structure primarily as a communicative phenomenon.* The thrust of these views is that structures are constituted by and operate through communication. The FSC and textual theories of organizations explore how more substantial features of organizations, such as hierarchies or rules, are produced and reproduced in communicative processes. FSC, grounded in the theory of structuration, emphasizes the actions of agents such as managers and design units in promulgating written or diagrammatic representations that project structures and how they should be taken. The textual theory of organization, grounded in theories of language and discourse, locates organization in the cycling between reified and interactive discourses. Both views encourage researchers to focus on the evanescent processes in which structures unfold and on the texts in which they are preserved to be drawn on at a later time to mobilize and to reproduce structural features in action. This is an intriguing move, which could uncover the processes by which structures influence activity, rather than simply reifying structure into variables whose mode of action is left unarticulated. A major disadvantage of these theories is that they create a tendency to see everything as fluid and continuously being reconstituted. However, language is a much more flexible medium than, for example, physical layout. While likening organizations to physical systems can overstate their stability, likening them to language can lead researchers to assume more fluidity and flexibility than is possible given the physical and economic constraints placed on organizations in actual contexts.

Directions for Future Research

Based on this review, we can make several suggestions for future research in organizational communication. We believe that it is counterproductive for organizational communication theory and research to reduce formal structure simply to a set of variables such as centralization. Exploring structural configurations or the communicative nature of formal structure offers much more promising routes of inquiry. The work reviewed in the third section represents an extensive effort to set a foundation for a theory of communication and organizational structure. However vague and sketchy it may seem, it explores fundamental issues and makes some initial choices that seem productive. The elusive nature of the communicative underpinnings of structure presents a continuing temptation to start over again and again, producing analyses that essentially repeat earlier efforts but use somewhat different terminology. We believe it is important for the next generation of scholarship to push past these initial efforts and to flesh out, evaluate, and revise our understanding of how communication constitutes, enacts, or enforces structure and of structure's discursive nature.

One way this might be done is to focus on some specific areas that have a high probability of exposing the dynamic influence of communication on structure: communication tech-

nology, the surveillance/control nexus, interorganizational and societal influences on organizational form (i.e., institutionalization and diffusion of "faddish" structural forms), the role of trust in the formation and maintenance of structures, and conflicts over structure. Other productive avenues for research might focus on processes of structural creation/change, the "expression" of structure in communication, and its interpretive application and effects in work practice and politics.

Most previous explanations of the communication-structure relationship have posited a single mechanism, however complex. It seems quite likely, however, that this relationship is multiply determined by several different mechanisms. Van de Ven and Poole (1995) argue that organizational patterns are often generated by more than one explanatory mechanism. They suggest several ways in which different types of generative mechanisms might interact to produce seemingly complex patterns. Different generative mechanisms may operate at different levels of abstraction or in different parts of a complex system, or they may operate on different temporal clocks or alternate in their influence on the system. Given the complexity of structure and communication, considering multiple generative mechanisms (each of which might be rather simple in its own right) offers a way to build a theory commensurate with the phenomenon. Of course, such theoretical systems must be elaborated with care to avoid loss of integrated explanatory power, parsimony, testability, and generality.

Finally, we believe there may be a tendency in organizational communication research to overemphasize socially created or symbolic features at the expense of material aspects of structure (cf. the similar argument by Tompkins, 1987). The material nature of organizations provides a matrix that preserves and provides resources for communication and interaction processes. It is important not to overemphasize communication to the point that we delude ourselves into thinking communication is really everything. An important issue for organizational communication theory is the relation of the material and symbolic/interactional aspects of structuring.

REFERENCES

Alexander, J. (Ed.). (1987). *The micro-macro link.* Berkeley: University of California Press.

Alter, C. (1990). An exploratory study of conflict and coordination in interorganizational service delivery systems. *Academy of Management Journal, 33,* 478-502.

Althusser, L. K. (1972). *For Marx.* London: NLB.

Axley, S. (1984). Managerial and organizational communication in terms of the container metaphor. *Academy of Management Review, 9,* 428-437.

Baker, W. (1992). An introduction to network analysis for managers. *Connections, 12,* 29-48.

Barker, J. (1993). Tightening the iron cage: Concertive control in self-managing teams. *Administrative Science Quarterly, 38,* 408-437.

Barnard, J. (1991). The information environment of new managers. *Journal of Business Communication, 28,* 312-325.

Baxter, L. A. (1993). "Talking things through" and "putting it in writing": Two codes of communication in an academic institution. *Journal of Applied Communication Research, 23,* 303-326.

Beniger, J. R. (1986). *The control revolution.* Cambridge, MA: Harvard University Press.

Benjamin R. I., & Scott-Morton, M. S. (1988). Information technology, integration, and organizational change. *Interfaces, 18,* 86-98.

Brass, D. J., & Burkhardt, M. E. (1993). Potential power and power use: An investigation of structure and behavior. *Academy of Management Journal, 36,* 441-470.

Breton, A., & Wintrobe, R. (1982). *The logic of bureaucratic conduct: An economic analysis of competition, exchange, and efficiency in private and public organizations.* New York: Cambridge University Press.

Burns, T., & Stalker, G. M. (1961). *The management of innovation.* London: Tavistock.

Child, J. (1972). Organizational structure, environment, and performance: The role of strategic choice. *Sociology, 6,* 1-32.

Child, J. (1987). Information technology, organization, and the response to strategic challenges. *California Management Review, 29,* 33-50.

Clampitt, P. G., & Downs, C. W. (1993). Employee perceptions of the relationship between communication and productivity: A field study. *Journal of Business Communication, 30,* 5-28.

Colling, T., & Ferner, A. (1992). The limits of autonomy: Devolution, line managers, and industrial relations in privatized companies. *Journal of Management Studies, 29,* 209-228.

Comer, D. R. (1991). Organizational newcomers' acquisition of information from peers. *Management Communication Quarterly, 5,* 64-89.

Connor, P. E. (1992). Decision making participation patterns: The role of organizational context. *Academy of Management Journal, 35,* 213-231.

Conrad, C., & Poole, M. S. (1998). *Strategic organizational communication: Into the twenty-first century.* Fort Worth, TX: Harcourt Brace.

Cooper, R. (1992). Formal organization as representation: Remote control, displacement, and abbreviation. In M. Reed & M. Hughes (Eds.), *Rethinking organization: New directions in organizational theory and analysis* (pp. 254-272). Newbury Park, CA: Sage.

Cooper, R., & Burrell, G. (1988). Modernism, postmodernism, and organizational analysis: An introduction. *Organization Studies, 9,* 96-112.

Cooren, F., & Taylor, J. R. (1997). Organization as an effect of mediation: Redefining the link between organization and communication. *Communication Theory, 7,* 219-261.

Cushman, D. P., & King, S. S. (1993). High-speed management: A revolution in organizational communication in the 1990s. In S. A. Deetz (Ed.), *Communication yearbook 16* (pp. 209-236). Newbury Park, CA: Sage.

Cushman, D. P., & King, S. S. (1995). *Communication and high-speed management.* Albany: State University of New York Press.

Dandeker, C. (1990). *Surveillance, power, and modernity: Bureaucracy and discipline from 1700 to the present day.* New York: Cambridge University Press.

Davidow, W., & Malone, M. (1992, December 7). Virtual corporation. *Forbes, 150*(13), 102-108.

DiMaggio, P. J., & Powell, W. W. (1983). The iron cage revisited: Institutional isomorphism and collective rationality in organizational fields. *American Sociological Review, 48,* 147-160.

Doty, D. H., & Glick, W. H. (1994). Typologies as a unique form of theory building: Toward improved understanding and modeling. *Academy of Management Review, 18,* 230-251.

Doty, D. H., Glick, W. H., & Huber, G. P. (1993). Fit, equifinality, and organizational effectiveness: A test of two configurational theories. *Academy of Management Journal, 36,* 1196-1250.

Driskell, L. P., & Salas, E. (1991). Group decision making under stress. *Journal of Applied Psychology, 76,* 473-478.

Drucker, P. (1994, September). The age of transformation. *Atlantic Monthly, 274*(5), 49-56.

Durkheim, É. (1938). *The rules of sociological method.* Chicago: Free Press.

Eccles, R. G., & Crane, D. B. (1987). Managing through networks in investment banking. *California Management Review, 30,* 176-195.

Evans, B. K., & Fischer, D. G. (1992). A hierarchical model of participative decision-making, job autonomy, and perceived control. *Human Relations, 45,* 1169-1189.

Finlay, M. (1987). *Powermatics: A discursive critique of new communications technology.* London: Routledge and Kegan Paul.

Foucault, M. (1977). *Discipline and punish: The birth of the prison.* New York: Vintage.

Fox, S. (1989). The panopticon: From Bentham's obsession to the revolution in management learning. *Human Relations, 42,* 717-739.

Galbraith, J. (1973). *Designing complex organizations.* Reading, MA: Addison-Wesley.

Garson, B. (1988). *The electronic sweatshop.* New York: Penguin.

Giddens, A. (1976). *New rules of sociological method: A positive critique of interpretative sociologies.* New York: Harper & Row.

Giddens, A. (1984). *The constitution of society.* Cambridge, UK: Polity.

Giddens, A. (1991). *Modernity and self-identity: Self and society in the late modern age.* Cambridge, UK: Polity.

Gilsdorf, J. W. (1992). Written corporate policy on communicating: A delphi survey. *Management Communication Quarterly, 5,* 316-347.

Golding, D. (1991). Some everyday rituals in management control. *Journal of Management Studies, 28,* 569-583.

Gouldner, A. (1970). *The coming crisis of Western sociology.* New York: Avon.

Grandori, A., & Soda, G. (1995). Interfirm networks: Antecedents, mechanisms and forms. *Organization Studies, 16,* 183-214.

Hage, J. (1965). An axiomatic theory of organizations. *Administrative Science Quarterly, 10,* 289-320.

Hage, J., & Aiken, M. (1967). Relationship of centralization to other structural properties. *Administrative Science Quarterly, 12,* 71-92.

Hammer, M., & Champy, J. (1993). *Reengineering the corporation.* New York: HarperCollins.

Handy, C. (1989). *The age of unreason.* Boston: Harvard Business School Press.

Hassard, J. (1991). Aspects of time in organization. *Human Relations, 44,* 105-126.

Heckscher, C. (1994). Defining the post-bureaucratic type. In C. Heckscher & A. Donnellon (Eds.), *The post-bureaucratic organization: New perspectives on organizational change* (pp. 14-62). Thousand Oaks, CA: Sage.

Hoffman, A. N., Stearns, T. M., & Shrader, C. B. (1990). Structure, context, and centrality in interorganizational networks. *Journal of Business Research, 20,* 333-347.

House, R., Rousseau, D., & Thomas-Hunt, M. (1995). The meso paradigm: A framework for integration of micro and macro organizational behavior. In L. Cummings & B. Staw (Eds.), *Research in organizational behavior* (Vol. 17, pp. 71-114). Greenwich, CT: JAI.

Huber, G. (1984). The nature and design of post-industrial organizations. *Management Science, 30,* 928-951.

Ilinitch, A., D'Aveni, R., & Lewin, A. Y. (1996). New organizational forms and strategies for managing in hypercompetitive environments. *Organization Science, 7,* 211-220.

Jablin, F. M. (1987). Formal organization structure. In F. M. Jablin, L. L. Putnam, K. H. Roberts, & L. W. Porter (Eds.), *Handbook of organizational communication: An interdisciplinary perspective* (pp. 389-419). Newbury Park, CA: Sage.

Jarvenppa, S. L., & Ives, B. (1994). The global network organization of the future: Information management opportunities and challenges. *Journal of Management Information Systems, 10,* 25-57.

Jermier, J. M., Slocum, J. W., Fry, L., & Gaines, J. (1991). Organizational substructures in a soft bureaucracy: Resistance behind the myth and facade of an official culture. *Organization Science, 2,* 170-194.

Johnson, J. D. (1993). *Organizational communication structure.* Norwood, NJ: Ablex.

Kant, I. (1970). *Critique of pure reason* (N. K. Smith, Trans.). London: Macmillan.

Kanter, R. M. (1977). *Men and women of the corporation.* New York: Basic Books.

Kanter, R. M. (1983). *The change masters: Innovations for productivity in the American corporation.* New York: Simon & Schuster.

Katovich, M. A. (1985). Ceremonial openings in bureaucratic encounters: From shuffling feet to shuffling papers. *Studies in Symbolic Interactionism, 6,* 307-333.

Katz, F. E. (1965). Explaining informal work groups in complex organizations: The case for autonomy in structure. *Administrative Science Quarterly, 10,* 204-223.

Konsynski, B. R., & Sviokla, J. J. (1994). Cognitive reapportionment: Rethinking the location of judgment in managerial decision-making. In C. Heckscher & A. Donnellon (Eds.), *The post-bureaucratic organization: New perspectives on organizational change* (pp. 91-107). Thousand Oaks, CA: Sage.

Kontopoulos, K. M. (1993). *The logics of social structure.* New York: Cambridge University Press.

Krone, K. J. (1986, May). *The effects of decision type, message initiation, and perceptions of centralization of authority on subordinates' use of upward influence message types.* Paper presented at the annual meeting of the International Communication Association, Chicago.

Krone, K. J. (1992). A comparison of organizational, structural, and relationship effects on subordinates' upward influence choices. *Communication Quarterly, 40,* 1-15.

Krone, K. J. (1994). Structuring constraints on perceptions of upward influence and supervisory relations. *Southern Communication Journal, 59,* 215-226.

Lammers, C. J. (1988). Transience and persistence of ideal types in organization theory. *Research in the Sociology of Organizations, 6,* 205-224.

Langley, A. (1990). Patterns in the use of formal analysis in strategic decisions. *Organization Studies, 11,* 17-45.

Larson, A. (1992). Network dyads in entrepreneurial settings: A study in the governance of exchange processes. *Administrative Science Quarterly, 37,* 76-104.

Lawrence, P., & Lorsch, J. (1967). *Organization and environment.* Cambridge, MA: Harvard Graduate School of Business Administration.

Lucas, H. C. (1996). *The T-form organization.* San Francisco: Jossey-Bass.

Lucas, H. C., & Baroudi, J. (1994). The role of information technology in organizational design. *Journal of Management Information Systems, 10,* 9-23.

Macey, B., Peterson, M. F., & Norton, L. W. (1989). A test of participation theory in a work redesign field setting: Degree of participation and comparison site contrasts. *Human Relations, 42,* 1095-1165.

MacLeod, L., Scriven, J., & Wayne, F. S. (1992). Gender and management level differences in the oral communication patterns of bank managers. *Journal of Business Communication, 29,* 343-365.

McCauley, C. D., Ruderman, M. N., Ohlcott, P. J., & Morrow, J. F. (1994). Assessing the developmental components of managerial jobs. *Journal of Applied Psychology, 79,* 544-560.

McKelvey, B. (1982). *Organizational systematics—Taxonomy, evolution, classification.* Berkeley: University of California Press.

McPhee, R. (1985). Formal structure and organizational communication. In R. D. McPhee & P. K. Tompkins (Eds.), *Organizational communication: Traditional themes and new directions* (pp. 149-177). Beverly Hills, CA: Sage.

McPhee, R. (1988). Vertical communication chains: Toward an integrated view. *Management Communication Quarterly, 1,* 455-493.

McPhee, R. (1989). Organizational communication: A structurational exemplar. In B. Dervin, L. Grossberg, B. O'Keefe, & E. Wartella (Eds.), *Rethinking communication: Vol. 2. Paradigm exemplars* (pp. 199-212). Newbury Park, CA: Sage.

McPhee, R. (1998). Giddens' conception of personal relationships and its relevance to communication theory. In R. Conville & E. Rogers (Eds.), *The meaning of "relationship" in interpersonal communication* (pp. 83-106). Westport, CT: Praeger.

McPhee, R., Habbel, D., & Fordham-Habbel, T. (1987, May). *Process theories of organizational structure.* Paper presented at the annual meeting of the International Communication Association Convention, Montreal.

Meyer, H. D. (1995). Organizational environments and organizational discourse: Bureaucracy between two worlds. *Organization Science, 6,* 32-43.

Meyer, J. W., & Rowan, B. (1977). Institutionalized organizations: Formal structure as myth and ceremony. *American Journal of Sociology, 83,* 340-363.

Miles, R. E., & Snow, C. C. (1986). Organizations: New concepts for new forms. *California Management Review, 28,* 62-73.

Miller, D. (1987). Strategy making and structure: Analysis and implications for performance. *Academy of Management Journal, 30,* 7-32.

Miller, D. (1990). Organizational configurations: Cohesion, change, and prediction. *Human Relations, 43,* 771-789.

Miller, D., Droje, C., & Toulouse, J.-M. (1988). Strategic process and content as mediators between organizational context and structure. *Academy of Management Journal, 31,* 544-569.

Miller, D., & Mintzberg, H. (1983). The case for configuration. In G. Morgan (Ed.), *Beyond method: Strategies for social research* (pp. 57-73). Beverly Hills, CA: Sage.

Mintzberg, H. (1979). *The structuring of organizations.* Englewood Cliffs, NJ: Prentice Hall.

Mintzberg, H. (1983a). *Power in and around organizations.* Englewood Cliffs, NJ: Prentice Hall.

Mintzberg, H. (1983b). *Structure in fives: Designing effective organizations.* Englewood Cliffs, NJ: Prentice Hall.

Mintzberg, H. (1989). *Mintzberg on management: Inside our strategic world of organizations.* New York: Free Press.

Morand, D. A. (1995). The role of behavioral formality and informality in the enactment of bureaucratic versus organic organizations. *Academy of Management Review, 20,* 831-872.

Mowshowitz, A. (1994). Virtual organization: A vision of management in the information age. *Information Society, 10,* 267-288.

Mowshowitz, A. (1997). Virtual organization: Introduction. *Communications of the ACM, 40,* 30-37.

Mulgan, G. J. (1991). *Communication and control: Networks and the new economies of communication.* New York: Guilford.

Nohria, N., & Berkley, J. D. (1994). The virtual organization: Bureaucracy, technology, and the implosion of control. In C. Heckscher & A. Donnellon (Eds.), *The post-bureaucratic organization: New perspectives on organizational change* (pp. 108-128). Thousand Oaks, CA: Sage.

Olson, L. M. (1995). Record keeping practices: Consequences of accounting demands in a public clinic. *Qualitative Sociology, 18,* 45-70.

Orton, J. D., & Weick, K. E. (1990). Loosely coupled systems: A reconceptualization. *Academy of Management Review, 15,* 203-223.

Ostroff, C., & Schmitt, N. (1993). Configurations of organizational effectiveness and efficiency. *Academy of Management Journal, 36,* 1345-1361.

Parsons, T. (1960). *Structure and process in modern societies.* New York: Free Press.

Pearson, C. A. L. (1992). Autonomous workgroups: An evaluation at an industrial site. *Human Relations, 45,* 905-936.

Pelz, D. (1952). Influence: A key to effective leadership in the first-line supervisor. *Personnel, 29,* 209-217.

Perin, C. (1991). The moral fabric of the office: Panopticon, discourse, and schedule flexibilities. *Research in the Sociology of Organizations, 8,* 241-268.

Perrow, C. (1986). *Complex organizations: A critical essay* (3rd ed.). Glenview, IL: Scott, Foresman.

Peters, T. (1980). Management systems: The language of organization character and competence. *Organizational Dynamics, 9,* 3-26.

Peters, T., & Waterman, R. (1982). *In search of excellence.* New York: Harper & Row.

Pettigrew, A. M. (1973). *The politics of organizational decision making.* London: Tavistock.

Pettigrew, A. M. (1985). *The awakening giant: Continuity and change in ICI.* Oxford, UK: Basil Blackwell.

Poole, M. S. (1999). Organizational challenges for the new forms. In G. DeSanctis & J. Fulk (Eds.), *Shaping organization form: Communication, connection, and community.* Thousand Oaks, CA: Sage.

Poster, M. (1990). *The mode of information: Poststructuralism and social context.* Chicago: University of Chicago Press.

Powell, W. W. (1990). Neither market nor hierarchy: Network forms or organization. In L. L. Cummings & B. M. Staw (Eds.), *Research in organizational behavior* (Vol. 12, pp. 295-336). Westport, CT: JAI.

Prechel, H. N. (1994). Economic crisis and the centralization of control over the managerial process: Corporate restructuring and neo-Fordist decision-making. *American Sociological Review, 59,* 723-745.

Ragins, B. R., & Cotton, J. L. (1991). Easier said than done: Gender differences in perceived barriers to gaining a mentor. *Academy of Management Journal, 34,* 939-951.

Reynolds, P. D. (1971). *A primer in theory construction.* Indianapolis, IN: Bobbs-Merrill.

Rice, R., & Associates. (1984). *The new media: Communication research and technology.* Beverly Hills, CA: Sage.

Rice, R., Chang, S.-J., & Torobin, J. (1992). Communicator style, media use, organizational level, and evaluation of electronic messaging. *Management Communication Quarterly, 4,* 3-33.

Rice, R., & Shook, D. E. (1990). Relationships of job categories and organizational levels to use of communication channels, including electronic mail: A meta-analysis and extension. *Journal of Management Studies, 27,* 375-399.

Ring, P., & Van de Ven, A. (1994). Developmental processes of cooperative interorganizational relationships. *Academy of Management Review, 19,* 90-118.

Roethlisberger, F. J. (1941). *Management and morale.* Cambridge, MA: Harvard University Press.

Scott-Morton, M. S. (Ed.). (1991). *The company of the 1990s: Information technology and organizational transformation.* New York: Oxford University Press.

Shrader, C. B., Lincoln, J. R., & Hoffman, A. N. (1989). The network structures of organizations: Effects of task contingencies and distributional form. *Human Relations, 42,* 43-66.

Simon, H. A. (1976). *Administrative behavior* (3rd ed.). New York: Free Press.

Smeltzer, L. R., & Fann, G. L. (1989). Comparison of manager communication patterns in small entrepreneurial organizations and large, mature organizations. *Group and Organization Studies, 14,* 198-215.

Smith, D. E. (1990). *Texts, facts, and femininity: Exploring the relations of ruling.* New York: Routledge.

Smith, K., Grimm, C., Gannon, M., & Chen, M.-J. (1991). Organizational information processing, competitive responses, and performance in the U.S. domestic airline industry. *Academy of Management Journal, 34,* 60-85.

Smith, R. (1993, May). *Images of organizational communication: Root-metaphors of the organization-communication relation.* Paper presented at annual meeting of the International Communication Association, Washington, D.C.

Souder, W. E., & Moenaert, R. K. (1992). Integrating marketing and RD project personnel within innovation projects: An information uncertainty model. *Journal of Management Studies, 29,* 485-512.

Stevenson, W. B., & Gilly, M. C. (1991). Information processing and problem solving: The migration of problems through formal positions and networks of ties. *Academy of Management Journal, 34,* 918-928.

Stinchcombe, A. (1968). *Constructing social theories.* New York: Harcourt, Brace, and World.

Stohl, C., & Redding, W. C. (1987). Messages and message exchange processes. In F. M. Jablin, L. L. Putnam, K. H. Roberts, & L. W. Porter (Eds.), *Handbook of organizational communication: An interdisciplinary perspective* (pp. 451-502). Newbury Park, CA: Sage.

Taylor, J. R. (1993). *Rethinking the theory of organizational communication: How to read an organization.* Norwood, NJ: Ablex.

Taylor, J. R., Cooren, R., Giroux, H., & Robichaud, D. (1996, February). *Are organization and communication equivalent?* Paper presented at the conference

Organizational Communication and Change: Challenges in the Next Century, Austin, TX.

Taylor, J. R., & Van Every, E. J. (1993). *The vulnerable fortress: Bureaucratic organization and management in the information age.* Toronto, Canada: University of Toronto Press.

Thomas, J. B., Shankster, L. J., & Mathieu, J. E. (1994). Antecedents to organizational issue interpretation: The roles of single-level, cross-level and content cues. *Academy of Management Journal, 37,* 1252-1284.

Tompkins, P. K. (1987). Translating organizational theory: Symbolism over substance. In F. M. Jablin, L. L. Putnam, K. H. Roberts, & L. W. Porter (Eds.), *Handbook of organizational communication: An interdisciplinary perspective* (pp. 70-96). Newbury Park, CA: Sage.

Trombetta, J. J., & Rogers, D. P. (1988). Communication climate, satisfaction, and organizational commitment: The effects of information adequacy, communication openness, and decision participation. *Management Communication Quarterly, 1,* 494-515.

Turner, J. (1988). *A theory of social interaction.* Stanford, CA: Stanford University Press.

Van de Ven, A. H., & Poole, M. S. (1995). Explaining development and change in organizations. *Academy of Management Review, 20,* 510-540.

Volberda, H. W. (1996). Toward the flexible form: How to remain vital in hypercompetitive environments. *Organization Science, 7,* 359-374.

Watzlawick, P., Beavin, J., & Jackson, D. D. (1967). *The pragmatics of human communication.* New York: Norton.

Weber, M. (1946). *Essays in sociology.* New York: Oxford University Press.

Weber, M. (1949). *Methodology of the social sciences* (E. Shils & H. Finch, Trans.). Chicago: Free Press.

Weick, K. E. (1979). *The social psychology of organizing* (2nd ed.). Reading, MA: Addison-Wesley.

Weick, K. E. (1995). *Sensemaking in organizations.* Thousand Oaks, CA: Sage.

Wiley, N. (1988). The micro-macro problem in social theory. *Sociological Theory, 6,* 254-261.

Winter, S. J., & Taylor, S. L. (1996). The role of IT in the transformation of work: A comparison of post-industrial, industrial, and proto-industrial organizations. *Information Systems Research, 7,* 5-21.

Witte, J. F. (1980). *Democracy, authority, and alienation in work: Workers' participation in an American corporation.* Chicago: University of Chicago Press.

Yammarino, F. J., & Dubinsky, A. J. (1992). Superior-subordinate relationships: A multiple levels of analysis approach. *Human Relations, 45,* 575-600.

Yammarino, F. J., & Naughton, T. N. (1988). Time spent communicating: A multiple levels of analysis approach. *Human Relations, 41,* 655-676.

Yates, J. (1989). *Control through communication: The rise of system in American management.* Baltimore: Johns Hopkins University Press.

Zenger, T. R., & Lawrence, B. S. (1989). Organizational demography: The differential effects of age and tenure distribution on technical communication. *Academy of Management Journal, 32,* 353-376.

Zuboff, S. (1988). *In the age of the smart machine: The future of work and power.* New York: Basic Books.

14

New Media and Organizational Structuring

RONALD E. RICE
Rutgers University

URS E. GATTIKER
Obel Family Foundation, Denmark

Try to imagine how a person in 1850 might explain organizational communication and organizational structures of the mid-20th century. That person would have no familiarity with telephones, telegraphs, vertical files, paper clips, photocopies, elevators, electricity, and a whole host of other communication and information technologies. Now, imagine explaining to someone in 1950—before personal computers, desktop publishing, multi-

AUTHORS' NOTE: We would like to thank editors Fred Jablin and Linda Putnam, anonymous reviewers, and Claire B. Johnson for their comments, and Michelle Seeman for her editorial assistance. Financial support for this research project was provided to the second author in part by the Social Sciences and Humanities Research Council of Canada, as well as the Burns and Cleo Mowers Endowment Fund, Faculty of Management, University of Lethbridge. Conclusions (if any) of this chapter represent those of the authors and do not necessarily reflect the views of the sponsoring agencies. Due to space limitations, we provide no methodological qualifications of reviewed studies. We do not mean this as a reflection on the importance of such considerations when assessing research and implications. Further, we could cover only a limited range of relevant issues. Again, this does not reflect on the significance of those other concerns. Indeed, the original manuscript bellied up at around 150 pages, indicating at least a slightly less biased and ideologically blind approach, research program, or worldview than does this short (*sic*) version.

media, the Internet and the World Wide Web, online databases, facsimiles, electronic mail, voice mail, videoconferencing, electronic funds transfer, data communication networks, cellular phones, and credit cards in most organizations—developments in organizational communication and structures at the beginning of this new millennium. Finally, imagine either explanation without referring to any extant communication and information systems or any extant theories of organizational communication and structure before either time period.

There are so many assumptions built into our notions and experiences of organizational communication and structure that are based on how people interact and communicate within and across organizations with these technologies that both of these explanations would be highly flawed, if not impossible. The implication is that our understandings of organizational communication, structure, and media are all influenced by preexisting media and structures, and in turn influence the development of new structures and media. We cannot know the future, but we can attempt to better understand the iterative and reciprocal influence of existing structures, underlying processes, and new media.

Thus, four propositions motivate this chapter. First, in addition to traditional concepts (such as centralization or formal communication flow), organizational structures include meanings (such as about the appropriate uses of familiar and new media) and relations (among members and units, within and across organizations). Second, these structures can constrain or facilitate the development and use of a computer-mediated communication and information system (CIS). Third, processes of transformation in organizational and CIS structures may range from subtle evolutions of usage norms to formal metastructuring activities. Fourth, CISs can constrain or facilitate changes within and across organizational structures.

The first section briefly introduces CISs and suggests some basic conceptual dimensions of organizational media in general. It ar-

gues that common conceptualizations of new media may be highly constrained (thus structured) by idealizations of familiar media that have become structured into media artifacts. The section outlines traditional approaches to studying organizational structure, then it presents a simple structurational approach as one way of organizing this diverse literature and research. The next section surveys concepts and results from selected research within three broad structurational processes (development, transformation, institutionalization). The last section provides a brief conclusion.

COMPUTER-MEDIATED COMMUNICATION AND INFORMATION SYSTEMS

Overview of CISs

CISs combine four major components. *Computing* allows processing of content and structuring of communication participation. *Telecommunication networks* allow access and connectivity to many others and to varieties of information across space and time. *Information or communication resources* range from databases to communities of potential participants. *Digitization of content* allows the integration and exchange of multiple communication modes—such as graphics, video, sound, text—across multiple media and distribution networks (Rice, 1987). This review emphasizes computer-mediated communication systems (CMC), but also refers to some research where information systems are associated with organizational communication.

Such systems include, for example, audiotex; automatic teller machines (ATMs) that are redesigned as information services terminals; cellular phones and pagers; collaborative systems such as screen-sharing and joint document preparation; computer bulletin boards; computer conferencing; conversational and workflow processors; cyberphones; decision support systems with communication components; desktop publishing and document distribution; multimedia desktop conferencing and screen-sharing; electronic document interchange (EDI); electronic mail; facsimile; gophers/World Wide Web; group support systems and other groupware; home shopping and banking; hypertext and hypermedia; intelligent telephone systems; Internet listservers; local area networks; mobile personal communication devices; multimedia computing; online and portable databases; optical media such as CD-ROM and lasercards; optically scanned and networked documents; personal information assistants; personal locator badges; presentation devices such as computer screen projectors; telephone services such as call forwarding, redial until delivery, or automatically transferring a pager message to one's voice messaging system; teletext; video teleconferencing; videotex; virtual reality and cyberspace; voice mail; wide area networks; and word processing.

All Media Are Multidimensional and Artifactual Structures

Such lists of example CISs are not, by themselves, particularly enduring or insightful. Further, they tend to conceptually structure the particular combination of components and uses into a singular system that appears stable and coherent. This institutionalization via labeling fosters both technological determinism (the "system" represents and imposes causal necessity) and critical determinism (any negative aspects associated with this system are due to the technology).

Thus, crucial to the general argument that meanings of CISs are a part of organizational structures is the awareness that both traditional and new media embed a wide, overlapping range of technical and social capabilities and constraints. Typically, researchers and ordinary folk alike tend to lump communication media into familiar, binary, and mutually exclusive categories. Examples include mass media/interpersonal, objective/socially constructed, information rich/lean, organic/technological, traditional/new, democratizing/hegemonic, same/different times/places, content sources/users are institutions/individuals/computer systems, and so forth (see the review of such typologies by Rice, 1992; see also Culnan & Markus, 1987; Soe & Markus, 1993).

Yet media in general and CISs in particular are inherently ambiguous (because they can be interpreted in multiple and possibly conflicting ways), can rarely be fully understood, and continue to be adapted, reinvented, and redesigned (Fulk, 1993; Johnson & Rice, 1987; Rice, 1992). So taking a multidimensional perspective toward conceptualizing media seems necessary and appropriate. Table 14.1 proposes four dimensions of a wide variety of capabilities and attributes of media: constraints, bandwidth, interactivity, and network flow (Rice, 1987; Rice & Steinfield, 1994). Table 14.1 also compares two very different communication channels—face-to-face and asynchronous computer conferencing—across these attributes as an example of how limited simple oppositions of "familiar" and "new" media are (see Rice, 1987, and Rice & Steinfield, 1994, for similar comparisons involving other media). An intriguing exercise would be to use this table to analyze one's own use of a variety of media (letters, telephone, meetings, e-mail, informal conversation, voice mail) in two very different social contexts (work, home).

This and other multidimensional typologies serve to emphasize that (a) all media may be perceived, constrained, adopted, used, and evaluated in different ways within social and technological constraints; and (b) overemphasis or idealization of some characteristics of one medium can de-emphasize and limit perceived as well as actual characteristics of other media.

Three main conclusions follow from such a multidimensional perspective. First, media may be compared in many ways, so no medium is absolutely preferable or inherently "better" or "worse." A multidimensional approach generates better understandings of how both familiar and new media are structured in particular organizations (Culnan &

TABLE 14.1 Dimensions and Attributes of Media, Comparing Use of Face-to-Face to Asynchronous Computer Conferencing

Dimensions and Attributes	Face-to-Face	Computer Conferencing
Constraints		
Receiver can identify sender	y at least appearance	n listservs, anonymous, aliases
Have to know receiver's account/name/ address/number	y to find	y if private message n if posting
Address where person receives message is fixed to physical location/terminal	y	n
Users have varying participation modes	y	y
Source or centrality of control	often one person	usually dispersed
Can overcome selectivity	easier	harder
Can maintain privacy	depends on trust	trust and/or features
Organizational norms for use	y institutionalized	n developing
Need temporal proximity	y	n
Need geographical proximity	y	n
Ease of access to physical location, physical device	y once in contact n if not	n improving y with wireless
Ease of access to and use of interface, commands	y for familiar n for novel	n improving
Access costs (time, money, energy, knowledge)	highly variable	variable
Diversity of content available	depends on person	extensive
Diversity of content sequencing	n	y
Can store content (short term, long term)	limited	extensive
Limits to message length	y	n
Use to transfer documents	y	y
Can indicate priority of message	y	y not as much
Can ensure levels of privacy	n usually	y
Can retrieve by indexes or browse in random or other order	n	y
Can use filtering or allocation processes	n once contacted	y developing
Message can initiate other processes directly	y depends	y developing
Receiver can reprocess, edit for further use	n not accurately	y
Users can structure flow and privileges	y if great power asymmetry	y developing
Can easily convert content to other medium	n	y developing
Bandwidth		
Analog/digital	analog	both
Color, images, sound, text, numbers, motion, other senses	most	developing
Physical distance	y	n
Gestures	y	n developing icons
Tone, emphasis	y	n paralinguistics

(continued)

TABLE 14.1 Continued

Dimensions and Attributes	Face-to-Face	Computer Conferencing
Connotation/denotation	y high level possible	n low level typically
Symbolic aspects or connotations of medium	y	y
Social presence/media richness	can be high	usually low
"Personalize" greeting	y	y
Interaction		
Synchronous or asynchronous	synchronous	both
Symmetry of initiation and response	usually asymmetric	symmetric
Type of feedback	multiple	limited
Quickness of response by intended receiver	can be simultaneous if person there but that takes time	quicker than face-to-face if count meeting scheduling time
Control receiving pace	n	y
Confirm correct receiver, receipt	y	n developing
Mutual discourse	possible	possible
Quick-reply feature	interrupting	y
Network		
Information flow (one-to-one, one-to-few, one-to-many, few-to-few, many-to-many—both of users and of content, such as multiple copies)	one-to-one, perhaps one-to-few	all flows, depending
Usage domain (human system, individual, dyadic, group, intraorganizational, community, interorganizational, transnational)	mostly dyadic group	most forms possible
Distortion through overload	y	y unless moderator
Distortion through forwarding edited message	y	y usually available record, though
Role effect (can flow be easily controlled)	y	n difficult in computer conferencing
Critical mass necessary	n	y

NOTE: y = yes; n = no. These allocations are highly subjective and contextual. Many situations might generate other evaluations. However, this shows the wide range of possible attributes within a medium as well as the wide range of comparisons across media.

Markus, 1987; Rice, 1993a). For instance, interpersonal communication may have many disadvantages with respect to constraints (everyone has to be in a particular place at a particular time) and network flow (in larger groups, a few talk and most listen, and everyone has to respond to topics immediately or not at all) for certain social contexts (such as organizational meetings) or participants (such as the physically disadvantaged or culturally discriminated).

Second, CISs have many more capabilities than just the by-now familiar "overcoming constraints of time and space." It may well be that the ability to reprocess, combine, and analyze information in many forms from multiple sources has far more profound implications for organizing than "fast" or "asynchronous" interaction. For example, the telegraph allowed people to communicate across time and space at a pace and amount never before experienced but also enabled railroad companies to collect, associate, and analyze information from stations about the dynamics of trains, shipments, and passengers. This transformed how organizations collected and processed information, and how they learned from that information to develop effective schedules, routing algorithms and billing procedures that changed the domains and design of railroads (Beniger, 1986; Yates & Benjamin, 1991).

A third, more subtle, conclusion is that much of what we feel is "natural" about traditional media is largely an "artifact" resulting from the confounding of particular characteristics (such as material production, forms of access, social conventions, etc.) with a particular communication medium (such as interpersonal "voice") (Rice, 1993a; Shudson, 1978). As a consequence, new media are often critiqued from the position of a privileged, artifactual, idealized notion of interpersonal communication and traditional media (Carey, 1990). This interpretative structuring of both familiar and new media leads to assessments of new media as a source of utopian benefits as well as a destroyer of traditional values and ideals (Jensen, 1990). Some historical analyses of how prior artifacts and interpretations constrained the development of new media have considered (a) how the memo evolved through intraorganizational battles from personal diaries and reports of branch managers or colonial administrators (Yates & Benjamin, 1991); (b) how the telephone and electricity were first embedded in prior social conventions and fears (Marvin, 1988); and how the typewriter, its supporting institutions, and even its technological design were developed, critiqued, and restructured through social practices (David, 1985; Walker, 1984).

Thus, we can conceptualize media artifacts as a particular kind of organizational "structure." Artifacts are the structuring of communication media through use and interpretation, until they become perceived as "familiar" or "natural" and thus "idealized" in ways that constrain possible interpretations of both those current as well as new media. A later section will identify some of the factors that generate as well as restructure such media artifacts.

Organizational Structure and Structuring

Organizational structure is generally conceived of as "constraints that organization members face in the communication process" (Jablin, 1987, p. 390). Stevenson (1993) provides a parsimonious review of major approaches to conceptualizing organizational structure, while Monge and Contractor (Chapter 12, this volume) look specifically at network aspects of structure. Johnson (1993) reviews five approaches toward organizational structure. Communication *relationships* (interactions, exchanges, and flow) are typically the surface manifestations of deeper relational structures, such as work dependencies, power, commitments, and obstructed or absent relations. *Entities* are the units or actors involved, such as dyads, groups, work units, and higher-order systems such as organizations; these represent different kinds and levels of structure. *Context* is the local and global environment of norms, tasks, rules, and prior relations that structure ongoing actions and interpretations. *Configuration* concerns recurrent and recognizable patterns. Formal approaches to structure often portray configuration in an organizational chart or through indexes such as formalization, centralization, size, complexity, and span of control. Finally, *temporal stability* is the extent of enduring or consistent organizational patterning, ranging from an enduring headquarter-branch organization to changing project groups. Johnson integrates these five forms of structure into a single definition (intentionally emphasizing intraorganizational and communication structures): "Organizational communication structure refers to the relatively stable configuration of communication relationships between entities within an organizational context" (p. 11).

Such reviews of prior approaches to organizational structure generate several implications relevant to our argument. First, structure is best conceptualized as a process. This process involves meaning (as reflected in norms, interpretations, and artifacts from individual interpretations to international regulatory environments) and relations (as reflected in formal and informal communication networks, within and across physical and regulated boundaries). Second, structure both constrains and facilitates human action in organizational contexts. Third, new structures can arise or be suppressed. Fourth, most approaches to structure reject strict determinism, whether of an optimistic or a critical sort (i.e., technological utopias or technophobias). So relations between structure and technology are contextual and dynamic, but (theoretically at least) understandably so, and involve both "positive" and "negative" aspects. Given these assumptions, a structuration perspective provides a general theoretical framework for organizing a review of relationships among organizational structures and CISs.

A structuration perspective allows us to generalize the domain of organizational structure well beyond limited concepts such as "formalization" or "complexity." It focuses on the ongoing reciprocal association among structures and technologies (Giddens, 1976, 1984). In this view, structure is manifested in properties of actual social systems. These properties include rules and resources that both mediate action and are institutionalized by human action. Social interaction involves meaning (structures of signification), power (structures of domination via authority and allocation), and norms (structures of legitimation). Interaction patterns (human agency) become institutionalized (as structural properties) through repeated, habitual action, which

are then referred to or applied through subsequent agency. Structural properties are therefore abstract properties of, and exhibited by, social systems. They are sustained only through contextualized human action and interpretation that are enabled by structural rules and resources in the form of objective conditions (Giddens, 1976; Orlikowski, 1992).

Systems have structures because they are conditioned by rules and resources. But these systems depend on routines being reproduced by (more or less) knowledgeable actors applying structural properties (intentionally and unintentionally) (Haines, 1988). However, actors are embedded in ongoing social and technical structures, which may both constrain and facilitate their knowledgeability and intentionality, as well as influence their access to those rules and resources. Thus, structure involves subjective and objective components, is manifested in social relations, and requires multiple levels of analysis.

We can see, then, that organizational media artifacts are a specific source as well as consequence of structuration. Attitudes toward and uses of current organizational media become institutionalized in the form of media artifacts. These structures of acceptable norms, evaluations, and resources of familiar media then constrain and facilitate the adoption and implementation of new media. Social actions, organizational policies, user attitudes, technology developments, and so on may interact in transformational processes that may or may not institutionalize new structures that themselves may well become artifacts over time.

Orlikowski refers to this as the *duality of technology* (1992; Orlikowski & Robey, 1991; see also Contractor & Eisenberg, 1990; Dutton & Danzinger, 1982; Kling & Jewett, 1994; Markus & Robey, 1988). Orlikowski's summary of this duality of technology involves four major propositions:

1. Technology is the product of human action.
2. Technology is the medium of human action (both constraining and facilitating action

through interpretations, capabilities, norms, use).

3. Institutional conditions provide the context for interaction with technology (such as professional standards, resources, implementation policies).

4. There are institutional consequences of interaction with technology (through structures of signification, domination, and legitimation).

Her model thus proposes two kinds of conditions for use (institutional and technological) and two kinds of consequences of use (technological and institutional), mediated through individuals' actions, specifically the use of technology (Orlikowski, Yates, Okamura, & Fujimoto, 1995).

Orlikowski et al. (1995) extend this model by identifying a metastructuring or transformational process: technology-use mediation. This explicit and ongoing adaptation of CISs in their changing use contexts, not just at formal implementation or maintenance periods, can facilitate ongoing changes in technology designs, social norms, and organizational forms. Technology-use mediation occurs through deliberate reinforcement and adjustment between institutional properties, with occasional periods of episodic change. Thus, metastructuration adds conditions for mediation and consequences for mediation to the model proposed by Orlikowski and colleagues. So institutions, technologies, and mediation present conditions as well as undergo consequences through the structuration process.

Thus, CISs—and the meanings and relations associated with them—are particular instances of some rules and resources representing organizational structure. The interpretations of new systems are constrained by earlier interpretations, perhaps by exaggeration or misunderstanding of its potential characteristics, comparisons to media artifacts, even by rationales for design choices that are now lost to the new users (such as reduced labor costs, a visionary supervisor, or strategic initiatives; see Johnson & Rice, 1987). Particular mani-

festations of CISs may be rejected or continually restructured through agency, or may remain stable through continued unreflective use, institutionalized procedures, or even considered choice. CISs may in turn be a catalyst or occasion for organizational restructuring. Thus, the structuring of CISs is manifested in widely diverse interpretations, uses, and outcomes (Dubinskas, 1993; Ehrlich, 1987; Johnson & Rice, 1987; Mackay, 1988; Markus, 1992).

Structuration of a CIS involves ongoing microprocesses, as individuals working together appropriate the technology in various ways, both consciously and unconsciously, intentionally and unintentionally, within organizational, social, and technological structures (Lea, O'Shea, & Fung, 1995; Poole & DeSanctis, 1990) such as preferences and abilities of users, design choices, and implementation and management strategies (Perio & Prieto, 1994). Lea et al. (1995) argue that "actors" may include both humans and other entities (such as technological infrastructure or industry regulations) that are co-constructed through interactions to constantly renegotiate both content and context. Taking a more macro view, Gattiker (1990) proposed that the forms and implications of technology in organizations are based on the mutual interaction among (a) internal labor markets (rules and regulations pertaining to human resources), (b) strategic choices by the firm (or how much planning may take advantage of environmental opportunities and constraints), and (c) the socially construed work environment.

We now turn to summarizing, within this structuration framework, some prior research on CISs and organizations.

REVIEWS WITHIN GENERAL STRUCTURATIONAL PHASES

The following sections generalize the structuration process somewhat by identifying three processes of CIS structuration: adoption/implementation, transformation, and institutionalization (Orlikowski, 1992; Rice, 1987). There is debate as to the temporal location of structuration processes. Lea et al. (1995), for instance, say that unpacking context and action into "temporal cycles of alternating cause and effect" somewhat weakens the power of structuration theory. Nonetheless, we agree with Haines's (1988) characterization of Giddens's position that actors are primarily motivated to integrate habitual practices across place and time, and thus do not perceive structuration as a constantly simultaneous process. So organizing our review by three general structurational processes is both parsimonious as well as general. Across these three processes, the following illustrative research identifies ways in which organizational structures (both meaning and relations) and CISs may constrain or facilitate each other. Of course, almost none of the CIS research traditions grouped within each of these three processes was developed and studied with structuration theory in mind. And many of them may well be implicated in one or more of the three processes. However, we propose that the various research traditions may be thought of as ways of framing different aspects and microprocesses of a general structuration process, and we summarize them within the process that best characterizes their underlying argument.

Structural Influences on Adoption/Implementation of CISs

The following subsections summarize several prominent research traditions that consider how organizational structures constrain or facilitate the adoption/implementation of CISs. To the extent that each of these processes reflects differential control over and access to material resources, influence, and forms of discourse, these also represent sites of organizational power. However, we defer discussion of power to the institutionalization section. The subsections are ordered, somewhat arbitrarily, from a greater emphasis on structuring through structures of meaning

(genres and norms, culture, and perceptions of CISs) to a greater emphasis on structuring through structures of relations (social influence through networks, critical mass, and physical location). More macrostructural relations such as environmental factors, unions, and regulatory policies—both domestic and international—also influence CIS use and related changes in organizations (Gattiker, 1990; Gattiker & Paulson, 1999). And new CISs generate occasions for restructuring such policies and organizational environments. But these topics are beyond the scope of this chapter.

Media Genres and Usage Norms

As one way of understanding the adoption and evolution of familiar and new media forms and uses, Yates and Orlikowski (1992) introduced the concept of *organizational communication genres*. Genres are specific variants of a general form of a medium, associated with identifiable formats, circumscribed content, established practices, and a specific community of users. One example is the moderated online listserv (with a boilerplate masthead, brief summary of entries, edited contributions by listserv members) as a genre from the general CIS medium of e-mail messages. These genres are invoked in response to commonly recognized recurrent situations, involving the "history and nature of established practices, social relations, and communication policies within organizations," as well as accepted rights and responsibilities of participants.

Examples of how meaning in the form of social conventions structures media genres include rules about appropriate communication behavior (when is a voice mail response "too late"?), taboos (you can't send an e-mail directly to the CEO), expectations (how much detail is required in e-mail responses?), and roles (how much message communication filtering should listserv moderators perform?) (Ehrlich, 1987). McKenney, Zack, and Doherty's (1992) study of a programming team's use of various media found that as people develop routines for solving initially new problems and organizational challenges, they also develop shared understandings and expectations for future interactions that include issues such as topics, timing, participants, and medium. Thus, they argue that face-to-face "effectively serves as a context-creating medium, while [e-mail] is a context-reliant medium" (p. 285). As CISs become more familiar and institutionalized, they too will be appropriated into new genres, and become context-creating media.

Orlikowski and Yates (1993) studied nearly 1,500 messages from an e-mail system used by 17 members of a distributed group in a three-year computer language design project, and followed up with personal interviews. The use of traditional genres (memo, proposal, and ballot) declined, while the use of a new genre ("dialogues"—chained conversations, identified by associated content in the subject line, and including portions of the message being referred to) increased. Influences on the development of the new genre included the group's social history, the project life cycle, and the capabilities of the system.

One implication of the genre approach is that how CISs are conceptualized strongly influences their adoption, application, and success/failure. For example, conceptualizing, implementing, and using voice mail as a single, fixed genre similar to a telephone with recording capabilities stifles the emergence of the possibly new organizational genre of voice messaging (Adams, Todd, & Nelson, 1993; Rice & Danowski, 1993; Rice & Tyler, 1995; Stewart, 1992). Bikson and Law (1993) described how technical constraints in the World Bank's e-mail system strongly limited its conceptualization and application (such as integrating several documents, preparing letters and envelopes, sharing of structured files, storing messages in different electronic file categories). Learning, experimentation, awareness of initial adoption rationales, expanded or new system capabilities, and sharing new ways of using systems with others all facili-

tate the development of new media genres (Johnson & Rice, 1987; Orlikowski, 1992).

Culture

Johnson (1993) argues that meanings and cultural elements are consequential organizational structures: "Communication rituals themselves, in addition to being reflections of culture, are also elements of communication structure, since they represent relatively stable configurations of communication relationships between entities within an organization" (p. 79). Configurational and cultural structures may well overlap, such as when a charismatic leader manages through bureaucratic forms. So both formal configuration and cultural meanings facilitate and constrain each other, promoting both temporal stability and change through different forms of structure.

The more traditional and formal aspects of organizational structures may initially look similar across national borders. However, different cultural myths, attitudes, and opinions will generate different interpretations, applications, social networks, and communication patterns within these structures (Gattiker & Willoughby, 1993). The enhanced ability of individuals using group support systems to offer comments that are anonymous and not necessarily embedded in ongoing group conversational threads are presumed by much of the CIS literature to be a positive capability. However, this interpretation is usually grounded in the context of "individualist" cultures. Such implementations may be not only counterproductive, but inherently distasteful, to more "collectivist" and "high power distance" cultures (Hofstede, 1993). Maurice, Sorge, and Warner (1980) showed that organization processes develop within an institutional logic that is unique to a society. For example, French manufacturing firms have a more hierarchical structure, whereby decisions are often made by technicians or engineers. Britain seems to be in the middle, while in Germany the decision about work-related matters is made whenever possible by the journeyperson at the bottom of the organizational hierarchy. So the range of adoption and implementation decisions about CISs is likely to be differentially constrained and interpreted in different organizational and national cultures (Gattiker & Kelley, 1999; Gattiker, Kelley, Paulson, & Bhatnagar, 1996; Gattiker & Nelligan, 1988).

As Acker (1990) argues, the typical implementation of CISs leaves technology in men's control because skilled work is defined as men's work, creating more negative outcomes for women (Gutek, 1994). Such relations may vary cross-nationally. Whereas women from the United States differed from men in how they assessed quality of work life, Canadian women differed from men in how they perceived communication and control by working with computers (Gattiker & Nelligan, 1988; Pazy, 1994). While more and more CISs are used by managers regardless of gender, male managers in today's Russia still refuse to take advantage of CISs since using a keyboard has the typing stigma attached to it; consequently, assistants (primarily female) use the manager's workstation. Firms and managers are less likely to support additional training required for skill upgrading for women than for men in Israel (Pazy, 1994) and New Zealand (Murray, 1994).

Media Richness and Social Presence

These two theoretical perspectives can be construed as identifying structures of meaning in which CIS adoption and implementation processes are embedded. Social presence (Short, Williams, & Christie, 1976) and media richness (Daft & Lengel, 1986) theories both emphasize how communication media differ in the extent to which (a) they can overcome various communication constraints of time, location, permanence, distribution, and distance; (b) transmit the social, symbolic, and nonverbal cues of human communication; and (c) convey equivocal information. The essential underlying principle in both theoretic traditions is contingency theory. A good match (generally, but not necessarily, implying con-

sciousness and intention) between the characteristics of a new medium (such as relatively high social presence in multimedia conferencing) and one's communication activities (such as equivocal tasks like strategic decision making) will lead to "better" (more effective, less time-consuming, satisfying, etc.) communication performance. The primary argument of media richness theory is that the relation between CIS use and performance is likely to be mediated by task equivocality and by users' "media awareness" of the suitability of new media to these tasks. Theoretically, CISs may not only be "too lean" for particular tasks, but also may be "too rich" (McGrath & Hollingshead, 1992). Proposed rankings of media on richness or social presence scales, and proposed associations of those perceptions with evaluations of new organizational media, are generally but weakly supported by study results (Rice, 1993b; Rice, with Hart et al., 1992; Rice, Hughes, & Love, 1989).

Critiques of this approach include: (a) the strength of the empirical support for media richness has usually been greatly exaggerated or nonexistent (especially concerning CISs), (b) media richness concepts have been well developed theoretically but poorly operationalized, (c) CISs can foster equivocal organizational innovations, (d) some higher-level managers seem to use e-mail contrary to media richness predictions, (e) CMC can support considerable socioemotional content, and (f) media use does not have to be nor is necessarily intentional (Lea, 1991; Rice, 1987, 1993b; Rice, Chang, & Torobin, 1992; Rice, with Hart et al., 1992; Rice & Love, 1987; Trevino, Lengel, & Daft, 1987). The negative effects associated with media low in information richness or social presence may be limited to a narrow set of situations including laboratory experiments, zero-history groups, and short initial usage periods (Walther, 1992).

The initial theories have spawned a variety of extensions. These include emphases on usage contexts (Moore & Jovanis, 1988), social influences (Fulk, 1993; Rice & Aydin, 1991; Rice, Grant, Schmitz, & Torobin, 1990; Rice,

Kraut, Cool, & Fish, 1994), symbolic aspects (Bozeman, 1993; Sitkin, Sutcliffe, & Barrios-Choplin, 1992; Trevino et al., 1987), time and knowledge specificity (Choudhury & Sampler, 1997), timeliness and sequential relations among different media (Valacich, Paranka, George, & Nunamaker, 1993), status differences across lines of authority and organizational boundaries (D'Ambra & Rice, 1995), expansion of perceptions of media richness with experience (Carlson & Zmud, 1994), distinctions between initiator and responder (Zmud, Lind, & Young, 1990), and the extent to which problem solving becomes routinized over time (Dawson, 1995; McKenney et al., 1992).

Both the original theoretical formulations and these extensions represent some ways in which the meanings (such as social presence or media richness) of CISs are structured in light of past meanings and uses of familiar media, potentially influencing if and how CISs are adopted and evaluated. For example, due to processes of "idealization" discussed in the beginning of this chapter, face-to-face interactions become social artifacts that seem necessarily and universally "rich." Conversely, due to the role of technology, especially the computer, voice mail becomes implicated as necessarily "lean." These two structurings of meaning are based on emphasizing one or two characteristics of each medium instead of the wide variety of capabilities and constraints of both. Thus, native theories of "media richness," forming preexisting interpretive structures, often stifle innovative and personal uses of voice mail (as Rice & Shook, 1990, and Rice & Danowski, 1993, found).

Communication Networks

Potential adopters of CISs are embedded in various formal and informal organizational networks (see Monge & Contractor, Chapter 12, this volume). These relational structures both limit and enable people's access to resources (such as potential communication partners on a new system, or expertise as to how to use the system) and to rules (such as attitudes toward, and usage norms for, a new medium). These structures may indeed be aspects of the media artifacts themselves, such as a well-established voice mail distribution list that fosters a self-supporting decision-making elite.

For example, Papa and Papa (1992) reported that greater network diversity and size, but not sheer frequency of communication, influenced how and the rate at which employees learned to increase their performance using an insurance information query system. Pava (1983) described how informal communication coalitions dynamically develop around topics of contention such as new CIS development and influence subsequent decisions and support for different solutions. Adoption of e-mail by lower-level users is often stimulated by higher-level employees (who are sources of greater initial resources) adopting e-mail first (Kaye & Byrne, 1986; Rice & Case, 1983). Asynchronous media such as electronic mail compared to, say, the telephone may not be as useful for weak relations, because of the preexisting social as well as substantive content of these infrequent but important ties (Hinds & Kiesler, 1995). At the interorganizational level, Newell and Clark (1990) suggested that one of the reasons why British inventory and control system manufacturers were less innovative than comparable U.S. manufacturers was that they had less communication with external organizations, conferences, and associations.

Social Influence Networks

Social influence models are one conceptualization of the microprocesses whereby organizational communication networks play a role in the structuration of CIS interpretation, adoption, use, and evaluation. One's perceptions of ambiguous phenomena such as a new CIS are likely to be influenced by the opinions, information, uncertainty reduction, behaviors, and rewards or sanctions of others accessible through one's communication structures, such as work groups, supervisors, and informal relations (Albrecht & Hall, 1991; Fulk, 1993; Fulk, Steinfield, & Schmitz, 1990; Howell & Higgins, 1990; Rice, 1993c; Rice & Aydin, 1991; Salancik & Pfeffer, 1978).

There is some empirical evidence of a network-based social influence on CIS adoption and evaluation. Rice and Aydin (1991) found a weak positive influence on one's attitude toward a hospital information system only from those with whom one communicated directly, and a weak negative influence from those who shared one's organizational position. This second result implies that social influence from others with whom one occupies an organizational position but with whom one may have no communication may lead to discrepant, rather than converging, attitudes. Anderson, Jay, Schweer, and Anderson (1987) found a more pervasive effect of social influence, as measured by the "normative values" of other physicians with whom one communicated frequently. These values of salient others predicted adoption time of, use of, attitude toward, and time between when the organization adopted and the physician started using a hospital information system. Schmitz and Fulk (1991) showed that the attitudes of a respondent's supervisor and the five closest communication partners positively influenced the respondent's attitude toward an e-mail system. Self-reported usage of the system by these significant others predicted the respondent's self-reported usage.

Social influences on CIS use and evaluation may be heightened by how those very influences themselves are structured. Factors moderating structural influence include greater attraction to one's group (Fulk, 1993), lower self-monitoring (Burkhardt, 1994), negative word-of-mouth (Galletta, Ahuja, Hartman, Teo, & Peace, 1995), subordinates' task-related skills, and lower innovativeness (Leonard-Barton & Deschamps, 1988). In a longitudinal study of voice mail use (Rice & Shook, 1990), for those with more analyzable tasks, the number of voice mail messages sent by one's supervisor predicted the number of voice mail messages one received. However,

for those with less analyzable tasks, the number of voice mail messages sent by one's coworkers reciprocally predicted the number of voice messages one sent and received. These results implied a more iterative and collaborative use of voice mail for more ambiguous tasks, providing some support for media richness theory, but not in its treatment of voice mail as a necessarily lean medium.

However, Rice and Aydin (1991) did not find any influence of group integration on one's susceptibility to social influence on attitudes about a medical information system, and reviewed other studies that failed to find any evidence of direct or moderated social influence on attitudes toward, or use of, CISs. Finally, analyzing a variety of media in four organizations, Rice (1993b) found a small social information processing effect only for the newest medium (desktop videoconferencing), and then only for organizational newcomers who communicated with each other through the new medium itself.

Theoretically, then, social influence in general is one microprocess of organizational structuring of the adoption and implementation of CISs. However, such influence does not seem to be a strong factor, and seems highly contingent on other structural contexts. Research might do well to better specify which contingent conditions structure how, why, and whether social influence affects the adoption and implementation of CISs, rather than make sweeping assertions about the pervasive role of social influence.

Critical Mass

The value of a CIS rises, and the relative cost of each person's potential adoption of the CIS decreases, as a critical mass develops. A *critical mass* is enough initial users to stimulate rapid later adoption by others (Markus, 1990; Rice, 1982, 1990). The greater the structural heterogeneity of interests and resources (such as task interdependence, centralization of resources, group size, and geographic dispersion) among potential users, the more likely it is that there will be initial users for whom the system initially has sufficient worth, or who can afford the start-up costs. These initial adopters then decrease the costs and increase the value of adoption for later users (Markus, 1990). Local critical masses of other users are especially crucial to the successful diffusion of group CISs precisely because they are more likely to share similar benefits and costs (Rice, 1990). We distinguish critical mass from social influence as structural processes for two reasons, though some do not (Fulk et al., 1990). One is that critical mass theory does not usually posit a role for others' perceptions. The second is that it operates at a fundamentally different level of analysis: the network as a whole rather than individuals.

Rice et al. (1990) found that the best predictor of an individual's adoption of an e-mail system nine months after implementation was the extent to which that individual communicated with others in the office network before implementation. The best predictor of some communication-related outcomes after adoption was the extent to which individuals communicated with others who had also adopted the system. Comparing usage of two email systems in a multinational high-tech firm, Kaye and Byrne (1986) found that the benefits of an e-mail system were not realizable until almost all members within each user's local critical mass (about 15-30 others) used it as a normal mode of communication. Several studies of voice mail have emphasized the importance of implementation policies that foster a general overall critical mass of users or several local critical masses within relevant groupings (Ehrlich, 1987; Finn, 1986; Rice, 1990; Rice & Danowski, 1993; Trevino & Webster, 1992).

E-mail use at the World Bank was more strongly influenced by critical mass measures than by social pressure measures of e-mail use (Bikson & Law, 1993). Soe and Markus's (1993) study of the use of several new media in two organizations found that social utilities (especially critical mass) were better predictors of use of voice mail and facsimile, though not of e-mail, than were technological utilities

(functionality, convenience, and appropriateness for one's tasks, barriers to use such as technological and physical accessibility, and substitutability with other media). These two analyses (and that by Rice et al., 1990) controlled for social influence, providing empirical grounds for distinguishing between these two processes, and for proposing that critical mass is a more influential structural factor than social influence in CIS adoption.

In a study of desktop videoconferencing among R&D workers, critical mass and task factors were initially strong influences on one's later usage, but habituation of one's own usage patterns over time removed those influences as predictors (Rice et al., 1994). This implies that some structurational microprocesses play a role primarily during the early stages of adoption, eventually becoming subsumed by and embedded in individuals' institutionalized behaviors and attitudes. The study also identified four forms of critical mass factors that do overlap with social influences: (a) local critical masses must involve relevant others, (b) a critical mass of others' experiences is necessary to institutionalize new norms and behaviors and leads to the development and subsequent awareness of new ways to use a CIS, (c) widespread usage may critically reduce system resources, and (d) widespread usage may also decrease trust among users because of lower personal familiarity among all the newer participants (Fish, Kraut, Root, & Rice, 1993; Johnson & Rice, 1987).

Macrolevel studies of large computer networks have also found support for critical mass propositions (Gurbaxani, 1990; Schaefermeyer & Sewell, 1988). New group media such as computer bulletin boards are classic public goods that represent problems for achieving critical mass and ongoing adoption. Rafaeli and LaRose (1993) reported that critical mass characteristics (such as diversity of content and symmetry of participation in 126 computer bulletin boards) of collaborative mass media were more important than management policies (such as access fees, time limits, etc.) in predicting patterns of use.

Interorganizational aspects of critical mass affecting CIS adoption include symmetric and asymmetric relations between and among vendors, users, and innovations. These forms of critical mass contribute to the development of media artifacts, such as the persistence of the originally intentionally inefficient typewriter keyboard layout known as the QWERTY system (David, 1985). National and cross-national programming and transmission compatibilities, and general communication infrastructure, are other forms of critical mass in telecommunications (Gattiker, in press; Gattiker, Kelley, & Janz, 1996).

Thus, critical mass seems a conceptually general, and empirically robust, aspect of CIS structuring. It embeds both social and technological factors, and it is both an influence on as well as an outcome of adoption and implementation processes.

Physical Location

Few researchers other than Allen (1977) have seriously considered the ways in which physical structures constrain or facilitate organizational communication. Physical environments within organizations represent material, though subtle, constraints on behavior, interaction, and possible interpretations. Influential aspects of physical environments include social density, proximity, access, exposure, privacy, mobility, time-space paths, physical structure (architectural and construction choices), physical stimuli (artwork, noise), and symbolic artifacts (office size and windows) (Archea, 1977; Davis, 1984; Johnson, 1993). Physical elements not only facilitate and constrain activities and relations but often represent particular resources and contexts (consider the familiar concept of the influence of "the water cooler" on emergent relations and communication climate). Physical and temporal distances constrain network relations, increasing the costs of signaling one's interests and of finding other people with similar interests (Feldman, 1987). Indeed, some researchers "view space as equivalent to context in providing the medium within which so-

cial interaction is embedded" (Johnson, 1993, p. 93).

Visual access to a terminal reduces some uncertainty associated with the costs of checking for e-mail messages and thus influences CISs' later use and evaluation (Rice & Shook, 1988). The fact that nearly half of the e-mail messages sent by employees of one R&D organization were exchanged among close coworkers was explained by factors such as cost, access, and task interdependencies (Eveland & Bikson, 1987; Markus, 1990). Thus, physical locations clearly structure access to, adoption of, use of, and outcomes associated with CISs. But as we shall see, CISs in turn have major consequences for those physical and temporal aspects of organizational structures. So adoption and use (as well as nonuse) of new media such as electronic mail may well be heavily constrained/facilitated by prior physical structures (old buildings that cannot be easily networked, or small project groups who work together closely), and in turn, pervasively restructure access to others, potential interactions, and shared meanings.

Summary

This section has summarized some of the more frequent and influential microprocesses that structure how CISs are interpreted, adopted, and implemented. Previously institutionalized conceptions of media usage, such as traditional media genres or initial adoption rationales, can prevent CISs from fostering new ways of doing work. Organizational communication research should consider these preexisting yet difficult-to-identify factors in studies of CIS adoption and use. Organizational and cultural norms represent boundaries around acceptable ways of implementing CISs and communicating through CISs. They may well be deeply embedded in media artifacts, heavily structuring how CISs are conceptualized and implemented. Alternatively, many implementations of CISs are so decoupled from an understanding of cultural structures that they foster limited adoption and negative outcomes. Social presence, media richness, and social influence theories, while not strongly supported by the data, do emphasize how interpretations of old and new media are structured, and how social influence itself operates through communication structures in shaping attitudes about new media. Their strength may be largely as manifestations of media artifacts, where "richness" or "influence" derive mainly from what's "familiar" and "natural." Various forms of critical mass influence the adoption and diffusion of CISs. For example, national telecommunications regulatory policies affect and structure not only domestic but also cross-national uses, perhaps stifling the emergence of a critical mass of international users. While CISs can overcome physical constraints, sometimes these boundaries of time and space are characteristics of real task interdependencies that cannot be ignored. However, those task interdependencies may themselves be restructured to take advantage of the other positive characteristics of CISs.

Transformations of Structures and CISs

The following subsections review studies that discuss processes whereby CISs and organizational structures are used, converted, reinvented, or integrated through their interaction. These may involve more or less emphasis on CISs or organizational structure. Again, the subsections are ordered from more emphasis on structuring through meaning (changes in the nature, form, and temporal aspects of content, and group communication), and through relations (group communication and metastructuring).

Nature of Content

Because of the potential capabilities of CISs suggested earlier in this chapter, content is processible. This allows for diverse entry, storage, massaging, retrieval, and distribution strategies (Mackay, 1988; Malone, Grant,

Turbak, Brobst, & Cohen, 1987; Rice & Case, 1983). Digitization structures information in CISs into a universal format (bits) so that content may appear in any communication mode (text, sounds, video, numbers) through any digital medium. Digitization also separates content from the traditional associations with specific media and institutional structures (e.g., words with books, accurate images with photography, music with records) (Brand, 1987; Mulgan, 1991; Rice, 1987). This detachment removes control of the content from the author, producer, publisher, custodian, librarian, and so forth. But it also creates contradictions and problems in the traditional policies and assumptions associated with those physical and institutional structures. Typically, individuals initially enact familiar genres with a new medium (such as conceptualizing word processing as a fancy typewriter, Johnson & Rice, 1987; or voice mail as a fancy telephone answering machine, Rice & Danowski, 1993). But they may develop or choose an entirely new genre (virtual reality) or develop new subgenres within a new medium (electronic novels), which changes the nature, form, and temporal aspects of that mediated content.

The *nature* of message content in CISs can differ from that of traditional organizational media. For example, e-mail communication among seven ad hoc programming task groups involved more discussion of scheduling, task assignment, and socioemotional topics, while face-to-face communication involved more consensus building and problem solving (Finholt, Sproull, & Kiesler, 1990). CISs may allow individuals to exchange messages, vote, or express preferences anonymously, supposedly separating content from identity and its attendant attributions and biases (Hayne & Rice, 1997; Hiltz, Turoff, & Johnson, 1989; Jessup, Connolly, & Tansik, 1990; Nunamaker, Dennis, Valacich, Vogel, & George, 1991). Craipeau (1994) notes one study that found electronic mail messages, compared to memos, placed less or no importance on closing signatures. There was decreased emphasis on hierarchical status and symbolic value, and increased emphasis on the content. While this reduces the role of organizational hierarchy in communicative content, it may also reduce the role of the social, as indicated and symbolized through closings, signatures, and position titles.

But the nature of the CIS content may be so strongly structured by the organizational context that it mirrors traditional media content, reinforced by and reinforcing the "artifact" of "familiar" organizational communication. Both Bikson and Law (1993) and Bizot, Smith, and Hill (1991) reported that over 90% of a sample of e-mail messages sent in each study's organization were clearly related to business, reflecting the strong intentional administration policies at both sites against social uses of the system, rather than technological causation. Among World Bank e-mail users, higher-level staff reported more substantive e-mail, while lower-level staff reported more administrative messages (Bikson & Law, 1993). Sherblom's (1988) study of the 157 e-mail messages to and from one middle-level manager found that messages sent upward in the hierarchy were more restricted in function (mostly involving exchange of information), functional categories were more evenly distributed among peer messages, and subordinates were more likely to "sign" their mail than were superiors. These aspects of e-mail content indicated that "an electronic paralanguage reflects, reinforces, and recontextualizes the organizational structural hierarchy" (p. 50).

Form of Content

The form of CIS content and message flow may also be different. "Multiple threads of conversation" occur in bulletin boards, computer conferencing, and listservs. These occur when e-mail postings are responses to an item added several entries ago by one user but just recently read by another user, a response to multiple previous topics, or conditional comments embedded in a message that reduce the likelihood of another person having to wait for a response from the original sender to a particular question before being able to provide some information or make a decision (Black, Levin, Mehan, & Quinn, 1983; Kolb, 1996). One consequence of such multiple threads is that online discussions can suffer from tangential comments and loss of coherence (Bump, 1990). Even regular private and synchronous e-mail messages may arrive at different users' screens in different order, due to different log-on schedules and different routings of the messages' packets through packet-switched computer networks.

On the other hand, the multiple threads identified in transcripts of online discussions can provide a visual structure of portions of an emerging virtual organization (Dubinskas, 1993). As an example of such analysis, Berthold, Sudweeks, Newton, and Coyne (1996) coded 3,000 messages from 30 newsgroups on three information services (Bitnet, Compuserve, Internet) over one month. They used neural network analysis to group 51 coded categories (such as emotion, gender, message was referenced later on) that highly co-occurred across the messages. Among other results, they found that messages that were part of conversational threads tended to have medium length, include an appropriate subject line, contain statements of fact, and not introduce a new topic. Organizational members interested in fostering enduring communication relations across otherwise diverse and distant teams or virtual firms might intentionally develop message genres with these thread attributes (see the discussion on metastructuring, below).

Hypertext links will relax our familiar notions of a sequential textual structuring even more. Users may now move from any content node (such as a word, picture, or reference) in a (possibly multimedia) document directly to associated content nodes in other documents, both within and across documents. They may also restructure hypertext documents by adding their own associations for other users to explore. Thus, an annual report posted as part of an organization's World Wide Web home page could allow stockholders to click on summary figures to inspect or reanalyze the full auditor's report, follow links to an industry association's home page for market comparisons of the organization's products and services, or discuss upcoming policy decisions with watchdog agencies. The structure of an organization's identity could be transformed repeatedly through mediated forms created by internal and external publics, many unknown to the organization. Note that hypertext structures are currently being conceptualized as novel or unique because the linear structuring of traditional printed documents has become institutionalized into media artifacts. Actually, hypertext and online relational/keyword searches share some characteristics of preprint oral culture (Grande, 1980) and the ongoing commentaries and annotations of early religious texts such as the Bible.

Temporal Aspects of Content

Time is another intrinsic aspect of the structure of communication that may be transformed within CISs. As well, changes in the use and meaning of time in CISs are transforming how people conceptualize media in general: consider evaluations of the interactivity or social presence of the traditional telephone in light of voice mail, cellular telephones, and videophones. Hesse, Werner, and Altman (1988) discuss a range of temporal aspects in CISs. These include how much communication can occur in a given synchronous period, how to sequence asynchronous contributions by multiple users, mismatches between communication pace of different participants, and the ability to recall prior contributions by participants. Kolb (1996) suggests that the limited length but rapid feedback inherent in CMC likely will foster discourse that builds up arguments over "point-for-point statements and rebuttals" (p. 16) rather than by lengthy linear arguments, and allows clarification and inquiries rather than unchallengeable pronouncements. However, the prevalence of conversational threads may make it difficult to keep the focus on a specific line of discourse and even suppress

discourse that arises out of thoughts long incubating. Temporal aspects that may be explicitly structured into group communication system capabilities, according to Johnson-Lenz and Johnson-Lenz (1991), might include identifiable stages, orientations, transitions, beginnings and endings, and rhythms such as patterns of periodic contact and participation. Conscious understanding of and attention to social aspects of how systems are used—open space, timing, rhythms, boundaries, containers, and procedures—can lead to "purpose-centered groupware." They propose that emphasis on these social aspects would allow users and designers to iteratively and continuously use the current state of groupware to design and implement the next state. Highlighting the duality of structure and technology, they argue for "the emergence of background processes that inform the next generation of foreground forms" (p. 402). Thus, even traditional artifacts of a temporally sequential design-build-implement-use system process may be transformed.

Group Communication

Considerable research has looked at how groupware may be used to structure group communication, processes, and outcomes (such as decision quality or consensus) (Kraemer & Pinsonneault, 1990; Rice, 1984; Valacich, Paranka, George, & Nunamaker, 1993) and how, in turn, groupware is structured through use and interpretation. Poole and DeSanctis (1990; DeSanctis & Poole, 1994) have developed a theoretical framework called adaptive structuration theory, and refined it through empirical coding schemes. The use and outcomes associated with groupware are influenced by (a) social structures of group processes, tasks, and organization, (b) how groups produce and reproduce their structures through their use and adaptation of technologies, and (c) technical features, limitations, and spirit of CISs (such as interface design). Teleconferencing, and group communication, are discussed elsewhere in this volume (Chapter 16).

Metastructuring

We have seen that transformation involving CISs and organizational structuring may involve the adaptation of an innovation during and after its initial adoption, sometimes called *reinvention.* An early application of the concept to CISs was a cross-organizational study showing how different management and user practices (sometimes intentional, sometimes not) involving word processing fostered or constrained different levels of reinvention (Johnson & Rice, 1987). For example, some units were managed by the supervisor into organization-wide consulting groups that restructured word processing as a foundation for document and transaction processing. Other units were administered strictly as industrial typing pools without proactive management, and eventually were disbanded.

Orlikowski et al. (1995) generalize this concept, labeled *metastructuring,* as part of their model of the duality of technology. They studied how a newsgroup and e-mail system were initiated, used, and iteratively redesigned by a team of software engineers. A few individuals influenced others' use of the medium, changed the system's features, and changed the context of system use. This mediation helped to establish norms and expectations for subsequent use, sometimes through major changes in either the system or the organization of project teams. There were four types of mediating activities: (a) establishment (such as shifting official announcements from a traditional lunchtime meeting to a new newsgroup), (b) reinforcement (such as promoting effective use), (c) adjustment (such as providing online feedback to clarify rules and resources), and (d) episodic change (such as adding a moderator). Indeed, without such ongoing metastructuring and reinvention, a CIS is likely to be irrelevant, damaging, unsatisfying, or rejected. Sure enough, when the engineers' organization was restructured, there was no formal provision for technology-use mediation, and the newsgroups and other services fell into disuse.

Summary

There are many dimensions of transformations involving CISs and organizations. CISs may be used in ways that transform the nature, form, and temporal aspects of content. To the extent that these microprocesses of communication influence the structuring of meaning and relations in organizational settings, they may be one of the primary ways in which new media genres emerge. These may possibly transform our ways of conceptualizing what has been considered "natural" conversational relations and meanings. Group CIS systems have been adapted to facilitate better group interaction, idea generation, and decision making—but also may be used to reinforce familiar group communication processes and structures. They may also seriously challenge traditional notions of organizational structure that presume most interaction is within the functional work group, rather than across organizational units or even across organizations themselves. Metastructuring may be designed into the implementation process as an ongoing, intentional transformation of social and technical aspects of CISs.

Institutionalization: CIS Influences on Organizational Structures

CISs may expand or reduce characteristics associated with traditional media, and alter the mix of available media. Associated patterns of communication and transactional processes are likely to change as well. New communication systems shorten the time between events and their consequences, reduce internal and external organizational buffers, and increase but also allow the management of interdependence (Rockart & Short, 1991). These processes may generate new behavioral and conceptual spaces, changing both actions in, and thinking about, organizations (Taylor & Van Every, 1993). That is, CISs provide occasions for institutionalization of changes in power, participation in communication networks, and meanings and relations within and across organizations.

Power

Organizational power is associated with access to and control over informal and formal rules and resources, such as communication flow, interaction norms, and hierarchical position (Blair, Roberts, & McKechnie, 1985). But *any* organizational medium (from memos to meetings) structures access to resources (intentionally or not). Current organizational information is already prefiltered, but largely in ways that we do not perceive, cannot control, or generally idealize rather than recognize as artifacts of how communication is structured and constrained. Pettigrew (1972) provides a classic case study of how differential access to interaction (involving pre-CIS media of face-to-face meetings, reports, memos, telephone calls, etc.) among organizational members was used to control the flow of information and the range of interpretations during the process of deciding on a new CIS. Moreover, differential structuring of access (by any particular medium) is neither universally good nor bad for an organization (Choo & Auster, 1993). Organizational members have always had opportunities to use unmediated and mediated interaction as ways to structure power, and will continue to do so with CISs. As Markus (1984) and others show, whether and how power is reallocated cannot be easily predicted because that depends considerably on personalities, internal organizational changes, and preexisting access to resources. For example, women are more likely to experience negative changes in work structures and skills, primarily because they hold jobs that have less power and in which CISs can play a greater role, such as routine processing (Gattiker, Gutek, & Berger, 1988; Gattiker & Howg, 1990; Gutek, 1994).

To the extent that CISs can alter some constraints—say, by reducing hierarchy, providing the occasion for development of expertise,

increasing one's centrality in online space, and allowing greater interaction and thus visibility through the network—more organizational members may share power (Blair et al., 1985; Sproull & Kiesler, 1991). And such outcomes are quite salient to those members: Joshi (1992) concluded that inequity with regards to the allocation of resources (measured in terms of role ambiguity and role conflict) was the single strongest predictor of users' reported dissatisfaction with a CIS.

CISs have the potential for changing power through providing new sources of organizational socialization and informational resources, such as ad hoc groups, distribution lists, and informal social interest groups (Eveland & Bikson, 1988; Finholt & Sproull, 1990; Rice & Steinfield, 1994; Sproull & Kiesler, 1991). For instance, increased network density, increased ability to recognize other members of the organization, less centralization of interaction, more cross-group communication, and quicker emergence of expertise were found in a group that used e-mail, compared with a comparable group of nonusers (Bikson & Eveland, 1990; see also Sproull & Kiesler, 1991). Several studies have found that over time, users in general, but early adopters in particular, increase their power and relational network centrality as they use a new CIS (Burkhardt & Brass, 1990; Hesse, Sproull, Kiesler, & Walsh, 1993; Huff, Sproull, & Kiesler, 1989).

CISs may well contribute to the erosion of organizational and even national hierarchies (Cleveland, 1985; Taylor & Van Every, 1993). Information via CISs flows easily across boundaries (so that many instead of few can be informed and participate). A CIS does not necessarily require a small set of leaders to coordinate decision making. But it may require greater cooperation among leaders. CISs may attenuate the influence of organizational legitimization and managerial trust by increasing the social space in which organizational members participate, and by emphasizing principles of self-management and semiautonomy (Perin, 1991). Indeed, Mulgan

(1991) argues that greater use and scale of telecommunications networking increases the decentralization of usage, with a corresponding loss of control and a rise in the costs of control.

Paradoxically, CISs themselves might be particularly vulnerable to changes in policy or concerns about power loss because they are not as visible or institutionalized as more traditional media structures (Perin, 1991). Perin suggests that new CIS structures may also obscure important differences in power and interests, and are not themselves necessarily free of hierarchy or conflict. Indeed, the very nature of organizational CISs may foster "strategic information behaviors" such as manipulation or distortion (Zmud, 1990). This may happen in two primary ways (in the content of a message that a system transmits/stores/distributes, or in how a message directs operations of the system itself) at a variety of system nodes (sensor, filter, router, carrier, interpreter, learner, and modifier). Zmud describes how information overload fosters the delegation, summary, or dilution of initial e-mail messages, increasing users' reliance on symbols of expertise and authority, and creating opportunities for manipulation and susceptibility to misrepresentation.

Bloomfield and Coombs (1992) emphasize "the potential role of computer-based information systems in the renegotiation of professional knowledge, discourses, and practices within organizations" (p. 461). Thus, to the extent that organizational activities involve technological terminology and jargon, and to the extent that these terms are differentially understood and valued by different members, a CIS is necessarily discursively associated with power relations (p. 467). Bloomfield and Coombs note that this power disciplines actors via norms (such as users being judged as more or less "competent" depending on their usage of technical terms). A CIS may foster a loss of power that is based on technical expertise and a weakening of group boundaries because of changes to in-group terminology

(Nelson, 1990). But it also empowers members by providing access to bodies of knowledge or discourses, enabling different kinds of action (such as technical staff members becoming internal consultants to high-level managers). Even *perceptions* of power may be influenced: In 27 CIS groups, users of "powerful" language were perceived as more attractive, credible, and persuasive relative to users of "powerless" language (Adkins & Brashers, 1995).

The potential for interconnectedness across boundaries of time and space may encourage the development of virtual communities (Rheingold, 1993) that in the long run reduce the power of geopolitical identities in politics (what Cleveland, 1985, calls the "passing of remoteness"). However, the openness of networked, participatory communication can also hinder innovation and bold initiatives, because they are then subject much earlier on to public scrutiny, defensiveness, and suspicion (Cleveland, 1985; Dutton, 1996). Cultural differences and identities may become blurred, with subsequent loss of diversity.

Communication Structures and Participation

Many studies show that CISs can overcome physical and temporal structural constraints and thereby facilitate more diverse communication (see, e.g., the early reviews by Rice & Associates, 1984). CISs may help solve some of the problems of traditional bureaucracies by reducing organizational complexity, hierarchical structures, and procedures; facilitating a better sense of members' opinions; and increasing participation and democratic interaction (Keen, 1991; Sackman & Nie, 1970; Taylor & Van Every, 1993).

In some cases, the empirical changes are considerable, such as the ability of organizational members to participate in ongoing multiple, overlapping committees because physical and temporal constraints have been reduced (Eveland & Bikson, 1988). Bishop (1993) found nearly two thirds of 950 aerospace engineers who used a variety of network applications reported increases in the amount of information available, exchange of information across organizational boundaries, and communication with others outside their own organizations. Kaye and Byrne's (1986) study of an organizational e-mail system revealed that ideas were recorded and circulated that would otherwise have been lost, opinions and decisions were better considered, information flow between organizational levels and departments increased, and more communication could be managed in the same time.

Simple increased access ("overcoming time and space") is not the whole story behind such changes, though. Lind and Zmud (1995) studied the influence of voice mail on the communication and sales performance of a multinational truck manufacturing firm by comparing sales regions that had used voice mail for nearly a year to regions that had not. They found increased and improved communication relations between sales representatives and dealership managers, primarily through direct benefits from the store-and-forward capabilities of voice mail. But voice mail was also used to signal a need for communication episodes between dealers and sales representatives, or to asynchronously establish a context for subsequent written exchanges, both of which increased dealers' satisfaction with their interactions with sales representatives.

Participation is usually less unequal in CISs than in face-to-face groups (Hiltz & Turoff, 1993; Kraemer & Pinsonneault, 1990; Rice, 1984). But users can participate more across vertical and external boundaries, as well. Online courses can foster more equal discussion among students than do traditional classrooms (Harasim, 1990; Hartman et al., 1991; Hiltz, 1986). Users in one organizational study sent 78% of their (computer-monitored) messages to others outside of their own work group, indicating extensive cross-

ing of traditional work boundaries (Bizot et al., 1991). Eveland and Bikson's (1987) study of 800 users in an R&D organization found that three quarters of the messages crossed departmental boundaries, while 40% of the messages crossed specific research project boundaries, indicating high cooperation on projects among research disciplines within broad organizational functions.

Such changes seem more likely in novel situations or new groups, when groups are not embedded in organizational structures, when other communication channels are not constrained, and when jobs are more technical than administrative. For example, Markus (1992) analyzed four field study groups that had access to groupware systems as well as participated in weekly face-to-face meetings. The groups' social contexts helped explain system usage—including one group using the system primarily so that two antagonistic members would not have to meet face-to-face! Rice (1994) found that initially the network of e-mail communication among new interns and their mentors in an R&D organization was strongly correlated with work and social networks. Over time, though, it diverged from those traditional structures as well as from formal mentor-intern relations. Eveland and Bikson (1988; Bikson & Eveland, 1990) provided strong evidence that CISs can influence the development and maintenance of both task and social networks among groups that had not interacted before, including fluctuating leadership patterns over three time periods, greater communication in all channels, greater connectedness, less centralization over time, more multiplex subcommittee relations, continued online communication after the report was completed, and considerable messaging across the task subgroups. Feldman's (1987) study of messages exchanged among 96 users indicated that 60% of the messages would not have been sent without the system, but this was even higher for people who did not know one another, who did not communicate other than by the CIS, who were spatially or organizationally distant, and who used distribution lists. Other reviews (Hiltz & Turoff, 1993; Rice, 1980, 1987, 1992; Rice & Associates, 1984; Sproull & Kiesler, 1991) summarize similar results from many studies.

Increases in horizontal and collaborative communication also seem more likely among certain types of users. An analysis of dyadic communications among administrators and technical workers found increased horizontal relations among technical workers who used e-mail. This was partially explained by the flatter internal structures of their project teams, more frequent boundary crossing to avoid extreme specialization, less analyzable tasks, and their professional socialization to work on projects in teams, and of course, e-mail use (Hinds & Kiesler, 1995). Such changes are even more likely among members of professional, dispersed occupational communities, such as academic researchers, whose values and perspectives transcend the norms of their employing organizations (Pickering & King, 1995). So organizations may have good reasons to be cautious about personnel using the Internet. These increased external network relations may weaken managerial control, provide access to unmonitored values and norms, increase external job opportunities, and allow leakage of organizational information (Gattiker, Janz, Kelley, & Schollmeyer, 1996).

Potential changes in communication associated with CISs may institutionalize new traditional organizational structures of meaning and relations, but may reinforce old ones. In one traditionally hierarchical R&D organization, 83% of all messages collected from 188 users over a three-day period were sent within a division, and 93% of messages were sent to a recipient either one job type above or below the sender, indicating little circumventing of the traditional organizational structure (Bizot et al., 1991). Eveland and Bikson (1987) found little evidence of changes in departmental or project communication clusters during 18 months of e-mail use in an R&D firm, indicating that the electronic mail system supported the intraorganizational structure of the R&D organization.

Mantovani (1994) underscores the strong organizational structurings of culture, social actors' goals, and local situations on the extent to which any democratization of participation through CISs may actually occur. He argues that access (physical, cultural, technical, and economic) to CISs is inherently unequally distributed. Equal participation does not necessarily mean equal attention from others (especially in noncooperative social contexts) because it is far easier to be selectively attentive in CISs than in face-to-face communication. Symbolic group norms may be stronger in CISs than in face-to-face contexts, and certain phases of group decision making such as negotiation and means-ends debates tend to be minimized in online discussions (Mantovani, 1994; McGrath, 1990; Rice, 1987, 1990; Spears & Lea, 1992).

Dutton (1996) suggests the possibility that the absence of formal as well as social norms that otherwise regulate online discussions may actually "undermine the very existence of such forums by chasing key individuals, such as opinion leaders and public officials, off the system" (p. 284). However, Ess (1996) applied Habermas's theory of communicative action to show that CISs have the potential to "facilitate the unconstrained discourse of communicative reasons, a discourse that leads to consensus over important norms" (p. 215), as represented by the "diverse plurality of democratic communities" of listservs and newsgroups.

Relationships among gender and participation in CISs have received considerable attention (Ebben & Mastronardi, 1993; Gattiker, 1994; Hackett, Mirvis, & Sales, 1991; Perry & Greber, 1990; Zimmerman, 1983). Because of their supposed limited bandwidth and the use of pseudonyms or anonymous accounts, CISs should reduce the influence of social and other status cues. Thus, discussion via a CIS would be expected to include more diversity of viewpoints, egalitarian participation, interpretative risk taking, and challenges to textual authority than in traditional face-to-face settings. Also, Internet connectivity can foster new organizational forms of particular interest to women, such as discussion groups centered around a specific professional interest (such as women's career development, sexual harassment awareness, or organizational mentoring).

Some studies do find evidence for empowerment and nondiscriminatory participation in CISs. Adoption of Santa Monica's Public Electronic Network (PEN) by women was encouraged by the free system and public terminals, public norms supporting community participation, system administrators' support for reinvention in design and implementation, and women's greater involvement in community politics (Collins-Jarvis, 1993).

However, some argue that the use of CISs in traditional ways may just reinforce existing gender inequities (Frissen, 1992; Sparks & van Zoonen, 1992). For example, women constitute small percentages (from 10% to 40%) of users on the major online systems (Brail, 1996). Selfe and Meyer's (1991) study of 56 teachers using a computer conference reported that men and high-profile members initiated more communications (although used fewer words per message) and disagreed more, and these differences were unaffected by options for using pseudonyms during a second 20-day usage period.

Precisely because context may be depersonalized due to anonymity and weak social feedback, online communication may be more disinhibited and critical, and lessen public awareness of social sanctions (Collins-Jarvis, 1996). This may lead to more, rather than fewer, gender-based stereotypical comments, especially when online social cues make groups' unequal and unstable power relations salient (Collins-Jarvis, 1996). Such content leads some women to drop out of, or never join, online discussions (Brail, 1996; Ebben, 1993). On the PEN system, initially, female users experienced instances of discrimination and harassment, so a few of these female users restructured some aspects of the system by forming a women's user group (Rogers, Collins-Jarvis, & Schmitz, 1994). Several of Brail's women respondents noted, however, that unpleasant disturbances occur in all communication environments (another instance of demythologizing the artifact of idealized interpersonal communication), and they would not let that discourage them from taking advantage of the Internet.

Intraorganizational Structures

Early studies of CISs and organizational structure concluded that computerization increased organizational centralization (Mowshowitz, 1976; Mumford & Banks, 1967; Whisler, 1970), increased number of job titles (Gerwin, 1981), or deskilled work by extracting local control (Braverman, 1974). Caufield's (1989) meta-analysis of technology as industrial process concluded that technology does have a direct effect on hierarchical and administrative structures. Outcomes such as increased consolidation of departments and reduced span of control occur, however, mostly within general subunits and not across broad organizational units (Perio & Prieto, 1994).

Later research included more contextual measures, such as the particular function of the system and environmental stability. These studies concluded that computerization primarily reinforced the status quo, whether that was a trend toward centralization or decentralization (Blau, Falbe, McKinley, & Tracy, 1976; Robey, 1981). Others found evidence of increased horizontal differentiation, but argued that increased differentiation does not necessarily mean a bureaucratic hierarchy: It can also support matrix and lateral relations (Bjorn-Andersen, Eason, & Robey, 1986). Along with Child (1986), they conclude that the primary influence is not technology per se but implementation and operational strategies, which are, however, typically decided by power elites.

Some familiar organizational communication roles will likely be restructured with the diffusion of CISs. For example, top managers can handle more of their correspondence through e-mail, voice mail, and word processing. One subtle consequence of this shift is the removal of secretaries from their accustomed informal role as gatekeepers and liaisons. Note, however, that in some ways this represents a reinstitutionalization of office roles before the typewriter separated secretarial from managerial activities, creating the "idealized" artifact of the now threatened executive secretary position (Johnson & Rice, 1987).

But the opposite role transformation may also occur. The unnecessary monitoring and filtering represented by middle management is being excised from many organizational structures. This change leads to a flattening of organizations' hierarchies, and new forms such as orchestration, group management, and teamwork, involving greater trust, motivation by more than pay, a willingness to change, and collaboration (Davidow & Malone, 1992; Wigand, 1985). Using CISs to access updates or relevant service processes, "lower-level" personnel now can solve nonroutine problems and take on informal guru roles, thus altering decision roles throughout the organization (Quinn & Paquette, 1990). (However, these informal roles rarely have their authority or resources restructured; Bikson & Law, 1993; Johnson & Rice, 1987.) Thus, different authority structures are being institutionalized—from one of control to one of interpersonal boundary management and empowerment (Johnson & Rice, 1987). But Hirschhorn and Gilmore (1992) warn that the loss of familiar internal organizational boundaries must be managed through formerly transparent but now exposed boundaries of authority, task, political, and identity. Such ongoing restructuring requires iterative communication within and across organization boundaries.

The physical structures of one's work, office, and organization are also evolving into new forms through the use of CISs (Fulk & DeSanctis, 1995). The physical structures of buildings and offices create considerable constraints on communication, and thus quality of work life, performance, and innovation (Al-

len, 1977; Johnson, 1993). Developments such as modular offices, shared drawing displays, wireless communication, and personal locator badges may overcome some of these constraints, while also generating others ("The New Workplace," 1996; Stone & Luchetti, 1985; Want, Hopper, Falcao, & Gibbons, 1992). Bikson and Eveland (1990) found that while there was a high negative association between the spatial distance network and the self-reported communication network for respondents of one ad hoc task force without an e-mail system, for the other task force that used the system there was little association. As many organizations are finding out, "the new work styles don't work in buildings designed for the old top-down corporation" ("The New Workplace," 1996, p. 108). Thus, traditional communication relations may, to some extent, be an artifact of "natural" physical structures, institutionalized into an "ideal" organizational communication context, which is being "threatened" by CISs. Consider, for example, how being in an elevator essentially silences all but the most ritualized interaction; compare that to anonymous brainstorming through group support systems. Integration of facsimile, mobile phone, voice messaging, rerouting of phone calls, and "smart buildings" may well foster changes in the familiar association of high organizational status with a large, remote office. Truly influential members may well become the most "virtual."

It is true, though, that the removal of these traditional aural and visual constraints can lead to a loss of sense of work privacy and an associated decline in job satisfaction (Sundstrom, Burt, & Kamp, 1980). But organizational norms of access and privacy have usually already been institutionalized for familiar media such as telephone, the office doorway, elevator interactions, and so on, creating "artifacts" that confound technological possibilities and limitations with social structuring. A case in point is a study of a networked desktop video conference system that showed that while it facilitated R&D workers' ability to make contacts and collaborate with others across offices, it still raised issues concerning norms of privacy, interruption, and access (Fish et al., 1993).

Certainly, telecommuting and telework are one form of restructuring organizations (Dürrenberger, Jaeger, Bieri, & Dahinden, 1995; Kraut, 1989; Nilles, Carlson, Gray, & Hanneman, 1976). New structures for telework range from prosaically working from home with visits to employer or client; to distance working enterprises, where enterprise workers provide information-based services to distant customers; to distributed business systems that are physically separated units (either part of same, or different enterprises) that are networked together to produce a final good or service (Dürrenberger et al., 1995; Holti, 1994, p. 263). Lower-level, female, and clerical workers, who might become even more disenfranchised through remote work (Calabrese, 1994; Soares, 1992), could decrease their isolation and simultaneously develop basic computer skills, through use of CISs (Matheson, 1992).

New organizational structures might include (a) answer networks, where networks of experts and databases can refer problems to the sufficient level of resolution; (b) overnight organizations, that assemble short-term project teams through a network, via a database of skills, evaluations, and availability; (c) internal labor markets, where services are allocated on the basis of project requirements, rather than by supervisory assignment; (d) computer-mediated decision networks that connect opinions and suggestions from multiple people at different decision phases; and (e) more effective and contextual information gatekeeping services (Malone & Rockart, 1993). Federal Express uses a CIS to avoid most middle organizational levels (an "infinitely flat" structure) and keep in constant communication with its vans and airplanes, leading to increased value-added services. This is an example of Mulgan's (1991) paradox that centralized CIS networks enable decentralized and customized decisions and service.

In the "spider's web" organization, relations among consultants and clients are supported by centralized CISs (such as expertise bulletin boards), allowing any participant to request information from, or make suggestions to, any other participant (Quinn & Paquette, 1990). As an example of "critical mass of expertise," this solution also reduces some of the potential loss to corporate memory that turnover by knowledge workers represents. Additionally, this increases switching costs for consultants considering jumping to firms that do not participate in the web, in turn allowing the more networked firms to invest more in specialized training.

Other new forms include "postmodern" (Bergquist, 1993) and "postbureaucratic" (Heydebrand, 1989) organizations. Such new organizational structures tend to involve fewer physical assets, customer information and communication as primary assets, increased informality, greater cross-organizational networking, and more permeable and transitory organizational boundaries. Crucial to their success is an increased dependence on strong cultures within, and trust and relationships across, organizations, implying increased interdependence. This in turn requires more mutual adjustment and cooperative mechanisms across suborganizations, such as cross-functional teams, ad hoc project teams, task rotation, overlapping electronic group memberships, and novel reward policies (Quinn & Paquette, 1990).

Interorganizational Structures

CISs can be used to restructure interorganizational boundaries, and these new structures also require and foster new forms of CISs. Such systems influence the transaction costs of acquiring knowledge, communicating, coordination, distribution, and producing and enforcing contracts, within and across organizations (Gurbaxani & Whang, 1991; Malone, Yates, & Benjamin, 1989; Monge & Contractor, Chapter 12, this volume).

The restructuring of organizations from clearly bounded, hierarchical structures to new forms has increased the possibilities for interorganizational relations. CISs can allow formerly separate and rival organizations to engage in new forms of cooperation, such as joint marketing partnerships (online services), intraindustry partnerships (electronic publishing ventures), customer-supplier partnerships (electronic document interchange), and CIS vendor-driven partnerships (using liaison CIS networks to enter new markets) as well as many other emerging structures (Cronin, 1994; Gale, 1994; Granstrand & Sjölander, 1990; Hart & Rice, 1988; Hepworth, 1989; Konsynski & McFarlan, 1990; Monge & Contractor, this volume).

Paradoxically, CISs may foster a return to small organizations, embedded in larger organizational networks involving long-term relationships with one or more suppliers (Ciborra, 1987; Davidow & Malone, 1992). These would be communication-rich environments where information flows blur traditional internal and external boundaries, perhaps leading to "boundaryless organizations" (Ashkenas, Ulrich, Jick, & Kerr, 1995; Rockart & Short, 1991). Other transformations include the creation of virtual electronic markets where customers, suppliers, and distributors interact in a largely seamless web (Dordick, Bradley, & Nanus, 1981). The Internet has ushered in the era of electronic commerce; online interactive sales are estimated to rise from the $350 million exchanged in 1995 to nearly $7 billion in 2000 (Kalakota & Whinston, 1996; Rupley, 1996). Another example is the French videotext network, where the national telephone system provides the transmission technology and the gateway software for information providers, individuals, or other businesses to exchange services and information (Steinfield, Caby, & Vialle, 1992).

Any discussion of the benefits or transcendence of the "network organization" should, however, consider the limitations and disadvantages of this new structure. These may include stifling of innovation, ambiguities in the nature of relationships, asymmetric commitment, conflict over control, personality and cultural differences, loss of autonomy and security, time lags, managing complexity, structural constraints, narrow managerial perspectives, manipulation and ulterior motives, mismatched or incomplete knowledge and competence, increased dependencies, and so on (Camagni, 1993; Nohria & Eccles, 1992).

Universities and academic professionals have always been a somewhat unique organizational form. They already incorporate various aspects of the "boundaryless organization" (conceptualized as "the invisible college"), but they, too, are undergoing transformations associated with CISs. The traditional cycle of scientific communication (conceptualization, documentation, and popularization, with some feedback loops) may change, by increased collaboration, diffusion, and feedback, through CISs, leading to an era of "telescience" (Lievrouw & Carley, 1990). CIS networks increase the intensity and diversity of communication and participants, the "stock" of ideas, and awareness of others' work (Hiltz, 1984; Hiltz & Turoff, 1993; Kerr & Hiltz, 1982).

The academic journal may evolve into new structures such as separate articles published and distributed on demand or retrieved by "intelligent agents," independently of other articles that have traditionally, but artifactually, been seen as constituting a regularly published "journal issue" (Kolb, 1996). Further, the content of the "article" may no longer be fixed, as readers and colleagues may provide ongoing feedback, evaluations, or addenda associated with the original material, through hypermedia linkages managed through World Wide Web interfaces. In the extreme, academic institutions may be restructured through direct distribution of materials from authors to readers via the Internet and personal or organizational Web pages. Readers may use on-demand publishing from optical archives, online databases, and Internet file transfer protocol (Gattiker, in press). Online courses, degrees, and educational organizations will not only challenge traditional organizational forms such as university campuses and classrooms but also redefine how learning itself is structured (Harasim, 1990; Harrison & Stephen, 1996). However, many boundaries in scholarly communication have been changing for some time, obscured by the "artifacts" of "familiar" academic media. For example, photocopying, microfilm, facsimile, and online databases have dramatically, but quietly, transformed relations among scholars, producers, publishers, vendors, libraries, and students (Schauder, 1994).

Summary

CISs can provide the occasion for the evolution of the fundamental basis of organizational power—the structuring of interaction—into new forms and locations. One way this may occur is through exposing hierarchy and authority as largely artifacts of traditional constraints on organizational structures. CISs have been associated with transformations in the communication flow within organizations when groups are less embedded in preexisting organizational structures (such as new or project-based groups, or cross-structural roles such as technical workers). A variety of social and organizational structures foster differences in men's and women's attitudes toward, and use of, CISs. To the extent that CISs, like other media, are malleable and socially adapted, they can be structured to foster positive or negative differences, or even mute differences, for good and ill.

CISs, by removing some structural constraints, will expose widely accepted communication norms as the artifacts they are, generating the need to develop and manage new norms. Unfortunately, limited conceptualizations of media will foster applying familiar norms to evaluating CISs, thus institutionalizing limited and constrained uses and interpretations of CISs. Managers may develop more integrated communication processing through CISs, and need to develop new ways of managing increasingly amorphous boundaries. At the same time, the role of "middle manager" may be largely deinstitutionalized from organizational structure. A wide diversity of orga-

nizational forms is emerging. New institutionalized structures associated with CIS networks are far more complex than the traditional opposition of "centralized or decentralized structures." This ongoing process probably best highlights the constant interactive and iterative relationships among CISs and organizational structuring. Academic institutions and communities, an early form of "virtual organization," are also undergoing structural changes associated with CISs.

CONCLUSION

This chapter has suggested both explicit and latent themes concerning theory and research on organizational structure and new communication and information systems.

Several explicit themes structured this review. Organizational structures include meanings and relations, within and across organizations. Such structures can constrain or facilitate the development and use of CISs. Transformations of structures of organizational communication and CISs may involve intentional processes of metastructuring, or nearly invisible evolutions of the form, nature, and temporal orientation of communication content. And CISs can constrain or institutionalize changes within and across organizational structures.

Table 14.2 summarizes these arenas of interaction between CISs and structure. This is not intended to portray a comprehensive, fully specified, or causal theoretical model, but rather to suggest various strands of research that seem to focus on different microprocesses of these three generalized processes involving CISs and organizational structuring of relations and meaning.

This framework may help to identify arenas for future research that would illuminate how microprocesses co-occur or moderate each other within each generalized process, and how microprocesses influence each other across generalized processes. For example,

TABLE 14.2 Summary Model of Macro- and Microprocesses of CISs and Organizational Structuring of Meaning and Relations

Structural influences on adoption and implementation of CISs
- Media genres and usage norms
- Culture
- Media richness and social presence
- Communication networks
- Critical mass
- Physical location

Transformations of organizational structures and CISs
- Nature of content
- Form of content
- Temporal aspects of content
- Group communication
- Metastructuring

CIS influences on organizational structures
- Power
- Communication networks and participation
- Intraorganizational forms
- Interorganizational forms

there has been increasing work on the contingent relations among media richness/social presence, communication networks, social influences, critical mass, and physical location in how they influence adoption, choice, and use of new media (Rice & Aydin, 1991; Rice et al., 1990). However, few of these and other prior structures have been considered in analyzing transformations of the nature, form, and temporal aspects of content, except perhaps in qualitative approaches to describing new media genres (Orlikowski et al., 1995). Only a few studies have considered how these transformations may be institutionalized into new intraorganizational forms, ranging from the role of signatures in e-mail messages (Sherblom, 1988) to forms of power embedded in participatory discourse enabled through organization-wide listservs (Sproull & Kiesler, 1991) and public computer conferences (Dutton, 1996).

This framework might be useful in developing implementation policies that emphasize metastructuring. For example, a better understanding of how new media can (though not necessarily) facilitate increased participation can be used to foster metastructuring discussion groups. These could then intentionally and consciously develop possible metastructuring procedures and roles to help shape transformations between prior structures and desired restructurings. This process itself, however, is a topic ripe for research. To what extent has the by-now familiar notion of "free agency" and "social construction of reality" become idealized into an invisible artifact of uninformed and unmanaged "social influences"? Once we have identified processes of adaptive structuration (Poole & DeSanctis, 1990), should these microprocesses be managed by participants in any conscious way? Can they be? Is the process of sociotechnical design inherently flawed because it must be intentional and conscious?

One latent theme of this chapter is that research on organizational structure and CISs—both supportive and critical—tends to be structured by past conventions about and research traditions in communication processes, new media, and organizational structure (for a review of perspectives, see Rice, 1992). In particular, organizational researchers and ordinary folk alike tend to compare the constraints and advantages of new media not to those of older media at similar stages of development, implementation, and structuring, but to idealizations and consequent artifacts of familiar media. Thus, we argue, one goal of a structurational approach toward CISs and organizational communication should be to "uncover" asymmetric assumptions about "old" and "new" media in organizational settings. It should force us to identify factors and processes that are conceptually distinguishable, but artifactually confounded, in familiar media and research practices. It seems fairly obvious that neither the determinism of technological utopianism nor the determinism of critical pessimism is free from constraining assumptions that limit our understanding of how CISs are embedded in organizational structures and in restructurings of organizational meanings and relations.

A second latent theme of this chapter is that pluralistic, multimethod approaches that involve triangulation of both method and analysis are necessary to better identify and understand the microprocesses of (re)structuring. A more subtle aspect of this theme, however, is that specific theoretical approaches that appear to be opposed may, in fact, be complementary approaches that just focus on different components of one of the three generalized processes. For example, some have tried to artificially characterize media richness theory as a "rational choice theory," which then obviously suffers in comparison to social influence models that are "social construction of reality theory." But this confounds structural facilitation with "meaning" and structural constraints with "technology." It may well be more enlightening to show how both objective and subjective influences both constrain and facilitate, so that media richness theory and social influence theory can both contribute to understanding structural influence on the adoption and implementation of CISs.

REFERENCES

Acker, J. (1990). Hierarchies, jobs, bodies: A theory of gendered organizations. *Gender & Society, 4*(2), 139-158.

Adams, D., Todd, P., & Nelson, R. (1993). A comparative evaluation of the impact of electronic and voice mail on organizational communication. *Information & Management, 24*(1), 9-22.

Adkins, M., & Brashers, D. (1995). The power of language in computer-mediated groups. *Management Communication Quarterly, 8*(3), 289-322.

Albrecht, T., & Hall, B. (1991). Relational and content differences between elites and outsiders in innovation networks. *Human Communication Research, 17*(4), 535-561.

Allen, T. (1977). *Managing the flow of technology.* Cambridge, MA: MIT Press.

Anderson, J. G., Jay, S. J., Schweer, H. M., & Anderson, M. M. (1987). Physician communication networks and the adoption and utilization of computer applications in medicine. In J. G. Anderson & S. J. Jay (Eds.), *Use and impact of computers in clinical medicine* (pp. 185-199). New York: Springer-Verlag.

Archea, J. (1977). The place of architectural factors in behavioral theories of privacy. *Journal of Social Issues, 33*(3), 116-137.

Ashkenas, R., Ulrich, D., Jick, T., & Kerr, S. (1995). *The boundaryless organization: Breaking the chains of organizational structure.* San Francisco: Jossey-Bass.

Beniger, J. (1986). *The control revolution: Technological and economic origins of the information society.* Cambridge, MA: Harvard University Press.

Bergquist, W. (1993). *The postmodern organization: Mastering the art of irreversible change.* San Francisco: Jossey-Bass.

Berthold, M., Sudweeks, F., Newton, S., & Coyne, R. (1996). "It makes sense": Using an autoassociative neural network to explore typicality in computer mediated discussions. In S. Rafaeli, F. Sudweeks, & M. McLaughlin (Eds.), *Network and netplay: Virtual groups on the Internet* (pp. 191-220). Cambridge, MA: AAAI/MIT Press.

Bikson, T., & Eveland, J. D. (1990). The interplay of work group structures and computer support. In J. Galegher, R. Kraut, & C. Egido (Eds.), *Intellectual teamwork: Social and technological bases of cooperative work* (pp. 245-290). Hillsdale, NJ: Lawrence Erlbaum.

Bikson, T., & Law, S. (1993). Electronic mail use at the World Bank: Messages from users. *Information Society, 9(2)*, 89-134.

Bishop, A. (1993). *The role of computer networks in aerospace engineering.* Urbana: University of Illinois, Graduate School of Library Science.

Bizot, E., Smith, N., & Hill, T. (1991). Use of electronic mail in a research and development organization. In J. Morell & M. Fleischer (Eds.), *Advances in the implementation and impact of computer systems* (Vol. 1, pp. 65-92). Greenwich, CT: JAI.

Bjorn-Andersen, N., Eason, K., & Robey, D. (1986). *Managing computer impact: An international study of management and organizations.* Norwood, NJ: Ablex.

Black, S., Levin, J., Mehan, H., & Quinn, C. (1983). Real and non-real time interaction: Unraveling multiple threads of discourse. *Discourse Processes, 6,* 59-75.

Blair, R., Roberts, K. H., & McKechnie, P. (1985). Vertical and network communication in organizations: The present and the future. In R. D. McPhee & P. K. Tompkins (Eds.), *Organizational communication: Traditional themes and new directions* (pp. 55-79). Beverly Hills, CA: Sage.

Blau, P., Falbe, C., McKinley, W., & Tracy, P. (1976). Technology and organization in manufacturing. *Administrative Science Quarterly, 21*(1), 20-40.

Bloomfield, B., & Coombs, R. (1992). Information technology, control and power: The centralization and decentralization debate revisited. *Journal of Management Studies, 29*(4), 459-484.

Bozeman, D. (1993). Toward a limited rationality perspective of managerial media selection in organizations. In D. Moore (Ed.), *Proceedings of the 1993 Academy of Management meeting* (pp. 278-282). Madison, WI: Omni.

Brail, S. (1996). The price of admission: Harassment and free speech in the wild, wild west. In L. Cherny & E. Weise (Eds.), *Wired-women: Gender and new realities in cyberspace* (pp. 157-182). Seattle, WA: Seal.

Brand, S. (1987). *The media lab: Reinventing the future at MIT.* New York: Viking.

Braverman, H. (1974). *Labor and monopoly capital: The degradation of work in the 20th century.* New York: Monthly Review Press.

Bump, J. (1990). Radical changes in class discussion using networked computers. *Computers and the Humanities, 24,* 49-65.

Burkhardt, M. (1994). Social interaction effects following a technological change: A longitudinal investigation. *Academy of Management Journal, 37*(4), 869-898.

Burkhardt, M., & Brass, D. (1990). Changing patterns or patterns of change: The effects of a change in technology on social network structure and power. *Administrative Science Quarterly, 35*(1), 104-127.

Camagni, R. (1993). Inter-firm industrial networks: The costs and benefits of cooperative behaviour. *Journal of Industry Studies, 1*(1), 1-15.

Calabrese, A. (1994). Home-based telework and the politics of private woman and public man: A critical appraisal. In U. E. Gattiker (Ed.), *Studies in technical innovation and human resources: Women and technology* (Vol. 4, pp. 161-199). Berlin and New York: Walter de Gruyter.

Carey, J. (1990). The language of technology: Talk, text, and template as metaphors for communication. In M. Medhurst, A. Gonzalez, & T. Peterson (Eds.), *Communication and the culture of technology* (pp. 19-39). Pullman: Washington State University Press.

Carlson, J., & Zmud, R. (1994). Channel expansion theory: A dynamic view of media and information richness perceptions. In D. Moore (Ed.), *Proceedings of the 1994 Academy of Management meeting* (pp. 280-284). Madison, WI: Omni.

Caufield, C. (1989). An integrative research review of the relationship between technology and structure: A meta-analytic synthesis (Ph.D. dissertation, University of Iowa, Ames). *Dissertation Abstracts International, 51,* 553A.

Child, J. (1986). New technology and developments in management organisation. In T. Lupton (Ed.), *Human factors: Man, machine and new technology* (pp. 137-156). Berlin: IFS Pub. Ltd., UK and Springer-Verlag.

Choo, C. W., & Auster, E. (1993). Environmental scanning: Acquisition and use of information by managers. In M. Williams (Ed.), *Annual review of information science and technology* (Vol. 28, pp. 279-314). Medford, NJ: Learned Information.

Choudhury, V., & Sampler, J. (1997). Information specificity and environmental scanning: An economic perspective. *MIS Quarterly, 21*(1), 25-54.

Ciborra, C. (1987). Reframing the role of computers in organizations—The transaction costs approach. *Office: Technology and People, 3,* 17-38.

Cleveland, H. (1985, January-February). The twilight of hierarchy: Speculations on the global information society. *Public Administration Review, 45,* 185-195.

Collins-Jarvis, L. (1993). Gender representation in an electronic city hall: Female adoption of Santa Monica's PEN system. *Journal of Broadcasting and Electronic Media, 37*(1), 49-65.

Collins-Jarvis, L. (1996, May). *Discriminatory messages in on-line discussion groups: The role of gender identity and social context.* Paper presented at International Communication Association, Chicago.

Contractor, N., & Eisenberg, E. (1990). Communication networks and new media in organizations. In J. Fulk & C. Steinfield (Eds.), *Organizations and communication technology* (pp. 143-172). Newbury Park, CA: Sage.

Craipeau, S. (1994). Telematics and corporate regulations. In J. E. Andriessen & R. Roe (Eds.), *Telematics and work* (pp. 289-311). Hillsdale, NJ: Lawrence Erlbaum.

Cronin, M. (1994). *Doing business on the Internet: How the electronic highway is transforming American companies.* New York: Van Nostrand Reinhold.

Culnan, M. J., & Markus, M. L. (1987). Information technologies. In F. M. Jablin, L. L. Putnam, K. H. Roberts, & L. W. Porter (Eds.), *Handbook of organizational communication: An interdisciplinary perspective* (pp. 420-443). Newbury Park, CA: Sage.

Daft, R. L., & Lengel, R. H. (1986). Organizational information requirements, media richness and structural design. *Management Science, 32,* 554-571.

D'Ambra, J., & Rice, R. E. (1994). The equivocality of media richness: A multi-method approach to analyzing selection of voice mail for equivocal tasks. *IEEE Transactions on Professional Communication, 37*(4), 231-239.

David, P. (1985). Clio and the economics of QWERTY. *American Economic Review, 75*(2), 332-337.

Davidow, W., & Malone, M. (1992). *The virtual corporation: Structuring and vitalizing the company for the 21st century.* New York: Burlingame/Harper.

Davis, T. R. (1984). The influence of the physical environment in offices. *Academy of Management Review, 9,* 271-283.

Dawson, K. (1995). Comments on "Read me what it says on your screen . . ." *Technology Studies, 2,* 80-85.

DeSanctis, G., & Poole, M. S. (1994). Capturing the complexity in advanced technology use: Adaptive structuration theory. *Organization Science, 5*(2), 121-147.

Dordick, H., Bradley, H., & Nanus, B. (1981). *The emerging network marketplace.* Norwood, NJ: Ablex.

Dubinskas, F. (1993). Virtual organizations: Computer conferencing and the technology-organization relationship. *Journal of Organizational Computing, 3*(4), 389-416.

Dürrenberger, G., Jaeger, C., Bieri, L., & Dahinden, U. (1995). Telework and vocational contact. *Technology Studies, 2,* 104-131.

Dutton, W. (1996). Network rules of order: Regulating speech in public electronic fora. *Media, Culture & Society, 18,* 269-290.

Dutton, W. H., & Danziger, J. N. (1982). Computers and politics. In J. N. Danziger, W. H. Dutton, R. Kling, & K. L. Kraemer (Eds.), *Computers and politics: High technology in American local governments* (pp. 1-21). New York: Columbia University Press.

Ebben, M. (1993, October). *Women on the net: An exploratory study of gender dynamics on the Soc.women computer network.* Paper presented at the 16th annual conference of the Organization for the Study of Communication, Language and Gender, Tempe, AZ.

Ebben, M., & Mastronardi, J. (1993). Women and information technology: An annotated bibliography. In J. Taylor, C. Kramarae, & M. Ebben (Eds.), *Women, information technology and scholarship* (pp. 78-121). Urbana-Champaign: University of Illinois, Center for Advanced Study.

Ehrlich, S. (1987). Strategies for encouraging successful adoption of office communication systems. *ACM Transactions on Office Information Systems, 5*(4), 340-357.

Ess, C. (1996). The political computer: Democracy, CMC, and Habermas. In C. Ess (Ed.), *Philosophical perspectives on computer-mediated communication* (pp. 197-230). Albany: State University of New York Press.

Eveland, J. D., & Bikson, T. E. (1987). Evolving electronic communication networks: An empirical assessment. *Office: Technology and People, 3,* 103-128.

Eveland, J. D., & Bikson, T. E. (1988). Workgroup structures and computer support: A field experiment. *ACM Transactions on Office Information Systems, 6*(4), 354-379.

Feldman, M. S. (1987). Electronic mail and weak ties in organizations. *Office: Technology and People, 3,* 83-101.

Finholt, T., & Sproull, L. (1990). Electronic groups at work. *Organization Science, 1*(1), 41-64.

Finholt, T., Sproull, L., & Kiesler, S. (1990). Communication and performance in ad hoc task groups. In J. Galegher, R. Kraut, & C. Egido (Eds.), *Intellectual teamwork: Social and technological bases of cooperative work* (pp. 291-325). Hillsdale, NJ: Lawrence Erlbaum.

Finn, T. A. (1986). An introduction to voice mail. In S. Guengerich (Ed.), *1986 office automation conference digest* (pp. 43-51). Washington, DC: American Federation of Information Processing Societies.

Fish, R., Kraut, R., Root, R., & Rice, R. E. (1993). Video as a technology for informal communication. *Communications of the ACM, 36*(1), 48-61.

Frissen, V. (1992). Trapped in electronic cages? Gender and new information technologies in the public and private domain: An overview of research. *Media, Culture & Society, 14,* 31-39.

Fulk, J. (1993). Social construction of communication technology. *Academy of Management Journal, 36*(5), 921-950.

Fulk, J., & DeSanctis, G. (1995). Electronic communication and changing organizational forms. *Organization Science, 6*(4), 337-349.

Fulk, J., Steinfield, C. W., & Schmitz, J. (1990). A social information processing model of media use in organizations. In J. Fulk & C. Steinfield (Eds.), *Organizations and communication technology* (pp. 117-140). Newbury Park, CA: Sage.

Gale, I. (1994). Price competition in noncooperative joint ventures. *International Journal of Industrial Organization, 12(1)*, 53-70.

Galletta, D., Ahuja, M., Hartman, A., Teo, T., & Peace, A. (1995). Social influence and end-user training. *Communications of the ACM, 38(7)*, 70-79.

Gattiker, U. E. (1990). *Technology management in organizations.* Newbury Park, CA: Sage.

Gattiker, U. E. (Ed.). (1994). *Studies in technical innovation and human resources: Women and technology* (Vol. 4). New York: Walter de Gruyter.

Gattiker, U. E. (in press). *Moral and economic issues on the information highway: Balancing interests.* Mahwah, NJ: Lawrence Erlbaum.

Gattiker, U. E., Gutek, B., & Berger, D. (1988). Office technology and employee attitudes. *Social Science Computer Review, 6*, 327-340.

Gattiker, U. E., & Howg, L. W. (1990). Information technology and quality of work life: Comparing users with non-users. *Journal of Business and Psychology, 5*, 237-260.

Gattiker, U. E., Janz, L., Kelley, H., & Schollmeyer, M. (1996). Information technology—The Internet and privacy: Do you know who's watching? *Business Quarterly, 60(4)*, 79-85.

Gattiker, U. E., & Kelley, H. (1999). Morality and computers: Attitudes and differences in moral judgments across populations. *Information Systems Research, 10*, 223-254.

Gattiker, U. E., Kelley, H., & Janz, L. (1996). The information highway: Opportunities and challenges for organizations. In R. Berndt (Ed.), *Global management* (pp. 417-453). Berlin and New York: Springer-Verlag.

Gattiker, U. E., Kelley, H., Paulson, D., & Bhatnagar, D. (1996). User information satisfaction: A comparison of three countries. *Journal of Organizational Behavior.*

Gattiker, U. E., & Nelligan, T. (1988). Computerized offices in Canada and the United States: Investigating dispositional similarities and differences. *Journal of Organizational Behavior, 9(1)*, 77-96.

Gattiker, U. E., & Paulson, D. (1999). Unions and new office technology. *Relations Industrielles, 54*, 245-276.

Gattiker, U. E., & Willoughby, K. (1993). Technological competence, ethics, and the global village: Cross-national comparisons for organization research. In R. Golembiewski (Ed.), *Handbook of organizational behavior* (pp. 457-485). New York: Marcel Dekker.

Gerwin, D. (1981). Relationships between structure and technology. In P. C. Nystrom & W. H. Starbuck (Eds.), *Handbook of organizational design: Vol. 2.*

Remodeling organizations and their environments (pp. 3-38). New York: Oxford University Press.

Giddens, A. (1976). *New rules of sociological method.* London: Hutchinson.

Giddens, A. (1984). *The constitution of society.* Berkeley: University of California Press.

Grande, S. (1980). Aspects of pre-literate culture shared by online searching and videotex. *Canadian Journal of Information Science, 5*, 125-131.

Granstrand, O., & Sjölander, S. (1990). The acquisition of technology and small firms by large firms. *Journal of Economic Behavior and Organization, 13*, 367-386.

Gurbaxani, V. (1990). Diffusion in computing networks: The case of Bitnet. *Communications of the ACM, 33(12)*, 65-75.

Gurbaxani, V., & Whang, S. (1991). The impact of information systems on organizations and markets. *Communications of the ACM, 34(1)*, 59-73.

Gutek, B. A. (1994). Clerical work and information technology: Implications of managerial assumptions. In U. E. Gattiker (Ed.), *Technological innovation and human resources: Women and technology* (Vol. 4, pp. 205-225). Berlin and New York: Walter de Gruyter.

Hackett, E., Mirvis, P., & Sales, A. (1991). Women's and men's expectations about the effects of new technology at work. *Group and Organization Studies, 16(1)*, 60-85.

Haines, V. (1988). Social network analysis, structuration theory and the holism-individualism debate. *Social Networks, 10(2)*, 157-182.

Harasim, L. (1990). *Online education: Perspectives on a new environment.* New York: Praeger.

Harrison, T., & Stephen, T. (Eds.). (1996). *Computer networking and scholarly communication in the twenty-first-century university.* Albany: State University of New York Press.

Hart, P., & Rice, R. E. (1988). Inter-industry relations in electronic news services. *Journal of the American Society for Information Science, 39(4)*, 252-261.

Hartman, K., Neuwirth, C., Kiesler, S., Sproull, L., Cochran, C., Palmquist, M., & Zubrow, D. (1991). Patterns of social interaction and learning to write. *Written Communication, 8(1)*, 79-113.

Hayne, S., & Rice, R. E. (1997). Accuracy of attribution in small groups using anonymity in group support systems. *International Journal of Human Computer Studies, 47*, 429-452.

Hepworth, M. (1989). *Geography of the information economy.* London: Belhaven.

Hesse, B., Sproull, L., Kiesler, S., & Walsh, J. (1993). Returns to science: Computer networks in oceanography. *Communications of the ACM, 36(8)*, 90-101.

Hesse, B., Werner, C., & Altman, I. (1988). Temporal aspects of computer-mediated communication. *Computers in Human Behavior, 4*, 147-165.

Heydebrand, W. (1989). New organizational forms. *Work and Occupations, 16*(3), 323-357.

Hiltz, S. R. (1984). *Online communities: A case study of the office of the future.* Norwood, NJ: Ablex.

Hiltz, S. R. (1986). The "virtual classroom": Using computer-mediated communication for university teaching. *Journal of Communication, 36*(2), 95-104.

Hiltz, S. R., & Turoff, M. (1993). *The network nation: Human communication via computer* (2nd ed.). Reading, MA: Addison-Wesley.

Hiltz, S. R., Turoff, M., & Johnson, K. (1989). Experiments in group decision making, 3: Dis-inhibition, de-individuation and group process in pen name and real name computer conferences. *Decision Support Systems, 5*(2), 217-232.

Hinds, P., & Kiesler, S. (1995). Communication across boundaries: Work, structure, and use of communication technologies in a large organization. *Organization Science, 6*(4), 373-393.

Hirschhorn, L., & Gilmore, T. (1992, May-June). The new boundaries of the "boundaryless" company. *Harvard Business Review, 70*(3), 104-116.

Hofstede, G. (1993). Cultural constraints in management theories. *Academy of Management Executive, 7*(1), 81-94.

Holti, R. (1994). Telematics, workplaces and homes: The evolving picture of teleworking. In J. E. Andriessen & R. Roe (Eds.), *Telematics and work* (pp. 261-288). Hillsdale, NJ: Lawrence Erlbaum.

Howell, J., & Higgins, C. (1990). Champions of technological innovation. *Administrative Science Quarterly, 35,* 317-341.

Huff, C., Sproull, L., & Kiesler, S. (1989). Computer communication and organizational commitment: Tracing the relationship in a city government. *Journal of Applied Social Psychology, 19,* 1371-1391.

Jablin, F. M. (1987). Formal organization structure. In F. M. Jablin, L. L. Putnam, K. H. Roberts, & L. W. Porter (Eds.), *Handbook of organizational communication: An interdisciplinary perspective* (pp. 389-419). Newbury Park, CA: Sage.

Jensen, J. (1990). *Redeeming modernity: Contradictions in media criticism.* Newbury Park, CA: Sage.

Jessup, L., Connolly, T., & Tansik, D. (1990). Toward a theory of automated group work: The deindividuating effects of anonymity. *Small Group Research, 21,* 333-348.

Johnson, B., & Rice, R. (1987). *Managing organizational innovation: The evolution from word processing to office information systems.* New York: Columbia University Press.

Johnson, J. D. (1993). *Organizational communication structure.* Norwood, NJ: Ablex.

Johnson-Lenz, P., & Johnson-Lenz, T. (1991). Post-mechanistic groupware primitives: Rhythms, boundaries and containers. *International Journal of Man-Machine Studies, 34,* 395-417.

Joshi, K. (1992). A causal path model of the overall user attitudes toward the MIS function: The case of user information satisfaction. *Information & Management, 22,* 77-88.

Kalakota, R., & Whinston, A. (1996). *Frontiers of electronic commerce.* Reading, MA: Addison-Wesley.

Kaye, A. R., & Byrne, K. E. (1986). Insights on the implementation of a computer-based message system. *Information & Management, 10,* 277-284.

Keen, P. (1991). *Shaping the future: Business design through information technology.* Boston: Harvard Business School Press.

Kerr, E., & Hiltz, S. R. (1982). *Computer-mediated communication systems.* New York: Academic Press.

Kling, R., & Jewett, T. (1994). The social design of worklife with computers and networks: An open natural systems perspective. *Advances in Computers, 39,* 239-293.

Kolb, D. (1996). Discourse across links. In C. Ess (Ed.), *Philosophical perspectives on computer-mediated communication* (pp. 15-41). Albany: State University of New York Press.

Konsynski, B., & McFarlan, W. (1990). Information partnerships—Shared data, shared scale. *Harvard Business Review, 68*(5), 114-120.

Kraemer, K., & Pinsonneault, A. (1990). Technology and groups: Assessments of the empirical research. In J. Galegher, R. Kraut, & C. Egido (Eds.), *Intellectual teamwork: Social and technological foundations of cooperative work* (pp. 373-404). Hillsdale, NJ: Lawrence Erlbaum.

Kraut, R. (1989). Telecommuting: The trade-offs of home work. *Journal of Communication, 39*(3), 19-47.

Lea, M. (1991). Rationalist assumptions in cross-media comparisons of computer-mediated communication. *Behaviour and Information Technology, 10*(2), 153-172.

Lea, M., O'Shea, T., & Fung, P. (1995). Constructing the networked organization: Content and context in the development of electronic communications. *Organization Science, 6*(4), 462-478.

Leonard-Barton, D., & Deschamps, I. (1988). Managerial influence in the implementation of new technology. *Management Science, 32*(10), 1252-1265.

Lievrouw, L., & Carley, K. (1990). Changing patterns of communication among scientists in an era of "telescience." *Technology in Society, 12,* 1-21.

Lind, M., & Zmud, R. (1995). Improving interorganizational effectiveness through voice mail facilitation of peer-to-peer relationships. *Organization Science, 6*(4), 445-461.

Mackay, W. (1988). Diversity in the use of electronic mail. *ACM Transactions on Office Information Systems, 6*(4), 380-397.

Malone, T., Grant, K., Turbak, F., Brobst, S., & Cohen, M. (1987). Intelligent information-sharing systems. *Communications of the ACM, 30*(5), 390-402.

Malone, T., & Rockart, J. (1993). How will information technology reshape organizations? Computers as co-ordination technology. In S. Bradley, J. Hausman, & R. Nolan (Eds.), *Globalization, technology, and competition: The fusion of computers and telecommunications in the 1990s* (pp. 37-56). Boston: Harvard Business School Press.

Malone, T., Yates, J., & Benjamin, R. (1989). The logic of electronic markets. *Harvard Business Review, 67*(3), 166-170.

Mantovani, G. (1994). Is computer-mediated communication intrinsically apt to enhance democracy in organizations? *Human Relations, 47*(1), 45-62.

Markus, M. L. (1984). *Systems in organizations: Bugs & features.* Boston: Pitman.

Markus, M. L. (1990). Toward a critical mass theory of interactive media: Universal access, interdependence and diffusion. In J. Fulk & C. Steinfield (Eds.), *Organizations and communication technology* (pp. 194-218). Newbury Park, CA: Sage.

Markus, M. L. (1992). Asynchronous technologies in small face-to-face groups. *Information Technology & People, 6*(1), 29-48.

Markus, M. L., & Robey, D. (1988). Information technology and organizational change: Causal structure in theory and research. *Management Science, 34*(5), 583-598.

Marvin, C. (1988). *When old technologies were new.* New York: Oxford University Press.

Matheson, K. (1992). Women and computer technology: Communicating for herself. In M. Lea (Ed.), *Contexts of computer-mediated communication* (pp. 66-88). New York: Harvester-Wheatsheaf.

Maurice, M., Sorge, A., & Warner, M. (1980). Societal differences in organizing manufacturing units: A comparison of France, West Germany, and Great Britain. *Organization Studies, 1,* 59-86.

McGrath, J. (1990). Time matters in groups. In J. Galegher, R. Kraut, & C. Egido (Eds.), *Intellectual teamwork: Social and technological foundations of cooperative work* (pp. 23-62). Hillsdale, NJ: Lawrence Erlbaum.

McGrath, J. E., & Hollingshead, A. B. (1992). Putting the "group" back in group support systems: Some theoretical issues about dynamic processes in groups with technological enhancements. In L. M. Jessup & J. S. Valacich (Eds.), *Group support systems: New perspectives* (pp. 78-96). New York: Macmillan.

McKenney, J., Zack, M., & Doherty, V. (1992). Complementary communication media: A comparison of electronic mail and face-to-face communication in a programming team. In N. Nohria & R. Eccles (Eds.), *Networks and organizations: Structure, form and action* (pp. 262-287). Boston: Harvard Business School Press.

Moore, A., & Jovanis, P. (1988). Modelling media choices in business organizations: Implications for analyzing telecommunications-transportation interactions. *Transportation Research, 22A,* 257-273.

Mowshowitz, A. (1976). *The conquest of will: Information processing in human affairs.* Menlo Park, CA: Addison-Wesley.

Mulgan, G. (1991). *Communication and control: Networks and the new economies of communication.* Oxford, UK: Polity.

Mumford, E., & Banks, O. (1967). *The computer and the clerk.* London: Routledge and Kegan Paul.

Murray, L. W. H. (1994). Women in science occupations: Some impacts of technological change. In U. E. Gattiker (Ed.), *Technological innovation and human resources: Women and technology* (Vol. 4, pp. 93-129). Berlin and New York: Walter de Gruyter.

Nelson, D. (1990, March). Individual adjustment to information-driven technologies. *MIS Quarterly, 14,* 79-98.

Newell, S., & Clark, P. (1990). The importance of extra-organizational networks in the diffusion and appropriation of new technologies. *Knowledge: Creation, Diffusion, Utilization, 12*(2), 199-212.

The new workplace. (1996, April 29). *Business Week,* pp. 106-117.

Nilles, J., Carlson, F., Gray, P., & Hanneman, G. (1976). *The telecommunication-transportation tradeoff: Options for tomorrow.* New York: Wiley Interscience.

Nohria, N., & Eccles, R. (1992). *Networks and organizations: Structure, form and action.* Boston: Harvard Business School Press.

Nunamaker, J., Dennis, A., Valacich, J., Vogel, D., & George, J. (1991). Electronic meeting systems to support group work. *Communications of the ACM, 34*(7), 40-61.

Orlikowski, W. (1992). The duality of technology: Rethinking the concept of technology in organizations. *Organization Science, 3*(3), 398-427.

Orlikowski, W., & Robey, D. (1991). Information technology and the structuring of organizations. *Information Systems Research, 2*(2), 143-169.

Orlikowski, W., & Yates, J. (1993, August). *From memo to dialogue: Enacting genres of communication in electronic media.* Paper presented at the annual meeting of the Academy of Management, Atlanta, GA.

Orlikowski, W., Yates, J., Okamura, K., & Fujimoto, M. (1995). Shaping electronic communication: The metastructuring of technology in the context of use. *Organization Science, 6*(4), 423-443.

Papa, W., & Papa, M. (1992). Communication network patterns and the re-invention of new technology. *Journal of Business Communication, 29*(1), 41-61.

Pava, C. (1983). *Managing new office technology.* New York: Free Press.

Pazy, A. (1994). Trying to combat professional obsolescence: The experience of women in technical careers. In U. E. Gattiker (Ed.), *Technological innovation and human resources: Women and technology*

(Vol. 4, pp. 65-91). Berlin and New York: Walter de Gruyter.

Perin, C. (1991). Electronic social fields in bureaucracies. *Communications of the ACM, 34*(12), 75-82.

Perio, J., & Prieto, F. (1994). Telematics and organizational structure and processes: An overview. In J. E. Andriessen & R. Roe (Eds.), *Telematics and work* (pp. 175-208). Hillsdale, NJ: Lawrence Erlbaum.

Perry, R., & Greber, L. (1990). Women and computers: An introduction. *Signs: Journal of Women in Culture and Society, 16*(1), 74-101.

Pettigrew, A. (1972). Information control as a power resource. *Sociology, 6*(2), 187-204.

Pickering, J., & King, J. L. (1995). Hardwiring weak ties: Interorganizational computer-mediated communication, occupational communities, and organizational change. *Organization Science, 6*(4), 479-486.

Poole, M. S., & DeSanctis, G. (1990). Understanding the use of group decision support systems: The theory of adaptive structuration. In J. Fulk & C. Steinfield (Eds.), *Organizations and communication technology* (pp. 173-193). Newbury Park, CA: Sage.

Quinn, J. B., & Paquette, P. (1990). Technology in services: Creating organizational revolutions. *Sloan Management Review, 31*(2), 67.

Rafaeli, S., & LaRose, R. (1993). Electronic bulletin boards and "public goods" explanations of collaborative mass media. *Communication Research, 20*(2), 277-297.

Rheingold, H. (1993). *The virtual community: Homesteading on the electronic frontier.* Reading, MA: Addison-Wesley.

Rice, R. E. (1980). Impacts of organizational and interpersonal computer-mediated communication. In M. Williams (Ed.), *Annual review of information science and technology* (Vol. 15, pp. 221-249). White Plains, NY: Knowledge Industry.

Rice, R. E. (1982). Communication networking in computer conferencing systems: A longitudinal study of group roles and system structure. In M. Burgoon (Ed.), *Communication yearbook* (Vol. 6, pp. 925-944). Beverly Hills, CA: Sage.

Rice, R. E. (1984). Mediated group communication. In R. E. Rice & Associates, *The new media: Communication, research and technology* (pp. 129-154). Beverly Hills, CA: Sage.

Rice, R. E. (1987). Computer-mediated communication systems and organizational innovation. *Journal of Communication, 37*(4), 65-94.

Rice, R. E. (1990). Computer-mediated communication system network data: Theoretical concerns and empirical examples. *International Journal of Man-Machine Studies, 30,* 1-21.

Rice, R. E. (1992). Contexts of research on organizational computer-mediated communication: A recursive review. In M. Lea (Ed.), *Contexts of computer-mediated communication* (pp. 113-144). London: Harvester-Wheatsheaf.

Rice, R. E. (1993a). Artifacts, freedoms, paradoxes and inquiries: Some ways new media challenge traditional mass media and interpersonal effects paradigms. *MultiMedia Review/Virtual Reality World, 4*(2), 30-35.

Rice, R. E. (1993b). Media appropriateness: Using social presence theory to compare traditional and new organizational media. *Human Communication Research, 19*(4), 451-484.

Rice, R. E. (1993c). Using network concepts to clarify sources and mechanisms of social influence. In W. Richards, Jr. & G. Barnett (Eds.), *Advances in communication network analysis* (pp. 43-52). Norwood, NJ: Ablex.

Rice, R. E. (1994). Relating electronic mail use and network structure to R&D work networks and performance. *Journal of Management Information Systems, 11*(1), 9-20.

Rice, R. E., & Associates. (1984). *The new media: Communication, research and technology.* Beverly Hills, CA: Sage.

Rice, R. E., & Aydin, C. (1991). Attitudes toward new organizational technology: Network proximity as a mechanism for social information processing. *Administrative Science Quarterly, 36,* 219-244.

Rice, R. E., & Case, D. (1983). Computer-based messaging in the university: A description of use and utility. *Journal of Communication, 33*(1), 131-152.

Rice, R. E., Chang, S., & Torobin, J. (1992). Communicator style, media use, organizational level, and use and evaluation of electronic messaging. *Management Communication Quarterly, 6*(1), 3-33.

Rice, R. E., & Danowski, J. (1993). Is it really just like a fancy answering machine? Comparing semantic networks of different types of voice mail users. *Journal of Business Communication, 30*(4), 369-397.

Rice, R. E., Grant, A., Schmitz, J., & Torobin, J. (1990). Individual and network influences on the adoption and perceived outcomes of electronic messaging. *Social Networks, 12*(1), 27-55.

Rice, R. E. (with Hart, P., Torobin, J., Shook, D., Tyler, J., Svenning, L., & Ruchinskas, J.). (1992). Task analyzability, use of new media, and effectiveness: A multi-site exploration of media richness. *Organization Science, 3*(4), 475-500.

Rice, R. E., Hughes, D., & Love, G. (1989). Usage and outcomes of electronic messaging at an R&D organization: Situational constraints, job level, and media awareness. *Office: Technology and People, 5*(2), 141-161.

Rice, R. E., Kraut, R., Cool, C., & Fish, R. (1994). Individual, structural and social influences on use of a new communication medium. In D. Moore (Ed.), *Proceedings of the 1994 Academy of Management meeting* (pp. 285-289). Madison, WI: Omni.

Rice, R. E., & Love, G. (1987). Electronic emotion: Socio-emotional content in a computer-mediated communication network. *Communication Research, 14*(1), 85-108.

Rice, R. E., & Shook, D. (1988). Access to, usage of, and outcomes from an electronic message system. *ACM Transactions on Office Information Systems, 6*(3), 255-276.

Rice, R. E., & Shook, D. (1990). Voice messaging, coordination and communication. In J. Galegher, R. Kraut, & C. Egido (Eds.), *Intellectual teamwork: Social and technological bases of cooperative work* (pp. 327-350). Hillsdale, NJ: Lawrence Erlbaum.

Rice, R. E., & Steinfield, C. (1994). New forms of organizational communication via electronic mail and voice messaging. In J. E. Andriessen & R. Roe (Eds.), *Telematics and work* (pp. 109-137). Hillsdale, NJ: Lawrence Erlbaum.

Rice, R. E., & Tyler, J. (1995). Innovativeness, organizational context, and voice mail use and evaluation. *Behaviour and Information Technology, 14*(6), 329-341.

Robey, D. (1981). Computer information systems and organization structure. *Communications of the ACM, 24*(10), 679-687.

Rockart, J., & Short, J. (1991). The networked organization and the management of interdependence. In M. S. Scott Morton (Ed.), *The corporation of the 1990s: Information technology and organizational transformation* (pp. 189-219). New York: Oxford University Press.

Rogers, E. M., Collins-Jarvis, L., & Schmitz, J. (1994). The PEN project in Santa Monica: Interactive communication, equality, and political action. *Journal of the American Society for Information Science, 45,* 401.

Rupley, S. (1996). Digital bucks? Stop here. *PC Magazine, 15*(10), p. 54ff.

Sackman, H., & Nie, N. (Eds.). (1970). *The information utility and social choice.* Montvale, NJ: American Federation of Information Processing Societies.

Salancik, G. R., & Pfeffer, J. (1978). A social information approach to job attitudes and task design. *Administrative Science Quarterly, 23,* 224-252.

Schaefermeyer, M., & Sewell, E. (1988). Communicating by electronic mail. *American Behavioral Scientist, 32*(2), 112-123.

Schauder, D. (1994). Electronic publishing of professional articles: Attitudes of academics and implications for the scholarly communication industry. *Journal of the American Society for Information Science, 45*(2), 73-100.

Schmitz, J., & Fulk, J. (1991). Organizational colleagues, information richness and electronic mail: A test of the social influence model of technology use. *Communication Research, 18*(4), 487-523.

Selfe, C., & Meyer, P. (1991). Testing claims for on-line conferences. *Written Communication, 8*(2), 163-192.

Sherblom, J. (1988). Direction, function and signature in electronic mail. *Journal of Business Communication, 25,* 39-54.

Short, J., Williams, E., & Christie, B. (1976). *The social psychology of telecommunications.* New York: John Wiley.

Shudson, M. (1978). The ideal of conversation in the study of mass media. *Communication Research, 5*(3), 320-329.

Sitkin, S., Sutcliffe, K., & Barrios-Choplin, J. (1992). A dual-capacity model of communication media choice in organizations. *Human Communication Research, 18*(4), 563-598.

Soares, A. S. (1992). Telework and communication in data processing centres in Brazil. In U. E. Gattiker (Ed.), *Studies in technological innovation and human resources: Technology-mediated communication* (Vol. 3, pp. 117-145). Berlin and New York: Walter de Gruyter.

Soe, L., & Markus, M. L. (1993). Technological or social utility? Unraveling explanations of email, vmail, and fax use. *Information Society, 9,* 213-236.

Sparks, C., & van Zoonen, L. (1992). Gender and technology. *Media, Culture and Society, 14,* 5-7.

Spears, R., & Lea, M. (1992). Social influence and the influence of the "social" in computer-mediated communication. In M. Lea (Ed.), *Contexts of computer-mediated communication* (pp. 30-65). London: Harvester-Wheatsheaf.

Sproull, L., & Kiesler, S. (1991). *Connections: New ways of working in the networked organization.* Cambridge, MA: MIT Press.

Steinfield, C., Caby, L., & Vialle, P. (1992). Internationalization of the firm and impacts of videotex networks. *Journal of Information Technology, 7,* 213-222.

Stevenson, W. (1993). Organization design. In R. Golembiewski (Ed.), *Handbook of organizational behavior* (pp. 141-168). New York: Marcel Dekker.

Stewart, C. (1992). Innovation is in the mind of the user: A case study of voice mail. In U. E. Gattiker (Ed.), *Studies in technological innovation and human resources: Technology mediated communication* (Vol. 3, pp. 151-185). New York: Walter de Gruyter.

Stone, P. J., & Luchetti, R. (1985, March-April). Your office is where you are. *Harvard Business Review, 63,* 102-117.

Sundstrom, E., Burt, R., & Kamp, D. (1980). Privacy at work: Architectural correlates of job satisfaction and job performance. *Academy of Management Journal, 23*(1), 101-117.

Taylor, J., & Van Every, E. (1993). *The vulnerable fortress: Bureaucratic organizations and management in the information age.* Toronto, Canada: University of Toronto Press.

Trevino, L. K., Lengel, R. H., & Daft, R. L. (1987). Media symbolism, media richness and media choice in organizations: A symbolic interactionist perspective. *Communication Research, 14*(5), 553-575.

Trevino, L., & Webster, J. (1992). Flow in computer-mediated communication: Electronic mail and voice mail evaluation and impacts. *Communication Research, 19,* 539-573.

Valacich, J., Paranka, D., George, J., & Nunamaker, J. (1993). Communication concurrency and the new media. *Communication Research, 20*(2), 249-276.

Walker, S. (1984). How typewriters changed correspondence: An analysis of prescription and practice. *Visible Language, 28*(2), 102-117.

Walther, J. (1992). Interpersonal effects in computer-mediated interaction: A relational perspective. *Communication Research, 19*(1), 52-90.

Want, R., Hopper, A., Falcao, V., & Gibbons, J. (1992). The active badge location system. *ACM Transactions on Information Systems, 10*(1), 91-102.

Whisler, T. (1970). *The impact of computers on organizations.* New York: Praeger.

Wigand, R. T. (1985). Integrated communications and work efficiency: Impacts on organizational structure and power. *Information Services and Use, 5,* 241-258.

Yates, J., & Benjamin, R. (1991). The past and present as a window on the future. In M. S. Scott Morton (Ed.), *The corporation of the 1990s: Information technology and organizational transformation* (pp. 61-92). New York: Oxford University Press.

Yates, J., & Orlikowski, W. (1992). Genres of organizational communication: A structurational approach to studying communication and media. *Academy of Management Review, 17,* 299-326.

Zimmerman, J. (Ed.). (1983). *The technological woman: Interfacing with tomorrow.* New York: Praeger.

Zmud, R. (1990). Opportunities for strategic information manipulation through new information technology. In J. Fulk & C. Steinfield (Eds.), *Organizations and communication technology* (pp. 95-116). Newbury Park, CA: Sage.

Zmud, R., Lind, M., & Young, F. (1990). An attribute space for organizational communication channels. *Information Systems Research, 1*(4), 440-457.

PART IV

Process: Communication Behavior in Organizations

15

Power and Politics

❖ DENNIS K. MUMBY
Purdue University

This chapter focuses on the relationships among communication, power, and organization. Its central premise is that organizations are intersubjective structures of meaning that are produced, reproduced, and transformed through the ongoing communicative activities of its members. As a critical organization scholar, however, I will argue that this process is fundamentally mediated by power, which I see as a defining, ubiquitous feature of organizational life. At the same time, and to be appreciated in all its complexities, power itself must be made sense of through a communication lens. From this perspective, communication, power, and organization are interdependent and coconstructed phenomena. The primary goal of this chapter is to explore this tripartite relationship, and to show how, as a field, we can contribute to an understanding of organizational power that is distinct from that offered by such disciplines as management studies, sociology, and political science.

Because of this distinctly communication focus, a secondary goal will be to examine noncommunication views of organizational power, and to show how such work both provides insights into, and places limitations on, our understanding of power. Indeed, given

AUTHOR'S NOTE: I thank George Cheney, Bob Gephart, Fred Jablin, Linda Putnam, and Cynthia Stohl for their constructive and challenging critiques of various drafts of this chapter.

that power has been a focus of research in various disciplines for several decades, it makes sense that such work will have loci of inquiry other than communication processes. Individual, interpersonal, and structural theories of power are all common in this vast and complex literature. However, many of these approaches contain implicit notions of communication that often remain untheorized. A tertiary goal of this chapter, then, will be to tease out, where relevant and appropriate, implicit perspectives on communication that are built into theories of power developed in other disciplines.

Given the complex terrain of the power literature, Table 15.1 provides definitions of constructs that will be central to the argument I develop. Definitions of each concept are drawn not from specific theorists (although in many ways each definition is the distillation of the work of many authors), but from my own attempt to privilege a communication orientation toward the literature reviewed in this chapter. Thus, each term reflects a perspective—rooted in my own work—that views communication as creating the very possibility for organizing, exercising power, engaging in political activity, and so forth. This conception of communication as *constitutive* of both organizing and power therefore serves as the benchmark against which we can review and critique the theory and research on organizational power and politics.

The structure of this chapter will unfold in the following manner. First is a brief historical and theoretical context for the study of power, focusing on Weber, Marx, and the sociological study of power since the 1950s. Second, I pick up the point at which power became an object of study in the management literature, beginning with the structural-functional tradition. Third, I delineate interpretive approaches to power and, fourth, examine the emergence of the critical perspective on organizations and power. Fifth, I discuss the recent emergence of postmodern conceptions of organizational power. Finally, I situate feminist studies as the latest contribution to understanding the relations among communication, power, and organization.

POWER AND POLITICS: IN THE BEGINNING . . .

It is difficult to make sense out of organizational power without reference to the works of Marx (1967) and Weber (1978). Both were concerned—albeit in different ways—with explaining how power is exercised under conditions of the division of labor. Neither paid much attention to power as a communication phenomenon, although Marx's theory of ideology presumes a process by which the ideas of the capitalist class are widely disseminated, and Weber envisions a bureaucratic system of rules, the communication and internalization of which legitimate a rational system of authority. For Marx, the focus was on the means by which capitalist relations of production extracted surplus value from expropriated labor through various coercive techniques, including the lengthening of the working day and the intensification of the labor process. Marx provides us with a class analysis of the capitalist relations of production as a means of critiquing bourgeois economic models and exposing the contradictions inherent in capitalism.

Weber, on the other hand, was more concerned with analyzing the system of rationality manifest in Western industrial societies. Weber (1978) situates his discussion of bureaucracy within the larger context of a general model of authority. Situating rational, bureaucratic authority in relation to traditional and charismatic forms of authority, Weber conceives of the former as "modernist" in its rejection of forms of power characterized by nepotism, raw force, and arbitrary decision making. As Cheney (personal correspondence) has suggested, Weber shows "how the bureaucratic ethos narrows our vision" to rationally, systematically—and perhaps most important—exercise authority in a nonarb-

TABLE 15.1   Definitions of Central Concepts

Communication: The process of creating intersubjective meanings through ongoing, interactional symbolic—verbal and nonverbal—practices, including conversation, metaphors, rituals, stories, dress, space, and so forth.

Organizational communication: The process of creating collective, coordinated structures of meaning through symbolic practices oriented toward the achievement of organizational goals.

Power: The production and reproduction of, resistance to, or transformation of relatively fixed (sedimented) structures of communication and meaning that support the interests (symbolic, political, and economic) of some organization members or groups over others.

Politics: The articulation of various individual and group interests through the everyday enactment of communicative processes that produce, reproduce, resist, and transform collective (intersubjective) structures of meaning. Politics is power enacted and resisted.

Ideology: The process of symbolically creating systems of meaning through which social actors' identities are constructed and situated within relations of power. Ideological struggle entails the attempts of various groups to "fix" and "naturalize" their worldview over others (Althusser, 1971; Therborn, 1980).

Hegemony: The ability of one class or group to link the interests and worldviews of other groups with its own. Hegemony does not refer to simple domination, but rather involves attempts by various groups to articulate meaning systems that are actively taken up by other groups (Gramsci, 1971).

Reification: The process through which humanly created structures take on an objective, "natural" existence, independent from those who constructed them. Reification leads to a sense of alienation, which engenders the possibility for self-reflection and social change (Lukács, 1971).

itrary fashion. Weber thus left us with both a structural and ideological legacy: a bureaucratic system of rules and regulations constitutive of authority, along with an ideology of rationality that shapes and constrains the behavior of actors in organizational contexts.

Both Marx and Weber were concerned with the direction in which modernity was moving: Marx focused on the exploitative nature of capitalism, while Weber expressed reservations with bureaucratic rationality and its eclipsing of other forms of rationality, particularly the charismatic, which he saw as an essential, magical feature of human collective action. Thus, while Weber articulated an "ideal type" of rational legal authority—

rooted in technical criteria and expertise—that overcame the capriciousness of other authority systems, he was concerned with the reification of this ideal type and its manifestation as an "iron cage" that imprisoned those it was intended to empower.

How does this translate into contemporary accounts of organizational power? While Marx's legacy has been fairly diverse in its spawning of a variety of Marxisms (neo, structural, functional, etc.), some of which impinge on organization studies (see below), Weber tends to be rather narrowly appropriated as *the* "theorist of bureaucracy," rather than as a social theorist in the wider sense (for exceptions, see Barker, 1993, 1999; Barker &

Cheney, 1994; Clegg, 1975, 1994b; O'Neill, 1986). Thus, although radical readings of Weber exist, most of management and organization studies read his work as a simple affirmation of bureaucratic rationality. For example, his work on *Verstehen* (understanding) as an interpretive method for analyzing human behavior is almost completely ignored. As such, most of the work on organizational power in the 1960s and 1970s was conducted in the context of this rather narrow reading of Weber. Power, then, is conceptualized largely within a systems-rational model of organizational structure, which sees decision making and the concomitant exercising of power as the logical, optimal, and adaptive response to changes in an organization's environment.

A debate in the field of political science that slightly predates such work implicitly embodies the tension between the conservative and radical readings of Weber. The "community power debate," conducted during the 1950s, 1960s, and 1970s addressed the status of power as an empirical phenomenon. That is, what is the structure and distribution of power in contemporary society? Attempts to answer this question developed roughly into two camps: the pluralists (Dahl, 1957, 1958, 1961; Wolfinger, 1971), and the elitists (Bachrach & Baratz, 1962, 1963; Hunter, 1953; Mills, 1956). The pluralists argued that power was equitably distributed throughout society and that no particular group had undue influence over decision-making processes. The elitists, on the other hand, claimed that power was concentrated in the hands of a privileged few who controlled political agendas.

In some respects, the two groups represent conservative (pluralist) and radical (elitist) readings of modernity, the former claiming that modernity/capitalism/bureaucracy has largely realized democracy, while the latter argues that modernity has emancipated only a privileged few. Dahl (1957) reflects this conservative reading of modernity with a rational, causal, behavioral model of power conceived in terms of decision-making processes. Thus, "A has power over B to the extent that he [or she] can get B to do something that B would

not otherwise do" (Dahl, 1957, pp. 202-203). This often cited definition focuses on the manifest *exercise* of power, and not on power as a potential or dispositional quality of actors. Such exercising can be identified only in explicit decision-making situations where overt conflict between parties is present.

On the other hand, Bachrach and Baratz (1962) criticize Dahl's exclusive focus on concrete decision-making situations, arguing that power is also exercised in situations of "non-decision making." They suggest that in this context, power is exercised when A is able to create and reinforce situations in which the political process is limited to the consideration of issues that do not endanger A's power. "To the extent that A succeeds in doing this, B is prevented, for all practical purposes, from bringing to the fore any issues that might in their resolution be seriously detrimental to A's set of preferences" (Bachrach & Baratz, 1962, p. 948). Quoting Schattschneider (1960), Bachrach and Baratz refer to this process as the "mobilization of bias":

> All forms of political organization have a bias in favour of the exploitation of some kinds of conflict and the suppression of other because *organization is the mobilization of bias*. Some issues are organized into politics while others are organized out. (Schattschneider, 1960, p. 71, emphasis in original)

While there is no explicit model of organizational *communication* operating here, Bachrach and Baratz set the stage for a rhetorical approach to organizational power taken up by theorists such as Tompkins and Cheney (Bullis & Tompkins, 1989; Cheney, 1983; Tompkins & Cheney, 1985) in which they examine the processes through which organizational identification and control are rhetorically managed. Further, Clegg (1989a, p. 75) suggests that Bachrach and Baratz's "two faces of power" is an attempt to make explicit the link between agency and structure, demonstrating that power resides not simply in relations of cause and effect (as Dahl suggests), but in the structured relations of autonomy and dependence that are an endemic feature of organizational life. In many respects, communication is the mediating link between agency and structure, as the process that functions as the constitutive element in relations of autonomy and dependence.

The last move in the community power debate is provided by Lukes's (1974) "radical," three-dimensional view of power that criticizes both Dahl's "one-dimensional" model and Bachrach and Baratz's "two-dimensional" model. Lukes argues that both models are problematic because they reduce power to a focus on decision-making processes and actual, observable conflict (p. 22). In contrast, he argues that power may be exercised in the absence of any observable conflict, suggesting that A exercises power over B "by influencing, shaping or determining his [sic] very wants" (Lukes, 1974, p. 23). In addition, Lukes rejects Bachrach and Baratz's notion that non-decision-making power exists only where grievances are denied access to the political process. Lukes disputes the idea that if a group has no grievances, then there must be a genuine consensus, and no one's interests are being hurt. Sounding remarkably like Habermas, Lukes (1974) argues that "to assume that the absence of grievance equals genuine consensus is simply to rule out the possibility of false or manipulated consensus by definitional fiat" (p. 24). Gaventa's (1980) analysis of the effects of landlord absenteeism on the local population in Appalachia provides an insightful application of this model to a real-world context.

Again, Lukes has no explicit conception of communication in his framework, but there is an implicit one that expands our view of power and makes muted connections to organizational communication studies. For example, his model clearly suggests that processes of socialization and identification—central concerns in our field—are important contexts for the exercise of power (Cheney, 1983; Tompkins & Cheney, 1985). That is, he suggests that power is exercised most effectively when social actors internalize and identify

with the interests of dominant groups—a process that is accomplished rhetorically. Further, his tying of power to false or manipulated interests prefigures critical studies of organizational communication, in which connections are made among communication, ideology, and power (see below). As such, the community power debate represents an important attempt to come to grips with how power functions in institutional settings, providing organizational scholars with insight into how to move beyond individual and relationally focused conceptions of power.

Power, Systems Rationality, and Management Studies

While power has clearly been a central analytic construct in sociology and political science for decades, its emergence as a focal point of research among management researchers is more recent. This is perhaps partly explainable by the field of management's rather narrow appropriation of Weber, resulting in an almost exclusive focus on organizations as sites of rational decision making. In other words, organizational behavior is viewed as explicable through mathematical, economic models of decision making, hence making power irrelevant as an explanatory construct.

This "classic" model of organizational behavior is somewhat modified by the work of the Carnegie group and its development of a model of "administrative man" that focuses on the cognitive and contextual limitations placed on "pure" forms of decision making (Cyert & March, 1963; March & Simon, 1958; Simon, 1976). In Simon's (1976) terms, an individual "satisfices" (makes decisions based on limited information) rather than "optimizes" (makes decisions based on the assessment of all available information). As March and Simon (1958) state:

This, then, is the general picture of the human organism that we will use to analyze organizational behavior. It is a picture of a choosing, decision-making, problem-solving, organism that can do only one or a few things at a time, and that can only attend to a small part of the information recorded in its memory and presented by the environment. (p. 11)

Cyert and March (1963) extend this model by shifting focus away from individual levels of decision making, and instead develop a decision-making coalition model. In this context, decision making is seen as a political process, resulting from the conflicts of interest characteristic of subgoal differentiation within organizational life.

As Pettigrew (1973) points out, however, the Carnegie group has a consistent bias in favor of psychological explanations of behavior, drawing heavily on learning theory and individual psychology. Little attention is paid to the larger, structural mechanisms that organizations use in making decisions and forming coalitions. Pettigrew argues that "critical questions related to the generation of support and how the structure of the organization might limit such a process are ignored. . . . [Further] they ignore role and communication structures and how they are devised and changed" (p. 10). Thus, for our purposes, the Carnegie group has little to say about the communicative dimensions of power and decision making. Although Simon (1976) does address the role of decision premises in shaping organizational behavior and decision making, there is no attempt to explicitly articulate this process as communication based.

Thompson's (1967) study extends the work of the Carnegie group through an early appropriation of the newly emergent systems perspective (Von Bertalanffy, 1968). Thompson (1967) defines complex organizations as "open systems, hence indeterminate and faced with uncertainty, but at the same time as subject to criteria of rationality and hence needing determinateness and certainty" (p. 10). The central problem of organization thus involves coping with uncertainty and assessing the impact of technologies and environments on the process of uncertainty absorption. Thompson's work is important not only because he fleshes out and extends the work of

the Carnegie group, but also because he situates power as a critical element in the process of problem solving and uncertainty absorption. He recognizes that the indeterminacy of organizational processes creates relations of dependence that shape organizational problem solving and task orientation. Bounded rationality cannot be explained through purely cognitive means, but must be understood as a fundamentally political phenomenon. Thompson's discussion of organizational systems, decision making, and power lays the groundwork for the emergence in the 1970s of two of the most widely adopted theories of organizational power: strategic contingencies theory (Hickson, Hinings, Lee, Schneck, & Pennings, 1971; Hinings, Hickson, Pennings, & Schneck, 1974) and resource dependency theory (Pfeffer, 1981; Pfeffer & Salancik, 1974, 1978; Salancik & Pfeffer, 1974, 1977).

The advent of these theories marks an intense period of study of organizational power in management studies proper, an intensity that has led some researchers to claim that "power is the cornerstone of both management theory and management practice . . . and . . . is a vital and ubiquitous reality in organizational life" (Cavanagh, Moberg, & Velasquez, 1981, p. 363). Some scholars claim that "power" is a better explanatory factor in organization studies than either "goals" or "rationality," given that organizations are not the paragons of logical decision making they were at one time conceived to be (Sunesson, 1985). This research marks a shift from a focus on individual power to departmental/structural power (Enz, 1988). Indeed, criticism of individual and interpersonal models of power is one of the most persistent features of the wave of research that began in the early 1970s:

The term [power] takes on different meanings when the unit, or power-holder, is a *formal group* in an *open system* with *multiple goals*, and the system is assumed to reflect a political-domination model of organization, rather than only a co-operative model. (Perrow, 1970, p. 84, emphasis in original)

Despite this shift in emphasis, much of the work carried out during this period still had little to do directly with communication (conceived as constitutive of the organizing process). Below I briefly adumbrate both strategic contingencies theory and resource dependency theory, suggesting why both have limited application to our understanding of the relationship between power and organizational *communication.*

Hickson et al. (1971; Hinings et al., 1974) pull together a number of different perspectives to create a theory that places power at the center of their definition of organization. Operating on the principle that organizations are fundamentally characterized by a division of labor, they argue that power must be examined as that which characterizes the relationships among functional subunits of organizations:

> Thus organizations are conceived of as interdepartmental systems in which a major task element is coping with uncertainty. . . . The essence of an organization is limitation of the autonomy of all its members or parts, since all are subject to power from the others; for subunits, unlike individuals, are not free to make a decision to participate, as March and Simon (1958) put it, nor to decide whether or not to come together in political relationships. They must. They exist to do so. (Hickson et al., 1971, p. 217)

Strategic contingencies theory is a structural theory of power, concerning itself not with the psychological attributes of individuals, but with the sources of power that result from the structural characteristics of collective, task-oriented behavior. For Hickson et al. (1971, p. 217), following Emerson (1962), the central question in the study of organizations is: What factors function to vary dependency, and thus to vary power? They identify uncertainty (and coping with uncertainty), substitutability, and centrality as the principal variables that determine the relations of power and dependence among organizational subunits. Hinings et al. (1974) provide a test of the initial formulation of this theory, concluding that coping with uncertainty does not in itself explain subunit power, but rather, as their initial theory suggests, such coping must be accompanied by workflow centrality (immediacy and pervasiveness) and low substitutability. Uncertainty is a theme common to the work of March and Simon (1958), Thompson, (1967), and Crozier (1964), the last theorist suggesting—in his study of maintenance engineers in French tobacco manufacturing plants—that power and uncertainty are closely interrelated. In Crozier's study, the maintenance engineers enjoyed a level of power out of all proportion with their positions in the bureaucratic hierarchy, due largely to the unpredictability of machine breakdowns. Crozier was able to assert that these engineers had "control over the last source of uncertainty remaining in a completely routinized organizational system" (p. 154).

The development of resource dependency theory is another important critique of the "rational choice" model of organizational behavior and, particularly, decision-making processes (Pfeffer, 1981; Pfeffer & Salancik, 1974, 1978; Salancik & Pfeffer, 1974, 1977). Drawing on the work of Cyert and March (1963), Pfeffer and Salancik develop a coalitional model of power, which argues that—especially with regard to resource allocation—organizational decision making is a political process that can be explained by considering the relative power of the various subunits within an organization. Resource dependency theory represents a variation of the strategic contingencies theory of power. As Pfeffer (1981) indicates, both perspectives "focus either on the dependence of the organization as a whole or of other subunits on the particular resources or certainty provided by other social actors within the organization" (p. 101). In addition, both theories view power as being derived from the ability of social actors or organizational subunits to address and to ameliorate objectively defined organizational exigencies.

Resource dependency theory studies power both within and between organizations (Pfeffer & Salancik, 1978). Organizations are viewed as open systems that are constantly in need of an ongoing supply of resources, and hence must engage in a continual series of transactions with their environments to secure these resources. Necessary organizational resources include money, prestige, legitimacy, rewards and sanctions, expertise, and the ability to deal with uncertainty. Two early studies by Pfeffer and Salancik (1974; Salancik & Pfeffer, 1974) examine the relative power of subunits (departments) within a university through an analysis of budget allocations. Both studies view organizational decision making as a political process that can be explained only through the analysis of relative subunit power. In addition, Pfeffer and Salancik adopt a coalitional view of organizations that emphasizes differences in the objectives and preferences of the various departments and attempts to demonstrate how conflict between competing preferences and beliefs are resolved. The political character of organization life is rooted in "nonbureaucratic decision mechanisms" (Salancik & Pfeffer, 1974, p. 454) that are used to resolve conflicts between subunits. For resource dependency theory, then, "power is first and foremost a structural phenomenon, and should be understood as such" (Pfeffer, 1981, p. x).

Both strategic contingencies theory and resource dependency theory have been heavily influential in the study of organizational power and politics. Recent literature in this area would suggest that, while modifications of the initial formulations of power have been fairly frequent, little related work has appeared that questions the fundamental assumptions of this early work. Rather, the tendency has been to build on and expand these perspectives (Astley & Sachdeva, 1984; Cobb, 1984; Enz, 1988; Lachman, 1989; Turow, 1984). For example, Astley and Sachdeva bemoan the theoretically fragmented character of work on power and suggest integration through a focus on the interdependent relationships among three structural sources of power: hierarchical authority, resource control, and network centrality. However, the three sources of power are each borrowed from different theoretical perspectives, and the connections between them are emphasized (hierarchical authority from bureaucratic theory, resource control from resource dependency theory, and network centrality from strategic contingencies theory). As such, Astley and Sachdeva's intervention represents not so much a theoretical synthesis as a theoretical aggregation.

With few exceptions (Pettigrew, 1973; Pfeffer, 1981), little attention has been paid to the relationship between communication and power in this body of research. This stems from rather primitive conceptions of the communication-organization relationship. As Axley (1984) has demonstrated, most managerial conceptions of communication function according to a "conduit" model in which communication involves the relatively unproblematic transmission of ideas and information between senders and receivers. In research on organizational power, communication is largely taken for granted. While a subunit's power is measured in terms of its centrality, autonomy, and access to resources, little or no attention is paid to how this power is communicated to other subunits. The presumption is that such communication occurs mechanically and unproblematically, simply relaying or representing the power of a subunit.

Pfeffer (1981) provides the most sophisticated resource dependence model of communication, examining political language and symbols as a way to mobilize organizational support and reduce opposition. Using Edelman (1964) as a conceptual foundation, Pfeffer discusses the various linguistic and symbolic practices that organizational actors draw on to solidify or enhance their influence in organizations. However, Pfeffer (1981) places strict parameters on the role of communicative processes in relation to organizational power:

The view developed here . . . is that language and symbolism are important in the *exercise* of power. It is helpful for social actors with power to use appropriate political language and symbols to legitimate and develop support for the decisions that are reached on the basis of power. However, in this formulation, language and the ability to use political symbols contribute only marginally to the development of the power of various organizational participants; rather, power derives from the conditions of resource control and resource interdependence. (p. 184, emphasis in original)

This representational view positions communication as auxiliary to power relations, rather than constituting them. For Pfeffer, relations of power are established prior to the communication of relations of autonomy and dependence. Despite the careful consideration of communication as an important organizational phenomenon, Pfeffer ultimately relegates it to the role of reproducing and legitimating already existing relations within the organization. Pfeffer privileges resource control over communication, failing to recognize that the latter constitutes a resource that controls organizational goals. Pfeffer thus neglects communication as an intersubjective process in which what counts as power involves struggles over meaning.

In sum, while the systems-rational approach established power as a legitimate area of research, its narrow conceptions of communication and power limit the kind of insights that can be developed about the political character of organizing. Table 15.2 outlines the principal strengths and weaknesses of this early research on organizational power and summarizes the other approaches to communication, power, and organizing to be discussed in this chapter. Readers are encouraged to refer back to this table as my argument unfolds.

The next section examines interpretive approaches to organizational power, a development that occurred in the wake of the so-called linguistic turn in philosophy and social theory (Rorty, 1967).

INTERPRETIVE APPROACHES TO ORGANIZATIONAL POWER

Interpretive research on power represents an important paradigm shift in organizational communication research and signals the point at which communication becomes central to our understanding of organizing processes. While the work reviewed in the previous section either ignored communication entirely or positioned it as an unproblematic extension of cognitive or structural factors, research conducted from an interpretive perspective sees communication as constitutive of organizing (Pacanowsky & O'Donnell-Trujillo, 1982; Putnam, 1983; Smith & Eisenberg, 1987). In other words, organizations have ontological status only insofar as members communicatively and collectively construct a shared reality.

Much of this literature develops out of the phenomenological, ethnomethodological, and hermeneutic traditions, where the central concern is intersubjectivity. That is, how does one articulate an alternative to the Cartesian bifurcation of subject and object, which positions knowledge as the mind's discovery of a preexisting reality? The interpretive approach shows how subject and world (including other subjects) are mutually constituted. In this perspective, communication is the process of creating an intersubjectively meaningful reality (Gadamer, 1989; Mehan & Wood, 1975; Merleau-Ponty, 1960; Schutz, 1962). It is not possible to review the entire sociological tradition that has emerged out of this work, but its orientation is perhaps expressed most forcefully by Gadamer's (1989) notion of *Sprachlichkeit* (linguisticality) and Heidegger's (1977) conception of language as the "house of being." In both perspectives, language is not merely a vehicle for the expression of already formed thoughts and identities, but is that which creates self, meaning, and the world as we know it.

The elements of this intersubjective approach to meaning have existed in the field of communication for more than 25 years

TABLE 15.2 Perspectives on Communication and Organizational Power

Theoretical Perspective	Conception of Power	Conception of Communication	Strengths	Limitations
Systems-Rationality	◆ Decision making ◆ Behavior of actors ◆ Control of resources ◆ Ability to create dependencies	◆ Representational ◆ Expresses existing power relations ◆ Groups translate power bases into effective communication	◆ View of actor as boundedly rational ◆ Legitimates "political" view of organizations ◆ Shift from interpersonal to structural view of power	◆ Power limited to struggle for scarce resources ◆ Ignores power exercised through consensus ◆ Role of communication peripheral
Interpretivism	◆ Normative system of shared meanings and values internalized by organization members	◆ Constitutes intersubjective systems of meaning ◆ Focus on relation between sensemaking and symbolic forms	◆ Communication central ◆ Focus on relation of power and meaning ◆ Links culture and control ◆ Power as socially constructed	◆ Fails to situate power in larger political and economic context ◆ No theory of society ◆ Inadequate view of contradiction and power
Critical theory	◆ Deep-structure group interests ◆ Relations of hegemony ◆ Dialectic of control ◆ Sovereign model	◆ Political; creates reality through ideological meaning systems ◆ Communication systematically distorted	◆ Communication central ◆ Links power to consent ◆ Ideology central to power ◆ "Thick" model of organizational power	◆ Totalizing view of power ◆ Most work studies domination, little on resistance
Postmodernism	◆ Dispersed in multiple sites ◆ Constituted through games of truth ◆ Discursive and nondiscursive practices ◆ Disciplinary model ◆ Positive rather than negative	◆ Produces multiple, fragmented positions and identities ◆ Linked intrinsically to power and knowledge ◆ Focus on "discursive formations"	◆ Focus on relation of power and subjectivity ◆ Critique of modernist, totalizing view of power ◆ Deconstructs dominant power/knowledge regimes ◆ Focus on discursive micropractices	◆ Resistance located at level of individual ◆ Limited theory of collective action ◆ Few empirical studies ◆ Many studies text based ◆ Undertheorizes politics
Feminism	◆ Embodied in gendered systems of exploitation and resistance ◆ Patriarchy as locus of power	◆ Communication creates gendered systems of meaning and identity ◆ Social actors "do gender" through communication	◆ "Genders" the study of power and identity ◆ Focus on alternative organizations ◆ Politicizes knowledge generation ◆ Critiques binary views	◆ Much research text based; little study of communication processes ◆ Limited development in organizational communication studies

(Deetz, 1973a, 1973b, 1978; Hawes, 1977), but the impact on organizational communication studies is more recent. The "interpretive paradigm" thus centers on the process of organizing as emerging from the intersubjective act of communication (Bittner, 1974; Burrell & Morgan, 1979; Gephart, 1978; Putnam, 1983; Putnam & Pacanowsky, 1983).

In studying power, the interpretive approach focuses on the relationships among communication, power, and meaning (Fowler, Hodge, Kress, & Trew, 1979). Kunda (1992) provides an insightful account of these relationships in his ethnographic study of the culture at a high-tech engineering company. Examining culture as a form of normative control (i.e., the process of shaping organization members' underlying experiences, feelings, and values in an effort to guide behavior), Kunda shows that employees do not simply *behave* in the corporation's interests, but actually develop a sense of identity through commitment to the organization and its goals. Such a commitment is not realized unproblematically, but occurs through a "struggle over meaning" in which the corporation and its members compete over definitions of organizational reality. As Kunda states: "The struggle between organizations bent on normative control and individuals subjected to it is over the definition of reality, and it is a difficult one, for meanings both personal and collective have become part of the contested terrain" (p. 227).

Kunda's study focuses on the communicative practices in which organization members engage, showing how organizing is produced in the moment to moment, as members "do" meetings, engage in hallway talk, and tell stories (Boden, 1994; Taylor, 1995; Taylor, Cooren, Giroux, & Robichaud, 1996). At issue, then, are the sensemaking practices of social actors. That is, how do organization members construct meanings—both collective and individual—out of communication processes that are inherently ambiguous and open to multiple interpretations? As Eisenberg (1984) has shown, such ambiguity can be used strategically by managers as forms of control. Sensemaking is not simply the product of mutually shared assumptions and interpretive procedures, but rather is shaped by the political context in which it occurs. Sensemaking and the creation of intersubjective structures of meaning exist in a dialectical relationship with organizational relations of power. Organizational power is defined in terms of the ability of individuals and groups to control and shape dominant interpretations of organizational events.

Although a ubiquitous feature of organizational life, control over meanings becomes particularly salient in organizational crises. At such times, dominant interpretations are challenged and taken-for-granted meanings are problematized. Gephart's (1988, 1992; Gephart, Steier, & Lawrence, 1990) study of inquiries into industrial accidents demonstrates this process at work, showing how various interest groups (the company, government investigators, families of employees) compete to shape interpretations of such events. For Gephart (1992), the key issue involves "determining how sensemaking practices are used to transform (varied) preliminary interpretations of disasters into culturally rational, sensible, and standardized interpretations assumedly shared by key inquiry participants" (p. 119). One of the most interesting features of this research is the extent to which dominant, institutionalized meanings appropriate and thus neutralize alternative, oppositional interpretations of events. For example, in his analysis of testimony at a public inquiry into a gas pipeline fire, Gephart (1992) shows how the official, "top-down," regulatory logic of the organization prevails over the "situated logic" (that developed on-site by workers) of work in action. The latter operates informally, makes sense to workers, and reflects an ad hoc, commonsense way of dealing with safety issues; however, it conflicts with the deductive, state-mandated logic employed by the company. In this context, the public inquiry is analyzed as a remedial process that attempts to relegitimate the state's role as the arbiter of "correct" organizational safety procedures, while simultaneously closing off alternative interpretations of events.

Gephart's work helps us to see the interconnections among communication, power, and meaning by showing how discourse can *construct* (as opposed to simply represent) meanings and sensemaking practices that legitimate certain interests over others. However, his studies focus on public discourse and its construction practices rather than the day-to-day communication in which organization members engage. In the latter case, focus is on the emergent, interactional, and often precarious character of organizing. In terms of power issues, the question is one of how organization members co-construct meanings that legitimate authority and control, moment to moment. Such research is relatively rare (given the difficulty of collecting interaction-based data), but the little that has been conducted provides insight into intersubjectivity as an ongoing process. For example, Boje's (1991) analysis of organizational storytelling—although not explicitly addressing power issues—shows that stories are co-constructed phenomena rather than symbolic artifacts produced by a single actor with a passive audience. This work contrasts with other research on organizational narrative that treats stories as self-contained events (e.g., J. Martin, 1990; Martin, Feldman, Hatch, & Sitkin, 1983; Mumby, 1987; Witten, 1993).

Fairhurst's (1993) discourse approach to the leader-member exchange (LMX) model of leadership is a further example of interpretive work that examines power and authority as an ongoing, situational accomplishment involving the management of meaning. Fairhurst operates from the premise that "as members of speech communities, leaders and members draw upon different strategies and use linguistic resources in particular ways because of the dilemmas they face at that moment and the meaningfulness of the social relation of which they are a part" (p. 322). Taking women leaders as the focus of her study, Fairhurst shows

that in high LMX situations (characterized by mutual trust, internalization of common goals, and mutual influence and support), leaders successfully manage interactions through particular communication strategies that enhance and, indeed, constitute the ongoing character of the relationship. Thus, leadership is conceived as the product of the interaction between leader and member. Fairhurst's focus on gender issues also points to important ways in which women leaders "do gender" interactionally by negotiating issues of power, conflict, and participation.

In sum, interpretive studies of organizational power provide important insight into the constitutive character of communication and the relationship of communication to both organizing and power. By treating power as socially constructed, researchers show how organization members employ interpretive procedures that produce, reproduce, or resist dominant organizational realities. However, such work often fails to address adequately the larger political and economic contexts within which relations of power develop. Issues such as ideology, hegemony, and contradiction go largely untheorized in the interpretive literature. In the next section, therefore, I address critical studies of organizational power, which draw extensively on Marxist and neo-Marxist traditions.

CRITICAL THEORIES OF ORGANIZATIONAL POWER

This section focuses on the ways that critical studies have helped to reshape conceptions of organizational power. Again, this approach will be examined from a communication perspective, with a focus on the processes through which systems of organizational power are produced, reproduced, and resisted. An appreciation of the richness of this work requires that one understands three of its central concepts: ideology, hegemony (Gramsci, 1971), and reification (Lukács, 1971). Thus, prior to examining the critical literature I briefly discuss these concepts. Then, I contextualize critical organizational communication studies with an examination of work that emanates from the sociological tradition. Finally, I examine the emergence of the critical perspective in organizational communication studies proper.

Central Concepts in the Critical Tradition

The concept of ideology plays a central role in neo-Marxist critiques of capitalism and, by extension, organizations (Eagleton, 1991; Geuss, 1981; Larrain, 1979; McClellan, 1986; Therborn, 1980; Thompson, 1984). Despite its slippery and contentious status, we can operate from a number of premises regarding this concept:

1. Ideology is most usefully conceived not as beliefs that are epiphenomenal to social actors' identities, but as that which constitutes those identities, or subjectivities (Althusser, 1971).
2. Ideology creates complex systems and chains of signification and interpretive schemas (Hall, 1985) through which people experience intersubjectively their social relations.
3. Ideology provides the framework for the privileging of certain interpretive schemas and interests over others. Hence, ideology has a strong legitimation function in its production and reproduction of the dominant relations of power (Habermas, 1975).
4. Ideology does not simply reflect the dominant relations of power in a straightforward manner, but rather transforms and hence obscures these relations, hiding them from immediate experience (Deetz & Kersten, 1983; Mumby, 1989).
5. Ideology is not simply ideational; rather, it is material insofar as (a) it is expressed in the everyday communication and behavioral practices of social actors, and (b) it has direct consequences in the construction of the lived experience of those actors.

6. Ideology is not monolithic, simply reproducing a seamless and totalizing reality. Rather, "ideology . . . sets limits to the degree to which a society-in-dominance can easily, smoothly, and functionally reproduce itself" (Hall, 1985, p. 113).
7. Social actors are thus never completely determined by ideology but are, in Therborn's (1980) terms, constantly implicated in the process of "subjection-qualification" whereby they are both "subjects" of (in the dual sense) and "qualified" by (in the dual sense) ideology.

For organizational communication studies, ideology concerns the ways in which the identities of organization members are constructed through everyday communicative practices, such that particular relations of power are produced, reproduced, or transformed (Deetz, 1982; Deetz & Kersten, 1983; Mumby, 1987, 1988). In this context, Gramsci's (1971) concept of hegemony plays an important role in critical organization studies.

Much confusion exists regarding the relationship between ideology and hegemony. In Gramsci's (1971) terms, hegemony involves not simple domination of one group by another, but rather the development of a "collective will" through "intellectual and moral reform" (pp. 60-61). Thus, hegemony explains "the ability of one class to articulate the interests of other social groups to its own" (Mouffe, 1979, p. 183) and is achieved through "the colonization of popular consciousness" (Grossberg, 1984, p. 412). Hegemony therefore includes the ideological but cannot be reduced to it. For Gramsci, hegemony places focus on the dialectical relation of various class forces not only in the ideological and cultural realms but also in the economic and political realms. Eagleton (1991) provides a useful way of distinguishing ideology and hegemony when he states:

Ideology refers specifically to the way power-struggles are fought out at the level of signification; and though such signification is involved in all hegemonic processes, it is not in all cases the *dominant* level by which rule is sustained. Singing the National Anthem comes as close to a "purely" ideological activity as one could imagine. . . . Religion, similarly, is probably the most purely ideological of the various institutions of civil society. But hegemony is also carried in cultural, political, and economic forms—in non-discursive practices as well as in rhetorical utterances. (p. 113)

Gramsci's notion of hegemony is important insofar as it marks a shift from ideology viewed as a relatively fixed, static "system of ideas" imposed on subordinate groups, to a dynamic conception of the lived relations of social groups and the various struggles that constantly unfold between and among these groups. As such, hegemony can be viewed as a process that is communicative in character, involving attempts by various groups to articulate systems of meaning that are actively taken up by other groups. By focusing on "civil society"—the "ensemble of organisms called 'private,' " including the media, family, religion, education, and so forth—as the primary realm where hegemony is exercised, Gramsci is able to conceptualize power as a consensual, noncoercive, and contested process.

Finally, the concept of reification is central to critical models of organizational communication. Lukács's (1971) *History and Class Consciousness* represents a restoration of the Hegelian influence in Marxism. He develops a humanist position that conceives of Marxism as an articulation of working-class, revolutionary consciousness. Extending Marx's analysis of the commodity form, which focuses primarily on the economic dimensions of the process of reification, Lukács asks the question, "How far is commodity exchange together with its structural consequences able to influence the *total* outer and inner life of society?" (p. 84). For him, the commodity form pervades every dimension of social life, mechanizing and dehumanizing experience such that "man's activity becomes estranged

from himself" (Lukács, 1971, p. 87) and develops a "phantom objectivity." This alienated existence provides the catalyst for a self-recognition in which the working class transcends itself. The moment of revolutionary recognition occurs "when the working class acknowledges this alienated world as its own confiscated creation, reclaiming it through political praxis" (Eagleton, 1991, p. 98).

The concept of reification figures prominently in critical approaches to organizational communication. Ranson, Hinings, and Greenwood (1980) develop a structurational approach to power in arguing that "interested action is typically oriented toward the framework of an organization, with members striving to secure their sectional claims within its very structure, which then operates to mediate or reconstitute those interests" (p. 7). In other words, groups strive to reify organizational structures that serve their interests. Deetz (1992a) discusses the various discursive strategies employed in the systematic distortion of communication (Habermas, 1970, 1979), showing how discourse "naturalizes" socially constructed, human creations, providing them with objective qualities that appear to be independent from their creators.

Critical Studies and the Sociology of Organizations

The critical sociological tradition has long attempted to come to grips with, and explain, the exploitative character of capitalism. For Marx, the expropriation of labor and the securing of surplus value was largely a coercive process. The ongoing accumulation of capital meant wresting more and more work from the laborer, either through lengthening the working day or by speeding up the labor process. Braverman's (1974) famous analysis of deskilling shows how 20th-century monopoly capitalism secures surplus value by simplifying and cheapening the cost of labor, reducing workers to abstract and undifferentiated elements in the labor process. While these methods are still ubiquitous in corporate America (studies suggest that the average employee now works longer hours for the same or less pay), much of the critical sociological literature—particularly that associated with the cultural studies tradition (Grossberg, 1984; Hall, 1985)—addresses the cultural and symbolic processes through which capitalism is produced and reproduced. This marks a shift from studying power as principally located within the system of economic production to a focus on power as situated mainly within communication and discourse processes.

Two studies that reflect this shift toward cultural, ideological conceptions of power and organizing are Willis's (1977) study of British working-class school-leavers and Burawoy's (1979) analysis of a shop floor culture of "making out." In his analysis of a group of "lads" in their final school year before going into the workplace, Willis shows how they resist the dominant educational culture of good behavior and studiousness by creating their own counterculture founded on "having a laff" and fighting. The lads intersubjectively construct an alternative system of meaning that radically inverts the values of the dominant culture, thus creating a space of resistance. Willis argues that, ironically, such resistance ultimately functions to prepare the lads for working-class jobs—their rejection of education condemns them to a life of manual labor. In this sense, opposition to the dominant system of ideas functions to reproduce those ideas along with the capitalist relations of production that undergird them.

Burawoy's (1979) critical ethnography of the labor process critiques 20th-century Marxism for reducing wage laborers to objects of manipulation and coercion, creating what he calls a "subjectless subject" (p. 77). In redressing this limitation, Burawoy is interested in exploring the dynamics of Gramsci's (1971, p. 285) claim that "hegemony is born in the factory" (Burawoy, 1979, p. xi). Thus, he focuses on the organization of relations of domination through consent. Arguing that

"the defining essence of the capitalist labor process is the simultaneous securing and obscuring of surplus value" (p. 30), Burawoy shows how the game of "making out" (played by workers as a way of maximizing wages under a modified piece-rate system) organizes consent and maintains a culture of cooperation with management in the production of surplus value. In this sense, the game functions ideologically and dialectically, embodying worker autonomy and resistance to management control over the labor process, while simultaneously obscuring the relations of production in response to which the game was originally constructed.

Interestingly, Collinson (1988, 1992, 1994) critiques both Willis and Burawoy for their lack of an adequate theory of the subject and an overly structuralist conception of power:

> In the absence of any theorizing of subjectivity, Burawoy cannot fully explain workers' active involvement in the game of making out or the subjective conditions that shape how and why workers routinely reproduce the conditions of their own subordination. Hence, whilst Willis exaggerates working-class resistance and penetrations, Burawoy, conversely, overstates consent and conformity on the shop floor. What unites these authors, however, is their failure to theorize subjectivity and their dualistic analyses that focus upon structuralist theories of power on the one hand and working-class culture on the other. (1992, pp. 150-151)

In his own study of a British engineering plant, Collinson (1988, 1992) reveals a complex system of meaning and identity formation that revolves around the deployment of humor by the engineers. Collinson interrogates the ways in which a working-class masculine identity is symbolically constructed through humor and how, ultimately, the particular form that this identity takes serves to undermine the possibilities for genuine resistance to capitalist alienation and reification processes. He argues that resistance is undermined through a use of humor that constructs a form of masculine identity—rooted in aggressive sexuality, a careful separation of private and work lives, and competitive individualism—that limits the possibilities for solidarity and collective action.

From a communication perspective, Collinson's study advances beyond Willis's and Burawoy's insofar as it focuses on the communicative construction of identity, power, and resistance. While both Willis and Burawoy present undertheorized and essentialist conceptions of subjectivity tied to class (even though their aim is to show how these subjectivities are socially constructed), Collinson demonstrates how subjectivity is constructed through complex and often contradictory processes of communication and meaning formation; in this sense, subjectivity itself is contradictory and fragmented. Just as important, Collinson avoids the production of a dualism between agency and structure insofar as communication is situated as central to both, providing the possibility for agency and defining structure in terms of routinized patterns of communication. For example, Collinson (1988, 1992) identifies humor as performing the three functions of resisting managerial authority, controlling workers perceived as lazy, and promoting consent to the prevailing form of masculine identity. These three functions simultaneously produce routinized behavior (workers are expected to exhibit masculine bravado or risk ostracism) and create possibilities for agency (workers "see through" and resist management attempts to co-opt them into a more informal "Americanized" corporate culture).

In summarizing the critical sociological approach to organizational power, then, three themes can be identified. First, power is conceived in dialectical terms (Benson, 1977; Brown, 1978; Clegg, 1975, 1981, 1987; Clegg & Dunkerley, 1980; Edwards, 1979; Goldman & Van Houten, 1977; Hindess, 1982; Ranson et al., 1980). This move situates power not as a purely structural, coalitional phenomenon, but as rooted in the dialectical interplay between conscious, acting subjects and the insti-

tutionalized, sedimented structures that reflect the underlying relations of production in the workplace. In other words, the relationship between agency and structure, first hinted at by Bachrach and Baratz in their two-dimensional model, becomes a central issue in institutional studies of power.

Second, power is not framed simply as a struggle over resources (economic, political, informational, etc.) but rather as a struggle over *meaning* (Clegg, 1989a). Against Pfeffer's (1981) explicit separation of symbolic and material resources, neo-Marxism theorizes the dialectical interplay among the economic, political, and ideological dimensions of social relations (Benson, 1977). Interest lies in examining how social actors construct a meaning environment that functions ideologically, simultaneously securing and obscuring the power relations that undergird everyday practices.

Third, critical sociology of organizations is concerned with what might be termed a "hermeneutics of suspicion" (Ricoeur, 1970). This orientation eschews the notion that organizations can be read by examining the surface, relatively visible features of organizational life and argues for a distinction between "surface" and "deep structure" dimensions of organizations. The concept of ideology is central to this distinction insofar as it functions to obscure deep-structure power relations, articulating a relatively coherent and orderly surface structure of organizational life. It is only through "ideology critique" that the pathological, contradictory, and coercive features of capitalist institutional forms can be unmasked.

Despite this shift to a meaning-centered, dialectical approach to power and organizing, little of this work explicitly examines communication as a constitutive feature of this relationship. Thus, studies do not center on language, discourse, or symbolic processes per se. Despite the occasional exception (e.g., Clegg, 1975; Collinson, 1992), most studies presume that organizations are constituted through social actors' practices, but the communicative dimension of these practices is afforded little scrutiny. Ironically, as long ago as the 1920s, Volosinov (1973) was arguing for "the sign" as the primary arena of class struggle: "Everything ideological possesses meaning: it represents, depicts, or stands for something lying outside itself. In other words, it is a *sign. Without signs there is no ideology*" (p. 9, emphasis in original). Thus, the most important exercise of power is at the level of signification (i.e., communication); the group that is best able to get a certain meaning system to "stick" is the group that has the most power. It is the study of the communicative dimensions of this process that provides critical organizational communication studies with its distinctive character.

Critical Approaches to Communication, Power, and Organization

I divide critical studies of organizational communication into two areas. First, there is a large body of work that is theory oriented, simultaneously challenging the managerial assumptions that undergird most organization studies and developing alternative perspectives that focus heavily on issues of power and politics (Alvesson, 1985; Alvesson & Willmott, 1992a, 1992b; Deetz, 1982, 1985; Frost, 1980, 1987; Mumby, 1993a, 1997; Steffy & Grimes, 1986). In terms of the connections among power, hegemony, ideology, and reification, critical theorists show how management theory functions ideologically by reifying and naturalizing a particular way of knowing, thus excluding as illegitimate other forms of representing knowledge claims. Here, the concern is to make explicit the politics of knowledge representation, and to demonstrate how managerially defined theories of knowledge serve to sustain the hegemony of management interests.

Second, there is a growing body of research that examines empirically the relationships among communication, power, and organization, focusing on the ways in which

power and resistance are manifested at the everyday level of organizing (Collinson, 1988, 1992; Graham, 1993; Huspek & Kendall, 1991; Markham, 1996; Murphy, 1998; Rosen, 1985, 1988; Scheibel, 1996; Witten, 1993; Young, 1989). This research takes seriously the notion that meaning, identity, and power relationships are produced, maintained, and reproduced through ongoing communicative practices. Researchers have examined specific forms of communication, including stories (Ehrenhaus, 1993; Helmer, 1993; Mumby, 1987, 1993b; Witten, 1993), rituals (Izraeli & Jick, 1986; Rosen, 1985, 1988), metaphors (Deetz & Mumby, 1985; McMillan & Cheney, 1996; Salvador & Markham, 1995; Wendt, 1994), corporate advertising (Fairclough, 1993), public announcements (Banks, 1994), conversational interaction (Clegg, 1975; Huspek & Kendall, 1991; Penkoff, 1995; van Dijk, 1993), work songs (Conrad, 1988), humor (Collinson, 1988, 1992), and organizational texts (Laird Brenton, 1993) as ways of getting at the complex dynamics that characterize the ideological structuring of organizations.

Given space limitations, I focus primarily on empirical work as a way of demonstrating the importance to critical studies of a communicative conception of organizational power. Here, power is conceptualized primarily as a struggle over meaning; the group that is best able to "fix" meaning and articulate it to its own interests is the one that will be best able to maintain and reproduce relations of power (Deetz, 1992a; Deetz & Mumby, 1990; Giddens, 1979; Gray, Bougon, & Donnellon, 1985; Hall, 1985; Mumby, 1987, 1988, 1989). As suggested above, issues of ideology, hegemony, and reification are central issues in this work, with critical researchers viewing language and communication as *constitutive* of organizational power relations.

The examination of this constitutive process has taken a number of different forms. Several critical scholars have used Giddens's (1976, 1979, 1984) structurational approach as a theoretical lens for explicating the relationship between agency (communication) and structure (rules and resources) (Banks & Riley, 1993; Mumby, 1987, 1988; Penkoff, 1995; Riley, 1983). Even though Giddens's work has been widely disseminated in our field, for the most part it has been appropriated in a rather conservative fashion, with emphasis on its compatibility with systems theory (e.g., Poole & DeSanctis, 1990). However, some organizational communication scholars have thematized the radical dimension of Giddens's work through a focus on the relationship between the notions of "duality of structure" and "dialectic of control." Giddens (1979, p. 69) argues that structure is both the medium and outcome of communicative practices. In this sense, structure is both enabling and constraining, simultaneously providing the possibility for agency and limiting its scope. Social actors draw on rules and resources to engage in communicative behavior and coordinated action, at the same time reproducing, resisting, or transforming that structure through social action. The dialectic of control thus addresses the extent to which a social actor could "act otherwise" (Giddens, 1979, pp. 145-150) as part of a structure of enablement and constraint.

Critical organization scholars have addressed the relationship between the structurational process and the communicative practices of organization members (Helmer, 1993; Howard & Geist, 1995; Mumby, 1987, 1988; Papa, Auwal, & Singhal, 1995; Ranson et al., 1980; Riley, 1983). Power, conceived as the ability to "act otherwise" in the context of the dialectic of control, is examined by focusing on how social actors draw on communication resources to privilege a structurational process that favors their interests. Researchers attempt to show the relationship between systems of signification and structures of domination. For example, Mumby (1987) provides an in-depth interpretation of an organizational story to demonstrate how it functions ideologically to maintain and reproduce relations of power. In analyzing the story, Mumby uses Giddens's (1979) three functions of ideology

and adds a fourth of his own. Thus, ideology functions to (1) transmute or deny contradictions, (2) naturalize the present through reification, (3) present sectional interests as universal, and (4) foster hegemonic forms of control.

While such an analysis is useful in drawing attention to the narrative-ideology-power constellation, it is limited insofar as (a) it is a secondary analysis (drawn from Martin et al., 1983); (b) the analysis is based on a single, fixed organizational story and must therefore make some large interpretive leaps (Boje, 1991); and (c) it lacks the context of naturally occurring storytelling events and is therefore limited in the kinds of conclusions it can draw. On the other hand, Helmer (1993) uses a structurational approach as the theoretical framework for his critical ethnography of a harness racing track. Through an analysis of the stories told by various groups (trainers, jockeys, etc.), he is able to provide insight into the system of legitimation and stratification that operates at the track, privileging some voices and marginalizing others. His analysis suggests that the discourse of the track is both characterized by, and understood through, three oppositional constructs: trainers versus administrators, "chemists" versus honest horsemen, and men versus women. Helmer shows how systems of signification (in this case, storytelling) connect to relations of domination by suggesting that these oppositional constructs function as sensemaking mechanisms, providing organization members with interpretive frames through which they produce, reproduce, or resist the dominant systems of meaning of the track as a capitalist site of profit making and labor exploitation.

While Giddens has provided critical scholars with a useful frame by which to examine organizational power, a number of researchers have taken up Habermas's (1979, 1984, 1987) critical theory of society as a way of critically exploring institutional power. The body of literature spawned by Habermas's work is voluminous, and it cannot be addressed fully here.

However, I will provide a sense of how it has been applied to organization studies.

Forester (1989, 1992, 1993) has applied Habermas's theory of communicative action to fieldwork settings, arguing that it "enables us to explore the continuing performance and practical accomplishment of relations of power. By refining Habermas's attention to a 'double structure of speech,' we come to examine specifically the micropolitics of speech and interaction" (1992, p. 62). Forester has used Habermas's "ideal speech situation" as a model for examining the ways in which discursive closure can occur in everyday organizational settings. Slightly reformulating Habermas's four claims to validity, he attempts to link them directly to issues of power and legitimation. Forester (1989) views organizations as structures of communicative interaction that reproduce particular social relations through relations of knowledge (truth), consent (rightness), trust (truthfulness), and comprehension (intelligibility). Placing these in a 3 by 4 matrix with three forms of power —decision making (Dahl, 1957), agenda setting (Bachrach & Baratz, 1962), and shaping felt needs (Lukes, 1974)—Forester (1989) comes up with 12 "forms of misinformation" that provide a map of the "micropolitics" of speech and interaction. Forester's work is unique in the extent to which it faithfully applies the principles of Habermas's work to ethnographies of organizational power.

Deetz (1992a, 1994, 1995) provides another important application of Habermas's work to the critical analysis of organizational power. Deetz's (1992a) work is particularly important in its development of a conception of power that is situated within a sociohistorical framework and that places issues of communication, identity, and meaning formation at its center. In brief, Deetz argues that the modern corporation has become the most important site of political decision making and, as such, plays a pivotal role in the development of our identities. Following Habermas (1984, 1987), Deetz argues that corporations have colonized the lifeworld (our sense of

community) and the institutional forms associated with it (e.g., education, interpersonal relations, family), such that any productive conceptions of communication, identity, and democracy have been appropriated and reframed in terms of managerial interests and technical forms of rationality (e.g., the reduction of communication to efficient information transmission). Deetz focuses on the ways in which organizational practices produce discursive closure and constitute the corporate individual. As an alternative to this view of modern organizational life, Deetz (1992a, 1995) argues for a communication-based model in which democracy is the product of open communication among a variety of stakeholders in organizations, rather than being the unproblematic product of a supposedly already existing democratic society, as narrowly defined through the politics of individual expression and voting rights.

Other critical studies of organizational power, while not as well developed as Deetz's, focus similarly on the connections among communication, meaning, identity, and the ongoing dialectic of control in the workplace. Rosen's (1985, 1988) critical ethnography of an advertising agency is a good example of such work, placing emphasis on the role of ritualized corporate behavior in the production and reproduction of capitalist relations of domination. His analyses of a corporate breakfast (1985) and an annual Christmas party (1988) reveal the ways that such events simultaneously provide workers with an interpretive frame by which they can make sense of their corporate identities and ideologically obscure the deep-structure power relations that secure their subordination to managerial corporate interests.

While critical organizational communication studies have focused primarily on the relationships among communication, ideology, and relations of hegemony (defined in terms of domination through consent), recent work has examined processes of resistance, arguing that such resistance does not have to be framed as ultimately reproducing relations of domination (as in, e.g., Burawoy, 1979, and Willis, 1977). Such work takes up the possibilities for genuine challenges to the "dominant hegemony," and the creation of spaces of resistance that provide alternative worldviews. Scott (1990) adopts this approach in his analysis of the resistant practices of subordinate groups. He argues that the reason why most critical and Marxist studies of power have focused on issues of domination rather than resistance (i.e., "power over" rather than "power to") is because such studies focus almost exclusively on the *public* contexts for the exercise of power. Distinguishing between "public transcripts" and "hidden transcripts," Scott suggests that much of the creative resistance of subordinate groups takes place not in public, but rather in discourse and behaviors that occur "offstage" and beyond the direct surveillance of those in power. Arguing that "relations of domination are, at the same time, relations of resistance" (p. 45), Scott (1990) focuses his attention on the "infrapolitics of subordinate groups" (p. 19), that is, low-profile forms of resistance that create dissident subcultures beyond the purview of "official," dominant political structures and systems of meaning.

Scott's analysis is extremely useful in its demonstration that surface-level "quiescence" or silence may actually function as a cover for deeper-level challenges to the apparent seamlessness of the dominant power structure. In this sense, his study provides a provocative reversal of the thesis suggested by both Willis and Burawoy. That is, rather than arguing that apparent resistance obscures deeper-level reproduction of relations of domination, Scott argues that the "manufacture of consent" provides a convenient cover for subordinate groups to create a space for resistance and the articulation of politically alternative worldviews. From this perspective, Scott (1990) offers "a way of addressing the issue of hegemonic incorporation" (p. 19) without ignoring the fundamentally dialectical character of power. Such a thesis is important from a critical communication perspective because it

suggests both that silence has important symbolic functions in terms of resistance and that public forms of communication may not provide researchers with a clear understanding of the dynamics of resistance and control.

In effect, critical studies have provided us with important insights into the relationships among identity, power, and everyday organizational practices. As mentioned earlier, critical studies attempt to explicate the agency-structure relationship, exploring the processes through which organizational actors both reproduce and resist the institutionalized meanings that are embedded in every act of communication. Importantly, critical studies have helped to contextualize discussions of ideology, hegemony, and reification and to situate organizing processes within larger social, political, and economic concerns. Critical studies have politicized organizational communication studies by exploring the intimate connections among communication, power, and identity formation and by suggesting possibilities for social change. However, the Marxist legacy of critical studies sometimes leads to rather totalizing, monolithic conceptions of power and resistance that overlook the multiple sites of struggle characteristic of modern social formations.

Partly in response to this limitation a development has occurred recently that has both enriched and complicated the terrain of critical studies, particularly in regards to our understanding of power as a pervasive, constitutive feature of organizational life. This development is the emergence of a postmodern perspective on organizations.

POWER, POSTMODERNISM, AND ORGANIZATIONAL COMMUNICATION

Postmodern analysis has emerged as an important and controversial mode of understanding and deconstructing contemporary human experience; it is the subject of a huge and ever-expanding body of literature in both the humanities and social sciences (Best & Kellner, 1991; Callinicos, 1989; Featherstone, 1988; Harvey, 1989; Rosenau & Bredemeier, 1993). A large corpus of literature has emerged in the past few years that directly addresses the impact of postmodern thought on organizational theory and research (Boje, Gephart, & Thatchenkery, 1996; Burrell, 1988; Cooper, 1989; Cooper & Burrell, 1988; Hassard, 1993a, 1993b; Hassard & Parker, 1993; Jeffcutt, 1994; Kilduff & Mehra, 1997; Parker, 1992a, 1992b; Tsoukas, 1992). My goal in this section is to map out the "basic contours" of postmodernism (recognizing that such a move is very unpostmodern!), articulating its relationship to organizational communication studies and the study of power. As in previous sections, I will examine the relationship between postmodernism and a conception of communication as constitutive of organizing.

Postmodernism is partly defined in terms of its relationship to modernism—it both comes after modernism and is a response to and critique of modernist sensibilities. In this sense, "the postmodern" characterizes both an epistemological break with "the modern" and a historical break with the epoch of modernity (Cooper & Burrell, 1988; Featherstone, 1988; Hassard, 1993a, 1993b). This distinction between an epistemological (modernism/postmodernism) and epochal (modernity/postmodernity) view of the modern-postmodern debate is also manifest in the literature of organization studies. Some scholars argue that the postmodern is a historical, ontological condition that demands new, postcapitalist, post-Fordist forms of organizing, characterized by small economies of scale, flexible production capabilities, and reintegration of the work process (e.g., Bergquist, 1993; Clegg, 1990; Harvey, 1989). On the other hand, a number of scholars pursue postmodern thought as a way to deconstruct the organization as a site of power that subjects members to various forms of disciplinary practice (Barker & Cheney, 1994; Burrell, 1992, 1993;

Daudi, 1986; Holmer-Nadesan, 1997, 1999: Jacques, 1996: Knights & Vurdubakis, 1994; Knights & Willmott, 1992; Linstead, 1993; Linstead & Grafton-Small, 1992). Given the focus of this chapter on the relationship between power and organizing, it is the latter perspective that will be explored here.

Postmodern thought has emerged in the context of a complex modernist landscape. Hassard (1993a, 1993b), for example, following Cooper and Burrell (1988), situates postmodernism in relation to two different and competing modernist orientations: systemic modernism and critical modernism. Systemic modernism represents the dominant orthodoxy in social thought today and, within organization studies, stands for progress in terms of the increasing rationalization of organizational life. From this perspective, "the main purposes of knowledge are to facilitate organizational control and to direct innovation and change" (Hassard, 1993a, p. 117). In most respects, the research discussed in this chapter under systems-rational perspectives falls under the rubric of systemic modernism.

Critical modernism, on the other hand, displays an ambiguous and ambivalent relationship with the Enlightenment project, simultaneously striving to maintain the emancipatory impulse of modernist thought and critiquing the direction that the Enlightenment has taken. It is the project of critical theory to oppose and deconstruct "traditional theory" (Horkheimer, 1986; Horkheimer & Adorno, 1988), and reappropriate self-consciousness and emancipation as the goals of knowledge. Critical modernism is thus both a deconstructive and reconstructive project, critiquing traditional science's lack of reflexivity and its connection to capitalist forms of power and domination, while at the same time developing a social theory that reclaims a sense of community and democracy (Habermas, 1979, 1984, 1987). The work discussed in the previous section falls under this domain.

Given this context, it is helpful to lay out some of the central issues that emerge across different postmodern writers:

1. Postmodernists challenge the very idea of rationality as it is developed in modernist thought. The idea of knowledge as progressive, cumulative, and continuous is rejected for a focus on discontinuity (Foucault, 1979).

2. Postmodernism rejects, or decenters, "the subject" as the origin of knowledge; instead, the subject is investigated as an effect of various power/knowledge regimes (Foucault, 1980b).

3. Following from this, language and discourse are conceived not as transparent, but rather as constitutive of knowledge and identity (Laclau, 1990; Laclau & Mouffe, 1985).

4. Postmodernism doesn't distinguish between truth and falsity, but rather attempts to understand how different kinds of power/knowledge relationships emerge at different historical conjunctures, thus laying out the rules for what counts as truth (Foucault, 1979, 1980b). Truth and power therefore implicate one another.

5. In contrast to the totalizing and universalizing tendencies of modernist thought, postmodern theorists view knowledge as ad hoc, local, and situational. Lyotard (1984) defines postmodernism as "incredulity toward metanarratives" (p. xxiv), arguing for paralogy, *petit récits* (little narratives), and "the search for instabilities" (p. 53) rather than for homology, grand narratives, and consensus.

6. The fomenting of a "crisis of representation" (Jameson, 1984) by postmodernism has translated into a concern with issues of marginality and otherness, and the articulation of worldviews that challenge the dominant orthodoxy (Clifford, 1988; Clifford & Marcus, 1986; Conquergood, 1991; West, 1993).

What impact have these developments had on our understanding of organizational power? While postmodern studies of organizations are still in a nascent state, there are some distinct trends. First, theorists such as Laclau and Mouffe (1985; Laclau, 1990), Foucault (1979, 1980a), and Derrida (1976) have provided radical organizational theorists and researchers with important understandings of organizations as sites of discursive power.

For example, Michel Foucault's (1975, 1979, 1980a, 1988) archaeological and genealogical studies of medicine, discipline, sexuality, and madness as well as his more philosophical writings on the status of knowledge (1973, 1980b) provide us with insight into the relationships among power, knowledge, subjectivity, and institutional forms and practices. Foucault's work has been adopted in organizational communication studies as a way of examining organizations as sites of disciplinary power (Barker, 1993, 1999; Clegg, 1989a, 1989b, 1994a, 1994b; Deetz, 1992a, 1992b; Holmer-Nadesan, 1997; Knights & Vurdubakis, 1994; Knights & Willmott, 1992; Marsden, 1993). In such a conception, power is not imposed from above (what Foucault critiques as a "sovereign" view of power), nor does it originate from a single source (e.g., as with Marxism's framing of all power relations within capitalist relations of domination—a position of which Foucault is highly critical); rather, power is widely dispersed, having multiple sites and modes of functioning. Social actors are "disciplined" to the extent that they become objects of knowledge of various discourses within these sites and thus come to know themselves (as subjects) in particular ways (e.g., as sexual, rule governed, normal). In Foucault's ("Florence," 1994) terms, "What are the processes of subjectivization and objectivization that allow the subject to become, as subject, an object of knowledge?" (p. 315). Discourses are thus texts and communicative practices that function within (and reproduce) certain "truth games" (rules for what counts as true or false), defining the subject and submitting him or her to processes of normalization.

For example, recent work on self-managing teams (Barker, 1993, 1999; Barker & Cheney, 1994; Mumby & Stohl, 1992) provides insight into how an ostensibly participative form of organizing has reconstituted the way power is exercised in "postbureaucratic" organizations. Barker (1993) shows how a shift from hierarchical, bureaucratic forms of control to "concertive control" (Tompkins & Cheney, 1985), in which locus of control shifts from managers to the workers themselves, is achieved through the establishment of work teams that engage in self-surveillance (what Foucault, 1979, calls "panopticism"). Power is produced from the bottom up through the everyday discursive practices that construct team members' identities. Similarly, Mumby and Stohl's (1992) analysis of work teams shows how absent members are labeled and identified as "deviant" by other team members and are required to provide an accounting of, or apology for, their deviant behavior. Both of these studies exemplify an important principle of Foucault's conception of power: it is positive rather than negative. Power does not forbid and negate, but rather produces identities, knowledge, and the possibilities for behavior. In this sense, power and knowledge are indissolubly linked, producing each other, and articulating what Foucault (1980a) calls "power/knowledge regimes."

Foucault's influence on the study of organizations as sites of disciplinary micropractices is complemented by work that evolves from Derrida's (1976, 1978) deconstructive approach to literary texts (Cooper, 1989). Derrida's deconstructive project is a critique of the "metaphysics of presence" as the privileged mode of rationality in Western thinking. This metaphysics is both logocentric and phonocentric, privileging the mind (logocentrism) and the speaking subject (phonocentrism) as that which validates human experience. Derrida (1976) deconstructs this metaphysics of presence by arguing that "there is nothing outside of the text" (p. 158); he shows how all attempts to impose meaning are rooted in hierarchically arranged binary oppositions, such that the stability and dominance of one term is dependent on a suppressed or marginalized opposite term (e.g., male/female, mind/body, public/private). De-

construction therefore involves a double movement of overturning these binary opposites (thus destabilizing the dominant term) and engaging in a process of "metaphorization," by which the opposing terms are shown to implicate and define one another in an endless play of signifiers (Cooper, 1989, p. 483). For example, Mumby and Putnam (1992) deconstruct the concept of "bounded rationality" by juxtaposing it with the notion of "bounded emotionality." However, rather than privileging the latter over the former as an alternate way of organizing, they metaphorically play the one against the other, speculating about "the rationality of emotions" and "the emotionality of the rational" as ways of thinking about organizing processes.

Derrida (1976) appropriates and transforms the Saussurian notion of *différence* (language as a system of difference) by coining the term *différance*. This term simultaneously conveys the ideas of deferring (or postponing) and differing. Meaning, then, involves a continuous play of différance, in which a text is never fully present to us, but derives its meaning from a system of signifiers that constantly defer to, and are different from, other absent signifiers. Meaning only appears fixed because of an apparently straightforward positive relationship between signifiers and signifieds. Derrida demonstrates that this positive relationship is chimerical by examining the play of presence and absence on which the meaning of a text depends. There is nothing outside of the text, then, in that there is no external referent to which a text refers, only other texts.

Derrida's work has been employed by a number of organization scholars to explore and critique the representational practices of canonical organizational texts (Calás & Smircich, 1991; Kilduff, 1993; Mumby & Putnam, 1992). Each of these researchers attempts to deconstruct the structures of presence and absence in such texts to expose the hierarchical oppositions that privilege certain meanings and forms of knowledge over others. Such deconstructive projects, like much of Foucault's work, draw attention to the relationships among representational practices, power, and institutionalized orthodoxies regarding what counts as "knowledge" in the field of organization studies. But deconstructionists have not focused purely on organization scholars. Deconstruction of the discursive practices of organizational life is also an emergent area of study. Linstead (1992), for example, argues for the development of a deconstructive ethnography by which to explore the tension between organization and disorganization. From this perspective, "organization . . . is continuously emergent, constituted and constituting, produced and consumed by subjects who, like organization, are themselves fields of the trace, sites of intertextuality" (Linstead, 1992, p. 60).

While it is hard to identify full-blown organizational ethnographies that take a deconstructive approach, several scholars have used deconstruction as a means to explore the tensions, absences, and contradictions that connect power and subjectivity (Burrell, 1993; Kondo, 1990; J. Martin, 1990). From this perspective, "organization always harbours within itself that which transgresses it, namely, disorganization" (Cooper, 1989, p. 480). One of the characteristics of such work is its tendency to engage in play, parody, and pastiche, undermining the reader's confidence in the authority of a conventional, linear, narrative style (Martin, 1992). For example, Burrell's (1993) whimsically titled "Eco and the Bunnymen" casts aside conventional academic form to question simultaneously the representational practices of academia and the structure of the modern university, and to provide a witty critique of the commodification of knowledge and bodies at the Academy of Management annual convention.

Finally, a considerable number of deconstructive and genealogical analyses of organizing practices are emerging from the field of accounting (Arrington & Francis, 1989; Hoskin & Macve, 1986, 1988; Miller & O'Leary, 1987; Power & Laughlin, 1992). This research provides an instance where the work of Derrida and Foucault coincide. Given Derrida's concern with writing, and Foucault's concern with professional discourse and its relationship to disciplinary practices and power/knowledge regimes, the critical study of accounting practices is an important area through which to examine the relationships between discursive micropractices, on the one hand, and the macrostructures of organizational power, on the other. Thus, this work deconstructs the notion that accounting is "only a techné of progress" (Arrington & Francis, 1989, p. 22), and instead argues that it is "an important calculative practice which is part of a much wider modern apparatus of power which emerges conspicuously in the early years of this [20th] century" (Miller & O'Leary, 1987, p. 234). Similarly, Hoskin and Macve (1988) conceptualize accounting as "a mode of 'writing the world' which, like the modern examination, embodies the power relations and the knowledge relations of a disciplinary and self-disciplinary culture" (p. 68).

In sum, postmodern thought has had a growing influence on the field of organizational communication. Its focus on the relationships among power, knowledge, and discourse provides important insights into how modern organizations function as disciplinary sites that structure meanings and identities. Postmodernism situates communication as central to the creation of multiple, contested, and fragmented subjectivities and power relations. As such, communication is not simply the creation of consensual meanings and communities but is also integral to normalization processes, power/knowledge regimes, and disciplined subjectivities, as well as the means by which such processes are resisted.

It would be wrong, however, to claim a complete disjuncture between critical and postmodern conceptions of power and discourse. While it is true that the more "skeptical" postmodernists (Rosenau, 1992) are deeply suspicious of theorists who invoke notions of emancipation from systems of oppression, many theorists view the relationship between critical theory and postmodernism as productive and dialectical rather than adversarial. For example, Smart (1986) highlights important connections between Gramsci's (1971) conception of hegemony and Foucault's analysis of disciplinary micropractices, arguing that "Foucault's work has revealed the complex multiple processes from which the strategic combination of forms of hegemony may emerge" (p. 160). Similarly, Lentricchia (1988) suggests that "if Marx gives us the theory of pure capitalism, then Foucault, on discipline, gives us the theory of practical capitalism whose essential category is *detail*" (p. 60, emphasis in original).

Perhaps one of the tasks of radical organization theorists is not to articulate disjunctures and oppositions between critical theory and postmodernism, but rather to conceptualize ways in which the two function dialectically, hence providing new and insightful means of exploring the relationships among communication, meaning, and organizational power. Although some writers believe no such rapprochement is possible (Callinicos, 1989; Eagleton, 1995), theorists such as Agger (1991), Best and Kellner (1991), and Deetz (1992a) have all suggested ways in which we can overcome both the foundationalism and potential elitism of critical theory, on the one hand (Alvesson & Willmott, 1992b), and the nihilism and relativism of postmodern thought, on the other.

In the next section, I present feminist thought as one perspective through which the study of communication and power can retain the emancipatory potential of critical theory, while simultaneously adopting a multiperspectival approach to knowledge claims and the process of critique.

FEMINIST STUDIES OF POWER, POLITICS, AND ORGANIZATIONS

I turn to feminism as a way of examining organizational power for two reasons. First, this move partly reflects my own intellectual development, and my recognition that it is impossible to study and theorize adequately about organizational power without addressing its gendered character. Organizations are "gendered" in the sense that "advantage and disadvantage, exploitation and control, action and emotion, meaning and identity, are patterned through and in terms of a distinction between male and female, masculine and feminine" (Acker, 1990, p. 146). Second, while critical theory and postmodernism provide robust analytic frameworks for studying power, their link to everyday practices is sometimes tenuous. Feminism, on the other hand, emerges directly from recognizing the institutional character of women's economic, political, and ideological subordination. In this sense, feminism never loses sight of the relationship between theory and practice.

In comparison with other disciplines the field of organizational communication has been slow to take up feminist perspectives, but the past decade has seen a distinct upsurge in feminist-oriented theory and research (Allen, 1996, 1998; Ashcraft, 1998, 2000; Bullis, 1993; Buzzanell, 1994; Clair, 1998; Gregg, 1993; Holmer-Nadesan, 1996; Marshall, 1993; Mumby, 1996; Sotirin & Gottfried, 1999; Spradlin, 1998; Trethewey, 1997, 1999a, 1999b). Similarly, in the 1990s management studies began to develop an identifiable body of feminist-influenced research (e.g., Acker, 1990, 1992; Alvesson & Billing, 1992; Calás, 1992; Calás & Smircich, 1991, 1992a, 1992b; Ferguson, 1984; Gherardi, 1994, 1995; Mills, 1995; Mills & Tancred, 1992; Mumby & Putnam, 1992). However, the general neglect of a systematic gendered approach to organizations has led Rothschild and Davies (1994) to claim that "the assumption of gender neutrality may be one of the great blind spots, and errors, of twentieth-century organizational theory" (p. 583).

Feminist perspectives on organizational power examine and critique the ways in which binary thinking (male/female, culture/nature, rational/emotional, etc.) lies at the root of all attempts to make sense of and to construct institutional forms, social practices, and actors' identities and experiences. In this context, gender is a "site of difference" that constructs relations of domination, marginalization, and resistance (Barrett, 1995), defined within a system of hegemonic masculinity (Connell, 1985, 1987). Even though there are multiple feminist perspectives that analyze these issues (Tong, 1989), the focus here centers on three areas of theory and research that directly address the intersection of communication, gender, and power: (1) feminist rereading/rewriting of organizational theory and research, (2) organizations as gendered sites of domination and resistance, and (3) feminist alternatives to patriarchal forms of organizing. Each of these areas is briefly discussed below (see Mumby, 1996, for a more detailed discussion).

Feminist Rereading/Rewriting of Organizational Theory and Research

Research from this perspective draws on postmodern theory to deconstruct the assumptions that underlie mainstream organizational communication studies. Such work demonstrates how theory and knowledge are built on patriarchal models of scholarship and rationality that systematically exclude alternative ways of theorizing organizational structures and practices (Acker & Van Houten, 1974; Calás & Smircich, 1991, 1992a; Ferguson, 1994; Holvino, 1997; Jacques, 1992; Mumby & Putnam, 1992; Nkomo, 1992; Putnam & Mumby, 1993). As in postmodern studies, feminist studies problematize the notion of "representation" and show how it embodies and obscures numerous political, epistemological, and gender issues.

Feminists appropriate postmodern theory to address the gendered relationship between the representational practices of the scholarly enterprise and those of the corporate enterprise, and the ways in which this relationship reproduces power. For example, the work of Calás and Smircich (1991, 1992a, 1992b) explores "how the idea of 'gender' can be a strategy through which we can question what *has been represented* as organization theory"

(1992a, emphasis in original). Their analyses are deconstructive, exploring the ways in which gender is "normally" written into organizational theorizing. Their strategy is to problematize gender, demonstrating the various ways in which it is represented, suppressed, marginalized, and made absent in the process of theory and research. In their (1991) deconstruction of organizational leadership texts, they juxtapose against "leadership" the notion of "seduction" (drawing on Braudrillard, 1990). By providing "seductive" readings of leadership texts (through the use of a split page) they "analyze the dependency of supposedly opposite concepts on one another and [show] how rhetoric and cultural conditions work together to conceal this dependency" (p. 569). (See Schwartz, 1993, and Calás & Smircich, 1993, for the aftermath of this article.)

The body of deconstructive work that is developing within postmodern feminist thought exemplifies what Gergen (1992) refers to as the "replacement of the real by the representational" (p. 213). That is, once we undermine the idea that language and communication are merely tools for representing the real, then the positivist modernist attempt to determine organizational reality through various forms of empirical investigation becomes increasingly suspect. As beginning points for feminist theories of organization, these studies break the silence implied by the idea that objective truth is the only possibility, and they show how various truths are communicatively constructed. By interrogating the intersection of discourse, power, knowledge, gender, and organizational practice, this work opens spaces for rethinking organizational analysis. However, one of the limitations of such work is its privileging of formal—usually scholarly—texts and its general neglect of the mundane, quotidian, and communication dimensions of gendered forms of power and domination. Although there is clearly a connection between theorizing about organizing and organizational processes themselves, there is clearly a need to examine gendered organizational practices empirically and in situ.

Organizations as Gendered Sites of Domination and Resistance

This second position focuses on the systematic "engendering" of organizational practices that constitute men's and women's identities and access to power in differential ways. This research is theoretically eclectic, drawing on both neo-Marxist theory and the poststructuralist focus on discourse. Analyses examine the relationships among capitalism, patriarchy, organization, and gendered communicative practices (Clair, 1993b, 1994, 1998; Cockburn, 1984; Collinson, 1992; Ferguson, 1984; Kondo, 1990; J. Martin, 1990; Pringle, 1989). A characteristic of this literature is a dual focus on (1) power-as-domination, and (2) (em)power(ment)-as-resistance.

In the former category are studies that examine the communicative and material processes through which patriarchy is produced and reproduced. Such work ranges from the discursive construction of hegemonic gender identities (e.g., Angus, 1993; Collinson, 1988, 1992; Connell, 1985, 1987; J. Martin, 1990, 1994; Pringle, 1989) to the symbolic and material dimensions of sexual harassment in the workplace (Clair, 1993a, 1993b; MacKinnon, 1979; Strine, 1992; Taylor & Conrad, 1992; Townsley & Geist, in press; Wood, 1992). For example, J. Martin (1990) provides a deconstruction of an organizational story (told to demonstrate the company's pro-employee maternity policy) to show how it reaffirms dominant understandings of sexuality and gender in the workplace. Through textual strategies such as dismantling dichotomies, examining silences in the story, and attending to disruptions and contradictions, Martin shows how a story that—at least ostensibly—affirms the importance of women to an organization can be read as maintaining and reproducing patriarchal modes of reasoning, showing how both women and men are structured by, and are the effects of, institutionalized discursive practices that reproduce gendered power relations.

Similar themes are taken up in Pringle's (1989) study of secretaries, Ferguson's (1984) critique of bureaucracy, and recent work that examines the discursive construction of masculinity (Angus, 1993; Collinson, 1988, 1992; Hearn, 1992, 1994). In each, the central issue is the communicative processes through which certain forms of gendered identity are articulated and constructed, thus reproducing dominant relations of power. Hearn's (1994) development of a "violence" perspective on gender and organizations forcefully brings home the extreme consequences of hegemonic masculinity.

On the other hand, feminist studies also examine the possibilities for gendered forms of resistance to organizational power relations. Again, this work is eclectic in its theoretical orientation. Feminist neo-Marxist research focuses on the possibilities for collective resistance and change and examines the ways in which community and egalitarianism can emerge within hierarchical and patriarchal structures (Benson, 1992; Boyce, 1995; Gottfried, 1994; Gottfried & Weiss, 1994; Lamphere, 1985; Zavella, 1985). Gottfried and Weiss (1994), for example, develop the notion of feminist "compound organizations" to demonstrate how women faculty at a major research university created their own collective, nonhierarchical, compound decision-making system that operated within, yet transcended the usual constraints of bureaucratic university life. The authors propose "compound" as a metaphor that incorporates multiplicity, allowing women with different agendas and perspectives to come together as a community within a large, potentially hostile, community. Similarly, Boyce (1995) and Spradlin (1998) adopt critical feminist perspectives to show the links among gender, sexuality, and power, simultaneously critiquing the pervasive homophobia of organizations and pointing to a diverse and inclusive model of organizing.

Other feminist studies have adopted a postmodern orientation toward issues of gender, organizing, and resistance (Bell &

Forbes, 1994; Clair, 1998; Gregg, 1993; Holmer-Nadesan, 1996; Trethewey, 1997, 1999a, 1999b). For example, Gregg's (1993) analysis of two activist women's groups draws on poststructuralist theory to problematize the notion of collective action as rooted in shared and homogeneous identities. Developing a "politics of location," she shows how political action and agency involve a negotiation among various "subject positions." Thus, in her analysis of a union organizing campaign, Gregg shows how the women who were the targets of the campaign attempted to maintain coherent identities in the face of multiple, competing, and unstable subjectivities available through discourses of race, class, and political position. From a communication perspective, "identity is a matter of negotiating the inconsistencies and contradictions between subject positions and everyday realities . . . available in both discourse and practices" (Gregg, 1993, p. 25).

Feminist postmodern views of gender, organizing, and resistance, therefore, reject efforts to articulate universal principles of identity and collective action rooted in women's common experience of oppression. Instead, resistance is complex, local, and often contradictory. For example, Bell and Forbes's (1994) analysis of "office graffiti" illustrates secretarial resistance to bureaucratic discipline as an example of individual "tactics" (De Certeau, 1984) that parody and subvert dominant institutional meanings without any pretensions to collective action or an identity politics. Such politics are much more visible, however, in the third area of feminist research.

Feminist Alternatives to Patriarchal Forms of Organizing

The third broad area of concern in feminist approaches to organization studies examines women's alternative organizations. Such organizations are premised on the recognition that traditional bureaucratic structures are not gen-

der neutral, but represent the institutionalization of patriarchy. Hence, egalitarian and participative organizational structures are realizable only in contexts where hierarchy and its attendant logics and forms of communication are transformed. Marshall (1989) uses the phrase "organizational heterarchy" to describe a structure that "has no one person or principle in command. Rather, temporary pyramids of authority form as and when appropriate in a system of mutual constraints and influences" (p. 289). While such an organizational structure rarely—if ever—sustains itself in pure form in the "real world," several scholars have studied attempts to enact this structure within the constraints of capitalist economic and political systems (Ferree & Martin, 1995; Hacker & Elcorobairutia, 1987; Lont, 1988; Maguire & Mohtar, 1994; P. Martin, 1990; Reinelt, 1994; Rodriguez, 1988; Rothschild-Whitt, 1979; Sealander & Smith, 1986).

Although collectivist and feminist organizations are not isomorphic, there appears to be considerable overlap in the values, structures, processes, goals, and outcomes of each. For example, Patricia Martin (1990) suggests that "feminist organizations are a unique species of the genus social movement organization [and are] pro-woman, political, and socially transformational" (pp. 183-184). Feminist values emphasize the importance of mutual caring, support, and empowerment, with work viewed as social rather than technical. Such values suggest a view of communication as focused on the construction of community rather than on the promotion of organizational efficiency. In addition, feminist outcomes revolve around both individual and societal transformation, aimed at the alleviation of women's oppression. Here, communication becomes a political act aimed at resisting patriarchy and articulating alternative, feminist realities.

For example, Maguire and Mohtar's (1994) study of a women's center shows how members discursively position themselves in opposition to state agencies and in solidarity with each other. However, Martin also notes the lack of consensus on the defining qualities of a feminist organization. For example, liberal feminists do not see hierarchy and bureaucracy as intrinsically patriarchal (Iannello, 1992), and many feminist organizations are for-profit rather than nonprofit, large/national rather than small/local, and dependent rather than autonomous. The National Organization for Women is the most visible example of an organization with a large membership (250,000) and extensive bureaucratic structure that works to improve the political and economic status of women.

In sum, feminist theory and research clearly provide important ways of understanding, critiquing, and transforming contemporary organizations. Feminist studies of organizational communication are critical to an appreciation of power as a central, constitutive feature of organizational life. To neglect feminism as a mode of analysis is to overlook the gendered character of organizational power and its relationship to "doing gender" (Gherardi, 1994; West & Zimmerman, 1987). However, the picture I have painted in this section contains its own elisions and aporia. For example, I have not addressed systematically the issue of race and its relationship to organizing processes. While black feminist theory has emerged as an important form of social critique (hooks, 1984, 1992; Wallace, 1992), little work of significance has emerged in organization communication studies that moves beyond the "race as variable" approach (see Allen, 1995, for an exception). Work by Calás (1992), Grimes (1994), and Nkomo (1992) begins to explore the representational practices through which race is constructed as a category in the organizational literature, but it is difficult to identify a distinct body of critical work in this area (although see Essed, 1991; van Dijk, 1993). One promising area of research involves "interrogating whiteness" (Frankenberg, 1993; hooks, 1992; Nakayama & Krizek, 1995). This work shows how "whiteness" as a racial and gendered category

is not neutral, but rather is socially constructed through various discursive practices.

Feminist studies thus examine organizational power in ways that are not easily reducible to other perspectives by virtue of their focus on gender as a constitutive feature of the power ↔ communication ↔ organization relationship. Its focus on praxis and the material implications of gender domination provides an important means of contextualizing critical and postmodern thought. At the same time, feminist studies must remain open to possibilities for transformation by previously marginalized voices. Feminism, by definition, avoids reification and the setting up of binary oppositions. Through the articulation of a multiplicity of voices, possibilities for critique and the development of inclusive communities are realized.

CONCLUSION AND FUTURE DIRECTIONS

Throughout this chapter, I have focused on the relationships among communication, power, and organization. Early models of organizational power focused largely on the cognitive, decision-making, and structural issues associated with the exercise of power. The most sophisticated of these perspectives elucidates a resource dependence approach in which power accrues to those groups that are able to position themselves as indispensable to the organization by virtue of resources held. In such models, communication plays a "handmaiden" role, functioning as the mechanism by which groups represent their power. This perspective, I have argued, neglects the extent to which power exists only as a product of the intersubjective systems of meaning that organization members create through their communication practices. The interpretive, critical, postmodern, and feminist perspectives on power represent varying attempts to explicate communication in its constitutive relationship to identity, power, and organizing. What, then, are the consequences of this work for the way we study organizational power?

First, it generates a much greater level of reflexivity in conceptualizing and researching organizational power. The metatheoretical issues addressed in this chapter make clear that we—as scholars of power—are never exempt from the processes that we analyze, but are always enmeshed in disciplinary practices that both enable and constrain our sensemaking attempts. We write about power, but we also are the "subject effects" of power/knowledge regimes. There is perhaps no clearer example of this process than Blair, Brown, and Baxter's (1994) stunning deconstruction of the blind review process in refereed journal publication. Their analysis exposes the fallacy of knowledge as somehow neutral, nonpolitical, and existing outside of the exercise of power. As scholars, we need to be aware of the extent to which we either produce or resist dominant discourses.

A second and related consequence of this view of power is that, in a basic sense, people are produced by power. Power is not something that can be taken up and used or discarded at will. This narrowly political sense of power overlooks the ways in which a subject's position exists through the intersection of discourses that "fix" meanings in certain ways. Power relations revolve around the production, maintenance, and transformation of those meanings. From a communication perspective, the study of organizational power requires theory and research that examine how communication practices construct identities, experiences, and ways of knowing that serve some interests over others. Part of our future agenda, then, is to engage in empirical analyses that explicate the ongoing, everyday character of this process. While Foucault, for example, has shown how this form of discipline has worked historically, we need to generate insight into its mundane (and perhaps most insidious) features.

Third, the shift to a focus on the relationships among communication, power, and organizing allows for a genuine move beyond the reification of organization-as-structure. If organizations are reconceptualized as discursive sites of identity formation and meaning creation, then the possibilities for what traditionally counts as "an organization" are greatly expanded. In such a move, organizations are viewed as communication communities in which the purpose of research is to understand how certain discourses get articulated to create systems of meaning and power. Organizations are reframed as constellations of intersubjective meaning and experience, that is, as "the sites where individuals 'inhabit' numerous discursive positions simultaneously, and those places in which established everyday discourses . . . give meaning to [inter]subjective experience by suggesting appropriate positions from which to make sense of one's life" (Gregg, 1993, p. 5).

Finally, we need to bring more theory, more voices, and more politics to the study of organization than most research addresses (Ferguson, 1994). This does not mean simply adding different voices and stirring, but rather developing alternative viewpoints and constructs as a way of fundamentally transforming our understanding of organizations and power. Opening the study of organizations to more voices is at one level concerned with addressing issues of race, class, gender, and sexuality as constitutive sites of organizational power, meaning, and identity formation. However, at another, related level, "other voices" highlight the study of noncorporate, nonbureaucratic organizational forms. For the most part, organizational research takes as its object of interest the business setting and industrial workplace. Given the connection of organizational scholars with managerial interests, this is hardly surprising. However, this chapter examines scholarship that questions extant organization theory and practice because it produces and reproduces systems of oppression that distort identity and meaning formation. In this context, future research needs to examine the ways in which social actors engage in identity formation through collective behavior that embodies alternative notions of community and that provides members with voices that make a difference in the ongoing life of the organization (Cheney, 1995, 1999; Rothschild-Whitt, 1979).

Given the amount of theory generated over the past few years in organizational communication studies, Ferguson's (1994) call for additional theory may seem strange. However, if we view theorizing not as a purely ideational, abstract process, but as ways of "thinking otherwise" and moving beyond common sense views of the world, then the ongoing theorizing of organizational life is indispensable. With the development of multiple perspectives on organizational power, it is important that we continue to explore their limitations and possibilities.

REFERENCES

Acker, J. (1990). Hierarchies, jobs, bodies: A theory of gendered organizations. *Gender & Society, 4,* 139-158.

Acker, J. (1992). Gendering organizational theory. In A. Mills & P. Tancred (Eds.), *Gendering organizational analysis.* Newbury Park, CA: Sage.

Acker, J., & Van Houten, D. (1974). Differential recruitment and control: The sex structuring of organizations. *Administrative Science Quarterly, 19,* 152-163.

Agger, B. (1991). *A critical theory of public life: Knowledge, discourse and politics in an age of decline.* London: Falmer.

Allen, B. J. (1995). "Diversity" and organizational communication. *Journal of Applied Communication Research, 23,* 143-155.

Allen, B. J. (1996). Feminist standpoint theory: A black woman's (re)view of organizational socialization. *Communication Studies, 47,* 257-271.

Allen, B. J. (1998). Black womanhood and feminist standpoints. *Management Communication Quarterly, 11,* 575-586.

Althusser, L. (1971). *Lenin and philosophy.* New York: Monthly Review Press.

Alvesson, M. (1985). A critical framework for organizational analysis. *Organization Studies, 6,* 117-138.

Alvesson, M., & Billing, Y. D. (1992). Gender and organizations. *Organization Studies, 13,* 73-102.

Alvesson, M., & Willmott, H. (Eds.). (1992a). *Critical management studies.* Newbury Park, CA: Sage.

Alvesson, M., & Willmott, H. (1992b). On the idea of emancipation in organization studies. *Academy of Management Review, 17,* 432-464.

Angus, L. B. (1993). Masculinity and women teachers at Christian Brothers College. *Organization Studies, 14,* 235-260.

Arrington, C. E., & Francis, J. E. (1989). Letting the chat out of the bag: Deconstruction, privilege and accounting research. *Accounting, Organizations and Society, 14,* 1-28.

Ashcraft, K. L. (1998). "I wouldn't say I'm a feminist, but . . .": Organizational micropractice and gender identity. *Management Communication Quarterly, 11,* 587-597.

Ashcraft, K. L. (2000). Empowering "professional" relationships: Organizational communication meets feminist practice. *Management Communication Quarterly, 13,* 347-392.

Astley, W. G., & Sachdeva, P. S. (1984). Structural sources of intraorganizational power: A theoretical synthesis. *Academy of Management Review, 9,* 104-113.

Axley, S. (1984). Managerial and organizational communication in terms of the conduit metaphor. *Academy of Management Review, 9,* 428-437.

Bachrach, P., & Baratz, M. (1962). Two faces of power. *American Political Science Review, 56,* 947-952.

Bachrach, P., & Baratz, M. (1963). Decisions and nondecisions: An analytical framework. *American Political Science Review, 57,* 641-651.

Banks, S. (1994). Performing flight announcements: The case of flight attendants' work discourse. *Text and Performance Quarterly, 14,* 253-267.

Banks, S., & Riley, P. (1993). Structuration theory as an ontology for communication research. In S. A. Deetz (Ed.), *Communication yearbook 16* (pp. 167-196). Newbury Park, CA: Sage.

Barker, J. (1993). Tightening the iron cage: Concertive control in self-managing teams. *Administrative Science Quarterly, 38,* 408-437.

Barker, J. (1999). *The discipline of teamwork: Participation and concertive control.* Thousand Oaks, CA: Sage.

Barker, J., & Cheney, G. (1994). The concept and practices of discipline in contemporary organizational life. *Communication Monographs, 61,* 19-43.

Barrett, F. J. (1995). Finding voice within the gender order. *Journal of Organizational Change Management, 8*(6), 8-15.

Baudrillard, J. (1990). *Seduction.* New York: St. Martin's.

Bell, E. L., & Forbes, L. C. (1994). Office folklore in the academic paperwork empire: The interstitial space of gendered (con)texts. *Text and Performance Quarterly, 14,* 181-196.

Benson, J. K. (1977). Organizations: A dialectical view. *Administrative Science Quarterly, 22,* 1-21.

Benson, S. (1992). "The clerking sisterhood": Rationalization and the work culture of saleswomen in American department stores, 1890-1960. In A. J. Mills &

P. Tancred (Eds.), *Gendering organizational analysis* (pp. 222-234). Newbury Park, CA: Sage.

Bergquist, W. (1993). *The postmodern organization: Mastering the art of irreversible change.* San Francisco: Jossey-Bass.

Best, S., & Kellner, D. (1991). *Postmodern theory: Critical interrogations.* New York: Guilford.

Bittner, E. (1974). The concept of organization. In R. Turner (Ed.), *Ethnomethodology* (pp. 69-81). Harmondsworth, UK: Penguin.

Blair, C., Brown, J. R., & Baxter, L. A. (1994). Disciplining the feminine. *Quarterly Journal of Speech, 80,* 383-409.

Boden, D. (1994). *The business of talk.* Cambridge, UK: Polity.

Boje, D. M. (1991). The storytelling organization: A study of story performance in an office-supply firm. *Administrative Science Quarterly, 36,* 106-126.

Boje, D. M., Gephart, R. P., & Thatchenkery, T. J. (Eds.). (1996). *Postmodern management and organization theory.* Thousand Oaks, CA: Sage.

Boyce, M. E. (1995). Solidarity and praxis: Being a change agent in a university setting. *Journal of Organizational Change Management, 8*(6), 58-66.

Braverman, H. (1974). *Labor and monopoly capital: The degradation of work in the twentieth century.* New York: Monthly Review Press.

Brown, R. H. (1978). Bureaucracy as praxis: Toward a political phenomenology of formal organizations. *Administrative Science Quarterly, 23,* 365-382.

Bullis, C. (1993). At least it is a start. In S. A. Deetz (Ed.), *Communication yearbook 16* (pp. 144-154). Newbury Park, CA: Sage.

Bullis, C. A., & Tompkins, P. K. (1989). The forest ranger revisited: A study of control practices and identification. *Communication Monographs, 56,* 287-306.

Burawoy, M. (1979). *Manufacturing consent: Changes in the labor process under monopoly capitalism.* Chicago: University of Chicago Press.

Burrell, G. (1988). Modernism, postmodernism and organizational analysis 2: The contribution of Michel Foucault. *Organization Studies, 9,* 221-235.

Burrell, G. (1992). The organization of pleasure. In M. Alvesson & H. Willmott (Eds.), *Critical management studies* (pp. 66-89). Newbury Park, CA: Sage.

Burrell, G. (1993). Eco and the bunnymen. In J. Hassard & M. Parker (Eds.), *Postmodernism and organizations* (pp. 71-82). Newbury Park, CA: Sage.

Burrell, G., & Morgan, G. (1979). *Sociological paradigms and organisational analysis.* London: Heinemann.

Buzzanell, P. (1994). Gaining a voice: Feminist organizational communication theorizing. *Management Communication Quarterly, 7,* 339-383.

Calás, M. (1992). An/other silent voice? Representing "Hispanic woman" in organizational texts. In A. J. Mills & P. Tancred (Eds.), *Gendering organizational analysis* (pp. 201-221). Newbury Park, CA: Sage.

Calás, M., & Smircich, L. (1991). Voicing seduction to silence leadership. *Organization Studies, 12,* 567-601.

Calás, M., & Smircich, L. (1992a). Re-writing gender into organizational theorizing: Directions from feminist perspectives. In M. Reed & M. Hughes (Eds.), *Rethinking organization: New directions in organization theory and analysis* (pp. 227-253). Newbury Park, CA: Sage.

Calás, M., & Smircich, L. (1992b). Using the "F" word: Feminist theories and the social consequences of organizational research. In A. J. Mills & P. Tancred (Eds.), *Gendering organizational analysis* (pp. 222-234). Newbury Park, CA: Sage.

Calás, M., & Smircich, L. (1993). Desperately seeking—? Or who/what was Howard's car? *Organization Studies, 14,* 282.

Callinicos, A. (1989). *Against postmodernism.* Cambridge, UK: Polity.

Cavanagh, G. F., Moberg, D. J., & Velasquez, M. (1981). The ethics of organizational politics. *Academy of Management Review, 6,* 363-374.

Cheney, G. (1983). On the various and changing meanings of organizational membership: A field study of organizational identification. *Communication Monographs, 50,* 342-362.

Cheney, G. (1995). Democracy in the workplace: Theory and practice from the perspective of communication. *Journal of Applied Communication Research, 23,* 167-200.

Cheney, G. (1999). *Values at work: Employee participation meets market pressure at Mondragón.* Ithaca, NY: Cornell University Press.

Clair, R. P. (1993a). The bureaucratization, commodification, and privatization of sexual harassment through institutional discourse. *Management Communication Quarterly, 7,* 123-157.

Clair, R. P. (1993b). The use of framing devices to sequester organizational narratives: Hegemony and harassment. *Communication Monographs, 60,* 113-136.

Clair, R. P. (1994). Resistance and oppression as a self-contained opposite: An organizational communication analysis of one man's story of sexual harassment. *Western Journal of Communication, 58,* 235-262.

Clair, R. P. (1998). *Organizing silence: A world of possibilities.* Albany: State University of New York Press.

Clegg, S. (1975). *Power, rule, and domination.* New York: Routledge and Kegan Paul.

Clegg, S. (1981). Organization and control. *Administrative Science Quarterly, 26,* 545-562.

Clegg, S. (1987). The language of power and the power of language. *Organization Studies, 8,* 61-70.

Clegg, S. (1989a). *Frameworks of power.* Newbury Park, CA: Sage.

Clegg, S. (1989b). Radical revisions: Power, discipline and organizations. *Organization Studies, 10,* 97-115.

Clegg, S. (1990). *Modern organizations: Organization studies in a postmodern world.* Newbury Park, CA: Sage.

Clegg, S. (1994a). Power relations and the constitution of the resistant subject. In J. M. Jermier, D. Knights, & W. R. Nord (Eds.), *Resistance and power in organizations* (pp. 274-325). London: Routledge.

Clegg, S. (1994b). Weber and Foucault: Social theory for the study of organizations. *Organization, 1,* 149-178.

Clegg, S., & Dunkerley, D. (Eds.). (1980). *Organization, class and control.* London: Routledge and Kegan Paul.

Clifford, J. (1988). *The predicament of culture.* Cambridge, MA: Harvard University Press.

Clifford, J., & Marcus, G. (Eds.). (1986). *Writing culture: The poetics and politics of ethnography.* Berkeley: University of California Press.

Cobb, A. T. (1984). An episodic model of power: Toward an integration of theory and research. *Academy of Management Review, 9,* 482-493.

Cockburn, C. (1984). *Brothers.* London: Verso.

Collinson, D. (1988). "Engineering humor": Masculinity, joking and conflict in shop-floor relations. *Organization Studies, 9,* 181-199.

Collinson, D. (1992). *Managing the shop floor: Subjectivity, masculinity, and workplace culture.* New York: Aldine de Gruyter.

Collinson, D. (1994). Strategies of resistance: Power, knowledge and resistance in the workplace. In J. M. Jermier, D. Knights, & W. M. Nord (Eds.), *Resistance and power in organizations* (pp. 25-68). London: Routledge.

Connell, R. W. (1985). Theorising gender. *Sociology, 19,* 260-272.

Connell, R. W. (1987). *Gender and power: Society, the person and sexual politics.* Cambridge, UK: Polity.

Conquergood, D. (1991). Rethinking ethnography: Toward a critical cultural politics. *Communication Monographs, 58,* 179-194.

Conrad, C. (1988). Work songs, hegemony, and illusions of self. *Critical Studies in Mass Communication, 5,* 179-201.

Cooper, R. (1989). Modernism, postmodernism and organizational analysis 3: The contribution of Jacques Derrida. *Organization Studies, 10,* 479-502.

Cooper, R., & Burrell, G. (1988). Modernism, postmodernism and organizational analysis: An introduction. *Organization Studies, 9,* 91-112.

Crozier, M. (1964). *The bureaucratic phenomenon.* Chicago: University of Chicago Press.

Cyert, R. M., & March, J. G. (1963). *A behavioral theory of the firm.* Englewood Cliffs, NJ: Prentice Hall.

Dahl, R. (1957). The concept of power. *Behavioral Science, 2,* 201-215.

Dahl, R. (1958). A critique of the ruling elite model. *American Political Science Review, 52,* 463-469.

Dahl, R. (1961). *Who governs? Democracy and power in an American city.* New Haven, CT: Yale University Press.

Daudi, P. (1986). *Power in the organisation.* Oxford, UK: Basil Blackwell.

De Certeau, M. (1984). *The practice of everyday life* (S. Rendall, Trans.). Berkeley: University of California Press.

Deetz, S. (1973a). An understanding of science and a hermeneutic science of understanding. *Journal of Communication, 23,* 139-159.

Deetz, S. (1973b). Words without things: Toward a social phenomenology of language. *Quarterly Journal of Speech, 59,* 40-51.

Deetz, S. (1978). Conceptualizing human understanding: Gadamer's hermeneutics and American communication research. *Communication Quarterly, 26,* 12-23.

Deetz, S. (1982). Critical interpretive research in organizational communication. *Western Journal of Speech Communication, 46,* 131-149.

Deetz, S. (1985). Critical-cultural research: New sensibilities and old realities. *Journal of Management, 11*(2), 121-136.

Deetz, S. (1992a). *Democracy in an age of corporate colonization: Developments in communication and the politics of everyday life.* Albany: State University of New York Press.

Deetz, S. (1992b). Disciplinary power in the modern corporation. In M. Alvesson & H. Willmott (Eds.), *Critical management studies* (pp. 21-45). Newbury Park, CA: Sage.

Deetz, S. (1994). The new politics of the workplace: Ideology and other unobtrusive controls. In H. W. Simons & M. Billig (Eds.), *After postmodernism: Reconstructing ideology critique* (pp. 172-199). Thousand Oaks, CA: Sage.

Deetz, S. (1995). *Transforming communication, transforming business: Building responsive and responsible workplaces.* Cresskill, NJ: Hampton.

Deetz, S., & Kersten, A. (1983). Critical models of interpretive research. In L. L. Putnam & M. E. Pacanowsky (Eds.), *Communication and organizations: An interpretive approach* (pp. 147-171). Beverly Hills, CA: Sage.

Deetz, S., & Mumby, D. K. (1985). Metaphors, information, and power. In B. Ruben (Ed.), *Information and behavior* (Vol. 1, pp. 369-386). New Brunswick, NJ: Transaction.

Deetz, S., & Mumby, D. K. (1990). Power, discourse, and the workplace: Reclaiming the critical tradition. In J. A. Anderson (Ed.), *Communication yearbook 13* (pp. 18-47). Newbury Park, CA: Sage.

Derrida, J. (1976). *Of grammatology* (G. Spivak, Trans.). Baltimore: Johns Hopkins University Press.

Derrida, J. (1978). *Writing and difference*. London: Routledge and Kegan Paul.

Eagleton, T. (1991). *Ideology: An introduction*. London: Verso.

Eagleton, T. (1995). Where do postmodernists come from? *Monthly Review, 47*(3), 59-70.

Edelman, M. (1964). *The symbolic uses of politics*. Urbana: University of Illinois Press.

Edwards, R. (1979). *Contested terrain: The transformation of the workplace in the twentieth century*. New York: Basic Books.

Ehrenhaus, P. (1993). Cultural narratives and the therapeutic motif: The political containment of Vietnam veterans. In D. K. Mumby (Ed.), *Narrative and social control* (pp. 77-96). Newbury Park, CA: Sage.

Eisenberg, E. (1984). Ambiguity as strategy in organizational communication. *Communication Monographs, 51*, 227-242.

Emerson, R. M. (1962). Power-dependence relations. *American Sociological Review, 27*, 31-41.

Enz, C. (1988). The role of value incongruity in intraorganizational power. *Administrative Science Quarterly, 33*, 284-304.

Essed, P. (1991). *Understanding everyday racism*. Newbury Park, CA: Sage.

Fairclough, N. (1993). Critical discourse and the marketization of public discourse: The universities. *Discourse & Society, 4*, 133-168.

Fairhurst, G. (1993). The leader-member exchange patterns of women leaders in industry: A discourse analysis. *Communication Monographs, 60*, 321-351.

Featherstone, M. (1988). In pursuit of the postmodern. *Theory, Culture & Society, 5*, 195-215.

Ferguson, K. (1984). *The feminist case against bureaucracy*. Philadelphia: Temple University Press.

Ferguson, K. (1994). On bringing more theory, more voices and more politics to the study of organization. *Organization, 1*, 81-99.

Ferree, M. M., & Martin, P. (Eds.). (1995). *Feminist organizations: Harvest of the new women's movement*. Philadelphia: Temple University Press.

"Florence, M." [Michel Foucault]. (1994). Foucault, Michel, 1926-. In G. Gutting (Ed.), *The Cambridge companion to Foucault* (pp. 314-319). Cambridge, UK: Cambridge University Press.

Forester, J. (1989). *Planning in the face of power*. Berkeley: University of California Press.

Forester, J. (1992). Fieldwork in a Habermasian way. In M. Alvesson & H. Willmott (Eds.), *Critical management studies* (pp. 46-65). Newbury Park, CA: Sage.

Forester, J. (1993). *Critical theory, public policy and planning practice*. Albany: State University of New York Press.

Foucault, M. (1973). *The order of things: An archaeology of the human sciences*. New York: Vintage.

Foucault, M. (1975). *The birth of the clinic: An archaeology of medical perception* (A. Sheridan, Trans.). New York: Vintage.

Foucault, M. (1979). *Discipline and punish: The birth of the prison* (A. Sheridan, Trans.). New York: Vintage.

Foucault, M. (1980a). *The history of sexuality: An introduction* (Vol. 1, R. Hurley, Trans.). New York: Vintage.

Foucault, M. (1980b). *Power/knowledge: Selected interviews and other writings 1972-1977* (C. Gordon, L. Marshall, J. Mepham, & K. Soper, Trans.). New York: Pantheon.

Foucault, M. (1988). *Madness and civilization: A history of insanity in the age of reason* (R. Howard, Trans.). New York: Vintage.

Fowler, R., Hodge, B., Kress, G., & Trew, T. (1979). *Language and control*. London: Routledge and Kegan Paul.

Frankenberg, R. (1993). *White women, race matters: The social construction of whiteness*. Minneapolis: University of Minnesota Press.

Frost, P. (1980). Toward a radical framework for practicing organization science. *Academy of Management Review, 5*, 501-508.

Frost, P. J. (1987). Power, politics, and influence. In F. M. Jablin, L. L. Putnam, K. H. Roberts, & L. W. Porter (Eds.), *Handbook of organizational communication: An interdisciplinary perspective* (pp. 503-548). Newbury Park, CA: Sage.

Gadamer, H.-G. (1989). *Truth and method* (2nd ed., J. Weinsheimer & D. G. Marshall, Trans.). New York: Continuum.

Gaventa, J. (1980). *Power and powerlessness: Quiescence and rebellion in an Appalachian valley*. Urbana: University of Illinois Press.

Gephart, R. P. (1978). Status degradation and organizational succession: An ethnomethodological approach. *Administrative Science Quarterly, 23*, 553-581.

Gephart, R. P. (1988). Managing the meaning of a sour gas well blowout: The public culture of organizational disasters. *Industrial Crisis Quarterly, 2*(1), 17-32.

Gephart, R. P. (1992). Sensemaking, communicative distortion and the logic of public inquiry. *Industrial Crisis Quarterly, 6*(2), 115-135.

Gephart, R. P., Steier, L., & Lawrence, T. (1990). Cultural rationalities in crisis sense-making: A study of public inquiry into a major industrial accident. *Industrial Crisis Quarterly, 4*(1), 27-48.

Gergen, K. (1992). Organization theory in the postmodern era. In M. Reed & M. Hughes (Eds.), *Rethinking organization: New directions in organization theory and analysis* (pp. 207-226). London: Sage.

Geuss, R. (1981). *The idea of a critical theory: Habermas and the Frankfurt school*. Cambridge, UK: Cambridge University Press.

Gherardi, S. (1994). The gender we think, the gender we do in our everyday organizational lives. *Human Relations, 47*, 591-610.

Gherardi, S. (1995). *Gender, symbolism and organizational cultures.* London: Sage.

Giddens, A. (1976). *New rules of sociological method: A positive critique of interpretative sociologies.* London: Hutchinson.

Giddens, A. (1979). *Central problems in social theory: Action, structure and contradiction in social analysis.* Berkeley: University of California Press.

Giddens, A. (1984). *The constitution of society: Outline of the theory of structuration.* Berkeley: University of California Press.

Goldman, P., & Van Houten, D. R. (1977). Managerial strategies and the worker: A Marxist analysis of bureaucracy. In J. K. Benson (Ed.), *Organizational analysis: Critique and innovation.* Beverly Hills, CA: Sage.

Gottfried, H. (1994). Learning the score: The duality of control and everyday resistance in the temporary-help service industry. In J. M. Jermier, D. Knights, & W. R. Nord (Eds.), *Resistance and power in organizations* (pp. 102-127). London: Routledge.

Gottfried, H., & Weiss, P. (1994). A compound feminist organization: Purdue University's Council on the Status of Women. *Women and Politics, 14*(2), 23-44.

Graham, L. (1993). Inside a Japanese transplant: A critical perspective. *Work and Occupations, 20,* 147-173.

Gramsci, A. (1971). *Selections from the prison notebooks* (Q. Hoare & G. Nowell Smith, Trans.). New York: International Publishers.

Gray, B., Bougon, M., & Donnellon, A. (1985). Organizations as constructions and destructions of meaning. *Journal of Management, 11*(2), 83-98.

Gregg, N. (1993). Politics of identity/politics of location: Women workers organizing in a postmodern world. *Women's Studies in Communication, 16*(1), 1-33.

Grimes, D. (1994, November). *Building community: Race, resistance and dialogue.* Paper presented at annual conference of the Speech Communication Association, New Orleans, LA.

Grossberg, L. (1984). Strategies of Marxist cultural interpretation. *Critical Studies in Mass Communication, 1,* 392-421.

Habermas, J. (1970). On systematically distorted communication. *Inquiry, 13,* 205-218.

Habermas, J. (1975). *Legitimation crisis* (T. McCarthy, Trans.). Boston: Beacon.

Habermas, J. (1979). *Communication and the evolution of society* (T. McCarthy, Trans.). Boston: Beacon.

Habermas, J. (1984). *The theory of communicative action: Vol. 1. Reason and the rationalization of society* (T. McCarthy, Trans.). Boston: Beacon.

Habermas, J. (1987). *The theory of communicative action: Vol. 2. Lifeworld and system* (T. McCarthy, Trans.). Boston: Beacon.

Hacker, S. L., & Elcorobairutia, C. (1987). Women workers in the Mondragón system of industrial cooperatives. *Gender & Society, 1,* 358-379.

Hall, S. (1985). Signification, representation, ideology: Althusser and the poststructuralist debates. *Critical Studies in Mass Communication, 2,* 91-114.

Harvey, D. (1989). *The condition of postmodernity: An enquiry into the origins of cultural change.* Oxford, UK: Basil Blackwell.

Hassard, J. (1993a). Postmodernism and organizational analysis: An overview. In J. Hassard & M. Parker (Eds.), *Postmodernism and organizations* (pp. 1-24). Newbury Park, CA: Sage.

Hassard, J. (1993b). *Sociology and organization theory: Positivism, paradigms and postmodernity.* Cambridge, UK: Cambridge University Press.

Hassard, J., & Parker, M. (Eds.). (1993). *Postmodernism and organizations.* Newbury Park, CA: Sage.

Hawes, L. (1977). Toward a hermeneutic phenomenology of communication. *Communication Quarterly, 25*(3), 30-41.

Hearn, J. (1992). *Men in the public eye: The construction and deconstruction of public men and public patriarchies.* New York: Routledge.

Hearn, J. (1994). The organization(s) of violence: Men, gender relations, organizations, and violences. *Human Relations, 47,* 731-754.

Heidegger, M. (1977). *Basic writings.* New York: Harper & Row.

Helmer, J. (1993). Storytelling in the creation and maintenance of organizational tension and stratification. *Southern Communication Journal, 59,* 34-44.

Hickson, D. J., Hinings, C. R., Lee, C. A., Schneck, R. E., & Pennings, J. M. (1971). A strategic contingencies' theory of intraorganizational power. *Administrative Science Quarterly, 17,* 216-229.

Hindess, B. (1982). Power, interests and the outcomes of struggles. *Sociology, 16,* 498-511.

Hinings, C. R., Hickson, D. J., Pennings, J. M., & Schneck, R. E. (1974). Structural conditions of intraorganizational power. *Administrative Science Quarterly, 19,* 22-44.

Holmer-Nadesan, M. (1996). Organizational identity and space of action. *Organization Studies, 17,* 49-81.

Holmer-Nadesan, M. (1997). Constructing paper dolls: The discourse of personality testing in organizational practice. *Communication Theory, 7,* 189-218.

Holmer-Nadesan, M. (1999). The discourses of corporate spiritualism and evangelical capitalism. *Management Communication Quarterly, 13,* 3-42.

Holvino, E. (1997). Reading organizational development from the margins: Outsider within. *Organization, 3,* 520-533.

hooks, b. (1984). *Feminist theory: From margin to center.* Boston: South End.

hooks, b. (1992). *Black looks: Race and representation.* Boston: South End.

Horkheimer, M. (1986). *Critical theory* (M. O'Connell et al., Trans.). New York: Continuum.

Horkheimer, M., & Adorno, T. (1988). *Dialectic of enlightenment* (J. Cumming, Trans.). New York: Continuum.

Hoskin, K. W., & Macve, R. H. (1986). Accounting and the examination: A genealogy of disciplinary power. *Accounting, Organizations and Society, 11,* 105-136.

Hoskin, K. W., & Macve, R. H. (1988). The genesis of accountability: The West Point connections. *Accounting, Organizations and Society, 13,* 37-73.

Howard, L. A., & Geist, P. (1995). Ideological positioning in organizational change: The dialectic of control in a merging organization. *Communication Monographs, 62,* 110-131.

Hunter, F. (1953). *Community power structure.* Chapel Hill: University of North Carolina Press.

Huspek, M., & Kendall, K. (1991). On withholding political voice: An analysis of the political vocabulary of a "nonpolitical" speech community. *Quarterly Journal of Speech, 77,* 1-19.

Iannello, K. P. (1992). *Decisions without hierarchy: Feminist interventions in organizational theory and practice.* New York: Routledge.

Izraeli, D. M., & Jick, T. D. (1986). The art of saying no: Linking power to culture. *Organization Studies, 7,* 171-192.

Jacques, R. (1992). Critique and theory building: Producing knowledge "from the kitchen." *Academy of Management Review, 17,* 582-606.

Jacques, R. (1996). *Manufacturing the employee: Management knowledge from the 19th to 21st centuries.* London: Sage.

Jameson, F. (1984). Foreword. In J.-F. Lyotard, *The postmodern condition: A report on knowledge* (pp. vii-xi). Minneapolis: University of Minnesota Press.

Jeffcutt, P. (1994). The interpretation of organization: A contemporary analysis and critique. *Journal of Management Studies, 31,* 225-250.

Kilduff, M. (1993). Deconstructing organizations. *Academy of Management Review, 18,* 13-31.

Kilduff, M., & Mehra, A. (1997). Postmodernism and organizational research. *Academy of Management Review, 22,* 453-481.

Knights, D., & Vurdubakis, T. (1994). Foucault, power, resistance and all that. In J. M. Jermier, D. Knights, & W. R. Nord (Eds.), *Resistance and power in organizations* (pp. 167-198). London: Routledge.

Knights, D., & Willmott, H. (1992). Conceptualizing leadership processes: A study of senior managers in a financial services company. *Journal of Management Studies, 29,* 761-782.

Kondo, D. (1990). *Crafting selves: Power, discourse and identity in a Japanese factory.* Chicago: University of Chicago Press.

Kunda, G. (1992). *Engineering culture: Control and commitment in a high-tech corporation.* Philadelphia: Temple University Press.

Lachman, R. (1989). Power from what? A reexamination of its relationships with structural conditions. *Administrative Science Quarterly, 34,* 231-251.

Laclau, E. (1990). *New reflections on the revolution of our time.* London: Verso.

Laclau, E., & Mouffe, C. (1985). *Hegemony and socialist strategy: Towards a radical democratic politics.* London: Verso.

Laird Brenton, A. (1993). Demystifying the magic of language: A critical linguistic case analysis of legitimation of authority. *Journal of Applied Communication Research, 21,* 227-244.

Lamphere, L. (1985). Bringing the family to work: Women's culture on the shop floor. *Feminist Studies, 11,* 519-540.

Larrain, J. (1979). *The concept of ideology.* London: Hutchinson.

Lentricchia, F. (1988). *Ariel and the police: Michel Foucault, William James, Wallace Stevens.* Madison: University of Wisconsin Press.

Linstead, S. (1993). Deconstruction in the study of organizations. In J. Hassard & M. Parker (Eds.), *Postmodernism and organizations* (pp. 49-70). Newbury Park, CA: Sage.

Linstead, S., & Grafton-Small, R. (1992). On reading organizational culture. *Organization Studies, 13,* 331-355.

Lont, C. M. (1988). Redwood Records: Principles and profit in women's music. In B. Bate & A. Taylor (Eds.), *Women communicating: Studies of women's talk* (pp. 233-250). Norwood, NJ: Ablex.

Lukács, G. (1971). *History and class consciousness: Studies in Marxist dialectics* (R. Livingstone, Trans.). Boston: MIT Press.

Lukes, S. (1974). *Power: A radical view.* London: Macmillan.

Lyotard, J.-F. (1984). *The postmodern condition: A report on knowledge* (G. Bennington & B. Massumi, Trans.). Minneapolis: University of Minnesota Press.

MacKinnon, C. (1979). *Sexual harassment of working women.* New Haven, CT: Yale University Press.

Maguire, M., & Mohtar, L. F. (1994). Performance and the celebration of a subaltern counterpublic. *Text and Performance Quarterly, 14,* 238-252.

March, J. G., & Simon, H. (1958). *Organizations.* New York: John Wiley.

Markham, A. (1996). Designing discourse: A critical analysis of strategic ambiguity and workplace control. *Management Communication Quarterly, 9,* 389-421.

Marsden, R. (1993). The politics of organizational analysis. *Organization Studies, 14,* 93-124.

Marshall, J. (1989). Re-visioning career concepts: A feminist invitation. In M. B. Arthur, D. Hall, & B. Lawrence (Eds.), *Handbook of career theory* (pp. 275-291). Cambridge, UK: Cambridge University Press.

Marshall, J. (1993). Viewing organizational communication from a feminist perspective: A critique and some offerings. In S. A. Deetz (Ed.), *Communication yearbook 16* (pp. 122-141). Newbury Park, CA: Sage.

Martin, J. (1990). Deconstructing organizational taboos: The suppression of gender conflict in organizations. *Organization Science, 1,* 339-359.

Martin, J. (1992). *Cultures in organizations: Three perspectives.* New York: Oxford University Press.

Martin, J. (1994). The organization of exclusion: Institutionalization of sex inequality, gendered faculty jobs and gendered knowledge in organizational theory and research. *Organization, 1,* 401-432.

Martin, J., Feldman, M., Hatch, M. J., & Sitkin, S. J. (1983). The uniqueness paradox in organizational stories. *Administrative Science Quarterly, 28,* 438-453.

Martin, P. Y. (1990). Rethinking feminist organizations. *Gender & Society, 4,* 182-206.

Marx, K. (1967). *Capital* (S. Moore & E. Aveling, Trans.). New York: International Publishers.

McClellan, D. (1986). *Ideology.* Minneapolis: University of Minnesota Press.

McMillan, J. J., & Cheney, G. (1996). The student as consumer: The implications and limitations of a metaphor. *Communication Education, 45,* 1-15.

Mehan, H., & Wood, H. (1975). *The reality of ethnomethodology.* New York: John Wiley.

Merleau-Ponty, M. (1960). *Phenomenology of perception* (C. Smith, Trans.). London: Routledge and Kegan Paul.

Miller, P., & O'Leary, T. (1987). Accounting and the construction of the governable person. *Accounting, Organizations and Society, 12,* 235-265.

Mills, A. J. (1995). Man/aging subjectivity, silencing diversity: Organizational imagery in the airline industry: The case of British Airways. *Organization, 2,* 243-270.

Mills, A. L., & Tancred, P. (Eds.). (1992). *Gendering organizational analysis.* Newbury Park, CA: Sage.

Mills, C. W. (1956). *The power elite.* Oxford, UK: Oxford University Press.

Mouffe, C. (1979). Hegemony and ideology in Gramsci. In C. Mouffe (Ed.), *Gramsci and Marxist theory* (pp. 168-204). London: Routledge and Kegan Paul.

Mumby, D. K. (1987). The political function of narrative in organizations. *Communication Monographs, 54,* 113-127.

Mumby, D. K. (1988). *Communication and power in organizations: Discourse, ideology, and domination.* Norwood, NJ: Ablex.

Mumby, D. K. (1989). Ideology and the social construction of meaning: A communication perspective. *Communication Quarterly, 37,* 291-304.

Mumby, D. K. (1993a). Critical organizational communication studies: The next ten years. *Communication Monographs, 60,* 18-25.

Mumby, D. K. (Ed.). (1993b). *Narrative and social control: Critical perspectives.* Newbury Park, CA: Sage.

Mumby, D. K. (1996). Feminism, postmodernism, and organizational communication: A critical reading. *Management Communication Quarterly, 9,* 259-295.

Mumby, D. K. (1997). The problem of hegemony: Rereading Gramsci for organizational communication studies. *Western Journal of Communication, 61,* 343-375.

Mumby, D. K., & Putnam, L. L. (1992). The politics of emotion: A feminist reading of bounded rationality. *Academy of Management Review, 17,* 465-486.

Mumby, D. K., & Stohl, C. (1992). Power and discourse in organization studies: Absence and the dialectic of control. *Discourse & Society, 2,* 313-332.

Murphy, A. G. (1998). Hidden transcripts of flight attendant resistance. *Management Communication Quarterly, 11,* 499-535.

Nakayama, T., & Krizek, R. (1995). Whiteness: A strategic rhetoric. *Quarterly Journal of Speech, 81,* 291-309.

Nkomo, S. (1992). The emperor has no clothes: Rewriting "race in organizations." *Academy of Management Review, 17,* 487-513.

O'Neill, J. (1986). The disciplinary society: From Weber to Foucault. *British Journal of Sociology, 37,* 42-60.

Pacanowsky, M., & O'Donnell-Trujillo, N. (1982). Communication and organizational cultures. *Western Journal of Speech Communication, 46,* 115-130.

Papa, M. J., Auwal, M. A., & Singhal, A. (1995). Dialectic of control and emancipation in organizing for social change: A multitheoretic study of the Grameen Bank in Bangladesh. *Communication Theory, 5,* 189-223.

Parker, M. (1992a). Getting down from the fence: A reply to Haridimos Tsoukas. *Organization Studies, 13,* 651-653.

Parker, M. (1992b). Post-modern organizations or postmodern organization theory. *Organization Studies, 13,* 1-18.

Penkoff, D. (1995, May). *Communication and recovery: Structuration as an ontological approach to organizational culture.* Paper presented at the annual conference of the International Communication Association, Albuquerque, NM.

Perrow, C. (1970). Departmental power and perspective in industrial firms. In M. Zald (Ed.), *Power in organizations* (pp. 59-89). Nashville, TN: Vanderbilt University Press.

Pettigrew, A. (1973). *The politics of organizational decision-making.* London: Tavistock.

Pfeffer, J. (1981). *Power in organizations.* Marshfield, MA: Pitman.

Pfeffer, J., & Salancik, G. (1974). Organizational decision making as a political process: The case of a university budget. *Administrative Science Quarterly, 19,* 135-151.

Pfeffer, J., & Salancik, G. (1978). *The external control of organizations: A resource dependence perspective.* New York: Harper & Row.

Poole, M. S., & DeSanctis, G. (1990). Understanding the use of group decision support systems: The theory of adaptive structuration. In J. Fulk & C. Steinfield (Eds.), *Organizations and communication technology* (pp. 173-193). Newbury Park, CA: Sage.

Power, M., & Laughlin, R. (1992). Critical theory and accounting. In M. Alvesson & H. Willmott (Eds.), *Critical management studies* (pp. 113-135). Newbury Park, CA: Sage.

Pringle, R. (1989). *Secretaries talk: Sexuality, power and work.* London: Verso.

Putnam, L. L. (1983). The interpretive perspective: An alternative to functionalism. In L. L. Putnam & M. E. Pacanowsky (Eds.), *Communication and organizations: An interpretive approach* (pp. 31-54). Beverly Hills, CA: Sage.

Putnam, L. L., & Mumby, D. K. (1993). Organizations, emotion, and the myth of rationality. In S. Fineman (Ed.), *Emotion in organizations* (pp. 36-57). London: Sage.

Putnam, L. L., & Pacanowsky, M. E. (Eds.). (1983). *Communication and organizations: An interpretive approach.* Beverly Hills, CA: Sage.

Ranson, S., Hinings, B., & Greenwood, R. (1980). The structuring of organizational structures. *Administrative Science Quarterly, 25,* 1-17.

Reinelt, C. (1994). Fostering empowerment, building community: The challenge for state-funded feminist organizations. *Human Relations, 47,* 685-705.

Ricoeur, P. (1970). *Freud and philosophy: An essay on interpretation* (D. Savage, Trans.). New Haven, CT: Yale University Press.

Riley, P. (1983). A structurationist account of political culture. *Administrative Science Quarterly, 28,* 414-437.

Rodriguez, N. M. (1988). Transcending bureaucracy: Feminist politics at a shelter for battered women. *Gender & Society, 2,* 214-227.

Rorty, R. (Ed.). (1967). *The linguistic turn: Recent essays in philosophical method.* Chicago: University of Chicago Press.

Rosen, M. (1985). "Breakfast at Spiro's": Dramaturgy and dominance. *Journal of Management, 11*(2), 31-48.

Rosen, M. (1988). You asked for it: Christmas at the bosses' expense. *Journal of Management Studies, 25,* 463-480.

Rosenau, P. M. (1992). *Post-modernism and the social sciences.* Princeton, NJ: Princeton University Press.

Rosenau, P. V., & Bredemeier, H. C. (1993). Modern and postmodern conceptions of social order. *Social Research, 60,* 337-362.

Rothschild, J., & Davies, C. (1994). Organizations through the lens of gender. *Human Relations, 47,* 583-590.

Rothschild-Whitt, J. (1979). The collectivist organization: An alternative to rational bureaucratic models. *American Sociological Review, 44,* 509-527.

Salancik, G., & Pfeffer, J. (1974). The bases and uses of power in organizational decision making: The case of a university. *Administrative Science Quarterly, 19,* 453-473.

Salancik, G., & Pfeffer, J. (1977). Who gets power—and how they hold on to it: A strategic contingency model of power. *Organizational Dynamics, 5*(3), 3-21.

Salvador, M., & Markham, A. (1995). The rhetoric of self-directive management and the operation of organizational power. *Communication Reports, 8,* 45-53.

Schattschneider, E. E. (1960). *The semi-sovereign people: A realist's view of democracy in America.* New York: Holt, Rinehart & Winston.

Scheibel, D. (1996). Appropriating bodies: Organ(izing) ideology and cultural practice in medical school. *Journal of Applied Communication Research, 24,* 310-331.

Schutz, A. (1962). *Collected papers I: The problem of social reality.* The Hague, Netherlands: Martinus Nijhoff.

Schwartz, H. (1993). Deconstructing my car at the Detroit airport. *Organization Studies, 14,* 279-281.

Scott, J. C. (1990). *Domination and the arts of resistance: Hidden transcripts.* New Haven, CT: Yale University Press.

Sealander, J., & Smith, D. (1986). The rise and fall of feminist organizations in the 1970s: Dayton as a case study. *Feminist Studies, 12,* 321-341.

Simon, H. (1976). *Administrative behavior* (3rd ed.). Glencoe, IL: Free Press.

Smart, B. (1986). The politics of truth and the problem of hegemony. In D. C. Hoy (Ed.), *Foucault: A critical reader* (pp. 157-174). Oxford, UK: Basil Blackwell.

Smith, R., & Eisenberg, E. (1987). Conflict at Disneyland: A root metaphor analysis. *Communication Monographs, 54,* 367-380.

Sotirin, P., & Gottfried, H. (1999). The ambivalent dynamics of secretarial "bitching": Control, resistance, and the construction of identity. *Organization, 6,* 57-80.

Spradlin, A. L. (1998). The price of "passing": A lesbian perspective on authenticity in organizations. *Management Communication Quarterly, 11,* 598-605.

Steffy, B., & Grimes, A. J. (1986). A critical theory of organization science. *Academy of Management Review, 11,* 322-336.

Strine, M. (1992). Understanding "how things work": Sexual harassment and academic culture. *Journal of Applied Communication Research, 20,* 391-400.

Sunesson, S. (1985). Outside the goal paradigm: Power and the structured patterns of non-rationality. *Organization Studies, 6,* 229-246.

Taylor, B., & Conrad, C. (1992). Narratives of sexual harassment: Organizational dimensions. *Journal of Applied Communication Research, 20,* 401-418.

Taylor, J. R. (1995). Shifting from a heteronomous to an autonomous worldview of organizational communication: Communication theory on the cusp. *Communication Theory, 5,* 1-35.

Taylor, J. R., Cooren, F., Giroux, N., & Robichaud, D. (1996). The communicational basis of organization: Between the conversation and the text. *Communication Theory, 6,* 1-39.

Therborn, G. (1980). *The ideology of power and the power of ideology.* London: NLB.

Thompson, J. (1967). *Organizations in action.* New York: McGraw-Hill.

Thompson, J. B. (1984). *Studies in the theory of ideology.* Berkeley: University of California Press.

Tompkins, P. K., & Cheney, G. (1985). Communication and unobtrusive control in contemporary organizations. In R. D. McPhee & P. K. Tompkins (Eds.), *Organizational communication: Traditional themes and new directions* (pp. 179-210). Beverly Hills, CA: Sage.

Tong, R. (1989). *Feminist thought.* Boulder, CO: Westview.

Townsley, N. C., & Geist, P. (in press). The discursive enactment of hegemony: Sexual harassment in academic organizing. *Western Journal of Communication, 64.*

Trethewey, A. (1997). Resistance, identity, and empowerment: A postmodern feminist analysis of clients in a human service organization. *Communication Monographs, 64,* 281-301.

Trethewey, A. (1999a). Disciplined bodies. *Organization Studies, 20,* 423-450.

Trethewey, A. (1999b). Isn't it ironic: Using irony to explore the contradictions of organizational life. *Western Journal of Communication, 63,* 140-167.

Tsoukas, H. (1992). Postmodernism, reflexive rationalism and organizational studies: A reply to Martin Parker. *Organization Studies, 13,* 643-650.

Turow, J. (1984). *Media industries: The production of news and entertainment.* New York: Longman.

van Dijk, T. A. (1993). *Elite discourse and racism.* Newbury Park, CA: Sage.

Volosinov, V. N. (1973). *Marxism and the philosophy of language.* Cambridge, MA: Harvard University Press.

Von Bertalanffy, L. (1968). *General system theory.* New York: George Braziller.

Wallace, M. (1992). Negative images: Towards a black feminist cultural criticism. In L. Grossberg, C. Nelson, & P. Treichler (Eds.), *Cultural studies* (pp. 654-671). New York: Routledge.

Weber, M. (1978). *Economy and society* (G. Roth & C. Wittich, Trans.). Berkeley: University of California Press.

Wendt, R. (1994). Learning to "walk the talk": A critical tale of the micropolitics at a total quality university. *Management Communication Quarterly, 8,* 5-45.

West, C., & Zimmerman, D. (1987). Doing gender. *Gender & Society, 1,* 125-151.

West, J. (1993). Ethnography and ideology: The politics of cultural representation. *Western Journal of Communication, 57,* 209-220.

Willis, P. (1977). *Learning to labor: How working class kids get working class jobs.* New York: Columbia University Press.

Witten, M. (1993). Narrative and the culture of obedience at the workplace. In D. K. Mumby (Ed.), *Narrative and social control: Critical perspectives* (pp. 97-118). Newbury Park, CA: Sage.

Wolfinger, R. E. (1971). Nondecisions and the study of local politics. *American Political Science Review, 65,* 1063-1080.

Wood, J. (1992). Telling our stories: Narratives as a basis for theorizing sexual harassment. *Journal of Applied Communication Research, 20,* 349-362.

Young, E. (1989). On the naming of the rose: Interests and multiple meanings as elements of organizational culture. *Organization Studies, 10,* 187-206.

Zavella, P. (1985). "Abnormal intimacy": The varying networks of Chicana cannery workers. *Feminist Studies, 11,* 541-564.

16

Wired Meetings

Technological Mediation of Organizational Gatherings

JANET FULK
University of Southern California

LORI COLLINS-JARVIS
Lieberman Research Worldwide

I deal with people all the time who talk about how videoconferencing is going to save time. It's going to save time on travel. It will be more effective and efficient. Every single person I've talked with, every white-collar worker I've asked, "What's the biggest waste of your time?" has said, "Meetings." And then they talk about videoconferencing. Geez, why would we recreate in cyberspace the single biggest waste of time we have in the physical world?

—Schrage (1996, p. 57)

Meetings are very common organizational communication events. They involve fundamental communication processes including sensemaking, control, power relations, structuration, and decision making. Theory and research on mediated meetings

AUTHORS' NOTE: We thank Alan Dennis, Linda Putnam and Fred Jablin for valuable comments on an earlier draft of this chapter. We thank the 3M Meeting Management Institute for support of the research on which this chapter is based. This chapter was completed in September 1997.

are growing exponentially as communication technologies have become critical to new organizational forms (Fulk & DeSanctis, 1998; McPhee & Poole, Chapter 13, this volume). This chapter organizes this theory and research and suggests new directions for investigation. We describe three theoretical perspectives and overview research on three types of technological support: teleconferencing, computer conferencing, and group support systems. We organize the research by commonly studied communication-related issues in groups: (a) equality of participation, (b) socioemotional expression, (c) conflict and consensus, (d) efficiency (time to complete a task), (e) decision quality, and (f) satisfaction. Finally, we overview several new developments in mediated meeting technology and suggest how they are linked to significant changes in organizational forms.

SCOPE AND FRAMEWORK OF THE CHAPTER

The term *meeting* (e.g., *gemetan* in Old English) has been in the English language since before *Beowulf* was written (approximately the first quarter of the eighth century; R. Fulk, 1992). Over the millennium, the concept of "meeting" has held a variety of meanings in both academic and lay contexts. We use the term to mean the act of gathering together for a limited period of time for the purpose of communication. We use the criterion of synchroneity not as a convenience, but rather as an observable demarcation for initiation and conclusion of a communication episode. Some scholars apply the term to asynchronous communication, particularly when it is technology mediated. However, the asynchronous criterion makes it difficult for researchers (and for participants themselves) to demarcate the meeting itself from ongoing communications extending over periods of days, months, and even years. The

synchronous criterion links the meeting concept to its centuries-long history. The concept also implies that participants construe the communication episode as "meeting." Meeting typically excludes, for example, the "synchronous" open radio frequencies on police patrols, which officers do not consider to be a meeting in the sense that the preshift briefing is a meeting.

Managerial time allocation to meetings varies from about 25% (Monge, McSween, & Wyer, 1989; Mosvick & Nelson, 1987) to more than 60% (McCall, Morrison, & Hannan, 1978; Mintzberg, 1973; Uhlig, Farber, & Bair, 1979). For each meeting hour, managers spend up to an additional hour of time preparing (Monge et al., 1989). Meetings are implicated in many communication-related organizational processes. Historically, meetings were used during the industrial revolution to inform management about plant-level activity, facilitate coordination across superintendents, humanize the new work procedures, and reduce hostility in the ranks of superintendents (Yates, 1989). Meetings also have been found to control organizational work flow by focusing managerial attention, targeting some problems and decisions as more salient than others, and offering legitimate forums for political processes (Oppenheim, 1987). Kling (1991) and Fulk and Monge (1995) argue that technological mediation of group processes is as deeply implicated in control and coercion as in collaboration and cooperation. Yates and Orlikowski (1992, p. 301) describe the meeting as a *genre*, a "typified communicative action in response to a current situation" that guides communication behavior.

Meetings are also sensemaking forums (Weick & Meader, 1992) that define, represent, and reproduce social entities and relationships and "produce" organization. They are the organization or community "writ small," yet they also help to create community or organizational identity (Schwartzman, 1989). Meetings serve ceremonial and symbolic functions (Trice, 1985), and as locales and mechanisms for impression management (Clapper & Prasad, 1993).

New and highly sophisticated electronic meeting support is widely available to organizations and includes three generic categories of meeting technologies. *Teleconferencing* includes meetings held through audioconferencing and videoconferencing systems. *Computer conferencing* allows multiple participants to interact by contributing to an ongoing computer file accessible to all. *Group support systems* (GSSs) supplement computer conferencing with information management capabilities, decision support tools, graphics displays, and meeting process management software. Multimedia systems have become available recently, although there is little research on group processes in multimedia meetings.

Most reviews of mediated meeting research cumulate findings by type of technology, and some combine synchronous and asynchronous forms. Teleconferencing findings were reviewed by Johansen, Vallee, and Spangler (1979), Fowler and Wackerbarth (1980), Williams (1977), and Johansen (1984). Studies of computer-conferenced meetings were reviewed by Kerr and Hiltz (1982), Rice (1984), and Sproull and Kiesler (1991). Culnan and Markus (1987) focused on teleconferencing and computer conferencing. GSS research was reviewed by Dennis, Nunamaker, and Vogel (1991), Dennis and Gallupe (1992), Benbasat, DeSanctis, and Nault (1993), Jessup and Valacich (1992), Benbasat and Lim (1993), Dennis, Haley, and Vandenberg (1996), and Nunamaker, Briggs, Mittleman, Vogel, and Balthazard (1996). Computer conferencing and GSS research was reviewed by McGrath and Hollingshead (1994), Hollingshead and McGrath (1995), and Pinsonneault and Kraemer (1990). Seibold, Heller, and Contractor (1994) crafted a review of reviews on GSS meetings. De-Sanctis (1992) and Poole and Jackson (1992) discuss assumptive foundations in GSS research.

Our purpose is to provide a historical perspective on the intellectual development of the field, one in which existing reviews may be situated. This approach chronicles how theory and research develop hand-in-hand and contextualizes theoretical developments to illustrate how new traditions are both constrained by and developed in opposition to existing thought. It illustrates Popper's (1962) contention that intellectual development proceeds as much through elimination of blind alleys as opening new doors. Due to space constraints, we limit our comparison to research that implicitly or explicitly contrasts mediated meetings with face-to-face. This delimitation may be unsatisfying to scholars interested in comparing the effects of different conditions in mediated meetings, such as group size (e.g., Valacich, Wheeler, Mennecke, & Wachter, 1995), anonymity (e.g., Connolly, Jessup, & Valacich, 1990; Hiltz, Turoff, & Johnson, 1989; Jessup, Connolly, & Tansik, 1990; Valacich, Dennis, & Nunamaker, 1992), interacting versus nominal groups (e.g., Dennis & Valacich, 1993, 1994; Valacich, Dennis, & Connolly, 1994), proximate versus distributed groups (e.g., Valacich, George, Nunamaker, & Vogel, 1994), facilitation and designated leadership effects (e.g., Gopal & Pollard, 1996; Hiltz, Johnson, & Turoff, 1991), and processes such as dialectical inquiry versus devil's advocate (e.g., Valacich & Schwenk, 1995). For reviews of research on different types of computer-based meeting support, see Dennis, George, Jessup, Nunamaker, and Vogel (1988), Easton, George, Nunamaker, and Pendergast (1990), and Kraemer and King (1988).

Comparison across technologies rather than specific features is a crude analysis, because features vary across implementations (Griffith & Northcraft, 1994). Seibold et al. (1994) argue that research should account not only for system features but also for use characteristics such as training and user characteristics, for example, computer expertise. Since prior research has not reported such variables, cumulating prior results on these bases is not possible.

Three main theoretical streams on mediated meetings developed over time: media capacity, input-process-output, and structuration. The next sections describe specific theories and research findings for each, and compare and critique underlying assumptions across the streams.

MEDIA CAPACITY THEORIES

The core premise is that media have different capacities to carry communicative cues. Simple cues can be communicated successfully using any medium, but complex interaction requires media with the capacity to transmit complex cues. This section (a) overviews two major theories, social presence and media richness; (b) discusses empirical research; and (c) critiques their assumptions.

Social Presence Theory

Statements on mediated meetings appeared in the 1970s, when audioconferencing was widely available and videoconferencing was in its early stages. An extensive series of experiments led to social presence theory (Short, Williams, & Christie, 1976). "Social presence" of a medium is linked to the nonverbal signals, including facial expression, direction of gaze, posture, dress, physical appearance, proximity, and orientation. Nonverbal cues relate to specific communication functions, including mutual attention and responsiveness, channel control, feedback, illustrations, emblems, and interpersonal attitudes.

A reasonable, but still naïve, hypothesis would thus be: we can predict the effects on interaction of varying medium of communication by listing the cues that are not transmitted via the different media, by discovering the functions of these cues by reference to research on face-to-face communication, and then deduc-

ing the way in which the outcome or processes of the conversation would be altered by the absence of these cues. (Short et al., p. 63)

Such an approach is inappropriate, they argued, for four reasons: (1) nonverbal cues occur in combination with verbal and with other nonverbal cues, which may compensate for or otherwise affect each other; (2) communicators may be aware of the reduced-cue situation and adjust by modifying behavior; (3) particular combinations of cues may mean different things in different contexts; and (4) we do not know enough about the tenuous relationship between visual cues and complex behavior.

The social presence concept responded to difficulties of developing predictions based on the presence or absence of single nonverbal cues in complex human interaction. Social presence is a single dimension that represents the *cognitive synthesis of combinations of cues* as attributed to the medium by the individual. Short et al. (1976) argue that social presence is a differential quality of each medium that describes "the degree of salience of the other person in the interaction and the consequent salience of the interpersonal relationships." Social presence is based on individual perceptions, and thus may vary somewhat across persons. On average across persons, however, the greatest social presence was found for face-to-face. Social presence decreased continuously as one moved to video, then audio forms of interaction.

Short et al. equivocate about medium effects in situations that require cooperation within a group, but they propose specific medium effects for negotiation and conflict situations. Drawing on a long history of the study of the bidimensional nature of group behavior (e.g., Argyle, 1957; Bales, 1955; Douglas, 1957), social presence theory proposes that interpersonal interactions involve both (1) acting out roles and (2) maintaining personal relationships. Depending on the nature of the interaction, the relationship maintenance dimension may be more or less important for the interaction compared with the role dimension.

> It is generally agreed that information transmission and cooperative problem-solving are activities in which interpersonal relationships are relatively unimportant; they are activities for which man-computer interaction is quite feasible. Since personal relationships are unimportant, it matters little whether interactors treat the other as a person or as an impersonal information source. (Short et al., 1976, p. 158)

By contrast, in conflict and negotiation situations each side's perception of the other's behavior is important to its own action choices: The relationship maintenance dimension is highly salient. Short et al. argue from existing research that removal of visual cues impairs the accuracy of person perception that is critical to development of trust. Where trust is impaired, there is more conflict. Specifically, the more types of cues the medium offers to person perception, the more cooperative the behaviors will be.

Thus, the theory proposed that mediated interaction would be less effective for highly interpersonally involving tasks, in proportion to the decreasing amount of social presence of the medium. Short et al.'s (1976) extensive research program investigated the hypothesized process changes in teleconferenced meetings, as well as the relative effectiveness of different levels of mediation (audio vs. video) for tasks that theoretically required high and low social presence media.

Social presence theory was explicitly a theory of interacting synchronous groups. Short et al. argued that the interactive factor was critical to limitations on their ability to generalize from social psychological research conducted in contexts that were not truly interactive. These include, for example, studies of anonymity effects in audio versus face-to-face where subjects only had knowledge of the judgment of others and were not permitted free verbal interaction. Nevertheless, the theory was applied by later researchers to asynchronous interaction, and came to be viewed simply as a theory of media effects.

Media Richness Theory

This theory draws on organizational information-processing premises. Theoretically, when tasks are simple and predictable (low uncertainty), preplanning is possible. Rules, standards, and procedures can achieve coordination without the need for direct communication among those whose activities need to be coordinated (Beniger, 1986; March & Simon, 1958). Under high task uncertainty, preplanning is not possible and direct communication is required for coordination, a process March and Simon called "coordination by feedback." A key premise is that the complexity of communication and information-processing mechanisms (e.g., rules vs. meetings) should match the uncertainty inherent in the task itself.

Later scholars proposed a distinction between uncertainty (lack of information) and equivocality (multiple possible meanings inherent in the information) (Daft & Lengel, 1984; Daft & Weick, 1984; Trevino, Daft, & Lengel, 1990; Weick, 1979). Uncertain situations can be made more certain through rationalization processes such as analysis routines (Perrow, 1970). Equivocal situations cannot be altered through rationalization, but must be managed by use of judgment strategies (Thompson & Tuden, 1959) or through "negotiation and construction of a mutually shared agreement" (Weick & Meader, 1992, p. 232).

Using this perspective, Daft and Lengel (1984) argued that media richness is the key to media capacity. A medium's richness is its information-carrying capacity, based on four criteria: (1) speed of feedback, (2) ability to communicate multiple cues such as body language and voice tone, (3) use of natural language rather than numbers, and (4) ability to readily convey feelings and emotions. Technological mediation restricts the capacity of meetings to handle tasks with the greatest complexity and equivocality (Daft & Lengel, 1984; McGrath & Hollingshead, 1992; Rice, 1984; Short et al., 1976). The fewer communication channels available (e.g., audio only vs. audio plus video) the more restricted is the medium's capacity, and the less uncertainty and equivocality it is able to manage. Media capacity decreases from face-to-face to teleconferencing, to computer-based systems.

Thus, the theory proposes that for equivocal communication tasks, face-to-face meetings are appropriate. And for unequivocal messages lean media such as written text should be used (Daft & Lengel, 1986, p. 560). The logic of "matching" media capabilities with task demands is similar to social presence theory, despite disparate theoretical underpinnings. Research testing media richness theory has focused heavily on asynchronous communication; research results are described in Rice and Gattiker (Chapter 14, this volume).

Empirical Evidence

Perceptions of social presence. Research indicates some perceived differences across media in salience of the other person and personal relationships. Short et al. (1976) report a series of studies in which the sense of social contact was greatest in face-to-face, less in video, and least in audio meetings. Reviews of teleconferencing research by Johansen et al. (1979) and Fowler and Wackerbarth (1980) and more recent studies (e.g., Dennis & Kinney, 1998; Dutton, Fulk, & Steinfield, 1982; Fulk & Dutton, 1984) generally support the conclusion that video dampens feelings of social contact and presence of the other party. This conclusion is reinforced by findings that coalitions tend to form within nodes (e.g., Weston, Kristen, & O'Connor, 1975; Williams, 1975). That is, people who are together face-to-face at one videoconferencing node develop a cohesion that does not extend to persons at the other node.

The strongest contrast in perceived social presence is for audio meetings, which are seen as less personal, less effective for getting to know someone, and communicate less affective content than face-to-face (Craig & Jull, 1974, cited in Johansen et al., 1979; Thomas & Williams, 1975; Williams, 1972). Yet the majority of studies suggest that audio is seen as no less effective than face-to-face in forming impressions of others (Johansen et al., 1979). One possible explanation for this apparent contradiction is that forming impressions may be less interactive than developing a personal relationship with someone. Whereas developing personal relationships may require the other party to be relatively salient in the interaction, impression formation can be more cognitive in focus (Fiske & Taylor, 1991).

Socioemotional content of teleconferenced meetings. The vast majority of studies found that compared to face-to-face meetings, both video and audio meetings were characterized by less emotional display (Champness, 1972; LaPlante, 1971; Weston et al., 1975; Williams, 1976). In addition, audio- and video-mediated meetings showed less conflict and unresolved disagreement (Barefoot & Strickland, 1982; Williams, 1976; Wilson, 1974). As discussed in the next section, subsequent research on computer conferencing produced a much more complicated set of findings, including some that show increased negative emotional display for that medium.

Participation. Johansen et al. (1979) argue that compared to mediated meetings, the personal nature of face-to-face meetings can inhibit broad participation across the participants. Face-to-face interaction conveys many visual status symbols that can cue deference behavior (Sproull & Kiesler, 1991), and it is easier for a single person to dominate. Research has consistently supported a finding of more equal participation in videoconferencing, with a single exception (Barefoot & Strickland, 1982). In videoconferenced meetings, participants are "more polite" and try to encourage participation among those who are reticent, leaders do not as readily emerge, and generally there is less developed hierarchy within the group (Dutton et al., 1982; Fulk & Dutton, 1984; George et al., 1975, cited in Johansen et al., 1979; Strickland, Guild, Barefoot, & Patterson, 1978). Equal participation has also been documented for audioconferencing (Champness, 1972), where participants were better able to exert control over domineering participants (Holloway & Hammond, 1976, and Short, 1973, cited in Johansen et al., 1979). The net effect is that audio meetings were more "orderly."

Conflict. Social presence theory predicts that when tasks are interpersonally involving, such as conflict and negotiation, more cooperation and agreement are likely with more communication channels. Short et al. (1976) report support for this prediction from four laboratory studies that involved two-person mixed-motive situations such as prisoner's dilemma; they also report one study that found no medium effects. Other studies have found mediated meetings to enhance agreement for audioconferencing (Williams, 1976; Wilson, 1974) and videoconferencing (Barefoot & Strickland, 1982). Rarely were *no* medium effects found in laboratory studies.

The central thesis of media capacity theories concerns how such process changes affect communication effectiveness and efficiency in mediated meetings. Theoretically, process changes have the greatest effect when tasks are complex, involving bargaining, negotiation, and personal relationships. The most thoroughly investigated effects are participant satisfaction, decision efficiency, and decision quality.

Satisfaction. Research has shown that participants are less satisfied in video- or audio-teleconferenced meetings (nine studies reported in Johansen et al., 1979; Korzenny & Bauer, 1979). Is satisfaction most affected when the tasks are more complex and personally involving? Field surveys and case research support this prediction for both audio (Albertson, 1977) and video (Albertson, 1977; Dutton et al., 1982; Fulk & Dutton, 1984; Noll, 1976) conditions. In direct contrast, laboratory studies found no differential effects on satisfaction by task complexity for either audio (Albertson, 1973; Champness & Davies, 1971; Korzenny & Bauer, 1979) or video (Dennis & Kinney, 1998; Korzenny & Bauer, 1979).

Efficiency. Many years of investigations in both lab and field have failed to demonstrate detrimental effects of teleconferencing versus face-to-face on efficiency in synchronous meetings. Indeed, the only efficiency effects have been in favor of teleconferenced meetings. In laboratory studies, no compromise in decision efficiency (time to complete the task) on high-complexity tasks has been found for video versus face-to-face meetings (Albertson, 1973; Barefoot & Strickland, 1982; Dennis & Kinney, 1998; Weeks & Chapanis, 1976). Valacich, Mennecke, Wachter, and Wheeler (1994) did find video meetings to be faster than face-to-face for a high-complexity task. Nor were differences in decision efficiency found for low-complexity tasks conducted via videoconferencing (Albertson, 1973; Dennis & Kinney, 1998; Ochsman & Chapanis, 1974; Valacich, Mennecke, et al., 1994; Weeks & Chapanis, 1976). Dennis and Kinney (1998) did find that video meetings were slower for both types of tasks when the meeting employed half-duplex technology (no feedback from the receiver was permitted during the sender's transmission, impeding true synchroneity). Dutton et al. (1982) and Johansen et al. (1979) also report results of three field surveys of managers in which video meetings were perceived to be shorter, although objective measures collected in one of the studies did not support the perceptions.

Similarly, no differences have been found for audioconferencing versus face-to-face for high-complexity tasks (Albertson, 1973; Weeks & Chapanis, 1976). For low-complexity tasks, although some research has shown no differences (Albertson, 1973; Ochsman & Chapanis, 1974; Weeks & Chapanis, 1976), most has shown greater decision efficiency for audio conditions (Davies, 1971: two experiments; Rawlins, 1989, and Johansen et al., 1979: six unpublished studies). One interpretation of these patterns is that the reduction in social presence achieved via mediation serves to limit the amount of distraction that "irrelevant" personal considerations inject into decision making for straightforward, low-complexity tasks. Without these distractions, groups may complete their work more quickly than if they needed to attend to and adjust to personal factors that are salient in each other's presence. Such an interpretation is consistent with Zajonc's (1965) "mere presence" hypothesis, on which social presence theory draws.

Quality. To recap, participants are less satisfied in teleconferenced meetings, especially in audio-only settings, and they participate more evenly. Further, teleconferenced meetings are at least as efficient and some save considerable time relative to face-to-face encounters. Assuming that participation and efficiency are generally valued in Western organizations, the findings for satisfaction appear somewhat curious. A partial explanation may relate to differences in perceived quality of decisions across media. Johansen et al. (1979) report ten studies in which respondents perceived teleconferencing as less effective for bargaining and negotiation (four video studies and six audio studies). These results suggest that despite some process-related benefits of mediation, the quality of work is perceived to suffer when complex interaction is required. Perceived quality decrements may counterbalance valuable process changes. An interesting aspect of the research on decision quality is that, in general, objective measures fail to support participant perceptions of reduced quality in teleconferenced meetings, even for complex tasks. With one exception for audioconferencing (Weston et al., 1975), no studies found a decrement in decision quality for complex tasks in a teleconferencing forum, although Lopez (1992) found lower-quality decisions in videoconferencing for a low-complexity

task. Most experiments found no differences in decision quality for face-to-face versus videoconferencing (Albertson, 1973; Dennis & Kinney, 1998) or audioconferencing (Albertson, 1973; Champness & Davies, 1971; Davies, 1971 [two studies], Harmon, Schneer, & Hoffman, 1995; Short, 1971; Williams, 1975). Rosetti and Surynt (1985) report higher quality under video than face-to-face for a complex task. Johansen et al. (1979) report empirical evidence from three experiments that showed no more breakdowns in audio negotiations than in face-to-face.

Divergences in perceptual versus objective measures of quality could result from researchers applying different criteria for decision quality than do meeting participants. Alternatively, meeting participants simply may prefer inclusion of those "irrelevant" personal considerations. Efficiency goals may be superseded by personal preferences for personalized contact and reinforcement of status cues. Participants may perceive a need for personal involvement in bargaining and negotiation situations to achieve a sense of personal satisfaction with the process.

Summary on Premises

A variety of critiques of the media capacity tradition have been published over the years. We review critiques of six types of premise; subsequent sections compare these media capacity premises to those from the other two dominant theoretical traditions that we review: input-process-output and structuration. The six areas are (1) group role in the meeting process, (2) task characteristics, (3) perspectives on processes in mediated meetings, (4) role of technology, (5) contextualization, and (6) nature of rationality. Table 16.1 summarizes the comparisons across the three theoretical traditions.

Group role in the meeting process. Media capacity theories offer little role for groups to actively manage the technology and context

TABLE 16.1 Evolution of Three Traditions

	Media Capacity	Input-Process-Output	Structuration
Intellectual heritage	Nonverbal communication Organizational information processing	Theories of groups Steiner's (1972) process losses	Structuration Self-organizing systems
Specific theories	Social presence Media richness	Input-Process-Output Time, interaction, and performance	Adaptive structuration Self-organizing systems
Premises			
Group role in the meeting process	Reacts passively to constraints	Responds to technological input factors	Proactively manages technology and group process
Task characteristics	Fixed	Partially altered by technology	Structured by groups in part via technology
Perspective on processes in mediated meetings	Process losses	Process gains and losses due to technological mediation	Articulation of group process with technology's structure and spirit
Role of technology	Connective	Constructive	Constructed and constructive
Contextualization	Minimal	Context as input factor	Context embedded in process through appropriation
Rationality	Objective	Objective	Subjective

of the meeting. Social presence theory, although built on theories of nonverbal communication and social psychology, portrays groups as responding relatively uncreatively to the situational constraints of mediation. Media richness theory follows its parent tradition in organizational information-processing theories in focusing on technology and tasks, largely devoid of human systems that interact through technology on specific tasks. An alternative assumption that situationally empowered groups actively manage task, technology, and context better fits findings that teleconferencing participants experienced process changes and lower satisfaction but no detrimental effects on performance. Groups may have actively altered their preferred processes to maintain performance under medium constraints, with the effect of depressing satisfaction with the experience.

Task characteristics. The media capacity perspective assumes that tasks are relatively unmalleable. Yet research on task design indicates that how tasks are interpreted varies considerably across individuals and groups and is subject to processes of social influence (Salancik & Pfeffer, 1978). Further, tasks that are uncertain but not equivocal may be modified and transformed by groups during the process of task accomplishment. One explanation for decision efficiency and effectiveness in teleconferenced groups with complex tasks is that the groups may have restructured and rationalized the tasks to a more manageable level. Such task rationalization to align task complexity with medium capacity could be incorporated within a revised social presence theory without violating the fundamental matching premise of the theory.

Perspective on processes. A central tenet of media capacity theories is that mediation involves losses in comparison to face-to-face interaction. The fewer the cues that are communicated through a medium, the less rich are the medium and the social presence involved in the interaction. Rice (1984) and

Culnan and Markus (1987) have criticized this perspective for assuming that face-to-face is the appropriate comparison and that mediated communication must involve losses. One could argue that channel capacity theorists of the 1970s could not have foreseen the future ability of computer support to provide improvements and as well decrements to interaction. However, even the established technology of speakerphone need not involve only losses in interactive capabilities. Culnan and Markus (1987, p. 433) point to mute buttons on speakerphones that allow unobtrusive private remarks that cannot be heard by listeners at another node—a capability not available in unmediated meetings. Fulk and Dutton (1984) also found that additional means of communication were available in teleconferenced meetings by people unobtrusively passing notes under the table outside the view of the camera.

Role of technology. Emphasis on process losses is linked to a 1970s perspective on communication processes as message transmission. Technology was seen to transmit cues to the maximum capacity of the pipe—if inflow exceeded a conduit's capacity, outflow would be reduced relative to inflow. As computing and telecommunications merged in the 1980s, researchers viewed media as capable of structuring interaction in ways other than simply filtering out cues. Culnan and Markus (1987) identify several factors available in computer-based meetings that make them substantively different from, rather than less capable than, face-to-face meetings. One feature is addressability, the ability to address communication selectively to some participants through distribution lists and private messaging features. A second is written memory, storage, and retrieval, which could inhibit opinion change or, as Fulk and Monge (1995) note, could exert control through collective sensemaking. A third is capabilities for controlling level of access and participation. Yet capabilities for structuring interaction need not rely on computing power. Fulk and Dutton (1984) found that voice-activated microphones structured interaction in a videoconference by eliminating talk-overs and favoring individuals with the stronger microphones. Virtually no theoretical development has been conducted to modify channel capacity theories to account for these capabilities of teleconference technologies to structure communication.

Contextualization. Media capacity theories largely seek explanations for meeting processes and effects within the mediated meeting itself. Little theoretical development focused on contextual factors beyond technology and task that could potentially affect meeting processes and effects. Short et al. (1976) briefly mention interpersonal attraction as potentially interacting with technology to affect meeting processes, indicating that evaluation of a medium may be "related to evaluation of people met via that medium" (p. 114). Yet they explain this contextual influence by reference to media factors: (1) people act more formally due to medium constraints and thus are viewed as displaying less warmth, and (2) people exhibit normal warmth cues but the reduced capacity of the medium inhibits transmission of such cues.

Social presence theory suggests several contextual factors that influence medium choice, including physical distance, status levels of participants, degree of acquaintance of participants, access to technology, and security needs. Media richness theory also proposes a list of factors, including physical distance, time pressures, and symbolic meanings of medium (e.g., use of written media symbolizes formality). Contextual effects on meeting processes per se are largely unexplicated in this tradition, however. This acontextual orientation is reflected in a body of research that is heavily based in controlled laboratory experiments, often with student subjects. Thus, one possible explanation for findings is that the artificial settings and contrived tasks may have produced atypical behavior. Culnan and Markus (1987, p. 430) argue that in most organizations people know each other, are fa-

miliar with and competent in using technologies they choose from a wide selection, and have a well-known and designated leader of higher status.

The consistent support in the few field studies contrasts markedly with the lack of support from many laboratory studies. Clearly, more investigations of channel capacity premises must be conducted in more naturally modeled contexts, whether these studies are laboratory experiments, field studies, or field experiments.

Rationality. Channel capacity models have been criticized for exhibiting a rationalist bias (Fulk, Schmitz, & Steinfield, 1990; Fulk, Steinfield, Schmitz, & Power, 1987; Lea, 1991). Scholars have argued that the efficiency and effectiveness purported to arise from properly matching task and medium are not the only or even the major goals of participants in interpersonal interaction. Participants have other goals, some of which may conflict with objectively rational choices toward efficiency and effectiveness. This criticism shares a conceptual heritage with Schwartzman's (1986) analysis of meetings as primary forums for playing out political processes and validating social relations rather than efficiently completing tasks.

A related issue is the theoretically ambiguous role of participant *perceptions* of media capabilities relative to "objective" features. Participants' perceptions of media limitations may not fit objective features as described by the theories. For example, pessimistic perceptions of medium constraints could serve as psychological barriers to creative solution seeking, whereas optimistic perceptions may guide a group to seek new and more successful approaches to their tasks. Conversely, optimistic perceptions by participants about the kinds of complex tasks that can be completed in a mediated meeting might produce unrealistic expectations and thus draw groups to attempt infeasible processes.

As documented in critiques, media richness theory is premised on objective media features. Social presence theory is more elusive. Short et al. (1976) stated, "We regard Social Presence as being a quality of the communications medium" (p. 65), which led some researchers to conclude that the concept is not based in perception (e.g., Walther, 1992, p. 55). Yet Short et al. also state, "Thus, when we said earlier that Social Presence is a quality of the medium we were not being strictly accurate. We conceive of Social Presence not as an objective quality of the medium, though it must surely be dependent upon the medium's objective qualities, but as a subjective quality of the medium . . . we believe that it is important to know how the user perceives the medium, what his [*sic*] feelings are and what his 'mental set' is" (pp. 65-66). The ambiguity of Short et al.'s statements is reflected in the differing measurement approaches across studies (some measured perceptions and some did not). The synthetic nature of the concept also poses challenges. It includes the capacity to transmit "facial expression, direction of looking, posture, dress, and nonverbal cues," and "the weights given to all these factors is determined by the individual" (p. 65). Rafaeli (1988) argues that because "there is no specification of how these qualities are achieved . . . it remains unclear whether social presence is a quality of the medium, channel, content, participants, or communication experience (Heeter, 1985; Rice, 1984). The multidimensional attraction of the 'social presence' construct is also its theoretical downfall" (p. 117).

INPUT-PROCESS-OUTPUT THEORIES

Computer-based meeting support was not widely available when social presence theory was originally formulated. Thus, social presence theorists had little to say about computer-based meeting support, arguing that "this medium is really too new to have been properly assessed" (Short et al., 1976, p. 8).

By the late 1970s, findings were beginning to accumulate on computer-conferencing systems, generally without the benefit of strong theoretical guidance (Johansen et al., 1979, provide a review). The availability of electronic text did not fit straightforwardly into social presence theory, due in part to potential improvements as well as decrements in nonverbal cues. Also, media richness theory originally focused on traditional written and telecommunication media and on computer-based reports, but not computer conferencing. With the increasing popularity of organizational computer-conferencing systems, researchers sought to develop theory that explained the ability of computer-based media not simply to transmit communicative cues but also to support and structure group interaction. Also, with the migration of social presence and media richness premises to asynchronous formats, it became evident that the interacting group had somehow been lost. In response, a new theoretical tradition that privileged the interacting, decision-making group was developed on a base of existing group communication theory.

The dominant model in this tradition is input-process-output (IPO) theory. Several variations of IPO theory exist, but all share several core premises that unite them in a theoretical tradition (e.g., Hiltz & Turoff, 1978; Kiesler, Siegel, & McGuire, 1984; Nunamaker, Dennis, Valacich, Vogel, & George, 1993; Rice, 1984). McGrath and Hollingshead's (1992, 1994) time, interaction, and performance theory integrates media richness theory into an IPO model, and thus is considered a separate IPO theory.

IPO Theory: Unified Formulation

Input-process-output theory proposes that the outcomes of a meeting depend on processes that occur in the meeting, which are significantly affected by input variables including contextual factors that frame the interaction. IPO research generally treats meeting technologies as an input factor (Hiltz & Turoff, 1978; McGrath & Hollingshead, 1992; Nunamaker, Dennis, George, Valacich, & Vogel, 1991), along with group characteristics, task characteristics, and broader contextual factors.

Drawing on Steiner (1972), IPO theory proposes that some aspects of the group's process improve outcomes (process gains) and some aspects impair outcomes (process losses) relative to individual decision makers. Achieving positive group outcomes depends on maximizing process gains while minimizing losses (Collins & Guetzkow, 1964; Hackman & Morris, 1975; Jarboe, 1988; Nunamaker et al., 1993). Process gains include such factors as more objective evaluation, synergy, more information availability, stimulation of individual performance, and learning effects across group members. Process losses occur due to "production blocking" because only one person can communicate at a time, and memory failures because when participants focus on their communication they may miss or forget others' contributions. Process losses include such factors as evaluation apprehension, domination of the group by a single member, coordination problems, information overload, conformance pressure, free riding, and incomplete task analysis (Nunamaker et al., 1993).

IPO and computer conferencing. IPO theory proposes that computer conferencing encourages certain process gains while avoiding other process losses. Because computer conferencing conveys information via written channels, it possesses limited ability to transmit cues about individual identities and relationships. By minimizing communication of non-task-related information, computer conferencing can reduce the importance of "unpredictable" interpersonal processes that often dominate face-to-face meetings (Hiltz & Turoff, 1978; Kiesler et al., 1984). For example, limiting information about individual identities could (1) encourage lower-status members to participate

more fully without fear of social retribution, and (2) constrain participants to evaluate each other's arguments based on quality rather than status of source (Hiltz & Turoff, 1978; Kiesler et al., 1984).

Parallel communication in computer conferencing reduces participants' real-time information-processing needs because they can ignore other members' contributions while they input their own ideas. The collective memory feature creates an instantaneous permanent record of information exchanged, and thus reduces process losses related to the failure to attend to and remember information (Hiltz & Turoff, 1978; Kiesler et al., 1984). Collective memory rationalizes the group process by standardizing the idea store available to participants (Hoffer & Valacich, 1992; Nunamaker et al., 1993).

Theoretically, these unique features result in higher-quality and more efficient decisions. However, IPO theorists also recognized that the limited ability of computer conferencing to transmit interpersonal information could contribute to process losses that diminish productivity. Reduction of social context cues could force computer-conferencing groups to spend more time processing information to analyze their tasks and coordinate their efforts. Reduction of social cues could also reduce social inhibitions, resulting in more negative socioemotional behavior and less consensus among group members. Thus, computer-conferencing groups could actually take longer to agree on a decision than face-to-face groups (Hiltz & Turoff, 1978; Kiesler et al., 1984; Rice, 1984). Jessup and George (1997) also propose that anonymity can lead to social loafing (e.g., Williams, Harkins, & Latane, 1981), cognitive loafing (Weldon & Mustari, 1988), and frivolous remarks (Jessup & Connolly, 1991). Shepherd, Briggs, Yen, and Nunamaker (1995) demonstrated that invocation of social comparison processes can dramatically improve GSS group performance. The net effect on meeting outcomes will depend on the relative balance of gains and losses that the group is able to maintain.

IPO and group support systems. One solution to some of these process losses is to offer the group more sophisticated tools for monitoring and controlling their meeting processes so as to maximize gains while minimizing losses. Theoretically, GSSs affect the balance of gains and losses through four mechanisms (Nunamaker et al., 1993):

1. *Process support* includes three mechanisms also available through computer conferencing: anonymity, parallel communication, and group memory.
2. *Process structure* includes techniques and rules that direct communication patterns (e.g., Robert's Rules of Order), timing (e.g., talk queues that determine who communicates next), or content (e.g., support for agenda setting).
3. *Task structure* includes techniques, rules, and models for analyzing task-related information (e.g., Bayesian analysis).
4. *Task support* refers to the communication and information infrastructure that embeds the task, such as access to databases or prior meeting notes.

The basic premise is that group support systems encourage more orderly and rationalized processes by structuring the way that communication flows and information is processed. The rationalizing abilities of group support systems are posited to compensate for process losses experienced with computer-conferenced meetings by helping participants cope with information overload and compensate for losses due to reduced social context cues. Thus, although participation equality should remain high for GSS meetings, there should be less negative socioemotional expression and conflict compared to computer-conferenced meetings (DeSanctis & Gallupe, 1987). The advantages of structural support should be greatest for groups using more sophisticated GSS technologies that provide more assistance in organizing the decision process (Poole, Holmes, & DeSanctis, 1991; Sambamurthy, Poole, & Kelly, 1993).

Time, Interaction, and Performance Theory

The most developed model of input factors is McGrath and Hollingshead's (1992, 1994) time, interaction, and performance (TIP) theory. The theory proposes that communication tasks can be classified into one or more of four types, in increasing order of complexity, and hence information richness requirements.

1. Idea generation tasks involve simple information transmission (e.g., brainstorming). "Evaluative and emotional connotations about message and source are not required and are often considered to be a hindrance" (McGrath & Hollingshead, 1992, p. 92).
2. Intellective tasks require solving problems that have correct answers.
3. Judgment tasks involve no right answer but the group can potentially arrive at a consensual judgment (e.g., jury verdict).
4. Negotiation tasks require resolution of conflicts of interest and "may require the transmission of maximally rich information, including not only 'facts' but also values, attitudes, affective messages, expectations, commitments, and so on" (p. 92).

Drawing on media richness theory, McGrath and Hollingshead (1992, 1994) argue that the more complex the task is, the richer the meeting system employed should be. The model also proposes that matching media to task complexity depends on group development, in that groups need richer media to process the equivocal information that characterizes the early developmental stages.

Most IPO theories recognize several phases of group problem solving that may require different support tools. Phase models typically propose a fixed series of phases in group development (e.g., Tuckman, 1965) that translates into fixed series of requirements for technological support (e.g., Kraut, Galegher, & Egido, 1990). TIP theory proposes that temporal aspects of groups are more complex. First, there is not a single series of phases, but rather several sets of phases each relating to one of three functions engaged in by groups: production, member support, and well-being. Second, groups do not necessarily pass through each phase for each function. Third, groups can engage in more than one task or project in a single meeting, and each project may progress at a different rate through each phase and function. Thus, although this perspective retains the linear model of input-process-output as its overall framework, it proposes that interactions among input factors are complex, interrelated, and dynamic.

Empirical Evidence

Socioemotional content of computer-supported meetings. A series of studies of student groups found more negative socioemotional expression within computer-conferencing groups for both low- and high-complexity tasks (Dubrovsky, Kiesler, & Sethna, 1991; Kiesler et al., 1984; Kiesler, Zubrow, Moses, & Geller, 1985; Siegel, Dubrovsky, Kiesler, & McGuire, 1986). This pattern was not consistently evoked, however. For example, Hiltz et al. (1978) found less negative emotion, Straus (1997) found higher rates of supportive communication and Walther (1995) found higher immediacy/affection, and other studies are divided between those showing more emotion of all types (e.g., Walther & Burgoon, 1992) and those showing less (e.g., Hiltz, Johnson, & Turoff, 1986), in no apparent relationship to task complexity. When groups used more structured GSSs rather than simple computer conferencing, the negative emotional effect was absent. Research has reported either no differences in negative affect exhibited (e.g., Poole et al., 1991) or less overall negative affect in GSS versus face-to-face meetings (e.g., Vician, DeSanctis, Poole, & Jackson, 1992).

If negative socioemotional behavior (also known as "flaming") results from limitations in interpersonal information exchange, why doesn't such behavior occur in teleconferencing meetings? Two explanations seem plausi-

ble. First, computer-conference participants may have difficulty monitoring socioemotional levels in the interaction. Audio cues are "leaky" (Ekman & Friesen, 1969), communicating a great deal about the mood and intention of the interaction partner. The loss of audio cues to regulate interaction may make it difficult to both encode and decode messages that transmit the emotional signals through subtle nonverbal behavior. Second, negative socioemotional behavior may be an artifact of the context in which computer-conferencing groups interacted. Theorists attribute flaming to reduced concerns regarding public self-presentation, which are most likely when participants are not identifiable to one another, do not maintain a preexisting relationship, and do not anticipate continuing their relationship with one another (Lea, O'Shea, Fung, & Spears, 1992; Olaniran, 1994; Walther, 1994; Walther, Anderson, & Park, 1994). Findings regarding flaming may be attributable to the fact that computer-conferencing experiments were mostly time limited and involved individuals who had no established (or anticipated) relational histories (Walther, 1992).

Walther (1992) posits two reasons why differential socioemotional expression was probably a coding artifact. First, studies did not code nonverbal behavior for face-to-face groups, where much socioemotional content lies. If nonverbal behavior were coded, "the overall ratio of socioemotional expressions to total messages may be no different in face-to-face than in CMC groups" (p. 63). Second, coding behavior as either task *or* socioemotional "is a notion contrary to axiomatic positions about the simultaneous content and relations functions of any message (Watzlawick, Beavin, & Jackson, 1967)" (p. 64). Walther argues that until both content and relational functions are adequately coded in all messages, one cannot draw conclusions about whether computer-supported meetings are more personal, less, or no different.

Participation. Participation patterns in computer-supported meetings have been heavily studied. Measures have focused primarily on leadership emergence, relative influence of each participant on the ultimate group decision, relative amounts of talk time, relative number of contributions by each participant, and participant perceptions of relative equity of participation. Groups have been studied in both identified and anonymous conditions, and in both field and laboratory. GSS research has studied both computerized support and equivalent paper-based support.

Field studies using either observation or self-report measures consistently document a participation equality effect for GSS groups relative to face-to-face (e.g., Tyran, Dennis, Vogel, & Nunamaker, 1992; Vician et al., 1992; Vogel & Nunamaker, 1989; Vogel, Nunamaker, Martz, Grohowski, & McGoff, 1989). Equality also was observed in some laboratory studies (Easton, 1988; Easton et al., 1990; George, Easton, Nunamaker, & Northcraft, 1990; Lewis, 1987; Nunamaker, Applegate, & Konsynski, 1987; Zigurs, Poole, & DeSanctis, 1988), but others found no differences in participation (Beauclair, 1987; Burke & Chidambaram, 1995; Gallupe, DeSanctis, & Dickson, 1988; McLeod & Liker, 1992; Poole et al., 1991; Poole et al., 1993; Walther, 1995; Watson, DeSanctis, & Poole, 1988). Findings on participation do not vary depending on task complexity. Finally, only one study found *greater* inequality in GSS groups, but this effect disappeared over time (Walther, 1995).

Virtually all computer-conferencing studies were conducted in controlled, laboratory contexts and show the same mixed trend as GSS laboratory studies. Regardless of task complexity, equalization was found in some studies (Dubrovsky et al., 1991; Hiltz, Johnson, & Agle, 1978; Hitz, Johnson, Aronovitch, & Turoff, 1980; Hitz et al., 1986 [high-complexity task only]; Johansen et al., 1979 [three studies]; Kiesler et al., 1984; McGuire, Kiesler, & Siegel, 1987; Siegel et al., 1986; Straus, 1996, 1997), but not in others (Hiltz et al., 1986 [low-complexity task only]; Jarvenpaa, Rao, & Huber, 1988; Walther & Burgoon, 1992; Weisband, Schneider, & Connolly, 1995 [three experiments]). No studies

showed a reverse effect for computer support, and the pattern is unrelated to how participation was measured.

Mixed laboratory findings may reflect that status hierarchies emerge over time as groups develop norms and social structure. Laboratory groups may not exhibit a strongly differentiated social structure even face-to-face, for the reasons Culnan and Markus (1987) stated: lack of prior acquaintance, no shared history, no shared organizational context with its attendant status hierarchies, and no formally assigned leader. Lack of participation differences may reflect that face-to-face groups had no status hierarchies that could cue unequal participation. The results may say more about face-to-face laboratory groups as a comparison condition than about computer support. Walther and Burgoon (1992) argue that as groups continue to meet over time and their attention turns toward more interpersonal issues, status hierarchies and norms may become more evident, even in laboratory groups. This logic is consistent with a meta-analysis of 13 GSS and computer-conferencing studies that showed greater equalization for ad hoc than established groups, even for time-limited tasks in the laboratory (Benbasat & Lim, 1993).

Weisband et al. (1995) argue, alternatively, that the failure of many laboratory studies to find an equalization effect may result from the availability of some status cues even in the computer-mediated condition. Their conclusion is consistent with research that found status differentials to persist in computer-mediated meetings (Saunders, Robey, & Vaverek, 1994; Spears & Lea, 1994). It is also consistent with findings that individuals with no knowledge of another person use whatever minimal cue information is available in reaching judgments about others, even irrelevant information.

There is much to be learned about how social stratification develops over time in previously unacquainted laboratory groups participating in mediated meetings. Research should focus on temporal aspects, cue availability, how individuals and groups recognize and process status-related cues, and how this translates to specific group processes and overall participation. In-depth research that monitors key developmental processes for computer-supported groups in relation to their face-to-face counterparts is essential to any determination of medium effects on meeting participation.

Consensus and conflict. A series of time-limited laboratory studies found that computer-conferencing groups were less likely to reach consensus, regardless of task complexity (Hiltz et al., 1978; Hiltz et al., 1980; Hiltz et al., 1986). These results have been interpreted as supporting the IPO proposition that slower rates of information exchange in computer conferencing leaves groups with insufficient time to work through decision-making issues (Hiltz & Turoff, 1978; Rice, 1984). Lea and Spears (1991) found the effects to be stronger for anonymous than identified groups. The effect disappeared totally, for both anonymous and identified groups, when research was conducted in a field setting (Hiltz et al., 1989).

With the addition of GSS structural and process support, the consensus decrement was moderated. Although sometimes less consensus was found (Gallupe et al., 1988; George et al., 1990; Poole et al., 1991), other research found either no differences (Watson et al., 1988) or more consensus for supported groups (Sambamurthy & DeSanctis, 1990; Steeb & Johnston, 1981). Benbasat and Lim's (1993) meta-analysis of eight studies showed a positive moderating effect for level of support: Greater task and process structure was associated with greater consensus. Sambamurthy et al. (1993) reported that consensus was positively related to the extent that groups exhibited procedural insight, ideational connection, critical examination of ideas, and productive use of formal evaluation, each of which was more commonly found in groups with higher-level support tools. These results offer a rationale for the divergent findings on consensus, suggesting that the processes that

evolve in meetings are determinants of whether consensus is likely and that these processes themselves may be influenced by the type of technology.

Poole et al. (1991) found that GSS groups engaged in more open expressions of conflict than unsupported face-to-face groups, while Miranda and Bostrom (1994) found the opposite. A longitudinal study suggested that GSS groups eventually develop more conflict than face-to-face groups (Chidambaram, Bostrom, & Wynne, 1991). Increased conflict may result from the combined effect of a depersonalized communication medium and a structural process that surfaces differences of opinion between members. The ability of groups to reach consensus given these conditions may well depend on how the group chooses to employ its structural support in the service of reaching agreement.

Satisfaction. Early experiments found that mediated meetings were less satisfying for complex tasks such as bargaining, persuasion, and resolving conflicts (Vallee, Johansen, Lipinski, Spangler, & Wilson, 1978, cited in Johansen et al., 1979; Pye & Williams, 1977; Hiltz, Johnson, & Turoff, 1981, cited in Rice, 1984; Vallee, Johansen, Randolph, & Hastings, 1974) and less satisfying overall compared to face-to-face (Hiltz et al., 1980; Hiltz et al., 1986). Satisfaction in computer-conferenced meetings may be dampened by negative socioemotional expression, problems in reaching consensus, and difficulties in completing the task in a timely manner (Hiltz et al., 1989; Straus, 1996). Recent research compared groups on both task type and medium, with mixed results. For low task complexity, Valacich, Paranka, George, and Nunamaker (1993) found no satisfaction differential between face-to-face and computer conferencing, while Straus (1996) found mediated groups to be less satisfied. However, Straus and McGrath (1994) found this difference only for high-complexity tasks, and Dennis and Kinney (1998) found no effect of task complexity on satisfaction. Hollingshead, McGrath, and O'Connor's (1993) results suggest a possible explanation. They found that although in general groups were less satisfied in mediated conditions, the effect was dynamic. During the first week that a group changed from face-to-face to a mediated condition, satisfaction decreased, but for the next two weeks there were no differences in satisfaction across conditions. Since most computer-conferencing studies were conducted in time-limited laboratory contexts, it is not possible to draw conclusions regarding the persistence of any satisfaction differentials.

Theoretically, advanced GSS features help manage process difficulties, countering any satisfaction decrement. Although some experiments have found a satisfaction decrement in GSS meetings compared to face-to-face (Easton et al., 1990; Gallupe et al., 1988; George et al., 1990; Watson et al., 1988), the bulk of studies found no differences relative to face-to-face (Beauclair, 1987; Bui, Sivansankaran, Fijol, & Woodburg, 1987; Easton, 1988; Gallupe & McKeen, 1990; George et al., 1990; Lewis, 1987; Sharda, Barr, & McDonnell, 1988). Some experiments even produced greater satisfaction for GSS meetings (Jessup, Tansik, & Laase, 1988; Steeb & Johnston, 1981). The compensating effects for GSS process structure should also lead to more satisfied GSS groups relative to computer conferencing. Benbasat and Lim (1993) tested this hypothesis in a meta-analysis of 16 laboratory studies. They found that GSS groups with more sophisticated tools were more satisfied with meeting processes and outcomes compared to groups with less sophisticated support, such as computer-conference tools.

In the field, users generally reported high satisfaction with GSS meetings (Dennis, Heminger, Nunamaker, & Vogel, 1990; DeSanctis, Poole, Lewis, & Desharnais, 1992; Martz, Vogel, & Nunamaker, 1992; Nunamaker et al., 1987; Tyran et al., 1992; Vogel et al., 1989). However, these studies did not compare satisfaction in GSS versus the same type of meeting face-to-face, nor were control conditions included. Thus, field research results must be interpreted cautiously.

Efficiency. Computer-conferencing groups are less efficient than face-to face groups for high-complexity tasks (Dennis & Kinney, 1998; Hiltz et al., 1978; Kiesler et al., 1984; McGuire et al., 1987; Siegel et al., 1986; Straus & McGrath, 1994). For low-complexity tasks, most studies found that computer-conferencing groups are less efficient (Dennis & Kinney, 1998; Hightower & Sayeed, 1995; Hiltz et al., 1978; Olaniran, 1994; Straus, 1996), with few exceptions (Gallupe et al., 1992; Johansen et al., 1979 [two field surveys]; Straus & McGrath, 1994). Results support contentions that computer-conferencing groups process information more slowly and experience information overload, particularly for high-complexity tasks. Problems reaching consensus may also contribute to inefficiency.

Field studies typically reported superior performance for GSSs; laboratory results were less consistent. GSS meetings were more efficient in ongoing organizations (Dennis et al., 1990; Martz et al., 1992; Nunamaker et al., 1987; Tyran et al., 1992; Valacich et al., 1993; Vogel & Nunamaker 1989; Vogel et al., 1989) and a few experiments (Bui & Sivansankaran, 1990; Sharda et al., 1988; Steeb & Johnston, 1981). However, some GSS experiments found that decisions take more time (Gallupe & McKeen, 1990; George et al., 1990). Benbasat and Lim's (1993) meta-analysis of eight experiments found that more sophisticated support was associated with greater decision efficiency than less sophisticated support.

Quality. Does more equal participation influence decision quality? Some experiments found higher quality for computer-conferencing groups performing high-complexity tasks (Hiltz et al., 1980; Hiltz et al., 1986). For less-complex tasks, some studies found greater quality for computer-conferencing groups (Gallupe et al., 1992; Jarvenpaa et al., 1988), but others found no difference (Burke & Chidambaram, 1995; Olaniran, 1994; Valacich & Schwenk, 1995). Experiments by Dennis and Kinney (1998) and Straus and McGrath (1994) found no difference in decision quality by task type or medium. An over-time study (Hollingshead et al., 1993) found that decision quality was consistently lower for high-complexity tasks but that decision quality increased over time with low-complexity tasks.

GSSs have been linked to higher decision quality in both field studies (Dennis et al., 1990; Martz et al., 1992; Nunamaker et al., 1987; Tyran et al. 1992; Vogel et al., 1989) and experiments (Bui & Sivansankaran, 1990; Bui et al., 1987; Lam, 1997, for complex tasks; Sharda et al., 1988; Valacich et al., 1993), although some experiments found no differences (Dennis, 1996; Gallupe & McKeen, 1990; George et al., 1990; Lam, 1997, for simple tasks; Steeb & Johnston, 1981). Benbasat and Lim's (1993) meta-analysis of 22 experimental studies found greater decision quality for low-complexity tasks and for more sophisticated support tools. No analyses assessed potential interactions between support level and task complexity.

Summary and Comparison of Premises

Group role in the meeting process. IPO theories model group processes as critical to task accomplishment. First, group characteristics are inputs that contribute to decision processes. Research investigated inputs such as size (Valacich et al., 1995), anonymity (Valacich et al., 1992), and stage of group development (Chidambaram & Bostrom, 1997a, 1997b; Hollingshead et al., 1993). Second, because some group processes may interfere with efficient and effective decision making, systems are designed to guide group processes by reducing "irrelevant" socioemotional content, encouraging broad participa-

tion, supporting consensus building and conflict resolution, and assisting decision analysis.

How effective is computer support in achieving these goals?'

1. Research suggests that system support reduces socioemotional content but also has some unintended effects, such as reducing cues that regulate interaction in computer-conferenced meetings. GSS support tools may resolve this problem.

2. Both types of support may encourage broader participation for established groups. With unacquainted groups, equalization occurs in some supported groups and not in others, although system support does not make participation *more* unequal compared to face-to-face.

3. Consensus can be impaired in computer conferencing, although GSS support moderates this effect somewhat. Conflict has not been extensively studied, but some groups experience more conflict and some less in GSS conditions.

4. Decision efficiency is not improved in computer-conferenced meetings, and some groups take considerable time to reach a decision. GSS support moderated this problem in some experiments, but not in others. Field studies consistently report improved efficiency in GSS meetings.

5. Decision quality is higher for low-complexity tasks and for GSS versus computer-conferenced support, consistent with TIP theory.

IPO theories assume that meeting processes can be constrained via technological support that directs groups toward more productive interaction. Groups respond to inputs that include task, technology, and their own characteristics. The failure of some laboratory groups to behave as predicted suggests that they respond to other factors as well or may act in ways inconsistent with technological guides.

Task characteristics. Compared to media capacity premises, IPO theories assume that tasks are more malleable, in that technological support rationalizes tasks. Tasks are also input variables, and TIP theory specifically includes task complexity as a critical contextual factor. TIP theory borrows premises from media capacity theory that tasks have specific inherent richness requirements. Thus, TIP theory proposes an interesting juxtaposition of assumptions regarding task malleability. A valuable future area of research is to assess how task characteristics change over time in relation to both technology use and group processes. If groups are not only responsive but also proactive, they may influence task structure for uncertain but not equivocal tasks.

Perspective on processes. A centerpiece of IPO theory and research is significant process *gains* as well as losses in computer-supported groups, an outcome not envisioned by media capacity theories. Some features that support gains may also support losses. For example, reduced interpersonal cues in anonymous computer conferencing not only support more equal participation but also remove some cues used to regulate interaction, contributing to less orderly and sometimes more negative communication. By focusing on gains in conjunction with losses, IPO theories offer richer views of mediated meeting processes.

Role of technology. Compared to media capacity theories, IPO theories view meeting technologies as more than transmission devices. The role of technological support is to *influence* decision processes, not simply to *carry* them. The findings suggest that different decision processes are found in many computer-supported meetings versus face-to-face groups and that more sophisticated support produces differences even from less supported groups. The mixed findings in laboratory studies, however, pose an important puzzle which structuration theory, discussed next, attempts to resolve.

Contextualization. IPO theories model several types of contextual factors as inputs: technological support, group attributes, task characteristics, member characteristics, and larger context. Research has focused primarily on type of support, task complexity, group size, anonymity, and presence or absence of a facilitator. Less attention has been paid to characteristics of the larger institutional context. IPO research shares with media capacity findings: (1) the heavy basis in laboratory contexts, and (2) markedly greater support for the theories from the relatively few field investigations. Even field studies, however, have not systematically measured or accounted for the kinds of organizational context factors that Culnan and Markus (1987) claim are critical to understanding meeting processes in ongoing organizations. Jessup and George (1997) note that the difficulties in understanding subject motivation in the laboratory, which approximates some real settings, argues for much greater attention to context in uncontrolled field settings.

Rationality. IPO theories posit "objective" rationality (Simon, 1957). First, meeting tools rationalize decision processes. Second, rationalization is designed to improve objectively measured group efficiency and effectiveness, regardless of the subjective goals participants hold. Third, the tools are posited to exert consistent effects on groups that have the same input factors. TIP theory adds the rationalist assumption that there is an optimal "match" between objectively described task characteristics and type of group support required. By retaining the concept of richness from media capacity premises, TIP theory has distinguished itself from other IPO theories regarding the critical assumption of an ideal task-media fit. Clapper and Prasad (1993) argue that the overemphasis on rationality that permeates most GSS research in this tradition neglects important political, symbolic, and interpersonal aspects of communication in organizational meetings. They argue for multimethod research that marries study of the rational processes with attempts to assess other dimensions of real-life organizational meetings.

STRUCTURATION THEORIES

Structuration premises have been applied to organizational technologies, including communication media (e.g., Barley, 1986; Orlikowski, 1992; Orlikowski, Yates, Okamura, & Fujimoto, 1995). Two versions have been crafted for mediated meeting technologies: adaptive structuration theory (DeSanctis & Poole, 1994; Poole & DeSanctis, 1990) and self-organizing systems theory (Contractor & Seibold, 1993).

Adaptive Structuration Theory

Adaptive structuration theory (AST) is described as an IPO theory by it proponents (DeSanctis & Poole, 1994; DeSanctis, Poole, Dickson, & Jackson, 1993; Poole & Jackson, 1992), yet its premises are sufficiently different from other IPO models to form a distinct theory. AST "attempts to explain how communication processes mediate and moderate input-output relationships" (Poole & Jackson, 1992, p. 287). Inputs include structural properties of the group support system, tasks, leader direction, and decision techniques. Processes are appropriation of technology structures and decision processes. Outcomes include meeting efficiency, decision quality, group attitudes, and emergent social structures, which feed back to influence processes. Three key features distinguish this theory from traditional IPO theory. First, AST proposes that technologies do not directly affect processes, but rather that processes will vary across groups based on how technology is appropriated during interaction. Second, group structures are emergent outcomes of the process phase, as well as inputs. Third, the process-outcome relationship is mutually causal.

Drawing on structuration theory (Giddens, 1979), AST proposes that GSSs offer groups both structural features and spirit. *Structural features* are specific technical protocols such as anonymity and decision modeling. *Spirit* includes the design metaphor underlying the system (e.g., promotion of democratic decision making), user interface, and training and help functions provided for the system (DeSanctis & Poole, 1994). Groups draw on spirit and structural features to create social structures during interaction ("structures-in-use.") Other sources of social structure include task, organizational environment, and structures that emerge while groups use the technology. *Structuration* is "the process through which groups select, adapt, and develop their own working structures from among those on the GDSS [group decision support system]" (Poole, DeSanctis, Kirsch, & Jackson, 1995, p. 303). Appropriation occurs as groups produce and reproduce their own customized structures and validate them through use.

Groups select not only which technology features to use but also how to use them. "Ironic" rather than "faithful" appropriations occur when groups use them in ways that violate the spirit of the technology. Appropriations are related to groups' internal system, such as style of interaction, experience, and degree of consensus on appropriations. Appropriations, in turn, are influential in structuring decision processes. Thus, groups exert control over use of technology and the new structures that emerge from their use (DeSanctis & Poole, 1994, p. 131). Technological features provide the opportunity, if the group chooses, to rationalize both task and group processes through mechanisms embedded in the system. Alternatively, rationalization can be accomplished by social processes, by modifications to system support options, or not at all. Poole et al. (1995) provide the example of a group that interprets a GSS not as reinforcing rationality but rather as a way to speed up meetings. The participants use the private messaging feature not for offline information sharing but rather to pressure participants to conform to keep the meeting moving.

The move away from technological determinism leads to contingent predictions. When the group sticks to the spirit of the technology and appropriates faithfully, the proposed positive outcomes of traditional IPO theory will likely result (DeSanctis & Poole, 1994). As the studies of paper-based manual systems indicate, the theory also proposes that nontechnological structures of the same type may also produce the proposed effects (Poole, Holmes, Watson, & DeSanctis, 1993). The theory also suggests that although groups vary greatly in how they use GSS technologies, successful groups hold several characteristics in common (DeSanctis et al., 1993; DeSanctis et al., 1992; Poole et al., 1995). First, they understand GSS features deeply. More successful groups comprehend the underlying operations that features are designed to support, rather than just learn "how to use" those features. Thus, such groups take advantage of features that promote more sophisticated thought processes (i.e., problem solving). Second, successful groups interpret the spirit of GSSs as a way to explore meanings and emotions that underlie group processes, rather than simply as a way to organize and record group process. Thus, they take advantage of features that help manage conflict, examine emotions, or reflect on activities. Third, aided by deeper understandings and interpretations, successful groups select appropriate tools by matching GSS structures to structures and procedures in other aspects of the group's work. "Matching" goes beyond fitting technological features to tasks; it refers to the ability to simultaneously redefine tasks to fit technological capabilities, and technological capabilities to fit task requirements.

Self-Organizing Systems Theory

Contractor and Seibold (1993) propose a theory that draws from work by Prigogine (Glansdorff & Prigogine, 1971). Their self-organizing systems theory (SOST) proposes a recursive mathematical model that offers three extensions to AST. First, it proposes conditions for stable appropriation. Second, it specifies boundary conditions for appropriation of a set of norms. Third, it identifies proposed effects of initial conditions on appropriation. Based on results of a simulation, they propose six hypotheses that relate three input variables (prior GSS expertise, level of GSS training, and initial awareness of norms regarding use of GSSs for task communication) to both communication activity and awareness of norms regarding use of GSSs for task communication.

Research Findings for Structuration Theories

Very few empirical studies have tested AST. Instead, most research has examined how different technological structures influence group outcomes and has found that structural support has a more positive impact on group performance than computer-conferencing features (Poole et al., 1993; Watson et al., 1988; Zigurs et al., 1988).

Media perceptions and social processes. Gopal, Bostrom, and Chin (1992) found that attitudes toward GSSs formed before the meeting had significant effects on group process and performance. Contractor, Seibold, and Heller (1996) tested predictions from both media capacity and structuration perspectives. The media capacity hypothesis was that members' perceptions of structures-in-use would be influenced by communication and decision support tools (GSS vs. no support). Results did not support this hypothesis, but did show that use of GSSs initially reduced social influence effects on perceptions of structures-in-use. The results are consistent with Walther and Burgoon's (1992) proposition that media influences on social processes change over time. The structuration hypotheses proposed that (1) interactions among participants would affect participants' perceptions, and (2) the effect would diminish over time. Significant social influences were found with both types of technological support, but the effects tended to stabilize over time rather than decrease. Sambamurthy and Chin (1994) similarly found that group attitudes toward the GSS, which were developed through processes of social influence, influenced decision performance over and beyond the effects of GSS capabilities. Chidambaram (1996) found a similar effect but it appeared only over time, with group outcomes improving even more slowly than group attitudes. These results are consistent with AST and with the social influence perspective, which suggests that media-related perceptions are significantly influenced by one's social network (Fulk, 1993; Fulk et al., 1990; Schmitz & Fulk, 1991) or by the overall collective of users of a collaborative technology (Fulk, Flanagin, Kalman, Ryan, & Monge, 1996).

Appropriation and participation, quality, effectiveness, and satisfaction. Studies of how AST works in dynamic environments of real-life organizations reveal the limitations of generalizing about the ability of GSSs to guide "rational" appropriations in all organizational settings (DeSanctis et al., 1993; DeSanctis et al., 1992; Poole et al., 1995). An experiment by Poole and DeSanctis (1992) suggests that groups who appropriate a GSS in manners that are faithful with the technology's "spirit" achieve more efficient and consensual decisions than groups appropriating technologies in ways inconsistent with the intended spirit. However, one organizational case suggests something quite different (DeSanctis et al., 1993). In this setting, two group leaders consistently violated the democratic spirit of the GSS by strictly controlling members' use of participatory features. In one team, the leader's actions exerted a negative impact on the group's performance, as predicted. In the other team, however, the same actions coincided with a more efficient group decision-making process. The inconsistencies in these findings suggest that ap-

propriations of GSSs influence information processing in very complex ways (DeSanctis et al., 1993).

Wheeler and Valacich (1996) found that three appropriation mediators (facilitation, GSS configuration, and training) did increase faithful use of GSSs and ultimate decision quality. Wheeler, Mennecke, and Scudder's (1993) results were more complex. They proposed that (1) group interaction style moderates appropriation, and (2) when GSS technology restricts groups from "invoking group processes that violate the spirit" (p. 509), appropriation will be more faithful and decisions will be higher quality. Their laboratory research using a highly complex problem showed that groups with low preference for procedural order (LPO) produced better decision quality overall, and best quality but lower satisfaction in the nonrestrictive condition. For groups with high preferences for procedural order (HPO), decision quality and satisfaction did not vary by condition, but participation was greater in the restricted condition. They concluded that restrictiveness could promote more faithful appropriation and more satisfied groups, but lower-quality outcomes. Also, the relatively high restrictiveness in most current GSS technologies "favor HPO communication styles and may be inadequate to support LPO individuals effectively" (p. 520). This conclusion is consistent with George, Dennis, and Nunamaker's (1992) finding of no differences between unrestricted groups and groups whose transitions between meeting phases were controlled by a facilitator.

Summary and Comparison of Premises

Applications of structuration theory to mediated meeting systems developed in part in response to mixed findings on effects of GSSs (DeSanctis & Poole, 1994). At times, these systems produced the effects posited by IPO theories, but at times the opposite or no effects were found. Structuration premises were designed in part to identify the conditions under which positive effects would emerge.

Role of groups and technology. Structuration premises differ from IPO theories most fundamentally on questions of technological determinism and the role of groups (DeSanctis & Poole, 1994). In AST, these two premises are highly interrelated. First, AST proposes that technological effects on decision processes depend on how groups appropriate technology during interaction. Outcomes will vary across meetings to the extent that groups differ in appropriations of GSS features and spirit, as the findings by DeSanctis et al. (1993) illustrate. Second, group structure is not simply an input factor. Group structures-in-use are created and recreated during employment of the technology. Groups play active roles in enabling structures that guide and constrain decision processes. From a structuration perspective, IPO premises are a special case that arises under (a) faithful appropriation, and (b) reproduction of structures that match initial structures or consistent use of stable, institutionalized structures.

Structuration premises were developed specifically for GSSs. Other meeting technologies such as teleconferencing have not come under this theoretical lens, in part because teleconferencing support has typically been viewed as simply a conduit. There are examples, however, of teleconference participants employing features to structure group interaction, such as providing the group leader with a stronger microphone. Voice-activated microphones can be used to influence interaction: By speaking, a person can automatically turn off the microphone of another speaker. These potentially constructive uses of teleconferencing could be investigated from a structuration perspective.

Task characteristics. Structuration theories share two premises with IPO theories regarding task characteristics. First, tasks are input variables. Second, tasks can be rationalized by use of meeting technology. Structuration premises depart from IPO in assumptions that (1) tasks can also be outputs, and (2) tasks can be altered in ways that do not rationalize them. For example, ironic appropriations of support tools may lead to tasks that are less rather than more structured. Even in successful cases based on faithful appropriations, technology and task are redefined in relation to each other.

Perspective on processes. Structuration premises concern how groups articulate their processes with the structural features and spirit of the technology. The key to such articulation is appropriation. Faithful appropriations are posited to increase process gains and reduce losses in ways predicted by IPO theories. Ironic appropriations are not expected to produce such results. The mixed results for IPO laboratory research could be explained by differences across groups in appropriation. Data about appropriations are not available for most prior GSS research. The contribution of structuration theories can be addressed by future research designed to investigate structuration and appropriations. DeSanctis and Poole (1994) describe the types of data and research designs needed. Appropriations are assessed by examining discourse; it is evident in "sentences, turns of speech, or other specific speech acts" (p. 133) at the microlevel, and should be studied over time. At the institutional level, appropriation is studied through longitudinal observation of organizational discourse about technology. Contractor and Seibold (1993, p. 536) also argue that AST research must be more precise regarding the *forms* and *dynamics* of production and reproduction related to faithful versus ironic appropriations and must "identify the boundary conditions under which these dynamics reflect gradual or major shifts in the structures." They also argue that although AST acknowledges the potential for ironic appropriations and unintended consequences, the main hypotheses focus on faithful appropriations and intended consequences.

Contractor and Seibold's (1993) formulation of SOST is designed, in part, to respond to this limitation in AST theory. George and Jessup (1997) also note that little research has been conducted on longer-term appropriation of meeting support tools into group processes, including which GSS tools are used for what purposes, and how appropriation of a tool emerges over time. If Chidambaram and Bostrom's (1997a) contention is correct that groups are more capable of effectively appropriating a GSS as they learn to use it and become more comfortable with it, over-time research to track processes is particularly critical. They suggest protocol analysis of audio- and videotapes, focusing on how naive versus experienced groups interact with technology and respond to alternative features.

Contextualization. Context is critical to the concept of appropriation, since it offers not only factors to appropriate but also influences on the appropriation process itself. Future research and conceptual development should target explanatory and predictive environmental variables for faithful versus ironic appropriations, such as group characteristics, level of training or experience, institutional environment, group history, time constraints, and decision type. Contextual influences on GSS success can be identified by research that attempts to explain how and when such attitudes are developed, and how they influence faithful versus ironic appropriation. AST's value will be enhanced when it offers testable contingent predictions about faithful appropriations.

An emerging area of context research focuses on group development. Chidambaram and Bostrom (1997b) argue that "the same group is capable of making high- or low-quality decisions, taking more or less time to reach consensus, and being satisfied or dissatisfied with its performance based on stage of development" (p. 250). They integrate the concept of entrainment from time-based theories (e.g., McGrath & Hollingshead, 1994) with AST to explain variations in group behavior. Based on an extensive review of group development

models (Chidambaram & Bostrom, 1997a), they present eight propositions on how GSS tools, if effectively appropriated, can assist group development. George and Jessup (1997) review results from 12 studies of computer-supported groups over time. They found that very few studies investigated appropriation, groups rarely had choices of which tools to employ, and groups worked primarily in the constraints of the laboratory. Further, what little attention was paid to group development focused on simple-stage models such as that of Tuckman (1965), rather than the more complex nonsequential models that dominate contemporary group development research (e.g., Gersick, 1989; Poole & Roth, 1989). They propose several research designs that overcome these limitations.

Rationality. Structuration premises retain two of the rationalizing assumptions of IPO theories. First, the structural features and spirit of the technology are designed as rationalizing mechanisms. Second, when appropriation is faithful, this rationalization should lead to greater efficiency and effectiveness. Structuration approaches depart from IPO in that (1) technology is not deterministic, (2) consistent efficiency effects are not expected unless groups employ the tools faithfully, and (3) compared to TIP theory, technologies and processes are not matched to unmalleable tasks. Rather, groups attempt to jointly optimize task, technology, and group structures through appropriation, production, and reproduction processes. Joint optimization is not designed to approach an objective standard for perfect match, but rather to meet each group's individual, subjective definitions of its goals. What is optimal for one group may not be for another, and in this sense rationality is subjective.

FUTURE RESEARCH CHALLENGES

As noted in the beginning of this chapter, meetings grew in importance as mechanisms for coordination and control with the growth of complex organizations in the late 1800s (Yates, 1989). Bureaucratic structures still dominated 25 years ago when research on mediated meetings began, although even then researchers predicted that mediated systems would stimulate new organizational configurations (Short et al., 1976). As the new millennium begins, these predictions are being realized through new technologies and new organizational forms (Fulk & DeSanctis, 1998; Rice & Gattiker, 1997). This section sketches some research issues linked to how meeting systems interact with trends in organizational form. Two technological trends include (1) advancements in integrated multimedia meeting technology, and (2) development of common communication infrastructures, primarily the Internet, that facilitate communication across globally dispersed organizational activities. Fulk and DeSanctis (1998) identify four changes in organizational form: (1) size, scope, and product domain; (2) vertical control; (3) horizontal coordination; and (4) forms of coupling.

Technological Developments in Mediated Meeting Systems

Integrated multimedia technology. Communication and computing continue to converge. Increasing integration of voice, video, and data into interactive systems offers significantly different capabilities than traditional media. First, multimedia systems are complex and multidimensional. Meeting support is increasingly ill fitted to unidimensional descriptions such as social presence or media richness. If voice, video, and data channels each has a different social presence, what social presence do we attribute to complex systems that integrate these features in nonadditive ways? Consider, for example, new systems for conferencing based on avatars (a graphic image designed to represent a person or object). Each user has a handheld "videophone" that displays the movements of the speaker's avatar, which is custom pro-

grammed to display specific behaviors associated with the speaker. How "rich" is avatar conferencing? Also, many other factors are relevant to how meetings are shaped, such as flow (Trevino & Webster, 1992) and reliability (Nass & Mason, 1990).

Second, newer meetings systems are flexible and readily customized to settings. Customization decreases comparability across implementations of a technology and poses important challenges for research design and causal inference regarding technological effects (Culnan & Markus, 1987). Comparability also is a problem with existing research, but it is exacerbated by dramatically increased system flexibility.

Third, systems are increasingly programmable and adaptable by users. System adaptability further reduces claims regarding unidimensional evaluations such as richness, which may vary depending on how systems are programmed and adapted by users. Adaptability to users limits comparability not only across implementations but also across uses of the "same" system over time and across meetings. Technological developments increasingly support assumptions that (1) group choices actively shape the technology as well as group process, and (2) meeting technologies not only construct group processes but also are constructed by them.

Public highways and global dispersion. Software developments support multimedia conferencing via local area networks or the Internet. For example, a program developed at the supercomputing center at the University of Illinois offers frameworks for sharing Java objects over the Internet (downloadable from http://www.ncsa.uiuc.edu/SDG/Software/Habanero). Such sophisticated tools support very complex interactions, such as real-time sharing of detailed 3D images of the human body among dispersed medical personnel, with each node using a low-power personal computer (*Wall Street Journal,* May 30, 1996, p. B-4). Downloadable Internet videoconferencing software such as Microsoft's Netmeeting™ (http://www.microsoft.

com) integrates voice, video, on-screen real-time graphics creation and data sharing. Users need only have an ordinary personal computer, Internet access, an inexpensive microphone ($10), and videocamera for the computer ($200). The availability of multimedia conferencing tools through public information highways has important implications for mediated meeting access, participation, and diffusion. In particular, this common infrastructure can facilitate meetings of multiple dispersed individuals rather than colocated participants situated in designated rooms. Although some research has focused on effects of co-located versus dispersed computer-supported meetings (e.g., Burke & Chidambaram, 1995; Jessup & Tansik, 1991), much more research is needed. Future research should assess how the new capabilities are linked to the conduct of mediated interorganizational meetings.

At this time, Internet conferencing (phone or video) has yet to achieve the critical mass (Markus, 1990) needed to initiate widespread adoption. The ability to connect to any other possible conference participant through a shared platform is a "public good" to which each individual can contribute by a modest investment in local hardware and expenditure of effort to develop the knowledge, skill, and motivation to employ conferencing software. When this public good is achieved in some reasonable measure, there will be increasing opportunities for (1) simultaneous inclusion of many widely dispersed participants through multipoint communication, (2) shared collaborative virtual environments (Schrage, 1989), and (3) increasing support for the emergent teams that characterize new organizational forms (DeSanctis & Poole, 1997).

Corporatewide conferencing tools on internal networks can contribute toward establishing widespread connectivity by permitting ready access to multimedia meetings by individuals at locations worldwide. The trend toward dispersed, global network forms of organization (e.g., Monge & Fulk, 1998; Nohria & Eccles, 1992; Powell, 1990) establishes conditions that require information sharing across far-flung organizational nodes. Much as the universal service aspect of the telephone has facilitated audio conferencing across organizations, Internet tools can facilitate multimedia conferencing with customers, suppliers, and alliance partners. "Virtual" corporations such as Verifone (http://www.verifone.com) already include customers in their internal electronic interactions (Tyabji, 1996). As technological solutions to security issues are developed further for the Internet, cross-organizational participation will be facilitated. The implications of cross-organizational participation in virtual meetings have not received either theoretical or empirical attention. (An exception is Dutton et al., 1982, who studied uses of a publicly available video-conferencing system, AT&T's now defunct Picturephone Meeting Service™, in which some meetings were cross-organizational.)

Existing research is of unknown generalizability to such new mediated meeting conditions. First, research to date lacks a cross-organizational component. Second, most GSS research lacks the dispersed component. Third, virtually all existing findings focus on predefined rather than emergent groups. Significant technological changes pose exciting new opportunities for theory and research on mediated meetings in organizations.

Mediated Meeting Systems and Changing Organizational Forms

Mediated meetings are intimately linked with changes in organizational forms, both as enablers and outcomes of form changes. Research on this linkage offers valuable new directions for organizational communication research.

Organizational size, scope, and product domain. Many researchers have observed the trend toward smaller, leaner, and more geographically dispersed organizational structures (Davidow & Malone, 1992; Heckscher, 1994; Heydebrand, 1989). Organizations redesign to create more integrated work processes and greater focus on the organization's core competencies, usually resulting in personnel reductions. Organizations can also reduce the scope of their production by changing their "value chain" or the integrated activities that produce a service or product (Fulk & DeSanctis, 1998).

Trends in meeting technologies accommodate the demands of smaller, more dispersed organizations. Desktop videoconferencing systems (DVSs) facilitate synchronous document and message sharing among multiple globally dispersed sites. Use of dispersed multimedia systems poses questions about how groups actively manage technology and group process to negotiate membership in meetings where perceptions of "who is participating" are variable. When meetings take place between fixed points such as two videoconferencing rooms, active participation in the meeting occurs between those members who are specifically invited, and who have a designated (and visible) "seat" equipped with support technology for communicating with all other participants. In contrast, dispersed systems such as DVSs can accommodate spontaneous meetings across multiple geographic sites (Alvear & Yaari, 1997, Brittan, 1995; Karpinski, 1997). For example, a study by Fish, Kraut, Root, and Rice (1993) examined how student interns and their engineering mentors used DVS technology to initiate spontaneous interactions. Although the technology was designed to support equal participation in spontaneous meetings, some individuals actively reduced participation by disconnecting from the system, while other individuals increased their participation by keeping their connections constantly open. Also, interns spontaneously contacted mentors more frequently than vice versa, suggesting that the organizational status structure was reproduced in the new technology (Fish et. al., 1993), rather than equalization.

In the area of product domain, movement to an information- and service-based economy is linked to a shift from creating products to manipulating information and symbols (Fulk & DeSanctis, 1998). An information product is difficult to distinguish from the process that created it (Heydebrand, 1989), especially when creation occurs online, rather than in physical space. The low cost and accessibility of the Internet overcome physical barriers to inclusion and thus allow for more diverse participation in virtual workspaces (Fulk & DeSanctis, 1998; Nohria & Berkley, 1994).

Virtual space may represent a "neutral" territory in which individuals from different organizational sites can meet with an equal degree of comfort. Yet ownership of the information product created within this neutral virtual space may not be clearly defined (Kumar & van Dissel, 1996). It could be jointly owned (Sudweeks & Rafaeli, 1996) or individual contributions and creations might be separately owned by their originators (Curtis, Dixon, Frederick, & Nichols, 1995; Curtis & Nichols, 1994). Ownership norms may depend on expectations that participants bring with them to virtual space, as well as the norms they produce and reproduce within the evolving culture of their online meetings.

Vertical control. New organizational forms are characterized by replacement of traditional vertical structures of control with flatter or more decentralized structures (Heckscher, 1994; Heydebrand, 1989). Organizations that redesign by reducing middle management and administrative support staff may decrease vertical control by delegating greater decision-making power to all members. For example, in a postbureaucratic structure (Heckscher, 1994) formal authority relationships are replaced with organization-wide dialogue and consensual decision making in which groups are guided by the organization's shared mission, as well as members' ability to personally influence one another. However, decentralization does not always reduce vertical control, since organizations can just as easily replace hierarchical control systems with information technology systems that perform the same functions (Zuboff, 1988), or can use technology to increase monitoring and control (Garson, 1988).

Future research should consider how technological features of mediated meetings are designed, implemented, and actively appropriated to enhance or resist the organization's structural control patterns. For example, Clement (1996) found that users of DVS in four research groups displayed relatively little concern that the technology would be employed as a centralized monitoring and control tool. Clement argued that this lack of resistance was attributable to users' control over the design of the technology, as well as the limited vertical control structures within the research-based organizations. Clement also proposed that as DVS use spreads to more hierarchical organizations, members will actively resist the technology as a perceived tool for centralized control (see also Dutton, 1998, for a discussion of the organizational control implications of new information and communication technologies in new organizational forms).

If new organizational forms rely on decision-making process based on personal influence, rather than formal authority (Heckscher, 1994), how do participants select particular features of multimedia systems to support these processes? TIP theory (McGrath & Hollingshead, 1994) proposes that in the early stages, decision-making groups should choose a richer channel (e.g., video) to undertake high-level information-processing tasks (such as judgment and negotiation tasks) that involve personal influence. How do groups make such choices when multiple channels are embedded in the technology in complex ways? Also, do participants follow media capacity premises to communicate more often through channels with the highest information-processing ability, or do they strategically appropriate channels to their personal influence goals (Markus, 1994)? For example, some participants could choose to use only audio-video channels to leverage their persuasive-speaking skills, whereas other members could use textual channels to support their persuasive-writing skills. How does the bal-

ance of channel use in multimedia systems change over time as groups develop norms and experience in meeting together? Future research should explore how meeting participants' personal influence goals affect the way that they use different media channels in multimedia meetings in new organizational forms.

Horizontal coordination. New organizational forms involve individuals from different expertise areas coordinating tasks, often in cross-functional teams (Fulk & DeSanctis, 1998). One example is concurrent engineering or parallel processing. Different stakeholders come together to work on different parts of a redesigned product simultaneously, instead of waiting for each functional unit (e.g., research and design) to finish its part and pass the design off to another unit (e.g., manufacturing) (Cushman & King, 1994; Davidow & Malone, 1992). Sometimes task coordination occurs between members who are geographically dispersed, such as in virtual organizations (Nohria & Berkley, 1994).

Horizontal coordination is supported by multimedia collaboration, particularly the ability for dispersed participants to manipulate shared documents, graphics, or simulated objects. Evidence suggests that work groups value information about their shared physical context (Brittan, 1995; Fish et al., 1993; Whittaker, 1995). In one study, individuals participating in cooperative design more frequently viewed images of the object being designed than images of their partner (Gaver, Sellen, Heath, & Luff, cited in Whittaker, 1995). However, researchers have yet to test how such channel choices affect the efficiency with which groups undertake tasks. Media richness theory (Daft & Lengel, 1984) would suggest that object sharing increases individuals' information-processing abilities, allowing them to undertake more uncertain work tasks. However, one interpretation of TIP theory (McGrath & Hollingshead, 1992) might be that focusing on object-sharing channels rather than channels that provide more interpersonal cues (e.g., voice and facial expressions) may delay the group development process. Future research based on the two perspectives should thus explore how multimedia choices such as object sharing influence the efficiency with which cross-functional teams complete their tasks.

Forms of connection. Changes in form occur with new types of connections or interorganizational couplings (Fulk & DeSanctis, 1998). One type involves organizations altering value chain connections by using information technology to support new forms of relationships with buyers and suppliers. Another type is the strategic alliance, whereby diverse firms form mutually beneficial associations, such as the complex interconnections between banking, travel, insurance, and telecommunications industries to offer such deals as frequent flier miles in exchange for other organizations' services (Ring & Van de Ven, 1994). Two other types are the federation, an organization that allows noncompetitive firms to pursue collective goals (Fulk, Flanagin, Kalman, Monge & Ryan, 1996), and the network organization (Monge & Fulk, 1998; Nohria & Eccles, 1992).

Kumar and van Dissel (1996) argue that dispersed multimedia systems are the appropriate mechanism for coordinating network organizations, because they allow members from globally dispersed organizations to meet frequently to exchange information and make decisions based on their evolving needs. However, they note that the task of electronically connecting different organizational sites is far simpler than the task of facilitating collaborative communication between members from vastly different organizational and national environments.

Future research from the IPO perspective should examine the impact of multimedia channel choices on the conflict management process in interorganizational meetings. For example, the task-media fit hypothesis proposes that conflict management tasks such as bargaining and negotiation will be performed more efficiently through richer communication channels, such as audio-/video-conferencing channels (Hollingshead & McGrath, 1995). However, some research suggests that even audio/video channels are insufficient to convey the subtle nonverbal cues and rapid conversational turn-taking that accompanies face-to-face negotiations (Dutton et al., 1982; Whittaker, 1995). Research from the IPO perspective suggests that GSS decision support tools can actually enhance conflict management in mediated meetings (Chidambaram et al., 1991; Miranda & Bostrom, 1994).

The choice of a particular mediated meeting system may itself become a source of sociopolitical conflict among participants of different national cultures, since Western assumptions about communication are embedded into the design of most mediated meeting systems. For example, the tendency for meeting systems to reduce contextual cues is more compatible with the American communication style, which relies relatively little on contextual cues, and therefore tends toward more direct (assertive, confrontational, explicit) conversation than many other cultures (Ma, 1996). The American value of individualism is also incorporated into GSS decision tools that rely on majority vote, rather than the consensual decision making practiced in more collectivist cultures (Ho, Raman, & Watson, 1989; Ishi, 1993). Serida-Nishimura (1994) adds that low power distance is implied by the focus on equal participation rather than status-based contributions, decision making is directed toward a rational rather than political process, and the focus on stages and sequences implies monochronic rather than polychronic approaches toward time. One consequence of these specific cultural assumptions embedded in meeting technologies may be that organizational members from other cultures will avoid communicating through mediated channels, particularly text-only channels. However, one study involving East Asian students suggests that participants from other cultures may adapt to computer-conferencing systems by adopting a more direct, self-disclosing style of communication than they normally adopt in face-to-face communication with Americans (Ma,

1996). Adaptiveness is also suggested by field research showing that Mexican users were more satisfied and produced more consensus and better-quality decisions in GSS meetings, whereas U.S. users reported no differences in any of these factors between manual and GSS meetings (Mejias, Shepherd, Vogel, & Lazeneo, 1996). Research should investigate how members from different cultural contexts actively structure both the technology and the group process to meet their particular needs.

CONCLUSION

As an embryonic field only a few decades old, the study of mediated meetings has made great strides. It has a solid base of strong theoretical perspectives that are integrated within a rich intellectual heritage of theory and research in organizations, technology, and social psychology. Each of the primary theories includes particular assumptions that shape advancements in theory and research on mediated meetings. These include assumptions about (1) the activeness of group role in the meeting process; (2) the degree to which group task characteristics are fixed or malleable; (3) the centrality of group processes; (4) the role of the technology as connective, constructive, and/or constructed; and (5) the influence of the environmental context. To advance the field, future research must take these differing assumptions into account when trying to synthesize theory and understand conflicting research findings.

Although meetings consume a large proportion of a manager's time (more than 60% by some estimates), mediated meetings are as yet a small proportion of all meetings conducted (as few as 13%; Volkema & Neederman, 1995). Nevertheless, there is every reason to believe that they will become much more prevalent. Advances in technology (e.g., multimedia capabilities and interconnected networks) are making such meeting support much more affordable and accessible at a time when it will be increasingly needed to facilitate the communication needs of new organizational forms (Fulk & DeSanctis, 1998). However, until the field of mediated meeting research can successfully investigate the complex world of real meetings within and between organizations, the potential of mediated meetings cannot be adequately assessed. Research on asynchronous meetings has a strong component of field studies, including studies of communication across organizations (see Rice & Gattiker, 1997). The challenge for synchronous meeting researchers is to expand the existing set of studies to these contexts. Even such field tests are limited, however, since it is difficult to assess how well results from firms that adopt mediated meetings early on will generalize to firms that adopt technologies once they become institutionalized. Leading firms often look quite different from firms later on the diffusion curve (Rogers, 1995). Nevertheless, with such a jump start on researching an innovation that is only beginning to take off, the field of mediated meetings is poised to provide even more valuable contributions to knowledge.

REFERENCES

Albertson, L. A. (1973). *The effectiveness of communication across media.* Melbourne: Telecom Australia Research Laboratories.

Albertson, L. A. (1977). Telecommunications as a travel substitute: Some psychological, organizational, and social aspects. *Journal of Communication, 27,* 32-43.

Alvear, J., & Yaari, R. (1997, February). You've got a video call . . . on your desktop. *Netguide,* pp. 149-150.

Argyle, M. (1957). Social pressure in public and private situations. *Journal of Abnormal Social Psychology, 54,* 172-175.

Badaracco, J. L., Jr. (1991). *The knowledge link: How firms compete through strategic alliances.* Boston: Harvard Business School Press.

Bales, R. F. (1955). How people interact in conferences. *Scientific American, 192*(3), 31-35.

Barefoot, J. C., & Strickland, L. H. (1982). Conflict and dominance in television-mediated interactions. *Human Relations, 35,* 559-566.

Barley, S. R. (1986). Technology as an occasion for structuring: Evidence from observations of CT scanners and the social ordering of radiology departments. *Administrative Science Quarterly, 31,* 78-108.

Beauclair, R. (1987). *An experimental study of the effects of group decision support system process support application on small group decision making.* Unpublished doctoral dissertation, University of Indiana, Bloomington.

Benbasat, I., DeSanctis, G., & Nault, B. (1993). Empirical research in managerial support systems: A review and assessment. In C. W. Holsapple & A. Whinston (Eds.), *Recent developments in decision support systems* (pp. 383-437). New York: Springer-Verlag.

Benbasat, I., & Lim, L. (1993). The effects of group, task, context, and technology variables on the usefulness of group support systems: A meta-analysis of experimental studies. *Small Group Research, 24,* 430-462.

Beniger, J. R. (1986). *The control revolution: Technological and economic origins of the information society.* Cambridge, MA: Harvard University Press.

Beniger, J. R. (1990). Conceptualizing information technology as organization, and vice versa. In J. Fulk & C. W. Steinfield (Eds.), *Organizations and communication technology* (pp. 29-45). Newbury Park, CA: Sage.

Biggart, N. W., & Hamilton, G. G. (1992). On the limits of a firm-based theory to explain business networks: The Western bias of neoclassical economics. In N. Nohria & R. Eccles (Eds.), *Networks and organizations: Structure, form and action* (pp. 471-490). Boston: Harvard Business School Press.

Brittan, D. (1995). Being there: The promise of multimedia communications. In R. M. Baecker (Ed.), *Groupware and computer-supported work* (pp. 57-65). San Mateo, CA: Morgan Kaufmann.

Bui, T., & Sivansankaran, T. R. (1990). Relation between GDSS use and group task complexity. In J. F. Nunamaker, Jr. (Ed.), *Proceedings of the Twenty-Third Hawaii International Conference on Systems Sciences* (Vol. 3, pp. 69-78). Los Alamitos, CA: IEEE Computer Society Press.

Bui, T., Sivansankaran, T., Fijol, Y., & Woodburg, M. (1987). Identifying organizational opportunities for GDSS use: Some experimental evidence. *Transactions of the Seventh Conference on Decision Support Systems* (pp. 68-75). San Francisco.

Burke, K., & Chidambaram, L. (1995). Developmental differences between distributed and face-to-face groups in electronically supported meeting environments: An exploratory investigation. *Group Decision and Negotiation, 4,* 213-233.

Champness, B. (1972). *The perceived adequacy of four communications systems for a variety of tasks* (Communication Studies Group Report No. E/72245/CH). London: University College.

Champness, B., & Davies, M. (1971). *The Maier pilot experiment* (Communication Studies Group Report No. E/71030/CH). London: University College.

Chidambaram, L. (1996). Relational development in computer-supported groups. *MIS Quarterly, 20,* 143-165.

Chidambaram, L., & Bostrom, R. P. (1997a). Group development I: A review and synthesis of development models. *Group Decision and Negotiation, 6,* 159-187.

Chidambaram, L., & Bostrom, R. P. (1997b). Group development II: Implications for GSS research and practice. *Group Decision and Negotiation, 6,* 231-254.

Chidambaram, L., Bostrom, R. P., & Wynne, B. E. (1991). The impact of GDSS on group development. *Journal of Management Information Systems, 7,* 325.

Clapper, D., & Prasad, P. (1993). The rationalization of the organizational meeting: Implications of group support systems for power, symbolism and face-work. *Proceedings of the Fourteenth International Conference on Information Systems* (pp. 321-329).

Clement, A. (1996). Considering privacy in the development of multi-media communications. In R. Kling (Ed.), *Computerization and controversy: Value conflicts & social choices* (2nd ed., pp. 907-931). San Diego, CA: Academic Press.

Collins, B. E., & Guetzkow, H. (1964). *A social psychology of group processes for decision-making.* New York: John Wiley.

Connolly, T., Jessup, L. M., & Valacich, J. S. (1990). Effects of anonymity and evaluative tone on idea generation in computer-mediated groups. *Management Science, 36,* 689-703.

Contractor, N. S., & Seibold, D. R. (1993). Theoretical frameworks for the study of structuring processes in group decision support systems: Adaptive structuration theory and self-organizing systems theory. *Human Communication Research, 19,* 528-563.

Contractor, N. S., Seibold, D. R., & Heller, M. A. (1996). Interactional influence in the structuring of media use in groups: Influence on members' perceptions of GDSS use. *Human Communication Research, 22,* 451-481.

Culnan, M. J., & Markus, M. L. (1987). Information technologies. In F. M. Jablin, L. L. Putnam, K. H. Roberts, & L. W. Porter (Eds.), *Handbook of organizational communication: An interdisciplinary perspective* (pp. 420-443). Newbury Park, CA: Sage.

Curtis, P., & Nichols, D. A. (1994, January). MUDs grow up: Social virtual reality in the real world. *Proceedings of the 1994 IEEE Computer Conference* [Online]. Available: ftp://parcftp.xerox.com/pub/MOO/papers/MUDsGrowUp.

Curtis, P., Dixon, M., Frederick, R., & Nichols, D. A. (1995). The Jupiter audio/video architecture: Secure multimedia in network places. *Proceedings of the*

1995 ACM International Conference on Multimedia [Online]. Available: ftp://parcftp.xerox.com/pub/MOO/papers/JupiterAV.ps.

Cushman, D. P., & King, S. S. (1994). High speed management: A revolution in organizational communication in the 1990's. In S. S. King & D. P. Cushman (Eds.), High speed management and organizational communication in the 1990's: A reader (pp. 5-41). Albany: State University of New York Press.

Daft, R. L., & Lengel, R. K. (1984). Information richness: A new approach to managerial information processing and organizational design. In L. L. Cummings & B. M. Staw (Eds.), Research in organizational behavior (Vol. 6, pp. 191-234). Greenwich, CT: JAI.

Daft, R. L., & Lengel, R. K. (1986). Organizational information requirements, media richness and structural design. Management Science, 32, 554-571.

Daft, R. L., & Weick, K. E. (1984). Toward a model of organizations as interpretation systems. Academy of Management Review, 9, 284-295.

Davidow, W. H., & Malone, M. S. (1992). The virtual corporation: Structuring and revitalizing the corporation of the 21st century. New York: HarperBusiness.

Davies, M. (1971). Cooperative problem solving (Communication Studies Group Report No. E/71159/DV). London: University College.

Dennis, A. R. (1996). Information exchange and use in small group decision-making. Small Group Research, 27, 532-550.

Dennis, A. R., & Gallupe, R. B. (1992). A history of group support systems empirical research: Lesson learned and future directions. In L. M. Jessup & J. S. Valacich (Eds.), Group support systems: New perspectives (pp. 59-77). New York: Macmillan.

Dennis, A. R., George, J. F., Jessup, L. M., Nunamaker, J. F., & Vogel, D. R. (1988). Information technology to support electronic meetings. MIS Quarterly, 12, 591-624.

Dennis, A. R., Haley, B. J., & Vandenberg, R. J. (1996). A meta-analysis of effectiveness, efficiency, and participant satisfaction in group support systems research. Proceedings of the International Conference on Information Systems (pp. 851-853). Cleveland, OH.

Dennis, A. R., Heminger, A. R., Nunamaker, J. F., & Vogel, D. R. (1990). Bringing automated support to large groups: The Burr-Brown experience. Information & Management, 18(3), 111-121.

Dennis, A. R., & Kinney, S. T. (1998). Testing media richness theory in the new media: The effects of cues, feedback, and task equivocality. Information Systems Research, 9(3), 256-274.

Dennis, A. R., Nunamaker, J. F., & Vogel, D. R. (1991). A comparison of laboratory and field research in the study of electronic meeting systems. Journal of Management Information Systems, 7, 107-135.

Dennis, A. R., & Valacich, J. S. (1993). Computer brainstorms: More heads are better than one. Journal of Applied Psychology, 78, 531-537.

Dennis, A. R., & Valacich, J. S. (1994). Group, subgroup, and nominal group idea generation: New rules for new media. Journal of Management, 20, 723-736.

DeSanctis, G. (1992). Shifting foundations in group support system research. In L. M. Jessup & J. S. Valacich (Eds.), Group support systems: New perspectives (pp. 97-111). New York: Macmillan.

DeSanctis, G., & Gallupe, R. B. (1987). A foundation for the study of group support systems. Management Science, 33, 589-609.

DeSanctis, G., & Poole, M. S. (1994). Capturing the complexity in advanced technology use: Adaptive structuration theory. Organization Science, 5, 121-147.

DeSanctis, G., & Poole, M. S. (1997). Transitions in teamwork in new organizational forms. Advances in Group Processes, 14, 157-176.

DeSanctis, G., Poole, M. S., Dickson, G. W., & Jackson, B. M. (1993). Interpretive analysis of team use of group technologies. Journal of Organizational Computing, 3, 1-29.

DeSanctis, G., Poole, M. S., Lewis, H., & Desharnais, G. (1992). Using computing in quality team meetings: Some initial observations from the IRS-Minnesota project. Journal of Management Information Systems, 8, 7-26.

Douglas, A. (1957). The peaceful settlement of industrial and intergroup disputes. Journal of Conflict Resolution, 1, 69-81.

Dutton, W. H. (1998). The virtual organization: Tele-access in business and industry. In G. DeSanctis & J. Fulk (Eds.), Shaping organizational form: Communication, connection, community. Thousand Oaks, CA: Sage.

Dutton, W. H., Fulk, J., & Steinfield, C. (1982, September). Utilization of video conferencing. Telecommunications Policy, 6, 164-178.

Dubrovsky, V. J., Kiesler, S., & Sethna, B. N. (1991). The equalization phenomenon: Status effects in computer-mediated and face-to-face decision-making groups. Human-Computer Interaction, 6, 119-146.

Easton, G. (1988). An experimental investigation of automated versus manual support for stakeholder identification and assumption surfacing in small groups. Unpublished doctoral dissertation, University of Arizona, Tucson.

Easton, G. K., George, J. F., Nunamaker, J. F., & Pendergast, M. F. (1990). Using two different electronic meeting system tools for the same task: An experimental comparison. Journal of Management Information Systems, 7, 85-100.

Ekman, P., & Friesen, W. V. (1969). Nonverbal leakage and clues to deception. Psychiatry, 32, 88-106.

Fish, R., Kraut, R., Root, R., & Rice, R. E. (1993). Video as a technology for informal communication. *Communications of the ACM, 36*(1), 48-61.

Fiske, S. T., & Taylor, S. E. (1991). *Social cognition.* New York: McGraw-Hill.

Fowler, G. D., & Wackerbarth, M. E. (1980). Audio teleconferencing versus face-to-face conferencing: A synthesis of the literature. *Western Journal of Speech Communication, 44,* 236-252.

Fulk, J. (1993). Social construction of communication technology. *Academy of Management Journal, 36,* 921-950.

Fulk, J., & DeSanctis, G. (1998). Articulation of communication technology and organizational form. In G. DeSanctis & J. Fulk (Eds.), *Shaping organizational form: Communication, connection, community.* Thousand Oaks, CA: Sage.

Fulk, J., & Dutton, W. (1984). Videoconferencing as an organizational information system: Assessing the role of electronic meetings. *Systems, Objectives, Solutions, 4,* 104-118.

Fulk, J., Flanagin, A., Kalman, M., Ryan, T., & Monge, P. (1996). Connective and communal public goods in interactive communication systems. *Communication Theory, 6,* 60-87.

Fulk, J., & Monge, P. R. (1995). *Control through computer-supported meetings.* Unpublished working paper, Annenberg School for Communication, University of Southern California, Los Angeles.

Fulk, J., Schmitz, J., & Steinfield, C. (1990). A social influence model for technology use. In J. Fulk & C. W. Steinfield (Eds.), *Organizations and communication technology* (pp. 117-140). Newbury Park, CA: Sage.

Fulk, J., Steinfield, C. W., Schmitz, J. A., & Power, J. G. (1987). A social information processing model of media use in organizations. *Communication Research, 14,* 529-552.

Fulk, R. D. (1992). *A history of Old English meter.* Philadelphia: University of Pennsylvania Press.

Gallupe, R. B., DeSanctis, G., & Dickson, G. W. (1988). Computer-based support for group problem-finding: An experimental investigation. *MIS Quarterly, 12,* 277-296.

Gallupe, R. B., Dennis, A. R., Cooper, W. H., Valacich, J. S., Bastianutti, L. M., & Nunamaker, J. F. (1992). Electronic brainstorming and group size. *Academy of Management Journal, 35,* 350-369.

Gallupe, R. B., & McKeen, J. D. (1990). Beyond computer-mediated communication: An experimental study into the use of a group decision support system for face-to-face versus remote meetings. *Information & Management, 18,* 113.

Garson, B. (1988). *The electronic sweatshop: How computers are transforming the office of the future into the factory of the past.* New York: Simon & Schuster.

George, J. F., Dennis, A. R., & Nunamaker, J. F. (1992). An experimental investigation of facilitation in an EMS decision room. *Group Decision and Negotiation, 1*(1), 57-70.

George, J. F., Easton, G. K., Nunamaker, J. F., & Northcraft, G. B. (1990). A study of collaborative group work with and without computer based support. *Information Systems Research, 1,* 394-415.

George, J. F., & Jessup, L. M. (1997). Groups over time: What are we really studying? *International Journal of Human Computer Studies, 47*(3), 497-511.

Gersick, C. (1989). Marking time: Predictable transitions in task groups. *Academy of Management Journal, 32,* 274-309.

Giddens, A. (1979). *Central problems in social theory.* Cambridge, UK: Cambridge University Press.

Glansdorff, P., & Prigogine, I. (1971). *Thermodynamic study of structure, stability and fluctuations.* New York: John Wiley.

Gopal, A., Bostrom, R. P., & Chin, W. W. (1992). Applying adaptive structuration theory to investigate the process of group support systems use. *Journal of Management and Information Systems, 9,* 45-69.

Gopal, A., & Pollard, C. E. (1996). Differences between workstation and keypad GSS facilitators. *Group Decision and Negotiation, 5,* 73-91.

Griffith, T. L., & Northcraft, G. B. (1994). Distinguishing between the forest and the trees: Media, features, and methodology in electronic communication research. *Organization Science, 5,* 272-285.

Hackman, J. R., & Morris, C. G. (1975). Group tasks, group interaction process, and group performance effectiveness: A review and proposed integration. In L. Berkowitz (Ed.), *Advances in experimental social psychology* (Vol. 8, pp. 47-99). New York: Academic Press.

Harmon, J., Schneer, J., & Hoffman, L. R. (1995). Electronic meetings and established decision groups: Audioconferencing effects on performance and structural stability. *Organizational Behavior and Human Decision Processes, 61,* 138-147.

Heckscher, C. (1994). Defining the postbureaucratic type. In C. Heckscher & A. Donnellon (Eds.), *The postbureaucratic organization: New perspectives on organizational change* (pp. 14-62). Thousand Oaks, CA: Sage.

Heeter, C. (1985). *Perspectives for the development of research on media systems.* Unpublished doctoral dissertation, Michigan State University.

Heydebrand, W. (1989). New organizational forms. *Work and Occupations, 16,* 323-357.

Hightower, R., & Sayeed, L. (1995). The impact of computer-mediated communication systems on biased group discussion. *Computers in Human Behavior, 11*(1), 33-44.

Hiltz, S. R., Johnson, K., & Agle, G. (1978). *Replicating Bales' problem-solving experiments on a computerized conferencing system* (Research Report No. 8). Newark: New Jersey Institute of Technology, Computerized Conferencing and Communications Center.

Hiltz, S. R., Johnson, K., Aronovitch, C., & Turoff, M. (1980). *Face-to-face vs. computerized conferences: A controlled experiment* (Research Report No. 12). Newark: New Jersey Institute of Technology, Computerized Conferencing and Communications Center.

Hiltz, S. R., Johnson, K., & Turoff, M. (1986). Experiments in group decision making: Communication process and outcome in face-to-face versus computerized conferences. *Human Communication Research, 13,* 225-252.

Hiltz, S. R., Johnson, K., & Turoff, M. (1991). Group decision support: The effects of designated human leaders and statistical feedback in computerized conferences. *Journal of Management Information Systems, 8,* 81-108.

Hiltz, S. R., & Turoff, M. (1978). *The network nation: Human communication via computer.* Reading, MA: Addison-Wesley.

Hiltz, S. R., Turoff, M., & Johnson, K. (1989). Experiments in group decision making, 3: Disinhibition, deindividuation, and group process in pen name and real name computer conferences. *Decision Support Systems, 5,* 217-232.

Ho, T. H., Raman, K. S., & Watson, R. T. (1989). Group decision support systems: The cultural factor. In J. I. Gross, J. C. Henderson, & B. R. Konsynski (Eds.), *Proceedings of the Tenth International Conference of Information Systems* (pp. 119-129). Baltimore: ACM.

Hoffer, J. A., & Valacich, J. S. (1992). Group memory in group support systems: A foundation for design. In L. M. Jessup & J. S. Valacich (Eds.), *Group support systems: New perspectives* (pp. 214-229). New York: Macmillan.

Hollingshead, A. B., & McGrath, J. E. (1995). The whole is less than the sum of its parts: A critical review of research on computer-assisted groups. In R. A. Guzzo & E. Salas (Eds.), *Team decision and team performance in organizations* (pp. 46-78). San Francisco: Jossey-Bass.

Hollingshead, A. B., McGrath, J. E., & O'Connor, K. M. (1993). Group task performance and communication technology: A longitudinal study of computer-mediated versus face-to-face work groups. *Small Group Research, 24,* 307-333.

Ishi, H. (1993). Cross-cultural communication and CSCW. In L. M. Harasim (Ed.), *Global networks: Computers and international communication* (pp. 143-151). Cambridge, MA: MIT Press.

Jarboe, S. (1988). A comparison of input-output, process-output, and input-process-output models of small group problem-solving effectiveness. *Communication Monographs, 55,* 121-142.

Jarvenpaa, S. L., Rao, V. S., & Huber, G. P. (1988). Computer support for meetings of groups working on un-

structured problems: A field experiment. *MIS Quarterly, 12,* 645-668.

Jessup, L., & Connolly, T. (1991). *The effects of GSS interaction frequency on group process and outcome.* Working paper, California State University, San Marcos.

Jessup, L. M., Connolly, T., & Tansik, D. A. (1990). Toward a theory of automated group work: The deindividuating effects of anonymity. *Small Group Research, 21,* 333-348.

Jessup, L. M., & George, J. F. (1997). Theoretical and methodological issues in group support systems research: Learning from groups gone awry. *Small Group Research, 28,* 394-413.

Jessup, L. M., & Tansik, D. A. (1991). Decision making in an automated environment: The effects of anonymity and proximity with a group decision support system. *Decision Sciences, 22,* 266-279.

Jessup, L. M., Tansik, D. A., & Laase, T. L. (1988). Group problem solving in an automated environment: The effects of anonymity and proximity on group process and outcome with a group decision support system. *Proceedings of the Forty-Eighth Annual Meeting of the Academy of Management* (pp. 237-241).

Jessup, L. M., & Valacich, J. S. (1992). *Group support systems: New perspectives.* New York: Macmillan.

Johansen, R. (1984). *Teleconferencing and beyond.* New York: McGraw-Hill.

Johansen, R. (1988). *Computer support for business teams.* New York: Free Press.

Johansen, R., Vallee, J., & Spangler, K. (1979). *Electronic meetings: Technical alternatives and social choices.* Reading, MA: Addison-Wesley.

Karpinski, R. (1997, April). Net videoconferencing in the real world. *Netguide,* pp. 139-140.

Kerr, E., & Hiltz, S. R. (1982). *Computer-mediated communication systems: Status and evaluation.* New York: Academic Press.

Kiesler, S., Siegel, J., & McGuire, T. (1984). Social psychological aspects of computer-mediated communication. *American Psychologist, 39,* 1123-1134.

Kiesler, S., Zubrow, D., Moses, A. M., & Geller, V. (1985). Affect in computer-mediated communications: An experiment in synchronous terminal-to-terminal discussion. *Human-Computer Interaction, 1,* 77-104.

Kling, R. (1991). Cooperation, coordination and control in computer-supported work. *Communication of the ACM, 34,* 83-88.

Kraemer, K. L., & King, J. (1988). Computer-based systems for cooperative work and group decision-making. *Computing Surveys, 20,* 115-146.

Kraut, R., Galegher, J., & Egido, J. (1990). Patterns of contact and communication in scientific research collaboration. In J. Galegher, R. E. Kraut, & C. Egido (Eds.), *Intellectual teamwork: Social and* technological foundations of cooperative work (pp, 149-170). Hillsdale, NJ: Lawrence Erlbaum.

Korzenny, F., & Bauer, C. (1979, May). *A preliminary test of the theory of electronic propinquity: Organizational teleconferencing.* Paper presented at the annual meeting of the International Communication Association, Philadelphia.

Kumar, K., & van Dissel, H. G. (1996). Sustainable collaboration: Managing conflict and cooperation in interorganizational firms. *MIS Quarterly, 20,* 279-300.

Lam, S. S. K. (1997). The effects of group decision support systems and task structures on group communication and decision quality. *Journal of Management Information Systems, 13,* 193-215.

LaPlante, D. (1971). *Communication, friendliness, trust and the prisoner's dilemma.* Unpublished master's thesis, University of Windsor.

Lea, M. (1991). Rationalist assumptions in cross-media comparisons of computer-mediated communication. *Behavior & Information Technology, 10,* 153-172.

Lea, M., O'Shea, T., Fung, P., & Spears, R. (1992). "Flaming" in computer-mediated communication: Observations, explanations, implication. In M. Lea (Ed.), *Contexts of computer-mediated communication* (pp. 89-112). London: Harvester-Wheatsheaf.

Lea, M., & Spears, R. (1991). Computer-mediated communication, de-individuation and group decision-making. *International Journal of Man-Machine Studies, 34,* 283-301.

Lewis, L. F. (1987). A decision support system for face-to-face groups. *Journal of Information Science, 13,* 211-219.

Lopez, M. G. M. (1992). Is interaction the message? The effect of democratizing and nondemocratizing interaction in videoconferencing small groups on social presence and quality of outcome. In U. E. Gattiker (Ed.), *Technology-mediated communication* (pp. 187-223). New York: Walter de Gruyter.

Ma, R. (1996). Computer-mediated conversations as a new dimension of inter-cultural communication between East Asian and North American college students. In S. Herring (Ed.), *Computer-mediated communication: Linguistic, social and cross-cultural perspectives* (pp. 173-186). Philadelphia: John Benjamins.

March, J. G., & Simon, H. A. (1958). *Organizations.* New York: John Wiley.

Markus, M. L. (1990). Toward a critical mass theory of interactive media: Universal access, interdependence and diffusion. In J. Fulk & C. W. Steinfield (Eds.), *Organizations and communication technology* (pp. 194-218). Newbury Park, CA: Sage.

Markus, M. L. (1994). Finding a happy medium: Explaining the negative effects of electronic communication on social life at work. *ACM Transactions on Information Systems, 12,* 119-149.

Martz, W. B. J., Vogel, D. R., & Nunamaker, J. F. (1992). Electronic meeting systems: Results from the field. *Decision Support Systems, 8,* 141-158.

McCall, M., Morrison, A., & Hannan, R. (1978). *Studies of managerial work: Results and methods* (Technical Report No. 9). Greensboro, NC: Center for Creative Leadership.

McGrath, J. E., & Hollingshead, A. B. (1992). Putting the "group" back in group support systems: Some theoretical issues about dynamic processes in groups with technological advancements. In L. M. Jessup & J. S. Valacich (Eds.), *Group support systems: New perspectives* (pp. 78-96). New York: Macmillan.

McGrath, J. E., & Hollingshead, A. B. (1994). *Groups interacting with technology: Ideas, evidence, issues and an agenda.* Thousand Oaks, CA: Sage.

McGuire, T. W., Kiesler S., & Siegel J. (1987). Group and computer-mediated discussion effects in risk decision-making. *Journal of Personality and Social Psychology, 52,* 917-930.

McLeod, P. L., & Liker, J. K. (1992). Electronic meeting systems: Evidence from a low structure environment. *Information Systems Research, 3,* 195-223.

Mejias, R. J., Shepherd, M. M., Vogel, D. R., & Lazaneo, L. (1996). Consensus and perceived satisfaction levels: A cross-cultural comparison of GSS and non-GSS outcomes within and between the United States and Mexico. *Journal of Management Information Systems, 13,* 137-161.

Miller, K., & Stiff, J. (1993). *Deceptive communication.* Newbury Park, CA: Sage.

Mintzberg, H. (1973). *The nature of managerial work.* New York: Harper & Row.

Miranda, S. M., & Bostrom, R. P. (1994). The impact of group support systems on group conflict and conflict management. *Journal of Management Information Systems, 10,* 63-95.

Monge, P. R., & Fulk, J. (1998). Global network organizations. In G. DeSanctis & J. Fulk (Eds.), *Shaping organizational form: Communication, connection, community.* Thousand Oaks, CA: Sage.

Monge, P., McSween, C., & Wyer, J. (1989). *A profile of meetings in corporate America: Results of the 3M Meeting effectiveness study.* Unpublished manuscript, Annenberg School for Communication, University of Southern California, Los Angeles.

Mosvick, R., & Nelson, R. (1987). *We've got to start a meeting like this! A guide to successful business meeting management.* Glencoe, IL: Scott, Foresman.

Nass, C., & Mason, L. (1990). On the study of technology and task: A variable-based approach. In J. Fulk & C. W. Steinfield (Eds.), *Organizations and communication technology* (pp. 46-67). Newbury Park, CA: Sage.

Nohria, N., & Berkley, J. D. (1994). The virtual organization: Bureaucracy, technology, and the implosion of control. In C. Heckscher & A. Donnellon (Eds.), *The postbureaucratic organization: New perspec-*

tives on organizational change (pp. 108-128). Thousand Oaks, CA: Sage.

Nohria, N., & Eccles, R. (1992). Face-to-face: Making network organizations work. In N. Nohria & R. Eccles (Eds.), *Networks and organizations: Structure, form, and action* (pp. 288-308). Boston: Harvard Business School Press.

Noll, A. M. (1976). Teleconferencing communications activities. *Communications Society, 14*(6), 8-14.

Nunamaker, J. F., Applegate, L. M., & Konsynski, B. R. (1987). Facilitating group creativity: Experience with a group decision support system. *Journal of Management Information Systems, 3*, 5-19.

Nunamaker, J. F., Briggs, R. O., Mittleman, D. D., Vogel, D. R., & Balthazard, P. A. (1996). Lessons from a dozen years of group support systems research: A discussion of lab and field findings. *Journal of Management Information Systems, 13*, 163-207.

Nunamaker, J. F., Dennis, A. R., George, J. F., Valacich, J. S., & Vogel, D. R. (1991). Electronic meeting systems to support group work: Theory and practice at Arizona. *Communications of the ACM, 34*(7), 40-61.

Nunamaker, J. F., Dennis, A. R., Valacich, J. S., Vogel, D. R., & George, J. F. (1993). Issues in the design, development, use, and management of group support systems. In L. M. Jessup & J. S. Valacich (Eds.), *Group support systems: New perspectives* (pp. 123-145). New York: Macmillan.

Ochsman, R. B., & Chapanis, A. (1974). The effects of 10 communication modes on the behavior of teams during cooperative problem-solving. *International Journal of Man-Machine Studies, 6*, 579-619.

Olaniran, B. A. (1994). Group performance in computer-mediated and face-to-face communication media. *Management Communication Quarterly, 7*, 256-281.

Oppenheim, L. (1987). *Making meetings matter: A report to the 3M Corporation.* Unpublished manuscript, Wharton Center for Applied Research, Philadelphia.

Orlikowski, W. J. (1992). The duality of technology: Rethinking the concept of technology in organizations. *Organization Science, 3*, 398-427.

Orlikowski, W. J., Yates, J., Okamura, K., & Fujimoto, M. (1995). Shaping electronic communication: The metastructuring of technology in the context of use. *Organization Science, 6*, 423-444.

Perrow, C. (1970). *Organizational analysis: A sociological view.* London: Tavistock.

Pinsonneault, A., & Kraemer, K. L. (1990). The effects of electronic meetings on group processes and outcomes: An assessment of the empirical research. *Decision Support Systems, 5*(2), 197-216.

Poole, M. S., & DeSanctis, G. (1990). Understanding the use of group decision support systems. In J. Fulk & C. W. Steinfield (Eds.), *Organizations and communi-*

cation technology (pp. 173-193). Newbury Park, CA: Sage.

Poole, M. S., & DeSanctis, G. (1992). Microlevel structuration in computer-supported group decision-making. *Human Communication Research, 19*, 5-49.

Poole, M. S., DeSanctis, G., Kirsch, L., & Jackson, M. (1995). Group decision support systems as facilitators of quality team efforts. In L. Frey (Ed.), *Innovations in group facilitation techniques: Case studies of applications in naturalistic settings* (pp. 299-322). Creskill, NJ: Hampton.

Poole, M. S., Holmes, R., & DeSanctis, G. (1991). Conflict management in a computer-supported meeting environment. *Management Science, 37*, 926-953.

Poole, M. S., Holmes, M., Watson, R., & DeSanctis, G. (1993). Group decision support systems and group communication: A comparison of decision-making in computer-supported and nonsupported groups. *Communication Research, 20*, 176-213.

Poole, M. S., & Jackson, M. H. (1992). Communication theory and group support systems. In L. M. Jessup & J. S. Valacich (Eds.), *Group support systems: New perspectives* (pp. 282-293). New York: Macmillan.

Poole, M. S., & Roth, J. (1989). Decision development in small groups IV: A typology of group decision paths. *Human Communication Research, 15*, 323-356.

Popper, K. (1962). *Conjectures and refutations.* New York: Basic Books.

Powell, W. W. (1990). Neither network nor hierarchy: Network forms of organization. In B. M. Staw & L. L. Cummings (Eds.), *Research in organizational behavior* (Vol. 12, pp. 295-336.). Greenwich, CT: JAI.

Pye, L., & Williams, E. (1977). Teleconferencing: Is video valuable or is audio adequate. *Telecommunications Policy, 1*, 230-241.

Rawlins, C. (1989). The impact of teleconferencing on the leadership of small decision-making groups. *Journal of Organizational Behavior Management, 10*, 37-52.

Rafaeli, S. (1988). Interactivity: From new media to communication. In R. P. Hawkins, J. M. Wiemann, & S. Pingree (Eds.), *Advancing communication science: Merging mass and interpersonal processes* (pp. 110-134). Newbury Park, CA: Sage.

Rice, R. E. (1984). Mediated group communication. In R. Rice (Ed.), *The new media* (pp. 129-154). Beverly Hills, CA: Sage.

Rice, R., & Gattiker, U. (1997). *New media and organizational structuring of media and relations.* Unpublished manuscript, Rutgers University, New Brunswick, NJ.

Ring, P., & Van de Ven, A. (1994). Developmental processes of cooperative interorganizational relationships. *Academy of Management Journal, 19*, 90-118.

Rogers, E. M. (1995). *Diffusion of innovations* (4th ed.). New York: Free Press.

Rosetti, D. K., & Surynt, T. J. (1985). Video teleconferencing and performance. *Journal of Business Communication, 22*, 25-31.

Salancik, G. R., & Pfeffer, J. (1978). A social information processing approach to job attitudes and task design. *Administrative Science Quarterly, 23*, 224-253.

Sambamurthy, V., & Chin, W. W. (1994). The effects of group attitudes toward alternative GDSS designs on the decision-making performance of computer-supported groups. *Decision Sciences, 25*, 215-241.

Sambamurthy, V., & DeSanctis, G. (1990). An experimental evaluation of GDSS effects on group performance during stakeholder analysis. In J. F. Nunamaker, Jr. (Ed.), *Proceedings of the Twenty-Third Annual Hawaii International Conference on Systems Sciences* (Vol. 3, pp. 79-88). Los Alamitos, CA: IEEE Computer Society Press.

Sambamurthy, V., Poole, M. S., & Kelly, J. (1993). The effects of variations in GDSS capabilities on decision-making processes in groups. *Small Group Research, 24*, 523-546.

Saunders, C. S., Robey, D., & Vaverek, K. A. (1994). The persistence of status differentials in computer conferencing. *Human Communication Research, 20*, 443-472.

Schmitz, J., & Fulk, J. (1991). Organizational colleagues, information richness, and electronic mail: A test of the social influence model of technology use. *Communication Research, 18*, 487-523.

Schrage, M. (1989). *No more teams! Mastering the dynamics of creative collaboration.* New York: Doubleday.

Schrage, M. (1996). Design for facilitation, facilitation for design: Managing media to manage innovation. In J. Kao (Ed.), *The new business of design* (pp. 46-63). New York: Allworth.

Schwartzman, H. (1986). The meeting as a neglected social form in organizational studies. In B. M. Staw & L. L. Cummings (Eds.), *Research in organizational behavior* (Vol. 8, pp. 233-258). Greenwich, CT: JAI.

Schwartzman, H. (1989). *The meeting: Gatherings in organizations and communities.* New York: Plenum.

Seibold, D. R., Heller, M. A., & Contractor, N. S. (1994). Group decision support systems (GDSS): Review, taxonomy, and research agenda. In B. Kovacic (Ed.), *New approaches to organizational communication* (pp. 143-168). Albany: State University of New York Press.

Serida-Nishimura, J. F. (1994). An organizational culture perspective for the study of group support systems. *Proceedings of the Fifteenth International Conference on Information Systems* (pp. 201-211).

Sharda, R., Barr, S. H., & McDonnell, J. C. (1988). Decision support system effectiveness: A review and an empirical test. *Management Science, 34*, 139-159.

Shepherd, M. M., Briggs, R. O., Yen, J., & Nunamaker, J. (1995). Invoking social comparison to improve electronic brainstorming: Beyond anonymity. *Journal of Management Information Systems, 12*, 155-170.

Short, J., Williams, E., & Christie, B. (1976). *The social psychology of telecommunications.* New York: John Wiley.

Short, J. A. (1971). *Conflicts of interest and conflicts of opinion in an experimental bargaining game conducted over the media* (Communication Studies Group Report No. E/71065/SH). London: University College.

Siegel, J., Dubrovsky, V., Kiesler, S., & McGuire, T. W. (1986). Group processes in computer-mediated communication. *Organizational Behavior and Human Decision Processes, 37*, 157-187.

Simon, H. (1957). *Administrative behavior.* New York: Macmillan.

Spears, R., & Lea, M. (1994). Panacea or panopticon? The hidden power in computer-mediated communication. *Communication Research, 21*, 427-459.

Sproull, L., & Kiesler, S. (1991). *Connections: New ways of working in the networked organization.* Cambridge, MA: MIT Press.

Steeb, R., & Johnston, S. C. (1981). A computer-based interactive system for group decision-making. *IEEE Transactions on Systems, Man, and Cybernetics, SMCII, 8*, 544-552.

Steiner, I. D. (1972). *Group process and productivity.* New York: Academic Press.

Straus, S. (1996). Getting a clue: Communication media and information distribution effects on group process and performance. *Small Group Research, 27*, 115-142.

Straus, S. (1997). Technology, group process, and group outcomes: Testing the connections in computer-mediated and face-to-face groups. *Human Computer Interaction, 12*, 227-266.

Straus, S. G., & McGrath, J. E. (1994). Does the medium matter? The interaction of task type and technology on group performance and member reactions. *Journal of Applied Psychology, 79*, 87-97.

Strickland, L., Guild, P., Barefoot, J., & Patterson, S. (1978). Teleconferencing and leadership emergence. *Human Relations, 31*, 583-596.

Sudweeks, F., & Rafaeli, S. (1996). How do you get a hundred strangers to agree? Computer-mediated communication and collaboration. In T. M. Harrison & T. Stephen (Eds.), *Computer networking and scholarly communication in the twenty-first century university* (pp. 115-136). Albany: State University of New York Press.

Thomas, H. B., & Williams, E. (1975). *The University of Quebec audioconferencing system: An analysis of users' attitudes* (Communication Studies Group Report No. P/75190/TH). London: University College.

Thompson, J. D., & Tuden, A. (1959). Strategies, structures and processes of organizational decisions. In J. D. Thompson (Ed.), *Comparative studies in admin-

istration (pp. 195-216). Pittsburgh, PA: University of Pittsburgh Press.

Trevino, L. K., Daft, R. L., & Lengel, R. H. (1990). Understanding managers' media choices: A symbolic interactionist perspective. In J. Fulk & C. W. Steinfield (Eds.), *Organizations and communication technology* (pp. 71-94). Newbury Park, CA: Sage.

Trevino, L. K., & Webster, J. (1992). Flow in computer-mediated communication. *Communication Research, 19,* 539-573.

Trice, H. (1985). Rites and ceremonials in organizational cultures. In S. B. Bacharach & S. M. Mitchell (Eds.), *Research in the sociology of organizations* (Vol. 4, pp. 221-270). Greenwich, CT: JAI.

Tuckman, B. W. (1965). Developmental sequence in small groups. *Psychological Bulletin, 64,* 384-399.

Tyabji, H. (1996). Managing the virtual company. In J. Kao (Ed.), *The new business of design* (pp. 64-79). New York: Allworth.

Tyran, C. K., Dennis, A. R., Vogel, D. R., & Nunamaker, J. F. (1992). The application of electronic meeting technology to support strategic management. *MIS Quarterly, 16,* 313-334.

Uhlig, R., Farber, D., & Bair, J. (1979). *The office of the future: Communication and computers.* New York: North Holland.

Valacich, J. S., Dennis, A. R., & Connolly, T. (1994). Idea generation in computer-based groups: A new ending to an old story. *Organizational Behavior and Human Decision Processes, 57,* 448-467.

Valacich, J. S., Dennis, A. R., & Nunamaker, J. F. (1992). Group size and anonymity effects on computer-mediated idea generation. *Small Group Research, 23,* 49-73.

Valacich, J. S., George, J. F., Nunamaker, J. F., & Vogel, D. R. (1994). Physical proximity effects on computer-mediated group idea generation. *Small Group Research, 25,* 83-104.

Valacich, J. S., Mennecke, B. E., Wachter, R., & Wheeler, B. C. (1994). Extensions to media richness theory: A test of the task-media fit hypothesis. *Proceedings of the Twenty-Third Hawaii International Conference on Systems Sciences* (Vol. 4, pp. 11-20). Los Alamitos, CA: IEEE Computer Society Press.

Valacich, J. S., Paranka, D., George, J. F., & Nunamaker, J. F. (1993). Communication concurrency and the new media: A new dimension for media richness. *Communication Research, 20,* 249-276.

Valacich, J. S., & Schwenk, C. (1995). Devil's advocacy and dialectical inquiry effects on face-to-face and computer-mediated group decision-making. *Organizational Behavior and Human Decision Processes, 63,* 158-173.

Valacich, J. S., Wheeler, B. C., Mennecke, B. E., & Wachter, R. (1995). The effects of numerical and logical group size on computer-mediated idea generation. *Organizational Behavior and Human Decision Processes, 62,* 318-329.

Vallee, J., Johansen, R., Randolph, R. H., & Hastings, A. C. (1974). *Group communication through computers, Vol. 2: A study of social effects.* Menlo Park: CA: Institute for the Future.

Vician, C., DeSanctis, G., Poole, M. S., & Jackson, B. M. (1992). Using group technologies to support the design of "lights out" computing systems: A case study. In K. E. Kendall, K. Lyytinen, & J. I. DeGross (Eds.), *The impact of computer supported technologies on information systems development* (pp. 151-178). New York: Elsevier Science.

Vogel, D. R., & Nunamaker, J. F. (1989, September). Automated planning support: Using computers to enhance group decision-making. *Administrative Radiology,* pp. 54-59.

Vogel, D. R., Nunamaker, J. F., Martz, W. B. J., Grohowski, R., & McGoff, C. (1989). Electronic meeting system experience at IBM. *Journal of Management Information Systems, 6,* 25-43.

Volkema, R. J., & Neederman, F. (1995). Organizational meetings: Formats and information requirements. *Small Group Research, 26,* 3-24.

Walther, J. B. (1992). Interpersonal effects in computer-mediated interaction: A relational perspective. *Communication Research, 19,* 52-90.

Walther, J. B. (1994). Anticipated ongoing interaction versus channel effects on relational communication in computer-mediated interaction. *Human Communication Research, 20,* 473-501.

Walther, J. B. (1995). Relational aspects of computer-mediated communication: Experimental observations over time. *Organization Science, 6,* 186-203.

Walther, J. B., Anderson, J. F., & Park, D. W. (1994). Interpersonal effects in computer-mediated interaction: A meta-analysis of social and antisocial communication. *Communication Research, 21,* 460-487.

Walther, J. B., & Burgoon, J. K. (1992). Relational communication in computer-mediated interaction. *Human Communication Research, 19,* 50-88.

Watson, R. T., DeSanctis, G., & Poole, M. S. (1988). Using a GDSS to facilitate group consensus: Some intended and unintended consequences. *MIS Quarterly, 12,* 463-477.

Watzlawick, P., Beavin, J. H., & Jackson, D. D. (1967). *Pragmatics of human communication: A study of interactional patterns, pathologies and paradoxes.* New York: Norton.

Weeks, G. D., & Chapanis, A. (1976). Cooperative versus conflictive problem solving in three telecommunication modes. *Perceptual and Motor Skills, 42,* 879-917.

Weick, K. E. (1979). *The social psychology of organizing* (2nd ed.). Reading, MA: Addison-Wesley.

Weick, K., & Meader, D. K. (1992). Sensemaking and group support systems. In L. M. Jessup & J. S. Valacich (Eds.), *Group support systems: New perspectives* (pp. 230-251). New York: Macmillan.

Weldon, E., & Mustari, E. L. (1988). Felt dispensability in groups of coactors: The effects of shared responsibility and explicit anonymity on cognitive effort. *Organizational Behavior and Human Decision Processes, 41,* 330-351.

Weisband, S., Schneider, S., & Connolly, T. (1995). Computer-mediated communication and social information: Status salience and status differences. *Academy of Management Journal, 38,* 1124-1151.

Weston, J. R., Kirsten, C., & O'Conner, S. (1975). *Teleconferencing: A comparison of group performance profiles in mediated and face-to-face interaction.* Ottawa, Ontario: University of Ottawa, Department of Communications.

Wheeler, B. C., Mennecke, B. E., & Scudder, J. N. (1993). Restrictive group support systems as a source of process structure for high and low procedural order groups. *Small Group Research, 24,* 504-522.

Wheeler, B. C., & Valacich, J. S. (1996). Facilitation, GSS, and training as sources of process restrictiveness and guidance for structured group decision-making: An empirical assessment. *Information Systems Research, 7,* 429-450.

Whittaker, S. (1995). Rethinking video as a technology for interpersonal communications: Theory and design implications. *International Journal of Human-Computer Studies, 42,* 501-529.

Williams, E. (1972). *Factors influencing the effect of medium of communication upon preferences for media, conversations and persons* (Communication Studies Group Report No. E/7227/WL). London: University College.

Williams, E. (1975). Coalition formation over telecommunications media. *European Journal of Social Psychology, 5,* 503-507.

Williams, E. (1976). *Chairmanships in audio-only teleconferencing* (Communication Studies Group Report No. E/76310/WL). London: University College.

Williams, E. (1977). Experimental comparisons of face-to-face and mediated communication: A review. *Psychological Bulletin, 84,* 963-976.

Williams, K., Harkins, S., & Latane, B. (1981). Identifiability as a deterrent to social loafing: Two cheering experiments. *Journal of Personality and Social Psychology, 40,* 303-311.

Wilson, C. (1974). *An experiment on the influence of the medium of communication on speech content* (Communication Studies Group Report No. E/74350/CW). London: University College.

Yates, J. (1989). *Control through communication: The rise of system in American management.* Baltimore: Johns Hopkins University Press.

Yates, J., & Orlikowski, W. (1992). Genres of organizational communication: An approach to studying communication and media. *Academy of Management Review, 17,* 299-326.

Zajonc, R. B. (1965). Social facilitation. *Science, 149,* 269-274.

Zigurs, I., Poole, M. S., & DeSanctis, G. (1988). A study of influence in computer-mediated group decision-making. *MIS Quarterly, 12,* 625-644.

Zuboff, S. (1988). *In the age of the smart machine: The future of work and power.* New York: Basic Books.

17

Participation and Decision Making

DAVID R. SEIBOLD
University of California, Santa Barbara

B. CHRISTINE SHEA
California Polytechnic State University

In most industrialized countries since World War II (Cole, 1985) and especially during the past five decades in America (Appelbaum & Batt, 1994; Mintzberg, 1991; Russell, 1988), traditional workplace designs and operations have been transformed to more "participative" work relationships and practices. Control by managers, pyramidal designs, stovepipe operational functions, vertical chain-of-command relationships, and rigid bureaucratic procedures have given way, increasingly, to workers' participation in managing, lattice organizations, cross-functional work arrangements, lateral collaborative relationships, and semiautonomous work teams (Fisher, 1993; Greenbaum & Query, 1999). Structurally, hierarchical organizations are be-

ing supplanted by "self-organizing," "shamrock," and "fishnet" organizations (DeSanctis & Poole, 1997; Seibold & Contractor, 1992). Many reasons have been offered for this change in organizations' structures and practices: the globalization of markets and resultant increases in international competition, economic turbulence, and pressures toward increased productivity; technological advances in the workplace, changes in workplace demographics, and the stance of organized labor toward these changes; and philosophical arguments and moral injunctions for workplace democracy, among other reasons (see Bachrach & Botwinick, 1992; Cheney, 1995, 1999; Cheney, Stohl, Dennis, & Harrison, 1998; Clegg, 1983; Fairhurst,

Green, & Courtright, 1995; Lawler, 1991; Stohl, 1995).

At root, this shift has entailed decreases in traditional forms of management and correlative increases in the extent and form of formal employee participation in organizational decision making and other organizational matters traditionally the province of managers (Seibold, 1995). Research reviews reveal equivocal findings with regard to the outcomes and effectiveness of various employee participation programs (Levine & Tyson, 1990; Locke & Schweiger, 1979; Miller & Monge, 1986; Schweiger & Leana, 1986; Wagner & Gooding, 1987b). As Cotton (1993) suggests, this may be because these reviews inappropriately combine several types of employee participation programs, since the type of involvement program and the level of participation it affords may determine its effectiveness (as well as other outcomes such as satisfaction). There is considerable controversy surrounding the claim that different involvement program outcomes are a function of the form(s) of employee participation organizations implemented (see Cotton, 1993; Cotton, Vollrath, Froggatt, Lengnick-Hall, & Jennings, 1988; Cotton, Vollrath, Lengnick-Hall, & Froggatt, 1990; Leana, Locke, & Schweiger, 1990; Wagner, 1994). The thesis undergirding this chapter is that the different effects are due, at least indirectly, to the *form* of employee participation implemented in the organization.

Further, since each type of program influences communication processes in the organization, this chapter focuses on the role of *communication* in mediating participation program outcomes and effectiveness as both an important theoretical and practical concern. "Communication is an integral part of participative processes in organizations" (Monge & Miller, 1988, p. 213), and evidence suggests that communication may moderate the effects of various types of participation or involvement programs (Marshall & Stohl, 1993; Stohl, 1989). Thus, it may be especially fruitful to examine the communication-related features of these programs, including their im-

pact on the communication processes in the organization, to determine how and why each program may have a different effect on relevant outcomes such as employee satisfaction and productivity.

Although space limitations preclude extensive discussion of a related argument entwined in this chapter, there also is evidence that the nature of communication within (and outside) the organization crucially affects the nature of the participation program implemented (Lawler, 1991; Margulies & Black, 1987; Pacanowsky, 1988; Stohl, 1987; Wagner & Gooding, 1987a). Of course, this is consistent with theoretical perspectives and research in other areas suggesting the *recursiveness* of communication and group/organizational structure (Barley, 1986; Contractor & Eisenberg, 1990; Contractor & Seibold, 1993; Pettigrew, 1990; Poole & DeSanctis, 1990; Poole, Seibold, & McPhee, 1996; Riley, 1983; Yates & Olikowski, 1992). Where evidence exists that communication processes and involvement program structures are recursively linked (each shaping the other), we shall integrate it into this review of five specific but pervasive organizational forms of employee participation in decision making: quality of work life, quality circles, self-directed work teams, gainsharing (and Scanlon plans in particular), and employee ownership programs (especially employee stock ownership plans).

It is difficult to do justice to the vast literature on political, economic, and social contexts for organizational change, including employee involvement (Deetz, 1994; Goll, 1991). Nor will we adequately address research findings concerning effects of employee participation programs that are government mandated or state sponsored, such as worker councils in European organizations (see Berggren, 1993; Clegg, 1983; Eijnatten, 1993; Kavcic & Tannenbaum, 1981; Koopman, Drenth, Bus, Kruyswijk, & Wierdsma, 1981; Stohl, 1993a, 1993b; Strauss, 1982), or other international and comparative national studies (e.g., Kavcic & Tannenbaum, 1981; Marsh, 1992; Veiga & Yanouzas, 1991). For the most part, the research we review is drawn from analyses of organizations "transitioning" (Lawler, 1990) to new or increased forms of participation, and we have not incorporated literature concerning organizations created around the principle of worker control and that define themselves in opposition to the "mainstream" (Ellerman, 1990; H. Glaser, 1994; Greenberg, 1980).

Finally, we will underscore in the final section of this chapter critical scholarship that focuses on workplace democracy, which has highlighted the possibilities for political "reordering" of the traditional workplace. Increasingly, communication scholars (e.g., Barker, 1993; Barker & Cheney, 1994; Cheney, 1995, in press; Cheney, Straub, et al., 1998; Deetz, 1992; Fairhurst, 1993; Fairhurst & Wendt, 1993; Frey, 1995; Harrison, 1994; Mumby & Putnam, 1992; Mumby & Stohl, 1992; Putnam, Phillips, & Chapman, 1996; Stohl, 1995) have critically addressed the values reflected in discourses and metaphors concerning the new workplace and, in doing so, have begun to balance the "people" inherent in participation programs with what has been a dominant focus on the "productivity" outcomes associated with them (e.g., Ahlbrandt, Leana, & Murrell, 1992; Blinder, 1990; Hoerr, 1989; Jones, Powell, & Roberts, 1990-1991; Lawler, 1995; Vandenberg, Richardson, & Eastman, 1999; Wellins, Byham, & Wilson, 1991). Before surveying the literature on five prevalent forms of employee involvement (quality circles, quality of work life, Scanlon plans, self-directed work teams, and employee stock ownership plans), we first examine the nature of participation in these programs, a matter that, in the research literature at least, has been inextricably tied to the effectiveness of these programs.

The preponderance of work on forms and effects of employee participation has been done by scholars outside of the communication discipline, especially organizational behavior, management, industrial and organizational psychology, and business administration researchers, who clearly endorse a managerial orientation. Thus, it is hardly sur-

prising that the literature produced by these researchers primarily focuses on how effective these participation programs are in furthering management's goals. As Locke and Schweiger (1979) have stated flatly, "Business organizations [do not] exist for the purpose of satisfying their employees since employee feelings have no market price; the goal of such organizations is to satisfy their customers and stockholders" (p. 327). More generally, since many organizations view employee satisfaction as a means to an end, not an end itself, this orientation also has been reflected in participation research (see Wagner & Gooding, 1987a), especially in researchers' assumptions about the goals of these programs, their choices of dependent measures, and the values embedded in how they assay the outcomes of participation programs. Given this prevailing "managerial" orientation, communication researchers, as well as those outside of the discipline, have viewed communication within the context of employee participation from a "functionalist" perspective (see Putnam, 1982, 1983), which emphasizes directionality of information flow, information processing, amount and frequency of information, sources of information, and networks. In the final section of this chapter, we shall turn to critical scholars'—especially communication researchers such as those noted above—concerns about those aspects of the participation literature and other matters.

CONCEPTUALIZING EMPLOYEE PARTICIPATION

Locke and Schweiger (1979) point out that although *employee participation* is difficult to define, it is essentially joint decision making with managers on work activities and other aspects of organizational functioning traditionally considered to be the responsibility or prerogative of management. Cotton (1993) argues that employee participation is too limiting a concept, since it does not include the majority of programs operating in organizations today. He offers a more inclusive term, *employee involvement,* defined as "a participative process to use the entire capacity of workers, designed to encourage employee commitment to organizational success. This process typically comes about by giving employees some combination of information, influence, and/or incentives" (p. 3). Researchers have also noted the conceptual confusion surrounding the notion of participation:

> Some researchers equate participation with organizational practices, programs, or techniques, while others view participation as an overarching philosophy of management. . . . Still others view participation as a broader social issue with a variety of underlying implications, such as manipulation, oppression, and control. (Glew, O'Leary-Kelly, Griffin, & Van Fleet, 1995, p. 400)

Regardless of the definition employed, there is general agreement on the major dimensions along which employee participation or involvement programs may vary. Participation programs may be *forced* by government or law (legally mandated); *voluntary,* where the organization initiates the idea of participation; or *contractually based,* where programs evolve from collective bargaining agreements. Participation also may be *formal,* where officially recognized decision-making groups are created, or *informal,* where managers and employees work together to make decisions without an established program (Locke & Schweiger, 1979).

Participation programs also vary according to degree or level of influence, content, and social range. The *degree* of participation (level of influence) falls somewhere in these areas: (1) *no participation* by employees; (2) *consultation,* where managers receive input from employees but they make the decision themselves; and (3) *full participation,* where employees and management vote as equals on decisions. The *content* of participation refers to the types of decisions with which employ-

ees might be involved, including routine personnel functions, the work itself, working conditions, and company policies (Locke & Schweiger, 1979, p. 276). *Social range* is the range of people involved in a participation program. For instance, in some cases only certain individuals or groups may be involved in decision making, but under other circumstances, all members of the organizations may provide input into the process (Dachler & Wilpert, 1978). Program dynamics along any or all of these dimensions may affect the outcomes of a particular program.

The majority of studies have focused on two major outcome areas: employee *satisfaction* or morale and *productivity.* Research reviews indicate that employee participation has a positive but small effect on satisfaction and very little, if any, impact on productivity (Levine & Tyson, 1990; Locke & Schweiger, 1979; Miller & Monge, 1986; Schweiger & Leana, 1986; Wagner, 1994; Wagner & Gooding, 1987b). However, these equivocal and relatively weak results may be due to methodological deficiencies, unclear distinctions among the forms of employee participation, or differing outcome measures.

Moreover, there are a variety of variables that may mediate the relationship between employee participation and outcomes, and these factors may be cognitive or affective (motivational) in nature (Locke & Schweiger, 1979; Miller & Monge, 1986). *Cognitive models* of variables mediating participation-outcome relationships consider the fact that employee involvement programs affect the flow of information in the organization. They assume that since subordinates know more about their work than does management, worker participation in the decision-making process may be valuable to the organization. Participation in decision making also gives employees the opportunity to learn more about the organization and its policies, which may ultimately enhance decision quality and productivity. Finally, participation in decision making may help employees develop more accurate perceptions of reward contingencies in the organization (Miller & Monge, 1987;

Monge & Miller, 1988). However, Miller and Monge (1986) emphasize that cognitive explanations assume participation must be in areas where employees are interested and knowledgeable to have concrete effects on productivity and satisfaction.

Affective or motivational models, on the other hand, assume that "participation need not be centered on issues of which employees are particularly knowledgeable, for it is the act, not the informational content, of participation that is the crucial mechanism" (Miller & Monge, 1986, p. 731). Generally, affective explanations expect that participation fulfills some higher-order needs of employees, which is the key to their satisfaction. Specifically, employee participation fosters increased feelings of control, trust, and identification with the organization, which lead to less resistance to change and greater motivation (Locke & Schweiger, 1979; Monge & Miller, 1988). In turn, this directly enhances satisfaction, which may ultimately influence productivity.

As noted earlier, research reviews indicate some support for both cognitive and affective models. For instance, in a meta-analysis of participation studies, Miller and Monge (1986) found minimal support for cognitive models and stronger support for affective explanations. Research reviews conducted by Locke and Schweiger (1979) and Schweiger and Leana (1986) also reported greater support for affective explanations, since overall results were stronger and more consistent for satisfaction variables than performance factors. However, these reviews neglected to distinguish among different forms of employee participation, so it may be difficult to conclude whether cognitive or affective models are better predictors of effects.

Some researchers suggest that the *form of participation* may affect the outcomes of employee involvement programs (Cotton, 1993; Cotton et al., 1988; Cotton et al., 1990; Guzzo, Jette, & Katzell, 1985). In a major review of 91 empirical studies examining participation in decision making, Cotton et al. (1988) found that different forms of employee participation have different effects on satisfac-

tion and productivity. Leana et al. (1990) criticized Cotton et al., claiming that their classification system was flawed, their reporting of the results of several studies was inaccurate, and they omitted relevant studies from their analysis. Leana et al. also noted that several of the studies analyzed by Cotton and colleagues confounded participative decision making (PDM) with quality circles or Scanlon plans.

In an attempt to help resolve some of the controversy surrounding the proposed effectiveness of employee participation, Wagner (1994) reanalyzed the results reported by Cotton et al. (1988) and examined other meta-analytic reviews of participation. He concluded that "research on participation has produced reliable evidence of statistically significant changes in performance and satisfaction that are positive in direction but limited in size" (p. 325). Although Wagner (1994) contends that his results do not support Cotton et al.'s claim about the differing effects of employee participation forms, he acknowledges that his own definition of participation is narrow and *excludes* the "concepts of delegation, consultation, and various multivariate interventions, many of which have been shown to have substantial effects on performance and satisfaction" (p. 326).

Scope of Review

Several reviews, even those that are critical of the research conducted by Cotton and colleagues, suggest that the form or type of employee participation may differentially affect outcomes, such as satisfaction and productivity (Beekun, 1989; Leana et al., 1990; Magjuka, 1989; Magjuka & Baldwin, 1991). Moreover, Leana et al. (1990) suggest there may be important intervening processes that influence how participation in decision making affects outcomes, and Cotton and colleagues (Cotton et al., 1988; Cotton et al., 1990) argue that researchers should consider contextual variables and the process through which the participation program operates.

Thus, to understand *why* certain forms of employee involvement may be more effective than others, we believe it is necessary to examine (a) the features of each program, (b) the contexts under which they are ordinarily implemented, and (c) the communication processes through which they function. Each of these foci will be addressed in our review of five types of employee involvement programs. Collectively, they provide a template for assessing the differential effectiveness of these programs, a template that will be summarized in the final section.

Cotton (1993) contends that the most effective forms of employee involvement are gainsharing plans (especially Scanlon plans) and self-directed work teams, while quality circles and representative participation are among the least effective. Quality of work life, job enrichment, and employee ownership programs have intermediate effects. The following sections examine five different types of employee involvement programs (Locke & Schweiger, 1979) that are *voluntarily* initiated by organizations and *formal* in status within the organization, yet have been found to vary in terms of effectiveness. The programs selected for analysis and comparison in this chapter are *quality circles* (QCs) (low effectiveness), *quality of work life* (QWL) programs and *employee stock ownership plans* (ESOPs) (moderate effectiveness), and both *self-directed work teams* (SDWTs) *in new-design plants* and *Scanlon gainsharing plans* (high effectiveness).

It also should be noted that the involvement programs to be reviewed differ in terms of the level of the organization at which they are introduced and their social range (Dachler & Wilpert, 1978) as defined previously. QCs are implemented at the group or department level. SDWTs may be implemented at the group or department level (especially when introduced on a pilot basis in "transitioning" organizations; Lawler, 1990), or they may be integral to "new plant" designs and thus employed throughout greenfield sites, which are new facilities specifically designed for SDWTs (Lawler, 1991). We shall emphasize the latter.

QWL programs, Scanlon plans, and ESOPs typically involve the entire organization.

Further, although the five types of involvement programs reviewed below are primarily "consultative" (Locke & Schweiger, 1979), they differ in terms of the degree of participation that they afford employees in (what is traditionally) managerial decision making, ranging from minimal participation (QC) to extensive participation (SDWT). As we shall see, degree of participation (or level of influence) is strongly related to program outcomes and effectiveness (see Table 17.1). Finally, as will be apparent, each type of program influences and is influenced by communication processes in the organization. In turn, this affords insights into the role of communication in mediating the effectiveness of involvement programs, an argument to which we return in the last section.

REVIEW OF EMPLOYEE INVOLVEMENT PROGRAMS

Quality Circles

Quality circles (QCs) have become the most popular employee involvement program in the world (Cotton, 1993), and hundreds of thousands of workers in the United States alone regularly participate in these programs (Lawler, 1986). The QC concept of using employee problem-solving groups to improve product quality originated in Japan in the late 1950s and early 1960s, and it spread in the early 1970s to the U.S. aerospace industry. As the QC movement grew in the United States, companies began viewing QCs not only as a way to improve product quality but also as a means of increasing employee participation, satisfaction, and productivity (Van Fleet & Griffin, 1989).

A QC is a small group of employees (generally 5-15 members) from the same work area who meet regularly to identify, discuss, and offer solutions to problems concerning product quality and productivity. QC mem-

TABLE 17.1 Form of Participation

	Quality Circles (QCs)	Quality of Work Life (QWL) Programs	Employee Stock Ownership Plans (ESOPs)	Scanlon Gainsharing Plans	Self-Directed Work Teams (SDWTs)/New Plant
Type of program	Voluntary Formal	Voluntary Formal	Voluntary Formal	Voluntary Formal	Voluntary Formal
Effectiveness	Low	Moderate	Moderate	High	High
Degree of participation	Low	Low	Low to moderate	Moderate to high	High
Type of influence	Consultative	Consultative	Varies with program	Consultative and full participation (can implement some decisions without management approval)	Consultative and full participation (can implement many decisions without management approval)
Content of decision making	Work itself Immediate work area	Work itself Working conditions Company policy (on occasion)	Varies (usually vote for representatives to sit on board of directors)	Work itself Working conditions Company policy Financial bonuses	Work itself Working conditions Schedules and budgets Hiring at team level Compensation
Social range of participation	Group/department (Employees from specific department or work area)	Group/organization (Employees, managers, union representatives across organization)	Individual/organization (Full-time employees, managers across organization)	Group/organization (Employees and managers work together across all levels)	Group/organization (Employees from specific areas across organization)
Financial component	No	No	Yes (indirect)	Yes (direct)	? (varies)

bers have volunteered to participate in the program and meet during regular working hours. Although QC members receive training in group process and problem-solving techniques, many companies appoint a group facilitator to meet with the group. After identifying and analyzing the problem, these groups prepare recommendations and present them to management, who may or may not implement the groups' suggestions. Lawler and Mohrman (1987) point out that QCs are "parallel" structures, separate from the organization's ongoing activities, and they have no formal authority in the organization (see also Herrick, 1985). Even if an organization saves money as a result of implementing the solutions proposed by the group, participants receive no direct financial rewards. Thus, using the dimensions outlined by Dachler and Wilpert (1978) and Locke and Schweiger (1979), QCs are voluntary, formal programs that are consultative in nature and have a limited social range (see Table 17.1). The types of decisions in which the members are involved deal primarily with the work itself (Bruning & Liverpool, 1993), where their creativity (DeToro, 1987) and problem-solving effectiveness (Greenbaum, Kaplan, & Metlay, 1988) have been foci of study.

Research findings on the outcomes and effectiveness of QC programs have been mixed; however, in general, studies indicate that most QCs eventually fail and the positive effects of successful QC programs are minimal (Cotton, 1993; Drago, 1988; Lawler, 1986; Lawler & Mohrman, 1987; Ledford, Lawler, & Mohrman, 1988; Steel & Lloyd, 1988; Van Fleet & Griffin, 1989). For instance, after reviewing numerous studies on QC outcomes, Cotton (1993) concluded that although participating in QC had a positive effect on program-specific attitudes, such as perceptions of influence and QC satisfaction, QC participation had little effect on general work attitudes, such as job satisfaction and organizational commitment. Additionally, researchers have found that QCs have had little impact on worker performance and productivity (Cotton, 1993; Steel, Jennings, & Lindsey, 1990; Steel

& Lloyd, 1988; Steel, Mento, Dilla, Ovalle, & Lloyd, 1985). However, Steel and Shane (1986) caution that in light of the methodological deficiencies in the QC research (e.g., lack of control groups, small sample sizes, few baseline measures, experimental mortality), it is difficult to conclude whether QCs are effective or ineffective.

Researchers have attempted to isolate the factors that may determine the effectiveness of QC programs. Lawler and Mohrman (1987) offer several reasons why QCs may be ineffective, including the in-group/out-group dynamics associated with implementing QCs only in some areas, which may cause negative backlash by nonparticipants; competition among circles for management attention; middle management's resistance to QC programs; upper management's failure to implement circle suggestions; and circles' limited range of decision-making tasks. Lawler and Mohrman contend that the primary barrier to QC program effectiveness is the fact that QCs are not well integrated into the organizational structure. Circle members often lack the information or knowledge needed to make viable suggestions. For instance, "circles often come up with good ideas that are not practical because of strategy changes or business decisions they don't know about" (Lawler & Mohrman, 1987, p. 52).

Other researchers have found empirical support for both the cognitive and attitudinal factors suggested by Lawler and Mohrman (1987). In a study of military and civilian employees at a U.S. Air Force base, Steel and Lloyd (1988) found that participating in a QC significantly affected cognitive factors, including perceptions of influence, competence, and interpersonal trust. However, QC participation did not lead to an increase in perceived participation. Steel and Lloyd found weak support for attitudinal outcomes, such as employee intention to remain with the organization. Also, Marks, Mirvis, Hackett, and Grady (1986) found that employees in a manufacturing firm who participated in a QC program did not experience a change in QWL variables (e.g., perceived opportunities to participate in decision making, quality of organizational and work group communication, feelings of accomplishment, and hopes for advancement), while employees who did not participate experienced a significant *decline* in these variables. Although QC participants experienced an increase in productivity, and both participants and nonparticipants had lower absenteeism rates after the program was implemented, this QC program resulted in some negative attitudinal and cognitive outcomes.

Other variables that may affect the survival rate and effectiveness of QCs include job insecurity, amount of participation in decision making, and presence of a union (Drago, 1988); self-esteem of QC members (Brockner & Hess, 1986); and willingness to participate in a QC program (Stohl & Jennings, 1988).

Although it appears as if participating in QCs may have inconsistent or little influence in overall work attitudes and productivity levels, research suggests that QC programs do affect the communication processes and patterns within the organization. For instance, Buch (1992) argues that QC programs can open once-closed or unidirectional boundaries between employees and management. She reports that QC members and management perceived that communication and teamwork improved after implementing a QC program. Stohl (1986) points out that "circle meetings introduce new communication links, and new channels of communication are opened. As workers remain in the circles and work on a variety of problems, they develop a richer, more diverse, and ever-expanding communication network" (p. 514).

In a study of manufacturing plants in New Zealand, Stohl (1986) found that once employees joined a QC, they talked to more people across hierarchical levels of the organization, which increased their knowledge of the organization. Compared to nonmembers and former circle members, currently active circle members also perceived a more positive communication climate. The positive effects of QC involvement were particularly strong for those members who were well integrated into

the organizational network. Interestingly, former circle members reported the lowest level of organizational commitment and felt disillusioned about their input on job-related issues. Stohl points out that most of the circle dropouts were nonlinkers, which suggests that the members' communication patterns and level of integration into the organizational network affected whether or not they would remain in the QC program.

Moreover, the circle's level of connection with the rest of the organization may influence the effectiveness of the program. Stohl (1987) found that "circles that transcend their parallelism and cross over into the larger organization have more of their proposals accepted and implemented" (p. 426). Specifically, she found that solution effectiveness was strongly related to the number of different groups in the organization with which the circle was linked (network range) and that managers' perceptions of circle effectiveness were strongly correlated with the number of relationships that circle participants had with other organizational members (extended network). Despite the fact that communication networks seemed to influence solution effectiveness and managers' perceptions of program effectiveness, Stohl (1987) found that only group cohesion factors influenced the circle members' perceptions of program effectiveness. These findings are consistent with Lawler and Mohrman's (1987) points on the problems with parallel structures, as well as their suggestion that changes in the organization's information system may make QC programs more effective. Moreover, Buch's (1992) discussion of the boundary-tightening effects of QCs may shed some additional light on Stohl's (1987) findings on group cohesion. Buch contends that "the formation of circles introduces new boundaries around work groups, thereby increasing members' feelings of identity and inclusion and strengthening group cohesiveness" (p. 64). She suggests that these effects may be particularly strong in underbounded organizations, which have unclear boundaries between groups, lack clear communication channels, and have few mechanisms to bring people together. Buch's analysis is consistent with Putnam and Stohl's (1990) theoretical postulate that such effects are quite predictable given the embedded nature of bona fide groups (like QCs) but which vary in the degree to which their boundaries are permeable. Putnam and Stohl point out that individuals typically belong to several different groups within an organization, which may result in divided loyalties, or may facilitate information sharing among groups. QCs are indeed bona fide groups, since each QC member is also a member of some department, unit, or division within the organization and each individual holds a formal position other than "QC group member."

QC programs may have effects on microlevel communication variables as well. Berman and Hellweg (1989) found that compared to nonparticipants, participants in QCs that included their supervisor were more satisfied with their supervisor and perceived that he or she was more communicatively competent. Also, QC participants' perceptions of their supervisor's communication competence was strongly related to how satisfied they were with him or her. From this, Berman and Hellweg conclude that "quality circles provide opportunities for supervisors and subordinates to improve their communication relationship by joint participation in a decision-making process" (p. 114). Margulies and Black (1987) found similar results in a study of a QC program implemented at a large public transit agency, where management perceived that the program improved communication channels between supervisors and employees.

Thus, although a review of the research indicates that QCs may not be particularly effective in increasing productivity and satisfaction, a growing number of studies suggest that QC programs can influence and are influenced by communication processes and patterns within the organization. Moreover, research findings suggest that for QCs to be effective, circle members must be well integrated into the communication network, and organizations that have implemented these programs must make appropriate changes in their information system.

Quality of Work Life Programs

In the early 1970s, concerns for worker well-being expressed by researchers, labor unions, and the federal government sparked the quality of work life (QWL) movement in the United States. Two events encouraged the spread of QWL programs: an agreement between the United Automobile Workers of America (UAW) and General Motors to institute a cooperative quality-of-work-life program in that company (Lawler, 1986), and a major government-sponsored University of Michigan Quality of Work Life study (Nadler & Lawler, 1983). For a short time during the late 1970s, interest in QWL programs waned until international competition and a desire to increase productivity in U.S. companies renewed the concern with QWL issues.

QWL is a broad concept that has been used to describe a wide range of employee development approaches and methods (Cotton, 1993; Efraty & Sirgy, 1990; Mohrman, Ledford, Lawler, & Mohrman, 1986; Nadler & Lawler, 1983). QWL programs often include QCs and gainsharing plans as well as other organizational intervention methods that expand beyond the scope of employee participation, including job enrichment and plant redesign. However, to avoid conflating QWL with other employee involvement programs, this section will limit its discussion to QWL programs that are "joint labor-management cooperative projects, particularly those aimed at improving outcomes for both the individual and the organization" (Nadler & Lawler, 1983, p. 22).

Lawler (1986) points out that QWL programs have several participation-related features in common. First, all QWL programs rely on a joint committee structure, where committees consisting of both union and company officials oversee the program. Several "lower level" committees or groups, which resemble QCs, are formed to deal with improving work methods. Occasionally, these groups may choose to focus on organization-wide issues as well. Although the QWL committees have no official power to implement their ideas, Lawler contends that "if members are representatives of the key power groups of the organization, then it is highly probable that QWL committee recommendations will be implemented" (p. 129).

Next, there is usually a formal agreement between the union and management specifying that the QWL program will not deal with issues typically covered under the collective bargaining contract. This agreement also may include a list of union, management, and joint objectives to be achieved through the implementation of the program. The company usually shares information about the company with the union and the employees and, as with QC programs, participants receive training in problem solving. Often, a third-party consultant will assist the company and the union with setting up the QWL program and with training.

Thus, QWL programs are formal participation approaches that, although consultative in nature, give employees more influence through representation than QCs do. Since committees include members of union and management groups that represent different levels of the organization, the social range is wider than that of QCs. Finally, compared to QCs, QWL committees make decisions about a wider range of issues. Although these decisions usually concern working conditions and the work itself, sometimes QWL committees are involved in making decisions about company policies (see Table 17.1).

Research indicates generally positive results in the areas of labor-management relations, employee satisfaction, and product or service quality (Cotton, 1993; Lawler, 1986). However, their impact on productivity is less certain. A review of QWL studies suggests that factors relating to the levels of union involvement and employee participation as well as the employees' desire for participation seem to moderate the effects somewhat. For instance, Cooke (1989) found that compared to less active QWL teams, active teams who met regularly positively affected productivity and quality.

Other researchers have examined the effects of direct versus indirect participation in QWL programs. Nurick (1982) studied 380 utility company employees who either directly participated in a QWL program as a member of a QWL committee or a task force, or were indirect participants who merely received information about the program. Compared to indirect participants, direct participants perceived that they had more influence and that their suggestions were considered. They also indicated higher levels of job satisfaction, organizational involvement, and trust. Nurick also noted that some employees felt isolated from the change process, and the lack of communication between the direct and indirect participants fostered feelings of program mistrust among those who were not directly involved.

The type of employees who participate in a QWL program may differ from those who choose not to participate. Miller and Prichard (1992) compared a group of manufacturing plant employees who were interested in volunteering to serve on a QWL committee with those employees who were not interested. They found that those who were interested also were more satisfied with their jobs and the company, were younger and more educated, were more involved with the union and interested in advancement, and had higher expectations about the potential benefits of employee participation. However, these employees did not actually participate in a program but simply expressed an interest in doing so. Research indicates differences between those who volunteer to become involved and those who actually do participate.

For example, Leana, Ahlbrandt, and Murrell (1992) studied a medium-size steel manufacturing organization and found that employees who had indicated a desire to participate in a QWL program but had not yet done so (volunteers) were more satisfied with the union and had higher levels of job involvement and organizational commitment compared to nonparticipants. The employees in this group also were more satisfied with their supervisors than were the employees who actually participated in the program, and they "reported greater differences between the level of influence they would like to have in decision making and the level they perceived themselves to have" (Leana et al., 1992, p. 870). However, program participants did not perceive themselves to have greater influence in decision making, so Leana et al. concluded:

> The program may not be living up to its promise in the eyes of participants because it does not permit employees to exercise their enhanced desire for influence; in addition, it may arm them with information and knowledge that enable them to see how little influence they actually have. (pp. 870-871)

Organizational factors may also influence the effectiveness of QWL programs. In a study of five Canadian petrochemical plants, Ondrack and Evans (1987) found no differences between plants with QWL programs and those without these programs. However, compared to employees at redesign plants that had implemented QWL, those at greenfield sites with QWL programs perceived greater autonomy, feedback, work collaboration, and satisfaction with coworkers and supervisors. This suggests that it may be easier to introduce employee involvement programs in newer facilities, where employees and management may be less resistant to change. Goll (1991) also found that an organization's emphasis on participative decision making was positively related to amount of employee influence.

The union may be a key factor in the success of a QWL program. Cooke (1989) found that the intensity of collaboration between union and management affected productivity and quality. Compared to steering committees with less union leader participation, those with greater union involvement were associated with greater improvements in quality and productivity. Ellinger and Nissen (1987) studied an unsuccessful QWL program implemented in a large manufacturing facility. At first, people were convinced of the program's success:

> Representatives of the company and the union claimed that QWL had led to improved communications, more employee interest in the business, an end to adversarial relationships, better mutual respect and cooperation, greater efficiency, better product quality, lower absenteeism, improved morale, and the like. (p. 200)

Yet the QWL program was causing internal problems within the local union, including interference with collective bargaining and other union activities. Also, some members felt that employees were shifting their loyalties from the union to management.

As a result of these and similar findings, Ellinger and Nissen (1987) advise practitioners to be aware of the potential problems QWL programs can pose for unions. Many unions are already aware of these problems, and as a result, union attitudes toward QWL have been mixed. Some union officials may be uncomfortable with or even suspicious of QWL since many employee participation programs have been viewed as a threat to unionization or as a means to dilute union power (see Parker, 1985). Parker warns that companies may use QWL programs to increase employee commitment to management goals, and that "QWL is carefully designed so that any sense of power an individual gets from the experience is company power—not union power" (p. 44). On the other hand, in a major study assessing the effects of worker participation and QWL programs on trade unions and collective bargaining, Kochan, Katz, and Mower (1984) found that unions had a very positive attitude toward these programs, and a vast majority believed that "the union should support and actively participate in running the program with management" (p. 149).

Research on successful QWL programs suggests that in addition to guaranteeing union participation, QWL activities should involve all levels of the organization (Kanter, Stein, & Brinkerhoff, 1982; Nadler & Lawler, 1983). Nadler and Lawler argue, for example, that middle managers may block suggestions made by the involved groups if the managers feel excluded from the program. Also, as with QC programs, intergroup conflict and competition may occur when there are differences in the level of involvement among groups at the same level of the organization.

Although most of the studies on QWL do not elaborate on how these programs affect organizational communication patterns, Lawler (1986) asserts that QWL programs have a major effect on information sharing in the organization:

> The major impact of a QWL project is often in the area of information sharing. In many, but not all cases, the creation of committee structures and task forces causes an array of communication channels to open. As a result, people often come to understand the business better and to participate more effectively in problem-solving activities. (p. 130)

Further, the parallel structure that QWL programs may bring to the organization "cuts across the hierarchy and existing functional distinctions," which opens new communication channels (Kanter et al., 1982, p. 379). Since QWL programs have greater potential than do QCs to provide employees with the means to transcend hierarchical divisions within the organization, Stohl's (1986, 1987, 1989) findings on the positive relationship between QC participation and integration into the organizational network may apply to QWL projects as well. Moreover, since QWL programs involve virtually the entire organization and allow group and committee members to participate in decisions about broader company issues, macro-organizational communication variables such as those Stohl

studied (e.g., communication climate, communication problems, knowledge of the corporation, communication networks) may be even more salient. Additional research is needed to examine the relationship between employee participation in QWL programs and their integration into the communication network.

Scanlon Gainsharing Plans

Gainsharing has been used for more than 60 years and has expanded beyond manufacturing settings to service and nonprofit organizations (Miller & Schuster, 1987b). A "gainsharing plan is an organizational system of employee involvement with a financial formula for distributing organization-wide gains" (Bullock & Lawler, 1984, pp. 23-24). Lawler (1988) adds that some "gainsharing plans are as much an approach to participative management as they are a pay plan" (p. 324). Many gainsharing plans exist, including Scanlon, Rucker, Improshare, DARCOM, Group/Plant, and Productivity and Waste programs (e.g., see Kaufman, 1992; Welbourne & Gomez-Mejia, 1995). However, although "gainsharing always includes a financial system to reinforce gains in organizational performance . . . the inclusion of a participation system of employee committees to generate and evaluate cost-saving ideas has not been used by all programs" (Gowen, 1990, p. 79).

The Scanlon plan, in particular, is concerned with establishing a strong link between employee participation and financial rewards. Developed in 1938 by company accountant Joseph Scanlon "as a cost-saving employee suggestion system to turn around the nearly bankrupt Empire Steel" (Gowen, 1990, p. 79), the profit-sharing component of the plan was not added to the suggestion system until ten years later. Scanlon plans are based on the assumption that

> all people have needs of psychological growth and development and are capable of and willing to fulfill those needs in their employer's

service if they are allowed the opportunity to participate in organizational decision making and if they are equitably compensated for the participation. (Hammer, 1988, p. 337)

Compared with other gainsharing programs, especially the pervasive Improshare plan and other productivity gainsharing (PG) programs that have *excluded* a formal employee involvement system (Graham-Moore & Ross, 1983; Miller & Schuster, 1987b), Scanlon gainsharing provides for a relatively high level of employee participation and involvement. Given the results of Bullock and Tubbs's (1990) meta-analysis of 33 studies of gainsharing plans (i.e., that plans with formal involvement structures had more successful gainsharing overall, especially high employee innovativeness, and higher levels of employee satisfaction and labor-management cooperation), gainsharing programs that *include* employee participation (especially Scanlon plans) will be emphasized in this section.

Companies implementing Scanlon programs form production committees that meet regularly to review employee suggestions and to discuss ways to cut costs and improve productivity. Ordinarily, these production committees include supervisors and employees from all areas of the organization who are elected by their coworkers. These committees solicit, review, and implement employees' ideas concerning how to improve performance and productivity. Scanlon plan programs also include a screening committee consisting of members from many areas of the organization. This committee approves production committee suggestions that exceed cost guidelines or affect multiple departments, reviews appeals from employees whose suggestions were rejected by the production committees, and reviews the bonus formula (Miller & Schuster, 1987b). Bonus formulas vary across organizations, but generally the steering committee sets a standard based on past performance, and when the company exceeds this baseline and "gains" are realized, employees receive a financial bonus.

Typically, these bonuses are based on a percentage of the employees' wages and are paid monthly or quarterly. In some organizations, bonuses are distributed on a team basis to reward and encourage collective performance (DeBettengies, 1989).

Lawler (1986) points out that Scanlon plan committee structures are similar to the parallel structure approach used in QC and QWL programs but, unlike QCs and QWL groups, Scanlon committees have a small budget and can implement certain suggestions without management approval. Thus, Scanlon plans are formal participation programs that are basically consultative but, compared with QC and QWL programs, give employees more latitude in implementing some suggestions on their own. These programs have a more expansive social range since interaction among employees cuts across department lines, and all employees have the opportunity to make suggestions and receive financial bonuses. The content of participation is more comprehensive than that of QCs, because Scanlon plans allow employees to be involved in decisions about broader company policies as well as issues relating to their immediate work area (see Table 17.1).

Studies indicate that gainsharing plans produce generally positive results, including improvements in individual attitudes, labor-management relations, teamwork and decision making, work methods, service or product quality, and productivity, as well as increases in financial decision-making and group process skills (Bullock & Lawler, 1984; Bullock & Tubbs, 1990; Gowen, 1990; Hatcher, Ross, & Collins, 1991; Lawler, 1986; Welbourne & Gomez-Mejia, 1995). In a study of a large, unionized manufacturing firm, Miller and Schuster (1987a) found that implementation of a Scanlon plan resulted in long-term employment stability, increases in productivity, and significant improvements in the relationship between union and management. Doherty, Nord, and McAdams (1989) examined different gainsharing programs in manufacturing and nonmanufacturing environments and found that these programs improved productivity, safety, and attendance. These programs also improved communication between workers and management and increased employee understanding of operations.

Additional findings indicate that these positive effects may persist over time (Schuster, 1984). For example, Hatcher and Ross (1991) examined a U.S. manufacturing company two months prior to the implementation of a gainsharing plan and 15 months later. Results revealed significant increases in organizational members' concern for performance and in perceptions of teamwork (coordination, open communication, helpfulness, friendliness). Interrupted time series analyses of more than 4 years of objective data indicated a significant decrease in grievances and a significant increase in product quality.

Although the majority of published studies on gainsharing conclude that this type of employee involvement program is quite effective, some researchers have been critical of this body of research (see Cotton, 1993; Hanlon, Meyer, & Taylor, 1994; Hanlon & Taylor, 1991; Lawler, 1986, 1988). They point out the methodological limitations of research, including the lack of control groups and the less than rigorous statistical procedures used in most of the studies. In addition to criticizing the measures of effects of these programs, researchers have argued that studies are too limited in scope and should examine how and why gainsharing works (Bullock & Lawler, 1984; Cotton, 1993; Gowen, 1990; Hanlon et al., 1994; Hanlon & Taylor, 1991; Lawler, 1988; Welbourne & Gomez-Mejia, 1995). Moreover, there may be important intervening processes that mediate and explain the effectiveness of gainsharing programs. Hanlon and colleagues (Hanlon et al., 1994; Hanlon & Taylor, 1991) posit that communication is a key intervening variable in gainsharing plan outcomes:

A major intervening effect of the implementation of gainsharing is a change in organizational communication content, quality, and climate. . . . [Specifically] changes in work group communication behaviors (the extent to which they talk about work and share job-related knowledge and ideas for performance improvement) increase group members' job knowledge or cognitions, which improves their ability to do their jobs and in turn partially accounts for improved job performance and economic gains for the employees and employer. (Hanlon & Taylor, 1991, pp. 242-243)

These researchers explain that since most members of organizations with gainsharing plans are economically motivated to improve their performance, they will increase the frequency and amount of interaction with one another to learn more about their job and the organization. This increase in job-related information leads to better job performance and organizational "gains," which are ultimately translated into financial bonuses in which employees "share." The relationship between performance and financial rewards increases the likelihood that employees will value their membership in the organization, which will lead to positive attitudinal outcomes as well.

Hanlon and Taylor (1991) found empirical support for this explanation of how gainsharing works. In a quasi-experimental field study of a modified Scanlon plan, they compared a regional facility of a priority package delivery company that had implemented a Scanlon plan with a primary facility of the same company that did not implement the program. Hanlon and Taylor found that compared to those employees at the nonparticipating facility, those at the Scanlon plan facility reported positive effects on communication. Specifically, "gainsharing participants perceived that they received useful and accurate information, had frank discussions about work situations, were encouraged to discuss problems, and talked about ideas for improving their work methods and environment more often than nonparticipants" (p. 258).

These findings are consistent with Lawler's (1986) suggestion that gainsharing influences the information flow in the organization, where information-seeking efforts are directed from employees to management, and financial information moves downward from management to the employees, resulting in increased knowledge about the economics of the business. Other studies suggest that gainsharing plans may improve communication and cooperation between supervisors and their employees as well (Bullock & Lawler, 1984; Bullock & Tubbs, 1990; Gowen, 1990).

Both cognitive and motivational models may explain these effects. For instance, Miller and Monge (1987) found a strong and direct link between employee cognitive factors and organizational commitment, and Hanlon and Taylor (1991) argued that cognitive models offered a useful explanation for their findings on gainsharing effects. This also is consistent with the claim that employee participation can help employees form more accurate perceptions of reward contingencies in the organization (Miller & Monge, 1987; Monge & Miller, 1988). Further, motivation is a factor, since the potential for financial gain may encourage employee interest in obtaining information.

In addition to affecting immediate changes in work group and organizational communication, gainsharing programs may have long-term attitudinal effects. A follow-up study conducted by Hanlon et al. (1994) found that even three months after the priority package delivery company eliminated the financial bonus component of the program, the facility that had participated in the plan exhibited higher levels of moral commitment and prosocial behavior and fewer turnover intentions than did the nonparticipating facility. Hanlon et al. assert that the bonus formula accounted for changes in communication behavior, and prosocial behavior became a group norm.

These findings are consistent with comments made by other researchers on the factors contributing to gainsharing program success. For instance, Lawler (1986, 1988) states that employee trust, understanding, acceptance, input, and cooperation are important to plan effectiveness. Other conditions that increase the likelihood of program success include an open communication policy, a man-

agement that is technically and communicatively competent and is able to deal with suggestions, a work force that is technically and financially knowledgeable and is interested in participation and higher pay (Lawler, 1988, p. 328), and involving members in the creation of a fair distribution rule (Cooper, Dyck, & Frohlich, 1992).

Thus, it is clear that managerial communication competence and willingness to share information are antecedents to effective Scanlon plan outcomes. Implementing these programs also may result in improved communication relationships between supervisors and employees, better information flow in the organization, and increased employee access to information about his or her job and the company. Further, gainsharing programs with higher levels of employee involvement (e.g., participation in the design of the plan and involvement in fair allocation rules) are associated with the most favorable outcomes in terms of innovativeness, performance, teamwork, climate and labor-management cooperation (Bullock & Tubbs, 1990; Hatcher & Ross, 1991).

Self-Directed Work Teams and New-Design Plants

Self-directed work teams (SDWTs) have their roots in human relations initiatives in the United States beginning in the 1930s, European coal mine and factory sociotechnical studies in the 1940s and 1950s, and Japanese quality circles following World War II. Beginning with their implementation in U.S. organizations in the 1960s and 1970s (Pasmore, Francis, Haldeman, & Shani, 1982; Walton, 1977), the discursive warrant for implementing "teams"—especially as they have been used in U.S. core manufacturing organizations—is organizational performance: improved quality, increased productivity, and decreased operating costs. Fisher (1993) reported that 7% of U.S. workers were organized in such teams, and more than 200 major corporations relied on them in at least one company location. In fact, the popularity of work teams continues to increase. As of 1999, 78% of U.S. corporations used self-managing teams (Lawler, 1999).

Typically, SDWTs are intact groups of employees who have collective responsibility for managing themselves and their work with minimal direct supervision. Usually, they plan and schedule work, order materials and handle budget expenditures, make production/service-related decisions, monitor productivity, and act on matters once reserved for management (Versteeg, 1990). Viewed in terms of Dachler and Wilpert's (1978) categories, SDWTs are voluntarily initiated by organizations, implemented at the group level and often throughout the entire organization, with direct and maximal participation by all employees involved in the SDWTs (see Table 17.1). Consider the SDWTs in a case study of a team-managed manufacturing plant (Seibold, 1995):

> Whereas production functions in traditional organizations are handled by some workers, and functions such as maintaining the equipment and assuring quality control and safety are handled by others, the organizational structure at BFSI cuts across those responsibilities. Multi-skilled blue-collar workers (technicians), working in "area teams" of 4-5 persons, rotate jobs within and across areas to handle *all* aspects of the production process. There are also no foremen or supervisors at BFSI. The technicians, with two-year technical degrees and training in electronics and mechanics, are self-directed. They monitor and maintain the production process machinery with specialized support from a small team of certified engineers, who act more as consultants than quality control overseers. (pp. 288-289)

It is difficult to separate SDWTs from their organizational context, frequently "new-design plants" (Lawler, 1986). New-design plants and the SDWTs at their core are outgrowths of sociotechnical systems theory (Emery & Trist, 1965). Patterned after self-regulating work teams in England and Norway (Burns & Stalker, 1968; Rice, 1958), as well as well-publicized participative management plants created in America during the 1970s by Procter & Gamble and by General Foods, U.S. corporations designed "new plants" in the 1980s that transferred to employees power, information, knowledge, and intrinsic rewards traditionally associated with management (Lawler, 1986). Walton (1985) noted that 200 new-design plants were in operation by the mid-1980s.

Characteristic of the participative practices common to new-design plants are coworker teams' selection of new employees, work team participation in the physical layout of the plant, design of jobs by employees, lack of much hierarchy in organizational structure, implementation of egalitarian pay and incentive systems, and the development of management philosophies that emphasize participation and shared decision making. In one study, the organization is designed to foster group participation in planning work, coordinating tasks, and solving problems. Each day, each shift begins with a meeting of everyone working in the plant during that rotation. Meetings of subunits or standing committees may follow or be held throughout the day. Standing committees, such as the Safety Committee, the Good Practices Committee, and the Design Committee, exist to address a variety of organization-wide issues. Personnel functions have been absorbed by other groups of employees, including preparation of an employee handbook, development of applicant screening/selection procedures, and monitoring compensation. Team members also administer most aspects of the reward system, including establishing skill-based pay levels, determining raises and bonuses, and monitoring a gainsharing program. All members are cross-trained in every aspect of the production process. Although there is a plant manager and an accountant, they primarily serve liaison roles in interfacing with the parent companies. A strong egalitarian culture . . . is reflected in the absence of formal hierarchies (team members rotate as "area leaders") and the absence of status markers (e.g., there are no eating areas, restrooms, offices, recreational facilities, parking places, and the like that cannot be used by all members). Training is emphasized: on-the-job and paid off-site technical training is provided for everyone on a regular basis, as is training in interpersonal and group process skills, career planning, and other personal development. (Seibold, 1995, p. 289)

As Lawler (1986) summarized, "New-design plants are clearly different from traditional plants. . . . The reward system, the structure, the physical layout, the personnel management system, and the nature of jobs are all changed in significant ways. Because so many features are altered, in aggregate they amount to a new kind of organization" (p. 178).

The literature on SDWTs is replete with research on factors associated with degree of members' identification with the organization (Barker & Tompkins, 1994), external activity and performance in organizational teams (Ancona & Caldwell, 1992), job switching (Blumberg, 1980), work group characteristics and effectiveness (Campion, Medsker, & Higgs, 1993), the social structure of the organization (Carnall, 1982), teamwork and communication (S. Glaser, 1994), frontline members' views of SDWTs (Berggren, 1993; Katz, Laughlin, & Wilson, 1990), organizational factors that enable and constrain team effectiveness (Hackman, 1990), obstacles to team-based performance (Katzenbach & Smith, 1993), dysfunctional decision dynamics (Manz & Sims, 1982), leadership dynamics (Manz, 1986; 1992; Manz, Keating, & Donnellon, 1990; Manz & Sims, 1984, 1987), personal control (Manz & Angle, 1986), member selection (Neuman, 1991), design and activation (Pearce & Ravlin, 1987; Sundstrom, DeMeuse, & Futrell, 1990), evaluation (Pearson, 1992), restructuring (Poza & Markus, 1980), peer assessment (Saavedra &

Kwun, 1993), member requisites for teamwork (Stevens & Campion, 1994), and training (Swezey & Salas, 1992). In an often cited research program, Kemp, Wall, Clegg, and Cordery (1983) and Wall, Kemp, Jackson, and Clegg (1986) compared employees in SDWTs to employees in the same factory on another shift and at another of the company's plants. Members of the SDWTs had significantly higher satisfaction with factors intrinsic to the job (opportunities to use abilities, amount of responsibility and autonomy), an effect that endured over 30 months of the study. SDWT members also were more satisfied with extrinsic factors of the work (pay, work conditions), although this lessened over time. Neither work motivation nor performance was found to differ, although cost savings were highest in the SDWTs.

However, in new-design plants in particular, research has revealed a number of positive outcomes associated with SDWTs: improvements in work methods and procedures due to team problem solving, enhanced recruitment and retention of team members due to increased involvement and pay, high-quality work due to team motivation, fewer supervision requirements because teams are self-managing, improved decision making resulting from increased input, higher levels of skill development and staffing flexibility due to cross-training, and lower levels of grievances because teams resolve issues (Lawler, 1986, 1990). These effects may be due to the fact that the range of the SDWTs extends to the entire organization (Dachler & Wilpert, 1978). Seibold (1995) found that SDWT members perceived four advantages to working at their new design plant (compared with nonparticipative organizations in which some had been employed, and organizations in which SDWTs were on a "trial basis" and were restricted to one area of the plant): (1) greater opportunities to elicit input from all members of the organization, (2) better utilization of both human and technical resources, (3) freedom to express their opinions and ideas increased their morale and satisfaction with the organization, and (4) cross-training as a major opportunity and advantage. He also found the following performance outcomes: nearly on-time start up and at less than projected cost, output equivalent to comparable plants but with 60% less labor, 80% less rework, more frequent inventory turns, less production machinery downtime than normal, and near-zero turnover in personnel. Compared to a traditionally managed organization, SDWT members also felt that they had a greater sense of ownership, greater satisfaction and better decision making, greater autonomy and self-motivation, good communication and a high level of interaction among members, more opportunity to talk directly to managers, greater tolerance for individual differences, more flexibility in scheduling work hours, an increase in coworkers' helpfulness and honesty, and the acknowledgment of individual contributions by others in the organization. Cotter's (1983) review of organizations in seven countries that transitioned from traditional work systems to SDWTs revealed similar outcomes: 93% reported improved productivity, 86% reported decreased operating costs, 86% reported improved quality, and 70% reported improved employee attitudes.

However, as writers have reported about the "pitfalls" and "dilemmas" of employee involvement programs in general (Baloff & Doherty, 1989; Connors & Romberg, 1991; Kanter, 1982, 1986; Magjuka, 1991), SDWTs in new-design plants are prone to a variety of problems as well: member expectations can be too high because of the philosophy and selection process; surveillance by other areas of the organization (e.g., management in "parent" companies) can produce pressure and conflict; training costs are high due to the need for cross-training and team training; team meetings take more time and decision processes can be slow; establishing standards can be difficult in the absence of a "history" and meaningful benchmarks; and the timing of new decisions regarding compensation, schedule, and production changes is difficult (Lawler, 1986). Further, members may revert

to the practices of traditional workplaces and hierarchical management during times of information overload, environmental uncertainty, decision difficulty, work pressure, and interpersonal conflict (Barker, Melville, & Pacanowsky, 1993). Interpersonal and group-level difficulties have been observed in self-directed teams in general: conflict, decision making, efficiency, performance feedback, inter-area relationships, and the like. Too, many problems can be found in organizations making a transition to self-managing teams: first-line supervisors, middle managers, or union representatives who resist the teams; reductions in existing work force size; SDWTs may be limited to select units of the organization or introduced on an "experimental" basis; changes in preexisting organizational roles or patterns of communication that need to be facilitated; dysfunctional correlates to increased "permissiveness" within units suddenly given greater autonomy (for discussion of these problems, see Barker et al., 1993; Cordery, Mueller, & Smith, 1991; Cummings, 1978; Lawler, 1986). Further, when *self*-managed *teams* occur in the context of a *team*-managed *organization* (especially new-design plants), SDWT outcomes such as member satisfaction and team performance may interact with a number of other organizational contingencies including the timing of start-up decisions about shift work, bonuses, and production schedules; establishing plantwide standards; interfacing with parent companies; and negotiating the unique role of the plant manager.

Employee Stock Ownership Plans

Toscano (1983) distinguished among three types of employee ownership, which we can conceptualize as forming a continuum. At one end, *direct ownership* refers to the typical situation in which employees individually own stock in their company. At the other end are *worker cooperatives,* in which a group of individuals working in a company both own and personally operate the firm. Somewhere between these poles are *employee stock ownership plans,* formed when the company creates a plan in which all employees acquire stock as a part of their benefits. We shall emphasize this form of employee ownership for several reasons. First, although direct ownership can be important in smaller organizations (where percentage of stock owned may be sufficient to significantly involve employees and to influence the organization), this is not usually the case in large organizations. Further, as Cotton (1993) notes, research attention to direct ownership has been sparse, in part because it is operationally difficult "to draw a line between the employee-owned corporation and the publicly owned corporation where some of the stockholders are also employees" (p. 203). Second, although worker cooperatives are easy to identify, they represent the fewest in number of organizations with employee ownership. Drawing comparisons is difficult because the organizations tend to be concentrated in certain sectors and certain countries (for an excellent communication-based treatment of cooperatives, see Cheney, 1995).

Employee stock ownership plans (ESOPs) are the most prevalent and popular form of employee ownership, with more than 10,000 plans in existence in the United States involving more than 10 million employees (Pierce & Furo, 1990). In essence, an ESOP is a legal trust that must invest in the company's stock by contributing stock or cash to the trust and allocating stock to employees. It usually takes employees five to ten years to become vested, and they typically cannot take possession of their shares until they retire or otherwise leave the organization. ESOPs differ from direct ownership in important ways: employees need not invest their own funds since they automatically receive shares from the firm, and they have more limited voting rights than employees with direct ownership of stock.

Viewed from the standpoint of Dachler and Wilpert's (1978) typology, ESOPs are a *formal* method of employee participation involv-

ing members of the entire organization. Employees' potential for influence is high, although this can vary from plan to plan. Since they own a portion of the company, it is assumed that they will be more involved in it—leading to increased employee satisfaction and organizational performance (Buchko, 1992).

However, researchers have pointed out that only some ESOP firms have actually instituted formal participation mechanisms for their employees. In a review of several studies, Rosen (1991) found that between one third and one half of the ESOP firms provided opportunities for joint worker-management decision making on job-related issues. This may be due, in part, to the fact that in addition to serving as an employee benefit plan and as a way to increase employee participation, ESOPs traditionally have been used to save failing firms, reap tax advantages for companies, finance corporate growth, and prevent takeovers (Harrison, 1994; McWhirter, 1991; Rosen, Klein, & Young, 1986). However, more recent sources suggest that the *primary* motivations for forming ESOPs in larger firms have changed from preventing takeovers and reaping tax benefits in the 1980s to providing postretirement benefits to employees and increasing worker participation in the 1990s ("ESOPs, Employee Ownership Evolve," 1993). For example, according to E. W. Purcell, senior associate with a firm specializing in structuring and implementing ESOPs, "the basis of the ESOP concept . . . is to create more employee participation and empowerment [meaning that] employees are more involved in the department in which they work and in the day-to-day operations of the business" ("ESOPs, Employee Ownership Evolve," 1993, p. 30).

Although much of the evidence is anecdotal, introducing ESOPs may foster a change in the company's culture, where "there is more communication and more freedom for employees to make decisions" (Taplin, 1989, p. 53). "Along with the implementation of an employee stock ownership plan (ESOP) frequently comes a change in corporate culture that includes better management/employee communications and increased employee participation and involvement" ("ESOP Brings Change," 1992, p. 25). At the very least, ESOPs influence information flow in the organization. Most ESOP firms share with their employees via newsletters, reports, company-wide and department meetings, and one-on-one discussions, information about company finances, budget, and performance (Burzawa, 1992, 1993; Rosen et al., 1986; Taplin, 1989). Further, even without a formal participation program in place, research suggests that employees' increased financial stake may lead to informal interaction about managerial decisions (see Lewis & Seibold, 1993, 1996, for arguments and evidence on the positive relationship between the introduction of new programs and increased informal communication among coworkers).

Research results concerning the effectiveness of ESOPs have been positive but mixed. In terms of organizational performance, studies have found increased sales and growth in companies that have converted to ESOPs (e.g., Rosen & Quarrey, 1987). However, as Cotton (1993) has summarized, "although no studies found employee-owned companies to have lower performance than conventional firms, several studies found no differences" (p. 210). With regard to the effects of ESOPs and direct ownership on employees' attitudes and behaviors, Cotton (1993) also concluded a review of relevant studies with a "mixed" assessment:

The studies of ESOPs and direct ownership found primarily positive, but also negative and null, results. To add to the confusion, most conversions to employee ownership are accompanied by a variety of other events (changes in worker population, financial rewards, sales and profits, etc.). Examples of positive changes in attitudes or the lack of changes can often be explained by these confounding effects. Overall, positive attitudes generally are found to be related to employee ownership. The attitude (sat-

isfaction, commitment, etc.) may vary, however, and in several cases the conversion to employee ownership produced more negative results. (p. 215)

Several explanations have been offered for why ownership influences employee attitudes and firm performance, controlling for factors such as those noted above. Proponents of a "financial investment" explanation (e.g., French, 1987; Sockell, 1985) contend that effects of this form of employee participation are a function of the financial rewards that members receive from their involvement. While considerable research has investigated the financial ownership hypothesis, according to Cotton (1993) results have been "extremely mixed": "Some research indicates that measures of financial stake (e.g., size of contribution by the company) are related to employee attitudes and/or organizational performance, yet the most obvious measure (amount of stock owned) shows few positive effects" (p. 233). Alternatively, some researchers (e.g., Buchko, 1992; Long, 1981; Paul, Ebadi, & Dilts, 1987; Pierce & Furo, 1990; Pierce, Rubenfeld, & Morgan, 1991) have proposed that the effects of employee ownership are moderated by the "psychological ownership" afforded by that form of participation in the organization. In an influential study of how employee attitudes are influenced by ESOPs, Klein (1987) used results from 2,804 employees in 37 ESOP firms to investigate organizational commitment, turnover intentions, satisfaction with the ESOP, ESOP philosophy, perception of work influence, and stock return performance. Findings revealed that employee satisfaction and commitment were positively related to strong contributions by the firm to the ESOP, a strong philosophy of employee ownership within management, and full and frequent communication by management. Cotton (1993) concluded that while there is less research concerning the psychological ownership hypothesis and ESOP effects, it has produced "more consistent evidence that perceptions of involvement or some type of employee participation program is related to more positive attitudes and/or organizational performance" (p. 222).

Other researchers also have concluded that ESOPs combined with employee participation in decision making are more effective in changing attitudes and performance than are ESOPs or participation alone (e.g., Blasi & Kruse, 1991; Burzawa, 1992, 1993; Long, 1982; Rosen, 1989; Rosen et al., 1986; Taplin, 1989; Turpin-Forster, 1989; Young, 1990, 1991). For instance, Young (1990) points out:

> Our research has very clearly shown that the most participative employee ownership companies have growth rates 11% to 17% per year higher than the least participative companies. Moreover, employees in the most participative companies were significantly more satisfied with their work and their ESOP, were more committed to their company, and were more likely to stay with their firm than workers in the less participative companies. (p. 177)

Some have even suggested that implementing ESOPs without encouraging employee participation in decision making may backfire (Blasi & Kruse, 1991; Turpin-Forster, 1989). For instance, ESOPs may make employees more responsible and committed to their jobs, but if they perceive that management is operating in a manner that is wasteful to the company and employees are not in a position to help change it, then frustrations may increase and employees may develop more negative attitudes (Turpin-Forster, 1989).

Unfortunately, as Cotton (1993) and others have noted, it is difficult to disentangle the participation effects from the financial ones. This is made even more difficult by the fact that the type of employee participation associated with ESOPs seems to vary somewhat among companies. The research reveals that the participation component of ESOPs may include one or more of the following techniques: suggestion boxes, employee commit-tees, QCs, interdepartmental task forces, same-department work groups, joint problem-solving teams, and representative boards (Blasi & Kruse, 1991; Taplin, 1989; Young, 1990). Many of these programs differ in terms of how much influence employees are accorded, the types of decision making in which they are involved, and the social range required. This is perhaps why ESOPs have been found to be only moderately effective in changing employee attitudes and behaviors. More research certainly is needed in this area to separate the effects of participation and to distinguish the varying outcomes among the different types of participation programs associated with each ESOP. We now turn to a number of dynamics embedded in a "psychological" explanation for employee participation effects, and we explore their communication implications.

COMMUNICATION AND PARTICIPATION EFFECTS

Although some researchers have expressed a concern for understanding *why* different types of employee participation programs work (Leana & Florkowski, 1992), few have attempted to answer this question empirically. Leana and Florkowski argue, "The research based on intrinsic models of participative decision making has often been analyzed with little regard for differences among the types of participation programs and various aspects of its implementation" (p. 263). As noted earlier, methodological and conceptual problems make it difficult to isolate specific factors that account for each program's differing outcomes. However, reviews of numerous studies on QCs, QWL programs, gainsharing plans, SDWTs, ESOPs, and employee participation in general suggest that *communication* functions as an intervening variable in participation outcomes. Further, this chapter has maintained that the type of employee participation program influences the communication patterns and processes in the organization, which mediates the cognitive and affective (motivational) effects of participation. The following section briefly explains the relationship between information flow and the cognitive and motivational effects of participation.

Cognitive and Motivational Effects

Researchers have suggested that there is an important connection between message flow and decision making in the organization (O'Reilly, Chatman, & Anderson, 1987). Moreover, there is a strong link between employee participation and information-processing capabilities, and this significantly affects organizational effectiveness and quality of work life (Castrogiovanni & Macy, 1990, p. 314). These claims are consistent with the findings on the relationship between involvement in one of the employee participation programs outlined in this chapter and organizational communication patterns. Castrogiovanni and Macy (1990) found that the degree of employee participation positively affected information-processing capabilities. Specifically, compared to indirect participants, direct participants (members of QWL committees and task forces) perceived greater influence over work and integrating activities as well as increased improvements in coordination, external feedback, and organizational communication.

Researchers have attempted to explain how participation in decision making, and hence, involvement in organizational communication networks, influences outcomes. This participation often entails an increase in downward and upward information dissemination, which in turn provides employees at various organizational levels greater access to information. Monge and Miller (1988) explain:

Participation in decision making will result in the individual employee having increased knowledge about the organization and his or her part in the organization. . . . Participative employees will have a greater understanding of the entire organization, its standing in the marketplace, and the part that individual employees play in the greater scheme of things. (p. 220)

Although these claims ordinarily are used to explain the cognitive influences of participation, they may offer insight into motivational and attitudinal forces as well. For instance, research suggests that employee participation in decision making and the corresponding involvement in communication networks may enhance employee feelings of empowerment and self-efficacy (Conger & Kanungo, 1988; Hammer, 1988; Jackson, 1983; Marshall & Stohl, 1993; Thomas & Griffin, 1989).

Within the vast literature on power sharing (Leana, 1987) and employee empowerment (Thomas & Velthouse, 1990), several researchers have elaborated on the relationship between access to other members of the organization, information, and empowerment. Conger and Kanungo (1988) define empowerment as a "process of enhancing feelings of self-efficacy among organizational members" (p. 474). Organizational conditions that may hamper empowerment or feelings of personal efficacy include poor network-forming and communications systems, lack of role clarity and network-forming opportunities, limited participation in decisions that have a direct impact on job performance, and limited contact with senior management (Conger & Kanungo, 1988, p. 477). Pacanowsky (1988) states that maintaining an open communication system and using integrative problem solving can empower employees. General adequacy of communication channels also enhances empowerment (Albrecht, 1988).

Marshall and Stohl (1993) expand the notion of empowerment to mean "the process of developing key relationships in the organization in order to gain greater control over one's own organizational life" (p. 141), and they found that empowerment was related to feelings of satisfaction. These findings are consistent with the suggestion made by Conger and Kanungo (1988) that increasing the number of communication opportunities and employee participation systems can be empowering; however, employees must also receive information that confirms their feelings of self-efficacy.

These points suggest that employee perceptions of control, personal influence, or self-efficacy may influence outcomes such as satisfaction. Based on a meta-analysis of studies examining the effects of perceived employee control, Spector (1986) concluded that employees who perceived high levels of control at work scored high on job satisfaction, organizational commitment, job involvement, and motivation.

This chapter has established that QCs, QWL programs, ESOP, SDWTs, and Scanlon plans differ somewhat in terms of the content and scope of decision making and the social range of participation, but they differ considerably in terms of the degree of participation and level of influence they afford members. As noted earlier, the differing dimensions of each employee involvement program influence the communication patterns within the organization, which subsequently affects organizational outcomes such as satisfaction and performance (Marshall & Stohl, 1993).

Participation Dimensions and Communication Patterns

Monge and Eisenberg (1987) argue that organizational change (i.e., implementing an employee participation program) may affect communication network participation, and the literature offers overwhelming support for this claim in general (Eisenberg, Monge, & Miller, 1983) and in the employee involvement area in particular (Buch, 1992; Hanlon et al., 1994; Hanlon & Taylor, 1991; Lawler, 1986, 1988; Marshall & Stohl, 1993; Stohl, 1986, 1987, 1989). However, no researchers have used this approach to explain the different effects of various employee involvement programs, such as QCs, QWL programs, SDWTs, ESOPs, and Scanlon plans.

The level of program effects may depend on the degree to which it influences and is influenced by information use. As mentioned earlier, the conditions necessary for beneficial participation outcomes include a supportive and participative organizational climate, a management that is willing and able to share relevant information, and employees who are interested in participation (see also Shadur, Kienzle, & Rodwell, 1999; Tesluk, Vance, & Mathieu, 1999). Lawler (1986) points out that information is "a source of power and effectiveness in organizational coordination and cooperation. Without considerable information moving downward, employee participation and involvement become impractical and even dangerous" (p. 24). The literature suggests that QCs may be less effective in this area than are QWL programs, which in turn are less effective than SDWTs and Scanlon plan programs. Further, each type of employee participation program discussed in this chapter differs with regard to level of influence, decision content, and social range. These differences affect the communication patterns and relationships in the organization.

QCs may have weaker and less consistent effects due to the limitations on decision content, lower levels of influence, and limited social range. Since QC members deal primarily with issues concerning the work itself, they may have less of a need to communicate with many members outside of their work area or department. If the need arises, however, QC members may not have the ability or the connections to reach others in the organization. "Usually, the group is provided with no systematic information about company performance, costs, long-range plans, and other matters" (Ledford et al., 1988, p. 259). This lack of information may result in poor decisions or management unwillingness to implement circle suggestions, which could reduce members' feelings of empowerment or self-efficacy. That, in turn, may ultimately undermine satisfaction and performance.

This is not to suggest, however, that QC members are unable to communicate with others outside of their group. Rather, as Stohl (1986, 1987, 1989) points out, QC members' level of integration in the organizational network affects circle members' intention to withdraw and overall QC effectiveness. More specifically, Stohl (1989) states:

> The greater number of diverse groups from which a circle received relevant information, resources, and support, the more influential that group was in (a) convincing management that its proposal was sound and worthwhile, (b) gaining commitment of resources to carry out the solution, and (c) assuring implementation of the solution by those members of the organization who had to carry out the new plan. (p. 357)

Thus, the communication network perspective may explain the inconsistent findings with regard to QC program outcomes as well as predict why, as Cotton (1993) concludes, QCs are less effective than QWL programs and Scanlon plans.

QWL and Scanlon programs, on the other hand, include committees and groups that represent a wider range of employees. This makes it much easier for these groups to access the information they might need from other areas in the organization. Moreover, compared to QCs, these groups deal with broader organizational issues. This expanded scope of decision making requires that they communicate with employees across the entire organization.

Scanlon plans may have particularly strong effects because of the financial reward component. Leana and Florkowski (1992) state that "offering bonus payments may increase the perceived job outcomes flowing from greater inputs on the part of employees in ways that intrinsic benefits cannot" (p. 251). Moreover, since the monetary incentive may motivate employees to work harder and smarter, employees will have a greater desire to obtain and to share information. For instance, "because employees receive financial information and their pay depends on effectiveness, they will challenge managers and demand change in ways that do not occur with QCs. For example, I have seen employees ask vice-presidents about accounts receivable and marketing issues" (Lawler, 1986, p. 166).

Hammer (1988) suggests that gainsharing facilitates employee empowerment by increasing access to management-level information. Additionally, "a sense of personal control develops among members of the organization when opportunities are afforded for the individual to attain rewards in sensible ways" (Albrecht, 1988, p. 385). As mentioned previously, participation gives employees information about which behaviors are likely to be rewarded, and the financial bonuses offered as part of the Scanlon plan certainly provide some tangible information about the results of the program.

As noted earlier, ESOPs may vary in their effectiveness because (1) although information flow (i.e., amount of financial information about the firm) is increased from management to employees, not all ESOPs include a formal employee participation component; and (2) even ESOP firms that do increase employee participation in decision making can differ with regard to both the type of participation program they implement and the type of formal involvement created. As with gainsharing, the financial incentive combined with participation may have powerful effects. However, some authors note that gainsharing plans may be more effective in increasing employee work effort than are ESOPs with a participation component, since ESOPs do not provide the same immediate financial rewards for employees as do annual gainsharing distributions (Rosen et al., 1986).

SDWTs may be most effective because the employees' level and scope of influence is high and the social range (Dachler & Wilpert, 1978) of the program extends to the entire organization in new-design plants. A parallel study of organizational work teams by Hirokawa and Keyton (1995) revealed that characteristics internal to the team (motivated members and competent group leadership) combined with organization-based factors (compatible work schedules, organizational assistance) and adequate informational resources best distinguished perceived volunteer-based work team effectiveness. It is precisely this combination of team, organizational, and informational factors that may inhere in the relative efficacy of SDWTs.

CRITICAL RESPONSES TO PARTICIPATION RESEARCH

As indicated earlier in this chapter, the five employee participation programs on which most previous research has focused are among the most popular choices of management (especially in North America) but are not necessarily the most "democratic." Among a variety of critical responses to these programs, critics have argued that managers' primary motivation is to increase profits rather than to relinquish control to workers. For instance, Rothschild-Whitt and Lindenfeld (1982) argue:

What identifies such participative models is that the permissible level of workers' participation is strictly controlled and limited by management. Employees may be afforded some measure of decisional control over immediate work tasks and environments, but the primacy of managerial control is left intact. . . . In the end, it is top management that has the authority to order and to halt experiments in workers' participation and job enlargement. (p. 5)

Other critics, including communication scholars (e.g., Barker, 1997; Barker & Cheney, 1994; Barker & Tompkins, 1992, 1994; Cheney, 1995; Conrad & Ryan, 1985; Deetz, 1992; Deetz & Kersten, 1983; Harrison, 1994), have leveled similar criticisms. For instance, Deetz and Kersten (1983) point out:

First, organizational goals are commonly viewed in terms of economic growth, profit, or continued organizational survival. Other goals, such as welfare of organizational participants, are subordinate to these goals and have only instrumental importance. Humanistic and participatory programs, for example, are valued only for their ability to increase productivity. (p. 153)

To a great extent, this is indicative of what Alvesson and Deetz (1996) term the "universalization of managerial interests," or the tendency for the interests of organizational subpopulations to be rationalized and interpreted in terms of the interests of privileged managerial groups in organizations where those practices are located.

Critical theorists contend that the type of participation promoted by the programs so predominant in North American organizations and so prevalent in the participation literature cannot foster a truly democratic and humane workplace. Rather, these forms of employee participation are merely "a tool for handling dissatisfaction, absenteeism, and alienation, problems that are detrimental to the accomplishment of organizational objectives" (Deetz & Kersten, 1983, p. 169). The limited form of participation afforded organizational members by these programs differs markedly from "political participation" (Abrahamsson, 1977; Deetz & Kersten, 1983) or "democratic participation" (Rothschild-Whitt & Lindenfeld, 1982). Political participation is grounded in the value of equality (Deetz & Kersten, 1983) and thus involves meaningful employee participation in decision making across all levels of the organization (Bachrach & Botwinick, 1992; Cheney, 1995; Deetz & Kersten, 1983; Mason, 1982; Rothschild-Whitt & Lindenfeld, 1982). According to Bernstein (1982), there are five conditions that must be present for participation to be meaningful and maintained over a long period of time: (1) adequate employee access to management-level information, (2) employee protection from reprisals, (3) an independent adjudicator to resolve disputes, (4) a participatory-democratic consciousness, and (5) a share in the profits resulting from participation.

In addition to widespread, meaningful, and sustained employee participation in decision making, there are factors that distinguish the democratic workplace from the management-controlled one. Democratic workplaces do not maintain a traditional hierarchical structure of managers and workers; rather, "in one way or another, everyone manages and everyone works" (Rothschild-Whitt & Lindenfeld, 1982, p. 6). Harrison (1994) notes that democratic organizations provide members unhindered access to information and equal access to resources. Also, organization members' interaction is less restricted and is regulated more by knowledge and technical expertise than by formal position or status. Ultimately, as Cheney and Carroll (1996) observe, democratic organizations transcend necessary concerns with the *organization's* performance, productivity, efficiency, and the like with attention to *members'* happiness, fair treatment, and well-being, among other values.

It is clear that none of the programs reviewed in this chapter meet the conditions needed to achieve the "democratic" participation described by these scholars. With the exception of SDWTs in (greenfield site) new-design plants, the programs discussed herein do very little—if anything—to change the basic hierarchical structure of the organization in which the participatory program is introduced. Moreover, it appears as if these employee participation programs fail to meet the five conditions for sustained democratic participation that were outlined by Bernstein (1982). First, each program reviewed in this chapter appears to vary with regard to the amount of management-level information provided to employees, but probably none ensures employees adequate access to such information. QC members probably receive the least and SDWTs acquire the most, while Scanlon plan and QWL participants receive a moderate amount. Although ESOP consultants recommend that managers in ESOP firms should provide their employees with financial and company performance information, there is no evidence suggesting that all firms follow this advice. Second, of the programs reviewed in this chapter, none appear to protect employees from reprisals, nor, third, do any of the five programs, about which so much research has been conducted, provide a neutral third-party to resolve disputes or even guarantee employee rights. Although the participation research reviewed here neglects to address the notion of employee rights, the organizational justice literature reflects a growing concern with fairness issues in the workplace (see Greenberg, 1990, 1996; Shea, 1995).

Fourth, there also is no clearly specified level of democratic consciousness associated with the employee participation programs reviewed here. As noted earlier, QC programs are often implemented by companies that are not necessarily concerned with worker fulfillment, except as a means to increase productivity. Indeed, Grenier (1988) has supplied compelling evidence of the way in which employee participation vis-à-vis quality circles has been a ruse for union-busting activities. New-design plants with SDWTs, and to some extent Scanlon plan companies, are far more likely to espouse a democratic philosophy. Even in these cases, as Cheney and Carroll (1996) note, the top-most level of such organizations are often filled with managers who situate themselves above the very team-based practices that they are promoting—including seeking to be free of bureaucratic (or team) constraints in exercising their latitude in decision making, while subordinates must work within team structures. This sort of rationalization by leaders (see Ritzer, 1993) is antithetical to the democratic consciousness necessary for meaningful and sustained workplace participation (Bernstein, 1982). Fifth, of the programs reviewed here, only Scanlon plans and SDWTs provide direct, financial rewards based on employee participation. Of course ESOPs are a financial plan, but the financial benefits are not tied directly to employee participation in decision making.

Some critical scholars even have suggested that most employee participation programs not only curtail employees' opportunity to exercise an equal voice in decision making, but these programs may be used to dominate and control workers (Fairhurst & Wendt, 1993; Mumby, 1988; Stohl, 1995; Stohl & Jennings, 1988). Cheney (1995) points out that participation programs may be used to pacify workers, diffuse resistance, and suppress potential opposition. Further, and this is most likely an unintended effect, some employee participation programs may actually increase concertive control over workers (Barker & Cheney, 1994; Tompkins & Cheney, 1985). Especially in SDWTs, concertive control "represents a key shift in the locus of control from management to the workers themselves, who collaborate to develop the means of their own control" (Barker, 1993, p. 411). In a study of self-managing teams, Barker (1993) examined how workers actually "developed a system of value-based normative rules that controlled their actions more powerfully and completely than the former system" (p. 408). Barker argued that concertive control, based on normative rules and peer pressure, paradoxically is far less apparent but much more powerful than are traditional forms of managerial control. Therefore, although SDWTs in new-design plants are probably the most democratic of all of the programs reviewed in this chapter, based on Barker's analysis, they may offer the greatest potential for worker control. To what degree are workers "controlling" other workers via mutually agreed-on norms, rules, and procedures antithetical to the notions of democracy advanced by the critical theorists? Although Barker and Tompkins (1992) acknowledge that a "communal-rational" system inheres in the transfer of authority from a hierarchical system to a team-based rules approach—which does not resemble the bureaucracy it has replaced—they concede

that the resulting concertive system fuses the peer pressure of team-based norms with the team's emergent rational rules to form a more powerful system of control (or what Barker, 1993, following Weber, termed a "tighter" iron cage). Given the pervasiveness of management approaches that propose to manage and control worker values, including the types of participation programs reviewed in this chapter, sustained critique may be needed to ensure that participants' dignity, happiness, sense of justice, and equality are maintained. As Cheney (1995) has summarized:

> The simple but profound question, "How do we implement democratic practices in work organizations?" leads us to think about the goals of organizations, the goals of the individuals who inhabit them, and the goals of the larger society, recognizing that those sets of aspirations can and perhaps should overlap even if not coincide perfectly. . . . Above all, I wish to promote the ideal of a humane workplace, a workplace not just for work but also for people, especially at a time when a simplistic form of the market principle and a crude impulse for greater productivity seem to preoccupy our factories, offices, schools, hospitals and universities. (p. 169)

RESEARCH AGENDA

As this review has emphasized, when the form of employee involvement studied is at the level of work *group* participation, there has been considerable imprecision and conflation of what are distinct forms of participation. For example, despite differences in the degree of participation, type of influence, and decision-making scope, semiautonomous and self-managing work teams have not only been treated as conceptually synonymous, but they often have been aggregated in empirical analyses of "teams." Careful taxonomic work is needed to provide precise conceptual and operational distinctions among these and related forms of group participation (e.g., self-directed teams, continuous process improvement teams, and the like). For example, Denison, Hart, and Kahn (1996) have distinguished cross-functional teams (CFTs) from other forms of organizational participation groups in terms of the greater role strain CFT members experience, greater expectations of CFTs than groups with longer-term goals, and the shorter life span of CFTs in which to accomplish those more immediate goals. In turn, Denison et al. demonstrate how these differences from other types of organizational teams will be associated with differences in interpersonal processes (development, collaboration, decision making, among others) these types of participation groups experience. Researchers also must be careful not to appropriate the label used by the host organization(s) for whatever involvement programs are studied. Instead, independent assessment of the form of work group should lead researchers to more accurately characterize their foci if comparison with other studies is sought.

A closely related concern should be the distinction between short-lived and long-term forms of employee participation. Continuous process improvement teams, cross-functional teams, and other teams created for the (brief) life of a project, for example, are likely to have communication-related processes and outcomes that are different from perennial agenda teams (e.g., ESOP and Scanlon oversight teams), SDWTs in a new-design plant, and so forth. Developmental changes in teams, to use but one area, underscore the potential import of this distinction. On one hand, research by Gersick (1988) with project teams, fund-raising committees, health care teams, and university groups has led to the repudiation of phasic models of group development—often borne of studies of short-lived laboratory groups—that emphasize a singular sequence of periods of defined group activity. Rather, Gersick found that the groups she studied experienced a "punctuated equilibrium" (periods of seeming inertia broken by burst of energy and transformation) and a "midpoint crisis" (a precipitating event at the midpoint of its life). However, it is important to note that even Gersick's foci were relatively short-lived teams, when compared with the long-term participative work arrangements noted above. Research on the developmental dynamics in those involvement structures could do much to confirm the applicability of the punctuated equilibrium model to participation forms with longer life spans, or to offer new understandings of the nature of group development in those arrangements.

Reviews of work group research repeatedly emphasize that work group performances are dependent on organizational contexts (Ancona & Caldwell, 1988; Denison et al., 1996; Guzzo & Dickson, 1996; Levine & Moreland, 1990; Shulman, 1996; Sundstrom et al., 1990). In the area of employee involvement programs, studies are needed that systematically relate the forms of individual and group participation to the culture of the organizations in which those involvement programs are embedded. Although case study research on workplace participation has underscored the inherent and recursive relationship between organizational culture and the processes and outcomes of their forms of participation, large-scale investigations have not studied this link explicitly (for a notable exception, see Lawler, Mohrman, & Ledford, 1992). Further, there has been a tendency by both individual researchers and reviewers to assume that the trans-bureaucratization of most forms of employee involvement somehow neutralizes or minimizes the effects of the organization's culture on those forms. There is evidence to the contrary. For example, Kornbluh (1984) chronicled the problems associated with the implementation of QCs and QWL programs in organizations that did not implement commensurate democratic forms of management. Research on employee participation could profit from efforts to link concerns with the dynamics and effects of involvement programs to theoretical perspectives on organizational culture and control. For instance, Walton and Hackman (1986) distinguished among control-strategy organizations (traditional, hierarchical, power-driven, controlling), commitment-strategy organizations (innovative, more flat, widely distributed power, participative), and mixed-strategy organizations (in transition from control- to commitment-strategy). We would expect not merely the range of employee participation to covary inversely with the degree of control inherent in these types of organizations, but important differences in the processes and success of the involvement programs to be determined by correlative dynamics in the degree of control in those cultures.

Also desperately needed are longitudinal studies of the over-time dynamics and outcomes of employee participation in organizations. As reviewed in this chapter, the overwhelming majority of studies on forms of employee involvement have been cross-sectional comparisons of organizations at single points in time. This is unfortunate when one considers studies that underscore the problems of such "snapshots" at specific points in time. For example, Hanlon et al. (1994) found that the positive effects of a Scanlon plan at a priority packaging company on employee participation endured even after a key financial component of the plan had been eliminated. Without that follow-up, the researchers, and readers, would have been led to inaccurate conclusions regarding the relative importance of the financial component. Similarly, a longitudinal field study of the impact of work teams on manufacturing performance (Banker, Field, Schroeder, & Sinha, 1996) demonstrated that quality and productivity improved over time after the introduction of teams. More studies of communication and various forms of employee participation, such as Monge, Cozzens, and Contractor's (1992) over-time analyses of Scanlon plans, are needed.

Indeed, as this review has demonstrated, broadly speaking, more research on the communication determinants, corollaries, and outcomes of organization participation programs is needed. For example, efforts at implementing various forms of organizational involve-ment are often yoked communicatively to those organizations' mission statements. Ample research has underscored the problems surrounding communication of mission statements (e.g., Ackoff, 1987; Collins & Porras, 1991; Ledford, Wendenhof, & Strahley, 1995; Swales & Rogers, 1995), and Fairhurst, Jordan, and Neuwirth (1997) have offered preliminary evidence that communication about a company's mission statement is a function of an organizational member's information environment, level of work unit commitment, trust in management, and organizational role. To the degree that implementation of an organizational involvement program is yoked to the organization's mission statement, we hypothesize that the four variables identified by Fairhurst et al. also affect organizational members' communication surrounding involvement in participation programs.

More generally, and paralleling Lewis and Seibold's (1998) agenda for the study of communication and the implementation of planned organizational change, researchers interested in communication and organizational participation programs might profitably pursue answers to the following questions concerning (a) *formal* organizational communication efforts related to participation programs and (b) members' *informal* communication surrounding the programs. With regard to information dissemination, (a) how are these programs formally announced, and what channels are used to provide information about them? and (b) what meanings do members assign to these formal communications, with whom do they share these impressions informally, and what additional information is sought and from whom? In terms of persuasive communication, (a) what formal "campaign" tactics are used to engender involvement? and (b) are these messages met with informal support, neutrality, or resistance—and through what communicative means is collective response offered, if at all? Concerning social support, (a) what communicative efforts do organizations employ, if any, to monitor and to ease members' anxieties concerning new involvement programs? and (b) how are members' support and comforting informally communicated during the implementation of the programs? With regard to reward structures (whose effects on organizations, as we observed, need to be separated from the involvement programs with which they are combined—e.g., ESOPs), (a) what channels are most frequently used to communicate information concerning rewards? and (b) how do members' informal interactions concerning rewards affect involvement in, and outcomes of, organizational participation programs? Finally, in the area of roles and role relations, (a) what are the formal communication dynamics surrounding selection and socialization of involvement program members? and (b) through what informal processes do members adopt new roles associated with these programs, and what communicative influence is associated with their emergent status?

Scholarship on participation often has been concerned with *either* how its various forms are evidenced in practice *or* what it means as an ideal to be valued. As in notable exceptions (see Cheney, 1995, 1997; Stohl, 1993), more analyses are needed that examine how workplace participation is manifested in practice *and* discursively. To paraphrase a similar suggestion by Cheney, Straub, et al. (1998) with regard to research on democracy in the workplace, future empirical studies need to consider not only what practices *count* as participation but also what the *meanings* of participation are.

Scholars interested in participation and decision making must continue to examine the dialectical tension between participation and control identified by critical theorists (and apparent in their juxtaposition in preceding sections in this chapter). Alvesson (1993) has offered a cultural-ideological perspective for understanding labor processes through four frames: collective control, performance-related control, ideological control, and perceptual control. This approach compels analysis of the control of work in terms of the ideological framework in which work is achieved (i.e.,

respectively, these entail sense of community, norms for performance, values concerning importance, and perceptions of reality). Frameworks such as this encourage investigation of the ways in which communication functions in organizations, even in participatory forms, to provide, suppress, or distort members' voice (Putnam et al., 1996).

Finally, the reordering of the workplace, vis-à-vis downsizing, reengineering, and lean production, emphasizes not merely increased employee involvement but increased productivity, integrative coordination, and speed of performance (Rifkin, 1995). Communication researchers have formulated theoretical propositions concerning speed requirements, communication, and coordination in contemporary organizations—and their implications for employee participation (see Cushman & King, 1993), although considerable research is needed to test these claims. Perhaps more significant is the emphasis on advanced communication technology as an infrastructure for sustaining participation. Set against overarching debates concerning whether computer-mediated communication in the workplace will effect new democratic structures or more centralized control (e.g., Mantovani, 1994; Sclove, 1995; Sproull & Kiesler, 1991), the emerging realities are that network forms of organizing—involving high coordination among strong but ad hoc relationships—will become increasingly prevalent (Monge, 1995; Powell, 1990), that the communication media by which members participate in an organization can shape the nature and the extent of participation (Collins-Jarvis, 1997), and that one of the principal consequences of introducing new information technologies in organizations "has not been better communications, only faster misunderstandings" (Shulman, 1996, p. 367). Although there is a burgeoning literature linking organizational structures and new media (see Rice & Gattiker, Chapter 14, this volume) and mediated meetings in organizations (see Fulk & Collins-Jarvis, Chapter 16, this volume), considerably more research is required to understand the recursive relationships among communication technologies, organizational structuring, and specific forms of employee participation (Poole, Putnam, & Seibold, 1997; Seibold, 1998).

REFERENCES

Abrahamsson, B. (1977). *Bureaucracy or participation: The logic of organization.* Beverly Hills, CA: Sage.

Ackoff, R. L. (1987). Mission statements. *Planning Review, 15,* 30-31.

Ahlbrandt, R. S., Leana, C. R., & Murrell, A. J. (1992). Employee involvement programmes improve corporate performance. *Long Range Planning, 25*(5), 91-98.

Albrecht, T. L. (1988). Communication and personal control in empowering organizations. In J. A. Anderson (Ed.), *Communication yearbook 11* (pp. 380-390). Newbury Park, CA: Sage.

Alvesson, M. (1993). *Cultural perspectives on organizations.* Cambridge, UK: Cambridge University Press.

Alvesson, M., & Deetz, S. (1996). Critical theory and postmodern approaches to organizational studies. In S. R. Clegg, C. Hardy, & W. R. Nord (Eds.), *Handbook of organization studies* (pp. 191-217). London: Sage.

Ancona, D. G., & Caldwell, D. F. (1988). Beyond task and maintenance: Defining external functions in groups. *Group and Organization Studies, 13,* 468-494.

Ancona, D. G., & Caldwell, D. F. (1992). Bridging the boundary: External activity and performance in organizational teams. *Administrative Science Quarterly, 37,* 634-665.

Appelbaum, E., & Batt, R. (1994). *The new American workplace: Transforming work systems in the United States.* Ithaca, NY: Cornell University Press.

Bachrach, P., & Botwinick, A. (1992). *Power and empowerment: A radical theory of participatory democracy.* Philadelphia: Temple University Press.

Baloff, N., & Doherty, E. M. (1989). Potential pitfalls in employee participation. *Organizational Dynamics, 17*(3), 51-62.

Banker, R. D., Field, J. M., Schroeder, R. G., & Sinha, K. K. (1996). Impact of work teams on manufacturing performance: A longitudinal field study. *Academy of Management Journal, 39,* 867-890.

Barker, J. R. (1993). Tightening the iron cage: Concertive control in self-managing teams. *Administrative Science Quarterly, 38,* 408-437.

Barker, J. R. (1997). *The team makes the rules: Culture and control in self-managing teams.* Thousand Oaks, CA: Sage.

Barker, J. R., & Cheney, G. (1994). The concept and practices of discipline in contemporary organizational life. *Communication Monographs, 61,* 19-43.

Barker, J. R., Melville, C. W., & Pacanowsky, M. E. (1993). Self-directed teams at Xel: Changes in communication practices during a program of cultural transformation. *Journal of Applied Communication Research, 21,* 297-312.

Barker, J. R., & Tompkins, P. K. (1992, October). *Organizations, teams, control, and identification.* Paper presented at the University of Helsinki and the Helsinki University of Technology, Helsinki, Finland.

Barker, J. R., & Tompkins, P. K. (1994). Identification in the self-managing organization: Characteristics of target and tenure. *Human Communication Research, 21,* 223-240.

Barley, S. R. (1986). Technology as an occasion for structuring: Observations on CT scanners and the social order of radiology departments. *Administrative Science Quarterly, 31,* 78-108.

Beekun, R. I. (1989). Assessing the effectiveness of sociotechnical interventions: Antidote or fad? *Human Relations, 42,* 877-897.

Berggren, C. (1993). *Alternatives to lean production.* Ithaca, NY: Cornell University Press.

Berman, S. J., & Hellweg, S. A. (1989). Perceived supervisor communication competence and supervisor satisfaction as a function of quality circle participation. *Journal of Business Communication, 26,* 103-122.

Bernstein, P. (1982). Necessary elements for effective worker participation in decision-making. In F. Lindenfeld & J. Rothschild-Whitt (Eds.), *Workplace democracy and social change* (pp. 51-86). Boston: Porter Sargent.

Blasi, J. R., & Kruse, D. L. (1991). *The new owners: The mass emergence of employee ownership in public companies and what it means to American business.* New York: HarperCollins.

Blinder, A. S. (1990). Pay, participation, and productivity. *Brookings Review, 8*(1), 33-38.

Blumberg, M. (1980). Job switching in autonomous work groups: An exploratory study in a Pennsylvania coal mine. *Academy of Management Journal, 23,* 287-306.

Brockner, J., & Hess, T. (1986). Self-esteem and task performance in quality circles. *Academy of Management Journal, 29,* 617-623.

Bruning, N. S., & Liverpool, P. R. (1993). Membership in quality circles and participation in decision making. *Journal of Applied Behavioral Science, 29,* 76-95.

Buch, K. (1992). Quality circles and employee withdrawal behaviors: A cross-organizational study. *Journal of Applied Behavioral Science, 28,* 62-73.

Buchko, A. A. (1992). Employee ownership, attitudes, and turnover: An empirical assessment. *Human Relations, 45,* 711-733.

Bullock, R. J., & Lawler, E. E. (1984). Gainsharing: A few questions and fewer answers. *Human Resource Management, 23,* 23-40.

Bullock, R. J., & Tubbs, M. E. (1990). A case meta-analysis of gainsharing plans as organization development interventions. *Journal of Applied Behavioral Science, 26,* 383-404.

Burns, T., & Stalker, G. M. (1961). *The management of innovation* (2nd ed.). London: Tavistock.

Burzawa, S. (1992, July). Sharing financial info with employees: Three employee-owned firms tell how. *Employee Benefit Plan Review, 47*(1), 23-25.

Burzawa, S. (1993, August). Employee ownership = governance: Panel. *Employee Benefit Plan Review, 48*(2), 32-36.

Campion, M. A., Medsker, G. J., & Higgs, A. C. (1993). Relations between work group characteristics and effectiveness: Implications for designing effective work teams. *Personnel Psychology, 46,* 823-850.

Carnall, C. A. (1982). Semi-autonomous work groups and the social structure of the organization. *Journal of Management Studies, 19,* 277-294.

Castrogiovanni, G. J., & Macy, B. A. (1990). Organizational information-processing capabilities and degree of employee participation. *Group and Organization Studies, 15,* 313-336.

Cheney, G. (1995). Democracy in the workplace: Theory and practice from the perspective of communication. *Journal of Applied Communication Research, 23,* 167-200.

Cheney, G. (in press). Interpreting interpretive research: Toward perspectivism without relativism. In S. R. Corman & M. S. Poole (Eds.), *Paradigm dialogues in organizational communication.* New York: Guilford.

Cheney, G. (1997). The many meanings of "solidarity": The negotiation of values in the Mondragón worker-cooperative complex under pressure. In B. D. Sypher (Ed.), *Contemporary case studies in organizational communication* (2nd ed.). New York: Guilford.

Cheney, G. (1999). *Values at work: Employee participation meets market pressure at Mondragón.* Ithaca, NY: Cornell University Press.

Cheney, G., & Carroll, C. (1996, May). *Persons as objects in discourses in and about organizations.* Paper presented at the preconference The New Social Contract Between Individuals and Organizations, annual meeting of the International Communication Association, Chicago.

Cheney, G., Stohl, C., Dennis, M., & Harrison, T. M. (Eds.). (1998). Communication et democratic organisationnelle [Communication and organizational democracy]. *La revue Electronique de communication* [*The electronic journal of communication*], *8*(1).

Cheney, G., Straub, J., Speirs-Glebe, L., Stohl, C., DeGooyer, D., Whalen, S., Garvin-Doxas, K., & Carlone, D. (1998). Democracy, participation, and communication at work: A multi-disciplinary review. In M. E. Roloff (Ed.), *Communication yearbook 21* (pp. 35-91), Thousand Oaks, CA: Sage.

Clegg, S. (1983). Organizational democracy, power and participation. In C. Crouch & F. Heller (Eds.), *Organizational democracy and political processes* (pp. 3-34). New York: John Wiley.

Cole, R. E. (1985). The macropolitics of organizational change: A comparative analysis of the spread of small-group activities. *Administrative Science Quarterly, 30,* 560-585.

Collins, J. C., & Porras, J. I. (1991). Organizational vision and visionary organizations. *California Management Review, 34,* 30-52.

Collins-Jarvis, L. (1997). Participation and consensus in collective action organizations. *Journal of Applied Communication Research, 25,* 1-16.

Conger, J. A., & Kanungo, R. N. (1988). The empowerment process: Integrating theory and practice. *Academy of Management Review, 13,* 471-482.

Connors, J. L., & Romberg, T. A. (1991). Middle management and quality control: Strategies for obstructionism. *Human Organization, 50,* 61-65.

Conrad, C., & Ryan, M. (1985). Power, praxis, and self in organizational communication theory. In R. D. McPhee & P. K. Tompkins (Eds.), *Organizational communication: Traditional themes and new directions* (pp. 235-255). Beverly Hills, CA: Sage.

Contractor, N. S., & Eisenberg, E. M. (1990). Communication networks and new media in organizations. In C. Steinfield & J. Fulk (Eds.), *Organizations and communication technology* (pp. 145-174). Newbury Park, CA: Sage.

Contractor, N. S., & Seibold, D. R. (1993). Theoretical frameworks for the study of structuring processes in group decision support systems: Adaptive structuration theory and self-organizing systems theory. *Human Communication Research, 19,* 528-563.

Cooke, W. N. (1989). Improving productivity and quality through collaboration. *Industrial Relations, 28,* 299-319.

Cooper, C. L., Dyck, B., & Frohlich, N. (1992). Improving the effectiveness of gainsharing: The role of fairness and participation. *Administrative Science Quarterly, 37,* 471-490.

Cordery, J. L., Mueller, W. S., & Smith, L. M. (1991). Attitudinal and behavioral effects of autonomous group working: A longitudinal field study. *Academy of Management Journal, 34,* 464-476.

Cotter, J. J. (1983). *Designing organizations that work: An open sociotechnical systems approach.* Cambridge, MA: J. J. Cotter and Associates.

Cotton, J. L. (1993). *Employee involvement: Methods for improving performance and work attitudes.* Newbury Park, CA: Sage.

Cotton, J. L., Vollrath, D. A., Froggatt, K. L., Lengnick-Hall, M. L., & Jennings, K. R. (1988). Employee participation: Diverse forms and different outcomes. *Academy of Management Review, 13,* 8-22.

Cotton, J. L., Vollrath, D. A., Lengnick-Hall, M. L., & Froggatt, K. L. (1990). Fact: The form of participation does matter—A rebuttal to Leana, Locke, and Schweiger. *Academy of Management Review, 15,* 147-153.

Cummings, T. G. (1978). Self-regulating work groups: A socio-technical synthesis. *Academy of Management Review, 3,* 625-634.

Cushman, D. P., & King, S. S. (1993). High-speed management: A revolution in organizational communication in the 1990s. In S. A. Deetz (Ed.), *Communication yearbook 16* (pp. 209-236). Newbury Park, CA: Sage.

Dachler, H. P., & Wilpert, B. (1978). Conceptual dimensions and boundaries of participation in organizations: A critical evaluation. *Administrative Science Quarterly, 23,* 1-39.

Deetz, S. (1992). *Democracy in an age of corporate colonization.* Albany: State University of New York Press.

Deetz, S. (1994, November). *Economic and political contexts for organizational democracy.* Paper presented at the annual meeting of the Speech Communication Association, New Orleans, LA.

Deetz, S. A., & Kersten, A. (1983). Critical models of interpretive research. In L. L. Putnam & M. E. Pacanowsky (Eds.), *Communication and organizations: An interpretive approach* (pp. 147-171). Beverly Hills, CA: Sage.

DeBettignies, C. W. (1989). Improving organization-wide teamwork through gainsharing. *National Productivity Review, 8,* 287-294.

Denison, D. R., Hart, S. L., & Kahn, J. A. (1996). From chimneys to cross-functional teams: Developing and validating a diagnostic model. *Academy of Management Journal, 39,* 1005-1023.

DeSanctis, G., & Poole, M. S. (1997). Transitions in teamwork in new organizational forms. *Advances in Group Processes, 14,* 157-176.

DeToro, I. J. (1987). Quality circles and the techniques of creativity: A case history. *Journal of Creative Behavior, 21,* 137-140.

Doherty, E. M., Nord, W. R., & McAdams, J. L. (1989). Gainsharing and organization development: A productive synergy. *Journal of Applied Behavioral Science, 25,* 209-229.

Drago, R. (1988). Quality circle survival: An exploratory analysis. *Industrial Relations, 27,* 336-351.

Efraty, D., & Sirgy, M. J. (1990). The effects of quality of working life (QWL) on employee behavioral responses. *Social Indicators Research, 22,* 31-47.

Eijnatten, F. M. (1993). *The paradigm that changed the workplace.* Stockholm: Swedish Center for Working Life.

Eisenberg, E. M., Monge, P. R., & Miller, K. I. (1983). Involvement in communication networks as a predic-

tor of organizational commitment. *Human Communication Research, 10,* 179-201.

Ellerman, D. (1990). *The democratic worker-owned firm: A new model for East and West.* Boston: Unwin Hyman.

Ellinger, C., & Nissen, B. (1987). A case study of a failed QWL program: Implications for labor education. *Labor Studies Journal, 11*(3), 195-219.

Emery, F. E., & Trist, E. L. (1965). The causal texture of organizational environments. *Human Relations, 18,* 21-32.

ESOP brings change in corporate culture. (1992, July). *Employee Benefit Plan Review, 47*(1), 25-26.

ESOPs, employee ownership evolve. (1993, August). *Employee Benefit Plan Review, 48*(2), 28-30.

Fairhurst, G. T. (1993). Echoes of the vision: When the rest of the organization talks total quality. *Management Communication Quarterly, 6,* 331-371.

Fairhurst, G. T., Green, S., & Courtright, J. (1995). Inertial forces and the implementation of a socio-technical systems approach: A communication study. *Organization Science, 6,* 168-185.

Fairhurst, G. T., Jordan, J. M., & Neuwirth, K. (1997). Why are we here? Managing the meaning of an organizational mission statement. *Journal of Applied Communication Research, 25,* 243-263.

Fairhurst, G. T., & Wendt, R. F. (1993). The gap in total quality: A commentary. *Management Communication Quarterly, 6,* 441-451.

Fisher, K. (1993). *Leading self-directed work teams.* New York: McGraw-Hill.

French, J. L. (1987). Perspectives on employee stock ownership: Financial investment of mechanism of control? *Academy of Management Review, 12,* 427-435.

Frey, L. R. (1995). Magical elixir or what the top tells the middle to do to the bottom? The promises and paradoxes of facilitating work teams for promoting organizational change and development. In R. Cesaria & P. Shockley-Zalabak (Eds.), *Organization means communication: Making the organizational communication concept relevant to practice* (pp. 199-215). Rome: Sipi Editore.

Gersick, C. J. G. (1988). Time and transition in work teams: Toward a new model of group development. *Academy of Management Journal, 31,* 9-41.

Glaser, H. (1994). *Structure and struggle in egalitarian groups: Reframing the problems of time emotion and inequality as defining characteristics.* Unpublished Ph.D. dissertation, University of Illinois at Urbana–Champaign.

Glaser, S. R. (1994). Teamwork and communication: A three-year case study of change. *Management Communication Quarterly, 7,* 282-296.

Glew, D. J., O'Leary-Kelly, A. M., Griffin, R. W., & Van Fleet, D. D. (1995). Participation in organizations: A preview of the issues and proposed framework for future analysis. *Journal of Management, 21*, 395-421.

Goll, I. (1991). Environment, corporate ideology, and employee involvement programs. *Industrial Relations, 30*, 138-149.

Gowen, C. R., III. (1990). Gainsharing programs: An overview of history and research. *Journal of Organizational Behavior Management, 11*(2), 77-99.

Graham-Moore, B. E., & Ross, T. L. (Eds.). (1983). *Productivity gainsharing.* Englewood Cliffs, NJ: Prentice Hall.

Greenbaum, H. H., Kaplan, I. T., & Metlay, W. (1988). Evaluation of problem-solving groups: The case of quality circle programs. *Group and Organization Studies, 13*, 133-147.

Greenbaum, H. H., & Query, J. L. (1999). Communication in organizational work groups: A review and synthesis of natural work group studies. In L. R. Frey, D. S. Gouran, & M. S. Poole (Eds.), *The handbook of group communication theory and research* (pp. 539-564). Thousand Oaks, CA: Sage.

Greenberg, E. S. (1980). Participation in industrial decision making and work satisfaction: The case of producer cooperatives. *Social Science Quarterly, 60*, 551-569.

Greenberg, J. (1990). Organizational justice: Yesterday, today, and tomorrow. *Journal of Management, 16*, 399-432.

Greenberg, J. (1996). *The quest for justice on the job: Essays and experiments.* Thousand Oaks, CA: Sage.

Grenier, G. J. (1988). *Inhuman relations: Quality circles and anti-unionism in American industry.* Philadelphia: Temple University Press.

Guzzo, R. A., & Dickson, M. W. (1996). Teams in organizations: Recent research on performance and effectiveness. *Annual Review of Psychology, 47*, 307-340.

Guzzo, R. A., Jette, R. D., & Katzell, R. A. (1985). The effects of psychologically based intervention programs on worker productivity: A meta-analysis. *Personnel Psychology, 38*, 275-291.

Hackman, J. R. (1990). *Groups that work (and those that don't): Creating conditions for effective teamwork.* San Francisco: Jossey-Bass.

Hammer, T. H. (1988). New developments in profit sharing, gainsharing, and employee ownership. In J. P. Campbell, R. J. Campbell, & Associates (Eds.), *Productivity in organizations: New perspectives from industrial and organizational psychology* (pp. 328-366). San Francisco: Jossey-Bass.

Hanlon, S. C., Meyer, D. G., & Taylor, R. R. (1994). Consequences of gainsharing: A field experiment revisited. *Group & Organization Management, 19*, 87-111.

Hanlon, S. C., & Taylor, R. R. (1991). An examination of changes in work group communication behaviors following installation of a gainsharing plan. *Group and Organization Studies, 16*, 238-267.

Harrison, T. M. (1994). Communication and interdependence in democratic organizations. In S. A. Deetz (Ed.), *Communication yearbook 17* (pp. 247-274). Thousand Oaks, CA: Sage.

Hatcher, L., & Ross, T. L. (1991). From individual incentives to an organization-wide gainsharing plan: Effects on teamwork and product quality. *Journal of Organizational Behavior, 12*, 169-183.

Hatcher, L., Ross, T. L., & Collins, D. (1991). Attributions for participation and nonparticipation in gainsharing-plan involvement systems. *Group and Organization Studies, 16*, 25-43.

Herrick, N. Q. (1985). Parallel organizations in unionized settings: Implications for organizational research. *Human Relations, 38*, 963-981.

Hirokawa, R. Y., & Keyton, J. (1995). Perceived facilitators and inhibitors of effectiveness in organizational work teams. *Management Communication Quarterly, 8*, 424-446.

Hoerr, J. (1989, July 10). The payoff from teamwork. *Business Week*, pp. 56-62.

Jackson, S. E. (1983). Participation in decision making as a strategy for reducing job-related strain. *Journal of Applied Psychology, 68*, 3-19.

Jones, S. D., Powell, R., & Roberts, S. (1990-1991). Comprehensive measurement to improve assembly-line work group effectiveness. *National Productivity Review, 10*, 45-55.

Kanter, R. M. (1982). Dilemmas of managing participation. *Organizational Dynamics, 11*(1), 5-27.

Kanter, R. M. (1986). The new workforce meets the changing workplace: Strains, dilemmas, and contradictions in attempts to implement participative and entrepreneurial management. *Human Resource Management, 25*, 515-537.

Kanter, R. M., Stein, B. A., & Brinkerhoff, D. W. (1982). Building participatory democracy within a conventional corporation. In F. Lindenfeld & J. Rothschild-Whitt (Eds.), *Workplace democracy and social change* (pp. 371-382). Boston: Porter Sargent.

Katz, A. J., Laughlin, P., & Wilson, J. (1990, December). Views on self-directed workteams from the line to the front office. *Journal for Quality and Participation*, pp. 48-51.

Katzenbach, J. R., & Smith, D. K. (1993). *The wisdom of teams.* Boston: Harvard Business School Press.

Kaufman, R. T. (1992). The effects of Improshare on productivity. *Industrial and Labor Relations Review, 45*, 311-322.

Kavcic, B., & Tannenbaum, A. S. (1981). A longitudinal study of the distribution of control in Yugoslav organizations. *Human Relations, 34*, 397-417.

Kemp, N. J., Wall, T. D., Clegg, C. W., & Cordery, J. L. (1983). Autonomous work groups in a greenfield site: A comparative study. *Journal of Occupational Psychology, 56*, 271-288.

Klein, K. J. (1987). Employee stock ownership and employee attitudes: A test of three models. *Journal of Applied Psychology, 72,* 319-332.

Kochan, T. A., Katz, H. C., & Mower, N. R. (1984). *Worker participation and American unions.* Kalamazoo, MI: W. E. Upjohn Institute for Employment Research.

Koopman, P. L., Drenth, P. J. D., Bus, F. B. M., Kruyswijk, A. J., & Wierdsma, A. F. M. (1981). Content, process, and effects of participative decision making on the shop floor: Three cases in the Netherlands. *Human Relations, 34,* 657-676.

Kornbluh, H. (1984). Workplace democracy and quality of worklife: Problems and prospects. *Annals of the American Academy of Political and Social Science, 473,* 88-95.

Lawler, E. E. (1986). *High-involvement management.* San Francisco: Jossey-Bass.

Lawler, E. E. (1988). Gainsharing theory and research: Findings and future directions. In W. A. Pasmore & R. W. Woodman (Eds.), *Research in organizational change and development* (Vol. 2, pp. 323-344). Greenwich, CT: JAI.

Lawler, E. E. (1990). The new plant revolution revisited. *Organizational Dynamics, 19*(2), 5-15.

Lawler, E. E. (1991). The new plant approach: A second generation approach. *Organizational Dynamics, 20*(1), 5-14.

Lawler, E. E. (1995). *Creating high-performance organizations.* San Francisco: Jossey-Bass.

Lawler, E. E. (1999). Employee involvement makes a difference. *Journal for Quality and Participation, 22*(5), 18-20.

Lawler, E. E., & Mohrman, S. A. (1987). Quality circles: After the honeymoon. *Organizational Dynamics, 15*(4), 42-54.

Lawler, E. E., Mohrman, S. A., & Ledford, G. E., Jr. (1992). *Employee involvement and total quality management: Practices and results in Fortune 1000 companies.* San Francisco: Jossey-Bass.

Leana, C. R. (1987). Power relinquishment versus power sharing: Theoretical clarification and empirical comparison of delegation and participation. *Journal of Applied Psychology, 72,* 228-233.

Leana, C. R., Ahlbrandt, R. S., & Murrell, A. J. (1992). The effects of employee involvement programs on unionized workers' attitudes, perceptions, and preferences in decision making. *Academy of Management Journal, 35,* 861-873.

Leana, C. R., & Florkowski, G. W. (1992). Employee involvement programs: Integrating psychological theory and management practice. In G. R. Ferris & K. M. Rowland (Eds.), *Research in personnel and human resources management* (Vol. 10, pp. 233-270). Greenwich, CT: JAI.

Leana, C. R., Locke, E. A., & Schweiger, D. M. (1990). Fact and fiction in analyzing research on participative decision making: A critique of Cotton, Vollrath, Froggatt, Lengnick-Hall, and Jennings. *Academy of Management Review, 15,* 137-146.

Ledford, G. E., Lawler, E. E., & Mohrman, S. A. (1988). The quality circle and its variations. In J. P. Campbell, R. J. Campbell, & Associates (Eds.), *Productivity in organizations: New perspectives from industrial and organizational psychology* (pp. 255-294). San Francisco: Jossey-Bass.

Ledford, G. E., Wendenhof, J. R., & Strahley, J. T. (1995). Realizing a corporate philosophy. *Organizational Dynamics, 23,* 5-19.

Levine, D. I., & Tyson, L. D. (1990). Participation, productivity, and the firm's environment. In A. S. Blinder (Ed.), *Paying for productivity: A look at the evidence* (pp. 183-243). Washington, DC: Brookings Institution.

Levine, J. M., & Moreland, R. L. (1990). Progress in small group research. *Annual Review of Psychology, 41,* 585-634.

Lewis, L. K., & Seibold, D. R. (1993). Innovation modification during intra-organizational adoption. *Academy of Management Review, 18,* 322-354.

Lewis, L. K., & Seibold, D. R. (1996). Communication during intraorganizational innovation adoption: Predicting users' behavioral coping responses to innovations in organizations. *Communication Monographs, 63,* 131-157.

Lewis, L. K., & Seibold, D. R. (1998). Reconceptualizing organizational change implementation as a communication problem: A review of literature and research agenda. In M. E. Roloff (Ed.), *Communication yearbook 21* (pp. 93-151). Thousand Oaks, CA: Sage.

Locke, E. A., & Schweiger, D. M. (1979). Participation in decision-making: One more look. In B. M. Staw (Ed.), *Research in organizational behavior* (Vol. 1, pp. 265-339). Greenwich, CT: JAI.

Long, R. J. (1981). The effects of formal employee participation in ownership and decision making on perceived and desired patterns of organizational influence: A longitudinal study. *Human Relations, 34,* 847-876.

Long, R. J. (1982). Worker ownership and job attitudes: A field study. *Industrial Relations, 21,* 196-215.

Magjuka, R. J. (1989). Participative systems: Toward a technology of design. *Research in the Sociology of Organizations, 7,* 79-115.

Magjuka, R. J. (1991). Examining barriers to integrating EIP into daily operations. *National Productivity Review, 10,* 327-337.

Magjuka, R. J., & Baldwin, T. T. (1991). Team-based employee involvement programs: Effects of design and administration. *Personnel Psychology, 44,* 793-812.

Mantovani, G. (1994). Is computer-mediated communication intrinsically apt to enhance democracy in organizations? *Human Relations, 47,* 45-62.

Manz, C. C. (1986). Self-leadership: Toward an expanded theory of self-influence process in organizations. *Academy of Management Review, 11,* 585-600.

Manz, C. C. (1992). Self-leading work teams: Moving beyond self-management myths. *Human Relations, 45,* 1119-1140.

Manz, C. C., & Angle, H. (1986). Can group self-management mean a loss of personal control: Triangulating a paradox. *Group and Organization Studies, 11,* 309-334.

Manz, C. C., Keating, D. E., & Donnellon, A. (1990). Preparing for an organizational change to employee self-management: The managerial transition. *Organizational Dynamics, 19*(2), 15-26.

Manz, C. C., & Sims, H. P. (1982). The potential for "groupthink" in autonomous work groups. *Human Relations, 35,* 773-784.

Manz, C. C., & Sims, H. P. (1984). Searching for the "unleader": Organizational member views on leading self-managed groups. *Human Relations, 37,* 409-424.

Manz, C. C., & Sims, H. P. (1987). Leading workers to lead themselves: The external leadership of self-managing work teams. *Administrative Science Quarterly, 32,* 106-128.

Margulies, N., & Black, S. (1987). Perspectives on the implementation of participative approaches. *Human Resource Management, 26,* 385-412.

Marks, M. L., Mirvis, P. H., Hackett, E. J., & Grady, J. F. (1986). Employee participation in a quality circle program: Impact on quality of work life, productivity, and absenteeism. *Journal of Applied Psychology, 71,* 61-69.

Marsh, R. M. (1992). The difference between participation and power in Japanese factories. *Industrial and Labor Relations Review, 45,* 250-257.

Marshall, A. A., & Stohl, C. (1993). Participating as participation: A network approach. *Communication Monographs, 60,* 137-157.

Mason, R. M. (1982). *Participatory and workplace democracy.* Carbondale: Southern Illinois University Press.

McWhirter, D. A. (1991). Employee stock ownership plans in the United States. In C. Rosen & K. M. Young (Eds.), *Understanding employee ownership* (pp. 43-73). Ithaca, NY: ILR.

Miller, C. S., & Schuster, M. (1987a). A decade's experience with the Scanlon plan: A case study. *Journal of Occupational Behavior, 8,* 167-173.

Miller, C. S., & Schuster, M. (1987b). Gainsharing plans: A comparative analysis. *Organizational Dynamics, 16*(1), 44-67.

Miller, K. I., & Monge, P. R. (1986). Participation, satisfaction, and productivity: A meta-analytic review. *Academy of Management Journal, 29,* 727-753.

Miller, K. I., & Monge, P. R. (1987). The development and test of a system of organizational participation and allocation. In M. L. McLaughlin (Ed.), *Commu-*

nication yearbook 10 (pp. 431-455). Newbury Park, CA: Sage.

Miller, R. W., & Prichard, F. N. (1992). Factors associated with workers' inclination to participate in an employee program. *Group & Organization Management, 17,* 414-430.

Mintzberg, H. (1991). The effective organization: Forces and forms. *Sloan Management Review, 32*(2), 54-67.

Mohrman, S. A., Ledford, G. E., Lawler, E. E., & Mohrman, A. M. (1986). Quality of worklife and employee involvement. In C. L. Cooper & I. Robertson (Eds.), *International review of industrial and organizational psychology* (pp. 189-216). New York: John Wiley.

Monge, P. R. (1995). Global network organizations. In R. Cesaria & P. Shockley-Zalabak (Eds.), *Organization means communication: Making the organizational communication concept relevant to practice* (pp. 131-151). Rome: Sipi Editore.

Monge, P. R., Cozzens, M. D., & Contractor, N. S. (1992). Communication and motivational predictors of the dynamics of organizational innovations. *Organization Science, 3,* 250-274.

Monge, P. R., & Eisenberg, E. M. (1987). Emergent communication networks. In F. M. Jablin, L. L. Putnam, K. H. Roberts, & L. W. Porter (Eds.), *Handbook of organizational communication: An interdisciplinary perspective* (pp. 304-342). Newbury Park, CA: Sage.

Monge, P. R., & Miller, K. I. (1988). Participative processes in organizations. In G. M. Goldhaber & G. A. Barnett (Eds.), *Handbook of organizational communication* (pp. 213-229). Norwood, NJ: Ablex.

Mumby, D. K. (1988). *Communication and power in organizations: Discourse ideology and domination.* Norwood, NJ: Ablex.

Mumby, D., & Putnam, L. (1992). The politics of emotion: A feminist reading of bounded rationality. *Academy of Management Review, 17,* 465-486.

Mumby, D., & Stohl, C. (1992). Power and discourse in organization studies: Absence and dialectic of control. *Discourse & Society, 2,* 313-332.

Nadler, D. A., & Lawler, E. E. (1983). Quality of work life: Perspectives and directions. *Organizational Dynamics, 11*(3), 20-30.

Neuman, G. A. (1991). Autonomous work group selection. *Journal of Business and Psychology, 6,* 283-291.

Nurick, A. J. (1982). Participation in organizational change: A longitudinal field study. *Human Relations, 35,* 413-430.

Ondrack, D. A., & Evans, M. G. (1987). Job enrichment and job satisfaction in greenfield and redesign QWL sites. *Group and Organization Studies, 12,* 5-22.

O'Reilly, C. A., Chatman, J. A., & Anderson, J. C. (1987). Message flow and decision making. In F. M. Jablin, L. L. Putnam, K. H. Roberts, & L. W. Porter (Eds.), *Handbook of organizational communication:*

An interdisciplinary perspective (pp. 600-623). Newbury Park, CA: Sage.

Pacanowsky, M. (1988). Communication in the empowering organization. In J. A. Anderson (Ed.), *Communication yearbook 11* (pp. 356-379). Newbury Park, CA: Sage.

Parker, M. (1985). *Inside the circle: A union guide to QWL*. Boston: South End.

Pasmore, W., Francis, C., Haldeman, J., & Shani, A. (1982). Sociotechnical systems: A North American reflection on empirical studies of the seventies. *Human Relations, 35*, 1179-1204.

Paul, R. J., Ebadi, Y. M., & Dilts, D. A. (1987). Commitment in employee-owned firms: Involvement or entrapment? *Quarterly Journal of Business and Economics, 26*(4), 81-99.

Pearce, J. A., & Ravlin, E. C. (1987). The design and activation of self-regulating work groups. *Human Relations, 40*, 751-782.

Pearson, C. A. L. (1992). Autonomous workgroups: An evaluation at an industrial site. *Human Relations, 45*, 905-936.

Pierce, J. L., & Furo, C. A. (1990). Employee ownership: Implications for management. *Organizational Dynamics, 18*(3), 32-43.

Pierce, J. L., Rubenfeld, S. A., & Morgan, S. (1991). Employee ownership: A conceptual model of process and effects. *Academy of Management Review, 16*, 121-144.

Pettigrew, A. M. (1990). Longitudinal field research on change: Theory and practice. *Organization Science, 1*, 267-292.

Poole, M. S., & DeSanctis, G. (1990). Understanding the use of group decision support systems: The theory of adaptive structuration. In C. Steinfield & J. Fulk (Eds.), *Organizations and communication technology* (pp. 175-195). Newbury Park, CA: Sage.

Poole, M. S., Putnam, L. L., & Seibold, D. R. (1997). Organizational communication in the 21st century. *Management Communication Quarterly, 11*, 127-138.

Poole, M. S., Seibold, D. R., & McPhee, R. D. (1996). The structuration of group decisions. In R. Y. Hirokawa & M. S. Poole (Eds.), *Communication and group decision making* (pp. 114-146). Thousand Oaks, CA: Sage.

Powell, W. (1990). Neither market nor hierarchy: Network forms of organization. *Research in Organizational Behavior, 12*, 295-336.

Poza, E. J., & Markus, L. (1980). Success story: The team approach to work restructuring. *Organizational Dynamics, 8*(3), 3-25.

Putnam, L. L. (1982). Paradigms for organizational communication research: An overview and synthesis. *Western Journal of Speech Communication, 46*, 192-206.

Putnam, L. L. (1983). The interpretive perspective: An alternative to functionalism. In L. L. Putnam & M. E. Pacanowsky (Eds.), *Communication and organizations: An interpretive approach* (pp. 31-54). Beverly Hills, CA: Sage.

Putnam, L. L., Phillips, N., & Chapman, P. (1996). Metaphors of communication and organization. In S. R. Clegg, C. Hardy, & W. R. Nord (Eds.), *Handbook of organization studies* (pp. 375-408). London: Sage.

Putnam, L. L., & Stohl, C. (1990). Bona fide groups: A reconceptualization of groups in context. *Communication Studies, 41*, 248-265.

Rice, A. K. (1958). *Productivity and social organization: The Ahmedabad experiments*. London: Tavistock.

Rifkin, J. (1995). *The end of work*. Los Angeles: Jeremy Tarcher/Putnam.

Riley, P. (1983). A structurationist account of political culture. *Administrative Science Quarterly, 28*, 414-437.

Ritzer, G. (1993). *The McDonaldization of society*. Thousand Oaks, CA: Pine Forge.

Rosen, C. (1989). Ownership, motivation, and corporate performance: Putting ESOPs to work. In G. Kalish (Ed.), *ESOPs: The handbook of employee stock ownership plans* (pp. 271-289). Chicago: Probus.

Rosen, C. (1991). Employee ownership: Performance, prospects, and promise. In C. Rosen & K. M. Young (Eds.), *Understanding employee ownership* (pp. 1-42). Ithaca, NY: ILR.

Rosen, C. M., Klein, K. J., & Young, K. M. (1986). *Employee ownership in America: The equity solution*. Lexington, MA: Lexington Books.

Rosen, C. M., & Quarrey, M. (1987). How well is employee ownership working? *Harvard Business Review, 65*(5), 126-132.

Rothschild-Whitt, J., & Lindenfeld, F. (1982). Reshaping work: Prospects and problems of workplace democracy. In F. Lindenfeld & J. Rothschild-Whitt (Eds.), *Workplace democracy and social change* (pp. 1-18). Boston: Porter Sargent.

Russell, R. (1988). Forms and extent of employee participation in the contemporary United States. *Work and Occupations, 15*, 374-395.

Saavedra, R., & Kwun, S. (1993). Peer evaluation in self-managing work groups. *Journal of Applied Psychology, 78*, 450-462.

Schuster, M. (1984). The Scanlon plan: A longitudinal analysis. *Journal of Applied Behavioral Science, 20*, 23-38.

Schweiger, D. M., & Leana, C. R. (1986). Participation in decision making. In E. A. Locke (Ed.), *Generalizing from laboratory to field settings* (pp. 147-166). Lexington, MA: Lexington Books.

Sclove, R. E. (1995). *Democracy and technology*. New York: Guilford.

Seibold, D. R. (1995). Developing the "team" in a team managed organization: Group facilitation in a new-design plant. In L. Frey (Ed.), *Innovations in group facilitation: Applications in natural settings* (pp. 282-298). Cresskill, NJ: Hampton.

Seibold, D. R. (1998). Groups and organizations: Premises and perspectives. In J. S. Trent (Ed.), *Communication: View from the helm for the 21st century* (pp. 162-168). Needham Heights, MA: Allyn & Bacon.

Seibold, D. R., & Contractor, N. S. (1992). Issues for a theory of high-speed management. In S. A. Deetz (Ed.), *Communication yearbook 16* (pp. 237-246). Newbury Park, CA: Sage.

Shadur, M. A., Kienzle, R., & Rodwell, J. J. (1999). The relationship between organizational climate and employee perceptions of involvement. *Group & Organization Management, 24,* 479-503.

Shea, B. C. (1995). *Non-union grievance systems: The effects of procedural fairness, distributive fairness, outcome, and supervisor relationship on employee perceptions of organizational fairness and support.* Unpublished doctoral dissertation, University of California, Santa Barbara.

Shulman, A. D. (1996). Putting group information technology in its place: Communication and good work group performance. In S. R. Clegg, C. Hardy, & W. R. Nord (Eds.), *Handbook of organization studies* (pp. 357-374). London: Sage.

Sockell, D. (1985). Attitudes, behavior, and employee ownership: Some preliminary data. *Industrial Relations, 24,* 130-138.

Spector, P. E. (1986). Perceived control by employees: A meta-analysis of studies concerning autonomy and participation at work. *Human Relations, 39,* 1005-1016.

Sproull, L., & Kiesler, S. (1991). *Connections: New ways of working in the networked organization.* Cambridge, MA: MIT Press.

Steel, R. P., Jennings, K. R., & Lindsey, J. T. (1990). Quality circle problem solving and common cents: Evaluation study findings from a United States federal mint. *Journal of Applied Behavioral Science, 26,* 365-381.

Steel, R. P., & Lloyd, R. F. (1988). Cognitive, affective, and behavioral outcomes of participation in quality circles: Conceptual and empirical findings. *Journal of Applied Behavioral Science, 24,* 1-17.

Steel, R. P., Mento, A. J., Dilla, B. L., Ovalle, N. K., & Lloyd, R. F. (1985). Factors influencing the success and failure of two quality circle programs. *Journal of Management, 11,* 99-119.

Steel, R. P., & Shane, G. S. (1986). Evaluation research on quality circles: Technical and analytical implications. *Human Relations, 39,* 449-468.

Stevens, M. J., & Campion, M. A. (1994). The knowledge, skill, and ability requirements for teamwork: Implications for human resource management. *Journal of Management, 20,* 503-530.

Stohl, C. (1986). Quality circles and changing patterns of communication. In M. McLaughlin (Ed.), *Com-*

munication yearbook 9 (pp. 511-531). Beverly Hills, CA: Sage.

Stohl, C. (1987). Bridging the parallel organization: A study of quality circle effectiveness. In M. L. McLaughlin (Ed.), *Communication yearbook 10* (pp. 416-430). Newbury Park, CA: Sage.

Stohl, C. (1989). Understanding quality circles: A communication network perspective. In B. Dervin, L. Grossberg, B. O'Keefe, & E. Wartella (Eds.), *Rethinking communication: Vol. 2. Paradigm exemplars* (pp. 346-360). Newbury Park, CA: Sage.

Stohl, C. (1993a). European managers' interpretations of participation: A semantic network analysis. *Human Communication Research, 20,* 97-117.

Stohl, C. (1993b). International organizing and organizational communication. *Journal of Applied Communication Research, 21,* 377-384.

Stohl, C. (1995). Paradoxes of participation. In R. Cesaria & P. Shockley-Zalabak (Eds.), *Organization means communication: Making the organizational communication concept relevant to practice* (pp. 199-215). Rome: Sipi Editore.

Stohl, C., & Jennings, K. (1988). Volunteerism and voice in quality circles. *Western Journal of Speech Communication, 52,* 238-251.

Strauss, G. (1982). Workers' participation in management: An international perspective. In L. L. Cummings & B. Staw (Eds.), *Research in organizational behavior* (Vol. 4, pp. 173-265). Greenwich, CT: JAI.

Sundstrom, E., DeMeuse, K. P., & Futrell, D. (1990). Work teams: Applications and effectiveness. *American Psychologist, 45,* 120-133.

Swales, J. M., & Rogers, P. S. (1995). Discourse and the projection of corporate culture: The mission statement. *Discourse & Society, 6,* 223-242.

Swezey, R., & Salas, E. (1992). *Teams: Their training and performance.* Norwood, NJ: Ablex.

Taplin, P. T. (1989, August). Successful ESOPs include participatory management. *Employee Benefit Plan Review, 44*(2), 52-54.

Tesluk, P. E., Vance, R. J., & Mathieu, J. E. (1999). Examining employee involvement in the context of participative work environments. *Group & Organization Management, 24,* 271-299.

Thomas, J. G., & Griffin, R. W. (1989). The power of social information in the workplace. *Organizational Dynamics, 18*(2), 63-75.

Thomas, K. W., & Velthouse, B. A. (1990). Cognitive elements of empowerment: An "interpretive" model of intrinsic task motivation. *Academy of Management Review, 15,* 666-681.

Tompkins, P. K., & Cheney, G. (1985). Communication and unobtrusive control in contemporary organizations. In R. D. McPhee & P. K. Tompkins (Eds.), *Organizational communication: Traditional themes and new directions* (pp. 179-210). Beverly Hills, CA: Sage.

Tosçano, D. J. (1983). Toward a typology of employee ownership. *Human Relations, 36,* 581-602.

Turpin-Forster, S. C. (1989). Communicating the message of employee stock ownership. In G. Kalish (Ed.), *ESOPs: The handbook of employee stock ownership plans* (pp. 253-269). Chicago: Probus.

Vandenberg, R. J., Richardson, H. A., & Eastman, L. J. (1999). The impact of high-involvement work processes on organizational effectiveness: A second-order latent variable approach. *Group & Organization Management, 24,* 300-339.

Van Fleet, D. D., & Griffin, R. W. (1989). Quality circles: A review and suggested further directions. In C. L. Cooper & I. Robertson (Eds.), *International review of industrial and organizational psychology* (pp. 213-233). New York: John Wiley.

Veiga, J. F., & Yanouzas, J. N. (1991). Differences between American and Greek managers in giving up control. *Organization Studies, 12,* 95-108.

Versteeg, A. (1990). Self-directed work teams yield long-term benefits. *Journal of Business Strategy, 11,* 9-12.

Wagner, J. A. (1994). Participation's effects on performance and satisfaction: A reconsideration of research evidence. *Academy of Management Review, 19,* 312-330.

Wagner, J. A., & Gooding, R. Z. (1987a). Effects of societal trends on participation research. *Administrative Science Quarterly, 32,* 241-262.

Wagner, J. A., & Gooding, R. Z. (1987b). Shared influence and organizational behavior: A meta-analysis of situational variables expected to moderate participation-outcome relationships. *Academy of Management Journal, 30,* 524-541.

Wall, T. D., Kemp, N. J., Jackson, P. R., & Clegg, C. W. (1986). Outcomes of autonomous workgroups: A long-term field experiment. *Academy of Management Journal, 29,* 280-304.

Walton, R. E. (1977). Work innovations at Topeka: After six years. *Journal of Applied Behavioral Science, 13,* 422-433.

Walton, R. E. (1985). From control to commitment: Transformation of workforce management strategies in the United States. In K. B. Clark, R. H. Hayes, & C. Lorez (Eds.), *The uneasy alliance: Managing the productivity-technology dilemma.* Boston: Harvard Business School Press.

Walton, R. E., & Hackman, J. R. (1986). Groups under contrasting management strategies. In P. S. Goodman et al. (Eds.), *Designing effective work groups* (pp. 168-201). San Francisco: Jossey-Bass.

Welbourne, T. M., & Gomez-Mejia, L. R. (1995). Gainsharing: A critical review and a future research agenda. *Journal of Management, 21,* 559-609.

Wellins, R. S., Byham, W. C., & Wilson, J. M. (1991). *Empowered teams: Creating self-directed work groups that improve quality, productivity, and participation.* San Francisco: Jossey-Bass.

Yates, J., & Orlikowski, W. J. (1992). Genres of organizational communication: An approach to studying communication and media. *Academy of Management Review, 17,* 299-326.

Young, K. M. (1990). Managing an employee ownership company. In K. M. Young (Ed.), *The expanding role of ESOPs in public companies* (pp. 159-188). Westport, CT: Quorum.

Young, K. M. (1991). Theory O: The ownership theory of management. In C. Rosen & K. M. Young (Eds.), *Understanding employee ownership* (pp. 108-135). Ithaca, NY: ILR.

18

Learning in Organizations

KARL E. WEICK

SUSAN J. ASHFORD
University of Michigan

Organizations often discover faulty learning when they experience failures on a large or small scale. Here are three examples of failure in communication that imply faulty prior learning and the necessity for further learning:

1. In response to a warning of enemy attack, which later proved to be false, a base commander is ordered to "be prepared for possible launch of your interceptors." The communiqué is heard as "launch interceptors!" The base commander does.

2. An aircraft is landing too low to make it to the runway, and the pilot asks the engineer for "takeoff power" so the plane can go around and try again. The engineer hears the request as "take off power" so he reduces power, and the aircraft crashes.

3. A ship commander facing a potentially hostile ship that is closing on his position says, "I'm not going to shoot first, but if he fires one then I'll fire one." "Fire One!" commands an ensign (examples are paraphrased from Sagan, 1993, pp. 241-242).

Each of these examples represents communication and interaction in an organizational context with unintended consequences and inadequate learning. Something needs to be understood more fully and corrected, which is not all that easy since communication and learning are intertwined. For example, these three misunderstandings could be seen as a problem of poor language use within a speech community. The specific problem common to these three examples is an inadequate differentiation between messages to prepare and messages to execute. The current language is poor because it is equivocal. The same word has more than one meaning. Time is used up trying to discover which meaning is intended, and different frames of reference generate different presumptions of intention.

Learning can occur in such systems, however. In the case of "takeoff power," for example, that phrase has now been dropped and the less equivocal phrase "maximum power" has been substituted. That substitution represents learning, but it also implies additional linkages between communication and learning. There are hints that richer language generates fewer problems, that languages create phenomena as well as represent them, that learning occurs when people change frames of reference as well as when they reaffirm them, that words and interactions can inhibit learning, and that words are central to the learning that occurs when people are socialized into an organizational culture.

Our goal in this chapter is to describe the nature of learning as it unfolds in organizational settings. We want to develop a picture of the individual and interpersonal processes inherent in organizational learning. Our intent is not to present a formal review of the literature on organizational learning (those interested in such reviews should see Cohen & Sproull, 1996; Huber, 1991; Levitt & March, 1988; Miller, 1996). Rather, we hope to highlight the essential elements of learning as it takes place in organizational settings that are sensitive to variations in communication.

This undertaking, it should be noted, is new to the handbook. The topic of organizational learning does not appear in the first edition of this handbook, there is no chapter by that name, and the phrase "organizational learning" is not in the index. The same thing might happen in the third edition. But for the moment, our purpose, in this second edition, is to explore whether scholars of organizational communication are better off with the concept "organizational learning" than they are without it. While this may be an open question, we believe that without doubt organizational learning scholars are better off considering communication issues. Indeed, we see communication as central to learning at the organizational level. This suggests an important role for communication research in the unfolding empirical effort to gain insights into organizational learning. One goal for this chapter is to highlight potential contributions in order to prompt research in this area.

There is no question that learning is a hot topic as of this edition. It is discussed in special issues of both practitioner (*Organizational Dynamics* in 1993) and researcher (*Organization Science* in 1991) journals, and the journal *Management Learning*, now in its 31st volume, continues to publish an increasing number of influential and significant contributions. Organizational learning is reviewed in the prestigious *Annual Review of Sociology* (Levitt & March, 1988), reviews of reviews are beginning to appear (e.g., Dodgson, 1993), proceedings of conferences devoted to learning have been published (Crossan, Lane, Rush, & White, 1993), and traditional concepts of organizational development and systems theory are being repackaged and sold as if they had been about learning all along (Senge, 1990).

To complement these existing resources, we intend to show how a communication perspective can deepen our understanding of the process of organizational learning. To do this we will develop the following argument. First, we define *organizational learning* by positioning it as an aspect of culture grounded in individual know-how. With that overview in place, we highlight selected properties of individual learning such as punctuation, reflection, action, categorization, and extrapolation. We then show how these properties are modified by organizational contexts and pay special attention to conflict, hierarchy, attribution, turnover, discontinuity, ambiguity, and speed. Next, we show how these organizational contexts are modified by language and communication processes. We conclude by examining a seemingly innocuous communication practice—NASA's use of "Monday Notes" as a communication system—and find that this practice has a powerful effect on learning through its effect on individuals and groups.

DEFINITIONS OF ORGANIZATIONAL LEARNING

Phenomena of organizational learning discussed could be subsumed under any one of the following three definitions. English and English (1958) argued that "the sign of learning is not a shift of response or performance as a consequence of a change in stimulus-situation or in motivation, but rather a shift in performance when the stimulus-situation and the motivation are essentially the same" (p. 289). This definition implies that learning occurs when an entity is able to respond differently to an identical stimulus over time. But as Weick (1991) demonstrated, these conditions rarely occur in organizations suggesting either that organizations don't learn or that their learning takes a different form. Furthermore, this definition seems to rule out strengthening of a response over time as an instance of learning (e.g., responding with more of the same to a constant stimulus). This definition also implies that learning should be difficult in ambiguous environments where stimuli are unclear and where action is necessary to create stimuli from which to learn. For these reasons, we see the English and English definition as problematic.

A second definition is offered by Weiss (1990): "Learning is a relatively permanent change in knowledge or skill produced by experience" (p. 172). However, the environments facing today's organization pose new challenges for this definition of learning. Specifically, in a rapidly changing world, how crucial is the permanent learning suggested by this definition? Are there instances where

such permanence might be a hindrance rather than an organizational benefit?

Finally Duncan and Weiss (1979), in a widely cited definition, proposed that learning is the "process within the organization by which knowledge about action-outcome relationships and the effect on the environment of these relationships is developed" (p. 84). This definition is attractive in that it highlights the theories of action and cause maps that are developed via a process of organizational learning. Knowledge, rather than any particular action pattern (same or new), is the outcome of learning. This suggests that inaction or continuing with the same action can be as much a reflection of learning as are new actions. Further, by giving action-outcome links center stage, this definition begins to point to organizational realities that should affect the learning process. In particular, Jaques (1989) has proposed that the link between actions and outcomes becomes more tenuous and more separated in time as one moves up the corporate hierarchy. Does this imply that learning will be more difficult at the upper levels of an organization? If action-outcome links become less directly observable as one moves up the organizational hierarchy, then do substitutes for direct observation and task feedback become more important to the learning process? What might those substitutes be?

While all three definitions are adequate, none of them portray learning in a way that incorporates communication as a core determinant. To do so, we can pursue Normann's (1985) intriguing suggestion that the flurry of interest in organizational culture was actually an interest in organizational learning. Normann (1985) states:

I would interpret the increasing interest in the concept of culture as really an increasing interest in organizational learning—in understanding and making conscious and effective as much as possible all the learning that has taken place in an organization. To be aware of culture is to come to know that which the organization has learned. Promoting awareness of culture within the organization increases the likelihood of subsequent learning. Thus, to be aware of culture is to increase the likelihood of learning. Only when the basic assumptions, beliefs, and success formulas are made conscious and visible do they become testable and open to reinforcement or modification. (p. 231)

The relevance of a culture perspective (e.g., Bantz, 1993) for communication scholars is that "culture has two absolutely crucial functions in any organization: It acts as a symbol and storage of past learning, and it works as an instrument to communicate this learning throughout the organization" (Normann, 1985, p. 23). While culture is changing continuously at the margin, at any point in time it represents the accepted ways of thinking and interpretations of reality. D'Andrade's description of culture underscores the importance of communication. Culture consists of "learned systems of meaning, communicated by means of natural language and other symbol systems, having representational, directive (task) and affective (socio-emotional) function, and capable of creating cultural entities and particular senses of reality" (D'Andrade, 1984, p. 116, cited in Barnett, 1988, p. 104).

To bring these descriptions of culture back to the topic of learning, we need to emphasize that a culture perspective is less about what happens in people's heads (e.g., the organization is a brain) and more about what happens between people and among their actions, practices, and narrative interpretations of practice (e.g., the organization is a tribe). The importance of action for a cultural perspective was implied by Duncan and Weiss's definition and is made explicit by Eisenberg and Goodall (1993):

An action is an interpretation of a situation and it sums up the actor's understanding of the culture as well as the actor's place in it. Everything an individual does and says is an action. An action is, therefore, a strategic performance within a culture that has called for or shaped that performance in some way. It is a strategy for dealing with news of the day by using the interpretive tools the culture has provided, and it is a performance enacted within a particular situation or context that is constructed within that culture. (p. 136)

Actions reflect an individual's learning. Actions also serve as cues to others regarding appropriate responses. Thus, actions—like cultures—both embody learning and promote learning, as is evident in Sitkin, Sutcliffe, and Weick's (1999) definition of *learning* as "a change in an organization's response repertoire" (p. 7-70).

To highlight action and practice is to foreground know-how (knowledge-informed performance improvement, i.e., practices, skills, and routines) and "know-that" (knowledge acquisition) as central content for learning (Tetlock, 1991, p. 31). A focus on action and practice also legitimizes trial and error as a fundamental sequence in learning. Actions and practices are subject to the sequence, trial-failure-learning-revision-retrial (von Hippel & Tyre, 1993, p. 4). Such a focus on action also helps us clarify that organizational learning can be unsuccessful as well as successful. That is, organizations sometimes can learn the wrong lesson.

Culture, communication, learning, and organization are brought together informally if we treat organizational learning as the

capacity of an organization to learn how to do what it does, where what it learns is possessed not only by individual members of the organization but by the aggregate itself. That is, when a group acquires the know-how associated with its ability to carry out its collective activities, that constitutes organizational learning. (Cook & Yanow, 1993, p. 378)

Stated more formally, organizational learning is the "acquiring, sustaining, or changing of intersubjective meanings through the artifactual vehicles of their expression and transmission and the collective actions of the group" (Cook & Yanow, 1993, p. 384).

The "artifactual vehicles" that carry the products of learning in the form of meanings are plentiful and diverse, as is evident in this description by Eisenberg and Goodall (1993):

> A culture is full of itself. That is, its values (always competing) are performed (Trujillo, 1985) and displayed (Goodall, 1990) *everywhere*—in symbols, language, stories, work routines, rituals, rites, advertisements, brochures, newsletters, parking lots, memos, cartoons, dress codes, office artifacts, and corporate histories. Thus, culture is not something an organization *has;* it is something an organization *is.* (p. 143)

Numbered among the key artifacts are the routines of a culture, which means that March's (1994) influential argument that rules and routines encode learning is included.

Three related definitional issues require attention before we explore individuals, contexts, and communication. The first deals with unlearning. There have been occasional efforts (e.g., Hedberg, 1981; Huber, 1991, pp. 104-105) to specify the dialectic of learning through conceptualization of its opposite, unlearning. Unlearning, indexed by the discarding of knowledge (Hedberg) or a decrease in the potential range of behaviors (Huber), has generated relatively little attention for reasons that seem fairly clear. Data suggest that there is some spontaneous loss of learning over time regardless of intervening activities (Estes, 1988, p. 383); rehearsal of any one behavior or routine necessarily reduces the time available to rehearse others' items, which means the unrehearsed tends to be unlearned. Data further suggest that the source of unlearning cannot unequivocally be pinned down to other learning that occurred before it and interfered proactively or occurred after it and interfered retroactively (Estes, 1988). If, to these relationships, we add the observation that most organizational learning is subject to intermittent reinforcement, which slows extinction; the observation that arousal tends to favor regression to and expression of older, more rehearsed actions; and finally the observation that there is continuous change, mean-

ing that antecedents are never literally the same, then we arrive at a composite picture in which newer learning overlays older learning, older learning is never fully forgotten, and learning is a perennial necessity since situations seldom repeat themselves. Hence, we concentrate on learning rather than unlearning in the belief that people in organizations distribute their attention in the same way.

The second definitional issue concerns the relationship between individual and organizational learning, an issue on which we find the thrust of Simon's (1991) argument to be persuasive. He proposed:

1. All learning takes place inside individual human heads.
2. An organization learns by the learning of its members or by the insertion of new members with new knowledge.
3. An important component of organizational learning is the transmission of information from one organizational member or group to another.
4. "Human learning in the context of an organization is very much influenced by the organization, has consequences for the organization, and produces phenomena at the organizational level that go beyond anything we could infer simply by observing learning processes in isolated individuals" (p. 126).

Of these four points, we feel the fourth is most useful and the first least useful. The first needlessly precludes the relational infrastructure of learning (e.g., Gergen, 1994; Wegner, 1987; Weick & Roberts, 1993). In the context of our definition here, individuals learn and they translate that learning into actions or routines. Their individual learning is influenced by others at the outset and is amended based on feedback from others. Individual learnings are also shared via verbal communication or by action patterns that send messages. They are shared in the new or altered cultural artifacts that manifest the new learning. Finally, individual learnings are collectively retained—in the memory of others and in the "organizational memory" (e.g., in files, standard operating procedures) (Walsh & Ungson, 1991). Thus, we believe that individual learning is both influenced by the collective (as represented by the culture, and the actions and communications of others), is transmitted to the collective, and is represented in the collective in the form of culture, action patterns (including coordinated actions), and standard operating procedures.

The third definitional issue concerns the relationship between learning and change. We want to make it clear that learning can be preservative as well as innovative. Cook and Yanow (1993, p. 384) show how people, in their case the craftsmen who make Powell flutes, learned to reaffirm existing patterns of coordination while experimenting with a new scale that threatened to undermine the distinctiveness of their product. The learning was subtle. Cook and Yanow (1993) describe it this way:

> The organization learns how to maintain the style and quality of its flutes through the particular skills, character, and quirks of a new individual. The organization engages in a dynamic process of maintaining the norms and practices that assure the constancy of its product. This is learning in a sense quite different from change-oriented learning: it is active reaffirmation or maintenance of the know-how that the organization already possesses. (pp. 381-382)

Notice two things. First, the organization is focused on what it does right, not on what it does wrong. This learning is not about the detection and correction of error but about things gone right and how to preserve them. Second, the organization learns to take on a new situation, not a new identity. People want to adopt a new innovation, in this case a new scale, yet remain who they are. It is not mandatory that both situations and identities change if learning is to occur. Observers who are mindful of culture and know-how as incentives for participation and as sources of competitive advantage are unlikely to equate

persistence with poor learning. Instead, they will entertain the hypothesis that persistent identity is a learned accomplishment in turbulent environments that lure firms toward entropy and the loss of distinctiveness.

To sum up this definitional overview, when people have experiences with the artifacts of an organization's culture or the artifacts of an organization's environment, they learn. They strengthen responses, they reaffirm the ways in which the artifacts fit together, they confront and temporarily resolve competing interpretations that arise from new coalitions or unsocialized newcomers, they wrestle with whether to exploit what they already know or to explore new possibilities. They undertake trials of new behaviors. These experiences are organized around know-how (practices, routines), which suggests that knowledge acquisition (know-that) operates in the service of these routines.

NATURE OF INDIVIDUAL LEARNING

Now that we have made culture central to our definition of learning, but also have argued that a learning analysis has its surest footing at the individual and small-group levels of analysis, we begin our elaboration of key learning dynamics with individual learning. In this section, we discuss a representative rather than exhaustive set of properties and look at those that seem to be especially susceptible to influence from organizational contexts and communication.

First, learning occurs within an ongoing stream that the individual can partition and label in a variety of ways. This is beautifully illustrated in Pye's (1994) elaboration of the insight that

> learning is a process by which we make a particular kind of sense of social life; that is, giving a particular significance to "an episode," by isolating a pattern or form and translation this

"duraction" into "an experience" from which one might conceive of lessons or learning and ultimately change one's behavior as a consequence. (p. 156)

Winograd and Flores (1986) provide a vivid account of just what it means to be thrown into ongoing situations that require structuring if any learning is to be extracted. When people are caught up in an ongoing situation, they cannot avoid acting, cannot step back and reflect on their actions, cannot predict accurately, cannot create stable representations, are at the mercy of interpretation, and resort to language as their primary resource for coping. Cohen, March, and Olsen (1972) preserve some of this ongoing character in their proposal that streams of problems, solutions, people, and choices flow through organizations and converge and diverge independent of human intention. What they overlook is that labels such as "problems" and "solutions" do not inhere in the streams but rather are differentially and opportunistically applied in response to such things as context, prevailing labels, social pressure, image concerns, and salience. The diversity of these influences can muddy appreciably action-outcome linkages that are actually learned.

Despite these challenges, people do continue to break ongoing streams into connected units that tell plausible stories within local subcultures. These punctuations are the raw material for learning.

A second property of individual learning is that it is primarily a controlled, mindful activity that is supplemented by tacit knowledge acquisition and operant conditioning. This mix of learning mechanisms was implied earlier in Normann's (1985) argument that an interest in culture is really an interest in learning. Recall that he refers to an interest in culture as "understanding and making conscious" learning that has taken place. He refers repeatedly to "awareness" of culture as a precursor to learning. And he concludes that only when assumptions "are made conscious and visible" can they be modified. While individuals are thought to do several things un-

consciously to adapt to their environments (Skinner, 1971), the essence of learning seems to be its conscious nature. Individuals monitor their environments, interpret what they see and formulate responses, all with some degree of consciousness regarding what they are doing. One implication of this observation is that to learn, individuals need to know that there is a need for learning. They also need to have a sense of what capabilities they have and what kind of environment they face. In other words, learners need to know who they are, what kind of situation they are in, and that there is a need for learning and possibly change (adaptation). This requirement holds whether the actor is attempting to learn something about his or her individual performance or about the organization and its situation. Recognizing the need for adaptation or learning is not always straightforward. Ashford and Taylor (1990), for example, cite the case of newcomers, who are often unaware of some of the dimensions along which they will be evaluated in a new setting. Given this awareness gap, they fail to see cues suggesting that some change in their personal style or behavior would make their contribution more acceptable and more effective. In a similar fashion, individuals charged with attending to an organization's performance might fail to account for all relevant aspects or performance demands. Because these executives fail to see the need to learn about, say, some emerging trend in their environment, the learning that they can do on behalf of the organization is limited.

Although considerable individual learning is primarily mindful, there is evidence that knowledge is also picked up tacitly, as a by-product of experience (Wagner & Sternberg, 1985). Tacit or implicit learning has several characteristics. Knowledge gained via implicit learning tends to be more complex; it is not fully accessible to consciousness; and the act of learning does not involve processes of conscious hypothesis testing (Seger, 1994). For example, Ashford and Black's (1996) work on organizational newcomers suggests that individuals learn in large part through conversations. Learning is often not the explicit goal of these interactions, but is an important by-product. Wagner and Sternberg (1985) place similar emphasis on the tacit learning that goes on during interactions between individuals in organizations. These examples suggest an important connection between learning and communication that involves the transmittal of tacit knowledge and the act of implicit learning. Indeed, scholars argue that implicit learning plays an important role in the development of procedural knowledge (Cohen & Bacdayan, 1994) of how complex, real-world systems function (Senge & Sterman, 1992), and in the development of skills, habits, and routines (Squire, Knowlton, & Musen, 1993). While scholars can attest to the existence and importance of implicit learning, just how implicit learning interacts with explicit learning and other cognitive processes is complex and less well studied (see Nonaka & Takeuchi, 1995, for a significant advance in explicating this relationship). For our purposes, it is sufficient to recognize that implicit or tacit learning occurs and that individuals may be unable to provide a full verbal account of what they have learned via this mechanism. This later recognition may make implicit learning more relevant for individual rather than organizational learning, given that an organization learns only when individual learnings are communicated and codified in some way.

A third observation is that in individual learning, activity often paves the way for thinking (e.g., Raelin, 1997). That is, one of the things that individual learners are conscious about is their own and others' activities. By seeing what I do, I learn. This observation suggests that contexts that offer individuals room to experiment, free from potential stigma, should promote learning. The idea that people learn by doing lies behind the long tradition of learning curve research in organizations (e.g., Arrow, 1962), which demonstrates that manufacturing performance improves with cumulative production experience. Pisano (1994) has recently suggested, using data from the pharmaceutical industry, that learning by doing may be more likely

"when organizations lack the underlying knowledge needed to simulate and predict effects 'off-line'" (p. 98). Firms with deep knowledge of cause-effect relationships tend to learn *before* doing.

Learning by doing does not require the presence of others nor does it require any abstract "environment." Individuals can learn by watching their own actions. This suggests that learning involves both a situational and a self-understanding. As such, learning may have the same preconditions that White (1974) associates with adaptability (the need to maintain adequate information about the environment, the need to maintain adequate internal conditions necessary to responding, and the need to maintain flexibility). The first two needs are often in tension. Thus, individuals learning about their own performance or that of their organization often make trade-offs between the desire for accurate information and the desire to defend the ego. Information often lowers self-esteem or threatens decision makers' sense of their good judgment, particularly if it is information that suggests that the organization's course of action or typical routines are incorrect. The manner in which individuals resolve these pressures will affect their level of learning and their ability to respond to changing environmental conditions. The third condition, flexibility, is crucial in fashioning a response to that which is detected. For example, in the Mann Gulch disaster (Weick, 1993) a group of young firefighters failed to maintain the internal condition necessary to respond (e.g., calmness, the internal organization of their group) and also lost flexibility as they engaged the explosive fire while remaining committed to their traditional ways of tackling small fires.

The need for accurate information noted in the last observation raises a further issue: Accuracy regarding what? Whether one finds learning to be a valuable concept or not may depend on one's belief in the existence of a reality and realism of some sort, and one's resourcefulness and creativity in selecting a reality in which one is willing to believe. Indeed, as we will see later, many observers treat organizational culture and environment as social facts (realities), which means that actions that accommodate more fully to them can be said to reflect learning (e.g., this is the central assertion in studies of socialization). Others argue that culture and environment are constituted by actions. They are not simply something out there to which actions accommodate. Instead, people create that to which they then respond. Different interests result in different communities of people who vouch for different creations. These multiple communities are clearly arenas for conflict, argument, and persuasion. But it is unclear what is learned other than rhetorical skill used to persuade others of the viability of one's view of the environment and skills at reaccomplishing structures that unravel.

We believe that both perspectives have merit. Organizational realities are socially constructed and some environmental imperatives do exist. Thus, if organizational learners socially construct an environment that is grossly out of tune with the actual demands imposed by powerful others, then performance should deteriorate. Within these limits, however, social construction does occur and is functional. That is, an organization that can socially construct an adequate reality and act on it ought to be better off than one that devotes an equivalent amount of time to developing an accurate sense of its environment and delays acting.

Individual learning is also dependent on cues, and it is this dependency that brings communication into discussions of learning. Individuals who are aware of the need for learning can learn by explicitly attending (to cues) offered by and punctuated from the environment regarding demands, requirements, and opportunities. Such attention gives the learner a sense of what ought to be done. To learn how adequate their (or their organization's) routines and practices are, individuals also need to attend to feedback cues offered by the environment. Such cues will suggest whether an individual performer or the organization is moving toward success or failure. Ashford's (1993) study of feedback cues sug-gests that these cues range from direct (someone provides the performer with an assessment) to indirect (actions occur that can be interpreted as performance feedback) and from positive to negative. For example, IBM lags Apple in a particular quarter. Is this feedback worth attending to by decision makers at either company, or is this quarter's performance due to some exogenous event? Cues are also provided by many sources, including one's relevant stakeholders and the task, and often are complex combinations of many of these (e.g., one's supervisor recognizes one's peers' performance on a similar but not exactly the same task in a public setting, but fails to recognize one's own performance—a feedback cue?). In reading the environment for cues regarding what the individual or the organization should be doing and how well it has been done, Ashford's (1989) research on self-assessments suggests that the individual learner needs to make three assessments about any available cue: Is this event, action, subtle gesture, and so forth a cue? Is this cue meant for me? What does this cue mean? For example, a firm loses market share. Is this a feedback cue from customers? If so, what does it mean (a lessening of desire for products of this type or for this firm's particular brand)?

Bandura (1986) suggested that individuals can use the actions of others as cues from which they learn vicariously. By watching what happens to individuals when they engage in different behavioral patterns, the learner comes to understand that a certain strategy leads to success while another leads to failure, without engaging in either strategy personally. Institutional theory suggests that a similar process occurs at the organizational level. Organizations learn what practices to adopt by watching successful firms in their industries (Zucker, 1987).

When neither environmental cues nor cues from models are available, learners can still resort to proactive action to obtain information and can create cues by trial and error. The individual or organization can try some action in an uncertain domain and monitor carefully the results.

Summary of Individual Learning

To sum up, organizational learning is grounded in several predispositions of humans including their tendency to break the ongoing stream of experience into meaningful units; their tendency to perceive and conduct learning as an explicit, controlled activity in which they engage intentionally; their tendency to overlook the reality that considerable learning also remains tacit and unexplicated; their tendency to learn by acting first in order to discover the consequences of that action; their tendency to use any occasion of learning as information about at least two things, the situation and the self; and their tendency to learn from cues that are treated as surrogates for more complex events. Organizational contexts and communication processes influence learning through their effect on these individual processes of punctuating, reflecting, acting, categorizing, and extrapolating. Variation in activities such as these, induced by variation in contexts and communication, should result in learning that is more or less adaptive, more or less permanent, and more or less positive to the learners themselves. To explore these variations in more detail, we turn next to the effects of organizational context on individual learning.

ORGANIZATIONAL CONTEXT

If organizational learning is about acquiring, sustaining, and revising action-outcome linkages that take the form of know-how embedded in culture, if that know-how is built up from interaction with artifacts and with other actors within and outside the organization, and if know-how is fleshed out when people learn new information (know-that) and beliefs (believe-that), then it is reasonable to view organizations as a context for learning (e.g., Tyre & von Hippel, 1997). What may be most characteristic of this context is its

multiple realities and combination of shared and unshared meanings. Eisenberg and Goodall (1997) quoting Conquergood (1991) put it this way:

> Cultures are composed of ongoing dialogues that are variously complicit or engaged. A dialogue is complicit when the individuals or groups participating in it go along with the dominant interpretation of meaning. It is engaged when the individuals and groups struggle against a dominant interpretation and try to motivate action based on an alternative explanation. In most organizations most of the time you can find both complicit and engaged resources for dialogues. For this reason, an organizational culture is necessarily a conflicted environment, a site of multiple meanings engaged in a constant struggle for interpretive control. (p. 142).

These notions prompt the idea of context as market.

Context: A Marketplace for Ideas

If people see things differently and learn different lessons from the "same" data, then persuasion and advocacy are critical to most organizational learning situations. In fact, it seems appropriate to think of an organization as a learning arena within which meanings compete in a marketplace of ideas. Like any marketplace, we believe that competition occurs for the time and attention of others, particularly for that of those in the top ranks of the organization. In organizations, there are multiple potential learners with multiple points of contact with the environment, the organization's task, or each other (i.e., multiple learning opportunities, and a high likelihood that learners will learn different things). Individuals also have a motivation to promote their particular "learning." For example, certain tangible rewards accrue to the sellers of particular issues (learnings/interpretations) (Dutton & Ashford, 1993; Kingdon, 1984).

These rewards may include a boost to the seller's image should the issue be looked on favorably by those at the top of the organization or a potential gain in tangible resources for the seller's department that may come with winning the competition for meaning in the organization. Given the potential rewards for those who can most influence the interpretation of or "lesson" drawn from the available data, we believe that a true marketplace exists in which sellers informally compete for the ability to define how the world is interpreted. Clearly, communication is critical to this process as individuals with more developed persuasion skills ought to be particularly adept at shaping the content of their organization's learning.

We also believe (as this last paragraph attests) that organizational learning is stratified. It takes place across the hierarchical and inclusionary boundaries defined by Van Maanen and Schein (1979). Whose meaning will be accepted will be partially a function of those boundaries: Old-timers' definitions of reality will be more influential than those offered by newcomers, and the power to define reality will be loosely correlated with one's place in the organization's hierarchy. This suggests that certain voices will be lost in the organizational learning process, and it allows us to specify the likely focus and direction of persuasion and influence attempts. Thus, newcomers will be particularly interested in influencing old-timers (and will need to in order to have their voices heard) and lower-level employees ought to be particularly interested in influencing higher-ups regarding how to interpret changing "realities."

This observation increases our confidence in the applicability of the marketplace metaphor and also suggests some likely dysfunctions in the organizational learning process. That is, it is difficult to get news across boundaries, especially hierarchical ones. Thus, it is hard to bring any news to the top of an organization. Individuals' concerns regarding their image (no one wants to look bad by bringing what might be bad news to the top) and the communication problems inherent in multiple layers (where each sender reinterprets the message slightly and delays its transmission somewhat) make communication upward difficult (e.g., the Hubble telescope failure). While the image concerns may be unique to the transmission of bad news, the problem of multiple layers mitigates against getting *any* news to the top. A quote attributed to Jack Welch, CEO of General Electric, exemplifies this problem: "Layers are like sweaters, you wear enough of them and you can't even tell what the weather is like outside."

In general, the communication literature has found that the more links in a communication chain, the more likely that information passed along the chain will be distorted (e.g., Fulk & Mani, 1986; O'Reilly & Roberts, 1974). One interesting question to pursue in the next several decades as organizations downsize and delayer is: What happens to difficulties of upward communication when organizational hierarchies flatten? Do they still exist but on a smaller scale? Do they disappear? Are they replaced by new, perhaps as yet unanticipated and perhaps more insidious, difficulties?

It is also worth noting that the marketplace for ideas, in which individual learning occurs and is communicated to others, takes place within a particular organizational culture. This culture affects preferred labels, interpretations, and attributions. These, in turn, affect learning. Not only do individual learners need to translate their findings into acceptable language (and by doing so, often shape and alter the learning slightly), but also the organization's culture affects the ability to learn. These comments suggest that the movement from individual to collective learning is by no means smooth and barrier free. In fact, we believe there are several predictable impediments to organizational learning. We now turn to an explicit discussion of these. Following this section, we will comment briefly on two other aspects of collective learning: the impact of movements of people in and out of the collective, and the dynamics of speedy learning in a collective context.

Context as Impediment to Learning

Sometimes the conflicts, alternative explanations, and subcultures in organizations operate at such cross-purposes that it is hard to believe that learning of any kind could occur. The impediments to organizational learning need to be kept in mind when assessing the potential value of a learning analysis. One impediment is the complexity of the environment. For example, in the domain of international politics, learning is slow because the environment is so causally complex. "Even when we sense that one factor or another contributed to outcomes, it is daunting to assign relative weights and to distinguish decisive from contributory-but-not-decisive causes, or to distinguish between necessary and sufficient conditions" (Breslauer & Tetlock, 1991, pp. 3-4). Compounding the difficulty of untangling causality is fact that people are unable to see what would have happened had they done something else (the problem of counterfactuals) and the fact that people are often motivated to misrepresent their intentions and capabilities. Add to that a labile environment capable of sudden qualitative discontinuities, field operators who give incomplete or inaccurate information, people concerned with protecting their own interests, and the temptation to "learn only the lessons that confirm their preconceptions, attribute success to their own actions and fit into their long-standing sense of mission" (Sagan, 1993, pp. 207-208), and it becomes clearer why the topic of organizational learning was not included in the first edition of this handbook. As Scott (1987) puts it, "We should not underestimate how difficult it is for organizational systems to learn anything useful, given a rapidly changing environment, selective attention and inattention processes, inertia, cognitive limits, and ambiguity of feedback" (p. 282).

Beyond ambiguity, contexts are also arenas of accountability in which people are, to a greater or lesser degree across contexts, held accountable for their actions (Tetlock, 1985). These variations should affect preoccupation with one's image, which in turn should affect learning. These dynamics are visible in Van de Ven and Polley's (1992) study of a new product team. The feedback and "experience" that the team had to learn from was largely a function of the team's own "impression management and 'sugar coated' administrative reviews" (p. 106). Van de Ven and Polley (1992, p. 107) concluded that in judging a new product, administrative reviews that are open to influence by the party being reviewed are a poor substitute for the "acid test of the market" in promoting learning. We believe that much of the "experience" from which individuals attempt to learn in organizations is similarly tainted by the learner's own and others' attempts to socially construct a positive image or scenario to help maximize their images. These realities make learning from experience difficult.

But image concerns as an impediment to learning go beyond simply looking good. Staw and Ross (1980, 1987) found, for example, that leaders who maintained a consistent course of action were seen as more effective than those who changed their course of action. This finding suggests some limitations on a learner's ability to try out various actions to see their effect. These self-imposed limits stem from the actors' needs to behave in self-consistent ways and their fears that inconsistency will tarnish their image with stakeholders. Staw and Ross (1980) interpreted their results as suggesting that experimentation would be problematic for those at the top of organizations. That is, experimentation may be a good way to gain information on how various strategies work (i.e., learn), but it may carry too high a price tag in terms of costs to the leader's image (unless you are Herb Kelleher of Southwest Airlines). These costs also may exist throughout the organization, where it may be more important to be right or predictable than to create opportunities for learning via experimenting with possible effective strategies. Indeed, our image of the good employee may be one who can foresee the results of various actions ahead of time and pick effective strategies consistently.

Thus, organizational norms regarding failure should affect organizational learning. The meaning of failure in a given organization affects the likelihood that people working within that organization will engage in trial-and-error learning. If failures are seen as catastrophic, then trial-and-error learning becomes less likely.

An additional complication associated with accountability occurs when people seek information and feedback in order to learn. Ashford and her colleagues (Ashford & Northcraft, 1992; Ashford & Tsui, 1991) have documented the pervasive fear that individuals seem to have about seeking feedback from others about the efficacy of their actions. That fear is based on concerns about how such seeking might be interpreted by others (i.e., as a sign of weakness). A key impediment to organizational learning, then, may be individuals' fears and concerns regarding how the primary activities involved in learning will "look" to others. These fears should reduce both information/feedback seeking on the part of organizational decision makers and constrain the variance in actions taken based on the information/feedback attained.

These impression-management or image concerns are different from the ego-defense concern mentioned earlier. Ego defense comes into play because some learning is unpleasant, as when one learns that a chosen course of action is failing. Given the need to maintain internal conditions adequate for response mentioned earlier, people exposed to failure information are likely to react in ways that undermine learning. People motivated by ego defense often restrict social comparisons (presumably in an attempt to avoid painful information) and to choose comparison referents with whom they would compare favorably (Festinger, 1954). Favorable comparison means that nothing much needs to be learned. In many organizational contexts, others may routinely aid and abet each other's ego defense. For example, Janis (1972) documented the tendency for subordinates of more senior managers to defend their managers' egos for them by preventing them from hearing disquieting information. Not only do executives often prefer to hear good news but, in fact, subordinates often get promoted up the career ladder because they tell only good news. Thus, as managers move up in the organization, it becomes more difficult for them to get honest feedback on their efforts as their subordinates are busily portraying every effort as a success. These processes in which learners defend their own egos or their subordinates do it for them would seem to impede organizational learning since they create an impoverished and distorted information base from which to take action.

Thus, a context of accountability can undermine learning either through image concerns or ego concerns. Image concerns focus on how actions will be interpreted by others and ego concerns focus on how the lesson learned will feel to the learner. Either concern can filter out substantial information from which people might learn.

Organizational contexts also vary in the amount of ambiguity that is typical, the form this ambiguity takes, and the resources made available to reduce it. These too act as impediments to organizational learning. Consider an organization undergoing a culture shift from a warm but complacent company to an aggressive, "take no prisoners" type culture. The cues regarding the new behaviors required in the new environment are likely to be a mix of direct instructions, indirect hopes for new types of behavior, and lingering cues reinforcing the old way of doing things (given that these changes are profound and must stem from the value level). Individuals who try to learn how to act within the new aggressive culture are faced with a problem: What in the sometimes bewildering actions that I see around me should I take as a guide for my behavior, and what do these guides mean? What should I try to learn from? Answering these questions involves at least two types of interpretation problems. First, superstitious learning is possible. For example, learning during munificent periods is noisy since almost any cue and action is associated with success. In the munificent period following World War II, many companies "learned" that they needed large staffs and many organizational layers to survive when these factors may have been incidental (if not counterproductive) to their success (Peters & Waterman, 1982). Superstitious learning is especially troublesome when such learning creates schemes that are then used by organization members to screen further information.

Second, the environments that most organizations face today are characterized as much by equivocality (synonymous with ambiguity in this discussion) as by uncertainty. Uncertainty, or ignorance understood as the absence of information, can be resolved by acquiring and analyzing more data. Indeed, uncertainty is seen as the primary motivation for learning at the individual or organizational level. Equivocality, however, presents a different set of issues. Equivocality involves the existence of multiple and conflicting interpretations about an organizational situation. Equivocality is often characterized by confusion, disagreement, and lack of understanding. As Daft, Lengel, and Trevino (1987) put it: "Managers are not certain what questions to ask, and if questions are posed there is no store of objective data to provide the answer." Rather than search for more data, people manage equivocality by exchanging views in order to define adequately the situation they presume to face. Equivocality poses a much more difficult problem for organizations because there are fewer established routines to reduce it, which means organizations prefer to treat it as an issue of uncertainty. To deal with confusion requires extensive communication among key organizational participants to resolve disagreements, formulate a collective definition of the situation, and enact a response.

Ambiguity is also important for learning because newer inputs tend to be filtered through existing categories, which tend to favor constraint over creativity and to reduce learning. Henry Kissinger put it this way: "It is an illusion to believe that leaders gain in profundity while they gain in experience. . . . The convictions that leaders have formed be-

fore reaching high office are the intellectual capital they will consume as long as they continue in office" (quoted in Breslauer & Tetlock, 1991, p. 4). If current events fit a prior point of view, then there is nothing to learn. March, Sproull, and Tamuz (1991) provide a wonderful example of ambiguity, in the context of air safety and near misses between aircraft:

> Every time a pilot avoids a collision, the event provides evidence for the threat and for its relevance. It is not clear whether the learning should emphasize how close the organization came to disaster, thus the reality of danger in the guise of safety, or the fact that disaster was avoided, thus the reality of safety in the guise of danger. (p. 10)

A near miss is ambiguous and with ambiguity comes increased pressures to reduce it. As Kissinger hints, it is usually easier to resolve ambiguity by imposing old constraints rather than by creating new ones. If that happens, an opportunity for learning is lost. If people see a near miss as vindication of their past experience with accident avoidance (the reality of safety in the guise of danger), this interpretation will inhibit learning because it discourages "more thorough investigations, more accurate reporting, deeper imagination, and greater sharing of information" (Sagan, 1993, p. 247).

Given the tendency of interpretation under ambiguity to favor constraints rather than creativity and tactical changes rather than changes in strategy, communication can promote learning only if it openly encourages novel interpretations. Failure to do this can result in disaster, as in the case of the Mann Gulch disaster mentioned earlier. The wildland fire at Mann Gulch was ambiguous (it appeared to be both a major and minor fire) but communication was blocked (leader and co-leader gave contradictory messages, noise blocked vocal communication, communication language was inappropriate, firefighters were relative strangers), which led to an ineffective collective solution (individuals tried to outrun an exploding fire by going up a slippery 76% hill).

A final impediment to organizational learning is the organizational culture itself. For example, an organizational culture with a typical behavioral pattern that encourages external attributions for failure reduces the need for and ability to learn. If, as culture researchers contend, these typical behavioral patterns are tacit, accepted, and occur without notice (Schein, 1985), then learning opportunities (and the organization's failure to take advantage of them) may similarly be overlooked. Thus, in addition to the marketplace for ideas and the inclusionary and hierarchical stratification of organizations, it is important to recognize that strong cultural forces affect learning. As we will see in the next section, organizational culture sets a prescribed language for discussing learning that may or may not facilitate communication from some learners (their voices may not fit and may, therefore, be unattended to) on some topics. The culture also entails a set of tacit norms regarding how the environment is engaged. These norms, like the tendency toward external attribution of failure noted above, may both hinder or prevent organizational learning and go undetected by those who take culture for granted.

Despite these formidable impediments, it does remain true that there are pockets of people in organizations and moments in their everyday lives when know-how and artifacts shed some meanings and acquire new ones and when newer skills and understandings come to dominate older ones. These learnings are the result of change in features of organizational context such as patterns of competing ideas, stratification, attributional style, turnover, accountability, tolerance of ambiguity, and preoccupation with speed in decision making. Of these seven, two aspects have received recent research attention and may be fruitful avenues around which to design interventions to enhance learning. These two are the role that turnover and the rate of learning play in organizational learning. Before exploring each of these features, we want to emphasize that context is both something that people enact and something to which they react. They enact the marketplace of ideas that then constrains the options to which they react. They enact the levels of hierarchy that filter their communication, which filtering then rearranges the hierarchy, and so on. Learning is not simply a reactive event even though phrases such as "learnings are the result of changes" encourage just such an interpretation. Communication is just as important for its capability to enact a learnable environment as it is for its capability to mediate learning from something already enacted.

Context: The Impact of Personnel Movements

When we consider organizations as a collective context for learning, we also have to consider the effect of personnel movements in and out of that collective. Most treatments of organizational learning presume that organizations rely on experience and that experience is preserved in the memories of individuals (Johnson & Hasher, 1987; Steinbruner, 1974). Supporting these contentions is a simulation study conducted by Carley (1992). She found that organizations with a higher turnover rate learned less and learned more slowly. This effect was less pronounced, however, in larger organizations and organizations engaged in simpler tasks. According to Carley, this effect occurs because turnover removes part of the organization's memory and because with a high turnover rate, personnel leave before they are fully trained. Consequently, the organization's final level of learning is lower.

Of note, however, is one of the model limitations that Carley (1992) specifies. Her simulation assumes a relatively stable environment and, therefore, a stable task. She points out that turnover might be less costly in a less stable environment and that "in turbulent environments turnover even may be beneficial to the organization" (p. 41). Indeed Virany,

Tushman, and Romanelli (1992) make a similar argument with respect to executive turnover. These findings and theoretical statements raise several questions regarding the effect of personnel turnover on organizational learning. First, how can organizations maintain learning in a high turnover world (or does the high turnover help if the environment is turbulent)? Alternatively, does turnover help learning because the communication required in the continuous resocializing of newcomers reminds old-timers of what they once knew but have forgotten (Sutton & Louis, 1987)?

Some have argued that in situations of high turnover, organizations cope by institutionalizing memory (e.g., create handbooks, policies, and standard operating procedures; Bluedorn, 1982; McCain, O'Reilly, & Pfeffer, 1983; Walsh & Ungson, 1991). However, we feel that formalization is a poor substitute for individuals' memories and experiences especially when individual and collective know-how is salient. We suspect that managers rarely consult files and that standard operating procedures rarely are sufficiently nuanced to depict expert performance. In fact, the real compensation for the loss of "memory" represented by turnover lies in the newcomers brought in as replacements. Newcomers represent fresh views and insights that may be more important for an organization facing turbulence than long historical memories. Organizations interested in promoting learning, however, need to consider how they bring newcomers on board. In this regard, March (1991, p. 76) suggests that slower-learning newcomers may actually be better for the organization over the long run than fast learners. With slow learners, organizational codes (i.e., the languages, beliefs, and practices of an organization) are exposed longer to deviant behavior and, consequently, there are more opportunities to consider code changes. A crucial irony in a fast-changing world, then, is that slow individual learners accelerate organizational learning because organization-level codes remain exposed longer to new inputs. In a fast-changing world, organiza-

tions with many newcomers (higher turnover), slow-learning newcomers, and strong-minded newcomers (who are more willing to deviate from organizational codes in the first place) may be at an adaptive advantage as they are more likely to modify their codes. If such changes bring the codes more in line with environmental demands, effective collective learning has occurred. This finding also suggests the importance of communication. In fast-changing environments, organizations with cultures that promote expressions of deviance (disagreement, etc.) from slow learners should be better off than those without such cultures. However, recall from above that organizational contexts vary in the degree to which people are held accountable for their actions (Tetlock, 1985) and feel free to express divergent views.

Context: A Crucible for Speedy Learning?

The final property of organizational context that affects individual learning through its effect on communication is the emphasis on speed and high-velocity decision making (Cushman & King, 1994; Eisenhardt, 1989). Again, Henry Kissinger's experience frames the issue. Larson (1991) commented on Kissinger's inability and unwillingness to change his ideas about the Soviet Union while serving in the Nixon administration, with the following observation:

> Policy makers must make quick decisions without having time to think. As Kissinger recalled, "There is little time for leaders to reflect. They are locked in an endless battle in which the urgent constantly gains on the important." Policy makers assimilate what is new to what they already know. They act first, and rationalize later. (p. 388)

The consequences for learning of a culture that values speed can be inferred from Fiske's (1992, p. 885) comparison of information processing that is accuracy oriented and that which is decision oriented. A concern with accuracy is evidence driven and bottom-up, and closure is resisted in the interest of acquiring more information. A concern with speed is driven by expectancy confirmation rather than evidence, and is top-down with closure being sought in the interest of action. Fast learning that occurs in conjunction with decision-oriented goals should be mindless, single-loop, often superstitious, unreflective, tactical, superficial. It could also be adaptive if fast, small learnings match fast, small environmental changes. The problem is, fast learning is expectancy driven rather than evidence driven, which means that even small environmental changes may be missed if they are unexpected. In their place, expectancies may provide the map of what appears to be needed.

The potential differences in the kind of learning expected with a mindset favoring speed rather than accuracy shed new light on prescriptions for practice that emphasize the value of "fast failures" (Peters, 1987, p. 259), rapid prototyping (von Hippel & Tyre, 1993), and the value of learning quickly in ways that are hard to imitate. Each of these prescriptions for better adaptation should actually reinforce the presumptions people bring to a situation. Perceptions are filtered through those presumptions in ways that appear to confirm them. What is sacrificed is accuracy—and the very adaptation that was supposed to be facilitated.

Except that in a socially constructed world constituted and held together by communication, accuracy may be a moot issue. Accuracy is a vestige of the view that communication represents, whereas expectancy is a vestige of the view that communication constitutes. Of course, communication does both. But if the constraints to be represented are socially constituted, and if they are driven by expectancies as much as by perceptions, then what people really need to learn is more about the self and the group that generates the expectancies, how those expectancies are generated, and how to improve that process, rather than learning

about the environment on which those expectancies are imposed.

What managers need is confidence as much as accuracy (Steinbruner, 1974). They need confidence to create and impose expectations that produce a more preferred set of constraints. Viewed this way, communication enhances the conditions for learning when it involves rich disclosive discourse about the self and about the conditions under which stronger expectations and more confident action occur. To learn about self and confident action, rather than about the world, is to learn ways to alter that world so that it eventually imposes constraints that are more satisfying. An altered world is no less an outcome of learning than is an altered learner.

Summary

To sum up, we have argued that individuals tend to punctuate, reflect, act, categorize, and extrapolate in order to learn and that these tendencies unfold more or less successfully depending on the degree of ambiguity, conflict, hierarchy, accountability, external attribution, turnover, and preoccupation with speed found in the context where unfolding takes place. In a very crude sense, as these features of context increase in their frequency and intensity, individual learning decreases. The decrease in learning is brought about because these contextual changes tend to induce arbitrary punctuation, intermittent reflection, interrupted action, meaningless categorization, and faulty extrapolation, all of which preclude learning or encourage superstitious learning of that which is salient rather than that which is basic.

COMMUNICATION AND LEARNING

Up to this point, we have focused on organizational learning as figure and communication as ground. Now we intend to reverse that emphasis and bring communication to the forefront by asking what it adds to our understanding of learning. We attack this question in two ways. First, we suggest that an inadequate "communication language," in this case preoccupation with the language of finance, precludes learning. Second, we suggest that a communication process that does not adequately capture the complexities of the ongoing flow of events both internal and external to the organization also precludes learning. A remedy for both communication shortcomings is found in the communication practice adopted by NASA in the early 1960s —the Monday Notes—that created both a flexible communication language and an adaptive communication process.

Communication Language

To see the interdependence of communication and learning, we can look at poor communication language in an organizational setting. Normann (1985) observed that most organizations are dominated by

> a poor figure-oriented language, focusing on budgets, profits-and-loss performance, and procedures but not on the substance of the business. As one of the key officials of a large multinational company told me, suddenly getting a flash of insight: "We had this long and nice dinner with the managing directors of two of our largest subsidiaries, one corporate vice-president, and myself. And suddenly I realized that we had been together for three hours, talking about the company every minute, but not once had anybody used the words *clients, product,* or *people.* The only things we talked about were budgets, return on investment, and the company's long-range planning procedure. We do have profit problems—but *talking* about profits and procedures will not solve any of them!" (p. 229)

This executive's insight suggests that to learn better procedures for profit-maximization in competition, people need to communicate about something else. They need to talk about clients, what is delivered to them, and when, in the case of competition. When people are unable to shift their frames of reference or enrich the ones they have, they get caught in what Normann calls "a vicious learning circle maintained by poor communication language." Such a vicious circle is depicted in Figure 18.1.

This diagram illustrates several points that are crucial if we want to understand the joint effects of organization, communication, and learning. First, communication can conceal and silence and thereby inhibit learning, as is shown in variable B. That is, people use the company's philosophy to tell them what to bring up and what to keep silent about. If individuals keep silent, organizations cannot learn effectively (they may be able to interpret individuals' silence, but not usually with any degree of accuracy). Second, Figure 18.1 shows how communication about planning (as a function of the choices made in variable B) drive out communication about substance, which blocks attention to substance and learning more about it (variable C). Individual learning is thereby impaired. The figure also suggests that organizational learning is affected by the distribution of communication (variable D). Communication affects who knows what and how quickly they know it. If all we are talking about is planning and controls, then we aren't sharing learnings about business substance. Further learning is shaped by interpretations driven by particular frames of reference (described in variable H). These frames, in turn, can vary depending on the performance they need to explain (EH linkage) and on the firm's "philosophy" or culture embedded in frames and explanations (HA reciprocal linkage). For example, if a firm faces low and uneven performance, managers may interpret this as a need for formal and administrative solutions (such as incentive pay systems). Interpretations, culture, and learning tend to be self-perpetuating (HA reciprocal link). That is, once the incentive system in the above example is put into place, people talk more and more about the incentive system

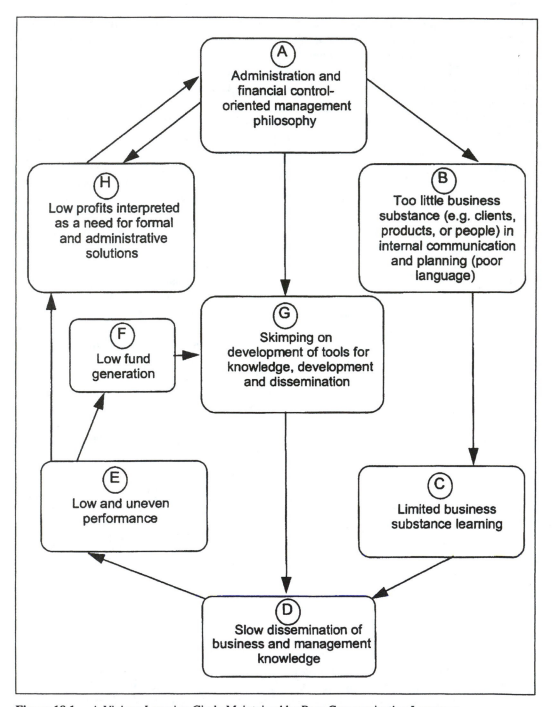

Figure 18.1. A Vicious Learning Circle Maintained by Poor Communication Language

SOURCE: Figure 1, p. 230, in Richard Normann, "Developing Capabilities for Organizational Learning," in J. M. Pennings & Associates, *Organizational Strategy and Change*. Copyright 1985 Jossey-Bass, Inc. Used with permission.

rather than about clients, products or people. Low performance is interpreted as a need for formal and administrative solutions, and this interpretation is reinforced by a philosophy that emphasized administration and financial controls in the first place and by continual talk and action involving controls.

The basic reason Normann calls this a "vicious" circle is because there is no way within this system to step outside, reexamine, and change its basic assumptions (the DEFGD loop is self-sealing). Said differently, this is what single-loop learning (Argyris & Schon, 1978) looks like. However, since this structure is a circle, it also means that if the direction in which any one of the variables is moving is reversed, for example, a retreat is convened to focus attention on business substance, which increases business substance learning thereby reversing the direction in which variable C (the amount of business substance learning) is moving, then each variable connected to C would also begin to move in the opposite direction. Thus, the circle is vicious only if control language is increased (as a manifestation of variable A), which then increases everything else. A movement of control language in the opposite direction (i.e., by its replacement with the rhetoric of self-regulation) has the opposite effect. Given the profit-oriented mindset of business practice, we expect that people will be preoccupied with financial controls and that this focus will be amplified. Nevertheless, theoretically this structure is capable of overriding this focus widely and swiftly, which makes it as much a volatile circle as one that is vicious.

There are two other ways this system could be changed and its language made more adequate. As depicted in Figure 18.1, the system is deviation-amplifying with an even number of inverse relationships (there are two, one between A and B, one between E and H). The system would become less dominated by the poor communication language of organizational control if one of these two inverse relationships were made direct (e.g., if lower performance led to less rather than more

interpretation of that lowered performance as demonstrating the need for even more formal solutions, the system would be stabilized), or if a third inverse relationship were created in the loop (e.g., if slower dissemination of knowledge [variable D] led to higher rather than lower performance [E], perhaps in a manner similar to March's slow-learning newcomers mentioned earlier, who accelerate adaptation).

Regardless of which form learning might take to increase the attention to substance and decrease the attention to financial controls, the learning will involve changes in communication at the relatively microlevel of words, conversation (Ford & Ford, 1995), and artifacts. Communication created the original blindspot toward business substance and it perpetuated this blindspot in ways that precluded learning. But communication also provides the means to dissolve the blindspot and the language to restructure the system and the medium for new learning.

Communication Process

Communication shapes learning through language as we have just seen, but also through process. While the role of process was implicit in the preceding discussion, here we make it more explicit. Freese's (1980) description, crafted in the context of a discussion of cumulative theorizing, provides the necessary tools. To describe the experiences that are the grist for learning, people have to use language:

> Constructing sentences to express statements about experience imposes discrete definitions on a subject matter that is continuous. One cannot report in a sentence an observation about experience without a concept that structures what one is observing. Observation statements describe not perceptions but planned perceptions. Data are not given by experience, but by the concept of the language used to interpret it.

Observational language imposes discrete boundaries on the continuity of the phenomenal world so as to define concrete, individual events in that world. Such events may be simple, solid objects like snowballs or complex, nontactile events like behavior sequences. Whether simple or complex, phenomenal events possess two properties whose significance for scientific inquiry cannot be overstated: They are unique and transitory. (Freese, 1980, p. 28)

Freese's description is a wonderful summary of the field for learning that is created by communication. It describes resources for learning when it refers to such things as sentences, discrete definitions, concepts, and interpretations that are imposed on observations, continuous subject matter, experiences, perception, and phenomenal events. It describes potential slippage between experience and the data that are available for learning when it suggests the kinds of simplifications produced by communication. Communication edits continuity into discrete categories, observations into interpretations, experience into bounded events, and perceptions into preexisting plans and frameworks. But most important, Freese's description pinpoints the difficulty that these simplifications create for learning. The clue to this difficulty is in the last sentence. If phenomenal events are unique, then how can knowledge of one unique event be used to deal with another unique event? If phenomenal events are transitory, why even bother with transfer of knowledge anyway?

Unique, transient phenomenal events are of no value for learning until they are made less unique and more enduring. These alternations are accomplished by discrete images and categories, imposed with some degree of consensus, as a result of coordinated communication practices and actions. To impose conversations on the world is to reconstitute that world in a form that is more learnable, because it has become more typical, more repetitive, more stable, and more enduring. However, the world of continuous flows to which that learning is directed has not itself become any less unique or transient simply because people choose to see it that way. Thus, there remains a chronic disjunction between the discrete products of communication and the continuous realities to which they refer, or in the language of learning, there is a disjunction between the reality an organization faces and the words used to represent that reality as organization members communicate with each other.

Learning has to bridge this disjunction. And its success in doing so is heavily dependent on the adequacy with which discrete communications approximate the continuity that ultimately validates or invalidates the learning. These approximates take at least three forms. First, successful learning depends on the adequacy with which the content of communication represents the flow and continuity in which learning is embedded. Content that is rich in dynamics, process imagery, verbs, possibilities, and unfolding narratives represents flows more accurately than does content that is dominated by statics, structures, nouns, the impractical, and arguments. Second, success also depends on the adequacy with which communication practices enact boundaries and categories into the world, thereby making its subject matter less continuous. Enacting boundaries into the world is what happens when discrete expectations trigger behavioral confirmation (e.g., Snyder, 1984, 1992). And third, success is also dependent on the adequacy with which communication practices themselves, not just their content, become isomorphic with the flows of which they are a part. Weick and Browning (1991, p. 7) describe an example of isomorphism when they discuss "pacing," a style of emotional contact among strangers consisting of precise and deliberate matching of micromovements in posture, gestures, language, voice pitch, and tempo, intended to accelerate familiarity, understanding, and deeper levels of rapport. Pacing appears to accelerate the evolution of cooperation.

Other efforts to bridge the disjunction between the continuous and the discrete in the service of learning are evident in work such as the dialogue project (Isaacs, 1993), which aims to create "a field of genuine meeting and inquiry." Isaacs (1993) defined dialogue as "a sustained collective inquiry into the processes, assumptions, and certainties that compose everyday experience" (p. 25). Conceivably, as dialogue develops, it will combine pacing, the imposition of learnable boundaries, and process imagery thereby improving the match between ongoing conversation and ongoing streams of events, and thereby improve learning. It is too early to tell. What interests us is the question of whether much of the recent repackaging of organizational development into the newer container of organizational learning may, either intentionally or unintentionally, create contexts in which communication matches referent events more closely and in doing so facilitates learning. For us the crucial issue is the degree to which that communication is compatible with reality both in form and content, the degree to which the communication is flexible and able to balance creativity and constraint (Eisenberg & Goodall, 1993), and the degree to which the communication replaces, at least temporarily, continuity and flow with bounded, self-contained, nameable, typical, recurrent events. Communication that can both represent flows by means of content and practice and create bounded events by means of self-fulfilling discrete definitions should be able to make the unique more typical and the transient more stable. Both of those changes promote learning. And both of these changes are the direct result of communication.

Learning, Communication, and the Monday Notes

The preceding theoretical answer to the question of what communication adds to our understanding of learning can be supplemented with an example that covers the same ground. This example comes from Tompkins's (1977, 1993) experience as a faculty communication consultant to the Marshall Space Flight Center in 1967 at the time Wernher von Braun was its director. As part of his interviews with engineers at the center, Tompkins asked the question, "What works well?" With surprising regularity, the interviewees answered, "The Monday Notes" (Tompkins, 1977, pp. 8-10; 1993, pp. 62-66). Von Braun had asked approximately 24 key managers, spread across several units, who were at least one layer removed from him, to send him a one-page memo every Monday morning in which they described the preceding week's progress and problems. As von Braun read the notes, he initialed them and added marginalia in the form of questions, suggestions, and praise. "These collected and annotated notes, arranged in alphabetical order by the authors' surnames, were reproduced and returned as a package to all of the contributors" (p. 63). Tompkins then goes on to report an intriguing discovery:

> Curious about how the 24 contributors generated the content of their weekly notes, I systematically asked about their procedures. In most cases the lab director would ask his subordinates, the division chiefs, to provide him with a Friday Note about their activities. . . . Moreover, some of the directors and managers organized meetings to determine what should be put in next week's notes and to discuss von Braun's responses to the most recent packet of notes. Relevant portions of the notes were reproduced for distribution down the line. In short, von Braun's simple request for a weekly note had generated a *rigorous and regularly recurring discipline of communication within the organization.* (pp. 64-65)

As Tompkins noted, the practice of Monday Notes kept people informed; tied groups together laterally; provided feedback; created a personalized substitute for face-to-face communication; could be used as a quick, frank, and informal forum for conflicts and arguments; and provided redundant communication channels thereby improving reliability. Since the notes were written weekly, they are closely attuned to the flow of events that occur in a relatively short period and, therefore, accurately represent continuity. Since drafting the notes is done in part by people who are actually doing the work to be represented, the drafting is constitutive as well as representative. People do things they can talk about, which begins to enact discrete categories directly into the flow of phenomenal events. And since the content of the notes is about ongoing progress, process, and problems, the content itself is more about process than structure. In the Monday Notes, the flow of events through Marshall is mapped accurately by communication practices that mirror them. The result should be faster learning. Learning should slow down if the memos become less frequent, more detached from everyday action, drafted by fewer people, more filled with outcomes than process, less conversational, less crucial to the director, and if each memo is returned to its author and no one else.

There are other points worth noting about these notes. The notes came both from R&D Operations housed in 12 laboratories organized by science and engineering disciplines and from Industrial Operations, which had responsibility to direct and monitor prime contractors. Because the notes spanned units with quite different missions and know-how, their communication languages also differed. Therefore, when people read the notes they are reminded of several different ways to frame common problems. This guards against some of the traps mentioned earlier where groups get stuck in a narrow language, such as the language of profits, and are unable to see any other meanings that could help them dissolve or solve their problems. The Monday Notes also potentially enlarge the domain of what is discussible, and bring strategies and assumptions into play, as well as tactics. Thus, learning can engage more fundamental understandings.

The frequency with which the notes are written and the cascading process of drafting them also guards against distortions of hindsight. Hindsight bias, which involves the use of knowledge about outcomes to edit reconstructions of the antecedents of those outcomes, should lead people to learn the wrong things. Bukszar and Connolly (1988), for example, documented the tendency of those told that an organization's strategic outcomes were favorable to rate the initial decision on which those outcomes were based as less risky, and the decision process as more successful on a variety of dimensions, than did those told that the outcomes were unfavorable.

Hindsight bias should be reduced by the practice of Monday Notes for reasons outlined by Starbuck and Milliken (1988): "In the present people can distinguish their perceptions from the alternative actions they are considering, but in the past it is difficult to do so because people change their perceptions to fit what they did" (p. 44). As we move from the present to the past, options, possibilities, and alternatives are lost in the interest of justification. The action taken becomes reconstructed in hindsight as sensible, necessary, and fitting, in light of perceptions now edited to justify it. The fact that other perceptions present at the time of action might have supported other actions is lost. In hindsight, there appears to be one best way and nothing much to learn. This conclusion is troublesome because it was arrived at through severe editing out of complexity and ambiguity present at the time the action originally unfolded. Those complexities might suggest the wisdom of different choices in the future. Unfortunately, those complexities can't be retrieved once justification has masked them. However, frequent communicating, such as is represented by the Monday Notes, is one way to prevent such masking. Neither much history nor much justification are allowed to build up around a choice before it is subjected to weekly public scrutiny, criticism, praise, and alternative constructions by von Braun and his associates. It is easier to keep perceptions and actions separated when progress is reported frequently. If they are kept separate, this should make it easier to experiment with new perception-action linkages and improve performance.

CONCLUSIONS

This chapter's goal was to present a portrait of the individual and interpersonal processes inherent in organizational learning, to describe individual and organizational impediments to those processes and to specify the inherent link between communication and learning and how communication can help overcome some of the barriers described. We conclude by highlighting what we see as the key themes of this discussion and describing their implications for future research.

First, organizational learning is primarily about individuals learning within their organizations (about themselves and their performance or about how the collective does or should operate) and interacting and competing with others to get their learnings "heard" within the organization. If we take this perspective seriously, then literatures on individual learning, communication, and persuasion should all provide critical insights into organizational learning. This theme also suggests that we add to the literature a new focus. In addition to focusing on how managers process information in the learning process, we should also study the processes by which information is moved around within the organization and "reality" or "learnings" are created. We have described these processes as interpersonal ones involving competition among different definitions of reality. We believe that these processes are at least as important as those describing how the individual manager comes to know something in the first place.

Second, decision makers' natural tendencies in organizations (to move quickly, to judge learning in terms of current images and constraints, etc.) may be problematic. At various points in the chapter, we have offered case examples of how such tendencies have gotten decision makers in trouble (see Klein, 1998,

for a fuller set of examples and principles). Research that fully documents the natural tendencies of organizational learners and begins to specify the conditions under which those tendencies are problematic would be valuable.

Third, we have described several impediments to learning. This reflects our belief that the power to enhance learning in organizations stems from a good understanding of what blocks it (and the motivation to do something about those blocks). Thus, understanding that learning from continuous experience is problematic or that feedback regarding the efficacy of various organizational actions is not typically sought gives those in organizations with an interest in promoting learning some guidance as to where and how to intervene. Research that goes beyond simply documenting the various ways in which individuals have trouble learning and begins, instead, to describe the conditions necessary to maximize their learning effectiveness will be particularly important.

Fourth, a key to understanding an organization's learning potential and its limitations (biases, etc.) lies in a study of its culture. Culture is the embodiment of past learning and serves as a constraint for future learning. Culture (and therefore learnings and frameworks for future learnings) is conveyed in many ways, but of central importance for communication scholars is how culture is conveyed through the firm's formal and informal communication and through artifacts that embody messages. What norms are conveyed about the acceptability of experimentation or the seeking of feedback? How do cultural norms facilitate or inhibit communication, and how are those norms conveyed via communication within the organization? These and related questions might help ground the organizational learning research and to move it forward.

Finally, organizational learning appears to be enhanced in settings where conflicting forces are tolerated; where decision makers can live with tension and paradox. Throughout this chapter we have highlighted the tensions involved in organizational learning.

Whether the tension is between the need for certainty and the necessity of disorder in learning, between the desire for speed and the need for accuracy, or between the need to show a consistent pattern of behavior and the advantages of experimentation, settings that not only can live with the tension but can maximize both aspects should develop enhanced organizational learning capabilities. Research that sheds light on practices that enable organizations to do this will be particularly valuable. Our goal has been to point out the forces in tension and to specify the impediments that prevent one force or another from flourishing in organizational life.

REFERENCES

Argyris, C., & Schon, D. (1978). *Organizational learning: A theory of action perspective.* Reading, MA: Addison-Wesley.

Arrow, K. (1962, April). The economic implications of learning by doing. *Review of Economic Studies, 29,* 166-170.

Ashford, S. J. (1989). Self-assessments in organizations: A literature review and integrative model. In B. M. Staw & L. L. Cummings (Eds.), *Research in organizational behavior* (Vol. 11, pp. 133-174). Greenwich, CT: JAI.

Ashford, S. J. (1993). The feedback environment: An exploratory study of cue use. *Journal of Organizational Behavior, 14,* 143-157.

Ashford, S. J., & Black, J. S. (1996). Proactivity during organizational entry: Antecedents, tactics and outcomes. *Journal of Applied Psychology, 81*(2), 199-214.

Ashford, S. J., & Northcraft, G. B. (1992). Conveying more (or less) than we realize: The role of impression-management in feedback-seeking. *Organizational Behavior and Human Decision Processes, 53,* 310-334.

Ashford, S. J., & Taylor, M. S. (1990). Adaptation to work transition: An integrative approach. In G. R. Ferris & K. M. Rowland (Eds.), *Research in personnel and human resource management* (Vol. 10, pp. 1-41). Greenwich, CT: JAI.

Ashford, S. J., & Tsui, A. S. (1991). Self-regulation for managerial effectiveness: The role of active feedback seeking. *Academy of Management Journal, 34,* 251-280.

Bandura, A. (1986). *Social foundations of thought and action: A social cognitive theory.* Englewood Cliffs, NJ: Prentice Hall.

Bantz, C. R. (1993). *Understanding organizations: Interpreting organizational communication cultures.* Columbia: University of South Carolina Press.

Barnett, G. A. (1988). Communication and organizational culture. In G. M. Goldhaber & G. A. Barnett (Eds.), *Handbook of organizational communication* (pp. 101-103). Norwood, NJ: Ablex.

Bluedorn, A. C. (1982). A unified model of turnover from organizations. *Human Relations, 35*(2), 135-153.

Breslauer, G. W., & Tetlock, P. (1991). Introduction. In G. W. Breslauer & P. E. Tetlock (Eds.), *Learning in U.S. and Soviet foreign policy* (pp. 3-19). Boulder, CO: Westview.

Bukszar, E., & Connolly, T. (1988). Hindsight bias and strategic choice: Some problems in learning from experience. *Academy of Management Journal, 31,* 628-641.

Carley, K. (1992). Organizational learning and personnel turnover. *Organization Science, 3,* 20-46.

Cohen, M. D., & Bacdayan, P. (1994). Organizational routines are stored as procedural memory: Evidence from a laboratory. *Organization Science, 5,* 554-568.

Cohen, M. D., March, J. G., & Olsen, J. P. (1972). A garbage can model of organizational choice. *Administrative Science Quarterly, 17,* 1-25.

Cohen, M. D., & Sproull, L. S. (Eds.). (1996). *Organizational learning.* Thousand Oaks, CA: Sage.

Conquergood, D. (1991). Rethinking ethnography: Towards a critical cultural politics. *Communication Monographs, 58,* 179-194.

Cook, S. D. N., & Yanow, D. (1993). Culture and organizational learning. *Journal of Management Inquiry, 2,* 373-390.

Crossan, M. M., Lane, H. M., Rush, J. C., & White, R. E. (1993). *Learning in organizations.* London, Ontario: Western Business School.

Cushman, D. P., & King, S. S. (Eds.). (1994). *High-speed management and organizational communication in the 1990's: A reader.* Albany: State University of New York Press.

D'Andrade, R. G. (1984). Cultural meaning systems. In R. A. Shweder & R. A. LeVine (Eds.), *Cultural theory: Essays on mind, self, and emotion.* Cambridge, UK: Cambridge University Press.

Daft, R. L., Lengel, R. H., & Trevino, L. K. (1987). Message equivocality, media selection, and manager performance: Implications for information systems. *MIS Quarterly, 11,* 355-366.

Dodgson, M. (1993). Organizational learning: A review of some literature. *Organization Studies, 14,* 375-394.

Duncan, R., & Weiss, A. (1979). Organizational learning: Implications for organizational design. In B. M. Staw (Ed.), *Research in organizational behavior* (Vol. 1, pp. 75-123). Greenwich, CT: JAI.

Dutton, J. E., & Ashford, S. J. (1993). Selling issues to top management. *Academy of Management Review, 18,* 397-428.

Eisenberg, E. M., & Goodall, H. L., Jr. (1993). *Organizational communication: Balancing creativity and constraint.* New York: St. Martin's.

Eisenberg, E. M., & Goodall, H. L., Jr. (1997). *Organizational communication: Balancing creativity and constraint* (2nd ed.). New York: St. Martin's.

Eisenhardt, K. M. (1989). Making fast strategic decisions in high-velocity environments. *Academy of Management Journal, 32,* 543-576.

English, H. B., & English, A. C. (1958). *A comprehensive dictionary of psychological and psychoanalytical terms.* New York: Longmans, Green.

Estes, W. K. (1988). Human learning and memory. In R. C. Atkinson, R. J. Herrnstein, G. Lindzey, & R. D. Luce (Eds.), *Stevens handbook of experimental psychology* (Vol. 2, 2nd ed., pp. 351-415). New York: John Wiley.

Festinger, L. (1954). A theory of social comparison processes. *Human Relations, 7,* 117-140.

Fiske, S. T. (1992). Thinking is for doing: Portraits of social cognition from daguerreotype to laserphoto. *Journal of Personality and Social Psychology, 63,* 877-889.

Ford, J. D., & Ford, L. W. (1995). The role of conversations in producing intentional change in organizations. *Academy of Management Review, 20,* 541-570.

Freese, L. (1980). The problem of cumulative knowledge. In L. Freese (Ed.), *Theoretical methods in sociology: Seven essays* (pp. 13-69). Pittsburgh, PA: University of Pittsburgh.

Fulk, J., & Mani, S. (1986). Distortion of communication in hierarchical relationships. In M. L. McLaughlin (Ed.), *Communication yearbook 9* (pp. 483-510). Beverly Hills, CA: Sage.

Gergen, K. J. (1994). *Realities and relationships.* Cambridge, MA: Harvard University Press.

Goodall, H. L. (1990). Interpretive context for decision-making: Toward an understanding of the physical, economic, dramatic, and hierarchical interplays of language in groups. In G. M. Phillips (Ed.), *Teaching how to work in groups* (pp. 197-224). Norwood, NJ: Ablex.

Hedberg, B. (1981). How organizations learn and unlearn. In P. C. Nystrom & W. H. Starbuck (Eds.), *Handbook of organizational design* (Vol. 1, pp. 3-27). New York: Oxford University Press.

Huber, G. P. (1991). Organizational learning: The contributing processes and the literature. *Organization Science, 2,* 88-115.

Isaacs, W. N. (1993). Taking flight: Dialogue, collective thinking, and organizational learning. *Organizational Dynamics, 22*(2), 24-39.

Janis, I. (1972). *Victims of group think.* Boston: Houghton Mifflin.

Jaques, E. (1989). *Requisite organization: The CEO's guide to creative structure and leadership.* Arlington, VA: Cason Hall.

Johnson, M. K., & Hasher, L. (1987). Human learning and memory. *Annual Review of Psychology, 38,* 631-668.

Kingdon, J. W. (1984). *Agendas, alternatives, and public policies.* Boston: Little, Brown.

Klein, G. (1998). *Sources of power.* Cambridge, MA: MIT Press.

Larson, D. W. (1991). Learning in U.S.-Soviet relations: The Nixon-Kissinger structure of peace. In G. W. Breslauer & P. E. Tetlock (Eds.), *Learning in U.S. and Soviet foreign policy* (pp. 350-399). Boulder, CA: Westview.

Levitt, B., & March, J. G. (1988). Organizational learning. *Annual Review of Sociology, 14,* 319-340.

March, J. G. (1991). Exploration and exploitation in organizational learning. *Organization Science, 2,* 71-87.

March, J. G. (1994). *A primer on decision making.* New York: Free Press.

March, J. G., Sproull, L. S., & Tamuz, M. (1991). Learning from samples of one or fewer. *Organization Science, 2,* 1-13.

McCain, B. E., O'Reilly, C., & Pfeffer, J. (1983). The effects of departmental demography on turnover: The case of a university. *Academy of Management Journal, 26,* 626-641.

Miller, D. (1996). A preliminary typology of organizational learning: Synthesizing the literature. *Journal of Management, 22,* 485-505.

Nonaka, I., & Takeuchi, H. (1995). *The knowledge-creating company.* New York: Oxford University Press.

Normann, R. (1985). Developing capabilities for organizational learning. In J. M. Pennings & Associates (Eds.), *Organizational strategy and change* (pp. 217-248). San Francisco: Jossey-Bass.

O'Reilly, C. A., & Roberts, K. H. (1974). Information filtration in organizations: Three experiments. *Organizational Behavior and Human Performance, 11,* 253-265.

Peters, T. J. (1987). *Thriving on chaos: Handbook for a management revolution.* New York: Knopf, Random House.

Peters, T. J., & Waterman, R. H., Jr. (1982). *In search of excellence: Lessons from America's best-run companies.* New York: Harper & Row.

Pisano, G. P. (1994). Knowledge, integration, and the locus of learning: An empirical analysis of process development. *Strategic Management Journal, 15,* 85-100.

Pye, A. (1994). Past, present, and possibility: An integrative appreciation of learning from experience. *Management Learning, 25,* 155-173.

Raelin, J. A. (1997). A model of work-based learning. *Organization Science, 8,* 563-578.

Sagan, S. D. (1993). *The limits of safety.* Princeton, NJ: Princeton University Press.

Schein, E. H. (1985). *Organizational culture and leadership.* San Francisco: Jossey-Bass.

Scott, W. R. (1987). *Organizations: Rational, natural, and open systems.* Englewood Cliffs, NJ: Prentice Hall.

Seger, C. A. (1994). Implicit learning. *Psychological Bulletin, 115,* 163-196.

Senge, P. M. (1990). *The fifth discipline: The art and practice of the learning organization.* New York: Doubleday/Currency.

Senge, P. M., & Sterman, J. D. (1992). Systems thinking and organizational learning: Acting locally and thinking globally in the organization of the future. In T. Kochan & M. Useem (Eds.), *Transforming organizations* (pp. 353-371). New York: Oxford University Press.

Simon, H. A. (1991). Bounded rationality and organizational learning. *Organization Science, 2,* 125-134.

Sitkin, S. B., Sutcliffe, K. M., & Weick, K. E. (1999). Organizational learning. In R. C. Dorf (Ed.), *The technology management handbook* (pp. 7-70–7-76). Boca Raton, FL: CRC Press.

Skinner, B. F. (1971). *Beyond freedom and dignity.* New York: Knopf.

Snyder, M. (1984). When belief creates reality. In L. Berkowitz (Ed.), *Advances in experimental social psychology* (Vol. 18, pp. 248-305). Orlando, FL: Academic Press.

Snyder, M. (1992). Motivational foundation of behavioral confirmation. In M. Zanna (Ed.), *Advances in experimental social psychology* (Vol. 25, pp. 67-114). San Diego, CA: Academic Press.

Squire, L. R., Knowlton, B., & Musen, G. (1993). The structure and organization of memory. *Annual Review of Psychology, 44,* 453-495.

Starbuck, W. H., & Milliken, F. J. (1988). Executives' perceptual filters: What they notice and how they make sense. In D. C. Hambrick (Ed.), *The executive effect: Concepts and methods for studying top managers* (pp. 35-65). Greenwich, CT: JAI.

Staw, B. M., & Ross, J. (1980). Commitment of an experimenting society: An experiment on the attribution of leadership from administrative scenarios. *Journal of Applied Psychology, 65,* 249-260.

Staw, B. M., & Ross, J. (1987). Understanding escalation situations: Antecedents, prototypes, and solutions. In B. M. Staw & L. L. Cummings (Eds.), *Research in organizational behavior* (Vol. 9, pp. 39-78). Greenwich, CT: JAI.

Steinbruner, J. D. (1974). *A cybernetic theory of decision: New dimensions of political analysis.* Princeton, NJ: Princeton University Press.

Sutton, R. I., & Louis, M. R. (1987). How selecting and socializing newcomers influences insiders. *Human Resource Management, 26,* 347-361.

Tetlock, P. E. (1985). Accountability: The neglected social context of judgment and choice. In L. L. Cummings & B. M. Staw (Eds.), *Research in organizational behavior* (Vol. 7, pp. 297-332). Greenwich, CT: JAI.

Tetlock, P. E. (1991). Learning in U.S. and Soviet foreign policy: In search of an elusive concept. In G. W. Breslauer & P. E. Tetlock (Eds.), *Learning in U.S. and Soviet foreign policy* (pp. 20-61). Boulder, CO: Westview.

Tompkins, P. K. (1977). Management qua communication in rocket research and development. *Communication Monographs, 44,* 1-26.

Tompkins, P. K. (1993). *Organizational communication imperatives: Lessons of the space program.* Los Angeles: Roxbury.

Trujillo, N. (1985). Organizational communication as cultural performance: Some managerial considerations. *Southern Speech Communication Journal, 50,* 201-224.

Tyre, M. J., & von Hippel, E. (1997). The situated nature of adaptive learning in organizations. *Organization Science, 8,* 71-83.

Van de Ven, A. H., & Polley, D. (1992). Learning while innovating. *Organization Science, 3,* 92-116.

Van Maanen, J., & Schein, E. H. (1979). Toward a theory of organizational socialization. In B. M. Staw (Ed.), *Research in organizational behavior* (Vol. 1, pp. 209-269). Greenwich, CT: JAI.

Virany, B., Tushman, M. L., & Romanelli, E. (1992). Executive succession and organization outcomes in turbulent environments: An organization learning approach. *Organization Science, 3,* 72-91.

von Hippel, E., & Tyre, M. (1993, January). *How learning by doing is done: Problem identification in novel process equipment.* Working paper, Sloan School of Management, MIT. SSM WP BPS 3521-93.

Wagner, R. K., & Sternberg, R. J. (1985). Practical intelligence in real world pursuits, the role of tacit knowledge. *Journal of Personality and Social Psychology, 49,* 436-458.

Walsh, J. P., & Ungson, G. R. (1991). Organizational memory. *Academy of Management Review, 16,* 57-91.

Wegner, D. M. (1987). Transactive memory: A contemporary analysis of the group mind. In B. Mullen & G. R. Goethals (Eds.), *Theories of group behavior* (pp. 185-208). New York: Springer-Verlag.

Weick, K. E. (1991). The non-traditional quality of organizational learning. *Organization Science, 2,* 116-124.

Weick, K. E. (1993). The collapse of sense-making in organizations: The Mann-Gulch disaster. *Administrative Science Quarterly, 38,* 628-652.

Weick, K. E., & Browning, L. D. (1991). Fixing with the voice: A research agenda for applied communication. *Journal of Applied Communication Research, 19,* 1-19.

Weick, K. E., & Roberts, K. H. (1993). Collective mind in organizations: Heedful interrelating on flight decks. *Administrative Science Quarterly, 38,* 357-381.

Weiss, H. M. (1990). Learning theory and industrial and organizational psychology. In M. D. Dunnette & L. M. Hough (Eds.), *Handbook of industrial and organizational psychology* (Vol. 1, pp. 171-222). Palo Alto, CA: Consulting Psychologists Press.

White, R. E. (1974). Strategies for adaptation: An attempt at systematic description. In G. V. Coelho, D. A. Hamburg, & J. E. Adams (Eds.), *Coping and adaptation* (pp. 47-68). New York: Basic Books.

Winograd, T., & Flores, F. (1986). *Understanding computers and cognition: A new foundation for design.* Reading, MA: Addison-Wesley.

Zucker, L. G. (1987). Institutional theories of organization. *Annual Review of Sociology, 13,* 443-464.

19

Organizational Entry, Assimilation, and Disengagement/Exit

FREDRIC M. JABLIN
University of Richmond

Research exploring the nature of communication processes associated with organizational entry, assimilation, and exit has burgeoned over the past decade. Not only has empirical research become more extensive, but discussions of communication and assimilation processes have been integrated into many undergraduate textbooks (e.g., Conrad, 1994; Hickson, Stacks, & Padgett-Greely, 1998; Miller, 1995), and the literature and its various underlying foundations, models, and terminology have been the focus of critical scrutiny (e.g., B. Allen, 1996; Bullis, 1993, 1999; Clair, 1999; Kramer & Miller, 1999; Miller & Kramer, 1999; Smith & Turner, 1995; Turner, 1999).[1] Thus, if one judges the development of the area in terms of the typi-cal, "normal" science indicators (Kuhn, 1970) its health appears quite robust. However, appearances can be deceiving and although certain systems of an entity may appear vigorous, their vigor may merely reflect the process of treading water versus progressing toward and achieving goals. In turn, the vigor of selective systems of an entity may also deflect attention away from other of its systems that may be struggling to perform their functions. To what extent do these conditions describe the state of research and theory exploring communication and the organizational entry, assimilation, and exit process? A major goal of this chapter is to address this question.

To assess the literature, this chapter will use the author's review and analysis of organizational entry, assimilation, and exit published in the earlier *Handbook of Organizational Communication* as a primary template for evaluating progress (Jablin, 1987). In that chapter, I described organizational entry/assimilation/exit as a life-span developmental process and thus began by "tracing" from childhood through employment in one's "chosen" vocation the development of an individual's work career. I will follow the same approach here. In addition, the focus of the present analysis, as was that of the earlier one, is on individuals' entry, assimilation, and exit into/from organizations in which they are paid for their labor. This focus is not intended to diminish the importance and legitimacy of nonpaid work in the family, assimilation into jobs in volunteer and nonprofit organizations (e.g., McComb, 1995), and the like, but merely reflects a means to limit the scope of the chapter. This approach also allows us to consider experiences prior to full-time, paid work as setting the stage for that experience. For some, this period may be quite traditional (paid work begins after formal education or training), while for others this period may be less conventional (e.g., paid work begins after a period of formal education, working to raise a family, and another period of formal training). In addition, and again for boundary-setting purposes, the discussion that follows will consider all experiences prior to one's first full-time employment in an organization (even if this first job is not exactly in one's preferred career area) as within the domain of vocational anticipatory socialization; subsequent experiences (including career changes) will be considered in terms of the more general, lifelong, vocational development/socialization process (for a discussion of the ideological implications of considering one period of socialization as anticipatory of another, see Clair, 1996).

Thus, the first section of this chapter examines how communication functions in the vocational and organizational entry processes. Generally, these processes serve as a form of "anticipatory socialization" for new organizational recruits, providing them with certain expectations (often of questionable accuracy) of the communication characteristics of their occupations and work environments. This discussion is followed by an examination of the organizational assimilation process, and in particular, how people become socialized into the communication cultures of organizations and concomitantly attempt to change these environments to better suit their needs and goals. Materials in this section are organized around basic communication-related processes associated with organizational assimilation—orienting, socialization, training, formal mentoring, informal mentoring, information seeking, information giving, relationships development, and role negotiation—rather than stages of the assimilation process. Subsequently, the role of communication in the organizational exit process is examined; however, unlike my 1987 discussion of research in this area, I do not focus on delineating communication antecedents of the voluntary turnover process but rather on "unpacking" communication processes and behaviors associated with disengaging from work environments in situations of voluntary organizational exit.

In assessing the status of research and theory, I attempt to discern what we know today that we didn't know in 1987, identifying specific areas in which we have achieved significant gains in understanding and those areas in which our knowledge remains limited. In addition, I suggest new or alternative directions for the study of communication in the organizational entry, assimilation, and disengagement/exit processes. The reader will note that in some sections of this chapter I have extrapolated material from my 1987 review and analysis; however, in these sections more recent research, if available, is cited to support conclusions and/or to develop ideas that were stated in the earlier chapter. Most sections of the chapter are new and reflect changes in my own thinking, recent developments in research and theory, and transformations in the nature of individual-organizational relationships that have occurred over the past decade (e.g., changes in the nature of the "psychological contract" between employer and employee, and growth in the size of the "contingent" workforce).

ANTICIPATORY SOCIALIZATION

Socialization to work and preparation to occupy paid organizational positions commences in early childhood (Crites, 1969). As part of this conditioning, most of us have developed, prior to entering any particular organization, a set of expectations and beliefs concerning how people communicate in particular occupations and in formal and informal work settings. Jablin (1985a) proposed that this anticipatory socialization contains two interrelated phases, one that encompasses the process of vocational choice/socialization and the second that involves the process of organizational choice/entry. Since vocational choice usually precedes organizational entry for those beginning their first full-time job (e.g., Wanous, 1977), research exploring the vocational anticipatory socialization process is considered here first, followed by a review and analysis of socialization processes that usually precede entry into paid organizational positions.

Vocational Anticipatory Socialization

The most widely accepted approaches to the vocational development process (e.g., Brown, Brooks, & Associates, 1996; Osipow, 1983; Walsh & Osipow, 1983) suggest that as individuals mature from childhood to young adulthood they intentionally and unintentionally are gathering occupational information from the environment, comparing this information against their self-concept, "weighing the factors and alternatives involved in choosing an occupation and finally making a series of conscious choices which determine the direction of [their] career" (Van Maanen, 1975,

p. 82). Individuals acquire vocational information during the occupational choice/socialization process through a variety of sources including (1) family members, (2) educational institutions, (3) part-time job experiences, (4) peers and friends (including nonfamilial adults), and (5) the media (Jablin, 1985b; Vangelisti, 1988). Each of these sources represents a "microsystem" (a direct context of influence) in the maturing person's career development environment/ecology (Bronfenbrenner, 1979; Moen, Elder, & Luscher, 1995). At the same time, however, these contexts are usually interconnected with one another (e.g., involvement in a part-time job may affect performance in school), as well as embedded within larger suprasystems (e.g., legal and social contexts) that indirectly affect a person's vocational development (Bronfenbrenner, 1986; Vonracek, Lerner, & Schulenberg, 1986). Unfortunately, most research has tended to treat each microsystem as an independent source of influence. As a consequence, research related to how each of the sources affects individuals' perceptions and behaviors with respect to communicating in work settings and different occupations is reviewed and interpreted below in relative isolation of the other sources.

Family

Family members, and in particular parents, are usually very influential in the career choices of children and adolescents (e.g., Bigelow, Tesson, & Lewko, 1996; Blyth, Hill, & Thiel, 1982; Sebald, 1986; Wilks, 1986; Young & Friesen, 1992). Thus, it is not surprising that adolescents and young adults frequently believe that their "parents were the primary determiners of their occupational choices" (Leifer & Lesser, 1976, p. 38).

Communication-related occupational and organizational information may be shared in families in a variety of ways. First, research findings indicate that in most families children participate in task-oriented organizing activity (e.g., Goldstein & Oldham, 1979; Larson, 1983; White & Brinkerhoff, 1981), typically in the form of performing household chores. Among others, Goodnow and her colleagues (Bowes & Goodnow, 1996; Goodnow, 1988; Goodnow, Bowes, Dawes, & Taylor, 1988; Goodnow, Bowes, Warton, Dawes, & Taylor, 1991; Goodnow & Delaney, 1989; Goodnow & Warton, 1991) have conceptualized the doing of household chores as involving the exchange of distinctive kinds of messages between parents and their children. Thus, for example, Ahlander and Bahr (1995) suggest that the manner in which family members, and especially parents, talk about household work can devalue it and make it drudgery or value it and use it to reinforce a sense of identification and community within the family. Thus, what household work *means* in any particular family is produced and reproduced in the everyday discourse of family members.

Findings from studies exploring children's household work suggest a number of interesting conclusions:

1. By the age of five, children know how to respond to requests for work and in particular know how to use justifications and accounts as excuses for refusing to perform a task (Dunn, 1988; Leonard, 1988).
2. Children learn early on how to solicit the help of others to perform tasks (e.g., remarking about the efficiency and expertise with which the other could perform the task; see Goodnow et al., 1988).
3. At a young age, children understand which chores they must do themselves and which tasks they can ask others to perform (Goodnow & Warton, 1991).
4. Many parents assign, label, and discuss tasks in terms of "boys'" or "girls'" work, thereby reinforcing traditional sex role stereotypes (e.g., boys perform outside chores and girls indoor ones; Peters, 1994). As Bowes and Goodnow (1996) note, children quickly learn a "set of criteria by which they can classify any activity as 'male' or 'female,' regardless of specific experience" (p. 306).
5. Fathers and mothers may differ in the manner in which they solicit their children to

perform tasks, with fathers more likely to tell their children to do something and mothers relying more on reminders and requests (Goodnow et al., 1988). Also, fathers tend to be more directive, interrupt more often, and experience more "communication breakdowns" than mothers (Bellinger & Gleason, 1982; Gleason, 1975; Malone & Guy, 1982; McLaughlin, White, McDevitt, & Raskin, 1983). At the same time, however, the difficulties that children may experience communicating with their fathers may be beneficial in that they encourage them to develop the sorts of communication skills required to be understood when interacting with persons in the "outside world" (Mannle & Tomasello, 1987).
6. Parents often communicate work principles to children through the use of metaphors (Goodnow & Warton, 1991).
7. A considerable amount of what children learn about work may focus on communication-related "procedures," including "the possibilities and the methods for raising questions or negotiating a change, the forms of talk or silence that are expected to accompany the work one does, and the extent to which people make decisions for themselves or need to follow orders" (Bowes & Goodnow, 1996, p. 308).
8. At least one study has found that while girls (14-18 years old) do not perceive differences in the procedures used to delegate a job (e.g., spelling out the details, the ways reminders are given) at home from in paid work, boys do perceive differences; boys believe that in paid work, "they just tell you" (Goodnow & Warton, 1991).

For a variety of reasons, caution is warranted in evaluating the above generalizations. In particular, the studies cited above tend to examine traditional, two-parent families (with neither party having been divorced) and may not generalize to single-parent households and families in which children live with a stepparent, which today is quite common (e.g., Barber & Eccles, 1992). Such variations in family structure create distinctive ambient and discretionary message environments for children (Jablin, 1987). For example, Asmussen and Larson (1991) report that in single-parent, mother-led families children's interactions with their mothers are more focused on household chores than in traditional, two-parent families. Relatedly, Barber and Eccles (1992) posit that "children in single-mother homes who participate in many required household tasks, and who have more household responsibility, may have more control in negotiations over rules" (p. 119).

Although children may implicitly learn about the communication characteristics of work relationships by participating in family-related organizing activity, discussions with their parents and other family members about work and careers provide such information in a more explicit fashion (e.g., Piotrkowski & Stark, 1987; Tucker, Barber, & Eccles, 1997; Young, Friesen, & Pearson, 1988). For example, in a study comparing the relative importance of work socialization agents in Colombia (in the city of Cali) and the United States, Laska and Micklin (1981) found that youths in both countries had fairly frequent discussions with their parents about the parents' jobs, though the frequency of such discussions was greater with mothers than with fathers. Similarly, in a study involving 82 children (ages 10-17) and their employed parents (fathers worked at an aerospace factory or for the postal service; mothers worked for a wide variety of employers), Piotrkowski and Stark (1987) found that 28% of the children reported their fathers spoke "often" to them about their jobs, while 53% reported their mothers "often" talked about work. This same pattern was also evident with respect to the children's reports of the frequency with which they visited their mothers and fathers at work. However, the children claimed to know similar amounts of information about their mothers' and fathers' jobs, and the more knowledge they claimed the more frequently they reported talking to their parents about work. It is also of interest to note that children's assessments of their

parents' job satisfaction were positively correlated with their parents' self-reports, suggesting that parents' general affective reactions to work were also being communicated fairly accurately to their children.

Parents' discussions about their jobs may be limited in scope, however, and in particular center on people and interpersonal relationships (Bowes & Goodnow, 1996; Crossen, 1985). Along these lines, Piotrkowski and Stark (1987), in the study noted above, compared children's descriptions of their parents' job conditions with their parents' self-reports. Results indicated that the children's descriptions were accurate only with respect to the physical work environment, fathers' relationships with supervisors, job effort required, and job insecurity (the researchers were not able to conduct similar analyses for mothers and their children). In addition, it is likely that from a very young age children may be cued to attend to and remember information about people and relationships in task settings, since these are frequent issues that parents ask them about with respect to their own daily activities (e.g., relationships with teachers and peers at preschool; see Flannagan & Hardee, 1994).

Discussions about work and careers may often occur in inveterate family interaction contexts such as dinner or in after-dinner conversations. Along these lines, a 1990 *New York Times*/CBS News poll showed that 80% of the respondents with children reported their family eating dinner together on most weeknights, with close to 60% reporting the main activity (besides eating) as conversation (Kleiman, 1990). In particular, dinnertime conversations between parents (in their children's presence but in which the children may not actively participate) frequently focus on the general day's events at work; company news; and relationships with supervisors, customers, and coworkers (Jablin, 1993). Children may also learn communication-related work principles from listening to their parents and other relatives telling family stories in which work is the central theme. In exploring the nature of family stories, Martin, Hagestad, and Diedrick (1988) found that 22% of family stories had work themes and in most of these stories (74%) a male family member was the hero. More generally, dinnertime talk represents a key source of children's socialization to how to tell stories and develop arguments (Blum-Kulka, 1997).

"Spillover" from parents' job settings to the family may occur in other ways as well. Greenberger, O'Neil, and Nagel (1994) report that parents whose jobs require "artfully persuading, reasoning, and explaining" may increase their use of these methods in managing their male but not necessarily their female children. Distressing interactions with supervisors and coworkers at work, as well as parental job insecurity, may also spill over to parents' after-work interactions with their children and affect their parenting behavior and their children's beliefs (Barling, Dupre, & Hepburn, 1998; Repetti, 1994; Repetti & Wood, 1997; Stewart & Barling, 1996). Other research suggests that the communication styles learned by parents at work as part of their involvement in participative management teams may influence their communication behavior in the family setting (Crouter, 1984).

In sum, it appears quite evident that children learn a considerable amount about communication at work in the family setting. As Stark (1992) observes, our homes may be one of the most important sources of on-the-job training (albeit we may be learning dysfunctional as well as functional ways of communicating and interacting that may carry over to our behavior in other task settings; e.g., Loraine, 1995; Oglensky, 1995).

Educational Institutions

As Jablin (1985a) suggests, schools and school-related activities are important sources of vocational information for children since (1) educational institutions have an explicit mandate to socialize people (e.g., Gecas, 1981); (2) school is typically the first socializing institution in a child's life that institutionalizes status differentiation and the hierarchical division of labor (e.g., Bowles & Gintis,

1976; Eccles, 1993); (3) for most individuals, school is a transitional institution between childhood and full-time work (e.g., Dreeban, 1968; Gecas, 1981); (4) school provides students with standards so that they can compare their competencies with others and develop realistic career aspirations; (5) school is probably the first formal context in which a child interacts in regular organizing activity (in the classroom as well as in extracurricular activities; e.g., Mihalka, 1974); and (6) the learning strategies developed in the classroom, and in particular the ways in which students learn to seek and interpret information in ambiguous situations, may be related to the strategies they later use to reduce uncertainty in the workplace (Hanson & Johnson, 1989).

Even in their earliest experiences in educational institutions (e.g., day care centers and preschools), children are learning about communicating with others in task settings. For instance, Meyer and Driskill (1997), in an observational study of children in a university child care center, found that the children were using a set of recurring communication strategies in developing and managing their relationships with others (strategies included appeal to rules, use of control, taking roles). Based on their findings, Meyer and Driskill (1997) suggest that "young children placed in day care centers are already developing and practicing the means for influencing and developing relationships" (p. 83), and in particular are experimenting with ways to balance their own needs with the needs of others in organizational environments. In like fashion, Corsaro (1990) discovered that children attending preschool know how to avoid "work" (e.g., cleaning up) by enacting a variety of communication strategies, including pretending not to hear the request, pleading a personal problem, or leaving the immediate area.

By the time students are in high school and college, they are acquiring distinctive forms of information about occupations in the specialized classes in which they are enrolled (Jablin, 1985a). For example, Cordes, Brown, and Olson (1991) collected data from university students enrolled in introductory accounting classes concerning their perceptions of the amount of social information conveyed in their classes (via teachers' comments, discussions with classmates, etc.) regarding the levels of autonomy, skill variety, and task significance in an accountant's job and the extent to which they expected these characteristics to typify an accountant's job. Results revealed the students perceived a moderate amount of classroom talk as focused on job characteristics, although those who intended to pursue accounting as a career perceived more sharing of information than those students who intended to enter other fields. Findings also showed a positive relationship between students' perceptions of the amount of information sharing about the job characteristics in their classes and their expectations that the characteristics would be present in an accountant's job. Similarly, Taylor (1985) found that college students' self-reports of the extent to which they talked to others (e.g., professors, peers) about careers to be predictive of their occupational knowledge.

Several studies have also shown that co-op experiences and internships help students clarify ideas about their fields, assess their competencies and interest in particular occupations, and develop basic protocols for interacting and communicating in the workplace (Feldman & Weitz, 1990; Gabriel, 1997; Moore, 1986; Staton-Spicer & Darling, 1986; Strom & Miller, 1993; Taylor, 1985, 1988). For example, in an enthnographic study, Moore (1986) found that internships can teach students "social procedures" (e.g., how to ask and answer questions) as well as expose them to different occupations.

In sum, as I concluded in 1987, it is likely that the information educational institutions (prior to professional or trade school) directly and indirectly disseminate to students focuses more on general job characteristics and the "ways" people communicate in different occupational/organizational roles, than with the specific content characteristics of such roles (e.g., DeFleur & Menke, 1975; Jablin, 1985a; Leifer & Lesser, 1976). However, it also seems clear that once a student has selected a

vocation and receives specific education in that field, the manner in which he or she communicates with other members of the field, the public, clients, and so on is somewhat constrained by the "occupational rhetoric" (e.g., Nelson & Barley, 1997) and implicit interaction norms (including norms associated with the expression of emotion) learned during his or her occupational or professional education (e.g., Brown, 1991; Bucher & Stelling, 1977; Cahill, 1999; Enoch, 1989; Fine, 1996; Fisher & Todd, 1987; Fogarty, 1992; Hafferty, 1988; Kressin, 1996; Martin, Arnold, & Parker, 1988; Nicholson & Arnold, 1989; Oseroff-Varnell, 1998; Stradling, Crow, & Tuohy, 1993; Trice, 1993; Van Maanen, 1984). As Van Maanen and Barley (1984) observe, "Becoming a member of an occupation always entails learning a set of codes that can be used to construct meaningful interpretations of persons, events, and objects commonly encountered in the occupational world" (p. 300).

Part-Time Employment

Approximately one half of all persons of high school age are employed in part-time jobs, and about 80% of the nation's high school students will have been employed in part-time jobs prior to graduating from high school (Greenberger & Steinberg, 1986; Stern, McMillion, Hopkins, & Stone, 1990). Exactly what do adolescents learn about communication at work from these experiences, and how might these jobs affect their communication-related occupational expectations? Unfortunately, scant research exists directly exploring these issues. Moreover, few new studies have been completed in recent years that build on the seminal work of Greenberger and Steinberg and their colleagues discussed in this chapter in 1987 (Greenberger, Steinberg, & Ruggiero, 1982; Greenberger, Steinberg, Vaux, & McAuliffe, 1980; Ruggiero, Greenberger, & Steinberg, 1982; Ruggiero & Steinberg, 1981; Steinberg, Greenberger, Vaux, & Ruggiero, 1981). The results of the series of studies conducted by Greenberger, Steinberg et al. suggested that adolescent part-time workers do not have close communication relationships with others (especially their supervisors) at work, and often work unsupervised and in jobs that vary greatly with respect to the opportunities they provide young adults to interact with others and develop their communication skills. Thus, it seems clear that "all jobs do not provide young workers with identical experiences and as such are not likely to be equally facilitative of adolescents' development and socialization" (Greenberger et al., 1982, p. 93; see also Barling, Rogers, & Kelloway, 1995; Mortimer, Finch, Owens, & Shanahan, 1990; Stern & Nakata, 1989). At the same time, however, findings from various studies in this area also suggest that "adolescents who work are learning a good deal about relationships" (Greenberger et al., 1980, p. 200) and are often developing basic communication skills required in work settings (Charner & Fraser, 1988; Phillips & Sandstrom, 1990).

In summary, it seems apparent that certain types of part-time jobs (e.g., those that require workers to influence others) provide adolescents with opportunities to learn and apply relational communication skills that may generalize to other work contexts. However, the specific manner and extent to which these early job experiences may contribute to the relational communication styles individuals adopt when they eventually enter their chosen occupations remains to be explored.

Peers and Friends

Although most adolescents spend over 50% of their time during a typical week with their peers (Csikszentmihalyi & Larson, 1984), often talk with peers and friends about their educational and occupational plans and aspirations (e.g., Blyth et al., 1982; Montemayer & Van Komen, 1980), and consider peers "as significant others who confirm or disconfirm the desirability of occupations" (Peterson & Peters, 1983, p. 81), we know little of what adolescents and younger children learn from their conversations with their friends about the nature of communication in

work/organizational relationships and occupations. However, it is important to recognize that while children and adolescents may learn about work and occupations in their explicit conversations with friends, other characteristics of peer relationships may be equally important in helping them learn about communicating in organizational contexts. In particular, in comparison to other relationships adolescents are involved in, friendships with other adolescents are "coconstructed" and are not guided by outside rules or regulations (Bigelow et al., 1996; Lewko, 1996; Youniss & Smollar, 1985). Peer relationships are characterized by mutual trust, symmetricality, respect, and openness (Larson, 1983; Raffaelli & Duckett, 1989; Zarbatany, Hartmann, & Rankin, 1990). As Burleson, Delia, and Applegate (1995) observe, "Peers prefer to be treated in person-centered ways that acknowledge their points of view, take their goals and motivations into account, and display concern for interpersonal relationships as well as instrumental goals" (p. 66). Thus, for instance, since friends rarely go to higher authorities to resolve conflicts among themselves, it is likely that they learn a great deal about regulating the expression of emotions and negotiating solutions to problems and conflicts in the process of maintaining their relationships (Gecas, 1981; Hartup, 1996; Larson & Kleiber, 1993; Newcomb & Bagwell, 1995). In addition, since peers interact more with one another as equals than in other of their relationships (e.g., at home or in school), their roles tend to be more fluid and as a consequence they do more role making than role taking (Gecas, 1981; Hartup & Moore, 1990).

Children and adolescents may also learn a great deal about communicating in task settings from their participation in voluntary, organized, non-school-related activities (e.g., Eccles & Barber, 1999). For example, it is very common for preadolescents as well as adolescents to participate in youth organizations (e.g., Girl Scouts; Auster, 1985) and organized sports teams that represent combinations of work and play and allow peers to communicate with one another, as well as with non-familial adult leaders or coaches (Larson & Verma, 1999). Thus, for instance, in Little League baseball (even when competitiveness is not stressed), attributes not typically associated with "play" such as "hustle," mental concentration and attention, control and discipline, "taking the game seriously," and acceptance and respect for rules and authority are stressed (Fine, 1987). In other words, a major focus of these activities is teaching young people to behave and communicate "properly" in working with others (e.g., controlling emotions, displaying team spirit/unity, and managing impressions). The specific nature of the effects of such activities and other forms of peer interaction/socializing on adolescents' perceptions and expectations of communication at work and in occupations, however, awaits determination by future research.

Media

As Huston, Wright, Rice, Kerkman, and St. Peters (1990) observe, "By the time American children are 18 years old, they have spent more time watching television than in any other activity except sleep. Moreover, their experiences with television begin long before exposure to school or, in many cases, any socialization agent other than the family" (p. 409). Unfortunately, research also suggests that television programs (including network news shows and cartoons; e.g., Potts & Martinez, 1994; Ryan & Sim, 1990) often transmit distorted, stereotypic images of occupations and how people communicate in them and that children's beliefs about these images "may well persist into adulthood" (Christenson & Roberts, 1983, p. 88). Television has not only been criticized for representing people in sex-role-stereotyped occupations (e.g., Gunter & McAleer, 1990; Huston & Alvarez, 1990; Signorielli, 1991), although there is some evidence that this is improving (Atkin, Moorman, & Lin, 1991; Moore, 1992), and overrepresenting managerial and professional

occupations and underrepresenting jobs of lesser prestige (e.g., Greenberg, 1982; Katzman, 1972; Signorielli, 1993), but also for frequently portraying persons who are successful in their occupational roles as involved in exciting and glamorous activities (Signorielli, 1993; Steenland, 1990), spending the bulk of their conversational time giving orders and/or advice to others (e.g., Chesebro, 1991), and in general engaging in fairly aggressive communication behaviors (e.g., Turow, 1974, 1980). Results of studies also suggest that business characters in prime-time television shows are frequently (at least 60% of the time) portrayed negatively (e.g., antisocial, criminal, or greedy) when performing their occupational activities (Lichter, Lichter, & Amundson, 1997; Theberge, 1981). In fact, in their analysis of prime-time shows over a 30-year period, Lichter et al. (1997) found that "no other occupation or institution was criticized as heavily as business, in terms of either the frequency or proportion of negative thematic portrayals" (p. 79). In turn, findings from other investigations indicate that in television representations of the workplace, little of the content of conversations among role occupants concerns work-related issues; rather, discussions focus on such topics as romantic relationships, family and marriage problems, and similar forms of small talk (Katzman, 1972; Turow, 1974). In essence, "television's representation of occupational roles, as with other roles, is both a wider perspective than everyday experience and a caricature of the actual world of work" (Peterson & Peters, 1983, p. 81).

It is also of interest to note that prime-time television shows frequently focus on conflicts of authority in the workplace. In particular, since the mid-1960s programs have increasingly depicted bosses as less authoritative, and subordinates as more likely to ridicule their bosses and to prevail in conflicts (Lichter, Lichter, & Rothman, 1994). In brief, many contemporary television programs depict organizations as places "where workers tell off bosses and warm personal relationships are infinitely more important that economic productivity" (Lichter et al., 1994, p. 418; see also Taylor, 1989).

Though some studies suggest that frequent exposure to television may influence how children and adolescents view occupational roles, and in particular their beliefs about "actual" interpersonal and task behavior in the work setting (e.g., Signorielli & Lears, 1992; Wroblewski & Huston, 1987), the nature of these relationships is still somewhat unclear, and as a consequence additional study of these issues will be required before definitive conclusions about causality can be drawn (e.g., Christenson & Roberts, 1983; Kubey & Csikszentmihalyi, 1990; Wright, Huston, Reitz, & Piemyat, 1994). In particular, given research findings that suggest the influence of television representations of jobs on children's (and adults') beliefs may be most potent for jobs that are outside of their everyday contacts (e.g., Pfau, Mullen, Deidrich, & Garrow, 1995), the extent to which television characters provide children with "surrogate experience" to know how to behave and communicate in work situations before such situations have been encountered in real life still requires intensive investigation (e.g., Berg & Trujillo, 1989; Noble, 1983; Wroblewski & Huston, 1987).

Finally, it should be realized that in addition to television other of the mass media may also be providing distorted depictions of the occupational behavior/communication of persons in work settings. For example, studies suggest that even award-winning children's books contain distorted or out-of-date occupational, racial, and sexual stereotypes (e.g., Ingersoll & Adams, 1992, 1976; Purcell & Stewart, 1990). Similarly, in a content analysis of fiction stories in magazines primarily written for and marketed to adolescent girls (e.g., *Teen, Seventeen*), Pierce (1993) found that occupations were portrayed in a sex-role-stereotyped manner and that in more than half the stories "the main character did not actively solve her own problems but depended on someone else to do it for her" (p. 59).

In sum, the messages conveyed by the media, and especially television, with respect to communication in organizations and in various occupations do not appear to be random in nature; rather, these messages are frequently patterned and presented in persuasive ways. Thus, while television may be entertaining young people, it also "selectively reinforces certain types of communication" (Chesebro, 1991, p. 219). The specific nature and effects of this reinforcement on individuals' communication behavior once they enter the world of work remain unknown.

Summary

In 1987, I noted that research exploring the vocational organizational communication socialization (VOCS) process was still in its infancy. With notable exceptions (research exploring family and media influences), studies investigating the VOCS process are still few in number. Thus, we continue to be unable to (1) indicate the degree to which various VOCS sources reinforce or conflict with one another (i.e., their interactive effects), or (2) draw conclusions about long-term VOCS effects on organizational communication behavior and attitudes. Clearly, one major reason for the scarcity of VOCS research is that scholarship in this area often involves elaborate, multiyear, longitudinal studies, which are rare in the study of organizational communication generally. Further, disentangling the influences of the various VOCS sources on children's and adolescents' developing communication-related cognitions and behaviors represents a formidable challenge to those who conduct research in this area.

In light of the above noted challenges, perhaps future research should proceed in a somewhat different direction than extant efforts. More specifically, we might focus more attention on identifying consistencies across sources with respect to the basic foci and content of their explicit and implicit messages about communicating in task settings and occupations. For example, based on the research reviewed in the preceding pages, it seems reasonable to hypothesize that children and adolescents will be learning from the various sources ways of communicating in procedural communication "predicaments" that are common in task settings (e.g., Bowes & Goodnow, 1996), such as how to request information or help, how to decline others' requests, how to express emotions, and the like. If we focus on communication functions that permeate most task settings (e.g., Stohl & Redding, 1987), we could determine if commonalities exist across sources with respect to how they promote enactment of these functions. Alternatively, given that recent studies of the organizational selection process indicate that one of the best predictors of the success of newcomers is the "match" between their values and those of their organizations (e.g., Cable & Judge, 1997), we might examine the sorts of basic communicative values that are promoted by each source during the VOCS process. For instance, we might expect each of the sources to communicate about what honesty and credibility means in organizations and in different occupations. Is there consistency across sources with respect to these messages? Do the messages of each source about communicative values remain invariant as a person matures from childhood to young adulthood? Exploration of issues such as these can be pursued with longitudinal research designs and cross-sectional ones, in which messages associated with each source are examined in samples involving different age cohorts.

The research directions suggested here are not intended to oversimplify the VOCS process but rather to encourage research in the area, especially in relation to the study of VOCS and messages exchanged among peers and friends, coworkers and supervisors in part-time jobs, and students and teachers. Indeed, the VOCS process is quite complex and individuals actually experience the influence of the sources in combination with each other (Jablin & Krone, 1994). Moreover, children and adolescents should not be viewed as merely passive recipients of VOCS messages but rather as active agents who can seek out communication-related vocational information (e.g., individuals can obtain prevocational information and experience in particular fields by their involvement in volunteer and paid work; e.g., Birnbaum & Somers, 1991). Further, it is important to realize that they may acquire information directly in conversations with others or indirectly by listening to the talk of parents, siblings, and others (Jablin, 1987).

In closing this discussion, I would be remiss if I failed to address one other issue that future research should address: the impact that recent changes in the nature of work and organizations is having on VOCS. For example, how has organizational downsizing, the increasing use of "temporary" versus permanent employees in organizations, the phenomenal increase of individuals who work out of their homes versus the sites of their formal organizations, the aggregation of professionals who traditionally worked as sole proprietors or in partnerships into large corporate entities (e.g., medical doctors), and the increasing demands for self-management that organizations are asking of their employees affected what young people are learning about the nature of communication in organizations and occupations? How are these changes reflected in the messages communicated by different VOCS sources? Is the deception and meaninglessness of organizational life displayed in popular television shows such as *Friends* and *Seinfeld* (Zurawik, 1996) and in celebrated comic strips such as "Dilbert" and "Doonesbury" different from the VOCS messages communicated by the media in earlier eras? Do the "made up" games children play today such as "Outplacement Barbie" and "You're Fired" (Shellenbarger, 1995) reflect important changes in VOCS as compared to prior decades? Do the many children who today have parents who work at home experience a different kind of VOCS than children whose parents perform their job duties at the site of their employers? Clearly, questions such as these warrant consideration in our future research endeavors.

Organizational Anticipatory Socialization

Subsequent to deliberately or accidentally choosing a career direction and receiving the education and training required to competently perform tasks associated with the occupation, most individuals will attempt to find positions in which to perform the jobs for which they have been trained. In the process of seeking jobs, individuals will concomitantly develop expectations about the organizations and respective jobs for which they have applied for employment. Job seekers typically acquire information that may affect their job/organizational expectations from two basic sources: (1) organizational literature (e.g., job advertisements, annual reports, training brochures, job preview booklets), and (2) interpersonal interactions with other applicants, organizational interviewers, teachers, current employees, and other direct and indirect social network ties (e.g., Bian, 1997; Granovetter, 1995). Generally speaking, studies exploring each of these sources of information have focused on one of three broad areas of research: (1) the relative effectiveness of each of the information sources in recruiting/attracting newcomers, (2) the realism or accuracy of job/organizational expectations that result from individuals' contacts with each source, and (3) the role of the employment interview as a recruiting and selection device. Research findings relevant to each of these areas of study are briefly reviewed below.

Recruiting Source Effects

Although over 30 years have passed since researchers first started to explore the relative effectiveness of different recruiting sources in attracting and subsequently retaining new-comers to organizations (Ullman, 1966), it is still very difficult to draw any firm conclusions from this corpus of study. Although some research (e.g., Conard & Ashworth, 1986; Decker & Cornelius, 1979; Gannon, 1971; Kirnan, Farley, & Geisinger, 1989; Reid, 1972; Saks, 1994; Taylor, 1994) suggests that newcomers recruited from informal (e.g., employee referrals, "walk ins") sources experience lower turnover than those recruited from more formal (e.g., newspaper ads, employment agencies) sources, the findings from other studies have brought this generalization into question. Not only have a number of investigations found minimal differences in the job survival and/or tenure of persons recruited via informal as compared to formal sources (Caldwell & Spivey, 1983; Griffeth, Hom, Fink, & Cohen, 1997; Swaroff, Barclay, & Bass, 1985; Werbel & Landau, 1996; Williams, Labig, & Stone, 1993), but the results from some recent studies suggest that in certain situations newcomers recruited through formal sources may have higher job survival rates than those recruited through informal sources (Rynes, Orlitzky, & Bretz, 1997; Saks & Ashforth, 1997). Further, with respect to recruiting source effects on newcomers' job performance, research results have been very inconsistent with some studies showing no differences among sources (e.g., Breaugh, 1981; Hill, 1970; Kirnan et al., 1989; Swaroff et al., 1985; Taylor, 1994; Williams et al., 1993), others indicating that personnel recruited via informal sources have higher performance than those recruited via formal sources (e.g., Blau, 1990; Breaugh, 1981; Breaugh & Mann, 1984), and still others suggesting that newcomers recruited via formal sources are the best performers (e.g., Caldwell & Spivey, 1983; Taylor & Schmidt, 1983; Werbel & Landau, 1996). Studies examining the impact of referral sources on job attitudes (such as job satisfaction and organizational commitment; e.g., Breaugh, 1981; Griffeth et al., 1997; Latham & Leddy, 1987; Saks, 1994; Saks & Ashforth, 1997; Taylor, 1994; Vecchio, 1995) and absenteeism (Breaugh, 1981; Griffeth et al., 1997; Taylor & Schmidt, 1983) have also produced equivocal results.

The generalizability of much of the research in this area is also clouded by evidence showing that many job applicants (upwards of 33%) rely on multiple versus singular sources for recruitment information (e.g., Vecchio, 1995; Williams et al., 1993), more prehire knowledge results from the use of multiple versus single sources, and combinations of sources may include mixes of formal and informal sources. Since the great majority of extant studies have asked respondents to identify only one recruitment source, their findings may not accurately reflect the manner in which recruitment sources affect potential job applicants. Moreover, if applicants obtain information from multiple sources, a variety of issues need to be explored including the manner in which they deal with inconsistencies in information obtained among sources and how variability across sources in the content, specificity, and amount of information they provide affects potential recruits.

Two basic explanations have been posited for the recruiting source effects described above. The "individual differences" hypothesis (Schwab, 1982) suggests differential source effectiveness is linked to individual differences in the applicant populations that are attracted to each communication/recruiting source. On the other hand, the "realistic information" hypothesis proposes that "individuals recruited via sources which provide more accurate information will be able to self-select out of jobs which do not meet their needs" (Breaugh & Mann, 1984, p. 261). In essence, this latter position suggests that recruiting sources vary with respect to the degree to which they provide "realistic job previews" (Wanous & Colella, 1989; see discussion below). Results from studies examining these explanations for recruiting source effects have not provided consistent support for either hypothesis and suggest that there may be other factors (for instance, applicants' perceptions of job fit; e.g., Saks &

Ashforth, 1997; Werbel & Landau, 1996) mediating the influence of recruiting sources on posthire outcomes (Blau, 1990; Griffeth et al., 1997; Vecchio, 1995; Werbel & Landau, 1996; Williams et al., 1993). In addition, studies in this area suffer from a variety of methodological problems (e.g., most studies have collected retrospective data and assume no within-source variation), and other potential confounds (e.g., one possible explanation for individual-differences effects may be differences in the realism of information provided by sources to different applicant populations [Wanous & Colella, 1989]; alternatively, several studies suggest that individual differences in race and self-esteem may moderate applicants' use of different recruiting sources [Blau, 1990; Caldwell & Spivey, 1983; Ellis & Taylor, 1983; Kirnan et al., 1989]).

In brief, research associated with recruiting source effects on job applicants appears ready for a shift in focus, and more specifically a shift that concentrates attention on message exchange processes associated with job candidates' contacts with recruiting sources. Basic descriptive research needs to be conducted to determine the content domains (e.g., information about organizational values and culture, supervision, company policies), specificity, consistency, valence, and so forth of messages provided by different sources (e.g., Saks, 1994). The likelihood that a source might be able to provide abundant, accurate information in some areas and not others needs to be considered (i.e., source credibility may vary with content domain). The extent to which a potential applicant may engage in one-way versus two-way communication with a source (for instance, newspaper ads can't answer questions) warrants study, since the latter (e.g., conversation with a current employee) allows an applicant to seek information about the job and/or organization that is most salient to him or her. At the same time, we need to recognize that face-to-face interaction between applicants and a recruiting source will result in considerable variability across applicants in the information they receive. If this is the case, then it may be important for us to also reconsider the relevance of the outcome variables that typify research in this area. Perhaps it makes more sense to evaluate the impact of recruiting sources in terms of their ability to generate pools of applicants who meet minimum job qualifications than to expect meaningful relationships between recruiting sources and criteria such as turnover and job performance, which may be more affected by organizational training and socialization practices (e.g., Werbel & Landau, 1996).

Finally, it seems apparent that changes in communication technology as well as in labor markets need greater consideration in future research. Potential job applicants can now obtain, 24 hours a day, information about job openings from an organization's homepage on the Internet and from participating in electronic chat groups and bulletin boards (forms of communication networks; e.g., Kilduff, 1990), or simply by contacting someone in the organization via electronic mail. Are these formal or informal recruiting sources, or a combination of the two? Also, we need to consider the extent to which "direct experience" may be replacing other recruiting sources in attracting applicants to organizations. For example, statistics suggest that 20% of the new jobs created between 1991 and 1993 were temporary ones and that 90% of companies use temporary employment agencies to meet some of their labor needs (Feldman, Doerpinghaus, & Turnley, 1994; Golden & Appelbaum, 1992). Given that most temporary employees consider their temporary jobs as temporary, it is of little surprise that about half report that they see these positions as a mechanism to find job leads and to examine companies without having to commit themselves (von Hippel, Mangnum, Greenberger, Heneman, & Skoglind, 1997). Does temporary employment represent a new, major recruiting source? To what extent are internships in which college students participate serving the same function (e.g., Taylor, 1988)? What, if anything, distinguishes the

nature of communication between job applicants and these recruiting sources in comparison to more traditional ones? Consideration of questions such as these represent exciting areas for future research.

Realism of Job/Organizational Expectations

Generally speaking, job applicants have unrealistic, typically positively "inflated" expectations about the organizations in which they are seeking employment (e.g., Jablin, 1984; Wanous, 1980). In part, it has been suggested that job candidates' expectations are unrealistic because organizations tend to follow traditional recruitment strategies in which they focus on primarily communicating the positive features of organizational membership to applicants (Wanous, 1977, 1980). Thus, the recruitment literature organizations provide students at college placement centers usually attempts to project companies as exciting and prestigious places to work (attraction) and typically focuses on extrinsic versus intrinsic job features (Herriot & Rothwell, 1981; "Recruiting Literature," 1981; Shyles & Ross, 1984). Given current and projected labor shortages in selective fields, evidence that qualified applicants respond most favorably to catchy employment advertisements that portray organizations in a positive manner and focus attention on extrinsic job characteristics (Barber & Roehling, 1993; Belt & Paolillo, 1982; Gatewood, Gowan, & Lautenschlager, 1993; Kaplan, Aamodt, & Wilk, 1991; Mason & Belt, 1986), and the increasing adoption by organizations of strategic marketing orientations to recruit and attract applicants (e.g., Martin & Franz, 1994; Maurer, Howe, & Lee, 1992; Palkowitz & Mueller, 1987), dramatic changes in contemporary (traditional) organizational recruitment strategies are probably unlikely in the immediate future.

As noted above, it also appears that applicants prefer traditional (positive focus) recruitment approaches (e.g., Saks, Wiesner, & Summers, 1994; Wiesner, Saks, & Summers,

1991), which may not present realistic views of jobs and organizations and inflate applicants' expectations. In theory, the desirability of recruits developing inflated job and organizational expectations, however, is problematic, since the more inflated the job candidates' preentry expectations are, the more difficult it usually is for them to meet these expectations once on the job. Along these lines, in a meta-analysis of 31 "met expectations" studies, Wanous, Poland, Premack, and Davis (1992) found fairly strong support for hypothesized relationships between unmet expectations and job satisfaction (mean $r = .39$) and organizational commitment (mean $r = .39$), but somewhat weaker relationships between unmet expectations and job survival (mean $r = .19$) and job performance (mean $r = .11$). As Wanous and his colleagues (Colella, 1989; Wanous & Colella, 1989; Wanous et al., 1992) have noted, however, an assumption underlying the met-expectations hypothesis, which remains to be tested, is that newcomers receive clear and consistent messages from insiders about the validity of their expectations. In other words, in work environments in which newcomers receive ambiguous or conflicting messages about job expectations from incumbents, it may not be possible for them to either confirm or disconfirm their expectations, and as a consequence the met-expectations hypothesis may not operate as predicted.

Although they have not been widely adopted by organizations, over the past several decades a considerable amount of research has been devoted to the study of realistic job previews (RJPs). Building on the met-expectations hypothesis, RJPs are intended to deflate applicants' expectations to more realistic levels (much like medical vaccinations) by providing them with a "dose of organizational reality" (Popovich & Wanous, 1982). Thus, it is believed that by presenting job applicants with RJP booklets, videotapes, films, work sample simulations, job visits, or oral presentations, job candidates' expectations will be deflated to more realistic levels, self-selection will occur among "marginal" applicants, and recruits will be better prepared to cope with their jobs once they start work; because they are provided with accurate job/organizational information prior to making their employment decisions, newcomers are also expected to feel greater commitment to their jobs, exhibit higher levels of job satisfaction, and have lower rates of turnover.

Although over 40 studies have explored the reasons why RJPs should work and the relative effectiveness of RJPs in reducing turnover and enhancing recruits' job attitudes, their results have frequently been inconsistent (e.g., McEvoy & Cascio, 1985; Premack & Wanous, 1985; Rynes, 1991; Wanous, 1977, 1980; Wanous & Colella, 1989). In fact, one recent study suggests that newcomers' early work experiences may be more potent than their preentry expectations in predicting turnover, job satisfaction, and organizational commitment (Irving & Meyer, 1994). However, it does appear that RJPs can lower expectations and increase job survival (e.g., Buckley, Fedor, Veres, Wiese, & Carraher, 1998; Hom, Griffeth, Palich, & Bracker, 1998; Premack & Wanous, 1985; Wanous et al., 1992), although the decrease in turnover is typically small (yet even small decreases in turnover can produce big savings for organizations) and we still do not have an adequate understanding as to why RJPs have this effect (Saks et al., 1994; Wanous & Colella, 1989). A number of reasons have been posited for inconsistencies in research findings among RJP studies. Factors that have been suggested as "causes" of variant results include inconsistent operational definitions of *realism* across studies; disparities across studies with respect to the timing of RJP presentations (e.g., before or after an employment interview or job offer); inadequate sample sizes to afford sufficient statistical power in testing hypotheses; overreliance on laboratory versus field studies; variability among the organizational roles/positions in which RJPs have been tested; inconsistencies in the time periods at which turnover data have been collected by researchers; differences across studies in methods/modes of presenting RJP; and the general failure to adequately consider other source (e.g., credibility, trustworthiness), message (e.g., content, amount, specificity), and audience (receiver) characteristics in preparing RJPs (e.g., Breaugh, 1983; Jablin, 1987; Phillips, 1998; Popovich & Wanous, 1982; Reilly, Brown, Blood, & Malatesta, 1981).

To unravel some of the inconsistencies in research findings, recent studies have focused on identifying factors that might mediate the effects of RJPs on outcomes. In particular, it appears that the complexity of the job being previewed (Breaugh, 1983; McEvoy & Cascio, 1985; Reilly et al., 1981), applicants' self-efficacy (Pond & Hay, 1989; Saks et al., 1994), job alternatives available to applicants (Saks et al., 1994; Saks, Wiesner, & Summers, 1996; Wiesner et al., 1991), and communication characteristics of previews (e.g., Colarelli, 1984; Green, 1991; Saks & Cronshaw, 1990) mediate effects associated with RJPs. With respect to communication-related mediators, studies suggest that the adequacy (amount), descriptiveness, valence, and accuracy of information applicants receive from RJPs may influence their attraction to a firm and their knowledge about job and organizational characteristics, and as a result affect their ability to determine the extent to which a job and organization match their needs (Dilla, 1987; Phillips, 1998; Saks & Cronshaw, 1990; Saks et al., 1994; Vandenberg & Scarpello, 1990). In addition, at least one study has also shown that previews allowing for two-way communication (after initial interviews with recruiters) between job incumbents (high-credibility sources) and applicants may be more effective in reducing turnover than written previews (Colarelli, 1984).

In assessing the literature over a decade ago, I argued that the employment interview is probably the setting in which most job previews actually occur (Jablin, 1985b, 1987). I suggested this because of the frequent discussion of job/organizational topics in these interaction settings and the domination of "talk time" by recruiters (research has shown that applicants speak for only about 10 minutes in the average 30-minute interview and that recruiters spend considerable amounts of time

telling applicants about themselves, the job, and the organization and in answering applicants' questions, which typically focus on job/organizational topics; e.g., Babbitt & Jablin, 1985; Tengler & Jablin, 1983). Thus, I concluded that the "interview is important not only as an interpersonal communication event, but because of the role it plays in communicating job/organizational expectations to potential employees" (Jablin, 1985b, p. 621). While others have subsequently recognized that the interview is likely "the most popular means for RJPs in practice" (Wanous & Colella, 1989, p. 75) and may be "the method of choice for the future" (Wanous, 1989, p. 130), researchers have yet to adequately investigate the interview as a method to communicate RJPs. Rather, RJP researchers continue to focus on the preview as a formal, standardized, one-way form of communication in which applicants are viewed as "passive receptors of new information" (Wanous & Colella, 1989, p. 76).

However, two studies have explicitly considered the interview as a method of communicating RJPs. In the first study, Saks and Cronshaw (1990) examined RJPs in the laboratory using students participating in simulated, role-play employment interviews (applicants were applying for a summer job) in which the interviewer followed a script that included ten standard interview questions. In one condition, applicants received a written RJP before their interviews, in another condition RJPs were presented orally during the interviews, and in a control condition applicants received only general job information in their interviews. Findings indicated that both the written and oral RJPs lowered applicants' job expectations and increased role clarity, but did not affect commitment to job choice or job acceptance. In addition, those receiving the oral RJP had more positive perceptions of the honesty of their interviewers and their organizations than those in the other conditions. In the second study, Barber, Hollenbeck, Tower, and Phillips (1994) examined the interaction of interview focus (recruitment only, a combination of recruitment and selection) and interview content (traditional, realistic preview) on applicants' retention of information and desire to pursue an actual opening for a part-time, temporary office assistant position at a university research center. Two doctoral students conducted the interviews and "followed detailed scripts" (p. 890). The combined recruitment and selection interviews were highly structured and about 25 minutes in duration. Applicants in the recruitment condition were told that their interviews (which lasted about 15 minutes) were not part of the selection process but rather were for informative purposes only. Results revealed no significant effects for interview content (type of preview); however, the researchers suggest this may have been the result of a weak RJP manipulation (i.e., the negative attributes of the job may not have been sufficient to produce effects).

While the studies described above are laudable, the extent to which the previews employed in these investigations reflects the manner in which they occur in naturally occurring interviews is highly questionable. In light of current knowledge about communication in selection interviews (see next section), it is unlikely that job previews are as formal, standardized, and one way in communication as those incorporated in these studies. Rather, it is more likely that in naturally occurring interviews previews are less structured and are embedded into communication exchanges taking place throughout the duration of the interview (i.e., they are not just one-shot presentations). In other words, previews are coconstructed by interviewers and applicants as a by-product of discourse processes (e.g., question, answer, statements sequences) that evolve over the course of the interview (e.g., Jablin, Miller, & Sias, 1999). Assuming this is the case, then future research should focus on identifying how previews are constructed in actual interviews and then explore how variations in discourse processes and preview content affect applicants' subsequent attitudes and behaviors.

To review, several communication-related propositions appear tenable about RJPs and applicants' expectations. First, if RJPs are to have any effect then applicants need to obtain accurate, ample, and salient information about job and organizational characteristics. Second, it is possible that RJPs have a greater impact on applicants' assessment of the match between their needs and the ability of organizations to fulfill those needs, and on newcomers' initial job and organizational adjustment, than on long-term outcomes such as turnover and job satisfaction. Third, "in studying realistic recruitment as transmitted through booklets, films, or rehearsed recruiter presentations, we are studying a phenomenon that probably occurs in a very small percentage of recruitment efforts" (Rynes, 1991, p. 428; see also Phillips, 1998). Finally, although the employment interview is likely the most common context in which all forms of job previews are communicated, we know little of how this is accomplished in this interaction setting.

The Selection Interview

Although we may not know much about how job previews are jointly constructed by interviewers and applicants in selection interviews, a vast number of studies have been conducted exploring other communication-related characteristics and processes of the interview (see Eder & Ferris, 1989; Harris, 1989; Jablin & Krone, 1994; Jablin & McComb, 1984; Jablin & Miller, 1990; Jablin et al., 1999). Building on the generalizations that Jablin and Krone (1994, pp. 627-628) have suggested, as well as more recent research in the area, Table 19.1 summarizes major findings of studies exploring communication in the employment interview.

Caution should be exercised in generalizing the findings listed in Table 19.1 since a considerable number of methodological problems and conceptual biases have been associated with selection interview research (e.g., Eder & Ferris, 1989; Eder & Harris, 1999; Jablin & McComb, 1984; Ralston & Kirkwood, 1995). At the same time, the quality (and, it is hoped, the generalizability) of communication research in this area has improved

TABLE 19.1 Summary of Research Findings on Communication in the Selection Interview

1. Applicants' interview outcome expectations (including likelihood of accepting job offers) appear related to their perceptions of and affective reactions to their recruiters as trustworthy, competent, composed, empathic, enthusiastic, and well-organized communicators (see Alderfer & McCord, 1970; Fisher, Ilgen, & Hoyer, 1979; Jablin, Tengler, & Teigen, 1982; Liden & Parsons, 1986; Ralston, 1993; Ralston & Brady, 1994; Rynes & Miller, 1983; Schmitt & Coyle, 1976; Taylor & Bergmann, 1987; Teigen, 1983).

2. Recruiters and applicants tend to have differential expectations and perceptions of communication behaviors displayed in interviews, including levels of talkativeness, listening, questioning, and topics of discussion (see Cheatham & McLaughlin, 1976; Connerley, 1997; Connerley & Rynes, 1997; Engler-Parish & Millar, 1989; Herriot & Rothwell, 1981, 1983; Posner, 1981; Shaw, 1983; Taylor & Sniezek, 1984).

3. Applicants do not particularly like or trust interviewers and appear hesitant to accept job offers if their only sources of information are recruiters; however, interviewers who are job incumbents are perceived as presenting more realistic job and organizational information than are interviewers who are personnel representatives (see Downs, 1969; Fisher et al., 1979; Jablin, Tengler, & Teigen, 1985; Rynes, Bretz, & Gerhart, 1991; Taylor & Bergmann, 1987).

4. Interviewee satisfaction, attraction to an organization, and perceptions of recruiter effectiveness appear related to the quality and amount of organizational and job information the recruiter provides and the degree to which the recruiter asks the interviewee open-ended questions that are high in "face validity," allows him or her sufficient "talk time," and shows warmth toward and interest in the applicant (see DeBell, Montgomery, McCarthy, & Lanthier, 1998; Golitz & Giannantonio, 1995; Herriot & Rothwell, 1983; Jablin, Tengler, McClary, & Teigen, 1987; Karol, 1977; Powell, 1991; Tengler, 1982; Turban & Dougherty, 1992).

5. Interviewees who display high versus low levels of nonverbal immediacy (operationalized by eye contact, smiling, posture, interpersonal distance, and body orientation), who are high in vocal activity and engage their interviewers in more "response-response" than "question-response" interactions, tend to be favored by interviewers (see Anderson & Shackleton, 1990; Burnett & Motowidlo, 1998; Byrd, 1979; Einhorn, 1981; Forbes & Jackson, 1980; Imada & Hakel, 1977; Keenan, 1976; Keenan & Wedderburn, 1975; McGovern & Tinsley, 1978; Mino, 1996; Trent, 1978).

6. Recruiters find interviewees more acceptable if they receive favorable information about them prior to or during their interviews; while recruiters may adopt confirmatory questioning strategies to test positive preinterview impressions, they do not necessarily use confirmatory questioning to validate negative preinterview impressions (Binning, Goldstein, Garcia, & Scattaregia, 1988; Dougherty, Turban, & Callender, 1994; Herriot & Rothwell, 1983; Lindvall, Culberson, Binning, & Goldstein, 1986; Macan & Dipboye, 1990; McDonald & Hakel, 1985; Phillips & Dipboye, 1989; Sackett, 1982).

7. Interviewers may more positively evaluate applicants who display assertive, self-enhancing impression management techniques, including agreeing with the interviewer, emphasizing positive traits, self-promotion and the use of personal stories to support assertions, asking positive-closed questions, and claiming fit with the organization. In general, applicants try to convey that they are competent, hardworking, goal oriented, confident, adaptable and flexible, interpersonally skilled, and effective leaders (see Baron, 1989; Gilmore & Ferris, 1989; Kacmar, Delery, & Ferris, 1992; Stevens, 1997; Stevens & Kristof, 1995).

8. Spoken attributions (somewhat similar to "accounts"; see Morris, 1988) are fairly frequent elements of applicants' interview communication; applicants tend to offer unstable and universal attributions for negative events and internal and controllable attributions for positive events. In general, interviewers attribute applicant "social rule" breaking in interviews more to situational than personal causes (see Ramsey, Gallois, & Callan, 1997; Silvester, 1997; Struthers, Colwill, & Perry, 1992).

(continued)

TABLE 19.1 Continued

9. Most questions applicants ask their interviewers are closed-ended, singular in form, typically not phrased in the first person, asked after interviewers ask applicants for inquiries, and seek job-related information (Babbitt & Jablin, 1985; Einhorn, 1981).

10. Applicants' perceptions of their interviewers as empathic listeners appear to be negatively related to the degree to which interviewers interject "interruptive statements" while the interviewees are speaking (see McComb & Jablin, 1984).

11. Interviewers tend to rate more highly and be more satisfied with applicants who talk more of the time in their interviews (though this talk is not necessarily in response to interviewers' questions), who elaborate on answers, and whose discussion of topics more nearly matches interviewers' expectations (Einhorn, 1981; Herriot & Rothwell, 1983; Tengler & Jablin, 1983; Tullar, 1989; Ugbah & Majors, 1992).

12. Interviewers tend to employ inverted-funnel question sequences (they begin with closed questions and then progress to more open-ended questions), thus limiting applicant talk time during the opening minutes of interviews. Recruiters also tend to "hold the floor" more after answering questions (Axtmann & Jablin, 1986; Tengler & Jablin, 1983).

13. Relational control analyses of employment interviews suggest that applicants are "pushed" into dominance by interviewers' questions, while interviewers are "pulled" into giving information (dominance or one-across moves) by the support statements of applicants (see Engler-Parish & Millar, 1989; Kacmar & Hochwarter, 1995; Tullar, 1989).

14. Structured interview question formats (e.g., behavior description interviews, situational interviews, comprehensive structured interviews, and structured behavioral interviews) appear more valid than unstructured approaches (see Campion, Palmer, & Campion, 1997; Campion, Pursell, & Brown, 1988; Dipboye, 1994; Huffcutt & Roth, 1998; Janz, 1989; Janz, Hellervik, & Gilmore, 1986; Latham, 1989; Latham, Saari, Pursell, & Campion, 1980; Motowidlo et al., 1992; Pursell, Campion, & Gaylord, 1980; Williamson, Campion, Roehling, Malos, & Campion, 1997).

15. Applicants relatively high in communication apprehension prepare for and think about employment interviews differently than those low in apprehension; applicants high in communication apprehension also tend to be judged lower by interviewers than applicants relatively low in apprehension. It is possible, however, that interviewer behavior (e.g., displays of "warmth" vs. "coldness") may interact with applicants' level of anxiety to affect interviewers' ratings of applicants (see Ayres & Crosby, 1995; Ayres, Ayres, & Sharp, 1983; Ayres, Keereetaweep, Chen, & Edwards, 1998; Liden, Martin, & Parson, 1993).

16. Applicant communication ability/skill (e.g., fluency of speech, composure, appropriateness of content, ability to express ideas in an organized fashion) is frequently reported by interviewers to be a critical factor in their decisions (see Bretz, Rynes, & Gerhart, 1993; Graves & Karren, 1992; Hollandsworth, Kazelskis, Stevens, & Dressel, 1979; Kinicki & Lockwood, 1985; Kinicki, Lockwood, Hom, & Griffeth, 1990; Mino, 1996; Peterson, 1997; Posner, 1981; Riggio & Throckmorton, 1988; Spano & Zimmermann, 1995; Ugbah & Majors, 1992).

NOTE: Generalizations are extrapolated from Jablin and Krone (1994) and Jablin and Miller (1990), and from the findings of recent studies.

greatly in recent years. Thus, while most studies still focus on examining interviews of graduating students in university placement centers or the interviews of students involved in role-play situations, and rarely consider the effects of situational variables (e.g., labor market conditions) on results, an increasing number of studies have centered on collecting behavioral (as compared to perceptual) forms of communication data and have focused attention on investigating processual dimensions of interview communication (see Jablin et al., 1999). These studies usually involve audio- or videotaping interviews, coding behavior, and analyzing patterns of communicative acts (e.g., spoken attributions [Silvester, 1997], impression management tactics [Stevens & Kristof, 1995], and information-gathering tactics [Dougherty, Turban, & Callender, 1994]) and patterns of interacts, double interacts, and transition sequences (e.g., patterns of question, answer, and statement interacts [Axtmann & Jablin, 1986] and patterns of relational control and transaction structures [Engler-Parish, & Millar, 1989; Kacmer & Hochwarter, 1995; Tullar, 1989]). In turn, researchers studying nonverbal interview communication have asked judges to listen to audiotapes or view videotapes of actual interviews and rate the extent to which applicants have displayed such behaviors as smiling, eye contact, and upright body posture (Burnett & Motowidlo, 1998; Jablin, Hudson, & Sias, 1997; Liden, Martin, & Parsons, 1993; Riggio & Throckmorton, 1988). Moreover, researchers are increasingly combining the quantitative coding of interview communication behavior with qualitative analyses aimed at understanding how behaviors are enacted. Thus, for instance, Stevens and Kristof (1995) not only report the frequency with which applicants use self-promotion as an impression management tactic but also delineate the content themes applicants use to describe themselves and the discourse devices (e.g., elaborations, stories) they use to construct these images. In sum, the above trends represent important developments that portend significant advances in our understanding of communication in the selection interview.

Although nascent, a shift also appears to be occurring in what researchers consider to be the central goal of the selection interview. Traditionally, the selection interview has been considered a mechanism for determining person-job (P-J) fit (i.e., as a method of determining if an applicant has the requisite skills, knowledge, and abilities to perform a job; see Adkins, Russell, & Werbel, 1994; Jablin, 1975). This purpose is reflected in research exploring various forms of highly structured interviews; that is, regardless of specific format, highly structured interviews are job focused and are grounded in the assumption that by concentrating on such matters the validity of the interview as a selection device can be enhanced (e.g., Dipboye, 1994). An alternative perspective to the purpose of the selection interview has evolved from recent work exploring organizations as cultures (see Eisenberg & Riley, Chapter 9, this volume) and Schneider's (1987) attraction-selection-attrition (ASA) model of organizational behavior (which maintains that organizations and applicants are attracted to one another because of shared values, interests, and other attributes). These approaches propose that person-organization (P-O) fit may be more crucial than P-J fit for individual success in organizations, as well as long-term organizational effectiveness (e.g., Bowen, Ledford, & Nathan, 1991; Kristof, 1996; O'Reilly, Chatman, & Caldwell, 1991; Saks & Ashforth, 1997). In other words, these models are founded on the notion that people join and leave whole organizations/cultures, not just jobs, "whether they realize it or not" (Schneider, Goldstein, & Smith, 1995, p. 764), and as a consequence, selection processes should largely focus on assessing the fit between job seekers' values and those that characterize the organizations in which they are seeking employment. In light of the popularity of the employment interview as a selection device, it is not surprising that scholars have suggested that the interview may be a viable method for establishing P-O fit (e.g., Adkins et al., 1994; Bretz, Rynes, & Gerhart, 1993; Cable & Judge, 1997; Chatman, 1991; Judge & Ferris, 1992; Rynes & Gerhart, 1990).

To date, only a handful of studies has examined the potential of the interview for establishing P-O fit, and it is difficult to aggregate their findings into generalizable conclusions. Although some studies have shown that interviewers recognize and seek organization-specific values and qualities (e.g., leadership and warmth) in job candidates (Adkins et al., 1994; Rynes & Gerhart, 1990; Turban & Keon, 1993), other research suggests that recruiters are more interested in applicants with "universally" desirable values and traits than ones specific to organizations (Bretz et al., 1993). Evidence also indicates that interviewers' evaluations of P-O fit are based more on their *perceptions* of congruence between applicants' values and organizational values (typically assessed via responses to the Organizational Culture Profile; see O'Reilly et al., 1991) than on actual value congruence and that these perceptions influence interviewers' assessments of applicants and their hiring recommendations (Cable & Judge, 1997). In turn, research exploring *applicants' perceptions* has found that their perceptions of the congruence between their own values and those of the organizations in which they are seeking employment are related to their own P-O fit assessments and that their P-O fit assessments predict their job choice decisions and later levels of job satisfaction, organizational identification, and other outcomes (Cable & Judge, 1996; Moss & Frieze, 1993; Saks & Ashforth, 1997). With respect to how applicants develop their perceptions of P-O fit, job seekers report that their perceptions develop from their interviews with recruiters and informal contacts with other organizational members (Rynes, Bretz, & Gerhart, 1991) and that the more sources (especially formal ones) from whom applicants obtain information the greater their perceptions of P-J and P-O fit (Saks & Ashforth, 1997).

To review, employment interviews may be important settings in which recruiters and applicants exchange information that is relevant to their respective assessments of P-O fit, as well as P-J fit. However, at this juncture we do not know the kinds of messages that are exchanged in interviews that are interpreted by each party as value or culture related, the ex-

tent to which "accurate" information is shared (or even available), the sorts of value-related information recruiters and applicants would like to obtain from each other, or how each party's general verbal and nonverbal communicative performance, including their questioning and answering behavior, among other factors, affect their respective perceptions of P-O fit. In addition, it is important to note that a shift to using employment interviews to judge P-O fit brings into question the use by organizations of job-focused, highly structured interviews to assess applicants. As Cable and Judge (1997) observe, "Job-based structured interviews appear to be somewhat incompatible with assessing applicants' values and P-O fit, because these criteria extend well beyond immediate job-related factors. . . . In fact, subjective fit impressions typically are what structured interviews remove from interviewer decision making" (p. 558). This may explain, in part, interviewers' resistance to the use of structured interviews (e.g., Dipboye, 1994); they do not allow interviewers to obtain information related to the match between applicants' values and beliefs and the values and assumptions that are central to their organizations.

If the employment interview is more suited to assess P-O fit than P-J fit (e.g., Jablin, 1975; Cable & Judge, 1996), and P-O fit is predictive of positive outcomes for both applicants and organizations, then it is essential that applicants and recruiters share accurate information with one another in the interview. However, contemporary approaches to employment interviewing tend to emphasize competitive as compared to collaborative approaches to communication (e.g., Jablin & McComb, 1984; Ralston & Kirkwood, 1995), which do not necessarily encourage "dialogue" but rather "monologue," "parroting," and other forms of "distorted" communication (Cable & Judge, 1996; Ferris & Judge, 1991; Habermas, 1970; Kirkwood & Ralston, 1999; Ralston & Thomason, 1997). In part, the use of highly structured interviews attempts to limit these tendencies by focusing discussion on specific, job-focused behavior (including ethical work behavior; e.g., Hollwitz & Pawlowski, 1997) and by constraining the nature of the information exchange process. However, if, as Cable and Judge (1997) suggest, highly structured approaches to interview communication are not especially effective in generating information useful for assessing individual and organizational values and P-O fit, then we may need to consider alternative approaches to generating valid information in employment interviews. Research along these lines should consider relevant communication processes not only in screening interviews but in (1) second or on-site interviews as well, since these interactions are fairly distinct from screening interviews (e.g., in location of interview, length, number of interviewers, display of "scripted" behavior, and appropriate topics of discussion; see Fink, Bauer, & Campion, 1994; Miller & Buzzanell, 1996) yet appear central to applicants' and employers' assessments of P-O fit (e.g., Turban, Campion, & Eyring, 1995); and (2) explore how *both* interviewers and applicants use communication to coconstruct meanings/generate valid information, and produce and reproduce interview structure (e.g., Dipboye, 1994; Jablin et al., 1999).

Finally, we need to more extensively explore the nature of communication between organizations and applicants, as well as among applicants, subsequent to screening and on-site interviews, but prior to applicants' receiving and accepting job offers. Although at present we know that delays in an organization's postinterview communications with job candidates are perceived negatively by applicants and often "signal" to them that something is wrong with the organization (Rynes et al., 1991) and that after their interviews applicants talk to peers and others about their experiences and that these conversations may affect their own and other applicants' organizational attitudes (Miller, Susskind, & Levine, 1995), little is known about the characteristics and effects of the message strategies applicants and organizational representatives use to negotiate employment conditions associated with job offers (e.g., Powell & Goulet, 1996).

Preentry

Although the period of time between when a person is offered and accepts a position and actually begins working in a new organization (which for new college graduates may last several months) has been an infrequent object of investigation, it is one deserving of study and likely represents "a distinct and under-researched phase of newcomer socialization" (Barrios-Choplin, 1994, p. 265). Three issues in particular warrant examination: (1) the nature and effects of the messages newcomers receive from their new employers prior to their first day of work; (2) how newcomers manage their "reputations" (others' impressions of them) prior to beginning work in their organizations; and (3) how "insiders" converse about and make sense of new hires during this period, and in particular how they socially construct or create a reputation for newcomers in their everyday conversations.

With respect to the first issue, research should explore the kinds of messages that new hires receive from their prospective employers prior to beginning work and how these messages may affect their initial job/organization expectations and attitudes. Future studies might build on the work of Barrios-Choplin (1994), who, in exploring the nature of the "surprises" (Louis, 1980) organizational newcomers experience, found that of all the surprises individuals reported, about 11% occurred during the preentry period and that the nature of these surprises were distinct from those associated with postentry. In particular, his research showed that (1) the types of surprises new hires experienced in the preentry period tended to be more pleasant than those they experienced later in the assimilation process (see also Gundry & Rousseau, 1994), and (2) one of the most common types of pleasant surprises was the "expression of caring" by members of the organization. For example, new hires reported being pleasantly surprised to receive a personal note from the boss welcoming the person to the organization and offering assistance in the relocation process. Although not explored in this research, this kind of symbolic activity (which might be conceived of as a form of impression management) may set a trajectory for newcomers' communication relationships with managers and overall identification with the organization (e.g., Allen, 1995; Myers & Kassing, 1998), affect their images of and commitment to the organization (e.g. Treadwell & Harrison, 1994), and the manner in which they interpret other messages they receive from members of the organization prior to and after they begin work.

While organizational insiders may communicate with newcomers prior to the recruit's first day of work, it is not unusual for newcomers to communicate with selective members of the organization as well. Thus, for example, a newcomer might send an e-mail message to those the newcomer met during the on-site interview expressing appreciation of their confidence and support and expounding on how he or she is looking forward to working with them. This might be conceptualized as a form of "anticipatory" impression management (Elsbach, Sutton, & Principe, 1997) that is aimed at insiders and employs messages designed to project a positive image of the newcomer. At the same time, new hires may also engage in "self-handicapping" (e.g., Greenberg, 1996) in their communications with insiders by offering disclaimers to manage others' attributions and expectations of their skills and performance capabilities (e.g., "I've never really performed X before, so it will probably take me some time to do it well"), and thereby engage in an "anticipatory" form of role negotiation/accommodation (e.g., Moreland & Levine, in press). In sum, we should realize that "a newcomer might arrange for word of his or her reputation to be spread in advance, so that people are prepared for what is to come" (Bromley, 1993, p. 23).

Finally, it is important to recognize that organizational members converse about and make sense of new hires during the preentry period (Sutton & Louis, 1984). They engage in collective sensemaking to reduce uncertainty about the newcomer, to make him or her

"comprehensible and manageable" (Bromley, 1993). Thus, prior to their first day of work newcomers are preceded by one or more reputations that they may have had little or no role in creating. As Bromley (1993) has observed, in most cases "when we join a group or interact with someone for the first time, people will have heard something about us and will have formed attitudes and expectations on the basis of the information" (p. 23). In the organizational context, it is likely that those persons involved in the selection and recruitment process are key sources of information for others about the newcomer, since they have observed or interacted with the person and have firsthand information about him or her. However, their impressions will be affected by what others involved in the selection and recruitment process say about the person. In other words, others' impressions of the new person may unconsciously become assimilated into one's own beliefs and subsequently be communicated to other employees in everyday conversations about the new hire. As a consequence of this process of selecting, editing, and even inventing information about the newcomer, one or more newcomer reputations may be created. While what organizational insiders may communicate to others about the newcomer may be detailed, most of the time that will not be the case; rather, information that is shared will "take the form of simple stereotypes encapsulated in a few words or phrases; 'A hard-working, no-nonsense chap,' 'A real bitch,' 'Quiet and aloof' " (Bromley, 1993, p. 23). In brief, it is likely that insiders' preentry collective sensemaking about the newcomer will revolve around the expression of stereotypic categories and labels shared among employees through systems of social networks.

The social construction of newcomers' reputations by old-timers during the preentry period has its benefits in terms of reducing uncertainty about new hires, but it also may create difficulties for newcomers. "The effect of reputation is that our expectations about other people, based on hearsay, influence our behavior when we come into face-to-face contact with them . . . possibly in a way that makes our expectation a self-fulfilling prophecy" (Bromley, 1993, p. 23). In other words, consistent with social information processing theory (Salancik & Pfeffer, 1978), the general "character" of a person that has been created in socially constructing his or her reputation may serve as the "template" against which the person is viewed and judged when insiders first interact with the person. However, it is also possible that insiders' conversations about newcomers may result in the creation of a "prototypical" newcomer reputation (e.g., Niedenthal, Cantor, & Kihlstrom, 1985) that becomes a template against which *all* newcomers are viewed. Thus, even though newcomers may not have actively participated in the creation of their reputations, they may find it difficult to change the way others talk and think about them once they actually begin work in the organization.

To date, we know little of the communication and sociocognitive processes (e.g., Levine, Resnick, & Higgins, 1993; Resnick, Levine, & Teasely, 1991) insiders use in the social construction of newcomers' preentry organizational reputations. Seemingly, task interdependence and the extent to which insiders are motivated to achieve consensus and accuracy in their impressions about newcomers will affect the substance of the information they share in conversations about them, as well as the degree to which they question and explore one another's impressions and seek new or more complete information about the new hires (e.g., Fiske & Neuberg, 1990; Ruscher, Hammer, & Hammer, 1996).

Summary

The preceding discussion has provided an overview of communication processes relevant to anticipatory organizational socialization. The focus of this presentation was on how job seekers and employers acquire and use information that affects their respective application/recruitment and employment decisions and expectations about one another.

The specific topics discussed in this section —recruiting sources, realism of expectations, the selection interview, and the preentry period—were examined in relative isolation of one another. In reality, many of these activities and processes are more overlapping, seamless, and fluid. In addition, in considering the literature presented here it is important to recognize that our knowledge of anticipatory organizational socialization is based primarily on data gathered from new college graduates—entry-level employees—and not seasoned veterans (e.g., Rynes et al., 1997). Further, many problems and limitations were noted in the communication between job candidates and organizations during anticipatory organizational socialization. As a consequence, employment decisions made by applicants and organizations are often based on less-than-perfect information and may result in ill-formed beliefs and expectations of each party's employment duties, implicit obligations, and identities, among other things. Regardless of the sources of these inaccurate, often inflated beliefs and expectations, their effects seems very clear: Discrepancies between expectations and reality increase the surprises (Louis, 1980) newcomers *and* incumbents experience as the new recruits enter the organization and engage in the organizational assimilation process.

ORGANIZATIONAL ENTRY AND ASSIMILATION

Organizational assimilation concerns the processes by which individuals become integrated into the culture of an organization (Jablin, 1982). It is generally considered to be composed of two dynamic interrelated processes: (1) planned as well as unintentional efforts by the organization to "socialize" employees, and (2) the attempts of organizational members to "individualize" or change their roles and work environments to better satisfy their values, attitudes, and needs (Jablin, 1987). To a large extent, these two reciprocal processes are also central components of the organizational "role-making" process (Graen, 1976; Jablin, 1982), since it is "through the proactive and reactive communication of expectations to and from an individual by members of his or her 'role set' (Katz & Kahn, 1966) that organizational roles are negotiated and individuals share in the socially created 'reality' of organizations" (Jablin, 1987, p. 694).

For most newcomers, organizational entry is a time for learning "pivotal" behaviors, values, and beliefs associated with their job and organization (Schein, 1968). In other words, it is a time for learning what insiders consider to be "normal" patterns of thinking and behaving (Van Maanen, 1975), and in particular what things *mean* to members of the organization (including what the newcomer means to insiders). Much of what must be learned will eventually become mundane aspects of communication for newcomers, including such things as how to address others (e.g., Morand, 1996), how to dress (e.g., Pratt & Rafaeli, 1997; Rafaeli, Dutton, Harquail, & Mackie-Lewis, 1997; Rafaeli & Pratt, 1993), the uses and functions of humor (e.g., Meyer, 1997), norms associated with the communication of emotion (e.g., Conrad & Witte, 1994; Morris & Feldman, 1996; Waldron, 1994), formal and informal rules of communicating (e.g., Gilsdorf, 1998), and appropriate media to use in communicating with others (e.g., Donabedian, McKinnon, & Bruns, 1998), among other things. How does the newcomer acquire this knowledge? The recruit develops initial interpretation schemes and scripts for his or her new work environment primarily through formal and informal communication, in both ambient and discretionary forms, with others in the organization including message exchanges with supervisors, peers/coworkers, and management sources (e.g., Harris, 1994; Teboul, 1997).

To a substantial extent, newcomers learn what things mean in the organization by learning the labels that insiders apply to actions, objects, and people. As Ashforth and Humphrey (1997) suggest, labels are critical devices for "interpreting, organizing, and communicating experience within organizations, and, in turn, for guiding experience. . . . Thus, to the extent that specific labels and cognitions are shared, labels constitute a parsimonious means of understanding and communicating about an object" (p. 43). In brief, organizational members usually assign labels to people, objects, and activities to reduce uncertainty and make sense of their experiences. However, in most organizational environments it is unlikely that all insiders use identical labels to categorize and assign meaning to the same referents; rather, many different and often contradictory labels may be used by veterans to assign meaning to phenomena in any particular situation. Consequently, the labels that insiders use, and the labels that newcomers adopt, are not "neutral"; since they denote and connote distinct definitions of "reality" they represent forms of social control and power (Ashforth & Humphrey, 1995). Thus, to a considerable degree, recruits make sense of their new environments by observing and participating in the ongoing "labeling contest" (Ashforth & Humphrey, 1995) in which organizational members, in general, engage.

As noted in the discussion of the preentry period, newcomers enter into organizations with some sort of reputation, usually concisely packaged in the form of one or more labels. At a minimum, they will be labeled "new" by insiders, which has both advantages and disadvantages. Being labeled new may be advantageous in that oldtimers may not expect newcomers to perform well and perceive it to be "OK" for them to make numerous errors on the job (e.g., Greenberg, 1996); however, veterans' use and acceptance of this label may also lead them to view the new person as just a member of a category—newcomers—and as a result to deindividuate or reify the newcomer and set in motion a "Pygmalion effect" (e.g., Ashforth & Humphrey, 1997). Thus, it is likely newcomers are not passive recipients of all the labels others assign to them; rather, from their earliest days in the organization they may engage in self-labeling and other forms of sense/information giving directed at conveying preferred images about themselves that they wish others to accept.

To review, newcomers do not begin work in organizations *tabula rasa*; they not only have experienced some form of vocational and organizational anticipatory socialization that has affected their expectations, but they find themselves entering a discourse milieu in which the way others talk and think about them may already be somewhat established. At the same time, as noted several times in the preceding discussion, the process of entering into a new organization is usually one of surprise and uncertainty for both newcomers and incumbents (e.g., Falcione & Wilson, 1988; Louis, 1980).

Newcomers often experience surprises because of differences in their expectations and the reality they experience in their organizations (e.g., Danielson, 1995; Dean, Ferris, & Konstas, 1988; Feij, Whitely, Peiró, & Taris, 1995; Holton & Russell, 1997; Nelson, Quick, & Eakin, 1988; Nelson & Sutton, 1991; Nicholson & Arnold, 1989, 1991). For example, it is not uncommon for newcomers to report that they receive significantly less feedback from others in the organization then they had expected (Dean et al., 1988) or are surprised at the way "communications" are handled at higher levels of the organization (Nicholson & Arnold, 1989). Unfortunately, while research has identified the areas in which newcomers experience expectation-reality "gaps" and has shown that interactions with and social support from insiders help newcomers make sense of these experiences and reduce levels of distress (Fisher, 1986; Major, Kozlowski, Chao, & Gardner, 1995; Nelson & Quick, 1991; Reichers, 1987), we know little of how newcomers talk to others about these incongruencies in their efforts to resolve or manage them (with some notable exceptions as discussed below).

When one enters the organization, the initial "psychological contracts" between the organization and the newcomer also unfold and may be actively negotiated (Nelson, Quick, & Joplin, 1991; Robinson, 1996; Tsui, Pearce, Porter, & Hite, 1995). Rousseau and Parks (1993) note that both contracts and expectations serve to reduce uncertainty, but that contracts are special forms of expectations: expectations or beliefs that include promises (the communication of a commitment to do something). Employees' expectations, if not fulfilled, tend to result in moderate levels of emotional arousal (e.g., disappointment; see Nelson et al., 1991) whereas perceived violations in psychological contracts often arouse more intense emotions such as anger, aggression, or hostility (e.g., Morrison & Robinson, 1997). To some degree, the terms established in the psychological contracts of newcomers affect veterans as well (Feldman, 1994), since new terms may create "drift" in "normative" elements (aspects shared among employees) of the contracts of incumbents (Rousseau & Parks, 1993). In particular, this may be true in situations where elements of the contract are communicated publicly or can be observed by veterans. Such drift may be considered as a breach of contract by incumbents and diminish their willingness to abide by the new contract's terms or it may result in their adopting new contract "scripts," among other alternatives. Thus, "it is quite common to find newcomers and veterans working side by side holding different psychological contracts" (Rousseau, 1996, p. 52).

Expectations and contracts lay the groundwork for the role negotiation process; in other words, these dynamic cognitions represent templates by which assimilation experiences are understood. Yet we still know little of the communication processes and activities associated with how newcomers and organizational agents construct psychological contracts. Moreover, we need to recognize that unrealistic and unmet expectations and promises are not just phenomena experienced by newcomers but by all organizational members as they are continuously negotiating the assimilation process (e.g., Lawson & Angle, 1998; Pearson, 1995). As Rousseau and Parks (1993) have suggested:

> Organizations and individuals create contracts through communications at critical junctures

or personnel actions in the employment relationship: recruitment, job change (including promotion and lateral moves), and organizational change and development (e.g., team building, restructuring). . . . Messages containing employer promises come from organizational history and reputation, formal commitments (Rousseau & Anton, 1988, 1991), the interpretations of procedures and policies (Parks & Schmedemann, 1992), and the experiences of fellow employees (Brockner, 1988). Contracts emerge from experience as well as observation and may in fact be continuously created and renegotiated. (p. 29)

In sum, organizational entry is typified by relatively high levels of uncertainty, surprise, discrepancies between expectations and reality, and related efforts to make sense of these experiences through reformulating cognitive schemas, scripts, and behavioral models; categorizing and labeling people, activities, and objects; and related methods of interpreting and constructing social reality. Traditionally, the entry period has been conceptualized as the "breaking-in" period or "encounter" stage of assimilation, at the end of which time newcomers are supposed to have a sufficient understanding of the organization, the job, and the people they work with so that they are capable of negotiating or individualizing their roles with members of their role set (e.g., Jablin, 1987; Schein, 1968; Van Maanen, 1975). In other words, the entry period is often viewed as a discrete stage or phase of the assimilation process.

Stage Models of Assimilation Reconsidered

In recent years, researchers have focused a considerable amount of attention on developing stage or phase models of the organizational assimilation process (e.g., Feldman, 1976; Jablin, 1987; Van Maanen, 1975). Most of these models include (1) an anticipatory socialization phase; (2) an entry or "encounter" stage; and (3) a long-term period of "meta-morphosis" in which role conflicts are managed, and role negotiation and resocialization occur, among other activities. Although none of these models has been thoroughly tested, extant studies have produced mixed results with respect to the notion that most newcomers exhibit particular kinds of behaviors and develop specific kinds of attitudes at discrete stages of the assimilation process. There are a number of likely reasons for these results.

First, a common problem faced by researchers is determining when one stage of assimilation is ending and another beginning. Generally speaking, researchers have adopted a chronological approach to depicting when one stage of the process ends and another begins (e.g., Bauer, Morrison, & Callister, 1998). For example, it has become somewhat of a convention to assume that the organizational encounter or entry stage ends sometime between three and six months after a newcomer has been employed in an organization. However, just because an organization, for example, chooses to consider the first six months of employment a "probationary period" does not mean that the encounter stage of assimilation did not end months before this point or may end sometime later. Thus, while most stage models of the assimilation process posit certain kinds of behavioral and attitudinal "markers" as indicative of transitions from one phase to another, few studies have actually employed these criteria to determine shifts across stages. Rather, studies have been driven more by practical methodological issues; that is, one chooses particular points in time to collect data from *all* newcomers and then attempts to discern their attitudes and behaviors at those "stages" (vs. determining if there are any commonalities among newcomers with respect to the chronological points in time at which transitions occur based on shifts in their attitudes and behaviors).

A second problem associated with testing stages of the assimilation process is that few investigations have actually collected data from newcomers for more than two or three points in time (usually the first few days a person is on the job and then three to six months later). In other words, it is possible that studies have not been as longitudinal as required to adequately test stage models.

A final issue related to problems associated with stage models is conceptual in nature. Specifically, it is likely that stages of the assimilation process are not quite as discrete as some models posit (e.g., Bullis & Bach, 1989; Hess, 1993) and that newcomers' attitudes and behaviors differ more in degree than kind over time. In fact, research suggests that for many newcomers aspects of organizational assimilation happen very quickly and that within days of their initial employment some patterns of behavior and attitudes have already stabilized (e.g., Bauer & Green, 1994; Liden, Wayne, & Stilwell, 1993; Ostroff & Kozlowski, 1992; Teboul, 1997). It is even possible that newcomers may engage in role innovation as early as the first few days of work through their asking incumbents "dumb"/ naive questions that encourage oldtimers to reconsider their expectations about newcomers' roles.

To review, while it is apparent that newcomers are learning over time about the people, policies, language, history, and values of their organizations (Chao, O'Leary-Kelley, Wolf, Klein, & Gardner, 1994), among other things, whether or not discrete points exist at which newcomers move from the organizational encounter phase to the metamorphosis phase of assimilation remains debatable. Further, since it is unlikely that newcomers develop competence in and acquire knowledge of each of the various facets of their jobs/organizations at the same rate across time, it may be more useful to view the assimilation process as involving "layered" (Lois, 1999), intersecting stages of development. Along these lines, the following discussion of organizational assimilation is founded on the notion that assimilation involves a chain of events, activities, message exchanges, interpretations, and related processes—essentially "links"—in which individuals use what they have learned in the past (the extant chain of sensemaking moments) to understand new organizational situations and contexts, and as

appropriate realign, reshape, reorder, overlap, or fabricate new links so they can better adapt to their own and their organizations' requirements in the present and future (e.g., Van Maanen, 1984). Thus, in the discussion that follows I will not suggest that certain communication activities, processes, and outcomes are distinct to particular stages of assimilation; rather, I assume that these phenomena are ongoing in nature and to some degree are relevant to understanding the assimilation process from the time a newcomer enters an organization to the time she or he formally leaves the organization. However, as in other of my work, this presentation does focus on newcomers' communication relationships with essential sources of information during the assimilation processes, including the organization/management, supervisors, and coworkers (Jablin, 1982, 1987).

The sections that follow are organized in terms of communication-assimilation processes. The first set of processes—orienting, socialization, training, formal mentoring—tends to focus on newcomers' communication interactions with organization/management sources of information, and to some degree represents "planned" activities (although this varies widely from organization to organization and among the processes). The remainder of the processes focus on interpersonal communication interactions between newcomers and their supervisors and coworkers, and tend to be more discretionary in nature (i.e., not part of any formal, planned assimilation activities). Rather than discuss communication and noncommunication "outcomes" associated with assimilation, at the conclusion of the presentation of the communication-assimilation processes (as I did in my 1987 model), outcomes are discussed along with each of the processes to better reflect their dynamic nature. In addition, I have attempted wherever possible to reflect the processes in terms of dual perspectives and behaviors, that is, to consider the processes in terms of insiders/incumbents as well as newcomers. Finally, I would like to stress that the communication-assimilation processes developed in the following sections are not exhaustive of all relevant processes (and might not be grouped by others as I have done), but focus on what appear to be some of the most basic ones.

Communication-Assimilation Processes

Orienting

Almost all organizations provide newcomers with some sort of oral and written orientation to their jobs and companies (e.g., Arthur, 1991; Cook, 1992; Jerris, 1993). Many formal orientations are very brief, lasting no more than a day, and may merely involve the distribution of an employee handbook; discussion of organizational rules, policies, and the like; and the completion of paperwork related to employee benefits. In light of the brevity of most orientations programs, yet the tendency for these programs to offer new hires extensive amounts of information, it is of little surprise that the "how-to" literature frequently warns practitioners to avoid information overload in designing these activities (e.g., Jerris, 1993). However, some formal orientation programs may last weeks or months and are considered to be part of an ongoing process of assimilating newcomers into the organization. Departmental orientations are usually provided to newcomers as well and are typically the responsibility of the recruit's supervisor or senior coworkers with whom the new employee will work (e.g., Noe, 1999). Along these lines, practitioners often suggest that supervisors and line managers have the "ultimate responsibility for orienting new employees" (Jerris, 1993, p. 101).

Formal orientation programs may serve a variety of objectives, including welcoming the new employee and helping him or her feel comfortable; providing the person with information on organizational history, products and services, policies, rules, mission, and philosophy and the interpretation of these principles; introducing the recruit to key staff in other units and departments in the organiza-tion; review of compensation and benefits plans and safety rules; orientation to the physical plant of the company; and in organizations that view orientation as an ongoing process, providing support for the newcomer beyond the first days on the job by assigning the person a "mentor" or "buddy" (e.g., Davis, 1994). Programs often use line employees to assist human resource professionals in teaching classes since these workers may be perceived of as high-credibility sources by newcomers and more easily "connect" with them (e.g., Kennedy & Berger, 1994). In general, orientation programs involve the presentation of many "checklists," which are completed by the newcomer to indicate that he or she understands the information provided (e.g., Arthur, 1991; Jerris, 1993). The use of checklists as part of orientation programs is sensible since as forms of communication lists legitimate particular beliefs and techniques, provide rules of thumb to guide and evaluate behavior, and order preferences of the organization (Browning, 1992).

Unfortunately, while an elaborate how-to literature exists pertaining to the planning, administration, and evaluating of new-employee orientation programs, little empirical research has explored the efficacy of these programs in achieving their goals. However, studies by Louis, Posner, and Powell (1983) and Nelson and Quick (1991) indicate that about two thirds of organizational newcomers (samples of MBAs and bachelor degree graduates) participate in formal orientations and view them as moderately helpful in learning about their organizations. At the same time, these investigations did not find any significant relationships between the availability of the orientation programs and newcomers' job attitudes and adjustment. In contrast, Gates and Hellweg (1989), in research examining employee orientation programs presented to newcomers during their first week of work ($n = 5$ organizations), found that those who participated in orientation programs reported higher levels of organizational identification but similar levels of job satisfaction in comparison to those who did not participate in programs ($n = 2$ organizations). Cawyer and Friedrich's (1998) research, however, showed that the number of hours new college faculty spent in institutional and department orientation sessions were predictive of their satisfaction with organizational entry/socialization.

Building on Gomersall and Myers (1966) often cited finding that informal, "anxiety-reduction" sessions following formal, conventional personnel department orientation briefings can dramatically shorten the length of time it takes for employees to obtain minimal job competency, several recent studies have explored the effects of orienting newcomers on ways of coping with their new jobs. Waung (1995), in a field experiment involving new hires ($n = 61$) to entry-level service jobs (in a fast-food chain and hospital), compared the effects of two orientation approaches on newcomers' adjustment and job survival. One group "received information warning of negative aspects of the job and about specific coping behaviors," and the other group received the same information plus self-regulatory training, that is, "training in cognitive restructuring, positive self-talk, and statements to bolster self-efficacy" (Waung, 1995, p. 633). Orientations were presented to newcomers in individual sessions. After four weeks of work, analyses showed the opposite of what was predicted: Those who received orientations that included training in self-regulatory coping behaviors exhibited more turnover than those who received just the "realistic" orientation. Other findings showed that newcomers in the self-regulatory training treatment also perceived they had received more negative information in their orientation sessions than those assigned to the "realistic" orientation condition, although they actually were presented with identical information concerning negative features of their jobs. Waung (1995, p. 645) speculated that the additional information and training provided to those in the self-regulatory condition may have increased their apprehension, reduced their self-efficacy, and caused them to rethink their job choices. Future research should explore this possibility and attempt to determine newcom-

ers' "threshold levels for negative information" in orientation sessions (Waung, 1995, p. 645).

Buckley et al. (1998) also explored how lowering job expectations in orientation sessions may influence job-related outcomes among newcomers. In this field experiment, new hires participated in one of four conditions: (1) control group (received no orientation program, just an employee handbook and a welcoming talk); (2) traditional group (received normal orientation program consisting of distribution of employee handbook and presentation of an organization film); (3) RJP group (received and discussed a written realistic job preview, watched organization film, and were given employee handbook); and (4) ELP group (participated in an expectation-lowering procedure [ELP], watched the organization film, and were given the employee handbook). In contrast to the RJP, the ELP included no specific *job* information; rather, in this seminar "discussion was focused on expectations and their effects on subsequent organizational outcomes: that expectations were set early, that they were usually inflated, and that violated expectations resulted in negative organizational outcomes" (Buckley et al., 1998, p. 455). Results showed the RJP and ELP to be more effective than the other conditions in lowering newcomers' initial job expectations; in addition, after six months employees in the RJP and ELP groups also had significantly lower turnover rates and higher levels of satisfaction than those in the other conditions. In sum, results from the above experiments suggest that what is talked about in orientation sessions can affect newcomers' job attitudes and turnover, and as a consequence represents an assimilation activity deserving of further study.

As noted above, most orientation programs involve the distribution and review of a wide variety of organizational publications, including official house organs, indoctrination and orientation booklets, and the employee handbook (Arthur, 1991; Jerris, 1993; Kennedy & Berger, 1994). With respect to this latter kind of publication (many of which are now online and electronic in form; e.g., Duff, 1989), Cohen (1991) suggests that a handbook should "educate, inform, and guide employees toward qualities of behavior and performance that will be beneficial both to themselves and the company" (p. 9). In terms of specific content, most handbooks appear to focus on three basic issues: (1) organizational history, mission, and policies; (2) work rules and related procedures and practices; and (3) employee benefits and services (Anson, 1988; Arthur, 1991). Given the problems most organizations experience in effectively communicating benefits-related information to new and continuing employees (e.g., Barocas, 1993; Driver, 1980; Huseman & Hatfield, 1978), it is not surprising that up to half the information in employee handbooks often focuses on communicating information related to compensation and benefits plans (Wolfe & Baskin, 1985).

Curiously, we know little of the relative effectiveness of company publications in orienting newcomers or whether or not they provide accurate depictions of their respective organizational environments. Thus, while printed orientation materials may be effective in informing newcomers of general organizational procedures and policies, they may be quite limited in their ability to inform them about an organization's culture (Briody, 1988). Moreover, while it is important for legal reasons that organizational members understand the content of the employee handbook (courts in over half the states have ruled that the contents of handbooks represent legally binding contracts), these documents have historically been plagued by readability problems (Davis, 1968). Yet it is not unusual for organizations to require all employees to sign a statement indicating that they "have received a copy of the company handbook, have read its contents, and understand them" (Arthur, 1991, p. 257).

Many large organizations also use expository videos as a key element in their orientation programs. For example, Berger and Huchendorf (1989) describe an orientation program at Metropolitan Life Insurance in which newcomers view a series of documentary style videotapes over the course of their first year of employment that are designed to introduce them to the traditions, customers, products, businesses, and future plans of the organization. Along these lines, Thralls (1992), in a qualitative analysis of organizational videos, concludes that orientation videos serve as rites of passage for new members by providing them with "visualized enactments" that socialize them to behaviors and attitudes compatible with key organizational identities and goals. Similarly, Pribble (1990), in a rhetorical case study of a medical technology firm's formal orientation program, found that a slide and audiotape presentation about the company, its products, and employees, followed by a speech by the firm's CEO, were strategically designed to foster shared values, organizational identification, and in the long run commitment to the company and its objectives.

To conclude, although it seems apparent that organizational members, not just newcomers, are continuously being oriented to organization-wide changes and initiatives, little attention has focused on "orientation" as an ongoing process (e.g., Jerris, 1993). For example, when an organization develops a new mission statement it is not unusual for employees to receive both written and oral orientations (often presented by organizational leaders) designed to unpack its meaning (e.g., Fairhurst, Jordan, & Neuwirth, 1997). Future research should explore potential linkages between newcomer orientation programs and communication processes associated with the ongoing efforts of organizations to orient their members to such things as new objectives, employment policies (e.g., layoffs, sexual harassment), and organizational citizenship behaviors (e.g., Allen, 1992; Organ, 1990).

Socialization Strategies

A substantial number of studies have been completed in recent years examining relationships between organizational socialization strategies and the adjustment of newcomers (typically assessed in terms of "adjustment" outcomes such as role ambiguity, role conflict, stress, intent to quit, organizational commitment, and job satisfaction). Most of this work has explored organizational socialization in terms of Van Maanen and Schein's (1979) "people processing strategies" and has used variations of Jones' (1986) self-report questionnaire of these strategies as a means to do so (e.g., Allen & Meyer, 1990; Ashforth & Saks, 1996; Ashforth, Saks, & Lee, 1998; Baker & Feldman, 1990, 1991; Black, 1992; Black & Ashford, 1995; Blau, 1988; Cooper, Graham, & Dyke, 1993; Fogarty, 1992; Fullagar, McCoy, & Shull, 1992). Results of these studies suggest that Van Maanen and Schein's typology of socialization strategies (formal-informal, individual-collective, sequential-nonsequential, fixed-variable, serial-disjunctive, investiture-divestiture) are interrelated with one another and tend to describe two basic ways of processing people into organizations: Batch/institutional/structured (formal, collective, sequential, fixed, serial) and unit/individualized/unstructured (informal, individual, nonsequential, variable, disjunctive). Research has also shown that investiture and divestiture socialization tactics are either not highly intercorrelated with the other tactics or they are not correlated with the same tactics in a consistent fashion (Allen & Meyer, 1990; Ashforth & Saks, 1996; Baker & Feldman, 1990; Black & Ashford, 1995; Jones, 1986). However, since most research in this area has relied on data gathered from new college graduates, who usually experience investiture rather than divestiture socialization tactics (e.g., Miller, 1996), the above results may be an artifact of the kinds of samples studied.

Several communication issues associated with socialization strategy/tactic research warrant discussion. First, the general adoption by researchers of the Van Maanen and Schein (1979) typology of socialization strategies implies the acceptance of a fairly one-way (organizations "process people") versus two-way or interactional view of socialization pro-

cesses. Granted that organization agents may be highly proactive in their endeavors to socialize newcomers, the participation and engagement of newcomers is required for these tactics to be "successfully" enacted. Thus, while it is clear that socialization strategies and tactics are cocreated by organizational agents *and* newcomers, the typologies used to study socialization processes tend to be one-sided in nature (Bauer et al., 1998; Feldman, 1994; Saks & Ashforth, 1997).

Second, although a considerable amount of research has been directed at testing typologies of socialization strategies and tactics, few studies have explicitly focused on unpacking the communication attributes and the specific kinds of messages associated with the enactment of the strategies and tactics. Rather, most studies focus on identifying associations between the frequency of use of particular strategies and tactics and selective communication outcomes, including relationships between the use of socialization tactics and newcomers' levels of communication satisfaction (Mignerey, Rubin, & Gordon, 1995), organizational identification (Ashforth & Saks, 1996), and communication-related variables such as role clarity (Jones, 1986) and role innovation (Ashforth & Saks, 1996; Black & Ashford, 1995; West, Nicholson, & Rees, 1987). Although research along these lines is of value, it does not reveal much about communication processes associated with the enactment of organizational socialization strategies and tactics. Thus, while we may know that in certain contexts organizations tend to use institutionalized socialization, we know little of how such strategies are communicatively performed by organizational agents; "the content of socialization—the values, norms, beliefs, skills, and knowledge—that is communicated through the medium of the socialization tactics" (Ashforth et al., 1998, p. 921; see also Chao et al., 1994); the communication behaviors (with notable exceptions) of newcomers' coconstructing the socialization process with organizational agents; or if the messages communicated via the various strategies and tactics are done so in a consistent, persuasive manner such that they are believed by newcomers.

Third, as briefly noted above, we have little understanding of how the content of messages exchanged between organizational agents and newcomers varies among socialization strategies. Although Chao et al. (1994) recently developed and tested an instrument designed to measure socialization content (as compared to process), the instrument's focus is not on the content of messages exchanged in the socialization process but rather on what newcomers are supposed to learn as a result of socialization. In other words, this instrument measures outcomes of socialization, including newcomers' perceptions of their performance/task proficiency; understanding of organizational goals, values, and history; knowledge of organizational politics and power structures; the extent to which they feel like they fit in and have developed relationships with other people in the organization; and their comprehension of organizational jargon, acronyms, and professional terminology. Although this information is useful, it does not enunciate the types of messages and message exchange processes that typify learning socialization content, or how these processes might vary among socialization strategies. For example, studies suggest that stories are a frequent vehicle via which newcomers learn about their organizations (e.g., Brown, 1985). Are stories a more common means by which newcomers acquire information about certain of the Chao et al. (1994) socialization content areas than others? Are the kinds of stories that are shared with newcomers (including who or what they are about, how they are framed, and their morals), when they are told and by whom, and the involvement (passive/active) of newcomers in the storytelling process related to an organization's socialization strategy (or the interaction of an organization's socialization strategy and the extent to which it emphasizes particular socialization content areas)? Posing and answering these sorts of questions are central to furthering our understanding of how messages and message exchange processes are related to socialization strategies and newcomers' acquisition of socialization content.

Research along the above lines might benefit from findings of investigations that have explored the sorts of memorable messages (Stohl, 1986), turning points (Bullis & Bach, 1989), and critical incidents (Gundry & Rousseau, 1994) newcomers report during their socialization experiences. These studies have identified events, activities, and interactions —messages—that newcomers perceive had important effects on their understandings of "appropriate" organizational behavior and beliefs, the development of relationships, and the like (socialization content). To what extent do memorable messages/turning points/critical incidents vary across types of socialization strategies and areas of learning? Findings from Gundry and Rousseau's (1994) research suggest that variations are likely. Specifically, they found that newcomers entering into organizational cultures typified by high satisfaction norms (humanistic-helpful, affiliative, achievement oriented, emphasis on self-actualization) reported different types and interpretations of critical incidents than new hires working in task security-oriented (oppositional, competitive) and people security-oriented (approval oriented, conventional, dependent) organizational cultures. Although these cultures are not isomorphic with the organizational socialization strategies or socialization content areas discussed above, overlap among them is evident; thus, it is possible that recurrent patterns exist between the memorable messages/turning points/critical incidents newcomers experience and their organizations' formal and informal socialization efforts.

Training

Feldman (1989), among others, has suggested that organizational training programs have become one of the primary processes for socializing new employees. These programs are typically formal (occur away from the work setting and present newcomers with activities specifically designed for them), experienced collectively by newcomers as a group (Van Maanen & Schein, 1979), and vary in the extent to which they positively affect newcomers (e.g., Chatman, 1991; Nicholson & Arnold, 1989). More specifically, results of studies evaluating newcomer-training programs suggest that they are available to about one third of employees (Nelson & Quick, 1991); their effects can be enhanced by providing trainees with realistic information about the nature of the programs prior to their participation in them (Hicks & Klimoski, 1987); training may have its greatest effects on newcomers with low levels of initial work-related self-efficacy who may be experiencing difficulty coping and are in need of job and organizational information (Saks, 1995); pretraining motivation "may prepare participants to receive the maximum benefits from training" (Tannenbaum, Mathieu, Salas, & Cannon-Bowles, 1991, p. 765); training manuals and recruits' conversations about training programs may articulate and reinforce "root metaphors" that are central organizational guiding principles (Smith & Eisenberg, 1987; Suchan, 1995); newcomers' perceptions of the amount of training they have received are positively related to their perceptions of the helpfulness of that training and to their supervisors' ratings of their communicative performance (among other outcomes) once on the job (Saks, 1996); group training in comparison to individual training can enhance "transactive memory" (i.e., one's own knowledge and an awareness of what other specific members know) within a work group (Liang, Moreland, & Argote, 1995); and contradictions often exist between the messages newcomers receive in training about adhering to established rules and procedures and the application of these policies once they begin work (DiSanza, 1995; Fielding, 1986).

A rather rare field experiment exploring the differential effects of formal/collective as compared to informal/individual training warrants special attention. In this study, Zahrly and Tosi (1989) examined the early work adjustment of blue-collar workers in a startup manufacturing facility in which employees were assigned to semiautonomous work teams. All newcomers experienced the same selection process and then about one half of the employees ($n = 40$) experienced formal, collective training while the other half ($n = 40$) did not receive any systematic training or orientation. Each work team to which newcomers were assigned contained roughly an equal number of persons from each induction mode. Beta weights from regression analyses showed that after four months on the job, those employees who had experienced the collective training were higher in job satisfaction and lower in work-family and role conflict than those who were trained individually. While only approaching statistical significance ($p < .10$), employees who experienced collective training also reported lower levels of role ambiguity and higher levels of group cohesion than those who were trained on an individual basis. Although the organization, situation, and sample examined in this research are rather unique, results of the study suggest that in certain contexts the group interaction fostered by collective training may enhance newcomers' sensemaking abilities and early work role adjustment (see also Liang et al., 1995). Future studies of the communication characteristics and effects of newcomers' training experiences would profit from the use of research designs similar to the one used by Zahrly and Tosi (1989).

Finally, those studying communication and organizational assimilation would benefit from broadening their view of the functions and goals of training beyond the initial employment period. Formal (and informal) training has become a part of the "continuous learning" movement in organizations (e.g., Goldstein & Gilliam, 1990), and thus training is an ongoing experience for most employees. (In 1995, over $52 billion was budgeted for formal training in U.S. organizations with 100 or more employees; "1995 Industry Reports," 1995.) In fact, research suggests that "senior executives are now as likely to be the target of training initiatives as entry or technical employees" (Martocchio & Baldwin, 1997, p. 5).

Some organizations now even train their vendors and business partners to the organization's work methods, procedures, and culture; in part this is done to facilitate operations, but it also serves to encourage (socialize) stakeholders to share in the organization's vision, values, and strategy. In addition, as organizations pursue major changes, develop new strategies, and attempt to reinforce existing ones, training presents a venue for the corporation to persuade employees to accept and support these activities, as well as learn about new technical and nontechnical developments (Drobrynski, 1993, cited in Martocchio & Baldwin, 1997). Moreover, the availability, type, content, and extent of training made available to organizational members represent "messages" to them about their membership status and can affect their perceptions of organizational support (e.g., Shore & Shore, 1995; Wayne, Shore, & Liden, 1997). As Abelson (1993) observes, "Those who receive training to help them more effectively function in the organization most likely interpret that to mean the organization values their membership and wants to help them succeed. Those not receiving development opportunities, through training or other means, frequently perceive an opposite message" (p. 354). In brief, training represents a mode of cultural transmission (Harrison & Carroll, 1991) and "resocialization" (e.g., Bullis & Clark, 1993; Kossek, Roberts, Fisher, & DeMarr, 1998) and thus is deserving of study as a part of the assimilation process across the entirety of an individual's tenure in an organization.

Formal Mentoring

Since it is often suggested that "mentoring speeds up socialization into the work role, encourages social interaction, provides an opportunity for high-quality interpersonal interactions, and enhances identification with and commitment to the organization" (Wigand & Boster, 1991, p. 16), it is not surprising that organizations have tried to formalize the

mentoring relationship to facilitate the assimilation of newcomers (e.g., Zey, 1991). A formal mentoring relationship is not a spontaneous relationship that naturally develops between an incumbent and a newcomer, but rather is a "deliberative pairing of a more skilled or experienced person with a lesser skilled or experienced one, with the agreed-upon goal of having the lesser skilled or experienced person grow and develop specific competencies" (Murray & Owen, 1991, p. xiv). Although formal, "assigned" mentoring relationships aim to fulfill a specific set of organizational functions and goals, formal mentors may also fulfill career-related (e.g., coaching, protection, exposure) and psychosocial (e.g., counseling, role-modeling, acceptance) functions for their protégés (similar to informal mentoring relationships; e.g., Kram, 1988; Noe, 1988). However, as Evans (1994) notes, formal mentoring relationships are distinct from informal ones in that "formal mentors are selected and trained by the organization while informal mentors are not likely to have had any mentoring training prior to the mentoring relationship" (p. 26).

Formal mentoring programs usually have one of two general goals: "grooming" experienced incumbents for advancement in the organization (e.g., Klauss, 1981; Noe, 1988; Ostroff & Kozlowski, 1993) or facilitating the adjustment of organizational newcomers (e.g., Chao, Walz, & Gardner, 1992; Wigand & Boster, 1991). In this section, our attention is focused on the latter goal.

Although many organizations have established formal mentorship programs for new employees, only a handful of empirical studies have explored the nature and effects of these programs on the assimilation of *newcomers* into organizations. The results of these studies provide mixed, but tentative support with respect to the benefits of these programs (e.g., Allen, McManus, & Russell, 1999; Seibert, 1999). For example, Chao et al. (1992), in a survey of college graduates, found no significant differences between newcomers involved in formal versus informal mentoring programs with respect to psychosocial benefits, and only a slight career-related benefit for those involved in informal mentoring relationships. In addition, results showed that while those involved in informal mentorships scored higher on all "outcome" measures (socialization, satisfaction, and salary) compared with nonmentored individuals, newcomers involved in formal mentorships scored higher than nonmentored individuals on only three socialization subscales: establishing satisfying work relationships with others, knowledge of organizational politics, and understanding of organizational goals and values.

More recently, Heimann and Pittenger (1996), in a study examining a formal mentorship program among new and senior faculty at a university ($n = 22$), found newcomers' perceptions of the "closeness" of their mentoring relationship (e.g., open, supportive, helpful) to be strongly associated with their self-reported levels of organizational socialization and organizational commitment, as well as their perceptions of the value of the mentoring program (see also Blau, 1988). Newcomers' perceptions of their opportunity to interact with their mentor were also positively related to their perceptions of each of the outcome measures. However, in a study of a formal peer mentoring program among MBA students (groups of second-year students served as mentors to teams of first-year students), Allen, Russell, and Maetzke (1997) found, after controlling for the extent of mentoring functions served, time spent interacting with mentors and protégés' satisfaction with their experiences were not significantly related. These findings led Allen et al. (1997) to conclude that "it is not so much the amount of time spent together as it is the quality of the mentor-protégé relationship that creates a satisfactory mentoring experience (at least from the perspective of the protégé)" (p. 500). Overall, their results led them to suggest, as have others (e.g., Seibert, 1999), that different mentoring functions may be more important at some stages of a protégé's career than other functions, and in particular that psychosocial

functions may be more important than career-related functions early in a worker's organization tenure.

In one of the only studies to date to specifically explore communication issues associated with formal mentoring programs, Evans (1994) collected communication network data from individuals participating in nursing "preceptor" programs at two large hospitals. Among other things, results of her research revealed that (1) protégés ($n = 23$) spent more time talking with their formal mentors than with coworkers (especially about organizational topics); (2) multiplexity of the protégé-mentor link was a predictor of newcomer organizational commitment; (3) protégés and formal mentors differed in many of their perceptions concerning communication with each other (including specific topics and functions of messages); (4) social support provided by the mentor was related to a number of protégé socialization outcomes (e.g., critical care and communication effectiveness); and (5) nonmentored newcomers ($n = 10$) were more connected in the communication networks of their groups while mentored newcomers evidenced higher levels of multiplexity in their network links.

In sum, the results of the studies discussed above provide tentative support for the notion that newcomers who participate in formal mentoring programs, in comparison to those who are not involved in any form of mentoring, experience a variety of benefits. In particular, involvement in a formal mentoring program can enhance a newcomer's understanding of organizational issues and potentially his or her level of satisfaction. However, given the paucity of research in this area, and differences in methods used across the few studies that have been conducted (e.g., variation in when data were collected in the assimilation process, differences in the operationalization of variables, variations in the occupations of those included in samples), it is difficult to determine if formal mentoring programs are more effective in facilitating newcomers' assimilation than informal mentoring processes. In particular, although "mentoring is essentially a communicative activity" (Evans, 1994, p. 2), we still know little of the communication characteristics and outcomes of formal mentoring processes in comparison to informal ones.

Informal Mentoring

Although conceptualizations vary across studies (e.g., Merriam, 1983; Noe, 1988), informal mentors are usually considered to be "experienced personnel who respect, guide, protect, sponsor, promote, and teach younger less experienced personnel—the protégés" (Pollock, 1995, p. 114). They are distinct from formal mentors in that they are not assigned to employees by the organization. Thus, informal mentoring relationships develop naturally at the discretion of the mentor and protégé and persist as long as the parties involved experience sufficient positive outcomes (e.g., career development and success).

Although informal mentoring is an interaction process, most of the research related to the dynamics of these relationships has *not directly* examined the nature of *communication* between mentor and protégé; rather, studies have focused on such issues as individuals' motivation and willingness to mentor others (e.g., Aryee, Chay, & Chew, 1996; Olian, Carroll, & Giannantonio, 1993), the organizational and personal characteristics of mentors and protégés (e.g., Eagen, 1996; Fagenson, 1992; Koberg, Boss, Chappel, & Ringer, 1994; Olian, Carroll, Giannantonio, & Feren, 1988), similarities and distinctions in the mentoring experiences of men and women (e.g., Dreher & Ash, 1990; Ragins & Cotton, 1999; Ragins & Scandura, 1997; Scandura & Ragins, 1993), and the experiences of those in diversified mentoring relationships (e.g., diverse in terms of race, ethnicity, and class; see Ibarra, 1993; Koberg, Boss, & Goodman, 1998; Ragins, 1997) and situations (Dreher & Cox, 1996; Kalbfleisch & Davies, 1991; Thomas, 1990). When communication processes and issues are considered, they are usu-

ally explored implicitly via respondents' retrospective reports of the frequency with which they have experienced mentoring "functions" (e.g., Noe, 1988; Riley & Wrench, 1985; Scandura & Katterberg, 1988), and in particular, psychosocial support (e.g., the extent to which a mentor offered coaching, acceptance, confirmation) and career-related guidance (e.g., the extent to which the mentor provided exposure and visibility, protection, sponsorship, and challenging assignments).

What do the few studies that have specifically focused on newcomers, and/or followed new organizational members over time, suggest about communication in informal mentoring relationships? First, it appears that mentors are most instrumental in providing newcomers with information about the organizational domain (for instance, information about organizational power and politics, history, culture) relative to the other content domains, such as information about job features and work groups (Dirsmith & Covaleski, 1985; Ostroff & Kozlowski, 1993). Second, protégés in informal mentoring relationships tend to receive more career-related support and at least equivalent amounts of psychosocial support when compared to those in formal mentoring relationships (Chao et al., 1992; Ragins & Cotton, 1999). Third, despite these benefits, informal mentors are not always available or easy for newcomers to establish relationships with (Nelson & Quick, 1991; Waldeck, Orrego, Plax, & Kearney, 1997). Fourth, it is likely that one of the best ways to initiate informal relationships with mentors is to ensure contact with the person, that is, be visible to the target and regularly meet and talk with him or her (Waldeck et al., 1997). Fifth, mentors do not necessarily provide the types of information and display the sorts of communication behaviors that are proposed by stages models (e.g., Kram, 1983; Missirian, 1982) of the mentoring process (e.g., Bullis & Bach, 1989; Green & Bauer, 1995; Pollock, 1995). For example, Pollock (1995) found that protégés report that their mentors provide the full range of mentoring functions (with at least moderate frequency) from early in their relationships and continue to do so as their relationships progress.

Recent studies that have not necessarily focused on organizational newcomers and mentor-protégé relationship development but have examined communication issues associated with informal mentoring also suggest several conclusions:

1. Generally speaking, protégés perceive that the more they communicate with their mentors, the more psychosocial benefits, career guidance, and role modeling they receive (Fagenson, 1992, 1994).

2. Protégés with higher levels of self-esteem and communication competence, and "who perceive less risk in intimacy, are more likely to participate in mentoring relationships than those with reduced communication competence and self-esteem, and perceptions of greater risk in intimacy" (Kalbfleisch & Davies, 1993, pp. 412-413).

3. Differences may exist in the communication patterns displayed by male and female protégés, and between protégés whose mentors are male as compared to female (Bahniuk, Dobos, & Hill, 1990; Bahniuk, Hill, & Darius, 1996; Burke, McKeen, & McKenna, 1990; Ragins & Scandura, 1997).

4. Those without mentors tend to rely more on coworkers for information (Ostroff & Kozlowski, 1993).

5. Protégés involved in informal supervisory mentorships (relationships in which the mentor is supervisor of the protégé) in comparison to those involved in formal supervisory mentorships, nonsupervisory mentorships, or nonmentoring supervisory relationships may differ in their communication behaviors, and in particular may use more direct and less regulative and contractual communication tactics to maintain relational stability (Burke, McKenna, & McKeen, 1991; Tepper, 1995).

In conclusion, from the perspective of understanding assimilation processes, extant research exploring informal mentoring pres-

ents several dilemmas. Most studies have not employed longitudinal research designs; in fact, few have even collected data from organizational newcomers. Rather, the typical research design is retrospective and cross-sectional in nature and includes a sample of persons who range from those with little career and organizational experience to those with decades of tenure in their organizations. In addition, most studies relying on self-reports of behavior have not distinguished among mentoring relationships at different phases of individuals' careers and in general have failed to explore relationship development issues. As a consequence, our understanding of the sorts of communication behaviors protégés and mentors display as their relationships develop, and the functions these behaviors serve, remain somewhat muddled. Even if research reveals there are no clear-cut, linear stages associated with the development of informal mentorships, there still may be foundational patterns of communication behavior that are requisite for the initiation and maintenance of these relationships. Along these lines, future research might elaborate on the results of Pollock's (1995, p. 159) study, in which she found that "challenging and respecting the subordinate seems to form the foundation of mentor-protégé relationships and this foundation is not subsequently taken for granted" as the relationship progresses.

Information Seeking

Founded on the notion that newcomers are active agents in their organizational assimilation, researchers have devoted a considerable amount of attention in the past decade to exploring new hires' proactive information-seeking tactics and behaviors. Much of this work has explored elements of Miller and Jablin's (1991) model of information seeking during organizational entry, which posits that newcomers' information seeking is influenced by their perceptions of uncertainty and the social costs involved in seeking information, the type/content of information sought (referent—information required to function/perform on the job; appraisal—feedback on the degree one is functioning successfully on the job; and relational—information on the nature of one's relationships with others), the source from whom the information is sought, and several individual difference (e.g., self-esteem, tolerance for ambiguity) and contextual (e.g., organizational socialization strategy) factors.

Expanding on research exploring feedback-seeking behavior in organizations (e.g., Ashford, 1986; Ashford & Cummings, 1985) and information seeking in interpersonal relationships generally (e.g., Berger & Bradac, 1982), Miller and Jablin (1991) argued that the factors noted above will influence newcomers to seek information via use of one or more of the following tactics:

Overt: Asking for information in a direct manner

Indirect: Getting others to give information by hinting and use of noninterrogative questions

Third party: Asking someone else rather than the primary information target

Testing: Breaking a rule, annoying the target, and so on and then observing the target's reaction

Disguising conversations: Use of jokes, verbal prompts, self-disclosure, and so on to ease information from the target without the person's awareness

Observing: Watching another's actions to model behavior or discern meanings associated with events

Surveillance: Indiscriminately monitoring conversations and activities to which meaning can retrospectively be attributed.

In subsequent empirical research, Miller (1996) found the "disguising conversations" and "indirect" information-seeking approaches to be closely associated and therefore grouped them together to represent one general "indirect" information-seeking tactic; for similar reasons, "observing" and "surveillance" were collapsed to form an index of "observing."

Other research has provided support for many of the propositions associated with the Miller and Jablin (1991) model. However, since researchers have not been consistent in the ways in which they have conceptualized and operationalized constructs, it is difficult to draw generalizations across studies. For example, whereas Miller and Jablin conceptualized technical and procedural information associated with role demands and task performance as elements of "referent" information, others have considered these to be unique content areas and have measured them as such (e.g., Comer, 1991; Morrison, 1993a, 1993b, 1995; Ostroff & Kozlowski, 1992). Albeit these distinctions, the results of studies suggest the following tentative conclusions:

1. As newcomers' perceptions of the social costs of seeking information increase, their use of overt/direct information seeking decreases and their use of "covert" tactics (e.g., indirect, observing) increases (e.g., Fedor, Rensvold, & Adams, 1992; Holder, 1996; Miller, 1996; Teboul, 1995).

2. The most frequent kinds of information sought by newcomers concern referent/task/technical issues (e.g., Morrison, 1993b, 1995; Ostroff & Kozlowski, 1992; Teboul, 1994), and they tend to seek such information through overt/direct information seeking (Comer, 1991; Morrison, 1995).

3. In general, the most frequent information-seeking tactics used by newcomers are overt/direct and observing, with some studies reporting overt/direct as the most frequent approach (Comer, 1991; Holder, 1996; Kramer, 1994; Kramer, Callister, & Turban, 1995; Miller, 1989, 1996; Myers, 1998; Teboul, 1994, 1995) and others monitoring (Morrison, 1993b; Ostroff & Kozlowski, 1992).

4. Supervisors and coworkers are the most common targets of newcomers' information seeking (as compared to subordinates,

friends, spouses, and impersonal organizational sources such as reports and training manuals; e.g., Morrison, 1993b; Teboul, 1994).

5. When seeking relational/social information newcomers most frequently employ observation and monitoring (Miller, 1996; Morrison, 1995), whereas when seeking appraisal information they most often use overt and monitoring tactics (Miller, 1996; Morrison, 1995).

6. The frequency and use by newcomers of particular information-seeking behaviors are associated with outcomes such as role ambiguity, role conflict, task mastery, role orientation, organizational commitment, job involvement, intent to leave, performance, and job satisfaction, although these relationships are not consistent across studies and rarely account for large amounts of variance (Ashford & Black, 1996; Holder, 1996; Kramer, 1994; Kramer et al., 1995; Mignerey et al., 1995; Miller, 1989; Morrison, 1993a; Ostroff & Kozlowski, 1992).

7. Newcomers' perceptions of target social support (Miller, 1996; Teboul, 1995), levels of self-esteem (Miller, 1989; Teboul, 1995), tolerance for ambiguity (Fedor et al., 1992; Teboul, 1995), value of feedback (Mignerey et al., 1995), and organizational domain/field of study (Comer, 1991; Miller, 1996) are related to their information-seeking behavior.

8. Newcomers' information-seeking behaviors vary with their experience of "institutional" as compared to "individualized" organizational socialization (Mignerey et al., 1995; Miller, 1996; Teboul, 1995).

In addition, initial evidence suggests that over time newcomers seek less normative (information about expected behaviors and attitudes in the organization) and social information and more referent and appraisal information (Morrison, 1993b) and that newcomers find the appraisal and referent/technical information they obtain as most useful and the organizational and social/relational information they acquire the least

useful (Morrison, 1995). Further, although researchers have experienced difficulty in gathering data reflective of the range of uncertainty newcomers experience on the job (e.g., Miller, 1996; Teboul, 1994), at least one investigation has reported correlational data showing that as uncertainty increases newcomers use observing, third-party, and indirect tactics more and overt/direct information seeking less (Holder, 1996).

Several studies of newcomers' information-seeking behavior have also explored the extent to which they passively obtain information. Passively acquired information is information that is not actively sought by newcomers but is voluntarily provided to them by others in the organization (either formally via organizational activities such as training programs or informally on the job). For example, Comer (1991) found that about one third of the technical and social information newcomers obtain from *peers* is acquired in a passive/explicit manner (explicit in the sense that the information is provided in verbal vs. nonverbal form). In contrast, Morrison's (1995) research showed that while newcomers obtain social, technical, political, referent, and appraisal information more actively, they acquire organizational information more passively, and normative information about equally through active and passive means. Ironically, she also discovered that newcomers rated the organizational information they received as the least useful of all information types, yet the kind of information they received more than any other type. In turn, in two different studies Kramer (1994; Kramer et al., 1995) discovered that newcomers' receipt of unsolicited feedback from peers and supervisors had a greater impact on their adjustment than information acquired through more active means (e.g., requests, monitoring). Unfortunately, the results of these studies do not provide much insight into the interrelationships between newcomers' active and passive information acquisition, although a theme underlying the research is the notion that if others in the organization volunteer useful information to newcomers then the new hires will feel more comfortable (perceive lower social costs) in actively seeking information from those sources. In brief, while research in this area appears promising, future studies should investigate sequential relationships that may exist between newcomers' passive information acquisition and their active information-seeking behavior.

As noted above, it is difficult to draw many firm conclusions from research exploring newcomers' information-seeking behavior. All extant studies have relied on self-report methods of data collection, including interviews, open-ended descriptions of information-seeking incidents, and questionnaires (the latter the most common data-gathering technique). While these methods have their advantages, their use assumes that people are highly conscious of their information-seeking behavior (e.g., Miller & Jablin, 1991) and can easily provide accurate self-reports of their use of all tactics. However, this assumption may be problematic and requires testing, especially with respect to implicit tactics (e.g., surveillance, indirect), which newcomers may be less conscious of using. Our choice of research methods has also hampered our ability to understand information-seeking behaviors and tactics as part of the ongoing stream of communication activity in which newcomers engage; in other words, we have yet to "examine the dialogue of newcomers seeking information" (Miller, 1996, p. 20), that is, how information seeking unfolds in discourse. In addition, with notable exceptions, research has tended to focus on the frequency with which newcomers report their use of information-seeking tactics, and not the value or usefulness of the information they acquire. In some situations, it may require only one information-seeking effort to acquire desired information while in others acquiring information may be a long-term endeavor. Along these lines, we also need to focus more attention on how newcomers' information seeking develops over time; to date, only a few studies have collected data over at least two points in time, and none beyond a period of six months.

Rather, most studies are cross-sectional in design and some even ask persons who have been working in their organizations for many years to provide retrospective accounts of their information seeking during their first few months on the job.

Also, given the inconsistent results evident across studies examining relationships between newcomers' information seeking and various outcomes (e.g., performance, role ambiguity), it might be useful to revisit some of our assumptions about relationships among these variables. In many cases, it might be possible to predict both positive as well as negative relationships between newcomers' information seeking and their adjustment to their jobs and organizations (e.g., Ashford & Black, 1996; Fedor et al., 1992). For example, we might predict a negative relationship between newcomers' information seeking and their performance, arguing that because they are performing well they will require less feedback, job instructions, and the like. However, it is also reasonable to predict that those who are high performers achieve that status because they seek information and feedback from those around them; consequently, we would predict a positive association between information seeking and performance. In sum, greater attention needs to be focused on studying the mutual influences of newcomers' information seeking on relevant outcomes and the effects of those outcomes on newcomers' information seeking.

Findings from the studies reviewed here also suggest several other areas that future research should explore including possible distinctions in newcomers' information seeking and their gender, race, and ethnicity (e.g., evidence indicates that in some organizations it is easier for white males to access information than other persons; see Holder, 1996; Lovelace & Rosen, 1996; Teboul, 1995); relationships that may exist between how newcomers are recruited and their information-seeking behavior (e.g., Saks, 1994, suggests that those who are recruited through informal means may already have "inside" contacts when they begin their jobs, thus facilitating their ability to acquire information); the extent to which newcomers' information-seeking behavior is stable over time (e.g., Morrison, 1993b; Ostroff & Kozlowski, 1992); and the information-seeking behavior of other career entrants besides new college graduates. Finally, although the preceding discussion has focused on how newcomers' information seeking may facilitate their adjustment, future studies need to consider what incumbents do with the information they acquire about new hires (and themselves) from the newcomers' information-seeking efforts. In other words, we should explore how newcomers' information-seeking behavior affects insiders' efforts to seek information from and make sense of newcomers.

In summary, it appears that newcomers are active agents in their assimilation in part due to their proactive information-seeking behaviors. Not surprisingly, we find that newcomers use monitoring-like tactics across almost all situations and that most of the variation in their behavior occurs in the use of more overt/direct information-seeking tactics. Further, it is also not surprising that newcomers tend to seek more information when the social costs of information seeking are low, and focus a considerable amount of attention on seeking referent and appraisal information, types of information that are crucial in their becoming competent in the performance of their jobs. The notion that the more information newcomers *seek* about their social and normative environments the more competent they will be in their jobs is not fully supported in the research. Does this imply that newcomers are not acquiring considerable amounts of information about these issues, or that acquisition of this information is not related to their development of job competence (or other outcomes)? Not necessarily; rather, it is possible that newcomers are obtaining social and normative information through other mechanisms, including formal and informal mentoring, and from incumbents who volunteer this information to them.

Information Giving

Although researchers have begun to explore newcomers' information-seeking behavior, scant research has focused on their information-giving behavior (i.e., utterances either initiated by newcomers or solicited of newcomers by another party) and its goals, functions, and effects in the assimilation process. There are several basic reasons for exploring newcomers' information giving. First, studying newcomers' information-giving behavior acknowledges that newcomers can and do play active communication roles (display "voice"; e.g., Gorden, Infante, & Graham, 1988) as they begin their new jobs (Reichers, 1987). While a portion of a newcomer's voice is evident in his or her information-seeking behavior, information seeking only addresses the manner in which a newcomer can proactively "receive" additional information about his or her new role. The newcomer can also be a source of information. Along these lines, Jablin (1984) found that even during the earliest days of newcomers' organizational tenure information giving comprised at least 25% of their total communication behavior. Second, a newcomer's information giving represents an important indicator of his or her sensemaking and ability to cope with the stress of the organizational entry process. In other words, the degree to which newcomers are making sense of and effectively coping with the new organizational environment will, to some extent, be reflected in the communication they initiate with others in the organization as well as the responses they give to others' questions. Moreover, a newcomer's information giving can provide others with signals as to how the newcomer's construction of self, role, and orientation to the new social and work environment may be changing (e.g., Arnold & Nicholson, 1991; Fournier, 1997; Fournier & Payne, 1994; Morrison, 1994).

Jablin's (1984) study of the assimilation of nursing assistants (*n* = 44) over the first 24 weeks of their employment was the first to detail both newcomers' information-giving and information-seeking behaviors. A portion of the data collected included communication logs completed by a third of the nursing assistants during their third and ninth weeks on the job (the first two weeks of employment involved a training program). Results showed that information giving comprised about a quarter of a newcomer's total communication during the initial weeks of work (Week 3 = 25.6%; Week 9 = 28.1%). Of their interactions with superiors, about 15% involved newcomers' giving information; of their interaction with peers, about one third involved newcomer information giving; of their interactions with patients, about 25% involved information giving. Findings also indicated that about one fourth of all newcomers' interactions were for the purpose of giving instructions. Not surprisingly, most of the instructions given by newcomers were to patients within the nursing homes. Unfortunately, this research did not attempt to identify the specific content areas associated with newcomers' information giving.

Building on Jablin's (1984) research, Hudson and Jablin (1992) proposed a descriptive model of the context and factors that influence newcomers' information-giving behavior and a scheme for categorizing these messages. They suggest that newcomers' information-giving behavior reflects the surprise or shock they are experiencing in relation to their expectations, the uncertainty and emotions they are experiencing in the new environment, the extent to which the newcomers are learning work group and organizational norms and values, and the level of development of their relationships with others in the work setting.

Accordingly, they developed the Information-Giving Message Categorization Scheme consistent with these four experiences, as well as with two basic dimensions in which "content" is frequently framed in organizational message typologies: work/nonwork and evaluative/nonevaluative (e.g., Gioia & Sims, 1986; Komaki, Zlotnick, & Jensen, 1986). Evaluative work information includes utterances expressing opinions or judgments related to discrepancies between expectations and experiences (overt surprises), job stress,

self-evaluation of performance, qualities and attributes of the work role, and evaluations of individuals affiliated with the organization and the organization itself. Evaluative nonwork information includes utterances that express opinions or judgments on such things as participation in nonwork activities and the pressures or conflicts experienced by the newcomer outside the organization. Descriptive work information includes nonevaluative utterances related to such matters as task understanding, causes for task performance, task goals, and task instructions. Descriptive nonwork information includes nonevaluative utterances focused on issues unrelated to the organization or task including information about one's interests, hobbies, family, and personal goals (e.g., I hope to run the marathon).

Although the Hudson and Jablin (1992) model and message categorization scheme has yet to be fully tested, two studies have explored issues related to it. In a survey study of the employment experiences of new college graduates, Ashford and Black (1992) asked newcomers to respond to a scale associated with providing others with task- or project-related information. Although this measure did not distinguish evaluative from nonevaluative information giving or determine if the information was solicited by others or volunteered by newcomers, results showed positive association between the extent to which newcomers provided others with information and their organizational commitment and organizational knowledge. More recently, Kramer et al. (1995) examined the information-receiving and information-giving behaviors of new hires and experienced employees (transfers) beginning work at a new location of a retail food store. Again information giving focused on task issues and did not distinguish evaluative from nonevaluative messages. Specifically, respondents indicated the extent to which they answered information requests from others concerning "tasks, making decisions, and improving the work setting," modeled appropriate actions and behaviors, and provided unrequested suggestions to peers and supervisors "for improving the work setting." Results showed modeling to be negatively associated with intent to quit; not surprisingly, veterans who transferred to the new store reported more information giving than newcomers. In addition, findings revealed that newcomers' answering of information requests from others and their providing unsolicited information to others were fairly strongly correlated ($r = .63$), suggesting that there may be some reciprocity between these two forms of information giving.

In brief, the above studies provide some support for the importance of newcomers' *task/work* information giving in the assimilation process. Unfortunately, neither of these investigations explored non-work-related information giving nor distinguished between evaluative and nonevaluative information giving and newcomers' adjustment. Future research should do so. In addition, we need to explore how the information-giving (and -seeking) behavior of incumbents is related to the information-giving (and -seeking) behavior of newcomers. Support for such a relationship is evident in the results of Kramer et al.'s (1995) research, in which they found a positive association ($r = .42$) between newcomers' receipt of unsolicited information from others and newcomers' providing unrequested information to others.

Studies should also consider information giving in terms of written and nonverbal as well as oral, verbal messages (the emphasis to date). For example, in the written reports and e-mail messages that newcomers send to others they are providing information that allows incumbents to make attributions about the newcomers' substantive, rhetorical, and social competence (e.g., Katz, 1998; Larson, 1996). Newcomers give information to others in the work setting via their nonverbal behavior as well. For instance, in light of the uncertainty they face when they begin their jobs, newcomers may act in awkward ways or make task-related and communication "mistakes" (e.g., Gilsdorf, 1998) that cause them to experience embarrassment (e.g., Keltner & Buswell, 1997; Miller, 1992). When a newcomer's face turns bright red with embarrassment, the newcomer may be sharing information about his

or her affective state, what makes the person self-conscious, his or her cognitive limitations (e.g., forgetfulness, stupidity), and his or her understanding of scripts that guide interaction or task performance (e.g., the newcomer's understanding of forms of work group and organizational humor [e.g. Meyer, 1997; Vinton, 1989], appropriate forms of address [e.g., Morand, 1996], and norms for expressing emotions [e.g., Waldron, 1994] and telling stories [e.g., Stevenson & Bartunek, 1996]). Such forms of nonverbal information giving are important indicants of how newcomers are making sense of and adjusting to their new work environments and are deserving of study from both the perspectives of newcomers and insiders.

Situations in which newcomers experience embarrassment may also initiate other forms of information giving, including the presentation of excuses, justifications, and accounts as means of saving face/identity and managing impressions. Accordingly, some forms of newcomers' (and insiders') information giving may be conceptualized in terms of impression management, an "inherently communicative process" (Bozeman & Kacmar, 1997, p. 10) that is concerned with how individuals attempt to control the image they are projecting to others by manipulating information (Schlenker, 1980). Thus, for example, in conversations with other organizational members newcomers may blame their poor performance on external sources, or use apologies, deception, and the "relabeling" of their actions (for instance, as successful) to disguise their failures (e.g., Bozeman & Kacmar, 1997; Caldwell & O'Reilly, 1982; Fandt & Ferris, 1990; Greenberg, 1996). Moreover, since newcomers are often more conscious of their behavior than oldtimers, future research should also consider the extent to which newcomers' use of impression management tactics may be tied to particular message design logics (O'Keefe, 1988, 1990) and plans to promote desired identity goals (e.g., Bozeman & Kacmar, 1997). Investigations might also explore if a newcomer's frequent use of highly manipulative impression management tactics communicates to incumbents that the newcomer is manipulative (Snyder, 1985), and how this may affect the willingness of others to share information with the newcomer. However, since a newcomer's use of impression management tactics does not necessarily mean that the newcomer is trying to "score points" with others, it is important that we also consider how these forms of information giving may represent attempts at building positive relationships (e.g., Wayne & Kacmar, 1991). As Bozeman and Kacmar (1997) suggest, impression management tactics may serve a variety of identity functions (e.g., identity enhancement, protection, or adjustment) and may be content or relationship oriented.

To conclude, to date few studies have explored newcomers' information-giving behavior (and its interrelationship with the communication behavior of incumbents). If we are to more fully understand how and with what effects (positive and negative) newcomers and oldtimers share information, we need to supplement our studies of information-seeking behavior with research exploring information-giving behavior as well.

Relationship Development

As evident in the earlier discussion of formal and informal mentoring, it is usually vital for newcomers to develop relationships with others in the work setting, especially with leaders and peers (including other newcomers). Among other things, relationships with peers and leaders provide newcomers with support that facilitates the learning process and reduces stress associated with adjusting to the new work environment (e.g., Allen, McManus, & Russell, 1999; Cawyer & Friedrich, 1998; Comer, 1992; Feij et al., 1995; McCauley, Ruderman, Ohlott, & Morrow, 1994; Myers, 1998; Nicholson & Arnold, 1989; Oseroff-Varnell, 1998; Ostroff & Kozlowski, 1992). At the same time, however, our knowledge of the communication processes associated with the development and maintenance of newcomers' relationships

with others in the work setting is very limited. Thus, we are in the curious position of being able to identify the types and characteristics of interpersonal relationships in work settings (e.g., Boyd & Taylor, 1998; Bridge & Baxter, 1992; Graen & Uhl-Bien, 1995; Kram & Isabella, 1985; Myers, Knox, Pawlowski, & Ropog, 1999) but know relatively little about how these relationships form and are maintained. However, it is apparent that the communication-assimilation processes discussed in the preceding pages (e.g., information seeking and information giving) provide newcomers and incumbents with information that facilitates the process of building relationships with one another beyond the basic interdependencies associated with their work roles.

Peer relationships. Since most newcomers have numerous peers in their work groups but typically just one immediate supervisor, they tend to have more contact with coworkers and as a consequence more opportunities to share information with them and develop relationships (e.g., Comer, 1992; Teboul, 1994). However, it is important to recognize that most interpersonal relationships formed in organizations are not close but rather acquaintance type in nature (Fritz, 1997). The manner in which coworker relationships may develop from acquaintances to "best friends" has recently been explored by Sias and Cahill (1998). They proposed that a variety of contextual factors, including shared tasks and group cohesion (e.g., Fine, 1986), physical proximity (e.g., Griffin & Sparks, 1990), lack of supervisor consideration (Odden & Sias, 1997), and life events outside the workplace, as well as individual factors (e.g., perceived similarity in attitudes and beliefs as well as demographic similarity; Adkins, Ravlin, & Meglino, 1996; Duck, 1994; Glaman, Jones, & Rozelle, 1996; Kirchmeyer, 1995), may affect the development of relationships with peers. However, the influence of these factors was not explored in a longitudinal manner in the research. Rather, retrospective interviews were conducted between pairs of coworkers ($n = 19$ pairs) exploring their relationships with one another (average length of relationships = 4.7 years). Respondents were asked to identify points at which their relationships changed across time, factors that caused these developments, and communication changes that were associated with transitions in their relationships.

Respondents in the Sias and Cahill (1998) study reported that the move from acquaintance to friend averaged 12 months from initially meeting, the passage from friend to close friend averaged an additional 19 months, and the transition from close friend to best friend another 17 months (total of four years). Factors that were important in the transition from acquaintance to friend included proximity, shared tasks, socializing outside the work settings (e.g., having lunch together), and perceived similarity. This transition was accompanied by increased discussion of personal topics and non-work-related issues, some decrease in caution in sharing opinions and information, but not much intimacy.

> Relationships developed into close friendships usually because of important personal or work-related problems, although perceived similarity and extra-organizational socializing continued to impact relational development. At this point, the coworker became a trusted source of support with communication becoming increasingly more intimate and less cautious. (Sias & Cahill, 1998, p. 289)

The same factors were associated with the transition from close friend to best friend; that is, communication continued to decrease in caution and increase in intimacy and discussion of work- and non-work-related problems.

Several other findings from the Sias and Cahill (1998) research are of interest. In particular, results showed moderate levels of agreement between coworkers with respect to the factors affecting, and the communication changes that characterized, their relationship development. Further, their results suggest that relational development among coworkers

may be driven by frustrations and problems they experience with their supervisors (consistent with the research of Gundry & Rousseau, 1994, who found the most frequent "critical incident" that made an impression on newcomers was a conflict between the supervisor and subordinate). Finally, findings in the Sias and Cahill study also revealed that some employees were reluctant to leave what they considered to be less than desirable work environments because of close friendships with coworkers. These data reiterate the notion that the close relationships that newcomers develop with peers implicitly involve commitments that "pose constraints when the need to alter behavior becomes apparent" (Ashford & Taylor, 1990, p. 10).

Although newcomer-coworker relationships typically develop in the context of work groups, few studies have explored how group communication processes and norms affect the development of relationships between newcomers and particular group members. However, it does seem apparent that the more role and interpersonal conflict within work groups, the longer it takes for newcomers to develop friendships with members of their groups and role sets (Katz, 1985). It is also likely that communication processes associated with the development of relationships between newcomers and oldtimers in their work groups will be affected by other group characteristics, including level of group cohesiveness, characteristics of social networks, team member exchange quality, the length of time group members have been working together, stage of group development, group initiation activities, diversity in group membership, and the frequency with which new members enter the group (e.g., Arrow & McGrath, 1995; Gersick, 1988, 1989; Hautaluoma, Enge, Mitchell, & Rittwager, 1991; Jackson, Stone, & Alvarez, 1993; Katz, 1980; Larkey, 1996; Levine & Moreland, 1991; Seers, 1989; Shah, 1998; Ziller, Behringer, & Jansen, 1991). In addition, while we know that in many circumstances (e.g., collective, formal socialization) newcomers frequently develop relationships with one another and provide each other with support and assistance, little is known about communication processes associated with the development and maintenance of these relationships.

Supervisory relationships. Research has shown that a newcomer's communication relationship with his or her initial supervisor is a crucial factor in the newcomer's assimilation, since the supervisor frequently communicates with the newcomer, may serve as a role model (e.g., Ben-Yoav & Hartman, 1988; Javidan, Bemmels, Devine, & Dastmalchian, 1995; Weiss, 1977), filters and interprets formal downward-directed management messages, has positional power to administer rewards and punishments, is a central source of information related to job and organizational expectations as well as feedback on task performance, and is pivotal in the newcomer's ability to negotiate his or her role, among other things (e.g., Jablin, 1982, 1987). Given the importance of the newcomer-supervisor relationship in the assimilation process, several models have recently been proposed describing stages of the relationship development process. Generally speaking, these models represent variations of Altman and Taylor's (1973) social penetration theory of relationship development integrated with research related to leader-member exchange (LMX) theory (e.g., Graen & Scandura, 1987; Graen & Uhl-Bien, 1995).

Graen and Uhl-Bien (1995) proposed a three-stage leadership making model. In this model, the leader-newcomer relationship begins with a "stranger" phase, in which the leader and follower come together because of their task interdependence and display forms of exchange that are contractual in nature; in other words, "leaders provide followers only with what they need to perform, and followers behave only as required and do only their prescribed job" (p. 230). The second stage of relationship development is the "acquaintance" phase and is chiefly characterized by one of the parties making an "offer for an improved working relationship through career-oriented social exchange" (p. 230); at this point there is increased interaction, and although exchanges are still limited they are characterized by the "return of favors" and "testing" in the relationship. Graen and Uhl-Bien (1995) describe the third phase of the relationship development process as "maturity," or the establishment of mature partnerships. They suggest that these exchanges are highly developed and that the parties rely on each other for loyalty, mutual respect, and support. In brief, "they are exchanges 'in kind' and many have a long time span of reciprocation" (p. 230). Unfortunately, little empirical research has explored the leadership making model, nor does the model provide much detail with respect to the communication processes associated with transitions in the development of newcomer-leader relationships.

More recently, Boyd and Taylor (1998) presented a developmental four-stage model of friendships in leader-follower relationships in which they propose that the development of a high LMX "does not depend on the development of a close leader-follower friendship relationship" (p. 4). However, they do suggest that the "highest quality work experience for both leader and follower potentially occurs when both a close leader-follower friendship and a high LMX are present" (p. 4).

Somewhat similar to the coworker friendship development work of Sias and Cahill (1998), Boyd and Taylor (1998) propose that leaders and followers begin their relationships at a stage at which the parties explore the potential for friendship and that such factors as physical proximity and attitudinal and demographic similarity are important factors affecting relationship development at this point (e.g., Bauer & Green, 1996; Liden et al., 1993; Sparrowe & Liden, 1997). The second stage is concerned with exploration and orientation, and the leader and follower consider the costs and rewards of developing the relationship. According to Boyd and Taylor (1998), this stage is "characterized by caution and tentativeness. There is little open evaluation, criticism, or expression of conflict and information is exchanged only at a superficial level" (p. 10). However, they posit that during this period value congruence and perceived similarities between the parties become evident, along with displays of liking and positive affect (e.g., Dockery & Steiner, 1990; Meglino, Ravlin, & Adkins, 1989, 1991). During the third stage, the leader and follower become casual friends and test their relationship; relations are thought to be "superficial in nature, lacking the intimacy, sense of uniqueness, strength of affective bond, and reciprocal obligations of more personal friendship relations" (Boyd & Taylor, 1998, p. 12). This stage is characterized by medium LMX, role making versus role taking (Graen, 1976), and increased and more open communication and is similar to the acquaintance stage of Graen and Uhl-Bien's (1995) leadership making model. In the fourth and final stage, the leader and follower develop a stable exchange and become close friends. Boyd and Taylor (1998) suggest that this kind of relationship is characterized by mutual reciprocal influence, intimacy, support, frequent interaction across a variety of settings, high levels of understanding, and efficient communication. They believe these types of relationships are rare in organizations and that the communication patterns associated with high LMX relationships may facilitate the development of close friendships between leaders and followers.

Several other issues are noteworthy about the Boyd and Taylor (1998) model. First, to date, no empirical research has explored the validity of its assumptions and propositions. Second, the model focuses on the development of leader-newcomer relationships in isolation of the work group. Third, the model recognizes that relationship development processes are not necessarily linear. Thus, for example, Boyd and Taylor suggest that relationships escalate as well as deteriorate over time, and in most cases never advance beyond casual friendships (characterized by moderate to high levels of LMX).

Findings from two recent empirical studies associated with the development of leader-newcomer relationships are also of interest. In the first investigation, Bauer and Green

(1996) expanded on and tested a model of LMX originally developed by Graen and Scandura (1987). This model posits that leader-follower relationships involve three phases: (1) role taking, during which time the parties make cognitive evaluations of one another's trustworthiness; (2) role making (the acquaintance stage in Graen & Uhl-Bien's model), a period where behavioral trustworthiness is determined in large part through a leader's taking a risk in delegating work to the newcomer; and (3) role routinization, a phase in which the behaviors of each member of the dyad are fairly predictable and the leader and follower experience affective trust as an outcome of their high LMX relationship. In general, results of the study showed that variables that were expected to be associated with trust building were related to leader-member relationship development. However, the research did not directly measure trust building or its many communication correlates (e.g., Jablin, 1979). The second investigation explored superior-subordinate communication during job transfers over the course of one year. In this research, Kramer (1995) reported results that suggest that transferees were "reliant on supervisors' actions in defining the relationship rather than being proactive in their communication" (p. 58); in other words, their relationship resulted from the leader's "typical style." Further, findings revealed patterns between the types of supervisory relationships transferees developed and their communication relationships with peers (e.g., those who had "overseer" relationships with their supervisors tended to have more "informational" than "collegial" or "special" peer relationships). In brief, Kramer's (1995) work supports the notion that there are interdependencies between the quality of the developing communication relationships transferees experience with their supervisors and the quality of their developing communication relationships with peers.

Finally, it is important to note that scholars have also begun to explore how leader-follower relationships are maintained over time (Bridge & Baxter, 1992; Lee, 1997, 1998a, 1998b; Lee & Jablin, 1995; Tepper, 1995;

Waldron, 1991; Waldron & Hunt, 1992; Winstead, Derlega, Montgomery, & Pilkington, 1995). Unfortunately, none of this research traces the development of newcomer-leader relationships from their initiation, thereby exploring maintenance communication processes and relationship development over time. However, results of these studies do suggest that leader-follower relationships may alter trajectory (escalate or deteriorate) and that leaders and followers employ distinctive maintenance communication tactics to keep their relationships at a steady state or intact (e.g., avoidance of interaction, refocusing conversations, openness, procrastination, deception, self-promotion, circumspectiveness, small talk, and supportiveness). In addition, a variety of factors have been found to affect how the parties enact maintenance communication behaviors, including quality of LMX, interactional context and relationship state, hierarchical position, group social context (cooperative-competitive), and perceived effectiveness in relationship maintenance. The results of Lee's (1997, 1998a, 1998b) studies are of particular importance, in that they indicate that leader-follower communication maintenance processes are affected not only by the context of the work group but also by perceptions of the leader's relationship with his or her superiors (a variation of the Pelz effect; e.g., Jablin, 1980).

In summary, while a number of valuable models have been posited detailing relationship development processes during organizational assimilation, few empirical studies have been conducted exploring these models generally, and with respect to communication processes and issues in particular. Rather, the focus of most extant research has been on identifying the communication characteristics of various forms of posttransition relational states that may exist between newcomers and other organizational members. Clearly, more longitudinal research exploring how newcomers and their leaders and coworkers communicate in the process of developing relationship states is required. In addition, it also seems apparent that we should direct more of our efforts into exploring newcomer-leader, new-comer-coworker, and if applicable, newcomer-subordinate (e.g., Kramer & Noland, 1999) communication and relationship development processes in combination with one another, rather than in isolation of each other. Within organizations, specific types of relationships develop and are embedded within networks of organizational relationships (e.g., McPhee, 1988; Sias & Jablin, 1995; Zorn, 1995). Further, since it is becoming increasingly common for organizational members to no longer work in the co-presence of their supervisors and coworkers, but rather communicate with each other via computer-mediated communication and information technologies from off-site locations (see Rice & Gattiker, Chapter 14, this volume), the manner in which newcomers develop relationships with others in their organizations may also be evolving (e.g., Sias & Cahill, 1998; Walther, 1992, 1996) and represents an important area for future research.

Role Negotiation

Role negotiation "occurs when two or more persons consciously interact with the express purpose of altering the others' expectations about how a role should be enacted and evaluated" (Miller, Jablin, Casey, Lamphear-Van Horn, & Ethington, 1996, p. 296). Most theories of organizational assimilation (e.g., Graen & Scandura, 1987) posit that during their early days in new jobs/organizations newcomers are more involved in "taking" (learning others' expectations of them) than in negotiating or generating coorientation about their roles (Jablin & Krone, 1987). In other words, although newcomers can actively attempt to "individualize" their roles to better satisfy their own needs, values, and beliefs at any time, for most this will not occur until they have reached a threshold level of adaptation to their new work environments. In addition, it is believed that the newcomer-leader role negotiation process is key to the newcomer's success in the role negotiation process generally; that is, if a newcomer is not successful in role negotiation with the immediate supervisor, the newcomer's chances of successfully individualizing his or her role in the organization become problematic (e.g., Jablin, 1987). As Graen (1976) has observed, "Although other members of the new person's role set can enter the negotiation of the definition of the new person's role . . . only the leader is granted the authority to impose formal sanctions to back up his [her] negotiations" (p. 1206).

Although newcomers' ability and success in negotiating their roles with leaders and co-workers appear central to the newcomers' success in satisfying their own needs and meeting organizational requirements, little research has focused on exploring the interaction that occurs among the relevant parties during the role negotiation process. Rather, most research that is typically associated with role negotiation focuses on subordinates' use of different kinds of upward influence tactics in various kinds of leader-member and peer relationships (e.g., Barry & Bateman, 1992; Deluga & Perry, 1994; Judge & Bretz, 1994; Krone, 1992; Maslyn, Farmer, & Fedor, 1996; Thacker & Wayne, 1995; Yukl, Guinan, & Sottolano, 1995); factors associated with employees' willingness to "voice" to their supervisors (e.g., Ashford & Taylor, 1990; Janssen, de Vries, & Cozijnsen, 1998; Saunders, Sheppard, Knight, & Roth, 1992); and newcomers' perceptions of their role innovation, role development, and personal/self change as they become assimilated into their organizations (e.g., Ashforth & Saks, 1996; Jones, 1986; Nicholson, 1984; Nicholson & West, 1988; Van Maanen & Schein, 1979; West, 1987). Thus, while it is evident that we need to conceptualize and study role negotiation in terms of the interdependent influence and negotiation strategies that newcomers and other organizational members use in the process of negotiating roles over time, research has not assumed that approach. Moreover, few studies have explored how the role negotiation strategies of newcomers and the sorts of issues or areas they attempt to negotiate change (if at all) as they progress from the initial stages of the formation of their roles to later periods in their organizational assimilation.

As noted above, only a few empirical studies have explored role negotiation processes and organizational assimilation. Dockery and Steiner (1990), in a laboratory study lasting only a few minutes in duration, assessed followers' use of upward influence tactics in their initial interactions with their leader. They found positive relationships between followers' use of ingratiation and rationality as strategies in their upward influence attempts and their perceptions of LMX; in addition, results showed a negative association between respondents' self-reports of assertiveness as an influence tactic and their perceptions of LMX. However, it is also important to observe that the researchers found assertiveness used so infrequently by followers that they suggest that newcomers may be reluctant to use this tactic in initial interactions with their leaders.

Jablin and Miller (1993) conducted a longitudinal study of newcomer-supervisor role negotiation processes, in which data ($n = 65$ across all time periods) were collected from newcomers (recent college graduates) at their 6th and 18th months of employment. Generally speaking, results did not show that newcomers were attempting to negotiate many role changes with their supervisors (an average of two attempts in the preceding 6 months), although they perceived themselves as very successful in these negotiations. Frequent topics newcomers attempted to negotiate with their supervisors concerned job responsibilities and duties, issues related to job procedures and scheduling tasks, and human resources/personnel matters. Other findings revealed that the more newcomers used a particular influence strategy (rationality, exchange, ingratiation, coalitions) in their negotiation efforts at 6 months of employment, the more they used it at 18 months of work; newcomers' use of ingratiation and to some degree rationality and coalitions as negotiation strategies decreased over time; and newcomers who perceived themselves as more communicatively competent or worked in groups high in cohesiveness increased their use of the exchange strategy in their role negotiations between their 6th and 18th months of employment. In addition, Jablin, Miller, and Keller (1999) found, in data collected from a sample of new college graduates ($n = 24$) employed for 6 months, no differences between newcomers' use of influence methods in their successful as compared to relatively unsuccessful role negotiations with their supervisors (and as in the Jablin & Miller, 1993, study, findings indicated that rationality was the most commonly reported influence tactic).

Using a sample of newly promoted (average time in position = 4.5 months) restaurant employees (not fast food), Kramer and Noland (1999) also provide data relevant to role negotiation processes subsequent to job transitions. Results derived from interviews with the new managers ($n = 20$) indicated that almost two thirds had attempted to negotiate changes in others' expectations of their roles. Negotiations usually occurred during informal discussions; involved a wide range of issues, including procedures, policies, and responsibilities related to their roles; and most frequently involved attempts to change the role expectations of subordinates (persons who had previously been the newly promoted employees' peers) and supervisors. In brief, these role negotiations usually involved people the newly promoted person already knew, and thus tended to focus on developing mutual understandings of the new leader-follower relationship and the person's role in social networks. Results also suggested that "testing" might have been used by subordinates and leaders in negotiating the newly promoted employee's role. In addition, Kramer and Noland found that only about half of the new managers explicitly negotiated role-related issues with their supervisors and that when such negotiations did occur, they were not always successful.

Another group of studies is also noteworthy, in that they suggest communication-related factors that may affect a newcomer's ability to negotiate his or her role with others in the organization. Exploring factors that increase the probability that workers will voice to their supervisors (e.g., offer suggestions,

discuss grievances and problems), Saunders et al. (1992) found that when workers changed supervisors they were less likely to exhibit voice with their new bosses and that employees' perceptions of their supervisors as "voice managers" (responsive and approachable communicators) affected their propensity to voice. In turn, Janssen et al. (1998) also found that employees are more likely to voice to their supervisors if they perceive them as effective voice managers, but in addition, they discovered that employees whose cognitive styles are more adaptive (oriented to work within established paradigms) than innovative (oriented to shifting paradigms) are more likely to voice ideas when they are dissatisfied, whereas innovators are more likely to voice ideas when they are satisfied with their jobs. In other words, it is possible that innovators tend to negotiate changes in their roles even when they are generally satisfied with them.

The notion that a supervisor's voice management skills are central to employee role negotiation is also evident in the results of a recent study by Miller, Johnson, Hart, and Peterson (1999). These researchers found that "open and facilitative supervisory relationships and the perception of the leader as facilitating work in the unit are central to employees' evaluation of their role negotiation ability" (p. 39). Although some research has found that an individual's need for feedback is associated with his or her self-change at work (Black & Ashford, 1995), Miller et al. did not find an employee's need for feedback or self-esteem related to perceptions of role negotiation ability. In elaborating on their results, Miller et al. also suggest that employees who work for supervisors who are open and responsive and facilitate work in their groups may actually experience less need to negotiate their roles, since their bosses tend to be more aware of problems and opportunities and therefore manage issues as they arise. Future research should explore this possibility.

To review, it is clear that our understanding of the manner in which newcomers negotiate their roles with their supervisors and others in organizations is rudimentary, at best. Although negotiation is an interactive process in which the parties involved usually make provisional offers and counteroffers and work together to generate compromises or alternative solutions to sources of dissatisfaction or conflict (Thompson, 1990), we have tended to study role negotiation during organizational assimilation from just the perspective of the newcomer and in terms of unidirectional influence attempts despite the fact that so much of the literature associated with work in this area is based on role negotiation as a social exchange process (e.g., Blau, 1964; Settoon, Bennett, & Liden, 1996). Future research should focus more on identifying the discourse patterns that emerge over time in the role negotiations between newcomers and other organizational members. Along these lines, Fairhurst's (1993) study of the discourse patterns of a small sample of women leaders and their followers in various LMX relationships is instructive. Through the application of discourse analysis methods (see Putnam and Fairhurst, Chapter 3, this volume) to audio-taped records of conversations, she was able to uncover subtleties in the communication behaviors and patterns of leaders and followers in informal, routine role negotiations. Among other things, she found that those in medium and high LMX relationships displayed a "pattern of politely acknowledging and responding to the other before revealing one's own expectations for the role" and this helped create "the give-and-take dynamic of a negotiation with multiple goals in the areas of task and relationship" (Fairhurst, 1993, p. 336).

Future research should also explore distinctions and commonalities that may exist in the formal versus informal, everyday role negotiations that occur between newcomers and other members of their role sets. Generally speaking, in research exploring role negotiation there has been insufficient integration of research and theory exploring negotiation and bargaining (e.g., Putnam & Roloff, 1992) with

studies of how individuals attempt to influence one another in organizations. In addition, since newcomers frequently experience unmet role expectations upon entering organizations (see earlier discussion in this chapter), researchers might begin to track over time how and under what conditions newcomers attempt to negotiate these discrepancies. Conversely, similar issues might be explored from the perspective of organizational insiders who also experience unmet and unexpected expectations about newcomers' roles. Finally, as inferred earlier, research is still required that (1) directly examines LMX and the influence/negotiation tactics that newcomers and leaders use in their role negotiations as their relationships develop over time, (2) the interaction patterns associated with the negotiations of those who enact distinctive types of organizational role orientations (e.g., custodial vs. innovative), and (3) the communication strategies that newcomers use to negotiate their roles with members of their work groups (e.g., Jablin, 1987).

Summary

The preceding discussion of role negotiation highlights one of the central issues that I have attempted to stress in this section: Assimilation-communication processes overlap and are linked to one another in an evolving, intersecting manner. Thus, as pertains to exploring communication processes associated with how newcomers and organizational incumbents negotiate their roles with one another, it is necessary to consider other of the assimilation-communication processes I have developed here, including relationship development, information-seeking and information-giving behaviors, mentoring activities, and organizational socialization. In addition, it is important to reiterate that I have not necessarily enunciated all of the relevant communication processes associated with organizational assimilation. In fact, most of the variables that I have previously identified as dynamic communication outcomes of the assimilation process—for example, involvement in communication networks, development of cultural knowledge and shared meaning, communication competence (e.g., Jablin, 1987; Jablin & Krone, 1994)—could easily be conceptualized as links in the unfolding and mutating chain of assimilation-communication processes.

ORGANIZATIONAL DISENGAGEMENT/EXIT[2]

In light of the centrality of work in our lives, and the important functions that relationships in the work setting play in the development and maintenance of our self-identities, it is clear that organizational disengagement, regardless of its form, is a stressful experience for most of us (e.g., Latack, Kinicki, & Prussia, 1997). Certainly, it is as difficult to become an "ex" as it is to become a part of a social group. Organizational disengagement is not only a challenge for the leaver, but also for those who remain in the old work environment. The exit of a coworker induces uncertainty (usually at multiple levels of analysis, such as dyadic, group, organizational, extraorganizational; e.g., Shaw & Barrett-Power, 1997) into the social fabric of the organization. It brings the temporal nature of almost all facets of our lives into the forefront of consciousness.

In 1987, I offered a preliminary model of the communication antecedents of the voluntary turnover process, along with a number of propositions about the communication correlates of withdrawal and the communication consequences of voluntary turnover in organizations (Jablin, 1987). Since that time, relatively little research has been conducted exploring communication issues associated with the voluntary turnover process generally, although two empirical studies have explored selected relationships suggested in the model (M. Allen, 1996; Scott et al., 1999). Results

from these investigations supported predicted indirect (as well as direct) relationships between coworker communication, supervisory communication, and organization-wide/top management communication and turnover intentions (see also Johnson, Bernhagen, Miller, & Allen, 1996). Further, findings in the Scott et al. (1999) study showed complex relationships between targets of identification in organizations (e.g., Scott, Corman, & Cheney, 1998) and intent to leave. In related research, and consistent with the general predictions of the Jablin (1987) model, Feeley and Barnett (1997) found that those highly connected in communication networks or more central to networks were less likely to leave their jobs than individuals less connected/central in their networks (unfortunately, this study did not clearly distinguish voluntary from involuntary turnover). More recently, Cox (1999) reported that the most common strategy coworkers use to encourage voluntary turnover among peers is to avoid communication with them, which he suggests should cause those peers to become more decentralized in communication networks, consistent with Feeley and Barnett's (1997) research and the Jablin (1987) model.

Given the limited amount of research that has explored the 1987 model, and the focus of these few studies on just one part of the model—relationships between communication antecedents and turnover—my purpose here is to develop those aspects of the model that have received little research attention (withdrawal and communication consequences of turnover) and to develop a general perspective about the roles and functions of communication in situations involving *voluntary* disengagement/exit (i.e., voluntary turnover, transfers, retirement). However, the ideas presented here are based on a broad examination of previous research exploring communication and organizational disengagement in a variety of contexts (e.g., Jablin & Krone, 1994), not just voluntary turnover. In particular, I reviewed recent research exploring communication and organizational disengagement in *retirement* (e.g., Avery & Jablin, 1988; Beehr & Nelson, 1995; Cude & Jablin, 1992; Shultz, Morton, & Weckerle, 1998; Sonnenfeld, 1988; van Tilburg, 1992), *transfers* (e.g., Briody & Chrisman, 1991; Campion, Cheraskin, & Stevens, 1994; Jablin & Kramer, 1998; Kramer, 1989, 1993a, 1993b; Toliver, 1993), *promotions* (e.g., Cooper et al., 1993; Kilduff & Day, 1994; Kramer & Noland, 1999; Rudin & Boudreau, 1996), *job changes resulting from mergers and acquisitions* (e.g., Bastien, 1987, 1992; Cornett-DeVito & Friedman, 1995; Haunschild, Moreland, & Murrell, 1994; Howard & Geist, 1995; Schweiger & DeNisi, 1991), *layoffs as a result of downsizing* (e.g., Folger & Skarlicki, 1998; Johnson et al., 1996; Mishra & Spreitzer, 1998; O'Neill & Lenn, 1995; Skarlicki, Ellard, & Kelln, 1998), and the *dismissal* of individual employees (e.g., Cox & Kramer, 1995; Klaas & Dell'omo, 1997).

In sum, my goal is to use the results of a fairly broad analysis of the literature to build a perspective about communication phenomena/processes that are associated with voluntary organizational disengagement/exit. In particular, my focus is on this process as the communication antecedents of turnover reach a threshold point, that is, when employees begin to have sufficient negative affective responses to their jobs and organizations to consider turnover (see Jablin, 1987). Accordingly, this section unfolds as follows. First, I offer a brief conceputalization of the notion of organizational disengagement/exit. Second, I develop a general perspective about the roles and functions of communication during the voluntary disengagement/exit process. Given that empirical research is quite limited with respect to communication phenomena in many of the areas in which I offer propositions, much of the discussion that follows is highly speculative; in other words, the material presented here is intended to stimulate research exploring communication and organizational disengagement/exit processes and not to present a series of well-supported research generalizations.

Conceptualizing Organizational Disengagement/Exit

Organizational disengagement is a process, not an event. What we might normally associate with exit—the public, physical activity of leaving a particular job and organization—is something that happens midway through the process. The processual nature of exit is noted by Ebaugh (1984, p. 10), who offers a general model of the disengagement process based on Cumming and Henry's (1961) conception of disengagement as "mutual withdrawal": "[Disengagement] . . . involves both the individual's decreased association with a group and, simultaneously, the group's decreased demands on and involvement with the individual. As a group expects less from an individual, the rewards of belonging also decrease, such that withdrawal from the group becomes a viable option."

Given that work roles are embedded within role sets, work groups, departments, and divisions, disengagement at one level of analysis (e.g., the work group) will affect the individual's relationships and functions at other levels of analysis (e.g., at the organizational level). One does not necessarily disengage from all levels of analysis at once. Thus, one may seek a lateral transfer to a new work group to leave a dissatisfying work situation, yet remain a part of the organization and perform more or less the same tasks. In addition, as Ebaugh (1984) observes, it is essential to realize that disengagement is a mutual process—to fully understand the roles and functions of communication in the disengagement process we must study both those who leave and those who stay. Relatedly, although disengagement may be a mutual process between leavers and stayers, this does not imply that the disengagement process occurs at the same pace or manner for each party. Disengagement processes between leavers and stayers are interdependent, not equivalent. In brief, since organizations are "open systems" (Katz & Kahn, 1966), the exit of an organizational member, for whatever reasons, requires the organization to achieve a revised state of homeostasis among its various sub- and supra-systems.

Disengagement/Exit Process

Since it is not my purpose to explore the antecedents of voluntary organizational exit, but rather to explore the roles and functions of communication in the process of disengagement/exit, my approach includes unpacking three basic phases that appear indigenous to all forms of voluntary disengagement/exit: (1) preannouncement, (2) announcement and actual exit, and (3) postexit. Depending on the phase of the disengagement process, this discussion incorporates distinctive theoretical perspectives, such as open systems theory (e.g., Katz & Kahn, 1966), uncertainty reduction theory (e.g., Berger, 1979), attribution theory (e.g., Kelley, 1971), balance theory (Heider, 1958), cognitive dissonance theory (e.g., Festinger, 1957), social information processing theory (e.g., Salancik & Pfeffer, 1978), and theory and research related to social justice and the use of accounts and justifications in organizations (e.g., Bies, 1987; Scott & Lyman, 1968).

In considering each of the phases, I attempt to develop the process in communicative terms from both the vantages of leavers and stayers. However, I have minimized discussion of communication phenomena that tend to be unique to specific forms of voluntary disengagement; rather, I focus on communication issues common to multiple forms of disengagement. At the same time, even though this integrative approach is designed to be applicable to most forms of voluntary disengagement, it will be evident to the reader that depending on the form of disengagement, some elements of the model may be more or less relevant.

Preannouncement

All forms of voluntary organizational disengagement are preceded by cues, signals, or even "shocks" (e.g., Lee, Mitchell, Wise, & Fireman, 1996) that are evident in the form of discretionary and ambient messages in the work setting. The specific kinds and timing of cues may vary according to the form of disengagement. For example, specific cues may be shared with coworkers and supervisors for many months before the announcement of the employee's departure from the organization (for instance, in the leaver's messages suggesting an unwillingness to perform organizational citizenship behaviors [see Chen, Hui, & Sego, 1998] or in coworkers' messages to motivate a peer to exit [Cox, 1999]). Some of the leaver's cues may be communicated in an active, intentional manner (e.g., Hirschman's [1970] notion of "voice"), whereas other cues may be passive and unintentional in nature (e.g., Ferris & Mitchell, 1987). Certain cues may be readily available to most members of the work group (poor performance, lateness, or absenteeism of a coworker), while others may be communicated to specific targets (for instance, discretionary messages to supervisors and/or coworkers; e.g., Cox, 1999; Jablin, 1987). Some cues are communicated to third parties or organizational outsiders (customers, members of competing organizations), who may be more receptive to them than other targets (e.g., Cox, 1999; Kydd, Ogilvie, & Slade, 1990). Cues may convey explicit dissatisfaction or disidentification with particular people, the work group, and organization, or they may focus on more indirect, mundane matters, for example, the quality of supplies the organization provides to employees; concern about the quality of the firm's products or services; distinctions between one's attitudes about particular issues and those of other members of the organization (Wilson, 1983). Depending on the nature of the cue, it may be directed at just one target or a variety of targets (e.g., coworkers, bosses, clients, family members, the community). Cues may be noticed by significant others (including peers and customers) and acted on, noticed by significant others but ignored or given low priority as action items, or never noticed by members of target audiences (e.g., Cox & Kramer, 1995; Withey & Cooper, 1989). In turn, cues may be noticed and acted on by some targets sooner (e.g., family members may recognize cues of burnout before work associates) and with greater intensity than other targets.

Who attends to and responds to an individual's disengagement cues may be extremely important (e.g., Feeley & Barnett, 1997). In many respects, it is likely that "weak ties" (Granovetter, 1973, 1995), or ties embedded in networks with "structural holes" (Burt, 1992), who recognize and respond to cues may have a greater impact on the potential leaver than will his or her strong communication ties (Podolny & Baron, 1997). By definition, it would seem likely that the source of disengagement cues already knows the attitudes and feelings of strong ties because of his or her frequent interaction with them. However, the beliefs of weak ties (especially those high in credibility) concerning the person's disengagement are probably less well understood. Hence, communication with weak ties, especially with those who are not relied on for organizational identity information/support or role expectations (e.g., Podolny & Baron, 1997), may be very useful for the potential leaver in reducing uncertainty related to disengagement.

As suggested above, the manner in which feedback targets respond to disengagement cues will vary considerably across targets. Targets may respond with feedback that varies in sign (positive, negative, equivocal), intensity, choice of media, consistency, explicitness, and so on. In addition, responses may be made in public or private. For example, if a manager recognizes cues that one of her employees feels taken for granted, expressing appreciation for the worker's efforts in a public meeting may be more meaningful to the employee and have greater impact on his attitudes than expression of these sentiments in a private conversation.

Responses to disengagement cues may be "scripted" or created in a conscious, mindful manner (mindful responses are especially likely in situations where individuals are try-

ing to motivate another person to exit; e.g., Cox, 1999). The extent to which targets respond to disengagement cues with "socially acceptable" scripts may be problematic. In particular, it is quite possible that socially acceptable responses to disengagement cues may often be counterproductive in situations involving undesired (from the perspective of the organization) voluntary turnover. For example, in such contexts targets of disengagement cues may frequently respond to the feedback seeker in very neutral, sometimes equivocal ways. In other words, targets are cautious in expressing their feelings because they do not want to stand in the way of another person's opportunity to advance his or her career, achieve a higher standard of living, and so on. For instance, the target may not specifically state an opinion (stay, leave) but reverts the issue back to the person seeking feedback (e.g., the respondent might say, "It's difficult to know what to do," "I'm glad you have choices," "Have you considered all the possibilities?"). Although these responses are socially acceptable, they also can be conceived of as disconfirming forms of response (Watzlawick, Beavin, & Jackson, 1967), in that they provide equivocal content and relational feedback. Given the generally negative consequences of disconfirmation on the maintenance of organizational relationships (e.g., Jablin, 1978), such forms of response to disengagement cues may decrease the feedback seeker's attraction to the organization. Equally important, by its very nature equivocal feedback from targets does not provide the potential leavers with specific enough information to help them reduce the uncertainty they may be experiencing with respect to voluntarily exiting the organization.

Although an equivocal response by a target to the voluntary disengagement cues of another organizational member may have a negative impact on the feedback seeker's attitudes, such a response may help the target cope with the cognitive imbalance he or she may experience as a consequence of the cues. An equivocal response does not commit the target to any position concerning the other's potential exit from the organization. In contrast, a statement of support for leaving the organization may cause the target to question his or her own employment in the organization (create dissonance; e.g., Steers & Mowday, 1981); in turn, a statement encouraging the other party to remain in the organization may cause the target to feel somewhat responsible if the other party remains in the job and experiences increased levels of discontent (or diminished employment opportunities in the future).

The disengagement cues/feedback-seeking efforts of potential job changers, regardless of how (or if) they are responded to by targets, serve other functions for targets. In particular, they may allow targets to make attributions about the disengagement behavior of their colleague (e.g., Judge & Martocchio, 1996). In many situations, it likely that work group members will share with one another the disengagement cues they have detected in their interactions with a peer (i.e., they will engage in collective sensemaking; e.g., Isabella, 1990). Subsequently, group members may develop similar attributions to explain the peer's actions and comments (for instance, attributions about why person X is going on job interviews). Depending on the circumstances, group members may also develop accounts to share with "outsiders." These collectively constructed preexit accounts or disclaimers (e.g., Bennett, 1990) may provide the group/organization with an opportunity to "test the waters" or rehearse accounts that allow the group/organization to save face in light of its losing a member (e.g., Goffman, 1971; Scheff, 1988).

Clearly, the nature of disengagement cues will vary in terms of their substance and enactment as the individual moves closer to (or away from) exiting the organization. For example, we might hypothesize that as one enters into advanced stages of disengagement cues will be constructed and performed in ways that validate the accounts and justifications that the leavers and stayers have formed to support organizational exit (e.g., Eden, 1984). Thus, for instance, in the context of

voluntary turnover, cues may contain more negative affect toward those with whom one works, thereby eliciting more negative affect in the responses of targets toward the source of the cues.

Certainly, there are other ways in which targets of cues could respond in the sample situations described above; the point, however, is that as individuals move closer to exiting an organization, there will be distinctive changes in the conscious and unconscious exit cues that they emit and concomitant changes in the ways they process any feedback that is received from targets. The nature of how a potential leaver's exit cues change over time, how targets' responses vary over time, and how both the source and receivers of cues alter the manner in which they process disengagement messages over time warrants attention in our research.

Studies exploring issues such as those described above will not be easy since it is likely that the preannouncement stage of disengagement cannot be characterized in simple, linear terms (for either potential leavers or stayers) but involves numerous reverse-causality cycles (e.g., Jablin, 1987), which may or may not result in sufficient arousal levels (threshold points) to consciously or unconsciously push or pull those involved to advance in the exit process (e.g., Somers, 1999). In addition, if we accept the notion that all members of organizations are to some degree experiencing organizational disengagement (e.g., Kahn, 1990), identification of "normal" kinds and levels of disengagement cues is a necessary prerequisite for recognizing patterns of cue enactment that are suggestive of movement along the disengagement continuum. Along these lines, it seems essential that we explore the cue patterns of work groups (and in some cases even organizations) as well as individuals, since in accordance with social information processing theory, it may be the collective pattern of disengagement cues and responses that pushes and pulls individuals along the disengagement continuum (e.g., Abelson, 1993; Blau, 1995; Cox, 1999; Harrison & Shaffer, 1994; Markham & McKee, 1995).

Finally, it is important to stress that disengagement cues are not direct causes of organizational exit; rather, these cues are signals (often progressive in nature; e.g., Cox & Kramer, 1995; Rosse, 1988) that can help all parties involved better understand the status of their respective states of organizational disengagement (obviously, in some cases such knowledge may also facilitate interventions designed to deal with the underlying factors associated with disengagement; e.g., Chen et al., 1998).

Announcement of Exit and Actual Exit

The announcement and exit stage is quite distinct from the preannouncement period. In particular, the announcement and exit stage focuses (relatively speaking) on public versus private events (though it is important to recognize that private announcements may occur weeks before public announcements, which is often the case in job transfers); announcements are often accompanied by written statements (which can be subjected to rhetorical and textual analysis; e.g., Allen & Tompkins, 1996; to some degree there are always some groups (internal and/or external to the organization) who are "surprised" by the announcement; it is socially acceptable to "publicly" talk about those who are leaving and why they are leaving once their exit has been announced; and as those involved move toward actually exiting the organization their impending boundary passage is often associated with numerous rites and rituals, such as office parties, gift giving, and speeches (e.g., Kramer, 1989, 1993a).

Curiously, other than in the context of major job layoffs, few studies have examined the content of announcements of organizational exit. It seems clear, however, based on research concerned with job layoffs that formal layoff announcements are communicated to employees and other stakeholders in impersonal, written documents, which may include many details but minimal amounts of information justifying or accounting for the layoffs

(e.g., Brockner, 1994; Folger & Skarlicki, 1998; Jablin & Krone, 1994; Skarlicki et al., 1998). In addition, research in this area indicates that the announcement of a layoff (or merger; e.g., Cornett-DeVito & Friedman, 1995) is often anticlimactic, since rumors are usually widespread prior to formal announcements (e.g., Smelzter & Zener, 1992). To what degree are these characteristics typical of formal announcements of forms of voluntary exit? Formal announcements that individuals are quitting their jobs, retiring, or transferring to another site of the organization are, in most circumstances, variations of "bad news" messages (e.g., Tesser & Rosen, 1975). Such messages are most frequently constructed to convey their respective content in "polite," diplomatic ways (e.g., Lee, 1993); thus, these missives may not always be frank and explanatory. At the same time, however, it is important to recognize that distinctions in the cultures of organizations, the extent to which managers are perceived as trustworthy and credible, and norms associated with legitimate accounts may moderate this generalization (e.g., Bies, 1987; Brockner, Siegel, Daly, Tyler, & Martin, 1997; Rousseau & Tijoriwala, 1999). In addition, as stressed in the discussion of the preannouncement period, disengagement cues are inherent in all forms of organizational exit. Thus, for most (but not all) internal and external constituents the formal announcement that a particular individual or group of workers is leaving an organization is often anticlimactic.

Like the preannouncement stage, the communication activities associated with the announcement and exit phase function, in part, to reduce uncertainty for leavers and stayers. However, as argued above, the formal announcement itself does not necessarily function in that manner. Rather, uncertainty is reduced by interpersonal communication between those who are leaving and staying (e.g., Kramer, 1993b). In particular, these individuals will share job-related information with one another and generate accounts and justifications to explain the exit of the employee. In line with Nicholson and West's (1988) research on the motives individuals report for job changes, it is likely that exit accounts will fall into one of four broad categories: (1) exit will facilitate the person's achieving long-term goals (future orientation), (2) exit allows one to avoid a bad situation/problems at work, (3) exit is due to unique circumstances (e.g., organizational restructuring, spouses' job, unique opportunity), or (4) some mixture of the above kinds of accounts.

Stayers can accept the account offered by the leaver, incorporate the leaver's account into the preannouncement account that may have been generated by the group, totally reject the validity of the leaver's account, construct a new account that is different from but compatible with the account of the person who is leaving, or negotiate a new common account that allows both the leaver and stayers to maintain face (essentially a form of impression/image management; e.g., Schlenker & Weigold, 1992). Even in the situation where an employee quits his or her job in a spontaneous, emotional fit of anger, it is very rare for an individual to "burn the bridges" behind him or her; rather, the parties involved usually negotiate an acceptable common account that allows all those involved to maintain an adequate amount of face (e.g., Theus, 1995).

The manner in which stayers and leavers communicate with each other during the period between the announcement of the exit and actual exit will vary considerably depending on the form of exit. In particular, the amount of time available for interaction will be highly dependent on the kind of exit. In addition, interactions between the parties will be tempered by the group's experience with turnover and the frequency with which it has occurred (e.g., Abelson, 1993; Arrow & McGrath, 1995). Groups that are fairly "open" (periodic turnover) will likely have established scripts for interacting with the leaver during his or her tenure as a "lame duck"; on the other hand, fairly "closed" groups will not have established norms or scripts to guide their communication behavior and may experience more awkwardness in their interactions with the leaver (Ziller, 1965).

In the latter case, it is possible that uncertainty will not be measurably reduced for the leaver or stayers during this stage of the disengagement process; rather, it is possible uncertainty will remain the same or even increase since those involved may avoid each other because they don't have established scripts to guide their behavior. In such cases, postexit dissonance may be high for stayers and the leaver since they may not have said to each other "what they needed to say." In like fashion, even activities (e.g., parties) designed to celebrate and acknowledge the leaver's contributions to the organization and wish the person bon voyage may fail to perform those functions if the parties involved don't possess appropriate scripts to guide their communicative behavior. Maladroit enactment of exit ceremonies may be especially problematic for stayers, since these rites of passage often function more to help them bring closure to the leaver's departure than to facilitate the leaver's disengagement from the organization.

While stayers and leavers may initially adopt a common account for the leaver's exit, it is important to recognize that the ways in which the two parties communicate the accounts to others may be quite distinct. Moreover, each time someone presents the account it will be somewhat different from the last time he or she discussed the situation. The person will actively reinterpret what happened and incorporate these insights as revisions to the account the next time it is told (e.g., Boje, 1991; Brown, 1990). In addition, when leavers present their accounts for exiting the organization it will usually be in narrative form, in comparison to a list of reasons for their actions (Riessman, 1990). Leavers might tell stories that include information that extends back to why they joined the organization in the first place, the feelings of what the organization was like back then, events that made the workplace change, and "what could have been" if things had worked out differently (e.g., Beach & Japp, 1983; Folger, 1986). In brief, leavers usually face a rhetorical situation, which requires them to draw the listener into their world so that the moral of the tale (the need to leave) goes without saying (though it is likely that the teller will help the listener reach this point by providing commentary about specific aspects of the narrative as it unfolds; e.g., Boje, 1991). In contrast, those who remain in the organization are unlikely to account for a coworker's exit by presenting the reasons in the form of a narrative. Rather, they may rationalize the situation by delineating in listlike fashion the reasons someone is leaving (e.g., Browning, 1992; Sheehan, 1991, 1995). This rational approach allows stayers to limit their emotional involvement in the situation, tends to cap the level of dissonance they may experience about remaining in the organization, and reduces the likelihood that they will question the values that form the foundation of the organization's ongoing story/culture.

Finally, it is possible that in some organizations the interval of time between the formal announcement of an individual's departure from an organization and the actual exit provides those involved (especially stayers) with an opportunity to discuss numerous topics that are usually taboo to openly talk about (e.g., Roth, 1991), such as problems with the firm's products or services, management's lack of understanding of what is "really" going on in the organization, examples of bad decision making by the boss, fairness and equity in salaries, and so forth (e.g., Abelson, 1993). While these conversations may help stayers make sense of what is happening, they may also have a hidden implication: the notion that if things had been different, person X would not be leaving to go to work at another company, or person Y would not be taking early retirement or be seeking a job transfer. Even as leavers and stayers reminisce about the past, they cannot escape the question of whether the future will be as good as the past. In brief, the impending exit of a colleague provides members of his or her role set with an ephemeral window in time to publicly vent their frustrations about their jobs, work groups, and organization. At the same time, however, these discussions also represent op-

portunities for those who remain in the organization to consider ways to improve their work environments and promote their own careers (e.g., Dalton & Tudor, 1979; Ford & Ford, 1995). Thus, in many work environments lamenting and overt displays of frustration among stayers will be brief in nature, followed by increased levels of social support among those involved as they prepare to cope with the loss of one of their associates and the concomitant changes that will occur in the social dynamics and communication patterns of their group/organization.

Postexit

Once an employee has left the organization, his or her "physical" and "symbolic" absence is experienced by those who remain. Similarly, assuming the leaver enters into a new organizational milieu, he or she will experience the contrast of being a relatively isolated node in a world of established communication networks. In brief, both the person exiting the organization and those remaining usually experience uncertainty as a consequence of the changes in their work environments. Thus, the postexit phase is usually a fairly stressful one for all those involved. For stayers, stress can be reduced as they acquire information that allows them to assess the actual absence of the leaver on the group/organization, and if necessary, locate a replacement for the leaver; for the leaver, stress can be reduced by clarifying/seeking information from the new colleagues about their expectations of the newcomer's role in the group/organization (e.g., Miller & Jablin, 1991). In addition, social support from significant others will also play a role in reducing stress for the leaver and stayers (e.g., Lim, 1996). At the same time, however, it is important to recognize that different kinds of social support may be required from different sources and the failure of the "right" sources to provide appropriate kinds of support for the target will yield problematic results. For example, a spouse who provides skill-based social support (endorsement of an individual's skills/abilities to perform a task) to his or her partner may have little impact on the level of skill-related stress experienced by the other party; rather, skills-based social support from a worker's boss is more likely to reduce a worker's concerns about job-related self-efficacy (Brett, 1984).

Once the leaver has exited the organization, his or her physical absence will serve as a stimuli for stayers to again converse about the causes of the person's departure from the organization (collective sensemaking), as well as to reminisce about their former coworker (e.g., Moreland & Levine, 1982). The period of remembrance may focus on retrospective evaluation of the leaver to arrive at a consensus about what the leaver contributed to the group while he or she was a member (Moreland & Levine, 1982). Depending on the nature of the disengagement, stayers may experience "counterfactual thinking" (Roese & Olson, 1995), betrayal (e.g., Moreland & McMinn, 1999; Morrison & Robinson, 1997), envy (e.g., Bedeian, 1995; Vecchio, 1995), guilt, insecurity, and other emotions as they engage in remembrance. The leaver is also likely to reminisce about and evaluate his former colleagues and the old work setting. For the leaver, reminiscence (and concomitant affective cognitive responses such as regret; e.g., Lawson & Angle, 1998) may be intrapersonal in nature or it may involve communication with others who are familiar with the old setting (e.g., others who once worked in the organization or one's spouse).

In situations where the leaver will be replaced in the old work group, a considerable amount of the stayers' time will be focused on finding a replacement for the leaver. In other words, stayers will center their energy on the recruitment and selection of a new worker (e.g., assessing resumes, interviewing prospective employees). During the process of selecting an individual to replace the leaver, it is likely that stayers will discover they possess many unconscious expectations of the leaver's role (e.g., questions asked by job applicants in the interviewing process will make incum-

bents aware of taken-for-granted assumptions about the role). In addition, in some cases stayers will be faced with the difficult rhetorical problem of explaining to potential recruits the reasons the leaver exited the organization. Along these lines, it would be interesting to assess the degree to which internal accounts for the leaver's exit are similar to the ones recruiters offer to job applicants. Once a replacement is hired, stayers will engage in information-giving (Hudson & Jablin, 1992) and information-seeking behaviors to make sense of the newcomer (figure out the newcomer's "story," reduce uncertainty). At the same time, stayers will adapt to the loss of a node in their communication networks by developing linkages with the newcomer (though these may not be the same as existed with the leaver).

The leaver will also be entering into some form of new role upon exit from former employer. As Jablin and Krone (1994) suggest, the realism of communication expectations "that individuals hold prior to their disengagement from work/organizational relationships appears to affect their ability to adapt successfully to the environments they are entering" (p. 656). The more realistic the expectations formed during anticipatory socialization, the easier the role adjustment upon entry into the new setting. At the same time, however, the leaver will experience some form of "encounter" upon organizational entry, during which time he or she must learn about the requirements of the new role (e.g., Jablin & Kramer, 1998). In addition, it is important to stress that significant variations in some types of newcomers' communication behavior may exist depending on the form of disengagement/entry considered (for instance, the reasons retirees offer to members of their new role set to account for leaving their organizations [e.g., Hanisch, 1994] may be quite distinct from those generated by individuals who voluntarily leave their old employers to take a job in a different organization). Communication may continue between the leaver and stayers at the old organization after the individual's departure from the firm. It is likely that initial communication will focus on work-related matters, but over time interactions will likely become focused only on personal issues and the maintenance of personal friendships/links (e.g., Kramer, 1989). In most situations, communication contact will greatly diminish over a period of time, as those involved become focused on maintaining the new organizational relationships they have formed. Thus, to some extent, many communication relationships that once were characterized as strong ties become weak ones. Also, different forms of disengagement/entry have distinctive effects on the extraorganizational communication networks of both stayers and leavers, as well as their families. For instance, disengagement that also involves geographic relocation (e.g., international transfers; see Arthur & Bennett, 1995; Black, Gregersen, & Mendenhall, 1992; Caligiuri, Hyland, Joshi, & Bross, 1998) will have a greater impact on stayers, leavers, and their respective families than disengagements in which individuals remain in the same community.

Finally, it is likely that a significant turning point signaling the consummation of the postexit phase for the leaver and stayers is when individuals internal and external to their respective organizations no longer show surprise (e.g., "I didn't know you [he/she] left X organization!") as to the leaver's change in employment status. In other words, when network links (especially weak ties) cease asking why the leaver no longer works at his or her former employer, ensuing conversations will no longer be framed by the past, but by the present and future. Thus, for example, stayers would no longer be offering accounts for why the leaver exited the organization (focus on the past), but would converse about the new person who was hired, future opportunities, and the like. In turn, leavers would no longer be telling the story of their departure from their former employer, but would talk about new colleagues, challenges associated with the new job, how they like the boss, and similar present- and future-oriented topics. In

sum, it is quite likely that the leaver and stayers have some control over the duration of the postexit period; however, the persistence of this stage is also partially determined by the speed with which "the word" of the leaver's exit from the organization is diffused through relevant communication networks and the frequency with which the leaver and stayers have contact with nodes in these networks.

Conclusion

In the preceding pages, I have attempted to build an integrative perspective about the roles and functions of communication in the voluntary organizational disengagement/exit process. As with most initial efforts I have likely failed to recognize or even excluded certain communication phenomena that should have been included here. At the same time, I may have included certain communication activities and processes that future research will show are not relevant across disengagement contexts. Despite these limitations, I hope the perspective presented here serves to stimulate future research in this area. As noted in the opening of this section, the corpus of existing research exploring communication and voluntary organizational disengagement remains rudimentary in nature. In conclusion, it is important to recognize that regardless of the form of organizational disengagement, the process of exiting an organization presents numerous communication dilemmas for all those involved. For both leavers and stayers as they progress through the process, they face "teller's problems" (Riessman, 1990), as well as listener's/receiver's problems. How they choose to manage (not necessarily solve) these problems will likely influence the stress they experience in adapting to the many changes that often are associated with the disengagement process. In fact, effective management of the communication dynamics of the process can just as easily result in "eustress" (positive stress that enriches us; see Selye, 1956) as it does problematic forms of stress that are often associated with organizational disengagement. Organizational disengagement is an opportunity for both stayers and leavers to reconstruct the "stories" they have constructed to explain the dynamics of their organizations, as well as numerous dimensions of their careers and identities.

CONCLUDING STATEMENT

As noted in the opening of this chapter, a major goal of the preceding review and analysis was to discern our progress since 1987 in developing our understanding of communication processes and phenomena associated with organizational entry, assimilation, and disengagement/exit. In the process of exploring this issue, a number of areas have been identified where we have achieved significant gains in understanding; at the same time, other areas have been identified where progress in building knowledge has been more limited or where alternative research strategies for generating knowledge may be useful. New directions for communication research have also been suggested with respect to each of the major foci of this chapter: anticipatory vocational and organizational socialization, organizational entry and assimilation, and voluntary organizational disengagement/exit.

It is hoped that these suggestions will be helpful in guiding future studies in these areas, and thereby further our understanding of communication processes and behaviors associated with organizational entry, assimilation, and disengagement/exit. As I concluded in 1987, the perspective presented in this chapter reiterates the notion that one of the keys to understanding human communication in organizations is to recognize its developmental nature.

NOTES

1. A useful discussion of the underlying foundations, models, and terminology used in communica-

tion-related organizational assimilation research was developed in a series of articles published in late 1999, subsequent to the preparation of this chapter. These essays explore a variety of issues central to the study of organizational assimilation, and I urge those interested in this area to read the original article by Kramer and Miller (1999) and the responses that it generated.

2. Some of the ideas presented here were originally outlined in an earlier paper by Jablin, Grady, and Parker (1994).

REFERENCES

Abelson, M. A. (1993). Turnover cultures. In G. R. Ferris (Ed.), *Research in personnel and human resources management* (Vol. 11, pp. 339-376). Greenwich, CT: JAI.

Adkins, C. L., Ravlin, E. C., & Meglino, B. M. (1996). Value congruence between co-workers and its relationship to work outcomes. *Group & Organization Management, 21*, 439-460.

Adkins, C. L., Russell, C. J., & Werbel, J. D. (1994). Judgments of fit in the selection process: The role of work value congruence. *Personnel Psychology, 47*, 605-623.

Ahlander, N. R., & Bahr, K. S. (1995). Beyond drudgery, power and equity: Toward an expanded discourse on the moral dimensions of housework in families. *Journal of Marriage and the Family, 57*, 54-68.

Alderfer, C. P., & McCord, C. G. (1970). Personal and situational factors in the recruitment interview. *Journal of Applied Psychology, 54*, 377-385.

Allen, B. J. (1996). Feminist standpoint theory: A black woman's (re)view of organizational socialization. *Communication Studies, 47*, 257-271.

Allen, B. J., & Tompkins, P. K. (1996). Vocabularies of motives in a crisis of academic leadership. *Southern Communication Journal, 61*, 321-322.

Allen, M. W. (1992). Communication and organizational commitment: Perceived organizational support as a mediating factor. *Communication Quarterly, 40*, 357-367.

Allen, M. W. (1995). How employees see the boss: Communication concepts related to perceived organizational support. *Western Journal of Communication, 59*, 326-346.

Allen, M. W. (1996). The relationship between communication, affect, job alternatives, and voluntary turnover intentions. *Southern Communication Journal, 61*, 198-209.

Allen, N. J., & Meyer, J. P. (1990). Organizational socialization tactics: A longitudinal analysis of links to newcomers' commitment and role orientation. *Academy of Management Journal, 33*, 847-858.

Allen, T. D., McManus, S. E., & Russell, J. E. A. (1999). Newcomer socialization and stress: Formal peer relationships as a source of support. *Journal of Vocational Behavior, 54,* 453-470.

Allen, T. D., Russell, J. E. A., & Maetzke, S. B. (1997). Formal peer mentoring: Factors related to protégés' satisfaction and willingness to mentor others. *Group & Organization Management, 22,* 488-507.

Altman, I., & Taylor, D. (1973). *Social penetration: The development of interpersonal relationships.* New York: Rinehart & Winston.

Anderson, N., & Shackleton, V. (1990). Decision making in the graduate selection interview: A field study. *Journal of Occupational Psychology, 63,* 63-76.

Anson, E. M. (1988). *How to prepare and write your employee handbook* (2nd ed.). New York: AMACOM.

Arnold, J., & Nicholson, N. (1991). Construing of self and others and work in the early years of corporate careers. *Journal of Organizational Behavior, 12,* 621-639.

Arrow, H., & McGrath, J. E. (1995). Membership dynamics in groups at work: A theoretical framework. In L. L. Cummings & B. M. Staw (Eds.), *Research in organizational behavior* (Vol. 17, pp. 373-411). Greenwich, CT: JAI.

Arthur, D. (1991). *Recruiting, interviewing and orienting new employees* (2nd ed.). New York: American Management Association.

Arthur, W., Jr., & Bennett, W., Jr. (1995). The international assignee: The relative importance of factors perceived to contribute to success. *Personnel Psychology, 48,* 99-114.

Aryee, S., Chay, Y. W., & Chew, J. (1996). The motivation to mentor among managerial employees. *Group & Organization Management, 21,* 261-277.

Ashford, S. J. (1986). The role of feedback seeking in individual adaptation: A resource perspective. *Academy of Management Journal, 29,* 465-487.

Ashford, S. J., & Black, J. S. (1992). *Self-socialization: Individual tactics to facilitate entry.* Paper presented at the annual meeting of the Academy of Management, Las Vegas, NV.

Ashford, S. J., & Black, J. S. (1996). Proactivity during organizational entry: The role of desire for control. *Journal of Applied Psychology, 81,* 199-214.

Ashford, S. J., & Cummings, L. L. (1985). Proactive feedback seeking: The instrumental use of the information environment. *Journal of Occupational Psychology, 58,* 67-79.

Ashford, S. J., & Taylor, M. S. (1990). Adaptations to work transitions: An integrative approach. In G. R. Ferris & K. M. Rowland (Eds.), *Research in personnel and human resources management* (Vol. 8, pp. 1-39). Greenwich, CT: JAI.

Ashforth, B. E., & Humphrey, R. H. (1995). Labeling processes in the organization: Constructing the individual. In L. L. Cummings & B. M. Staw (Eds.), *Research in organizational behavior* (Vol. 17, pp. 413-461). Greenwich, CT: JAI Press.

Ashforth, B. E., & Humphrey. (1997). The ubiquity and potency of labeling in organizations. *Organizational Science, 8,* 43-58.

Ashforth, B. E., & Saks, A. M. (1996). Socialization tactics: Longitudinal effects of newcomer adjustment. *Academy of Management Journal, 39,* 149-178.

Ashforth, B. E., Saks, A. M., & Lee, R. T. (1998). Socialization and newcomer adjustment: The role of organizational context. *Human Relations, 51,* 897-926.

Asmussen, L., & Larson, R. (1991). The quality of family time among young adolescents in single-parent and married-parent families. *Journal of Marriage and the Family, 53,* 1021-1030.

Atkin, D. J., Moorman, J., & Lin, C. A. (1991). Ready for prime time: Network series devoted to working women in the 1980s. *Sex Roles, 25,* 677-685.

Auster, C. J. (1985). Manuals for socialization: Examples from Girl Scout handbooks 1913-1984. *Qualitative Sociology, 8,* 359-367.

Avery, C. M., & Jablin, F. M. (1988). Retirement preparation programs and organizational communication. *Communication Education, 37,* 68-80.

Axtmann, L., & Jablin, F. M. (1986, May). *Distributional and sequential interaction structure in the employment screening interview.* Paper presented at the annual meeting of the International Communication Association, Chicago.

Ayres, J., Ayres, D. M., & Sharp, D. (1993). A progress report on the development of an instrument to measure communication apprehension in employment interviews. *Communication Research Reports, 10,* 87-94.

Ayres, J., & Crosby, S. (1995). Two studies concerning the predictive validity of the Personal Report of Communication Apprehension in Employment Interviews. *Communication Research Reports, 12,* 145-151.

Ayres, J., Keereetaweep, T., Chen, P., & Edwards, P. A. (1998). Communication apprehension and employment interviews. *Communication Education, 47,* 1-17.

Babbitt, L. V., & Jablin, F. M. (1985). Characteristics of applicants' questions and employment screening interview outcomes. *Human Communication Research, 11,* 507-535.

Bahniuk, M. H., Dobos, J., & Hill, S. E. K. (1990). The impact of mentoring, collegial support, and information adequacy on career success: A replication. *Journal of Social Behavior and Personality, 5,* 431-451. (Special issue, J. W. Neuliep, Ed., *Handbook of replication research in the behavioral and social sciences*)

Bahniuk, M. H., Hill, S. E. K., & Darius, H. J. (1996). The relationship of power-gaining communication strategies to career success. *Western Journal of Communication, 60,* 358-378.

Baker, H. E., & Feldman, D. C. (1990). Strategies of organizational socialization and their impact on newcomer adjustment. *Journal of Managerial Issues, 2,* 198-212.

Baker, H. E., & Feldman, D. C. (1991). Linking organizational socialization tactics with corporate human resource management strategies. *Human Resource Management Review, 1,* 193-202.

Barber, A. E., Hollenbeck, J. R., Tower, S. L., & Phillips, J. (1994). The effects of interview focus on recruitment effectiveness: A field experiment. *Journal of Applied Psychology, 79,* 886-896.

Barber, A. E., & Roehling, M. V. (1993). Job postings and the decision to interview: A verbal protocol analysis. *Journal of Applied Psychology, 78,* 845-856.

Barber, B. L., & Eccles, J. S. (1992). Long-term influence of divorce and single parenting on adolescent family- and work-related values, behaviors, and aspiration. *Psychological Bulletin, 111,* 108-126.

Barling, J., Dupre, K. E., & Hepburn, C. G. (1998). Effects of parents' job insecurity on children's work beliefs and attitudes. *Journal of Applied Psychology, 83,* 112-118.

Barling, J., Rogers, K., & Kelloway, E. K. (1995). Some effects of teenagers' part-time employment: The quantity and quality of work make the difference. *Journal of Organizational Behavior, 16,* 143-154.

Barocas, V. S. (1993). *Benefit communications: Enhancing the employer's investment.* New York: Conference Board.

Baron, R. A. (1989). Impression management by applicants during employment interviews: The "too much of a good thing" effect. In R. W. Eder & G. R. Ferris (Eds.), *The employment interview: Theory, research and practice* (pp. 204-215). Newbury Park, CA: Sage.

Barrios-Choplin, J. R. (1994). *Newcomers' surprise: An extension and exploratory study of Louis' conceptualization.* Unpublished doctoral dissertation, University of Texas at Austin.

Barry, B., & Bateman, T. S. (1992). Perceptions of influence in managerial dyads: The role of hierarchy, media, and tactics. *Human Relations, 45,* 555-574.

Bastien, D. T. (1987). Common patterns of behavior and communication in corporate mergers and acquisitions. *Human Resource Management, 26,* 17-23.

Bastien, D. T. (1992). Change in organizational culture: The use of linguistic methods in a corporate acquisition. *Management Communication Quarterly, 5,* 403-442.

Bauer, T. N., & Green, S. G. (1994). Effect of newcomer involvement in work-related activities: A longitudinal study of socialization. *Journal of Applied Psychology, 79,* 211-223.

Bauer, T. N., & Green, S. G. (1996). Development of leader-member exchange: A longitudinal test. *Academy of Management Journal, 39,* 1538-1567.

Bauer, T. N., Morrison, E. W., & Callister, R. R. (1998). Organizational socialization: A review and directions for future research. In G. R. Ferris & K. M. Rowland (Eds.), *Research in personnel and human resources management* (Vol. 16, pp. 149-214). Greenwich, CT: JAI.

Beach, W. A., & Japp, P. (1983). Storifying as time-traveling: The knowledgeable use of temporally structured discourse. In R. Bostrom (Ed.), *Communication yearbook 7* (pp. 867-888). Beverly Hills, CA: Sage.

Bedeian, A. G. (1995). Workplace envy. *Organizational Dynamics, 23*(4), 49-56.

Beehr, T. A., & Nelson, N. L. (1995). Descriptions of job characteristics and retirement activities during the transition to retirement. *Journal of Organizational Behavior, 16,* 681-690.

Bellinger, D. C., & Gleason, J. B. (1982). Sex differences in parental directives to young children. *Sex Roles, 8,* 1123-1139.

Belt, J. A., & Paolillo, J. G. (1982). The influence of corporate image and specificity of candidate qualifications on response to recruitment advertisements. *Journal of Management, 8,* 105-112.

Bennett, M. (1990). Children's understanding of the mitigating function of disclaimers. *Journal of Social Psychology, 130,* 29-47.

Ben-Yoav, O., & Hartman, K. (1988). Supervisors' competence and learning of work values and behaviors during organizational entry. *Journal of Social Behavior and Personality, 13,* 23-36.

Berg, L. V., & Trujillo, N. (1989). *Organizational life on television.* Norwood, NJ: Ablex.

Berger, C. R. (1979). Beyond initial understandings: Uncertainty, understanding, and the development of interpersonal relationships. In H. Giles & R. N. St. Clair (Eds.), *Language and social psychology* (pp. 122-144). Oxford, UK: Basil Blackwell.

Berger, C. R., & Bradac, J. J. (1982). *Language and social knowledge: Uncertainty in interpersonal relations.* London: Edward Arnold.

Berger, S., & Huchendorf, K. (1989, December). Ongoing orientation at Metropolitan Life. *Personnel Journal,* pp. 28, 30, 32, 34-35.

Bian, Y. (1997). Bringing strong ties back in: Indirect ties, network bridges, and job searches in China. *American Sociological Review, 62,* 366-385.

Bies, R. B. (1987). The predicament of injustice: The management of moral outrage. In L. L. Cummings & B. M. Staw (Eds.), *Research in organizational behavior* (Vol. 9, pp. 289-319). Greenwich, CT: JAI.

Bigelow, B. J., Tesson, G., & Lewko, J. H. (1996). *Learning the rules: The anatomy of children's relationships.* New York: Guilford.

Binning, J. F., Goldstein, M. A., Garcia, M. F., & Scattaregia, J. H. (1988). Effects of preinterview impressions on questioning strategies in same- and opposite-sex employment interviews. *Journal of Applied Psychology, 73*, 30-37.

Birnbaum, D., & Somers, M. J. (1991). Prevocational experience and post-entry behavior: Occupational influences on job attitudes and turnover. *Journal of Applied Social Psychology, 21*, 508-523.

Black, J. S. (1992). Socializing American expatriate managers overseas. *Group & Organization Management, 17*, 171-192.

Black, J. S., & Ashford, S. J. (1995). Fitting in or making jobs fit: Factors affecting mode of adjustment for new hires. *Human Relations, 48*, 421-437.

Black, J. S., Gregersen, H. B., & Mendenhall, M. E. (1992). *Global assignments: Successfully expatriating and repatriating international managers.* San Francisco: Jossey-Bass.

Blau, G. (1988). An investigation of the apprenticeship organizational socialization strategy. *Journal of Vocational Behavior, 32*, 176-195.

Blau, G. (1995). Influence of group lateness on individual lateness: A cross-level examination. *Academy of Management Journal, 38*, 1483-1496.

Blau, G. J. (1990). Exploring the mediating mechanisms affecting the relationship of recruitment source to employee performance. *Journal of Vocational Behavior, 37*, 303-320.

Blau, P. (1964). *Exchange and power in social life.* New York: John Wiley.

Blum-Kulka, S. (1997). *Dinner talk: Cultural patterns of sociability and socialization in family discourse.* Mahwah, NJ: Lawrence Erlbaum.

Blyth, D. A., Hill, J. P., & Thiel, K. S. (1982). Early adolescents' significant others: Grade and gender differences in perceived relationships with familial and nonfamilial adults and young people. *Journal of Youth and Adolescence, 11*, 425-450.

Boje, D. M. (1991). The storytelling organization: A study of story performance in an office-supply firm. *Administrative Science Quarterly, 36*, 106-126.

Bowen, D. E., Ledford, G. E., & Nathan, B. R. (1991). Hiring for the organization, not the job. *Academy of Management Executive, 5*, 35-51.

Bowes, J. M., & Goodnow, J. J. (1996). Work for home, school, or labor force: The nature and sources of changes in understanding. *Psychological Bulletin, 119*, 300-321.

Bowles, S., & Gintis, H. (1976). *Schooling in capitalist America: Educational reforms and the contradictions of economic life.* New York: Basic Books.

Boyd, N. G., & Taylor, R. R. (1998). A developmental approach to the examination of friendship in leader-follower relationships. *Leadership Quarterly, 9*, 1-25.

Bozeman, D. P., & Kacmar, K. M. (1997). A cybernetic model of impression management processes in organizations. *Organizational Behavior and Human Decision Processes, 69*, 9-30.

Breaugh, J. A. (1981). Relationship between recruiting sources and employee performance, absenteeism, and work attitudes. *Academy of Management Journal, 24*, 142-147.

Breaugh, J. A. (1983). Realistic job previews: A critical appraisal and future research directions. *Academy of Management Review, 8*, 612-619.

Breaugh, J. A., & Mann, R. B. (1984). Recruiting source effects: A test of two alternative explanations. *Journal of Occupational Psychology, 57*, 261-267.

Brett, J. M. (1984). Job transitions and personal development. In K. M. Rowland & G. R. Ferris (Eds.), *Research in personnel and human resources management* (Vol. 2, pp. 155-185). Greenwich, CT: JAI.

Bretz, R. D., Rynes, S. L., & Gerhart, B. (1993). Recruiter perceptions of applicant fit: Implications for individual career preparation and job search behavior. *Journal of Vocational Behavior, 43*, 310-327.

Bridge, K., & Baxter, L. A. (1992). Blended relationships: Friends as work associates. *Western Journal of Communication, 56*, 200-225.

Briody, E. K. (1988). Fitting in: Newcomer adaptation in a corporate research setting. *Central Issues in Anthropology, 7*(2), 19-38.

Briody, E. K., & Chrisman, J. B. (1991). Cultural adaptation on overseas assignments. *Human Organization, 50*, 264-282.

Brockner, J. (1988). The effect of work layoffs on survivors. In B. M. Staw & L. L. Cummings (Eds.), *Research in organizational behavior* (Vol. 10, pp. 213-255). Greenwich, CT: JAI.

Brockner, J. (1994). Perceived fairness and survivors' reactions to layoffs, or how downsizing organizations can do well by doing good. *Social Justice Research, 7*, 345-371.

Brockner, J., Siegel, P. A., Daly, J. P., Tyler, T., & Martin, C. (1987). When trust matters: The moderating effect of outcome favorability. *Administrative Science Quarterly, 42*, 558-583.

Bromley, D. B. (1993). *Reputation, image and impression management.* Chichester, UK: Wiley.

Bronfenbrenner, U. (1979). *The ecology of human development: Experiments by nature and design.* Cambridge, MA: Harvard University Press.

Bronfenbrenner, U. (1986). Ecology of the family as a context for human development: Research perspectives. *Developmental Psychology, 22*, 723-742.

Brown, D., Brooks, L., & Associates. (1996). *Career choice and development* (3rd ed.). San Francisco: Jossey-Bass.

Brown, J. D. (1991). Preprofessional socialization and identity transformation: The case of the professional ex-. *Journal of Contemporary Ethnography, 20*, 157-178.

Brown, M. H. (1985). That reminds me of a story: Speech action in organizational socialization. *Western Journal of Speech Communication, 49*, 27-42.

Brown, M. H. (1990). Defining stories in organizations: Characteristics and functions. In J. A. Anderson (Ed.), *Communication yearbook 13* (pp. 162-190). Newbury Park, CA: Sage.

Browning, L. D. (1992). Lists and stories as organizational communication. *Communication Theory, 2,* 281-302.

Bucher, R., & Stelling, J. G. (1977). *Becoming professional.* Beverly Hills, CA: Sage.

Buckley, M. R., Fedor, D. B., Veres, J. G., Wiese, D. S., & Carraher, S. M. (1998). Investigating newcomer expectations and job-related outcomes. *Journal of Applied Psychology, 83,* 452-461.

Bullis, C. (1993). Organizational socialization research: Enabling, constraining, and shifting perspectives. *Communication Monographs, 60,* 10-17.

Bullis, C. (1999). Mad or bad: A response to Kramer and Miller. *Communication Monographs, 66,* 368-373.

Bullis, C., & Bach, B. W. (1989). Are mentor relationships helping organizations? An exploration of developing mentee-mentor-organizational identifications using turning point analysis. *Communication Quarterly, 37,* 199-213.

Bullis, C., & Clark, C. L. (1993, November). *A longitudinal study of employee resocialization.* Paper presented at the annual meeting of the Speech Communication Association, Miami Beach, FL.

Burke, R. J., McKeen, C. A., & McKenna, C. S. (1990). Sex differences and cross-sex effects on mentoring: Some preliminary data. *Psychological Reports, 67,* 1011-1023,

Burke, R. J., McKenna, C. S., & McKeen, C. A. (1991). How do mentorships differ from typical supervisory relationships? *Psychological Reports, 68,* 459-466.

Burleson, B. R., Delia, J. G., & Applegate, J. L. (1995). The socialization of person-centered communication. In M. A. Fitzpatrick & A. L. Vangelisti (Eds.), *Explaining family interactions* (pp. 34-76). Thousand Oaks, CA: Sage.

Burnett, J. R., & Motowidlo, S. J. (1998). Relations between different sources of information in the structured selection interview. *Personnel Psychology, 51,* 963-983.

Burt, R. S. (1992). *Structural holes: The social structure of competition.* Cambridge, MA: Harvard University Press.

Byrd, M. L. V. (1979). *The effects of vocal activity and race of applicant on the job selection interview decision.* Unpublished doctoral dissertation, University of Missouri, Columbia.

Cable, D. M., & Judge, T. A. (1996). Person-organization fit, job choice decisions, and organizational entry. *Organizational Behavior and Human Decision Processes, 67,* 294-311.

Cable, D. M., & Judge, T. A. (1997). Interviewers' perceptions of person-organization fit and organizational selection decisions. *Journal of Applied Psychology, 82,* 546-561.

Cahill, S. E. (1999). Emotional capital and professional socialization: The case of mortuary science students (and me). *Social Psychology Quarterly, 62,* 101-116.

Caldwell, D., & O'Reilly, C. (1982). Responses to failure: The effects of choice and responsibility on impression management. *Academy of Management Journal, 25,* 121-136.

Caldwell, D. F., & Spivey, W. A. (1983). The relationship between recruiting source and employee success: An analysis by race. *Personnel Psychology, 36,* 67-72.

Caligiuri, P. M., Hyland, M. M., Joshi, A., & Bross, A. S. (1998). Testing a theoretical model for examining the relationship between family adjustment and expatriates' work adjustment. *Journal of Applied Psychology, 83,* 598-614.

Campion, M. A., Cheraskin, L., & Stevens, M. J. (1994). Career-related antecedents and outcomes of job rotation. *Academy of Management Journal, 37,* 1518-1542.

Campion, M. A., Palmer, D. K., & Campion, J. E. (1997). A review of structure in the selection interview. *Personnel Psychology, 50,* 655-702.

Campion, M. A., Pursell, E. D., & Brown, B. K. (1988). Structured interviewing: Raising the psychometric properties of the employment interview. *Personnel Psychology, 41,* 25-42.

Cawyer, C. S., & Friedrich, G. W. (1998). Organizational socialization: Processes for new communication faculty. *Communication Education, 47,* 234-245.

Chao, G. T., Walz, P. M., & Gardner, P. D. (1992). Formal and informal mentorships: A comparison on mentoring functions and contrast with nonmentored counterparts. *Personnel Psychology, 45,* 619-636.

Chao, G. T., O'Leary-Kelly, A. M., Wolf, S., Klein, H. J., & Gardner, P. D. (1994). Organizational socialization: Its content and consequences. *Journal of Applied Psychology, 79,* 730-743.

Charner, I., & Fraser, B. S. (1988). *Youth and work: What we know, what we don't know, what we need to know.* Washington, DC: W. T. Grant Foundation Commission on Youth and America's Future.

Chatman, J. (1991). Matching people and organizations: Selection and socialization in public accounting firms. *Administrative Science Quarterly, 36,* 459-484.

Cheatham, T. R., & McLaughlin, M. L. (1976). A comparison of co-participant perceptions of self and others in placement center interviews. *Communication Quarterly, 24,* 9-13.

Chen, X.-P., Hui, C., & Sego, D. J. (1998). The role of organizational citizenship behavior in turnover: Conceptualization and preliminary tests of key hypotheses. *Journal of Applied Psychology, 83,* 922-931.

Chesebro, J. W. (1991). Communication, values, and popular television series—A seventeen-year assessment. *Communication Quarterly, 39,* 197-225.

Christenson, P. G., & Roberts, D. F. (1983). The role of television in the formation of children's social attitudes. In M. J. A. Howe (Ed.), *Learning from television: Psychological and educational research* (pp. 79-99). New York: Academic Press.

Clair, R. P. (1996). The political nature of the colloquialism, "a real job": Implications for organizational socialization. *Communication Monographs, 63,* 249-267.

Clair, R. P. (1999). A review of Kramer and Miller's manuscript. *Communication Monographs, 66,* 374-381.

Cohen, P. (1991, May 9-10). Confessions of a handbook writer. *Personnel, 68*(5), 9.

Colarelli, S. M. (1984). Methods of communication and mediating processes in realistic job previews. *Journal of Applied Psychology, 69,* 633-642.

Colella, A. (1989). *A new role for newcomer pre-entry expectations during organizational entry: Expectation effects on job perceptions.* Unpublished doctoral dissertation, Ohio State University, Columbus.

Comer, D. R. (1991). Organizational newcomers' acquisition of information from peers. *Management Communication Quarterly, 5,* 64-89.

Comer, D. R. (1992). Factors that make peers effective information agents for organizational newcomers. *Journal of Management Systems, 4,* 13-27.

Conard, M. A., & Ashforth, S. D. (1986). *Recruiting source effectiveness: A meta-analysis and reexamination of two rival hypotheses.* Paper presented at the first annual meeting of the Society of Industrial/Organizational Psychology, Chicago.

Connerley, M. L. (1997). The influence of training on perceptions of recruiters' interpersonal skills and effectiveness. *Journal of Occupational and Organizational Psychology, 70,* 259-272.

Connerley, M. L., & Rynes, S. L. (1997). The influence of recruiter characteristics and organizational recruitment support on perceived recruiter effectiveness: Views from applicants and recruiters. *Human Relations, 50,* 1563-1586.

Conrad, C. (1994). *Strategic organizational communication: Toward the twenty-first century* (3rd ed.). Fort Worth, TX: Harcourt Brace.

Conrad, C., & Witte, K. (1994). Is emotional expression repression oppression? Myths of organizational affective regulation. In S. A. Deetz (Ed.), *Communication yearbook 17* (pp. 417-428). Thousand Oaks, CA: Sage.

Cook, M. F. (1992). *The AMA handbook for employee recruitment and retention.* New York: American Management Association.

Cooper, W. H., Graham, W. J., & Dyke, L. S. (1993). Tournament players. In G. Ferris (Ed.), *Research in personnel and human resources management* (Vol. 11, pp. 83-132). Greenwich, CT: JAI.

Cordes, C., Brown, J., & Olson, D. E. (1991). The role of social information processing in the career selection process. *Akron Business and Economic Review, 22,* 7-19.

Cornett-DeVito, M. M., & Friedman, P. G. (1995). Communication processes and merger success: An exploratory study of four financial institution mergers. *Management Communication Quarterly, 9,* 46-77.

Corsaro, W. A. (1990). The underlife of the nursery school: Young children's social representations of adult rules. In G. Duveen & B. Lloyd (Eds.), *Social representations and the development of knowledge* (pp. 11-26). Cambridge, UK: Cambridge University Press.

Cox, S. A. (1998, April). *A social exchange model of employee satisfaction, voice and exit.* Paper presented at the annual convention of the Southern Communication Association, San Antonio, TX.

Cox, S. A. (1999). Group communication and employee turnover: How coworkers encourage peers to voluntarily exit. *Southern Communication Journal, 64,* 181-192.

Cox, S. A., & Kramer, M. W. (1995). Communication during employee dismissals: Social exchange principles and group influences on employee. *Management Communication Quarterly, 9,* 156-190.

Crites, J. O. (1969). *Vocational psychology.* New York: McGraw-Hill.

Crossen, C. (1985, March 19). Kids of top executives are crazy about dad–especially his money. *Wall Street Journal,* Sec. 2, p. 33.

Crouter, A. C. (1984). Spillover from family to work: The neglected side of the work-family interface. *Human Relations, 37,* 425-442.

Cude, R. L., & Jablin, F. M. (1992). Retiring from work: The paradoxical impact of organizational commitment. *Journal of Managerial Issues, 4,* 31-45.

Cumming, E., & Henry, W. E. (1961). *Growing old: The process of disengagement.* New York: Basic Books.

Csikszentmihalyi, M., & Larson, R. (1984). *Being adolescent: Conflict and growth in the teenage years.* New York: Basic Books.

Dalton, D. R., & Tudor, W. D. (1979). Turnover turned over: An expanded and positive perspective. *Academy of Management Review, 4,* 225-235.

Danielson, M. A. (1995). *A taxonomy of newcomer university professors' expectancy violations during organizational assimilation.* Paper presented at the annual meeting of the Speech Communication Association, San Antonio, TX.

Davis, H. S. (1994). *New employee orientation.* New York: Neal-Schuman.

Davis, K. (1968). Readability changes in employee handbooks of identical companies during a fifteen-year period. *Personnel Psychology, 21,* 413-420.

Dean, R. A., Ferris, K. R., & Konstas, C. (1988). Occupational reality shock and organizational commitment: Evidence from the accounting profession. *Accounting, Organizations and Society, 13,* 235-250.

DeBell, C. S., Montgomery, M. J., McCarthy, P. R., & Lanthier, R. P. (1998). The critical contact: A study of recruiter verbal behavior during campus interviews. *Journal of Business Communication, 35,* 202-223.

Decker, P. J., & Cornelius, E. T., III. (1979). A note on recruiting sources and job survival rates. *Journal of Applied Psychology, 64,* 463-464.

DeFleur, L. B., & Menke, B. A. (1975). Learning about the labor force: Occupational knowledge among high school males. *Sociology of Education, 48,* 324-345.

Deluga, R. J., & Perry, J. T. (1994). The role of subordinate performance and ingratiation in leader-member exchanges. *Group & Organization Management, 19,* 67-86.

Dilla, B. L. (1987). Descriptive versus prescriptive information in a realistic job preview. *Journal of Vocational Behavior, 30,* 33-48.

Dipboye, R. L. (1994). Structured and unstructured selection interviews: Beyond the job-fit model. In G. R. Ferris (Ed.), *Research in personnel and human resources management* (Vol. 12, pp. 79-123). Greenwich, CT: JAI.

Dirsmith, M. W., & Covaleski, M. A. (1985). Informal communications, nonformal communications and mentoring in public accounting firms. *Accounting, Organizations and Society, 10,* 149-169.

DiSanza, J. R. (1995). Bank teller organizational assimilation in a system of contradictory practices. *Management Communication Quarterly, 9,* 191-218.

Dockery, T. M., & Steiner, D. D. (1990). The role of the initial interaction in leader-member exchange. *Group and Organization Studies, 15,* 395-413.

Donabedian, B., McKinnon, S. M., & Bruns, W. J. (1998). Task characteristics, managerial socialization, and media selection. *Management Communication Quarterly, 11,* 372-400.

Dougherty, T. W., Turban, D. B., & Callender, J. C. (1994). Confirming impressions in the employment interview: A field study of interviewer behavior. *Journal of Applied Psychology, 79,* 659-665.

Downs, C. W. (1969). Perceptions of the selection interview. *Personnel Administration, 32,* 8-23.

Dreeban, R. (1968). *What is learned in school.* Reading, MA: Addison-Wesley.

Dreher, G. F., & Ash, R. A. (1990). A comparative study of mentoring among men and women in managerial, professional and technical positions. *Journal of Applied Psychology, 75,* 539-546.

Dreher, G. F., & Cox, T. H. (1996). Race, gender, and opportunity: A study of compensation attainment and the establishment of mentoring relationships. *Journal of Applied Psychology, 81,* 297-308.

Driver, R. W. (1980). A determination of the relative efficacy of different techniques for employee benefit communication. *Journal of Business Communication, 17,* 23-37.

Duck, S. (1994). *Meaningful relationships: Talking, sense, and relating.* Thousand Oaks, CA: Sage.

Duff, K. (1989, February). An electronic employee handbook. *Personnel,* pp. 12-14, 17.

Dunn, J. (1988). *The beginnings of social understanding.* Cambridge, MA: Harvard University Press.

Eagen, K. S. (1996). Flexible mentoring: Adaptations in style for women's ways of knowing. *Journal of Business Communication, 33,* 401-425.

Ebaugh, H. R. F. (1984). *Becoming an ex: The process of role exit.* Chicago: University of Chicago Press.

Eccles, J. S. (1993). School and family effects on the ontogeny of children's interests, self-perceptions, and activity choices. *Nebraska Symposium on Motivation: Developmental Perspectives on Motivation, 40,* 145-208.

Eccles, J. S., & Barber, B. L. (1999). Student council, volunteering, basketball, or marching band: What kind of extracurricular involvement matters? *Journal of Adolescent Research, 14,* 10-43.

Eden, D. (1984). Self-fulfilling prophesy as a management tool: Harnessing Pygmalion. *Academy of Management Review, 9,* 64-73.

Eder, R. W., & Ferris, G. R. (Eds.). (1989). *The employment interview: Theory, research and practice.* Newbury Park, CA: Sage.

Eder, R. W., & Harris, M. M. (1999). *The employment interview handbook.* Thousand Oaks, CA: Sage.

Einhorn, L. J. (1981). An inner view of the job interview: An investigation of successful interview behaviors. *Communication Education, 30,* 217-228.

Ellis, R. A., & Taylor, M. S. (1983). Role of self-esteem within the job search process. *Journal of Applied Psychology, 68,* 632-640.

Elsbach, K. D., Sutton, R. I., & Principe, K. E. (1997). Averting expected challenges through anticipatory impression management: A study of hospital billing. *Organization Science, 9,* 68-86.

Engler-Parish, P. G., & Millar, F. E. (1989). An exploratory relational control analysis of the employment screening interview. *Western Journal of Speech Communication, 53,* 30-51.

Enoch, Y. (1989). Change of values during socialization for a profession: An application to the marginal man theory. *Human Relations, 42,* 219-239.

Evans, C. P. (1994). *Analysis of formal mentoring communication and subsequent socialization of newcomers into work groups.* Unpublished master's thesis, University of Texas at Austin.

Fagenson, E. A. (1992). Mentoring—Who needs it? A comparison of proteges' and nonproteges' needs for power, achievement, affiliation, and autonomy. *Journal of Vocational Behavior, 41,* 48-60.

Fagenson, E. A. (1994). Perceptions of proteges' vs. nonproteges' relationships with their peers, superiors, and departments. *Journal of Vocational Behavior, 45,* 55-78.

Fairhurst, G. T. (1993). The leader-member exchange patterns of women leaders in industry: A discourse analysis. *Communication Monographs, 60,* 321-351.

Fairhurst, G. T., Jordan, J. M., & Neuwirth, K. (1997). Why are we here? Managing the meaning of an organizational mission statement. *Journal of Applied Communication Research, 25,* 243-263.

Falcione, R. L., & Wilson, C. E. (1988). Socialization processes in organizations. In G. M. Goldhaber & G. A. Barnett (Eds.), *Handbook of organizational communication* (pp. 151-169). Norwood, NJ: Ablex.

Fandt, P. M., & Ferris, G. R. (1990). The management of information and impressions: When employees behave opportunistically. *Organizational Behavior and Human Decision Processes, 45,* 140-158.

Fedor, D. B., Rensvold, R. B., & Adams, S. M. (1992). An investigation of factors expected to affect feedback seeking: A longitudinal field study. *Personnel Psychology, 45,* 779-803.

Feeley, T. H., & Barnett, G. A. (1997). Predicting employee turnover from communication networks. *Human Communication Research, 23,* 370-387.

Feij, J. A., Whitely, W. T., Peiró, J. M., & Taris, T. W. (1995). The development of career-enhancing strategies and content innovation: A longitudinal study of new workers. *Journal of Vocational Behavior, 46,* 231-256.

Feldman, D. C. (1976). A practical program for employee socialization. *Organizational Dynamics, 5,* 64-80.

Feldman, D. C. (1989). Socialization, resocialization, and training: Reframing the research agenda. In I. L. Goldstein (Ed.), *Training and development in organizations* (pp. 376-416). San Francisco: Jossey-Bass.

Feldman, D. C. (1994). Who's socializing whom? The impact of socializing newcomers on insiders, workgroups, and organizations. *Human Resource Management Review, 4,* 213-233.

Feldman, D. C., Doerpinghaus, H. I., & Turnley, W. H. (1994, Fall). Managing temporary workers: A permanent HRM challenge. *Organizational Dynamics, 23,* 49-63.

Feldman, D. C., & Weitz, B. A. (1990). Summer interns: Factors contributing to positive development experiences. *Journal of Vocational Behavior, 37,* 267-284.

Ferris, G. R., & Judge, T. A. (1991). Personnel/human resource management: A political influence perspective. *Journal of Management, 17,* 447-488.

Ferris, G. R., & Mitchell, T. R. (1987). The components of social influence and their importance for human resources research. In K. M. Rowland & G. R. Ferris (Eds.), *Research in personnel and human resources management* (Vol. 5, pp. 103-128). Greenwich, CT: JAI.

Festinger, L. (1957). *A theory of cognitive dissonance.* Stanford, CA: Stanford University Press.

Fielding, N. G. (1986). Evaluating the role of training in police socialization: A British example. *Journal of Community Psychology, 14,* 319-330.

Fine, G. A. (1986). Friendships in the work place. In V. J. Derlega & B. A. Winstead (Eds.), *Friendship and social interaction* (pp. 185-206). New York: St. Martin's.

Fine, G. A. (1987). *With the boys: Little League baseball and preadolescent culture.* Chicago: University of Chicago Press.

Fine, G. A. (1996). Justifying work: Occupational rhetorics as resources in restaurant kitchens. *Administrative Science Quarterly, 41,* 90-115.

Fink, L. S., Bauer, T. N., & Campion, M. A. (1994, Spring). Job candidates' views of site interviews. *Journal of Career Planing and Development,* pp. 32-38.

Fisher, C. D. (1986). Organizational socialization: An integrative review. In B. Rowland & G. Ferris (Eds.), *Research in personnel and human resources management* (Vol. 4, pp. 101-145). Greenwich, CT: JAI.

Fisher, C. D., Ilgen, D. R., & Hoyer, W. D. (1979). Source of credibility, information favorability, and job offer acceptance. *Academy of Management Journal, 22,* 94-103.

Fisher, S., & Todd, A. D. (1987). *Discourse in institutional authority: Medicine, education and law.* Norwood, NJ: Ablex.

Fiske, S. T., & Neuberg, S. L. (1990). A continuum model of impression formation from category-based to individuating processes: Influence of information and motivation on attention and interpretation. In M. P. Zanna (Ed.), *Advances in experimental and social psychology* (pp. 1-74). New York: Academic Press.

Flannagan, D., & Hardee, S. D. (1994). Talk about preschoolers' interpersonal relationships: Patterns related to culture, SES, and gender of child. *Merrill-Palmer Quarterly, 40,* 523-537.

Fogarty, T. J. (1992). Organizational socialization in accounting firms: A theoretical framework and agenda for future research. *Accounting, Organizations and Society, 17,* 129-149.

Folger, R. (1986). Rethinking equity theory: A referent cognitions model. In H. W. Bierhoff, R. L. Cohen, & J. Greenberg (Eds.), *Justice in social relations* (pp. 145-162). New York: Plenum.

Folger, R., & Skarlicki, D. P. (1998). When tough times make tough bosses: Managerial distancing as a function of layoff blame. *Academy of Management Journal, 41,* 79-87.

Forbes, R. J., & Jackson, P. R. (1980). Non-verbal behavior and the outcome of selection interviews. *Journal of Occupational Psychology, 53,* 65-72.

Ford, J. D., & Ford, L. W. (1995). The role of conversations in producing intentional change in organizations. *Academy of Management Review, 20,* 541-570.

Fournier, V. (1997). Graduates' construction systems and career development. *Human Relations, 50,* 363-391.

Fournier, V., & Payne, R. (1994). Changes in self construction during the transition from university to employment: A personal construct psychology approach. *Journal of Occupational and Organizational Psychology, 67,* 297-314.

Fritz, J. H. (1997). Men's and women's organizational peer relationships: A comparison. *Journal of Business Communication, 34,* 27-46.

Fullagar, C., McCoy, D., & Shull, C. (1992). The socialization of union loyalty. *Journal of Organizational Behavior, 13,* 13-26.

Gabriel, Y. (1997). Meeting God: When organizational members come face-to-face with the supreme leader. *Human Relations, 50,* 315-342.

Gannon, M. J. (1971). Sources of referral and employee turnover. *Journal of Applied Psychology, 55,* 226-228.

Gates, L. R., & Hellweg, S. A. (1989, February). *The socializing function of new employee orientation programs: A study of organizational identification and job satisfaction.* Paper presented at the annual meeting of the Western Speech Communication Association, Spokane, WA.

Gatewood, R. D., Gowan, M. A., & Lautenschlager, G. J. (1993). Corporate image, recruitment image, and initial job choice decisions. *Academy of Management Journal, 36,* 414-427.

Gecas, V. (1981). Contexts of socialization. In R. Rosenberg & R. H. Turner (Eds.), *Social psychology: Sociological perspectives* (pp. 165-199). New York: Basic Books.

Gersick, C. J. G. (1988). Time and transition in work teams: Toward a new model of group development. *Academy of Management Journal, 31,* 9-41.

Gersick, C. J. G. (1989). Marking time: Predictable transitions in task groups. *Academy of Management Journal, 32,* 274-309.

Gilsdorf, J. W. (1998). Organizational rules on communicating: How employees are and are not learning the ropes. *Journal of Business Communication, 35,* 173-201.

Gilmore, D. C., & Ferris, G. R. (1989). The effects of applicant impression management tactics on interviewer judgments. *Journal of Management, 15,* 557-564.

Gioia, D. A., & Sims, H. P., Jr. (1986). Cognition-behavior connections: Attribution and verbal behavior in leader-subordinate interactions. *Organizational Behavior and Human Decision Processes, 37,* 197-229.

Glaman, J. M., Jones, A. P., & Rozelle, R. M. (1996). The effects of co-worker similarity on the emergence of affect in work teams. *Group & Organization Management, 21,* 192-215.

Gleason, J. B. (1975). Fathers and other strangers: Men's speech to young children. In D. P. Dato (Ed.), *Devel-opmental psycholinguistics: Theory and application* (pp. 289-297). Washington, DC: Georgetown University Press.

Goffman, E. (1971). *Relations in public.* New York: Basic Books.

Golden, L., & Appelbaum, E. (1992). What was driving the 1982-88 boom in temporary employment? Preference of workers or decisions and power of employers. *American Journal of Economics and Sociology, 51,* 473-493.

Goldstein, B., & Oldham, J. (1979). *Children and work: A study of socialization.* New Brunswick, NJ: Transaction Books.

Goldstein, I. L., & Gilliam, P. (1990). Training systems in the year 2000. *American Psychologist, 45,* 134-143.

Golitz, S. M., & Giannantonio, C. M. (1995). Recruiter friendliness and attraction to the job: The mediating role of inferences about the organization. *Journal of Vocational Behavior, 46,* 109-118.

Gomersall, E. R., & Myers, M. S. (1966). Breakthrough in on-the-job training. *Harvard Business Review, 44*(4), 62-72.

Goodnow, J. J. (1988). Children's household work: Its nature and functions. *Psychological Bulletin, 103,* 5-26.

Goodnow, J. J., Bowes, J. M., Dawes, L. J., & Taylor, A. J. (1988, August). *The flow of work in families.* Paper presented at the fifth Australian Developmental Conference, Sydney.

Goodnow, J. J., Bowes, J. M., Warton, P. M., Dawes, L. J., & Taylor, A. J. (1991). Would you ask someone else to do this task? Parents' and children's ideas about household work requests. *Developmental Psychology, 27,* 817-828.

Goodnow, J. J., & Delaney, S. (1989). Children's household work: Task differences, styles of assignment, and links to family relationships. *Journal of Applied Developmental Psychology, 10,* 209-226.

Goodnow, J. J., & Warton, P. M. (1991). The social bases of social cognition: Interactions about work and their implications. *Merrill-Palmer Quarterly, 37,* 27-58.

Gorden, W. I., Infante, D. A., & Graham, E. E. (1988). Corporate conditions conducive to employee voice: A subordinate perspective. *Employee Responsibilities and Rights Journal, 1,* 101-111.

Graen, G. B. (1976). Role-making processes within complex organizations. In M. D. Dunnette (Ed.), *Handbook of industrial and organizational psychology* (pp. 1201-1245). Chicago: Rand McNally.

Graen, G. B., & Scandura, T. A. (1987). Toward a psychology of dyadic organizing. In L. L. Cummings & B. M. Staw (Eds.), *Research in organizational behavior* (Vol. 9, pp. 175-208). Greenwich, CT: JAI.

Graen, G. B., & Uhl-Bien, M. (1995). Development of leader-member exchange (LMX) theory of leadership over 25 years: Applying a multi-level multi-domain perspective. *Leadership Quarterly, 62,* 219-247.

Granovetter, M. (1973). The strength of weak ties. *American Journal of Sociology, 78,* 1360-1380.

Granovetter, M. (1995). *Getting a job: A study of contacts and careers* (2nd ed.). Chicago: University of Chicago Press.

Graves, L. M., & Karren, R. J. (1992). Interviewer decision processes and effectiveness: An experimental policy-capturing investigation. *Personnel Psychology, 45,* 313-340.

Green, S. G. (1991). Professional entry and the adviser relationship: Socialization, commitment, and productivity. *Group and Organization Studies, 16,* 387-407.

Green, S. G., & Bauer, T. N. (1995). Supervisory mentoring by advisers: Relationships with doctoral student potential, productivity, and commitment. *Personnel Psychology, 48,* 537-561.

Greenberg, B. S. (1982). Television and role socialization. In D. Pearl, L. Bouthilet, & J. Lazar (Eds.), *Television and behavior: Ten years of scientific progress and implications for the eighties* (Vol. 2, pp. 179-190). Rockville, MD: U.S. Department of Health and Human Services.

Greenberg, J. (1996). "Forgive me, I'm new": Three experimental demonstrations of the effects of attempts to excuse poor performance. *Organizational Behavior and Human Decision Processes, 66,* 165-178.

Greenberger, E., O'Neil, R., & Nagel, S. K. (1994). Linking workplace and homeplace: Relations between the nature of adults' work and their parenting behaviors. *Developmental Psychology, 30,* 990-1002.

Greenberger, E., & Steinberg, L. D. (1986). *When teenagers work: The psychological and social costs of adolescent employment.* New York: Basic Books.

Greenberger, E., Steinberg, L. D., & Ruggiero, M. (1982). A job is a job is a job . . . or is it? *Work and Occupations, 9,* 79-96.

Greenberger, E., Steinberg, L. D., Vaux, A., & McAuliffe, S. (1980). Adolescents who work: Effects of part-time employment on family and peer relations. *Journal of Youth and Adolescence, 9,* 189-202.

Griffeth, R. W., Hom, P. W., Fink, L. S., & Cohen, D. J. (1997). Comparative tests of multivariate models of recruiting source effects. *Journal of Management, 23,* 19-36.

Griffin, E., & Sparks, G. G. (1990). Friends forever: A longitudinal exploration of intimacy in same-sex pairs and platonic pairs. *Journal of Social and Personal Relationships, 7,* 29-46.

Gundry, L. K., & Rousseau, D. M. (1994). Critical incidents in communicating culture to newcomers: The meaning is the message. *Human Relations, 47,* 1063-1088.

Gunter, B., & McAleer, J. L. (1990). *Children and television: The one eyed monster?* London: Routledge.

Habermas, J. (1970). Towards a theory of communicative competence. In H. P. Dreitzel (Ed.), *Recent Sociology, 2,* 115-148.

Hafferty, F. W. (1988). Cadaver stories and the emotional socialization of medical students. *Journal of Health and Social Behavior, 29,* 344-356.

Hanisch, K. A. (1994). Reasons people retire and their relations to attitudinal and behavioral correlates in retirement. *Journal of Vocational Behavior, 45,* 1-16.

Hanson, D. A., & Johnson, V. A. (1989). Classroom lesson strategies and orientations toward work. In D. Stern & D. Eichorn (Eds.), *Adolescence and work: Influences of social structure, labor markets, and culture* (pp. 75-99). Hillsdale, NJ: Lawrence Erlbaum.

Harris, M. M. (1989). Reconsidering the employment interview: A review of recent literature and suggestions for future research. *Personnel Psychology, 42,* 691-726.

Harris, S. G. (1994). Organizational culture and individual sensemaking: A schema-based perspective. *Organization Science, 5,* 309-321.

Harrison, D., & Schaffer, M. (1994). Comparative examination of self-reports and perceived absenteeism norms: Wading through Lake Wobegon. *Journal of Applied Psychology, 79,* 240-251.

Harrison, J. R., & Carroll, G. R. (1991). Keeping the faith: A model of cultural transmission in formal organizations. *Administrative Science Quarterly, 36,* 552-582.

Hartup, W. W. (1996). The company they keep: Friendships and their developmental significance. *Child Development, 67,* 1-13.

Hartup, W. W., & Moore, S. G. (1990). Early peer relations: Developmental significance and prognostic implications. *Early Childhood Research Quarterly, 5,* 1-17.

Haunschild, P. R., Moreland, R. L., & Murrell, A. J. (1994). Sources of resistance to mergers between groups. *Journal of Applied Social Psychology, 24,* 1150-1178.

Hautaluoma, J. E., Enge, R. S., Mitchell, T. M., & Rittwager, F. J. (1991). Early socialization into a work group: Severity of initiations revisited. *Journal of Social Behavior and Personality, 6,* 725-748.

Heider, F. (1958). *The psychology of interpersonal relationships.* New York: John Wiley.

Heimann, B., & Pittenger, K. K. S. (1996). The impact of formal mentorship on socialization and commitment of newcomers. *Journal of Managerial Issues, 8,* 108-117.

Herriot, R., & Rothwell, C. (1981). Organizational choice and decision theory: Effects of employers' literature and selection interview. *Journal of Occupational Psychology, 54,* 17-31.

Herriot, R., & Rothwell, C. (1983). Expectations and impressions in the graduate selection interview. *Journal of Occupational Psychology, 56*, 303-314.

Hess, J. A. (1993). Assimilating newcomers into an organization: A cultural perspective. *Journal of Applied Communication Research, 12*, 189-210.

Hicks, W. D., & Klimoski, R. J. (1987). Entry into training programs and its effects on training outcomes: A field experiment. *Academy of Management Journal, 30*, 542-552.

Hickson, M., III, Stacks, D. W., & Padgett-Greely, M. (1998). *Organizational communication in the personal context: From interview to retirement.* Boston: Allyn & Bacon.

Hill, R. E. (1970). New look at employee referrals as a recruitment channel. *Personnel Journal, 49*, 144-148.

Hirschman, A. O. (1970). *Exit, voice, and loyalty: Responses to decline in firms, organizations, and the state.* Cambridge, MA: Harvard University Press.

Holder, T. (1996). Women in nontraditional organizations: Information-seeking during organizational entry. *Journal of Business Communication, 33*, 9-26.

Hollandsworth, J. G., Kazelskis, R., Stevens, J., & Dressel, M. E. (1979). Relative contributions of verbal, articulative and nonverbal communication to employment interview decisions in the job interview setting. *Personnel Psychology, 32*, 359-367.

Hollwitz, J. C., & Pawlowski, D. R. (1997). The development of a structured ethical integrity interview for pre-employment screening. *Journal of Business Communication, 34*, 203-219.

Holton, E. F., & Russell, C. J. (1997). The relationship of anticipation to newcomer socialization processes and outcomes: A pilot study. *Journal of Occupational and Organizational Psychology, 70*, 163-172.

Hom, P. W., Griffeth, R. W., Palich, L. E., & Bracker, J. S. (1998). An exploratory investigation into theoretical mechanisms underlying realistic job previews. *Personnel Psychology, 51*, 421-451.

Howard, L. A., & Geist, P. (1995). Ideological positioning in organizational change: The dialectic of control in a merging organization. *Communication Monographs, 62*, 110-131.

Hudson, D. C., & Jablin, F. M. (1992, May). *Newcomer information-giving during organizational entry: Conceptualization and the development of a message categorization scheme.* Paper presented at the annual meeting of the International Communication Association, Miami, FL.

Huffcutt, A. I., & Roth, P. L. (1998). Racial group differences in employment interview evaluations. *Journal of Applied Psychology, 83*, 179-189.

Huseman, R. C., & Hatfield, J. D. (1978). Communicating employee benefits: Directions for future research. *Journal of Business Communication, 15*, 3-17.

Huston, A. C., & Alvarez, M. M. (1990). The socialization context of gender role development in early adolescence. In R. Montemayor, G. Adams, & T. Gullotta (Eds.), *From childhood to adolescence: A transitional period?* Newbury Park, CA: Sage.

Huston, A. C., Wright, J. C., Rice, M. L. Kerkman, D., & St. Peters, M. (1990). Development of television viewing patterns in early childhood: A longitudinal investigation. *Developmental Psychology, 26*, 409-420.

Ibarra, H. (1993). Personal networks of women and minorities in management: A conceptual framework. *Academy of Management Review, 18*, 56-87.

Imada, A. S., & Hakel, M. D. (1977). Influence of nonverbal communication and rater proximity on impressions and decisions in simulated employment interviews. *Journal of Applied Psychology, 62*, 295-300.

Ingersoll, V. H., & Adams, G. B. (1992). The child is "father" to the manager: Images of organizations in U.S. children's literature. *Organization Studies, 13*, 497-519.

Irving, P. G., & Meyer, J. P. (1994). Reexamination of the met-expectations hypothesis: A longitudinal analysis. *Journal of Applied Psychology, 79*, 937-949.

Isabella, L. A. (1990). Evolving interpretations as a change unfolds: How managers construe key organizational events. *Academy of Management Journal, 33*, 7-41.

Jablin, F. M. (1975). The selection interview: Contingency theory and beyond. *Human Resource Management, 14*, 2-9.

Jablin, F. M. (1978). Message-response and "openness" in superior-subordinate communication. In B. D. Ruben (Ed.), *Communication yearbook 2* (pp. 293-309). New Brunswick, NJ: Transaction.

Jablin, F. M. (1979). Superior-subordinate communication: The state of the art. *Psychological Bulletin, 86*, 1201-1222.

Jablin, F. M. (1980). Superior's upward influence, satisfaction, and openness in superior-subordinate communication: A re-examination of the "Pelz effect." *Human Communication Research, 6*, 210-220.

Jablin, F. M. (1982). Organizational communication: An assimilation approach. In M. E. Roloff & C. R. Berger (Eds.), *Social cognition and communication* (pp. 255-286). Beverly Hills, CA: Sage.

Jablin, F. M. (1984). Assimilating new members into organizations. In R. N. Bostrom (Ed.), *Communication yearbook 8* (pp. 594-626). Beverly Hills, CA: Sage.

Jablin, F. M. (1985a). An exploratory study of vocational organizational communication socialization. *Southern Speech Communication Journal, 50*, 261-282.

Jablin, F. M. (1985b). Task/work relationships: A life-span perspective. In M. L. Knapp & G. R. Miller (Eds.), *Handbook of interpersonal communication* (pp. 615-654). Beverly Hills, CA: Sage.

Jablin, F. M. (1987). Organizational entry, assimilation, and exit. In F. M. Jablin, L. L. Putnam, K. H. Roberts, & L. W. Porter (Eds.), *Handbook of organizational communication: An interdisciplinary perspective* (pp. 679-740). Newbury Park, CA: Sage.

Jablin, F. M. (1993). *Dinner-time talk: Ambient messages from parents to children about work.* Unpublished manuscript, University of Texas at Austin.

Jablin, F. M., Grady, D. P., & Parker, P. S. (1984). *Organizational disengagement: A review and integration of the literature.* Paper presented at the annual meeting of the Speech Communication Association, New Orleans, LA.

Jablin, F. M., Hudson, D., & Sias, P. (1997). *Verbal and nonverbal correlates of communication satisfaction in employment screening interviews.* Unpublished manuscript, University of Richmond, Richmond, VA.

Jablin, F. M., & Kramer, M. W. (1998). Communication-related sense-making and adjustment during job transfers. *Management Communication Quarterly, 12,* 155-182.

Jablin, F. M., & Krone, K. J. (1987). Organizational assimilation. In C. R. Berger & S. H. Chaffee (Eds.), *Handbook of communication science* (pp. 711-746). Newbury Park, CA: Sage.

Jablin, F. M., & Krone, K. J. (1994). Task/work relationships: A life-span perspective. In M. L. Knapp & G. R. Miller (Eds.), *Handbook of interpersonal communication* (2nd ed., pp. 621-675). Thousand Oaks, CA: Sage.

Jablin, F. M., & McComb, K. B. (1984). The employment screening interview: An organizational assimilation and communication perspective. In R. N. Bostrom (Ed.), *Communication yearbook 8* (pp. 137-163). Beverly Hills, CA: Sage.

Jablin, F. M., & Miller, V. D. (1990). Interviewer and applicant questioning behavior in employment interviews. *Management Communication Quarterly, 4,* 51-86.

Jablin, F. M., & Miller, V. D. (1993). *Newcomer-supervisor role negotiation processes: A preliminary report of a longitudinal investigation.* Paper presented at the annul convention of the Speech Communication Association, Miami, FL.

Jablin, F. M., Miller, V. D., & Keller, T. (1999). *Newcomer-leader role negotiations: Negotiation topics/issues, tactics, and outcomes.* Paper presented at the annual conference the International Leadership Association, Atlanta, GA.

Jablin, F. M., Miller, V. D., & Sias, P. M. (1999). Communication and interaction processes. In R. W. Eder & M. H. Harris (Eds.), *The employment interview handbook* (pp. 297-320). Thousand Oaks, CA: Sage.

Jablin, F. M., Tengler, C. D., McClary, K. B., & Teigen, C. W. (1987, May). *Behavioral and perceptual correlates of applicants' communication satisfaction in employment screening interviews.* Paper presented at the annual convention of the International Communication Association, Montreal, Canada.

Jablin, F. M., Tengler, C. D., & Teigen, C. W. (1982, May). *Interviewee perceptions of employment screening interviews: Relationships among perceptions of communication satisfaction, interviewer credibility and trust, interviewing experience, and interview outcomes.* Paper presented at the annual meeting of the International Communication Association, Boston.

Jablin, F. M., Tengler, C. D., & Teigen, C. W. (1985, August). *Applicant perceptions of job incumbents and personnel representatives as communication sources in screening interviews.* Paper presented at the annual meeting of the Academy of Management, San Diego, CA.

Jackson, S. E., Stone, V. K., & Alvarez, E. B. (1993). Socialization amidst diversity: The impact of demographics on work team old-timers and newcomers. In L. L. Cummings & B. S. Staw (Eds.), *Research in organizational behavior* (Vol. 15, pp. 45-109). Greenwich, CT: JAI.

Janssen, O., de Vries, T., & Cozijnsen, A. J. (1998). Voicing by adapting and innovating employees: An empirical study on how personality and environment interact to affect voice behavior. *Human Relations, 51,* 945-967.

Janz, T. (1989). The patterned behavior description interview: The best prophet of the future is the past. In R. W. Eder & G. R. Ferris (Eds.), *The employment interview: Theory, research, and practice* (pp. 158-168). Newbury Park, CA: Sage.

Janz, T., Hellervik, L., & Gilmore, D. C. (1986). *Behavior description interviewing.* Boston: Allyn & Bacon.

Javidan, M., Bemmels, B., Devine, K. S., & Dastmalchian, A. (1995). Superior and subordinate gender and acceptance of superiors as role models. *Human Relations, 48,* 1271-1284.

Jerris, L. A. (1993). *Effective employee orientation.* New York: American Management Association.

Johnson, J. R., Bernhagen, M. J., Miller, V., & Allen, M. (1996). The role of communication in managing reductions in work force. *Journal of Applied Communication Research, 24,* 139-164.

Jones, G. R. (1986). Socialization tactics, self-efficacy, and newcomers' adjustments to organizations. *Academy of Management Journal, 29,* 262-279.

Judge, T. A., & Bretz, R. D. (1994). Political influence behavior and career success. *Journal of Management, 20,* 43-65.

Judge, T. A., & Ferris, G. R. (1992). The elusive criterion of fit in human resource staffing decisions. *Human Resource Planning, 15*(4), 47-67.

Judge, T. A., & Martocchio, J. J. (1996). Dispositional influences on attributions concerning absenteeism. *Journal of Management, 22,* 837-861.

Kacmar, K. M., Delery, J. E., & Ferris, G. R. (1992). Differential effectiveness of applicant impression management tactics on employment interview decisions. *Journal of Applied Social Psychology, 22,* 1250-1272.

Kacmar, K. M., & Hochwarter, W. A. (1995). The interview as a communication event: A field examination of demographic effects on interview outcomes. *Journal of Business Communication, 32,* 207-232.

Kahn, W. A. (1990). Psychological conditions of personal engagement and disengagement at work. *Academy of Management Journal, 33,* 692-724.

Kalbfleisch, P. J., & Davies, A. B. (1991). Minorities and mentoring: Managing the multicultural institution. *Communication Education, 40,* 266-271.

Kalbfleisch, P. J., & Davies, A. B. (1993). An interpersonal model for participation in mentoring relationships. *Western Journal of Communication, 57,* 399-415.

Kaplan, A. B., Aamodt, M. G., & Wilk, D. (1991). The relationship between advertisement variables and applicant responses to newspaper recruitment advertisements. *Journal of Business and Psychology, 5,* 383-395.

Karol, B. L. (1977). *Relationship of recruiter behavior, perceived similarity, and prior information to applicants' assessments of the campus recruitment interview.* Unpublished doctoral dissertation, Ohio State University.

Katz, D., & Kahn, R. L. (1966). *The social psychology of organizations.* New York: John Wiley.

Katz, R. (1980). Time and work: Toward an integrative perspective. In B. M. Staw & L. L. Cummings (Eds.), *Research in organizational behavior* (Vol. 2, pp. 81-128). Greenwich, CT: JAI.

Katz, R. (1985). Organizational stress and early socialization experiences. In T. Beehr & R. Bhagat (Eds.), *Human stress and cognition in organization: An integrative perspective* (pp. 117-139). New York: John Wiley.

Katz, S. M. (1998). A newcomer gains power: An analysis of the role of rhetorical expertise. *Journal of Business Communication, 35,* 419-441.

Katzman, N. (1972). Television soap operas: What's been going on anyway? *Public Opinion Quarterly, 36,* 200-212.

Keenan, A. (1976). Effects of non-verbal behaviour on candidates' performance. *Journal of Occupational Psychology, 49,* 171-176.

Keenan, A., & Wedderburn, A. A. I. (1975). Effects of non-verbal behaviour on candidates' impressions. *Journal of Occupational Psychology, 48,* 129-132.

Kelley, H. (1971). *Attribution in social interaction.* Morristown, NJ: General Learning Press.

Keltner, D., & Buswell, B. N. (1997). Embarrassment: Its distinct form and appeasement functions. *Psychological Bulletin, 122,* 250-270.

Kennedy, D. J., & Berger, F. (1994). Newcomer socialization: Oriented to facts or feelings. *Cornell Hotel and Restaurant Administration Quarterly, 35*(6), 58-71.

Kilduff, M. (1990). The interpersonal structure of decision making: A social comparison approach to organizational choice. *Organizational Behavior and Human Decision Processes, 47,* 270-288.

Kilduff, M., & Day, D. V. (1994). Do chameleons get ahead? The effects of self-monitoring on managerial careers. *Academy of Management Journal, 37,* 1047-1060.

Kinicki, A. J., & Lockwood, C. A. (1985). The interview process: An examination of factors recruiters use in evaluating job applicants. *Journal of Vocational Behavior, 26,* 117-125.

Kinicki, A. J., Lockwood, C. A., Hom, P. W., & Griffeth, R. W. (1990). Interviewer predictions of applicant qualifications and interviewer validity: Aggregate and individual analyses. *Journal of Applied Psychology, 75,* 477-486.

Kirchmeyer, C. (1995). Demographic similarity to the work group: A longitudinal study of managers at the early career stage. *Journal of Organizational Behavior, 16,* 67-83.

Kirkwood, W. G., & Ralston, S. M. (1999). Inviting meaningful applicant performances in employment interviews. *Journal of Business Communication, 36,* 55-76.

Kirnan, J. P., Farley, J. A., & Geisinger, K. F. (1989). The relationship between recruiting source, applicants' quality, and hire performance: An analysis by sex, ethnicity, and age. *Personnel Psychology, 42,* 293-308.

Klaas, B. S., & Dell'Omo, G. G. (1997). Managerial use of dismissal: Organizational-level determinants. *Personnel Psychology, 50,* 927-953.

Klauss, R. (1981). Formalized mentor relationships for management and executive development programs in the federal government. *Public Administration Review, 41,* 489-496.

Kleiman, D. (1990, December 6). Dinner still family time. *Austin-American Statesman,* Sec. A, p. 6.

Koberg, C. S., Boss, R. W., Chappel, D., & Ringer, R. C. (1994). Correlates and consequences of protégé mentoring in a large hospital. *Group & Organization Management, 19,* 219-239.

Koberg, C. S., Boss, R. W., & Goodman, E. (1998). Factors and outcomes associated with mentoring among health-care professionals. *Journal of Vocational Behavior, 53,* 58-72.

Komaki, J. L., Zlotnick, S., & Jensen, M. (1986). Development of an operant-based taxonomy and observational index of supervisory behavior. *Journal of Applied Psychology, 71,* 260-269.

Kossek, E. E., Roberts, K., Fisher, S., & DeMarr, B. (1998). Career self-management: A quasi-experimental assessment of the effects of a training intervention. *Personnel Psychology, 51,* 935-962.

Kram, K. E. (1983). Phases of the mentor relationship. *Academy of Management Journal, 26,* 608-625.

Kram, K. E. (1988). *Mentoring at work: Developmental relationships in organizational life.* New York: University Press of America.

Kram, K. E., & Isabella, L. A. (1985). Mentoring alternatives: The role of peer relationships in career development. *Academy of Management Journal, 28,* 110-132.

Kramer, M. W. (1989). Communication during intraorganizational transfers. *Management Communication Quarterly, 3,* 213-248.

Kramer, M. W. (1993a). Communication after job transfers: Social exchange processes in learning new roles. *Human Communication Research, 20,* 147-174.

Kramer, M. W. (1993b). Communication and uncertainty reduction during job transfers: Leaving and joining processes. *Communication Monographs, 60,* 178-198.

Kramer, M. W. (1994). Uncertainty reduction during job transitions: An exploratory study of the communication experiences of newcomers and transferees. *Management Communication Quarterly, 7,* 384-412.

Kramer, M. W. (1995). A longitudinal study of superior-subordinate communication during job transfers. *Human Communication Research, 22,* 39-46.

Kramer, M. W., Callister, R. R., & Turban, D. B. (1995). Information-receiving and information-giving during job transitions. *Western Journal of Communication, 59,* 151-170.

Kramer, M. W., & Miller, V. D. (1999). A response to criticisms of organizational socialization research: In support of contemporary conceptualizations of organizational assimilation. *Communication Monographs, 66,* 358-367.

Kramer, M. W., & Noland, T. L. (1999). Communication during job promotions: A case of ongoing assimilation. *Journal of Applied Communication Research, 27,* 335-355.

Kressin, N. R. (1996). The effect of medical socialization on medical students' need for power. *Personality and Social Psychology Bulletin, 22,* 91-98.

Kristof, A. L. (1996). Person-organization fit: An integrative review of its conceptualizations, measurement, and implications. *Personnel Psychology, 49,* 1-49.

Krone, K. J. (1992). A comparison of organizational, structural, and relationship effects on subordinates' upward influence choices. *Communication Quarterly, 40,* 1-15.

Kubey, R., & Csikszentmihalyi, M. (1990). *Television and the quality of life: How viewing shapes everyday experiences.* Hillsdale, NJ: Lawrence Erlbaum.

Kuhn, T. (1970). *The structure of scientific revolutions* (2nd ed.). Chicago: University of Chicago Press.

Kydd, C. T., Ogilvie, J. R., & Slade, L. A. (1990). "I don't care what they say, as long as they spell my name right": Publicity, reputation and turnover. *Group and Organization Studies, 15,* 53-43.

Larkey, L. K. (1996). Toward a theory of communicative interactions in culturally diverse workgroups. *Academy of Management Review, 21,* 463-491.

Larson, M. H. (1996). Patterns in transition: A writing teacher's survey of organizational socialization. *Journal of Business and Technical Communication, 10,* 352-368.

Larson, R. W. (1983). Adolescents' daily experience with family and friends: Contrasting opportunity systems. *Journal of Marriage and the Family, 45,* 739-750.

Larson, R. W., & Kleiber, D. (1993). Daily experience of adolescents. In P. Tolan & B. Cohler (Eds.), *Handbook of clinical research and practice with adolescents* (pp. 125-145). New York: John Wiley.

Larson, R. W., & Verma, S. (1999). How children and adolescents spend time across the world: Work, play and developmental opportunities. *Psychological Bulletin, 125,* 701-736.

Laska, S. B., & Micklin, M. (1981). Modernization, the family and work socialization: A comparative study of U.S. and Columbian youth. *Journal of Comparative Family Studies, 12,* 187-203.

Latack, J. C., Kinicki, A. J., & Prussia, G. E. (1995). An integrative process model of coping with job loss. *Academy of Management Review, 20,* 311-342.

Latham, G. P. (1989). The reliability, validity and practicality of the situational interview. In R. W. Eder & G. R. Ferris (Eds.), *The employment interview: Theory, research and practice* (pp. 169-182). Newbury Park, CA: Sage.

Latham, G. P., Saari, L. M., Pursell, E. D., & Campion, M. A. (1980). The situational interview. *Journal of Applied Psychology, 65,* 422-427.

Latham, V. M., & Leddy, P. M. (1987). Source of recruitment and employee attitudes: An analysis of job involvement, organizational commitment, and job satisfaction. *Journal of Business and Psychology, 1,* 230-235.

Lawson, M. B., & Angle, H. L. (1998). Upon reflection: Commitment, satisfaction, and regret after a corporate relocation. *Group & Organization Management, 23,* 289-317.

Lee, F. (1993). Being polite and keeping mum: How bad news is communicated in organizational hierarchies. *Journal of Applied Social Psychology, 23,* 1124-1149.

Lee, J. (1997). Leader-member exchange, the "Pelz effect," and cooperative communication between group members. *Management Communication Quarterly, 11,* 266-287.

Lee, J. (1998a). Effective maintenance communication in superior-subordinate relationships. *Western Journal of Communication, 62,* 181-208.

Lee, J. (1998b). Maintenance communication in superior-subordinate relationships: An exploratory investigation of group social context and the "Pelz effect." *Southern Communication Journal, 63,* 144-157.

Lee, J., & Jablin, F. M. (1995). Maintenance communication in superior-subordinate work relationships. *Human Communication Research, 22,* 220-257.

Lee, T. S., Mitchell, T. R., Wise, L., & Fireman, S. (1996). An unfolding model of voluntary employee turnover. *Academy of Management Journal, 39,* 5-36.

Leifer, A. D., & Lesser, G. S. (1976). *The development of career awareness in young children.* Washington, DC: National Institute of Education.

Leonard, R. (1988, August). *Ways of studying early negotiations between children and parents.* Paper presented at the fifth Australian Developmental Conference, Sydney.

Levine, J. M., & Moreland, R. L. (1991). Culture and socialization in work groups. In L. B. Resnick, J. M. Levine, & S. D. Teasley (Eds.), *Perspectives on socially shared cognition* (pp. 257-279). Washington, DC: American Psychological Association.

Levine, J. M., Resnick, L. B., & Higgins, E. T. (1993). Social foundations of cognition. *Annual Review of Psychology, 44,* 585-612.

Liang, D. W., Moreland, R., & Argote, L. (1995). Group versus individual training and group performance: The mediating role of transactive memory. *Personality and Social Psychology Bulletin, 21,* 384-393.

Lichter, S. R., Lichter, L. S., & Amundson, D. (1997). Does Hollywood hate business or money? *Journal of Communication, 47,* 68-84.

Lichter, S. R., Lichter, L. S., & Rothman, S. (1994). *Prime time: How TV portrays American culture.* Washington, DC: Regnery.

Liden, R. C., Martin, C. L., & Parsons, C. K. (1993). Interviewer and applicant behaviors in employment interviews. *Academy of Management Journal, 36,* 372-386.

Liden, R. C., & Parsons, C. K. (1986). A field study of job applicant interview perceptions, alternative opportunities, and demographic characteristics. *Personnel Psychology, 39,* 109-122.

Liden, R. C., Wayne, S. J., & Stilwell, D. (1993). A longitudinal study on the early development of leader-member exchanges. *Journal of Applied Psychology, 78,* 662-674.

Lim, V. K. G. (1996). Job insecurity and its outcomes: Moderating effects of work-based and nonwork-based social support. *Human Relations, 49,* 171-194.

Lindvall, D. C., Culberson, D. K., Binning, J. F., & Goldstein, M. A. (1986, April). *The effects of perceived labor market condition and interviewer sex on hypothesis testing in the employment interview.* Paper presented at the annual meeting of the Midwest Academy of Management.

Lois, J. (1999). Socialization to heroism: Individualism and collectivism in a voluntary search and rescue group. *Social Psychology Quarterly, 62,* 117-135.

Loraine, K. (1995). Leadership—Where does it come from? *Supervision, 56,* 14-16.

Louis, M. R. (1980). Surprise and sense making: What newcomers experience in entering unfamiliar organizational settings. *Administrative Science Quarterly, 25,* 226-251.

Louis, M. R. (1990). Acculturation in the workplace: Newcomers as lay ethnographers. In B. Schneider (Ed.), *Organizational culture and climate* (pp. 85-129). San Francisco: Jossey-Bass.

Louis, M. R., Posner, B. Z., & Powell, G. N. (1983). The availability and helpfulness of socialization practices. *Personnel Psychology, 36,* 857-866.

Lovelace, K., & Rosen, B. (1996). Differences in achieving person-organization fit among diverse groups of managers. *Journal of Management, 22,* 703-722.

Macon, T. H., & Dipboye, R. L. (1990). The relationship of interviewers' preinterview impressions to selection and recruitment outcomes. *Personnel Psychology, 43,* 745-768.

Major, D. A., Kozlowski, S. W. J., Chao, G. T., & Gardner, P. D. (1995). A longitudinal investigation of newcomers' expectations, early socialization outcomes, and the moderating effects of role development factors. *Journal of Applied Psychology, 80,* 418-431.

Malone, M. J., & Guy, R. (1982). A comparison of mothers' and fathers' speech to their 3-year-old sons. *Journal of Psycholinguistic Research, 11,* 599-608.

Mannle, S., & Tomasello, M. (1987). Fathers, siblings, and the bridge hypothesis. In K. E. Nelson & A. Van Kleek (Eds.), *Children's language* (Vol. 6, pp. 23-42). Hillsdale, NJ: Lawrence Erlbaum.

Markham, S. E., & McKee, G. H. (1995). Group absence behavior and standards: A multilevel analysis. *Academy of Management Journal, 38,* 1174-1190.

Martin, J. H., & Franz, E. B. (1994). Attracting applicants from a changing labor market: A strategic marketing framework. *Journal of Managerial Issues, 6,* 33-53.

Martin, P., Hagestad, G. O., & Diedrick, P. (1988). Family stories: Events (temporarily) remembered. *Journal of Marriage and the Family, 50,* 533-541.

Martin, S. C., Arnold, R. M., & Parker, R. M. (1988). Gender and medical socialization. *Journal of Health and Social Behavior, 29,* 333-343.

Martocchio, J. J., & Baldwin, T. B. (1997). The evolution of strategic organizational training: New objectives and research agenda. In G. R. Ferris (Ed.), *Research in personnel and human resources management* (Vol. 15, pp. 1-46). Greenwich, CT: JAI.

Maslyn, J. M., Farmer, S. M., & Fedor, D. B. (1996). Failed upward influence attempts: Predicting the nature of subordinate persistence in pursuit of organizational goals. *Group & Organization Management, 21,* 461-480.

Mason, N. A., & Belt, J. A. (1986). Effectiveness of specificity in recruitment advertising. *Journal of Management, 12,* 425-432.

Maurer, S. D., Howe, V., & Lee, T. W. (1992). Organizational recruiting as marketing management: An interdisciplinary study of engineering graduates. *Personnel Psychology, 45,* 807-833.

McCauley, C. D. Ruderman, M. N., Ohlott, P. J., & Morrow, J. E. (1994). Assessing the developmental components of managerial jobs. *Journal of Applied Psychology, 79,* 544-560.

McComb, K. B., & Jablin, F. M. (1984). Verbal correlates of interviewer empathic listening and employment interview outcomes. *Communication Monographs, 51,* 353-371.

McComb, M. (1995). Becoming a Travelers Aid volunteer: Communication in socialization and training. *Communication Studies, 46,* 297-316.

McDonald, T., & Hakel, M. D. (1985). Effects of applicant race, sex, suitability, and answers on interviewer's questioning strategy and rating. *Personnel Psychology, 38,* 321-334.

McEvoy, G. M., & Cascio, W. F. (1985). Strategies for reducing turnover: A meta-analysis. *Journal of Applied Psychology, 70,* 342-353.

McGovern, T. V., & Tinsley, H. E. A. (1978). Interviewers' evaluations of interviewee nonverbal behavior. *Journal of Vocational Behavior, 13,* 163-171.

McLaughlin, B., White, D., McDevitt, T., & Raskin, R. (1983). Mothers' and fathers' speech to their young children: Similar or different. *Journal of Child Language, 10,* 245-252.

McPhee, R. D. (1988). Vertical communication chains: Toward an integrated approach. *Management Communication Quarterly, 1,* 455-493.

Meglino, B. M., Ravlin, E. C., & Adkins, C. L. (1989). A work values approach to corporate culture: A field test of the value congruence process and its relationship to individual outcomes. *Journal of Applied Psychology, 74,* 424-432.

Meglino, B. M., Ravlin, E. C., & Adkins, C. L. (1991). Value congruence and satisfaction with a leader: An examination of the role of interaction. *Human Relations, 22,* 481-495.

Merriam, S. (1983). Mentors and protégés: A critical review of the literature. *Adult Education Quarterly, 33*(3), 161-173.

Meyer, D. C. (1997). Humor in member narratives: Uniting and dividing at work. *Western Journal of Communication, 61,* 188-208.

Meyer, J., & Driskill, G. (1997). Children and relationship development: Communication strategies in a day care center. *Communication Reports, 10,* 75-85.

Mignerey, J. T., Rubin, R. R., & Gordon, W. I. (1995). Organizational entry: An investigation of newcomer communication behavior and uncertainty. *Communication Research, 22,* 54-85.

Mihalka, J. A. (1974). *Youth and work.* Columbus, OH: Charles E. Merrill.

Miller, K. (1995). *Organizational communication: Approaches and processes.* Belmont, CA: Wadsworth.

Miller, R. S. (1992). The nature and severity of self-reported embarrassing circumstances. *Personality and Social Psychology Bulletin, 18,* 190-198.

Miller, V. D. (1989, May). *A quasi-experimental study of newcomers' information seeking behaviors during organizational entry.* Paper presented at the annual convention of the International Communication Association, San Francisco.

Miller, V. D. (1996). An experimental study of newcomers' information seeking behaviors during organizational entry. *Communication Studies, 47,* 1-24.

Miller, V. D., & Buzzanell, O. M. (1996). Toward a research agenda for the second employment interview. *Journal of Applied Communication Research, 24,* 165-180.

Miller, V. D., & Jablin, F. M. (1991). Information seeking during organizational entry: Influences, tactics, and a model of the process. *Academy of Management Review, 16,* 92-120.

Miller, V. D., Jablin, F. M., Casey, M. K., Lamphear-Van Horn, M., & Ethington, C. (1996). The maternity leave as a role negotiation process. *Journal of Managerial Issues, 8,* 286-309.

Miller, V. D., Johnson, J. R., Hart, Z., & Peterson, D. L. (1999). A test of antecedents and outcomes of employee role negotiation ability. *Journal of Applied Communication Research, 27,* 24-48.

Miller, V. D., & Kramer, M. K. (1999). A reply to Bullis, Turner, and Clair. *Communication Monographs, 66,* 390-392.

Miller, V. D., Susskind, A., & Levine, K. (1995). *The impact of interviewer behavior and reputation on job candidates.* Unpublished manuscript, Michigan State University.

Mino, M. (1996). The relative effects of content and vocal delivery during a simulated employment interview. *Communication Research Reports, 13,* 225-238.

Mishra, A. K., & Spreitzer, G. M. (1998). Explaining how survivors respond to downsizing: The roles of trust, empowerment, justice and work redesign. *Academy of Management Review, 23,* 567-588.

Missirian, A. K. (1982). *The corporate connection: Why executive women need mentors to reach the top.* Englewood Cliffs, NJ: Prentice Hall.

Moen, P., Edler, G. H., & Luscher, K. (Eds.). (1995). *Examining lives in context: Perspectives on the ecology of human development.* Washington, DC: American Psychological Association.

Montemayer, R., & Van Komen, R. (1980). Age segregation of adolescents in and out of school. *Journal of Youth and Adolescence, 9,* 371-381.

Moore, D. T. (1986). Knowledge at work: An approach to learning by interns. In K. M. Borman & J. Reisman (Eds.), *Becoming a worker* (pp. 116-139). Norwood, NJ: Ablex.

Moore, M. L. (1992). The family as portrayed on prime-time television, 1947-1990: Structure and characteristics. *Sex Roles, 26,* 41-61.

Morand, D. A. (1996). What's in a name? An exploration of the social dynamics of forms of address in organizations. *Management Communication Quarterly, 9,* 422-451.

Moreland, R. L., & Levine, J. M. (1982). Socialization in small groups: Temporal changes in individual-group relations. In L. Berkowitz (Ed.), *Advances in experimental social psychology* (Vol. 15, pp. 137-191). New York: Academic Press.

Moreland, R. L., & Levine, J. M. (in press). Socialization in organizations and work groups. In M. Turner (Ed.), *Groups at work: Advances in theory and research.* Hillsdale, NJ: Lawrence Erlbaum.

Moreland, R. L., & McMinn, J. G. (1999). Gone but not forgotten: Loyalty and betrayal among ex-members of small groups. *Personality and Social Psychology Bulletin, 25,* 1476-1486.

Morris, G. H. (1988). Accounts in selection interviews. *Journal of Applied Communication Research, 16,* 82-98.

Morris, J. A., & Feldman, D. C. (1996). The dimensions, antecedents, and consequences of emotional labor. *Academy of Management Review, 21,* 986-1010.

Morrison, E. W. (1993a). Longitudinal study of the effects of information seeking on newcomer socialization. *Journal of Applied Psychology, 78,* 173-183.

Morrison, E. W. (1993b). Newcomer information seeking: Exploring types, modes, sources, and outcomes. *Academy of Management Journal, 36,* 557-589.

Morrison, E. W. (1994). Role definitions and organizational citizenship behavior: The importance of the employee's perspective. *Academy of Management Journal, 37,* 1543-1567.

Morrison, E. W. (1995). Information usefulness and acquisition during organizational encounter. *Management Communication Quarterly, 9,* 131-155.

Morrison, E. W., & Robinson, S. L. (1997). When employees feel betrayed: A model of how psychological contract violations develop. *Academy of Management Review, 22,* 226-256.

Mortimer, J. T., Finch, M. D., Owens, T. J., & Shanahan, M. (1990). Gender and work in adolescence. *Youth & Society, 22,* 201-224.

Moss, M. K., & Frieze, I. H. (1993). Job preferences in the anticipatory socialization phase: A comparison of two matching models. *Journal of Vocational Behavior, 42,* 282-297.

Motowidlo, S. J., Carter, G. W., Dunnette, M. D., Tippins, N., Werner, S., Burnett, J. R., & Vaugh, M. (1992). Studies of the structured behavioral interview. *Journal of Applied Psychology, 77,* 571-587.

Murray, M., & Owen, M. (1991). *Beyond the myths and magic of mentoring: How to facilitate an effective mentoring program.* San Francisco: Jossey-Bass.

Myers, S. A. (1998). GTAs as organizational newcomers: The association between supportive communication relationships and information seeking. *Western Journal of Communication, 60,* 54-73.

Myers, S. A., & Kassing, J. W. (1998). The relationship between perceived supervisory communication behaviors and subordinate organizational identification. *Communication Research Reports, 15,* 81-82.

Myers, S. A., Knox, R. L., Pawlowski, D. R., & Ropog, B. L. (1999). Perceived communication openness and functional communication skills among organizational peers. *Communication Reports, 12,* 71-83.

Nelson, B. J., & Barley, S. R. (1997). For love or money? Commodification and the construction of an occupational mandate. *Administrative Science Quarterly, 42,* 619-653.

Nelson, D. L., & Quick, J. C. (1991). Social support and newcomer adjustment in organizations: Attachment theory at work? *Journal of Organizational Behavior, 12,* 543-554.

Nelson, D. L., Quick, J. C., & Eakin, M. E. (1988). A longitudinal study of newcomer role adjustment in US organizations. *Work and Stress, 2,* 239-253.

Nelson, D. L., Quick, J. C., & Joplin, J. R. (1991). Psychological contracting and newcomer socialization: An attachment theory foundation. *Journal of Social Behavior and Personality, 6*(7), 55-72.

Nelson, D. L., & Sutton, C. D. (1991). The relationship between newcomer expectations of job stressors and adjustment to the new job. *Work and Stress, 5,* 241-251.

Newcomb, A. F., & Bagwell, C. L. (1995). Children's friendship relations: A meta-analytic review. *Psychological Bulletin, 117,* 306-347.

Nicholson, N. (1984). A theory of work role transitions. *Administrative Science Quarterly, 29,* 172-191.

Nicholson, N., & Arnold, J. (1989). Graduate entry and adjustment to corporate life. *Personnel Review, 18*(3), 23-35.

Nicholson, N., & Arnold, J. (1991). From expectation to experience: Graduates entering a large corporation. *Journal of Organizational Behavior, 12,* 413-429.

Nicholson, N., & West, M. A. (1988). *Managerial job change: Men and women in transition.* Cambridge, UK: Cambridge University Press.

Niedenthal, P. M., Cantor, N., & Kihlstrom, J. F. (1985). Prototype-matching: A strategy for social decision-making. *Journal of Personality and Social Psychology, 48,* 575-584.

1995 industry reports: Training budgets. (1995, October). *Training, 21*(10), 42.

Noble, G. (1983). Social learning from everyday television. In M. J. A. Howe (Ed.), *Learning from television: Psychological and education research* (pp. 101-124). New York: Academic Press.

Noe, R. A. (1988). An investigation of the determinants of successful assigned mentoring relationships. *Personnel Psychology, 41,* 457-479.

Noe, R. A. (1999). *Employee training and development.* New York: Irwin McGraw-Hill.

Odden, C. M., & Sias, P. M. (1997). Peer communication relationships and psychological climate. *Communication Quarterly, 45,* 153-166.

Oglensky, B. D. (1995). Socio-psychoanalytic perspectives on the subordinate. *Human Relations, 48,* 1029-1054.

O'Keefe, B. J. (1988). The logic of message design: Individual differences in reasoning about communication. *Communication Monographs, 55,* 80-103.

O'Keefe, B. J. (1990). The logic of regulative communication: Understanding the rationality of message designs. In J. P. Dillard (Ed.), *Seeking compliance: The production of interpersonal influence messages* (pp. 87-105). Scottsdale, AZ: Gorsuch Scarisbrick.

Olian, J. D., Carroll, S. J., & Giannantonio, C. M. (1993). Mentor reactions to proteges: An experiment with managers. *Journal of Vocational Behavior, 43,* 266-278.

Olian, J. D., Carroll, S. J., Giannantonio, C. M., & Feren, D. B. (1988). What do proteges look for in a mentor? Results of three experimental studies. *Journal of Vocational Behavior, 33,* 15-37.

O'Neill, H. M., & Lenn, D. J. (1995). Voices of survivors: Words that downsizing CEOs should hear. *Academy of Management Executive, 9,* 23-33.

O'Reilly, C., Chatman, J., & Caldwell, D. F. (1991). People and organizational culture: A profile comparison approach to assessing person-organization fit. *Academy of Management Journal, 34,* 487-516.

Organ, D. W. (1990). The motivational basis of organizational citizenship behavior. In B. M. Staw & L. L. Cummings (Eds.), *Research in organizational behavior* (Vol. 12, pp. 43-72). Greenwich, CT: JAI.

Oseroff-Varnell, D. (1998). Communication and the socialization of dance students: An analysis of the hidden curriculum in a residential arts school. *Communication Education, 47,* 101-119.

Osipow, S. H. (1983). *Theories of career development* (3rd ed.). Englewood Cliffs, NJ: Prentice Hall.

Ostroff, C., & Kozlowski, S. W. J. (1992). Organizational socialization as a learning process: The role of information acquisition. *Personnel Psychology, 45,* 849-874.

Ostroff, C., & Kozlowski, S. W. J. (1993). The role of mentoring in the information gathering processes of newcomers during early organizational socialization. *Journal of Vocational Behavior, 42,* 170-183.

Palkowitz, E., & Mueller, M. (1987). Agencies foresee change in advertising's future. *Personnel Journal, 66,* 124-128.

Parks, J. M., & Schmedemann, D. (1992). *Pine River promises: A policy-capturing analysis of the legal and organizational properties of employee handbook provisions on job security.* Paper presented at the annual meeting of the Academy of Management, Las Vegas, NV.

Pearson, C. A. L. (1995). The turnover process in organizations: An exploration of the role of met-unmet expectations. *Human Relations, 48,* 405-420.

Peters, J. F. (1994). Gender socialization of adolescents in the home: Research and discussion. *Adolescence, 29,* 914-934.

Peterson, G. W., & Peters, D. F. (1983). Adolescents' construction of social reality: The impact of television and peers. *Youth & Society, 15,* 67-85.

Peterson, M. S. (1997). Personnel interviewers' perceptions of the importance and adequacy of applicants' communication skills. *Communication Education, 46,* 287-291.

Pfau, M., Mullen, L. J., Deidrich, T., & Garrow, K. (1995). Television viewing and public perceptions of attorneys. *Human Communication Research, 21,* 307-330.

Phillips, A. P., & Dipboye, R. L. (1989). Correlational tests of predictions from a process model of the interview. *Journal of Applied Psychology, 74,* 41-52.

Phillips, J. M. (1998). Effects of realistic job previews on multiple organizational outcomes: A meta-analysis. *Academy of Management Journal, 41,* 673-690.

Phillips, S., & Sandstrom, K. L. (1990). Parental attitudes toward youth work. *Youth & Society, 22,* 160-183.

Pierce, K. (1993). Socialization of teenage girls through teen-magazine fiction: The making of a new woman or an old lady? *Sex Roles, 29,* 59-68.

Piotrkowski, C. S., & Stark, E. (1987). Children and adolescents look at their parents' jobs. In J. H. Lewko (Ed.), *How children and adolescents view the world of work* (pp. 3-20). San Francisco: Jossey-Bass.

Podolny, J. M., & Baron, J. S. (1997). Resources and relationships: Social networks and mobility in the workplace. *American Sociological Review, 62,* 673-693.

Pollock, R. (1995). A test of conceptual models depicting the developmental course of informal mentor-protégé relationships in the work place. *Journal of Vocational Behavior, 46,* 144-162.

Pond, S. B., & Hay, M. S. (1989). The impact of task preview information as a function of recipient self-efficacy. *Journal of Vocational Behavior, 35,* 17-29.

Popovich, P., & Wanous, J. P. (1982). The realistic job preview as a persuasive communication. *Academy of Management Review, 7,* 570-578.

Posner, B. Z. (1981). Comparing recruiter, student and faculty perceptions of important applicant job characteristics. *Personnel Psychology, 34,* 329-339.

Potts, R., & Martinez, I. (1994). Television viewing and children's beliefs about scientists. *Journal of Applied Developmental Psychology, 15,* 287-300.

Powell, G. N. (1991). Applicant reactions to the initial employment interview: Exploring theoretical and methodological issues. *Personnel Psychology, 44*, 67-83.

Powell, G. N., & Goulet, L. R. (1996). Recruiters' and applicants' reactions to campus interviews and employment decisions. *Academy of Management Journal, 39*, 1619-1640.

Pratt, M. G., & Rafaeli, A. (1997). Organizational dress as a symbol of multilayered social identities. *Academy of Management Journal, 40*, 862-898.

Premack, S. L., & Wanous, J. P. (1985). A meta-analysis of realistic job preview experiments. *Journal of Applied Psychology, 70*, 706-719.

Pribble, P. T. (1990). Making an ethical commitment: A rhetorical case study of organizational socialization. *Communication Quarterly, 38*, 255-267.

Purcell, P., & Stewart, L. (1990). Dick and Jane in 1989. *Sex Roles, 22*, 177-185.

Pursell, E. D., Campion, M. A., & Gaylord, S. R. (1980). Structured interviewing: Avoiding selection problems. *Personnel Journal, 59*, 907-912.

Putnam, L. L., & Roloff, M. E. (Eds.). (1992). *Communication and negotiation*. Newbury Park, CA: Sage.

Rafaeli, A., Dutton, J., Harquail, C. V., & Mackie-Lewis, S. (1997). Navigating by attire: The use of dress by female administrative employees. *Academy of Management Journal, 40*, 9-45.

Rafaeli, A., & Pratt, M. G. (1993). Tailored meanings: On the meaning and impact of organizational dress. *Academy of Management Review, 18*, 32-55.

Raffaelli, M., & Duckett, E. (1989). "We were just talking . . . ": Conversations in early adolescence. *Journal of Youth and Adolescence, 18*, 567-582.

Ragins, B. R. (1997). Diversified mentoring relationships in organizations: A power perspective. *Academy of Management Review, 22*, 482-521.

Ragins, B. R., & Cotton, J. L. (1999). Mentor functions and outcomes: A comparison of men and women in formal and informal mentoring relationships. *Journal of Applied Psychology, 84*, 529-550.

Ragins, B. R., & Scandura, T. A. (1997). The way we were: Gender and the termination of mentoring relationships. *Journal of Applied Psychology, 82*, 945-953.

Ralston, S. M. (1993). Applicant communication satisfaction, intent to accept second interview offers, and recruiter communication style. *Journal of Applied Communication Research, 21*, 53-65.

Ralston, S. M., & Brady, R. (1994). The relative influence of interview communication satisfaction on applicants' recruitment interview decisions. *Journal of Business Communication, 31*, 61-77.

Ralston, S. M., & Kirkwood, W. G. (1995). Overcoming managerial bias in employment interviewing. *Journal of Applied Communication Research, 23*, 75-92.

Ralston, S. M., & Thomason, W. R. (1997). Employment interviewing and postbureaucracy. *Journal of Business and Technical Communication, 11*, 83-94.

Ramsay, S., Gallois, C., & Callan, V. J. (1997). Social rules and attributions in the personnel selection interview. *Journal of Occupational and Organizational Psychology, 70*, 189-203.

Recruiting literature: Is it accurate? (1981). *Journal of College Placement, 42*, 56-59.

Reichers, A. E. (1987). An interactionist perspective on newcomer socialization rates. *Academy of Management Review, 12*, 278-287.

Reid, G. L. (1972). Job search and the effectiveness of job-finding methods. *Industrial and Labor Relations Review, 25*, 479-495.

Reilly, R. R., Brown, R., Blood, M. R., & Malatesta, C. Z. (1981). The effects of realistic previews: A study and discussion of the literature. *Personnel Psychology, 34*, 823-834.

Repetti, R. L. (1994). Short-term and long-term processes linking job stressors to father-child interaction. *Social Development, 3*, 1-15.

Repetti, R. L., & Wood, J. (1997). Effects of daily stress at work on mothers' interactions with preschoolers. *Journal of Family Psychology, 11*, 90-108.

Resnick, L. B., Levine, J. M., & Teasley, S. D. (Eds.). (1991). *Perspectives on social shared cognition*. Washington, DC: American Psychological Association.

Riessman, C. K. (1990). *Divorce talk: Women and men make sense of personal relationships*. New Brunswick, NJ: Rutgers University Press.

Riggio, R. E., & Throckmorton, B. (1988). The relative effects of verbal and nonverbal behavior, appearance, and social skills on evaluations made in hiring interviews. *Journal of Applied Social Psychology, 18*, 331-348.

Riley, S., & Wrench, D. (1985). Mentoring among female lawyers. *Journal of Applied Social Psychology, 15*, 374-386.

Robinson, S. L. (1996). Trust and breach of the psychological contract. *Administrative Science Quarterly, 41*, 574-599.

Roese, R. J., & Olson, J. M. (1995). Counterfactual thinking: A critical overview. In N. J. Roese & J. M. Olson (Eds.), *What might have been: The social psychology of counterfactual thinking* (pp. 1-55). Mahwah, NJ: Lawrence Erlbaum.

Rosse, J. G. (1988). Relations among lateness, absence and turnover: Is there a progression of withdrawal? *Human Relations, 41*, 517-531.

Roth, N. L. (1991, February). *Secrets in organizations: Addressing taboo topics at work*. Paper presented at the annual meeting of the Western Speech Communication Association, Phoenix, AZ.

Rousseau, D. M. (1996). Changing the deal while keeping the people. *Academy of Management Executive, 10*(1), 50-61.

Rousseau, D. M., & Anton, R. J. (1988). Fairness and implied contract obligations in job terminations: A policy-capturing study. *Human Performance, 1,* 273-289.

Rousseau, D. M., & Anton, R. J. (1991). Fairness and implied contract obligations in job terminations: The role of contributions, promises, and performance. *Journal of Organizational Behavior, 12,* 287-299.

Rousseau, D. M., & Parks, J. M. (1993). The contracts of individuals and organizations. In L. L. Cummings & B. M. Staw (Eds.), *Research in organizational behavior* (Vol. 15, pp. 1-43). Greenwich, CT: JAI.

Rousseau, D. M., & Tijoriwala, S. A. (1999). What's a good reason to change? Motivated reasoning and social accounts in promoting organizational change. *Journal of Applied Psychology, 84,* 514-528.

Rudin, J. P., & Boudreau, J. W. (1996). Information acquisition in promotion decisions. *Human Relations, 49,* 313-325.

Ruggiero, M., Greenberger, E., & Steinberg, L. D. (1982). Occupational deviance among adolescent workers. *Youth & Society, 13,* 423-448.

Ruggiero, M., & Steinberg, L. D. (1981). The empirical study of teenage work: A behavioral code for the assessment of adolescent job environments. *Journal of Vocational Behavior, 19,* 163-174.

Ruscher, J. B., Hammer, E. Y., & Hammer, E. D. (1996). Forming shared impressions through conversation: An adaptation of the continuum model. *Personality and Social Psychology Bulletin, 22,* 705-720.

Ryan, J., & Sim, D. H. (1990). When art becomes news: Portrayals of art and artists on network television news. *Social Forces, 68,* 869-889.

Rynes, S. L. (1991). Recruitment, job choice, and post-hire consequences: A call for new research directions. In M. D. Dunnette & L. M. Hough (Eds.), *Handbook of industrial and organizational psychology* (2nd ed., Vol. 2, pp. 399-444). Palo Alto, CA: Consulting Psychologists.

Rynes, S. L., Bretz, R. D., & Gerhart, B. (1991). The importance of recruitment in job choice: A different way of looking. *Personnel Psychology, 44,* 487-521.

Rynes, S. L., & Gerhart, B. (1990). Interviewer assessments of applicant "fit": An exploratory investigation. *Personnel Psychology, 43,* 13-35.

Rynes, S. L., & Miller, H. E. (1983). Recruiter and job influences on candidates for employment. *Journal of Applied Psychology, 68,* 147-154.

Rynes, S. L., Orlitzky, M. O., & Bretz, R. D. (1997). Experienced hiring versus college recruiting: Practices and emerging trends. *Personnel Psychology, 50,* 309-339.

Sackett, P. R. (1982). The interviewer as hypothesis tester: The effects of impressions of an applicant on interviewer questioning strategy. *Personnel Psychology, 35,* 789-804.

Saks, A. M. (1994). A psychological process investigation for the effects of recruitment source and organization information on job survival. *Journal of Organizational Behavior, 15,* 225-244.

Saks, A. M. (1995). Longitudinal field investigation of the moderating and mediating effects of self-efficacy on the relationship between training and newcomer adjustment. *Journal of Applied Psychology, 80,* 211-225.

Saks, A. (1996). The relationship between the amount and helpfulness of entry training and work outcomes. *Human Relations, 49,* 429-451.

Saks, A. M., & Ashforth, B. E. (1997). A longitudinal investigation of the relationships between job information sources, applicant perceptions of fit, and work outcomes. *Personnel Psychology, 50,* 395-426.

Saks, A. M., & Cronshaw, S. F. (1990). A process investigation of realistic job previews: Mediating variables and channels of communication. *Journal of Organizational Behavior, 11,* 221-236.

Saks, A. M., Wiesner, W. H., & Summers, R. J. (1994). Effects of job previews on self-selection and job choice. *Journal of Vocational Behavior, 44,* 297-316.

Saks, A. M., Wiesner, W. H., & Summers, R. J. (1996). Effects of job previews and compensation policy on applicant attraction and job choice. *Journal of Vocational Behavior, 49,* 68-85.

Salancik, G., & Pfeffer, J. (1978). A social information processing approach to job attitudes and task design. *Administrative Science Quarterly, 23,* 224-253.

Saunders, D. M., Sheppard, B. H., Knight, V., & Roth, J. (1992). Employee voice to supervisors. *Employee Responsibilities and Rights Journal, 5,* 241-259.

Scandura, T. A., & Katterberg, R. J. (1988). *Much ado about mentors and little ado about measurement: Development of an instrument.* Paper presented at the annual meeting of the Academy of Management, Anaheim, CA.

Scandura, T. A., & Ragins, B. R. (1993). The effects of sex and gender role orientation on mentorship in male-dominated occupations. *Journal of Vocational Behavior, 43,* 251-265.

Scheff, T. J. (1988). Shame and conformity: The deference-emotion system. *American Sociological Review, 53,* 395-406.

Schein, E. H. (1968). Organizational socialization and the profession of management. *Industrial Management Review, 9,* 1-16.

Schlenker, B. R. (1980). *Impression management: The self-concept, social identity, and interpersonal relations.* Belmont, CA: Brooks/Cole.

Schlenker, B. R., & Weigold, M. F. (1992). Interpersonal processes involving impression regulation and management. *Annual Review of Psychology, 43,* 133-168.

Schmitt, N., & Coyle, B. W. (1976). Applicant decisions in the employment interview. *Journal of Applied Psychology, 61,* 184-192.

Schneider, B. (1987). The people make the place. *Personnel Psychology, 40,* 437-453.

Schneider, B., Goldstein, H. W., & Smith, D. B. (1995). The ASA framework: An update. *Personnel Psychology, 48,* 747-773.

Schwab, D. P. (1982). Recruiting and organizational participation. In K. Rowland & G. Ferris (Eds.), *Personnel management: New perspectives* (pp. 103-128). Boston: Allyn & Bacon.

Schweiger, D. M., & DeNisi, A. S. (1991). Communication with employees following a merger: A longitudinal field experiment. *Academy of Management Journal, 34,* 110-135.

Scott, C. R., Connaughton, S. L., Diaz-Saenz, H. R., Maguire, K., Ramirez, R., Richardson, B., Shaw, S. P., & Morgan, D. (1999). The impacts of communication and multiple identifications on intent to leave. *Management Communication Quarterly, 12,* 400-435.

Scott, C. R., Corman, S. R., & Cheney, G. (1998). Development of a structurational model of identifications in organizations. *Communication Theory, 8,* 298-336.

Scott, M. B., & Lyman, S. M. (1968). Accounts. *American Sociological Review, 33,* 46-62.

Sebald, H. (1986). Adolescents' shifting orientation toward parents and peers: A curvilinear trend over recent decades. *Journal of Marriage and the Family, 48,* 5-13.

Seers, A. (1989). Team-member exchange quality: A new construct for role-making research. *Organizational Behavior and Human Decision Processes, 43,* 118-135.

Seibert, S. (1999). The effectiveness of facilitated mentoring: A longitudinal quasi-experiment. *Journal of Vocational Behavior, 54,* 483-502.

Selye, H. (1956). *The stress of life.* New York: McGraw-Hill.

Settoon, R. P., Bennett, N., & Liden, R. C. (1996). Social exchange in organizations: Perceived organizational support, leader-member exchange, and employee reciprocity. *Journal of Applied Psychology, 81,* 219-227.

Shah, P. P. (1998). Who are employees' social referents? Using a network perspective to determine referent others. *Academy of Management Journal, 41,* 249-268.

Shaw, J. B., & Barrett-Power, E. (1997). A conceptual framework for assessing organization, work group, and individual effectiveness during and after downsizing. *Human Relations, 50,* 109-127.

Shaw, M. R. (1983). Taken-for-granted assumptions of applicants in simulated selection interviews. *Western Journal of Speech Communication, 47,* 138-156.

Sheehan, E. P. (1991). Reasons for quitting: Their effects on those who stay. *Journal of Social Behavior and Personality, 6,* 343-354.

Sheehan, E. P. (1995). Affective responses to employee turnover. *Journal of Social Psychology, 135,* 63-69.

Shellenbarger, S. (1995, November 15). Work and family. *Wall Street Journal,* Sec. B, p. 1.

Shore, L. M., & Shore, T. H. (1995). Perceived organizational support and organizational justice. In R. Cropanzano & K. M. Kacmar (Eds.), *Organizational politics, justice and support: Managing social climate at work* (pp. 149-164). Westport, CT: Quorum.

Shultz, K. S., Morton, K. R., & Weckerle, J. R. (1998). The influence of push and pull factors on voluntary and involuntary early retirees' retirement decision and adjustment. *Journal of Vocational Behavior, 53,* 45-58.

Shyles, L., & Ross, M. (1984). Recruitment rhetoric in brochures advertising the all volunteer force. *Journal of Applied Communication Research, 12,* 34-49.

Sias, P. M., & Cahill, D. J. (1998). From coworkers to friends: The development of peer friendships in the workplace. *Western Journal of Communication, 62,* 273-299.

Sias, P. M., & Jablin, F. M. (1995). Differential superior-subordinate relations, perceptions of fairness, and coworker communication. *Human Communication Research, 22,* 5-38.

Signorielli, N. (1991). *A sourcebook on children and television.* New York: Greenwood.

Signorielli, N. (1993). Television and adolescents' perceptions about work. *Youth & Society, 24,* 314-341.

Signorielli, N., & Lears, M. (1992). Children, television, and conceptions about chores: Attitudes and behaviors. *Sex Roles, 27,* 157-170.

Silvester, J. (1997). Spoken attributions and candidate success in graduate recruitment interviews. *Journal of Occupational and Organizational Psychology, 70,* 61-73.

Skarlicki, D. P., Ellard, J. H., & Kelln, B. R. C. (1998). Third-party perceptions of a layoff: Procedural, derogation, and retributive aspects of justice. *Journal of Applied Psychology, 83,* 119-127.

Smeltzer, L. R., & Zener, M. F. (1992). Development of a model for announcing major layoffs. *Group & Organization Management, 17,* 446-472.

Smith, R. C., & Eisenberg, E. M. (1987). Conflict at Disneyland: A root metaphor analysis. *Communication Monographs, 54,* 367-380.

Smith, R. C., & Turner, P. K. (1995). A social constructionist reconfiguration of metaphor analysis: An application of "SCMA" to organizational socialization theorizing. *Communication Monographs, 62,* 152-181.

Snyder, C. R. (1985). The excuse: An amazing grace? In B. R. Schlenker (Ed.), *The self and social life* (pp. 235-289). New York: McGraw-Hill.

Somers, M. J. (1999). Application of two neural network paradigms to the study of voluntary employee turnover. *Journal of Applied Psychology, 84,* 177-185.

Sonnenfeld, J. (1988). *The hero's farewell: What happens when CEOs retire.* New York: Oxford University Press.

Spano, S., & Zimmermann, S. (1995). Interpersonal communication competence in context: Assessing performance in the selection interview. *Communication Reports, 8,* 18-26.

Sparrowe, R. T., & Liden, R. C. (1997). Process and structure in leader-member exchange. *Academy of Management Review, 22,* 522-552.

Stark, A. (1992). *Because I said so.* New York: Pharos.

Staton-Spicer, A. Q., & Darling, A. L. (1986). Communication in the socialization of preservice teachers. *Communication Education, 35,* 215-230.

Steenland, S. (1990). *What's wrong with this picture? The status of women on screen and behind the camera in entertainment TV.* Washington, DC: National Commission on Working Women and of Wider Opportunities for Women.

Steers, R. M., & Mowday, R. T. (1981). Employee turnover and post-decision accommodation processes. In L. L. Cummings & B. M. Staw (Eds.), *Research in organizational behavior* (Vol. 3, pp. 235-281). Greenwich, CT: JAI.

Steinberg, L. D., Greenberger, E., Vaux, A., & Ruggiero, M. (1981). Early work experience: Effects on adolescent occupational socialization. *Youth & Society, 12,* 403-422.

Stern, D., McMillion, M., Hopkins, C., & Stone, J. (1990). Work experience for students in high school and college. *Youth & Society, 21,* 355-389.

Stern, D., & Nakata, Y. (1989). Characteristics of high school students' paid jobs, and employment experience after graduation. In D. Stern & D. Eichorn (Eds.), *Adolescence and work: Influences of social structure, labor markets, and culture.* Hillsdale, NJ: Lawrence Erlbaum.

Stevens, C. K. (1997). Effects of preinterview beliefs on applicants' reactions to campus interviews. *Academy of Management Journal, 40,* 947-966.

Stevens, C. K., & Kristof, A. L. (1995). Making the right impression: A field study of applicant impression management during job interviews. *Journal of Applied Psychology, 80,* 587-606.

Stevenson, W. B., & Bartunek, J. M. (1996). Power, interaction, position and the generation of cultural agreement in organizations. *Human Relations, 49,* 75-104.

Stewart, W., & Barling, J. (1996). Fathers' work experiences affect children's behaviors via job-related effect and parenting behaviors. *Journal of Organizational Behavior, 17,* 221-232.

Stohl, C. (1986). The role of memorable messages in the process of organizational socialization. *Communication Quarterly, 34,* 231-249.

Stohl, C., & Redding, W. C. (1987). Messages and message exchange processes. In F. M. Jablin, L. L. Putnam, K. H. Roberts, & L. W. Porter (Eds.), *Handbook of organizational communication: An interdisciplinary perspective* (pp. 451-502). Newbury Park, CA: Sage.

Stradling, S. G., Crowe, G., & Tuohy, A. P. (1993). Changes in self-concept during occupational socialization of new recruits to the police. *Journal of Community and Social Psychology, 3,* 131-147.

Strom, S. A., & Miller, V. (1993, November). *Socialization experiences of college co-ops and interns.* Paper presented at the annual meeting of the Speech Communication Association, Miami, FL.

Struthers, C. W., Colwill, N. L., & Perry, R. P. (1992). An attributional analysis of decision making in a personnel selection interview. *Journal of Applied Social Psychology, 22,* 801-818.

Suchan, J. (1995). The influence of organizational metaphors on writers' communication roles and stylistic choices. *Journal of Business Communication, 32,* 7-29.

Sutton, R. I., & Louis, M. R. (1984). *The influence of selection and socialization on insider sense-making.* Paper presented at the annual meeting of the Academy of Management, Boston.

Swaroff, P. G., Barclay, L. A., & Bass, A. R. (1985). Recruiting sources: Another look. *Journal of Applied Psychology, 70,* 720-728.

Tannenbaum, S. I., Mathieu, J. E., Salas, E., & Cannon-Bowles, J. A. (1991). Meeting trainees' expectations: The influence of training fulfillment on the development of commitment, self-efficacy, and motivation. *Journal of Applied Psychology, 76,* 759-769.

Taylor, E. (1989). *Prime-time families: Television culture in postwar America.* Berkeley: University of California Press.

Taylor, G. S. (1994). The relationship between sources of new employees and attitudes toward the job. *Journal of Social Psychology, 134,* 99-110.

Taylor, M. S. (1985). The roles of occupational knowledge and vocational self-concept crystallization in students' school-to-work transition. *Journal of Counseling Psychology, 32,* 539-550.

Taylor, M. S. (1988). Effects of college internships on individual participants. *Journal of Applied Psychology, 73,* 393-401.

Taylor, M. S., & Bergmann, T. J. (1987). Organizational recruitment activities and applicants' reactions at different stages of the recruitment process. *Personnel Psychology, 40,* 261-285.

Taylor, M. S., & Schmidt, D. W. (1983). A process-oriented investigation of recruitment source effectiveness. *Personnel Psychology, 36,* 343-354.

Taylor, M. S., & Sniezek, J. A. (1984). The college recruitment interview: Topical content and applicant reactions. *Journal of Occupational Psychology, 57,* 157-168.

Teboul, J. C. B. (1994). Facing and coping with uncertainty during organizational encounter. *Management Communication Quarterly, 8,* 190-224.

Teboul, J. C. B. (1995). Determinants of new hire information-seeking during organizational encounter. *Western Journal of Communication, 59,* 305-325.

Teboul, J. C. B. (1997). "Scripting" the organization: New hire learning during organizational encounter. *Communication Research Reports, 14,* 33-47.

Teigen, C. W. (1983). *Communication of organizational climate during job screening interviews: A field study of interviewee perceptions, "actual" communication behavior and interview outcomes.* Unpublished doctoral dissertation, University of Texas at Austin.

Tengler, C. D. (1982). *Effects of question type and question orientation on interview outcomes in naturally occurring employment interviews.* Unpublished master's thesis, University of Texas at Austin.

Tengler, C. D., & Jablin, F. M. (1983). Effects of question type, orientation, and sequencing in the employment screening interview. *Communication Monographs, 50,* 245-263.

Tepper, B. J. (1995). Upward maintenance tactics in supervisory mentoring and nonmentoring relationships. *Academy of Management Journal, 38,* 1191-1205.

Tesser, A., & Rosen, S. (1975). The reluctance to transmit bad news. In L. Berkowitz (Ed.), *Advances in experimental social psychology* (Vol. 8, pp. 193-232). New York: Academic Press.

Thacker, R. A., & Wayne, S. J. (1995). An examination of the relationship between upward influence tactics and assessments of promotability. *Journal of Management, 21,* 739-756.

Theberge, L. (1981). *Crooks, conmen and clowns: Businessmen in TV entertainment.* Washington, DC: Media Institute.

Theus, K. T. (1995). Communication in a power vacuum: Sense-making and enactment during crisis-induced departures. *Human Resource Management, 34,* 27-49.

Thomas, D. A. (1990). The impact of race on managers' experiences of developmental relationships (mentoring and sponsorship): An intra-organizational study. *Journal of Organizational Behavior, 11,* 479-492.

Thompson, L. (1990). Negotiation behavior and outcomes: Empirical evidence and theoretical issues. *Psychological Bulletin, 108,* 515-532.

Thralls, C. (1992). Rites and ceremonials: Corporate video and the construction of social realities in modern organizations. *Journal of Business and Technical Communication, 6,* 381-402.

Toliver, S. D. (1993). Movers and shakers: Black families and corporate relocation. *Marriage and Family Review, 19,* 113-130.

Treadwell, D. F., & Harrison, T. M. (1994). Conceptualizing and assessing organizational image: Model images, commitment and communication. *Communication Monographs, 61,* 63-85.

Trent, L. W. (1978). *The effects of varying levels of interviewee nonverbal behavior in the employment interview.* Unpublished doctoral dissertation, Southern Illinois University.

Trice, H. M. (1993). *Occupational subcultures in the workplace.* Ithaca, NY: ILR.

Tsui, A. S., Pearce, J. L., Porter, L. W., & Hite, J. P. (1995). Choice of employee-organization relationship: Influence of external and internal organizational factors. In G. R. Ferris (Ed.), *Research in personnel and human resources management* (Vol. 13, pp. 117-151). Greenwich, CT: JAI.

Tucker, C. J., Barber, B. L., & Eccles, J. S. (1997). Advice about life plans and personal problems in late adolescent sibling relationships. *Journal of Youth and Adolescence, 26,* 63-76.

Tullar, W. L. (1989). Relational control in the employment interview. *Journal of Applied Psychology, 74,* 971-977.

Turban, D. B., Campion, J. E., & Eyring, A. R. (1995). Factors related to job acceptance decisions of college recruits. *Journal of Vocational Behavior, 47,* 193-213.

Turban, D. B., & Dougherty, T. W. (1992). Influence of campus recruiting on applicant attraction to firms. *Academy of Management Journal, 35,* 739-765.

Turban, D. B., & Keon, T. L. (1993). Organizational attractiveness: An interactionist perspective. *Journal of Applied Psychology, 78,* 184-193.

Turner, P. K. (1999). What if you don't? A response to Kramer and Miller. *Communication Monographs, 66,* 382-389.

Turow, J. (1974). Advising and ordering in daytime, primetime. *Journal of Communication, 24,* 138-141.

Turow, J. (1980). Occupation and personality in television dramas: An industry view. *Communication Research, 7,* 295-318.

Ugbah, S. D., & Majors, R. E. (1992). Influential communication factors in employment screening interviews. *Journal of Business Communication, 29,* 145-159.

Ullman, J. C. (1966). Employee referrals: Prime tools for recruiting workers. *Personnel, 43,* 30-45.

Van Maanen, J. (1975). Breaking in: Socialization to work. In R. Dubin (Ed.), *Handbook of work, organization and society* (pp. 67-120). Chicago: Rand McNally.

Van Maanen, J. (1984). Doing new things in old ways: The chains of socialization. In J. L. Bass (Ed.), *College and university organization: Insights from the behavioral sciences* (pp. 211-247). New York: New York University Press.

Van Maanen, J., & Barley, S. R. (1984). Occupational communities: Culture and control in organizations. In B. M. Staw & L. L. Cummings (Eds.), *Research in organizational behavior* (Vol. 6, pp. 287-365). Greenwich, CT: JAI.

Van Maanen, J., & Schein, E. H. (1979). Toward a theory of organizational socialization. In B. M. Staw & L. L. Cummings (Eds.), *Research in organizational behavior* (Vol. 1, pp. 209-264). Greenwich, CT: JAI.

van Tilburg, T. (1992). Support networks before and after retirement. *Journal of Social and Personal Relationships, 9,* 433-455.

Vandenberg, R. J., & Scarpello, V. (1990). The matching model: An examination of the processes underlying realistic job previews. *Journal of Applied Psychology, 75,* 60-67.

Vangelisti, A. L. (1988). Adolescent socialization into the workplace: A synthesis and critique of current literature. *Youth & Society, 19,* 460-484.

Vecchio, R. P. (1995). The impact of referral sources on employee attitudes: Evidence from a national sample. *Journal of Management, 21,* 953-965.

Vinton, K. L. (1989). Humor in the workplace: It is more than telling jokes. *Small Group Behavior, 20,* 151-166.

von Hippel, C., Mangnum, S. L., Greenberger, D. B., Heneman, R. L., & Skoglind, J. D. (1997). Temporary employment: Can organizations and employees both win? *Academy of Management Executive, 11,* 93-104.

Vonracek, F. W., Lerner, R. M., & Schulenberg, J. E. (1986). *Career development: A life-span developmental approach.* Hillsdale, NJ: Lawrence Erlbaum.

Waldeck, J. H., Orrego, V. O., Plax, T. G., & Kearney, P. (1997). Graduate student/faculty mentoring relationships: Who gets mentored, how it happens, and to what end. *Communication Quarterly, 45,* 93-109.

Waldron, V. R. (1991). Achieving communication goals in superior-subordinate relationships: The multi-functionality of upward maintenance tactics. *Communication Monographs, 58,* 289-306.

Waldron, V. R. (1994). Once more, with feeling: Reconsidering the role of emotion in work. In S. A. Deetz (Ed.), *Communication yearbook 17* (pp. 388-416). Thousand Oaks, CA: Sage.

Waldron, V. R., & Hunt, M. D. (1992). Hierarchical level, length, and quality of supervisory relationship as predictors of subordinates' use of maintenance tactics. *Communication Reports, 5,* 82-89.

Walsh, W. B., & Osipow, S. H. (Eds.). (1983). *Handbook of vocational psychology: Foundations* (Vol. 1). Hillsdale, NJ: Lawrence Erlbaum.

Walther, J. B. (1992). Interpersonal effects in computer-mediated communication: A relational perspective. *Communication Research, 19,* 52-90.

Walther, J. B. (1996). Computer-mediated communication: Impersonal, interpersonal and hyperpersonal interaction. *Communication Research, 23,* 3-43.

Wanous, J. P. (1977). Organizational entry: Newcomers moving from outside to inside. *Psychological Bulletin, 84,* 601-618.

Wanous, J. P. (1980). *Organizational entry: Recruitment, selection and socialization of newcomers.* Reading, MA: Addison-Wesley.

Wanous, J. P. (1989). Installing a realistic job preview: Ten tough choices. *Personnel Psychology, 42,* 117-133.

Wanous, J. P., & Colella, A. (1989). Organizational entry research: Current status and future directions. In G. R. Ferris & K. M. Rowland (Eds.), *Research in personnel and human resources management* (Vol. 7, pp. 59-120). Greenwich, CT: JAI.

Wanous, J. P., Poland, T. D., Premack, S. L., & Davis, K. S. (1992). The effects of met expectations on newcomer attitudes and behaviors: A review and meta-analysis. *Journal of Applied Psychology, 77,* 288-297.

Watzlawick, P., Beavin, J., & Jackson, D. (1967). *The pragmatics of human communication.* New York: Norton.

Waung, M. (1995). The effects of self-regulatory coping orientation on newcomer adjustment and job survival. *Personnel Psychology, 48,* 633-650.

Wayne, S. J., & Kacmar, K. M. (1991). The effects of impression management on the performance appraisal process. *Organizational Behavior and Human Decision Processes, 48,* 70-88.

Wayne, S. J., Shore, L. M., & Liden, R. C. (1997). Perceived organizational support and leader-member exchange: A social exchange perspective. *Academy of Management Journal, 40,* 82-111.

Weiss, H. M. (1977). Subordinate imitation of supervisor behavior: The role of modeling in organizational socialization. *Organizational Behavior and Human Performance, 19,* 89-105.

Werbel, J. D., & Landau, J. (1996). The effectiveness of different recruitment sources: A mediating variable analysis. *Journal of Applied Social Psychology, 26,* 1337-1350.

West, M. A. (1987). Role innovation in the world of work. *British Journal of Social Psychology, 26,* 304-315.

West, M. A., Nicholson, N., & Rees, A. (1987). Transitions into newly created jobs. *Journal of Occupational Psychology, 60,* 97-113.

White, L. K., & Brinkerhoff, D. B. (1981). Children's work in the family: Its significance and meaning. *Journal of Marriage and the Family, 43,* 789-798.

Wiesner, W. H., Saks, A. M., & Summers, R. J. (1991). Job alternatives and job choice. *Journal of Vocational Behavior, 38,* 198-207.

Wigand, R. T., & Boster, F. S. (1991). Mentoring, social interaction, and commitment: An empirical analysis of a mentoring program. *Communications, 16,* 15-31.

Wilks, J. (1986). The relative importance of parents and friends in adolescent decision making. *Journal of Youth and Adolescence, 15,* 323-334.

Williams, C. R., Labig, C. E., & Stone, R. H. (1993). Recruitment sources and posthire outcomes for job applicants and new hires: A test of two hypotheses. *Journal of Applied Psychology, 78,* 163-172.

Williamson, L. G., Campion, J. E., Roehling, M. V., Malos, S. B., & Campion, M. A. (1997). Employment interview on trial: Linking interview structure with litigation outcomes. *Journal of Applied Psychology, 82,* 900-912.

Wilson, C. E. (1983). *Toward understanding the process of organizational leave-taking.* Paper presented at the annual meeting of the Speech Communication Association, Washington, DC.

Winstead, B. A., Derlega, V. J., Montgomery, M. J., & Pilkington, C. (1995). The quality of friendships and work and job satisfaction. *Journal of Social and Personal Relationships, 12,* 199-215.

Withey, M. J., & Cooper, W. H. (1989). Predicting exit, voice, loyalty, and neglect. *Administrative Science Quarterly, 34,* 521-539.

Wolfe, M. N., & Baskin, O. W. (1985, August). *The communication of corporate culture in employee indoctrination literature: An empirical analysis using content analysis.* Paper presented at the annual meeting of the Academy of Management, San Diego, CA.

Wright, J. C., Huston, A. C., Reitz, A. L., & Piemyat, S. (1994). Young children's perceptions of television reality: Determinants and developmental differences. *Developmental Psychology, 30,* 229-239.

Wroblewski, R., & Huston, A. C. (1987). Televised occupational stereotypes and their effects on early adolescents: Are they changing? *Journal of Early Adolescence, 7,* 283-297.

Young, R. A., & Friesen, J. D. (1992). The intentions of parents in influencing the career development of their children. *Career Development Quarterly, 40,* 198-207.

Young, R. A., Friesen, J. D., & Pearson, H. M. (1988). Activities and interpersonal relations as dimensions of parental behavior in the career development of adolescents. *Youth & Society, 20,* 29-45.

Youniss, J., & Smollar, J. (1985). *Adolescent relations with mothers, fathers, and friends.* Chicago: University of Chicago Press.

Yukl, G., Guinan, P. J., & Sottolano, D. (1995). Influence tactics used for different objectives with subordinates, peers, and superiors. *Group & Organization Management, 20,* 272-296.

Zahrly, J., & Tosi, H. (1989). The differential effect of organizational induction process on early work adjustment. *Journal of Organizational Behavior, 10,* 59-74.

Zarbatany, L., Hartmann, D. P., & Rankin, D. B. (1990). The psychological functions of pre-adolescent peer activities. *Child Development, 61,* 1067-1080.

Zey, M. (1991). *The mentor connection.* Homewood, IL: Dow Jones-Irwin.

Ziller, R. C. (1965). Toward a theory of open and closed groups. *Psychological Bulletin, 64,* 164-182.

Ziller, R. C., Behringer, R. D., & Jansen, M. J. (1961). The minority member in open and closed groups. *Journal of Applied Psychology, 45,* 55-58.

Zorn, T. E. (1995). Bosses and buddies: Constructing and performing simultaneously hierarchical and close friendship relationships. In J. T. Woods & S. Duck (Eds.), *Under-studied relationships: Off the beaten track* (pp. 122-147). Thousand Oaks, CA: Sage.

Zurawik, D. (1996, March 6). What we watch may reflect our attitudes about work. *Richmond Times-Dispatch,* Sec. D, pp. 1, 3.

20

Communication Competence

FREDRIC M. JABLIN
University of Richmond

PATRICIA M. SIAS
Washington State University

As Spitzberg and Cupach (1984), among others, have observed, "Competence is an issue both perennial and fundamental to the study of communication" (p. 11). However, although communication competence has been an object of study in Western cultures since the time of the ancient Greeks (Fisher, 1978), it remains a "fuzzy" concept that both scholars and practitioners have struggled to conceptualize and operationalize (e.g., Bochner & Kelley, 1974; Bostrom, 1984; Habermas, 1970; Hart, Olsen, Robinson, & Mandleco, 1997; Hymes, 1972; Parks, 1994; Rubin, 1990; Wiemann, 1977). Not surpris-

ingly, difficulties associated with the study of communication competence generally, including its tendency to be viewed as a "hybrid" concept (part social science/part art), are reflected in research focused on exploring organizational communication competence, in particular (e.g., Jablin, Cude, House, Lee, & Roth, 1994).

Our goal in this chapter is not to resolve all the controversies associated with the conceptualization of organizational communication competence. Nor is our goal to provide a complete review of empirical research focused on organizational communication competence,

AUTHORS' NOTE: We would like to thank Dave Seibold and Ted Zorn for their helpful comments on an earlier draft of this chapter.

since this literature has been the subject of recent review (see Jablin et al., 1994). Rather, our purpose here is to (1) describe the ways organizational communication competence has been viewed by those who have studied it, (2) discuss a series of assumptions and premises associated with extant conceptualizations and investigations of organizational competence that we believe have hampered research in the area, and (3) propose a developmental-ecological framework for organizing and critiquing existing competence research and suggest how this framework might help guide future investigation of the fuzzy concept we have come to call organizational communication competence.

CONCEPTUALIZATIONS OF ORGANIZATIONAL COMMUNICATION COMPETENCE

Communication competence has been conceptualized in a variety of ways. In fact, there are almost as many definitions of communication competence as there are researchers interested in the construct. One frequent approach to conceptualizing competence has been to focus on *goal achievement*. Monge, Bachman, Dillard, and Eisenberg (1981), for example, equate competence with effectiveness and argue that "competent communicators are those who are effective at achieving their goals" (p. 506). Parks (1994) is more specific in his goal/control-oriented conceptualization of communication competence:

> Communication competence represents the degree to which individuals satisfy and perceive that they have satisfied their goals within the limits of a given social situation without jeopardizing their ability or opportunity to pursue other subjectively more important goals. (p. 595)

Other conceptualizations of communication competence concentrate on the ability to display *appropriate communication behaviors* in given situations (without direct consideration of whether or not one obtains one's objectives). Along these lines, one of the most popular conceptualizations of competence is that of Spitzberg and Cupach (1984), who state that "communication competence refers to the ability to demonstrate appropriate communication in a given context" (p. 66). Obviously, the nature of "appropriate" communication behavior needs to be identified if one uses this approach. As applied to the organizational context, this requires at least an elemental analysis of how tasks, situations, and person(s) interact to affect what is considered to be appropriate communication behavior.

In contrast to the above conceptualizations, McCroskey (1984), among others, views communication competence as distinct from behavior/performance. In particular, he distinguishes among "understanding," "ability," and "doing" (performance) and points out that "communication competence requires not only the ability to perform adequately certain communication behaviors, it also requires an understanding of those behaviors and the cognitive ability to make choices among behaviors" (p. 264). For McCroskey, however, competence does not require the actual performance of adequate behaviors, just the knowledge and ability to do so.

Jablin et al. (1994) build on these perspectives in developing a *resource-oriented* view of competence that reflects the linkages of competence with the related concepts of behavior/performance and effectiveness/goal achievement. Accordingly, they define competence as "the set of abilities, henceforth, termed *resources,* which a communicator has available for use in the communication process" (p. 125, emphasis in original). These resources include strategic communication knowledge (e.g., knowledge of appropriate communication rules and norms) and communication capacities (e.g., traits and abilities such as cognitive differentiation, perspective taking, and general encoding and decoding skills). In turn, they conceptualize "communication *performance* as the display of communication behaviors, upon which attributions of competence are based" (Jablin et al., 1994, p. 125). Thus, they stress the necessity of recognizing the fundamental interrelationship between communicative performance and communication competence, but also suggest the importance of distinguishing between the two in our research. In addition, Jablin et al. do not consider effectiveness/goal achievement as necessary or sufficient conditions for one to be perceived of as a relatively competent communicator. Rather, they support McCroskey's (1982, p. 3) position that "one may be effective without being competent and one may be competent without being effective," a notion that is unfortunately a truism in many organizations (see, e.g., Luthans, 1988).[1]

Another rather unique feature of the Jablin et al. (1994) approach to competence is their proposition that organizational communication competence should be analyzed at multiple levels of analysis, rather than at just the individual level, which typifies extant research in the area. They suggest that groups and organizations can be characterized with respect to unique group and organizational forms of communication knowledge and capacities and that these resources are not necessarily a mere aggregate of the competencies of their respective constituent parts (consistent with the systems notion that the whole is greater than the sum of its parts). Further, by conceptualizing communication competence at multiple levels of analysis Jablin et al. focus attention on the dynamic interdependence among the various levels of analysis. Curiously, while communication research exploring higher-order forms of competence is still scarce, the notion that groups and organizations possess "core competencies" has become popular in other areas of organizational studies (e.g., the study of strategic management; see Lei, Hitt, & Bettis, 1996; Marino, 1996; Nadler & Tushman, 1999; Prahalad & Hamel, 1990; Ulrich & Lake, 1990). To conclude, our purpose in this section is not to argue that one approach to conceptualizing communication competence is superior to another; rather, we suggest that

each approach emphasizes a different sort of dynamic relative to understanding competence.

In general, however, when one examines the conceptualizations of communication competence discussed above, two primary dimensions of the construct are reflected: behavior and cognition. Behavioral studies seek to identify the specific communication behaviors and skills that organizational members associate with competence. Research conceptualizing competence as "appropriate behavior" or "goal achievement" often falls into this category (e.g., Hirokawa, 1988; Snavely & Walters, 1983; Wheeless & Berryman-Fink, 1985). Cognitive research examines the various types of social knowledge and cognitive abilities associated with communication competence. Many of these studies conceptualize (though often implicitly) competence as represented by cognitive "resources" (e.g., Harris & Cronen, 1979; Sypher & Sypher, 1981). Within each of these two general categories of research, we find some studies that seek to identify behaviors or cognitive factors, respectively, associated with "effective" communication. As might be expected, few cognition-oriented studies directly explore relationships between cognition and communicative performance. However, this is also true for most behaviorally oriented studies as well—the focus of investigation is individuals' *perceptions* of competent communication behaviors.

EMPIRICAL COMPETENCE RESEARCH: THE STATE OF THE ART

To orient the reader to empirical organizational communication competence research, as well as the strengths and weaknesses of research in the area, this section presents a brief but representative literature review. We summarize major findings from previous reviews of the literature, and we survey results from studies reported in the 1990s according to (1) basic conceptual orientation (i.e., behavioral or cognitive), and (2) level of analysis examined (i.e., individual, group, or organization). Before proceeding further, it is important to stress that although we discuss behavioral and cognitive approaches to communication competence in relative isolation of each other, we do so only to highlight salient features of the literature. As noted above, there are often close interrelations between cognitive and behavioral approaches to the study of competence, and the literature is not always as neatly divided as we present it here. For example, one might easily argue that implicitly embedded within all communication skills are elements of communication knowledge and that the two are in a constant state of development. Unfortunately, most studies do not reflect this mutuality between skills/behavior and knowledge/cognition. Our review of the literature is followed by a critique organized in terms of a series of problematic assumptions that we believe have characterized organizational communication competence research.

Individual-Level Competence

Behavioral/skill studies. The bulk of existing research at the individual level of analysis has examined competence from a behavioral orientation. A great deal of attention, for example, has been directed toward developing inventories of what organizational members (very frequently managers) or students perceive to be communication behaviors indicative of a competent organizational communicator (e.g., Cooper, 1997; DiSalvo, 1980; DiSalvo & Larsen, 1987; Maes, Weldy, & Icenogle, 1997; Morse & Piland, 1981; Rader & Wunsch, 1980; Wheeless & Berryman-Fink, 1985). Skills frequently reported in such inventories include behaviors such as listening, giving feedback, advising, persuading, instructing, interviewing, and motivating (Jablin et al., 1994). More recent studies report findings in line with earlier research (Maes et al., 1997). For example,

Reinsch and Shelby (1996, 1997) found that MBA students perceived their most pressing work-related communication needs to include enhanced self-confidence, persuasiveness, ability to clearly express ideas, and control of communication anxiety. Research in this area reflects a common problem evident in studies that attempt to develop inventories of communication competencies: It is often quite difficult for respondents to describe the specific *communication* skills they require on the job. For example, the most frequent communication need identified by Reinsch and Shelby (1996) was labeled "enhanced self-confidence," a notion that could have innumerable possibilities with respect to specific communication skills, affective and motivational states, and the like.

Researchers have not only sought to identify specific communication behaviors associated with competence but also to ascertain the basic dimensions or "simple structure" of the competence construct. Along these lines, Wheeless and Berryman-Fink (1985) found individual-level communication competence in organizations to be reflected by two behavioral dimensions: altercentrism (empathy, listening, supportiveness, other-orientation) and interaction management (including appropriate turn taking and episode punctuation). Others, such as Snavely and Walters (1983), have identified a larger number of basic behavioral dimensions of competence (Snavely and Walters's research resulted in five dimensions: empathy, listening, self-disclosure, social anxiety, and versatility). More recently, Scudder and Guinan (1989) proposed a four-factor model of supervisor communication competence. The first two factors were extrapolated from the work of Monge et al. (1981) and included encoding abilities (e.g., getting to the point, writing ability, clarity of expression) and decoding abilities (e.g., listening, attentiveness, sensitivity). Their third and fourth factors were related to special characteristics associated with their sample of systems developers and included "maintaining communication" with others generally and "maintaining user relationships" specifically (e.g., keeping users updated on project status, soliciting user input).

Other scholars have examined relationships between individuals' perceptions of the communicative behaviors of supervisors, coworkers, and others in the workplace and their attributions about the communication competence of those persons. Berman and Hellweg (1989), for instance, found that supervisor participation in quality circles enhanced subordinates' perceptions of their supervisor's communicative competence, as well as the supervisor's perceptions of his or her own communication competence. Also investigating subordinates' perceptions of their supervisors' communication competence, Johnson (1992) determined that subordinates' perceptions were significantly influenced by the compliance-gaining strategies used by the supervisor. In particular, supervisors using "prosocial" compliance-gaining tactics were perceived as more communicatively competent than those who used "antisocial" tactics (negative altercasting). In a study focused on peer competence, Haas and Arnold (1995) discovered that perceptions of listening-related behaviors accounted for about 32% of the attributes associated with judgments of communication competence in coworkers.

Finally, consistent with a long tradition of pedagogically oriented studies of competence, recent research has also assessed the effectiveness of a variety of training methods and programs in enhancing individuals' development of organizational communication skills (e.g., public speaking, listening, giving presentations, and interviewing; see Cooper & Husband, 1993; Ford & Wolvin, 1993; Goodall, 1982; Seibold, Kudsi, & Rude, 1993). Questioning the degree to which workers really benefit from such training, and assuming a more "critical" stance to competence research generally, other scholars have begun to debate the extent to which oral and written communication skills training in organizations is inherently manipulative and thereby another form of "unobtrusive" managerial control (e.g., Elmes & Costello, 1992; Hargie & Tourish, 1994; Thompson, 1996).

Cognitive studies. Research examining individual-level competence as a cognitive construct assumes that to be a competent communicator an individual must possess certain traits, knowledge, and cognitive abilities. Beverly Sypher, Ted Zorn, and their colleagues, for instance, have investigated a variety of cognitive traits and abilities associated with communication competence, including cognitive differentiation (Sypher, 1981; Sypher & Sypher, 1981; Sypher, Sypher, & Leichty, 1983; Sypher & Zorn, 1986; Zorn, 1991; Zorn & Violanti, 1996), perspective taking (Sypher, 1981), and self-monitoring (Sypher & Sypher, 1983). Overall, results of this program of research suggest that the more developed a person's social-cognitive abilities are, the more successful he or she is in organizations (success operationalized as frequency of promotion and level in the organizational hierarchy; see Sypher & Zorn, 1986; Zorn & Violanti, 1996).

Others have employed tenets of symbolic interactionism as a basis for exploring communication competence, and in particular have focused on exploring how individuals develop the communicative knowledge that allows them to negotiate meaning with others in the organization (Harris & Cronen, 1979; Wellmon, 1988). Based on rules theory (e.g., Cushman & Whiting, 1972; Shimanoff, 1980), this line of research considers communication competence to be "a by-product of an individual's understanding of the organization's 'master contract' [shared beliefs or culture that define the organization], as well as the constitutive rules [that allow members to assign meaning to communicative acts] and regulative rules [standards for 'appropriate' action to bring about outcomes] which guide interaction" (Jablin et al., 1994, p. 118).

Although it has not yet been tested in the organizational context and is still in its early stages of development, Duran and Spitzberg's (1995) work on a measure of cognitive communicative competence warrants discussion, since it integrates several approaches to the study of competence. More specifically, initial results of their studies (exploring interpersonal communication generally) support the position that "cognitive communication competence entails anticipating potentially influential contextual variables, monitoring the manner in which a conversation transpires, and reflecting upon one's performance for the purpose of eliminating unsuccessful communication tacts" (Duran & Spitzberg, 1995, p. 270). In brief, their work suggests that cognitive communication competence should be viewed as a "cyclical process that leads to the continual refinement of one's social communication repertoire" (p. 270). This refinement process may lead communicators to develop particular "message design logics" (O'Keefe, 1988), which influence the ways they create messages. O'Keefe (1988), for instance, suggests that "the level of message design logic a person has achieved reflects the acquisition and integration of knowledge about communication processes" (p. 97). Thus, cognitive communication competence may enable communicators to develop the complex cognitive resources (e.g., higher-order message design logics) necessary for designing situationally appropriate and effective messages.

To summarize, cognitive studies of individual-level communication competence indicate that competent communicators possess traits such as cognitive differentiation, perspective taking, and self-monitoring. They also are knowledgeable about communication rules and norms, and they have the ability to anticipate and reflect on the interaction of situational factors and their own communicative behavior.

Group-Level Competence

As noted earlier, to date few studies have explicitly explored communication competence at the group and organizational levels of analysis. Rather, we find studies framed in terms of communication skills/behaviors associated with "effectiveness." Since the skills/behaviors and forms of communication knowledge that groups and organizations use

in the pursuit of their goals also can be conceptualized as communication capacities or resources, in the sections that follow we extricate relevant competence findings from the results of effectiveness studies.

Behavioral studies. Among other processes, Jablin et al. (1994) suggest that behavioral studies of group communication competence frequently focus on a group's internal and external ability to gather, transmit, and interpret information. Hence, they suggest that many of the variables traditionally associated with the study of communication and group process can be recast "in terms of the functions they serve in providing groups with the capability of responding to the information requirements of their information environments" (p. 130). Thus, for example, a group's internal feedback structures, intergroup communication networks, and the communication practices and structures that help it maintain successful collaboration (e.g., Health & Sias, 1999) can be considered elements of the group's communication resources. Along these lines, the program of research of Randy Hirokawa and his colleagues investigating communication behaviors associated with "competent" group decision making and effective work teams is germane. For instance, Hirokawa (1988) found that effective decision-making groups display a variety of "vigilant" communication behaviors including capabilities associated with problem analysis, assessment of decision criteria, and critical evaluation of alternative courses of action. In subsequent research, Hirokawa and Rost's (1992) data showed that effective decision-making groups pay more attention to the procedures they use to solve problems (the "process") than do ineffective groups.

Finally, in a recent test of the ecological validity of Gouran and Hirokawa's (1983) "functional" theory of effective decision making, Propp and Nelson (1996) found that members' "analysis of the problem," "orientation/establishment of operating procedures," and "evaluation of the positive consequences of alternatives" each had independent effects on the level of decision utility (effectiveness) of 29 work groups in a midwestern manufacturing firm. In brief, such processes and functions represent group-level communication resources that may aid a group in the pursuit of its goals.

Similarly, recent research investigating the extent to which the use of computer-mediated group communication systems, such as group support systems (GSSs), can augment a group's capabilities can be considered in terms of communication competence. GSSs were designed to facilitate group communication and, thus, a group's communication capabilities, by allowing parallel communication, enhancing "group memory" (i.e., most systems record electronically all comments and ideas that are generated), and providing structure to enable a group to remain focused on the task at hand (Andrews & Herschel, 1996, pp. 120-121). In particular, several studies that have examined the extent to which the use of a GSS helps groups manage conflict (e.g., Nunamaker, Dennis, Valacich, Vogel, & George, 1991; Poole, Holmes, & DeSanctis, 1991; Sambamurthy & Poole, 1992) are of interest, since their findings suggest that GSSs can hinder group communication competence by slowing down the communication process (typing words on a computer terminal is slower than speaking) and by reducing the availability of nonverbal cues (Nunamaker et al., 1991). At the same time, however, results from these studies also generally indicate that GSSs can facilitate conflict management by helping members identify and resolve differences (including conflicts of interest).

Cognitive studies. As at the individual level of analysis, cognitive studies of group-level competence tend to employ resource-based conceptualizations of communication competence. In particular, group-level competence is often viewed as residing in cognitive resources associated with group rules, structures, culture, history, and the like (Jablin et al., 1994). Thus, phenomena such as group

"synergy" and "mentality" (Bion, 1959), history, rituals and culture, value structures, languages/codes, fantasy themes (e.g., Bormann, Pratt, & Putnam, 1978), distributed cognition (e.g., Cole & Engeström, 1993; Hinz, Tindale, & Vollrath, 1997), "group knowledge structures" (Walsh, 1995), "transactive memory" (Liang, Moreland, & Argote, 1995), and the like all have embedded within them forms of group-level communication knowledge/competence. As Schein (1985, p. 149) observed with respect to group culture, culture implies "shared solutions, shared understandings, and consensus," all of which are inherently associated with knowledge of a group's communication "rules" (e.g., Schall, 1983). However, as Jablin et al. (1994, p. 129) note, it does not necessarily follow that groups with "stronger" cultures are more communicatively competent than groups with "weaker" cultures, since groups with very strong cultures may fall into a "competency trap often experienced in the form of 'groupthink' [Janis, 1972]."

The notion that group-level communication knowledge may be embedded in the fantasy themes that "spin out" in groups has been investigated in a recent study by Baron and Clair (1996). A fantasy theme is "the creative interpretation of events that fulfills a group's psychological or rhetorical need" (Baron & Clair, 1996, p. 17) and serves to help members make sense of the realities of their groups and organizations. Accordingly, fantasy themes become interpretive resources for groups, which frame knowledge structures regarding effective communication. Through inspection of archival records, direct observation, and interviews with organizational members, Baron and Clair were able to identify four fantasy themes associated with communication competence in a small, primarily female staffed, not-for-profit organization. Among the themes that were identified across groups, one suggested that stereotypical forms of male communication (e.g., communication should be efficient, objective, clear, and task oriented) versus female communication (which organizational members tended to define in opposite terms) were "conceived as being the most effective way to communicate" (Baron & Clair, 1996, p. 21).

Group-level cognitive resources such as knowledge structures and shared understandings have also been shown to influence the degree to which GSS technology (mentioned above as a group competence resource) is appropriated and used effectively by groups. Poole and DeSanctis (1992), for example, examined the structurational processes associated with the use of a group decision support system and found that effective appropriation of the technology by the group was influenced by the group's interpretations of the "spirit" and the features of the technology. Specifically, groups whose interpretations were consistent with (i.e., "faithful to") the spirit and features of the technology tended to be more effective than those whose interpretations were inconsistent ("unfaithful"). Accordingly, a group's ability to use technological resources depends on the quality of the group's cognitive resources such as group interpretations, knowledge, and understanding of the technology.

In summary, the fantasy themes, rules, language attributes, cultures, and structuration processes of groups guide their communication activity (e.g., Poole, Seibold, & McPhee, 1996), and thus can be analyzed and deconstructed to reveal the knowledge dimension of group-level communication competence.

Organizational Level of Analysis

Behavioral studies. Behaviorally oriented studies of communication competence at the organizational level of analysis focus "on the communication structures and programs which allow for the production, reception, and basic interpretation of messages exchanged with external and internal audiences" (Jablin et al., 1994, p. 133). Although rarely framed in terms of competence, orga-

nizational public relations and advertising activities and programs; participation in interorganizational communication networks; organizational recruiting methods; information data storage, retrieval, and processing systems (from the simplest filing system to elaborate computerized expert systems); and organizational house organs/publications and other forms of corporate communication all represent mechanisms that allow organizations to communicate with their internal and external environments. Hence, these activities, programs, and media all represent resources that organizations as entities can use in the communication process. For example, the intra- and interorganizational networks and media available to an organization to use in communicating with its environment during times of crisis reflect a distinct set of organizational communication capacities (e.g., Krackhardt & Stern, 1988). Thus, it would seem that the more behavioral choices available to an organization (or the size of its communication "genre repertoire"; Orlikowski & Yates, 1994), the more competent the organization (assuming related forms of knowledge to guide behavior and sufficient motivation to initiate and sustain communicative actions). In addition, an organization's behavioral competence may be reflected in the extent to which messages communicated via various media and representatives are consistent across one another (especially in times of crisis).

Cognitive studies. Jablin et al. (1994) suggest that communication knowledge at the organizational level of analysis is evident in resources such as organizational "knowledge bases" (Johnston & Carrico, 1988), "knowledge structures" (Walsh, 1995), organizational culture (e.g., Friedman, 1989; Sackmann, 1991), and mental maps and memories (Walsh & Ungson, 1991) and reflects "both the collective knowledge of groups and individuals within an organization and the strategies which guide the interpretation of situational and environmental cues" (p. 132). Moreover, Jablin et al. propose that it is these memories, embedded within communication processes such as an organization's "semantic networks" (Hutchins, 1991; Monge & Eisenberg, 1987), that allow an organization to "interpret as a system" (Daft & Weick, 1984, p. 285). Not surprisingly, there is a close overlap between the development of organization-level communication knowledge and organizational learning processes (see Miller, 1996; Raelin, 1997; Weick & Ashford, Chapter 18, this volume).

Organization-level communication knowledge also can be embedded within organizational routines, which represent ways of doing things (Winter, 1986) but do not necessarily represent activity that is performed in a mindless fashion; rather, organizational routines are continuously "worked at" in day-to-day conduct (Cohen & Bacdayan, 1994; Giddens, 1984). Along these lines, for example, Pentland and Rueter (1994) studied characteristics of supposedly nonroutine service interactions and discovered these interactions were "highly regular" in nature (when analyzed in terms of grammars of action—the normative rules and processes that set the possibilities for acting in the organization; see Pentland, 1995). More specifically, their research showed that organizational routines do not represent single patterns of action but "rather a set of possible patterns—enabled and constrained by a variety of organizational, social, physical, and cognitive structures—from which organizational members enact particular performances" (Pentland & Rueter, 1994, p. 491). In other words, similar to the ways in which knowledge of the grammar associated with a particular language allows one to construct innumerable sentences, organizational routines can be analyzed in terms of how they enable organizational members to enact a wide variety of communicative performances (and to improvise; e.g., Moorman & Miner, 1998).

To summarize, organization-level communication knowledge is embedded within organizational routines, procedures, policies, and values and in the collective knowledge of organizational members. Research exploring organization-level communication knowledge is still in its infancy, and we are just beginning to understand how organizations create and recreate their meaning systems so as to maximize their ability to interpret internal and external information, the consequences of their actions, and the like.

Underlying Assumptions in the Literature

Extant research reflects several underlying assumptions and problematic premises about organizational communication competence that we believe have hindered progress with respect to research in this area. This section provides a discussion of these issues, including some noted by Jablin et al. (1994), as well as others not considered in that review.

Discrete View of Competence

Although it is unlikely that most researchers believe communication competence is a dichotomous variable (i.e., that individuals can be classified as either competent or incompetent), with little variation between the two extremes, discussions of competence frequently present the construct in such terms. The heavy emphasis in the research literature on identifying communication skills associated with competent communicators, in part, accounts for the tendency to view competence as a discrete variable. More specifically, because researchers interested in developing skill inventories typically ask respondents to identify communication abilities associated with persons they perceive to be "competent" communicators, the issue of the "degree" to which one must evidence these qualities to be considered competent is not addressed; rather, it is assumed, by default, that if one does not possess the various skills, one is "incompetent." Relatedly, researchers often treat the various skills they associate with competence as if they are mutually exclusive of one another, whereas they may share considerable amounts of variance or be embedded within one another.

As evident from the above discussion, competence may be more fruitfully considered a continuous construct. Communicators should be viewed along a continuum as relatively more or less competent. Jablin et al. (1994) move toward this type of conceptualization with their distinctions between "threshold" and "proficient" levels of competence. Threshold competencies are "generic capabilities which are essential to performing jobs, but which are not sufficient to cause superior levels of effectiveness in communication" (Jablin et al., 1994, p. 120); they represent minimally required, role-related encoding and decoding capacities. Jablin et al. (1994, p. 120) argue that as a consequence of organizational selection, socialization, and training processes, most organizational newcomers are communicatively competent at the threshold level (although it must be recognized that what is considered threshold competence in one organization may be considered less than or more than the threshold level in another organization). Accordingly, although organizational newcomers may be considered competent, they are likely to be less competent communicators than veteran employees with several years tenure, who have developed proficient or above-threshold communication competencies (e.g., Jablin, 1994). Typically, those who are proficient communicators possess a "deep" versus "surface" level set of communication capabilities (e.g., they recognize messages that contain double meanings or require "reading between the lines" to understand), as well as a broader repertoire of communication resources to draw on in any given communication situation (e.g., they are capable of appropriately communicating a message via many available organizational media vs. a select few).

It is also important to recognize that it may not be appropriate to categorize a communicator as "incompetent" (relatively speaking) simply because she or he has not yet developed the capacities necessary to communicate competently in a particular environment. The absence of competence does not necessarily imply incompetence. Rather, it is possible for a communicator to be in a state of "precompetence," a notion that recognizes the person's potential for becoming competent (Langer & Parks, 1990). In other words, precompetence represents a temporary learning state in which the communicator is in the process of learning and developing the abilities necessary for competent organizational communication.

Competence as Static

In light of the preceding commentary, it is not surprising to discover that descriptions of organizational communication competence often fail to develop the dynamic, developmental nature of the construct; rather, competence is viewed in fairly static terms. On the whole, competence researchers have not adequately addressed the notion that levels of communication competence may change over time. For example, a newcomer who enters an organization with a threshold level of competence is likely to become increasingly more competent (or proficient) over time as he or she obtains more knowledge and skills (e.g., Jablin, 1994). However, competence levels also may *decrease* as communicators enter new situations (e.g., transfer jobs or move to different organizations) or experience the effects of broader societal developments (e.g., the proliferation of new computer-mediated communication technologies). Not only may a communicator's overall level of competence vary over time, but also the ways or strategies that she or he employs to achieve particular communicative goals. Consistent with the open-systems principle of equifinality (e.g., Katz & Kahn, 1978), communicators are capable of learning new ways to display their competence and perform their duties. Thus, a proficient communicator may not focus his or her efforts on determining the best communication strategy for any particular situation (a static orientation to competence), but rather focus on developing the capacity and knowledge to "enact several alternative strategies that might be equally appropriate for the situation" (Jablin et al. 1994, p. 124).

Extant research also tends to assume that once one learns a particular set of skills and abilities, one's level of competence with respect to those capabilities will remain constant over time. Although this may be true for some capabilities, especially those at the threshold level, it may not be true for other, more sophisticated forms of competence. In brief, research has focused on ways to develop communication competence (especially via skills training) and has neglected to consider how communicators can maintain their levels of competence over time. Clearly, the dynamic, processual nature of communication competence requires more attention in future research.

Assumption of Rationality

Consistent with most traditional approaches to organizational studies, research exploring organizational communication competence has tended to assume that organizational members think and behave rationally. However, as Jablin et al. (1994) caution, "in our conceptualizations of competence we need to recognize that people don't always use their communication capabilities in logical ways and that relationship history factors, motives, emotions, etc. can affect competence levels" (p. 123). For example, even though most managers are aware that punishment in the form of an angry reprimand of a subordinate in the presence of his or her coworkers is inappropriate (e.g., Cusella, 1987) and rarely solves any problems (if anything, it creates new problems), are there many managers who have not at one time or another acted in this manner?

It is also important to consider the notion of *mindless* versus mindful behavior when considering issues of competence (e.g.,

Langer, 1978). Research suggests that much behavior in organizations is guided by cognitive "scripts" (e.g., Gioia, 1986). These scripts are unconsciously triggered by situational cues that cause individuals to act automatically and without conscious thought ("mindlessly") in particular ways. These scripts are learned and developed over time, and their overuse may be an indication of "overcompetence." That is, an individual who finds herself frequently engaging mindlessly in behaviors may have surpassed the proficient level of competency and become overcompetent. At this point, such an individual is likely to have fallen into the "competency trap" (March, 1988) where overlearning undermines the potential for new learning. Although it may seem somewhat counter-rational, it may be necessary for communicators to periodically experience overcompetence to maintain, over the long run, consistently high levels of competence. In other words, occasional minor falls into the competency trap may jar communicators to reconsider how they are communicatively responding to what appear to be routine situations, thereby facilitating the development of new communication knowledge and abilities, and diminishing the likelihood of falling into a competency trap from which one cannot escape. Ultimately, as Jablin et al. (1994) have observed, the more proficient communicator "not only possesses a repertoire of scripted communication knowledge, but is also capable of knowing when to shift from mindless (script-guided) to mindful behavior (active consideration of multiple interpretations/meanings of the situation)" (p. 124).

Invariance in Motivation

"Applied to communication, motivation is what sets in motion our communicative efforts, directs us toward specific strategies, and impels us to continue" (Zorn, 1993, p. 517). On the whole, researchers have tended to assume that organizational members maintain fairly constant levels of motivation with respect to their desire to communicate and be perceived of as competent communicators. In other words, the assumption is that if someone has the ability to communicate competently, that person will want to do so in most situations. It is likely, however, that people differ in the extent to which they are motivated to display the communication behaviors they are able to perform (between-person variation). In addition, it is likely that across time and situations, any particular individual's motivation to communicate in a competent fashion may vary (within-person variation).

Although motivation is generally recognized as an important antecedent to performance, it has received little attention among scholars exploring organizational communication competence. In particular, Zorn (1993) points out that "the construct of motivation has largely been overshadowed by constructs such as ability, skill, and knowledge in the communication competence literature" (p. 517). Consistent with principles associated with goal-setting theory (e.g., Locke & Henne, 1986), Zorn (1993) maintains that goals have the greatest impact on motivation. Specifically, he proposes that the more difficult, specific, and highly valued the goal, the more motivated an individual will be to communicate. Thus, for a competent person to be motivated to communicate, he or she must be motivated to do so in pursuit of a desired goal. Zorn (1993) recognizes that while some communicative goals are often below the conscious awareness level of interactants, given the purposive nature of organizations, "individuals are consciously aware of at least *some* of their communicative goals" (p. 541). In addition, he also supports O'Keefe's (1988, p. 82) argument that while communicative goals are not necessarily as clear and consciously recognized as other kinds of goals (e.g., performance goals), they often "are socially constituted objectives that are implicit in the predefined activities of human cultures." Similarly, Kellermann, Reynolds, and Chen (1991) emphasize the importance of "metagoals" in motivation to communicate. According to metagoal theory, an individual may have a va-

riety of goals motivating him or her to communicate (e.g., information seeking, comforting). The goals, however, are constrained by metagoals such as efficiency and appropriateness. Thus, for instance, one may be motivated to perform particular communication behaviors to comfort another person *if* the behavior can be performed in an appropriate (i.e., polite) and efficient (i.e., "without expending unnecessary time, energy, or resources"; Kellermann et al., 1991, p. 364) manner.

The notion of self-efficacy is also important to consider when assessing an individual's motivation to communicate. Self-efficacy is "concerned with people's beliefs in their capabilities to mobilize the motivation, cognitive resources, and courses of action needed to exercise control over task demands" (Bandura, 1990, p. 316). We already have noted that communication competence primarily has been studied as a cognitive and/or behavioral construct. The notions of motivation and self-efficacy provide an important link between the two. That is, when individuals know what to do, whether or not they enact a communicative behavior depends in large part on their belief that they are able to enact the behavior successfully (Spitzberg & Cupach, 1984, p. 158). Thus, a person may possess the knowledge and skills necessary to communicate competently, yet because of a low level of self-efficacy in a particular task setting, he or she may not be motivated to enact the behaviors (or persevere with the behaviors in the face of obstacles that arise as a consequence of the initial display of the behaviors). In other words, the less individuals perceive they are able to communicate competently with respect to a particular task (i.e., "felt" competence), the less they are motivated to communicate (Zorn, 1993, p. 542).

In sum, rather than assuming within-individual and between-individuals levels of motivation to communicate are relatively constant, we need to recognize that motivation fluctuates and may differentially affect individuals' levels of organizational communication competence. In addition, we need to consider the extent to which conscious and unconscious communicative goals (and metagoals; see Kellermann et al., 1991), as well as individuals' beliefs of self-efficacy with respect to communicative tasks (regardless of the accuracy of those beliefs), are associated with displays and perceptions of organizational communication competence. Also, research should explore how the labels that coworkers and others in the task setting use to describe a person's ability (such as classifying a person as "incompetent" with respect to a particular communicative task) may affect the individual's self-efficacy, motivation to communicate, access to important forms of organizational discourse and knowledge, and quality of communicative performance. As Bandura (1990) noted in discussing the notion of competence in general, "Research shows that when people are cast in subordinate roles or assigned inferior labels, implying limited competence, they perform activities at which they are highly skilled less well than when they do not bear the negative labels" (p. 324).

Assumption of Objectivity

Many, although certainly not all, discussions of organizational communication competence treat competence as though it was an "objective" construct. This is unfortunate, because

> competence and incompetence represent labeling phenomena. They cannot be understood as entities in themselves, apart from the people who ascribe them. Although certain kinds of performance can be measured objectively, competence cannot be, because competence is not itself an objective phenomenon. What is competence in one culture may be incompetence in another, and not only levels but even dimensions of performance may differ across cultures in terms of the extent to which they are viewed as relevant for judging competence. (Sternberg, 1990, p. 144)

Thus, it is essential that research exploring competence recognizes it as an attributional

rather than objective phenomenon. That is, we make attributions regarding an individual's level of competence by comparing him or her (generally and with respect to particular communicative performances) to others, and the standards by which we make such comparisons vary across individuals, groups, organizations, and cultures.

Along these lines, Jablin et al. (1994) point out that values play an important role in perceptions of communication competence, and such values differ across organizations. As they explain, "The deep-structure values of the organization inform members of the capabilities they need to possess, beyond the threshold level, in order to be optimal communicators in the organization" (p. 121). Because value structures differ across organizations, what is perceived as competent communication (especially above the threshold level) may differ across organizations and should be explicitly considered in studies exploring competence (e.g., Zorn & Violanti, 1996).

Ideological Assumptions Ignored

Although rarely discussed, conceptualizations of organizational communication competence reflect varying underlying organizational and disciplinary ideologies. As Spitzberg and Duran (1993) observe, "The criteria and content of competence theories have consistently reflected ideological undercurrents, which reveal themselves in terms of cultural, cocultural, and contextual variations" (p. 1). In other words, theories of organizational communication competence are not "neutral" in nature, but privilege certain qualities of communication over others (Baron & Clair, 1996). For example, in many organizations "masculine" approaches and models of communication (e.g., a competent communicator controls the expression of emotions) are privileged over more "feminine" ones (e.g., in which the expression of emotions is considered appropriate). Thus, "the socio-historical context in which competence research has been conducted has determined the specific constituents of competence. These constituents often reflect ideological preferences" (Spitzberg & Duran, 1993, p. 7).

In addition, the fact that most theories of competence assume that competent communicators not only have the requisite skills to communicate but must also possess knowledge of appropriate ways of communicating to achieve goals suggests a connection between understanding the discursive practices of organizations and of obtaining power in organizations. Moreover, the notion that there are "appropriate" versus "inappropriate" ways of communicating in organizations may stifle the creativity of organizational members and serve to reinforce "the status quo, conformity, and the maintenance of the extant social order" (Spitzberg & Duran, 1993, p. 11).

Finally, it is also important for us to recognize the ideological baggage we have assumed by borrowing competence concepts and related research methodologies from other fields such as psychology, sociology, and management. Even notions associated with communication competence extrapolated from the study of interpersonal communication competence in nonorganizational settings may be problematic when applied to the organizational setting (e.g., the extent to which openness in communication should be valued; see Eisenberg & Witten, 1987). In brief, as Redding (1979, p. 321) cautioned, organizational communication scholars need to be aware that when we "import" concepts from other disciplines, we also import ideologies that may constrain our understanding of various communication phenomena, including the notion of communication competence.

Ethical Issues Overlooked

Generally speaking, competence research has failed to consider the relationship between communication competence and standards of ethical communication. For example, while researchers often conceptualize communication competence as the successful attainment of communicative goals (e.g., Monge et al., 1981; Parks, 1994), they less frequently con-

sider the questions: Do the ends justify the means? Should "truth" be the central criterion for determining standards of ethical communication (e.g., Habermas, 1970)? It is not difficult, for instance, to imagine a situation in which lying enhances one's ability to successfully achieve a goal, perhaps the goal of presenting a particular image (i.e., impression management; see Giacalone & Rosenfeld, 1991; Wexley, 1986). Thus, although goal attainment may indicate communication competence, as Jablin et al. (1994) argue, "as scholars we are obligated to consider the issue of whether or not a competent communicator is an ethical communicator" (p. 122).

Ethical issues are not only relevant considerations at the individual level of analysis but are also important at higher-order levels of analysis. For example, organizations that are highly institutionalized in nature often seek to communicate to their relevant external audiences/stakeholders that they use "legitimate" practices (e.g., Meyer & Rowan, 1977). However, the practices perceived as legitimate by an organization's external audiences may not always be the most practical or efficient for the organization. Accordingly, in communicating with their environments, "competent" organizations may "decouple" their internal practices from what they present to their external audiences (e.g., in information provided in annual reports and in related financial and accounting reports). Are such practices deceptive or merely signs of competent organizational communication? How important should honesty and ethics be in classifying an organization as (relatively speaking) communicatively competent?

Focus on the Individual
Level of Analysis

To date, most research exploring organizational communication competence has focused on competence at the individual/person level of analysis. However, as Jablin et al. (1994) explain, "workgroups and organizations as entities can be described in terms of their communication competence" (p. 119). Importantly, they also suggest that group and organizational competence each represents more than the aggregate competence of its constituent parts (i.e., individuals and groups). Thus, as reviewed earlier in this chapter, group competence may be evident in the mechanisms the group uses for processing information, the specialized languages and codes used for encoding and decoding messages, rituals for assimilating newcomers into communication networks, and so forth. At the same time, however, it is important to recognize that communication competence at any particular level of analysis influences, and is influenced by, competence at the other levels of analysis. In studying organizational communication competence, we need to explore the embeddedness of the various levels of competence within and between one another, and the degree to which the various levels mutually influence each other.

Perceptions of *individual* communication competence, for instance, are influenced by the behaviors valued and rewarded by the *organization*. At the same time, the types of behaviors valued by the organization are likely to be influenced by the communicative behavior of individuals. Similarly, *group* effectiveness is influenced by the knowledge and abilities of *individual* group members, as well as *organizational* factors such as reward and support systems (Hirokawa & Keyton, 1995). Concomitantly, group effectiveness exerts influence on attributes of individual and organizational communication competence. For example, being a member of a successful work group may influence the self-efficacy of an individual group member, providing that individual with more motivation to communicate in a competent manner.

In sum, we believe researchers studying organizational communication competence need to consider competence as a multiple-level construct, recognize that the various levels of competence are embedded within one another, and as a consequence, examine how the levels mutually influence each other with respect to what competence means.

AN ECOLOGICAL MODEL OF ORGANIZATIONAL COMMUNICATION COMPETENCE

In light of the limitations we have highlighted with respect to research exploring competence, we present an alternative model of organizational communication competence in this section. This model, which incorporates an ecological perspective (e.g., Bronfenbrenner, 1979; Johnson, Staton, & Jorgensen-Earp, 1995; Magnusson, 1995), proposes that human/group/organization development is best viewed as a product of the dynamic interaction of the environment and developing person/group/organization. That is, the development of communication competence (at the individual, group, or organizational level of analysis) is influenced by, and influences, the environment (and the various ecological systems that make up the environment) in which the process occurs. Accordingly, organizational communication competence may be profitably investigated by considering the influences of the environment or ecological systems in which the individual, group, or organization is embedded.

In particular, the model presented in Figure 20.1 conceptualizes organizational communication competence along three dimensions: competence assessment criteria, competence levels, and ecological systems. Such a conceptualization acknowledges the cognitive and behavioral components of communication competence, the developmental nature of communication competence, and the embeddedness of communication competence at various levels of analysis.

Communication Competence Indicators and Assessment Criteria

As suggested in the preceding sections, communication competence is generally conceptualized in terms of cognition (knowledge of communication rules, symbols, cognitive

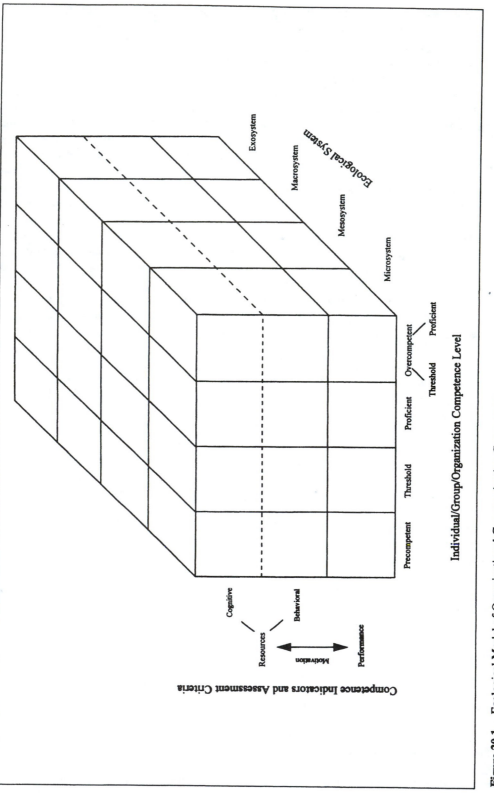

Figure 20.1. Ecological Model of Organizational Communication Competence

complexity, etc.), behavior/skill repertoire, and performance (actual display of communicative behavior upon which attributions of an entity's communication knowledge and skills are primarily based). In essence, the former two competence elements (which when considered together comprise the communication resources available to a communicator; see Jablin et al., 1994) represent the criteria used to evaluate communicative performance. As a consequence, one dimension of our model (the vertical dimension in Figure 20.1) focuses on organizational communication competence assessment criteria. Although these components can be conceptualized as representing distinct criteria, they are not necessarily mutually exclusive of one another; for example, judgments of a person's communication skills may be interrelated with judgments of the person's communicative knowledge.

In addition to communication resources, we include motivation to communicate as an assessment criterion, because it serves as a force linking the use of communicative resources with the actual performance of communicative behavior. In other words, the model reflects the possibility that communicators may have the necessary knowledge and skills to communicate competently, but may not always be motivated to do so. Thus, it is possible that even though a person may have performed inadequately, she or he may not be judged by others as communicatively incompetent (relatively speaking) unless the person is also judged to have expended a reasonable amount of effort in the communication process. The inclusion of motivation in our model also takes into consideration the possibility that a communicator may be perceived as possessing the necessary communication resources to perform competently, but does not do so because of low self-confidence/self-efficacy with respect to his or her capabilities (i.e., low "felt" competence). Finally, the reciprocal arrow linking resources and performance also recognizes that performance can affect resources; that is, how individuals perform certain communicative behaviors affects their motivation to enact the behaviors in the future and their willingness to learn new behaviors, thus increasing their resources.

Levels of Competence

As noted in the preceding section, communication competence is best represented as a continuum where communicators are relatively more or less competent. The horizontal dimension of our model presents varying levels of communication competence. As discussed earlier, in a move toward such a conceptualization, Jablin et al. (1994) offered the notions of *threshold* competence (e.g., "generic capabilities which are essential to performing jobs, but which are not sufficient to cause superior levels of effectiveness in communication"; p. 120) and *proficiency* (e.g., above-average or above-threshold communication knowledge and abilities). To these levels of competence, our model adds two additional levels: (1) precompetence and (2) overcompetence. *Precompetence* represents a temporary learning state where an individual obtains knowledge and develops the capabilities necessary to be a competent communicator. *Overcompetence* represents the state where an individual's communicative behavior in the organization is guided largely by cognitive scripts; that is, the person engages in communicative behavior in a largely "mindless," unconscious manner such that the individual is unable to recognize and process unique cues available in the task setting that should be considered in directing his or her communicative behavior. We further distinguish between threshold and proficient levels of overcompetence. Thus, just as an entity at the threshold level can engage in (essential) communicative behavior in a scripted, relatively mindless fashion, a communicator who is proficient and overcompetent can mindlessly perform communication behaviors, although these behaviors will be associated with superior as compared to essential communication effectiveness.

We therefore conceptualize communication competence as a continuum ranging from precompetence to overcompetence. Two issues are important to consider, however. First, we reemphasize here the notion that attributions or perceptions of competence are *relative,* not objective. That is, a communicator in a particular organization is perceived as relatively more or less competent compared to salient others (e.g., other employees in the same organization or work group), not compared to some objective "ideal" communicator (although attributions may, in part, be based on perceptions of prototypic or "average" communication competence in particular settings; e.g., Pavitt & Haight, 1986). Second, competence is a *local,* rather than global phenomenon; that is, one's level of communication competence likely varies across domains. For example, one may perform some communicative behaviors with little thought (e.g., is overcompetent when communicating with a customer), yet engage in other behaviors in a very *mindful* and proficient fashion (e.g., communicating with a supervisor about a work-related problem).

A developmental conceptualization of communication competence highlights the importance of two concepts: change and time (e.g., Magnusson, 1995). As mentioned earlier, levels of communication competence change as individuals (or groups or organizations) obtain knowledge and develop new abilities. Further, such change can be progressive or regressive. That is, competence does not always increase, but can decrease for a variety of reasons. Such change is also not likely to be a linear developmental process. One does not necessarily go from precompetence to threshold, proficient, and overcompetent levels in that order. Some communicators, for example, may never reach a proficient level of competence; rather, they vacillate between precompetent and threshold levels. On the other hand, one may be a proficient communicator and regress toward threshold or even precompetent levels.

As Magnusson (1995) notes, "Development always has a temporal dimension" (p.

20). Accordingly, the notion of time is important to consider. For instance, it is likely that changes in communication competency levels occur at different rates for different individuals, groups, and organizations. While some entities develop proficient communication competencies quickly, others may develop their competencies at a slower pace. Consistent with this notion, Alwin (1995) argues that an ecological perspective recognizes that "each individual is unique and that one aspect of this uniqueness is the heterogeneity of experience with the environment" (p. 220). Thus, individuals (and groups and organizations) in similar ecological systems are likely to be affected by those systems in unique ways, resulting in developmental variation between individuals (or groups or organizations).

Ecological Systems

The ecological perspective emphasizes the notion that "both individuals and environments change and interact as totalities [and] . . . changes do not take place in single aspects isolated from the totality" (Magnusson, 1995, p. 39). Consistent with this view, we suggest that the development of communication competence (progressive, maintenance, or regressive trajectories) and the rate at which such development occurs over time are likely to be influenced by individual, group, organizational, and sociocultural factors. In particular, our ecological model of organizational communication competence revolves around four systems represented along the depth dimension (z-axis) of Figure 20.1: (1) the microsystem, which contains the developing organizational member and other persons in the immediate work environment (e.g., supervisors, coworkers, and clients); (2) the mesosystem, which represents the interrelations among various microsystems (e.g., what individuals learn in their project teams may affect their competence in the functional work groups in which they are members); (3) the macrosystem, which does not represent the immediate context in which an individual works, but does impinge on him or her (i.e., major divisions of the organization and the organization itself as a whole); and (4) the exosystem, which represents the overarching cultural belief system, forms of knowledge, social, technological, and political ideologies, and so forth that manifest themselves in the form and content of the other subsystems (e.g., sex role stereotypes that are derived from societal beliefs but may be reflected in the other systems).[2]

In brief, an ecological perspective emphasizes system embeddedness. That is, the actions of one element of the system affect the other elements. Such impact is not unidirectional, however. Rather, our model highlights the notion of reciprocal influence (e.g., Bronfenbrenner, 1979). This notion acknowledges that each element in the total system is an active, not passive, participant in the overall functioning of that system. Accordingly, the various system levels influence, and at the same time are influenced by, each other (Friedman & Wachs, 1999; Moen, Elder, & Luscher, 1995).

In the following sections, we discuss characteristics of each ecological system and consider the potential influence of these systems on communication competence at individual, group, and organizational levels of analysis. In the interests of clarity, each section considers the influence of each ecological system on communication competence in relative isolation of the other systems. An example is then provided at the end of each section to illustrate the notions of mutual influence and the embeddedness of the levels of analysis discussed above. Many of our examples are speculative in nature and are designed merely to elucidate our developmental-ecological approach, and the ways in which the approach can be used to study communication competence. We begin by discussing the highest-order ecological system, the exosystem. We do this not to demonstrate higher-order determinism, but because it enables us to more clearly explain the characteristics of the model.

The Exosystem

The exosystem represents the overarching belief systems; forms of knowledge; and social, technological, and economic systems and trends as well as political ideologies of the larger society in which individuals, groups, and organizations exist. For the sake of brevity in discussing the exosystem, we consider only two recent trends in society that have important implications for communication competence in organizations. These trends, which have been highlighted throughout this volume, are the move toward a global economy and the rapid growth of information/communication technology.

Globalization

Industry is becoming increasingly global with more organizations doing business in other countries. As Eisenberg and Goodall (1993) point out, "About one-third of the profits of U.S. companies, as well as one-sixth of the nation's jobs, come from international business [Cascio, 1986; Offerman & Gowing, 1990]" (p. 9).

The move toward globalization carries a variety of expectations regarding what constitutes competent communication at the individual, group, and organizational levels of analysis. In general, a communicator "becomes interculturally competent when messages may be encoded and directed as if from within the new culture and when messages from the new culture may be decoded and responded to successfully" (Beamer, 1992). More specifically, to communicate competently in a global marketplace, individuals typically need adequate knowledge regarding the values, symbol systems, beliefs, and communication norms of cultures other than one's dominant culture, as well as knowledge about the economic situations of other countries (e.g., Adler & Bartholomew, 1992; Collier, 1994; Hogan & Goodson, 1990; Stohl, Chapter 10, this volume; Triandis, 1973; Triandis & Albert, 1987). Communication competence may also be enhanced if an individual is relatively high in tolerance for ambiguity, appreciates diversity, is capable of establishing relationships with those from other cultures, and has the ability to speak languages other than his or her native one (e.g., Barna, 1991; Hammer, 1987; Nishida, 1985; Ruben, 1977; Zimmermann, 1995). Other individual abilities often associated with intercultural communication competence include knowledge of ways to display respect in different cultures, empathy, flexibility, willingness to suspend judgment of others, and culture-specific knowledge of problem-solving methods and ways of managing interactions (e.g., Dinges & Lieberman, 1989; Koester, 1985; Koester & Olebe, 1988; Ruben & Kealey, 1979; Sell, 1983; Sriussadaporn-Charoenngam & Jablin, 1999).

Individuals who have never worked in a global context are likely to enter a new position in a precompetent state. This is often the case, for example, with newly expatriated employees in multinational organizations (e.g., Black, Gregersen, & Mendenhall, 1992; Wiseman & Shuter, 1994). Prior to leaving for an overseas assignment, these individuals are often provided with training covering topics such as language skills and overviews of cultural norms in the country to which they are dispatched. Presumably, once trained (though language skills may still require development), the expatriate employees are able to begin their new assignments with a threshold level of competence (e.g., basic encoding and decoding abilities appropriate to the new culture). Successful expatriate employees develop proficient levels of communication competence over time. Ratiu (1983), for instance, indicates that the most effective expatriate managers, whom he labels "internationals," demonstrate cognitive traits that go beyond the broad-based concepts of tolerance for ambiguity, flexibility, empathy, and knowledge of overall cultural communication norms. Rather, in communicating with others, internationals do not rely on overall cultural stereotypes but attempt to approach others as individuals and adjust to them accordingly.

The move toward globalization also has important implications for communication competence at the group level. Groups and teams in organizations are becoming more culturally diverse (e.g., Stohl, Chapter 10, this volume; Wiseman & Shuter, 1994). In light of the fact that national cultures vary among one another with respect to which they value "groupness" (as reflected in the cultural value of individualism-collectivism; see Hofstede, 1981), at a very basic level the move toward globalization and more culturally heterogeneous work groups creates new challenges for group process. For example, Americans, who tend to be individualistic, logical, and technical in decision making, and the Japanese, who tend to be more social/group oriented in decision making (Stewart, 1985), may experience difficulties when working together in teams. Other problems culturally diverse groups/teams face include differential conversational norms, expectations about work, face-saving practices, meanings associated with the physical workspace the group occupies, ways of managing conflict, language capabilities, and the like (e.g., Bantz, 1993; Stohl, this volume). Under these conditions, one path to competence may be reflected in the notions of "third culture" or "culturally synergistic" groups (Adler, 1980; Casmir, 1993; Moran & Harris, 1981; Stohl, this volume), in which group members enact communication systems that transcend the characteristics of any particular culture.

Levels of communication competence in culturally diverse work groups also may change over time. Milliken and Martins (1996), for instance, note that cultural diversity tends to decrease group effectiveness at the early stages of the group's life. As they explain, this is "presumably because it takes some time for group members to get over their interpersonal differences on observable dimensions that tend to be associated with lower levels of initial attraction and social integration [O'Reilly, Caldwell, & Barnett, 1989]" (Milliken & Martins, 1996, p. 407). Research indicates that after this early stage group performance can be enhanced by diversity, particularly in terms of the group's ability to generate a variety of perspectives and ideas (Milliken & Martins, 1996). The development of group-level *communication* competence may parallel that of overall group competence. That is, group communication competence may lie at a fairly low, perhaps precompetent, level early on. As group members gain knowledge, particularly knowledge regarding how to communicate with the other members (which should develop as a by-product of working together), group-level communication competence is likely to increase to threshold or proficient levels.

Competence at the organizational level also is influenced by globalization. To succeed in a global marketplace, organizations must display a variety of capabilities. An organization must have knowledge about the global aspects of its particular industry, as well as knowledge of the cultures and communication norms and practices of the host countries in which it operates. An organization may also need to understand the communication implications of related issues, such as each country's political and ideological system, labor regulations, tax policies, and energy and safety regulations, to communicate in a competent manner (Teboul, Chen, & Fritz, 1994). Globalization and increased diversity also require that organizations prepare their employees for communication in a global world. Accordingly, competent organizations might include a commitment to diversity in their mission statements and provide instructional seminars for members on topics such as intercultural communication, diversity, and the global marketplace (Cox & Blake, 1991).

In addition, competent organizations need the resources to communicate on a global scale with their various constituents. Accordingly, competent organizations must have access to and the ability to use a wide variety of communication media and telecommunication systems, fax systems, the Internet and electronic mail, formal and informal interorganizational communication networks, and the like (e.g., Kovacic, 1994, p. 11). Such systems can serve as mechanisms through which global organizations can communicate messages to foster a common identity and vision (which when internalized can unobtrusively guide communication behavior) among its geographically disparate members (see Cheney & Christensen, Chapter 7, this volume). These resources also provide organizations with a skill identified by King and Cushman (1994) as vital for organization-level communication competence in today's global society: high-speed management. In particular, King and Cushman suggest that for organizations to communicate effectively in a global economic environment, they must not only communicate appropriately but also quickly. These communication methods and media can also help the multinational organization manage one of its greatest challenges: coordination and control (e.g., Adler, 1980). Along these lines, a wide variety of organizational structures and forms have been developed to allow global organizations to coordinate their efforts. Because each organizational structure has rather unique communication values, patterns, policies, and properties associated with it, each structure fosters the development of distinctive kinds of organization-level communication knowledge and capability (e.g., Triandis & Albert, 1987).

While many organizations now operate facilities or conduct business across the globe, in recent years some firms have taken globalization one step further: They have established partnerships with organizations in other countries for the purpose of working together to found and operate new organizations (see McPhee & Poole, Chapter 13, this volume). Such arrangements (e.g., a multi-billion-dollar partnership between a German manufacturer and an American manufacturer of semiconductors) represent enormous challenges, since communication competence criteria associated with distinctive national as well as organizational cultures may clash and require reconciliation. In brief, it is apparent that the move toward globalization has important implications for the nature of communication competence at the individual, group, and organizational levels of analysis.

Technology

Another societal trend relevant to organizational communication competence, and related to the move toward a global economy, is a greater reliance on computer-mediated communication technology. By all accounts, we currently are living in the information age (see Fulk & Collins-Jarvis, Chapter 17, and Rice & Gattiker, Chapter 14, this volume). Recent technological advances such as the Internet and the World Wide Web provide access to more information than ever before.

Cetron, Rocha, and Luchins (1988) predicted that by the year 2000 approximately one half of all service jobs will involve collecting, analyzing, synthesizing, structuring, or retrieving information; five of the ten fastest-growing careers will be computer-related; and the typical large business will be "information-based" (Andrews & Herschel, 1996). In short, communication competence in the information age requires an understanding of and ability to use computer-mediated communication systems to send and receive messages and to obtain, process, and interpret information at all levels in an organization.

In the information age, individual communication competence requires that individuals possess a variety of relevant capabilities. Szajna (1994), for instance, suggests that "computer aptitude" (defined as the aptitude for accomplishing computer-related tasks other than programming, such as word processing, spreadsheets, and data tasks) consists of the following abilities: (1) logical reasoning, (2) alphabetic and numeric sequencing, (3) alphanumeric translation, (4) general quantitative abilities, and (5) visiospatial abilities (p. 928). Certain affective-cognitive characteristics also may enhance an individual's communication competence in the computer age. For example, individuals who report high levels of "computer anxiety" (generally defined as a fear of using computers) tend to avoid using computer-mediated communication systems. Thus, high levels of computer anxiety are likely to diminish individual communication competence. In particular, computer anxiety may affect an individual's motivation to communicate. Individuals high in computer anxiety tend to perceive themselves as being unable to use computers (i.e., low self-efficacy) (Kernan & Howard, 1990). Computer anxiety, therefore, may reduce motivation to communicate via computer, thus moderating the relationship between communication capabilities and actual performance.

Previous research also indicates that competence in computer-mediated communication is something that one develops over time. Results from studies consistently demonstrate, for instance, that computer anxiety decreases significantly as one gains experience using computers (e.g., Kernan & Howard, 1990; Szajna, 1994). Individuals high in computer anxiety, therefore, are likely to be precompetent (rather than incompetent) with respect to using computer-mediated communication technology. With more experience with the technology, they may increase their computer aptitude to threshold or proficient levels of competence. If most urban Americans are computer literate within the next decade, then within a few years employees are likely to enter organizations with at least threshold levels of computer-related communication competence. Thus, those who are considered proficient communicators will most likely have the ability to effectively use a variety of communication media and communication-related computer software and have the ability to choose the media and/or software appropriate to any particular situation.

Information technology also has important implications for group-level communication competence. As mentioned earlier, many groups are able to improve their overall performance by using group communication technology such as GSSs. Accordingly, group-level competence in today's business climate may be increased by having access to various forms of "groupware" (group communication software that allows for multiple users to simultaneously access and work in the same database; e.g., Wohlert, 1995). In addition, group-level communication competence may be enhanced if members understand how these systems affect group processes, and in particular, structuring and decision-making activities (e.g., Poole & DeSanctis, 1990), and develop ways to access group knowledge stored within the system itself.

As organizations increase their global operations, many of their constituent work groups and teams will be composed of members who rarely communicate in a face-to-face manner. For example, among software engineers and programmers it is not uncommon today for group members to be located in different countries around the world, for work to be conducted on a project 24 hours a day (one advantage of the use of global work groups), and for participants to communicate with one another via modem using asynchronous computer-mediated message systems. While these systems present challenges to work group effectiveness (e.g., Walther, 1995), related group processes, structures, practices, rules, and so forth that allow such groups to achieve their goals represent communication-related resources associated with competence.

At both the group and organizational levels of analysis the use of the new media can also facilitate the development of a wide array of unique group and organizational communication networks (Finholt & Sproull, 1990). These networks are important in that they not only allow for messages to be exchanged among network participants but also because each network represents a distinctive semantic knowledge structure that may augment a group's and/or organization's communication competence and power (e.g., Monge & Eisenberg, 1987).

Group and organizational communication competence may also be affected by the extent to which a "critical mass" of members use available communication technologies (Markus, 1987). Extrapolating from "critical mass theory," it is likely that groups using particular communication technologies such as groupware cannot exceed the threshold level of competence until a sufficient number (a critical mass) of members have access to and use the system. In turn, it is possible that a group's communication competence may be negatively affected by overuse/saturation of its mediated communication systems, since overuse may result in a state of overload, thereby inhibiting the group's ability to process information (Wohlert, 1995).

To be competent in the information age, organizations also must have knowledge regarding communication technology relevant to their particular industry. Because information technology changes at a very fast rate, organizations must be able to keep up with technological innovations and understand their organizational and human resources consequences (e.g., Beer, Spector, Lawrence, Mills, & Walton, 1985). It may be the ability to constantly update or reinvent these knowledge bases (and the interpretive systems associated with them; e.g., Griffith, 1999) that increases an organization's competence level from threshold to proficient. An organization's communication competence is also associated with its use of various kinds of computerized internal and external communication systems including Internet access, Web pages, electronic bulletin boards, and mail systems. Large organizations may even create departments ("information technology" or "network support") and positions ("chief information officer") to organize, implement, and maintain the organization's computer-mediated communication and information systems. While the creation of such units and positions centralizes knowledge and capabilities with respect to the use of organizational computer-mediated communication systems, centralization of these resources may also affect the "balance of power" among departments, and as a consequence the character of their communication relationships (e.g., Frost, 1987; Hickson, Hinings, Lee, Schneck, & Pennings, 1971).

Level Embeddedness

Individuals, groups, and organizations do not exist in isolation of each other. Rather, they affect one another in a variety of ways; hence, communication competence at any one level of analysis has an impact on communication competence at the other levels. We mentioned above, for example, that organization-level communication competence in a global economy requires the ability to develop global communication networks. One way to develop such networks is by assigning employees to overseas organizational branches (e.g., expatriate managers). Accordingly, to increase its level of communication competence, a multinational organization may dispatch an employee to an overseas branch in an attempt to enhance the quality of its global communication networks (e.g., Black et al., 1992). The expatriate employee may have problems adjusting to the new culture, however. In fact, adjustment problems are fairly common. Research indicates that approximately 40% of expatriate managers return to the United States before completing their overseas assignment (Hogan & Goodson, 1990). A common reason for the failure of expatriates to successfully adjust to overseas assignments is the failure of the employee and his or her family members to positively adjust to the new culture (e.g., Hogan & Goodson, 1990; Thornburg, 1990). Many organizations (approximately 65%) do not provide any predeparture cultural training for their expatriate employees (Hogan & Goodson, 1990; Tung, 1988). Moreover, most organizations do not help prepare the expatriate's family members for the new culture (Stohl, 1995). Simply put, the employee and his or her family members may lack the threshold communication competencies (e.g., knowledge about the other culture, ability to speak the language of the host culture) necessary for successful adjustment to the new culture. Consequently, the employee fails to complete the assignment, decreasing the organization's overall level of communication competence. This example highlights the role of the individual as an active participant in the functioning of the overall organizational system (i.e., the reciprocal influence of the individual and the organization). In particular, this example demonstrates how communication competence at the organizational level may be impaired by the communication competence of an individual employee and the employee's immediate family members.

An example also helps illustrate the notion of embeddedness with respect to the societal trend toward reliance on communication technology. In the preceding section, we suggested that a group's level of communication competence may be closely associated with its use of various forms of group communication technology, such as group decision support systems. We also noted that some individuals experience high levels of computer anxiety. The successful implementation of group communication technology requires, at a minimum, that most group members use the technology. If several group members experience computer anxiety, they are less likely to use the technology, hampering the ability of the group to use the software effectively (insufficient critical mass). Consequently, it is evident that low levels of communication competence at the individual level can impair the development of threshold communication competence at the group level.

The Macrosystem

Included in the macrosystem are elements of the overall system that do not directly contain the individual or immediate work group but that impinge on those entities. Thus, the macrosystem includes major divisions of the organization and the organization as a whole. Consistent with this conceptualization, our discussion below considers the potential impact of a variety of organizational forms and their related managerial philosophies (especially their beliefs and assumptions about people) on communication competence at the individual, group, and organizational levels of analysis.

Organizational Forms and Managerial Philosophies

Organizations, and major organizational divisions, often differ significantly among one another with respect to their forms and managerial philosophies. Although a number of schemes have been proposed to classify organization forms (see McPhee & Poole, this volume) and managerial philosophies (e.g., Barley & Kunda, 1992), these classification systems tend to examine issues related to organizational forms and managerial philosophies in relative isolation of one another. Miles and Creed (1995), in contrast, have developed a configurational approach to organizational analysis that classifies organizations in terms of both form and managerial philosophy (in part based on the argument that certain philosophies are more supportive of particular organizational forms than other ones). In the discussion that follows, we have adopted their model and classification scheme since "it creates bridges across traditional micro and macro concepts and theories" (p. 133), consistent with our orientation to the study of communication competence. Below we consider relationships between communication competence at various levels of analysis and in terms of three of the four organizational form/managerial philosophy configurations identified by Miles and Creed (1995): (1) the centralized/traditional organization, (2) the functional/human relations organization, and (3) the divisional (and matrix)/human resources organization. Due to space limitations and its still evolving character, we do not discuss the fourth configuration proposed by Miles and Creed, the network/human investment organization (e.g., Powell, 1990; Snow, Miles, & Coleman, 1992; see also McPhee & Poole, Chapter 13, and Monge & Contractor, Chapter 12, this volume). Finally, we wish to emphasize that our focus on these particular form/philosophy configurations does not reflect a belief that other configurations do not exist (there are many hybrid configurations). Rather, our concern is with suggesting possible relationships between characteristics of communication competence and organizational forms/philosophies; as a consequence, the particular configurations we discuss and the hypothetical examples we offer should be viewed as only a means to achieve that end.

Centralized/traditional. The centralized/traditional organization is one in which control is centralized at the top of the hierarchy, employees are expected to adhere to formal rules and regulations, and close supervision of employees is the norm. Large and well-established organizations in stable environments typify the centralized form (Andrews & Herschel, 1996; Miles & Creed, 1995). According to Miles and Creed (1995), centralized organizations are usually managed according to traditional philosophies and, in particular, are guided by variations of the principles of bureaucracy (e.g., Weber, 1947) and scientific management (e.g., Taylor, 1911), which emphasize order and authority. As Miles and Creed (1995) observe, the traditional philosophy assumes that "managers and workers [are] cut from a different cloth" (p. 338). In particular, workers are seen to have limited capability (thus the need for close supervision) and to be motivated primarily by extrinsic rewards. Because of the assumed stability of the external environment, adaptability to external environmental turbulence or change is not emphasized. Communication in centralized/traditional organizations tends to be downward, formal, and written, mainly used for the dissemination of policies, rules, and instructions. Given the above characteristics, the types of resources required for communication competence in a centralized/traditional organization are likely somewhat distinct from those required in other organizational forms.

At the individual level of analysis, communication competence resources include knowledge of the organization's rules and regulations governing communication. Managers in centralized organizations must be aware of the requirements of their own tasks, as well as the requirements of their subordinates' tasks. Individual skills required for managerial competence revolve around the ability to give instructions and orders, and monitor compliance to communication policies. On the other hand, workers need knowledge of the requirements of their jobs and of appropriate (usually formal) ways of communicating in the organization (Morand, 1995). Because individual staff members are typically supervised closely and upward communication is not encouraged, in this configuration the primary abilities necessary for communication competence are related to the decoding of messages, and in particular "discriminative" listening (listening to acquire information for future use) and "evaluative" listening (listening to assess arguments and evidence; e.g., Wolff, Marsnik, Tacey, & Nichols, 1983). We hypothesize that because of the routineness of their communication environments and the limited use of their overall competencies, individuals in centralized/traditional organizations may easily become overcompetent with respect to their threshold communication capabilities.

In general, the communication competencies required at the group level in centralized/traditional organizations will be fairly restricted as well. At most, employees belong to functional groups and departments, whose efforts are coordinated through scheduled (planned) forms of communication (e.g., Hage, Aiken, & Marrett, 1971). Informal communication among department members is typically not strongly encouraged, and in some cases may even be discouraged. During group meetings, fairly formal means will be employed to guide interaction and discussion (e.g., agendas, parliamentary procedures). Hence, communication knowledge at the group level will be embedded within a group's rules, policies, and procedures and readily available to all group members. In brief, in comparison to the other organizational configurations discussed below, group communication competence in centralized/traditional firms may be reflected in relatively fewer, and more basic, resources. At the same time, however, it is important to note that because of the bureaucratic character of centralized/tradi-

tional organizations, groups and their members may develop informal/emergent communication networks and cliques to accomplish their tasks and to meet members' needs (e.g., Schein, 1980); although not officially sanctioned, such informal cliques and networks can be considered communication resources available for use in the communication process.

Given the fairly predictable and stable environments in which centralized/traditional organizations operate, organization-level competence will rest in well-defined structures such as the chain-of-command/hierarchy and in standard operating procedures for communication. As a consequence, communication competence will be centered on capabilities associated with use of "lean" media (Daft & Lengel, 1986) and knowledge of correct protocol for organization-wide communication. Thus, internal (mostly downward, one-way) communication mechanisms such as house organs, employee manuals, and internal memoranda represent key communication resources associated with organization-level communication competence in centralized/traditional organizations. In addition, because of the accuracy and relatively fast speed in which they disseminate information, organizational grapevines (although not "official" communication resources) may constitute an important part of a centralized/traditional organization's communication capabilities (e.g., Hellweg, 1987).

Functional/human relations. In functional organizations, control is delegated from top management to managers of various functional departments such as sales, finance, and production. According to Miles and Creed (1995), functional organizations work best with a human relations management philosophy. This philosophy assumes that workers are "motivated by social as well as economic factors" (Miles & Creed, 1995) and emphasizes the importance of informal interaction and working in groups. Managers focus attention on the satisfaction of individual employees, since the human relations perspective assumes (somewhat problematically) that, by satisfying the needs of individual workers, productivity will increase. Although control is not delegated to lower-level employees, managers seek input from staff, mainly as a way to satisfy the members' intrinsic involvement and personal growth needs.

Communication competence resources in functional organizations will likely differ significantly from those found in centralized/traditional organizations, primarily due to different assumptions about people. Because of the human relations emphasis on individual satisfaction, managers in functional organizations will need knowledge regarding not only the formal communication-related rules and regulations of the organization and their respective departments but also knowledge regarding informal group communication norms and of the character of emergent group communication networks. In addition, the human relations model recommends that managers be cognizant of individual staff members' personalities, and information and motivational needs (e.g., feedback needs). Consistent with this form of organization, competent managers will also likely be skilled in empathic as well as discriminative and evaluative listening, the use of feedback to motivate employees (e.g., Cusella, 1987), the use of persuasion (vs. authority) as a means of compliance-gaining, and supportive communication practices (e.g., Euske & Roberts, 1987). In sum, in the functional/human relations organization the hallmark of managerial communication competence will be a robust repertoire of communication knowledge and skills (thus allowing managers to be flexible and adaptive in their communication behavior).

In this type of organization, competent communicators will also be highly aware of the substantive and relational dimensions of their interactions with others (e.g., Watzlawick, Beavin, & Jackson, 1967; Zorn & Violanti, 1996). In addition, given that functional/human relations organizations stress the importance of work groups and informal

communication, those who are considered competent communicators will be capable of sharing information and opinions, managing conflict, involving others in decision making, and tolerating disagreement, and in general, will be highly skilled in face-to-face communication (e.g., Euske & Roberts, 1987).

In contrast to groups in centralized/traditional organizations, group competence in functional/human relations organizations will be reflected more in the emergent norms, languages, codes, informal role expectations, stories, rituals, symbols, and other cultural artifacts of the ongoing process of group development. A considerable amount of group communicative knowledge will be generated through everyday communication and collective sensemaking and feedback processes and will be shared among members via informal, emergent communication networks. Group (vs. individual) goals and rewards, shared sentiments, and feelings of potency (e.g., Homans, 1950; Shea & Guzzo, 1987; Zander, 1980) will serve as important sources of motivation to communicate in a competent manner, and groups will possess informal mechanisms to hold members accountable for undesirable communicative behavior (e.g., social loafing; see Latane, Williams, & Harkins, 1979). However, group communication norms and related pressures to conform may be quite strong and lead to overcompetence, similar in form to what Janis (1972) describes as "groupthink."

Capabilities associated with organization-level competence will include those characteristic of centralized/functional organizations, but will also involve numerous upward communication mechanisms (e.g., electronic mail, suggestion boxes, "open door" policies, employee attitude surveys). Organization-wide communication (e.g., house organs, company meetings) will emphasize identification with the organization's mission and goals and seek to encourage employees to internalize decision premises and attitudes conducive to the organization's objectives; hence, the ability of an organization to "unobtrusively control" (Barker & Tompkins, 1994; Cheney, 1983; Tompkins & Cheney, 1985) its members might be conceptualized as an element of communication competence. Formal "linking pin" roles and units (e.g., Likert, 1967) will often be used to build efficient communication networks among groups and departments, and training programs might be offered to help organizational members develop their communication skills, thus enhancing the organization's overall communication competence. To some extent, organizations operate under a "norm of reciprocity" assumption; that is, if they develop the communication abilities of their members, their members will be motivated to reciprocate by using their new competencies in the best interest of the organization.

Divisional (and matrix)/human resources. Divisional organizations tend to be larger and more decentralized than functional firms. The divisional organization is "essentially a collection of similar, special purpose machines, each independently serving its respective markets" (Miles & Creed, 1995, p. 337). These divisions enjoy a great deal of autonomy. According to Miles and Creed (1995), the divisional form is most consistent with the human resources management philosophy (they suggest this is also true for matrix organizations, which meld characteristics of both the functional and divisional forms). The human resources perspective is similar to human relations in its emphasis on the primacy of individual development and satisfaction and acknowledgment of the importance of informal communication. The main difference between the two is that while the human relations perspective stresses the importance of making employees feel important and providing them with ways to express their views, the human resources perspective views workers as not only wanting to share their views but also possessing untapped capabilities that can enhance organizational performance (Kreps, 1990). Accordingly, in organizations adhering to the human re-

sources perspective members are not just consulted when management makes decisions, but they are encouraged to actively participate in making decisions that affect their tasks and organizations. In this type of environment, management supports employees' efforts to broaden their self-direction, influence, and self-control (Miles, 1975); management's role is "one of facilitating employees' performance rather than controlling their behaviors" (Miles & Creed, 1995, p. 341).

Knowledge and skill requirements for communication competence at the organizational, group, and individual levels in a divisional organization are similar to the requirements in a functional organization. However, additional capabilities will likely be required. As mentioned earlier, managers adhering to the human resources philosophy listen to their employees not only to make them feel cared for and appreciated (as with the human relations perspective), but because they believe their employees' contributions can best be maximized if they are in control of their own decisions, behavior, and so on. Thus, for example, if a subordinate were to come to a supervisor with a work-related problem, a communicatively competent supervisor would not tell the worker how to solve the dilemma but rather ask the individual a series of questions that might help him or her frame the problem, develop criteria to assess solutions, and the like. Through the use of inquiry the supervisor would not only help the follower discover for himself or herself a viable solution to the problem, but would also model ways of approaching problem solving in general (the process), thereby facilitating the follower's ability to engage in self-directed problem-solving behavior in the future (e.g., Manz & Sims, 1989; Sims & Lorenzi, 1992). Competent leaders would also be capable of facilitating group discussions in a similar manner (e.g., they would be skilled at seeking information and opinions, providing meta-informational cues, and fostering meeting environments in which participants feel supported, included, and empowered; McGee, 1994).

Since organizational members are highly involved in decision-making processes, conflict within and between groups is quite common in divisional/human resources organizations. Thus, the ability to effectively manage conflict is an indicator of group-level communication competence in divisional (and matrix) organizations. Further, competent groups likely pay close attention to the decision-making process. According to "vigilant interaction theory," effective decision-making groups are skilled at analyzing their task, assessing the criteria used for evaluation, and distinguishing alternative choices in terms of their good and bad qualities (Hirokawa & Rost, 1992, p. 284).

Because of the emphasis on participative management (e.g., Follett, 1940; Likert, 1961), competent divisional (and matrix) organizations require mechanisms that enable communication among various organizational members for the purpose of problem solving, information sharing, and decision making. Mechanisms that might be used to solve problems and coordinate activities include quality circles, task forces, and self-managed teams (see Seibold & Shea, this volume). In a divisional/human resources organization, information about decisions and policies would not just be open and readily available (as it might in a functional/human relations organization), but also include explanations as to why particular decisions were made, the implications of decisions, and so on. Moreover, communication mechanisms would be available for those who disagree to voice their concerns with respect to particular actions and decisions. In sum, a communicatively competent divisional (or matrix)/human resources organization will have the capability of building and maintaining trust and confidence with its various stakeholders.

Level Embeddedness

The discussion above suggests that communication competence at the individual, group, and organizational levels is influenced, to some degree, by the overarching form and managerial philosophy of the organization itself. Consistent with the notion of embeddedness incorporated in our model of communication competence, we illustrate here how competence at one level is embedded in competence at other levels of analysis. To do so, we elaborate further on the notion of communication competence in a human resources/participatory organization or unit.

In participatory organizations, individual-, group-, and organization-level communication competence is tightly intertwined. We suggested above, for instance, that organization-level competence is indicated by the use of problem-solving groups such as quality circles. The communication competence of such groups is highly dependent on the ability (competence) and willingness (motivation) of individual group members to participate (Glew, O'Leary-Kelly, Griffin, & Van Fleet, 1995). Thus, a quality circle composed of many individuals who lack competencies related to group communication and decision-making processes is likely to experience numerous problems (e.g., Cotton, 1993). Similarly, if the individual members of a quality circle have the capabilities (e.g., knowledge and skills) necessary for competent communication, but are not sufficiently motivated to perform, group-level competence will be impaired. Employees invited to participate in quality circles often harbor doubts regarding the amount of influence the quality circle will actually have, for example (see Stohl & Jennings, 1988). Such doubts may result from having previously worked in an environment where employee opinions were sought but never considered for implementation (e.g., Cotton, 1993). Regardless of the source of the skepticism, however, the skepticism is likely to decrease a competent individual's motivation to be an active (rather than passive) quality circle participant. Accordingly, low levels of individual communication competence decrease group-level communication competence, leading to decreased organization-level communication competence.

The Mesosystem

Because of the multiple roles an individual occupies both in and out of the workplace (e.g., an employee may simultaneously be a subordinate, a supervisor, a functional group member, a work team member, a spouse, and a parent), that employee participates in multiple microsystems (e.g., the supervisor-subordinate microsystem, the work group microsystem, the work team microsystem, the marriage microsystem, and the family microsystem). The mesosystem represents the interrelations among these various microsystems. As will become evident in our later discussion of microsystems, the "primary building blocks of the mesosystem are the same as those for the microsystem: molar activities, interpersonal relations, and role transactions" (Vondracek, Lerner, & Schulenberg, 1986, p. 57). However, the mesosystem is distinct from the microsystem in that activities associated with the mesosystem occur across rather than within particular microsystem settings. Although individual organizational members typically serve as the linking pins between microsystems, what is learned as a consequence of these linkages may affect communication competence at the individual, group, and organizational levels of analysis.

Individual Microsystem Linkages

Individuals in organizations occupy a variety of roles both in and out of the workplace. In these roles, the individual often becomes a "linking pin" (a means for intersetting communication and knowledge sharing) among various microsystems. Many individuals, for instance, occupy both a supervisor and a subordinate role in their organization. Thus, they "link" the vertical relationship in which they are the subordinate to the vertical relationship in which they are the supervisor. Some research suggests the possibility that the communication resources developed as part of one's experiences in one of these dyadic relationships (or microsystems) can influence the development of communication competencies in the other relationship/microsystem. Weiss (1977), for example, found that subordinates often imitate or model the communication behavior of their supervisor (assuming that the supervisor is perceived of as a credible and expert source of information and behavior). Thus, in some cases communication resources learned in an upper-level leader-follower relationship may be transferred to a lower-level leader-follower relationship. Similarly, a lower-level supervisor may learn the sorts of communication behaviors that are inappropriate to enact with his or her own followers (what not to do), by observing the boss' problematic display of those behaviors. In addition, it is possible that upper-level leaders may develop their own communication competence by modeling the behaviors of lower-level leaders who are (formally speaking) their followers.

The roles an individual holds outside the workplace can also affect that person's communication competence in workplace microsystems (e.g., Crouter, 1984; Jones & Fletcher, 1996). The notion of "sex role spillover" (Gutek & Morasch, 1982) provides an excellent illustration. Sex role spillover refers to the ways gender-based behavioral expectations developed outside the organizational sphere carry over into the workplace. For instance, a man may become accustomed to communicating with women outside the workplace (e.g., his spouse) in a particular way. He may find his communication knowledge, skills, and behavior to be appropriate and effective within those extraorganizational microsystems. In other words, he is a fairly competent communicator when interacting in extraorganizational microsystems. In a similar vein, Metts and Spitzberg (1996) argue that individuals' sexual communicative behavior is guided largely by scripts—the traditional sexual script being "one in which males play the role of initiator and females the role of regulator" (p. 73). Communicating with a female colleague at work the same scripted way you communicate with your spouse, however, is likely to be inappropriate. In fact, sex role spillover has been linked to sexual harassment (Gutek, 1985; Gutek & Morasch, 1982). Accordingly, sex role spillover can lead to reduced levels of communication competence in the workplace. That is, expectations regarding competent communication developed in one microsystem can affect (in this case, decrease) one's level of communication competence in another microsystem.

Group Microsystem Linkages

Organizations can be composed of many types of groups, ranging from functional work groups (e.g., a group of employees who work in a particular department or unit of an organization, but whose level of interdependence may be quite low) to work teams. In contrast to functional work groups, teams represent "an intact group of employees who are responsible for a 'whole' work process or segment that delivers a product or service to an internal or external customer" (Wellins, Byham, & Wilson, 1991, p. 3). An individual can be simultaneously a member of a functional work group and a team. Matrix organizations, for instance, often create multifunctional teams (MFTs) composed of employees from a variety of functional work groups (e.g., engineering, manufacturing, and sales departments) who work together on particular projects. Thus, an employee may link a functional work group with a project work team.

Recent research indicates that teams often develop shared cognitive knowledge structures. Klimoski and Mohammed (1994), for instance, discuss "team mental models," which represent emergent, shared, organized knowledge reflecting beliefs, assumptions, and perceptions. As Klimoski and Mohammed (1994) explain, these models reflect "how the group members *as a collectivity* think or characterize phenomena" (p. 426, emphasis added). Mental models also include the ways group members collectively think

about or characterize *communication* phenomena. Accordingly, teams likely develop shared beliefs, assumptions, and perceptions regarding the requirements for communication competence. Individual team members may carry these beliefs, assumptions, and perceptions back to their functional work groups, thus affecting the functional group's knowledge/mental models regarding the characteristics of competent communication.

At the same time, an individual may bring to a project team the shared/collective knowledge of his or her functional work group regarding communication, thereby influencing the team's mental models with respect to communication competence. As suggested earlier, the transfer of communication resources across intersetting linkages is often reciprocal in nature.

Organizational Microsystem Linkages

A variety of microsystem linkages exist at the organizational level of analysis (e.g., Eisenberg et al., 1985). Organizations participate in many types of interorganizational relationships, for example, including interlocking directorates, trade associations, joint ventures, and research and development partnerships. Powell, Koput, and Smith-Doerr (1996) suggest that "what is learned is profoundly linked to the conditions under which it is learned" (p. 118). They further argue that sources of learning and innovation typically reside outside, rather than inside, the organization. As they explain, these sources "are commonly found in the interstices between firms, universities, research laboratories, suppliers, and customers" (p. 118). Consequently, the sources of learning and innovation reside in interorganizational networks or relationships. We suggested earlier in this chapter that a sign of organization-level communication competence is the ability to keep up with rapidly changing innovations in communication technology. Along these lines, Powell et al. (1996) maintain that participation in external networks or alliances is vital for staying current in a rapidly changing field because "external collaboration provides access to news and resources that cannot be generated internally" (p. 119). This suggests that organizations can increase their communication competence by selectively transferring into their own systems communication-related knowledge and skills they learn about from their interorganizational relationships (e.g., Powell, 1990). For example, an organizational member who participates in a multiorganizational research and development consortium formed to develop new communication technologies will obtain competence resources (in this case, knowledge regarding communication technologies as well as knowledge about communicating in a consortium), which can be transferred back to his or her company for use, thus enhancing the organization's overall level of communication competence.

Level Embeddedness

Within the mesosystem, communication competence at the individual, group, and organizational levels is embedded within and mutually influences each other. For example, if an individual is a member of both a functional work group and a cross-functional project team (as one might find in a matrix organization), he or she is likely to develop communication relationships with some of the members of the project group that persist even after the team has completed its project and disbanded. These continuing relationships/linkages, many of which might be characterized as "weak ties" (Granovetter, 1973), represent organization-level communication resources since they allow for the exchange (albeit infrequently) of messages across diverse parts/networks of the organization. In particular, they represent important communication resources since innovations, which might affect the communication capabilities of numerous groups and individuals in an organization, are often first learned about through interactions with weak ties (e.g.,

Monge & Eisenberg, 1987). Hence, individual-level competence in developing and maintaining communication relationships with persons met through mesosystem activities can affect organizational as well as group-level competence.

The Microsystem

The microsystem includes the organizational member and most directly considers his or her communication with others in the immediate work environment. More specifically, a microsystem is "a pattern of activities, roles, and interpersonal relations experienced by the developing person in a given setting with particular physical and material characteristics" (Bronfenbrenner, 1979, p. 22). Below we discuss two elements of the microsystem we believe have important implications for communication competence at the individual, group, and organizational levels of analysis: (1) gender expectations and related gender-related patterns of behavior, and (2) the employment status—permanent or contingent—of microsystem members and the impact of this status on interpersonal relationships. Clearly, there are numerous microsystem characteristics that we might have discussed in this section (e.g., differences among microsystem members in terms of race, occupation, education, and tenure; characteristics of leader-follower exchanges; interdependence among workers with respect to task performance; and emergent work group cliques and network roles). However, we chose the above noted characteristics to discuss because one represents a traditional focus of microlevel competence research (gender), whereas the latter issue (employment status) represents an area of growing interest among those studying organizations. Hence, the following discussion shows how a traditional microsystem element might be recast in terms of our model, while also demonstrating how the model might be used to study an emerging microsystem factor.

Gender

Communication competence is often conceptualized as the use of appropriate communication behaviors (e.g., Spitzberg & Cupach, 1984). Although recent research indicates that actual differences in the communication behavior of men and women are minimal (e.g., Wilkins & Andersen, 1991), the literature also indicates that others' perceptions of an individual's communication competence can be influenced by his or her gender. As Hearn (1993) points out, " 'Men at work' are generally not expected to display certain categories of emotion, especially those associated with women or those that are conventionally assumed to be 'what women show' " (p. 143). A man, therefore, who expresses his emotions (other than anger; see Hearn, 1993, p. 143) may be perceived by others to be incompetent because he communicates inappropriately.

Gender expectations can be particularly problematic for women. Organizations tend to be portrayed as rational, unemotional arenas where individuals are expected to behave in a rational, unemotional manner. As Putnam and Mumby (1993) explain, "In organizations, rationality is revered while emotions are illegitimate or inappropriate" (p. 40). Women, in general, however, are expected by society to be emotional beings. As a consequence, women are often faced with a double-bind with respect to being perceived as competent communicators. Communicating without emotion violates society's expectations of competent female behavior. Communicating with emotion, however, violates society's expectations of competent organizational behavior. Along these lines, research indicates that women who attempt to communicate "like men" (e.g., unemotional, competitive) are often perceived as hard-edged, aggressive, and shrill. At the same time, communication behaviors perceived as "feminine" are often perceived as "too soft," particularly for managers and higher-level organizational members (Mize, 1992). Accordingly, communicating in

a "feminine" manner can lead to perceptions that women are unable to succeed in management positions.

Consistent with the notion of embeddedness, however, it is important to note that expectations regarding competent male and female communication may be affected by the organizational role of the individual and the managerial philosophy of the organization or department in which the individual works. Women in "caretaking" roles, for example, are expected to communicate in an emotional, supportive manner (see Burleson, Albrecht, & Sarason, 1994). Accordingly, emotional, supportive communication abilities would enhance a woman's communication competence in those roles. The same skills would likely lead to perceptions of a woman manager as having a low level of competence. Rosener (1990), however, indicates that many women have been very successful using these types of communication behaviors in organizations or units guided by "participatory" or human resources management philosophies. Thus, it is likely that women who are proficient communicators have a large repertoire of communication skills and abilities and keen insight into how gender expectations, organizational role, managerial philosophy, and related situational factors interact to affect what others in the microsystem consider to be appropriate communication behavior.

The issue of sexual harassment is also pertinent to any discussion of employee gender and communication competence. In particular, it is noteworthy that the U.S. Equal Employment Opportunity Commission (EEOC) considers sexual harassment that occurs in any organizational microsystem to be illegal (among other actions, sexual harassment includes conduct that interferes with an employee's work or creates an intimidating, hostile, or offensive work environment; see Sheffey & Tindale, 1992). Though sexual harassment has likely occurred since the first time men and women worked together in organizations, it has received increasing attention over the past two decades. Some estimate that as many as 40% of women in organizations experience some form of sexual harassment (Bingham & Burleson, 1989). Men also experience sexual harassment, though to a far lesser extent (estimates suggest that approximately 5%-15% of men encounter sexual harassment in the workplace; see Clair, 1993). Because it is also inappropriate (as well as illegal), an individual who communicates with another employee in a sexually harassing manner displays a precompetent level of communication competence. To communicate competently, individuals must be knowledgeable about sexual harassment law and policies. In particular, employees must have an understanding of what constitutes sexually harassing communication behavior and be motivated to communicate in ways consistent with the law. As mentioned earlier, Gutek and Morasch (1982) suggest that sex role spillover can cause confusion when men perceive their female coworkers as women rather than coworkers. In addition, because some men have developed rigid ways of interacting with women outside the workplace (e.g., with their spouses, partners), it may be difficult for them to develop appropriate ways of communicating with women in the workplace. However, it is apparent that such capabilities are required if one is to display situationally appropriate (i.e., competent) ways of communicating with both male and female coworkers.

Work group communication competence may also be affected by the development of informal communication networks and cliques that exclude males or females, respectively, from membership (e.g., Kanter, 1977). Although the members of these cliques and networks may not realize that during their informal interactions (e.g., during lunch), important information is often exchanged about issues related to appropriate and effective communication behavior, intra- and extraorganizational links that might be valuable sources of information, and the like, such activities do occur during their meetings (e.g.,

Brass, 1985; Moore, 1992), and if not shared with all members of the group diminishes the group's overall communication competence. Similarly, beliefs that develop at the group level that support the notion that female coworkers who become pregnant will not return to their jobs after their maternity leaves, and/or show bias against working mothers generally (e.g., Gueutal & Taylor, 1992; Miller, Jablin, Casey, Lamphear-Van Horn, & Ethington, 1996), can negatively affect group communication competence by treating women as "temporary" team members, who are not committed to the group and thus are excluded from participation in selective communication networks, not provided with helpful "insider" knowledge about ways of communicating in the organization, and so on.

Organization-level communication competence can also be negatively affected by the organization's unwillingness to recognize the existence of gender-related stereotypes and bias. For example, organizations that implicitly permit sexual harassment to occur or sanction retaliation of employees who voice charges of harassment may not only lose credibility with many employees, but they may also demotivate workers generally from voicing issues of concern, thereby diminishing the organization's overall communication competence. In addition, failure to respond to gender bias may lessen the organization's credibility and legitimacy with respect to its external stakeholders, and as a consequence limit the organization's access to information from key sources in its environment(s).

In brief, competent organizations will develop and communicate to their constituents policy statements outlining definitions of sexual harassment and the organizational consequences facing harassers, create mentoring programs that allow women as well as men access to the informal "ins and outs" of communication in the organization (e.g., Noe, 1988), offer workshops or seminars designed to help employees understand the nature and definition of sexual harassment, and in general, learn to communicate in a manner free of gender bias (Hulin, Fitzgerald, & Drasgow, 1996). As Hulin et al. (1996) explain,

> Establishing and communicating contingencies between sexually harassing behaviors and negative outcomes for harassers, establishing procedures that minimize the risk of reporting sexual harassment (i.e., retaliation), and establishing procedures that ensure complainants, or grievants, will be taken seriously can do a great deal to improve the climate for sexual harassment in an organization. (p. 148)

Permanent Versus Contingent Employment Status

Business has seen a fundamental change over the past ten years in the relationship between individuals and their jobs (e.g., Chilton & Weidenbaum, 1994; Rousseau & Parks, 1993). Traditionally, workers entered organizations with the assumption that they would remain with the organization for the duration of their career. This was particularly true until the 1970s and early 1980s. In other words, permanent employment was the norm. The mid-1980s and the 1990s saw a dramatic change with a considerable portion of the workforce becoming what has been labeled "contingent," that is, "workers who do not have a long-term attachment to their employers (for example, temporary, part-time, and subcontracted workers)" (Belous, 1989, p. 7).

The growth of the contingent workforce has, indeed, been dramatic. Experts estimate that approximately one fourth of the American workforce now consists of contingent workers (Fierman, 1994, p. 30). The number of temporary workers, in particular, has almost tripled since 1980 (Rogers, 1995). In essence, the United States and selective other countries may be moving toward a "two-tier" workforce "in which a core of essential full-time employees is supplemented by contingent workers" ("Economic Factors," 1995).

In other words, a relatively new type of "individual difference" has emerged as a factor distinguishing among workers: status as a permanent or contingent/temporary employee.

This difference among workers implies some equally fundamental changes in the nature of role expectations and interpersonal relationships in organizations (e.g., Tsui, Pearce, Porter, & Hite, 1995), and concomitantly the knowledge and skills required for organizational communication competence (at all levels). Competent contingent workers, for instance, may require knowledge regarding a variety of organizational/management styles and the ability to communicate effectively in various environments (e.g., the ability to listen critically in a traditional organization, the ability to be assertive and engage in "dialogue" in functional/human relations or divisional/human resources organizations). To be competent communicators, contingent workers also need to be highly flexible (Tsui et al., 1995) and, given the ever-changing demands of their work, have a high tolerance for ambiguity and uncertainty (Rogers, 1995). In addition, because of the brief length of their time in any particular job or organization, they may need to be proficient in skills associated with seeking information and developing communication relationships/linkages quickly and efficiently.

The growth of the contingent workforce may also have profound implications for the use of groups and teams in organizations (see Seibold & Shea, this volume). Because effective groups tend to have a history and share a "group mentality," growing reliance on contingent workers may result in fundamental changes in the substance of group-level communication competence, a decreased use of teams, or the use of teams with only permanent employees performing highly complex and interdependent tasks in which the maintenance of knowledge structures is essential for effectiveness (e.g., Davis-Blake & Uzzi, 1993; Thompson, 1967). On the other hand, we may see organizations hiring "temporary teams"—teams composed of individuals who have worked together before in a team capacity, but are not permanent members of the organization (in line with Toffler's [1970] notion of groups in "adhocracies").

However, the two-tier employee system can, at times, create a type of "caste" system within groups in which core (permanent) workers resent and look down on contingent workers who are hired to work on "temporary" projects (it is important to recognize that in some situations temporary may mean a few months, while in other cases it may mean a year or more; Belous, 1989). Accordingly, groups must either develop capabilities that allow for effective communication relationships between "in-group" and "out-group" members or act to prevent the development of caste systems. With respect to this latter point, permanent group members may need to be educated about the benefits of a contingent workforce, and in particular, how contingent workers benefit core employees in the long run (in theory, contingent workers help the overall health of the group and organization, making core workers' jobs more secure; Belous, 1989). In addition, some groups (and organizations) may use mentor or coaching programs to encourage the development of communication relationships between permanent and contingent workers (Belous, 1989).

At the organizational level, the use of both permanent and temporary employees provides the organization with the flexibility to produce a mix of labor that has the skills and knowledge (including communication resources) to meet needs associated with shifting workloads and special projects (e.g., Davis-Blake & Uzzi, 1993). At the same time, however, the use of temporary workers means that the quality and extent of the organization's communication competence may be highly variable, and to some degree unpredictable. Special mechanisms may be required to enable the organization to maintain communication ties with contingent workers external to the company. In essence, organizations must be able to establish long-term relationships with either individual contingent workers (perhaps through the maintenance of weak ties with them; e.g., Granovetter, 1973) or the providers of contingent workers including temporary agencies and professional associations (Belous, 1989).

In addition, competent organizations may need to develop distinctive internal systems of communication with permanent and contingent workers. In particular, it is likely that the sorts of organizational messages that might serve to motivate permanent employees will be irrelevant to temporary employees, who have contracts that clearly spell out their duties and responsibilities.

Many organizations provide formal socialization/orientation programs for newly hired permanent employees in which the employees receive information regarding the organization, their tasks, employee benefits, and so forth. Little is known, however, about the ways in which contingent workers are socialized into their temporary positions. It seems likely that communicatively competent organizations would have knowledge regarding the sorts of information contingent workers actually need to accomplish their tasks effectively and have the capacities to provide them with that information. Along these lines, Feldman, Doerpinghaus, and Turnley (1994, p. 60) suggest that organizations can more effectively employ contingent workers if they provide them with extensive training and orientation. Moreover, Feldman et al.'s research indicates that organizations should communicate with temporary employees before their assignments begin so as to provide clear expectations regarding the length of the assignment (p. 58).

Finally, because they have experience working in a variety of positions and organizations, contingent workers are likely to have a large array of skills and abilities with respect to task performance. Consequently, contingent workers may be a source of innovative ideas. Thus, a possible indicator of organization-level communication competence may be the development of ways to use contingent workers as a resource for innovation. This may require major "attitude" changes on the part of companies, since research suggests that organizations rarely seek information from temporary employees (Sias, Kramer, & Jenkins, 1997). However, organizations that nurture cultures that encourage permanent members to communicate with and learn from contingent workers may be more communicatively competent (perhaps proficient) than organizations that do not adopt this approach, since they will be reinforcing the process of continuous learning, which is central to organizational survival.

Level Embeddedness

In the preceding sections, we have implicitly highlighted the embeddedness of the effects of gender and employment status on communication competence within each of our three levels of analysis. Thus, for instance, we suggested that for an individual to be a competent communicator, he or she must understand the behaviors that constitute sexually harassing communication. However, if an organization does not have the threshold communication resources or motivation (e.g., to develop and disseminate policy statements and training programs to provide employees with such information, as well as develop methods to ensure compliance and to fairly process complaints), the ability of individual employees to communicate in a nonharassing manner may be impaired (primarily out of ignorance). In other words, if sexual harassment is tolerated at the organizational level (a sign of a low level of organizational communication competence), individual employees are more likely to engage in sexually harassing behavior (Hulin et al., 1996).

CONCLUDING STATEMENT

Although the discussion and examples we have offered to explicate our model of orga-

nizational communication competence highlighted the importance of considering how the characteristics of the various ecological systems may affect the nature of communication competence at the individual, group, and organizational levels, to conserve space we did not explicitly discuss how the interaction of the ecological systems affects the character of competence. This is an important issue, and we hope that some of the examples we have presented in the preceding pages have indirectly demonstrated that the ecological systems are in continuous, mutual interaction with one another. As a final, explicit example, we note that gender stereotypes and expectations that influence communication competence in various kinds of microsystems are derived, in part, from larger societal biases and socialization processes in the exosystem (e.g., Wood, 1994). At the same time, the increased number of women in leadership positions in organizations over recent decades has affected managerial philosophies, and consequently, communication expectations within macrosystems. Rosener (1990), for example, argues that "feminine" communication styles are at the core of transformational and interactive managerial philosophies. Thus, although not emphasized in detail in this chapter, we hope that the reciprocal influence of the various ecological systems and their possible effects on organizational communication competence are plainly evident and become more of a focus of study in future research.

In conclusion, we wish to emphasize that the model we have developed to consider extant research, as well as guide the future study of communication competence in organizations, does not frame the study of competence from any particular philosophical or methodological perspective. Rather, the developmental-ecological approach serves as framework that facilitates the process of "owning up" to underlying, value-laden, ideological assumptions about competence. Thus, for example, in the process of speculating about the nature of competence in functional/traditional organizations, we suggested that a hallmark of competence (at least from one viewpoint) might be the organization's capabilities to "unobtrusively control" its members through its use of organization-level communication resources. Is this desirable? Is this ethical? Our purpose here was not to answer those questions, but rather to provide a framework that inherently mandates that such issues be addressed in our research. We stated in the opening of this chapter that communication competence might be described as a hybrid construct (part social science, part art). Its elusive, fuzzy nature does not make it easy to study, but if competence is as fundamental to the study of organizational communication as many scholars claim, then we need to keep our eyes, ears, and minds open when pursuing research in this area.

NOTES

1. This is not to say that goal achievement is irrelevant to communication competence. Having a large repertoire of competence resources, for instance, may increase the likelihood that one will achieve one's goals. Similarly, consistent goal achievement is likely to enhance self-efficacy and, consequently, increase one's motivation to communicate, thereby increasing the likelihood of subsequent goal achievement.

2. For purposes of clarity, we have adapted Bronfenbrenner's (1979) labels with respect to the macrosystem and exosystem. Specifically, whereas Bronfenbrenner refers to the organizational level as the exosystem, we refer to it as macrosystem (which is more consistent with the use of the term *macro* in organizational studies), and whereas he labels the broader overarching environment (cultural and societal beliefs systems, political ideologies, etc.) the macrosystem we label it the exosystem.

REFERENCES

Adler, N. J. (1980). *Cultural synergy: The management of cross-cultural organizations*. San Diego, CA: University Associates.

Adler, N. J., & Bartholomew, S. (1992). Managing globally competent people. *Academy of Management Executive, 6*, 52-65.

Alwin, D. F. (1995). Taking time seriously: Social change, social structure and human lives. In P. Moen, G. H. Elder, Jr., & K. Luscher (Eds.), *Examining lives in context: Perspectives on the ecology of human development* (pp. 211-264). Washington, DC: American Psychological Association.

Andrews, P. H., & Herschel, R. T. (1996). *Organizational communication: Empowerment in a technological society*. Boston: Houghton Mifflin.

Bandura, A. (1990). Conclusion: Reflections on nonability determinants of competence. In R. J. Sternberg & J. Kolligian, Jr. (Eds.), *Competence considered* (pp. 315-362). New Haven, CT: Yale University Press.

Bantz, C. (1993). Cultural diversity and group cross-cultural team research. *Journal of Applied Communication Research, 20*, 1-19.

Barker, J. R., & Tompkins, P. K. (1994). Identification in the self-managing organization: Characteristics of target and tenure. *Human Communication Research, 21*, 223-240.

Barley, S. R., & Kunda, G. (1992). Design and devotion: Surges of rational and normative ideologies of control in managerial discourse. *Administrative Science Quarterly, 37*, 363-399.

Barna, L. M. (1991). Stumbling blocks in intercultural communication. In L. A. Samovar & R. E. Porter (Eds.), *Intercultural communication: A reader* (6th ed., p. 345-352). Belmont, CA: Wadsworth.

Baron, S., & Clair, R. P. (1996, May). *From coercion to manipulation: Communication competence as disciplinary discourse in the organization*. Paper presented at the annual meeting of the International Communication Association, Chicago.

Beamer, L. (1992). Learning intercultural communication competence. *Journal of Business Communication, 29*, 285-303.

Beer, M., Spector, B., Lawrence, P. R., Mills, D. Q., & Walton, R. E. (1985). *Human resource management: A general manager's perspective*. New York: Free Press.

Belous, R. S. (1989). *The contingent economy: The growth of the temporary, part-time, and subcontracted workforce*. Washington, DC: National Planning Association.

Berman, S. J., & Hellweg, S. A. (1989). Perceived supervisor communication competence and supervisor satisfaction as a function of quality circle participation. *Journal of Business Communication, 26*, 103-122.

Bingham, S. G., & Burleson, B. R. (1989). Multiple effects of messages with multiple goals: Some perceived outcomes of responses to sexual harassment. *Human Communication Research, 16*, 184-216.

Bion, W. R. (1959). *Experiences in groups.* London: Tavistock.

Black, J. S., Gregersen, H. B., & Mendenhall, M. E. (1992). *Global assignments: Successfully expatriating and repatriating international managers.* San Francisco: Jossey-Bass.

Bochner, A., & Kelly, C. (1974). Interpersonal communication competency: Rationale, philosophy and implementation of a conceptual framework. *Speech Teacher, 23,* 279-301.

Bormann, E. G., Pratt, J., & Putnam, L. (1978). Power, authority, and sex: Male response to female leadership. *Communication Monographs, 45,* 119-155.

Bostrom, R. N. (Ed.). (1984). *Competence in communication: A multidisciplinary approach.* Beverly Hills, CA: Sage.

Brass, D. (1985). Men's and women's networks: A study of interaction patterns and influence in an organization. *Academy of Management Journal, 28,* 327-343.

Bronfenbrenner, U. (1979). *The ecology of human development: Experiments by nature and design.* Cambridge, MA: Harvard University Press.

Burleson, B. R., Albrecht, T. L., & Sarason, I. G. (Eds.). (1994). *Communication of social support: Messages, interactions, relationships and community.* Thousand Oaks, CA: Sage.

Cascio, W. (1986). *Managing human resources.* New York: McGraw-Hill.

Casmir, F. (1993). Third-culture building: A paradigm shift for international intercultural communication. In S. A. Deetz (Ed.), *Communication yearbook 16* (pp. 407-428). Newbury Park, CA: Sage.

Cetron, M. J., Rocha, W., & Luchins, R. (1988). Into the 21st century: Long-term trends affecting the United States. *The Futurist, 22*(5), 29-40.

Cheney, G. (1983). The rhetoric of identification and the study of organizational communication. *Quarterly Journal of Speech, 69,* 143-158.

Chilton, K., & Weidenbaum, M. (1994). *A new social contract for the American workplace: From paternalism to partnering* (Policy Study No. 123). St. Louis, MO: Washington University, Center for the Study of American Business.

Clair, R. P. (1993). The use of framing devices to sequester organizational narratives: Hegemony and harassment. *Communication Monographs, 60,* 113-136.

Cohen, M. D., & Bacdayan, P. (1994). Organizational routines are stored as procedural memory: Evidence from a laboratory study. *Organization Science, 5,* 554-568.

Cole, M., & Engeström, Y. (1993). A cultural-historical approach to distributed cognition. In G. Salomon (Ed.), *Distributed cognitions: Psychological and education considerations* (pp. 1-46). Cambridge, UK: Cambridge University Press.

Collier, M. J. (1994). Cultural identity and intercultural communication. In L. A. Samovar & R. E. Porter (Eds.), *Intercultural communication: A reader* (7th ed., pp. 36-44). Belmont, CA: Wadsworth.

Cooper, L. O. (1997). Listening competency in the workplace: A model for training. *Business Communication Quarterly, 60*(4), 75-84.

Cooper, L. O., & Husband, R. (1993). Developing a model of organizational listening competency. *Journal of the International Listening Association, 7,* 6-34.

Cotton, J. L. (1993). *Employee involvement: Methods for improving performance and work attitudes.* Newbury Park, CA: Sage.

Cox, T. H., & Blake, S. (1991). Managing cultural diversity: Implications for organizational competitiveness. *Academy of Management Executive, 5,* 45-56.

Crouter, A. C. (1984). Spillover from family to work: The neglected side of the work-family interface. *Human Relations, 37,* 425-442.

Cushman, D., & Whiting, G. C. (1972). An approach to communication theory: Toward a consensus on rules. *Journal of Communication, 22,* 217-238.

Cusella, L. P. (1987). Feedback, motivation, and performance. In F. M. Jablin, L. L. Putnam, K. H. Roberts, & L. W. Porter (Eds.), *Handbook of organizational communication: An interdisciplinary perspective* (pp. 624-678). Newbury Park, CA: Sage.

Daft, R. L., & Lengel, R. H. (1986). Organizational information requirements, media richness and structural design. *Management Science, 32,* 554-571.

Daft, R. L., & Weick, K. E. (1984). Toward a model of organizations as interpretation systems. *Academy of Management Review, 9,* 284-295.

Davis-Blake, A., & Uzzi, B. (1993). Determinants of employment externalization: A study of temporary workers and independent contractors. *Administrative Science Quarterly, 38,* 195-223.

Dinges, N. G., & Lieberman, D. A. (1989). Intercultural communication competence: Coping with stressful work situations. *International Journal of Intercultural Relations, 13,* 371-385.

DiSalvo, V. S. (1980). A summary of current research identifying communication skills in various organizational contexts. *Communication Education, 29,* 283-290.

DiSalvo, V. S., & Larsen, J. K. (1987). A contingency approach to communication skill importance: The impact of occupation, direction, and position. *Journal of Business Communication, 24,* 3-22.

Duran, R. L., & Spitzberg, B. H. (1995). Toward the development and validation of a measure of cognitive communication competence. *Communication Quarterly, 43,* 259-275.

Economic factors fuel growth of two-tier workforce in U.S. (1995, April 17). *Spokane Spokesman-Review,* pp. E1, E3.

Eisenberg, E. M., Farace, R. V., Monge, P. R., Bettinghaus, E. P., Kurchner-Hawkins, R., Miller, K., & Rothman, L. (1985). Communication linkages in interorganizational systems. In B. Dervin & M. Voight (Eds.), *Progress in the communication sciences* (Vol. 6, pp. 231-261). New York: Ablex.

Eisenberg, E. M., & Goodall, H. L. (1993). *Organizational communication: Balancing creativity and constraint.* New York: St. Martin's.

Eisenberg, E. M., & Witten, M. (1987). Reconsidering openness in organizational communication. *Academy of Management Review, 12,* 418-426.

Elmes, M., & Costello, M. (1992). Mystification and social drama: The hidden side of communication skills training. *Human Relations, 45,* 427-445.

Euske, N. A., & Roberts, K. H. (1987). Evolving perspectives in organization theory: Communication implications. In F. M. Jablin, L. L. Putnam, K. H. Roberts, & L. W. Porter (Eds.), *Handbook of organizational communication: An interdisciplinary perspective* (pp. 41-69). Newbury Park, CA: Sage.

Feldman, D. C., Doerpinghaus, H. I., & Turnley, W. H. (1994). Managing temporary workers: A permanent HRM challenge. *Organizational Dynamics, 23,* 49-63.

Fierman, J. (1994, January 4). The contingency work force. *Fortune, 129*(2), 30-36.

Finholt, T., & Sproull, L. (1990). Electronic groups at work. *Organization Science, 1*(1), 41-64.

Fisher, B. A. (1978). *Perspectives on human communication.* New York: Macmillan.

Follett, M. P. (1940). The giving of orders. In H. C. Metcalf & L. Urwick (Eds.), *Dynamic administration: The collected papers of Mary Parker Follett* (pp. 50-70). New York: Harper.

Ford, W. S. Z., & Wolvin, A. D. (1993). The differential impact of a basic communication course on perceived communication competencies in class, work and social contexts. *Communication Education, 42,* 215-223.

Friedman, R. A. (1989). Interaction norms as carriers of organizational culture: A study of labor negotiations at International Harvester. *Journal of Contemporary Ethnography, 18,* 3-29.

Friedman, S. L., & Wachs, T. D. (Eds.). (1999). *Measuring environment across the life span: Emerging methods and concepts.* Washington, DC: American Psychological Association.

Frost, P. J. (1987). Power, politics, and influence. In F. M. Jablin, L. L. Putnam, K. H. Roberts, & L. W. Porter (Eds.), *Handbook of organizational communication: An interdisciplinary perspective* (pp. 503-548). Newbury Park, CA: Sage.

Giacalone, R. A., & Rosenfeld, P. (Eds.). (1991). *Impression management in organizations.* Hillsdale, NJ: Lawrence Erlbaum.

Giddens, A. (1984). *The constitution of society: Outline of a theory of structuration.* Berkeley: University of California Press.

Gioia, D. A. (1986). Symbols, scripts, and sensemaking: Creating meaning in the organizational experience.

In H. Sims, D. Gioia, & Associates (Eds.), *The thinking organization: Dynamics of organizational social cognition* (pp. 49-74). San Francisco: Jossey-Bass.

Glew, D. J., O'Leary-Kelly, A. M., Griffin, R. W., & Van Fleet, D. D. (1995). Participation in organizations: A preview of the issues and proposed framework for future analysis. *Journal of Management, 21,* 395-421.

Goodall, J. L., Jr. (1982). Organizational communication competence: The development of an industrial simulation to teach adaptive skills. *Communication Quarterly, 30,* 282-295.

Gouran, D. S., & Hirokawa, R. Y. (1983). The role of communication in decision-making groups. In M. S. Mander (Ed.), *Communication in transition* (pp. 168-185). New York Praeger.

Granovetter, M. (1973). The strength of weak ties. *American Journal of Sociology, 78,* 1360-1380.

Griffith, T. L. (1999). Technology features as triggers for sensemaking. *Academy of Management Review, 24,* 472-488.

Gueutal, H. G., & Taylor, E. M. (1992). Employee pregnancy: The impact on organizations, pregnant employees and co-workers. *Journal of Business and Psychology, 5,* 59-476.

Gutek, B. A. (1985). *Sex and the workplace.* San Francisco: Jossey-Bass.

Gutek, B. A., & Morasch, B. (1982). Sex ratios, sex role spillover, and sexual harassment of women at work. *Journal of Social Issues, 38,* 55-74.

Haas, J. W., & Arnold, C. L. (1995). An examination of the role of listening in judgments of communication competence in co-workers. *Journal of Business Communication, 32,* 123-140.

Habermas, J. (1970). Toward a theory of communicative competence. In H. P. Dreitzel (Ed.), *Recent Sociology, 2,* 115-148.

Hage, J., Aiken, M., & Marrett, C. B. (1971). Organizational structure and communications. *American Sociological Review, 36,* 860-871.

Hammer, M. (1987). Behavioral dimensions of intercultural effectiveness: A replication and extension. *International Journal of Intercultural Relations, 11,* 65-88.

Hargie, O., & Tourish, D. (1994). Communication skills training: Management manipulation or personal development. *Human Relations, 47,* 1377-1389.

Harris, L., & Cronen, V. E. (1979). A rules-based model for the analysis and evaluation of organizational communication. *Communication Quarterly, 27,* 12-28.

Hart, C. H., Olsen, S. F., Robinson, C. C., & Mandleco, B. L. (1997). The development of social and communicative competence in childhood: Review and model of personal, familial, and extrafamilial processes. In B. R. Burleson (Ed.), *Communication yearbook 20* (pp. 305-373). Thousand Oaks, CA: Sage.

Hearn, J. (1993). Emotive subjects: Organizational men, organizational masculinities and the (de)construction of "emotions." In S. Fineman (Ed.), *Emotion in organizations* (pp. 142-166). London: Sage.

Health, R. G., & Sias, P. M. (1999). Communicating spirit in a collaborative alliance. *Journal of Applied Communication Research, 27,* 356-376.

Hellweg, S. (1987). Organizational grapevines: A state of the art review. In B. Dervin & M. Voight (Eds.), *Progress in communication sciences* (Vol. 8, pp. 213-230). Norwood, NJ: Ablex.

Hickson, D. J., Hinings, C. R., Lee, C. A., Schneck, R. J., & Pennings, J. M. (1971). A strategic contingencies theory of intraorganizational power. *Administrative Science Quarterly, 16,* 216-229.

Hinz, V. B., Tindale, R. S., & Vollrath, D. A. (1997). The emerging conceptualization of groups as information processors. *Psychological Bulletin, 121,* 43-64.

Hirokawa, R. Y. (1988). Group communication and decision-making performance: A test of a functional perspective. *Human Communication Research, 14,* 487-515.

Hirokawa, R. Y., & Keyton, J. (1995). Perceived facilitators and inhibitors of effectiveness in organizational work teams. *Management Communication Quarterly, 8,* 424-446.

Hirokawa, R. Y., & Rost, K. M. (1992). Effective group decision making in organizations: Field test of the vigilant interaction theory. *Management Communication Quarterly, 5,* 267-288.

Hofstede, G. (1981). *Culture's consequences: International differences in work-related values.* Beverly Hills, CA: Sage.

Hogan, G. W., & Goodson, J. R. (1990). The key to expatriate success. *Training and Development Journal, 44,* 50-52.

Homans, G. C. (1950). *The human group.* New York: Harcourt, Brace.

Hulin, C. L., Fitzgerald, L. F., & Drasgow, F. (1996). Organizational influences on sexual harassment. In M. S. Stockdale (Ed.), *Sexual harassment in the workplace: Perspectives, frontiers, and response strategies: Vol. 5. Women and work* (pp. 127-150). Thousand Oaks, CA: Sage.

Hutchins, E. (1991). The social organization of distributed cognition. In L. B. Resnick, J. M. Levine, & S. D. Teasley (Eds.), *Perspectives on socially shared cognition* (pp. 283-307). Washington, DC: American Psychological Association.

Hymes, D. (1972). *On communication competence.* In J. B. Pride & J. Holmes (Eds.), *Sociolinguistics: Selected readings* (pp. 269-293). Baltimore: Penguin.

Jablin, F. M. (1994). Communication competence: An organizational assimilation perspective. In L. van Waes, E. Woudstra, & P. van den Hoven (Eds.), *Functional communication quality* (pp. 28-41). Amsterdam: Rodopi.

Jablin, F. M., Cude, R. L., House, A., Lee, J., & Roth, N. L. (1994). Communication competence in organizations: Conceptualization and comparison across multiple levels of analysis. In L. Thayer & G. Barnett (Eds.), *Organization-communication: Emerging perspectives* (Vol. 4, pp. 114-140). Norwood, NJ: Ablex.

Janis, I. L. (1972). *Victims of group think.* Boston: Houghton Mifflin.

Johnson, G. M. (1992). Subordinate perceptions of superior's communication competence and task attraction related to superior's use of compliance-gaining tactics. *Western Journal of Communication, 56,* 54-57.

Johnson, G. M., Staton, A. Q., & Jorgensen-Earp, C. R. (1995). An ecological perspective on the transition of new university freshmen. *Communication Education, 44,* 336-352.

Johnston, H. R., & Carrico, S. R. (1988). Developing capabilities to use information strategically. *MIS Quarterly, 12,* 37-48.

Jones, F., & Fletcher, B. (1996). Taking work home: A study of daily fluctuations in work stressors, effects on moods and impacts on marital partners. *Journal of Occupational and Organizational Psychology, 69,* 89-106.

Kanter, R. M. (1977). *Men and women of the corporation.* New York: Basic Books.

Katz, D., & Kahn, R. (1978). *The social psychology of organizations* (2nd ed.). New York: John Wiley.

Kellermann, K., Reynolds, R., & Chen, J. B. (1991). Strategies of conversational retreat: When parting is not sweet sorrow. *Communication Monographs, 58,* 362-383.

Kernan, M. C., & Howard, G. S. (1990). Computer anxiety and computer attitudes: An investigation of construct and predictive validity. *Educational and Psychological Measurement, 50,* 681-690.

King, S. S., & Cushman, D. P. (1994). High speed management as a theoretic principle for yielding significant organizational communication behaviors. In B. Kovacic (Ed.), *New approaches to organizational communication* (pp. 87-116). Albany: State University of New York Press.

Klimoski, R., & Mohammed, S. (1994). Team mental model: Construct or metaphor? *Journal of Management, 20,* 403-437.

Koester, J. (1985). *A profile of the U.S. student abroad.* New York: Council on International Educational Exchange.

Koester, J., & Olebe, M. (1988). The Behavioral Assessment Scale for Intercultural Communication Effectiveness. *International Journal of Intercultural Relations, 12,* 233-246.

Kovacic, B. (1994). New perspectives on organizational communication. In B. Kovacic (Ed.). *New approaches to organizational communication* (pp. 1-37). Albany: State University of New York Press.

Krackhardt, D., & Stern, R. N. (1988). Structuring of information organizations and the management of crises. *Social Psychological Quarterly, 51,* 123-140.

Kreps, G. L. (1990). *Organizational communication* (2nd ed.). New York: Longman.

Langer, E. J. (1978). Rethinking the role of thought in social interaction. In J. H. Harvey, W. J. Ickes, & R. F. Kidd (Eds.), *New directions in attribution research* (Vol. 2, pp. 35-58). Hillsdale, NJ: Lawrence Erlbaum.

Langer, E. J., & Parks, K. (1990). Incompetence: A conceptual reconsideration. In R. J. Sternberg & J. Kolligian, Jr. (Eds.), *Competence considered* (pp. 149-166). New Haven, CT: Yale University Press.

Latane, B., Williams, K., & Harkins, S. (1979). Many hands make light the work: The causes and consequences of social loafing. *Journal of Personality and Social Psychology, 12,* 144-150.

Lei, D., Hitt, M. A., & Bettis, R. (1996). Dynamic core competencies through meta-learning and strategic context. *Journal of Management, 22,* 549-569.

Liang, D., Moreland, R., & Argote, L. (1995). Group versus individual training and group performance: The mediating role of transactive memory. *Personality and Social Psychology Bulletin, 21,* 384-393.

Likert, R. (1961). *New patterns of management.* New York: McGraw-Hill.

Likert, R. (1967). *The human organization.* New York: McGraw-Hill.

Locke, E. A., & Henne, D. (1986). Work motivation theories. In C. L. Cooper & I. Robertson (Eds.), *International review of industrial and organizational psychology* (Vol. 1, pp. 1-35). Chichester, UK: Wiley.

Luthans, F. (1988). Successful vs. effective real managers. *Academy of Management Executive, 11,* 127-132.

Maes, J. D., Weldy, T. G., & Icenogle, M. L. (1997). A managerial perspective: Oral communication competency is most important for business students in the workplace. *Journal of Business Communication, 34*(1), 67-80.

Magnusson, D. (1995). Individual development: A holistic, integrated model. In P. Moen, G. H. Elder, Jr., & K. Luscher (Eds.), *Examining lives in context: Perspectives on the ecology of human development* (pp. 19-60). Washington, DC: American Psychological Association.

Manz, C. C., & Sims, H. P., Jr. (1989). *Super-leadership: Leading others to lead themselves.* New York: Berkley.

March, J. G. (1988, April). *Learning and taking risks.* Keynote address at the annual Texas Conference on Organizations, Lago Vista.

Marino, K. E. (1996). Developing consensus on firm competencies and capabilities. *Academy of Management Executive, 10*(3), 40-51.

Markus, M. L. (1987). Toward a "critical mass" theory of interactive media: Universal access, interdependence and diffusion. *Communication Research, 14,* 491-511.

McCroskey, J. C. (1982). Communication competence and performance: A pedagogical perspective. *Communication Education, 31,* 1-8.

McCroskey, J. C. (1984). Communication competence: The elusive construct. In R. N. Bostrom (Ed.), *Competence in communication* (pp. 259-268). Beverly Hills, CA: Sage.

McGee, D. S. (1994, November). *Classroom discussion competence: A preliminary model.* Paper presented at the annual meeting of the Speech Communication Association, New Orleans, LA.

Metts, S., & Spitzberg, B. H. (1996). Sexual communication in interpersonal contexts: A script-based approach. In B. R. Burleson (Ed.), *Communication yearbook 19* (pp. 49-92). Thousand Oaks, CA: Sage.

Meyer, J., & Rowan, B. (1977). Institutionalized organizations: Formal structure as myth and ceremony. *American Journal of Sociology, 83,* 340-363.

Miles, R. E. (1975). *Theories of management: Implications for organizational behavior and development.* New York: McGraw-Hill.

Miles, R. E., & Creed, W. E. D. (1995). Organizational forms and managerial philosophies: A descriptive and analytical review. In L. Cummings & B. Staw (Eds.), *Research in organizational behavior* (Vol. 17, pp. 333-372). Greenwich, CT: JAI.

Miller, D. (1996). A preliminary typology of organizational learning: Synthesizing the literature. *Journal of Management, 22,* 485-505.

Miller, V. D., Jablin, F. M., Casey, M. K., Lamphear-Van Horn, M., & Ethington, C. (1996). The maternity leave as a role negotiation process. *Journal of Managerial Issues, 8,* 286-309.

Milliken, F. J., & Martins, L. I. (1996). Searching for common threads: Understanding the multiple effects of diversity in organizational groups. *Academy of Management Review, 21,* 402-433.

Mize, S. (1992). Shattering the glass ceiling. *Training and Development Journal, 46,* 60-62.

Moen, P., Elder, G. H., Jr., & Luscher, K. (Ed.). (1995). *Examining lives in context: Perspectives on the ecology of human development.* Washington, DC: American Psychological Association.

Monge, P. R., Bachman, S. G., Dillard, J. P., & Eisenberg, E. M. (1981). Communicator competence in the workplace: Model testing and scale development. In M. Burgoon (Ed.), *Communication yearbook 5* (pp. 505-527). Beverly Hills, CA: Sage.

Monge, P. R., & Eisenberg, E. M. (1987). Emergent communication networks. In F. M. Jablin, L. L. Putnam, K. H. Roberts, & L. W. Porter (Eds.), *Handbook of organizational communication: An interdisciplinary perspective* (pp. 304-342). Newbury Park, CA: Sage.

Moore, G. (1992). Gender and informal networks in state government. *Social Science Quarterly, 73,* 46-61.

Moorman, C., & Miner, A. S. (1998). Organizational improvisation and organizational memory. *Academy of Management Review, 23,* 698-723.

Moran, R., & Harris, P. (1981). *Managing cultural synergy.* Houston, TX: Gulf.

Morand, D. A. (1995). The role of behavioral formality and informality in the enactment of bureaucratic versus organic organizations. *Academy of Management Review, 20,* 831-872.

Morse, B. W., & Piland, R. N. (1981). An assessment of communication competencies needed by intermediate-level health care providers: A study of nurse-patient, nurse-doctor, nurse-nurse communication relationships. *Journal of Applied Communication Research, 9,* 30-41.

Nadler, D. A., & Tushman, M. L. (1999). The organization of the future: Strategic imperatives and core competencies for the 21st century. *Organizational Dynamics, 28*(1), 45-60.

Nishida, H. (1985). Japanese intercultural communication competence and cross-cultural adjustment. *International Journal of Intercultural Relations, 9,* 247-269.

Nunamaker, J., Dennis, A., Valacich, J., Vogel, D., & George, J. (1991). Group support systems research: Experience from the lab and field. In L. M. Jessup & J. S. Valacich (Eds.), *Group support systems: New perspectives* (pp. 78-96). New York: Macmillan.

Noe, R. A. (1988). Women and mentoring: A review and research agenda. *Academy of Management Review, 13,* 65-78.

Offerman, L., & Gowing, M. (1990). Organizations of the future: Changes and challenges. *American Psychologist, 45,* 95-108.

O'Keefe, B. J. (1988). The logic of message design: Individual differences in reasoning about communication. *Communication Monographs, 55,* 80-103.

O'Reilly, C. A., Caldwell, D. F., & Barnett, W. P. (1989). Work group demography, social integration, and turnover. *Administrative Science Quarterly, 34,* 21-37.

Orlikowski, W. J., & Yates, J. (1994). Genre repertoire: The structuring of communicative practices in organizations. *Administrative Science Quarterly, 39,* 541-574.

Parks, M. R. (1994). Communicative competence and interpersonal control. In M. L. Knapp & G. R. Miller (Eds.), *Handbook of interpersonal communication* (2nd ed., pp. 589-620). Thousand Oaks, CA: Sage.

Pavitt, C., & Haight, L. (1986). Implicit theories of communicative competence: Situational and competence level differences in judgments of prototype and target. *Communication Monographs, 53,* 221-235.

Pentland, B. T. (1995). Grammatical models of organizational processes. *Organization Science, 6,* 541-556.

Pentland, B. T., & Rueter, H. H. (1994). Organizational routines as grammars of action. *Administrative Science Quarterly, 39,* 484-510.

Poole, M. S., & DeSanctis, G. (1990). Understanding the use of group decision support systems. In J. Fulk & C. Steinfield (Eds.), *Organizations and communication technology* (pp. 173-193). Newbury Park, CA: Sage.

Poole, M. S., & DeSanctis, G. (1992). Microlevel structuration in computer-supported group decision making. *Human Communication Research, 19,* 5-49.

Poole, M. S., Holmes, M., & DeSanctis, G. (1991). Conflict management in a computer-supported meeting environment. *Management Science, 8,* 926-953.

Poole, M. S., Seibold, D. R., & McPhee, R. D. (1996). The structuration of group decisions. In R. Hirokawa & M. S. Poole (Eds.), *Communication and group decision making* (2nd ed., pp. 114-146). Thousand Oaks, CA: Sage.

Powell, W. W. (1990). Neither market nor hierarchy: Network forms of organization. In B. Staw & L. Cummings (Eds.), *Research in organizational behavior* (Vol. 12, pp. 295-336). Greenwich, CT: JAI.

Powell, W. W., Koput, K. W., & Smith-Doerr, L. (1996). Interorganizational collaboration and the locus of innovation: Networks of learning in biotechnology. *Administrative Science Quarterly, 41,* 116-145.

Prahalad, C. K., & Hamel, G. (1990, May-June). The core competence of the organization. *Harvard Business Review, 68,* 79-91.

Propp, K. M., & Nelson, D. (1986). Problem-solving performance in naturalistic groups: The ecological validity of the functional perspective. *Communication Studies, 47,* 35-45.

Putnam, L. L., & Mumby, D. K. (1993). Organizations, emotion and the myth of rationality. In S. Fineman (Ed.), *Emotion in organizations* (pp. 36-57). London: Sage.

Rader, M., & Wunsch, A. (1980). A survey of communication practices of business school graduates by job category and undergraduate major. *Journal of Business Communication, 17*(4), 33-41.

Raelin, J. A. (1997). A model of work-based learning. *Organization Science, 8,* 563-578.

Ratiu, I. (1983). Thinking internationally: A comparison of how international executives learn. *International Studies of Management and Organization, 8,* 139-150.

Redding, W. C. (1979). Organizational communication theory and ideology: An overview. In D. Nimmo (Ed.), *Communication yearbook 3* (pp. 309-341). New Brunswick, NJ: Transaction.

Reinsch, L., & Shelby, A. N. (1996). Communication challenges and needs: Perceptions of MBA students. *Business Communication Quarterly, 59,* 36-53.

Reinsch, L., & Shelby, A. N. (1997). What communication abilities do practitioners need? Evidence from MBA students. *Business Communication Quarterly, 60*(4), 7-29.

Rogers, J. K. (1995). Just a temp: Experience and structure of alienation in temporary clerical employment. *Work and Occupations, 22,* 137-166.

Rosener, J. B. (1990, November-December). Ways women lead. *Harvard Business Review, 68,* 119-125.

Rousseau, D. M., & Parks, J. M. (1993). The contracts of individuals and organizations. In L. Cummings & B. Staw (Eds.), *Research in organizational behavior* (Vol. 14, pp. 1-43). Greenwich, CT: JAI.

Ruben, B. D. (1977). Human communication and cross-cultural effectiveness. *International Journal of Intercultural Relations, 4,* 95-105.

Ruben, B. D., & Kealey, D. H. (1979). Behavioral assessment of communication competency and the prediction of cross-cultural adaptation. *International Journal of Intercultural Relations, 3,* 15-48.

Rubin, R. B. (1990). Communication competence. In G. M. Phillips & J. T. Wood (Eds.), *Speech communication: Essays to commemorate the 75th anniversary of the Speech Communication Association* (pp. 94-129). Carbondale: Southern Illinois University.

Sackmann, S. A. (1991). *Cultural knowledge in organizations: Exploring the collective mind.* Newbury Park, CA: Sage.

Sambamurthy, V., & Poole, M. S. (1992). The effects of variations in capabilities of GDSS designs on management conflict in groups. *Information Systems Research, 3,* 224-251.

Schall, M. S. (1983). A communication-rules approach to organizational culture. *Administrative Science Quarterly, 28,* 557-581.

Schein, E. H. (1980). *Organizational psychology* (3rd ed.). Englewood Cliffs, NJ: Prentice Hall.

Schein, E. H. (1985). *Organizational culture and leadership.* San Francisco: Jossey-Bass.

Scudder, J. N., Guinan, P. J. (1989). Communication competencies as discriminators of superiors' ratings of employee performance. *Journal of Business Communication, 26,* 217-229.

Seibold, D. R., Kudsi, S., & Rude, M. (1993). Does communication training make a difference? Evidence for the effectiveness of a presentation skills program. *Journal of Applied Communication Research, 21,* 111-131.

Sell, D. K. (1983). Research on attitude change in U.S. students who participate in foreign study experience: Past findings and suggestions for future research. *International Journal of Intercultural Relations, 7,* 131-138.

Shea, G. P., & Guzzo, R. A. (1987). Group effectiveness: What really matters? *Sloan Management Review, 28,* 25-31.

Sheffey, S., & Tindale, R. S. (1992). Perceptions of sexual harassment in the workplace. *Journal of Applied Psychology, 22,* 1502-1520.

Shimanoff, S. B. (1980). *Communication rules: Theory and research.* Beverly Hills, CA: Sage.

Sias, P. M., Kramer, M. W., & Jenkins, E. (1997). A comparison of the communication behavior of temporary employees and new hires. *Communication Research, 24,* 731-754.

Sims, H. P., Jr., & Lorenzi, P. (1992). *The new leadership paradigm: Social learning and cognition in organizations.* Newbury Park, CA: Sage.

Snavely, W. B., & Walters, E. V. (1983). Differences in the communication competence among administrator social styles. *Journal of Applied Communication Research, 11*(2), 120-135.

Snow, C. C., Miles, R. E., & Coleman, H. J. (1992). Managing 21st century network organizations. *Organizational Dynamics, 20*(3), 5-20.

Spitzberg, B. H., & Cupach, W. R. (1984). *Interpersonal communication competence.* Beverly Hills, CA: Sage.

Spitzberg, B. H., & Duran, R. L. (1993, July). *Toward an ideological deconstruction of competence.* Paper presented at the annual meeting of the International Communication Association, Sydney, Australia.

Sriussadaporn-Charoenngam, N., & Jablin, F. M. (1999). An exploratory study of communication competence in Thai organizations. *Journal of Business Communication, 36,* 382-412.

Sternberg, R. J. (1990). Prototypes of competence and incompetence. In R. J. Sternberg & J. Kolligian, Jr. (Eds.), *Competence considered* (pp. 117-145). New Haven, CT: Yale University Press.

Stewart, E. (1985). Culture and decision making. In W. Gudykunst, L. Stewart, & S. Ting-Toomey (Eds.), *Communication, culture and organizational processes* (pp. 177-211). Beverly Hills, CA: Sage.

Stohl, C. (1995). *Organizational communication: Connectedness in action.* Thousand Oaks, CA: Sage.

Stohl, C., & Jennings, K. (1988). Volunteerism and voice in quality circles. *Western Journal of Speech Communication, 52,* 238-251.

Sypher, B. D. (1981). *A multimethod investigation of employee communication abilities, communication satisfaction and job satisfaction.* Doctoral dissertation, University of Michigan.

Sypher, B. D., & Sypher, H. E. (1981, May). *Individual differences and perceived communication abilities in an organizational setting.* Paper presented at the annual meeting of the International Communication Association, Minneapolis, MN.

Sypher, B. D., & Sypher, H. E. (1983). Perceptions of communication ability: Self-monitoring in an organizational setting. *Personality and Social Psychology Bulletin, 9,* 297-304.

Sypher, B. D., Sypher, H. E., & Leichty, G. B. (1983). *Cognitive differentiation, self-monitoring and indi-*

vidual success in organizations. Paper presented at the Fifth International Congress on Personal Construct Psychology, Boston.

Sypher, B. D., & Zorn, T. (1986). Communication-related abilities and upward mobility: A longitudinal investigation. *Human Communication Research, 12,* 420-431.

Szajna, B. (1994). An investigation of the predictive validity of computer anxiety and computer aptitude. *Educational and Psychological Measurement, 54,* 926-934.

Taylor, F. W. (1911). *The principles of scientific management.* New York: Harper.

Teboul, J., Chen, L., & Fritz, L. (1994). Communication in multinational organizations in the United States and Western Europe. In R. Wiseman & R. Shuter (Eds.), *Communicating in multinational organizations* (pp. 12-29). Thousand Oaks, CA: Sage.

Thompson, I. (1996). Competence and critique in technical communication: A qualitative content analysis of journal articles. *Journal of Business and Technical Communication, 16,* 48-80.

Thompson, J. D. (1967). *Organizations in action.* New York: McGraw-Hill.

Thornburg, L. (1990, September). Transfers need not mean dislocation. *Human Resources Magazine,* pp. 46-48.

Toffler, A. (1970). *Future shock.* New York: Bantam.

Tompkins, P. K., & Cheney, G. (1985). Communication and unobtrusive control in contemporary organizations. In R. D. McPhee & P. K. Tompkins (Eds.), *Organizational communication: Traditional themes and new directions* (pp. 179-210). Beverly Hills, CA: Sage.

Triandis, H. (1973). Dimensions of cultural variation as parameters of organizational theories. *International Studies of Management and Organization, 12,* 139-169.

Triandis, H. C., & Albert, R. D. (1987). Cross-cultural perspectives. In F. M. Jablin, L. L. Putnam, K. H. Roberts, & L. W. Porter (Eds.), *Handbook of organizational communication: An interdisciplinary perspective* (pp. 264-296). Newbury Park, CA: Sage.

Tsui, A. S., Pearce, J. L., Porter, L. W., & Hite, J. P. (1995). Choice of employee-organization relationship: Influence of external and internal organizational factors. In G. Ferris (Ed.), *Research in personnel and human resources management* (Vol. 13, pp. 117-151). Greenwich, CT: JAI.

Tung, R. (1988). *The new expatriates: Managing human resources abroad.* New York: Ballinger.

Ulrich, D., & Lake, D. (1990). *Organizational capability.* New York: John Wiley.

Vondracek, F. W., Lerner, R. M., & Schulenberg, J. E. (1986). *Career development: A life-span developmental approach.* Hillsdale, NJ: Lawrence Erlbaum.

Walsh, J. P. (1995). Managerial and organizational cognition: Notes from a trip down memory lane. *Organization Science, 6,* 280-321.

Walsh, J. P., & Ungson, G. R. (1991). Organizational memory. *Academy of Management Review, 16,* 57-91.

Walther, J. B. (1995). Relational aspects of computer-mediated communication: Experimental observations over time. *Organization Science, 6,* 186-203.

Watzlawick, P., Beavin, J., & Jackson, D. (1967). *The pragmatics of human communication.* New York: Norton.

Weber, M. (1947). *The theory of social and economic organizations* (A. A. M. Henderson & T. Parsons, Trans.). New York: Oxford University Press.

Weiss, H. M. (1977). Subordinate imitation of supervisor behavior: The role of modeling in organizational socialization. *Organizational Behavior and Human Performance, 19,* 89-105.

Wellins, R., Byham, W., & Wilson, J. (1991). *Empowered teams.* San Francisco: Jossey-Bass.

Wellmon, T. (1988). Conceptualizing organizational communication competence: A rules-based perspective. *Management Communication Quarterly, 1,* 515-534.

Wexley, M. N. (1986). Impression management and the new competence: Conjecture for seekers. *Et cetera, 43,* 247-258.

Wheeless, V. E., & Berryman-Fink, C. (1985). Perceptions of women managers and their communicator competencies. *Communication Quarterly, 33,* 137-148.

Wiemann, J. A. (1977). Explication and test of a model of communication competence. *Human Communication Research, 3,* 195-213.

Wilkins, B. M., & Andersen, P. A. (1991). Gender differences and similarities in management communication: A meta-analysis. *Management Communication Quarterly, 5,* 6-35.

Winter, S. G. (1986). The research program of the behavioral theory of the firm: Orthodox critique and evolutionary perspective. In B. Gilad & S. Kaish (Eds.), *Handbook of behavioral economics* (Vol. A, pp. 151-188). Greenwich, CT: JAI.

Wiseman, R., & Shuter, R. (Eds.). (1994). *Communicating in multinational organizations.* Thousand Oaks, CA: Sage.

Wohlert, K. L. (1995). *A longitudinal, multilevel analysis of the implementation and non-mandated use of a group communication technology: The case of Lotus Notes.* Unpublished doctoral dissertation, University of Texas at Austin.

Wolff, F. I., Marsnik, N. C., Tacey, W. S., & Nichols, R. G. (1983). *Perceptive listening.* New York: Holt, Rinehart & Winston.

Wood, J. T. (1994). *Gendered lives: Communication, gender, and culture.* Belmont, CA: Wadsworth.

Zander, A. W. (1980). The origins and consequences of group goals. In L. Festinger (Ed.), *Retrospections on social psychology*. New York: Oxford University Press.

Zimmermann, S. (1995). Perceptions of intercultural communication competence and international student adaptation to an American campus. *Communication Education, 44,* 321-335.

Zorn, T. E. (1991). Construct system development, transformational leadership and leadership messages. *Southern Communication Journal, 56,* 178-193.

Zorn, T. E. (1993). Motivation to communicate: A critical review with suggested alternatives. In S. A. Deetz (Ed.), *Communication yearbook 16* (pp. 515-549). Newbury Park, CA: Sage.

Zorn, T. E., & Violanti, M. T. (1996). Communication abilities and individual achievement in organizations. *Management Communication Quarterly, 10,* 139-167.

Name Index

Subject Index

About the Editors

Fredric M. Jablin (Ph.D., Purdue University) is the E. Claiborne Robins Chaired Professor of Leadership Studies in the Jepson School of Leadership Studies at the University of Richmond. He joined the faculty in the Jepson School in 1994, after having served for many years as a Professor of Speech Communication and Management (in the Graduate School of Business) at the University of Texas at Austin. His research, which has been published in a wide variety of communication, psychology, personnel and management journals, and scholarly books, has examined various facets of leader-member communication in organizations, group problem-solving, communication competence, and communication processes associated with organizational entry, assimilation and exit. He has been a member of the editorial boards of over a dozen different professional journals, the recipient of numerous awards for his research and teaching, and has served as a researcher and/or consultant to organizations in both the public and private sectors. He is currently working on a research symposium and book project related to communication processes and paradoxes associated with leadership/followership in organizations.

Linda L. Putnam (Ph.D., University of Minnesota) is Professor of Organizational Communication in the Department of Speech Communication at Texas A&M University. Her current research interests include negotiation and organizational conflict, metaphors of organizational communication, and language analysis in organizations. She is coeditor of *Communication and Negotiation* (1992), *Handbook of Organizational Communication* (1987), and *Communication and Organizations: An Interpretive Approach* (1983). She has published over 80 articles and book chapters in the areas of organizational communication, conflict management, negotiation, and organizational studies. She is the 1993 recipient of the Charles H. Woolbert Research Award for innovative research in communication, the 1999 recipient of the Distinguished Scholar Award from the National Communication Association, and a Fellow and Past President of the International Communication Association and the International Association for Conflict Management.

About the Contributors

Susan J. Ashford (M.S. and Ph.D. in organizational behavior, Northwestern University) is currently the Michael and Susan Jandernoa Professor of Organizational Behavior at the University of Michigan Business School. She joined the Michigan faculty in 1991 after spending eight years at Dartmouth College's Amos Tuck School of Business Administration. Her research focuses on the ways that individuals are proactive in their organizational lives. Her work has been published in *Administrative Science Quarterly, Academy of Management Review, Academy of Management Journal, Journal of Applied Psychology, Organizational Behavior and Human Decision Processes, Research in Organizational Behavior,* and *Strategic Management Journal,* among others. Professor Ashford was the consulting editor for the *Academy of Management Journal,* 1990-1993, has served on the editorial board since 1984 and is currently a board member for *Organizational Behavior and Human Decision Processes.*

George Cheney (Ph.D., Purdue University, 1985) is Professor and Director of Graduate Studies in Communication at the University of Montana–Missoula. Also, he is Adjunct Professor of Management Communication at the University of Waikato, Hamilton, New Zealand. He specializes in the study of contemporary organizational life, focusing on such issues as human identity, the exercise of power, democracy at work, business and organizational ethics, the analysis of corporate public discourse, and quality of worklife. He has developed courses on, and has published in, nearly all these topics. He has published over 50 journal articles, book chapters, and reviews. He is author of two books: *Rhetoric in an Organizational Society: Managing Multiple Identities* (1991) and *Values at Work: Employee Participation Meets Market Pressure at Mondragón* (1999). Recognized for both teaching and research, he has lectured and consulted in the United States, Europe, Latin America, and Australasia.

Lars Thøger Christensen (Pd.D., Odense University) is Research Professor of Corporate Communication at the Department of Intercultural Communication and Management, The Copenhagen Business School, Denmark. Previously, he has held positions at The Southern Denmark Business School and at Odense University where he was department chair at the Department of Marketing. He specializes in the study of market-related communications—in the broadest sense of the term—issued and organized by corporate bodies. His theoretical perspective is meaning based and rooted in the socio-anthropological tradition. His primary research and teaching interests are in public discourse, corporate communications, advertising, semiotics, image/identity formation, strategy, and issue management. He is author of *Markedskommunikation som organiseringsmåde: En kulturteoretisk analyse* (Market Communication as a Way of Organizing: A Cultural Analysis). His current work continues to integrate "internal" and "external" dimensions of organizational communication. His research is published in *Organization Studies, European Journal of Marketing, Consumption, Markets and Culture,* and elsewhere.

Lori Collins-Jarvis (Ph.D., University of Southern California) currently works as a Senior Project Director in the Entertainment Division of Lieberman Research Worldwide (Los Angeles, CA), specializing in new media market research. Her early work focused on social and equity issues in implementation of the Public Electronic Network in Santa Monica, California and communication issues in nonprofit organizations. She has published articles in the *Journal of Broadcasting and Electronic Media* and *The Journal of the American Society for Information Science.* As Assistant Professor at Rutgers University, she advised a local consortium of libraries, public schools, and colleges in the development of a public computer-conferencing network.

Charles Conrad (Ph.D., Kansas University, 1980) is Professor of Speech Communication at Texas A&M University. His research focuses on the relationship between communi-

cation and social/organizational power and on organizational rhetoric. He is author or editor of five books, and his research has appeared in the *Quarterly Journal of Speech, Communication Monographs, Journal of Applied Communication Research,* and elsewhere.

Noshir S. Contractor (http://www.spcomm. uiuc.edu/contractor) is Associate Professor of Speech Communication and Psychology at the University of Illinois at Urbana-Champaign. His research interests include applications of complex adaptive systems theory to communication, the role of emergent communication and knowledge networks in organizations, and collaboration technologies in the workplace. He is currently investigating factors that lead to the formation, maintenance, and dissolution of dynamically linked knowledge networks in work communities. He is the principal investigator on a major three-year grant from the National Science Foundation's Knowledge and Distributed Intelligence Initiative to study the coevolution of knowledge networks and 21st-century organizational forms. He and Peter Monge have written a book, *Theories of Communication Networks and Flows,* which will be published next year.

Stanley Deetz, Ph.D., is Professor of Communication at the University of Colorado, Boulder, where he teaches courses in organizational theory, organizational communication, and communication theory. He is coauthor of *Leading Organizations Through Transition: Communication and Cultural Change* and *Doing Critical Management Research* and author of *Transforming Communication, Transforming Business: Building Responsive and Responsible Workplaces* and *Democracy in an Age of Corporate Colonization: Developments in Communication and the Politics of Everyday Life,* as well as editor or author of 8 other books. He has published nearly 100 essays in scholarly journals and books regarding stakeholder representation, culture, and communication in corporate organizations. He has served as a consultant on culture, diversity, and participatory decision making for several major corporations. He is a Fellow of the International Communication Association and served as its President, 1996-1997.

Eric M. Eisenberg is Professor and Chair of the Department of Communication at the University of South Florida. He received his doctorate in organizational communication from Michigan State University in 1982. After leaving MSU, he directed the master's program in applied communication at Temple University before moving to the University of Southern California. Over a ten-year period at USC, he twice received the Speech Communication Association award for outstanding publication in organizational communication, as well as the Burlington Foundation award for excellence in teaching. In 1994, his textbook *Organizational Communication: Balancing Creativity and Constraint* (with H. L. Goodall, Jr.) won the Academic Textbook Author award for best textbook of the year. This past year, he received the Florida State Legislature Teaching Incentive Award for Excellence in Teaching. He is an internationally recognized researcher, teacher, and consultant specializing in the strategic use of communication to promote organizational change.

Gail T. Fairhurst (Ph.D., University of Oregon) is Professor in the Department of Communication at the University of Cincinnati. Her research interests focus primarily on leadership communication and language analysis in organizational contexts. She has published in several communication and organizational science journals including *Hu-*

man Communication Research, Communication Monographs, Organization Science, Academy of Management Journal, Academy of Management Review, and *Organizational Behavior and Human Decision Processes,* as well as in *Communication Yearbooks* (8, 9, and 10). She is coauthor (with Bob Sarr) of *The Art of Framing: Managing the Language of Leadership,* which received the 1996-97 National Communication Association award for outstanding book in organizational communication. She has received an NCA Best Article Award for organizational communication as well as numerous top paper honors at the annual conferences of the International Communication Association. In addition to serving on a number of editorial boards, she has served as a consultant on leadership and organizational communication for several major corporations.

Dayna Finet (Ph.D., University of Southern California) taught at the University of Texas, Austin, and State University of New York, Albany, where she specialized on topics of social issues in organizational communication and organizational communication ethics. Now a writer based in Austin, Texas, she concentrates on biography, autobiography, and memoir. Her book, *With Courage and Common Sense,* a collection of memoirs from Texas women of the Depression/World War II generation, is scheduled for 2001 publication by the University of Texas Press. With grant support from the Texas Commission on the Arts, she is currently writing *Age and Youth in Action: An Oral History of the Gray Panthers.* She also writes biographical literature for children.

Janet Fulk is Professor of Communications in the Annenberg School for Communication and Professor of Management & Organization in the Marshall School of Business at the University of Southern California. She holds

M.B.A. and Ph.D. degrees in administrative sciences from The Ohio State University. A series of recent projects sponsored by the National Science Foundation examines how communication and information systems are employed to foster collaboration and knowledge distribution within and between organizations. A recently completed research project sponsored by the Annenberg Center for Communication examines the development of new virtual" organizational forms for global competition. Recent publications include *Shaping Organizational Form: Communication Connection and Community* (1999, with Gerardine DeSanctis), and *Organizations and Communication Technology* (1990, with Charles Steinfield), which won an award from the National Communication Association. Recent articles on organizations and communication technology have appeared in *Human Relations, Communication Theory,* and *Organization Science,* and an award-winning article appeared in *Academy of Management Journal.* She serves on several editorial boards and has completed a term on the Board of Governors of Academy of Management, where she was also elected Fellow in 1997.

Urs E. Gattiker (Ph.D., Management and Organization, Claremont Graduate School) is Professor of Technology and Innovation Management, Department of Production, at the Obel Family Foundation in Denmark. Formerly, he was Associate Professor of Organizational Behaviour and Technology Management at the University of Lethbridge, Alberta, Canada. He has edited the book series *Technological Innovation and Human Resources* and the journal *Technological Studies,* and he authored *Technology Management in Organization* (1990) and *Moral and Economic Issues on the Information Highway: Balancing Interests* (1996). He has published widely in management, technology, and information systems journals and

books. His research interests include skill acquisition and human capital theory, technological change, career development, quality-of-work-life issues, and privacy and ethical issues on the Internet. He has been an officer of two divisions in the Academy of Management.

Julie Haynes received her master's degree in speech communication from Texas A&M University under the direction of Charles Conrad. She is a doctoral candidate in speech communication at Penn State University and teaches in the Department of Communication Studies at Rowan University.

Robert D. McPhee (Ph.D., Michigan State University, 1978) is Herberger Professor in the Hugh Downs School of Human Communication at Arizona State University. Specializing in organizational communication and communication theory, he has served as the Chair of the Organizational Communication Division of the National Communication Association and as Associate Editor for *Human Communication Research.* His special interests are formal/hierarchical communication and structuration theory.

Katherine Miller (Ph.D., University of Southern California) is Professor of Speech Communication at Texas A&M University. Her research interests center on communication within human service organizations. In particular, her work has considered the effects of participation in human service agencies, the role of emotional communication in service provision, interorganizational coordination for service provision, and the development of stress and burnout among human service workers. She is author of *Organizational Communication: Approaches and Processes,* and her research has been published in such journals as *Human Communication Research, Journal of Applied Communication*

Research, Communication Monographs, Communication Research, Academy of Management Journal, and Management Communication Quarterly.

Peter R. Monge is Professor of Communication at the Annenberg School for Communication, University of Southern California. He has published Communicating and Organizing (with Vince Farace and Hamish Russell), Multivariate Techniques in Human Communication Research (with Joe Cappella), Policing Hawthorne (with Janet Fulk and Gregory Patton), and Reasoning With Statistics (5th ed., with Fred Williams). His research interests include organizational communication and knowledge networks, coevolutionary communication systems, globalization and communication processes, and research methods. He served as editor of Communication Research from 1986 to 1993 and as president of the International Communication Association, 1997-1998. He and Noshir Contractor have written a book, Theories of Communication Networks and Flows, which will be published next year.

Dennis K. Mumby (Ph.D., Southern Illinois University—Carbondale) is Professor of Communication at Purdue University. He has published in journals such as Communication Monographs, Communication Theory, Academy of Management Review, Discourse & Society, and Management Communication Quarterly. He is author of Communication and Power in Organizations and editor of Narrative and Social Control. His research focuses on the relationships among communication, organizing, identity, and power and their intersection in the dialectics of domination and resistance. His current research interests include an examination of the relationship between feminism and postmodernism, and its application for the development of di-

alectical conceptions of organizational power. He is currently working on a book for Sage titled Organizing Gender: Feminism, Postmodernism, and Organization Studies.

Marshall Scott Poole (Ph.D., University of Wisconsin, 1980) is Professor of Speech-Communication at Texas A&M University. He has conducted research and published extensively on the topics of group and organizational communication, computer-mediated communication systems, conflict management, and organizational innovation. He has coauthored or edited four books, including Communication and Group Decision-Making, Working Through Conflict, and Research on the Management of Innovation. He has published in a number of journals, including Management Science, MIS Quarterly, Human Communication Research, Academy of Management Journal, and Communication Monographs. He is currently a senior editor of Information Systems Research and Organizational Science.

Ronald E. Rice (M.A., Ph.D., Stanford University) is Professor in the School of Communication, Information & Library Studies, Rutgers University. He has coauthored or coedited The Internet and Health Communication; Public Communication Campaigns; The New Media: Communication, Research and Technology; Managing Organizational Innovation; and Research Methods and the New Media. He has conducted research and published widely in communication science, public communication campaigns, computer-mediated communication systems, methodology, organizational and management theory, information systems, information science and bibliometrics, and social networks. His publications have won awards as best dissertation from the American Society for Information Science, half a dozen times as best paper from International Communication Association divisions, and twice as best paper from Academy of Management divisions. He has been elected a divisional officer in both the International Communication Association and the Academy of Management and is currently on the ICA Publications Board. He has served as associate editor for *Human Communication Research* and *MIS Quarterly*.

Patricia Riley (Ph.D., University of Nebraska) is Associate Professor of Organizational Communication and Director of the School of Communication in the Annenberg School for Communication at the University of Southern California. Her work focuses on communication and institutional politics, organizational culture change, business process reengineering and organizational transformation. Her research has appeared in such books as *Organizational Culture Advances in Leadership Research*, and in *Communication Quarterly, Journal of Management, Argument and Advocacy, New Management,* and *Communication Reports.* She is presently working on a grant to study the role of communication and information systems in reengineering projects and a book with Warren Bennis called *Organizational Redevelopment.* An experienced organizational consultant, she conducts workshops and seminars for top executives in areas such as reengineering, leadership, advocacy, strategic communication, and managing cultural change.

David R. Seibold (Ph.D., Michigan State University) is Professor and Chair, Department of Communication, University of California, Santa Barbara. He is author of 100 publications on organizational communication, group dynamics, and interpersonal influence and has received numerous research and teaching awards. He is recent editor of the

Journal of Applied Communication Research and serves on the boards of many other journals. Former Chair of the Interpersonal Communication Division of both the National Communication Association and the International Communication Association, he currently is Chair of the Organizational Communication Division of the International Communication Association. He also works closely with many business, government, and health organizations.

B. Christine Shea (Ph.D., University of California, Santa Barbara) is Lecturer in Speech Communication at California Polytechnic State University, San Luis Obispo. She is author of more than 30 papers, articles, and book chapters on organizational communication, interpersonal relationships, and argumentation. She has served as a reviewer for several journals, including *Management Communication Quarterly* and *Journal of Applied Communication Research.* Her current research interests include organizational justice and fairness, non-union due process systems, and sex and gender issues in organizations.

Patricia M. Sias is Associate Professor of Communication in the Edward R. Murrow School of Communication at Washington State University. Her research centers primarily on workplace relationships. In particular, her work focuses on the development of peer relationships and workplace friendships and the ways such relationships influence, and are influenced by, the organizational context. She has published articles in a variety of journals including *Communication Monographs, Human Communication Research, Communication Research, Western Journal of Communication, Communication Quarterly,* and *Journal of Applied Communication Research.* She received the W. Charles Redding

Award for outstanding dissertation in organizational communication in 1993.

Cynthia Stohl (Ph.D., Purdue, 1982) is the Margaret Church Distinguished Professor of Communication and Head of the Department of Communication at Purdue University. She teaches a variety of courses at both the graduate and undergraduate levels in organizational, global, and group communication and has published widely in these areas. She is author of more than 45 articles in management, communication, and sociology journals and handbooks. Her book *Organizational Communication: Connectedness in Action* received the National Communication Association Award (1995) for the best book in organizational communication, and her article (coauthored with George Cheney, Joe Straub, Laura Speirs, Dan DeGooyer, Susan Whalen, Kathy Garvin-Doxas, and David Carlone) "Democracy, Participation, and Communication at Work" (1997) received the 1998 NCA Award for best article. She has also been the recipient of several departmental, school, and university teaching awards.

Kathleen M. Sutcliffe (Ph.D. in management, University of Texas–Austin) is a member of the Organizational Behavior and Human Resources Management faculty at the University of Michigan Business School. Her current research is focused both on understanding top management team perception and learning processes and how management teams can be designed to better sense and cope with changing contextual requirements, and on understanding how organizations remain reliable under uncertain and changing conditions. Her work has appeared in many journals including the *Academy of Management Journal, Academy of Management Review, Organization Science, Research in Organizational Behavior, Research in the Sociology of Organizations,* and *Strategic Management Journal.*

Bryan C. Taylor (Ph.D., Utah, 1991) is Associate Professor in the Department of Communication at the University of Colorado at Boulder. His interests include critical theory and interpretive methods associated with the study of organizational culture and symbolism. He is particularly interested in the culture of nuclear weapons production, and in developing potential relationships between the fields of organizational communication and cultural studies.

Phillip K. Tompkins is Professor Emeritus of Communication, University of Colorado at Boulder. For the past 18 months, he has worked as a volunteer at the St. Francis Center, a shelter for the homeless in Denver, Colorado. He is now doing research on poverty and homelessness and is the co-leader of the Affordable Housing Study Group within St. John's Episcopal Cathedral in Denver. He is at work on a book about these subjects with a working title of *Down, Out, and Up Again in Denver: A Theological Ethnography of Homelessness and Housing.*

Nick Trujillo (Ph.D., University of Utah, 1983) is Professor of Communication Studies at California State University, Sacramento. He is author of two books (*Organizational Life on Television,* with Leah Vande Berg, and *The Meaning of Nolan Ryan*) and of over 40 scholarly and popular articles. He conducts research on organizational communication, ethnography, and media sports, and he is currently finishing a book about the life and death of his grandmother. He can be contacted at nickt@csus.edu.

Maryanne Wanca-Thibault is Assistant Professor of Communication at the University of Colorado at Colorado Springs. Her teaching and research interests include changing organizational forms, women in organizations, and domestic violence.

Karl E. Weick (Ph.D., Ohio State University) is Rensis Likert Collegiate Professor of Organizational Behavior and Psychology at the University of Michigan. He has been associated with the faculties at Purdue University, the University of Minnesota, Cornell University, and the University of Texas at Austin. He is a former editor of *Administrative Science Quarterly* and author of a num-

ber of books including *The Social Psychology of Organizing* and *Sensemaking in Organizations*. He has also written numerous journal articles, book chapters, and book reviews and has received a variety of awards for his scholarship. He studies such topics as how people make sense of confusing events, the social psychology of improvisation, high-reliability systems, the effects of stress on thinking and imagination, indeterminacy in social systems, social commitment, small wins as the embodiment of wisdom, and linkages between theory and practice.